The Reader's Adviser

The Reader's Adviser
14th EDITION
Marion Sader, Series Editor

Volume 1
The Best in Reference Works, British Literature, and American Literature
David Scott Kastan and Emory Elliott, Volume Editors

Books About Books • Bibliography • Reference Books: General • Reference Books: Literature • Medieval Literature • Renaissance Literature • Shakespeare • Restoration and Eighteenth-Century Literature • The Romantic Period • The Victorian Period • Modern British and Irish Literature • British Literature: Popular Modes • Early American Literature: Beginnings to the Nineteenth Century • Early Nineteenth-Century American Literature • Middle to Late Nineteenth-Century American Literature • Early Twentieth-Century American Literature • Middle to Late Twentieth-Century American Literature • Modern American Drama • American Literature: Some New Directions • American Literature: Popular Modes

Volume 2
The Best in World Literature
Robert DiYanni, Volume Editor

Introduction to World Literature • Hebrew Literature • Yiddish Literature • Middle Eastern Literatures • African Literatures • Literature of the Indian Subcontinent • Chinese Literature • Japanese Literature • Korean Literature • Southeast Asian Literatures • Greek Literature • Latin Literature • Italian Literature • French Literature • Spanish Literature • Portuguese Literature • German Literature • Netherlandic Literature • Scandinavian Literatures • Russian Literature • East European Literatures • Latin American Literatures • Canadian Literature • Literature of the Caribbean • Australian Literature • New Zealand Literature • Comparative Literature

Volume 3
The Best in Social Sciences, History, and the Arts
John G. Sproat, Volume Editor

Social Sciences and History: General Reference • Anthropology • Economics • Geography • Political Science • Psychology • Sociology • Education • World History • Ancient History • European History • African History • Middle Eastern History • History of Asia and the Pacific • United States History • Canadian History • Latin American History • Music and Dance • Art and Architecture • Mass Media • Folklore, Humor, and Popular Culture • Travel and Exploration

Volume 4
The Best in Philosophy and Religion
Robert S. Ellwood, Volume Editor

Philosophy and Religion: General Reference • General Philosophy • Greek and Roman Philosophy • Medieval Philosophy • Renaissance Philosophy • Modern Western Philosophy, 1600–1900 • Twentieth-Century Western Philosophy • Asian and African Philosophy, 1850 to the Present • Contemporary Issues in Philosophy • Ancient Religions and Philosophies • Eastern Religions • Islam • Judaism • Early and Medieval Christianity • Late Christianity, 1500 to the Present • The Bible and Related Literature • Minority Religions and Contemporary Religious Movements • Contemporary Issues in Religious Thought

Volume 5
The Best in Science, Technology, and Medicine
Carl Mitcham and William F. Williams, Volume Editors

Science, Technology, and Medicine: General Reference • A General View: Science, Technology, and Medicine • History of Science, Technology, and Medicine • Philosophy of Science, Technology, and Medicine • Ethics in Science, Technology, and Medicine • Science, Technology, and Society • Special Issues in Science, Technology, and Society • Engineering and Technology • Agriculture and Food Technology • Energy • Communications Technology • Medicine and Health • Illness and Disease • Clinical Psychology and Psychiatry • Mathematics • Statistics and Probability • Information Science and Computer Science • Astronomy and Space Science • Earth Sciences • Physics • Chemistry • Biological Sciences • Ecology and Environmental Science

THE
Reader's Adviser®

14th EDITION

Volume 5

The Best in Science, Technology, and Medicine

Carl Mitcham and William F. Williams, Volume Editors

Marion Sader, Series Editor

R. R. Bowker®

A Reed Reference Publishing Company
New Providence, New Jersey

Published by R. R. Bowker
A Reed Reference Publishing Company
Copyright © 1994 by Reed Publishing (USA) Inc.

Printed and bound in the United States of America

International Standard Book Numbers
0-8352-3320-0 (SET)
0-8352-3321-9 (Volume 1)
0-8352-3322-7 (Volume 2)
0-8352-3323-5 (Volume 3)
0-8352-3324-3 (Volume 4)
0-8352-3325-1 (Volume 5)
0-8352-3326-X (Volume 6)
International Standard Serial Number 0094-5943
Library of Congress Catalog Card Number 57-13277

The paper used in this publication meets the minimum requirements
of American National Standard for Information Sciences—Permanence
of Papers for Printed Library Materials, ANSI Z39.48-1984.

ISBN 0-8352-3320-0

9 780835 233200

Contents

Preface

Libraries are busy places and rarely is there time for the reader and the librarian to sit down, discuss and analyze the reader's book problem, direct his interest or locate the book he wants. . . . In answer to this demand readers' advisers are appearing on many library staffs.

—JENNIE M. FLEXNER

When Jennie M. Flexner, founder of the New York Public Library's famous Reader's Advisory service, wrote those words in *Library Journal* in 1938, R. R. Bowker's own *Reader's Adviser* had already been a Baedeker for overwhelmed library patrons for nearly a generation. Known then as *The Bookman's Manual*, it had, as its name suggests, actually been conceived, not by a librarian, but by a bookseller, Bessie Graham. Graham's first edition, published in 1921, was based on an enormously popular bookselling course she had recently taught at the William Penn Evening High School in Philadelphia. Just over 400 pages, that first *Bookman's Manual* was intended to give novice book retailers a basic inventory of essential in-print titles, both to stock and to recommend to customers. (It did, admittedly, fail to mention Shakespeare—a shortcoming that so appalled Mildred C. Smith, the young Bowker employee who had been asked to organize Graham's material, that more than four decades later, as editor of *Publishers Weekly*, Smith still vividly recalled the omission.) Not surprisingly, however, *The Bookman's Manual* was quickly adopted by librarians facing much the same task with their own patrons—and through 13 editions the work, in its various guises, has been successfully matching good books with grateful readers for more than 70 years.

Because of its roots in bookselling, *The Reader's Adviser* has always been far more than a guide to "the classics"—those time-honored treasures that, as Mark Twain once insisted, "everybody talks about but nobody reads." From the very first edition, its chapters reflected current literary, social, and political trends, embracing not only such mainstream categories as "Great Names in English Poetry" and "Essays and Letters" but also, as befitted the new era of universal suffrage, "American Fiction—Contemporary *Men* Writers" and "American Fiction—Contemporary *Women* Writers." Modern British authors experienced the same sexual differentiation in the second edition, published three years later, by which time Shakespeare had returned from exile and books on such extraliterary subjects as "Nature," "Music," and "Travel" had also been added.

Throughout the 1920s and 1930s, *The Bookman's Manual* continued to grow explosively—so much so that, by the time Bessie Graham bid farewell to her "lifework" (as she called it in her preface to the fifth edition of 1941), it had nearly doubled in size. "I commend its future editions to my unknown successor," she wrote, "and take leave of a task that holds only pleasant associations for me now that I pass 'Out of the stress of the doing, Into the peace of the done.'" Sadly, the United States's entry into World War II would soon interrupt that peace as well as the arrival of "future editions."

With the war near an end in June 1945, Bowker's Mildred Smith recommended Hester R. Hoffman, a bookseller with nearly 30 years' experience at the Hampshire Bookshop in Northampton, Massachusetts, to compile the next peacetime edition of Graham's *The Bookman's Manual*. Unfortunately, Hoffman's start was frustrated by more than a wartime paper shortage; Bowker's proposal reached her (as she later put it) while she was "lying flat in a room in a South Boston Hospital recovering from, of all things, a broken neck." Undaunted by her predicament, by the dearth of current titles on publishers' lists, and even by her typesetter's utter lack of foreign accents for the chapter on French literature, she succeeded in pulling together the sixth edition of *The Bookman's Manual* by 1948. The war, though, had taken its toll: despite a seven-year hiatus between editions, Hoffman's first effort was 62 pages *shorter* than Graham's last.

As the 1950s unfolded and the nuclear age cast a lengthening shadow, Hester Hoffman strove to keep *The Bookman's Manual* at the forefront of breaking literary and nonliterary events worldwide. A new chapter on science in the seventh edition of 1954 helped readers make sense of the profound legacy of such diverse theorists as Einstein and Freud. Thanks to Russian literature editors Helen Muchnic and Nicolai Vorobiov, anyone searching for contemporary Soviet novelists could have discovered the great Boris Pasternak (then known in the West only as a poet) fully three years before *Doctor Zhivago* made him an international sensation. In the eighth edition of 1958, the chapter on bibles updated readers who were eager to learn more about one of the seminal discoveries in Judeo-Christian history: a tattered collection of Hebrew and Aramaic parchments, concealed in pottery jars in caves near Qumran, that soon became known as the Dead Sea Scrolls.

Renamed *The Reader's Adviser and Bookman's Manual*, in 1960, the work continued to grow precipitously—struggling to reward the newfound postwar affluence, leisure, and cosmopolitan curiosity of American readers. With the baby boom at that time came a publishing boom, and, as Americans opened the New Frontier, they hungered for books about everything from rockets and space travel to parapsychology to segregation and the South. Indeed, just a glimpse of the new reading lists added during this heady and tumultuous era recaptures a time when readers were discovering ideas, arts, peoples, and places as perhaps they never had discovered before. There were books on the North American Indian and the opening of the West, Soviet history and policy, and the Civil War (as it reached its centenary); there were books by authors from Africa, Japan, China, India, Latin America, and, at long last, black America, as well as books about the lively arts of jazz, cinema, children's theater, and, yes, McLuhan's "cool medium," television.

By 1968, when Winifred F. Courtney guided the eleventh edition to press, one volume could no longer hold it all: It took two. The twelfth edition, published from 1974 to 1977, then blossomed to three volumes. As Bowker's own *Books in Print* continued to document a book market that was all but doubling in size every 10 years (from 245,000 titles in 1967 to 750,000 in 1987), the thirteenth edition, published in two installments, in 1986 and 1988, swelled to five volumes (plus a separately bound index). *The Reader's Adviser*, which always had been a reference tool built on the contributions of subject specialists, now had become virtually an encyclopedia—requiring separate editors for the set, for the individual volumes, for the sections . . . and even for the chapters!

As little as today's *Reader's Adviser* may resemble Bessie Graham's once modest *Bookman's Manual*, the work still adheres to tradition. More than ever the essential starting point for anyone who is setting out to read about the world of literary, artistic, philosophical, or scientific endeavor, the work's individual volumes are designed to carry users from the general to the specific—from overarching reference guides, critical histories, and anthologies about a genre or a field to the lives and works of its leading exemplars. As always, booksellers, reference and acquisitions librarians, lay readers, teachers, academics, and students alike can readily use it to identify the best of nearly everything available in English in the United States today, from the poetry of the ancients to Renaissance philosophy to meditations on the ethics of modern medicine.

Choosing what to include and what to leave out is never easy. As specialists, the volume and chapter editors know their field's most noted and popular figures, current and historic, and the body of literature on which the reputations of those individuals stand. Although I have asked each editor, when possible, to revise an "out of vogue" author's profile and bibliography rather than simply to eliminate it, paring is inevitable with any new edition. Then, too, the mere availability of an author's work can play its own editorial role. Although it is customary to list only titles published as books and (according to the latest monthly release of *Books in Print* on CD-ROM) currently for sale in the United States, exceptions are made for invaluable out-of-print works deemed likely to appear in the stacks of an established, modest-sized municipal library.

Revisions to the fourteenth edition have been judicious. Most noticeably, the set itself is longer and has a larger trim size—up from 6" x 9" to 7" x 10"—to give the pages a more open look. As the heart of *The Reader's Adviser*, the bibliographies have been more extensively annotated than ever before, and the lists of "books by" that accompany each profiled author in Volumes 1 and 2 are now helpfully subcategorized into genres (fiction, nonfiction, poetry, plays, etc.). Furthermore, ISBNs have been added to the usual bibliographic data (again, drawn from the latest monthly release of *Books in Print* on CD-ROM) of publisher, price, and year of publication. In addition, on the sensible assumption that the author profiles preceding bibliographies should be a tantalizing appetizer for the entrée to come, the editors have done their best to season them all with rich, lively biographical detail. Finally, the reader should be aware that not all in-print editions of a work are necessarily listed but, rather, only those editions selected because of their quality or special features.

Another change in this edition is the addition of a "Chronology of Authors" section before the alphabetical arrangement of profiled authors in each chapter—a complement to the chronology that appears at the outset of each volume and a quick and easy means of placing each chapter's profiled entrants in historical perspective. Finally, to boost *The Reader's Adviser*'s reference utility, the subject index of each volume has been greatly expanded, and the chapters on "Books about Books," "General Bibliography," and "General Reference" (which were previously split between Volumes 1 and 2) have been brought together and now appear at the beginning of Volume 1.

Of course, much about this new edition of *The Reader's Adviser* remains uniquely similar to the previous edition. The six-volume organization begun with the thirteenth edition continues: Volume 1 encompasses general reference works and American and British literature; Volume 2, world literature in translation; Volume 3, the social sciences, history, and the arts; Volume 4, the literature of philosophy and world religions; and Volume 5, the literature of science, technology, and medicine. Similarly, Volume 6 incorporates the name, title, and subject indexes of each of the previous volumes. Also retained are convenient cross-references throughout, which guide inquiring readers to related authors, chapters, sections, or volumes. A "see" reference leads the reader to the appropriate volume and chapter for information on a specific author. "See also" refers the reader to additional information in another chapter or volume. Within any sections of narrative, the name of an author who appears as a main listing in another chapter or volume is printed in large and small capital letters. If the chapter cross-referenced is to be found in a different volume from the one being consulted, the volume number is also given. Furthermore, to make basic research easier, the annotated bibliographies accompanying profiled individuals separately list works "by" and "about" those authors.

To assure that all volumes of the fourteenth edition are compiled concurrently and arrive together, I have relied on the contributions of countless authorities. Special thanks are due to both *The Reader's Adviser*'s team of volume editors and the chapter contributors, whose names are listed in each volume. The book production experts at Book Builders Incorporated directed the almost Herculean task of coordinating the 110 chapters by 120 authors through numerous editing and production stages; to everyone's satisfaction, the system succeeded, as the reader can affirm from a glance at these six volumes. In particular, I must recognize Book Builders' Lauren Fedorko, president and guiding spirit, for her unfailing good spirits and intelligent decisions; Diane Schadoff, editorial coordinator; and Paula Wiech, production manager. Many thanks to them and their staffs for the extra hours and care that they lavished on our "magnum opus." Very special appreciation is due to Charles Roebuck, managing editor *extraordinaire*, whose concerns for accuracy, detail, and style made perfection almost attainable. Charles's contributions are countless, and much of the success of this edition is due to his tact and diplomacy in managing many people, many deadlines, and many pages of manuscript. Here at Bowker, I am especially grateful to my assistant, Angela Szablewski, who has had the monumental responsibility of coordinating all stages of the books' production.

In her 1938 article, Ms. Flexner wrote that "libraries are made up of good, old books as well as good, new books." In agreement with her view, I have continued in the *Reader's Adviser* tradition by including in this new fourteenth edition titles that are timeless, as well as those that are timely; the aim is to provide the user with both a broad and a specific view of the great writings and great writers of the past and present. I wish you all satisfaction in your research, delight in your browsing, and pleasure in your reading.

Marion Sader
Publisher
Professional & Reference Books
R.R. Bowker
September 1993

Contributing Editors

Judith A. Adams, SCIENCE, TECHNOLOGY, AND SOCIETY
Director of Lockwood Library, State University of New York at Buffalo

Peter Bohn, AGRICULTURE AND FOOD TECHNOLOGY
Editor and Publisher, *The Nutrient Management Report;* Member of the American
Society of Agronomy and the Soil Science Society of America

Edward S. Cassedy, ENERGY
Professor of Electrical Engineering, Polytechnic University, Brooklyn, New York

John Ciciarelli, EARTH SCIENCES
Geologist and Assistant Professor of Environmental Sciences, The Pennsylvania State
University (Beaver Campus)

Stephen H. Cutcliffe, SCIENCE, TECHNOLOGY, AND SOCIETY
Associate Professor of Science, Technology, and Society and History; Director,
Science, Technology, and Society Program, Lehigh University (Pennsylvania)

Joseph W. Dauben, MATHEMATICS
Professor of History and the History of Science, Herbert H. Lehman College, and
Ph.D. Program in History, The Graduate Center, City University of New York

Richard A. Deitrich, SPECIAL ISSUES IN SCIENCE, TECHNOLOGY, AND SOCIETY
Assistant Professor of Science, Technology, and Society, The Pennsylvania State
University

Paul T. Durbin, PHILOSOPHY OF SCIENCE, TECHNOLOGY, AND MEDICINE
Professor, Philosophy Department; Director of the Center for Science and Culture;
Professor in the College of Urban Affairs and Public Policy, University of Delaware;
Visiting Scholar, Jefferson Medical College (Philadelphia, Pennsylvania)

Heyward Ehrlich, INFORMATION AND COMPUTER SCIENCE
Associate Professor, English Department, Rutgers University at Newark, New Jersey

Jean Dickinson Gibbons, STATISTICS AND PROBABILITY
Russell Professor of Applied Statistics, University of Alabama

Amedeo Giorgi, CLINICAL PSYCHOLOGY AND PSYCHIATRY
Professor, Department of Psychology, University of Quebec at Montreal, and at The
Saybrook Institute, San Francisco, California

Kathleen Kehoe Glass, BIOLOGY AND GENETICS
Biology and Physics Librarian, Columbia University

Harold Groff, COMMUNICATIONS TECHNOLOGY
Assistant Professor and Program Chair, Department of Telecommunications
Technology, The Pennsylvania State University (Wilkes-Barre Campus)

Stephen Kcenich, PHYSICS
Graduate student in Mathematical Science, The Pennsylvania State University

Henry Lowood, HISTORY OF SCIENCE, TECHNOLOGY, AND MEDICINE
Bibliographer for History of Science and Technology Collections, Stanford University

Maureen Welling Matkovich, CHEMISTRY
Manager, Library Services, American Chemical Society, Washington, D.C.

Robert Meredith, ECOLOGY AND ENVIRONMENTAL SCIENCE
Writer and Editor, Pennsylvania Groundwater Policy Education Project, The
Pennsylvania State University

Carl Mitcham, VOLUME EDITOR; ETHICS IN SCIENCE, TECHNOLOGY, AND MEDICINE;
SPECIAL ISSUES IN SCIENCE, TECHNOLOGY, AND SOCIETY
Director of the Science, Technology, and Society Program, The Pennsylvania State
University

Mohammad Nouri, PHYSICS
Professor of Mathematics and Science, Technology, and Society, The Pennsylvania
State University

Bonnie Osif, SCIENCE, TECHNOLOGY, AND MEDICINE: GENERAL REFERENCE;
A GENERAL VIEW: SCIENCE, TECHNOLOGY, AND MEDICINE
Assistant Engineering Librarian, The Pennsylvania State University

Daniel T. Richards, MEDICINE AND HEALTH; ILLNESS AND DISEASE
Director of Biomedical Libraries, Dartmouth College

Harry L. Shipman, ASTRONOMY AND SPACE SCIENCE
Professor of Physics and Astronomy, University of Delaware

Joyce Williams, SPECIAL ISSUES IN SCIENCE, TECHNOLOGY, AND SOCIETY
Assistant Professor of Science, Technology, and Society, The Pennsylvania State
University

William F. Williams, VOLUME EDITOR; COMMUNICATIONS TECHNOLOGY;
ENGINEERING AND TECHNOLOGY
Professor of Science, Technology, and Society, The Pennsylvania State University;
Director of Combined Studies in Science (retired), The University of Leeds (England)

Abbreviations

abr.	abridged
A.D.	in the year of the Lord
annot(s).	annotated, annotator(s)
B.C.	before Christ
B.C.E.	before the common era
B.P.	before the present
Bk(s)	Book(s)
c.	circa
C.E.	of the common era
Class.	Classic(s)
coll.	collected
comp(s).	compiled, compiler(s)
ed(s).	edited, editor(s), edition(s)
fl.	flourished
fwd.	foreword
gen. ed(s).	general editor(s)
ill(s).	illustrated, illustrator(s)
intro.	introduction
Lit.	Literature
o.p.	out-of-print
Pr.	Press
pref.	preface
pt(s).	part(s)
repr.	reprint
rev. ed.	revised edition
Ser.	Series
Supp.	Supplement
trans.	translated, translator(s), translation
U. or Univ.	University
Vol(s).	Volume(s)

Throughout this series, publisher names are abbreviated within bibliographic entries. The full names of these publishers can be found listed in Volume 6, the Index to the series.

Chronology of Authors

Main author entries appear here chronologically by year of birth. Within each chapter, main author entries are arranged alphabetically by surname.

Rolston, Holmes, III. 1932–
Stone, Christopher. 1937–
Beauchamp, Thomas L. 1939–
Veatch, Robert M. 1939–
Engelhardt, H. Tristram. 1941–
Hargrove, Eugene. 1944–
Shrader-Frechette, Kristin S. 1944-
Winner, Langdon. 1944–

6. Science, Technology, and Society
Mumford, Lewis. 1895–1990
Bronowski, Jacob. 1908–1974
Ellul, Jacques. 1912–
Kranzberg, Melvin. 1917–
Barbour, Ian. 1923–
Roy, Rustum. 1924–
Florman, Samuel C(harles). 1925–
Meadows, Donella H. 1931–
Nelkin, Dorothy. 1933–
Roszak, Theodore. 1933–
Petroski, Henry. 1942–
Latour, Bruno. 1947–

7. Special Issues in Science, Technology, and Society
Bush, Vannevar. 1880–1974
Tillich, Paul. 1886–1965
Gilkey, Langdon B. 1919–
Jaki Stanley L. 1924–
Rothschild, Joan. 1928–
Kemp, Martin. 1942–
Tichi, Cecilia. 1942–
Haraway, Donna. 1944–
Rothman, Barbara Katz. 1948–

8. Engineering and Technology
Brindley, James. 1716–1772
Smeaton, John. 1724–1792
Telford, Thomas. 1757–1834
Rennie, John. 1761–1821
Rennie, Sir John. 1794–1874
Brunel, Sir Isambard Kingdom. 1806–1859
Edison, Thomas A(lva). 1847–1931
Vincenti, Walter Guido. 1917–

Florman, Samuel C(harles). 1925–
Bugliarello, George. 1927–

9. Agriculture and Food Technology
Columella, Lucius Junius Moderatus. fl. 1st century A.D.
Boussingault, Jean-Baptiste. 1802–1887
Liebig, Justus von. 1803–1873
Lawes, John B. 1814–1900
Gilbert, Joseph H. 1817–1901
Wallace, Henry. 1836–1916
Benson, Ezra Taft. 1899–
Borlaug, Norman. 1914–
Rodale, Robert David. 1930–1990
Berry, Wendell. 1934–
Jackson, Wes. 1936–

10. Energy
Adelman, Morris A. 1917–
Rose, David J. 1921–
Duffie, John A. 1925–
Boer, Karl W. 1926–
Holdren, John P. 1944–
Munasinghe, Mohan. 1945–
Yergin, Daniel. 1947–

11. Communications Technology
Cherry, Colin. 1914–1979
Freeman, Roger L. 1928–
Keiser, Bernhard E(dward). 1928–
Hiltz, Starr Roxanne. 1942–
Tomasi, Wayne. 1946–

12. Medicine and Health
Vesalius, Andreas. 1514–1564
Harvey, William. 1578–1657
Nightingale, Florence. 1820–1910
Gray, Henry. 1825–1861
Osler, William. 1849–1919
Pavlov, Ivan Petrovich. 1849–1936

13. Illness and Disease
Fauchard, Pierre. 1678–1761
Virchow, Rudolf Karl. 1821–1902
Pasteur, Louis. 1822–1895
Lister, Joseph. 1827–1912

Fleming, Sir Alexander. 1881–1955

Banting, Sir Frederick Grant.
1891–1941

14. Clinical Psychology and Psychiatry

James, William. 1842–1910

Freud, Sigmund. 1856–1939

Ellis, Havelock. 1859–1939

Adler, Alfred. 1870–1937

Brill, A(braham) A(rden).
1874–1948

Jung, C(arl) G(ustav). 1875–1961

Binswanger, Ludwig. 1881–1966

Klein, Melanie. 1882–1960

Rank, Otto. 1884–1939

Horney, Karen. 1885–1952

Reik, Theodor. 1888–1969

Straus, Erwin. 1891–1975

Sullivan, Harry Stack. 1892–1949

Menninger, Karl Augustus.
1893–1990

Perls, Frederick. 1893–1970

Freud, Anna. 1895–1982

Winnicott, Donald Woods.
1896–1971

Allport, Gordon W(illard).
1897–1967

Fromm, Erich. 1900–1980

Erickson, Milton H. 1901–1980

Lacan, Jacques. 1901–1981

Erikson, Erik H. 1902–

Rogers, Carl Ransom. 1902–1987

Bettelheim, Bruno. 1903–1990

Boss, Medard. 1903–

Frankl, Viktor. 1905–

Maslow, Abraham H(arold).
1908–1970

May, Rollo. 1909–

Berne, Eric Lennard. 1910–1970

Ellis, Albert. 1913–

Kohut, Heinz. 1913–1981

Van den Berg, J. H. 1914–

Bugental, James F. T. 1915–

Wolpe, Joseph. 1915–

Beck, Aaron T. 1921–

Schafer, Roy. 1922–

Glasser, William. 1925–

Foucault, Michel. 1926–1984

Laing, R(onald) D(avid). 1927–1989

Lazarus, Arnold A. 1932–

15. Mathematics

Pythagoras. c.580 B.C–c.500 B.C.

Euclid. fl. c.300 B.C.

Archimedes. c.287–212 B.C.

Diophantus. fl. c.250

Apollonius of Perga. fl. 247–205
B.C.

Descartes, René. 1596–1650

Fermat, Pierre de. 1601–1665

Newton, Sir Isaac. 1642–1727

Euler, Leonhard. 1707–1783

Gauss, Carl Friedrich. 1777–1855

Cauchy, Augustin Louis, Baron.
1789–1857

Boole, George. 1815–1864

Weierstrass, Karl Wilhem Theodor.
1815–1897

Cantor, Georg. 1845–1918

Klein, Christian Felix. 1849–1925

Poincaré, Jules Henri. 1854–1912

Hilbert, David. 1862–1943

Russell, Bertrand Arthur William,
3rd Earl Russell. 1872–1970

Noether, Emmy. 1882–1935

Gödell, Kurt. 1906–1978

Gardner, Martin. 1914–

Robinson, Abraham. 1918–1974

Bourbaki, Nicolas. 20th century

16. Statistics and Probability

Bernoulli, Jakob. 1654–1705

DeMoivre, Abraham. 1667–1754

Laplace, Marquis Pierre Simon de.
1749–1827

Gauss, Carl Friedrich. 1777–1855

Galton, Francis. 1822–1911.

Pearson, Karl. 1857–1936

Gosset, William Sealy. 1876–1937

Fisher, Ronald Aylmer. 1890–1962

Pearson, Egon Sharpe. 1895–1980

Kapitza, Peter Leonidovich.
1894-1984
Pauli, Wolfgang. 1900-1958
Fermi, Enrico. 1901-1954
Heisenberg, Werner. 1901-1976
Dirac, Paul Adrien Maurice.
1902-1984
Wigner, Eugene Paul. 1902-
Gamow, George. 1904-1968
Oppenheimer, J. Robert.
1904-1967
Bloch, Felix. 1905-1983
Mott, Sir Nevill Francis. 1905-
Bethe, Hans Albrecht. 1906-
Tomonaga, Sin-Itiro. 1906-1979
Yukawa, Hideki. 1907-1981
Bardeen, John. 1908-
Chandrasekhar, Subrahmanyan.
1910-
Fowler, William A. 1911-
Wheeler, John Archibald. 1911-
Lamb, Willis Eugene, Jr. 1913-
Townes, Charles H(ard). 1915-
Feynman, Richard P(hillips).
1918-1988
Schwinger, Julian Seymour. 1918-
Yang, Chen Ning. 1922-
Anderson, Philip W. 1923-
Fitch, Val Logsdon. 1923-
Salam, Abdus. 1926-
Gell-Mann, Murray. 1929-
Mössbauer, Rudolf Ludwig. 1929-
Cronin, James W(ilson). 1931-
Penrose, Roger. 1931-
Glashow, Sheldon Lee. 1932-
Weinberg, Steven. 1933-
Josephson, Brian David. 1940-
Hawking, Steven William. 1942-
Binnig, Gerd. 1947-

21. Chemistry
Paracelsus, Philippus Aureolus.
1493?-1541
Boyle, Robert. 1627-1691
Priestley, Joseph. 1733-1804
Lavoisier, Antoine Laurent.
1743-1794

Dalton, John. 1766-1844
Davy, Sir Humphry. 1778-1829
Gay-Lussac, Joseph-Louis.
1778-1850
Berzelius, Jons Jakob. 1779-1848
Faraday, Michael. 1791-1867
Wöhler, Friedrich. 1800-1882
Cannizzaro, Stanislao. 1826-1910
Mendeleev, Dmitrii Ivanovitch.
1834-1907
Perkin, Sir William Henry.
1838-1907
Gibbs, Josiah Willard. 1839-1903
Ramsay, Sir William. 1852-1916
Arrhenius, Svante. 1859-1927
Lewis, Gilbert Newton. 1875-1946
Langmuir, Irving. 1881-1957
Beckman, Arnold Orville. 1900-
Pauling, Linus. 1901-
Libby, Willard Frank. 1908-1980
Flory, Paul John. 1910-1985
Calvin, Melvin. 1911-
Seaborg, Glenn Theodore. 1912-
Woodward, Robert Burns.
1917-1979
Djerassi, Carl. 1923-
Corey, Elias James. 1928-
Ernst, Richard Robert. 1933-
Hoffmann, Roald. 1937-

22. Biological Sciences
Pliny the Elder. c.A.D. 23-A.D. 79
Leeuwenhoek, Anton von.
1632-1723
Linnaeus, Carolus. 1707-1778
Lamarck, Jean Baptiste. 1744-1829
Cuvier, Baron Georges. 1769-1832
Audubon, John James. 1785-1851
Agassiz, Louis. 1807-1873
Darwin, Charles Robert. 1809-1882
Bernard, Claude. 1813-1878
Mendel, Gregor Johann. 1822-1884
Pasteur, Louis. 1822-1895
Fabre, Jean Henri. 1823-1915
Wallace, Alfred Russel. 1823-1913
Huxley, Thomas Henry. 1825-1895
Koch, Robert. 1843-1910

Ramon y Cajal, Santiago.
  1852–1934
Bailey, Liberty Hyde. 1858–1954
Morgan, Thomas Hunt. 1866–1945
Frisch, Karl von. 1887–1982
Huxley, Julian Sorrell. 1887–1975
Sinnott, Edmund Ware. 1888–1968
Muller, Hermann Joseph.
  1890–1967
Haldane, John Burdon Sanderson.
  1892–1964
Krebs, Hans Adolf. 1900–1981
Dubos, René Jules. 1901–1982
McClintock, Barbara. 1902–1992
Beadle, George Wells. 1903–1989
Levi-Montalcini, Rita. 1909–1989
Crick, Francis Harry Compton.
  1916–
Wilkins, Maurice Hugh Frederick.
  1916–
François, Jacob. 1920–

Cohen, Stanley. 1922–
Watson, James Dewey. 1928–
Bishop, John Michael. 1936–

23. Ecology and Environmental Science

Darwin, Charles Robert. 1809–1882
Thoreau, Henry David. 1817–1862
Muir, John. 1838–1914
Frisch, Karl von. 1887–1982
Leopold, Aldo. 1887–1948
Krutch, Joseph Wood. 1893–1970
Lorenz, Konrad. 1903–1989
Carson, Rachel Louise. 1907–1964
Tinbergen, Nikolaas. 1907–1988
Abbey, Edward. 1927–1989
Ehrlich, Paul Ralph. 1932–
Ehrlich, Anne. 1933–
Brown, Lester Russell. 1934–
Goodall, Jane van Lawick. 1934–

Introduction

In his book *The Two Cultures* (1959), English physicist C. P. Snow remarked that "[t]he intellectual life of the whole of Western society is increasingly split into two polar groups . . . at one pole we have the literary intellectuals . . . at the other scientists." With the publication of the thirteenth edition of *The Reader's Adviser* in 1988, an attempt was made to try to bridge the gap between what Snow saw as the unwarranted distinctions between literary and scientific intellectuals (what he termed the "two cultures") by including a separate volume on "The Best in the Literature of Science, Technology, and Medicine."

Volume 5 of the fourteenth edition of *The Reader's Adviser* constitutes only the first revision of that approach. As with the revision of other volumes in *The Reader's Adviser*, we are fortunate to be able to build on the considerable achievements of the contributors to the previous edition. In this case, because of the uniqueness of the venture, this new volume rests particularly strongly on the work of Paul T. Durbin, the volume editor of the thirteenth edition, who remains a contributor to the fourteenth edition. In his introduction to the thirteenth edition, Durbin correctly observed that

> When people think of science, it is often to the medical sciences . . . that their thoughts turn. But students of the sciences, . . . cognizant of the contributions of pharmaceutical research . . . or of biomedical engineering . . . as well as of public health initiatives, . . . spread their thought-net more widely. . . .
>
> Increasingly, the complexity of the interactions among scientists, engineers, and technical personnel . . . and the public in modern society suggests something of the massive impact of science, technology, and medicine on society today. No one can be considered an enlightened citizen in today's world who does not know something about science and technology . . . .
>
> [And general education about science and technology] is important because citizens in a modern democracy are called on with increasing frequency to make value decisions about major technological developments. . . . These issues . . . will be better addressed if ordinary citizens are aware of the best literature on science, technology, and medicine—including the literature of criticism and challenge.

What Durbin wrote six years ago is, if anything, even more true today, and we have attempted to follow his thinking as we revised the thirteenth edition. This volume is not without major changes, however, which are largely twofold. The first major change concerns author profiles. As with other volumes, the number of author profiles has been greatly expanded, and the profiles themselves have been enlarged. Readers thus are presented with a broader range of individuals, both past and present, who have made significant contributions to their fields. The second and more significant change concerns the basic organization of the volume. In this edition, Volume 5 has been fundamentally restructured. The previous edition began with chapters on science, continued with chapters on technology, and concluded with several chapters on the social context of science and technology. Our contention, however, is that both science and technology exist first and foremost in a social context, and that technology is, in fact, more fundamental than science. Much of the literature on science, technology, and medicine, for example, generally is concerned not only with the technical literature within these three branches of human knowledge and practice, but also with the relationship of science, technology, and medicine to society. The organization of this edition thus has been changed to reflect the primacy of social relations and practice.

Given the importance of this structural framework, it is appropriate to comment on each of the primary divisions of the volume. The volume begins with two new introductory chapters: one is general reference, and the other is a general view of science, technology, and medicine. These chapters are followed by Part One, which contains revised and updated chapters on the history, philosophy, and ethics of science, technology, and medicine. Each of these chapters emphasizes the unity of perspective provided by historical, philosophical, and ethical studies, and the ways in which science, technology, and medicine constitute common and mutually reinforcing endeavors. (Ethics is separated from philosophy because of the special ethical challenges engendered by science, technology, and medicine.) Medicine today generally is viewed as a kind of technology; and both technology and medicine today are closely linked to science. Modern scientific theory, too, from Galileo's telescope to the superconducting supercollider, is heavily indebted to technological developments. Moreover, the ethical issues raised by both science and technology are focused by increasingly overlapping issues of responsibility, assessment, risk, and related concerns. The history, philosophy, and ethics of science, technology, and medicine would not be complete without a recognition of such interrelationships.

The last two chapters in Part One make this point even more emphatically. Whereas the first three chapters in Part One approach science, technology, and medicine from the traditional perspectives of history and philosophy, the last two chapters introduce the new interdisciplinary field of science, technology, and society (STS) studies. Here the emphasis is on interdisciplinary approaches that bridge and unite the disciplines of history and philosophy, as well as sociology, political science, cultural studies, and other disciplines, with the unique STS context in which we now live. Chapter 6, "Science, Technology, and Society," does this for STS in general; a new Chapter 7, "Special Issues in Science, Technology, and Society," does it with regard to four special STS themes. These two chapters complement the preceding ones, and the five chapters as a whole provide the contextual framework within which to appreciate the literatures of technology and science that follow in Part Two and Part Three.

Part Two begins with a general overview of engineering and technology, followed by chapters that focus in more detail on the most fundamental technologies of communications, agriculture, and energy, as well as on the different aspects of the technology known as medicine. Of these chapters, the ones on communications technology and agriculture technology are completely new. Part Three begins with the most abstract and pure of the sciences—

mathematics, followed by two chapters on specialized mathematical disciplines—statistics and probability, and information science and computer
science. The remaining chapters in Volume 5 survey the other major sciences—
astronomy, earth sciences, physics, chemistry, biological sciences, and ecology
and environmental science.

It should be noted that many of the chapters in this volume possess special
linkages to material in other volumes. Obvious examples include the chapter on
communications technology and the chapter on the mass media in Volume 3,
the chapter on earth sciences and the chapter on geography in Volume 3, and
the chapters on the philosophy of science, technology, and medicine and on
contemporary issues in philosophy in Volume 4. Even beyond such obvious
connections, because the world in which we live is now permeated and to some
extent defined by science and technology, literature, social sciences, history,
philosophy, and religion, insofar as they reflect on this world, we must also take
science and technology into account. This volume may help provide, in fact, a
context for a substantive unity that pervades the other four volumes as the
material they reference approaches the contemporary. This volume thus
constitutes not only an excursion into C. P. Snow's second culture of science
and technology, but also a bridge to the culture of the humanities and social
sciences.

In conclusion, it is important to note that a number of chapters in this volume
have been written by a community of scholars associated with the Pennsylvania
State University program in Science, Technology, and Society (STS). Nine
contributors are directly associated with the STS Program at Pennsylvania
State, and another four are close colleagues in STS programs at other
universities. This is, therefore, not simply the work of scholars isolated at
diverse institutions, each pursuing his or her own special areas of research;
rather, the intent has been to share insight and understanding, and to produce a
volume with a coherent and unified perspective.

Finally, we would like to acknowledge the help of our research assistant, Mary
Paliotta, secretaries Karen Snare and Pam Kachik, and Paul Rosen, who did
research for the chapter on special issues in science, technology, and society.
We would like to extend a special thanks to all the contributors who worked on
the chapters of this volume for their hard work and diligence in bringing the
volume to fruition.

Carl Mitcham and William F. Williams

CHAPTER 1

Science, Technology, and Medicine: General Reference

Bonnie A. Osif

> The world today is made, it is powered by science; and for any man to abdicate an interest in science is to walk with open eyes toward slavery.
> —JACOB BRONOWSKI, *Science and Human Values*

Science and technology pervade our lives. Topics related to science, technology, and medicine are covered in newspapers and magazines, are alluded to in advertisements, and are the subject of popular television documentaries. Many of our workplaces rely on the products of science and technology. Even our homes are centers of science and technology. We use microwave radiation to cook food in minutes; infrared radiation to switch the television set on and off; personal computers to write and draw; and interactive videos for educational and entertainment purposes.

At the same time, science, technology, and medicine are often regarded as activities of specialists, of an intellectual elite, who use computers and communicate in a language that most people have difficulty understanding. Few of us understand scientific-technological methods or the social contexts within which they are practiced. But insofar as science and its methods provide people with the understanding necessary for making rational decisions, science should not remain the private domain of a privileged elite, but must be made accessible to everyone.

Because science and technology influence people daily, there is a need to understand its basic ideas, processes, and limitations. The decisions concerning foods to buy, implications of medical diagnostics and treatments, and the future uses of nuclear energy will be made by consumers and voters rather than by scientists in lab coats.

The books described in this chapter are general references that can help the reader understand and appreciate science. Chapter 2, as a complement, describes books that provide a general view of science, technology, and medicine. In general, the references listed here do not have to be read from cover to cover, but instead can be used to locate relevant information. To aid the reader in locating sources quickly, the references are divided into several sections, including dictionaries and encyclopedias, directories, guides and indexes, a special section on medicine, and one on otherwise unclassified works. The reference works in these sections should provide the reader with a solid foundation for further scientific study.

DICTIONARIES AND ENCYCLOPEDIAS

Dictionaries and encyclopedias are excellent sources of background information. Whether a scientific novice or an experienced researcher, a person can find in dictionaries and encyclopedias the essential terminology, formulas, and related information necessary for further study. Encyclopedias provide explanations, diagrams, and additional sources of information. Dictionaries listed, especially the *Academic Press Dictionary of Science and Technology* and the *McGraw-Hill Dictionary of Scientific and Technical Terms*, provide thorough, clear definitions for easier reading of scientific books and articles. More specialized science dictionaries are listed within appropriate chapters in this volume.

Academic Press Dictionary of Science and Technology. Acad. Pr. 1992 $115.00. ISBN 0-12-200400-0. Excellent coverage and understandable definitions of more than 125,000 terms in all areas of science and technology.

Blackburn, David, and Geoffrey Holister, eds. *G. K. Hall Encyclopedia of Modern Technology.* Macmillan 1988 $40.00. ISBN 0-8161-9056-9. Thorough descriptions of technologies with many illustrations, diagrams, and photographs.

Brennan, Richard P. *Dictionary of Scientific Literacy.* Wiley 1991 $22.95. ISBN 0-471-53214-2. Current vocabulary clearly defined; includes other sources of information.

Concise Science Dictionary. OUP 1991 $39.95. ISBN 0-19-866167-3. Easy-to-understand explanations of major scientific terms.

Considine, Douglas M., ed. *Van Nostrand's Scientific Encyclopedia.* Van Nos. Reinhold 1989 $195.00. ISBN 0-442-21750-1. Reliable and useful reference for the scientist and the layperson.

Facts on File Scientific Yearbook. 1986–1990. Bks. Demand 1986–1990 $59.70.–$60.30. ISBNs 0-7837-1220-0, 0-7837-1221-9, 0-7837-1569-2, 0-7837-1367-3. Presents illustrated articles on current popular science topics; includes an index and glossary.

Hunt, Candida, and Monica Byles, eds. *The Encyclopedia Dictionary of Science.* Facts on File 1988 $35.00. ISBN 0-8160-2021-3. Broadly covers science; includes definitions, some historical references, and illustrations.

McGraw-Hill Concise Encyclopedia of Science and Technology. McGraw 1989 $110.00. ISBN 0-07-045512-0. Shorter version of the basic reference work listed below.

McGraw-Hill Yearbook of Science and Technology, 1992. McGraw 1991 $80.00. ISBN 0-07-046707-2. Provides annual updates of the *Concise Encyclopedia of Science and Technology.*

Meyers, Robert A., ed. *Encyclopedia of Physical Science and Technology.* 15 vols. Acad. Pr. 1987 $2,500.00. ISBN 0-12-226901-2. Features signed articles by specialists; includes cross references, bibliographies, and indexes.

Mount, Ellis. *Milestones in Science and Technology.* Oryx Pr. 1993 $34.50. ISBN 0-89774-671-6. Provides useful information, dates, people, and describes more than 1,000 scientific discoveries.

New Illustrated Science and Invention Encyclopedia. Stuttman 1987 $207.48. ISBN 0-87475-450-X. Provides useful information on a wide range of inventions.

Oxford Illustrated Encyclopedia of Invention and Technology. OUP 1992 $49.95. ISBN 0-19-869138-6. Presents illustrated articles with a historical focus.

Parker, Sybil P., ed. *McGraw-Hill Dictionary of Scientific and Technical Terms.* McGraw 1989 $90.00. ISBN 0-07-042570-9. Defines more than 100,000 terms for the layperson; includes abbreviations, synonyms, and acronyms.

———, ed. *McGraw-Hill Encyclopedia of Science and Technology.* 20 vols. McGraw 1992 $2,639.00. ISBN 0-07-909206-3. A standard reference with clear articles; uses annual yearbooks for updating information between editions.

Rose, J. *Quick Scientific Terminology.* Wiley 1988 $12.95. ISBN 0-471-85763-7. A self-teaching guide that covers scientific terminology; examines word segments and their meanings.

Rycroft, Michael, ed. *Cambridge Encyclopedia of Space*. Cambridge U. Pr. 1990 $79.50. ISBN 0-521-36426-4. Provides detailed summaries of international space programs, missions, and individuals; well illustrated.

Science Year, 1993: The World Book Annual Science Supplement. World Bk. 1992 ISBN 0-7166-0592-9. Annual supplement to *The World Book Encyclopedia;* especially useful for students.

Sheppard, Helen E., and Julie E. Towell, eds. *International Acronyms, Initialisms and Abbreviations Dictionary*. Gale 1987 $165.00. ISBN 0-8103-2196-3. Helps the reader decipher abbreviations used in science and other subjects.

_____. *Reverse International Acronyms, Initialisms and Abbreviations Dictionary*. Gale 1987 $180.00. ISBN 0-8103-2197-1. Companion to *International Acronyms, Initialisms and Abbreviations Dictionary;* lists 110,000 terms followed by their meanings, abbreviations, and other useful information.

Uvarov, E. B., and Alan Isaacs. *The Penguin Dictionary of Science*. Viking Penguin 1986 $9.95. ISBN 0-14-051156-3. A standard pocket dictionary for students and laypersons.

Walker, Peter M. B. *Cambridge Dictionary of Science and Technology*. Cambridge U. Pr. 1990 $39.50. ISBN 0-521-39441-4. Defines 45,000 terms in 100 fields of science and technology.

The World Book Encyclopedia of Science. 8 vols. World Bk. 1991 $120.00. ISBN 0-7166-3226-8. Quality coverage of the sciences; especially useful for students.

DIRECTORIES

Directories provide easy access and succinct entries for information on important people, organizations, and places. Organizational directories provide addresses, statistical information, and descriptions. Biographical directories may be general, subject-oriented, historical, or geographical. Like other directories, biographical directories provide a great deal of personal and professional information in brief entries.

Organizational Directories

Armstrong, Chris, ed. *World Databases in Medicine*. Bowker-Saur 1993 $165.00. ISBN 0-86291-613-5. Provides a comprehensive source of databases available in the medical field.

Directory of Technical and Scientific Directories: A World Bibliographic Guide to Medical, Agricultural, Industrial, and Natural Science Directories. Oryx Pr. 1988 ISBN 0-582-00602-3. Includes directories published within the past six years—a current tool.

European Research Centres. 2 vols. Gale 1992 $545.00. ISBN 0-8103-9726-9. Profiles more than 17,000 laboratories and science departments.

European Sources of Scientific and Technical Information. Gale 1993 $217.00. ISBN 0-8103-9658-0. An index to sources of scientific information; includes patent offices as well as scientific and technical organizations.

Guide to American Scientific and Technical Directories. Todd Pubns. 1993 $75.00. ISBN 0-915344-15-7. Guide to directories in the physical sciences, life sciences, social sciences, and technology.

Morton, Leslie, and Shane Godbolt, eds. *Information Sources in the Medical Sciences*. 4th ed. Bowker-Saur 1992 $100.00. ISBN 0-86291-596-1. Identifies and reviews literature on all aspects of medicine.

Research Center Directory. 2 vols. Gale 1993 $420.00. ISBN 0-8103-8159-1. Describes more than 12,000 university and nonprofit research centers in North America.

Research Services Directory. Gale 1992 $305.00. ISBN 0-8103-7631-8. Describes 74,400 research sites in the United States and Canada; includes information on facilities and staff.

World Guide to Scientific Associations and Learned Societies. Comp. and ed. by Michael
    Sachs. K. G. Saur 1990 $275.00. ISBN 3-598-20530-9. International coverage of the
    sciences and technology; includes a useful subject index.
Young, Margaret, ed. *Scientific and Technical Organizations and Agencies Directory.* 2
    vols. Gale 1987 $195.00. ISBN 0-8103-2103-3. Guide to more than 12,000 agencies
    involved in scientific or technological research.

Biographical Directories

Abbott, David, ed. *The Biographical Dictionary of Scientists.* 6 vols. P. Bedrick Bks,
    1984–86 $28.00 ea. Vol. 1 *Engineers and Inventors.* ISBN 0-87226-009-7. Vol. 2
    Mathematicians. ISBN 0-87226-008-9. Vol. 3 *Astronomers.* ISBN 0-911745-80-7. Vol. 4
    Biologists. ISBN 0-911745-82-3. Vol. 5 *Chemists.* ISBN 0-911745-81-5. Vol. 6
    Physicists. ISBN 0-911745-79-3. Brief biographies with a historical perspective.
*American Men and Women of Science: A Biographical Directory of Today's Leaders in
    Physical, Biological and Related Sciences, 1992–93.* 8 vols. Bowker 1992 $750.00.
    ISBN 0-8352-3074-0. A basic reference that provides information on scientists in the
    United States and Canada; includes educational background, degrees, and honors for
    more than 125,000 scientists.
Bertsch, Sharon McGrayne. *Nobel Prize Women in Science: Their Lives, Struggles and
    Momentous Discoveries.* Carol Pub. Group 1992 $24.00. ISBN 1-55972-146-4.
    Biographies of women who have won (or helped men win) the Nobel prize; includes
    excellent references for further study.
Bond, Peter. *Heroes in Space: From Gagarin to Challenger.* Blackwell Pubs. 1987 $29.95.
    ISBN 0-631-15349-7. Presents a historical account of the specific missions and
    individuals connected with the space program of the United States and the former
    Soviet Union.
Daintith, John, and others, eds. *Biographical Encyclopedia of Scientists.* 2 vols. Facts on
    File 1981 $125.00. ISBN 0-87196-296-5. Covers 2,000 important scientists from
    antiquity to the present; includes a chronology of the history of science and a list of
    important books and papers.
Davis, Gordon. *Who's Who in Engineering.* AAES 1988 $200.00. ISBN 0-87615-015-6.
    Presents biographies of 12,000 engineers worldwide; includes information on
    engineering societies.
Gillispie, Charles C., ed. *Dictionary of Scientific Biography.* 8 vols. and Supplements 1 and
    2 (1990). Scribner $1080.00. ISBN 0-684-16962-2. Present scientific biographies
    modeled after the *Dictionary of National Biography.* Originally published as 16
    volumes; all essays are signed and include bibliographies.
Ireland, Norma O. *Index to Scientists of the World from Ancient to Modern Times:
    Biographies and Portraits.* Faxon 1962 $13.00. ISBN 0-87305-090-8. Provides infor-
    mation on notable scientists; for example, it lists more than 50 books on Isaac
    Newton (without annotation).
Ogilvie, Marilyn B. *Women in Science: Antiquity through the Nineteenth Century.* MIT Pr.
    1990 $13.50. ISBN 0-262-65038-X. Presents biographies of women scientists to 1910.
Pelletier, Paul A. *Prominent Scientists: An Index to Collective Biographies.* Neal-Schuman
    1992 $49.95. ISBN 1-55570-114-0. Useful as an index to other biographical indexes.
Schlessinger, Bernard, and June H. Schlessinger. *Who's Who of Nobel Prize Winners,
    1901–1990.* Oryx Pr. 1991 $39.50. ISBN 0-89774-599-X. Presents biographies, a short
    list of publications, and commentary on Nobel Prize-winning scientists and their
    accomplishments.
Who's Who in Science and Engineering, 1992-1993. Marquis 1992 $199.00. ISBN 0-8379-
    5751-6. Provides personal, academic, and career information for scientists and
    engineers in the United States and Canada.
Who's Who in Science in Europe. 4 vols. Gale 1992 $885.00. ISBN 0-582-08658-2. Profiles
    more than 26,000 government, industry, and academic scientists in Europe.
Who's Who in Technology. 2 vols. Gale 1989 $380.00. ISBN 0-8103-4950-7. Biographical
    and professional information on more than 37,000 individuals.

GUIDES AND INDEXES

The following works can help the reader locate and use resources in the sciences. In general, guides are written for librarians, students, and practitioners in the specific subject described. A guide describes useful references and indicates where the needed information can be found. Indexes provide access to magazine and journal information. They are especially useful for current information and for subjects in which books are not available. Bibliographical indexes list books and, frequently, other materials, with purchasing information. Some include evaluative descriptions of the items. Guides and indexes are useful in locating and evaluating published material in science, technology, and medicine.

Applied Science and Technology Index. 1958–87. Wilson 1958–79 $215.00. ea. (write for price information on other volumes). Annual subscription also available. Basic subject index to technological subjects, complements *General Science Index.*

Chen, Ching-chih. *Scientific and Technical Information Sources.* 2nd ed. MIT Pr. 1987 $55.00. ISBN 0-262-03120-5. Offers an essential guide to current sources of information; includes 5,300 sources, most published since 1980.

General Science Index. 9 vols. Wilson 1978–1979 $175.00 ea. Annual subscription also available. Basic subject index to the sciences; similar to *Reader's Guide.*

Malinowsky, H. Robert. *Science and Technology Annual Reference Review.* Oryx Pr. 1991 $74.50. ISBN 0-89774-608-2. Useful collection of book reviews on science and technology.

Pure and Applied Science Books, 1876–1982. 6 vols. Bowker 1982 $345.00. ISBN 0-8352-1437-0. Comprehensive; lists 220,000 titles under 56,000 subject categories.

Scientific and Technical Books and Serials in Print, 1994. 3 vols. Bowker 1993 $285.00. ISBN 0-8352-3400-2. Subset of the basic reference for in-print books available in the United States; lists more than 140,000 books and 25,000 periodicals published worldwide.

Walker, Richard D., and C. D. Hurt. *Scientific and Technical Literature: An Introduction for Communication.* ALA 1990 $44.00. ISBN 0-8389-0539-0. Describes the types and purposes of science references.

Wolff, Kathryn, and others. *AAAS Science Book List, 1978–1986.* AAAS 1986 $25.00. ISBN 0-87168-315-6. Part of a AAAS series listing quality books for the student and layperson.

MEDICINE

The following list includes books that describe medical issues clearly for the general reader. The books examine diseases, medical procedures and diagnostics, drugs, terminology, abbreviations, and personal health regimens. Specialized material is discussed in Chapters 12 through 14.

American Medical Association Encyclopedia of Medicine. Random 1989 $44.45. ISBN 0-394-56528-2. Describes diagnostic tests, medical procedures, and health care.

Columbia University College of Physicians and Surgeons Complete Home Medical Guide. Crown Pub. Group 1989 $39.95. ISBN 0-517-57216-8. Well-written guide that describes diseases, tests, first aid, and related medical information.

Complete Drug Reference. 1993 ed. Consumers Reports 1992 $39.95. ISBN 0-89043-587-1. Presents clearly written information on drugs.

Firkin, B. G., and J. A. Whitworth, eds. *Dictionary of Medical Eponyms.* Prthenon Pub. 1987 $48.00. ISBN 0-940813-15-7. Presents definitions of eponyms in medicine; includes a brief historical note in many cases.

Franck, Irene, and David Brownstone. *The Parent's Desk Reference.* P-H Gen. Ref. &
Trav. 1991 $29.95. ISBN 0-13-649989-9. Provides a combination of nutritional and
medical advice; includes other useful information for parents.

Hamilton, Betty, and Barbara Guidos. *Medical Word Finder: A Reverse Medical Dictionary.* Neal-Schuman 1987 $45.00. ISBN 1-55570-011-X. Lists and defines 10,000
words and phrases; includes equivalent technical terms.

————, eds. *MASA: Medical Acronyms, Symbols and Abbreviations.* Neal-Schuman 1988
$55.00. ISBN 1-55570-012-8. Lists and describes more than 732,000 medical terms.

Logan, Carolynn M., and M. Katherine Rice. *Logan's Medical and Scientific Abbreviations.* Lippincott 1987 $28.95. ISBN 0-397-54589-4. Defines abbreviations widely
used in science and medicine.

Medical and Health Information Directory. 3 vols. Gale 1991 $485.00. ISBN 0-8103-
7524-9. Lists and describes more than 40,000 hospitals, associations, and centers.

Merck Manual of Diagnosis and Therapy. Ed. by Robert Berkow. Merck 16th ed. 1992
$26.00. ISBN 0-911910-16-6. The world's most widely used comprehensive reference
book of medicine.

Personal Health Reporter. Gale 1992 $95.00. ISBN 0-8103-8392-6. Summarizes informa-
tion about medical disorders, procedures, and other health-related topics; information gathered from authoritative sources.

Rees, Alan M., and Catherine Hoffman. *Consumer Health Information Source Book.* Oryx
Pr. 1989 $39.50. ISBN 0-89774-408-X. Lists and evaluates health materials; written
for the general reader.

Stanaszek, Mary, and others. *The Inverted Medical Dictionary.* Technomic 1991 $75.00.
ISBN 0-87762-825-4. Provides the correct medical term from either a definition or a
description.

ADDITIONAL REFERENCES

The books described below are useful additions to the reference collection.
Although they cannot be easily classified into any of the above categories, these
references provide helpful information related to science, technology, and
medicine. Additional reference materials that go into these subjects in more
depth can be found throughout the other chapters in this volume.

Asimov, Isaac. *Asimov's Chronology of Science and Discovery.* HarpC 1989 $29.95. ISBN
0-06-015612-0. Provides a historical perspective of major scientific discoveries from
4,000,000 B.C. to 1988.

Bunch, Bryan. *Henry Holt Handbook of Current Science and Technology.* H. Holt & Co.
1992 $50.00. ISBN 0-8050-1829-8. Examines recent advances in the sciences.

Curtis, Anthony R., ed. *Space Almanac.* Gulf Pub. 1992 $36.95. ISBN 0-88415-030-5.
Presents a compilation of useful information on space programs throughout the
world.

Durbin, Paul T., ed. *A Guide to the Culture of Science, Technology, and Medicine.* Free Pr.
1980 o.p. Perhaps the single best reference to the different disciplines that comprise
the field of science, technology, and medicine.

Golob, Richard. *Almanac of Science and Technology: What's New and What's Known.*
HarBraceJ 1990 $59.95. ISBN 0-15-105050-3. Presents a clear account of discov-
eries, theories, and scientific breakthroughs; described in clear articles.

MacKay, A. L. *Dictionary of Scientific Quotations.* Am. Inst. Physics 1991 o.p. Provides an
interesting and useful collection of quotes about science by notable scientists.

Parkinson, Claire L. *Breakthroughs: A Chronology of Great Achievements in Science and
Mathematics. 1200–1930.* Macmillan 1985 $40.00. ISBN 0-8161-8706-1. Chronologi-
cal arrangement of scientific discoveries; includes a brief discussion of the
importance and applications of some discoveries.

Ruffner, James A., and Frank E. Bair. *Weather Almanac*. Gale 1991 $120.00. ISBN 0-8103-2843-7. Provides weather statistics, explanations of important terms, and weather profiles for selected cities in the United States.

Science and Technology Desk Reference: Answers to Frequently Asked and Difficult to Answer Reference Questions in Science and Technology. Gale 1992 $39.95. ISBN 0-8103-8884-7. Presents about 1,500 questions with accompanying answers; includes sources of information.

CHAPTER 2

A General View: Science, Technology, and Medicine

Bonnie A. Osif

I feel that science has come to play such a large role in our lives that it is absolutely crucial that the general public know what is happening.
—JAMES TREFIL

Science and technology permeate everyday life in the twentieth century, and knowledge empowers those who are informed. As JAMES S. TREFIL indicates, there is a responsibility for the general public to become involved in science, to understand scientific research and its practical implications.

Since it is undeniable that science and technology play an invaluable role in the lives of most people, it is surprising that scientific knowledge is not always viewed as essential to a liberal education. Many studies continue to show that most Americans know little about science and technology, and do not seem to show much interest in attaining this knowledge. Instead, people often seem more interested in pseudosciences such as astrology, parapsychology, and creation science. In fact, popular books written about these pseudosciences often are bestsellers in contrast to books about the sciences. A notable exception is STEPHEN HAWKING's *A Brief History of Time*, which did make the bestseller lists. (There is skepticism, however, concerning the number of people who actually read the book.) This also applies to other science books for the general reader.

Many of the books listed in the following sections offer fascinating, well-written descriptions of science. In many cases, they are written by leading scientists and researchers who not only have expertise in their field, but also are enthusiastic spokespeople for their subjects. They provide scientific information at a level that enables laypersons to make informed decisions, and they provide motivation for further study in a particular science.

The scientifically and technologically literate person must understand not only something about science and technology, but also the social context of these disciplines and their consequences on people and society. They must understand the connections among science, technology, and medicine; the impact these fields have on the laboratory, industry, the marketplace, and the political arena; who the practitioners of these fields are; the history of the fields; and the potential implications and influence of these fields on society.

In recent years, it has become easier for people to learn about issues in science, technology, and medicine as the scientific–technical community increasingly has recognized the need to explain its accomplishments through books, articles, and television programs. These presentations usually are understandable to the layperson and tend to highlight areas of significant interest. But the idea that science is an accumulation of facts to be memorized is outdated. Instead, there is greater emphasis today on understanding general scientific and technical concepts. Indeed, science and technology have become an important factor related to social and ethical issues.

The books listed below describe science, technology, and medicine from several viewpoints. Some are firsthand accounts of life in science. Some are accounts of how a particular science or technology has affected human beings. Still others provide a historical perspective on a particular science or technology. Critiques of science, technology, and medicine also are included to illustrate the value of a field to the individual and to society as a whole. All of the books support the underlying theme of advancing scientific and technological literacy in order to foster an informed citizenry, and they provide a good start toward becoming a scientifically and technologically literate person.

SCIENCE

General Science

This section includes books about a variety of sciences. They emphasize breadth of scientific knowledge rather than in-depth study, interdisciplinary study, or explanations of the methods and domain of science. Books on policy and procedural aspects of science also are included in this section. In addition, there are some books on science education that emphasize the broad, societal implications of achieving scientific literacy.

Bauer, Henry H. *Scientific Literacy and the Myth of the Scientific Method.* U. of Ill. Pr. 1992 $24.95. ISBN 0-252-01856-7. Examines the debate over scientific literacy and support for more emphasis on scientific knowledge.

Bell, Robert. *Impure Science: Fraud, Compromise and Political Influence in Scientific Research.* Wiley 1992 $24.95. ISBN 0-471-52913-3. Describes the problem of fraud in science; includes a discussion of defective weaponry and dangerous drugs.

Bowen, Elizabeth, and Beverly E. Schneller. *Writing about Science.* OUP 2nd ed. 1991 $14.95. ISBN 0-19-506274-4. Anthology of scientists who also have been great science writers; includes Rachel Carson, Isaac Asimov, and Richard Feynman.

Brockman, John, ed. *Doing Science.* P-H 1990 $11.95. ISBN 0-13-795097-7. Essays that consider the nature, processes, and domain of science.

Calder, Nigel, and John Newell, eds. *On the Frontiers of Science: How Scientists See Our Future.* Facts on File 1989 $35.00. ISBN 0-8160-2205-4. Examines the implications of science on our lives—today and in the future.

Carr, Joseph J. *The Art of Science: A Practical Guide to Experiments, Observations, and Handling Data.* HighText Pubs. 1992 $19.95. ISBN 1-878707-05-1. A very useful text exploring the "how-to" of science.

Collins, Harry, and Trevor Pinch. *The Golem: What Everyone Should Know about Science.* Cambridge U. Pr. 1993 $19.95. ISBN 0-521-35601-6. Provides a provocative alternative interpretation of the character of science.

Crick, Francis. *What Mad Pursuit: A Personal View of Scientific Discovery.* Basic 1990 $10.00. ISBN 0-465-09138-5. A Nobel Prize-winning biological researcher describes the scientific process.

Darius, Jon. *Beyond Vision: One Hundred Historic Scientific Photographs.* OUP 1984 $39.95. ISBN 0-19-853245-8. Fascinating survey (covering 150 years) that examines the importance of photography to science; claims that some discoveries can be made only through photography.

Dickinson, John P. *Science and Scientific Researchers in Modern Society.* UNIPUB 2nd ed. 1986 $21.00. ISBN 92-3-102427-2. Easy-to-read study of ethical codes and institutional support for scientific workers throughout the world.

Dyson, Freeman. *From Eros to Gaia*. HarpC 1990 $25.00. ISBN 0-06-039111-1. Collection of essays on a variety of science topics; includes a plea for preservation of the Earth's environmental quality.

————. *Infinite in All Directions*. HarpC 1989 $10.00. ISBN 0-06-091569-2. Text of Dyson's Gifford Lecture on science, politics, and several other subjects.

Excitement and Fascination of Science. 3 vols. Annual Reviews 1965-1990. Vol. 1 $25.00. ISBN 0-8243-1602-9. Vol. 2 $25.00. ISBN 0-8243-2601-6. Vol. 3 $90.00. ISBN 0-8243-2603-2. Collection of *Annual Review* articles selected for the general reader.

Fruton, Joseph S. *A Skeptical Biochemist*. HUP 1992 $27.95. ISBN 0-674-81077-5. Perspective on biochemistry and the scientific process.

Gornick, Vivian. *Women in Science: Portraits from a World in Transition*. S&S Trade 1990 $8.95. ISBN 0-671-69592-4. Interviews with women scientists; reveals why they became scientists and what factors contributed to their success.

Grinnell, Frederick. *The Scientific Attitude*. Guilford Pr. 2nd ed. 1992 $16.96. ISBN 0-8962-018-X. Describes how science is practiced.

Groen, Janny, Eefke Smit, and Juurd Eijsvoogel, eds. *The Discipline of Curiosity: Science in the World*. Elsevier 1990 $25.00. ISBN 0-444-88861-6. Good collection of readings by scientists about how they understand their work.

Hatton, John, and Paul P. Plouffe. *The Culture of Science: Essays and Issues for Writers*. Macmillan 1993. ISBN 0-02-351705-0. General essays by a broad spectrum of writers; includes technology despite the title.

Karplus, Walter J. *The Heavens Are Falling: The Scientific Predictions of Catastrophes in Our Time*. Plenum 1992 $24.95. ISBN 0-306-44130-6. Examines the science of prediction for the general reader; discusses how scientific prediction is applied to potential catastrophe.

Keen, Richard A. *Skywatch East: A Weather Guide*. Fulcrum Pub. 1992 $19.95. ISBN 1-55591-091-2. Covers weather phenomena for the general reader.

LaFollette, Marcel C. *Making Science Our Own: Public Images of Science, 1910–1955*. U. Ch. Pr. 1990 $45.00. ISBN 0-226-46778-3. Examines the public view of science by focusing on science coverage in magazines during the first half of the twentieth century.

Mozans, H. J. *Woman in Science*. U. of Notre Dame Pr. 1991 $14.95. ISBN 0-268-01946-0. Profiles notable women in the sciences—from antiquity to the beginning of the twentieth century.

Olby, Robert, and Geoffrey Cantor, eds. *Companion to the History of Modern Science*. Routledge 1989 $89.95. ISBN 0-415-01988-5. Comprehensive perspective on the history of science from 1500 to the present.

Park, David. *The How and the Why: An Essay on the Origins and Development of Physical Theory*. Princeton U. Pr. 1990 $49.50. ISBN 0-691-08492-0. Easy-to-read, interesting account of "What is science?"

Perutz, Max. *Is Science Necessary? Essays on Science and Scientists*. OUP 1991 $9.95. ISBN 0-19-286118-2. Several essays on scientists and the impact of science on society.

Raymo, Chet. *The Virgin and the Mousetrap: Essays in Search of the Soul of Science*. Viking Penguin 1991 $18.95. ISBN 0-670-83315-0. Covers the "experience" of science.

Redner, Harry. *The Ends of Science: An Essay in Scientific Authority*. Westview 1987 $66.00. Examines the sociology of science, paying special attention to political aspects.

Root-Berstein, Robert S. *Discovering*. HUP 1989 $35.00. ISBN 0-674-21175-8. Imaginative examination of the scientific process using the journals of fictional characters as they study the work of several scientists.

Rothman, Milton A. *The Science Gap: Dispelling the Myths and Understanding the Reality of Science*. Prometheus Bks. 1991 $24.95. ISBN 0-87975-710-8. Exposes some common misconceptions about science.

Rothman, Tony. *Science à la Mode: Physical Fashions and Fictions*. Princeton U. Pr. 1991 $29.95. ISBN 0-691-08484-X. Six essays examining the sociology of science.

Rutherford, F. James, and Andrew Ahlgren. *Science for All Americans.* OUP 1991 $24.95. ISBN 0-19-506770-3. Comprehensive overview of what all high school graduates should know about science and technology.

Schwartz, Joseph. *The Creative Moment: How Science Made Itself Alien to Modern Culture.* HarpC 1992 $25.00. ISBN 0-06-016788-2. Presents historical examples illustrating how modern science has alienated itself from the general public.

Science Education in the United States: Issues, Crises, Priorities. Pa. St. U. Pr. 1991 $45.00. ISBN 0-945809-04-2. Describes science education and presents information for reflection on critical school issues.

Tobias, Sheila, and Carl T. Tomizuka. *Breaking the Science Barrier: How to Explore and Explain the Sciences.* College Entrance Examination Board 1992 $14.00. ISBN 0-87447-441-8. Includes considerable concrete knowledge about the fundamentals of science.

Zuckerman, Harriet, and others, eds. *The Outer Circle: Women in the Scientific Community.* Norton 1991 $24.95. ISBN 0-393-02773-2. Excellent study of women in science; includes a comprehensive bibliography.

Physical Sciences

"Physical sciences" is a general term for material that covers a combination of physics, astronomy, meteorology, geology, and chemistry. Distinct from "general science," it is thus listed separately in this chapter. This section lists books on a broad range of generalized subjects within the physical sciences. Specialized books in each discipline can be found in subsequent chapters in this volume.

Barrow, John D. *The World within the World.* OUP 1990 $13.95. ISBN 0-19-286108-5. Examines the philosophical aspects of physics; written for the general reader and the scientist.

Emiliani, Cesare. *Dictionary of the Physical Sciences: Terms, Formulas, Data.* OUP 1987 $19.95. ISBN 0-19-503651-4. Broad coverage, with illustrations, for the attentive general reader.

Gingerich, Owen. *The Album of Science: The Physical Sciences in the Twentieth Century.* Scribner 1989 $80.00. ISBN 0-684-15497-8. Well-illustrated historical examination of the physical sciences, designed for the technically oriented reader.

Knight, David. *A Companion to the Physical Sciences.* Routledge 1989 $25.00. ISBN 0-415-00901-4. Easy-to-read essays on various aspects of the physical sciences.

Magill, Frank N., ed. *Magill's Survey of Science: Physical Science Ser.* 6 vols. Salem Pr. 1992 $475.00. ISBN 0-89356-618-7. Offers 380 articles on a wide range of topics; includes definitions, applications, history, and bibliographies.

Peat, F. David. *Cold Fusion: The Making of a Scientific Controversy.* Contemp. Bks. 1990 $8.95. ISBN 0-8092-4085-8. Account of the Pons and Fleischmann cold fusion episode.

Shapiro, Gilbert. *Physics without Math: A Descriptive Introduction.* P-H 1979 ISBN 0-13-674317-X. Useful introduction to physics, emphasizing concepts rather than mathematics.

Young, Louise B. *The Unfinished Universe.* OUP 1993 $10.95. ISBN 0-19-508039-4. Survey of research findings that seek meaning in the universe.

TECHNOLOGY

Technology mirrors the science section of this chapter. General and understandable books explain a multitude of subjects, items, and issues that can baffle anyone but an engineer in our technological world. Some of these works can be read as novels, providing interesting and informative stories. Others are more likely to be used as references providing information on some specific technological issue.

Brennan, Richard P. *Levitating Trains and Kamikaze Genes: Technological Literacy for the 1990's.* Wiley 1990 $18.95. ISBN 0-471-62295-8. An eclectic but nonetheless interesting and informative collection of articles.

Ferguson, Eugene S. *Engineering and the Mind's Eye.* MIT Pr. 1992 $24.95. ISBN 0-262-06147-3. Argues that good design is not based solely on technical knowledge; includes recent interesting examples, such as the Hubble space telescope.

Fost, Norman, ed. *Science and Technology. Opposing Viewpoints Ser.* Greenhaven 1987. ISBN 0-89908-533-4. Informative readings on many aspects of science and technology, especially their social context.

Gebo, Sue. *What's Left to Eat?* McGraw 1992 $24.95. ISBN 0-07-023534-1. Easy-to-read discussion of food safety, nutrition, pesticides, and additives.

How Things Work in Your Home and What to Do When They Don't. H. Holt & Co. 1987 $16.95. ISBN 0-8050-0126-3. Quality "how to fix it" guide for the homeowner.

Lewis, H. W. *Technological Risk.* Norton 1992 $11.95. ISBN 0-393-30829-4. Examines the risks of technology in everyday life.

Macaulay, David. *The Way Things Work.* HM 1988 $24.95. ISBN 0-395-42857-2. Funny but informative examination of how things are assembled and how they work.

Nickerson, Raymond, and Philip Zodhiates. *Technology in Education: Looking toward 2020.* L. Erlbaum Assocs. 1988 $59.95. ISBN 0-8058-0214-2. Discusses the increasing importance of technology in schools; especially relevant for teachers.

Petroski, Henry. *To Engineer Is Human: The Role of Failure in Successful Design.* Random 1985 $17.95. ISBN 0-312-80680-9. Argues that engineering is more a trial-and-error endeavor than a science; examines such failures as the Tacoma Narrows Bridge and the Hyatt Regency skywalks.

Pierce, John R., and Michael A. Noll. *Signals: The Science of Communications.* W. H. Freeman 1990 $32.95. ISBN 0-7167-5026-0. Interesting description of the rapidly changing field of communications.

Salvadori, Mario, and Matthys Levy. *Why Buildings Fall Down: How Structures Fail.* Norton 1992 $24.95. ISBN 0-393-03356-2. Clearly written explanations of structural failures; includes many illustrations.

Sclar, Deanna. *Auto Repair for Dummies.* Ten Speed Pr. 2nd rev. ed. 1989 $26.95. ISBN 0-89815-341-7. Illustrated, standard guide to help nonmechanical people repair their cars.

Toenjes, Leonard P. *Building Trades Dictionary.* Am. Technical 1989 $34.96. ISBN 0-8269-0403-3. Definitions of terms, tools, equipment, and processes for the building trades or anyone concerned with home repairs.

MEDICINE

Medicine as a specialized technology is covered in greater depth in chapters 12 through 14 in this volume. The books listed below include some basic information, conforming to the "science literacy," "informed citizen" theme of this chapter. In addition, several books are listed that offer practical sources of information for the layperson.

Alster, Kristine B. *The Holistic Health Movement.* U. of Ala. Pr. 1989 $26.95. ISBN 0-8173-0416-9. Comprehensive examination of holistic health practice, care, and business implications.

American Red Cross First Aid and Safety Handbook. Little 1992 $14.95. ISBN 0-316-73646-5. Basic guide to first aid.

Bronzino, Joseph, and Vincent Smith. *Medical Technology and Society: An Interdisciplinary Perspective.* MIT Pr. 1990 $37.50. ISBN 0-262-02300-8. Describes new medical techniques; includes an examination of the social and ethical implications of these techniques.

Cassedy, James H. *Medicine in America: A Short History.* Johns Hopkins 1991 $36.00. ISBN 0-8018-4207-7. Clearly written, interesting book describing the history of medicine in America.

Daintith, John, and Amanda Isaacs, eds. *Medical Quotes: A Thematic Dictionary.* Facts on File 1989 o.p. Collection of quotes on various aspects of medicine and science.

Gevitz, Norman, ed. *Other Healers.* Johns Hopkins 1988 $13.95. ISBN 0-8018-3710-3. Clearly written examination of nontraditional medical practices.

Jonsen, Albert R. *The New Medicine and the Old Ethics.* HUP 1990 $18.95. ISBN 0-674-61725-8. Interesting examination of the historical basis for medical ethics, status, and other related issues.

McBride, David. *Integrating the City of Medicine.* Temple U. Pr. 1988 $39.95. ISBN 0-87722-546-X. Describes African American health care providers in Philadelphia during the twentieth century.

Medicine. Time-Life 1991 $25.93. ISBN 0-8094-7871-4. Provides useful medical information; includes many color illustrations.

Miles, Agnes. *Women, Health and Medicine.* Taylor & Francis 1991 $75.00. ISBN 0-335-09906-8. Survey of health and medical care by and for women.

Oppenheim, Michael. *A Doctor's Guide to the Best Medical Care: A Practical No-Nonsense Evaluation of Your Treatment Options for over 100 Conditions and Diseases.* Rodale Pr. Inc. 1991 $24.95. ISBN 0-87857-982-6. List of medical disorders and treatments, including a graded scale that helps the reader determine the possibility of successful treatment.

Rosenfeld, Isadore. *Second Opinion.* Bantam 1991 $5.99. ISBN 0-553-20562-5. Patient-oriented perspective on medical treatment.

Rosser, Sue V., ed. *Feminism within the Science and Health Care Professions: Overcoming Resistance.* Pergamon 1988 $36.50. ISBN 0-08-035558-7. Examines the resistance that feminism has met in various fields; includes an excellent bibliography.

Szumski, Bonnie, ed. *The Health Crisis: Opposing Viewpoints.* Greenwood 1988 $17.95. ISBN 0-89908-369-2. Various perspectives on medical issues; includes additional references.

Weatherall, M. *In Search of a Cure: A History of the Pharmaceutical Discovery.* OUP 1990 $45.00. ISBN 0-19-261747-8. Historical look at various diseases, drugs, and future prospects.

CHRONOLOGY OF AUTHORS

Thomas, Lewis. 1913–
Cohen, I. Bernard. 1914–
Medawar, Sir Peter Brian. 1915–1987
Asimov, Isaac. 1920–1992
Holton, Gerald. 1922–

Ziman, John M. 1925–
Trefil, James S. 1938–
Gould, Stephen Jay. 1941–
Hawking, Stephen William. 1942–
Davies, Paul. 1946–

ASIMOV, ISAAC. 1920–1992

Science lost one of its most prolific and effective spokespersons when Isaac Asimov died on April 6, 1992. Asimov leaves a legacy of almost 500 books on diverse subjects, from the Bible and SHAKESPEARE (see Vol. 1) to biochemistry and the *How Did We Find Out About* science series for children. Asimov is best remembered as one of the great science fiction writers of the twentieth century. However, he also will be remembered by many as someone who could explain science intelligibly to the general reader in an accurate and enjoyable style.

During his life, Asimov actively worked against the influence of pseudoscience and superstition.

Asimov moved to New York City from Russia at the age of 3. He earned his Ph.D. in chemistry from Columbia University and later taught biochemistry at Boston University's School of Medicine. Asimov's life was devoted mainly to writing, lecturing, and introducing countless people to the wonders and joys of science. He holds the distinction of contributing the word *robotics* to the English language.

Books by Asimov

Asimov's Biographical Encyclopedia of Science and Technology. 1964. Doubleday 2nd rev. ed. 1982 $29.95. ISBN 0-385-17771-2. Compilation of more than 1,500 vignettes of scientists, from ancient Greece to the present day, arranged chronologically, according to the birth date of each major scientist. Each vignette is followed by biographies of other scientists who worked in the same field or a closely related field. The index is organized by biographical number to illustrate the interrelation of the sciences.

Asimov's Chronology of Science & Discovery: How Science Has Shaped the World and How the World Has Affected Science from 4,000,000 B.C. to the Present. HarpC 1989 $29.95. ISBN 0-06-015612-0. Historical perspective on many scientific discoveries.

Asimov's New Guide to Science. Basic rev. ed. 1984 $34.95. ISBN 0-465-00473-3. Easy-to-read, excellent popularization of the life and physical sciences.

How Did We Find Out about Atoms? How Did We Find Out Ser. Walker & Co. 1976 $12.85. ISBN 0-8027-6248-4. One of a series of about 30 informative science books written primarily for school children.

In Joy Still Felt: Autobiography of Isaac Asimov, 1954–1978. Doubleday o.p. Account of Asimov's life from adolescence to adulthood.

In Memory Yet Green: The Autobiography of Isaac Asimov, 1920–1954. Doubleday o.p. Detailed account of Asimov's early years.

A Short History of Biology. Greenwood 1980 repr. of 1964 ed. $35.00. ISBN 0-313-22583-4. Easy-to-read look at the history of biology.

A Short History of Chemistry. Greenwood 1979 repr. of 1964 ed. $45.00. ISBN 0-313-20769-0. Easy-to-read examination of the history of chemistry; similar to his history of biology.

Book about Asimov

Erlanger, Ellen. *Isaac Asimov: Scientist and Storyteller.* Lerner Pubns. 1986 $13.50. ISBN 0-8225-0482-0. A very readable biography, especially for younger readers.

Miller, Marjorie M. *Isaac Asimov: A Checklist of Works Published in the United States.* Bks. Demand 1972 $29.70. ISBN 0-8357-5574-4. List of American, Canadian, and British books and articles; also includes some personal background references on Asimov.

BRONOWSKI, JACOB. 1908–1974

[See Chapter 6 in this volume.]

BUSH, VANNEVAR. 1880–1974

[See Chapter 7 in this volume.]

COHEN, I. BERNARD. 1914–

Born in Far Rockaway, New York, I. Bernard Cohen earned his degrees from Harvard University. He holds the distinction of being the first person in the United States to earn a Ph.D. in the history of science. Later, he established the History of Science Department at Harvard. Cohen has received many fellowships and has won the George Sarton Medal, awarded by the History of Science

Society. Cohen is a prolific author and editor, widely known for his books about SIR ISAAC NEWTON (see also Vol. 4) and BENJAMIN FRANKLIN (see Vol. 1).

BOOKS BY COHEN

Benjamin Franklin's Science. HUP 1990 $35.00. ISBN 0-674-06658-8. Comprehensive account of Franklin's discoveries and role in the history of science.

The Birth of a New Physics. Norton rev. ed. 1985 $19.95. ISBN 0-393-01994-2. Classic book examining the importance of discoveries by Kepler, Galileo, Newton, and Copernicus in the development of modern physics.

Puritanism and the Rise of Modern Science: The Merton Thesis. Rutgers U. Pr. 1990 $45.00. ISBN 0-8135-1529-7. Discusses Robert Merton's ideas about the influence of Protestantism on science and on his critics.

Revolution in Science. HUP 1985 $14.95. ISBN 0-674-76776-0. Scholarly examination of major events in the history of science and the changes that resulted from them.

DAVIES, PAUL. 1946–

Paul Davies received degrees in physics from University College, London. He is now both professor of mathematical physics at the University of Adelaide, Australia, and a fellow of the Institute of Physics, London. Although Davies has continued his studies and research in physics, he also has written many books for the general reader in the fascinating fields of cosmology and physics. All of his books include a discussion of philosophy and encourage the reader to understand the concepts of modern physics and to speculate about the future of physics. Davies also considers the philosophical implications of physics, especially their relationship to religious ideas. Davies's books successfully present the author's excitement and awe to the reader.

BOOKS BY DAVIES

The Cosmic Blueprint: New Discoveries in Nature's Creative Ability to Order the Universe. S&S Trade 1989 $9.95. ISBN 0-671-67561-3. Davies's ideas about the universe.

God and the New Physics. S&S Trade 1983 $9.95. ISBN 0-671-52806-8. New ideas in physics and their relationship to religion.

The Matter Myth: Dramatic Discoveries That Challenge Our Understanding of Physical Realities. (coauthored with John Gribbin). S&S Trade 1992 $25.00. ISBN 0-671-72840-7. Examines physics from Newton's clockwork-based universe to the strange features of our current quantum-based universe.

The Mind of God: The Scientific Basis for a Rational World. S&S Trade 1992 $22.00. ISBN 0-671-68787-5. Philosophical aspects and implications of science for the general reader.

The New Physics. Cambridge U. Pr. 1989 $49.95. ISBN 0-521-30420-2. Clearly written account of the complex ideas of modern physics.

Superforce: The Search for a Grand Unified Theory of Nature. S&S Trade 1985 $9.95. ISBN 0-671-60573-9. Describes the attempt to unify the laws of physics into one theory; written for the general reader.

Superstrings: A Theory of Everything? Cambridge U. Pr. 1988 $39.95. ISBN 0-521-35741-1. Clearly written account of the "superstring" concept.

GOULD, STEPHEN JAY. 1941–

Born in New York City, Stephen Jay Gould received his Ph.D. in paleontology from Columbia University. He is currently Alexander Agassiz Professor of Zoology at Harvard University. Gould has served on the advisory boards of the Children's Television Workshop and *Nova* and is editor of the professional journal *Evolution*. His popular column for *Natural History* illustrates his depth and breadth of scientific knowledge, as well as his wit and graceful writing style.

Many of these essays have been collected and made into popular books, including *The Panda's Thumb, The Flamingo's Smile,* and *Hen's Teeth and Horse's Toes.* Gould has an ability to make science come alive for the general reader, and he is passionate about the value of science. In fact, he is admired equally for the quality of his writing and for his scientific knowledge. An ardent enemy of pseudoscience, Gould is well known as an articulate spokesperson for evolutionary science.

BOOKS BY GOULD

Bully for "Brontosaurus": Reflections in Natural History. Norton 1991 $22.95. ISBN 0-393-02961-1. Gould's fifth collection of articles from *Natural History.*
Ever since Darwin: Reflections in Natural History. Norton 1979 $19.95. ISBN 0-393-06425-5. Broad-ranging essay on themes related to Darwinian evolution; originally published in *Natural History.*
The Flamingo's Smile: Reflections in Natural History. Norton 1987 $17.95. ISBN 0-393-02228-5. Another collection of articles from *Natural History;* includes an essay that describes Gould's research on Bahamian snails.
Hen's Teeth and Horse's Toes: Further Reflections in Natural History. Norton 1984 $6.95. ISBN 0-393-30200-8. Gould's third collection of articles from *Natural History;* compiled and published on the centennial of Darwin's death.
The Individual in Darwin's World. Col. U. Pr. 1991 $7.00. ISBN 0-7486-0227-5. Lecture on the nature of individuals, featuring Gould's viewpoint on evolutionary theory.
The Mismeasure of Man. 1981. Norton 1983 $8.95. ISBN 0-393-30056-0. Refutation of biological determinism and IQ testing; witty but somewhat difficult reading.
Ontogeny and Phylogeny. HUP 1977 $30.50. ISBN 0-674-63940-5. Technical essay on the theme "phylogeny recapitulates ontogeny."
The Panda's Thumb: More Reflections in Natural History. 1982. Norton 1992 $9.95. ISBN 0-393-30819-7. Another collection of articles from *Natural History,* focusing on the evidence for evolution.
An Urchin in the Storm: Essays about Books and Ideas. Norton 1988 $18.95. ISBN 0-393-002492-X. Collection of book reviews as the basis for examining nature, science, and human life.

HAWKING, STEPHEN W. 1942–

Stephen Hawking generally is considered one of the most famous scientists of the twentieth century. A graduate of Oxford (B.S. in mathematics and physics) and Cambridge (Ph.D. in cosmology) universities, Hawking has a brilliant academic record, which has earned him a reputation as the "new Einstein" or the "new Newton." Hawking was honored in 1979, becoming the prestigious Lucasian Professor of Mathematics at Cambridge. He also authored the best-selling book *A Brief History of Time,* which has been made into a movie. Because Hawking has suffered from amyotrophic lateral sclerosis (Lou Gehrig's disease) for more than 30 years, he must use a computer-synthesized voicebox and a motorized wheelchair. His humor, the quality of his lectures, his scientific insight, and his refusal to allow his physical limitations to deter him have brought him great respect, both for his intellect and for his persona.

BOOKS BY HAWKING

Black Holes and Baby Universes and Other Essays. Bantam 1993 $21.95. ISBN 0-553-09523-4. Contains 14 of the physicist's lectures and essays; very readable for the layperson.
A Brief History of Time: From the Big Bang to Black Holes. Bantam 1988 $19.95. ISBN 0-553-05340-X. Bestseller that clearly describes fundamental concepts of the new physics.

Illustrated Companion to a Brief History of Time. Bantam 1992 $25.00. ISBN 0-553-07772-4. Helps the general reader understand the bestseller listed above.

BOOKS ABOUT HAWKING

Ferguson, Kitty. *Stephen Hawking: Quest for a Theory of the Universe.* Bantam 1992 $5.99. ISBN 0-553-29895-X. Conveys an exciting sense of Hawking the man and his role in modern-day theoretical physics.

White, Michael, and John Gribben. *Stephen Hawking: a Life in Science.* NAL-Dutton 1992 $23.00. ISBN 0-525-93447-2. Biography of Hawking, with an explanation of his scientific insights.

HOLTON, GERALD. 1922–

Born in Berlin, Germany, Gerald Holton received his Ph.D. in physics from Harvard University in 1946. Shortly afterward, he launched into what has become a major part of his career—directing a well-known program that originally was developed to teach physical science to liberal arts majors at Harvard. This program, called Harvard Project Physics, became the model for an ambitious program to teach physics in a similar historical manner in colleges and high schools throughout the United States. Later, Holton used this model in a somewhat different manner, establishing a program for the public understanding of science that eventually grew into a journal, *Science, Technology and Human Values.* For many years, Holton was a coeditor of *Daedalus,* the journal of the American Academy of Arts and Sciences. Recently he has gained recognition as a biographer of ALBERT EINSTEIN, and he has worked tirelessly to demonstrate that science requires as much creative imagination as do the arts and humanities.

BOOKS BY HOLTON

The Advancement of Science and Its Burdens: The Jefferson Lecture and Other Essays. Cambridge U. Pr. 1986 $54.95. ISBN 0-521-25244-X. Scholarly book on modern science and its influence on the world.

Albert Einstein, Historical and Cultural Perspectives: The Centennial Symposium in Jerusalem. (coedited with Yehuda Elkana). Princeton U. Pr. 1982 $57.50. ISBN 0-691-08299-5. Presents the major symposium on the centennial of Einstein's birth; this volume includes provocative essays about Einstein's professional and personal life.

Introduction to Concepts and Theories in Physical Science. Princeton U. Pr. 1985 $24.95. ISBN 0-691-08384-3. One of the first (and probably still the best) introductions to physical science for nonscience students; an updated version, revised by Stephen G. Brush.

Science and Its Public: The Changing Relationship. (coedited with William Blanpied). *Boston Studies in the Philosophy of Science.* Kluwer Ac. 1975 $12.50. ISBN 90-277-0657-3. Important collection of essays on the new limits some people want to place on science.

The Scientific Imagination. Cambridge U. Pr. 1978 $49.50. ISBN 0-521-21700-8. Features a new thesis about thematic origins; states that science requires as much imagination as the arts.

Thematic Origins of Scientific Thought: Kepler to Einstein. 1973. HUP rev. ed. 1988 $14.95. ISBN 0-674-87748-9. Case studies illustrating Holton's "thematic" interpretation of the history of science.

MEDAWAR, SIR PETER BRIAN. 1915–1987

Peter Medawar was born as a British citizen in Rio de Janeiro, Brazil. His mother was British and his father was Lebanese. He graduated from Oxford

University in 1939 with a degree in zoology. Medawar taught at the University of Birmingham, England, and University College, London, before becoming the director of the National Institute for Medical Research in Great Britain. He then became head of the division of surgical science at the Clinical Research Centre, as well as professor of experimental medicine at the Royal Institution. A cowinner of the Nobel Prize in physiology and medicine (with Macfarlane Burnet) in 1960, Medawar focused his research mainly on tissue compatibility and the immune system. Although known as a scholar, administrator, and one of the world's great immunologists, he is equally famous for his popularizations of science, listed below.

BOOKS BY MEDAWAR

Advice to a Young Scientist. Basic 1981 $12.00. ISBN 0-465-00092-4. Admirably captures the essence of Medawar's attitude toward the meaning of scientific work.

Aristotle to Zoos: A Philosophical Dictionary of Biology. (coedited with J. S. Medawar). HUP 1983 $25.00. ISBN 0-674-04535-1. Collection of topical and in-depth essays for both browsing and reference; includes more than 150 biological entries.

Induction and Intuition in Scientific Thought. Am. Philos. 1980 $10.00. ISBN 0-87169-075-6. Describes the logical way scientists work in their scientific activities.

The Limits of Science. OUP 1988 $9.95. ISBN 0-19-505212-9. Three essays on the nature and limits of science; somewhat critical, but mostly favorable.

Memoir of a Thinking Radish: An Autobiography. OUP 1986 $19.95. ISBN 0-19-217737-0. Describes Medawar's reflections on his life.

Pluto's Republic: Incorporating "The Art of the Soluble" and "Induction and Intuition in Scientific Thought." OUP 1982 $29.95. ISBN 0-19-217726-5. Essays reprinted from earlier books as well as from *Encounter* and *The Times Literary Supplement;* features a remarkable range of science-related topics.

Structure in Science and Art: Proceedings of Taunus, May 1979. (coedited with J. H. Shelley). Elsevier 1980 $53.00. ISBN 0-444-90150-7. Important essay on D'Arcy Thompson, plus other interesting essays on the role of structure in art and science.

The Threat and the Glory: Reflections on Science and Scientists. Ed. by David Pyke. OUP 1991 $9.95. ISBN 0-19-286128-X. Collection of interviews, book reviews, and essays on a wide range of science topics.

The Uniqueness of the Individual. Dover 1981 $6.95. ISBN 0-486-24042-8. Thought-provoking collection of essays on a variety of subjects, including aging and evolution.

BOOK ABOUT MEDAWAR

Medawar, Jean. *A Very Decided Preference: Life with Peter Medawar.* Norton 1990 $19.95. ISBN 0-393-02820-8. Medawar's life from his college days at Oxford until his death in 1987, written by his wife.

NELKIN, DOROTHY. 1933–

[SEE Chapter 6 in this volume.]

SAGAN, CARL. 1934–

[SEE Chapter 18 in this volume.]

SNOW, SIR CHARLES PERCY. 1905–1980

[SEE Volume 1.]

THOMAS, LEWIS. 1913–

Lewis Thomas was born in Flushing, New York, and received his medical degree from Harvard University, with a specialization in internal medicine and pathology. He has been a professor at several medical schools, as well as dean of the Yale Medical School. Most recently Thomas has been chancellor and president emeritus of the Memorial Sloan-Kettering Cancer Center in New York City and professor of medicine at the Cornell Medical School. His erudite books have earned him a wide audience, making him one of the best-known advocates of science in the United States during the past 20 years. For example, *The Lives of a Cell* won the National Book Award in arts and letters in 1974, and *The Medusa and the Snail* won the American Book Award for science in 1981.

BOOKS BY LEWIS

The Fragile Species: Notes of an Earth Watcher. Macmillan 1992 $20.00. ISBN 0-684-19420-1. Clearly written collection of essays covering topics in medicine and science and their influence on society.

Late Night Thoughts on Listening to Mahler's Ninth Symphony. Bantam 1984 $8.95. ISBN 0-553-34533-8. Collection of broad-ranging essays, mostly from *Discover* magazine.

The Lives of a Cell: Notes of a Biology Watcher. Bantam 1984 $4.95. ISBN 0-553-27580-1. Collection of essays that appeared originally in *The New England Journal of Medicine* (1971–73).

The Medusa and the Snail: More Notes of a Biology Watcher. Viking Penguin 1979 o.p. More essays that originally were published in *The New England Journal of Medicine* (1974–79).

The Youngest Science: Notes of a Medicine Watcher. Bantam 1984 $6.95. ISBN 0-553-34066-2. Partly autobiographical survey of twentieth-century medicine; includes some of Thomas's earlier essays.

TREFIL, JAMES S. 1938–

James Trefil was born in Chicago and educated at the University of Illinois, Oxford University, and Stanford University, where he earned a Ph.D. in physics. Currently Clarence H. Robinson Professor of physics at George Mason University, he is among the well-respected scientists who have the skill to translate physics for the general reader into prose worthy of an English major. For example, his "meditation trilogy," described below, recounts interesting examples, clear explanations, and the wonder of science in Trefil's beautiful and lively language.

BOOKS BY TREFIL

Dark Side of the Universe. Doubleday 1989 $9.95. ISBN 0-385-26212-4. Discusses astronomical dark matter in Trefil's personal, clear style.

Meditations at Sunset: A Scientist Looks at the Sky. Macmillan 1987 $16.95. ISBN 0-684-18787-6. Part of the "meditation trilogy," along with *Meditations at 10,000 Feet* and *A Scientist at the Seashore.*

Meditations at 10,000 Feet: A Scientist in the Mountains. Macmillan 1987 $8.95. ISBN 0-02-025890-0. Trefil's thoughts on geology are used to explain science.

The Moment of Creation: Big Bang Physics from before the First Millisecond to the Present Universe. Macmillan 1984 $10.95. ISBN 0-02-096770-5. The main ideas of cosmology in a readable, comprehensive format.

One Thousand and One Things Everyone Should Know about Science. Doubleday 1992 $20.00. ISBN 0-385-24795-8. Contains 1,001 brief entries on science; designed for informative browsing.

Reading the Mind of God. Macmillan 1989 $18.95. ISBN 0-684-18796-5. Clear explanation of physical science topics, including spectroscopy, radioactivity, and the principle of universality; for the general reader.

A Scientist at the Seashore. Macmillan 1987 $8.95. ISBN 0-02-025920-4. Trefil focuses on the seashore as a springboard for musings on such topics as waves, tides, and aerodynamics.

ZIMAN, JOHN M. 1925–

A British thereotical physicist and philosopher of science, John Ziman was educated in New Zealand and at Balliol College, Oxford University. He has taught at several British universities, including Oxford, Cambridge, the University of Bristol, and the Imperial College of Science and Technology, London (Science Policy Support Group). Throughout his career, Ziman has been involved primarily with the social dimensions of science. He was an early interdisciplinary researcher who not only studied the effects of science on society, but also examined the social aspects of science. While at the University of Bristol, Ziman developed a course on the social relations of science and technology. He was also an early member of a "leftist" group of scientists who established the Society for Social Responsibility in Science.

Ziman is well known for a series of lucid books on the nature of science. His *An Introduction to Science Studies* (1985) is regarded as one of the best overviews and presentations of science/technology/society studies. This and other works have earned him a reputation as the best British interpreter of science for college students—comparable to GERALD HOLTON of the United States. An active member of the Council for Science and Society, Ziman remains an influential supporter of the formulation of a social model of science for use by science educators.

BOOKS BY ZIMAN

The Force of Knowledge: The Scientific Dimension of Society. Cambridge U. Pr. 1976 o.p. Excellent perspective on science, technology, and society, based on a lecture series for undergraduate science students at Bristol University.

An Introduction to Science Studies: The Philosophical and Social Aspects of Science and Technology. Cambridge U. Pr. 1987 $19.95. ISBN 0-521-34680-0. Remarkable tour de force, covering all aspects of this field.

Knowing Everything about Nothing: Specialization and Change in Research Centres. Cambridge U. Pr. 1987 $39.95. ISBN 0-521-32385-1. Examines the increasing specializations in science careers, based on interviews with scientists; a British perspective.

Public Knowledge: An Essay Concerning the Social Dimension of Science. Cambridge U. Pr. 1976 o.p. An introductory sociological analysis of science. Argues that science is a form of public knowledge based on a consensus of rational opinion and contrasts scientific and nonscientific disciplines.

Puzzles, Problems and Enigmas: Occasional Pieces on the Human Aspects of Science. Cambridge U. Pr. 1981 $34.95. ISBN 0-521-23659-2. Book reviews, radio programs, public lectures, and essays on a wide variety of science topics.

Reliable Knowledge: An Exploration of the Grounds for Belief in Science. Cambridge U. Pr. 1991 $8.95. ISBN 0-521-40670-6. Scholarly but clear discussion on the nature of science and how science can be communicated effectively.

Teaching and Learning about Science and Society. Cambridge U. Pr. 1980 $29.95. ISBN 0-521-23221-X. Describes the essential components of a course on science, technology, and society.

PART ONE

SCIENCE, TECHNOLOGY, AND SOCIETY

CHAPTER 3

History of Science, Technology, and Medicine

Henry Lowood

Considering the part played by the sciences in the story of our Western
civilization, it is hardly possible to doubt the importance which the history of
science will sooner or later acquire both in its own right and as the bridge
which has been so long needed between the Arts and the Sciences.
—HERBERT BUTTERFIELD, *The Origins of Modern Science, 1300–1800*

All history is relevant, but the history of technology is the most relevant.
—MELVIN KRANZBERG, *Technology and Culture*

Those who study the historical development of science, medicine, and
technology have benefited greatly from the rapid growth of institutions and
disciplines engaged in technical and scientific endeavors since the mid-
twentieth century. From a handful of seminars and chairs in the 1930s, each of
these scholarly communities now comprises dozens of academic journals,
professional societies, and doctoral programs. At the same time, historians of
science, technology, and medicine have expanded their scope and research
strategies. In the 1990s, research and publication in these fields transcends
many areas of cultural, social, economic, and political history. Moreover, the
perspectives gained by these studies have enriched discourse in philosophy,
sociology, anthropology, communications, and many other disciplines.

There has been increasing eclecticism within the communities formulating
research programs in the history of science, technology, and medicine. Thus,
the mutual influences of these multidisciplinary specializations with each other
and with other fields, such as the social sciences, concerned with the growing
complex of modern "techno-science" have blurred the clear purposes of the
first several generations of scholars (a few of whom are profiled in this chapter).
As young disciplines, the histories of science, technology, and medicine focused
on heroic moments and the sequence of path-defining discoveries and
inventions. The earliest generation of scholars who studied these issues, such as
GEORGE SARTON in the early twentieth century, tended to agree on the
cumulative and progressive nature of the growth of knowledge in Western
civilization. Consequently, they organized their research around moments that
defined the course of a developmental path. By the 1970s, many of the
embedded assumptions in this view of progress in science, technology, and
medicine had been challenged. The ensuing debates about the autonomy,
contingency, and institutional matrix of technical and scientific activities set the
stage for new syntheses, as well as for divergence and eclecticism. To date, the
"new" histories of science, technology, and medicine have not been presented
to the general reader with quite the vigor of the older generation of

proselytizing scholars. As a result, popular treatments, surveys, and television documentaries generally present the progress of knowledge as linear, continuous, and relatively independent of social and political factors.

This chapter is devoted to general historical studies of the natural sciences, technology, and medicine. Related materials can be found in the chapters that focus on specific disciplines, especially Chapter 4, "Philosophy of Science, Technology, and Medicine"; Chapter 5, "Ethics in Science, Technology, and Medicine"; and Chapter 6, "Science, Technology, and Society." In general, this chapter follows the topical and chronological organization of the *Isis Current Bibliography* for the history of science and the *Current Bibliography in the History of Technology*, which are the primary bibliographic resources in their respective fields.

GENERAL WORKS

Science, technology, and medicine are woven into the fabric of Western civilization. Given the complexity of this rich tapestry, historians have narrowed their scope by selecting specific strands to trace through individual disciplines, time periods, and countries. In contrast, the following general works have been selected for their breadth and worldwide scope, often linking several subjects and surveying long spans of time.

Adas, Michael. *Machines as the Measure of Man: Science, Technology, and Ideologies of Western Dominance*. Cornell Univ. Pr. 1990 $15.95. ISBN 0-8014-9760-4. Outstanding survey of the relationship between Western science, technology, and colonialism; seminal work in an emerging specialization in the history of science and technology.

Bernal, J. D. *Science in History*. 4 vols. MIT Pr. 1971 $40.00. ISBN 0-262-52082-6. Survey of the social context of science, written by one of England's most prominent Marxist historians.

Bijker, Wiebe, and others, eds. *The Social Construction of Technological Systems*. MIT Pr. 1989 $13.95. ISBN 0-262-52137-7. Features a pioneering collection of articles outlining an approach to the history of technology, emphasizing the significant connections between the processes of social negotiation and technological innovation.

Boorstin, Daniel J. *The Discoverers: A History of Man's Search to Know His World and Himself*. Random 1985 $12.95. ISBN 0-396-72625-1. Offers an easy to read and broad interpretation of the role of science in Western civilization, written by a Pulitzer Prize-winning historian and former Librarian of Congress.

Bronowski, Jacob. *The Ascent of Man*. Little 1976 $29.95. ISBN 0-316-10933-9. Interesting, "personal view" of the history of science in the broader context of Western culture.

Burke, James. *The Day the Universe Changed*. Little 1987 $22.95. ISBN 0-316-11706-4. A provocative and witty (though at times overly glib) interpretation of science for the general readers; companion to the television series of the same title. Includes lively images.

Butterfield, Herbert. *The Origins of Modern Science*. Free Pr. 1965 $14.95. ISBN 0-02-905070-7. Classic study, emphasizing the central role of science in Western civilization and the discontinuity associated with the scientific revolution.

Bynum, W. F., and others. *Dictionary of the History of Science*. Princeton U. Pr. 1981 $17.95. ISBN 0-691-02384-0. Useful dictionary of concepts that have been prominent in the development of scientific ideas since antiquity.

Cohen, I. Bernard. *Album of Science: From Leonardo to Lavoisier, 1450–1800*. Scribner 1980 $80.00. ISBN 0-684-15377-7. An attractive, pictorial overview of science from the Renaissance to the Enlightenment.

————. *Revolution in Science*. HUP 1985 $34.95. ISBN 0-674-76777-2. Ambitious study of the concept of scientific revolution, arguing for incremental transformations in scientific thought rather than discontinuous paradigm shifts.

Dampier, William C. *A History of Science*. Cambridge U. Pr. 1948 $29.95. ISBN 0-521-09366-X. Presents a useful, but somewhat dated, single-volume survey of science.

Daumas, Maurice, ed. *A History of Technology and Invention: Progress through the Ages*. 3 vols. Crown Pub. Group 1978 o.p. An encyclopedic, multi-authored survey that covers all aspects of technology; well illustrated. Includes Vol. 1 *The Origins of Technological Civilization*; Vol. 2 *The First Stages of Mechanization*; Vol. 3 *The Expansion of Mechanization, 1725–1860*.

Dijksterhuis, E. J. *The Mechanization of the World Picture*. Trans. by C. Dikshoorn. Princeton U. Pr. 1986 $19.95. ISBN 0-691-02396-4. Examines the development of physical science from antiquity to Newton, arguing that the mechanization of nature led to the mathematization of science.

Duhem, Pierre. *To Save the Phenomena: An Essay on the Idea of Physical Theory from Plato to Galileo*. Midway Repr. Ser. U. Ch. Pr. 1985 $9.95. ISBN 0-226-16921. Brief, pioneering study that applies Duhem's instrumentalist philosophy of science to examine the historical rift between descriptive astronomy and physical cosmology.

Giedion, Siegfried. *Mechanization Takes Command: A Contribution to Anonymous History*. Norton 1969 $16.95. ISBN 0-393-00489-9. A provocative survey of the impact of mechanization on culture.

Gillispie, Charles C. *The Edge of Objectivity: An Essay in the History of Scientific Ideas*. Princeton U. Pr. 1960 $15.95. ISBN 0-685-04159-X. Argues that science created an objective world described by measurement rather than penetrated by sympathy. Fundamental study of the development of modern science, written with wit and insight.

Hall, A. R., and Maria Boas Hall. *A Brief History of Science*. Iowa St. U. Pr. 1988 repr. of 1964 ed. o.p. Compact survey of science, written by respected science historians of their generation.

Harding, Sandra. *The Racial Economy of Science: Toward a Democratic Future*. Ind. U. Pr. 1993 ISBN 0-253-20810-6. Provocative analysis of the history of science and its future role in society by a noted feminist scholar.

Holton, Gerald. *Thematic Origins of Scientific Thought: Kepler to Einstein*. HUP 1988 $14.95. ISBN 0-674-87748-9. Examines thematic threads that illustrate the role of individual creativity in the physical sciences.

Inkster, Ian. *Science and Technology in History: An Approach to Industrial Development*. Rutgers U. Pr. 1991 $50.00. ISBN 0-8135-1680-3. Offers a useful introduction to show the relationship between economics and economic growth and research and development.

Jaffe, Bernard. *Men of Science in America: The Story of American Science Told Through the Lives and Achievements of Twenty Outstanding Men from Earliest Colonial Times to the Present Day*. Ed. by Bernard I. Cohen. *Three Centuries of Science in Amer. Ser.* Ayer 1980 repr. of 1958 ed. $62.00. ISBN 0-405-12551-8. Introductory survey from colonial times to the early twentieth century; somewhat dated.

Kitcher, Philip. *Advancement of Science: Science Without Legend, Objectivity Without Illusions*. OUP 1993 $39.95. ISBN 0-19-504628-5. Insightful analysis of the history of science focusing on dispelling traditional "myths" of scientific knowledge.

Kuhn, Thomas S. *The Essential Tension: Selected Studies in Scientific Tradition and Change*. U. Ch. Pr. 1979 $13.95. ISBN 0-226-45806-7. Includes a selection of articles, essays, and lectures written between 1959 and 1974 on historiographic and historical themes.

————. *The Structure of Scientific Revolutions. Foundations of the Unity of Science Ser.* U. Ch. Pr. 1970 $9.95. ISBN 0-226-45804-0. Argues that science normally develops cumulatively, but periodically undergoes discontinuous and radical transformations of the conceptual paradigms underlying scientific research. Appealing and highly influential study of scientific change.

Layton, E. T., and others, eds. *The Dynamics of Science and Technology*. Kluwer Ac. 1978 $72.50. ISBN 90-277-0880-0. Features a collection of cross-disciplinary essays on the interactions of science, technology, and medicine.

Lindberg, David C. *The Beginnings of Western Science: The European Scientific Tradition in Philosophical, Religious and Institutional Context, 600 B.C. to A.D. 1450*. U. Ch. Pr. 1992 $57.00. ISBN 0-226-48231-6. Studies the origins of science as an activity in Western society; destined to be a classic.

McNeil, Ian, ed. *An Encyclopedia of the History of Technology*. Routledge 1990 o.p. Presents 21 detailed articles on broad areas within the historical development of technology, such as "ferrous metals" and "electricity"; emphasizes technical development of these topics rather than contextual factors.

Mason, Stephen F. *A History of the Sciences*. Macmillan 1962 $10.95. ISBN 0-02-093400-9. A comprehensive, single-volume survey of the sciences from antiquity to the twentieth century, originally titled *Main Currents of Scientific Thought*.

Needham, Joseph. *Science and Civilisation in China*. 6 vols. Cambridge U. Pr. 1954–91. Vol. 1 *Introductory Orientations*. $84.95. ISBN 0-521-05799-X. Vol. 2 *History of Scientific Thought*. $130.00. ISBN 0-521-05800-7. Vol. 3 *Mathematics and the Sciences of the Heavens and the Earth*. $185.00. ISBN 0-521-05801-5. Vol. 4 *Physics and Physical Technology*. 3 pts. Pt. 1. *Physics* $110.00. ISBN 0-521-05802-3. Pt. 2 *Mechanical Engineering*. $150.00. ISBN 0-521-05803-1. Pt. 3 *Engineering and Nautics*. $185.00. ISBN 0-521-07060-0. Vol. 5 *Chemistry and Chemical Technology*. 6 pts. Pt. 1 *Paper and Printing*. $120.00. ISBN 0-521-08690-6. Pt. 2 *Spagyrical Discovery and Invention: Magisteries of Gold and Immortality*. $120.00. ISBN 0-521-08571-3. Pt. 3 *Spagyrical Discovery and Invention: Historical Survey from Cinnabar Elixirs to Synthetic Insulin*. $120.00. ISBN 0-521-21028-3. Pt. 4 *Spagyrical Discovery and Invention: Apparatus and Theory*. $150.00. ISBN 0-521-08573-X. Pt. 5 *Spagyrical Discovery and Invention: Physiological Alchemy*. $130.00. ISBN 0-521-08574-8. Pt. 7 *Military Technology: The Gunpowder Epic*. $130.00. ISBN 0-521-30358-3. Vol. 6 *Biology and Biological Technology. Agriculture* $130.00. ISBN 0-521-25076-5. Presents a monumental study of Chinese science and technology by an acknowledged authority; collaborators include colleagues with expertise in selected areas.

Olby, R. C., and others. *Companion to the History of Modern Science*. Routledge 1990 $89.95. ISBN 0-415-01988-5. Presents 67 topical articles that illustrate new interpretative viewpoints and approaches to the history of science. Useful, single-volume orientation to the state of historical writing and recent historiography.

Ronan, Colin, and Joseph Needham, eds. *The Shorter Science and Civilisation in China*. Cambridge U. Pr. 1986 $24.95. ISBN 0-521-29286-7. Useful abridgment of Needham's multivolume survey.

Schiebinger, Londa. *The Mind Has No Sex? Women in the Origins of Modern Science*. HUP 1991 $12.95. ISBN 0-674-57625-X. Presents an important contribution to the growing field of gender and feminist studies; highlights women and science.

Singer, Charles. *A Short History of Scientific Ideas to 1900*. OUP 1959 $9.95. ISBN 0-19-881049-0. Offers a useful, but dated, survey by a pioneer in the history of science.

Singer, Charles, and others, eds. *A History of Technology*. 8 vols. OUP 1955–84. Vols. 1–7 $98.00 ea. Vol. 8 $45.00. ISBNs 0-19-858105-X, 0-19-858106-8, 0-19-858107-6, 0-19-858108-4, 0-19-858109-2, 0-19-858151-3, 0-19-858155-6, 0-19-822905-4. An encyclopedic survey that covers the breadth and depth of the technical arts, technics, and technology from antiquity to the mid-twentieth century.

Taton, Rene, ed. *A General History of the Sciences*. 4 vols. Thames & Hudson 1963–66 o.p. Useful multiauthored survey translated from the original French edition.

Thorndike, Lynn. *A History of Magic and Experimental Science*. 8 vols. Col. U. Pr. 1923–64 $98.00 ea. ISBNs 0-231-08794-2, 0-231-08795-0, 0-231-08796-9, 0-231-08797-7, 0-231-08798-5, 0-231-08799-3, 0-231-08800-0, 0-231-08801-9. Features a detailed compilation of information, particularly focusing on minor figures and primary sources; places the occult sciences and pseudosciences in historical context.

Whitehead, Alfred North. *Science and the Modern World.* Free Pr. 1967 $12.95. ISBN 0-02-935190-1. Provocative, philosophical perspective on the role of science in Western thought and culture.

Wightman, William. *The Growth of Scientific Ideas.* Greenwood 1974 repr. of 1966 ed. $65.00. ISBN 0-8371-7484-8. Survey of the development of science from antiquity to the twentieth century.

Williams, Trevor I. *The History of Invention: From Stone Axes to Silicon Chips.* Facts on File 1987 $40.00. ISBN 0-8160-1788-3. Features a fast-paced introduction to the history of technology, focusing on inventions; designed for the general reader.

REFERENCE WORKS

The following reference works are useful to readers with specialized interests in the history of science, technology, and medicine. Included are general reference works, bibliographies, and sources of biographical information in the history of science, technology, and medicine.

Asimov, Isaac. *Asimov's Biographical Encyclopedia of Science and Technology.* Doubleday 1982 $29.95. ISBN 0-385-17771-2. Biographical guide arranged by birth date; covers figures from antiquity to the twentieth century.

Batschelet, Margaret W. *Early American Scientific and Technical Literature: An Annotated Bibliography of Books, Pamphlets, and Broadsides.* Scarecrow 1990 $20.00. ISBN 0-8108-2318-7. Lists more than 800 titles on scientific, medical, and technical topics published in the British-ruled North American colonies (excluding Canada) between 1665 and 1799.

Black, George W., Jr. *American Science and Technology: A Bicentennial Bibliography.* So. Ill. U. Pr. 1979 $15.95. ISBN 0-8093-0898-3. Lists more than 1,000 articles published during the American bicentennial that examine the history of science and technology.

Blackburn, David, and Geoffrey Holister, eds. *The G.K. Hall Encyclopedia of Modern Technology.* Macmillan 1987 $40.00. ISBN 0-8161-9056-9. Beautifully illustrated survey covering nine fields of technology throughout history. Includes bibliography.

Brennan, Richard P. *Dictionary of Scientific Literacy.* Wiley 1991 $22.95. ISBN 0-471-53214-2. More than 650 scientific definitions designed to relate technical terms to laypeople.

Brush, Stephen G. *The History of Modern Science: A Guide to the Second Scientific Revolution, 1800–1950.* History of Technology and Science Ser. Iowa St. U. Pr. 1988 $41.95. ISBN 0-8138-0883-9. Presents an overview, introduction, and guide to sources; designed for general readership, particularly useful for secondary teachers.

Brush, Stephen G., and Lanfranco Belloni. *The History of Modern Physics: An International Bibliography.* History of Science and Technology Ser. Garland 1983 o.p. Annotated bibliography of scholarship that focuses on physics since Röntgen's discovery of X-rays in 1895.

Brush, Stephen G., and others. *The History of Meteorology and Geophysics: An Annotated Bibliography.* History of Science and Technology Ser. Garland 1985 o.p. Includes carefully annotated entries on all aspects of the history of these geosciences.

Bynum, William F., and others, eds. *Dictionary of the History of Science.* Princeton U. Pr. 1985 $75.00. ISBN 0-691-02384-0

Channell, David F. *The History of Engineering Science: An Annotated Bibliography.* Garland 1990 o.p. Good selection with useful annotations.

Concise Dictionary of Scientific Biography. Scribner 1981 $70.00. ISBN 0-684-16650-X. Handy reference work derived from the definitive biographical encyclopedia listed under Gillispie below.

Cortada, James W. *A Bibliographic Guide to the History of Computing, Computers, and the Information Processing Industry.* Greenwood 1990 $69.50. ISBN 0-313-26810-X. Extensive compilation by a diligent bibliographer.

Daintith, John, and others. *A Biographical Encyclopedia of Scientists*. 2 vols. Facts on File 1981 $125.00. ISBN 0-87196-396-5. Contains some 2,000 entries on scientists, both living and dead; emphasis is on the modern and contemporary periods.

Dauben, Joseph W. *The History of Mathematics from Antiquity to the Present: A Selective Bibliography*. Garland 1985 o.p. Provides more than 2,000 annotated entries compiled by "49 scholars on five continents."

Debus, A. G., ed. *World Who's Who in Science: A Biographical Dictionary of Notable Scientists from Antiquity to the Present*. Western Pub. 1968 o.p. Comprehensive dictionary containing brief entries for some 30,000 scientists, most from the twentieth century.

DeVorkin, David H. *The History of Modern Astronomy and Astrophysics: A Selected, Annotated Bibliography*. Garland 1985 o.p. Covers research from the invention of the telescope to the mid-twentieth century; includes about 1,500 annotated entries.

Dunbar, Gary S. *The History of Modern Geography: An Annotated Bibliography of Selected Works*. Garland 1985 o.p. Reflects scholarship in most major Western languages from 1750 to the present; includes more than 1,700 annotated entries.

Durbin, Paul T., ed. *A Guide to the Culture of Science, Technology, and Medicine*. Free Pr. 1984 o.p. Introductory essays and useful bibliographies for all the major specialties within the history of science, technology, and medicine.

Elliott, Clark A. *Biographical Dictionary of American Science: The Seventeenth through the Nineteenth Centuries*. Greenwood 1979 $65.00. ISBN 0-313-20419-5. Provides detailed entries on about 600 American scientists.

Erlen, Jonathon. *The History of the Health Care Sciences and Health Care, 1700–1980: A Selective Annotated Bibliography*. Garland 1984 o.p. Reflects historical scholarship in a variety of medical sciences and specialties; includes more than 5,000 annotated entries.

Gibilisco, Stan. *The Concise Illustrated Dictionary of Science and Technology*. TAB Bks. 1992 $36.95. ISBN 0-8306-4152-1. Designed for high school students; more than 5,000 easy-to-understand definitions.

Gillispie, Charles C., ed. *Dictionary of Scientific Biography*. 16 vols. Scribner 1970–80 $1,080.00. ISBN 0-684-16962-2. Presents alphabetized biographical articles written by specialists; often with useful bibliographies. A monumental reference source for the history of science, which includes important figures from the history of philosophy, medicine, and technology.

Harkányi, Katalin. *The Natural Sciences and American Scientists in the Revolutionary Era*. Greenwood 1990 $65.00. ISBN 0-313-26547-X. Extensive bibliography covering a broad range of topics and formats.

Herzenberg, Caroline L. *Women Scientists from Antiquity to the Present: An Index*. Locust Hill Pr. 1986 $30.00. ISBN 0-933951-01-9. Biographical index for about 2,500 women active in the development of the natural and social sciences, engineering, and medicine.

Home, R. W. (with the assistance of Mark J. Gittins). *The History of Classical Physics: A Selected, Annotated Bibliography*. History of Science and Technology Ser. Garland 1984 o.p. Focuses on the period from Sir Isaac Newton to the end of the nineteenth century; includes annotated entries for about 1,200 books and articles.

Isis Cumulative Bibliography, 1966–1975. Ed. by John Neu. Cassell Vol. 1 *Personalities and Institutions*. 1980 $200.00. ISBN 0-7201-1515-9. Vol. 2 *Subjects, Periods and Civilizations*. 1985 $200.00. ISBN 0-7201-1516-7. Provides an authoritative index of articles and books in the history of science and related fields, drawn from the annual bibliographies published in the scholarly journal *Isis*.

Kren, Claudia. *Medieval Science and Technology: A Selected, Annotated Bibliography*. Ed. by Ellen Wells. *History of Science and Technology Ser*. Garland 1985 o.p. Provides more than 1,400 annotated entries, emphasizing Latin-oriented Western society.

Kronick, David A. *Scientific and Technological Periodicals of the Seventeenth and Eighteenth Centuries: A Guide*. Scarecrow 1991 $39.50. ISBN 0-8108-2492-2. Presents a straightforward, informative bibliographic guide to the topic; covers the period from the founding of the *Philosophical Transactions* of the Royal Society of London to the end of the eighteenth century.

McGraw-Hill Concise Encyclopedia of Science and Technology. McGraw 1989 $114.50. ISBN 0-07-045512-0. Condensed version of the original 20-volume set.

Macmillan Encyclopedia of Science. 12 vols. Macmillan $325.00. ISBN 0-02-941346-X. Written for students grades 6–12 with basic science information as well as articles on applied science topics of current interest.

Messadie, Gerald. *Great Scientific Discoveries.* Chambers 1992 $9.95. ISBN 0-550-17002-2

Meyers, Robert A. *Encyclopedia of Physical Science and Technology.* 15 vols. Acad. Pr. 1987 $2,500.00. ISBN 0-685-18138-3

Molloy, Peter M. *The History of Metal Mining and Metallurgy: An Annotated Bibliography.* Garland 1986 $65.00. ISBN 0-8240-9065-9. Covers, primarily from the late nineteenth century through the twentieth century, the history of metal mining, assaying, smelting, and related subjects.

Morris, C., ed. *Academic Press Dictionary of Science and Technology.* Acad. Pr. 1992 $115.00. ISBN 0-12-200400-0. Outstanding work covering 124 different fields of science and technology and providing the most comprehensive coverage of terminology available.

Multhauf, Robert P. *The History of Chemical Technology: An Annotated Bibliography.* Garland 1983 o.p. Features more than 1,500 annotated entries on all aspects of chemical technology.

Ogilvie, Marilyn B. *Women in Science: Antiquity through Nineteenth Century.* MIT Pr. 1986 $35.00. ISBN 0-262-15031-X. Brief, but well-researched biographical entries; includes an introduction and useful bibliography.

Oleson, John Peter. *Bronze Age, Greek and Roman Technology: A Select, Annotated Bibliography.* Garland 1986 o.p. Reflects scholarship on all aspects of early technologies and technics; includes more than 2,000 annotated entries.

Osen, Lynn M. *Women in Mathematics.* MIT Pr. 1974 $10.95. ISBN 0-262-65009-6. Popular, biographical treatment of women mathematicians from Hypatia to Emmy Noether.

Overmier, Judith. *The History of Biology: An Annotated Bibliography.* Garland 1986 o.p. A bibliographic survey that includes useful annotations.

Parker, Sybil P. *McGraw Hill Encyclopedia of Science and Technology.* 2 vols. McGraw 1992 $1,900.00. ISBN 0-07-909206-3. The only general purpose, multivolume scientific encyclopedia currently on the market for adults.

Pelletier, Paul A., ed. *Prominent Scientists: An Index to Collective Biographies.* Neal-Schuman 1992 $49.95. ISBN 1-55570-114-0. Provides an alphabetical index of some 12,000 names with coded keys to books published in English between 1960 and 1983.

Porter, Roy S. *The Earth Sciences: An Annotated Bibliography.* Garland 1983 o.p. Reflects recent scholarship on the history of the earth sciences; thematically organized, with more than 800 annotated entries.

Rothenberg, Marc. *The History of Science and Technology in the United States: A Critical and Selective Bibliography.* Garland 1982 o.p. Presents a survey of scholarship on the history of American science and technology, excluding medicine; includes 832 annotated entries.

Salvat Encyclopedia of Science and Technology. 14 vols. Fr. & Eur. 1990 $19.95. ISBN 0-8288-8237-1

Stapleton, Darwin H. (with the assistance of Roger L. Shumaker). *The History of Civil Engineering since 1600: An Annotated Bibliography.* Garland 1986 o.p. Lists secondary literature from 1600 to the present; includes 1,200 entries on various fields of civil engineering.

Wellcome Institute for the History of Medicine, London. *Subject Catalogue of the History of Medicine and Related Sciences.* 18 vols. Kraus Intl. 1980 $2,400.00. ISBN 3-601-00000-8. A useful, multivolume guide to secondary sources in medicine and the life sciences.

Who Was Who in American History: Science and Technology. Marquis 1976 o.p. Contains
  over 10,000 brief sketches on Americans prominent in all fields of science,
  invention, and technology.
Williams, Trevor I., ed. *A Biographical Dictionary of Scientists.* Wiley 1982 o.p. Provides
  excellent entries for some 1,000 scientists, emphasizing the period since 1800.
  Includes brief lists of suggested readings.

HISTORIES OF THE SPECIAL SCIENCES

The following subsections comprise general works devoted to particular
scientific disciplines or subject areas, namely, mathematics, physical sciences,
geosciences, biological sciences, social sciences, medicine and health care, and
technology and engineering. In each of these areas, historians have sought to
trace the development of ideas and techniques shaping distinct disciplinary
trajectories, rather than the broader advance of scientific or technical culture.
The history of medicine and the history of technology have evolved through
journals, professional societies, bibliographies, and academic appointments
into established disciplines alongside the history of science, rather than
subcategories of it.

The works cited in these subsections are general surveys or monographs
pertaining to particular scientific or technical disciplines that also cut across at
least two of the chronological divisions to be found later in this chapter. Studies
limited to a single chronological division are to be found in the appropriate
sections devoted to those divisions. The reader should also refer to the
appropriate chapters in this volume for discussion of the distinctive nature of
each of the specific disciplines treated here, as well as to the chapter on the
philosophy of science, technology, and medicine for philosophical issues
limited to a particular discipline, such as the philosophy of mathematics.

Mathematics

Bell, E. T. *The Development of Mathematics.* Dover 1992 repr. of 1945 ed. $12.95. ISBN 0-
  486-27239-7
Boyer, Carl B. *A History of Mathematics.* Wiley 1991 $24.95. ISBN 0-471-54397-7.
  Venerable survey for students, covering primitive times to the twentieth century;
  includes problem exercises.
———. *The History of the Calculus and Its Conceptual Development.* Dover 1959 $7.95.
  ISBN 0-486-60509-4. Comprehensive introduction to the history of the calculus.
Cajori, Florian. *History of Mathematical Notations.* 2 vols. Open Court 1951–52 o.p.
  Includes Vol. 1: *Notations in Elementary Mathematics*; Vol. 2: *Notations Mainly in
  Higher Mathematics.* The best historical introduction to mathematical notations and
  the controversy surrounding their acceptance.
David, Florence N. *Games, Gods and Gambling: The Origins and History of Probability and
  Statistical Ideas from the Earliest Times to the Newtonian Era.* OUP 1962 $45.00.
  ISBN 0-19-520566-9. Excellent introduction to the origins and early history of
  probability and statistical thought.
Edwards, C. H., Jr. *The Historical Development of the Calculus.* Spr.-Verlag 1982 $49.00.
  ISBN 0-387-90436-0. Introductory text for students; includes problem exercises.
Fauel, John, and Jeremy Gray, eds. *The History of Mathematics: A Reader.* Macmillan
  1988 $29.95. ISBN 0-333-42791-2. A survey that includes many original documents;
  initially prepared for an Open University course.
Grattan-Guinness, Ivor. *The Development of the Foundation of Mathematical Analysis
  from Euler to Riemann.* MIT Pr. o.p. Examines the contributions of Euler,
  d'Alembert, Lagrange, Cauchy, and others; includes an excellent bibliography.

Katz, Victor J. *A History of Mathematics*. HarpC 1992 $56.50. ISBN 0-673-38039-4. Comprehensive overview of the field of mathematics, from the ancient Greeks to the present.

Kline, Morris. *Mathematical Thought from Ancient to Modern Times*. OUP 1972 $75.00. ISBN 0-19-501496-0. Comprehensive, single-volume introduction to the concept of mathematics.

———. *Mathematics and the Search for Knowledge*. OUP 1986 $24.95. ISBN 0-19-504230-1. Thematic survey, illustrating the importance of mathematics and mathematical imagination for the natural sciences.

———. *Mathematics in Western Culture*. OUP 1964 $15.95. ISBN 0-19-500716-X. Portrays mathematics as central to the development of Western culture; a lively and well-written introduction for the general reader.

Restivo, Sal. *Mathematics in Society and History: Sociological Enquiries*. Kluwer Ac. 1992 $89.00. ISBN 0-7923-1765-3. Examines the role mathematics has played in societies throughout history.

Smith, David Eugene, and Jekuthiel Ginsberg. *A History of Mathematics in America Before Nineteen Hundred*. Ed. by I. Bernard Cohen. *Three Centuries of Science in Amer. Ser*. Ayer 1980 repr. of 1934 ed. $19.00. ISBN 0-405-12578-X. Introduction to the work of America's earliest mathematicians.

Struik, Dirk J., ed. *Source Book in Mathematics: Twelve Hundred to Eighteen Hundred*. *Source Bks. in the History of the Sciences Ser*. Princeton U. Pr. 1986 repr. of 1969 ed. $55.00. ISBN 0-691-02397-2. Offers a useful selection of primary documents in algebra, geometry, and forms of analysis.

Todhunter, Isaac. *History of the Calculus of Variations in the Nineteenth Century*. Chelsea Pub. 1961 $29.50. ISBN 0-8284-0164-0. A useful introduction to the subject; somewhat dated.

Van Heijenoort, Jean, ed. *From Frege to Godel: A Source Book in Mathematical Logic, 1879–1931*. *Source Bks. in the History of the Sciences Ser*. HUP 1967 $42.50. ISBN 0-674-32450-1. Provides useful primary readings for the half-century, centering on the turn of the twentieth century.

Physical Sciences: Astronomy, Physics, and Chemistry

Berry, Arthur. *A Short History of Astronomy: From Earliest Times Through the 19th Century*. Dover 1961 repr. of 1898 ed. $10.95. ISBN 0-486-20210-0. Excellent, single-volume survey of the field.

Cantor, G. N., and M. J. S. Hodge, eds. *Conceptions of Ether: Studies in the History of Ether Theories, 1740–1900*. Cambridge U. Pr. 1981 $74.95. ISBN 0-521-22430-6. A multiauthored volume that includes ten original essays and a useful bibliography.

Dick, Steven J. *Plurality of Worlds: The Extraterrestrial Life Debate from Democritus to Kant*. Cambridge U. Pr. o.p. Provocative survey of the philosophic, religious, and scientific issues in the history of this debate.

Dreyer, John L. *A History of Astronomy from Thales to Kepler*. Dover 1953 repr. of 1906 ed. $9.95. ISBN 0-486-60029-3. Reliable, single-volume survey of the history of planetary theory through the mid-seventeenth century.

Harre, Rom, ed. *A History of the Physical Sciences since Antiquity*. St. Martin 1986 $35.00. ISBN 0-312-38174-3. A collection of nine essays on the development of the science of matter from social and intellectual perspectives.

Heilbron, J. L. *Electricity in the Seventeenth and Eighteenth Centuries: A Study of Early Modern Physics*. U. CA Pr. 1979 $67.50. ISBN 0-520-03478-3. Presents a standard, comprehensive account of the subject.

———. *Elements of Early Modern Physics*. U. CA Pr. 1982 $15.95. ISBN 0-520-04554-8. Condensed version for general readers of *Electricity in the Seventeenth and Eighteenth Centuries*.

Herrmann, Dieter B. *The History of Astronomy from Herschel to Hertzsprung*. Trans. and ed. by Kevin Krisciunas. Cambridge U. Pr. 1984 $29.95. ISBN 0-521-25733-6. Examines classical astronomy, the development of astrophysics, and related developments in instrumentation since the discovery of electromagnetic energy (c.1780–1930).

Ihde, Aaron J. *The Development of Modern Chemistry.* Dover 1983 repr. of 1964 ed. $17.95. ISBN 0-486-64235-6. Authoritative, encyclopedic survey; includes an informative bibliographic essay.

King, Henry C. *The History of the Telescope.* Dover 1979 repr. of 1955 ed. $12.95. ISBN 0-486-23893-8. Excellent, single-volume study of telescopes, observational instruments, and techniques from antiquity to the twentieth century.

King, Henry C., and John R. Millburn. *Geared to the Stars: The Evolution of Planetariums, Orreries and Astronomical Clocks.* U. of Toronto Pr. 1978 o.p. Presents a comprehensive and well-illustrated study of clocks and clock-driven instruments; includes an excellent bibliography.

Leicester, Henry M., and Herbert S. Klickstein, eds. *A Source Book in Chemistry 1400–1900.* HUP 1952 o.p. Useful collection of excerpts from original sources in the history of chemistry.

Nye, Mary J., and others, eds. *The Invention of Physical Science: Intersections of Mathematics, Theology and Natural Philosophy Since the Seventeenth Century.* Kluwer Ac. 1992 $99.00. ISBN 0-7923-1753-X

Pannekoek, A. *A History of Astronomy.* Dover 1989 repr. of 1961 ed. $11.95. ISBN 0-686-65994-1. Presents a comprehensive, single-volume survey.

Partington, James R. *A History of Chemistry.* 4 vols. St. Martin o.p. A useful reference for the general reader or student.

Toulmin, Stephen, and June Goodfield. *The Architecture of Matter.* Phoenix Ser. U. Ch. Pr. 1982 $15.95. ISBN 0-226-80840-8. Study of theories of matter, alchemy, and the emergence of physical theories in chemistry and physics.

————. *Fabric of the Heavens: The Development of Astronomy and Dynamics.* HarpC $13.00. ISBN 0-06-130599-0. Provocative survey of astronomy, physical cosmology, and the emergence of modern dynamics.

Van Helden, Albert. *Measuring the Universe: Cosmic Dimensions from Aristarchus to Halley.* Bks. Demand repr. of 1985 ed. $54.90. ISBN 0-8357-8947-0. A superb study that examines the evolution of ideas and observations about the planets and the limits of the cosmos; highlights contributions after Kepler.

Earth Sciences: Geology, Geography, Meteorology, Oceanography, and Related Fields

Adams, Frank D. *The Birth and Development of the Geological Sciences.* Dover 1900 $10.95. ISBN 0-486-26372-X. Surveys geological thought from antiquity to the early nineteenth century.

Blouet, Brian W., and Teresa L. Stitcher, eds. *The Origins of Academic Geography in the United States.* Shoe String 1981 $42.50. ISBN 0-208-01881-6. Presents 20 essays on the early intellectual and institutional history of academic geography in the United States.

Bowen, Margarita. *Empiricism and Geographical Thought: From Francis Bacon to Alexander Von Humboldt.* Cambridge U. Pr. 1981 o.p. Examines the impact of modern scientific methods on geography from 1600 to 1860.

Carey, S. Warren. *Theories of the Earth and Universe: A History of Dogma in the Earth Sciences.* Stanford U. Pr. 1988 $49.50. ISBN 0-8047-1364-2. Comprehensive history of geology and its theories.

James, Preston E., and G. J. Martin. *All Possible Worlds: A History of Geographical Ideas.* Wiley 1981 $59.95. ISBN 0-471-06121-2. Introductory survey from antiquity through the twentieth century, focusing on recent developments in geography.

Kish, George, ed. *A Source Book in Geography.* HUP 1978 $40.00. ISBN 0-674-82270-6. Excerpts with notes and commentary of original geographical writings from Hesiod to von Humboldt.

Mather, Kirtley F., and Shirley L. Mason, eds. *A Source Book in Geology, 1400–1900*. HUP 1939 $43.00. ISBN 0-674-82277-3. Excerpts of original writings from da Vinci to Van Hise, covering topics such as the origin of Earth and glaciation.

Middleton, W. E. Knowles. *The History of the Barometer*. Bks. Demand repr. of 1964 ed. $127.80. ISBN 0-317-08446-1. Presents a standard survey based on primary sources.

———. *A History of the Thermometer and Its Use in Meteorology*. Bks. Demand repr. of 1966 ed. $65.50. ISBN 0-317-51975-1. Comprehensive account of the development of the thermometer from the seventeenth century to the present.

Porter, Roy. *The Making of Geology: Earth Science in Britain, 1660–1815*. Cambridge U. Pr. 1980 $75.00. ISBN 0-317-27575-5. Offers an authoritative study, describing important changes in fundamental attitudes toward Earth that preceded the introduction of geology as a science in the nineteenth century.

Shirley, R. W. *Mapping of the World, 1472–1700: Early Printed World Maps*. Saifer $200.00. ISBN 0-87556-671-5. A superbly illustrated review of the early history of cartography.

Tinkler, Keith J. *A Short History of Geomorphology*. B & N Imports 1985 o.p. A compact and useful survey.

Biological Sciences: Biology, Botany, Zoology, and Related Fields

Andrews, Henry N. *The Fossil Hunters: In Search of Ancient Plants*. Cornell Univ. Pr. 1980 $49.95. ISBN 0-8014-1248-X. Examines paleobotany from the seventeenth century to the present; well illustrated.

Clay, Reginald S., and T. H. Court. *The History of the Microscope*. Longwood 1977 repr. of 1932 ed. o.p. Provides an excellent introduction to the history of microscopy.

Cole, Francis J. *History of Comparative Anatomy: From Aristotle to the 18th Century*. AMS Pr. repr. of 1944 ed. $42.50. ISBN 0-404-13245-6. Chronicles the emergence of comparative anatomy through three stages: the recognition of the importance of the minutiae of anatomy, the development of techniques for investigating and accumulating minutiae, and the integration of the data into coherent patterns.

Farber, Paul. *The Emergence of Ornithology as a Scientific Discipline: 1760–1850*. Kluwer Ac. 1982 $75.50. ISBN 90-277-1410-X. Presents the development of ornithology in relation to the history of natural history, as well as to broader social and institutional developments.

Greene, John C. *The Death of Adam: Evolution and Its Impact on Western Thought*. Iowa St. U. Pr. 1959 $14.95. ISBN 0-8138-0390-X. Examines the idea of evolution from the seventeenth century through the nineteenth century.

Gruter, Margaret, and Paul Bohannon, eds. *Law, Biology, and Culture: The Evolution of Law*. Gruter Inst. 1983 $10.95. ISBN 0-915520-63-X. Multidisciplinary attempt at setting up behavioral models which link biological principles, behavior, and the values of modern social and legal systems.

Hall, Thomas S. *History of General Physiology, 600 B.C. to A.D. 1900*. 2 vols. U. Ch. Pr. 1975 $6.50 ea. ISBNs 0-226-31353-0, 0-226-31354-9. Vol. 1 examines the development of physiology from ancient Greece through the eighteenth century. Vol. 2 continues the survey through the late twentieth century.

———. *Source Book in Animal Biology*. Source Bks. in the History of the Sciences Ser. HUP 1951 $48.00. ISBN 0-674-82141-6. Features a comprehensive selection of topically and chronologically arranged excerpts from original sources; discusses all phases of animal research from antiquity to the twentieth century.

Haraway, Donna J. *Primate Visions: Gender, Race and Nature in the World of Modern Science*. Routledge 1989 $35.00. ISBN 0-415-90294-0. Brilliant exposition of the influence of human social theories on the development of primatology.

———. *Simians, Cyborgs, and Women: The Reinvention of Nature*. Routledge 1990 $55.00. ISBN 0-415-90386-6. Essays applying modern feminist theory to various perspectives on science and perceptions of human culture.

Leicester, Henry M. *Development of Biochemical Concepts from Ancient to Modern Times*. *Monographs in the History of Science Ser*. HUP 1974 $25.00. ISBN 0-674-20018-7.

Discusses concepts of organisms and the emergence of biochemistry as a science; emphasizes developments after 1800.

Mayr, Ernst. *The Growth of Biological Thought: Diversity, Evolution, and Inheritance.* HUP 1982 $45.00. ISBN 0-674-36445-7. A useful survey that covers biology from antiquity to the twentieth century; emphasizes the background, triumph, and defense of Darwinism.

Mayr, Ernst, and William B. Provine. *The Evolutionary Synthesis: Perspectives on the Unification of Biology.* HUP 1980 $37.50. ISBN 0-674-27225-0. Essays from a symposium, examining the background and emergence of the evolutionary synthesis.

Medvei, Victor C. *A History of Endocrinology.* Kluwer Ac. 1982 $155.00. ISBN 0-85200-245-9. An extensive, useful survey of endocrinology.

Needham, Joseph. *A History of Embryology.* Ayer 1975 $30.00. ISBN 0-405-06607-4. Classic study written by a pioneer historian of science.

Nordenskiold, Erik. *The History of Biology: A Survey.* Trans. by L. B. Eyre. Scholarly 1988 repr. of 1935 ed. $85.00. ISBN 0-403-1788-2. Venerable, single-volume survey of the field.

Persaud, T. V. N. *Early History of Human Anatomy: From Antiquity to the Beginning of the Modern Era.* C. C. Thomas 1984 o.p. A brief, but useful survey of anatomical observation and investigation from antiquity to Vesalius; profusely illustrated.

Rothschuh, Karl E. *History of Physiology (Geschichte Der Physiologie).* Trans. by G. B. Risse. Krieger 1973 $31.50. ISBN 0-88275-069-0. An introductory survey of the development of physiology from antiquity to the early twentieth century, highlights German contributions during the nineteenth century.

Rudwick, Martin J. S. *The Meaning of Fossils: Episodes in the History of Palaeontology.* U. Ch. Pr. 1985 $14.95. ISBN 0-226-73103-0. Offers an imaginative, lively interpretation of the evolving understanding of the nature of fossils and the meaning of the fossil record from sixteenth-century curiosities through eighteenth- and nineteenth-century scientific debates.

Singer, Charles. *A History of Biology: A General Introduction to the Study of Living Things.* Iowa St. U. Pr. 1989 repr. of 1959 ed. $22.95. ISBN 0-8138-0937-1. Survey that covers biology from Hippocrates to Mendel; dated, but still useful as an introduction for nonspecialists.

Stresemann, Erwin. *Ornithology: From Aristotle to the Present.* Trans. by H. J. Epstein and C. Epstein. HUP 1975 o.p. Defines the role of ornithology in the development of systematics, evolutionary theory, and the emergence of modern biology; standard single-volume survey.

Thorpe, W. H. *The Origins and Rise of Ethnology.* Praeger 1979 $42.95. ISBN 0-275-90431-8. Discusses the origins of ethnology from classical natural history to current research on animal behavior.

Social Sciences

Barnes, Harry E., ed. *Introduction to the History of Sociology.* U. Ch. Pr. 1948 o.p. A comprehensive, collaborative study that examines the development of sociological thought from antiquity through the early twentieth century; emphasizes nineteenth-century contributions.

Boring, Edwin G. *A History of Experimental Psychology.* P-H 1950 $60.00. ISBN 0-13-390039-8. Standard, but dated, single-volume survey, covering the period from 1860 to 1940.

Ellenberger, Henri F. *The Discovery of the Unconscious: The History and Evolution of Dynamic Psychiatry.* Basic 1981 $35.00. ISBN 0-465-01673-1. Comprehensive study of dynamic psychiatry, focusing on contributions made by Janet, Freud, Adler, and Jung.

Harris, Marvin. *The Rise of Anthropological Theory: A History of Theories of Culture.* HarpCollege 1990 $49.50. ISBN 0-690-70322-8. Interpretive survey of cultural

anthropology from the Enlightenment through twentieth-century cultural materialism.

Herrnstein, Richard J., and Edwin G. Boring, eds. *Source Book in the History of Psychology. Source Bks. in the History of the Sciences Ser.* HUP 1965 $35.50. ISBN 0-674-82410-5. Includes selections from original sources that reflect all phases of psychology from Aristotle to the early twentieth century.

Hothersall, David. *History of Psychology.* McGraw 1989 $29.82. ISBN 0-07-030509-9. Covers psychology from antiquity to the neobehaviorists; designed as an introductory survey for students.

Hunt, Morton. *The Story of Psychology: Humankind's Ultimate Adventure—the Exploration of the Universe Within.* Doubleday 1993 $29.95. ISBN 0-385-24762-1. Narrative history of psychology from Ancient Greece to present.

Klein, D. B. *A History of Scientific Psychology: Its Origins and Philosophical Backgrounds.* Basic 1970 o.p. Covers the emergence of psychology as a science from antiquity through the modern period.

Leahey, Thomas H. *A History of Psychology.* P-H 1987 $46.00. ISBN 0-13-391764-9. Covers psychology from antiquity to the twentieth century; designed as an introductory survey for students.

Leakey, Louis S. B., and William S. Bester, eds. *Adam or Ape: A Sourcebook of Discoveries about Early Man.* Schenkman Bks. Inc. 1986 $16.95. ISBN 0-87073-701-5. Presents selections from primary sources and essays on anthropology and paleontology from Darwin through the twentieth century.

Lewellen, T. C. *Political Anthropology: An Introduction.* Greenwood 1983 $42.95. ISBN 0-89789-028-0

Reisman, John M. *A History of Clinical Psychology: Enlarged Edition of the Development of Clinical Psychology.* Irvington 1983 $19.95. ISBN 0-8290-0873-X. Describes themes in clinical theory, technique, practice, and professional organization from the late eighteenth through the twentieth centuries.

Richards, Graham. *Mental Machinery: The Origins and Consequences of Psychological Ideas, 1600–1850.* Johns Hopkins 1992 $49.95. ISBN 0-8018-4544-0. A history of the emergence of a metaphorical construct that has come to be called "the psychological" from the ideas of European thinkers from the seventeenth to the mid-nineteenth centuries, including Descartes, Hobbes, Locke, Hartley, Hume, and Mill.

Robins, R. H. *A Short History of Linguistics.* Longman 1990 $20.95. ISBN 0-582-29145-3. Compact survey of linguistics from classical Greece to the mid-twentieth century.

Smith, Dennis. *The Rise of Historical Sociology.* Temple U. Pr. 1992 $49.95. ISBN 0-87722-920-1. Cogently argues that the postwar resurgence of historical sociology are related to changes in the political and ideological context.

Swingewood, Alan. *A Short History of Sociological Thought.* St. Martin 1984 $29.95. ISBN 0-312-72151-X. Concise, useful survey of the origins and development of sociology.

Watson, Robert I. *The Great Psychologists: From Aristotle to Freud.* HarpC 1978 $53.50. ISBN 0-06-041919-9. Includes excerpts of primary sources from antiquity to the twentieth century.

MEDICINE AND HEALTH CARE

Castiglioni, Arturo. *A History of Medicine.* Aronson 1973 o.p. Excellent survey of the history of medicine from antiquity to the twentieth century; emphasizes Italian and British medicine.

Clendening, Logan, ed. *Source Book of Medical History.* Dover 1942 $14.95. ISBN 0-486-20621-1. Presents selected readings in the history of medical philosophy and practice.

Earle, A. S. *Surgery in America: From the Colonial Era to the Twentieth Century.* Greenwood 1983 $75.00. ISBN 0-275-91389-9. Covers the early history of American surgery from primitive amputation techniques through the development of anesthesiology and improved surgical procedures.

Hopkins, Donald R. *Princes and Peasants: Smallpox in History.* U. Ch. Pr. 1983 o.p. Describes the history of smallpox and its virtual eradication from Elizabethan times through the twentieth century.

Leavitt, Judith W., and Ronald L. Numbers, eds. *Sickness and Health in America: Readings in the History of Medicine and Public Health.* U. of Wis. Pr. 1985 $32.50. ISBN 0-299-10274-2. Features a selection of reprints and excerpts from the writings of American physicians.

Macleod, Roy, and Milton Lewis. *Disease, Medicine and Empire.* Routledge 1989 $79.95. ISBN 0-415-00685-6. Attempts to outline the ways in which colonial medicine obscured the relationships between disease and social structure.

Rosen, George. *A History of Public Health.* Johns Hopkins 1958 $18.95. ISBN 0-8018-4645-5. Chronicles the field from classical Greece to the mid-twentieth century.

Rosenberg, Charles E., and Janet Golden, eds. *Framing Disease: Studies in Cultural History.* Rutgers U. Pr. 1992 $48.00. ISBN 0-8135-1756-7. Collection of essays on the social mediations in the construction and management of disease.

Shryock, Richard H. *Developments of Modern Medicine: An Interpretation of the Social and Scientific Factors Involved.* U. of Wis. Pr. 1980 $13.95. ISBN 0-299-07536-6. Describes medical developments in Europe and America from 1600 to the early twentieth century.

_____. *Medicine and Society in America: 1660–1860.* Cornell Univ. Pr. 1962 $9.95. ISBN 0-8014-9093-6. Presents a compact introduction to the origins of the medical profession in the United States; the development of medical theory and practice; concepts of disease; and the transition to modern medical practice in the mid-nineteenth century.

Sigerist, Henry E. *A History of Medicine.* 2 vols. OUP 1951–61 Vol. 1 *Primitive and Archaic Medicine.* $39.95. ISBN 0-19-500102-8. Vol. 2 *Early Greek, Hindu and Persian Medicine.* $39.95. ISBN 0-19-500103-6. An introductory survey of medical practice from prehistory through antiquity.

Singer, Charles, and Ashworth E. Underwood. *Short History of Medicine.* OUP 1962 o.p. Standard, though outdated, survey of the practice and science of medicine from prehistory to the early twentieth century.

Spink, Wesley W. *Infectious Diseases: A History of Their Control.* U. of Minn. Pr. 1979 o.p. Useful survey of the medical and social control of infectious disease.

TECHNOLOGY AND ENGINEERING

Agassi, Joseph. *Technology: Philosophical and Social Aspects.* Kluwer Ac. 1985 $87.00. ISBN 90-277-2044-4. Examines the social and intellectual impact of technological change.

Buchanan, R. A. *The Power of the Machine: The Impact of Technology from 1700 to the Present Day.* Viking Penguin 1993 $30.00. ISBN 0-670-83656-7. Basic introduction to how technology has transformed human society and the earth.

Calhoun, Daniel H. *The American Civil Engineer: Origins and Conflict.* MIT Pr. 1962 o.p. A pioneering study that examines the emergence of the profession and institutions of civil engineering in the United States; includes an excellent bibliography.

Calvert, Monte. *The Mechanical Engineer in America, 1830–1910; Professional Cultures in Conflict.* Bks. Demand repr. of 1967 ed. $79.30. ISBN 0-317-42068-2. Overview and social analysis of the process of professionalization in mechanical engineering; emphasizes the conflict between activists and their opponents.

Derry, T. K., and Trevor Williams. *A Short History of Technology: From the Earliest Times to 1900 A.D.* Dover 1993. ISBN 0-486-27472-1

Eisenstein, Elizabeth L. *The Printing Press as an Agent of Change: Communications and Cultural Transformations in Early Modern Europe.* 2 vols. Cambridge U. Pr. 1980 $42.95. ISBN 0-521-29955-1. Influential study of the print technology in early modern Europe and its impact on Western culture, especially religion and science.

Emme, Eugene M., ed. *Two Hundred Years of Flight in America*. Univelt 1979 $35.00. ISBN 0-87703-101-0. Presents collected essays on the history of flight through the age of space exploration in the United States.

Goldstine, Herman H. *The Computer from Pascal to Von Neumann*. Princeton U. Pr. 1980 $55.00. ISBN 0-691-08104-2. A comprehensive survey of computational mathematics and the development of computer technology from the seventeenth to the twentieth century.

Hughes, Thomas P. *Networks of Power: Electrification in Western Society, 1880–1930*. Johns Hopkins 1993 $34.95. ISBN 0-8018-4614-5. An excellent, comparative study of the development of power networks in the United States and Europe; represents the foundation for subsequent studies of large technological systems.

Klemm, Friedrich. *History of Western Technology*. Trans. by Dorothea W. Singer. Iowa St. U. Pr. 1991 repr. of 1964 ed. $17.95. ISBN 0-8138-0499-X. A concise survey in one volume.

Kranzberg, Melvin, and Carroll W. Pursell, Jr., eds. *Technology in Western Civilization*. 2 vols. OUP 1967 Vol. 1 *The Emergence of Modern Industrial Society, Earliest Times to 1900*. $29.95. ISBN 0-19-500938-X. Vol. 2 *Technology in the Twentieth Century*. $24.95. ISBN 0-19-500939-8. Features the first important survey in the history of technology built on the foundation of postwar research.

Landes, David S. *Revolution in Time: Clocks and the Making of the Modern World*. HUP 1983 $27.50. ISBN 0-674-76800-0. A comprehensive survey of horology, timekeeping, and changing attitudes about time.

Pacey, Arnold. *The Maze of Ingenuity: Ideas and Idealism in the Development of Technology*. MIT Pr. 1992 $10.95. ISBN 0-262-16128-1. Presents a wide-ranging survey of the role of ideas in the history of technology, from medieval cathedrals to contemporary technology.

Pursell, Carroll W., Jr., ed. *Technology in America: A History of Individuals and Ideas*. MIT Pr. 1990 $12.95. ISBN 0-262-66067-9. Presents a collection of articles that describe American technology from colonial times to the space age.

Rosenblum, Naomi. *A World History of Photography*. Ed. by Walton Rawls. Abbeville Pr. 1989 $60.00. ISBN 1-55859-054-4. Solid, illustrated survey.

Rothschild, Joan, ed. *Machina Ex Dea: Feminist Perspectives on Technology*. Pergamon 1983 $48.50. ISBN 0-08-029404-9. A collection of provocative essays that cover the emerging field of research on women and technology in Western culture.

Von Braun, Wernher, and Frederick I. Ordway, III. *History of Rocketry and Space Travel*. Harper & Row 1985 o.p. Offers a well-illustrated survey for the general reader.

Williams, Michael R. *A History of Computing Technology*. P-H 1985 $40.00. ISBN 0-13-389917-9. Brief introduction to computational techniques and computing, emphasizing modern computing.

CHRONOLOGICAL DIVISIONS

The following subsections comprise writings in the history of science, technology, and medicine limited to a particular chronological period. Topical themes and geographical limits within these periods vary widely, for a variety of reasons: the common tendency of some fields of study to "lead" or "lag"; the ever-changing mix of influences resulting from social, political, cultural, and economic context; and the persistent framework fixed long-established traditions of historical writing. The chronological divisions used below, like important bibliographical resources such as the *Isis Current Bibliography* and the *Current Bibliography in the History of Technology*, are clearly influenced by such deep-seated traditions in the humanities, although, in fact, many have acquired their own special meaning for the history of science, technology, and medicine. Thus, the eighteenth century, the Age of Enlightenment, is associated, in the history of science, with the post-Newtonian evolution of the mathematical and physical sciences and, in the history of technology, for example, with the Industrial Revolution. The chronological divisions used here are: ancient and classical period, Middle Ages, Renaissance and Reformation; seventeenth century, eighteenth century, nineteenth century, and twentieth century.

Ancient and Classical Period

Aaboe, A. *Episodes from the Early History of Mathematics.* Math. Assn. 1964 $12.00. ISBN 0-88385-613-1. Standard introduction designed for students.

Aristotle. *The Complete Works of Aristotle: The Revised Oxford Translation.* 2 vols. Ed. by Jonathan Barnes. *Bollingen Ser.* Princeton U. Pr. 1984 $79.00. ISBN 0-691-09950-2. Features the most accessible collection of Aristotle's writings.

Bowen, Alan C., ed. *Science and Philosophy in Classical Greece.* Garland 1991 $58.00. ISBN 0-8153-0214-2. Essays by historians of ancient Greek philosophy exploring definitions and the demarcation of particular sciences.

Brock, Arthur J., ed. *Greek Medicine: Being Extracts Illustrative of Medical Writing from Hippocrates to Galen.* AMS Pr. 1977 repr. of 1929 ed. $29.50. ISBN 0-404-07806-0. Offers a useful anthology of primary texts.

De Camp, L. Sprague. *Ancient Engineers: Technology and Invention from the Earliest Times to the Renaissance.* Marboro 1990 $19.95. ISBN 0-88029-456-6. Solid introduction, especially regarding coverage of antiquity.

De Santillana, Giorgio. *Origins of Scientific Though from Anaximander to Proclus, 600 B.C.–500 A.D.* NAL-Dutton 1955 o.p. Offers a brisk, breezy, but often brilliant, survey of early scientific ideas.

Dicks, D. R. *Early Greek Astronomy to Aristotle. Aspects of Greek and Roman Life Ser.* Cornell Univ. Pr. 1985 $15.95. ISBN 0-8014-9310-2. Philosophical and textual, rather than technical analysis of the field.

Euclid. *The Elements.* 3 vols. Trans. by Thomas L. Heath. Dover 1956 repr. of 1926 ed. $9.95 ea. ISBNs 0-486-60088-2, 0-486-60089-0, 0-486-60090-4. Standard edition of this timeless work of ancient science and foundation of the history of mathematics.

Gillings, Richard J. *Mathematics in the Time of the Pharaohs.* Dover 1982 $6.95. ISBN 0-486-24315-X. Offers a solid, nontechnical introduction.

Heath, Thomas L. *Aristarchus of Samos: The Greek Copernicus.* Dover 1981 $9.95. ISBN 0-486-24188-2. Brilliant study of ancient Greek astronomy, by highlighting Aristarchus.

————. *A History of Greek Mathematics.* Dover 1981 $12.95. ISBN 0-486-24073-8. Remains an outstanding introduction to Greek mathematics.

Lloyd, Geoffrey E. *Early Greek Science: Thales to Aristotle.* Ed. by M. I. Finley. Norton 1974 $7.95. ISBN 0-393-00583-6. The standard work by the dean of historians of Hellenistic science.

————. *Greek Science after Aristotle.* Norton 1975 $9.95. ISBN 0-393-00780-4. A companion to *Early Greek Science*; standard work on Hellenistic science.

————. *Magic, Reason and Experience: Studies in the Origin and Development of Greek Science.* Cambridge U. Pr. 1979 $79.95. ISBN 0-521-22373-3. A bold, but balanced, attempt to understand the emergence of Greek scientific thought in respect to social, political, and anthropological models of development.

————. *Science, Folklore, and Ideology: Studies in the Life Sciences in Ancient Greece.* Cambridge U. Pr. 1983 o.p. Imaginative, insightful attempt to place ancient medicine and biology in the context of the experience and knowledge of midwives and herbalists.

Neugebauer, Otto. *The Exact Sciences in Antiquity.* Dover 1969 repr. of 1957 ed. $6.95. ISBN 0-486-22332-9. Authoritative introduction to the technical rudiments of the exact sciences in antiquity.

————. *A History of Ancient Mathematical Astronomy.* 3 vols. Spr.-Verlag 1975 $341.00. ISBN 0-387-06995-X. A definitive, scholarly study written by a master of the subject.

Sarton, George. *Ancient Science Through the Golden Age of Greece.* Dover 1993 repr. of 1970 ed. $14.95. ISBN 0-486-27695-0

Scarborough, John. *Roman Medicine.* Ed. by H. H. Scullard *Aspects of Greek and Roman Life Ser.* Cornell Univ. Pr. 1970 o.p. Solid introduction to the field.

Singer, Charles J. *Greek Biology and Greek Medicine.* AMS Pr. 1979 repr. of 1922 ed. $20.00. ISBN 0-404-13366-5. Offers useful, but dated, treatment of the field.

Stahl, William H. *Roman Science: Origins, Development, and Influence to the Later Middle Ages.* Greenwood 1978 repr. of 1962 ed. $69.50. ISBN 0-313-20473-X. Comprehensive introduction to the development and legacy of science in the Roman Empire.

Van der Waerden, Bartel L. *Science Awakening I: Egyptian, Babylonian, and Greek Mathematics.* Scholar Bookshelf 1988 $40.00. ISBN 0-945726-04-X. Valuable, technical introduction to science in antiquity.

———. *Science Awakening 2: The Birth of Astronomy.* OUP 1974 $45.00. ISBN 0-19-519753-4. In combination with Neugebauer's *Exact Sciences in Antiquity,* it represents the definitive work on the technical aspects of ancient science.

White, K. D. *Greek and Roman Technology.* Cornell Univ. Pr. 1983 $48.95. ISBN 0-8014-1439-3. Survey of all aspects of technology in ancient Greece and Rome; includes informative illustrations and diagrams.

Middle Ages

Al-Andalusi, Sa'id. *Science in the Medieval World: "Book of the Categories of Nations."* Trans. by Salem Sema'an and Alok Kumov. U. of Tex. Pr. 1991 $35.00. ISBN 0-292-71139-5. Translation of 1068 essay on history of science in Muslim Spain.

Clagett, Marshall. *The Science of Mechanics in the Middle Ages.* U. of Wis. Pr. 1959 $50.00. ISBN 0-299-01900-4. A fundamental, scholarly study that describes developments in mechanics; emphasizes medieval impetus theory.

Gimpel, Jean. *The Medieval Machine: The Industrial Revolution of the Middle Ages.* Viking Penguin 1977 $7.95. ISBN 0-14-004514-7. Presents an introduction to medieval technology, focusing on the claim that inventions in the Middle Ages constituted an early "industrial revolution."

Grant, Edward. *Physical Science in the Middle Ages. History of Science Ser.* Cambridge U. Pr. 1978 $15.95. ISBN 0-521-29294-8. Standard introduction to medieval science; designed for students.

———. *A Source Book in Medieval Science. Source Bks. in the History of the Sciences Ser.* HUP 1974 $186.00. ISBN 0-7837-4152-9. Surveys the Middle Ages from the encyclopedia tradition to writers of the fifteenth century; compiled from more than 150 authors.

Haskins, Charles H. *The Renaissance of the Twelfth Century.* HUP 1927 $12.50. ISBN 0-674-76075-1. Classic study on the revival of learning in Latin-based Western cultures.

Knowles, David. *The Evolution of Medieval Thought.* Longman 1988 $19.95. ISBN 0-582-49426-5. Standard introduction to the intellectual traditions and context of medieval science and learning.

Lang, Helen S. *Aristotle's Physics and Its Medieval Varieties.* State U. NY Pr. 1992 $57.50. ISBN 0-7914-1083-8. Presents Aristotlean ideas and their interpretation by Aquinas, Buriden and Duns Scotus, inter alia.

Lindberg, David C., ed. *Science in the Middle Ages.* U. Ch. Pr. 1979 $20.00. ISBN 0-226-48233-2. Features a collection of essays by authorities on all aspects of medieval science and learning.

Murdoch, John E. *Antiquity and the Middle Ages.* Scribner 1984 o.p. Superb compilation of images, including an explanatory text.

Nasr, Hosein. *Science and Civilization in Islam.* Bks. Demand repr. of 1968 ed. $107.50. ISBN 0-7837-4122-7. Presents the major developments of Islamic science and their influence on medieval Latin-based western cultures.

Sarton, George. *Introduction to the History of Science.* 5 vols. Krieger 1975 $425.00. ISBN 0-88275-172-7. An encyclopedic reference work that chronicles science from Homer through the late fourteenth century; somewhat dated, but still useful as a source of bibliographic and other historical details.

Weisheipl, James A. *The Development of Physical Theory in the Middle Ages.* U. of Mich. Pr. 1971 $8.95. ISBN 0-472-06181-X. Covers themes in physical theory; emphasizes the work of Albertus Magnus and Thomas Aquinas.

White, Lynn, Jr. *Medieval Technology and Social Change.* OUP 1962 $9.95. ISBN 0-19-500266-0. Classic study, tracing the social impact of medieval innovations, such as the horse stirrup, collar, and the three-field crop rotation.

Renaissance and Reformation, 1450–1600

Boas Hall, Maria. *The Scientific Renaissance 1450–1630.* HarpC 1966 $10.95. ISBN 0-06-130583-9. Presents a one-volume survey of Renaissance science; remains the standard treatment.

Copernicus, Nicholas. *Three Copernican Treatises: The Commentariolus and the Letter against Werner of Copernicus and the Narratio Prima of Rheticus.* Ed. and trans. by Edward Rosen. Hippocrene Bks. 1971 repr. of 1939 ed. o.p. Features brief, primary readings that provide an excellent introduction to Copernican astronomy.

Debus, Allen G. *Man and Nature in the Renaissance.* History of Science Ser. Cambridge U. Pr. 1978 $39.95. ISBN 0-521-21972-8. Standard introduction to Renaissance science designed for students; focuses on the impact of occult natural philosophy on the emergence of modern science.

Drake, Stillman, and I. E. Drabkin, trans. *Mechanics in Sixteenth Century Italy: Selections from Tartaglia, Benedetti, Guido Ubaldo and Galileo.* Bks. Demand repr. of 1969 ed. $119.40. ISBN 0-7857-1657-5. Excellent introduction to sixteenth-century mechanics and science during Galileo's time.

Dreyer, John L. *Tycho Brahe: A Picture of Scientific Life and Work in the Sixteenth Century.* Peter Smith 1977 o.p. Classic biography of the sixteenth-century Danish astronomer.

Johnson, Francis R. *Astronomical Thought in Renaissance England.* Hippocrene Bks. 1968 o.p. A standard, although dated, introduction to Tudor astronomy and cosmology; includes much information on the reception of Copernican astronomy in England.

Mandrou, Robert. *From Humanism to Science, 1480–1700.* Gordon & Breach 1992. ISBN 2-88124-568-4. Analyzes the changes that occurred in scientific knowledge and study as a result of rebirth of rationalism during the Renaissance.

O'Malley, C. D. *Andreas Vesalius of Brussels 1514–1564.* U. CA Pr. 1964 o.p. Standard study of the famous Belgian anatomist.

Popkin, Richard H. *The History of Scepticism from Erasmus to Spinoza.* U. CA Pr. 1979 $15.00. ISBN 0-520-03876-2. Argues that modern science was partly an intellectual compromise between dogmatism and skepticism; a brilliant study of the skeptical crisis of the late Renaissance and its impact on theology, philosophy, and science.

Pumfrey, Stephen, and others, eds. *Science, Culture and Popular Belief in Renaissance Europe.* St. Martin 1991 $79.95. ISBN 0-7190-2925-2. Scholarly analyses on the influence of the state, the church, the supernatural, rhetoric, and mathematics on emerging science.

Rosen, Edward. *Copernicus and the Scientific Revolution.* Krieger 1984 $9.50. ISBN 0-89874-573-X. Polemical introduction to achievements of Copernicus.

Sarton, George. *Six Wings: Men of Science in the Renaissance.* Bks. Demand repr. of 1957 ed. $86.90. ISBN 0-8357-6694-2. An influential, but dated, introduction to Renaissance science.

Swerdlow, Noel M., and Otto Neugebauer. *Mathematical Astronomy in Copernicus's De Revolutionibus.* 2 vols. Spr.-Verlag 1984 $131.00. ISBN 0-387-90939-7. Highly technical, scholarly analysis of Copernicus's revolutionary work.

Thoren, Victor E. *The Lord of Uraniborg: A Biography of Tycho Brahe.* Cambridge U. Pr. 1991 $59.95. ISBN 0-521-35158-8. Now considered the standard biography of the most important astronomer between the time of Copernicus and Kepler.

Wear, Andrew, and I. M. Lomie, eds. *The Medical Renaissance of the Sixteenth Century.* Cambridge U. Pr. 1985 $74.95. ISBN 0-521-30112-2. Conference proceedings that examine the Galenic tradition and medical education in sixteenth-century Europe.

Westman, Robert S., and J. E. McGuire. *Hermeticism and the Scientific Revolution.* U. CA Pr. 1977 o.p. Presents essays that reevaluate the so-called Yates thesis (see *Giordano Bruno and the Hermetic Tradition* below), which states that Hermeticism and other occult modes of thought substantially influenced Copernicanism and other important traditions in early modern science.

Wightman, William P. *Science and the Renaissance.* 2 vols. Hafner 1962 o.p. Standard survey of Renaissance science.

Yates, Frances. *Giordano Bruno and the Hermetic Tradition.* U. Ch. Pr. 1990 $16.95. ISBN 0-226-95007-7. Argues that the emergence of modern science was stimulated by Hermetic philosophy and natural magic; a controversial, but brilliant study.

Seventeenth Century

Boas-Hall, Marie. *Promoting Experimental Learning: Experiment and the Royal Society, 1660–1727.* Cambridge U. Pr. 1991 $64.95. ISBN 0-521-40503-3. An important monograph that combines a lifetime of scholarship on the scientific revolution and the expanding literature on experimental philosophy in the early Royal Society.

Brown, Harcourt. *Scientific Organizations in Seventeenth Century France, 1620–1680.* 1934 o.p. Classic study of the informal societies that culminated in the Paris Academy of Sciences.

Burtt, Edwin A. *The Metaphysical Foundations of Modern Physical Science.* Humanities 1980 $15.00. ISBN 0-391-01742-X. A classic examination of the philosophical and theological background to the scientific revolution.

Caspar, Max. *Kepler.* Trans. by C. Doris Hellman. Dover 1990 repr. of 1959 ed. $10.95. ISBN 0-486-26528-5. Standard biography of Johannes Kepler.

Chappell, Veve, ed. *Seventeenth-Century Natural Scientists.* Garland 1992 $60.00. ISBN 0-8153-0581-8. Fifteen essays on Newton, Boyle, and Huygens, showing how they were part of the philosophical milieu of the seventeenth century.

Christianson, Gale E. *In the Presence of the Creator: Isaac Newton and His Times.* Free Pr. 1984 $24.95. ISBN 0-02-905190-8. Accessible biography of Newton, highlighting his scientific achievements.

Cohen, I. Bernard. *The Birth of a New Physics.* Norton 1985 $19.95. ISBN 0-393-30065-5. Introduces the major themes in terrestrial and celestial physics during the scientific revolution.

Descartes, Rene. *Principles of Philosophy.* Trans. by Reese P. Miller and Valentine R. Miller. Kluwer Ac. 1984 $37.50. ISBN 90-277-1754-0. Describes Descartes's most comprehensive statement of his physical system.

Dobbs, Betty J. *The Foundations of Newton's Alchemy: Or "The Hunting of the Greene Lvon."* Cambridge U. Pr. 1983 $22.95. ISBN 0-521-27381-1. Provocative study by the leading historian of Newton's alchemical interests.

Dobell, C., ed. *Antony van Leeuwenhoek and His "Little Animals."* Dover 1960 repr. of 1932 ed. o.p. Standard introduction to Leeuwenhoek and his early microscopic studies.

Drake, Stillman. *Galileo at Work: His Scientific Biography.* U. Ch. Pr. 1978 o.p. An introduction to Galileo's scientific work by a prominent specialist in the field.

Frank, Robert G., Jr. *Harvey and the Oxford Physiologist: A Study of Scientific Ideas.* U. CA Pr. 1980 $52.50. ISBN 0-520-03906-8. Comprehensive study of the "English School" of physiology from Harvey to Lower; examined in an intellectual and institutional context.

Galilei, Galileo. *Dialogue Concerning the Two Chief World Systems, Ptolemaic and Copernican.* Trans. by Stillman Drake. U. CA Pr. 1967 $15.95. ISBN 0-520-00450-7. The standard translation of Galileo's scientific classic in an accessible literary style; designed for the general reader.

————. *Discoveries and Opinions of Galileo*. Trans. by S. Drake. Doubleday 1957 $7.95. ISBN 0-385-09239-3. Includes lively translations of Galileo's brief publications on telescopes, science, and religion.

————. *Sidereus Nuncius, Or the Sidereal Messenger*. Trans. by Albert Van Helden. U. Ch. Pr. 1989 $29.95. ISBN 0-226-27903-0. Includes Galileo's important and entertaining work on the results of his telescopic observations.

Gassendi, Pierre. *The Selected Works of Pierre Gassendi*. Ed. and trans. by Craig B. Brush. Johnson 1972 o.p. Includes selections from the writings of Descartes's contemporary and critic.

Hacking, Ian. *The Emergence of Probability: A Philosophical Study of Early Ideas about Probability, Induction, and Statistical Inference*. Cambridge U. Pr. 1975 $37.50. ISBN 0-521-31803-3. Examines the philosophical context of early probability theory.

Hall, Alfred Rupert. *Philosophers at War: The Quarrel between Newton and Leibniz*. Cambridge U. Pr. 1980 $47.95. ISBN 0-521-22732-1. Describes the war of words between the supporters of Newton and Leibniz caused by the battle over priority in the invention of the calculus.

————. *The Revolution in Science 1500–1750*. Longman 1983 o.p. Revised and expanded version of Hall's standard work on the scientific revolution.

Harvey, William. *De Motu Cordis: Anatomical Studies on the Motion of the Heart and Blood*. Trans. by Chauncey D. Leake. C. C. Thomas 1978 $25.50. ISBN 0-398-00793-4. Presents the text of Harvey's revolutionary *On the Motion of the Heart and Blood*; includes a commentary.

Hooykaas, R. *Religion and the Rise of Modern Science*. Eerdmans 1972 o.p. An outstanding study of the relationship between science and religion in the seventeenth century.

Jacob, Margaret. *The Newtonians and the English Revolution*. Gordon & Breach 1990 $32.00. ISBN 2-88124-400-9. Classic study of the interaction of Puritanism, politics, and Newtonian natural philosophy.

Jones, Richard F. *Ancients and Moderns: A Study of the Rise of the Scientific Movement in Seventeenth Century England*. Peter Smith 1961 $12.75. ISBN 0-8446-2340-7. A classic examination of the literary battle between those who supported the superiority of ancient learning and adherents of the new natural philosophy.

Kepler, Johannes. *The Secret of the Universe: Mysterium Cosmographicum*. Trans. by A. M. Duncan. Abaris Bks. 1981 o.p. Excellent translation of Kepler's first major work; includes useful notes.

King, Lester S. *The Road to Medical Enlightenment, 1650–1695*. Watson 1970 o.p. Standard study of seventeenth-century English medical thought; emphasizes the works of Sylvius, Sydenham, Hoffman, and others.

Koestler, Arthur. *The Sleepwalkers: A History of Man's Changing Vision of the Universe*. Viking Penguin 1990 $9.95. ISBN 0-14-019246-8. Argues that scientific discovery involves periods of intellectual "sleepwalking"; a controversial psychobiographical study of Copernicus, Kepler, and Galileo.

Koyre, Alexandre. *The Astronomical Revolution: Copernicus-Kepler-Borelli*. Trans. by R.E.W. Maddison. Dover 1992 repr. of 1973 ed. $12.95. ISBN 0-486-27095-5. Focuses on the problem of planetary motion as the central issue of the scientific revolution; important study in the tradition of intellectual history.

————. *From the Closed World to the Infinite Universe*. Johns Hopkins 1968 repr. of 1956 ed. $13.95. ISBN 0-8018-0347-0. Influential study of the "geometrization of space" that destroyed the closed Aristotelian cosmos.

Kuhn, Thomas S. *The Copernican Revolution: Planetary Astronomy in the Development of Western Thought*. HUP 1957 $11.95. ISBN 0-674-17103-9. Remains the essential introduction to the technical issues associated with this topic.

Manuel, Frank E. *A Portrait of Isaac Newton*. Da Capo 1990 $13.95. ISBN 0-306-80400-X. A provocative and controversial psychobiography that describes Newton's character and psychological development.

Mayr, Otto. *Authority, Liberty, and Automatic Machinery in Early Modern Europe.* Johns Hopkins 1989 $17.95. ISBN 0-8018-3939-4. Original synthesis of political, intellectual, and technological history.

Merton, Robert K. *Science, Technology and Society in Seventeenth Century England.* Fertig 1970 $40.00. ISBN 0-86527-178-X. Classic study of the so-called Puritan ethic and how it influenced support for scientific activities in seventeenth-century England.

Newton, Isaac. *Newton's Philosophy of Nature.* Trans. by H. S. Thayer. *Lib. of Class. Ser.* Free Pr. 1974 $12.95. ISBN 0-685-43029-4. Features selections from Newton's *Principia, Opticks,* and his correspondences.

_____. *Opticks, or a Treatise of the Reflections, Refractions, Inflections, and Colours of Light.* Dover 1952 $9.95. ISBN 0-486-60205-2. Standard treatment of Newton's classic and most widely read work.

Redondi, Pietro. *Galileo, Heretic.* Trans. by Raymond Rosenthal. Princeton U. Pr. 1990 $42.50. ISBN 0-691-02426-X. Offers a new interpretation of Galileo's trial; has rejuvenated scholarship on the subject.

Sabra, A. I. *Theories of Light from Descartes to Newton.* Cambridge U. Pr. 1981 $19.95. ISBN 0-521-28436-8. Describes the contributions of Descartes, Huygens, and Newton.

Santillana, Giorgio. *The Crime of Galileo. Midway Repr. Ser.* U. Ch. Pr. 1978 $8.95. ISBN 0-226-73681-1. Lively polemical account of the Catholic Church's condemnation of Galileo for his heliocentric beliefs.

Shea, William R. *Galileo's Intellectual Revolution: Middle Period, 1610–1632.* Watson Pub. Intl. 1977 o.p. A scholarly account that focuses on Galileo's creative years; emphasizes his Aristotelian leanings in contrast with the Platonic interpretation of Koyre and the positivism of Drake.

Webster, Charles. *The Great Instauration: Science, Medicine and Reform 1626–1660.* Holmes & Meier 1976 o.p. A comprehensive study that emphasizes the religious, social, and institutional underpinnings of the radical shift in mid-seventeenth century English science, which was mainly the result of Puritanism.

Westfall, Richard S. *The Construction of Modern Science: Mechanisms and Mechanics.* Cambridge U. Pr. 1978 $49.95. ISBN 0-521-29295-6. Introduction to the scientific revolution; designed primarily for undergraduate students.

_____. *Never at Rest: A Biography of Isaac Newton.* Cambridge U. Pr. 1981 $100.00. ISBN 0-521-23143-4. Definitive study of Newton's life and scientific achievements.

_____. *Science and Religion in Seventeenth-Century England.* Elliots Bks. 1958 o.p. Argues that English scientists were uncertain about aspects of Christianity but remained committed to the harmony of science and natural religion.

Wolf, Abraham. *A History of Science, Technology and Philosophy in the Sixteenth and Seventeenth Centuries.* 2 vols. Peter Smith repr. of 1952 ed. o.p. Useful compilation of detailed information on various subjects.

Yolton, John W., ed. *Philosophy, Religion and Science in the Seventeenth and Eighteenth Centuries.* Univ. Rochester Pr. 1990 $49.50. ISBN 1-878822-01-2. Essays advocating an interdisciplinary approach to the history of ideas.

Eighteenth Century

Anderson, Wilda C. *Between the Library and the Laboratory: The Language of Chemistry in Eighteenth Century France.* Johns Hopkins 1985 $32.00. ISBN 0-8018-3229-2. Centrally concerned with the philosopher-chemists Lavoisier and Macques.

Bedini, Silvio A. *Thinkers and Tinkers: Early American Men of Science.* Landmark Ent. 1983 repr. of 1975 ed. $25.00. ISBN 0-910845-19-0. A well-illustrated survey of colonial scientists and instrument-makers; emphasizes the importance of mathematical practitioners.

Burkhardt, Richard W., Jr. *The Spirit of System: Lamarck and Evolutionary Biology.* HUP 1977 o.p. Examines the structure and legacy of Lamarckian science.

Bury, John B. *The Idea of Progress: An Inquiry into Its Origin and Growth.* Dover 1987 $8.95. ISBN 0-486-25421-6. Classic study in the history of ideas; emphasizes the eighteenth-century intellectual shift from providence to the secular philosophy of progress.

Cohen, I. Bernard. *Franklin and Newton: An Inquiry into Speculative Newtonian Experimental Science and Franklin's Work in Electricity as an Example Thereof.* Am. Philos. 1957 o.p. A pioneering study that examines the impact of the Newtonian tradition as exemplified by the influence of Newton's *Opticks* on Benjamin Franklin's experimental science.

Darnton, Robert. *Mesmerism and the End of the Enlightenment in France.* HUP 1968 $20.00. ISBN 0-674-56950-4. Important study of science and pseudoscience in an intellectual, institutional, and political context preceding the French Revolution.

Daston, Lorraine. *Classical Probability in the Enlightenment.* Princeton U. Pr. 1988 $57.50. ISBN 0-691-08497-1. A broad, intellectual history of probability theory and notions of risk in the eighteenth century.

Dooley, Brendon M. *Science, Politics and Society in Eighteenth Century Italy: The Giornale de Letterati d'Italia and Its World.* Garland 1991 $53.00. ISBN 0-8153-0471-4

Frängsmyr, Tore, and others, eds. *The Quantifying Spirit in the Eighteenth Century.* U. CA Pr. 1990 $47.50. ISBN 0-520-07022-4. A collection of essays from an international collaboration of historians that examined the importance of a "quantitative spirit" in science and technology during the Enlightenment.

Gelfand, Toby. *Professionalizing Modern Medicine: Paris Surgeons and Medical Science and Institutions in the Eighteenth Century. Contributions in Medical History Ser.* Greenwood 1980 $39.95. ISBN 0-313-21488-3. Discusses the intellectual, social, and institutional elements that gave rise to the modern medical profession; uses Paris, France, as a case study.

Gillispie, Charles C. *Science and Polity in France at the End of the Old Regime.* Princeton U. Pr. 1980 $166.10. ISBN 0-7837-3408-5. Definitive study of the interactions of politics, the emergence of the modern state, and scientific activity in the eighteenth century.

Hahn, Roger. *The Anatomy of a Scientific Institution: The Paris Academy of Sciences, 1666–1803.* U. CA Pr. 1971 $50.00. ISBN 0-520-01818-4. Classic institutional study that illuminates the emergence of science as a profession.

Hankins, Thomas L. *Jean d'Alembert: Science and the Enlightenment.* Gordon & Breach 1990 $32.00. ISBN 2-88126-399-1. Informative study of a leading French scientist and mathematician in the intellectual context of his times.

————. *Science and the Enlightenment. History of Science Ser.* Cambridge U. Pr. 1985 o.p. Presents a brief introduction to eighteenth-century science; designed for undergraduate students.

Hindle, Brooke. *The Pursuit of Science in Revolutionary America, 1735–1789.* Norton 1974 o.p. A standard survey of the emergence of science during the colonial period and early history of the United States.

Holmes, Frederic L. *Lavoisier and the Chemistry of Life: An Exploration of Scientific Creativity. History of Science and Medicine Ser.* U. of Wis. Pr. 1985 $38.50. ISBN 0-299-09980-6. Important study of Lavoisier's research in animal chemistry.

Hufbauer, Karl. *The Formation of the German Chemical Community, 1720–1795.* U. CA Pr. 1982 $55.00. ISBN 0-520-04415-0. A comprehensive examination of the social and institutional development of German chemistry, culminating in the reception of Lavoisier's "new" chemistry.

King, Lester S. *The Philosophy of Medicine: The Early Eighteenth Century.* HUP 1978 $80.80. ISBN 0-7837-4161-8. Excellent introduction to trends and themes in eighteenth-century medical theory and practice.

Lavoisier, Antoine L. *Elements of Chemistry.* Trans. by R. Kerr. Dover 1984 repr. of 1790 ed. $14.95. ISBN 0-486-64624-6. The standard translation of Lavoisier's revolutionary work in chemistry.

Lyon, John, and Philip Sloan, eds. *From Natural History to the History of Nature: Readings from Buffon and His Critics*. U. of Notre Dame Pr. 1981 $26.95. ISBN 0-268-00955-6. Includes selections from Buffon's various scientific writings.

McClellan, James E., III. *Science Reorganized: Scientific Societies in the 18th Century*. Col. U. Pr. 1985 $65.00. ISBN 0-231-05996-5. Covers scientific academies and societies from the founding of the Royal Society of London in 1660 to the closing of the Paris Academy of Sciences in 1793.

Paul, Charles B. *Science and Immortality: The Eloges of the Paris Academy of Sciences (1699–1791)*. U. CA Pr. 1980 $34.95. ISBN 0-520-03986-6. Argues that published eulogies of the academy created a new hero and myth—the disinterested scientist.

Roe, Shirley A. *Matter, Life and Generation: Eighteenth Century Embryology and the Haller-Wolff Debate*. Cambridge U. Pr. 1981 $42.95. ISBN 0-521-23540-5. Covers the debates over the nature of life.

Rousseau, G. S., and R. Porter. eds. *The Ferment of Knowledge: Studies in the Historiography of Eighteenth-Century Science*. Cambridge U. Pr. 1980 $69.95. ISBN 0-521-22599-X. Presents a collection of essays appraising issues and historiographical themes in historical research of science during the Enlightenment.

Schofield, Robert S. *The Lunar Society of Birmingham: A Social History of Provincial Society and Industry in 18th Century England*. OUP 1963 o.p. Standard study of the informal group that sparked the English Industrial Revolution; covers Boulton, E. Darwin, Priestley, Watt, and others.

Spangenburg, Ray, and Diane K. Moser. *The History of Science in the Eighteenth Century*. Facts on File 1993 $17.95. ISBN 0-8160-2740-4. Traces the sometimes tortuous path of reasoning that underlies present scientific understandings. Includes an extensive annotated bibliography.

Thackray, Arnold. *Atoms and Power: An Essay on Newtonian Matter-Theory and the Development of Chemistry*. Bks. Demand 1970 $66.90. ISBN 0-8357-9153-X. Examines the development of Newtonian theories of matter through the eighteenth century.

Woolf, Harry. *The Transits of Venus: A Study of Eighteenth-Century Science*. Ayer 1981 $25.00. ISBN 0-405-13959-4. Classic case study of the emerging international character of eighteenth-century science; highlights institutions and expeditions.

Nineteenth Century

Appleman, Philip, ed. *Darwin*. Norton 1979 $24.95. ISBN 0-393-01192-5. A good anthology of primary sources on the background and impact of Darwin's ideas on science, theology, philosophy, society, and letters.

Bowler, Peter J. *Evolution: The History of an Idea*. U. CA Pr. 1989 $42.50. ISBN 0-520-06385-6. Excellent, introductory survey of the history and impact of evolution and evolutionary concepts.

Brooks, John L. *Just Before the Origin: Alfred Russel Wallace's Theory of Evolution*. Col. U. Pr. 1984 $50.00. ISBN 0-231-05676-1. Examines the scientific work of the co-proponent of evolution.

Bruce, Robert V. *The Launching of Modern American Science, 1846–1876*. Cornell Univ. Pr. 1988 $15.95. ISBN 0-8014-9496-6. Authoritative coverage of the social and institutional history of American science during this period.

Burchfield, Joe D. *Lord Kelvin and the Age of the Earth*. U. Ch. Pr. 1990 $15.95. ISBN 0-226-08043-9. Examines the controversy about the age of Earth.

Clark, Ronald W. *The Survival of Charles Darwin: A Biography of a Man and an Idea*. Avon 1986 $5.95. ISBN 0-380-69991-5. Offers a broad, clearly written introduction to Darwin's life, times, and accomplishments.

Clerke, Agnes M. *A Popular History of Astronomy in the Nineteenth Century*. Scholarly repr. of 1908 ed. $79.00. ISBN 0-403-01492-1. Classic introduction to nineteenth-century astronomy and astrophysics.

Coleman, William. *Biology in the Nineteenth Century*. History of Science Ser. Cambridge U. Pr. 1978 $15.95. ISBN 0-521-29293-X. Examines the emergence of modern biology through cell theory, the evolution debate, and issues surrounding form, function, and experiment; standard survey designed for undergraduate students.

Cooter, Roger. *The Cultural Meaning of Popular Science: Phrenology and the Organization of Consent in Nineteenth Century Britain.* Cambridge U. Pr. 1985 $69.95. ISBN 0-521-22743-7. An exposition of the political uses of the ostensible authority of science.

Crouch, Tom D. *A Dream of Wings: Americans and the Airplane, 1875–1905.* Smithsonian 1989 $19.95. ISBN 0-87474-325-7. An authoritative, well-illustrated book that describes the early history of flight in the United States; emphasizes nineteenth-century aeronautics and early gliders.

Daniels, George H. *American Science in the Age of Jackson.* Col. U. Pr. 1968 $46.50. ISBN 0-231-0373-8. Remains the best introduction for this period.

Darwin, Charles. *The Autobiography and Selected Letters.* Ed. by Francis Darwin. Dover repr. of 1892 ed. $6.95. ISBN 0-486-20479-0. Classic example of scientific autobiography.

———. *On the Origin of Species by Means of Natural Selection, or the Preservation of Favoured Races in the Struggle for Life.* HUP 1964 repr. of 1859 ed. $11.95. ISBN 0-674-63752-6. The best available version of Darwin's theory.

Eiseley, Loren. *Darwin's Century: Evolution and the Men Who Discovered It.* Doubleday 1961 $9.95. ISBN 0-385-08141-3. Intelligent, well-written account of Darwin's predecessors and influences.

Gillespie, Neal C. *Charles Darwin and the Problem of Creation.* U. Ch. Pr. 1979 o.p. Excellent study of Darwin's religious beliefs.

Gillispie, Charles C. *Genesis and Geology: A Study in the Relations of Scientific Thought, Natural Theology and Social Opinion in Great Britain, 1790–1850. Historical Monographs Ser.* HUP 1951 $25.50. ISBN 0-674-34480-4. Standard introduction to the topic.

Greene, John C. *American Science in the Age of Jefferson.* Iowa St. U. Pr. 1984 o.p. Excellent introduction to American science in the early history of the United States. Emphasizes the slow development of institutional support and the influence of Jefferson.

Greene, Mott T. *Geology in the Nineteenth Century: Changing Views of a Changing World.* Cornell Univ. Pr. 1982 $47.50. ISBN 0-8014-1467-9. Examines geological theories and controversies from Hutton and Werner to twentieth-century theories of continental drift and plate tectonics.

Gregory, Frederick. *Scientific Materialism in Nineteenth-Century Germany.* Kluwer Ac. 1979 o.p. Provides a detailed study of German materialism in the second half of the nineteenth century.

Hall, Marie B. *All Scientists Now: The Royal Society in the Nineteenth Century.* Cambridge U. Pr. 1985 $64.95. ISBN 0-521-26746-3. A chapter in the history of the oldest continuous scientific society in the world.

Harman, Peter M. *Energy, Force and Matter: The Conceptual Development of Nineteenth-Century Physics. History of Science Ser.* Cambridge U. Pr. 1982 $14.95. ISBN 0-521-28812-6. Introductory survey; designed primarily for undergraduate students.

Himmelfarb, Gertrude. *Darwin and the Darwinian Revolution.* Norton 1968 repr. of 1959 ed. $13.95. ISBN 0-393-00455-4. A controversial study that examines Darwin's method and the debate over modern evolutionary synthesis.

Hindle, Brooke, and Steven Lubar. *Engines of Change: The American Industrial Revolution, 1790–1860.* Smithsonian 1986 $15.95. ISBN 0-87474-539-X. Excellent introduction to the early history of technology and its links with industrial development in the United States.

Hofstadter, Richard. *Social Darwinism in American Thought.* Beacon 1955 o.p. Classic, but somewhat dated, study.

Holmes, Frederic L. *Claude Bernard and Animal Chemistry.* HUP 1974 $45.00. ISBN 0-674-13485-0. Detailed study of Bernard's life, work, and influence.

Hull, David L. *Darwin and His Critics: The Reception of Darwin's Theory of Evolution by the Scientific Community.* U. Ch. Pr. 1983 $17.00. ISBN 0-226-36046-6. Features selections and excerpts from Darwin's critics; includes brief introductions.

Huxley, Thomas H. *Autobiography and Essays*. Ed. by Brander Matthews. Kraus 1969 repr. of 1919 ed. o.p. A classic of scientific autobiography, written by "Darwin's Bulldog."

Jones, Ernest. *The Life and Work of Sigmund Freud*. 3 vols. Basic 1953–57 $85.00. ISBN 0-465-04015-2. Classic in the "life and letters" tradition of intellectual biography.

Lenoir, Timothy. *The Strategy of Life: Teleology and Mechanics in 19th-Century German Biology*. U. Ch. Pr. 1989 $14.95. ISBN 0-226-47183-7. Covers issues relating to the nature of life, materialism, and biological purpose in German physiology.

Merz, John Theodor. *A History of European Thought in the Nineteenth Century*. 4 vols. Peter Smith 1904–12 o.p. A pioneering survey (particularly innovative for its time) that examines institutional and national aspects of science; now somewhat dated.

Pernick, Martin S. *A Calculus of Suffering: Pain, Professionalism and Anesthesia in Nineteenth Century America*. Col. U. Pr. 1987 $55.00. ISBN 0-231-05186-7. Describes the reception of anesthesia among various ranks of American practitioners from its introduction in 1846 to the end of the nineteenth century.

Reingold, Nathan, ed. *Science in Nineteenth-Century America: A Documentary History*. U. Ch. Pr. 1985 $12.50. ISBN 0-226-70947-7. Standard introduction and collection of documentary sources.

Rothstein, William G. *American Physicians in the Nineteenth Century: From Sects to Science*. Bks. Demand 1972 $18.95. ISBN 0-8018-4427-4. Sociological interpretation of American medicine and medical practice in the nineteenth century.

Ruse, Michael. *The Darwinian Revolution: Science Red in Tooth and Claw*. U. Ch. Pr. 1981 $12.95. ISBN 0-226-73165-0. Outlines themes and controversies regarding the reception of Darwinism.

Sheets-Pyenson, Susan. *Cathedrals of Science: Development of Colonial Natural History Museums During the Late Nineteenth Century*. U. of Toronto Pr. 1988 $29.95. ISBN 0-7735-0655-1. Establishes connections between imperial and scientific enterprises.

Sulloway, Frank J. *Freud, Biologist of the Mind: Beyond the Psychoanalytic Legend*. HUP 1992 $19.95. ISBN 0-676-32335-1. Argues that many of Freud's ideas drew upon biological thought, particularly Darwinian evolution; stimulating introduction to Freud and his work.

Turner, Gerard L'E. *Nineteenth-Century Scientific Instruments*. U. CA Pr. 1984 $70.00. ISBN 0-520-05160-2. A standard work on the subject.

Williams, L. Pearce. *Album of Science: The Nineteenth Century*. Scribner 1978 $85.00. ISBN 0-684-15047-6. Presents a well-illustrated selection of images; includes explanatory text.

Twentieth Century

Allen, Garland E. *Life and Science in the Twentieth Century*. *History of Science Ser*. Cambridge U. Pr. 1978 o.p. A standard, introductory survey designed for undergraduate students.

Beyerchen, Alan D. *Scientists under Hitler: Politics and the Physics Community in the Third Reich*. Bks. Demand repr. of 1981 ed. $83.50. ISBN 0-7837-4526-5. Describes the range of responses among German physicists to National Socialism during the dictatorship of Adolph Hitler.

Bliss, Michael. *The Discovery of Insulin*. U. Ch. Pr. 1984 $13.50. ISBN 0-226-05898-0. Account of the discovery of insulin and the career of Frederick Banting, who received the Nobel Prize.

Braun, Ernest, and Stuart MacDonald. *Revolution in Miniature: The History and Impact of Semiconductor Electronics Re-Explored*. Cambridge U. Pr. 1982 o.p. Standard survey of the development of microelectronics and the semiconductor industry.

Clark, Ronald W. *Einstein: The Life and Times*. Avon 1972 $6.95. ISBN 0-380-01159-X. Popular biography for the general reader; includes hundreds of photographs.

Corn, Joseph, ed. *Imagining Tomorrow: History, Technology, and the American Future*. MIT Pr. 1988 $11.95. ISBN 0-262-03115-9. Features a collection of essays on technology in the American imagination.

Cravens, Hamilton. *Triumph of Evolution: American Scientists and the Heredity-Environment Controversy, 1900–1941.* Johns Hopkins 1988 $14.95. ISBN 0-8018-3742-1. Examines the nature/nurture controversy in the United States during the early decades of the twentieth century.

Dupree, A. Hunter. *Science in the Federal Government: A History of Policies and Activities to 1940.* Ed. by I. Bernard Cohen. Ayer 1980 repr. of 1957 ed. $39.00. ISBN 0-405-12540-2. Remains a valuable and informative reference despite the many new publications covering science and public policy in the United States.

Einstein, Albert. *Relativity: The Special and General Theory.* Trans. by Robert W. Lawson. Crown Pub. Group 1961 $4.95. ISBN 0-517-02530-2. Classic, nontechnical introduction to relativity theory.

Einstein, Albert, and Leopold Infeld. *The Evolution of Physics: The Growth of Ideas from Early Concepts to Relativity and Quanta.* Bks. Demand repr. of 1967 ed. $79.00. ISBN 0-685-17873-0. A classic example of the popular history of science, written by active scientists.

Franklin, Allan. *The Neglect of Experiment.* Cambridge U. Pr. 1989 $21.95. ISBN 0-521-37965-2. Combines philosophy and history to reveal the role of experimentation in modern physics.

Galison, Peter. *How Experiments End.* U. Ch. Pr. 1987 $39.95. ISBN 0-226-27914-6. Merges philosophical insights and historical methodology to produce informative case studies in the development of modern physics; emphasizes the importance of instrumention and laboratory practice.

Galison, Peter, and Bruce Hevly, eds. *Big Science: The Growth of Large-Scale Research.* Stanford U. Pr. 1992 $47.50. ISBN 0-8047-1879-2. Collection of essays by specialists on various aspects of "Big Science," government-sponsored research, and science-based technology in the postwar period.

Gingerich, Owen, ed. *Astrophysics and Twentieth-Century Astronomy to 1950. General History of Astronomy Ser.* Cambridge U. Pr. 1984 $42.95. ISBN 0-521-24256-8. A collection of papers covering all aspects of astronomy and astrophysics.

Heilbron, John L. *The Dilemmas of an Upright Man: Max Planck as Spokesman for German Science.* U. CA Pr. 1986 $32.50. ISBN 0-520-05710-4. Intellectual biography of the German physicist; focuses on his moral dilemmas in Germany under the National Socialist regime.

Hounshell, David A., and John Smith, Jr. *Science and Corporate Strategy: Du Pont R&D, 1902–1980.* Cambridge U. Pr. 1988 $47.95. ISBN 0-521-32767-9. Fascinating case study of the evolving role of basic laboratory research in modern corporate strategy.

Kevles, Daniel J. *In the Name of Eugenics: Genetics and the Uses of Human Heredity.* U. CA Pr. 1986 $15.00. ISBN 0-520-05763-5. Describes the development of eugenics and related social and ethical issues.

———. *The Physicists: The History of a Scientific Community in Modern America.* HUP 1987 $16.95. ISBN 0-674-66655-0. Covers the intellectual and institutional development of the American physics community from the late nineteenth century; particularly emphasizes the political dimension.

Kuhn, Thomas S. *Black-Body Theory and the Quantum Discontinuity, 1894–1912.* U. Ch. Pr. 1987 $18.95. ISBN 0-226-45800-8. Technical study of the origins of quantum physics, focusing on Max Planck's work on the early quantum theory.

Lang, Kenneth R., and Owen Gingerich, eds. *A Source Book in Astronomy and Astrophysics, 1900–1975.* HUP 1979 $80.00. ISBN 0-674-82200-5. Provides a useful selection of original papers that examines the emergence of contemporary astronomy and astrophysics.

Layton, Edwin T. *The Revolt of the Engineers: Social Responsibility and the American Engineering Profession.* Johns Hopkins 1986 repr. of 1971 ed. $37.50. ISBN 0-8018-3286-1. Classic study of the emergence of engineering as a profession in the United States.

McGowen, Tom. *The Great Monkey Trial: Science Versus Fundamentalism in America.* Watts 1990 $13.90. ISBN 0-531-10965-8. Recreation of the drama of the 1925 Scopes

Monkey Trial in the wider context of conflicts between science and faith from Copernicus to Creationism.

Metropolis, N., and others, eds. *A History of Computing in the Twentieth Century: A Collection of Essays.* Acad. Pr. 1980 $77.00. ISBN 0-12-491650-3. Provides a diverse collection of essays that includes hardware, software, and corporate warfare; includes contributions from historians as well as participants.

Miller, Arthur I. *Imagery in Scientific Thought: Creating Twentieth-Century Physics.* MIT Pr. 1986 repr. of 1984 ed. $13.95. ISBN 0-262-63104-0. Important study of the roots of scientific creativity.

Olby, Robert. *The Path to the Double Helix.* U. of Wash. Pr. 1974 o.p. Intellectual, institutional background to the discovery of DNA and the double helix.

Pais, Abraham. *Subtle Is the Lord: The Science and Life of Albert Einstein.* OUP 1982 $35.00. ISBN 0-19-853907-X. Intimate, yet scholarly biography; includes technical details and personal insights.

Provine, William B. *The Origins of Theoretical Population Genetics. History of Science and Medicine Ser.* U. Ch. Pr. 1987 $16.95. ISBN 0-226-68466-0. Examines the issues that formed population genetics at the beginning of the twentieth century.

Reingold, Nathan. *Science, American Style.* Rutgers U. Pr. 1992 $45.00. ISBN 0-8135-1660-9. Presents a collection of the lively essays from the dean of historians of twentieth-century American science; many essays were previously published.

_____. *Science in America: A Documentary History, 1900–1939.* U. Ch. Pr. 1981 $37.50. ISBN 0-226-70946-9. Useful selection of primary sources; includes commentary.

Rossiter, Margaret. *Women Scientists in America: Struggles and Strategies to 1940.* Johns Hopkins 1984 $14.95. ISBN 0-8018-2509-1. An important book that describes the contributions of women scientists in the United States.

Schilpp, Paul Arthur, ed. *Albert Einstein, Philosopher-Scientist.* 2 vols. Open Court 1970 $26.95. ISBN 0-87548-286-4. A collection of essays on Einstein's life, thought, and influence in science, philosophy, and culture.

Smith, Robert W. *The Expanding Universe: Astronomy's "Great Debate," 1900–1931.* Cambridge U. Pr. 1982 $34.50. ISBN 0-521-23212-0. A nontechnical treatment of the scientific debate on the nature of our galaxy and the size and structure of the universe; emphasizes the specific contributions of Eddington, Shapley, and Curtis.

Snow, C. P. *The Two Cultures: And a Second Look.* Cambridge U. Pr. 1993 repr. of 1964 ed. $9.95. ISBN 0-521-45730-0. A classic statement and reevaluation of the controversial claim that scientists and humanistically trained individuals represent distinct cultures.

Vincenti, Walter G. *What Engineers Know and How They Know It: Analytical Studies from Aeronautical History.* Johns Hopkins 1990 $48.50. ISBN 0-8018-3974-2. An updated revision of previously published studies, written by a creative historian of technology.

Watson, James D. *Double Helix: Being a Personal Account of the Discovery of the Structure of DNA.* Ed. by Gunther S. Stent. Atheneum 1980 $11.95. ISBN 0-689-70602-2. Gripping firsthand account of one of the most significant scientific discoveries of the twentieth century.

Will, Clifford M. *Was Einstein Right? Putting General Relativity to the Test.* Basic 1988 $13.00. ISBN 0-465-09087-7. Popular introduction to general relativity and the experimental ingenuity involved in its demonstration; written for the general reader.

Williams, Trevor I. *Science: A History of Discovery in the Twentieth Century.* OUP 1990 $40.00. ISBN 0-19-520843-9

_____. *A Short History of Twentieth-Century Technology, 1900–1950.* OUP 1982 $29.95. ISBN 0-19-858159-9. Surveys the development of technology in the first half of the twentieth-century; covers the economic, social, and political factors that shaped Western technological society.

CHRONOLOGY OF AUTHORS

Whewell, William. 1794–1866
Osler, Sir William. 1849–1919
Garrison, Fielding H. 1870–1935
Usher, Abbott Payson. 1883–1965
Sarton, George. 1884–1956
White, Lynn, Jr. 1907–

Kranzberg, Melvin. 1917–
Kuhn, Thomas S(amuel). 1922–
Hughes, Thomas P(arke). 1923–
Pursell, Carroll W(irth), Jr. 1932–
Thackray, Arnold W. 1939–

GARRISON, FIELDING H. 1870–1935

Medical historian Fielding Garrison was born in Washington, D.C., and studied at Johns Hopkins University and Georgetown University. After joining the Surgeon General's office in 1891, he served as assistant librarian (1899–1922) of its medical library, the largest in the world. It was there that he launched his outstanding career as librarian-scholar and medical historian.

Garrison served in the Army Medical Reserve Corps during World War I and remained in the army until 1930, when he was appointed head of the medical library at Johns Hopkins. Under his stewardship, the Johns Hopkins's medical collection was greatly strengthened and became one of the finest in the world.

Garrison also achieved prominence as America's leading medical historian with his steady output of scholarly works and textbooks. His most important volume, *An Introduction to the History of Medicine* (1913), became a standard reference and helped contemporary physicians and those of later generations understand the history of medicine and its importance in their own practices.

BOOKS BY GARRISON

History of Neurology. Thomas 1969 o.p.
Introduction to the History of Medicine. W. B. Saunders 1929 o.p. One of the most well-known standard reference works on the topic.
A Medical Bibliography. Grafton & Co. 1943 o.p.
Notes on the History of Military Medicine. Coronet Bks. repr. of 1922 ed. $47.50. ISBN 0-685-13790-2

HUGHES, THOMAS P(ARKE). 1923–

Born in Richmond, Virginia, the son of a lumber merchant, Thomas Parke Hughes is an eminent historian of science and technology, and perhaps the best writer in his discipline. His book *American Genesis* was a Pulitzer Prize finalist in 1989, and *Elmer Sperry* won the Dexter Prize in 1971. After serving in the United States Navy during World War II as a lieutenant commander, Hughes continued his education at the University of Virginia, receiving a Ph.D in history from the university in 1953. He then taught history at Washington and Lee University (1956–63)); MIT (1963–66); and Southern Methodist University (1969–73). From 1973 until 1988, he was professor of history and sociology of science at the University of Pennsylvania, and in 1988 he was appointed Visiting Research Professor at the Wissenshaftszentrum in Berlin.

In the 1980s and early 1990s, Hughes received important recognition for his work. In 1984 he was selected to serve on the Advisory Council of the Smithsonian Institution and awarded a Leonardo da Vinci medal. In addition to his books, Hughes has written extensively in professional journals. Several of his

articles examine how United States technological support built the former
Soviet Union into a twentieth-century superpower.

BOOKS BY HUGHES

American Genesis: A Century of Invention and Technological Enthusiasm, 1870–1970.
1989. Viking Penguin 1990 $12.95. ISBN 0-14-60974-4. Comprehensive look at the
dramatic scientific changes that occurred during the period and what effect these
changes have had on contemporary American society.

Elmer Sperry: Inventor and Engineer. 1971. Bks. Demand repr. of 1971 ed. $95.70. ISBN
0-8357-8115-1

Lewis Mumford: Public Intellectual. OUP 1990 $42.50. ISBN 0-19-506173-X. Sixteen
essays discuss the ideas and insights of Lewis Mumford.

Networks of Power: Electrification in Western Society, 1880–1930. Johns Hopkins 1983
$48.00. ISBN 0-8018-2873-2. Examines the history of electric power systems in the
United States, Great Britain, and Germany.

KRANZBERG, MELVIN. 1917–

Melvin Kranzberg is a historian known primarily for his contribution as
primary founder of the history of technology as a discipline. He also founded the
professional Society for the History of Technology (SHOT), serving as first
editor of its journal, *Technology and Culture*, as well as SHOT secretary
(1959–79) and president (1983–84). Kranzberg also has been an active
supporter and proponent of other STS professional organizations, such as the
Society of Philosophy and Technology and the National Association of Science,
Technology and Society, from which he was initial recipient of a NASTS
Honorary Lifetime Membership. Kranzberg enjoys an active retirement of
lecturing, writing, and serving on numerous professional organization advisory
boards, as well as being Callaway Professor Emeritus of the History of
Technology at Georgia Institute of Technology.

Kranzberg earned a Ph.D. in modern European history from Harvard
University in 1942. His initial books, *The Siege of Paris, 1870–71* (1950) and
1848: A Turning Point? (1959) reflect Kranzberg's Ivy League background. In his
teaching and research, however, Kranzberg increasingly realized the important
role that technology has played in historical development. His interests then
rapidly turned in that direction. Among his books, Kranzberg is perhaps best
known for the two-volume *Technology in Western Civilization* (1967), which has
served as a core text in the history of technology for a generation of students.
Kranzberg's broad interests are evident in other works, ranging from such
topics as work and technological innovation to energy and ethics. His central
theme has been "the significance in human affairs of the history of technology
and the value of the contextual approach in understanding technical developments," codified as Kranzberg's First Law: "Technology is neither good nor
bad; nor is it neutral." This theme and Kranzberg's role in its development are
reflected in two volumes. One is John M. Staudenmaier's *Technology's
Storytellers: Reweaving the Human Fabric* (1985), which analyzes the first 20
years of the journal *Technology and Culture*. The other is edited by Stephen H.
Cutcliffe and Robert C. Post, *In Context: History and the History of Technology—
Essays in Honor of Melvin Kranzberg* (1989), a Festschrift collection that reflects
on the history of technology as a discipline.

BOOKS BY KRANZBERG

By the Sweat of the Brow: Work in the Western World. (coauthored with Joseph Gries).
1975. Greenwood 1986 $45.50. ISBN 0-313-25323-4. Offers a popular overview that

examines the changing nature of work in the face of evolving technology—from the Stone Age to the present.

Bridge to the Future: A Centennial Celebration of the Brooklyn Bridge. (coedited with Brooke Hindle and Margaret Latimer). *Annals of the New York Academy of Sciences.* NY Acad. Sci. 1984 $75.00. ISBN 0-89766-246-6. Features papers from a conference that commemorates the Brooklyn Bridge and the broader relationship between technology and society, especially in terms of creativity.

Energy and the Way We Live. (coedited with Timothy A. Hall). Boyd & Fraser 1980 o.p. A study guide designed for a course by newspaper program; distributed nationwide, appearing in more than 400 newspapers.

Ethics in an Age of Pervasive Technology. Westview 1980 o.p. Presents an edited collection of conference papers treating ethics and values issues related to technology worldwide.

Innovation at the Crossroads between Science and Technology. (coedited with Yehuda Elkana and Zehev Tadwor). S. Neaman Pr. 1989 $46.75. ISBN 965-386-000-3. Presents proceedings of an international conference on technological innovation sponsored by the Samuel Neaman Institute for Advanced Studies in Science and Technology and the Van Leer Jerusalem Institute; includes historical case studies and analyses of contemporary issues.

Technological Education—Technological Style. San Francisco Pr. 1986 $15.00. ISBN 0-911302-59-X. Presents brief introductory case studies of technical and engineering education, mainly in the late nineteenth and early twentieth century; countries covered include the United States, Great Britain, Germany, France, India, and Romania.

Technological Innovation: A Critical Review of Current Knowledge. (coedited with Patrick Kelly). San Francisco Pr. 1978 $35.00. ISBN 0-911302-34-3. A mid-1970s state-of-the-art survey of knowledge on research and development and the innovation process; includes a lengthy overview, contributions by nine scholars, and an extensive, but dated, bibliography.

Technology and Culture: An Anthology. (coedited with William H. Davenport). Schocken 1972 o.p. Features a selection of some outstanding articles that were published during the first decade of *Technology and Culture.*

Technology in Western Civilization. (coedited with Carroll W. Pusell, Jr.). 1967. 2 vols. OUP 1967. Vol. 1 *The Emergence of Modern Industrial Society.* $29.95. ISBN 0-19-500938-X. Vol. 2 *Technology of the Twentieth Century.* $24.95. ISBN 0-19-500939-8. Includes contributions from experts in the history of technology; used for more than 25 years as the standard text in the field.

BOOK ABOUT KRANZBERG

Cutcliffe, Stephen H., and Robert Post, eds. *In Context: History and the History of Technology, Essays in Honor of Melvin Kranzberg.* Lehigh Univ. Pr. 1989 $38.50. ISBN 0-934223-03-3. Executes a tour de force of this field of inquiry; rich and varied fare.

KUHN, THOMAS S(AMUEL). 1922–

Born in Cincinnati, Ohio, and educated at Harvard University, Thomas Samuel Kuhn earned his doctorate in physics in 1949. His name is synonymous with the concept of scientific revolutions. Trained as a physicist, Kuhn made his mark in the history and philosophy of science. While a student at Harvard, he became interested in the philosophy of science and was introduced to the history of science by the historian (and president of Harvard) James B. Conant. With Leonard K. Nash, Kuhn was asked to teach a historically oriented course on science for nonscientists. Kuhn found that what he had learned in the philosophy of science did not fit the case studies that were central to the course in the history of science. For instance, the discovery of oxygen seen through the eyes of a historian looks different from the same episode seen from the point of view of present-day chemical theory. Kuhn explored this interdisciplinary area during a postdoctoral fellowship at Harvard. Subsequently, he made the professional shift to the history of science, but also retained his philosophical interests. By 1956 Kuhn was teaching the history of science at the University of California at Berkeley. He later taught at Princeton University and the Massachusetts Institute of Technology.

In the early 1960s, Kuhn was invited to contribute an essay on scientific revolutions for the *International Encyclopedia of Unified Science*. This resulted in a slim volume entitled *The Structure of Scientific Revolutions* (1962). Kuhn's book asks this question: If scientists proceed by a scientific method that is definite and decisive, why are there dramatic disagreements among scientists, both during revolutions and in such disciplines as the social sciences? Kuhn proposes ideas that might answer the question. Successful, stable sciences possess "paradigms," which are "universally recognized scientific achievements that for a time provide model problems and solutions to a community of practitioners." Revolutions are changes from one paradigm to another. Lack of consensus, which occurs in the social sciences, indicates the absence of a paradigm. Kuhn concludes that the philosophy of science needs to be supplemented by history. This view gradually took hold in academic philosophy of science—and also in many other fields. The Kuhnian historical revolution in the philosophy of science paved the way for later sociological theories, such as those of BRUNO LATOUR, that were even more critical, not only of the positivist philosophy of science, but also of any rationalist model of scientific thinking.

BOOKS BY KUHN

Black-Body Theory and the Quantum Discontinuity, 1894–1912. U. Ch. Pr. 1987 $18.95. ISBN 0-226-45800-8. A detailed history of science texts.

The Copernican Revolution: Planetary Astronomy in the Development of Western Thought. HUP 1957 $10.95. ISBN 0-674-17103-9. Earliest philosophical-historical treatise, written before his formulation of the scientific revolutions thesis.

The Essential Tension: Selected Studies in Scientific Tradition and Change. U. Ch. Pr. 1979 $13.95. ISBN 0-226-45806-7. Series of essays written both before and after *The Structure of Scientific Revolutions*; helpful in gaining a fuller understanding of Kuhn's thought.

The Structure of Scientific Revolutions. 1962. *Foundations of the Unity of Science Ser.* U. Ch. Pr. 1970 $19.95. ISBN 0-226-45804-0. Kuhn's most influential work, in which he applies lessons from the history of science to the philosophy of science.

Tradition and Change. U. Ch. Pr. 1979 $13.95. ISBN 0-226-45806-7. Series of essays written before and after *The Structure of Scientific Revolutions*; helpful in gaining a fuller understanding of Kuhn's thought.

BOOKS ABOUT KUHN

Barnes, Barry. *T. S. Kuhn and Social Science.* Col. U. Pr. 1982 $16.50. ISBN 0-231-05437-8. An attack on Kuhn by a leading sociologist of scientific knowledge.

Gutting, Gary, ed. *Paradigms and Revolutions: Appraisals and Applications of Thomas Kuhn's Philosophy of Science.* U. of Notre Dame Pr. 1980 o.p. Excellent studies by leading philosophers on various aspects of Kuhn's revolutionary thought.

Hoyningen-Huene, Paul. *Reconstructing Scientific Revolutions: Thomas S. Kuhn's Philosophy of Science.* U. Ch. Pr. 1993 $40.00. ISBN 0-226-35550-0. Attempts to provide a comprehensive and fair summary and critique of Kuhn's thought.

Lakatos, Imre, and Alan Musgrave, eds. *Criticism and the Growth of Knowledge.* Cambridge U. Pr. 1970 o.p. Includes introductory summary of his views by Kuhn, numerous criticisms by Popperian philosophers of science (and others), plus an extended reply by Kuhn.

Margolis, Howard. *Paradigms and Barriers: How Habits of Mind Govern Scientific Belief*. U. Ch. Pr. 1993 $40.00. ISBN 0-226-50522-7. A new study that attempts to apply Kuhn's approach.

Stove, D. C. *Popper and After: Four Modern Irrationalists*. B. Franklin 1982 $45.00. ISBN 0-08-026791-2. In addition to Popper, this work also investigates Kuhn, Imre Lakatos, and Paul Feyerabend. Only a critic could lump the four together.

MUMFORD, LEWIS. 1895-1990

[SEE Chapter 6 in this volume.]

OSLER, SIR WILLIAM. 1849-1919

Canadian physician, writer, and lecturer William Osler was born at Tecumseh, Ontario, the son of a clergyman. After graduating from Trinity College in Toronto, he decided to become a doctor. When he completed his medical work at McGill University in 1872, Osler traveled to Europe and continued his studies there in London, Berlin, and Vienna. On his return to Canada, he was appointed chair in physiology and pathology at McGill. During the 1870s at McGill, he avidly pursued research in pathology on parasites and freshwater polyzoa. From 1884 to 1889, Osler served as head of clinical medicine at the University of Pennsylvania. He then was invited to Johns Hopkins University as professor of the principles and practices of medicine. After an outstanding tenure at Johns Hopkins, in 1905 he accepted the post of regius professor of medicine at Oxford University.

A popular lecturer and a clear and insightful writer, Osler gained distinction as an outstanding medical historian and scholar. His writings included *Science and Immortality* (1904) and *A Way of Life* (1914). His best-known work, however, was his popular textbook *Principles and Practice of Medicine* (1892), which achieved numerous editions and was translated into several languages. During his lifetime, Osler amassed a large and impressive medical history library of rare books. This library was eventually transported and restored at the McGill Medical School, preserving intact this valuable collection.

BOOKS BY OSLER

Principles and Practice of Medicine. Appleton 1892 o.p.
Science and Immortality. Ayer 1977 repr. of 1904 ed. $14.00. ISBN 0-405-09581-3
A Way of Life. Lippincott 1937 $11.95. ISBN 0-06-141860-9

BOOKS ABOUT OSLER

Cushing, Harvey. *Life of Sir William Osler*. 2 vols. OUP 1940 $75.00. ISBN 0-19-500524-4
Golden, Richard L., and others. *Sir William Osler: An Annotated Bibliography*. Norman SF 1988 $125.00. ISBN 0-930405-00-5
Howard, R. Palmer. *The Chief: Doctor William Osler*. Watson Pub. Intl. 1983 $20.00. ISBN 0-88135-000-1
King, Lester S. *Transformations in American Medicine: From Benjamin Rush to William Osler*. Johns Hopkins 1990 $39.50. ISBN 0-8018-4057-0. Analysis of the transformation of medical theory from the eighteenth to nineteenth centuries with special emphasis on Osler's radically different theories.

PURSELL, CARROLL W(IRTH), JR. 1932-

Born in Visalia, California, the son of a salesman, Carroll Pursell currently ranks among the foremost American historians of science and technology. His research and writing has focused on the role of science and technology in shaping national policy in the United States. Pursell was educated at the University of California at Berkeley, receiving a B.A. in 1956 and a Ph.D. in 1961, and at the University of Delaware, where he earned a Master's degree in history in 1958. From 1963 to 1965, he taught history at Case Western Reserve University in Cleveland. Then he was appointed professor of history at the University of California at Santa Barbara, remaining there for more than 20 years. In 1988 he returned to Case Western Reserve University, where he is currently the Adeline Barry Davee Distinguished Professor of History.

Pursell has received widespread recognition for his contributions to the history of science and for the quality of his scholarly research. Appointed Visting Research Scholar at the Smithsonian Institution in 1970, he has also served as Andrew W. Mellon Professor of the Humanities at Lehigh University (1974–76) and Research Professor at the University of Wisconsin (1977). A Fellow of the American Association for the Advancement of Science, Pursell has also served as president of the Society of History and Technology (1990–92). In 1991 he was awarded the Leonardo da Vinci medal for his contributions in his field.

BOOKS BY PURSELL

Early Stationary Steam Engines in America: A Study in the Migration of Technology. Smithsonian 1969 o.p.

From Conservation to Ecology. Crowell 1973 o.p.

The Military Industrial Complex. HarpC 1972 o.p. Discusses the economic aspects of disarmament and defense contracts.

Technology in America: A History of Individuals and Ideas. MIT Pr. 1990 $12.95. ISBN 0-262-66067-9. A collection of essays that chronicle American technology from the colonial period to the space age.

Technology in Western Civilization 2 Vols. Ed. by Melvin Kranzberg. Vol. 1 *The Emergence of Modern Industrial Society.* OUP 1967 $29.95. ISBN 0-19-500938-X. Vol. 2. *Technology in the Twentieth Century.* OUP 1968 $24.95. ISBN 0-19-500939-8

SARTON, GEORGE. 1884–1956

George Sarton is generally considered the founder of the history of science as a scholarly discipline. He studied chemistry, celestial mechanics, and mathematics at the University of Ghent, where he earned a Ph.D. in mathematics (1911). In 1912, while still a resident of his native Belgium, he founded *Isis*, a "review dedicated to the history of science." Sarton immigrated to the United States in 1915, assuming a research position in the Widener Library at Harvard University in 1916. He remained at Harvard for the rest of his life, becoming a lecturer in 1920 and founding the History of Science Society in 1924. In 1940 Sarton was appointed professor of the history of science. Sarton also established the new discipline by example, writing more than 300 books, articles, and essays on ancient and medieval science; on early historians of the exact sciences, such as Jean Etienne Montucla (1725–99); and on the development of physics in the twentieth century. He nurtured his encyclopedic approach to the history of science, which he coupled to a broad vision of its potential contribution to what he called the "New Humanism," by editing *Isis* for almost four decades and compiling nearly 80 critical bibliographies. In published lectures and guides to the history of science, such as his *Study of the History of Science* (1936) and *Guide to the History of Science* (1952), as well as the editorial work for *Isis*, Sarton defined this emerging discipline while actively promoting teaching and research.

BOOKS BY SARTON

Ancient Science and Modern Civilization. Bks. Demand repr. of 1954 ed. $31.60. ISBN 0-8357-2950-8

A Guide to the History of Science. Ronald 1952 o.p. The first disciplinary handbook that covers research in the history of science; includes published versions of Sarton's characteristic lectures on "Science and Tradition" and methods of teaching the history of science.

The History of Science and the New Humanism. Transaction Pubs. 1988 repr. of 1962 ed. $14.95. ISBN 0-88738-703-9. Suggests the need to study the history of science as a step in elevating the "scientific spirit" to its rightful place in modern humanism.

Introduction to the History of Science. 3 vols. Krieger 1975 repr. of 1927–53 ed. $425.00. ISBN 0-88275-172-7. An encyclopedic and bibliographic survey of the history of science from antiquity through the fourteenth century.

Life of Science: Essays in the History of Civilization. Ayer repr. of 1948 ed. $16.00. ISBN 0-8369-2472-X

Six Wings: Men of Science in the Renaissance. Bks. Demand repr. of 1957 ed. $86.90. ISBN 0-8357-6694-2. Extends Sarton's survey of the development of modern science to the fifteenth and sixteenth centuries; posthumously published Patten Lectures of 1955.

THACKRAY, ARNOLD W. 1939–

Science historian Arnold Thackray was born and educated in England, receiving his B.S. degree at Bristol University and his doctorate in the history and philosophy of science at Cambridge University. After receiving his doctorate in 1965, Thackray served as a research fellow at Churchill College, Cambridge University, until 1968, when he joined the faculty of the University of Pennsylvania as a professor of history and of the history of science. In 1973 he became chair of the department of the history and sociology of science at Pennsylvania.

A leading authority in the history of science, Thackray has studied the development of modern science and the sociological and intellectual nexus of science and society. He focuses much of his attention on the field of chemistry, where his research has highlighted the role that ISAAC NEWTON's theory of matter and JOHN DALTON's atomic theory have had on developments in chemistry.

A member of the Institute of Advanced Study at Princeton, Thackray has served as visiting lecturer at Harvard University and Bryn Mawr College as well as visiting professor at the London School of Economics and Political Science.

BOOKS BY THACKRAY

Atoms and Power: An Essay on Newtonian Matter Theory and the Development of Chemistry. Bks. Demand repr. of 1970 ed. $66.90. ISBN 0-8357-9153-X

Chemistry in America, Eighteen Seventy-Six to Nineteen Seventy-Six: Historical Indicators. Kluwer Ac. 1988 $52.00. ISBN 90-277-2662-0

Classics, Staples, and Precursors in the History, Philosophy, and Sociology of Science. Arno Pr. 1972 o.p.

A Guide to the History of Science. Am. Hist. Assn. 1985 o.p.

John Dalton: Critical Assessments of His Life and Science. HUP 1972 $17.00. ISBN 0-674-47525-9

Science after Forty. (ed.) U. Ch. Pr. 1992 $39.00. ISBN 0-226-79374-5. Includes topics on big science in the last years of the Soviet Union, inventing the maser in postwar America, cold fusian, and Soviet lunar science.

USHER, ABBOTT PAYSON. 1883–1965

Abbott Payson Usher was born in Lynn, Massachusetts, and educated at Harvard University and the University of Paris. After receiving his Ph.D. from

Harvard, he joined the faculties of Cornell University, where he taught economics and economic history from 1914 to 1920, and Harvard, where he served as professor of economics until his retirement in 1949.

A historian of technology, Usher helped pioneer the study of industrial technology and its impact on the development of the world economy. He emphasized the role of inventions in technological change, focusing on the historical forces underlying the inventive process rather than viewing inventions as the isolated achievements of gifted individuals. He also addressed the question of creativity and change within the continuous flow of human history. His scholarly output of books, articles, and monographs helped define economic history and its role as an integral part of the field of economics. His best-known work, which remains a classic in the history of technology, is *A History of Mechanical Inventions* (1929). His other important writings include *An Introduction to the Industrial History of England* (1920) and *The History of Deposit Banking in Mediterranean Europe* (1943).

BOOKS BY USHER

An Economic History of Europe Since 1750. AMS Pr. 1970 repr. of 1937 ed. $16.00. ISBN 0-404-00962-X

The History of Deposit Banking in Mediterranean Europe. HUP 1943 o.p.

A History of Mechanical Inventions. 1929. Dover 1988 repr. of 1954 ed. $10.95. ISBN 0-486-25593-X

An Introduction to the Industrial History of England. 1920. Ayer repr. of 1920 ed. o.p.

WHEWELL, WILLIAM. 1794–1866

William Whewell was born in Lancaster, England, the son of a master carpenter. He was educated and spent virtually his entire career at Trinity College, Cambridge University. From 1841 until his death, he served as Master of Trinity. One of the most prolific scholars of his age, he was active in many fields, such as moral philosophy, theology, political economy, meteorology, and mineralogy. Beginning in the 1830s, Whewell focused his attention mainly on the history and philosophy of science, publishing the *History of the Inductive Sciences* in 1837 and *Philosophy of the Inductive Sciences* in 1840. These two books constituted the most significant survey of the development of the exact sciences published during the nineteenth century. Whewell also wrote sermons, poetry, and essays on a variety of subjects.

BOOKS BY WHEWELL

History of the Inductive Sciences. 3 vols. F. Cass Pub. 1967 repr. of 1857 ed. $85.00. ISBN 0-7146-1149-2. The result of a monumental project to reveal the best methods of discovering truth by a thorough examination of previous discoveries.

Philosophy of the Inductive Sciences. 2 vols. 1840. F. Cass Pub. 1967 repr. of 1847 ed. $95.00. ISBN 0-7146-1156-5. A remarkable effort to synthesize empirical and rational traditions in the philosophy of science.

Selected Writings on the History of Science. Ed. by Yehuda Elkana. U. Ch. Pr. 1984 $15.00. ISBN 0-226-89434-7. Offers a selection of texts; includes extensive excerpts from the *History* and *Philosophy of the Inductive Sciences*.

BOOKS ABOUT WHEWELL

Fisch, Menachem. *William Whewell, Philosopher of Science*. OUP 1991 $59.00. ISBN 0-19-8242490-9. Presents the best available intellectual biography of Whewell; emphasizes his philosophical importance.

Fisch, Menachem, and Simon Schaffer, eds. *William Whewell: A Composite Portrait.* OUP
    1991 $98.00. ISBN 0-19-824900-4. Offers a collection of essays about Whewell's
    personal and professional life.
Yeo, Richard. *Defining Science: William Whewell, Natural Knowledge and Public Debate
    in Early Victorian Britain.* Cambridge U. Pr. 1993 $54.95. ISBN 0-521-43182-4.
    Examines Whewell's contributions to the history and philosophy of science and how
    his work influenced the development of the field.

WHITE, LYNN, JR. 1907–

A historian of technology and a medieval specialist, Lynn White was born in
San Francisco and educated at Stanford University. He earned advanced
degrees at Union Theological Seminary and Harvard University, where he
earned an M.A. and Ph.D. in European medieval and Renaissance history. In
1934 White began his distinguished teaching career, first at Princeton University, then at Stanford University and Mills College, where he also served as
president from 1943 to 1958. Appointed professor of history at the University of
California, Los Angeles, in 1958, he taught there until he retired in 1972. Among
his numerous academic honors, White served as president of the History of
Science Society, the Society for the History of Technology, and the American
Historical Association.

White's research and writing emphasized the thrust of technology in the
transformation of Western culture from its medieval religious impulse to its
increasingly secular Renaissance concerns. In his classic study, *Machina ex
Deo: Essays in the Dynamism of Western Culture* (1969), he explored the
spiritual foundations of technological innovation in Western Europe.

BOOKS BY WHITE

Frontiers of Knowledge. HarpC 1956 o.p.
Latin Monasticism in Norman Sicily. Medieval Acad. 1967 repr. of 1938 ed. $25.00. ISBN
    0-910956-12-X
Machina ex Deo: Essays in the Dynamism of Western Culture. MIT Pr. 1969 o.p. Also
    published as *Dynamo and Virgin Reconsidered: Machina ex Deo.*
Medieval Religion and Technology. U. CA Pr. 1978 $15.00. ISBN 0-520-05896-8
Medieval Technology and Social Change. OUP 1962 $9.95. ISBN 0-19-500266-0

CHAPTER 4

Philosophy of Science, Technology, and Medicine

Paul T. Durbin

> Philosophy grows out of, and . . . is connected with, human affairs. . . . In effect, if not in profession, the great systems of Western philosophy all have been thus motivated and occupied.
> —JOHN DEWEY, *Reconstruction in Philosophy*

When ordinary people think about science, it is often to the medical sciences, with their phenomenal success in the twentieth century in discovering the causes and cures of various diseases, that their thoughts turn. Experts tend instead to think of something like the pure-thought experiments of a scientist such as ALBERT EINSTEIN—although they will also admit that relativity physics can lead to an atomic bomb and that scientific theories and good engineering practices, in general, can lead to products and processes useful to humanity.

The stereotype of philosophy is that it is concerned exclusively with the foundations of these and other human activities—with basic definitions, principles, and general theoretical formulations. The philosophy of science, among the fields discussed in this chapter, has certainly had this stereotyped focus throughout most of its history, although in recent decades the focus has come into question.

The philosophy of technology, with an equally long history going back to the late nineteenth century, has tended to challenge facile distinctions between the pure sciences and applied science and technology. From KARL MARX (see Vols. 3 and 4) on, critical philosophers and social theorists have tended to see science and technology as largely indistinguishable, embedded in society, and driven by historical social forces, differentially in different epochs. To many scientists, engineers, and philosophers of science, this leads to a suspicion that philosophers of technology are woolly-headed ruminators, akin to cultural historians, about ages and stages in the history of the modern world. As a result, another group of philosophers concerned with technology focuses more narrowly on particular technologies, from artificial intelligence to environmental ethics, from biotechnology to risk assessment.

These concretely focused philosophers of particular technologies would read JOHN DEWEY's (see Vols. 3 and 4) admonition to get involved in real-world practice as meaning involvement with the real world of practicing scientists and engineers. For their part, the more traditional philosophers of technology also claim that their work has a practical aim: to provide wise and farsighted direction for societies with shortsighted science and technology policies.

As for philosophers of medicine, they would seem to have chosen the most concrete focus of all. This is certainly true for bioethicists, medical ethicists, and related philosophers who focus on ethical issues and cases in hospitals and other health care settings.

For this volume there has been an organizational division of labor, and the ethics of medicine and health care (along with engineering ethics and similar fields) has been assigned to Chapter 5. In this chapter only the most abstract philosophical discussions of medicine—akin to the philosophy of science—are included. To receive a complete picture of the philosophy of science, technology, and medicine, the diligent reader will thus need to consult the two chapters.

REFERENCE BOOKS

Asimov, Isaac. *Asimov's New Guide to Science*. Basic rev. ed. 1984 $34.95. ISBN 0-465-00473-3. Probably the single best popularization of natural sciences available, widely accepted by working scientists in all fields; clinical science not included.

Asquith, Peter, and Henry Kyburg, eds. *Current Research in Philosophy of Science*. Philos. Sci. Assn. 1979 o.p. Presents surveys of past and projected future directions in the academic philosophy of science. A few chapters related to technology and medicine; somewhat technical.

Blackwell, Richard J., comp. *A Bibliography of the Philosophy of Science, 1945–1981*. Greenwood 1983 $95.00. ISBN 0-313-23124-9. Authoritative source on standard topics in the academic philosophy of science, lists over 7,000 works; includes appendixes and name index.

Bynum, W. F., E. J. Browne, and Roy Porter, eds. *Dictionary of the History of Science*. Princeton U. Pr. 1985 $75.00. ISBN 0-691-02384-0. Excellent sourcebook with many philosophical entries; includes medicine but almost no engineering or technology.

Cutcliffe, Stephen H., Judith A. Mistichelli, and Christine M. Roysdon, comps. *Technology and Values in American Civilization: A Guide to Information Sources*. Amer. Information Guide Ser. Gale 1980 $68.00. ISBN 0-8103-1475-4. Bibliographical survey of the literature on technology and values; includes over 2,400 well-annotated entries.

Durbin, Paul T. *Dictionary of Concepts in the Philosophy of Science. Reference Sources for the Social Sciences and Humanities Ser.* Greenwood 1988 $59.95. ISBN 0-318-32545-4. Focuses on 100 controversial concepts in the history of the philosophy of science. Alphabetical arrangement of topics; excellent bibliographies; little technology and no medicine.

———, ed. *A Guide to the Culture of Science, Technology, and Medicine*. Free Pr. rev. ed. 1984 $19.95. ISBN 0-02-907890-3. Important bibliographical and descriptive source for the philosophy of science, technology, and medicine, accompanied by history and social science discussions of the same fields; includes bibliographical update.

Edwards, Paul, ed. *The Encyclopedia of Philosophy*. 4 vols. Free Pr. 1973 $425.00. ISBN 0-02-894950-1. Standard reference work for philosophy generally, including excellent material on almost all aspects of philosophy of science before the late 1960s; includes little on the philosophies of technology and medicine.

Floistad, Guttorm, ed. *Contemporary Philosophy: A New Survey*. Vol. 2 *Philosophy of Science*. Kluwer Ac. 1982 $151.50. ISBN 90-247-2518-6. Good surveys of many aspects of the philosophy of science by leading experts from all over the world; one chapter on the philosophy of technology from an analytical perspective; technical.

Lineback, Richard H., ed. *The Philosopher's Index 1990 Cumulative Edition*. Vol. 24. Bowling Green Univ. 1991 $144.00. ISBN 0-912632-52-6. Most useful source available for students of any aspect of philosophy, including the philosophy of science, technology, and medicine. Books, book reviews, and journal articles indexed.

Mitcham, Carl, and Robert Mackey. *Bibliography of the Philosophy of Technology*. Bks. Demand 1985 $55.80. ISBN 0-8357-7201-2. Basic starting point for research in the field, concentrating on works of the period from 1925 to 1972. Includes an author index. This bibliography has been supplemented by updates in *Research in Philosophy of Technology*.

Olby, R. C., Geoffrey N. Cantor, J.R.R. Christie, and M. S. Hodge. *Companion to the History of Modern Science*. Routledge 1989 $89.95. ISBN 0-415-01988-5. Excellent source book for the history of science; includes discussions of the history of the philosophy of science by leading experts.

Reich, Warren T., ed. *Encyclopedia of Bioethics*. 4 vols. Free Pr. 1978 $250.00. ISBN 0-02-926060-4. Currently the best encyclopedic source on this rapidly developing field. Includes some philosophy of science and philosophy of technology related to medicine; covers much more on bioethics than on the philosophy of medicine in the foundational sense.

Spiegel-Rösing, Ina, and Derek de Solla Price, eds. *Science, Technology, and Society: A Cross-Disciplinary Perspective*. Russell Sage 1977 o.p. Excellent sourcebook on science and technology policy, although somewhat dated; includes much philosophy but almost nothing on medicine.

Walters, LeRoy, and Tamar J. Kahn, ed. *Bibliography of Bioethics*. Vol. 17. Georgetown U. Pr. 1991 $45.00. ISBN 0-9614448-7-8. Standard bibliographic source for bioethics books and articles; includes little on the philosophy of medicine beyond bioethics.

PHILOSOPHY OF SCIENCE

In terms of its representation in the universities, this is the best developed of the fields included here. The philosophy of science has its own journals, professional societies, and even a few separate university departments. Long dominated by a school called logical positivism (or logical empiricism), the traditional philosophy of science has focused primarily on a small set of problems: inductive inference, the confirmation or disconfirmation of hypotheses, the logical characteristics of scientific theories or laws, and so on. Beginning about 1960, historically oriented philosophers of science, led by THOMAS S. KUHN, began to attack the tradition. By the 1980s these attacks had been absorbed, with many philosophers of science adding a historical dimension to their logical, epistemological, and methodological studies—however much at odds this was with Kuhn's original intent radically to transform the philosophy of science. In the 1980s and 1990s, the philosophy of science again came under attack in the name of various postmodernisms, new social approaches, feminist critiques, and so on. In this section, books will be cited under three headings: Epistemological and Methodological Issues; Historical, Social, and Cultural Critiques; and Philosophical Treatments of Particular Scientific Disciplines.

Epistemological and Methodological Issues

This section includes books related to the dominant traditions in the academic philosophy of science, especially in the English-speaking world over roughly the past 50 years. Criticisms of the academic philosophy of science appear in the next section. Also included here are the small number of books attacking pseudo-science.

Achinstein, Peter, ed. *The Concept of Evidence*. Oxford Readings in Philosophy Ser. OUP 1984 $16.95. ISBN 0-19-875062-5. A useful collection introducing controversies about how experience supports scientific theories; technical.

Agassi, Joseph, and Ian C. Jarvie, eds. *Rationality: The Critical View.* Kluwer Ac. 1987 $54.00. ISBN 90-247-3455-X. Prominent students of Karl Popper collect examples of studies employing the critical rationality method, many of them highly technical.

Armstrong, D. M. *What Is a Law of Nature? Cambridge Studies in Philosophy Ser.* Cambridge U. Pr. 1985 $15.95. ISBN 0-521-31481-X. Discusses laws as relations among universals; technical.

Blake, Ralph M., Curt J. Ducasse, and Edward H. Madden. *Theories of Scientific Method: The Renaissance Through the Nineteenth Century. Classics in the History and Philosophy of Science Ser.* Gordon & Breach 1960 $32.00. ISBN 2-88124-351-7. Discusses major figures in the history of philosophy of science. One of the few good sources on the history of philosophy of science.

Boyd, Richard, Philip Gasper, and J. D. Trout, eds. *The Philosophy of Science.* MIT Pr. 1991 $55.00. ISBN 0-262-52156-3. Welcome addition to a field that until recently had few basic textbooks; somewhat technical.

Bunge, Mario. *Causality and Modern Science.* Dover 1979 repr. of 1963 ed. $9.95. ISBN 0-486-23728-1. Provides a useful survey of various concepts of causality in philosophy and science, along with a discussion of causal determinism and the role of causal concepts in modern physics.

Capek, Milic. *The New Aspects of Time: Its Continuity and Novelities.* Kluwer Ac. 1991 $94.00. ISBN 0-7923-0911-1. Longtime defender of flow of time collects papers spanning 40 years; some essays difficult.

Carnap, Rudolf. *Introduction to the Philosophy of Science.* Ed. by Martin Gardner. Basic 1966 o.p. For the general reader; the most readable introduction to the work of this most important leader of the positivist philosophy of science.

Cohen, Robert S., and Marx W. Wartofsky, eds. *A Portrait of Twenty-Five Years. Boston Studies in the Philosophy of Science Ser.* Kluwer Ac. 1985 $31.00. ISBN 90-277-1971-3. Selection of outstanding contributions to the leading philosophy of science series in the United States and probably in the world. Many papers technical but provide a remarkably broad picture of the philosophy of science over more than 20 years of diversity and change in the field.

Colodny, Robert G., ed. *Frontiers of Science and Philosophy. Univ. of Pittsburgh Ser. in the Philosophy of Science.* Bks. Demand repr. of 1962 ed. $77.00. ISBN 0-318-34736-9. First in the series edited by Colodny. Contributors include such well-known philosophers as Hempel, Sellars, Scriven, and Grünbaum.

——. *Mind and Cosmos: Essays in Contemporary Science and Philosophy. CPS Publications in Philosophy of Science.* U. Pr. of Amer. 1984 $52.00. ISBN 0-8191-3650-6. Includes discussions of scientific inference and conceptual change; technical.

——. *The Nature and Function of Scientific Theories: Essays in Contemporary Science and Philosophy. Philosophy of Science Ser.* U. of Pittsburgh Pr. 1970 o.p. Includes important articles by Shimony, Feyerabend, Maxwell, Hesse, Salmon, and Hanson; technical.

Earman, John. *Bayes or Bust? Critical Examination of Bayesian Confirmation Theory.* MIT Pr. 1992 $35.00. ISBN 0-262-05046-3. Technical discussion of the most important theory of theoretical confirmation.

——, ed. *Testing Scientific Theories. Minnesota Studies in the Philosophy of Science.* U. of Minn. Pr. 1984 $44.95. ISBN 0-8166-1159-9. Technical sampling of recent work in inductive reasoning with the Bayesian point of view represented by some of its major practitioners and a number of historical case studies rounding out the collection.

Fetzer, James H. *Philosophy of Science.* Paragon Hse. 1992 $16.95. ISBN 1-55778-481-7. Good introductory textbook.

——, ed. *Foundations of Philosophy of Science.* Paragon Hse. 1992 $28.95. ISBN 1-55778-480-9. Companion to the above textbook.

Fraassen, Bas van. *Laws and Symmetry.* OUP 1990 $65.00. ISBN 0-19-824860-1. Technical introduction to very difficult material on scientific theories, especially in physics.

———. *The Scientific Image*. OUP 1980 $22.50. ISBN 0-19-824427-4. Attacks scientific realism in the name of updated empiricism; technical.

Gale, George. *Theory of Science*. McGraw 1979 $32.52. ISBN 0-07-022680-6. A text reflecting 1970s developments in the philosophy of science.

Gardner, Martin. *Fads and Fallacies in the Name of Science*. Dover 1957 $6.95. ISBN 0-486-20394-8. A classic in the field of debunking crank theories.

Giere, Ronald N. *Explaining Science: A Cognitive Approach. Science and Its Conceptual Foundations Ser.* U. Ch. Pr. 1990 $17.95. ISBN 0-226-29306-1. The author's summary of his novel "naturalistic philosophy of science" approach.

———. *Understanding Scientific Reasoning*. HB Coll. Pubs. 1991 $25.00. ISBN 0-03-026419-7. Excellent textbook on the basic forms of reasoning in science.

Glymour, Clark. *Theory and Evidence*. Bks. Demand 1980 $103.00. ISBN 0-8357-3568-0. Technical discussion about how explanations and predictions support the theories from which they are derived.

Goodman, Nelson. *Fact, Fiction, and Forecast*. HUP 1983 $14.50. ISBN 0-674-29071-2. Goodman's presentation of his classic puzzle of inductive inference and his proposed solution; technical.

Grandy, Richard E., ed. *Theories and Observation in Science*. Ridgeview 1980 $27.00. ISBN 0-917930-19-3. Presents principal views on how theories affect observations.

Grim, Patrick, ed. *Philosophy of Science and the Occult*. State U. NY Pr. 1990 $12.95. ISBN 0-7914-0204-5. Includes articles, some critical, some not, on a wide range of pseudo-sciences.

Hacking, Ian M. *The Emergence of Probability: A Philosophical Study of Early Ideas about Probability, Induction, and Statistical Inference*. Cambridge U. Pr. 1984 $18.95. ISBN 0-521-31803-3. Excellent sourcebook on the items mentioned in the subtitle.

———. *Representing and Intervening: Introductory Topics in the Philosophy of Natural Science*. Cambridge U. Pr. 1983 $16.95. ISBN 0-521-28246-2. More advanced than the title suggests; technical.

———. *Scientific Revolutions. Oxford Readings in Philosophy Ser.* OUP 1981 $13.95. ISBN 0-19-875051-X. Balanced collection of the main contenders on the notion of revolutions in the history of science; includes Popper, Kuhn, Feyerabend, Lakatos, and Shapere.

Harré, Rom. *Principles of Scientific Thinking*. U. Ch. Pr. 1970 $22.50. ISBN 0-226-31708-0. Proposes a realist philosophy of science in opposition to the dominant view of logical empiricism. Valuable treatment of models in scientific thinking.

Harris, Errol E. *Formal, Transcendental, and Dialectical Thinking: Logic and Reality*. State U. NY Pr. 1987 $64.50. ISBN 0-88706-430-2. A leading defender of the dialectical philosophy of science challenges empiricism by contrasting different interpretations of the relationship between logic and reality.

Hempel, Carl. *Philosophy of Natural Science*. P-H 1966 ISBN 0-13-663823-6. The best introduction to the traditional academic philosophy of science. Clear and readable, even for those with little background.

Hesse, Mary B. *Models and Analogies in Science*. U. of Notre Dame Pr. 1966 o.p. Classic on the use of scientific models and analogies.

Holton, Gerald. *Thematic Origins of Scientific Thought: Kepler to Einstein*. HUP rev. ed. 1988 $14.95. ISBN 0-674-87748-9. A physicist-historian explores thinking processes in the history of scientific controversies.

Jeffrey, Richard C. *The Logic of Decision*. U. Ch. Pr. 1983 $14.95. ISBN 0-226-39582-0. An eminent defender supports a decision-theory doctrine of scientific reasoning; technical.

Kitcher, Philip. *Abusing Science: The Case Against Creationism*. MIT Pr. 1982 $9.95. ISBN 0-262-61037-X. Rebuttal of creationist arguments against modern evolutionary theory.

Kosso, Peter. *Reading the Book of Nature: An Introduction to the Philosophy of Science*. Cambridge U. Pr. 1992 $10.95. ISBN 0-521-42682-0. A very useful and basic introduction.

Kyburg, Henry E., Jr. *Epistemology and Inference*. U. of Minn. Pr. 1983 $44.50. ISBN 0-8166-1150-5. Technical.

LaFollette, Marcel C. *Making Science Our Own: Public Images of Science, 1910–1955*. U. Ch. Pr. 1990 $45.00. ISBN 0-226-46779-1. A student of science journalism covers the formative period of twentieth-century American science in terms of its public acceptance.

Lamb, David, ed. *New Horizons in the Philosophy of Science*. Ashgate Pub. Co. 1992 $55.95. ISBN 1-85628-296-1. Somewhat technical introduction to the philosophy of science.

Lambert, Karel, and Gordon G. Brittan, eds. *Introduction to the Philosophy of Science*. Ridgeview 1987 $35.00. ISBN 0-924922-10-9. A very popular work; suitable for a general audience.

Laudan, Larry. *Progress and Its Problems: Towards a Theory of Scientific Growth*. U. CA Pr. 1977 $42.00. ISBN 0-520-03330-2. Challenge to traditional logical-empiricist philosophies of science based on problem solving as the key to understanding science.

———. *Science and Relativism: Some Key Controversies in the Philosophy of Science*. U. Ch. Pr. 1990 $32.00. ISBN 0-226-46949-2. Interesting and informative introduction to key problems by way of a fictitious dialogue.

Laudan, Rachel. *From Mineralogy to Geology: The Foundations of a Science, 1650–1830*. *Science and Its Conceptual Foundations Ser*. U. Ch. Pr. 1987 $27.50. ISBN 0-226-46950-6. Excellent combination of history and the philosophy of science.

Levi, Isaac. *Decisions and Revisions: Philosophical Essays on Knowledge and Value*. Cambridge U. Pr. 1984 $49.95. ISBN 0-521-25457-4. Summary of the author's views on inductive logic and statistical inference presented as challenges to opposing views; technical.

Losee, John. *An Historical Introduction to the Philosophy of Science*. OUP 1980 $12.95. ISBN 0-19-289143-X. Useful history of the philosophy of science.

Margolis, Joseph. *Pragmatism without Foundations: Reconciling Realism and Relativism*. Blackwell Pubs. 1986 $45.00. ISBN 0-631-16584-3. Difficult but rewarding summary of author's defense of relativism; introduction to the multivolume set.

Maxwell, Grover, and Robert M. Anderson, Jr., eds. *Induction, Probability, and Confirmation*. *Studies in the Philosophy of Science Ser*. U. of Minn. Pr. 1975 $44.95. ISBN 0-8166-0736-2. Presents papers by leading logical empiricists; technical.

Michalos, Alex C. *Improving Your Reasoning*. P-H 1986 ISBN 0-13-453465-4. Excellent introduction to logic and scientific reasoning for students; recently updated.

Nagel, Ernest. *The Structure of Science*. Hackett Pub. 1979 $37.95. ISBN 0-915144-71-9. The classic advanced textbook in the philosophy of science; has stood up well over the decades, though some discussions now outdated.

Nersessian, Nancy. *Faraday to Einstein: Constructing Meaning in Scientific Theories*. *Science and Philosophy Ser*. Kluwer Ac. 1990 $32.50. ISBN 0-7923-0950-2. Presents an interesting combination of history and the philosophy of science.

Pitt, Joseph C. *Theories of Explanation*. OUP 1988 $14.95. ISBN 0-19-504971-3. Views classical problem through the lens of a series of papers from the 1940s to the 1980s; somewhat technical.

Popper, Karl R. *Objective Knowledge: An Evolutionary Approach*. OUP 1972 $16.95. ISBN 0-19-875024-2. Perhaps not most representative of the work of this important falsificationist philosopher of science, but the most accessible to the general reader.

Putnam, Hilary. *Philosophical Papers*. 3 vols. Cambridge U. Pr. 1986 $59.95. ISBN 0-521-31020-2. Includes widely respected contributions on several topics in the traditional philosophy of science. Presents some evidence of how the author's views have changed radically over the years; technical.

Quine, Willard van Orman. *From a Logical Point of View: Nine Lògico-Philosophical Essays*. HUP rev. ed. 1980 $16.95. ISBN 0-674-32351-3. A collection of previously published essays including the author's famous "Two Dogmas of Empiricism." Considered one of the most important books in the logical-empiricist tradition.

Radner, Daisie, and Michael Radner. *Science and Unreason*. Wadsworth Pub. 1982 ISBN 0-534-01153-5. Short, clearly written book presenting rules for identifying pseudo-sciences; illustrated with a number of historical examples.

Rosenkrantz, Roger D. *Foundations and Applications of Inductive Probability*. Ridgeview 1981 $36.00. ISBN 0-917930-03-7. Technical but excellent textbook for students of inductive probability.

Salmon, Merrilee, and others. *Introduction to the Philosophy of Science*. P-H 1992 ISBN 0-13-663345-5. Best textbook currently available. Favors traditional logical empiri-cism, but contrasts it with most recent anti-empiricist approaches. Written by faculty members from University of Pittsburgh.

Salmon, Wesley. *Scientific Explanation and the Causal Structure of the World*. Princeton U. Pr. 1984 $18.95. ISBN 0-691-10170-1. Ingenious explanation of a new theory of causality; technical.

Scheffler, Israel. *The Anatomy of Inquiry: Philosophical Studies in the Theory of Science*. Hackett Pub. 1981 $32.50. ISBN 0-915144-98-0. Summary of all the popular views in the philosophy of science before the field was challenged by Kuhn's historical approach; technical.

Schlagel, Richard. *Contextual Realism: A Meta-physical Framework for Modern Science*. Paragon Hse. 1986 o.p. Straightforward defense of scientific realism, but only within specific contexts; not difficult reading.

Shapere, Dudley. *Reason and the Search for Knowledge*. Kluwer Ac. 1983 $131.00. ISBN 90-277-1551-3. The author's theory of conceptual development challenges the logical-empiricist approach. Excellent incorporation of the history of science; somewhat technical.

Skyrms, Brian. *Choice and Chance: An Introduction to Inductive Logic*. Wadsworth Pub. 1986 ISBN 0-534-05190-1. Somewhat technical, though elementary, introduction to inductive reasoning.

Suppe, Frederick, ed. *The Structure of Scientific Theories*. U. of Ill. Pr. 1977 $49.95. ISBN 0-252-00634-8. Somewhat technical review of research on what theories are and how they relate to experiments; includes an extensive bibliography.

Suppes, Patrick, and others. *Foundations of Measurement*. Vol. 2. Acad. Pr. 1989 $89.50. ISBN 0-12-425402-0. Technical studies of the most important feature of science; lead author a foremost authority in the field.

Thagard, Paul. *Conceptual Revolutions*. Princeton U. Pr. 1992 $35.00. ISBN 0-691-08745-8. Presents an excellent challenge to Kuhn on scientific revolutions.

Toulmin, Stephen. *Foresight and Understanding: An Enquiry into the Aims of Science*. HarpC 1961 o.p. Important historical approach to scientific thinking that partially overlaps with postpositivist writers such as Kuhn.

Wallace, William A. *From a Realist Point of View: Essays on the Philosophy of Science*. U. Pr. of Amer. 1983 $26.25. ISBN 0-8191-3446-5. A philosopher-historian defends Thomistic realism against its opponents.

Wartofsky, Marx W., ed. *Models*. Kluwer Ac. 1979 $72.50. ISBN 90-277-0947-5. One of the founders of Boston Studies in Philosophy of Science collects contributions on models, an important but often neglected topic in the philosophy of science.

Watkins, John. *Science and Scepticism*. Princeton U. Pr. 1984 $55.00. ISBN 0-691-10171-X. Popperian attempt to go beyond Hume's skepticism about the possibility of scientific knowledge; technical.

Ziman, John M. *Reliable Knowledge: An Exploration of the Grounds for Belief in Science*. Cambridge U. Pr. 1991 $8.95. ISBN 0-521-40670-6. A physicist defends a sociologi-cally oriented philosophy of science.

Historical, Social, and Cultural Critiques of Standard Philosophy of Science

This section collects the main critiques of the academic philosophy of science that have been made over the past decade or so. They come from historicist, radical, feminist, and postmodernist perspectives, among others. Although the numbers of books of this sort have increased in recent years, these new perspectives have by no means supplanted the traditional philosophy of science in academic circles.

Ashmore, Malcolm. *The Reflexive Thesis: Wrighting Sociology of Scientific Knowledge.* U. Ch. Pr. 1989 $29.95. ISBN 0-226-02968-9. Encyclopedic survey of the new sociological challenge to the traditional philosophy of science.

Bloor, David. *Knowledge and Social Imagery.* U. Ch. Pr. 1991 $32.00. ISBN 0-226-06097-7. Leading spokesman for sociology of scientific knowledge school of thought.

Collins, Harry, and Trevor Pinch. *The Golem: What Everyone Should Know about Science.* Cambridge U. Pr. 1993 $19.95. ISBN 0-521-35601-6. Seven case studies arguing that scientific certainties do not come down to experimental method, but from the way ambiguous results are interpreted.

Feyerabend, Paul. *Against Method.* Routledge Chapman & Hall 1988 $50.00. ISBN 0-86091-934-X. An anarchist epistemologist challenges the conventional philosophy of science and suggests a more flexible and open "anything goes" alternative view that science is neither developed nor defended on rational grounds.

Fuller, Steve. *Philosophy, Rhetoric, and the End of Knowledge: The Coming of Science and Technology Studies.* Rhetoric of the Human Sciences Ser. U. of Wis. Pr. 1993 $54.00. ISBN 0-299-13774-0. The author goes a step beyond his earlier book, transforming social epistemology into studies of science and technology.

_____. *Social Epistemology.* Science, Technology, and Society Ser. Ind. U. Pr. 1988 $35.00. ISBN 0-253-35227-4. Argues that all epistemology of science ought to be social, in spite of appearances and objections.

Gutting, Gary, ed. *Paradigms and Revolutions: Appraisals and Applications of Thomas Kuhn's Philosophy of Science.* U. of Notre Dame Pr. 1980 o.p. Important selection of essays evaluating Kuhn's concepts and contributions.

Hanson, Norwood R. *Patterns of Discovery: An Enquiry into the Conceptual Foundations of Science.* Cambridge U. Pr. 1958 o.p. Along with Kuhn's approach, presents the first major challenge to the traditional philosophy of science; not difficult reading.

Harding, Sandra. *The Science Question in Feminism.* Cornell Univ. Pr. 1986 $11.95. ISBN 0-8014-9363-3. Summary of feminist critiques of science and the philosophy of science, including the author's own "standpoint epistemology."

Keller, Evelyn Fox. *Secrets of Life, Secrets of Death: Essays on Language, Gender, and Science.* Routledge 1992 $49.95. ISBN 0-415-90524-9. A radical feminist critic of science and the philosophy of science presents a collection of recent essays summarizing her views.

Kuhn, Thomas S. *The Essential Tension: Selected Studies in Scientific Tradition and Change.* U. Ch. Pr. 1979 $13.95. ISBN 0-226-45806-7. Selection of articles, essays, and lectures written between 1959 and 1974 on historiographic and metahistorical themes.

_____. *The Structure of Scientific Revolutions.* Foundations of the Unity of Science Ser. U. Ch. Pr. 1970 $19.95. ISBN 0-226-45804-0. Brilliant and highly influential study of scientific and historical change, arguing that science normally develops cumulatively but periodically undergoes discontinuous paradigm shifts or revolutions.

Lakatos, Imre, and A. E. Musgrave, eds. *Criticism and the Growth of Knowledge.* Cambridge U. Pr. 1970 $19.95. ISBN 0-521-09623-5. Report of conference proceedings in which Kuhn meets his critics, especially Popper and Popperians.

Longino, Helen. *Science as Social Knowledge: Values and Objectivity in Scientific Inquiry.* Princeton U. Pr. 1990 $35.00. ISBN 0-691-02051-5. Sophisticated attempt to mediate differences between the traditional philosophy of science and feminist and other criticisms with social perspective as the key.

Ormiston, Gayle, and Raphael Sassower. *Narrative Experiments: The Discursive Authority of Science and Technology.* U. of Minn. Pr. 1989 $39.95. ISBN 0-8166-1821-6. Direct challenge, in "postmodernist" terms, to the authority of science and technology.

Pickering, Andrew, ed. *Science as Practice and Culture.* U. Ch. Pr. 1992 $65.00. ISBN 0-226-66800-2. Presents the latest contributions from leaders in sociology of the school of scientific knowledge.

Proctor, Robert N. *Value-Free Science?: Purity and Power in Modern Knowledge.* HUP 1991 $34.95. ISBN 0-674-93170-X. A historian's version of the latest challenges to claims of scientific objectivity.

Rouse, Joseph. *Knowledge and Power: Toward a Political Philosophy of Science.* Cornell Univ. Pr. 1987 $34.50. ISBN 0-8014-9713-2. Uses European approaches to highlight the political dimension of science. Rethinks the traditional philosophy of science rather than challenges it directly.

Philosophical Treatments of Particular Scientific Disciplines

The fields covered here are the philosophy of physics, including cosmology, quantum mechanics, and relativity; the philosophy of biology; and the philosophy of social science. For philosophical treatments of artificial intelligence, see the section on Philosophical Studies of Particular Technological Developments. For the philosophy of psychology, see the section on Philosophy of Mind in Medicine.

Achinstein, Peter. *Particles and Waves: Historical Essays in the Philosophy of Science.* OUP 1991 $24.95. ISBN 0-19-506755-X. A well-known analytical philosopher of science traces the history of nineteenth-century controversies.

Agazzi, Evandro, and Albert Cordero, eds. *Philosophy and the Origin and Evolution of the Universe.* Kluwer Ac. 1991 $106.00. ISBN 0-7923-1322-4. An international set of authors considers the importance of cosmological and other scientific theories in relation to the philosophy of science.

Brandon, Robert N., and Richard M. Burian, eds. *Genes, Organisms, Populations: Controversies over the Units of Selection.* MIT Pr. 1984 $37.50. ISBN 0-262-52115-6. A collection of writings by well-known philosophers and biologists; includes bibliographies and index.

Braybrooke, David. *Philosophy of Social Science.* P-H 1987 ISBN 0-13-663394-3. Fairly technical, but good introduction to the topic.

Bub, Jeffrey. *The Interpretation of Quantum Mechanics.* Western Ontario Ser. Kluwer Ac. 1974 $50.50. ISBN 90-277-0466-X. A classical philosophical discussion of one of the most difficult fields of modern physics; technical.

Cartwright, Nancy. *How the Laws of Physics Lie.* OUP 1983 $21.00. ISBN 0-19-824704-4. The author defends a balanced view to the question: Are physical laws and theories correct representations of real processes or idealizations?

Cushing, James, and Ernan McMullin, eds. *Philosophical Consequences of Quantum Theory: Reflections on Bell's Theorem.* U. of Notre Dame Pr. 1989 $19.95. ISBN 0-268-01579-1. Written for philosophers unfamiliar with quantum theory.

Earman, John S. *World Enough and Space Time: Absolute vs. Relational Theories of Space and Time.* MIT Pr. 1992 $14.95. ISBN 0-262-55021-0. First-rate analysis of the controversy concerning absolute versus relational theories of space and time.

Fraassen, Bas C. van. *An Introduction to the Philosophy of Time and Space.* Columbia U. Pr. 1985 $39.50. ISBN 0-231-06132-3. Technical.

Friedman, Michael. *Foundations of Space-Time Theories: Relativistic Physics and Philosophy of Science.* Princeton U. Pr. 1986 $19.95. ISBN 0-691-02039-6. Technical but good introduction for those capable of dealing with the theory of relativity.

Griffiths, Paul, ed. *Trees of Life: Essays in Philosophy of Biology. Australasian Studies in History and Philosophy of Science.* Kluwer Ac. 1992 $96.00. ISBN 0-7923-1709-2. Proceedings of the Philosophical Problems in Evolutionary Biology Conference held in New Zealand in 1990.

Grünbaum, Adolf. *Philosophical Problems of Space and Time. Synthese Lib.* Kluwer Ac. 1973 $117.50. ISBN 90-277-0358-2. A leading empiricist summarizes his well-known views on the topic; includes arguments against opponents; technical.

Hughes, R.I.G. *The Structure and Interpretation of Quantum Mechanics.* HUP 1989 $39.50. ISBN 0-674-84392-4. Technical introduction to limited aspects of quantum mechanics.

Hull, David. *Science as a Process: An Evolutionary Account of the Social and Conceptual Development of Science.* U. Ch. Pr. 1990 $23.95. ISBN 0-226-36051-2. Presents the author's general approach to the philosophy of science based on detailed analyses of the history of biological-research communities.

Jammer, Max. *Concepts of Space: The History of Theories of Space in Physics.* Dover 1992 $6.95. ISBN 0-486-27119-6. A valuable sourcebook for students of space and time.

Kitcher, Philip. *Vaulting Ambition: Sociobiology and the Quest for Human Nature.* MIT Pr. 1987 $35.00. ISBN 0-262-61049-3. Detailed critique of sociobiology's attempt to explain human behavior on the basis of biology.

Lightman, Alan. *Ancient Light: Our Changing View of the Universe.* HUP 1991 $18.95. ISBN 0-674-03362-0. Popularization of recent cosmological theories; excellent introduction for the layperson.

MacKinnon, Edward M. *Scientific Explanation and Atomic Physics.* U. Ch. Pr. 1982 o.p. Gives a history of fundamental theories in physics and the concepts used to explain them. One of the best attempts to combine the history of science and the philosophy of science.

Margenau, Henry. *The Nature of Physical Reality: A Philosophy of Modern Physics.* Ox Bow 1977 $35.00. ISBN 0-918024-03-X. A reprint of the 1950 classic; includes bibliographies and indexes.

Margenau, Henry, and Roy Abraham Varghese. *Cosmos, Bios, Theos: Scientists Reflect on Science, Religion, and the Origins of the Universe.* Open Court 1992 $38.95. ISBN 0-8126-9186-5. Somewhat idiosyncratic attempt to find out what scientists today think about religious ideas in the context of the new cosmology and other fields.

Newton-Smith, W. H. *The Structure of Time.* Routledge 1984 $14.95. ISBN 0-7102-0389-6. Clear and readable book, with no more technical discussion than needed for clarity.

Prigogine, Ilya, and Isabelle Stengers. *Order Out of Chaos: Man's New Dialogue with Nature.* Bantam 1984 $8.95. ISBN 0-553-34363-7. How the Newtonian worldview is transformed by recent developments in theoretical mechanics and thermodynamics.

Ray, Christopher. *Time, Space and Philosophy. Philosophical Issues in Science Ser.* Routledge 1991 $55.00. ISBN 0-415-03222-0. Intended for people with little scientific background; covers historical as well as contemporary views.

Rosenberg, Alexander. *Philosophy of Social Science. Dimensions of Philosophy Ser.* Westview 1988 $62.00. ISBN 0-8133-0616-7. Good introduction and overview of the subject.

Ruse, Michael. *Philosophy of Biology. Philosophy Topics Ser.* Macmillan 1989 ISBN 0-02-404492-X. A prolific philosopher of biology provides a useful introductory textbook.

_____. *Philosophy of Biology Today. Philosophy and Biology Ser.* State U. NY Pr. 1988 $39.50. ISBN 0-88706-911-8. Survey of contemporary issues in the field.

_____. *What the Philosophy of Biology Is: Essays for David Hull.* Kluwer Ac. 1989 $107.50. ISBN 90-247-3778-8. Leaders in the field honor one of their colleagues.

Salmon, Wesley C. *Space, Time, and Motion: A Philosophical Introduction.* Bks. Demand rev. ed. 1981 $44.50. ISBN 0-318-39664-5. Though technical, a good introduction.

Schlesinger, George N. *Aspects of Time.* Hackett Pub. 1980 $27.50. ISBN 0-915144-69-7. An analytical philosopher discusses puzzles about time.

Sklar, Lawrence. *Philosophy and Spacetime Physics.* U. CA Pr. 1985 $45.00. ISBN 0-520-05374-5. Collection of reprinted articles on many aspects of the philosophy of space-time geometry.

Sober, Elliott. *Philosophy of Biology. Dimensions of Philosophy Ser.* Westview 1992 $49.95. ISBN 0-8133-0785-6. Basic introduction and overview of the field.

Whitrow, G. J. *The Natural Philosophy of Time.* OUP 1980 $37.50. ISBN 0-19-858215-3. Revision of a classic book on the subject.

PHILOSOPHY OF TECHNOLOGY

Although academic philosophers of science have claimed—in the 1970s, when the philosophy of technology was first emerging in U.S. universities—that there is no controlling paradigm for the philosophy of technology as an academic field, philosophical concerns over technology go gack over 100 years. KARL MARX (see Vols. 3 and 4), in fact, with his characterization of different periods in the history of humankind according to varying modes of production, has a legitimate claim to being called the first philosopher of technology, in what is now a long line. An anti-Marxist, ERNST KAPP, wrote the first book with an explicit philosophy of technology title, *Grundlinien einer Philosophie der Technik* (*Outlines of a Philosophy of Technology*), in 1877. One of the things that philosophers of science have objected to in the work of philosophers of technology is that so much of it is antiacademic, being opposed to the "scientific-rationalistic" model on which the departmental structure of the modern university is founded. In the set of books listed here, the first section, under the heading, The Nature of Technology in General, is devoted to studies of this sort. However, since some philosophers concerned with technology have paid attention to their critics and turned to more concrete and less nebulous topics, two other sets of books are cited under two other headings: The Politics of Technology and Philosophical Studies of Particular Technological Developments.

The Nature of Technology in General

This section is devoted to what most people think of when the phrase *philosophy of technology* comes up; that is, the books here focus on the nature of technology or technological society in general.

Agassi, Joseph. *Technology: Philosophical and Social Aspects.* Kluwer Ac. 1985 $87.00. ISBN 90-277-2044-4. One of the founding fathers of the philosophy of technology in the United States summarizes his views.

Ballard, Edward G. *Man and Technology: Toward the Measurement of Culture.* Duquesne 1978 $25.00. ISBN 0-391-01048-4. Early attempt to take the measure of a technological society as a whole from a broadly humanistic perspective.

Barrett, William. *The Illusion of Technique: The Search for Meaning in a Technological Civilization.* Doubleday 1979 $8.95. ISBN 0-385-11202-5. A prominent existentialist philosopher comments pungently on the shortcomings of technological culture.

Berger, Peter L., and others. *The Homeless Mind: Modernization and Consciousness.* Random 1974 $5.95. ISBN 0-394-71994-8. Major sociological and phenomenological study of the influence of technology and bureaucracy on developed cultures.

Boorstin, Daniel J. *Creators: A History of Heroes of the Imagination.* Random 1992 $30.00. ISBN 0-394-54395-5. An eminent historian defends the importance of technology for the progress of humankind through the ages, placing engineers and others alongside creative artistic geniuses.

Borgmann, Albert. *Crossing the Postmodern Divide.* U. Ch. Pr. 1992 $19.95. ISBN 0-226-06626-6. A recent update of his earlier work. Here, postmodern society confronts the fatal choice between hyper-reality and "focal" realism.

———. *Technology and the Character of Contemporary Life.* U. Ch. Pr. 1987 $14.95. ISBN 0-226-06629-0. Presents the author's thesis that contemporary society is dominated by devices serving convenience and that salvation can only be found in "focal things."

Bugliarello, George, and Dean Doner, eds. *The History and Philosophy of Technology*. U. of Ill. Pr. 1979 o.p. Proceedings of an important early conference introducing technology as a historical and philosophical problem to U.S. academic audiences.

Bunge, Mario. *Treatise on Basic Philosophy*. 8 vols. Kluwer Ac. 1990 $595.00. ISBN 0-7923-0551-5. The collected works of the founder of the philosophy of technology in North America. Volume 7 contains a distillation of 30 years of his analysis of technology in set-theory terms.

Casey, Timothy, and Lester Embree, eds. *Lifeworld and Technology*. U. Pr. of Amer. 1990 $46.00. ISBN 0-8191-7626-5. Conference proceedings focusing on the embeddedness of technology in everyday life; most of the included authors are well-known philosophers.

Christians, Clifford G., and Jay M. Van Hook, eds. *Jacques Ellul: Interpretive Essays*. U. of Ill. Pr. 1981 $29.95. ISBN 0-252-00890-1. Mostly favorable commentaries on the pessimistic French social critic.

Cutcliffe, Stephen H., and others. *New Worlds, New Technologies, New Issues*. Lehigh Univ. Pr. 1992 $36.50. ISBN 0-934223-24-6. English-language version of proceedings of a conference in Valencia, Spain, in December 1989. Includes the papers of several leading philosophers of technology.

Durbin, Paul T., ed. *Research in Philosophy and Technology*. Vol. 7. JAI Pr. 1984 $63.50. ISBN 0-89232-505-4. Volume focuses on technology and society associated with the dystopian prediction of George Orwell. The series highlights the most significant philosophers discussing technological issues in the United States, with some international contributions.

———, ed. *Technology and Responsibility*. Philosophy and Technology Ser. Kluwer Ac. 1987 $99.50. ISBN 90-277-2415-6. First conference-proceedings volume in a new series; includes many international contributions that focus on a key topic often ignored in discussions of technology and society.

Ellul, Jacques. *The Technological Society*. Trans. by J. Wilkinson. Random 1967 $7.95. ISBN 0-394-70390-1. Devastatingly detailed analysis of the technicization of every aspect of modern life in the manner of the grand social theorists; very influential.

Ferré, Frederick. *Philosophy of Technology*. P-H 1988 ISBN 0-13-662586-X. Introductory textbook that argues that an organic view can save technological society.

———, ed. *Research in Philosophy and Technology*. Vol. 12 *Technology and the Environment*. JAI Pr. 1992 $63.50. ISBN 1-55938-456-5. Collection of some of the best writing by philosophers of technology on environmental ethics and other environmental issues. Includes an excellent bibliographical update on environmental ethics by Eric Katz.

Florman, Samuel C. *Blaming Technology: The Irrational Search for Scapegoats*. St. Martin 1982 $6.95. ISBN 0-312-08363-7. Continues the author's attack on antitechnologists in gracefully written essays.

———. *The Existential Pleasures of Engineering*. St. Martin 1977 $7.95. ISBN 0-312-27546-3. Vigorous and critical defense of the engineering profession and an attack on antitechnologists.

Gouldner, Alvin W. *The Dialectic of Ideology and Technology*. OUP 1982 $8.95. ISBN 0-19-503064-8. A well-known American Marxist theoretician focuses on the role of technology in modern alienation.

Grant, George Parkin. *Technology and Justice*. U. of Notre Dame Pr. 1986 $8.95. ISBN 0-268-01863-4. Defense of traditional values in the face of what the Canada, and the United States have become under the influence of technology.

Habermas, Jürgen. *The Theory of Communicative Action*. 2 vols. Beacon Pr. Vol. 1 1985 $19.00. ISBN 0-8070-1507-5. Vol. 2 1989 $40.00. ISBN 0-8070-1401-X. His magnum opus; includes critiques of functionalist thinking and possibilities for transforming society; technical.

Hanks, Joyce M. *Jacques Ellul: A Comprehensive Bibliography*. JAI Pr. 1984 $63.50. ISBN 0-89232-478-3. First installment of a truly comprehensive bibliography on this pessimistic critic of our technological society.

Heidegger, Martin. *Basic Writings*. Ed. by D. F. Krell. HarpC rev. ed. 1992 $15.00. ISBN 0-685-56690-0. Includes "The Question Concerning Technology" and other essays important for understanding Heidegger's critique of modernity.

Hickman, Larry A., ed. *Technology as a Human Affair*. McGraw 1990 $19.32. ISBN 0-07-028688-4. Good collection of essays, many by well-known philosophers, covering a broad range of critiques of all aspects of technology.

Ihde, Don. *Existential Technics*. State U. NY Pr. 1983 $59.50. ISBN 0-87395-687-7. This second installment clarifies the relationship of the author's phenomenology of technology to Heidegger and Husserl.

———. *Philosophy of Technology: An Introduction*. Paragon Hse. 1992 $12.95. ISBN 1-55778-273-3. Somewhat difficult introductory textbook stressing that different cultural embodiments of technology have much to contribute to one another.

———. *Technics and Praxis*. Kluwer Ac. 1979 o.p. The author's first book-length formulation of the phenomenology of technology.

———. *Technology and the Lifeworld: From Garden to Earth*. Indiana Ser. in Philosophy of Technology. Ind. U. Pr. 1990 $35.00. ISBN 0-253-20560-3. Culmination of a series of books based on the premise that cultural lifeworlds and their technologies are inextricably intertwined.

Jonas, Hans. *The Imperative of Responsibility: In Search of an Ethics for the Technological Age*. U. Ch. Pr. 1985 $12.95. ISBN 0-226-40597-4. Major statement on responsibility by the person some have taken to be the leading critical philosopher of technology in the United States.

Kuhns, William. *The Post-Industrial Prophets: Interpretations of Technology*. HarpC 1973 o.p. Interesting summaries of the views of Jacques Ellul, Buckminster Fuller, Siegfried Giedion, Marshall McLuhan, Lewis Mumford, and Norbert Wiener.

Lovekin, David. *Technique, Discourse, and Consciousness: An Introduction to the Philosophy of Jacque Ellul*. Lehigh Univ. Pr. 1991 $38.50. ISBN 0-934223-01-7. More than just providing an introduction to Ellul's philosophy, the author defends Ellul as an ironic prophet of technological society.

Lovekin, David, and Donald Phillip Verene, eds. *Essays in Humanity and Technology*. Sauk 1978 o.p. One of the earliest collections of cultural critiques of technology in the United States.

Marcuse, Herbert. *One-Dimensional Man*. Beacon Pr. 1992 $12.95. ISBN 0-8070-1417-6. Most influential critique of technocapitalist society by the guru of the New Left in the 1970s; some parts difficult.

Mesthene, Emmanual G. *Technology and Social Change*. Macmillan 1967 o.p. An influential summary on the relationship between technology and society.

Mitcham, Carl. *Spanish-Language Philosophy of Technology*. Kluwer Ac. 1994. ISBN 0-7923-2567-2. Intriguing collection of papers presenting a long tradition of philosophical criticism of technology that has been virtually ignored in the English-speaking world.

Mitcham, Carl, and Robert Mackey, eds. *Philosophy and Technology: Readings in the Philosophical Problems of Technology*. Free Pr. 1983 $14.95. ISBN 0-02-921430-0. Includes several translations of European critiques and defenses of technology and the technological world with some heavy metaphysical speculation.

Morison, Elting E. *Men, Machines, and Modern Times*. MIT Pr. 1966 $9.95. ISBN 0-262-63018-4. Includes philosophical speculations by an eminent historian of technology.

Mumford, Lewis. *The Myth of the Machine*. 2 vols. Vol. 1 *Technics and Human Development* HarBraceJ 1967 $19.95. ISBN 0-15-662341-2. Vol. 2 *The Pentagon of Power*. HarBraceJ 1970 $19.95. ISBN 0-15-163974-4. Masterpiece of a critique of technology by a leading historian and critic; extremely influential.

Ormiston, Gayle L., ed. *From Artifact to Habitat: Studies in the Critical Engagement of Technology*. Lehigh Univ. Pr. 1990 $35.00. ISBN 0-934223-09-2. Interesting set of papers by leading philosophers of technology, with some focusing on particular technologies, such as artificial intelligence.

Pacey, Arnold. *The Culture of Technology*. MIT Pr. 1983 $11.95. ISBN 0-262-66056-3. Presents historical perspectives on the nature of technology.

Pirsig, Robert M. *Zen and the Art of Motorcycle Maintenance: An Inquiry into Values.* Bantam 1989 $5.95. ISBN 0-553-27747-2. Autobiographical and antitechnological novel in the form of a travel diary, with the journey as much spiritual as geographical. Filled with philosophical speculations; very popular in the United States in the early 1970s.

Rapp, Friedrich. *Analytical Philosophy of Technology.* Trans. by S. Carpenter and T. Langenbruch. Kluwer Ac. 1981 $55.00. ISBN 90-277-1221-2. A leading German philosopher of technology summarizes and synthesizes his views.

———, ed. *Contributions to a Philosophy of Technology: The Structure of Thinking in the Technological Sciences.* Reidel 1974 o.p. The most influential book in bringing technology to the attention of philosophers worldwide. Written by a leader of a group of German philosophers associated with the (then) West German society of engineers.

Rockmore, Tom, and Joseph Margolis. *The Heidegger Case: On Philosophy and Politics.* Temple U. Pr. 1992 $49.95. ISBN 0-87722-908-2. Philosophical reflections on Heidegger and the Nazis.

Roszak, Theodore. *Where the Wasteland Ends: Politics and Transcendence in Postindustrial Society.* Doubleday 1973 $4.95. ISBN 0-385-02738-9. The voice of the romantic antitechnologists of the early 1970s, Roszak should be compared with Pirsig (above).

Rothenberg, David. *Hand's End: Technology and the Limits of Nature.* U. CA. Pr. 1993 $30.00. ISBN 0-520-08054-8. This unique contribution to the phenomenology of technology considers the old artifice-nature contrast, reconfigures it in a way that makes of it a bipolar tension rather than a dichotomy. In doing so, he provides a new grounding for a philosophy of the environment that might change our attitude toward nature and the environment.

Schuurman, Egbert. *Technology and the Future: A Philosophical Challenge.* Trans. by H. D. Morton. Shiloh Bks. 1980 $19.95. ISBN 0-88906-111-4. Analysis of technology by an engineer-philosopher-theologian-politician, who is critical of a technological society but confident that Christian faith can use technology well. Intended specifically as an answer to Ellul (above).

Skolimowski, Henryk. *Living Philosophy: Eco-Philosophy as a Tree of Life.* Viking Penguin 1992 $10.00. ISBN 0-14-019308-1. A masterpiece summarizing decades of efforts to provide meaning for technological activity.

Stover, Carl F., ed. *The Technological Order.* Wayne St. U. Pr. 1963 o.p. Proceedings of a 1962 conference that helped bring the thought of Ellul and other critics to the attention of the American public.

Susskind, Charles. *Understanding Technology.* San Francisco Pr. 1985 $10.00. ISBN 0-911302-53-0. An engineering dean defends his field; includes bibliographical references.

Vonnegut, Kurt. *Player Piano.* Dell 1974 $5.99. ISBN 0-440-17037-0. Most explicitly antitechnological of Vonnegut's wildly imaginative satires on contemporary society. His novels were widely used in courses on technology and society in the 1970s.

Zimmerman, Michael. *Heidegger's Confrontation with Modernity: Technology, Politics, and Art.* Indiana Ser. in Philosophy of Technology. Ind. U. Pr. 1990 $39.95. ISBN 0-253-20558-1. Masterful synthesis of Heidegger's contributions to the philosophy of technology, written from a sympathetic perspective.

The Politics of Technology

This section collects those books that focus on the politics of technology from a philosophical perspective. Often more concrete or detailed in their focus than is the case with the traditional philosophy of technology, the authors here focus on topics such as Marxist critiques of technocapitalism or the politics of the engineering profession.

Baum, Robert J., and Albert Flores, eds. *Ethical Problems in Engineering*. 2 vols. RPI 1980 o.p. Important formative collection with a focus on ethics; helps the reader understand many political aspects of contemporary technology.

Byrne, Edmund. *Work, Inc.: A Philosophical Inquiry*. Temple U. Pr. 1990 $49.95. ISBN 0-87722-957-0. Defends union claims against multinational corporations in the name of justice. Attacks popular theories of justice for ignoring this problem.

Dickson, David. *The New Politics of Science*. U. Ch. Pr. 1988 $14.95. ISBN 0-226-14763-0. Critical examination of the way science and technology work in the real world.

Durbin, Paul T. *Social Responsibility in Science, Technology, and Medicine*. Lehigh Univ. Pr. 1992 $31.50. ISBN 0-934223-27-0. Argues for Dewey-based progressive social activism, especially on the part of technical professionals.

Feenberg, Andrew. *Critical Theory and Technology*. OUP 1991 $35.00. ISBN 0-19-506855-6. Post-Marxist defense of worker-controlled society. Extends theories of Marcuse and Foucault.

Gendron, Bernard. *Technology and the Human Condition*. St. Martin 1976 $18.65. ISBN 0-312-78925-4. Marxist critique of both critics and advocates of the role of technology in improving the human condition.

Gould, Carol. *Rethinking Democracy*. Cambridge U. Pr. 1989 $18.95. ISBN 0-521-38629-2. Another Marx-based defense of worker-controlled society.

Hamlett, Patrick W. *Understanding Technological Politics*. P-H 1991 $25.20. ISBN 0-13-947094-8. Framework for understanding and improving technological decision making.

Hickman, Larry. *John Dewey's Pragmatic Technology*. *Indiana Ser. in Philosophy of Technology*. Ind. U. Pr. 1990 $29.95. ISBN 0-253-20763-0. Excellent interpretation of Dewey as a philosopher of technology; includes arguments against opponents.

Man, Science, Technology: A Marxist Analysis of the Scientific and Technological Revolution. Academia 1973 o.p. Official publication stating the party line on technology and society from an unreconstructed Communist perspective. For that very reason, an important historical document.

Nelkin, Dorothy, ed. *Controversy: Politics of Technical Decisions*. Russell Sage 1992 $46.00. ISBN 0-8039-4467-5. Excellent set of case studies on the social aspects of science and technology.

Noble, David F. *America by Design: Science, Technology, and Corporate Capital*. OUP 1979 $10.95. ISBN 0-19-502618-7. Best neo-Marxist analysis of technocorporate capitalism available. Historical approach, but also deeply philosophical.

Stanley, Manfred. *The Technological Conscience: Survival and Dignity in an Age of Expertise*. U. Ch. Pr. 1981 $9.95. ISBN 0-226-77096-6. A political philosopher with leftist leanings highlights the difficulties of democracy in a technocapitalist society.

Teich, Albert. *Technology and the Future*. St. Martin 1989 $20.00. ISBN 0-312-01885-1. Very popular work stressing the political aspects of the control of technology.

Winner, Langdon. *Autonomous Technology: Technics-out-of-Control as a Theme in Political Thought*. MIT Pr. 1977 $12.95. ISBN 0-262-73049-9. A famous American critic of technocracy puts forth his thesis.

_____. *The Whale and the Reactor: A Search for Limits in an Age of High Technology*. U. Ch. Pr. 1988 $9.95. ISBN 0-226-90211-0. Essays on particular technological developments; tones down the author's earlier critique.

_____, ed. *Democracy in a Technological Society*. Kluwer Ac. 1992 $89.00. ISBN 0-7923-1995-8. Excellent collection of philosophical papers addressing the theme of technology and democracy, including an important paper by Jacques Ellul; from a conference in Bordeaux, France, in 1989.

Philosophical Studies of Particular Technological Developments

This section focuses on the philosophical studies of engineering, technology and risk assessment, environmental problems, and such special fields as nuclear power. Artificial intelligence and biotechnology—both enormous fields—are also included here, although the reader should also consult the section on Philosophy of Mind in Medicine.

Attfield, Robin. *The Ethics of Environmental Concern.* U. of Ga. Pr. 1991 $35.00. ISBN 0-8203-1344-0. Update of good discussion that focuses mostly on ethics.

Bains, W., and J. Raggett. *Artificial Intelligence from A to Z: A Glossary of Artificial Intelligence.* Chapman and Hall 1991 $36.95. ISBN 0-412-37950-3. Excellent reference dictionary, with an index.

Barbour, Ian. *Technology, the Environment, and Human Values.* Greenwood 1980 $29.95. ISBN 0-275-91483-6. A physicist active in interdisciplinary studies, including science and religion, focuses on problems of technology and the environment.

Blackstone, William T., ed. *Philosophy and Environmental Crisis.* U. of Ga. Pr. 1974 o.p. The first collection on this topic; helped form the basis for later discussions.

Boden, Margaret. *Philosophy of Artificial Intelligence.* OUP 1990 $16.95. ISBN 0-19-824854-7. Presents technical arguments in favor of computational and computer models of mental functioning.

Burnham, David. *The Rise of the Computer State.* Random 1984 $6.95. ISBN 0-394-72375-9. Discusses the impact of the computer on contemporary society.

Campbell, Jeremy. *The Improbable Machine: What New Discoveries in Artificial Intelligence Reveal about How the Mind Really Works.* S&S Trade 1990 $10.95. ISBN 0-671-72509-2

Collins, H. M. *Artificial Experts: Social Knowledge and Intelligent Machines.* MIT Pr. 1990 $24.50. ISBN 0-262-03168-X. A leader in the sociology of the scientific-knowledge movement examines the artificial-intelligence community.

Cranor, Carl F. *Regulating Toxic Substances: A Philosophy of Science and the Law. Environmental Ethics and Science Policy Ser.* OUP 1992 $39.95. ISBN 0-19-507436-X. Technical but excellent study of this important aspect of the environmental-technology philosophy.

Crosson, Frederick J. *Human and Artificial Intelligence.* Irvington 1970 $9.95. ISBN 0-89197-220-X. Classic balanced look at the artificial-intelligence question; holds up well.

Cummins, Robert E., and John Pollack. *Philosophy and AI: Essays at the Interface.* MIT Pr. 1991 $29.95. ISBN 0-262-03180-9. Presents technical studies by leaders in the field.

Dennett, Daniel C. *Brainstorms: Philosophical Essays on Mind and Psychology.* MIT Pr. 1980 $14.95. ISBN 0-262-54037-1. Collection of recent essays by a leading philosopher of artificial intelligence; demanding reading.

Dretske, Fred. *Explaining Behavior: Reasons in a World of Causes.* MIT Pr. 1991 $10.95. ISBN 0-262-54061-4. Expands on his earlier balanced arguments.

————. *Knowledge and the Flow of Information.* MIT Pr. 1981 o.p. Technical but still readable and balanced presentation of arguments for and against computer models of human information processing.

Dreyfus, Hubert L. *What Computers Still Can't Do: A Critique of Artificial Reason.* MIT Pr. 1992 $27.50. ISBN 0-262-54067-3. A leading critic of computers and artificial intelligence continues his 30-year attack.

Durbin, Paul T., ed. *Critical Perspectives on Nonacademic Science and Engineering. Research in Technology Studies Ser.* Lehigh Univ. Pr. 1991 $45.00. ISBN 0-934223-15-7. Essays on the philosophy of engineering and other aspects of nonacademic science. Tries to bring the philosophy of technology down to earth.

Feigenbaum, Edward A., and Pamela McCorduck. *The Fifth Generation: Artificial Intelligence and Japan's Computer Challenge to the World.* Addison-Wesley 1983 $16.30. ISBN 0-201-11519-0. Overblown predictions about the future of artificial intelligence.

Ferkiss, Victor. *Nature, Technology, and Society: Cultural Roots of the Current Environmental Crisis.* NYU Pr. 1992 $40.00. ISBN 0-8147-2611-9. An early critic of technological society turns his attention to the effects of technology on the environment.

Glymour, Clark, and others, eds. *Discovering Causal Structure: Artificial Intelligence, Philosophy of Science, and Statistical Modeling.* Acad. Pr. 1987 $54.50. ISBN 0-12-286961-3. Technical essays on statistical methods, data processing, and mathematical models used in the social sciences.

Graubard, Stephen R., ed. *The Artificial Intelligence Debate: False Starts, Real Foundations.* MIT Pr. 1988 $11.95. ISBN 0-262-57074-2. A reconsideration of the evidence for and against machine learning and artificial intelligence.

Gunderson, Keith. *Mentality and Machines.* Bks. Demand 1971 $77.00. ISBN 0-8357-2587-1. Classic defense of mental reduction in relation to problem solving, the intellect, and artificial intelligence.

Haugeland, John. *Artificial Intelligence: The Very Idea.* MIT Pr. 1989 $11.95. ISBN 0-262-58095-0. A leading proponent of artificial intelligence defends his views.

————, ed. *Mind Design: Philosophy, Psychology, Artificial Intelligence.* MIT Pr. 1981 $12.50. ISBN 0-262-58052-7. Somewhat technical collection of some of the best papers on artificial intelligence by philosophers and psychologists.

Hofstadter, Douglas R., and Daniel C. Dennett, eds. *The Mind's I: Fantasies and Reflections on Self and Soul.* Bantam 1982 $13.95. ISBN 0-553-34343-2. Provocative essays by leaders in the artificial-intelligence field.

Holtzman, Neil. *Proceed with Caution: Predicting Genetic Risks in the Recombinant DNA Era.* Johns Hopkins 1989 $43.50. ISBN 0-8018-3737-5. Excellent study and exploration of the civil liberties aspects of genetic testing by an eminent physician.

Krimsky, Sheldon. *Biotechnics and Society: The Rise of Industrial Genetics.* Greenwood 1991 $47.95. ISBN 0-275-93860-3. Extends his earlier study to the applications of genetic engineering.

————. *Genetic Alchemy: The Social History of the Recombinant DNA Controversy.* MIT Pr. 1982 $12.95. ISBN 0-262-61038-8. Outstanding study and survey of the history of a major biotechnical controversy.

Lovins, Amory B., and others. *Energy Unbound: A Fable for America's Future.* Sierra Club 1986 $17.95. ISBN 0-87156-820-9. Advocates of "soft energy paths" on the policies of the government-industry energy development establishment.

Lowrance, William W. *Modern Science and Human Values.* OUP 1985 $15.95. ISBN 0-19-504211-5. An expert on risk assessment broadens his perspective in order to weigh the role of values in a great number of cases of applied science and technology.

Margolis, Joseph. *Persons and Minds: The Prospects of Nonreductive Materialism.* Kluwer Ac. 1977 $63.50. ISBN 90-277-0863-0. Presents the arguments of a well-known critic of the reductionism rampant among philosophers of artificial intelligence; difficult reading.

Morone, Joseph G., and Edward J. Woodhouse. *Averting Catastrophe: Strategies for Regulating Risky Technologies.* U. CA Pr. 1986 $34.95. ISBN 0-520-05754-6. Discusses ways of managing technology in order to avoid such consequences as pollution and other hazards.

————. *The Demise of American Nuclear Power: Learning from the Failure of a Politically Unsafe Technology.* Yale U. Pr. 1989 $25.00. ISBN 0-300-04449-6. Puts forth the claim that nuclear power can be managed safely if redesigned.

Nelkin, Dorothy, and Laurence Tancredi. *Dangerous Diagnostics: The Social Power of Biological Information.* Basic 1991 $10.95. ISBN 0-465-01572-7. Another excellent study of genetics research and the moral and ethical dilemmas of genetic manipulation.

Nelkin, Dorothy, and Michael S. Brown. *Workers at Risk: Voices from the Workplace.* U. Ch. Pr. 1986 $20.00. ISBN 0-226-57128-9. One of numerous policy studies of particular technology-related issues by Nelkin and colleagues. Includes discussion of workplace enrivonments and stress, among other topics.

Noble, David F. *Forces of Production: A Social History of Industrial Automation.* OUP 1986 $15.95. ISBN 0-19-504046-5. Detailed historical analysis of the introduction of automated machine tools in U.S. industry by a noted neo-Marxist historian.

Nordquist, Joan, ed. *Biotechnology and Society: A Bibliography. Contemporary Social Issues: A Bibliographical Ser.* Ref. Rsch. Serv. 1987 $15.00. ISBN 0-937855-15-4. Compilation of bibliographical references in biotechnology, biotechnology industries, and genetic engineering.

Paehlke, Robert. *Environmentalism and the Future of Progressive Politics.* Yale U. Pr. 1989 $30.00. ISBN 0-300-04021-0. Argues that environmentalism can become the focus of a new progressive politics in the United States and Canada.

Penrose, Roger. *The Emperor's New Mind: Concern, Computers, Minds, and the Laws of Physics.* OUP 1989 $30.00. ISBN 0-19-851973-7. An eminent physicist puts forth his skepticism of artificial-intelligence claims.

Porter, Alan L., and others. *A Guidebook for Technology Assessment and Impact Analysis.* Elsevier 1980 o.p. Best available summary of technology assessment methods and their place in technological decision making; some technical parts.

Regan, Tom, ed. *Earthbound: New Introductory Essays in Environmental Ethics.* Temple U. Pr. 1984 $37.95. ISBN 0-87722-351-3. Excellent collection of essays on the moral and ethical aspects of human ecology.

Rolston, Holmes, III. *Environmental Ethics. Ethics and Action Ser.* Temple U. Pr. 1989 $44.95. ISBN 0-87722-628-8. Perhaps the most comprehensive philosophy of environmental ethics currently available.

Sagoff, Mark. *The Economy of the Earth.* Cambridge U. Pr. 1990 $13.95. ISBN 0-521-39566-6. Interesting attempt by a philosopher to transform economic theory to accommodate environmental concerns.

Schumacher, E. F. *Small Is Beautiful: Economics as if People Mattered.* Borgo Pr. 1991 $25.00. ISBN 0-8095-9115-4. The bible of the alternative-technology movement of the 1970s.

Searle, John. *The Rediscovery of the Mind.* MIT Pr. 1992 $22.50. ISBN 0-262-19321-3. A leading philosophical critic of artificial intelligence offers new versions of his arguments.

Shapiro, Stuart C., ed. *Encyclopedia of Artificial Intelligence.* 2 vols. Wiley 1992 $275.00. ISBN 0-471-50307-X. Classic source updated. Contains almost 300 alphabetically arranged articles written by experts; includes tables, cross-reference, indexes, and bibliographies.

Shrader-Frechette, Kristin S. *Nuclear Power and Public Policy: The Social and Ethical Problems of Fission Technology.* Kluwer Ac. 1980 o.p. Seminal philosophical discussion of nuclear power in the United States.

_____. *Risk Analysis and Scientific Method: Methodological and Ethical Problems with Evaluating Societal Hazards.* Kluwer Ac. 1985 o.p. Excellent analysis of social hazards related to technological decision making.

_____. *Risk and Rationality: Philosophical Foundations for Populist Reforms.* U. CA Pr. 1991 $39.95. ISBN 0-520-07289-8. Continues the author's efforts to understand the social aspects of risk in equity terms.

_____. *Science Policy, Ethics, and Economic Methodology: Some Problems of Technology Assessment and Environmental-Impact Analysis.* Kluwer Ac. 1985 $84.50. ISBN 90-277-1845-8. Examines the difficulties of assessing the impact of technology on the environment and how that affects science policy, ethics, and economic planning.

Simon, Herbert A. *The Sciences of the Artificial.* MIT Pr. 1981 $9.95. ISBN 0-262-69073-X. Broad statement of philosophy by a leading advocate and practitioner of artificial-intelligence research and development.

Stone, Christopher D. *Earth and Other Ethics: The Case for Moral Pluralism.* HarpC 1987 $19.95. ISBN 0-06-015731-3. A leading legal scholar makes a comprehensive case for broadening the ethics of environmentalism.

Taylor, Paul W. *Respect for Nature: A Theory of Environmental Ethics.* Princeton U. Pr. 1986 $14.95. ISBN 0-691-02250-X. A well-known environmental ethicist discusses the moral and ethical aspects of human ecology and environmental protection.

Van de Veer, Donald, and Christine Pierce, eds. *People, Penguins, and Plastic Trees: Basic Issues in Environmental Ethics.* Wadsworth Pub. 1986 ISBN 0-534-06312-8. A highly readable introductory work.

Weizenbaum, Joseph. *Computer Power and Human Reason: From Calculation to Judgment.* W. H. Freeman 1976 $14.95. ISBN 0-7167-0463-3. A computer scientist takes on his colleagues in a powerful argument against overexpectations of the computer revolution.

Wiener, Norbert. *The Human Use of Human Beings: Cybernetics and Society. Quality Paperback Ser.* Da Capo 1988 $9.95. ISBN 0-306-80320-8. Words of warning by one of the developers of computers and automation.

Woodhead, A. D., and B. Barnhart. *Biotechnology and the Human Genome: Innovations and Impact. Basic Life Science Ser.* Plenum Pub. 1988 $55.00. ISBN 0-306-42990-X. A helpful look at biotechnology and human genetic research, topics for which not enough good general studies are available.

PHILOSOPHY OF MEDICINE

Two well-known philosophers of medicine, H. TRISTRAM ENGELHARDT and Edmund L. Erde, claim that there is a long-standing tradition of philosophical reflection on the nature of medical practice distinct from medical ethics. This view is controverted by another well-known philosopher of medicine, Arthur L. Caplan, who claims that developments in the philosophy of medicine (apart from bioethics) have been sporadic and that the field lacks the sort of governing paradigm and distinctive debates that characterize other academic fields. While Caplan's skepticism might seem closer to reality than Engelhardt and Erde's optimism, quite a few interesting books on the philosophy of medicine have been published in recent years. They are listed here, following Englehardt and Erde's outline, under three headings: Medical Concepts and Theories, Analyses of Clinical Judgment and Medical Decision Making, and Philosophy of Mind in Medicine.

Medical Concepts and Theories

This section includes foundational critiques of medicine, mostly by philosophers. The foundational philosophy of medicine shares its approach with the academic philosophy of science. Only the focus is different because of the peculiarities of medicine involving both health care and scientific aspects.

Abercrombie, M. L. Johnson. *The Anatomy of Judgment: An Investigation into the Process of Perception and Reasoning.* Col. U. Pr. 1990 $14.00. ISBN 1-85343-106-0. Includes a discussion of what "normal" means when it is used as a criterion in medical judgments.

Caplan, Arthur, H. T. Engelhardt, and J. McCartney, eds. *Concepts of Health and Disease.* Addison-Wesley 1981 $42.95. ISBN 0-201-00973-0. Collection of addresses, essays, and lectures on the subjects of medicine, health, and disease; includes bibliographical references and indexes.

Cipolla, Carlo. *Public Health and the Medical Profession in the Renaissance.* Bks. Demand 1976 $37.50. ISBN 0-318-34771-7. Presentation is mostly historical but contains discussions of the earliest stages of the modern philosophy of medicine in the West.

Cohen, Henry. *Concepts of Medicine.* Ed. by Brandon Rush. Pergamon 1960 o.p. Historical perspectives on nineteenth-century debates on the philosophy of medicine.

Culver, Charles M., and Bernard Gert. *Philosophy in Medicine: Concepts and Ethical Issues in Medicine and Psychiatry.* OUP 1982 $35.00. ISBN 0-19-502979-8. Covers broader philosophical concerns than many books focused on bioethics.

Duffy, John. *The Healers: A History of American Medicine.* U. of Ill. Pr. 1979 $12.95. ISBN 0-252-00743-3. An eminent historian discusses the philosophies of leaders of the American medical establishment.

Engelhardt, H. Tristram, and Daniel Callahan, eds. *Science, Ethics, and Medicine.* Institute of Society, Ethics, and the Life Sciences 1976 o.p. The head of the Hastings Center and another leading bioethicist present the field of medical and professional ethics in a broader context.

Engelhardt, H. Tristram, and Stuart F. Spicker, eds. *Evaluation and Explanation in the Biomedical Sciences.* Kluwer Ac. 1975 o.p. The editors of the principal book series in the philosophy of medicine, including bioethics, bring together a set of well-known philosophers interested in the scientific aspects of medicine.

Foucault, Michel. *The Birth of the Clinic: An Archeology of Medical Perception.* Trans. by A. Smith. Random 1974 $9.00. ISBN 0-394-71097-5. Historical ruminations of the best-known French philosopher of medicine in recent decades.

Have, Henk ten, Gerrit Kimsma, and Stuart F. Spicker, eds. *The Growth of Medical Knowledge.* Kluwer Ac. 1990 $69.00. ISBN 0-7923-0736-4. Central section devoted to the philosophy of science and the philosophy of medicine; some contributions somewhat technical.

King, Lester. *Transformations in American Medicine: From Benjamin Rush to William Osler.* Johns Hopkins 1990 $38.00. ISBN 0-8018-4057-0. Focuses on the formative period in the development of the philosophy of modern medicine.

Laudan, Larry, ed. *Mind and Medicine: Problems of Explanation and Evaluation in Psychiatry and the Biomedical Sciences.* U. CA Pr. 1982 $45.00. ISBN 0-520-04623-4. Somewhat technical conference papers on the philosophy of science, psychoanalysis, psychology, and medicine.

Löwy, Ilana. *The Polish School of Philosophy of Medicine: From Titus Chalubinski (1820–1889) to Ludwig Fleck (1896–1961).* Kluwer Ac. 1990 $70.00. ISBN 0-7923-0958-8. Important historical overview of a prominent school of the philosophy of medicine.

Nordenfelt, Lennart. *On the Nature of Health: An Action-Theoretic Approach.* Kluwer Ac. 1987 $72.00. ISBN 1-55608-032-8. Fairly technical study combining concepts from action theory in analytical philosophy with more traditional concepts from the philosophy of medicine.

Nordenfelt, Lennart, and Ingemar B. Lindahl, eds. *Health, Disease, and Causal Explanations in Medicine.* Kluwer Ac. 1984 $71.00. ISBN 90-277-1660-9. Collection of philosophical analyses of key concepts in the philosophy of medicine and health care, including holistic health and medicine.

Spicker, Stuart F., ed. *Organism, Medicine, and Metaphysics.* Kluwer Ac. 1978 $58.50. ISBN 90-277-0823-1. Collection of essays, addresses, and lectures examining whether metaphysical conceptions of the organism are helpful in analyzing medical practice.

Van der Steen, Wim J., and P. J. Thung. *Faces of Medicine: A Philosophical Study.* Kluwer Ac. 1988 $69.00. ISBN 90-247-3673-0. Challenges standard conceptions in the philosophy of science and the philosophy of mind by contrasting them with medical practice; includes discussions of alternative medicine, spiritual healing, and related topics.

Wolff, H. R., S. A. Pedersen, and R. Rosenberg. *Philosophy of Medicine.* Blackwell Pubs. 1986 o.p. Useful introductory work; includes bibliography and index.

Zaner, Richard, ed. *Death: Beyond Whole-Brain Criteria.* Kluwer Ac. 1988 $93.50. ISBN 1-55608-053-0. An important issue in bioethics is submitted to philosophical analysis; edited by a leading phenomenologist of medicine.

Analyses of Clinical Judgment and Medical Decision Making

Whereas the previous section covers books that focus on the concerns of the philosophy of science as applied to medical science, this section includes books that focus on medical (and health care) practice. It should be noted, however, that the distinction is sometimes arbitrary because of the peculiar intermingling of science and health care in modern medicine.

Albert, Daniel A., Ronald Munson, and Michael D. Resnik. *Reasoning in Medicine: An Introduction to Clinical Inference.* Johns Hopkins 1988 $35.00. ISBN 0-8018-3426-0. A clinician, a philosopher of science, and a logician attempt to provide an introduction to the basic reasoning skills needed by physicians; includes somewhat technical discussions of decision analysis.

Bunker, J., Benjamin Barnes, and Frederick Mosteller, eds. *Costs, Risks, and Benefits of Surgery.* OUP 1977 $37.50. ISBN 0-19-502118-5. Classical application of probability and statistics measures to the evaluation of medical practices; technical.

Caplan, Arthur L. *When Medicine Went Mad: Bioethics and the Holocaust.* Humana 1992 $22.50. ISBN 0-253-31307-4. Although the perspective is bioethical, raises important issues in the philosophy of medicine.

Colodny, Robert G., and Leonard J. Savage, eds. *Logic, Laws, and Life.* Bks. Demand 1977 $70.80. ISBN 0-8357-8211-5. Includes some discussions of medicine within a framework of the academic philosophy of science.

Delkeskamp-Hayes, Corinna, and Mary A. Cutter, eds. *Science, Technology, and the Art of Medicine.* Kluwer Ac. 1993 $49.00. ISBN 0-7923-1869-2. Investigates the role and importance of new technologies in the practice of medicine.

Elstein, Arthur, Lee S. Shulman, and Sarah A. Sprafka. *Medical Problem Solving: An Analysis of Clinical Reasoning.* HUP 1978 $28.00. ISBN 0-674-56125-2. Classic study of clinical reasoning.

Engelhardt, H. Tristram, and Stuart F. Spicker, eds. *Clinical Judgment.* Kluwer Ac. 1979 $58.00. ISBN 90-277-0952-1. Collection of some of the best discussions of clinical judgment and medical decision making.

Feinstein, Alvan. *Clinical Epidemiology: The Architecture of Clinical Research.* Saunders 1985 $72.00. ISBN 0-7216-1308-X. Author is well known for arguing that clinical judgment cannot be reduced to physiological or biochemical analyses of functions.

Illich, Ivan. *Medical Nemesis: The Expropriation of Health.* Pantheon 1982 $11.96. ISBN 0-394-71245-5. Attack on the modern medical establishment for taking away the traditional abilities of laypersons to care for their own health.

Katz, Jay. *Experimentation with Human Beings.* Russell Sage 1972 $85.00. ISBN 0-87154-438-5. Classic study of the legal aspects of experimental medicine. Relevant to bioethics as well as the clash between clinical and scientific imperatives in clinical research.

_____. *The Silent World of Doctor and Patient.* Free Pr. 1986 $10.95. ISBN 0-02-918760-5. Excellent study of all aspects of the clinical encounter. Discusses physician-patient relations, informed consent, and trust issues.

Katz, Jay, and Alexander M. Capron. *Catastrophic Diseases: Who Decides What?* Russell Sage 1975 $29.95. ISBN 0-87154-439-3. Looks at medical decision making in such extreme cases as hemodialysis and transplantation.

Laor, Nathaniel, and Joseph Agassi. *Diagnosis: Philosophical and Medical Perspectives.* Kluwer Ac. 1990 $68.00. ISBN 0-7923-0845-X. Physician and philosopher discuss the bioethical and philosophical considerations of issues such as computer-assisted diagnosis.

Lasagna, Louis. *The Conflict of Interest between Physician as Therapist and as Experimenter.* Society for Health and Human Values 1975 o.p. Classic statement of the issue by a renowned physician.

Lifton, Robert J. *The Nazi Doctors: Medical Killing and the Psychology of Genocide.* Basic 1988 $14.95. ISBN 0-465-04905-2. A famous psychiatrist looks at the psychology of the physicians who collaborated in the Holocaust.

Menzel, Paul T. *Medical Costs, Medical Choices.* Yale U. Pr. 1983 $40.00. ISBN 0-300-03476-8. Serious study of fundamental issues facing medical practitioners today.

Murphy, Edmond. *Skepsis, Dogma, and Belief: Uses and Abuses in Medicine.* Johns Hopkins 1981 $28.00. ISBN 0-8018-2510-5. A physician looks at the philosophy of medicine.

Pellegrino, Edmund D., and David Thomasma. *A Philosophical Basis of Medical Practice.* OUP 1981 $29.95. ISBN 0-19-502789-2. A physician and philosopher collaborate to produce a comprehensive philosophy of medicine based on virtuous medical practice.

Proctor, Robert N. *Racial Hygiene: Medicine under the Nazis.* HUP 1988 $14.95. ISBN 0-674-74578-7. Detailed study of the same material addressed by Lifton (above), concluding that collaboration with the Nazis was not an aberration of only a few German physicians.

Ridderikhoff, J. *Methods in Medicine: A Descriptive Study of Physicians' Behaviour.* Kluwer Ac. 1989 $82.00. ISBN 1-5560-8080-8. Detailed analysis of problematic aspects of medical decision making, contrasting practice with science and discussing such new proposals as computer-assisted diagnoses.

Shelp, Earl E, ed. *The Clinical Encounter.* Kluwer Ac. 1983 $84.50. ISBN 90-277-1593-9. Collection focusing on the bioethical as well as philosophy-of-medicine concerns, related to this central feature of medical practice.

Shortliffe, Edward H., and others. *Medical Informatics: Computer Applications in Health Care.* Addison-Wesley 1990 $48.50. ISBN 0-201-06741-2. Useful compilation on this important new topic; includes bibliographical references and indexes.

Susser, Mervyn. *Epidemiology, Health, and Society: Selected Papers.* OUP 1987 $45.00. ISBN 0-19-505020-7. Collection of papers on social medicine and public health, with bibliographies and index.

U.S. National Commission for the Protection of Human Subjects. *The Belmont Report: Ethical Principles and Guidelines for the Protection of Human Subjects of Research.* USGPO 1978 o.p. Basic government document on the conflict between health care and research; followed in subsequent years by numerous volumes on specific bioethics issues related to research.

Philosophy of Mind in Medicine

This section focuses on mental health in medical practice and related philosophical theories. It is by no means a complete listing—obviously, many studies of the topic are technical—and the reader should also consult those books listed above, under Philosophical Studies of Particular Technological Developments, which discuss artificial intelligence and related technologies.

Engelhardt, H. Tristram, and Stuart F. Spicker, eds. *Mental Health: Philosophical Perspectives.* Kluwer Ac. 1977 $57.50. ISBN 90-277-0828-2. One in a long series of volumes based on conferences bringing philosophers and others together to discuss crucial issues—in this case, the concepts of mental health and mental illness.

Feigl, Herbert, Michael Scriven, and Grover Maxwell, eds. *Concepts, Theories, and the Mind-Body Problem.* U. of Minn. Pr. 1958 $39.95. ISBN 0-8166-0158-5. Discussions of an ancient philosophical controversy by influential logical positivists.

Grünbaum, Adolf. *The Foundations of Psychoanalysis: A Philosophical Critique.* U. CA Pr. 1984 $12.95. ISBN 0-520-05017-7. Devastating attack on the field of psychoanalysis by a prominent philosopher of science; technical.

Hook, Sidney, ed. *Psychoanalysis, Scientific Method, and Philosophy.* Transaction Pubs. 1990 $19.95. ISBN 0-88738-834-5. A collection of essays on philosophy and psychoanalysis, written by a number of prominent philosophers and doctors.

Jaynes, Julian. *The Origins of Consciousness in the Breakdown of the Bicameral Mind.* HM 1990 $22.45. ISBN 0-395-56352-6. Controversial study of the rise of human consciousness based on the then-recent discoveries about bilateral features of the brain.

Penfield, Wilder. *The Mystery of the Mind*. Bks. Demand 1975 $41.60. ISBN 0-7837-0102-0. Another study of human consciousness related to the physiology of the brain.

Popper, Karl R., and John C. Eccles. *The Self and Its Brain*. Spr-Verlag 1985 $67.00. ISBN 0-387-08307-3. Compares and contrasts Popper's views with those of a famous neuroscientist.

Skinner, B. F. *Beyond Freedom and Dignity*. Bantam 1984 $5.95. ISBN 0-553-25404-9. Best popular presentation of the famous behaviorist's arguments that freedom is an illusion and that democracy is not inconsistent with the widespread implementation of behavior control techniques.

Spicker, Stuart F., and H. Tristram Engelhardt, eds. *Philosophical Dimensions of the Neuro-Medical Sciences*. Kluwer Ac. 1976 $58.00. ISBN 90-277-0672-7. Collection of papers on the topic from the second Transdisciplinary Symposium on Philosophy of Medicine.

Szasz, Thomas. *Insanity: The Idea and Its Consequences*. Wiley 1990 $17.95. ISBN 0-471-52534-0. Update of 30 years of the author's arguments related to the philosophy and ethics of social psychiatry.

_____. *The Myth of Mental Illness: Foundations of a Theory of Personal Conduct*. HarpC 1984 $12.00. ISBN 0-06-091151-4. Update of his 1961 attack on the psychiatric and psychological professions, especially in terms of the grounds for involuntary commitment to mental institutions.

CHRONOLOGY OF AUTHORS

Russell, Bertrand Arthur William, 3rd Earl Russell. 1872–1970
Dessauer, Friedrich. 1881–1963
Ortega y Gasset, José. 1883–1955
Heidegger, Martin. 1889–1976
Carnap, Rudolf. 1891–1970
Marcuse, Herbert. 1898–1979
Nagel, Ernest. 1901–1985
Popper, Sir Karl Raimund. 1902–
Jonas, Hans. 1904–1993
Hempel, Carl Gustav. 1905–

Arendt, Hannah. 1906–1975
Quine, Willard van Orman. 1908–
Bunge, Mario A(ugusto). 1919–
Pellegrino, Edmund D. 1920–
Feyerabend, Paul Karl. 1924–
Salmon, Wesley Charles. 1925–
Foucault, Michel. 1926–1984
Rescher, Nicholas. 1928–
Habermas, Jürgen. 1929–
Callahan, Daniel J. 1930–
Ihde, Don. 1934–

ARENDT, HANNAH. 1906–1975

Hannah Arendt is acknowledged as one of the leading Jewish philosophers in the United States in the period following World War II. A refugee from Nazi Germany, Arendt had studied with MARTIN HEIDEGGER (see also Vol. 4) and KARL JASPERS (see also Vol. 4) at Heidelberg University, where she received a Ph.D. in philosophy in 1928. In the United States she taught at the University of Chicago and the New School for Social Research in New York City. Her field of specialty became cultural criticism. One of the most eminent political theorists of her time, Arendt was the author of penetrating studies of political action, totalitarianism, democracy, morality and the life of mind, anti-Semitism, and modernity. Arendt's book *The Human Condition* (1958) explored the human triad of labor, work, and action. This work, which displayed her mastery of philosophical anthropology and social philosophy and drew upon ancient ideas and ideals, has been an important focus of attention for many philosophers of technology. Many of Arendt's later books were devoted to the characteristic experiences, events, and persons of the times. However, she never abandoned investigations into the history of philosophy and other basic philosophical topics.

BOOKS BY ARENDT

Between Past and Future: Eight Exercises in Political Thought. Viking Penguin 1977. An insightful exploration of issues in political philosophy and practical politics.

Crises of the Republic. HarBraceJ 1971 $10.95. ISBN 0-15-623200-6. A collection of articles on pressing problems.

The Human Condition. 1958. U. Ch. Pr. 1970 $13.95. ISBN 0-226-02593-4. A profound philosophical work that has had a strong influence among philosophers of technology.

The Life of the Mind. HarBraceJ 1981 $12.95. ISBN 0-15-651992-5. Posthumously published, unfinished work of systematic philosophy.

The Origins of Totalitarianism. HarBraceJ 1973 $14.95. ISBN 0-15-670153-7. A classic in the field, this work established Arendt's reputation. It reveals psychological and social causes for the formation of human personalities compatible with, and supportive of, political dictatorships.

BOOKS ABOUT ARENDT

Bowen-Moore, Patricia. *Hannah Arendt's Philosophy of Natality.* St. Martin 1989 $24.95. ISBN 0-312-02831-8. Good study of an important aspect of Arendt's thought.

Bradshaw, Leah. *Acting and Thinking: The Political Thought of Hannah Arendt.* U. of Toronto Pr. 1989 $45.00. ISBN 0-8020-2625-7. Somewhat technical.

Canovan, Margaret. *Hannah Arendt: A Reinterpretation of Her Political Thought.* Cambridge U. Pr. 1992 $54.95. ISBN 0-521-41911-5. A fascinating discussion reevaluating Arendt's political philosophy.

Dossa, Shiraz. *The Public Realm and the Public Self: The Political Theory of Hannah Arendt.* Humanities 1989 $29.95. ISBN 0-88920-967-7. An important scholarly discussion.

Isaac, Jeffrey C. *Arendt, Camus, and Modern Rebellion.* Yale U. Pr. 1992 $30.00. ISBN 0-300-05203-0. Interesting discussion of the relation between two thinkers on totalitarianism and democracy in the twentieth century.

Kateb, George. *Hannah Arendt: Politics, Conscience, Evil. Philosophy and Society Ser.* Rowman 1984 $21.00. ISBN 0-8476-7558-0. An expository and sympathetic critical examination of the body of Arendt's work.

Nordquist, Joan, comp. *Hannah Arendt: A Bibliography. Social Theory: A Bibliographic Ser.* Ref. Rsch. Serv. 1989 $15.00. ISBN 0-937855-26-X. A useful place to begin research on Arendt.

Tlaba, Gabriel M. *Politics and Freedom: Human Will and Action in the Thought of Hannah Arendt.* U. Pr. of Amer. 1987 $40.50. ISBN 0-8191-6468-2. Another scholarly study.

Young-Bruehl, Elisabeth. *Hannah Arendt: For Love of the World.* Yale U. Pr. 1983 $17.95. ISBN 0-300-03099-1. Based on Arendt's papers and correspondence, the author's personal acquaintance with Arendt, and interviews with Arendt's family and friends, relates Arendt's childhood and adolescence, her friendship with Karl Jaspers, and her love affair with Martin Heidegger.

BUNGE, MARIO A(UGUSTO). 1919–

A prolific author on all aspects of the philosophy of science—from a self-proclaimed "exact" and "scientific" perspective—and a pioneer in philosophy of technology, Mario Augusto Bunge was born in Buenos Aires, Argentina, and educated at the Universidad Nacional de La Plata, receiving his Ph.D. in physics in 1952. He did research work in and taught theoretical physics in Argentina before moving to the United States in 1960, where he taught at several universities, including the Universities of Pennsylvania, Texas, and Delaware and Temple University. Later, he moved to Montreal in 1966, where he remains and has been Frothingham Professor of Logic and Metaphysics at McGill University since 1981.

Bunge's "exact" approach to philosophy means exactly what it says, and he is hard-nosed in insisting on describing both science and technology exactly as they are. His pioneering approach to the philosophy of technology follows this model, with a clear characterization of all the components of technological systems in systems-theory terms, including their value commitments and relationships to other institutions. Outspokenly critical of what he views as pseudo-science, including psychoanalysis, Bunge is equally strong in his defenses of democracy, although he also sees it as subject to much abuse.

BOOKS BY BUNGE

Causality and Modern Science. Dover 1979 $9.95. ISBN 0-486-23728-1. Early statement of Bunge's realist philosophy; includes a broad discussion of the meanings of causality in science. Somewhat technical.

Method, Model and Matter. Synthese Lib. Kluwer Ac. 1972 $50.50. ISBN 90-277-0252-7. Important, among other things, for its emphasis on scientific models.

The Mind-Body Problem: A Psycho-Biological Approach. Foundations and Philosophy of Science and Technology Ser. B. Franklin 1980 $26.00. ISBN 0-08-024719-9. Reveals Bunge's emergent materialism in operation.

Philosophy of Physics. Synthese Lib. Kluwer Ac. 1972 $63.50. ISBN 90-277-0253-5. Reveals a personal stamp on key issues; technical.

Philosophy of Psychology. (coauthored with Ruben Ardilla). Spr-Verlag 1987 $83.00. ISBN 0-387-96442-8. Continues in the same approach as *Philosophy of Science and Technology*, but with criticisms of other views.

Philosophy of Science and Technology. 2 vols. Kluwer Ac. 1985 Vol. 1 $44.00. ISBN 90-277-1904-7. Vol. 2 $51.00. ISBN 90-277-1914-4. Part of Bunge's *Treatise on Philosophy*, but the most relevant part for this chapter.

Scientific Materialism. Kluwer Ac. 1981 $80.00. ISBN 90-277-1304-9. An emergent, antireductive materialism is evident in this work.

Scientific Research. 2 vols. Spr-Verlag 1967 o.p. Important discussion of science, with a focus on the way it is actually done; also important as one of the first serious discussions of technology in the United States.

A Treatise on Basic Philosophy. 8 vols. Kluwer Ac. 1990 $295.00. ISBN 0-7923-0552-3. Bunge's masterpiece; covers every aspect of philosophy, from semantics to ethics.

BOOKS ABOUT BUNGE

Scientific Philosophy: Essays in Honor of Mario Bunge. Kluwer Ac. 1982 o.p. Leading philosophers of science develop their own views as well as refer to Bunge's contributions.

Weingartner, Paul, and Georg J. W. Dron, eds. *Studies on Mario Bunge's Treatise.* Rodopi 1990 o.p. Contains 32 papers with replies by Bunge and a short autobiography.

CALLAHAN, DANIEL J. 1930–

Daniel Callahan is the best known of American bioethicists and is the longtime director of the Hastings Institute—officially the Institute for Society, Ethics, and the Life Sciences. Born in Washington, D.C., he was educated at Yale and Georgetown universities and received his Ph.D. from Harvard University in 1965. From 1961 until 1968, he was executive editor of *Commonweal*, after which he worked for the Population Council. In 1970 he published *Abortion: Law, Choice, and Morality*; its sympathetic views toward abortion and pro-choice stances made him a controversial figure in Roman Catholic intellectual circles. In 1970 he was the primary mover in the establishment of the Hastings Institute. Over the next decades, he established himself as a leading thinker on a whole range of bioethics issues and other topics in the philosophy of medicine, not only in the United States, but also throughout the world. A prolific writer, he became most controversial in the late 1980s, when he began to espouse the setting of limits on health care for an aging population in an era of limits on health care spending.

BOOKS BY CALLAHAN

Abortion: Understanding Differences. (coedited with Sidney Callahan). *Hastings Center Ser. in Ethics.* Plenum 1984 $49.50. ISBN 0-306-41640-9. Attempts to bring reason to a very controversial issue.

Ethics and Population Limitation. Population Coun. 1971 $3.95. ISBN 0-87834-002-5. Early statement of an open-minded view on population control.

Ethics Teaching in Higher Education. (coedited with Sissela Bok). *Hastings Center Ser. in Ethics.* Plenum 1980 $45.00. ISBN 0-306-40522-9. The first volume in a series on ethics in various professions.

The Roots of Ethics: Science, Religion, and Values. (coedited with H. Tristram Engelhardt). Plenum 1981 $55.00. ISBN 0-306-40796-5. An important collection of essays.

Setting Limits: Medical Goals in an Aging Society. S&S Trade 1988 $9.95. ISBN 0-671-66831-5. The first proposal of a medical-rationing policy for the elderly.

The Troubled Dream of Life: Living with Mortality. S&S Trade 1993 $21.00. ISBN 0-671-70830-9. Argues for a materialistic acceptance of death.

The Tyranny of Survival: And Other Pathologies of Civilized Life. U. Pr. of Amer. 1985 $20.00. ISBN 0-8191-4636-6. Originally published in 1973, this work already showed more awareness of the import of technology than the works of most bioethicists.

What Kind of Life: The Limits of Medical Progress. S&S Trade 1990 $19.95. ISBN 0-671-67096-4. Continued discussion of the controversy over the rationing of medical care.

CARNAP, RUDOLF. 1891–1970

Rudolf Carnap is almost universally recognized as the greatest of the positivist philosophers of science of the early twentieth century. Born in Ronsdorf in northwest Germany, Carnap attended the Universities of Jena and Freiberg/Baden from 1910 to 1914, studying philosophy, mathematics, and physics. After World War I, he received his doctorate at Jena (1921) with a thesis on concepts of space. He then did research on his own until his appointment as instructor in philosophy at the University of Vienna in 1926. There he was a member of the Vienna Circle of Logical Positivists. Carnap then served as professor at the German University in Prague from 1931 to 1935. The rise of Hitler led to Carnap's emigration to the United States in 1936, where he was a professor of philosophy at the University of Chicago from 1936 to 1952. In 1954 Carnap moved to the University of California at Los Angeles, occupying the professorship left vacant by the death of his friend Hans Reichenbach. After retiring from teaching in 1962, he continued his own research until his death in 1970. Carnap's immense influence on the philosophy of science stems not only from his many technical contributions to the field but also from his method. Carnap was a student of GOTTLOB FREGE (see Vol. 4), a founder of the new symbolic logic, but BERTRAND RUSSELL (see also Vol. 4) had an even greater influence on him. Russell and ALFRED NORTH WHITEHEAD's (see Vol. 4) *Principia Mathematica* introduced Carnap to the new "logic of relations," wherein phrases such as *father of, greater than,* and *between* received adequate treatment for the first time. Thus, Russell's logic could express complex mathematical and scientific propositions. Carnap felt strongly that, outside of physics, the sciences do not attain sufficient clarity in their explanations of concepts and laws. Symbolic logic, however, offers the means to reach the desired clarity. The turning point for Carnap came in 1921, when he read Russell's *Our Knowledge of the External World, as a Field for Scientific Method in Philosophy*, in which Russell demonstrated how symbolic logic could transform vague philosophical problems into precise questions allowing definitive answers. All of Carnap's subsequent work follows this pattern. Carnap published several books on the logical structure of language and made fundamental contributions to the field of inductive inference. Much of his writing is technical, requiring knowledge of symbolic logic. His intellectual autobiography, edited by Paul Schilpp, provides an understandable survey of his thought.

BOOKS BY CARNAP

Dear Carnap, Dear Van: The Quine-Carnap Correspondence and Related Work. (coauthored with W. V. Quine). U. CA Pr. 1990 $34.95. ISBN 0-620-06847-5. An important documentary source revealing much about the formulation of Carnap's thoughts. Introduction by Richard Creath.

Introduction to the Philosophy of Science. Ed. by Martin Gardner. Basic 1966 o.p. Probably the most readable Carnap book for the nonspecialist, thanks to Martin Gardner's editing.

Logical Foundations of Probability. 1950. U. Ch. Pr. 1962 o.p. Carnap's great work on the logical relationship between evidence and theory. Mostly technical, though some parts are understandable without a familiarity with symbolic logic.

The Logical Structure of the World and Pseudoproblems in Philosophy. Trans. by Rolf A. George. U. CA Pr. 1967 $14.95. ISBN 0-520-01417-0. An early masterwork that builds knowledge statements from statements about slices of sensory experience.

Meaning and Necessity: A Study in Semantics and Modal Logic. U. Ch. Pr. 1988 $17.95. ISBN 0-226-09347-6. Technical discussion of semantics and symbolic logic.

BOOKS ABOUT CARNAP

Butrick, Richard, Jr. *Carnap on Meaning and Analyticity.* Mouton 1970 $12.00. ISBN 0-686-22409-4. Technical.

Schilpp, Paul A., ed. *The Philosophy of Rudolf Carnap.* Lib. of Living Philosophers. Open Court 1984 $44.95. ISBN 0-87548-130-2. Contains Carnap's intellectual autobiography along with critiques and replies.

DESSAUER, FRIEDRICH. 1881–1963

Friedrich Dessauer has been called the most broad-ranging philosopher of technology in Germany in the twentieth century, which is saying a great deal, considering the number of famous German philosophers who have discussed technology. Unfortunately, Dessauer is almost unknown outside Germany. Born in Aschaffenburg, he received his Ph.D. from the University of Frankfurt, where he also later taught. In addition to being a philosopher, he was also an engineer and scientist who did important research on X-rays, an inventor and businessman, and a theologian and political thinker. His writings include travel letters, scientific biography, and contributions to jurisprudence. In the philosophy of technology, Dessauer is a somewhat naive neo-Kantian, attempting to add to IMMANUEL KANT's (see Vol. 4) three critiques a fourth critique of the technological realm. For Dessauer, scientific and engineering creativity are primarily spiritual, sharing in divine creativity. His main work, *Streit um die Technik* (*Controversy over Technology*) (1956), situates this viewpoint in the history of controversies over the meaning of technology.

BOOKS BY DESSAUER

Controversy over Technology. (Streit um die Technik) 1956. Knecht 1956 o.p. Dessauer's masterpiece; a reworking of his comprehensive philosophy of technology, with arguments against other views.

Culture, Technology and Society. (Kultur, Technik und Gesellschaft) Westphal 1954 o.p.
Philosophy of Technology: The Problem of Its Realization. (Philosophie der Technik: Das Problem der Realisierung) Cohen 1927 o.p. First formulation of Dessauer's comprehensive philosophy of technology.
The Soul under the Influence of Technology. (Seele im Bannkreis der Technik) (coauthored with Friedrich and Xavier von Hornstein). Otto Walter 1945 o.p. More on the spiritual aspects of technological culture.
Technology as Meaning and Destiny. (Technik als Sinn und Bestimmung) Benziger 1944 o.p.

ELLUL, JACQUES. 1912–

[SEE Chapter 6 in this volume.]

FEYERABEND, PAUL KARL. 1924–

Paul Feyerabend, who began as an orthodox philosopher of science, has become the discipline's most bitter critic. Born in Vienna, Feyerabend served in the German army during World War II and then completed his education in philosophy and physics at the University of Vienna, receiving a Ph.D. in 1952. He absorbed logical-positivist doctrines and also KARL POPPER's philosophy. Beginning in the mid-1950s, Feyerabend taught in England at Bristol University and in the United States at the University of California at Berkeley. From 1957 to 1963, he held fellowships at the Minnesota Center for Philosophy of Science. Since 1962, Feyerabend has been professor at the University of California at Berkeley, concurrently holding a series of positions at the University of London, the Free University of Berlin, and the Federal Institute of Technology in Zurich. An advocate of freedom and diversity in science, Feyerabend disparages rules, rationality, and methodology. His views emerge from the mismatch between the logical-empiricist philosophy of science, with its emphasis on justification of theories, and the history of science, with its stress on differences and idiosyncrasies. Feyerabend maintains that, in fact, scientists do not generally argue rationally; instead, they resort to rhetoric and concoct new principles to back up their ideas. Thus, science does not operate by using a "scientific method." Feyerabend draws the moral that "anything goes," and anarchy is the best policy. He offers a stark choice between a rigid, oversimplified version of scientific method and total anarchy. Although it is not entirely clear that his purpose is not simply to stir up controversy, Feyerabend chooses the anarchical side.

BOOKS BY FEYERABEND

Against Method. 1975. Routledge Chapman & Hall 1988 $16.95. ISBN 0-86091-934-X. The original version (1975) appeared in the fourth volume of *Minnesota Studies in the Philosophy of Science.* In this work, Feyerabend challenges the conventional philosophy of science and suggests a more flexible and open alternative.
Farewell to Reason. 1978. Routledge Chapman & Hall 1988 $15.95. ISBN 0-86091-896-3. A more anarchic criticism of science.
Philosophical Papers. 2 vols. Cambridge U. Pr. Vol. 1 1985 $21.95. ISBN 0-521-31642-1. Vol. 2 1985 $21.95. ISBN 0-521-31641-3. In Volume 1, *Realism, Rationalism, and Scientific Method*, Feyerabend offers a variety of themes and treatments, from quite formidable technical discussions to informal, even breezy, essays. In Volume 2, *Problems of Empiricism: Philosophical Papers*, his long paper "Problems of Empiricism" shows how he makes the transition from a more orthodox doctrine of scientific knowledge to his later radical phase.
Three Dialogues on Knowledge. Blackwell Pubs. 1991 $42.95. ISBN 0-631-17918-6. Latest version of critiques of the standard philosophy of science.

FOUCAULT, MICHEL. 1926–1984

Born in Poitiers, France, the son of a doctor, Michel Foucault attended the École Normal Superieure and received his diploma from the Sorbonne in 1952. A social analyst and philosopher, he is one of the most controversial figures in the recent history of the three fields of the philosophy of science, the philosophy of technology, and the philosophy of medicine. When he died in 1984, he held the chair in the history of systems of thought at the Collège de France and was the reigning Parisian intellectual. Foucault's influential theory of knowledge is historically oriented. It is an "archaeology" laying bare the conceptual scheme that preconditions the rise and development of the particular sciences, especially the human sciences of biology, economics, and language, during a given period. Furthermore, Foucault's conceptual schemes are themselves the products of an infrastructure that is determined not so much by means of reason as by the power relations that prevail. Foucault's thought has affinities to both FRIEDRICH NIETZSCHE (see Vols. 2 and 4) and to KARL MARX (see Vols. 3 and 4). He pursued his historical (or "archaeological") investigations with regard to Western institutions and cultural phenomena that traditional historians have neglected—medicine, madness, the prison, and sexuality. As much a provocateur as a philosopher, Foucault deliberately challenged received views, inviting—even demanding—reconsideration by others of the roots of their disciplines.

BOOKS BY FOUCAULT

Archaeology of Knowledge. 1969. Pantheon 1982 $7.96. ISBN 0-394-71106-8. Foucault's fundamental approach to this concept is spelled out clearly here.

Birth of the Clinic: An Archaeology of Medical Perception. Random 1974 $9.00. ISBN 0-394-71097-5. A unique history of medicine illustrating Foucault's theses about the efficacy of concealed power relations.

The Care of the Self. Vol. 3 in *The History of Sexuality.* Trans. by Robert Hurley. Random 1988 $9.00. ISBN 0-394-74155-2. Posthumously published third volume of Foucault's comprehensive, historical study of sexuality.

Discipline and Punish: The Birth of the Prison. 1975.Trans. by Alan Sheridan. Random 1979 $11.00. ISBN 0-394-72767-3. A remarkable history of human conceptions and the purposes of the penal system.

The History of Sexuality: An Introduction. 1976. Vol. 1 in *The History of Sexuality.* Trans. by Robert Hurley. Random 1990 $10.00. ISBN 0-679-72469-9. First volume of a monumental, but idiosyncratic, history of sex in Foucault's mode.

Madness and Civilization: A History of Insanity in the Age of Reason. 1961. Random 1988 $11.00. ISBN 0-679-72110-X. A singular history of what constitutes insanity that reveals the intention of control.

The Order of Things: An Archaeology of the Human Sciences. 1966. Random 1973 $10.00. ISBN 0-394-71935-2. Foucault's most fundamental text on the theory of knowledge.

Power-Knowledge: Selected Interviews and Other Writings 1972–1977. Pantheon 1980 $14.00. ISBN 0-394-73954-X. A brilliant selection of Foucault's provocative pronouncements.

The Use of Pleasure. 1984. Vol. 2 in *The History of Sexuality.* Trans. by Robert Hurley. Random 1986 $6.95. ISBN 0-394-72952-8. The second volume of Foucault's historical investigations of sexuality.

BOOKS ABOUT FOUCAULT

Arac, Jonathan. *After Foucault: Humanistic Knowledge, Postmodern Challenges.* Rutgers U. Pr. 1988 $14.00. ISBN 0-8135-1330-8. The real focus is on postmodernism rather than Foucault.

Armstrong, T. J., ed. and trans. *Michel Foucault, Philosopher*. Routledge 1991 $35.00. ISBN 0-415-90333-5. A good introduction to his fundamental philosophy.

Ball, Stephen J., ed. *Foucault and Education: Disciplines and Knowledge*. Routledge 1990 $52.50. ISBN 0-415-05004-9. A series of scholarly studies on his philosophy of knowledge.

Bernauer, James W. *Michel Foucault's Force of Flight: Toward an Ethics for Thought. Contemporary Studies in Philosophy and the Human Sciences*. Humanities 1990 $15.00. ISBN 0-391-03740-4. Focuses on counterethics.

Bernauer, James W., and David Rasmussen. *The Final Foucault*. MIT Pr. 1988 $10.95. ISBN 0-262-52132-6. An odd title for a book on Foucault, for whom nothing is really final.

Boyne, Roy. *Foucault and Derrida: The Other Side of Reason*. Unwin Hyman 1990 $44.95. ISBN 0-685-33059-1. Deals with irrationality in regard to the works of the two leading French thinkers of postmodernism.

Gane, Mike, ed. *Towards a Critique of Foucault*. Routledge 1987 $15.95. ISBN 0-7102-0764-6. A good collection of essays.

Gutting, Gary. *Foucault's Archaeology: Science and the History of Reason*. Cambridge U. Pr. 1989 $47.95. ISBN 0-521-36698-4. An excellent discussion by a philosopher of science.

Mahon, Michael. *Foucault's Nietzschean Genealogy: Truth, Power, and the Subject. SUNY Ser. in Contemporary Continental Philosophy*. State U. NY Pr. 1992 $57.50. ISBN 0-7914-1150-8. Turns the tables on Foucault.

Miller, Peter. *Domination and Power*. Routledge 1987 $39.95. ISBN 0-7102-0624-0. Presents Foucault's key ideas.

Nordquist, Joan, comp. *Michel Foucault: A Bibliography. Social Theory: A Bibliographic Ser*. Ref. Rsch. Serv. 1986 $15.00. ISBN 0-937855-06-5. A good, basic source for research on Foucault.

Sawicki, Jana. *Disciplining Foucault: Feminism, Power, and the Body*. Routledge 1991 $42.50. ISBN 0-415-90188-X. One of many studies of Foucault from a feminist perspective.

HABERMAS, JÜRGEN. 1929–

Born and educated in Germany, Jürgen Habermas received his Ph.D. from the University of Bonn in 1954. In 1973 he received the Hegel Prize for his outstanding contribution to the advancement of human sciences. Professor of philosophy at the University of Frankfurt, Habermas is the leading figure in contemporary critical theory, a neo-Marxist philosophy that grew out of the earlier Frankfurt School. Habermas's version of critical theory, however, can be distinguished from the earlier Frankfurt School of Max Horkheimer, THEODOR ADORNO (see also Vol. 4), and HERBERT MARCUSE (see also Vol. 4). These philosophers and social scientists, while Marxist, adhere to a notion of critique that stems from IMMANUEL KANT (see Vol. 4) and GEORG HEGEL (see Vols. 3 and 4), and they share the conviction that, despite the historical conditioning of knowledge, reason possesses a measure of autonomy in the moment of criticism. In the 1950s Habermas set out to analyze contemporary society by means of the methods of empirical science, but, at the same time, he stressed that the critique be undertaken from a historical and practical standpoint. He stood against Marxists on the one hand and positivists on the other. In the course of furthering his critique of society, he has engaged in a cluster of research projects that have been published in separate works: a general theory of communication, which he calls "universal pragmatics"; a theory of how human beings are socialized to acquire the competence to communicate; and a theory of social evolution, which he maintains is a renovated historical materialism. The philosophy of technology owes important debts to the Frankfurt School in general and to Habermas in particular.

BOOKS BY HABERMAS

Communication and the Evolution of Society. Trans. by Thomas McCarthy. Beacon Pr. 1979 $16.00. ISBN 0-8070-1513-X. Habermas's account of the role of language in society; preliminary to his later masterpiece.

Justification and Application: Remarks on Discourse Ethics. Studies in Contemporary German Social Thought. MIT Pr. 1993 $22.50. ISBN 0-262-08217-9. A practical application of Habermas's basic approach.

Knowledge and Human Interests. Trans. by Jeremy J. Shapiro. Beacon Pr. 1971 $15.00. ISBN 0-8070-1541-5. Obscurely written but profound theory of knowledge; requisite to an understanding of Habermas's thought.

Legitimation Crisis. Trans. by Thomas McCarthy. Beacon Pr. 1975 $13.00. ISBN 0-8070-1521-0. A probing critique of the claims to authority by the establishment.

Moral Consciousness and Communicative Action. Studies in Contemporary German Social Thought. MIT Pr. 1990 $27.50. ISBN 0-262-08192-X. A compilation of recent studies.

On the Logic of the Social Sciences. Trans. by Sherry W. Nicholson and Jerry Stark. *Studies in Contemporary German Social Thought.* MIT Pr. 1990 $13.50. ISBN 0-262-58104-3. A somewhat technical treatment.

The Philosophical Discourse of Modernity: Twelve Lectures. Trans. by Frederick Lawrence. *Studies in Contemporary German Social Thought.* MIT Pr. 1990 $15.95. ISBN 0-262-58102-7. A good introduction to his thought.

Philosophical-Political Profiles. Trans. by Frederick Lawrence. MIT Pr. 1985 $13.95. ISBN 0-262-58071-3. A series of essays, sympathetic and critical, of leading twentieth-century thinkers.

Theory and Practice. Trans. by John Viertel. Beacon Pr. 1973 $14.00. ISBN 0-8070-1527-X. Covers the essentials of the philosophy of action.

The Theory of Communicative Action. Trans. by Thomas McCarthy. 2 vols. Beacon Pr. Vol. 1 1985 $40.00. ISBN 0-8070-1506-7. Vol. 2 1989 $40.00. ISBN 0-8070-1401-X. Habermas's most significant, mature work.

Toward a Rational Society: Student Protest, Science, and Politics. Trans. by Jeremy J. Shapiro. Beacon Pr. 1971 $11.00. ISBN 0-9070-4177-7. An important tract for understanding the student movement in the 1960s from the standpoint of critical theory.

BOOKS ABOUT HABERMAS

Bernstein, Richard, ed. *Habermas and Modernity.* MIT Pr. 1985 $25.00. ISBN 0-262-52102-4. A collection of essays by experts, edited and introduced by a leading American philosophical scholar of Continental thought.

Geuss, Raymond. *The Idea of a Critical Theory: Habermas and the Frankfurt School. Modern European Philosophy.* Cambridge U. Pr. 1981 $12.95. ISBN 0-521-28422-8. An important scholarly study; indispensable to the serious student of critical theory.

Held, David. *Introduction to Critical Theory: Horkheimer to Habermas.* U. CA Pr. 1980 $47.50. ISBN 0-520-04175-5. The purpose of this work is to determine historical context and empirical and theoretical concerns and to evaluate the key figures.

Ingram, David. *Habermas and the Dialectic of Reason.* Yale U. Pr. 1989 $12.95. ISBN 0-300-04613-8. A lucid, stimulating discussion of Habermas's ideas.

Keat, Russell. *The Politics of Social Theory: Habermas, Freud, and the Critique of Positivism.* U. Ch. Pr. 1981 $9.00. ISBN 0-226-42876-1. A probing examination of the central concerns in Habermas's philosophy.

McCarthy, Thomas A. *The Critical Theory of Jürgen Habermas.* MIT Pr. 1978 $17.50. ISBN 0-262-63073-7. A standard exposition and criticism of Habermas's philosophy.

Thompson, John B., and David Held. *Habermas: Critical Debates*. MIT Pr. 1982 $37.50.
    ISBN 0-262-700-23-9. Essays on various features of Habermas's social theory, with a
    reply to critics.
Seidman, Steven, ed. and trans. *Jürgen Habermas on Society and Politics*. Beacon Pr.
    1989 $18.00. ISBN 0-8070-2001-X

HEIDEGGER, MARTIN. 1889–1976

Although Martin Heidegger's early education was in scholastic philosophy, he
soon became interested in EDMUND HUSSERL's (see Vol. 4) phenomenology.
Whereas Husserl's phenomenological investigations centered on cognition and
bracketed existence, Heidegger expanded the subject matter for phenomenology, examining such noncognitive states as anxiety. Moreover, he employed the
phenomenological method to illuminate ontology and to resolve questions of
contemporary existence. After teaching at the University of Marburg, Heidegger
went to the University of Freiburg as the successor to Husserl. In 1933 he
became the first National Socialist rector there. Esteemed by many as the
foremost twentieth-century philosopher, Heidegger has been tainted by his
association with the Nazis. Heidegger's *Being and Time* (1927) is generally
acknowledged as one of the premier documents in the history of existentialism,
although Heidegger himself did not like the label. After a famous "turning" in
his thought, Heidegger devoted a great deal of attention to the negative
characterization of our technological age. Philosophers of technology who are
unimpressed by his earlier work continue to think of Heidegger as the leading
thinker in the contemporary critique of technological society.

BOOKS BY HEIDEGGER

Basic Writings. Ed. by David F. Krell. HarpC rev. ed. 1992 $15.00. ISBN 0-685-56690-0. A
    good place to begin.
Being and Time. 1927. Trans. by John Macquarrie and Edward Robinson. Harper SF 1962
    $24.45. ISBN 0-06-063850-8. The first translation into English of a book often called
    untranslatable. *Sein und Zeit* is one of the great classics of modern philosophy and a
    basic work in existentialism. A very difficult book even for a German reader because
    it is full of coined expressions, puns, and obsolete terms.
Nietzsche. 1961. 2 vols. Adlers Foreign Bks. 1982 $118.00. ISBN 0-3-7885-0115-4.
    Important volumes that reveal more about Heidegger than about Nietzsche.
The Question Concerning Technology and Other Essays. Trans. by William Lovitt. HarpC
    1982 $12.00. ISBN 0-06-131969-4. Most important of Heidegger's works on technolo-
    gy; difficult.
What Is a Thing? Trans. by W. B. Barton, Jr. and Vera Deutsch. Regnery Gateway 1968
    $5.95. ISBN 0-89526-979-1. Investigates Heidegger's thoughts on tools, art, the state,
    and the world.
What Is Called Thinking? Trans. by J. Glenn Gary and Fred D. Wieck. HarpC 1976 $12.00.
    ISBN 0-06090528-X. Lectures from 1952 that clearly reveal Heidegger's "turning."

BOOKS ABOUT HEIDEGGER

Dreyfuss, Hubert L. *Being-in-the-World: A Commentary on Heidegger's Being and Time*.
    MIT Pr. 1990 $30.00. ISBN 0-262-04106-5. Excellent and clear presentation of the
    nature of Heidegger's position as expounded in his classic work.
Ferry, Luc, and Alain Renaut. *Heidegger and Modernity*. U. Ch. Pr. 1990 $16.95. ISBN 0-
    226-24462-8. Argues that Heidegger's relation to the Nazis is complex because there
    is an irresolvable tension between his humanism and his anti-humanism.
Goldmann, Lucien. *Lukacs and Heidegger: Towards a New Philosophy*. Trans. by William
    Q. Boelhower. Routledge 1985 $12.95. ISBN 0-7100-8794-2. Comparison of Heideg-
    ger with a leading neo-Marxist.

Kockelmans, Joseph. *On the Truth of Being: Reflections on Heidegger's Later Philosophy. Studies in Phenomenology and Existential Philosophy*. Ind. U. Pr. 1985 $29.95. ISBN 0-253-34245-7. Focuses on Heidegger's later thought.

Kolb, David. *The Critique of Pure Modernity: Hegel, Heidegger, and After*. U. Ch. Pr. 1986 $15.95. ISBN 0-226-45029-5. A scholarly study of idealist and existentialist responses to modern life.

Nordquist, Joan, comp. *Martin Heidegger: A Bibliography. Social Theory: A Bibliographic Ser*. Ref. Rsch. Serv. 1990 $15.00. ISBN 0-9378550-33-2. The best place to begin research on Heidegger and his work.

Richardson, Joseph. *Heidegger. Phaenomenologica Ser*. Kluwer Ac. 1974 $76.00. ISBN 90-247-0246-1. Generally agreed to be the best available commentary.

Rockmore, Tom, and Joseph Margolis, eds. *The Heidegger Case: On Philosophy and Ethics*. Temple U. Pr. 1992 $49.95. ISBN 0-87722-908-2. An excellent series of essays; the central focus on Heidegger's relation to Nazism.

Zimmerman, Michael E. *Heidegger's Confrontation with Modernity: Technology, Politics, and Art. Indiana Ser. in Philosophy of Technology*. Ind. U. Pr. 1990 $39.95. ISBN 0-253-20558-1. Includes a discussion of Heidegger's relation to Nazism in a study focusing on technology.

HEMPEL, CARL GUSTAV. 1905–

Carl Gustav Hempel's work is essential for understanding the positivist philosophy of science. His explanation of scientific explanation and his "paradoxes of confirmation" have stimulated discussion for decades. Born in Oranienburg, Germany, Hempel has been a U.S. citizen since 1944. Like many other philosophers of science, he studied physics and mathematics at the Universities of Göttingen and Heidelberg. In Berlin he was a student of Hans Reichenbach and participated in the Society for Scientific Philosophy, the sister group of the Vienna Circle of Logical Positivists. Hempel left Germany for Brussels in 1934 and then went to the United States in 1937, where he held positions at the University of Chicago, the City College of New York, Queens College, and Yale University. Hempel became professor of philosophy at Princeton University in 1955 and held the title of Stuart Professor from 1956 until he retired in 1973. The University of Pittsburgh appointed him professor of philosophy in 1977.

Hempel writes in a scientific style: clear, matter of fact, free of personal idiosyncrasies. The reader always has a sense of the goals, problems, and permissible means of solving the problems. In effect, Hempel invites the reader to join him in research. Many philosophers of science have accepted his invitation. In conjunction with Paul Oppenheim, Hempel proposed the most influential model of scientific explanation: that events are explained by deducing their descriptions from universal scientific laws and "antecedent conditions." Ever since, sociologists, political scientists, and historians have agonized over the question of whether their disciplines can possess such explanations. In 1945 Hempel published "Studies in the Logic of Confirmation." *Confirmation* is the support that evidence confers on a scientific theory. Hempel's investigation uncovered fundamental difficulties, even paradoxes. In 1965 Hempel published a collection entitled *Aspects of Scientific Explanation*, which is the best summary of his thoughts on confirmation and scientific explanation.

BOOKS BY HEMPEL

Aspects of Scientific Explanation. 1965. Free Pr. 1970 $16.95. ISBN 0-02-914340-3. A collection of Hempel's most important writings; indispensable but technical.

Philosophy of Natural Science. P-H 1966 ISBN 0-13-663823-6. An excellent introduction to the traditional academic philosophy of science. Clear and readable, even for those with little background.

BOOK ABOUT HEMPEL

Rescher, Nicholas, ed. *Essays in Honor of Carl G. Hempel: A Tribute on the Occasion of His Sixty-Fifth Birthday. Synthese Lib.* Kluwer Ac. 1969 $22.00. ISBN 0-685-02824-0. Salmon, Jeffrey, Grünbaum, and Putnam are among the contributors. Includes reminiscences about Hempel and a bibliography of his writings up to 1964.

IHDE, DON. 1934–

Don Ihde is one of the founders of a distinctly North American approach to phenomenology in work that centers around technology. After completing his B.A. degree at the University of Kansas (1956), he earned a Master of Divinity degree at Andover Newton Theological School (1959) and a Ph.D. at Boston University (1964). His doctoral dissertation on the phenomenology of PAUL RICOEUR (see Vol. 4) set the stage for later original contributions to phenomenological analysis.

Ihde taught at Southern Illinois University before moving to the State University of New York at Stony Brook, where, since 1969, he has served at different times as Head of Philosophy and Dean of Liberal Arts and Humanities. In the mid-1970s, together with his colleagues at Stony Brook, Ihde developed an intentionally eclectic school of experienced-based "experimental phenomenology" with bridges to pragmatism, which has concentrated on elaborating the ways that instumentation mediates between human beings and the world. His book *Technics and Praxis* (1979) was the first real work on the philosophy of technology in English. In 1990 Ihde, together with Indiana University Press, initiated a new mongraph series in philosophy of techology that has since become one of the most influential collection of publications in the field.

BOOKS BY IHDE

Consequences of Phenomenology St. U. NY Pr. 1986 $59.50. ISBN 0-88706-141-9. Part two is devoted to technology.
Existential Technics. St. U. NY Pr. 1983 $59.50. ISBN 0-87395-687-7. Discusses how technologies influence not just perception but also self-understanding.
Experimental Phenomenology: An Introduction. St. U. NY Pr. 1986 $39.50. ISBN 0-88706-198-2. This programatic call for a new experiential-based phenomenology includes a number of phenomenological descriptions of science and the arts, and introduces the need for a careful analysis of the way machines mediate between human beings and the world.
Instrumental Realism: The Interface between Philosophy of Science and Philosophy of Technology. Ind. U. Pr. 1991 $29.95. ISBN 0-253-20626-X. An appendix to *Technology and the Lifeworld*; argues that philosphy of technology includes philosphy of science.
Philosophy of Technology: An Introduction. Paragon Hse. 1992 $12.95. ISBN 1-55778-273-3. Ihde's personal introduction to the field.
Technics and Praxis. 1979. Kluwer Ac. 1979 o.p. Focuses on the structure of human-machine-world relationships. Especially good on how instrumentation and technology transform perception in both science and everyday experience. Includes critical essays on other philosophers of technology such as Martin Heidegger and Hans Jonas.
Technology and the Lifeworld: From Garden to Earth. Ind. U. Pr. 1990 $35.00. IOSBN 0-253-32900-0. Ihde's most extended study of technology, this work begins with a reprise of the analysis of human-machine-world relations from *Technics and Praxis* and *Existential Technics.*

JONAS, HANS. 1904–1993

Hans Jonas was a well-known Jewish thinker, an early and influential biomedical ethicist, and an equally early and influential philosopher of technology in the United States and his native Germany. Born in 1904 in Mönchengladbach, Jonas studied under MARTIN HEIDEGGER (see also Vol. 4) at the University of Freiburg before Hitler came to power and Heidegger became chancellor of the university. He received his doctorate in 1928 from the University of Marburg. In 1933 he fled Germany and, in 1964, publicly repudiated Heidegger because of his Nazi connections. Jonas taught in Jerusalem and Canada before becoming a professor at the New School for Social Research in New York in 1955, where he was chair of the philosophy department (1957–63) and Johnson Professor of Philosophy (from 1966 until his retirement in 1976). Jonas is best known for his neo-Kantian ethics of responsible caution in the face of the awesome power of modern technology— especially the power of modern biotechnology, including genetic engineering. According to Jonas, we must consult our fears and not our hopes when understanding technological ventures that can have a potentially devastating impact on what it means to be human (and therefore ethical). More than half of Jonas's books were written in German, including an early version of his greatest work, *The Imperative of Responsibility* (1984).

BOOKS BY JONAS

Gnostic Religion: The Message of the Alien God and the Beginnings of Christianity. Peter Smith 1958 $24.25. ISBN 0-8446-2339-3. Examines the relations between Jewish and Christian thought.

The Imperative of Responsibility: In Search of an Ethics for the Technological Age. 1984. U. Ch. Pr. 1985 $12.95. ISBN 0-226-40597-4. Jonas's magnum opus, summarizing all his earlier views. An excellent place to begin an examination of his thought.

The Phenomenon of Life: Toward a Philosophical Biology. U. Ch. Pr. 1982 $8.95. ISBN 0-226-40595-8. An early formulation of Jonas's responsibility theme, with respect to modern biology.

Philosophical Essays: From Ancient Creed to Technological Man. U. Ch. Pr. 1980 $19.95. ISBN 0-226-40591-5. Focuses on technology in the context of biomedical ethics and related issues.

BOOK ABOUT JONAS

Spicker, Stuart, ed. *Organism, Medicine, and Metaphysics: Essays in Honor of Hans Jonas on his 75th Birthday, May 10, 1978.* Kluwer Ac. 1978 $58.00. ISBN 90-277-0823-1. Leading bioethicists honor Jonas in a series of interesting and insightful essays.

KUHN, THOMAS S(AMUEL). 1922–

[SEE Chapter 3 in this volume.]

LATOUR, BRUNO. 1947–

[SEE Chapter 6 in this volume.]

MARCUSE, HERBERT. 1898–1979

During his lifetime, Herbert Marcuse was the most famous exponent of critical theory, the neo-Marxism associated with the Frankfurt School of Max Horkheimer and THEODOR ADORNO (see also Vol. 4) and now headed by JÜRGEN HABERMAS (see also Vol. 4). Born in Berlin, Germany, Marcuse attended the Universities of Freiburg and Berlin. He emigrated to the United States in 1934, became a U.S. citizen in 1940, and served as a consultant to the U.S. government during World War II. He lectured at Harvard and Columbia universities and taught philosophy and political science at Brandeis University. At the end of his life, he was a professor of philosophy at the University of California at San Diego.

In the 1960s and 1970s, Marcuse became the acknowledged guru of the New Left. His thought is strongly influenced by SIGMUND FREUD (see also Vols. 3 and 4), KARL MARX (see Vols. 3 and 4), and GEORG HEGEL (see Vol. 2). Marcuse's *Eros and Civilization* (1955) attempts to document the psychic repression needed to survive in a capitalist culture (but also needing to be repudiated even if this is viewed as irrational). His *One-Dimensional Man* (1964), with its thesis that technology renders this repression even more pernicious, has been very influential among philosophers of technology.

BOOKS BY MARCUSE

The Aesthetic Dimension: Toward a Critique of Marxist Aesthetics. 1978. Beacon Pr. 1978 $11.00. ISBN 0-8070-1519-9. Somewhat difficult analysis of aesthetics from a leftist perspective.

Counterrevolution and Revolt. 1972. Beacon Pr. 1972 $10.95. ISBN 0-8070-1533-4. An important statement on the possibility of revolution in the 1970s.

Eros and Civilization: A Philosophical Inquiry into Freud. 1955. Beacon Pr. 1974 $14.00. ISBN 0-8070-1555-5. A revolutionary synthesis of Freud and Marx.

An Essay on Liberation. 1969. Beacon Pr. 1969 $11.00. ISBN 0-8070-0595-9. Focuses on the student portion of the New Left movement.

Negations. Col. U. Pr. 1989 $20.00. ISBN 1-85343-048-X. Comments on current issues from an abstract philosophical perspective.

One-Dimensional Man: Studies in the Ideology of Advanced Industrial Society. 1964. Beacon Pr. 1992 $12.95. ISBN 0-8070-1417-6. Marcuse's major statement on the pernicious influence of technology (including the media) on contemporary society; widely influential.

Reason and Revolution: Hegel and the Rise of Social Theory. 1941. Humanities 1954 $17.50. ISBN 0-391-02999-1. An influential study of Hegel that contributed to the restoration of his reputation as a positive force in free society.

Revolution or Reform: A Confrontation. (coauthored with Karl Popper). Transaction Pubs. 1976 $14.95. ISBN 0-89044-020-4. A polemical exchange between two important twentieth-century philosophers.

Soviet Marxism: A Critical Analysis. 1958. Col. U. Pr. 1985 $17.00. ISBN 0-231-08379-3. Always critical of the Soviet Union, Marcuse here summarizes his objections to Soviet Marxism.

BOOKS ABOUT MARCUSE

Alford, C. Fred. *Science and the Revenge of Nature: Marcuse and Habermas.* U. Press Fla. 1985 $29.95. ISBN 0-8130-0817-4. A useful comparison of the two most famous critical theorists.

Lind, Peter. *Marcuse and Freedom: The Genesis and Development of a Theory of Human Liberation.* St. Martin 1985 $27.50. ISBN 0-312-51445-X. An interesting study of one of Marcuse's favorite themes.

Lipshires, Sidney. *Marcuse's Dilemma: From Marx to Freud and Beyond.* Schenkman Bks. Inc. 1974 $11.95. ISBN 0-87073-677-9. A study of key sources and directions in Marcuse's thought.

Lukes, Timothy J. *The Flight into Inwardness: Herbert Marcuse and Liberatory Aesthetics.* Susquehanna U. Pr. 1985 $29.50. ISBN 0-941664-0-X. Explores an often missed dimension of Marcuse's thought.

Nordquist, Joan, comp. *Herbert Marcuse: A Bibliography.* Ref. Rsch. Serv. 1988 $15.00. ISBN 0-937855-16-2. A good, basic source for researchers.

Pippin, Robert, and others. *Marcuse: Critical Theory and the Promise of Utopia.* Greenwood 1987 $47.95. ISBN 0-89789-107-4. Scholarly essays on utopianism, another often missed dimension of Marcuse's thought.

Robinson, Paul. *The Freudian Left: Wilhelm Reich, Geza Roheim, Herbert Marcuse.* Cornell Univ. Pr. 1990 $10.95. ISBN 0-8014-9716-7. A scholarly study that provides useful comparisons of these leftist thinkers.

Schoolman, Morton. *The Imaginary Witness: The Critical Theory of Herbert Marcuse.* NYU Pr. 1984 $20.00. ISBN 0-8147-7833-X. The best intellectual biography of Marcuse.

Stuernagel, Gertrude. *Political Philosophy as Therapy: Marcuse Reconsidered. Contributions in Political Science Ser.* Greenwood 1979 $47.95. ISBN 0-313-20315-6. A critical evaluation of Marcuse's contributions to political thought.

MUMFORD, LEWIS. 1895–1990.

[SEE Chapter 6 in this volume.]

NAGEL, ERNEST. 1901–1985

Ernest Nagel was one of the most prominent philosophers of science in the United States during most of his professional career. A positivist, he nonetheless softened the edges of that school with elements of pragmatism and instrumentalism. Like the original logical positivists, Nagel was born in Central Europe (Nove Mesto, Czechoslovakia), but as a child of 10 he emigrated to the United States. His teachers included MORRIS R. COHEN (see Vol. 4), JOHN DEWEY (see Vols. 3 and 4), and Frederick Woodbridge. From these men and from his reading of such other great American philosophers as CHARLES SANDERS PEIRCE (see Vol. 4) and GEORGE SANTAYANA (see Vol. 4), Nagel established a firm grounding in the tradition of American naturalism and pragmatism. Naturalists try to explain everything in terms of natural laws and processes and deny that there is anything beyond the natural order.

Nagel earned his doctorate in philosophy from Columbia University in 1930, and he taught there from 1931 until his retirement four decades later. With Morris R. Cohen, he wrote *An Introduction to Logic and Scientific Method* (1934), the first logic text to incorporate the new thinking in the philosophies of science and mathematics. For 20 years it was the leading text in the field. Although much of the logical-empiricist philosophy of science is located in articles and volumes intended for specialists, Nagel put many of his ideas into readable form. The best example is *The Structure of Science* (1961), which not only summarizes contemporary work in the philosophy of science but also reflects Nagel's own philosophical orientation. Nagel shared the other positivists' interest in physics, and he made important contributions to the discussion of determinism and indeterminism. He was also interested in other fields—for instance, whether other sciences can be reduced to physics, whether biological-teleological explanations are valid, and whether historical explanations can be scientific.

BOOKS BY NAGEL

Gödel's Proof. (coauthored with James R. Newman). NYU Pr. 1958 $7.50. ISBN 0-8147-0325-9. Brief but important popularization of a famous scientific proof.

An Introduction to Logic and Scientific Method. (coauthored with Morris R. Cohen). 1934. HarBraceJ 1934 o.p. A pioneering and still highly readable work on deductive and inductive inference.

Sovereign Reason: And Other Studies in the Philosophy of Science. Free Pr. 1954 o.p. Difficult to find, this is the best introduction to Nagel's philosophy for the general reader. Feisty, easy reading.

The Structure of Science. 1961. Hackett Pub. 1979 $37.95. ISBN 0-915144-71-9. In this
   influential account of scientific explanation, Nagel combines pragmatism and
   logical empiricism.
Teleology Revisited and Other Essays in the Philosophy and History of Science. Col. U. Pr.
   1982 $18.50. ISBN 0-231-04505-0. Readable essays, some with a focus on biological
   topics. Includes pieces on the history of modern logic, the concept of determinism,
   and the title piece: the 1977 John Dewey Lectures at Columbia University.

BOOK ABOUT NAGEL

Morgenbesser, Sidney, Patrick Suppes, and Morton White, eds. *Philosophy, Science and
   Method: Essays in Honor of Ernest Nagel.* St. Martin 1969 o.p. Important philosophers
   (such as Hesse, Levi, and Black) discuss issues related to Nagel's approach, and
   scientists (such as Feinberg and Dobzhansky) discuss the philosophical aspects of
   their fields.

ORTEGA Y GASSET, JOSÉ. 1883–1955

Born in Madrid, José Ortega y Gasset was the initiator of a tradition of
philosophers of technology in the Spanish-speaking world, although he is better
known in the United States as an existentialist essayist. Ortega was professor of
metaphysics at the University of Madrid from 1910 until the outbreak of the
Spanish Civil War in 1936. His most famous work, *The Revolt of the Masses*
(1930), owes much to post-Kantian schools of thought, especially to FRIEDRICH
NIETZSCHE (see Vols. 2 and 4) and HENRI BERGSON (see Vol. 4). Ortega's
predominant thesis is the need for an intellectual aristocracy governing in a
spirit of enlightened liberalism. Although Franco, after his victory in the civil
war, offered to make Ortega the "official philosopher" of Spain and to publish a
deluxe edition of his works (with certain parts deleted), the philosopher refused.
Instead, he chose the life of a voluntary exile, first in Argentina and then in
Peru, where he was professor of philosophy at the University of San Marcos in
Lima. Ortega returned to Spain in 1945 and died in Madrid.

Ortega's reformulation of the Cartesian *cogito* displays the fulcrum of his
thought. While RENÉ DESCARTES (see also Vol. 4) declared *Cogito ergo sum* ("I
think, therefore I am"), Ortega maintained *Cogito quia vivo* ("I think because I
live"). He subordinated reason to life and to vitality. For Ortega, reason
becomes the tool of an individual existing biologically in a given time and place,
rather than an overarching sovereign. His philosophy consequently discloses
affinities in its metaphysics to both American pragmatism and European
existentialism (in spite of its elitism in social philosophy). In the philosophy of
technology, Ortega's thought shares some themes with that of MARTIN
HEIDEGGER (see also Vol. 4), although his politics were clearly different from
those of Heidegger.

BOOKS BY ORTEGA

History as a System. Norton 1962 $7.95. ISBN 0-393-00122-9. An important contribution
   to the philosophy of history.
Man and Crisis. Trans. by Mildred Adams. Norton 1922 $8.95. ISBN 0-393-00121-0
The Origin of Philosophy. Norton 1968 $6.95. ISBN 0-393-00128-8. Examines the history
   of philosophy, with significant focus on Greek philosophy.
The Revolt of the Masses. 1930. Norton 1964 $4.95. ISBN 0-393-09637-8. A major work;
   analyzes the revolutionary impulse of the masses from an existential perspective.
What Is Philosophy? Norton 1964 $7.95. ISBN 0-393-00126-1. A lesser-known work that
   can serve as a useful introduction to Ortega's fundamental thought.

BOOKS ABOUT ORTEGA

Gray, Rockwell. *The Imperative of Modernity: An Intellectual Biography of José Ortega y Gasset.* U. CA Pr. 1989 $45.00. ISBN 0-520-06201-9. An excellent study of the man and his philosophy.

Marias, Julian. *José Ortega y Gasset: Circumstances and Vocation.* Trans. by Frances M. Lopez-Morillas. Bks. Demand repr. of 1970 ed. $122.50. ISBN 0-8357-9729-5. A classic work on Ortega that has been reissued only recently.

Mattei, Carlos R. *Ethical Self-Determination in Don José Ortega y Gasset. American Univ. Studies.* P. Lang Pubs. 1987 $38.50. ISBN 0-8204-0473-X. An important scholarly study of Ortega, focusing on the development of his thought.

PELLEGRINO, EDMUND D. 1920–

Edmund D. Pellegrino is the leading physician-philosopher of medicine in the United States. Born in Newark, N.J., he was educated at St. John's University and received his M.D. from New York University in 1944. From 1959 to 1966 he was professor and chairman of the Department of Medicine at the University of Kentucky, where he was involved in introducing a medical-humanities curriculum. He then held a number of administrative positions: academic vice-president and dean of the School of Medicine at the State University of New York at Stony Brook (1966–73), chancellor and vice-president for health affairs at the University of Tennessee (1973–75), president of the Yale-New Haven Medical Center (1975–78), president of the Catholic University of America (1978–82), and director of the Kennedy Institute of Ethics at Georgetown University (1983–89). He is currently director of the Center for the Advanced Study of Ethics at Georgetown University.

During his career, Pellegrino has remained extremely active in professional societies for the medical humanities. He has also been a prolific author of medical articles, including articles on medical ethics and medical humanities, and he has written two books on the philosophy of medicine. Pellegrino is best known, however, as a dynamic lecturer to medical school faculties, medical students, and the general public on a wide variety of topics relevant to medical ethics and the philosophy of medicine. Although no books have been written about Pellegrino, the spring 1990 issue of the *Journal of Medicine and Philosophy* is devoted to a discussion of his philosophy.

BOOKS BY PELLEGRINO

For the Patient's Good: The Restoration of Beneficence in Health Care. (coauthored with David C. Thomasma). OUP 1988 $35.00. ISBN 0-19-504319-7. The most detailed presentation of a philosophy of medicine founded on the physician's primary commitment to the good of the patient.

Humanism and the Physician. U. of Tenn. Pr. 1979 $33.95. ISBN 0-87049-311-6

A Philosophical Basis of Medical Practice: Toward a Philosophy and Ethics of the Healing Professions. (coauthored with David C. Thomasma). OUP 1981 $29.95. ISBN 0-19-502789-2. The first formulation of a practice-based philosophy of medicine.

Teaching Ethics, the Humanities, and Human Values in Medicine. (coauthored with Thomas K. McElhinney). Society for Health and Human Values 1982 o.p. One of several efforts by Pellegrino to promote, but also to criticize, the introduction of medical humanities into the medical-school curriculum.

POPPER, SIR KARL RAIMUND. 1902–

Karl Raimund Popper's lively writing style, sharp wit, and strongly expressed views have made him one of the most widely read twentieth-century philosophers of science. Popper was born and educated in Vienna, but his academic career blossomed in England. He received his Ph.D. from the University of Vienna in 1928. Although he was not a member of the Vienna Circle of Logical Positivists and disagreed with some of their doctrines, there was a mutual influence between him and circle members. One of them, Herbert Feigl, encouraged Popper to put his ideas in book form. The manuscript that emerged became *The Logic of Scientific Discovery* (1935), considered to be the fundamental book for understanding Popper's thought.

Popper left Austria in 1937 to accept a post at Canterbury University College in New Zealand. After World War II, he moved to the London School of Economics, where he was professor of logic and scientific method from 1949 to 1969 and professor emeritus thereafter. He was knighted in 1965. Popper's prominence in the philosophy of science began with the publication of the English translation of *The Logic of Scientific Discovery* in 1959. A somewhat easier book of essays, *Conjectures and Refutations* (1962), followed soon after. Other works have appeared since, dealing with the evolutionary theory of knowledge and the philosophy of physics. While the logical positivists often stressed the experiential basis of scientific knowledge, Popper denies that there are absolute foundations for knowledge, and argues that science is essentially a self-correcting but progressive process in constant flux. He holds that science is not, properly speaking, inductive; scientists can only make bold conjectures and subject them to criticism. Science begins, in other words, with problems. To solve these problems, scientists first develop hypotheses and then try to prove them to be false. The hypotheses that survive testing are the ones accepted by science.

BOOKS BY POPPER

Conjectures and Refutations: The Growth of Scientific Knowledge. 1962. HarpC 1968 o.p. An informally written book that provides reasonably easy access to Popper's views.
In Search of a Better World: Lectures and Essays of Thirty Years. Routledge 1992 $25.00. ISBN 0-415-08774-0
The Logic of Scientific Discovery. 1935. Basic 1959 o.p. Popper's central ideas appear here; technical.
Objective Knowledge: An Evolutionary Approach. 1972. OUP 1972 $16.95. ISBN 0-19-875024-2. The best introduction to Popper's thought for the beginner; expounds his evolutionary theory.
The Open Society and Its Enemies. 1945. 2 vols. Princeton U. Pr. 1966 $16.95. ISBN 0-691-01972-X. The latest edition of Popper's most popular social and political philosophy book.
The Open Universe: An Argument for Indeterminism. Postscript to Logic of Scientific Discovery Ser. Ed. by W. W. Bartley III. Rowman 1982 $48.25. ISBN 0-8476-7388-X. Technical.
Popper Selections. 1985. Ed. by David Miller. Princeton U. Pr. 1985 $57.50. ISBN 0-691-02031-0. An excellent place to begin a study of Popper and his philosophy. Parts 1 and 2 reprint articles and sections of Popper's books on the theory of knowledge and philosphy of science. The collection has the advantage of juxtaposing abstracts from different periods so that the reader can see both the continuity and the development of Popper's thought.
Quantum Theory and the Schism in Physics. Postscript to Logic of Scientific Discovery Ser. Ed. by W. W. Bartley III. Rowman 1984 $21.00. ISBN 0-8476-7015-5. Technical.
Realism and the Aim of Science. Postscript to Logic of Scientific Discovery Ser. Ed. by W. W. Bartley III. Rowman 1983 $55.00. ISBN 0-8476-7015-5. Technical.
The Self and Its Brain: An Argument for Interactionism. 1977. (coauthored with John Eccles). Routledge 1984 $16.95. ISBN 0-7100-9584-8. A famous physiologist joins Popper in a debate about mind and body.

Unended Quest: An Intellectual Autobiography. 1976. Open Court rev. ed. 1982 $12.95. ISBN 0-87548-343-7. A revised edition of an autobiography that first appeared in a two-volume work by Paul Schilpp.

BOOKS ABOUT POPPER

Berkson, William, and John Wettersten. *Learning from Errors: Karl Popper's Psychology of Learning.* Open Court 1984 $29.95. ISBN 0-912050-74-8. Two of Popper's disciples summarize his thought.

Bunge, Mario, ed. *The Critical Approach to Science and Philosophy.* Free Pr. 1964 o.p. Scientists and scholars contribute essays that pertain to Popper's thought and interests. The Popper bibliography covers up to 1964.

Magee, Bryan. *Philosophy and the Real World: An Introduction to Karl Popper.* Open Court 1985 $7.95. ISBN 0-87548-436-0. Presents a vivid picture of Popper's philosophy, from the point of view of a believer; an excellent place to begin.

Schilpp, Paul A., ed. *The Philosophy of Karl Popper.* Lib. of Living Philosophers. 2 vols. Open Court 1974 $39.95. ISBN 0-87548-353-4. An invaluable sourcebook about Popper's thought. It begins with his intellectual autobiography, contains essays by distinguished scholars, and ends with replies by Popper.

QUINE, WILLARD VAN ORMAN. 1908–

W. V. Quine, a logician and philosopher, was born in Akron, Ohio, and educated at Oberlin College and Harvard University. He is one of the most respected academic American philosophers since the end of World War II. An accomplished and creative mathematical logician and professor of philosophy at Harvard University, he has made a lasting contribution to philosophy in the fields of epistemology and ontology.

Using the rigorous tools of formal logic but expressing himself in a clear prose style, Quine has analyzed the nature and function of language and has found that the epistemological principles on which positivism rests are defective. He undermined the sharp distinction between analytic and empirical statements and also brought into question the empiricist program of reducing empirical statements for meaningfulness to direct reports describing what is given in experience. This is the basis of his claims about the indeterminacy of translation, stressing the dependence of empirical meanings on the conceptual structures to which they belong. This holistic approach to knowledge is paralleled by an ontological commitment to nominalism. His nominalistic program has been modified in recent years, however. Quine first presented his highly influential views in several influential articles; these were subsequently collected and published in books; then in 1960 he provided a coherent and systematic statement of his thought in the book *Word and Object.*

BOOKS BY QUINE

Dear Carnap, Dear Van: The Quine-Carnap Correspondence and Related Work. U. CA Pr. 1990 $34.95. ISBN 0-520-06847-5. An important source that links the thought of Quine and Carnap.

From a Logical Point of View: Nine Logico-Philosophical Essays. HUP 1980 $16.95. ISBN 0-674-32351-3. A collection of previously published essays, including his famous paper, "Two Dogmas of Empiricism."

Ontological Relativity and Other Essays. Col. U. Pr. 1977 $16.00. ISBN 0-231-08357-2. A collection of essays pertinent to such central theses of Quine as the primacy of language for metaphysics.

Philosophy of Logic. 1969. HUP 1986 $9.00. ISBN 0-674-66563-5. Introduction to the foundations of logic.

Pursuit of Truth. HUP 1992 $19.95. ISBN 0-674-73950-7. A lucid and compelling summary of Quine's views.

Quiddities: An Intermittently Philosophical Dictionary. 1987. HUP 1987 $27.50. ISBN 0-674-74351-2. Contains playful entries dealing with philosophical, linguistic, and mathematical issues.

The Roots of Reference. Carus Lecture Ser. Open Court 1975 $22.95. ISBN 0-8126-9101-6. Penetrating investigation of the basic ideas of language and meaning.

Theories and Things. 1981. HUP 1981 $8.95. ISBN 0-674-87926-0. A review of language and ontology that offers clearer statements but no change of view.

The Time of My Life: An Autobiography. 1985. MIT Pr. 1985 $30.00. ISBN 0-262-17003-5. An autobiographical account distinguished by its mentions of persons and places.

The Ways of Paradox and Other Essays. HUP 1976 $25.50. ISBN 0-674-94837-8. A collection of essays previously published in specialist journals.

The Web of Belief. (coauthored with J. S. Ullian). Random 1978 $10.50. ISBN 0-394-32179-0. A lucid presentation of the holistic theory of knowledge.

Word and Object. 1960. MIT Pr. 1960 $12.95. ISBN 0-262-67001-1. Quine's most systematic work; a classic in recent American analytic philosophy.

BOOKS ABOUT QUINE

Barret, Robert B., and Roger Gibson, eds. *Perspectives on Quine.* Blackwell Pubs. 1989 $45.00. ISBN 0-631-16135-X

Dilman, Ilham. *Quine on Ontology, Necessity and Experience: A Philosophical Critique.* State U. NY Pr. 1984 $59.50. ISBN 0-87395-760-1. An important critical study.

Gibson, Roger F. *The Philosophy of W. V. Quine: An Expository Essay.* U. Press Fla. 1982 $19.50. ISBN 0-685-05101-3. A sympathetic introduction to Quine's philosophy.

Gochet, Paul. *Ascent to Truth: A Critical Examination of Quine's Philosophy.* Philosophia Pr. 1986 $39.00. ISBN 3-88405-076-1. Scholarly monograph by a leading European follower of Quine.

Hahn, Lewis, and Paul Arthur Schilpp, eds. *The Philosophy of W. V. Quine. Lib. of Living Philosophers.* Open Court 1986 $49.95. ISBN 0-8126-9012-5. A collection of original articles by leading experts on Quine's philosophy; preceded by Quine's intellectual autobiography and followed by responses to his critics. Concludes with a bibliography of Quine's writings.

Shahan, Robert W., and Chris Swoyer, eds. *Essays on the Philosophy of W. V. Quine.* U. of Okla. Pr. 1979 $19.50. ISBN 0-8061-1516-5. Articles by prominent philosophers that originally appeared in the *Southwest Journal of Philosophy.*

RESCHER, NICHOLAS. 1928–

A philosopher of science, Nicholas Rescher was born in Hagen, Germany, but fled that country and became a naturalized American citizen in 1944. Educated at Queens College, he received an M.A. and Ph.D. from Princeton University. He then became an instructor in philosophy there, followed by a position as a research mathematician with the Rand Corporation from 1954 to 1957. After leaving Rand, he taught at Lehigh University and then at the University of Pittsburgh, where he served as a professor of philosophy and, since 1981, as director of the Center of the Philosophy of Science.

A specialist in the theory of knowledge and metaphysics, Rescher is best known for his work in the philosophy of science. In his later writings, such as *Scientific Progress* (1977), he examined the ethical and external constraints on science and scientific research. He also studied the growing challenges and limits imposed on technological progress in modern society in his *Unpopular Essays on Technological Progress* (1980).

BOOKS BY RESCHER

Baffling Phenomena: And Other Studies in the Philosophy of Knowledge and Valuation. Rowman 1990 $46.50. ISBN 0-8476-7638-2. Collection of recent essays on the theory of knowledge and the nature of philosophic inquiry.

Empirical Inquiry. Roman & Littlefield 1981 o.p.

Human Interests: Reflections on Philosophical Anthropology. Stanford U. Pr. 1990 $32.50. ISBN 0-8047-1811-3. Collection of essays.

Hypothetical Reasoning. North-Holland Pub. 1964 o.p.

An Introduction to Logic. St. Martin 1964 o.p.

Introduction to Value Theory. U. Pr. of Amer. 1982 repr. of 1969 ed. $17.75. ISBN 0-8191-2474-5

The Logic of Commands. Routledge 1966 o.p.

On the Epistemology of the Inexact Sciences. Rand Corp. 1960 o.p.

The Philosophy of Leibniz. P-H 1967 o.p.

Rationality: A Philosophical Inquiry into the Nature and Rationale of Reason. OUP 1989 $49.95. ISBN 0-19-824435-5. Study of the various aspects of rationality.

Scientific Progress: A Philosophical Essay on the Economics of Research in the Natural Sciences. 1977. U. of Pittsburgh Pr. 1977 $49.95. ISBN 0-8229-1128-0

Unpopular Essays on Technological Progress. U. of Pittsburgh Pr. 1980 $49.95. ISBN 0-8229-3411-6

A Useful Inheritance: Evolutionary Aspects of the Theory of Knowledge. Rowman 1990 $43.50. ISBN 0-8476-7615-3. Well-written account of Rescher's view of the evolutionary basis of human intelligence.

BOOK ABOUT RESCHER

Sosa, Ernest, ed. *The Philosophy of Nicholas Rescher: Discussion and Replies.* Kluwer Ac. 1979 $50.50. ISBN 90-277-0962-9

ROSZAK, THEODORE. 1933–

[SEE Chapter 6 in this volume.]

RUSSELL, BERTRAND ARTHUR WILLIAM, 3rd EARL RUSSELL. 1872–1970 (NOBEL PRIZE 1950)

Bertrand Russell is one of the giants of twentieth-century philosophy. A more complete profile and listing of his works appears in Volume 4, but he is also profiled here because of the significant impact he had on academic philosophy of science in the English-speaking world—indeed, throughout the entire world.

Russell was born in what is now the county of Gwent, Wales, into an aristocratic family that had been prominent in British politics since the sixteenth century. After both his parents died, he went to live with his grandmother in England, where he was privately educated. In 1890 he entered Trinity College in Cambridge, receiving his B.A. in moral sciences in 1894. After spending several years in Paris and Berlin, he returned to England and began lecturing at Cambridge University; he remained associated with that university throughout his life.

Shortly after joining the faculty of Cambridge, Russell began a collaboration with ALFRED NORTH WHITEHEAD (see Vol. 4) that resulted in his most famous and influential work, *Principia Mathematica* (1910–13). This work was instrumental (especially through such Vienna Circle logical positivists as RUDOLF CARNAP) in revolutionizing philosophical discussions of science. Russell and Whitehead's new logic was directly applicable in the complex analysis of scientific theories and the methods by which they are validated. Russell was also influential in his skepticism toward metaphysical and religious claims, in his insistence on the importance for reliable knowledge of direct factual observations, and in his overall scientific outlook.

In addition to his tenure at Cambridge, Russell also taught for various lengths of time (and often under stormy conditions) at the University of Chicago, Harvard University, and the University of California. In 1940 he was appointed professor at the College of the City of New York, but the appointment was revoked by a Supreme Court justice on the ground that certain passages in his books carried moral contamination for the youth of New York. Russell succeeded to his earldom in 1931 and briefly took a seat in the House of Lords; but he claimed, on many occasions, that he had to support himself by lecturing and writing books. He authored nearly 100 books only some of which are relevant to his contributions to the philosophy of science. In terms of that field as an academic discipline, Russell always remained something of an outsider. Everyone read and reacted to his works on logic, mathematics, and various aspects of the theory of knowledge, but his own work was never academic. The best of his contributions, *Human Knowledge: Its Scope and Limits* (1948), in addition to being much broader in its sweep than any other academic studies of the time (and most later studies), defended unorthodox theories of perception, induction and probability, and similar topics. Russell was also an outstanding popularizer of scientific subjects, as in *The ABC of Atoms* (1923) and *The ABC of Relativity* (1925).

Despite his aristocratic background and upbringing, Russell was opposed to England's involvement in World War I. An ardent advocate of pacifism, he was imprisoned twice during the war for taking this stance. Although Russell put aside his pacifist leanings to support the British war effort after the Nazi invasion of Poland in 1939, he spent the last 20 years of his life as a peace activist working to promote nuclear disarmament.

BOOKS BY RUSSELL

The ABC of Relativity. 1925. NAL-Dutton 1985 $4.95. ISBN 0-451-62738-5. A philosophical analysis of scientific theory; a good, easily understandable exposition.

The Autobiography of Bertrand Russell. 1967-69. 3 vols. Unwin Hyman Vol. 1 1978 $16.95. ISBN 0-04-921022-X. Vol. 2 1968 $34.95. ISBN 0-04-921009-2. Vol. 3 1981 $34.95. ISBN 0-04-921010-6

The Basic Writings of Bertrand Russell 1903–1959. Ed. by Robert E. Egner and Lester E. Dennon. S&S Trade 1967 $12.95. ISBN 0-671-20154-9. Consists of 81 essays and chapters or passages from longer works selected to represent Russell as philosopher, mathematician, man of letters, historian, and analyst of international affairs.

An Inquiry into Meaning and Truth. 1940. Unwin Hyman 1980 $7.95. ISBN 0-04-121019-0. A technical work in philosophical semantics written during the early period of the field's development.

Logic and Knowledge: Essays 1901–50. Ed. by Robert Charles Marsh. Unwin Hyman 1988 $24.95. ISBN 0-04-440260-0. A selection of Russell's most significant essays on the technical subjects of logic and epistemology; prepared for the serious student.

My Philosophical Development. 1959. Unwin Hyman 1975 $9.95. ISBN 0-04-192030-9. An intellectual autobiography beginning when Russell was 16; written with his usual clarity and wit. Includes an appendix, "Russell's Philosophy," by Alan Wood.

Principia Mathematica. 1910–13. (coauthored with Alfred North Whitehead). 3 vols. Cambridge U. Pr. 1927 $500.00. ISBN 0-521-06791-X. Monumental treatise on the foundations of mathematics; a classic for all time, though accessible only to the expert.

The Principles of Mathematics. 1903. Norton 1964 $12.95. ISBN 0-393-00249-7. Introductory work presenting Russell's revolutionary theory that logic is the basis of mathematics.

BOOKS ABOUT RUSSELL

Ayer, A. J. *Bertrand Russell.* U. of Ch. Pr. 1988 $9.95. ISBN 0-226-03343-0. A leading positivist philosopher acknowledges Russell's contributions to philosophy.

Clark, Ronald. *The Life of Bertrand Russell. Quality Paperback Ser.* Da Capo 1990 $17.95. ISBN 0-306-80397-6. A noted biographer and popularizer of many twentieth-century intellectuals turns his attention to Russell in this very readable and interesting biography.

Hill, Claire O. *Word and Object in Husserl, Frege, and Russell: The Roots of Twentieth-Century Philosophy.* Ohio U. Pr. 1991 $34.95. ISBN 0-8214-1002-4. A good scholarly study of sources.

Oaklander, L. Nathan. *Temporal Relations and Temporal Becoming: A Defense of a Russellian Theory of Time.* U. Pr. of Amer. 1984 $43.75. ISBN 0-8191-4150-X

Rodriguez-Consuegra, F. A. *The Mathematical Philosophy of Bertrand Russell: Origins and Development.* Birkhauser 1991 $68.50. ISBN 0-8176-2656-5. A highly technical examination and analysis of Russell's philosophy of mathematics.

Sainsbury, Mark. *Russell. Arguments of Philosophers Ser.* Routledge 1979 $15.95. ISBN 0-7102-0536-8. A good summary for beginners; part of an excellent series.

Savage, C. Wade, and C. Anthony Anderson, eds. *Rereading Russell: Essays on Bertrand Russell's Metaphysics and Epistemology. Minnesota Studies in the Philosophy of Science.* U. of Minn. Pr. 1989 $39.95. ISBN 0-8166-1649-3. Fairly technical essays aimed at professional philosophers of science.

Schilpp, Paul A. *The Philosophy of Bertrand Russell.* Bks. Demand 1980 $160.00. ISBN 0-317-09085-2. Includes an intellectual autobiography, commentaries by famous philosophers, and replies by Russell; includes a bibliography.

SALMON, WESLEY CHARLES. 1925–

Born in Detroit, Michigan, the philosopher of science Wesley Charles Salmon received his M.A. from the University of Chicago, where he studied theology and metaphysics. He then shifted his interest to the philosophy of science at the University of California at Los Angeles, where he studied under Hans Reichenbach. After receiving his Ph.D. at UCLA in 1950, Salmon became an instructor at Washington State University, followed by appointments at Northwestern, Brown, and Indiana universities. From 1973 to 1981 he served on the faculty of the University of Arizona and then became professor of philosophy at the University of Pittsburgh.

Noted for his contributions to the philosophy of inductive inference, Salmon focused on causality and scientific explanation. His 1966 essay *The Foundations of Scientific Inference* offered a concise treatise on the problem of induction, its historical roots, and modern approaches to its solution. Later study and writings continued his efforts to strengthen locial empiricism in scientific thought. Salmon's fullest statement of his theory of inductive inference is found in *Scientific Explanation and the Causal Structure of the World* (1984).

BOOKS BY SALMON

The Foundations of Scientific Inference. 1966. U. of Pittsburgh Pr. 1967 $12.95. ISBN 0-8229-5118-5

Four Decades of Scientific Explanation. 1984. U. of Minn. Pr. 1990 $14.95. ISBN 0-8166-1825-9. Witty account of the pattern of recent developments in thought about the nature of scientific explanation.

Hans Reichenbach: Logical Empiricist. Kluwer Ac. 1979 $76.00. ISBN 90-277-0958-0

Logic. P-H 3rd ed. 1984 ISBN 0-13-540021-X

Scientific Explanation and the Causal Structure of the World. Princeton U. Pr. 1984 $18.95. ISBN 0-691-10170-1

Space, Time, and Motion: A Philosophical Introduction. Bks. Demand repr. of 1980 ed.
    $44.50. ISBN 0-318-39664-5
Statistical Explanation and Statistical Relevance. U. of Pittsburgh Pr. 1971 $10.95. ISBN
    0-8229-5225-4

WHEWELL, WILLIAM. 1794–1866
[SEE Chapter 3 in this volume.]

WINNER, LANGDON. 1944–
[SEE Chapter 5 in this volume.]

ZIMAN, JOHN M. 1925–
[SEE Chapter 2 in this volume.]

CHAPTER 5

Ethics in Science, Technology, and Medicine

Carl Mitcham

> The bomb . . . and other discoveries present us with . . . a problem not of physics but of ethics.
> —ALBERT EINSTEIN, *Einstein on Peace*

> Modern technology has introduced actions of such novel scale, objects, and consequences that the framework of former ethics can no longer contain them.
> —HANS JONAS, *The Imperative of Responsibility*

Ethics is the study and evaluation of human conduct. To some extent, ethics always has been related to science, technology, and medicine. For example, in the *Nicomachean Ethics* of ARISTOTLE (see Vols. 3 and 4), science and *techne* (the Greek root of *technics* and *technology*) are described as intellectual virtues. Moreover, illustrations often are drawn from the arts and medicine to explore the nature of such virtues. The Hippocratic Oath, which is a creation of Classical Greece, establishes general ethical principles for the conduct of medical practitioners. About 2,000 years later, IMMANUEL KANT (see Vol. 4) held a radically different view of the relationship between ethics and science and technology. He distinguished ethical from scientific knowledge and moral imperatives from technical ones.

Throughout history, there have been two broad ethical attitudes toward science, technology, and medicine. From PLATO (see Vols. 3 and 4) and Aristotle to the Renaissance, science and its correlates were subject to political and religious constraints. In general, science and technology were considered defective forms of knowledge, socially destablizing and morally pernicious.

Beginning in the Renaissance and becoming clearly evident by the Enlightenment, the political and religious constraints were removed and replaced by a new ethical commitment to the unfettered pursuit of science and technology for "the relief of man's estate" (FRANCIS BACON [see Vol. 4]). Science was promoted as the only true form of knowledge. Its proponents claimed that applications of science in medicine and industrial technology would produce unqualified material benefits for all people.

Since the mid-eighteenth century, there have been several ethical reevaluations of science, technology, and medicine—first, in reaction to modern science and then to the Industrial Revolution. Contemporary ethical reevaluation is also associated with technological developments such as nuclear energy, environmental pollution, genetic engineering, and powerful information technologies. The following bibliography highlights the latter developments as well as the literature on the ethics of science in general, professional engineering ethics, and the ethics of technology.

Many of the works listed require a basic knowledge of the history and philosophy of science, technology, and medicine (see Chapters 3 and 4). Moreover, they lead the reader toward more general studies of the relationship between science, technology, and society (see Chapter 6) and to special science, technology, and society issues (see Chapter 7). Civil court cases are another fertile source for developing moral perceptions, especially regarding environmental ethics and bioethics. The current ethical issues associated with technology include increasing corporate liability for industrial accidents; environmental legislation concerning enforcement of the U.S. Natural Environment Policy Act of 1969; consumer-protection legislation; and court decisions in biomedical cases (from Karen Ann Quinlan to Baby M). The present survey does not include books of legal case studies that relate to science, technology, and medicine.

ETHICS IN SCIENCE

There are three related but different themes concerning ethics in science. First, the distinction between science and ethics often has been expressed as one between facts and values; there are books that illustrate the "fact" that values are essential to human beings or state that promoting scientific facts is a "value." Second, there are books that examine the professional ethics of scientific research or the moral principles and values of scientific researchers. Third, there are books that focus on the social impact of modern science. These suggest that scientists should adopt social ethics, which crosses over into public policy analyses of science, technology, and medicine. The latter theme has been illustrated increasingly by recent books on science and education.

Bayles, Michael D. *Professional, Ethics.* Wadsworth Pub. 2nd ed. 1989 $13.00. ISBN 0-536-09546-1. Focuses on consulting professionals (physicians, lawyers, consulting engineers, architects) rather than on scholarly professionals (scientists, nonconsulting engineers, teachers); includes useful references and a bibliography.

Beauchamp, Tom L., and others, eds. *Ethical Issues in Social Science Research.* Johns Hopkins 1982 $70.00. ISBN 0-8018-2655-1. Essays by philosophers and social scientists examining moral dilemmas, the research imperatives that lead to conflicts, and proposals for regulation.

Bell, Robert. *Impure Science: Fraud, Compromise and Political Influence in Scientific Research.* Wiley 1992 $24.95. ISBN 0-471-52913-3. Argues that the three control mechanisms designed to prevent fraud and compromise in science (peer review of grant proposals, peer refereeing of publications, and replication of experiments) have all broken down. Includes a clear discussion of the "Baltimore case" and other examples of scientific misconduct, as well as new attempts at regulation.

Bronowski, Jacob. *Science and Human Values.* 1965. HarpC 1990 $9.00. ISBN 0-06-097281-5. Considered a classic text in the field.

Cattell, Raymond B. *Beyondism: Religion from Science.* Greenwood 1987 $67.95. ISBN 0-275-92431-9. Sequel to *A New Morality from Science: Beyondism* (1972). "[T]akes its momentum from Bacon, Bentham, Darwin, Mill, Comte, Haeckel, Spencer, and those who have seen with increasing clarity the integration of ethics possible through science." Suggests that science is the fundamental value. This work is beyond compare.

Chubin, Daryl E., and Ellen W. Chu, eds. *Science off the Pedestal: Social Perspectives on Science and Technology.* Wadsworth Pub. 1989. ISBN 0-534-09858-4. Fourteen articles discussing science in a social and technological context.

Dickinson, John P. *Science and Scientific Researchers in Modern Society*. UNESCO 1984 $21.00. ISBN 92-3-102427-2. An approach similar to but more general than that of Diener and Crandell; includes chapters on preparing for a career in scientific research, the scientist as a professional, and the scientist as a citizen.

Diener, Edward, and Rick Crandall. *Ethics in Social and Behavioral Research*. U. Ch. Pr. 1978 $4.50. ISBN 0-226-14824-6. Basic introduction to professional research ethics; for graduate students in the social sciences.

Dubos, René. *Reason Awake: Science of Man*. Col. U. Pr. 1970 $44.00. ISBN 0-231-03181-5. "[S]ocial constraints on the scientific enterprise have been made inevitable by the fact that science impinges with increasing effectiveness and violence on all aspects of human life." At the same time, science can "help man to examine objectively, rationally, and creatively the problems that are emerging." A scientist's critical defense of science.

Elzinga, Aant, and others, eds. *In Science We Trust? Moral and Political Issues of Science in Society*. Lund U. Pr. 1990 o.p. Discusses general theories about the relations among science, society, and ethics; includes specific cases on such topics as feminism, environmentalism, and militarization in relation to science.

Frazer, M. J., and A. Kornhauser, eds. *Ethics and Social Responsibility in Science Education*. Pergamon 1986 $27.00. ISBN 0-08-033912-3. More than 20 brief articles on the theme that ethics is "an unavoidable part of science education."

Glass, Hiram B. *Science and Ethical Values*. Greenwood repr. of 1965 ed. $45.00. ISBN 0-313-23141-9. Classic argument that "ethical values . . . grow out of the biological nature of man and his evolution."

Gosling, David, and Bert Musschenga, eds. *Science Education and Ethical Values: Introducing Ethics and Religion into the Classroom and Laboratory*. Wrld. Coun. Churches 1985 o.p. Examines how schools, teachers' colleges, universities, and churches can play a creative role.

Graham, Loren R. *Between Science and Values*. Col. U. Pr. 1983 $47.50. ISBN 0-231-05192-1. Historical study of how recent transformations in physics and biology have significantly influenced epistemological and ethical values.

Grinnell, Frederick. *The Scientific Attitude*. Guilford Pr. 1992 $16.95. ISBN 0-89862-018-X. General overview that briefly discussed secrecy and fraud in science in the first edition (1987). This edition adds an entirely new chapter, "Scientific Misconduct: Science at Risk."

Holton, Gerald, and Robert S. Morison, eds. *Limits of Scientific Inquiry*. o.p. Seminal discussion of the question, Should science be limited, for ethical or other reasons? Includes the responses of 15 scientists, philosophers, and historians; originally published as a special issue of *Daedalus* (1979).

Hook, Sidney, and others, eds. *The Ethics of Teaching and Scientific Research*. Prometheus Bks. 1977 $23.95. ISBN 0-87975-068-5. Contains, in its third section, 10 essays (mainly by scientists) on the ethical dimensions of scientific research.

Lehrer, Keith, ed. *Science and Ethics*. Rodopi 1988 o.p. Collection of articles covering the intersection between science and morality. Discusses topics that include the view that science is a responsible and rational human activity guided by its own normative system; ethical viewpoints derived from evolutionary biology and their hidden historical conditions; a defense of the Kantian argument that intellectual liberty is indispensable to integrity of persons; an examination of the position that scientific knowledge is intrinsically good; questions of morality and rationality in decisions regarding science; interpersonal practical reasoning; modern humanism's mission for world unity; a more rational and radical form of democracy; and rights/obligations as emergent entities.

Lowrance, William W. *Modern Science and Human Values*. OUP 1985 $24.95. ISBN 0-19-503605-0. Sophisticated study of the interactions between values (including ethics) and science technology. Argues that science can influence but cannot dictate values; considers the professional responsibility of scientists.

Miller, David J., and Michel Hersen, eds. *Research Fraud in the Behavioral and Biomedical Sciences*. Wiley 1992 $34.95. ISBN 0-471-52068-3. Twelve papers by practicing medical researchers focusing on "human factors" as well as problems caused by the system of scientific research.

Nelkin, Dorothy. *Science as Intellectual Property: Who Controls Scientific Research?* Free Pr. 1983 $7.95. ISBN 0-685-08671-2. Useful social, historical, and legal background for many ethical issues.

Newton, David E. *Science Ethics.* Modan-Adama Bks. 1987 o.p. Brief popular overview of the field; includes photographs and cartoons.

Proctor, Robert N. *Value-Free Science? Purity and Power in Modern Knowledge.* HUP 1991 $34.95. ISBN 0-674-93170-X. Explores the theory that "value neutrality, far from being a timeless or self-evident principle, has a distinctive geography; 'value-freedom' has meant different things to different people at different times."

Rescher, Nicholas. *The Limits of Science.* U. CA Pr. 1984 $42.50. Discusses the internal (cognitive) and external (economic) constraints on science.

Sperry, Roger W. *Science and Moral Priority: The Merging of Mind, Brain, and Values.* *Convergence Ser.* Greenwood 1984 $12.95. ISBN 0-275-91799-1. Argues for an ethics based on knowledge of the brain and the brain-mind relationship provided by scientific research; with an introduction by Ruth N. Anshen.

Stent, Gunther S., ed. *Morality as a Biological Phenomenon: The Presuppositions of Sociobiological Research.* U. CA Pr. 1980 $40.00. ISBN 0-520-04029-5. Focuses on the thesis that morality has an evolutionary basis in biology; includes proceedings from a critical symposium on Edward O. Wilson's *Sociobiology: The New Synthesis* (HUP 1975).

Weingartner, Paul, and Gerhard Zecha, eds. *Induction, Physics, and Ethics: Proceedings of the 1968 Salzburg Colloquium in the Philosophy of Science.* *Synthese Lib.* Kluwer Ac. 1970 $75.50. ISBN 90-277-0158-X. Section three contains six papers and a discussion on "Science and Ethics: The Moral Responsibility of the Scientist."

NUCLEAR ETHICS

The successful application of concepts from theoretical physics to the issue of harnessing nuclear energy for weapons and power generation has been the most significant stimulus for reevaluation of the Enlightenment faith in modern science. The resulting debate, which has included both scientists and the public, has gone through two major stages.

First, concern was voiced by nuclear scientists and engineers in the late 1940s and early 1950s, resulting in publication of the *Bulletin of the Atomic Scientists* and the Pugwash movement. The *Bulletin* (which briefly changed its name to *Science and Human Affairs*) remains a useful reference source; two valuable collections of articles from the *Bulletin* are listed below (see Grodzins and Rabinowitch, and Ackland and McGuire). The Pugwash movement takes its name from Pugwash, Nova Scotia, where its first conference was held in 1957 (see the book by Joseph Rotblat below). In the late 1950s and early 1960s, the *Bulletin* and the Pugwash movement led a public protest against nuclear weapons that eventually led to the limited nuclear test ban treaty of 1963.

The second major stage began during the late 1970s. At that time, the burgeoning environmental movement stimulated concern over nuclear power as well as a renewed protest against nuclear weapons. The issue concerning the safety of nuclear energy was dramatized by the partial meltdown of the reactor at Three Mile Island in the United States (1979) and the more serious disaster at Chernobyl in the former Soviet Union (1986). The nuclear weapons issue was highlighted by the breakdown of détente as a result of President Reagan's Strategic Defense Initiative (announced in March 1983) and by a pastoral letter of the United States Conference of Catholic Bishops that was critical of nuclear weapons (May 1983).

With the end of the cold war (1989), emphasis has shifted to problems of dismantling and disposing of nuclear weapons, problems of nonproliferation, and again the safety of nuclear power.

The fundamental ethical issues are whether or not nuclear weapons have altered the human condition; the moral status of deterrence theory and the potential use of nuclear weapons; and proper apportionment of responsibility and risk regarding nuclear weapons and nuclear power.

Ackland, Len, and Steven McGuire, eds. *Assessing the Nuclear Age.* U. Ch. Pr. 1986 $29.00. ISBN 0-226-03872-6. Important collection of more recent articles from the *Bulletin of the Atomic Scientists.*

Allison, Graham T., and others, eds. *Hawks, Doves, and Owls: An Agenda for Avoiding Nuclear War.* Norton 1985 $14.95. ISBN 0-393-01995-0. Nine studies discussing ways of assuring that the U.S. government's nuclear weapons policy defends and preserves our values and institutions by avoiding nuclear war; developed out of the Harvard Nuclear Study Group.

Anzovin, Steven, ed. *The Star Wars Debate. Reference Shelf Ser.* Wilson 1986 o.p. Collection of recent substantive journal articles; includes two presidential documents.

Babin, Ronald. *The Nuclear Power Game.* Paul & Co. Pubs. 1985 $39.95. ISBN 0-820057-30-6

Balogh, Brian. *Chain Reaction: Expert Debate and Public Participation in American Commercial Nuclear Power, 1945–1975.* Cambridge U. Pr. 1991 $37.95. ISBN 0-521-37296-8. A study of the commercial nuclear power industry. Deals with the formation of public policy and public opinion as well as the development of several nuclear power organizations.

Blake, Nige, and Kay Pole, eds. *Dangers of Deterrence: Philosophers on Nuclear Strategy.* Methuen 1984 o.p.

_____. *Objections to Nuclear Defence: Philosophers on Deterrence.* Methuen 1984 o.p. Both *Dangers of Deterrence* (above) and *Objections to Nuclear Defence* take a skeptical view of deterrence theory. *Dangers* contains seven essays on political and strategic questions and *Objections* contains nine essays on moral issues; all authors reflect the Anglo-American analytic philosophical tradition.

Bracken, Paul. *The Command and Control of Nuclear Forces.* Yale U. Pr. 1983 $15.00. ISBN 0-300-03398-2. Suggests that the proper management of nuclear weapons presents as many ethical issues as military issues.

Burns, Grant. *The Nuclear Present: A Guide to Recent Books on Nuclear War, Weapons, the Peace Movement, and Related Issues.* Scarecrow 1992 $69.50. ISBN 0-8108-2619-4. Offers a nuclear chronology and a periodical guide to journals, magazines, and newsletters relevant to nuclear and peace issues.

Carlton, David, and Carlo Schaerf, eds. *The Arms Race in the Era of Star Wars: Studies in Disarmament and Conflicts.* St. Martin 1988 $39.95. ISBN 0-312-00237-8. Contains 16 articles on the Soviet-American strategic arms race written by different international scholars. Deals with both technological and political aspects.

Castelli, Jim. *The Bishops and the Bomb: Waging Peace in a Nuclear Age.* Doubleday 1983 o.p. Approving account and analysis of the writing of the United States Conference of Catholic Bishops' pastoral letter "The Challenge of Peace: God's Promise and Our Response"; includes the text of the pastoral letter in an appendix.

Cohen, Avner, and Steven Lee, eds. *Nuclear Weapons and the Future of Humanity: The Fundamental Questions. Philosophy and Society Ser.* Rowman 1986 $65.00. ISBN 0-8476-7257-3. Twenty-four original essays on the history and dimensions of the nuclear arms race. Topics include living with nuclear threats; the paradoxes of nuclear strategy, morality, and deterrence; and future prospects. The two "fundamental questions" of the subtitle are: Do nuclear weapons alter the human condition and is deterrence theory morally justified? Both questions underlie specific concerns about MX deployment, the nuclear freeze, Strategic Defense Initiative, and other related issues; one of the two primary collections on nuclear weapons.

Davidson, Donald L. *Nuclear Weapons and the American Churches: Ethical Positions on Modern Warfare*. Westview 1983 o.p. Describes the positions on nuclear weapons and policies held by major religious denominations in the United States.

Depastas, Apostolos N. *Nuclear Age Thinking*. Vantage 1991 $13.95. ISBN 0-533-09149-7

Dwyer, Judith A., ed. *The Catholic Bishops and Nuclear War: A Critique and Analysis of the Pastoral, the Challenge of Peace*. Georgetown U. Pr. 1984 o.p. Five critical essays on the pastoral letter of the United States Conference of Catholic Bishops; introduction by Joseph Cardinal Bernardin.

Dyson, Freeman. *Weapons and Hope*. HarpC 1984 $17.95. ISBN 0-06-039031-X. A mathematician and physicist suggests ways of achieving a peaceful resolution of the nuclear weapons dilemma.

Dyson, Freeman, Raymond Aron, and Joan Robinson. *Values at War: Selected Tanner Lectures on the Nuclear Crisis*. Bks. Demand repr. of 1983 ed. $38.60. ISBN 0-8357-3273-8. Three lectures by Dyson on the theme that cultural patterns endure longer than weapons technologies and political arrangements; Aron concludes that peace research institutes have not been effective; Robinson discusses obstructions to peace, such as international economic complicity, nationalistic aspiration, and the lack of political morality.

Ehrlich, Paul R., and others. *The Cold and the Dark: The World after Nuclear War*. Norton 1984 o.p. Easy-to-read presentation of the "nuclear winter" thesis, which states that nuclear war would have long-term biological and climatic consequences; includes significant papers by Ehrlich and Sagan; the text of an exchange between Soviet and American scientists; and technical papers supporting the major conclusions. Foreword by Lewis Thomas.

English, Raymond, ed. *Ethics and Nuclear Arms: European and American Perspectives*. Ethics & Public Policy 1985 $13.50. ISBN 0-89633-095-8. Mainly supports American policies and criticizes the German Greens, British unilateralists, United States Catholic bishops, and the World Council of Churches.

Faulkner, Peter T., ed. *Silent Bomb: A Guide to the Nuclear Energy Controversy*. Random 1977 o.p. Adversarial collection of 23 articles criticizing nuclear energy; appendices include testimonies before the United States Atomic Energy Commission, as well as a bibliography, glossary, and a list of organizations and periodicals.

Feld, Bernard T. *A Voice Crying in the Wilderness: Essays on the Problem of Science and World Affairs*. 1979 Franklin $136.00. ISBN 0-08-026065-9. Collection of tables and articles on nuclear weapons and disarmament, by a renowned physicist.

Fisher, David. *Morality and the Bomb: An Ethical Assessment of Nuclear Deterrence*. St. Martin 1985 $27.50. ISBN 0-312-54796-6. Analysis of NATO deterrence police concluding that nuclear deterrence is morally justifiable, yet arguing for the simultaneous pursuit of complete disarmament as a utopian ideal.

Fox, Michael, and Leo Groarke, eds. *Nuclear War: Philosophical Perspectives*. P. Lang Pubs. 1985 $19.95. ISBN 0-8206-0209-5. The second of two primary collections on nuclear weapons (with Cohen and Lee's *Nuclear Weapons and the Future of Humanity*). The editors are Canadians, and more than half the contributors are not United States citizens, giving a special tone to the volume; includes 12 papers and 14 commentaries, followed by an unannotated but useful bibliography.

Goodwin, Geoffrey. *Ethics and Nuclear Deterrence*. St. Martin 1982 o.p. Eight essays commissioned by the Council on Christian Approaches to Defence and Disarmament of the British Council of Churches.

Grinspoon, Lester, ed. *The Long Darkness: Psychological and Moral Perspectives on Nuclear Winter*. Yale U. Pr. 1986 o.p. Eight essays, not all equally related to the theme. Carl Sagan summarizes the nuclear winter hypothesis; J. Bryan Hehir outlines the reasoning behind the United States Conference of Catholic Bishops' criticism of nuclear weapons; psychologists Robert Jay Lifton, John E. Mack, and Jerome D. Frank discuss nuclear weapons as a psychological phenomenon.

Grodzins, Morton, and Eugene Rabinowitch, eds. *The Atomic Age: Forty-Five Scientists and Scholars Speak.* S&S Trade 1965 o.p. The first collection of articles from the *Bulletin of the Atomic Scientists*; the best source reflecting views of scientists during the early nuclear period.

Hardin, Russell, and others, eds. *Nuclear Deterrence: Ethics and Strategy.* U. Ch. Pr. 1985 $29.95. ISBN 0-226-31702-1. Includes 20 articles collected from three different issues of the journal *Ethics.*

Hollenbach, David. *Nuclear Ethics: A Christian Moral Argument.* Paulist Pr. 1983 o.p. Part 1 examines "just war" theory and Part 2 discusses nuclear weapons policy from the viewpoint of theological ethics.

Jaspers, Karl. *The Atom Bomb and the Future of Man.* Trans. by E. B. Ashton. U. Ch. Pr. 1984 o.p. The first major philosophical attempt to argue that nuclear weapons alter the human condition, and as Einstein said, require people to develop a "new way of thinking." Originally published in German in 1958 (first trans. as *The Future of Mankind,* 1961).

Kahn, Herman. *On Thermonuclear War.* Greenwood 1978 repr. of 1961 ed. $85.00. ISBN 0-313-20060-2. Classic systems analysis of the military options during nuclear war; somewhat dated.

Kaku, Michio, and Jennifer Trainer, eds. *Nuclear Power, Both Sides: The Best Arguments for and against the Most Controversial Technology.* Norton 1982 o.p. Twenty original essays on the history of nuclear power, radiation dangers, reactor safety, nuclear waste disposal, economics, alternative reactor technologies, and future prospects; the best collection on nuclear power.

Kenny, Anthony. *The Logic of Deterrence.* U. Ch. Pr. 1985 $20.00. ISBN 0-226-43154-1. Analyzes the ethics of nuclear war and critiques deterrence theory and practice.

Lackey, Douglas P. *Moral Principles and Nuclear Weapons. Philosophy and Society Ser.* Rowman 1984 $22.50. ISBN 0-8476-7515-7. Comprehensive moral critique of nuclear weapons policies from a global utilitarian perspective.

Lawler, Philip F. *The Ultimate Weapon.* Regnery Gateway 1984 o.p. Traditionalist response to the United States Conference of Catholic Bishops' pastoral letter on nuclear weapons; suggests that the "ultimate weapon" is not bombs but prayer.

Lefever, Ernest W., and E. Stephen Hunt, eds. *The Apocalyptic Premise: Nuclear Arms Debated.* Ethics & Public Policy 1982 $40.00. ISBN 0-89633-063-X. Outlines alternative positions concerning the production and potential use of nuclear weapons.

MacLean, Douglas, ed. *The Security Gamble: Deterrence Dilemmas in the Nuclear Age. Maryland Studies in Public Philosophy.* IPPP 1984 $22.75. ISBN 0-317-05231-4. Part 1 discusses nuclear deterrence policies of the United States; part 2 contains eight essays that examine the moral justification of these policies.

Man-Machine Interface in the Nuclear Industry. Proceedings Ser. UNIPUB 1988 $290.00. ISBN 92-0-020588-7. Contains 69 papers and other materials from a 1988 international conference organized by the International Atomic Energy Agency, the Commission of European Communities, and the Nuclear Energy Agency of the OECD.

Nelkin, Dorothy, and Michael Pollak. *The Atom Besieged: Extraparliamentary Dissent in France and Germany.* MIT Pr. 1981 $9.95. ISBN 0-262-64021-X. Comparative study of the antinuclear power movements in France and West Germany; argues that these movements are part of a general socioethical critique of modern technology.

Novak, Michael. *Moral Clarity in the Nuclear Age.* Nelson-Hall 1983 o.p. Criticizes the United States Conference of Catholic Bishops' pastoral letter and defends deterrence; foreword by Billy Graham.

Nye, Joseph S., Jr. *Nuclear Ethics.* Free Pr. 1986 $22.95. ISBN 0-02-922460-8. Defines a moderate position between the extremes of nuclear advocacy and nuclear abolition, with a discussion of both consequences and intentions. Concludes by suggesting five ethical maxims to guide nuclear policymaking. Includes useful notes and a partially annotated bibliography; written by an ethicist and former deputy undersecretary of State.

Paul, Ellen Frankel, and others, eds. *Nuclear Rights, Nuclear Wrongs*. Blackwell Pubs. 1986 $24.95. ISBN 0-631-14964-3. Covers the fundamental ethical principles that should guide defense policies, obligations among nations, and the dilemmas created by advanced weapons technology and strategic theory.

Ramsey, Paul. *The Just War: Force and Political Responsibility*. Littlefield 1983 repr. of 1968 ed. $19.95. ISBN 0-8226-3014-1. Important argument by a conservative Protestant theologian; from an early stage of the nuclear weapons debate.

———. *War and the Christian Conscience: How Shall Modern War Be Conducted Justly?* Bks. Demand 1985 $88.30. ISBN 0-317-26099-5. Unlike most theologians, Ramsey argues that a just nuclear war might be possible under certain conditions.

Roberts, L.E.J. *Nuclear Power and Public Responsibility*. Cambridge U. Pr. 1984 $29.95. ISBN 0-521-26718-7. Argues that the nuclear power industry has responsibilities during normal operation to protect human beings against toxic emissions, accidents, and environmental pollution. Claims that the industry is failing its responsibility in all three areas; written by the director of the Atomic Energy Research Establishment at Harwell, England.

Rotblat, Joseph. *Scientists in Quest for Peace: A History of the Pugwash Conferences*. MIT Pr. 1972 o.p. The best coverage of the subject.

Russell, Bertrand. *Common Sense and Nuclear Warfare*. AMS Pr. 1985 repr. of 1959 ed. $18.00. ISBN 0-606-05465-X. Standard work from the initial public debate about nuclear weapons; written by a Nobel Prize-winning mathematician, philosopher, and critic of nuclear warfare.

Schell, Jonathan. *The Abolition*. Avon 1986 $3.95. ISBN 0-380-69912-5. Vigorous argument for the abolition of nuclear weapons.

———. *The Fate of the Earth*. Knopf 1982 $19.95. ISBN 0-396-52559-0. Graphic, popular account of the consequences of a full-scale nuclear war.

Schrader-Frechette, Kristin S. *Nuclear Power and Public Policy: The Social and Ethical Problems of Fission Technology*. Pallas Paperbacks Ser. Kluwer Ac. 1980 o.p. Covers reactor radiation emission standards and core meltdown dangers in relation to due process; nuclear waste disposal policy as exemplifying the argument from ignorance; the problem of externalities in nuclear economics; and nuclear safety and the naturalistic fallacy. The best monograph on ethical issues related to nuclear power.

———, ed. *Nuclear Energy and Ethics*. World Council of Churches 1991 o.p. Papers from a WCC consultation in Kinshasa, Zaire, in 1989.

Sider, Ronald J., and Richard K. Taylor. *Nuclear Holocaust and Christian Hope: A Book for Christian Peacemakers*. Inter Varsity 1982 $9.99. ISBN 0-87786-386-6. Action-oriented biblical analysis that is critical of nuclear weapons; appendices include a bibliography and lists of peace organizations, audiovisual materials, and study guides.

Skousen, Eric N. *The War against Nuclear Power*. Natl. Ctr. Constitutional 1981 $7.95. ISBN 0-88080-002-X. Presents a strong defense of nuclear power. Rejects "nuclear fairy tales" and the "radiation myth" and argues that nuclear power plants are both safe and important to the economy.

Sterba, James, ed. *The Ethics of War and Nuclear Deterrence*. Wadsworth Pub. 1985 $11.00. ISBN 0-534-03951-0. Nineteen reprinted articles covering "just war" theories, the history of ethical questions concerning whether nuclear weapons ever can be used legitimately, and whether threatening their use is justified.

Teller, Edward. *Better a Shield than a Sword: Perspectives on Defense and Technology*. Free Pr. 1987 $27.95. ISBN 0-02-932461-0. A nuclear physicist's views on nuclear technology, science and the military, and nuclear ethics.

Thompson, Kenneth W., ed. *Arms Control: Alliances, Arms Sales, and the Future*. U. Pr. of Amer. 1993 $46.50. ISBN 0-8191-8936-7. Shows how attitudes on arms control have undergone a decided shift since the period of the 1920s and 1930s, when several nations first met to negotiate limits to arms sales. Examines how international alliances have affected the results of negotiations in the Cold War and post-Cold War eras.

Van Der Pligt, J. *Nuclear Energy and the Public.* Blackwell Pubs. 1993 $29.95. ISBN 0-631-18732-4

Weinberg, Alvin, and others, eds. *The Nuclear Connection: A Reassessment of Nuclear Power and Nuclear Proliferation.* Paragon Hse. 1985 $27.95. ISBN 0-88702-204-9. Six essays evaluating the specific problems of nuclear proliferation; each essay includes a commentary. Preface by Peter Auer.

Woolsey, R. James, and Michael Quinlan, eds. *Nuclear Arms: Ethics, Strategy, Politics.* ICS Pubns. 1984 o.p. Fifteen original studies, three of which are devoted explicitly to ethics: Charles Krauthammer's "On Nuclear Morality," Patrick Glynn's "The Moral Case for the Arms Buildup," and Michael Quinlan's "Thinking Deterrence Through."

ENVIRONMENTAL ETHICS

The ethical discussion of nuclear weapons often has been promoted by and identified with Christian institutions. In contrast, environmental ethics, at its inception in the late 1960s was associated with an intense criticism of Christianity. In "The Historical Roots of Our Ecologic Crisis" (*Science*, 1967), an article that became a rallying cry of the early environmental movement, medieval historian LYNN WHITE, JR. claimed that the Judeo-Christian belief that human beings were created in the image of God to practice dominion over the Earth was a major factor contributing to environmental degradation. (It is ironic that the Apollo moon landing of 1969, which was a major achievement of the "domination project," provided photographs of a blue-green planet Earth rising above the barren lunar landscape. This successfully raised public consciousness of Earth as a complex but fragile ecosystem on which human life depends.)

Subsequent discussion—developed in conjunction with a plethora of analyses of natural ecology, the population explosion, resource depletion, pollution, and global climate change—has focused debate on the following ethical questions: Is nature intrinsically valuable or valuable only in relation to human use? Should environmental ethics be based on human nature and needs or on the natural order and requirements of all living things? Are human beings responsible for the well-being solely of future generations, or do they bear responsibility for all animals, plants, and the physical environment? Does morality involve individuals, species, or entire ecosystems? Is it possible to balance economic development with environmental preservation?

Catastrophic consequences could follow both current and future environmental practices. (Major climatic change and destruction of the ozone layer are two possibilities.) As a result, the field of environmental ethics has become particularly important and has experienced significant development during the past decade.

Two recent bibliographies on environmental ethics by Eric Katz are cited below under Frederick Ferré and under Carl Mitcham in the last section on "Engineering Ethics and Ethics of Technology." Also see Robert Merideth, listed below. A primary outlet for articles in the field is the journal *Environmental Ethics*, edited by EUGENE HARGROVE.

Attfield, Robin. *The Ethics of Environmental Concern.* U. of Ga. Pr. 2nd ed. 1991 $35.00. ISBN 0-8203-1346-0. Useful historically oriented overview covering many of the same themes as Passmore.

Berry, Wendell. *The Unsettling of America: Culture and Agriculture.* Sierra 1977 $9.00. ISBN 0-87156-772-5. Criticizes agribusiness and argues that the ecological crisis is "a crisis of character"; written by a poet and farmer.

Blackstone, William T., ed. *Philosophy and Environment Crisis*. U. of Ga. Pr. 1974 o.p. Eight papers from the proceedings of a 1971 conference; the first book on environmental ethics.

Burrill, Richard. *Protectors of the Land: An Environmental Journey to Understanding the Conservation Ethic*. Anthro. Co. 1993 $22.95. ISBN 1-878464-02-7. Presentation of the conservation ethic via a fictional Native American Californian storyteller/guide. Explores environments of several California sites. Geared toward a younger audience.

DesJardins, Joseph R. *Environmental Ethics: An Introduction to Environmental Philosophy*. Wadsworth Pub. 1993. ISBN 0-534-20046-X. General overview, using case studies.

Devall, Bill. *Living Richly in an Age of Limits*. Gibbs Smith 1993 $21.95. ISBN 0-87905-559-6. How to use deep ecology as a guide for living differently with nature.

Ehrenfeld, David. *Beginning Again: People and Nature in the New Millennium*. OUP 1993 $22.00. ISBN 0-19-507812-8. A biologist presents a succinct discussion of new guidelines for human-nature relationships; concludes with useful collection of suggested readings. An ecologist's vision.

Evernden, Neil. *The Natural Alien: Humankind and Environment*. U. of Toronto Pr. 1985 $18.95. ISBN 0-8020-6639-9. Examines affairs of the mind (art, literature, philosophy, biology, photography, etc.) that make it difficult to clearly espouse the causes of environmental crises. Not specifically crisis oriented, rather a subtle study of the worldview that underlies crises.

Ferré, Frederick, ed. *Technology and the Environment. Research in Philosophy and Technology*. Vol. 12. Jai Pr. 1990 o.p. Includes critiques from Europe and the United States, as well as Eric Katz's "Environmental Ethics: A Selected Annotated Bibliography II, 1987–1990."

Glacken, C. J. *Traces on the Rhodian Shore: Nature and Culture in Western Thought from Ancient Times to the End of the Eighteenth Century*. U. CA Pr. repr. of 1967 ed. $60.00. ISBN 0-520-02367-6. More detailed study than Passmore's.

The Global Ecology Handbook: What You Can Do about the Environmental Crisis. Global Tomorrow Coalition. Beacon Pr. 1990 $16.95. ISBN 0-8070-8501-4. Practical overview for the general reader.

Goldfarb, Theodore, ed. *Taking Sides: Clashing Views on Controversial Environmental Issues*. Dushkin Pub. 5th ed. 1993 $12.95. ISBN 1-56134-125-8. Good collection of alternative views; designed as a high school text.

Hardin, Garrett. *Filters against Folly: How to Survive despite Ecologists, Economists, and the Merely Eloquent*. Viking Penguin 1986 $9.95. ISBN 0-14-007729-4. Claims that environmental problems are caused not by vice but by foolishness and provides three ways to filter out the follies of our natural inclinations and simplified ideologies: literacy (examining the meanings of words), numeracy (quantifying information), and ecolacy (assessing complex interactions); criticizes both free market capitalism and radical ecology.

Hardin, Garrett, and John Baden, eds. *Managing the Commons*. W. H. Freeman 1977 $14.95. ISBN 0-7167-0476-5. Twenty-six essays, half of them written by the editors; includes Hardin's "The Tragedy of the Commons" (*Science*, 1968), a seminal influence on the ecology movement.

Hargrove, Eugene C., ed. *The Animal Rights-Environmental Ethics Debate: The Environmental Perspective*. State U. NY Pr. 1992 $44.50. ISBN 0-7914-0933-3. Describes the recent split between the animal rights and environmental movements.

_____. *Beyond Spaceship Earth: Environmental Ethics and the Solar System*. Environ. Ethics Bks. 1986 $14.95. ISBN 0-962807-1-0. Fifteen papers from a 1985 conference on the social, human, and political dimensions of space exploration; includes scientific-technological, philosophical, and theological perspectives.

_____. *Foundations of Environmental Ethics*. P-H 1989 $24.00. ISBN 0-13-329574-5. Discusses traditional attitudes, the risk of environmental consciousness, and philosophical-ethical implications of this new consciousness. Argues for the role of an aesthetic appreciation of nature in environmental ethics; the best monograph for the general reader.

———. *Religion and the Environmental Crisis.* U. of Ga. Pr. 1989 o.p. Eleven papers examining pagan, Amerindian, Jewish, Christian, Taoist, and Islamic environmental ethics.

Johnson, Lawrence E. *A Morally Deep World: An Essay on Moral Significance and Environmental Ethics.* Cambridge U. Pr. 1993 $16.95. ISBN 0-521-44706-2. Concludes by stating, "We live in a world of life, and all life processes, of whatever sort, define interests that count morally."

Kohak, Erazim. *The Embers and the Stars: A Philosophical Inquiry into the Moral Sense of Nature.* U. Ch. Pr. 1984 $17.50. ISBN 0-226-45022-8. Personal reflections on the experience of building and inhabiting an isolated mountain cabin; also discusses human beings as part of the order and unity of nature.

Leopold, Aldo. *A Sand County Almanac: With Other Essays on Conservation from Round River.* OUP 1966 $17.95. ISBN 0-19-500619-4. Chapter titled "The Land Ethic" has become the guiding statement of environmental ethicists. With introduction by Hal Borland.

Lewis, Martin W. *Green Delusions: An Environmentalist Critique of Radical Environmentalism.* Duke 1992 $24.95. ISBN 0-8223-1257-3. A rejection of environmental extremism offering a critique of current environmental discourse, philosophy, and action.

McCloskey, J. J. *Ecological Ethics and Politics. Philosophy and Society Ser.* Rowman 1983 o.p. Rejects scientific predictions of ecological disaster as too reliant on projections of past trends; argues for anthropocentric environmental ethics; and expresses optimism about international political solutions to environmental problems.

McKibben, Bill. *The End of Nature.* Doubleday 1990 $9.95. ISBN 0-385-41604-0. Suggests that human beings have turned the natural environment into an artifact.

MacLean, Douglas, and Peter G. Brown, eds. *Energy and the Future.* Rowman 1983 $59.50. ISBN 0-317-05223-3. Outstanding philosophical analysis of energy policy issues; stresses social justice, environmental ethics, and responsibilities to future generations.

Merideth, Robert. *The Environmentalist's Bookshelf: A Guide to the Best Books.* Macmillan 1993 $40.00. ISBN 0-8161-7359-1. Results of a survey of more than 200 environmentalists; includes extensive annotations and evaluations by critical readers.

Naess, Arne. *Ecology, Community, and Lifestyle: Outline of an Ecosophy.* Ed. and trans. by David Rothenberg. Cambridge U. Pr. 1990 $22.95. ISBN 0-521-34873-0. The most general statement by the founder of the "deep" (versus "shallow") ecology movement.

Nash, Rodrick. *The Risks of Nature: A History of Environmental Ethics.* U. of Wis. Pr. 1989 $35.00. ISBN 0-299-11840-1. Argues that rights properly have been extended from males to minorities and women—and now to animals and the environment.

Norton, Bryan G., ed. *The Preservation of the Species: The Value of Biological Diversity.* IPPP 1986 $45.00. ISBN 0-317-05211-X. Useful interdisciplinary collection of 11 original papers focused on the key question: Why preserve an endangered species? Includes a bibliography.

———. *Why Preserve Natural Variety?* Princeton U. Pr. 1987 $39.50. ISBN 0-691-07762-2. Defends natural variety as an intrinsic good.

Orr, David W. *Ecological Literacy: Education and the Transition to a Postmodern World.* State U. NY Pr. 1991 $49.50. ISBN 0-7914-0873-6. Broad, critical evaluation of the concept of sustainable development.

Partridge, Ernest, ed. *Responsibilities to Future Generations: Environmental Ethics.* Prometheus Bks. 1981 o.p. Twenty-five outstanding essays by philosophers focused on the question, What moral responsibilities do the living have to future generations?

Passmore, John. *Man's Responsibility for Nature: Ecological Problems and Western Traditions.* Macmillan 1978 o.p. Remains one of the best one-volume, historically oriented introductions to the field. Part 1 contrasts the "man as despot" and "cooperation with nature" traditions in Western societies; part 2 examines such problems as environmental pollution, resource depletion, species extinction, and human overpopulation; part 3 concludes that "if the world's ecological problems are to be solved . . . it can only be by that old-fashioned procedure, thoughtful action."

Regan, Tom, ed. *Earthbound: New Introductory Essays in Environmental Ethics.* Waveland Pr. 1990 $18.95. ISBN 0-88133-568-1. Ten original essays on significant topics by well-known figures in the field; includes good introduction to the field (Regan), analyses of pollution and political theory (Machan), energy and ethics (Schrader-Frechette), responsibilities to future generations (Baier), ethics in agriculture (Aiken), and environmental ethics theory (Johnson).

Rolston, Holmes, III. *Environmental Ethics: Duties to and Values in the Natural World.* Temple U. Pr. 1987 $44.95. ISBN 0-87722-501-X. Argues that human beings have a moral obligation to preserve and maintain natural ecosystems.

———. *Philosophy Gone Wild: Essays in Environmental Ethics.* Prometheus Bks. 1989 $17.95. ISBN 0-87975-556-3. Previously published essays by a philosopher-scientist; includes "Is There an Ecological Ethic?" (1975), which is considered a significant work in the field.

Santmire, H. Paul. *The Travail of Nature: The Ambiguous Ecological Promise of Christian Theology.* Augsburg Fortress 1991 $15.00. ISBN 0-8006-1806-8. The most comprehensive Protestant theological response to the challenge of Lynn White, Jr., and others; also includes a study of Christian attitudes and resources not covered by Passmore and Attfield.

Sax, Joseph L. *Mountains without Handrails; Reflections on the Natural Parks.* U. of Mich. Pr. 1980 o.p. Proposes an environmentally sensitive justification for the protection of national parks in the United States; includes such statements as "Parks are places where recreation reflects the aspirations of a free and independent people" and characterizes the parks as "an object lesson for a world of limited resources," "laboratories of successful natural communities," and "memorials of human history."

Scherer, Donald, and Thomas Attig, eds. *Ethics and the Environment.* P-H 1983. ISBN 0-13-290163-3. Introductory anthology on the field.

Seager, Joni. *Earth Follies: Coming to Feminist Terms with the Global Environmental Crisis.* Routledge 1993 $27.50. ISBN 0-415-90720-9

Shrader-Frechette, Kristin S. *Environmental Ethics.* Boxwood 2nd ed. 1991 $12.95. ISBN 0-90168-22-7. Both a monograph and a reader, consisting of 12 chapters, each followed by readings, a third of which are written by the author.

Stone, Christopher D. *The Gnat Is Older than Man: Global Environment and Human Agenda.* Princeton U. Pr. 1993 $21.95. ISBN 0-691-03250-5. Argues for a shift in focus from potential long-range problems (e.g., global warming) to practical institutional reforms for current ills (e.g., environmental destruction in Eastern Europe); written by a professor of international environmental law.

———. *Should Trees Have Standing? Toward Legal Rights for Natural Objects.* Tioga Pub. Co. 2nd ed. 1988 $7.95. ISBN 0-835382-69-0. The classic argument that nonhuman entities have natural rights and therefore "standing" in a court of law.

Taylor, Bob P. *Our Limits Transgressed: Environmental Political Thought in America.* U. Pr. of KS 1992 $25.00. ISBN 0-7006-0542-8. Explores the relationship between political and environmental values with reference to many classical and contemporary environmental writers.

Taylor, Paul W. *Respect for Nature: A Theory of Environmental Ethics. Studies in Moral, Political, and Legal Philosophy.* Princeton U. Pr. 1986 o.p. Monograph defending a biocentric theory of environmental ethics.

VanDeVeer, Donald, and Christine Pierce, eds. *People, Penguins, and Plastic Trees: Basic Issues in Environmental Ethics.* Wadsworth Pub. 1986. ISBN 0-534-06312-8. Well-organized brief volume, considered the best introductory anthology for the general reader. Focuses on the inherent value of wildlife and the environment; environmental ethics theory; and the conflicts between ethics, economics, and ecology; includes a select, unannotated bibliography.

White, Lynn, Jr. *Machina ex Deo: The Virgin and the Dynamo Reconsidered and Other Essays.* MIT Pr. 1969 o.p. Collection of influential popular essays by an important historian of technology.

Wilson, Edward O. *Biophilia.* HUP 1984 $18.95. ISBN 0-674-07441-6. A leading biologist testifies that "Modern biology has produced a genuinely new way of looking at the world [and] to the degree that we come to understand other organisms, we will place greater value on them, and on ourselves."

_____. *The Diversity of Life.* HUP 1992 $29.95. ISBN 0-674-21298-3. Personal vision of natural history, including "violent nature," the resiliency of biodiversity, and the problems created by human beings. Concluding chapter proposes environmental ethics "to preserve not only the health and freedom of our species, but [also] access to the world in which the human spirit was born"; includes fascinating remarks about the field of experience of this world-famous entomologist.

Worster, David. *The Wealth of Nature: Environmental History and the Ecological Imagination.* OUP 1993 o.p. Impressionistic essays examining the history of American attitudes toward the environment.

Zimmerman, Michael E., and others, eds. *Environmental Philosophy: From Animal Rights to Radical Ecology.* P-H 1992 $24.00. ISBN 0-13-666959-X. Collection of 23 articles on four themes: environmental ethics, "deep" ecology, ecofeminism, and social ecology; each theme introduced by a proponent.

ETHICS IN MEDICINE AND BIOETHICS

The United States spends more annually on health care than on nuclear weapons, nuclear power plants, or automobiles and gasoline (one of the primary sources of pollution). In fact, medicine is the field in which technological advancements have immediate impact on the greatest number of people. Thus, it is not surprising that biomedical ethics is the most highly developed area of interaction between ethics and technology. Bioethics has many good texts, an encyclopedia (*Encyclopedia of Bioethics*, edited by Warren T. Reich), and a voluminous list of publications, surveyed annually in *Bibliography of Bioethics*, edited by LeRoy Walters and others, listed below. (The reader can appreciate the diversity of relevant journals by perusing the annotations in this section.) Moreover, because of its traditional involvement with professional medical ethics, bioethics has deeper historical roots than other contemporary debates on aspects of technology and ethics.

Bioethics can be divided conveniently into the various moral issues associated with different stages of human life. Abortion, in vitro fertilization, fetal experimentation, and surrogate motherhood are associated with the beginning of life. The physician-patient relationship, issues of confidentiality and informed consent, and psychopharmacological behavior modification relate to the mature life. Organ transplants and euthanasia are associated with the end of life. The allocation of scarce medical resources and health care policy, the protocols of biomedical research (including experimentation on animals), and the special perspectives of nurses, psychologists, and social workers are issues that cover all stages of life. In each of these areas, bioethical issues are framed in terms of competing claims and their ethical theories appealing to personal rights, social utilities, or natural law.

Because of the wealth of books in this field, the following section is the most selective of this chapter. Consult also the section on Philosophy of Medicine in Chapter 4.

Abrams, Natalie, and Michael D. Buckner, eds. *Medical Ethics: A Clinical Textbook and Reference for the Health Care Professions*. MIT Pr. 1982 o.p. Articles discussing conceptual foundations, clinical ideals and behaviors, and issues in clinical cases. "The editors . . . have taken on—and succeeded at—the difficult task of compiling a book that is, at once, a practical handbook for clinical use, a reference work for scholars and theorists, and a collection of thoughtful philosophical discourses on the role of medicine" (*Science, Technology, and Human Values*).

Ackerman, Terrence F., and Carson Strong. *A Casebook of Medical Ethics*. OUP 1989 $45.00. ISBN 0-19-503916-5. Real-life view of the central issue involved in clinical medical ethics in a broad collection of case histories from the work of medical ethics educators and consultants; reflects the complex medical and psychosocial issues involved in the decision-making process.

Alpern, Kenneth D., ed. *The Ethics of Reproductive Technology*. OUP 1992 $19.95. ISBN 0-19-507435-1. Collection of essays on the ethical and social issues raised by in vitro fertilization, embryo transfer, surrogate motherhood, and other recent innovations in human reproduction; includes contributions from philosophers, legal scholars, health care professionals, scientists, and theologians.

Annas, George J., and Sherman Elias, eds. *Gene Mapping: Using Law and Ethics as Guides*. OUP 1992 $39.95. ISBN 0-19-507303-7. Covers the legal and ethical dimensions of genetics and the Human Genome Project; written by experts in genetics, medicine, history of science, health law, philosophy of science, and medical ethics.

Bach, Julie S., and others. *Biomedical Ethics*. Opposing Viewpoints Ser. Greenhaven 1987. o.p. Good selection of popular articles introducing alternative perspectives on organ transplants, fetal tissue research, reproductive technologies, and animal experimentation.

Beauchamp, Tom L., and James F. Childress. *Principles of Biomedical Ethics*. OUP 3rd ed. 1989 $45.00. ISBN 0-19-505901-8. Systematic philosophical discussion of basic principles presents biomedical ethics as the application of general ethical theories, principles, and rules to problems of therapeutic practice, health care delivery, and medical and biological research. Covers utilitarian and deontological theories of moral deliberation and analyzes four core principles—autonomy, beneficence, nonmaleficence, and justice. "Selections of principles, rules, and issues are apropos, and the cases are wide ranging and provocative" (*Journal of the American Medical Association*).

Beauchamp, Tom L., and Leroy Walters, eds. *Contemporary Issues in Bioethics*. Wadsworth Pub. 4th ed. 1994. ISBN 0-534-22314-1. One of the earliest, and still one of the best, collections of essays in the field.

Belkin, Lisa. *First, Do No Harm*. S&S Trade 1993 $23.00. ISBN 0-671-68538-4. True story of how Institutional Ethics Committees work in hospitals; covers priority of treatment, type of treatment, and whether or not treatment should be offered.

Benjamin, Martin, and Joy Curtis. *Ethics in Nursing*. OUP 2nd ed. 1986 $39.95. ISBN 0-19-504052-X. Details of nursing practice considered from the perspectives, methods, and resources of philosophical ethics. Examines the aspects of nursing that present special ethical problems, especially how nurses relate to physicians, patients, administrators, and other nurses; addresses such issues as deception, paternalism, confidentiality, conscientious refusal, nurse autonomy, compromise, and personal responsibility for institutional and public policy. "The first edition of this book was a welcome addition to the literature and this edition is even more welcome" (*Bioethics*).

Blank, Robert H., and Andrea Bonnicksen, eds. *Debates over Medical Authority and Challenges in Biomedical Experimentation*. Vol. 2 Col. U. Pr. 1993 $45.00. ISBN 0-231-08016-6. Seventeen essays on biomedical experimentation and authority in medical decision making.

Bloch, Sidney, and Paul Chodoff, eds. *Psychiatric Ethics*. OUP 2nd ed. 1991 $120.00. ISBN 0-19-261865-2. Authoritative and comprehensive text on complex ethical dilemmas faced by the clinician in everyday practice, including suicide, use of drug therapy, sex therapy and child psychiatry. Other topics considered are abuses in psychiatry in Japan and Nazi Germany; the conceptual analysis of mental illness; psychiatry as a profession; the ethical aspects of psychogeriatrics; and deinstitutionalization. "Nowhere has the richness of ethical issues been presented in such a comprehensive and meaningful way" (*Journal of the American Medical Association*).

Brock, Dan W. *Life and Death: Philosophical Essays in Biomedical Ethics*. Cambridge U. Pr. 1993 $54.95. ISBN 0-521-41785-6

Bronzino, Joseph D., and others. *Medical Technology and Society: An Interdisciplinary Perspective*. MIT Pr. 1990 $37.50. ISBN 0-262-02300-8. Contains chapters on the historical development of medical technology, economics, ethics, and the specific technologies of cardiac care, critical care, computers in medicine, and medical imaging.

Bullough, Vern L., and others, eds. *Issues in Nursing: An Annotated Bibliography*. Garland 1986 o.p. Includes primary and secondary sources from books, journals, and dissertations, with a broad scope that covers ethical, legal, educational, and professional issues.

Callahan, Daniel. *The Tyranny of Survival: And Other Pathologies of Civilized Life*. U. Pr. of Amer. 1985 repr. of 1973 ed. $20.00. ISBN 0-8191-4636-6. Suggests that obsessions with individualism and survival can lead to technological tyranny and proposes a resolution based on an ethic of public morality and knowledge of technological limits; draws on the work of Freud and Philip Rieff and uses the fields of population growth and genetic engineering as case studies.

Campbell, Alastair V., Grant Gillett, and D. Gareth Jones. *Practical Medical Ethics*. OUP 1992 $29.95. ISBN 0-19-558234-9. Covers traditional "end of life" issues as well as medical research and consent issues, confidentiality and AIDS, resource allocation, care of the mentally ill, and the doctor-patient relationship. Examines a diversity of ethical views, drawing from traditional philosophy and contemporary views; uses real and hypothetical examples.

Cassell, Eric J. *The Nature of Suffering: And the Goals of Medicine*. OUP 1991 $24.95. ISBN 0-19-50222-6. Argues that two patients with the same symptoms might need different treatment, because each has different needs and experiences a different type of suffering. "This is a book that clinicians and educators should read to understand better how the scientific and personal parts of medicine meet in the relationship between a doctor and a patient" (*New England Journal of Medicine*).

Childress, James F. *Who Should Decide? Paternalism in Health Care*. OUP 1982 $29.95. ISBN 0-19-503127-X. Claims that the conflict between professional paternalism and patient autonomy pervades health care and suggests that understanding might result from examining some of the underlying factors, such as the principles of beneficence and respect for persons, the metaphors of father or parent (from family life), and autonomy (from political life).

Christie, Ronald J., and C. Barry Hoffmaster. *Ethical Issues in Family Medicine*. OUP 1986 $29.95. ISBN 0-19-503637-9. Collaborative work by a physician and a philosopher examining the pervasive ethical questions of everyday medical practice, such as whether or not to impose changes on a patient's lifestyle and how to treat difficult patients.

Davis, John W., and others, eds. *Contemporary Issues in Biomedical Ethics*. Humana 1978 o.p. Collection of essays, mostly by philosophers, focusing on moral problems in genetics, professional responsibility, and informed consent.

Dubler, Nancy N., and David Nimmons. *Ethics on Call*. Random 1993 $12.00. ISBN 0-679-79538-6. Helps readers sort out the issues and choices involved with life/death situations in today's health care system.

Duncan, A. S., and others, eds. *Dictionary of Medical Ethics*. Crossroad NY 1981 o.p. "This volume aims simply to define and to serve as an introduction to the burgeoning and increasingly complex field of medical ethics. It provides both an informed guide for the layperson seeking information, and, for the professional, detailed bibliographies with cross references" (*Journal of Bioethics*).

Engelhardt, H. Tristram, Jr. *The Foundations of Bioethics*. OUP 1986 $37.50. ISBN 0-19-503608-5. Systematic treatment by an author who holds doctorates in medicine and philosophy, covering the history of secular bioethics, and discussing its foundations and applications. Suggests that the basic principle is a Kantian conception of "the person" as a moral agent: "Persons, not humans, are special." "An excellent book." (*Medical Humanities Review*).

Faden, Ruth R., and Tom L. Beauchamp. *A History of Theory of Informed Consent*. OUP 1986 $42.50. ISBN 0-19-503686-7. Definitive account of this topic.

Fletcher, Joseph. *Humanhood: Essays in Biomedical Ethics*. Prometheus Bks. 1979 $24.95. ISBN 0-87975-112-6. Collection of essays revealing an avowedly secular humanist position on a wide range of issues.

Glover, Jonathan. *What Sort of People Should There Be?* Viking Penguin 1984 o.p. Addresses issues raised by genetic engineering and technologies of brain manipulation. Presents a carefully argued defense of modifying human nature.

Glover, Jonathan, and others. *Ethics of New Reproductive Technologies: The Glover Report to the European Commission*. N. Ill. U. Pr. 1989 $26.00. ISBN 0-87580-147-1. Analyzes fundamental questions of value associated with new reproductive technologies; combines surveys of the available scientific and social evidence with rational arguments to offer a viable set of views and policies on these issues.

Goldstein, Doris Mueller. *Bioethics: A Guide to Information Sources*. Gale 1982 o.p. Excellent one-volume survey of organizations, library collections, journals, bibliographies, and textbooks; includes a selective, annotated index emphasizing publications prior to 1973.

Gorovitz, Samuel. *Doctors' Dilemmas: Moral Conflict and Medical Care*. OUP 1985 $9.95. ISBN 0-19-503695-6. Introduction to areas of health care frequently affected by moral issues, discussing how philosophical reflection can help resolve the problems; written for the general reader.

———. *Drawing the Line: Life, Death, and Ethical Choices in an American Hospital*. OUP 1991 $19.95. ISBN 0-19-504428-2. "Medical ethics is recovering an appreciation for the role of discretion in clinical judgment and health care politics. *Drawing the Line* puts Samuel Gorovitz in the vanguard of this reevaluation. This is analytically adept, commonsense philosophy, as concerned with the character of moral judgment as it is with the criteria and ends of moral action. It is also high-caliber practical philosophy, informed by ideas, deepened by experience, and attentive to practice" (Hastings Center Report).

Grubb, Andrew. *Choices and Decisions in Health Care*. Wiley 1993. ISBN 0-471-93621-9. On decision making in medical law and ethics. A series of essays.

Harris, John. *Wonderwoman and Superman: The Ethics of Human Biotechnology*. OUP 1992 $22.95. ISBN 0-19-217754-0. The first comprehensive analysis of moral dilemmas created by the revolutions in molecular biology; written for the general reader.

Holmes, Helen Bequaert, ed. *Issues in Reproductive Technology I: An Anthology*. Garland 1992 $60.00. ISBN 0-8153-0035-2. Collection of articles illustrating that the application of technological development in reproduction is not value-free. Asserts that the use of reproductive medical technology requires careful moral assessment and perceptive analysis; factual and thought-provoking book.

Holmes, Helen Bequaert, and Laura M. Purdy, eds. *Feminist Perspectives in Medical Ethics*. Ind. U. Pr. 1992 $39.95. ISBN 0-253-32848-9. Twenty articles analyzing medical ethics in general from a feminist perspective; includes the changing role of health care, clinical experiments on women, reproductive medicine, and contract pregnancy.

Holmstrom, Lynda Lytle, and Jeanne Guillemin. *Mixed Blessings: Intensive Care for Newborns*. OUP 1990 repr. of 1986 ed. $39.00. ISBN 0-19-504032-5. "In this inside account of the work accomplished in the neonatal intensive care unit, two medical sociologists focus on . . . medical decision making" in the United States, England, the Netherlands, and Brazil (*American Journal of Public Health*).

Hunter, Edna, and Daniel Hunter. *Professional Ethics and Law in the Health Sciences.* Krieger 1984 $21.50. ISBN 0-89874-711-2. Guidebook for the practitioner.

Jameton, Andrew. *Nursing Practice: The Ethical Issues.* P-H 1984. ISBN 0-13-627448-X. "At least the fourth book on nursing ethics in recent years, and . . . extremely rich in coverage and resources cited" (*Journal of Religious Ethics*).

Jennett, Bryan. *High Technology Medicine: Benefit and Burdens.* OUP 1986 $15.95. ISBN 0-19-261588-2. Descriptive but critical survey of medical technologies in diagnosis and treatment; includes an analysis of options in future assessment and use.

Jonsen, Albert R., and others. *Clinical Ethics: A Practical Approach to Ethical Decisions in Clinical Medicine.* McGraw 3rd ed. 1992 $22.00. ISBN 0-07-105392-1. Thoughtful text, widely used in the field. A clinician's handbook dealing with when to treat, how to involve patients, how to consider quality of life, and economic and legal contexts. Includes its own legal-liability disclaimer. For the theory behind the method, see Albert R. Jonsen and Stephen Toulmin, *The Abuse of Casuistry: A History of Moral Reasoning* (1988).

Kass, Leon R. *Toward a More Natural Science: Biology and Human Affairs.* Free Pr. 1985 $27.95. ISBN 0-02-918340-5. Discusses the ethics of new biomedical technologies of reproduction and genetics and the relation between modern medicine and the traditional art of healing. Proposes a new view of nature as the basis for an ethics of scientific technology. "Different in many ways from anything else in the field. Well written and provocative" (*Hastings Center Report*).

Kennedy, Ian. *Treat Me Right: Essays in Medical Law and Ethics.* OUP 1991 repr. of 1988 ed. $28.00. ISBN 0-19-825558-6. "It is a delight to read such a scholarly, well-written, and important presentation of very difficult concepts in medical ethics and medical law. This book is highly recommended to serious students of medical jurisprudence and to practitioners who wish to practice medicine with the highest regard for the concern and interest of their patients" (*New England Journal of Medicine*).

Kleinig, John. *Ethical Issues in Psychosurgery.* Allen & Unwin 1985 o.p. Discusses the problem of objective evaluation in psychosurgery by examining inadequate follow-ups, diversity of procedures, placebo effects, and other issues. "Kleinig's chief contribution is to pose clearly a series of relevant questions that permit intelligent ethical debate" (*Hastings Center Report*).

Kramer, Peter. *Listening to Prozac: A Psychiatrist Explores Mood-Altering Drugs and the New Meaning of the Self.* Viking-Penguin 1993 $22.50. ISBN 0-670-84183-8. Raises controversial social and ethical issues regarding the ability of the psychoactive drug Prozac not just to treat pathological states (clinical depression, obsessive-compulsive disorders, etc.) but also feelings previously taken as common to the human condition (low self-esteem, homesickness, etc.)

Lammers, Stephen, and Allen Verhey, eds. *On Moral Medicine: Theological Perspectives in Medical Ethics.* Eerdmans 1987 $35.00. ISBN 0-8028-3629-1. A large collection of readings that includes religious perspectives.

Lappe, Marc, and Robert S. Morrison, eds. *Ethical and Scientific Issues Posed by Human Uses of Molecular Genetics.* NY Acad. of Sci. 1976 $26.00. ISBN 0-89072-019-3. Early attempt to articulate the main ethical and scientific issues related to molecular genetics.

Lauritzen, Paul. *Pursuing Parenthood: Ethical Issues in Assisted Reproduction.* Ind. U. Pr. 1992 $19.95. ISBN 0-253-33261-3. Personal and scholarly assessment of the ethical dilemmas raised by methods of assisted reproduction; treats artificial insemination with husband and donor sperm, in vitro fertilization, surrogate motherhood, and adoption.

Levine, Carol, ed. *Taking Sides: Clashing Views on Controversial Bioethical Issues.* Dushkin Pub. 5th ed. 1993 $12.95. ISBN 1-56134-123-1. Well-edited collection of topical, popular, and provocative essays.

Levine, Robert J. *Ethics and Regulation of Clinical Research.* Yale U. Pr. 1988 $19.00. ISBN 0-300-04288-4. Comprehensive survey of the ethical and legal responsibilities of clinical investigations and institutional review boards.

Lewis, Marcia A., and Carol D. Tamparo. *Medical Law, Ethics, and Bioethics in the Medical Office*. Davis Co. 1993 $18.95. ISBN 0-8036-5624-6. An overview of legal and ethical questions in medical practices. Deals with community standards as well as medical office issues.

Lockwood, Michael, ed. *Moral Dilemmas in Modern Medicine*. OUP 1986 $29.95. ISBN 0-19-286056-9. Nine original papers from a seminar and lecture series. Mary Warnock, chair of the British Committee of Inquiry into Human Fertilization and Embryology, contributes reflections that became the "Warnock Report"; Lockwood analyzes some of the issues highlighted by the report; an appendix describes the legal and political ramifications in Great Britain resulting from this controversial inquiry.

Lynn, Joanne, ed. *By No Extraordinary Means: The Choice to Forgo Life-Sustaining Food and Water*. Ind. U. Pr. 1989 $35.00. ISBN 0-253-20517-4. Twenty-seven articles on a very controversial issue; an excellent resource.

Mabie, Margot C. *Bioethics and the New Medical Technology*. Macmillan Child Grp. 1993 $14.95. ISBN 0-689-31637-2. Addresses social and philosophical issues surrounding contemporary medical technology, such as genome research and care of terminal patients.

McCormick, Richard A. *How Brave a New World?: Dilemmas in Bioethics*. Georgetown U. Pr. 1985 repr. of 1981 ed. $12.95. ISBN 0-87840-417-1. Good introductory overview of the issues.

Mappes, Thomas A., and Jane S. Zembaty, eds. *Biomedical Ethics*. McGraw 3rd ed. 1993 $37.80. ISBN 0-07-040126-8. Good standard text with well-organized collection of readings in the field.

Meier, Levi, ed. *Jewish Values in Bioethics*. Human Sci. Pr. 1986 $35.95. ISBN 0-89885-299-4. Presents the Jewish perspective on the field.

Menzel, Paul T. *Strong Medicine: The Ethical Rationing of Health Care*. OUP 1990 $35.00. ISBN 0-19-505710-4. Addresses the issue of treating the individual patient with dignity and genuine respect in a system that values overall efficiency. This central idea is developed and applied to major issues of health policy and economics, including the notion of pricing life, the long-term cost of prevention, measuring the quality of life, imperiled newborns, adequate care for the poor, containing costs by market competition, malpractice suits, procuring organs for transplant, and dying expensively in old age. "A challenging and controversial book [to] be read by everyone concerned about the ethical implications of health-care rationing" (*Bioethics Books*).

Nelkin, Dorothy, and Lawrence Tancredi. *Dangerous Diagnostics: The Social Power of Biological Information*. Basic 1989 $18.95. ISBN 0-965-01573-5. The authors state that although "biological tests enhance institutional control, they can also conflict with . . . civil liberties, human integrity, or personal privacy."

Nicholson, Richard H., ed. *Medical Research with Children: Ethics, Law, and Practice*. OUP 1986 $29.95. ISBN 0-19-261528-9. Report of a British Institute of Medical Ethics working group of 19 physicians, lawyers, ministers, and hospital administrators. Identifies significant risks and benefits in pediatric research and discusses the dilemmas of child consent (age of competency and adequacy of parental or guardian consent). "As society moves further from the codes of an established religion, it looks increasingly to the moralist for a set of rules" (*Lancet*).

Overall, Christine, and William P. Zion, eds. *Perspectives on AIDS: Ethical and Social Issues*. OUP 1991 $29.95. ISBN 0-19-540799-0. Essays exploring the difficult questions related to AIDS and HIV infection in North America. Examines the culture and context of AIDS and HIV infection, as well as specific ethical and social issues, such as sexual ethics, AIDS education, and health care policy development.

Pence, George. *Classic Cases in Medical Ethics: Accounts of the Cases That Have Shaped Medical Ethics, with Philosophical, Legal, and Historical Backgrounds*. McGraw 1990 $18.65 ISBN 0-07-038092-9. A crucial resource.

Pence, Terry. *Ethics in Nursing: An Annotated Bibliography*. Natl. League Nurse 2nd ed. 1986 $16.95. ISBN 0-88737-192-2. Selected bibliography of articles in nursing journals explicitly on ethics, written by nurses.

Proctor, Robert N. *Racial Hygiene: Medicine under the Nazis.* HUP 1988 $14.95. ISBN 0-674-74578-7. Insightful historical study, with implications for understanding our own medical practices.

Rachels, James. *The End of Life: Euthanasia and Morality.* OUP 1986 $13.95. ISBN 0-19-286070-4. Criticizes the traditional (especially religious) arguments against euthanasia and supports an alternative, qualified acceptance. "The alternative view begins by pointing out that there is a deep difference between *having a life* and merely *being alive.*" Claims that the latter distinction is not crucial, as traditional arguments against euthanasia seem to imply.

Reich, Warren T., ed. *Encyclopedia of Bioethics.* 2 vols. Macmillan 1982 $200.00. ISBN 0-02-925910-X. The standard reference work in the field.

Reiser, Stanley J., ed. *Ethics in Medicine: Historical Perspectives and Contemporary Concerns.* MIT Pr. 1977 o.p. The best and most wide-ranging sourcebook available, including more than 100 classic and contemporary documents and articles and numerous illustrations of the physician-patient relationship, foundations of medical ethics, regulation and public health, truth-telling, human experimentation, procreation, suffering and death, and health care allocation.

Rodwin, Marc A. *Medicine, Money, and Morals: Physicians' Conflicts of Interest.* OUP 1993 $25.00. ISBN 0-19-508096-3. A constructive book with concrete proposals for reform in health care. Concentrates mainly on the need for financial and medical regulation of physicians.

Shannon, Thomas A., ed. *Bioethics: Basic Writings on the Key Ethical Questions That Surround Major, Modern Biological Possibilities and Problems.* Paulist Pr. 1987 $14.95. ISBN 0-8091-2805-5. An extensive and widely-used collection of readings.

Shannon, Thomas A., and James J. Walter, eds. *Quality of Life: The New Medical Dilemma.* Paulist Pr. 1991 $14.95. ISBN 0-8091-3191-9. Collection of 32 essays examining various definitions of quality of life, application of quality-of-life criteria in specific situations, and public policy in relation to quality of life.

Shannon, Thomas A., and Jo Ann Manfra. *Law and Bioethics: Selected Cases.* Paulist Pr. 1981 o.p. Texts of more than 20 major court cases in the United States; includes commentary.

Shelp, Earl E. *Theology and Bioethics: Exploring the Foundations and Frontiers.* Kluwer Ac. 1985 o.p. Eighteen original papers, mainly by leading religious ethicists who previously have contributed to the development of bioethics; concludes that "Christianity does not provide a set of moral principles distinct from [those of] post-Christian thinkers."

Silverman, William A. *Human Experimentation: A Guided Step into the Unknown.* OUP 1986 $24.95. ISBN 0-19-261636-6. Argues for randomized clinical trials before introducing any new therapy. "[A] clean, well-written exposition of the problems that face a clinical investigator" (*British Medical Journal*).

Singer, Peter, and Deane Wells. *Making Babies: The New Science and Ethics of Conception.* Macmillan 1985 o.p. A "valuable introduction to the new reproductive technologies and to at least some of the moral quandaries . . . they create" (*Ethics*); a revision of *The Reproduction Revolution* (1984).

Smith, Jane A., and Kenneth M. Boyd, eds. *The Ethics of Using Animals in Biomedical Research.* OUP 1991 $39.95. ISBN 0-19-854744-7. Detailed examination of moral issues related to the potential benefits of animal research. Also describes strategies for weighing these benefits against the harm caused to animals, as a basis for deciding whether or not particular research projects should be conducted; includes a variety of philosophical arguments concerning the use of animals in research.

Spicker, Stuart F., and others. *The Use of Human Beings in Research: With Special Reference to Clinical Trials.* Kluwer Ac. 1988 $90.50. ISBN 1-55608-043-3. Scholarly examination of ethical issues raised by the implementation of biomedical science and technology. Analyzes several current perspectives to increase understanding and influence future health policies.

Steere, Jane. *Ethics in Clinical Psychology.* OUP 1984 $15.95. ISBN 0-19-57073-1. The only book specifically addressing the ethical issues of clinical psychology; includes chapters on ethics in psychotherapy, psychological assessment, research, and "the South African context" (the author is a lecturer at the Child Guidance Clinic of the University of Cape Town); includes a good unannotated bibliography.

Steinbock, Bonnie. *Life before Birth: The Moral and Legal Status of Embryos and Fetuses.* OUP 1992 $29.95. ISBN 0-19-505494-6. Covers abortion, the legal status of the fetus, maternal-fetal conflict, fetal research, and the use and disposition of extracorporeal embryos that have been made available by new reproductive technologies; includes case studies.

Teichler-Zallen, Doris, and Colleen D. Clements, eds. *Science and Morality: New Directions in Bioethics.* Free Pr. 1982 $29.95. ISBN 0-669-04406-7. Supports a self-conscious "second generation" bioethics. Defines and addresses the purposes of bioethics as a special branch of ethics. Argues for "scientific value systems" that help individual human beings.

Thompson, Joyce, and Henry O. Thompson. *Bioethical Decision Making: Who Owns the Problem.* Appleton & Lange 1985 o.p. Part 2 provides a step-by-step process for decision making; includes a good annotated bibliography of more than 80 titles.

Tooley, Michael. *Abortion and Infanticide.* OUP 1984 $29.95. Philosophical defense of the liberal position on the morality of abortion.

Vaux, Kenneth, ed. *Powers That Make Us Human: The Foundations of Medical Ethics.* U. of Ill. Pr. 1986 $29.95. ISBN 0-19-924916-0. Examines such "powers" as morality (Leon Kass), honor (William May), subsistence (Ivan Illich), feelings (Willard Gaylin), reason (H. Tristram Engelhardt, Jr.), justice (Joseph Fletcher), hope (Vaux), and virtue (Stanley Hauerwas). "Draws our attention to the rich complexities of the moral life in medicine" (*Journal of Medicine and Philosophy*).

Veatch, Robert M. *A Theory of Medical Ethics.* Basic 1981 $20.95. ISBN 0-465-08937-0. Criticizes paternalism and argues that the theory of a social contract among equals produces the best medical decisions.

Verhey, Allen, and Stephen E. Lammers, eds. *Theological Voices in Medical Ethics.* Eerdmans 1993 $17.99. ISBN 0-8028-0664-3. Ten essays exploring the contributions of theologians to bioethics. Addresses topics such as reproductive ethics and euthanasia.

Walters, LeRoy, and others, eds. *Bibliography of Bioethics.* 3 vols. Geo. V. Kennedy Inst. 1984–86 $35.00. ISBN 0-9614448-0-0. This annual series is the most comprehensive index to the field, listing books from 1973; one weakness is the lack of annotations prior to Vol. 9 (1983, focusing on 1980–82), when annotations were added, but only for articles from 15 selected journals.

Weinstein, Bruce. *Dental Ethics.* Lea and Febiger 1993 $29.95. ISBN 0-8121-1444-2. Deals with ethical issues in dentistry such as rights to dentistry, treating people with AIDS, and confidentiality.

Weir, Robert F. *Selective Nontreatment of Handicapped Newborns: Moral Dilemmas in Neonatal Medicine.* OUP 1984 $35.00. ISBN 0-19-503396-5. Important and generally well-accepted study constituting "the first full-length analysis . . . since the famous Baby Doe case of 1982" (*New England Journal of Medicine*).

ETHICS IN COMPUTERS AND OTHER ELECTRONIC INFORMATION TECHNOLOGIES

The relation of ethics to computers and electronic information media often is called computer ethics. The term, however, is unnecessarily limiting, because the basic ethical issues in computer ethics also are associated with other information technologies—from print to television. The ethical issues include responsibility in information handling, fair public access, privacy, confidentiality, and security. These issues can be extended to encompass concerns for the character of our information-electronic society and culture.

Computer ethics initially focused on possible threats to individual privacy and corporate security. Recently, its scope has expanded to address the issues of ethics codes for computer professionals, liability for the malfunctioning of computer programs, computer decision making with expert systems, and the relations between computers and social power. Other issues with ethical connotations are the anthropological implications of artificial intelligence and the aesthetic-ontological interpretations of virtual realities.

Baber, Robert L. *Software Reflected: The Socially Responsible Programming of Computers.* Elsevier 1982 $51.50. ISBN 0-444-86372-9. Ethics in information technologies and computers.

Beniger, James R. *The Control Revolution.* HUP 1986 $32.50. ISBN 0-674-16985-9. Argues that the information age is not a postindustrial phenomenon but part of the "control revolution" that began in the mid-nineteenth century.

Brown, Geoffrey. *The Information Game: Ethical Issues in a Microchip World.* Humanities 1990 $49.50. ISBN 0-391-03545-4. Views information technology as presenting problems of moral character. Also discusses reliability, privacy, dehumanization, ownership of software, and the idea of computers as moral agents.

Chartrand, Robert L., ed. *Critical Issues in the Information Age.* Scarecrow 1991 $42.50. ISBN 0-8108-2402-7. Contains 11 essays plus 2 useful appendices: bibliography, and review of information technology legislation in the United States from the 95th to the 100th Congress.

Christians, Clifford, and others. *Media Ethics: Cases and Moral Reasoning.* Annenberg Communication Ser. Longman 1991 $22.95. ISBN 0-8013-0650-7. Covers news reporting, advertising, and entertainment in print and electronic media. Analyzes case studies to focus on issues of censorship, child education, confidentiality, conflicts of interest, deception, economic pressures, explicit sex, fairness, self-criticism, minorities and the elderly, privacy, sensationalism, stereotyping, and violence.

Ermann, M. David, Mary B. Williams, and Claudia Gutierrez, eds. *Computers, Ethics, and Society.* OUP 1990 $17.95. ISBN 0-19-505850-X. Thirty-four readings on basic ethical frameworks; computer impacts on privacy, personal life, work, and justice; and issues affecting computer professionals—from legal to moral responsibilities.

Ethical Conflicts in Information and Computer Science, Technology, and Business. QED Info. Sci. 1990 $34.95. ISBN 0-89435-313-6. Reports the opinions of 34 experts who were presented with ethical-conflict scenarios on which to construct fundamental principles.

Forester, Tom, and Perry Morrison. *Computer Ethics: Cautionary Tales and Ethical Dilemmas in Computing.* MIT Pr. 1990 $24.50. ISBN 0-262-06131-7. Covers ethical dilemmas for computer professionals and users, computer crime, software theft, hacking and viruses, unreliability in computers, invasions of privacy, AI and expert systems, and the computerized workplace.

Gould, Carol C., ed. *The Information Web: Ethical and Social Implications of Computer Networking.* Westview 1989 $48.50. ISBN 0-8133-0699-X. Extends ethical reflection into issues related to electronic networks.

Gross, Larry, and others, eds. *Image Ethics: The Moral Rights of Subjects in Photographs, Film, and Television.* OUP 1991 $35.00. ISBN 0-19-505433-4. Provocative exploration of an issue related to information property rights.

Hoffman, W. Michael, and Jennifer Mills Moore, eds. *Ethics and the Management of Computer Technology. Proceedings of the Fourth National Conference on Business Ethics.* Oelgeschlager 1982 o.p.

Johnson, Deborah. *Computer Ethics.* P-H 1985 $20.00. ISBN 0-13-164005-4. Opening chapter on ethical theory, followed by ethical codes for computer professionals, corporate liability for malfunctioning programs, privacy, influence of computers on centralization of power, and ownership of software; emphasizes legal issues.

Laudon, Kenneth C. *Dossier Society: Value Choices in the Design of National Information Systems.* Col. U. Pr. 1986 $63.00. ISBN 0-231-06188-9. Addresses the central question: "How can rational information systems . . . be held politically and socially accountable?" Describes the work of designers and operators of information systems and analyzes the concepts and laws used to control these systems.

Leonhardt, Thomas W., ed. *Information Technology: It's for Everyone!* ALA 1992 $22.00. ISBN 0-8389-7634-4. Papers from the Third National Conference of the Library and Information Technology Association (LITA) covering varied topics.

Mander, Jerry. *Four Arguments for the Elimination of Television.* Morrow 1978 $8.95. ISBN 0-688-08274-2. Argues that television mediates experience, centralizes power, can have negative psychological and even physiological effects on individuals, and is inherently biased.

Meadows, Jack, ed. *Information Technology and the Individual.* St. Martin 1992 $57.50. ISBN 0-86187-877-9. From the abstract concept of how the individual relates to information technology to its application in examples such as the mass media, banking, and retail trade.

Mintz, Anne P., ed. *Information Ethics: Concerns for Librarianship and the Information Industry.* McFarland & Co. 1990 $13.95. ISBN 0-89950-514-7. Four essays, along with ethical codes from various information professional organizations; includes a brief annotated bibliography of articles.

Mitcham, Carl, and Alois Huning, eds. *Philosophy and Technology II: Information Technology and Computers in Theory and Practice.* Kluwer Ac. 1986 $105.00. ISBN 90-277-1975-6. Covers automation and workers' rights, computers in medicine, privacy, responsibility for "data pollution," and other issues; includes a 40-page annotated bibliography.

Parker, Donn B. *A Manager's Guide to Computer Security.* P-H 1983 $19.50. ISBN 0-8359-4232-5. Outlines an approach to prevent computer crime; written by an internationally known computer security consultant.

Parker, Donn B., and others. *Ethical Conflicts in Information and Computer Science, Technology, and Business.* QED Info. Sci. 1990 $34.95. ISBN 0-89435-313-6. "Bottom-up," empirical study of ethical issues in the computer professional community that complements the "top-down," theoretical work of Deborah Johnson; based on surveyed responses to various real-world scenarios.

Poster, Mark. *The Mode of Information: Poststructuralism and Social Context.* U. Ch. Pr. 1990 $39.95. ISBN 0-226-67595-5. Discusses the influence of electronic information media on postmodern culture.

Rosenberg, Richard S. *The Social Impact of Computers.* Acad. Pr. 1992 $42.50. ISBN 0-12-5917530-3. Survey of impacts that computers are having on society.

Rossman, Parker, and Richard Kirby. *Christians and the World of Computers: Professional and Social Excellence in the Computer World.* TPI PA 1990 $12.95. ISBN 0-334-02468-4. Protestant perspective on computer-related ethical issues.

Roszak, Theodore. *The Cult of Information: The Folklore of Computers and the True Art of Thinking.* Pantheon 1986 $17.95. ISBN 0-394-75175-2. Rejects the cybernetic model of the human mind, debunks the notion of an information economy, and criticizes the computer industry for its opportunistic invasion of schools.

Schellenberg, Kathryn, ed. *Computer Studies: Computers in Society.* Dushkin Pub. 1994 $11.95. ISBN 1-56134-259-9. Reprints of a wide variety of articles, mostly from the popular press, on computer-related social and ethical issues.

Shallis, Michael. *The Silicon Idol: The Micro Revolution and Its Social Implications.* Schocken 1984 o.p. What is unique about Shallis is that he includes arguments about the moral dangers of computers from a religious orientation.

Tuman, Myron C., ed. *Literacy Online: The Promise (and Peril) of Reading and Writing with Computers.* U. of Pittsburgh Pr. 1992 $49.95. ISBN 0-8229-3701-8. Describes the new ethics of hypertexts.

Weizenbaum, Joseph. *Computer Power and Human Reason: From Judgment to Calculation.* W. H. Freeman 1976 $16.95. ISBN 0-7167-0463-3. Defines and describes the advantages and limitations of computers. Argues against the "imperialism of instrumental reason" and provides an eloquent, skeptical review of the potential substitution of computers for human interaction in such areas as counseling, law, and language translation.

Wriston, Walter B. *The Twilight of Sovereignty: How the Information Revolution Is Transforming Our World.* Macmillan $25.00. ISBN 0-684-19454-6. A positive view of the democratic global implications of information technology.

ENGINEERING ETHICS AND ETHICS OF TECHNOLOGY

Engineering ethics develops ethical principles for the profession most intimately involved with various modern technologies. The ethics of technology has a much broader scope, confronting the general field of technology. The ethics of technology is not limited to nuclear weapons and power plants, industries that create chemical pollutants, biomedical technologies that challenge traditional understandings of life, and machines designed to manipulate information. In fact, the ethics of technology seeks to find commonalities among the specific technologies. Because engineers also are involved across the whole spectrum of technologies, professional engineering ethics and the general ethics of technology are appropriately related. Both fields have undergone dramatic growth and development over the last 25 years.

The major developments in professional engineering ethics have occurred during the twentieth century. In the early 1900s, it was commonly assumed that the primary obligation of the engineer was to an employer. However, by the 1960s, this presumption began to be questioned. During the past two decades, it has been increasingly argued that an engineer's primary responsibility is to society as a whole. This shift in values is associated with the development of alternative technologies and with attempts to protect engineers from the abuses of unscrupulous employers.

The development of an ethics of technology has been influenced, like engineering ethics, by several factors. In addition to specific ethical issues already surveyed, other factors include the consumer advocacy movement, concerns about employee health in various industrial or office settings, and technological disasters (such as airplane accidents and bridge or dam failures). Consequently, the concepts of safety and risk have become increasingly characteristic of ethical discourse. The central transformation taking place in ethics (as a result of advanced technology) is the articulation and expansion of the notion of moral responsibility to meet the significant factors of safety and risk. In the developing countries, issues of social justice and cultural dislocation that result from technological transfer or development also play a prominent role.

Ballard, Edward G. *Man and Technology: Toward the Measurement of a Culture.* Duquesne 1978 $25.00. ISBN 0-391-00751-3. General critique of technological culture. Argues that an extreme involvement in technology ignores the psychological needs of human beings.

Barbour, Ian. *Ethics in an Age of Technology.* Harper SF 1992 $35.00. ISBN 0-06-060935-4. Comprehensive study examining general relations between technology and values (technical, human, environmental, religious); technology and values in agriculture, energy, and computers; and the future in the light of new technologies and forms of control.

Baum, Robert J. *Ethics and Engineering Curricula. Teaching of Ethics Ser.* Hastings Ctr. 1980 $4.00. ISBN 0-916558-12-6. Overview of instructional strategies in this field, with a preface by Sissela Bok.

Berger, Peter L. *Pyramids of Sacrifice: Political Ethics and Social Change.* Doubleday 1976 $3.50. ISBN 0-385-07101-9. Compares the development strategies of Brazil (capitalistic) and China (socialistic); concludes that both cause unjustified human suffering and proposes an alternative approach.

Douglas, Mary. *Risk Acceptability according to the Social Sciences. Social Science Perspectives: Occasional Reports of Current Topics.* Russell Sage 1986 $9.95. ISBN 0-87154-211-0. Critical overview based on the thesis that risk perception is influenced by social and cultural institutions as much as by personal or individual factors.

Durbin, Paul T., ed. *Technology and Responsibility. Philosophy and Technology,* Vol. 3 Kluwer A. 1987 $100.00. ISBN 90-277-2415-6. General analysis of technology and responsibility in relation to specific questions of technical autonomy, medicine, and religion; includes Carl Mitcham's "Responsibility and Technology: A Select, Annotated Bibliography."

Fischoff, Baruch, and others. *Acceptable Risk.* Cambridge U. Pr. 1984 $17.95. ISBN 0-521-27892-9. Best general overview of risk in a technological society; includes the various methods used to evaluate risk.

Flores, Albert, ed. *Ethics and Risk Management in Engineering.* U. Pr. of Amer. 1989 $56.50. ISBN 0-8191-7564-1. Fifteen papers on risk in relation to ethical and economic values, legal and institutional mechanisms, and engineering responses.

Germain, Gilbert G. *A Discourse of Disenchantment: Reflections on Politics and Technology.* State U. NY Pr. 1993 $49.50. ISBN 0-7914-1319-5. Argues Weber's disenchantment theory proposing an "embodied politics" that would diverge from an ethos of technological domination of humans and nature.

Goodpaster, K. E., and K. M. Sayre, eds. *Ethics and Problems of the 21st Century.* U. of Notre Dame Pr. 1980 o.p. Covers the concept of morality and methods of moral reflection, with applications to food distribution, technology and the sanctity of life, historical preservation, and the rights of other species.

Goulet, Denis. *The Cruel Choice: A New Concept in the Theory of Development.* U. Pr. of Amer. 1985 repr. of 1971 ed. $25.50. ISBN 0-8191-4612-9. "The aim of this work is to thrust debates over economic and social development into the arena of ethical values" (introduction). Develops the key concepts of "vulnerability" and "existence rationality" and describes a series of "ethical strategies for development" based on the principles of adequate means, universal solidarity, and popular participation.

Grant, George. *English-Speaking Justice.* U. of Notre Dame Pr. 1985 $7.95. ISBN 0-268-00915-5. Argues that modern technology is based on the English-speaking peoples' ideas of justice, freedom, and equality; criticizes this orientation.

Gunn, Alastair, and P. Aarne Vesilind. *Environmental Ethics for Engineers.* Lewis 1986 $30.95. ISBN 0-87371-074-6. Brief analysis and overview of environmental ethics and engineering practice; includes an anthology of nine readings.

Hickman, Larry A. *Technology as a Human Affair: Readings in the Philosophy of Technology.* McGraw 1990 $21.65. ISBN 0-07-028688-4. Broad-ranging collection of more than 30 short articles. Part 7, "Order and Change in Human Societies is especially useful, with readings from Langdon Winner, John Dewey, W. H. Lowrance, and others.

Iannone, A. Pablo, ed. *Contemporary Moral Controversies in Technology.* OUP 1987 $38.00. ISBN 0-19-50425-9. Contains 33 articles oriented toward specific problems, such as moral controversies in technology assessment, technology management, technology research and development, technology transfer, and technology policy-making. The extensive section on technology management has six subsections that include the technologies of information, gene splicing, health care, space development, energy, and materials; includes a select bibliography.

Illich, Ivan. *Tools for Conviviality.* HarpC 1980 $3.95. ISBN 0-06-090743-6. Classic and influential attempt to delineate moral standards for evaluating technological development.

Johnson, Deborah, ed. *Ethical Issues in Engineering.* P-H 1990. ISBN 0-13-290578-7. The best engineering ethics reader to date; includes more than 30 articles examining historical and social contexts; the role of professional codes; the responsibility of engineers to society, other engineers, and clients; and the future of the engineering profession.

Jonas, Hans. *The Imperative of Responsibility: In Search of an Ethics for the Technological Age*. U. Ch. Pr. 1985 $25.00. ISBN 0-226-40596-6. The most important philosophical text in the general ethics of technology. Argues that human behavior has been altered fundamentally by modern technology and that responsibility, especially toward future generations, requires a slowing of technological change; also proposes a theoretical basis for responsibility as a moral concept.

————. *Philosophical Essays: From Ancient Creed to Technological Man*. U. Ch. Pr. 1980 o.p. Part 1 contains eight essays on "Science, Technology, and Ethics." The first and fifth essays—"Technology and Responsibility: Reflections on the New Tasks of Ethics" and "Philosophical Reflections on Experimenting with Human Subjects"— are especially important; also examines the Jewish perspective on the ethics of technology.

Kranzberg, Melvin, ed. *Ethics in an Age of Pervasive Technology*. Westview 1980 o.p. Proceedings of a 1974 symposium held in Israel. Good collection of brief articles by such scholars as Gershom Scholem, Isaiah Berlin, Daniel Bell, Robert Gordis, René Dubos, Jacques Ellul, Hans Jonas, Alvin Weinberg, and others; includes the "Mount Carmel Declaration on Technology and Moral Responsibility."

Kyle, David T. *Human Robots and Holy Mechanics: Reclaiming Our Souls in a Machine World*. Swan Raven 1993 $14.95. ISBN 0-9632310-0-6. Addresses what the author views as a lack of spiritual awareness in the corporate-controlled world economy. The book aims at developing "holy mechanics" who work at fixing the world through spirituality.

Layton, Edwin T. *The Revolt of the Engineers: Social Responsibility and the American Engineering Profession*. Johns Hopkins 1986 $37.50. ISBN 0-8018-3286-1. Excellent and influential overview of the rise of engineering as a profession; includes professional codes and special values in the United States (originally published in 1971).

Lossing, Larry D., and Edward J. Bayer, eds. *Technological Powers and the Person: Nuclear Energy and Reproductive Technology*. Pope John Ctr. 1983 $15.95. ISBN 0-935372-12-1. Examines the moral status of nuclear power and reproductive techniques from a Catholic perspective; reflects a somewhat pronuclear and antiartificial insemination position.

Lyndberg, Steven D., and others. *Rating America's Corporate Conscience: A Provocative Guide to the Companies behind the Products You Buy Every Day*. Addison-Wesley 1987 $21.95. ISBN 0-201-15886-8. An example of the grass-roots ethics of technology.

MacLean, Douglas, ed. *Values at Risk*. Rowman 1986 $49.00. ISBN 0-8476-7414-2. Eight original essays that discuss risk and risk analysis in a technological society.

Mander, Jerry. *In the Absence of the Sacred: The Failure of Technology and the Survival of the Indian Nations*. Sierra 1991 $25.00. ISBN 0-87156-739-3. Broad ethical-religious critique that focuses on the relationship between electronic media and environmental ethics.

Martin, Michael, and Roland Schinzinger. *Ethics in Engineering*. McGraw 2nd ed. 1989 $23.30. ISBN 0-07-040719-3. A philosopher and an engineer cover a diversity of ethical issues from an analytic perspective.

Mitcham, Carl, ed. *Ethics and Technology. Research in Philosophy and Technology*. Vol. 9 Jai Pr. 1989 o.p. Fifteen articles that show the interrelationships among nuclear, environmental, biomedical, computer, and engineering ethics; includes Eric Katz's "Environmental Ethics: A Select Annotated Bibliography, 1983–1987."

Mitcham, Carl, and Robert Mackey, eds. *Philosophy and Technology: Readings in the Philosophical Problems of Technology*. Free Pr. 1983 repr. of 1972 ed. $16.95. ISBN 0-02-921430-0. Reprints important texts not readily available elsewhere by Jacques Ellul, Emmanuel Mesthene, Gunther Anders, C. S. Lewis, Yves Simm, George Grant, Nicholas Berdyaev, Eric Gill, Lynn White, Jr., and others; the largest section of the book is devoted to "Ethical and Political Critiques."

Mitcham, Carl, and Philip Siekevitz, eds. *Ethical Issues Associated with Scientific and Technological Research for the Military. Annuals of the NY Academy of Sciences.* Vol. 577 NY Acad. of Sci. 1989 o.p.

Monsma, Stephen V., and others. *Responsible Technology: A Christian Perspective.* Eerdmans 1986 o.p. The product of a year-long study group at Calvin College (Michigan) that analyzes the spiritual nature of technology and develops moral guidelines for Christian engineers and others; includes a good annotated bibliography.

Nef, Jorge, and others, eds. *Ethics and Technology: Ethical Choices in the Age of Pervasive Technology.* Wall & Thompson 1989 o.p. Proceedings of a major conference on public affairs, containing papers on global survival, sustainable resources, economic efficiency, quality of life and social justice, power and freedom, and culture and accessibility; companion volume to *Critical Choices! Ethics, Science, and Technology* (Henry Wiseman and others, eds.). Thompson Educational Pubs., 1991.

Nelkin, Dorothy, ed. *Controversy: Politics of Technical Decisions.* Sage 3rd ed. 1992 $46.00. ISBN 0-8039-4466-7. Core studies on the politics (and implicitly, the ethics) of technical decision making about nuclear power plants, automobile safety devices, and medical and other technologies.

Papanek, Victor. *Design for the Real World: Human Ecology and Social Change.* Academy Chi. Pubs. 2nd rev. ed. 1985 $17.00. ISBN 0-89733-153-2. Strongly worded moral argument by an industrial engineer, who states, "Design must become an innovative highly creative, cross-disciplinary tool responsive to the true needs of man. It must be more research oriented, and we must stop defiling the earth itself with poorly designed objects and structures."

Porter, A. R., and others. *A Guidebook for Technology Assessment and Impact Analysis.* Elsevier 1980 o.p. Reference book that provides an overview of technology assessment.

Postman, Neil. *Technopoly: The Surrender of Culture to Technology.* Random 1993 $11.00. ISBN 0-679-74540-8. General critique of the cultural-ethical influence of technology; covers medical technologies, computers, and other technologies.

Rescher, Nicholas. *Risk: A Philosophical Introduction to the Theory of Risk Evaluation and Management.* U. Pr. of Amer. 1983 o.p. Contains chapters on "The Ethical and Legal Dimension of Risk" and "Risk and Technology."

———. *Unpopular Essays on Technological Progress.* U. of Pittsburgh Pr. 1980 $49.95. ISBN 0-8229-3411-6. Examines the economic and social ramifications of technological progress.

Sapolsky, Harvey M. *Consuming Fears: The Politics of Product Risks.* Basic 1986 $18.95. ISBN 0-965-01411-9. Highlights problems but provides a very brief discussion of moral analysis or alternatives.

Schaub, James H., and others, eds. *Engineering Professionalism and Ethics.* Krieger 1986 repr. of 1983 ed. $36.50. ISBN 0-89874-954-9. Good general collection of more than 70 readings.

Shinn, Roger L. *Forced Options: Social Decisions for the Twenty-First Century.* Pilgrim Pr. 3rd ed. 1992 $16.95. ISBN 0-8298-0934-1. Suggests that a "forced option" is a choice that cannot be avoided because science, technology, and medicine force numerous choices upon us. (Thus, to avoid choosing is itself a choice.) Covers "the big problems" of energy, hunger, population, resource limits, genetic technology, and war; includes analysis of related social, ethical, and religious issues.

Shrader-Frechette, Kristin S. *Science-Policy, Ethics, and Economic Methodology: Some Problems of Technology Assessment and Environmental Impact Analysis.* Kluwer Ac. 1984 $85.00. ISBN 90-277-1806-7. Critical analysis that highlights the ethical issues embedded in these methodologies and discusses ways to improve them.

Taitte, W. L. *Traditional Moral Values in the Age of Technology.* U. of Tex. Pr. 1987 $16.50. ISBN 0-292-78098-2. Five papers: Hans Mark's "The *Challenger* and Chernobyl: Lessons and Reflections," Tom L. Beauchamp's "Medical Ethics in the Age of Technology," Jesse P. Luton's "Professional and Business Ethical and Moral Values in the Age of Technology," Martin E. Marty's "The Many Faces of Technology, The

Many Faces of Tradition," and Andrew R. Cecil's "The Unchanging Spirit of Freedom."

Teich, Albert H., ed. *Technology and the Future*. St. Martin 5th ed. 1992 $21.35. ISBN 0-312-06747-X. Twenty-five standard articles in a conventional anthology format, covering the 1970s and 1980s.

Tillich, Paul. *The Spiritual Situation in Our Technical Society*. Mercer Univ. Pr. 1988 $40.00. ISBN 0-86554-293-7. Collection of essays from the 1940s to the 1960s that examine structure and meaning in relation to such issues as technical progress, urbanization, space exploration, and nuclear power.

Unger, Stephen H. *Controlling Technology: Ethics and the Responsible Engineer*. Wiley 2nd ed. 1993. ISBN 0-471-59181-5. Illustrates (with case studies) that engineers often are forced to choose between loyalty to a corporate employer and loyalty to conscience. Argues that loyalty to conscience and the "whistle blowing" that often results must be supported by professional engineering organizations; appendices include several engineering ethics codes. "A book that must be read by all engineers" (*IEEE Technology and Society Magazine*).

Winner, Langdon. *The Whale and the Reactor: A Search for Limits in an Age of High Technology*. U. Ch. Pr. 1988 $9.95. ISBN 0-226-90211-0. Argues that technologies can be considered forms of life. Claims that choices about the kinds of technical systems we construct should be understood as choices about our future as individuals and what kind of future society we want to live in.

CHRONOLOGY OF AUTHORS

Jaspers, Karl. 1883–1969
Teller, Edward. 1908–
Hardin, Garrett. 1915–
Dyson, Freeman J. 1923–
Weizenbaum, Joseph. 1923–
Illich, Ivan. 1926–
Postman, Neil. 1931–
Rolston, Holmes, III. 1932–

Stone, Christopher. 1937–
Beauchamp, Thomas L. 1939–
Veatch, Robert M. 1939–
Engelhardt, H. Tristram. 1941–
Hargrove, Eugene. 1944–
Shrader-Frechette, Kristin S. 1944–
Winner, Langdon. 1944–

ABBEY, EDWARD. 1927–1989

[SEE Chapter 23 in this volume.]

BEAUCHAMP, THOMAS L. 1939–

A philosopher and writer in the field of biomedical ethics, Thomas Beauchamp was born in Austin, Texas. He was educated at Southern Methodist University, where he received his B.A. and M.A. degrees; at Yale University; and at Johns Hopkins, where he earned a Ph.D. in 1970. That same year Beauchamp joined the philosophy department at Georgetown University, becoming professor of philosophy in 1979. He also served as senior research scholar with the Center for Bioethics at Georgetown's Kennedy Institute.

Beauchamp is an influential leader and teacher in the emerging field of biomedical ethics, which deals with the interrelationship of ethics and the complex technology of modern medicine. His concerns have embraced the philosophical and ethical dimensions of health care, therapeutic practice, and medical and biological research. His best known work, *Principles of Biomedical Ethics* (1979), was the first of an impressive series of studies he produced in the field of bioethics.

BOOKS BY BEAUCHAMP

Case Studies in Business, Society, and Ethics. (ed.) P-H 1989 $30.60. ISBN 0-13-119355-4

Health and Human Values. (coauthored with Frank Harron and John Burnside). Yale U.
Pr. 1983 $32.00. ISBN 0-300-03026-6

A History and Theory of Informed Consent: A Guide to Making Your Own Decisions.
(coauthored with Ruth Faden and Nancy King). OUP 1986 $42.50. ISBN 0-19-
503686-7. A practical guide for thinking about abortion, euthanasia, informed
consent, health care rights, and related issues.

Medical Ethics: The Moral Responsibilities of Physicians. (coauthored with Laurence
McCullough). P-H 1984 $22.20. ISBN 0-13-572652-2. Straightforward guidance for
practicing doctors and other health care professionals.

Philosophical Ethics: An Introduction to Moral Philosophy. McGraw 1982 $26.26. ISBN 0-
07-004203-9. A general study with both text and readings.

Philosophy and the Human Condition. (coauthored with William T. Blackstone and Joel
Feinberg). P-H 1980 o.p. Presents philosophical problems that grow naturally out of
everyday concerns.

Principles of Biomedical Ethics. 1979. OUP 1979 $24.95. ISBN 0-19-502487-7. Systematic
philosophical discussion of basic principles presents biomedical ethics as the
application of general ethical theories, principles, and rules to medical ethical
problems.

The Virtuous Journalist. (coauthored with Stephen Klaidman). OUP 1987 $19.95. ISBN 0-
19-504205-0. Serves as a guide to where philosophy can improve media criticism and
where the field is better left to practicing journalists.

BERRY, WENDELL. 1934–

[SEE Chapter 9 in this volume.]

BRONOWSKI, JACOB. 1908–1974

[SEE Chapter 6 in this volume.]

BROWN, LESTER RUSSELL. 1934–

[SEE Chapter 23 in this volume.]

CALLAHAN, DANIEL J. 1930–

[SEE Chapter 4 in this volume.]

CARSON, RACHEL LOUISE. 1907–1964

[SEE Chapter 23 in this volume.]

DUBOS, RENÉ JULES. 1901-1982

[SEE Chapter 22 in this volume.]

DYSON, FREEMAN J. 1923–

Freeman Dyson is a British-American physicist, moral philosopher, and critic
of the political applications of postwar science. He is perhaps best known for his
speculations on the philosophical implications of science and its uses. Born in
Crowthorne, Berkshire, the son of a prominent composer and musician, Dyson
became interested in mathematics at an early age. In 1941 he enrolled at
Cambridge University, where he was recruited by C. P. SNOW (see Vol. 1) to
assist in studies of tactical bombing strategies for the Royal Air Force. These
studies aroused his moral concern with the uses of science in certain endeavors.
After graduating from Cambridge in 1945, Dyson became a fellow at Trinity
College. Then, in 1947, he was granted a fellowship to Cornell University, where

he studied under physicists HANS BETHE and RICHARD FEYNMAN, and made important contributions to the physics of quantum electrodynamics.

Some of his teachers at Cornell had played key roles in the development of the atomic bomb, and Dyson often discussed the moral and philosophical implications of this awesome new weapon. Increasingly, his interest focused on the ethical dimension of science and its applications. At this critical juncture, Dyson met J. ROBERT OPPENHEIMER, who invited him to study at the Institute for Advanced Study at Princeton. Dyson accepted and went there for a year (1950). In 1951 he returned to Cornell as a faculty member in physics; two years later, however, Dyson returned to Princeton, where he remained for many years.

In 1956 Dyson began a collaboration with EDWARD TELLER on constructing an inherently safe nuclear reactor, but their approach proved too costly to construct. Dyson then joined a research team in La Jolla, California, to design a nuclear-powered spacecraft for manned exploration. After this project was canceled by the government, Dyson again worked with Teller, this time in developing the neutron bomb. During this period, he became one of the leading critics of the proposed Soviet-American nuclear test ban, although he later repudiated his position. His moral concerns were also evidenced by his work with the American Federation of Scientists. As chair of that group (1962), he was a leading force in creating the Arms Control and Disarmament Agency. Dyson's honors include membership in the National Academy of Science, a fellow of the Royal Society of London, and a recipient of the Max Planck Medal.

BOOKS BY DYSON

Disturbing the Universe. Basic 1981 $13.00. ISBN 0-465-01677-4. An autobiography stressing the disruptive influence of modern science and technology. Of this work, Dyson says "I have collected . . . memories extending over fifty years."

From Eros to Gaia. Pantheon 1992 $24.50. ISBN 0-679-41307-3. An anthology that bridges the gulf between literature and science, between the public and the experts. Thirty-six essays from boyhood to NASA.

Infinite in All Directions. HarpC 1989 repr. of 1988 ed. $10.00. ISBN 0-06-091569-2. Revision of Dyson's Gifford lectures delivered in Aberdeen in 1985.

Origins of Life. Cambridge U. Pr. 1986 $14.95. ISBN 0-521-30949-2

Values at War: Selected Tanner Lectures on the Nuclear Crisis. Bks. Demand repr. of 1983 ed. $38.40. ISBN 0-8357-3273-8. Includes three essays by Dyson on the theme that cultural patterns endure longer than weapons technologies and political arrangements.

Weapons and Hope. HarpC 1985 $7.95. ISBN 0-06-039039-5. Suggests ways of achieving a peaceful resolution of the nuclear weapons dilemma.

EINSTEIN, ALBERT. 1879–1955

[SEE Chapter 20 in this volume.]

ELLUL, JACQUES. 1912–

[SEE Chapter 6 in this volume.]

ENGELHARDT, H. TRISTRAM. 1941–

Born in New Orleans, Louisiana, H. Tristram Engelhardt holds both a Ph.D. in philosophy from the University of Texas (1963) and an M.D. from the Tulane Medical School (1972). From 1972 until 1977, he taught bioethics at the University of Texas Medical School and then, for the next five years, served as Rosemary Kennedy Professor of the Philosophy of Medicine at Georgetown University and Senior Research Scholar at the Kennedy Center for Bioethics in

Washington, D.C. Since 1983 he has been professor of internal medicine, community medicine, and obstetrics-gynecology at the Baylor University College of Medicine. For his contributions to bioethics, especially related to the use of human beings in research, Engelhardt has received a Woodrow Wilson fellowship (1988) and a fellowship from the Institute for Advanced Studies in Berlin, Germany (1988–89).

BOOKS BY ENGELHARDT

Bioethics and Secular Humanism: The Search for a Common Morality. TPI PA 1990 $29.95. ISBN 1-56338-000-5

The Foundations of Bioethics. OUP 1986 $37.50. ISBN 0-19-503608-5. Presents the first systematic treatment of the field. Describes the origins and rise of secular bioethics and discusses its foundations and applications. Supports a Kantian conception of "the person" as a moral agent: "Persons, not humans, are special."

Mind and Body: A Categorical Relation. Martinus Nijhoff 1973 o.p.

Science, Ethics, and Medicine. Inst. of Society, Ethics & the Life Sciences 1976 o.p.

Scientific Controversies. (ed.) Cambridge U. Pr. 1987 $69.95. ISBN 0-521-25565-1. Addresses important issues in a sophisticated and readable manner. Debates discussed here range from continental drift to the desirability of nuclear power plants to homosexuality as a disease concept.

HARDIN, GARRETT. 1915–

Garrett Hardin, an American scientist and prominent human ecologist, was born in Dallas, Texas. A victim of polio as a child, Hardin and his family moved around to various cities in the midwest before finally settling in Chicago, where he attended the University of Chicago, receiving a degree in zoology in 1936. At Chicago, Hardin was greatly influenced by several prominent teachers, including geologist J. Harlan Bretz, ecologist W. C. Allee, and philosopher-educator MORTIMER ADLER (see Vol. 4).

Hardin did graduate work in biology at Stanford University, and he served as a teaching assistant there from 1939 to 1941, when he was awarded his Ph.D. He then became a researcher in plant biology at Stanford, investigating the culture of algae. In 1945 he was made an assistant professor of biology but resigned the following year, abandoning his research in the belief that his work was contributing to the expansion in food production, an outcome that could only increase world population pressures and hunger. Instead, he became assistant professor of bacteriology at a small college that soon grew into the University of California at Santa Barbara. He was given a full professorship there in 1957 and later was also appointed professor of human ecology. Shortly after going to Santa Barbara, Hardin revised the school's biology curriculum and wrote a popular college textbook, *Biology: Its Human Implications* (1949) (revised in 1966 as *Biology: Its Principles and Implications*). At the same time, his interest shifted increasingly to genetics and evolution.

In 1960 Hardin began teaching a course in human ecology at Santa Barbara, which examined the problem of population pressures on the earth's environment. He directly confronted the ethical implications of the problem, openly advocating legalizing abortion—then, as now, a highly charged and controversial topic. He lectured widely in the 1960s urging this cause, a campaign that helped pave the way for the later Supreme Court ruling in *Roe v. Wade* (1973). In a widely publicized article in *Science* magazine in 1968, Hardin insisted that the control of population growth and pollution was essential to human survival and thus required worldwide limits on the individual's freedom to reproduce and to degrade the environment. He expounded these views in greater detail in a later work, *Exploring New Ethics for Survival* (1972).

BOOKS BY HARDIN

Filters Against Folly: How to Survive Despite Ecologists, Economists, and the Merely Eloquent. Viking Penguin 1986 $9.95. ISBN 0-14-007729-4. Claims that environmental problems are caused not by vice but by foolishness. Criticizes both free market capitalism and radical ecology and provides suggestions for how to filter out the follies of human inclinations and simplified ideologies.

Managing the Commons. (Ed. with John Buden). W. H. Freeman 1977 $14.95. ISBN 0-7167-0476-5. Includes Hardin's classic article "The Tragedy of the Commons."

Mandatory Motherhood: The True Meaning of "Right to Life." Beacon Pr. 1974 o.p. A critique of the right-to-life movement as causing overpopulation.

Naked Emperors: Essays of a Taboo Stalker. Wm. Kaufman 1982 o.p. Thirty essays, mostly from popular periodicals.

Nature and Man's Fate. H. Holt & Co. 1959 o.p. A history of the development of the theory of evolution and examinations of its political and ethical implications. Considers such questions as: If evolution is dependent on genetic mutations, and nuclear weapons cause such mutations, why are nuclear weapons bad?

Population, Evolution, and Birth Control: A Collage of Controversial Issues. W. H. Freeman 1964 o.p. Over 100 readings from sources as diverse as the *Bible*, Aristotle, Charles Darwin, Benjamin Franklin, and Hardin himself.

Promethean Ethics: Living with Death, Competition, and Triage. U. of Wash. Pr. 1980 o.p. Promethean ethics is another name for the ethics of technology.

Science, Conflict, and Society. W. H. Freeman 1969 o.p. Almost 50 articles from *Scientific American* on the social impacts of modern science.

Voyage of the Spaceship Beagle: Exploring New Ethics for Survival. 1972. Viking Penguin 1972 o.p. The first book-length statement of Hardin's ethics of limits.

HARGROVE, EUGENE. 1944–

Eugene Hargrove received his Ph.D. from the University of Missouri, has done postdoctorate research at the University of Vienna, and has held a Rockefeller Foundation Fellowship in Environmental Affairs. He has taught at the University of New Mexico, the University of Georgia, and the University of North Texas, where he is now chair of the Philosophy Department. As the founding editor of the journal *Environmental Ethics*, Hargrove has exercised a leadership role in the development of that field. He has recently expanded his influence with a new series of books on environmental ethics. In his own environmental ethical studies, Hargrove emphasizes the importance of the aesthetic appreciation of nature.

BOOKS BY HARGROVE

The Animal Rights-Environmental Ethics Debate: The Environmental Perspective. State U. NY Pr. 1992 $44.50. ISBN 0-7914-0933-3. Reprints eleven articles analyzing the different and often conflicting perspectives of the animal rights and environmental movements.

Beyond Spaceship Earth: Environmental Ethics and the Solar System. Environ. Ethics Bks. $14.95. ISBN 0-9626807-1-0. Fifteen papers from a 1985 conference on the social, human, and political dimensions of space exploration; includes scientific-technological, philosophical, and theological perspectives.

Foundations of Environmental Ethics. P-H 1989 $24.00. ISBN 0-13-329574-5. Discusses traditional attitudes, the risk of environmental consciousness, and philosophical ethical implications of this new consciousness. Argues for the role of an aesthetic appreciation of nature in environmental ethics. The best monograph for the general reader.

Religion and the Environmental Crisis. U. of Ga. Pr. 1987 o.p. Eleven papers examining
   pagan, Amerindian, Jewish, Christian, Taoist, and Islamic environmental ethics.

HOLTON, GERALD. 1922–

[SEE Chapter 2 in this volume.]

ILLICH, IVAN. 1926–

Born in Vienna in 1926, Ivan Illich grew up in Europe. He studied theology,
philosophy, history, and natural science. During the 1950s he worked as a parish
priest among Puerto Ricans in the Hell's Kitchen section of New York City and
then served as rector of the Catholic University of Puerto Rico. During the 1960s
he founded centers for cross-cultural communication, first in Puerto Rico and
then in Cuernavaca, Mexico. Since the late 1970s, he has divided his time
among Mexico, the United States, and Germany. He currently is professor of
Science, Technology, and Society at Penn State University.

Illich's radical anarchist views first became widely known through a set of
four books published during the early 1970s—*Deschooling Society* (1971), *Tools
for Conviviality* (1973), *Energy and Equity* (1974), and *Medical Nemesis* (1976).
Tools is the most general statement of Illich's principles; the other three expand
on examples sketched in *Today* in order to critique what he calls "radical
monopolies" in the technologies of education, energy consumption, and
medical treatment. This critique applies equally to both the so-called developed
and the developing nations but in different ways.

Two subsequent collections of occasional pieces—*Toward a History of Needs*
(1978) and *Shadow Work* (1981)—stress the distorting influence on society and
culture of the economics of scarcity, or the presumption that economies
function to remedy scarcities rather than to share goods. *Toward a History of
Needs* also initiates a project in the history or archaeology of ideas that takes its
first full-bodied shape in *Gender* (1982), an attempt to recover social experiences of female-male complementarity that have been obscured by the modern
economic regime. *H₂O and the Waters of Forgetfulness* (1985) extends this
project into a history of "stuff."

ABC: The Alphabetization of the Popular Mind (1988) carries Illich's project
forward into the area of literacy, as does his most recent book, *In the Vineyard
of the Text* (1993). *In the Mirror of the Past* (1992) is a collection of occasional
essays and talks from the 1980s, linking his concerns with economics,
education, history, and the new ideological meaning of life.

Illich himself is a polymath who speaks at least six languages fluently and who
writes regularly in three of these (English, Spanish, and German); his books
have been translated into more than 15 other languages. He has had a strong
influence on a close circle of friends whose own insightful and independent
work has also begun to appear. Representative of what might be called the Illich
community of reflection are, for example, *The Woman beneath the Skin: A
Doctor's Patients in Eighteenth-Century Germany* by Barbara Duden and *The
Development Dictionary: A Guide to Knowledge as Power* edited by Wolfgang
Sachs.

BOOKS BY ILLICH

ABC: The Alphabetization of the Popular Mind. (coauthored with Barry Sanders). Random
   1989 $9.95. ISBN 0-679-72192-4. Discusses how printing has transformed thinking.
Celebration of Awareness: A Call for Institutional Revolution. Heyday Bks. 1988 repr. of
   1970 ed. $8.95. ISBN 0-930588-36-3. Critical reflections on protest against the

Vietnam War, the attitude of the Catholic Church toward Latin Americans (especially Puerto Ricans), institutional schooling, and the idea of economic-technological development.

Deschooling Society. HarpC 1989 repr. of 1971 ed. $9.00. ISBN 0-06-132086-2. A trenchant argument for the disestablishment of compulsory education. Influential on the alternative-schools movement of the 1970s, and probably Illich's most widely read book.

Gender. 1982 Heyday Bks. 1988 repr. of 1982 ed. $8.95. ISBN 0-930588-40-1. One of the first articulations of sexual (biological) and gender (social) distinctions. Argues that the historical transformation from vernacular and modern economic milieux has fundamentally transformed the second.

H_2O and the Waters of Forgetfulness: An Inquiry into Our Changing Perceptions of Urban Space and the Waters That Cleanse It. Heyday Bks. 1987 repr. of 1985 ed. ISBN 0-930588-25-8. Critical analysis of the typically modern attitude toward water and its urban uses.

In the Mirror of the Past: Lectures and Addresses 1978–1990. M. Boyars Pubs. 1992 $24.95. ISBN 0-7145-2937-0. Includes the texts of 19 occasional talks delivered in Asia, Europe, and North America.

In the Vineyard of the Text: A Commentary to Hugh's Didascalicon. U. Ch. Pr. 1993 $24.95. ISBN 0-226-37235-9. Explores the transformation of the text as a physical object and the experience of reading during the thirteenth century, by way of an extended commentary on Hugh of St. Victor's "Didascalicon."

Medical Nemesis: The Expropriation of Health. Pantheon 1982 repr. of 1976 ed. $11.96. ISBN 0-394-71245-5. Savage indictment of the health establishment, arguing that high-tech medical interventions now do more harm than good, especially when the good is conceived as something more than the simple prolongation of physical life.

Shadow Work. M. Boyars Pubs. 1981 $15.00. ISBN 0-7145-2711-4. "Shadow work" is work that is not paid for. The thesis of the title essay of this collection of five longer articles is that the functioning of the money economy depends on not paying for certain kinds of work.

Tools for Conviviality. HarpC 1988 repr. of 1973 ed. $8.95. ISBN 0-930588-37-1. Classic and influential attempt to delineate moral standards for evaluating technological development. Provides a kind of general theory for, and has become associated with, the alternative-technology movement.

Toward a History of Needs. Heyday Bks. 1987 repr. of 1978 ed. $8.95. ISBN 0-930588-26-6. A collection of essays, including the short monograph "Energy and Equity," published separately in 1974.

BOOKS ABOUT ILLICH

Cayley, David. *Ivan Illich: In Conversation.* Anansi 1992 o.p. A series of interviews, done originally for a radio broadcast by Cayley, who works for the Canadian Broadcasting Company. The long introduction by Cayley provides a good overview of Illich's thought.

Plessix Gray, Francine. *Divine Disobedience: Profiles in Catholic Radicalism.* Knopf 1970 o.p. The last of these four profiles, which first appeared in *The New Yorker* magazine, is devoted to Illich.

JASPERS, KARL. 1883–1969

Born in Oldenburg, Germany, the eminent philosopher and psychologist Karl Jaspers undertook a lifelong search for the meaning and purpose of human existence. While studying at the Universities of Heidelberg and Munich, Jaspers shifted his interest from law to medicine. He continued his studies in medicine at the Universities of Berlin and Göttingen until 1908, at which time he passed his examination to practice medicine. For the next six years, Jaspers served as a research assistant in a psychiatric clinic at the University of Heidelberg. Clinical psychiatry at that time focused on diagnosing the causes of mental illness;

Jaspers thus saw the need to view the field as a science and to research therapies that might be used in treating patients. He soon published a major textbook in the field, *General Psychopathology* (1911).

In 1913 Jaspers joined the faculty of the University of Heidelberg, shifting both his interests and affiliation from psychology and medicine to philosophy. A major study, *Psychology of World Views* (1919), which was intended to define the limits of psychology in human understanding, instead set forth a philosophical view of humanity. As his thinking developed, Jaspers abandoned efforts to delineate the relationships between science and philosophy. He concentrated instead on developing a philosophy independent of science that was not to be a substitute for religion, but was to explain the reality of humanity's existence beyond any scientific considerations. During the 1920s, Jaspers devoted his energies to defining this philosophy, which he based on the freedom of the individual and humanity's role as the center of all reality. This philosophy was explicated in *Man in the Modern Age* (1932) and his three-volume *Philosophy* (1933).

Hitler's rise to power curtailed Jasper's career because he was married to a Jew. Although he was allowed to continue teaching and writing for several years, he finally was removed from his teaching post and no longer allowed to write. Refusing to leave Germany without his wife, who was refused permission to emigrate, Jaspers waited out the war until the Allied occupation of Germany. His wartime experience disillusioned Jaspers. Yet with Germany's defeat, he set as his goals the renewal of German universities and the rebirth of the German people and devoted his energies toward accomplishing these tasks.

In 1948 Jaspers went to the University of Basel in Switzerland as professor of philosophy, a step many Germans viewed as a rebuke and betrayal. At Basel, Jaspers continued to refine his view of philosophy, largely in an effort to clarify and heal his own existence. In the last decades of his life, Jaspers's philosophy searched for a new way of thinking about humanity and existence that would ensure a new free world order. His search produced two major works of deep complexity—*The Perennial Shape of Philosophy* (1949) and *Philosophical Faith and Revelation* (1967)—that centered on philosophical abstraction as common ground among conflicting religious and metaphysical systems. In the latter years of his life, he centered his attention on German politics and the international scene.

BOOKS BY JASPERS

The Future of Mankind. Trans. by E. B. Ashton. U. Ch. Pr. 1961 o.p. Reflections on the challenges posed by nuclear weapons.

Man in the Modern Age. 1932. AMS Pr. repr. of 1933 ed. $28.50. ISBN 0-404-14558-2. Focuses on the moral problem of human life in a technical world.

Origin and Goal of History. Trans. by Michael Bullock. Greenwood 1977 repr. of 1953 ed. $41.50. ISBN 0-8371-8983-7. Touches on various issues and analyzes the place of modern technology in world history.

Philosophy. 1933. 3 vols. Trans by E. B. Ashton. U. Ch. Pr. 1971. Vol. 1 $19.00. ISBN 0-226- 39489-1. Vol. 2 $21.00. ISBN 0-226-39491-3. Vol. 3 $14.00. ISBN 0-226-39494-8

Philosophy and the World. Trans. by E. B. Ashton. Regnery Gateway 1989 repr. of 1963 ed. $10.95. ISBN 0-89526-757-8. An overview of philosophy and its practical, commonsense importance.

Philosophy of Existence. U. of Pa. Pr. 1971 $16.95. ISBN 0-8122-1010-7

Way to Wisdom: An Introduction to Philosophy. Trans. by Ralph Manheim. Yale U. Pr. 1954 $11.00. ISBN 0-300-00134-7

BOOKS ABOUT JASPERS

Schilpp, Paul A., ed. *The Philosophy of Karl Jaspers*. Open Court 1981 $39.95. ISBN 0-87548-361-5. An insightful analysis of Jaspers's thought and his significance to contemporary philosophy.

Wallraff, Charles F. *Karl Jaspers: An Introduction to His Philosophy*. Bks. Demand repr. of 1970 ed. $65.00. ISBN 0-8357-6173-8. Provides a useful and understandable look at Jaspers's basic philosophy.

JONAS, HANS. 1904–1993

[SEE Chapter 4 in this volume.]

KRUTCH, JOSEPH WOOD. 1893–1970

[SEE Chapter 23 in this volume.]

LEOPOLD, ALDO. 1887–1948

[SEE Chapter 23 in this volume.]

MUIR, JOHN. 1838–1914

[SEE Chapter 23 in this volume.]

NELKIN, DOROTHY. 1933–

[SEE Chapter 6 in this volume.]

PELLEGRINO, EDMUND D. 1920–

[SEE Chapter 4 in this volume.]

POSTMAN, NEIL. 1931–

Born in Brooklyn, New York, and educated at the State University of New York and Columbia University, Neil Postman is a communications theorist, educator, and writer who has been deeply involved with the issue of the impact of the media and advanced communications technology on American culture. In his many books, Postman has strongly opposed the idea that technology will "save" humanity. In fact, he has focused on the negative ways in which television and computers alter social behavior. In his book *Technopoly*, Postman argues that the uncontrolled growth of technology destroys humanity by creating a culture with no moral structure. Thus, technology can be a dangerous enemy as well as a good friend.

Postman, who is married and has three children, currently is a professor of media ecology at New York University and editor of *Et Cetera*, the journal of general semantics. In addition to his books, he has contributed to various magazines and periodicals, including *Atlantic* and *The Nation*. He has also appeared on the television program *Sunrise Semester*. Postman is the holder of the Christian Lindback Award for Excellence in Teaching from New York University.

BOOKS BY POSTMAN

Amusing Ourselves to Death: Public Discourse in the Age of Show Business. Viking Penguin 1986 $10.00. ISBN 0-14-009438-5. Contends that television has conditioned us to tolerate visually entertaining material to the detriment of rational public discourse.

Conscientious Objections: Stirring up Trouble about Language, Technology, and Educa-
   tion. Knopf 1988 $17.95. ISBN 0-394-57270-X. Collection of 18 essays, several
   satirical in nature, on various aspects of the mass media.
How to Watch TV News. (coauthored with Steve Powers). Viking Penguin 1992 $10.00.
   ISBN 0-14-013231-7. Critical view of television news broadcasting in which the
   authors advise readers to be on guard and read more about news stories rather than
   relying only on television coverage.
Teaching as a Conserving Activity. Dell 1987 $4.95. ISBN 0-440-38486-9
Teaching as a Subversive Activity. (coauthored with Charles Weingartner). Dell 1987
   $4.95. ISBN 0-440-38485-0. Originally published in 1969, this book presents a critical
   view of American education and ways that teachers can "subvert" and improve the
   system.
Technopoly: The Surrender of Culture to Technology. Random 1993 $11.00. ISBN 0-679-
   74540-8. General critique of the cultural-ethical influence of technology; covers
   medical technologies, computers, and other technologies. Defines the United States
   as a society in which technology is deified to a near-totalitarian degree.

ROLSTON, HOLMES, III. 1932–

Born in Staunton, Virginia, Holmes Rolston received both a theological and
secular education. After receiving a B.S. degree in philosophy from Davidson
University in 1953, he went on to earn a divinity degree from the Union
Theological Seminary (1956) and a Ph.D. in theology from the University of
Edinburgh (1958). Rolston initially taught philosophy at Hampden-Sydney
College in 1958, before becoming pastor of the Walnut Grove Presbyterian
Church in Bristol, Virginia, where he remained until 1967. Since 1968 he has
been professor of philosophy at Colorado State University. Rolston's main areas
of research and writing have focused on the interrelationship between ecology
and religion and on ecological ethics and environmental issues. He is the
associate editor of the *Journal of Environmental Ethics*, which is a primary
outlet for articles in the field of environmental ethics. One of Rolston's main
themes is that science can be used to promote religious experience, rather than
destroy it.

BOOKS BY ROLSTON

Environmental Ethics. Temple U. Pr. 1987 $44.95. ISBN 0-87722-201-X. Suggests ways for
   government, business, and the individual to make philosophical peace with the
   natural order. Brilliantly provocative.
Philosophy Gone Wild: Essays in Environmental Ethics. Prometheus Bks. 1989 $17.95.
   ISBN 0-87975-556-3. Argues that an "ecological ethic" is based on an individual's
   appreciation of nature; written from the perspective of a philosopher-scientist.
Science and Religion: A Critical Survey. Temple U. Pr. 1986 $39.95. ISBN 0-877-22-437-4.
   Discusses how science cannot answer all fundamental questions in life, and the
   religions that do.

RUSSELL, BERTRAND ARTHUR WILLIAM, 3rd EARL RUSSELL.
   1872–1970

[SEE Volume 4 and Chapter 4 in this volume.]

SHRADER-FRECHETTE, KRISTIN S. 1944–

Kristin Shrader-Frechette is distinguished research professor at the University
of South Florida. She received her undergraduate degree in mathematics and
physics, followed by a Ph.D. in philosophy from the University of Notre Dame in
1971. She has also done postdoctoral work in biology, economics, and

hydrogeology, and is currently editor of the Oxford University Press monograph series "Environmental Ethics and Science Policy."

Most of Shrader-Frechette's work is in philosophy of science, environmental ethics, probabilistic risk assessment, and science policy. From 1971 until 1985, her theoretical research was on methodological and ethical problems associated with high-energy physics and welfare economics. Since 1984 her theoretical work has focused on methods in hydrogeology and in community ecology. Her more applied research deals with applications of probabilistic risk assessment and community ecology to environmental and technological problems. As a result, Shrader-Frechette's work addresses issues in nuclear ethics, environmental ethics, and the general ethics of technology.

BOOKS BY SHRADER-FRECHETTE

Environmental Ethics. (ed.) Boxwood 1991 $12.95. ISBN 0-940168-22-7. This cross between a monograph and a reader is composed of 12 chapters, each followed by readings, a third of which are, in fact, by the author.

Nuclear Energy and Ethics. (ed.) Wrld. Coun. Churches 1991 o.p. A collection of 13 papers including also reports and appendices, from a WCC consultation in Kinshasa, Zaire, in 1989.

Nuclear Power and Public Policy: The Social and Ethical Problems of Fission Technology. Kluwer Ac. 1983 o.p. Covers reactor radiation emission standards and core meltdown dangers in relation to due process; nuclear waste disposal as exemplifying the argument from ignorance; the problem of externalities in nuclear economics; and unclear safety and the naturalistic fallacy. The best monograph on ethical issues related to nuclear power.

Policy for Land: Law and Ethics. (coauthored with Lynton K. Caldwell). Rowman 1993 $24.95. ISBN 0-8476-7779-6. Outlines a new national policy for land use and provides legal, political, and ethical justifications for proposed policies.

Risk Analysis and the Scientific Method: Methodological and Ethical Problems with Evaluating Societal Hazards. Kluwer Ac. 1985 o.p. Carries forward the analysis begun in *Science-Policy, Ethics, and Economic Methodology* into nonclassical methods for the assessment of social risks associated with the development of contemporary technologies.

Science Policy, Ethics, and Economic Methodology: Some Problems of Technology Assessment and Environmental Impact Analysis. Kluwer Ac. 1984 $92.00. ISBN 90-277-1806-7. A critical analysis of the classical economic methodologies that are used for formulating public policy, pointing up the ethical issues embedded in them, and looking for ways to improve them.

STONE, CHRISTOPHER. 1937–

Legal scholar and environmentalist Christopher Stone was born in New York City and educated at Harvard University and Yale University, where he received his law degree in 1962. A fellow in law and economics at the University of Chicago from 1962 to 1963, Stone then joined the law firm of Cravath, Swaine, and Moore. In 1965 he became associate professor of law at the University of Southern California and since 1969 has served as professor of law at the University of California at Los Angeles.

Stone's interests and writings have helped focus public attention on environmental law and the ethics of corporate practices concerning the environment. Two of his works in particular, *Should Trees Have Standing?* (1974) and *Where the Law Ends* (1975), were both highly controversial and received widespread publicity because of the strong advocacy positions they espoused. *Should Trees Have Standing?* was written as a rebuttal to the Supreme Court's ruling against the attempt by the Sierra Club to block the building of a recreational complex in a wilderness area of the Sierra Nevadas. In this work, Stone asserts that nature and natural objects can be regarded as subjects of legal rights. This unique argument was an early milestone in the emerging field of environmental law. In *Where the Law Ends*, Stone insists that the law must hold corporations fully accountable when they act irresponsibly, whether by producing faulty products or polluting the environment. To enforce such accountability, he argues that the courts can intrude into the internal affairs of a business and require changes in corporate policies and practices. His novel argument for the "social control" of corporate behavior had widespread impact on both corporate management and the law.

BOOKS BY STONE

Earth and Other Ethics. HarpC 1987 $19.95. ISBN 0-06-015731-3. Shows why traditional ethics and jurisprudence must be rethought. Argues for pluralism in ethics.

The Gnat is Older Than Man: Global Environment and the Human Agenda. Princeton U. Pr. 1993 $21.95. ISBN 0-691-03250-5. Contends that our environmental problems are real but often blown out of proportion, and that they are, in fact, treatable. Argues for a shift in focus from potential long-range problems to practical institutional reforms for current ills.

Law, Language, and Ethics. (coauthored with W. R. Bishin). Foundation Pr. 1972 o.p.

Should Trees Have Standing? 1974. Tioga Pub. Co. 1988 $7.95. ISBN 0-935382-69-0. Presents the classic argument that nonhuman entities have natural rights and therefore "standing" in a court of law.

Where the Law Ends: The Social Control of Corporate Behavior. 1975. HarpC 1978 $7.95. ISBN 0-06-131940-6

TELLER, EDWARD. 1908–

A prominent nuclear physicist and pragmatic advocate of political applications of scientific research, Edward Teller was a leading figure on the post-World War II international scene. Born in Budapest, Hungary, in his student years there he became friends with several young men who, like himself, were later to achieve fame in science and mathematics—Leo Szilard, EUGENE WIGNER, and JOHN VON NEUMANN.

In 1926, to escape anti-Semitism in his homeland, Teller went to Germany, where he enrolled at the Karlsruhe Institute of Technology for two years. He then attended the University of Munich and Leipzig University, where he received his Ph.D. in physical chemistry in 1930. From 1931 to 1933, he was research associate at the University of Göttingen. The following year, he attended the Institute of Theoretical Physics at the University of Copenhagen, where he studied under NIELS BOHR.

In 1935 Teller was appointed professor of physics at George Washington University in Washington, D.C., a position he maintained until 1946. While on leave during 1941–42, he served as professor at Columbia University in 1941. The year at Columbia was a significant one in Teller's life, for while there he made his "moral decision" to work on the atomic bomb project, and he also became an American citizen. While at Columbia, he worked with ENRICO FERMI on the problem of nuclear fission. He continued research on the atomic bomb at the University of Chicago from 1942 to 1943 and at the Los Alamos Scientific Laboratory in New Mexico from 1943 to 1944.

Present at the first experimental explosion of an atomic bomb at Alamogordo, New Mexico, a few weeks before the attack on Hiroshima, Teller searched his moral conscience, considering the implications of the research success he and his fellow scientists had achieved. In doing so, he became convinced that the

U.S. government's policy was morally justified, although he argued that the Japanese should be given an advance warning of the bomb.

Teller returned to the University of Chicago from 1946 to 1952 as professor of physics, but he was on leave much of the time at Los Alamos. His further research there helped develop the hydrogen bomb, which was authorized by President Truman as the superbomb needed to offset the Soviet Union's development of this weapon and to maintain a U.S.-Soviet nuclear balance in weaponry. Teller's work on the hydrogen bomb met strong opposition from J. ROBERT OPPENHEIMER and many other prominent scientists. Teller was not present when the United States successfully exploded the hydrogen bomb at Eniwetok in the Pacific on November 1, 1952. Although dubbed "the father of the H bomb," Teller believed that that title properly belonged to the entire team of scientists involved in its creation.

Teller's subsequent career was marked by a continuing split in the scientific community over the development of nuclear weapons. This schism deepened in 1954 when the government denied Oppenheimer security clearance in this field after hearings in which Teller testified against him. Oppenheimer was viewed by many as a martyr and Teller as his persecutor. Teller continued his work on government projects at the Lawrence Livermore Laboratory of the University of California, where he became director. He also was professor of physics at the University of California at Berkeley from 1953 to 1975 and then professor emeritus there. During the presidency of Ronald Reagan, Teller was a strong supporter of and adviser on the Strategic Defense Initiative, or "Star Wars" project, a project that again divided the scientific community and aroused partisan politics. Despite opposition, Teller forcefully argued his moral pragmatism, and he considered his position vindicated with the collapse of the Soviet Union in 1991.

BOOKS BY TELLER

Better a Shield Than a Sword: Perspectives on Defense and Technology. Free Pr. 1987 $27.95. ISBN 0-02-932461-0. Defends his role in the Manhattan Project and the aftermath of that atomic bomb project.
Energy from Heaven and Earth. W. H. Freeman 1979 $21.95. ISBN 0-7167-1063-3

BOOK ABOUT TELLER

Broad, William J. *Teller's War: The Top-Secret Story behind the Star Wars Deception.* S&S Trade 1993 $13.00. ISBN 0-671-86738-5. Critical look at Teller's role in the Strategic Defense Initiative (SDI), or "Star Wars" project of President Ronald Reagan.

THOREAU, HENRY DAVID. 1817–1862

[SEE Chapter 23 in this volume.]

VEATCH, ROBERT M. 1939–

Robert Veatch is currently a professor of medical ethics at the Kennedy Institute of Ethics and professor of philosophy at Georgetown University. For ten years previously, he was on the staff of the Hastings Center (formerly the Institute of Society, Ethics, and the Life Sciences). Veatch was born in Utica, New York, and received a B.S. degree from Purdue University (1961), an M.S. from the University of California at San Francisco (1962), and a B.D. (1964), M.A. (1970), and Ph.D. (1971) from Harvard University. A lecturer and writer, Veatch is the author of many important books on ethical issues in biology and medicine.

Veatch's areas of interest center on the relation of science to public policy, death and dying, and experimentation on human subjects. He has worked both to assemble numerous case studies and to advance general theoretical reflection in these areas. In *A Theory of Medical Ethics* (1981), he argues that current medical codes such as the Hippocratic Oath are too restrictive and lack sufficient support for comprehensive use in the medical profession. The solution, he argues, is that medicine can no longer be based on a professionally articulated code. Instead, Veatch proposes a "covenant" theory of medical ethics that resembles the traditional social contract of philosophers such as JOHN LOCKE (see Vol. 4), THOMAS HOBBES (see Vol. 4), and JEAN-JACQUES ROUSSEAU (see Vol. 4).

BOOKS BY VEATCH

Case Studies in Medical Ethics. HUP 1977 $35.00. ISBN 0-674-09932-X

Case Studies in Nursing Ethics. Lippincott 1987 o.p.

Cases in Bioethics: Selections from the Hastings Center Report. St. Martin 1993 $20.00. ISBN 0-312-06746-1. Edited by Veatch.

Cross Cultural Perspectives in Medical Ethics: Readings. Jones & Bartlett 1989 $33.75. ISBN 0-86720-075-8. A collection of historical and other readings is designed to complement the argument of *Medical Ethics.*

Death, Dying, and the Biological Revolution: Our Last Quest for Responsibility. Yale U. Pr. 1989 $17.00. ISBN 0-300-04365-7. The first edition of this book (1976) constituted Veatch's most general statement of medical ethics prior to *A Theory of Medical Ethics.* Written with the conviction "that the best hope for gaining insight into the complex dilemmas posed by the technological and biological revolution is an eclectic spirit combining contributions from many disciplines . . . I begin with a theoretical reflection . . . and move through a maze of technical, medical, and legal facts toward an examination of alternative public and personal policy."

The Foundations of Justice: Why the Retarded and the Rest of Us Have Claims to Equality. OUP 1986. ISBN 0-19-504076-7

Life Span: Values and Life-Extending Technologies. HarpC 1979 o.p. Edited by Veatch, these articles address the implications of new technologies that are vastly increasing people's life span through enhanced medical techniques, drugs, and genetic intervention. Gives guidelines for weighing the ethical and social questions of medical technology and points to the consideration of values that these choices pose.

Medical Ethics. Jones & Bartlett 1989 $41.25. ISBN 0-86720-074-X. An original collection of essays, edited by Veatch, on the main themes in medical ethics: normative principles, concepts of health and disease, the physician-patient relationship, limiting procreation, human experimentation, informed consent, genetics and reproductive technologies, organ transplantation, psychiatry, resource allocation, death and dying.

The Patient as Partner: A Theory of Human-Experimentation Ethics. Ind. U. Pr. 1987 $29.95. ISBN 0-253-35725-X. Presents the idea of partnership as a model for understanding the lay-professional relationship.

The Patient-Physician Relation: The Patient as Partner, Part 2. Ind. U. Pr. 1991 $27.50. ISBN 0-253-36207-5. Extends the argument of *The Patient as Partner* from research to clinical medicine.

A Theory of Medical Ethics. 1981. Basic 1983 $9.95. ISBN 0-465-08439-7. Criticizes paternalism and argues that the theory of a social contract among equals produces the best medical decisions. Provides a general theory for *The Patient as Partner* and *The Patient-Physician Relation.*

WEIZENBAUM, JOSEPH. 1923–

Born in Berlin, Germany, Joseph Weizenbaum immigrated to the United States as a child. He is among the world's foremost computer scientists, as well as a pioneer in the field of computer ethics. An outspoken critic of overdependence on and misuse of powerful new computers, Weizenbaum claims that individual privacy is being depleted rapidly by the computer revolution. He also is concerned about the increasing role of computer technology in warfare and claims that computers have made combat more deadly and potentially catastrophic. Weizenbaum worked for General Electric as a computer systems engineer in the late 1950s and early 1960s, before becoming an instructor in the Department of Computer Science at MIT in 1963. In 1970 he was appointed professor of computer science and engineering at MIT and also became editor of the *International Journal of Man-Machine Studies*. In his published work, Weizenbaum emphasizes the dangers associated with substituting computer technology for human to human contact in counseling, legal situations, and language translation. In 1973 Weizenbaum was honored as the Vinton Hays Senior Research Fellow at Harvard University.

BOOK BY WEIZENBAUM

Computer Power and Human Reason: From Judgment to Calculation. W. H. Freeman 1976 $14.95. ISBN 0-7167-0463-3. A basic introduction to how computers work, followed by a critical analysis of their social uses. Argues that there are some things that computers should not be allowed to do.

WHITE, LYNN, JR. 1907–

[SEE Chapter 3 in this volume.]

WINNER, LANGDON. 1944–

Langdon Winner spent his youth in the then agricultural San Luis Obispo on the California coast. His article "The Whale and the Reactor" relates a childhood experience of technological "progress" in the 1950s and early 1960s and the coming "freeways, supermarkets, jet airplanes, television, guided missiles . . . computers, prefabricated houses . . . plastics." Also formative in the development of his interest in the controlling nature of technology were experiences as an undergraduate summer intern systems analyst at the Pentagon and as an observer of the student rebellions at the University of California at Berkeley during the mid-1960s, where he received his Ph.D. in political science.

Winner's first book, *Autonomous Technology* (1977), considers the thesis that we do not control or form technologies but that technologies shape cultural and social activities. All spheres of human activity, from workplace and politics to personal relations, have been restructured to accommodate technical innovations and the myth of "progress."

Many of Winner's articles, published during the 1980s and collected in *The Whale and the Reactor* (1988), expand on this thesis in relation to specific technologies. "Do Artifacts Have Politics?" argues that certain technologies have inherent political traits, which are generally authoritative and centralized rather than democratic and individualistic. "Mythinformation" looks at the computer revolution and the politics that sold it to the world as a "democratic" force. "On Not Hitting the Tar-Baby" evaluates the practice of risk assessment and finds that it is designed to support new technologies, to complicate risk indicators, and to sustain the industrial status quo.

Currently, Winner is professor of political science at Rensselaer Polytechnic Institute. He also writes a regular column on "The Culture of Technology" for *Technology Review*.

BOOKS BY WINNER

Autonomous Technology: Technics-Out-of-Control as a Theme in Political Thought. MIT
    Pr. 1977 $12.95. ISBN 0-262-73049-9. Argues that technological change is out of
    human control and hence the political sphere is now being shaped by the needs of
    technological activity. Ordered progress is a myth, and innovation is moving in many
    directions toward highly uncertain destinations. The nature of technological effort
    has caused a complete restructuring of the work, political, and social environments
    to accommodate technological rather than social goals.
Democracy in a Technological Society. (ed.) *Philosophy and Technology Ser.* Kluwer Ac.
    1992 $89.00. ISBN 0-7923-1995-8. A collection of 13 papers from a 1989 conference,
    which focuses on technology and democratic values. Winner provides a good
    introduction to the issues.
The Whale and the Reactor: A Search for Limits in an Age of High Technology. U. Ch. Pr.
    1988 $9.95. ISBN 0-226-90211-0. Largely a collection of Winner's previously
    published and influential articles, this volume provides guidance in looking beyond
    the facts of objects of technologies to study their politics and to develop the wisdom
    of placing limits on the technologically possible.

CHAPTER 6

Science, Technology, and Society

Judith A. Adams and Stephen H. Cutcliffe

> [T]echnics . . . does not form an independent system, like the universe: it exists as an element in human culture and it promises well or ill as the social groups that exploit it promise well or ill.
> —LEWIS MUMFORD, *Technics and Civilization*

> If one observes how thoroughly our lives are shaped by interconnected systems of modern technology, how strongly we feel their influence, respect their authority and participate in their workings, one begins to understand that, like it or not, we have become members of a new order in human history.
> —LANGDON WINNER, *The Whale and the Reactor*

LEWIS MUMFORD's early recognition that technology "exists as an element in human culture" presaged our contemporary understanding that science, technology, and medicine are processes driven primarily by value judgments separate from the scientific- and technical-knowledge bases on which they draw. Science and technology also have societal impacts affecting human values. These societal impacts are reflected in cultural, political, and economic institutions, thereby forming a dynamic relationship of constant and complex recursive interactions. The academic study of this complex set of relationships has coalesced as the field of Science, Technology, and Society (STS) studies. STS is now a recognized field of graduate study and is widely diffused in undergraduate curriculums and in kindergarten-through-grade-12 education. STS also is making inroads, although more slowly, in the policy arena. For the past two decades, STS has been used by educators to raise our collective social consciousness regarding the complexity of relationships among science, technology, and society.

STS emerged in consort with, and in many ways out of, the widespread social upheavals of the 1960s and early 1970s. Simultaneously, cognate changes in several academic fields also took place. In large part, this approach evolved out of the work of THOMAS S. KUHN, especially his book *The Structure of Scientific Revolutions* (1962–70). It began to come together as historians, sociologists, and philosophers of science and technology increasingly moved away from internalist-oriented subdisciplines to progressively more externalist or "contextual" interpretations. As STS evolved, its central focus became the analysis and explication of science and technology as complex "social constructs" encompassing many political, ethical, and general theoretical questions.

The STS field approaches its subject matter from an interdisciplinary perspective, as well as from a variety of specific disciplinary perspectives, including history, philosophy, and ethics (as surveyed in Chapters 3, 4, and 5) as well as the social sciences. More specific contributions to the field of science, technology, and society come from science and technology policy studies,

147

gender studies, studies of science, technology, and art, and of science, technology, and religion (see chapter 7). In summary, the study of science, technology, and society is a broad and multifaceted field.

There are three main interdisciplinary research and educational approaches to STS. They are Science, Technology, and Public Policy; Science and Technology Studies; and Science, Technology, and Society programs. The Science, Technology, and Public Policy (STPP) approach is professionally oriented, focusing on analyses of large-scale sociotechnical interactions and their management. STPP has a strong scientific and technical orientation, stressing the need for training in appropriate policy and management fields. In contrast to the more career-oriented focus of the STPP approach, Science and Technology studies involve more theoretical investigations into the social and cultural context of science and technology, and how they function as social processes. Here, the interest is primarily explanatory and interpretive, an approach Steve Fuller has referred to as "High Church" in his book *Philosophy, Rhetoric, and the End of Knowledge: The Coming of Science and Technology Studies* (1993). He perceives Science, Technology, and Society (STS) programs as the more problem centered, social-activist oriented, or "Low Church." The STS approach arose out of the late 1960s and early 1970s concern for needed changes in undergraduate education. STS courses and programs emphasize general education for intelligent responsible citizenship in an increasingly scientific-technological society, scientific and technological literacy for practical citizenship, and the contextual analysis of science and technology.

STS examines the complexities of science and technology by noting their positive and negative (both expected and unexpected) impacts. This is accomplished by analyzing the modes by which scientists and engineers conduct their work, by scrutinizing the ways in which societal institutions (governmental, industrial, economic, communications, academic) employ science and technology to shape the environment, and by suggesting mechanisms for greater control over the scientific and technological process. Although sometimes "critical" of science and technology, STS is not "anti" science and technology. To perceive a critical approach as totally negative is somewhat akin to calling art critics "anti-art" (LANGDON WINNER, *The Whale and the Reactor*).

An extensive literature of monographs, journals, and other materials has evolved, which illuminates the societal context and complexities of science and technology. This chapter features interdisciplinary books that deal with science and technology in the context of societal values. It includes important works in the sociology of science and technology, which are critical to understanding how scientific knowledge, technological artifacts, and systems are "socially constructed." Much of the STS literature is found in periodicals. For that reason, several anthologies that contain important essays have been included. The goal of this chapter is to provide the reader with a cross section and balance of statements on specific issues, general attitudes, and theoretical approaches to STS studies.

OVERVIEWS AND REFERENCE WORKS

The titles in this section are overviews of science, technology, and society written from the unified perspective of a single author, and they are suggested as useful introductions to the field or as basic texts. Obviously, many titles in the

"General Bibliography" section and in the lists of books that accompany profiled authors could also function in similar or complementary capacities.

Cutcliffe, Stephen H., Judith A. Mistichelli, and Christine M. Roysdon. *Technology and Values in American Civilization: A Guide to Information Sources. Amer. Information Guide Ser.* Gale 1980 $68.00. ISBN 0-8103-1475-4. Presents an extensive interdisciplinary bibliography of more than 2,400 annotated entries covering both books and articles concerning the interactions of human values and technology.

Durbin, Paul T., ed. *A Guide to the Culture of Science, Technology, and Medicine.* Free Pr. rev. ed. 1984 o.p. Presents a useful guide to the field that includes descriptive essays on the history, philosophy, and sociology of science, technology, and medicine as well as a chapter on science and technology policy; extensive unannotated bibliographies supplement each chapter.

McGee, David. *Science in Society: An Annotated Guide to Resources.* Wall & Thompson 1989 o.p. Offers a brief introductory guide designed for students; divided into four sections: the nature of science, the nature of technology, humans in the environment, and current issues in science.

McGinn, Robert E. *Science, Technology and Society.* P-H 1991 $21.50. ISBN 0-13-794736-1. Argues that while science and technology are causative agents of social change, they also "exist and unfold in rich social contexts"; written by a philosopher.

Markert, Linda Rae. *Contemporary Technology: Innovations, Issues, and Perspectives.* Goodheart 1989 $30.00. ISBN 0-87006-730-3. Introductory work designed to increase awareness of technology's pervasive nature, covering both the promises and uncertainties associated with technology; includes topics such as genetic engineering, artificial intelligence, space exploration, medicine, manufacturing technology transfer, energy, environment, military defense, and social response to and responsibility for technological change.

Spieger-Rosing, Ina, and Derek de Solla Price, eds. *Science, Technology and Society: A Cross-Disciplinary Perspective.* 1977 o.p. Offers a significant collection of original papers on contextual values of science and technology, social studies of science and technology, and science-policy studies; includes useful bibliographies.

Volti, Rudi. *Society and Technological Change.* St. Martin 1992 $19.35. ISBN 0-312-05664-8. Easy-to-read work covering themes such as technology-society interactions, process of technological innovation, work, communications, military technology, and the politics of technology, including its control and regulation.

Webster, Andrew. *Science, Technology, and Society: New Directions.* Rutgers U. Pr. 1991 $36.00. ISBN 0-8135-1722-2. Presents an overview of new developments in science and technology and in the sociological study of them. Webster argues that the sociology of science and technology can help shape or enlighten the policy-making process.

Westrum, Ron. *Technologies and Societies: The Shaping of People and Things.* Wadsworth Pub. 1991 $24.50. ISBN 0-534-13644-3. An excellent work by a sociologist of science and technology that focuses on the mutual shaping of science and technology or how they intertwine; two chapters on the idea of technology "sponsorship," the social groups and institutions that "push along" certain technologies are especially interesting.

GENERAL BIBLIOGRAPHY

This listing includes representative relevant works from a number of disciplines, especially from the sociology of science and technology, as well as works that take a broad interdisciplinary perspective. Such a general bibliography readily blends into, and overlaps with, more disciplinary works (see Chapters 3, 4, and 5) and more specialized but interdisciplinary studies (see Chapter 7).

Adams, James L. *Flying Buttresses, Entropy and O-Rings: The World of an Engineer.* HUP 1991 $24.95. ISBN 0-674-30688-0. Presents a clearly written description of the role of an engineer in a broad societal context.

Agassi, Joseph. *Science and Society: Selected Essays in the Sociology of Science.* Kluwer Ac. 1981 $126.00. ISBN 90-277-1244-1. Presents 34 essays on scientific methodology, the nature of scientific revolutions, scientific discovery, science and culture, scientific publishing, science and religion, and science and technocracy.

———. *Technology: Philosophical and Social Aspects.* Kluwer Ac. 1985 $87.00. ISBN 90-277-2044-4. Offers a philosophical analysis of technology in which Agassi argues for a harmonization of social and physical technology involving broad public participation in the political process. "In brief, this book is meant to be one small addition to the campaign for the intensification of the search for better tools for the democratic control of technology."

Barnes, Barry. *About Science.* Blackwell Pubs. 1985 $39.95. ISBN 0-631-14157-X. Examines "science as an activity, the way science is ordered and organized, and particularly the relationship of science to the rest of society." Barnes refutes a simplistic notion of "technological determinism," suggesting that science and technology should be understood in the social context that engenders them.

Barnes, Barry, and David Edge, eds. *Science in Context: Readings in the Sociology of Science.* Taylor & Francis 1982 $32.50. ISBN 0-335-10054-6. Addresses five themes: scientific communication, scientific knowledge, science-technology interplay, the interaction of science and society, and science as expertise; written by scientists of the past, contemporary sociologists of science, and popular writers.

Bauer, Henry H. *Scientific Literacy and the Myth of the Scientific Method.* U. of Ill. Pr. 1992 $24.95. ISBN 0-252-01856-7. Debunks traditional positivist notions of the scientific method; written in response to recent calls for enhancing the public's scientific literacy.

Bell, Daniel. *Coming of Post-Industrial Society: A Venture in Social Forecasting.* Basic 1976 $17.00. ISBN 0-465-09713-8. Examines changes in the social framework of the United States caused by the transformation from a manufacturing society to an information society. Discusses how the preeminent position of industries relying on science and technology generates a technical elite that holds a central position in the political process, creating tension between populism and elitism.

Ben-David, Joseph. *Scientific Growth: Essays on the Social Organization and Ethos of Science.* Ed. by Gad Freudenthal. U. CA Pr. 1991 $60.00. ISBN 0-520-06925-0. Reveals how the author's historical approach to science, which focuses on the institutional factors integrating the social system of science, is actually compatible with contemporary emphases on the "extrascientific social contexts in which knowledge is produced."

———. *The Scientist's Role in Society: A Comparative Study.* U. Ch. Pr. 1984 2nd ed. $20.00. ISBN 0-226-04227-8. Presents a classic analysis of the transformation of the scientist from a leisured amateur (seventeenth century) to an academic professor (eighteenth and nineteenth centuries) to a member of an institutional or industrial team (twentieth century); states that recognition of these historical changes is crucial insofar as responsibility is related to a social role.

Bereano, Philip L., ed. *Technology as a Social and Political Phenomenon.* Bks. Demand repr. of 1976 ed. $144.10. ISBN 0-318-34745-8. Offers a collection of essays about general and theoretical concepts regarding the relationship between technology and society, essays are classified into seven themes: the nature of technology; technology and social change; technology and values; on being a technocrat and the alternatives; defining the problem; technology: the past and the future; and technological planning: the politics of choice.

Bijker, Wiebe E., and John Law, eds. *Shaping Technology/Building Society: Studies in Sociotechnical Change. Inside Technology Ser.* MIT Pr. 1992 $29.95. ISBN 0-262-02338-5. Offers 12 essays that extend and build upon Bijker and others' earlier *Social Construction of Technological Systems;* contributes toward development of a theory explaining how technologies become "stabilized" and take on "accepted" forms.

Bijker, Wiebe E., Thomas P. Hughes, and Trevor J. Pinch, eds. *The Social Construction of Technological Systems: New Directions in the Sociology and History of Technology.* MIT Pr. 1987 $13.95. ISBN 0-262-52137-7. Presents a collection of essays written by sociologists and historians of science and technology; attempts to conceptualize an integrated approach to the study of science and technology by discussing three trends in analysis: the "social constructivist" approach, a "systems metaphor," and the "actor-network" perspective.

Bleier, Ruth, ed. *Feminist Approaches to Science.* Pergamon 1986 $36.50. ISBN 0-08-032787-7. Features nine essays that examine "the nature of contemporary science and [attempt] to extend our visions toward a science that is different, better, feminist, and emancipating" (Preface).

Bloor, David. *Knowledge and Social Imagery.* U. Ch. Pr. 1991 $32.00. ISBN 0-226-06096-9. Supports a relativistic view of science, in which knowledge claims will embody, or reflect, social and political interests; Bloor is a proponent of the so-called "strong programme," or the Edinburgh School.

Brante, Thomas, Steve Fuller, and William Lynch, eds. *Controversial Science: From Content to Contention.* Science, Technology, and Society Ser. State U. NY Pr. 1993 $59.50. ISBN 0-7914-1473-6. Offers a collection of essays that examine alternative perspectives on the constructivist view of science and technology.

Brown, Lester R. *Building a Sustainable Society.* Norton 1981 $11.95. ISBN 0-393-30027-7. Presents a prescriptive outline of the steps to a sustainable society, in order to describe its essential character and provide direction for planners; Brown claims that creating such a society will require fundamental economic and social changes that will affect all aspects of human existence.

Chalk, Rosemary. *Science, Technology, and Society: Emerging Relationships.* Amer. Assoc. for the Advancement of Science 1988 $19.95. ISBN 0-087168-332-6. A collection of articles, editorials, and other brief pieces dealing with science, society, and value issues. Articles were originally published in *Science* magazine.

Cheek, Dennis W. *Thinking Constructively about Science, Technology, and Society Education.* Curriculum Issues and Inquiries Ser. State U. NY Pr. 1992 $49.50. ISBN 0-7914-0939-2. Presents a comprehensive analysis of STS education in the United States; concludes with a model for curriculum development in kindergarten through grade 12.

Chubin, Daryl E., and Edward J. Hackett. *Peerless Science: Peer Review and U.S. Science Policy.* State U. NY Pr. 1990 $64.50. ISBN 0-7914-0309-2. Examines the role of peer review in the governance of science and how it affects the relationship between the scientific and policy communities; argues that U. S. science cannot afford to conduct business as usual.

Chubin, Daryl E., and Ellen W. Chu, eds. *Science Off the Pedestal: Social Perspectives on Science and Technology.* Wadsworth Pub. 1989 $19.50. ISBN 0-534-09858-4. Designed as a textbook for undergraduate or graduate courses, science and technology are presented in a holistic framework as social phenomena influenced by cultural forces as well as economic, national, professional, and personal interests; includes the views of an academic social scientist and a biologist/science editor.

Collins, Harry M. *Changing Order: Replication and Induction in Scientific Practice.* Sage 1985 $47.50. ISBN 0-8039-9757-4. Examines the issue of replication of scientific findings in respect to analyzing the negotiation over what constitutes acceptable scientific knowledge; uses three cases: building TEA-lasers, gravitational-radiation detection, and paranormal experiments.

Cozzens, Susan E., and Thomas F. Gieryn, eds. *Theories of Science in Society.* Science, Technology, and Society Ser. Ind. U. Pr. 1990 $25.00. ISBN 0-253-31471-2. Demonstrates that the internalist-externalist dichotomy between science and society does not exist. The contributors (all sociologists of science) describe the theoretical basis of their thinking about science in society; their theories are then applied to concrete examples, such as pure mathematics, power in science, innovation, reproductive science, and the politics of knowledge.

Cutcliffe, Stephen H., Steven L. Goldman, Manuel Medina, and José Sanmartín, eds. *New Worlds, New Technologies, New Issues. Research in Technology Studies.* Lehigh Univ. Pr. 1992 $36.50. ISBN 0-934223-24-6. Addresses the cultural worlds that crystalize around new technologies, the democratic and political challenges posed by these technologies, and the public response and responsibility for precipitating new social and moral issues.

Dickson, David. *The New Politics of Science.* U. Ch. Pr. 1988 repr. of 1984 ed. $14.95. ISBN 0-226-14763-0. Examines the patterns of control over science; determines that decision-making power is concentrated in a class of corporate, banking, military, and university leaders who use this control for political as well as economic objectives. Describes how the removal of science policy from direct democratic control has been assisted by measures such as tax incentives, patent reform, and links between universities and business.

――――. *The Politics of Alternative Technology.* Universe 1977 $7.00. ISBN 0-87663-917-1. Interprets technological change as a political process; argues that the problems associated with technology result from social and political factors as well as the nature of technology. Claims that alternative technologies only can be developed within the framework of an alternative society.

Dubos, Rene. *So Human an Animal.* Macmillan 1968 $10.95. ISBN 0-684-71753-0. Examines the effects of the external world (not only the natural environment but also technologies, cities, and social attitudes) on a person's physical and mental health; concludes that a holistic understanding of environmental effects on human health and development provides a rational basis for resolving problems, especially the consequences of technology.

Durbin, Paul T., ed. *Critical Perspectives on Nonacademic Science and Engineering. Research in Technology Studies.* Lehigh Univ. Pr. 1991 $45.00. ISBN 0-934223-15-7. Features 11 philosophical essays that examine the daily work of scientists and engineers; contrasts the actual work of scientists to the abstract concept traditionally promoted.

――――. *Social Responsibility in Science, Technology, and Medicine.* Lehigh Univ. Pr. 1992 $31.50. ISBN 0-934223-27-0. Argues that social problems related to science, technology, and medicine can be resolved through engaged social activism; offers an excellent summary of Durbin's ideas.

Durning, Alan T. *How Much Is Enough? The Consumer Society and the Future of the Earth.* Norton 1992 $19.95. ISBN 0-393-03383-X. Focuses on rampant consumerism in the United States, typified by Bloomington, Minnesota's Mall of America; argues for a curtailment of consumption.

Elliott, Brian, ed. *Technology and Social Process.* Edinburgh U. Pr. 1988 o.p. Features eight essays by such major scholars as Tom Hughes, Bruno Latour, John Law, Trevor Pinch, and Donald Mackenzie that resulted from joint seminars on technological and social change at Edinburgh University and Queen's University.

Feenberg, Andrew. *Critical Theory of Technology.* OUP 1991 $35.00. ISBN 0-19-506854-8. Refutes the non-neutrality of technology while rejecting a simplistic either/or tradeoff between technology and human values; Feenberg argues that democratic reform of a technological society is possible.

Ferkiss, Victor. *Nature, Technology, and Society: Cultural Roots of the Current Environmental Crisis.* NYU Pr. 1993 $40.00. ISBN 0-8147-2611-9. Chronicles Eastern and Western cultural attitudes toward nature and technology from antiquity to the present; examines feminist, "green," and Marxist approaches related to the impact of various technologies on the environment.

Fuchs, Stephan. *The Professional Quest for Truth: A Social Theory of Science and Knowledge.* State U. NY Pr. 1992 $59.50. ISBN 0-7914-0923-6. Focuses on the scientific discipline as an organization encompassing the universities and laboratories in which scientists work and describes a framework of the social determinants of scientific production; refines an organizational theory of the sciences embracing laboratory life, scientific discourse, innovation, technology, and scientific controversy.

Fuller, Steve, and others, eds. *The Cognitive Turn: Sociological and Psychological Perspectives on Science. Sociology of the Sciences Ser.* Kluwer Ac. 1989 $84.00. ISBN 0-7923-0306-7. Presents selected papers from a 1987 conference that examined the different approaches of sociologists and psychologists of science.

_____. *Philosophy, Rhetoric and the End of Knowledge: The Coming of Science and Technology Studies. Rhetoric of the Human Sciences Ser.* U. of Wis. Pr. 1993 $54.00. ISBN 0-299-13770-8. Views the field of Science and Technology Studies as a way to break down the artificial barriers between disciplines and the rhetorical components of scientific-knowledge production; Fuller considers his approach as "social epistemology."

_____. *Philosophy of Science and Its Discontents. The Conduct of Science Ser.* Guilford Pr. 1992 $18.95. ISBN 0-89862-020-1. Features an up-to-date normative philosophical approach to the psychology and sociology of science; includes Fuller's "map of the field," a question-and-answer response to his critics, and a useful bibliography.

_____. *Social Epistemology. Science, Technology, and Society Ser.* Ind. U. Pr. 1988 $35.00. ISBN 0-253-35227-4. Argues that understanding the sciences requires recognizing the historical, social, and especially the "political" environments in which research is created; seeks to reconcile normative philosophy with empirical sociology in what Fuller calls "social epistemology," thereby enhancing communications between academic disciplines.

Galison, Peter. *How Experiments End.* U. Ch. Pr. 1987 $39.95. ISBN 0-226-27914-6. Offers a historical study of high-energy physics; focuses on the laboratory to determine how scientists develop and conclude a persuasive argument.

Gendron, Bernard. *Technology and the Human Condition.* St. Martin 1976 $18.65. ISBN 0-312-78925-4. Presents a critical review of three perspectives on the social role of technology: utopian, dystopian, and socialist; questions whether technology's impact is harmful or beneficial; concludes that the socialist perspective is most compelling, with the potential for societal benefit depending on optimum political conditions.

Gholson, Barry, and others, eds. *Psychology of Science: Contributions to Metascience.* Cambridge U. Pr. 1989 $64.95. ISBN 0-521-35410-2. Presents 16 essays that examine science from a psychological perspective; concludes with "A Preliminary Agenda for the Psychology of Science."

Gilbert, G. Nigel, and Michael Mulkay. *Opening Pandora's Box: A Sociological Analysis of Scientists' Discourse.* Cambridge U. Pr. 1984 o.p. Presents an investigation of the variability and conflicting motivations in scientific discourse by examining materials from practitioners in biochemical research. Rather than establishing a systematic set of concepts that govern scientific discourse the authors document various methods and forces that affect such communication.

Goldman, Steven L., ed. *Competitiveness in American Society. Research in Technology Studies.* Lehigh Univ. Pr. 1993 $39.50. ISBN 0-934223-28-9. Features 10 essays that examine the issue of competitiveness; discusses its meaning and implications as well as its economic, institutional, and social values.

_____. *Science, Technology, and Social Progress. Research in Technology Studies.* Lehigh Univ. Pr. 1989 $42.50. ISBN 0-934223-05-X. Features 12 essays that examine the traditional premise that associates science and technology with progress—from the perspective of related societal values.

Gorman, Michael E. *Simulating Science: Heuristics, Mental Models, and Technoscientific Thinking. Science, Technology, and Society Ser.* Ind. U. Pr. 1992 $45.00. ISBN 0-253-32608-7. A psychologist subjects his research program on the cognitive processes associated with scientific processes to reflexive scrutiny; claims that to understand techno-scientific thinking one must transcend traditional disciplinary and methodological ideologies.

Greenberg, Mark L., and Lance Schachterle, eds. *Literature and Technology. Research in Technology Studies.* Lehigh Univ. Pr. 1992 $45.00. ISBN 0-934223-20-3. Features 10 essays that examine technology as reflected by and revealed through literature; investigates such major authors as Chaucer, Blake, Romains, Pynchon, and Prigogine.

Grinnell, Frederick. *The Scientific Attitude. The Conduct of Science Ser.* Guilford Pr. 1992 $16.95. ISBN 0-89862-018-X. Presents the basic cognitive and social features of science in order to understand them in terms of daily practice.

Gross, Alan G. *The Rhetoric of Science.* HUP 1990 $29.95. ISBN 0-674-76873-6. Offers a rhetorical analysis of scientific texts, concluding that science is speculative knowledge and a matter of persuasion.

Harding, Sandra. *The Science Question in Feminism.* Cornell Univ. Pr. 1986 $11.95. ISBN 0-8014-9363-3. Examines major trends in feminist critiques of science and its culture; identifies inadequacies, tensions, obstacles, and gaps in these critiques in order to transform them into more powerful tools for the construction of emancipatory meanings and practices.

———. *Whose Science? Whose Knowledge? Thinking from Women's Lives.* Cornell Univ. Pr. 1991 $34.50. ISBN 0-8014-2513-1. Examines feminist theories about the methodology and epistemology of the natural and social sciences; emphasizes that scientists must be aware of the biases that influence their research and claims that new processes should be developed using the perspectives and insights of dominated groups.

Hardison, O. B., Jr. *Disappearing Through the Skylight: Culture and Technology in the Twentieth Century.* Viking Penguin 1990 $14.00. ISBN 0-14-011582-X. Argues that science and technology have an influence on modern culture; describes how forms of art, music, literature—even the way we perceive humanity—are disappearing "through the skylight."

Hickman, Larry, ed. *Technology as a Human Affair.* McGraw 1990 $19.32. ISBN 0-07-028688-4. Presents a diverse range of essays by philosophers, humanists, and social scientists; designed for classroom use.

Hopper, David H. *Technology and the Idea of Progress.* Westminster John Knox 1991 $14.95. ISBN 0-664-25203-6. Examines technology from a theological perspective, questioning the frequent equation of technology and progress; claims that if society is to regain a Christian "purpose of community building," there must be a "critical distancing" in public understanding of, and a corresponding increased involvement with, technology.

Keller, Evelyn Fox. *Reflections on Gender and Science.* 1985. Yale U. Pr. 1986 $9.95. ISBN 0-300-03636-1. Presents nine essays that examine the network of gender associations in the structure of scientific ideology and practice; divided into four perspectives: historical, psychoanalytic, scientific, and philosophical; the basic premise being that gender and science are socially constructed categories.

———. *Secrets of Life, Secrets of Death: Essays on Language, Gender, and Science.* Routledge 1992 $49.95. ISBN 0-415-90524-9. Presents a collection of Keller's recent essays on the role of language in science and how feminist theory, the insights of historians and philosophers of science, and the accomplishments of working scientists can be integrated.

Kidder, Tracy. *Soul of a New Machine.* Avon 1990 repr. of 1982 ed. $9.95. ISBN 0-380-71115-X. Explores the close-knit working relations of a group of engineers in this study of the development of a new super minicomputer at Data General in the late 1970s; describes the competition, obsession, camaraderie, and unique managerial and technical talents involved in high-pressure, high-tech projects.

Kipnis, David. *Technology and Power.* Spr.-Verlag 1990 $36.00. ISBN 0-387-97082-7. Demonstrates how technology changes social relations by examining managers and employees, physicians and patients, colonialists and native populations; shows how technological changes interact with psychological processes to transform such social values as the reduction of individual autonomy.

Knorr-Cetina, Karin, and Michael Mulkay, eds. *Science Observed: New Perspectives on the Social Study of Science.* Sage 1983 o.p. Features essays that discuss new empirical approaches to the sociology of science; focuses on scientific discourse and on the science laboratory to study the sociology and ethnography of scientific work.

Kraft, Michael E., and Norman J. Vig, eds. *Technology and Politics.* Duke 1988 $59.75. ISBN 0-8223-0838-X. Presents 14 essays that explore the governing of technology, such as philosophical discussions about whether technologies become a determining force in society or whether they should be considered instruments for problem solving, the regulation of technology, and the methodologies that should be applied to assess technological risks; addresses the adequacy of institutions to make public decisions and the role of the citizenry in respect to risky or personal technologies.

Kuhn, Thomas S. *The Structure of Scientific Revolutions. Foundations of the Unity of Science Ser.* U. Ch. Pr. 1970 $19.95. ISBN 0-226-45803-2. Scrutinizes how the scientific establishment reacts to anomalies that subvert the existing tradition of scientific practice; focuses special attention on the roles of apparently arbitrary or accidental personal, cultural, and historical elements in scientific revolutions.

LaFollette, Marcel C. *Stealing into Print: Fraud, Plagiarism and Misconduct in Scientific Publishing.* U. CA Pr. 1992 $30.00. ISBN 0-520-07831-4. Focuses on how recent revelations of scientific fraud have affected the communication practices and policies of scientific journals that disseminate research findings; claims that the issue of fraud "revolves ultimately around the concepts of *autonomy* and accountability . . . which are currently set in tension."

Lawless, Edward W. *Technology and Social Shock.* Rutgers U. Pr. 1977 $20.00. ISBN 0-8135-0781-2. Presents 45 case studies that examine "episodes of public alarm over technology-social shock" (Preface). Each case study provides an abstract of the events, author's comment, and references; final overview describes characteristics and commonalities of the case studies.

Lewenstein, Bruce V., ed. *When Science Meets the Public.* AAAS 1992 $18.00. ISBN 0-87168-440-5. Presents the proceedings of a 1991 AAAS workshop devoted to public understanding of science and technology.

Longino, Helen E. *Science as Social Knowledge: Values and Objectivity in Scientific Inquiry.* Princeton U. Pr. 1990 $35.00. ISBN 0-691-07342-2. Offers a good analysis of the supposed value-free nature of scientific inquiry, incorporates feminist theory to develop a view that reconciles the objectivity of science with its social construction, which Longino calls "contextual empiricism"; draws on research in the fields of human evolution and alleged gender differences.

Lowrance, William W. *Of Acceptable Risk: Science and the Determination of Safety.* Kaufmann 1976 o.p. Based on the premise that "risks to health and safety are becoming more acute in nature and degree," the book reviews the processes by which policy decisions on safety are reached; illustrated by a case study of DDT.

Mackenzie, Donald, and Judy Wajcman, eds. *The Social Shaping of Technology: How the Refrigerator Got Its Hum.* Taylor & Francis 1985 $69.00. ISBN 0-335-15027-6. Focuses on "the *social* factors that shape technological change;" begins with several general essays on this theme and concludes with sections devoted to production, domestic, and military technology.

Mayo, Deborah G., and Rachelle D. Hollander, eds. *Acceptable Evidence: Science and Values in Risk Management. Environmental Ethics and Science Policy Studies.* OUP 1991 $35.00. ISBN 0-19-506372-4. Presents 12 essays on the ethical and value-laden nature of assessing scientific evidence and evaluating risk.

Mazur, Allan. *The Dynamics of Technical Controversy.* Broadcasting Pubns. 1981 o.p. Identifies a general "life cycle" for controversies such as the antiballistic missile, fluoridation, and nuclear power; claims that technology-based controversies can be extremely useful for society by providing an effective means for identifying and evaluating the problems and advantages of technologies which are not always in clear view.

Meehan, Richard. *Getting Sued and Other Tales of the Engineering Life.* MIT Pr. 1981 $11.95. ISBN 0-262-63089-3. Captures the essence and spirit of the civil engineer through a series of autobiographical anecdotes; traces Meehan's career from his MIT student days through dam-building projects in Thailand and Chile to getting sued for his role in the construction of a California high school. Revealing and good reading at the same time.

Merton, Robert K. *The Sociology of Science: Theoretical and Empirical Investigations.* Ed. by Norman Storer. U. Ch. Pr. 1979 repr. of 1973 ed. $15.95. ISBN 0-226-52092-7.

Presents a chronological collection of Merton's significant papers on the social and cultural context of science; includes the reward system, normative structure, process of evaluation, and the sociology of knowledge.

Mesthene, Emanuel G. *Technological Change: Its Impact on Man and Society. Studies in Technology and Society.* HUP 1970 o.p. Based on his experience with the Harvard Program on Technology and Society, Mesthene argues that technology is a "neutral" force that can be used for good or harm. Mesthene is regarded as a conservative spokesperson in favor of technology's potential for good rather than for harm.

Morone, Joseph G., and Edward J. Woodhouse. *Averting Catastrophe: Strategies for Regulating Risky Technologies.* U. CA Pr. 1986 $34.95. ISBN 0-520-05723-6. Examines case studies that describe how certain technological risks such as toxic chemicals, nuclear power, recombinant DNA research, threats to the ozone layer, and the greenhouse effect are currently being handled. Suggests that the basic elements of a system for averting catastrophe—protection against severe risks, erring on the side of caution, advance testing, the setting of priorities, and learning from error—are already in place and proposes additional strategic improvements.

———. *The Demise of Nuclear Energy? Lessons for Democratic Control of Technology.* Yale U. Pr. 1989 $25.00. ISBN 0-300-04448-8. Analyzes decisions that have lead to the somewhat moribund state of the nuclear-power industry in the United States and how this affects democratic decision making regarding technology.

Mulkay, Michael J. *Sociology of Science: A Sociological Pilgrimage. Science, Technology, and Society Ser.* Ind. U. Pr. 1991 $39.95. ISBN 0-253-33933-2. Presents a survey of developments in the sociology of science from the Strong Program, which emphasizes the social interests centrally involved in scientific practice, to the more recent notion of "reflexivity."

Ogburn, William F. *On Culture and Social Change: Selected Papers. History of Sociology Ser.* U. Ch. Pr. 1964 o.p. Features a collection of several papers by a major sociologist that cover the relationship between technological and social change; includes topics such as technology and government, technology and standard of living, and technology as an environment.

Ormiston, Gayle L., ed. *From Artifact to Habitat: Studies in the Critical Engagement of Technology. Research in Technology Studies.* Lehigh Univ. Pr. 1990 $35.00. ISBN 0-934223-09-2. Features nine essays that examine technology not only as "artifact" but also as "habitat."

Ormiston, Gayle L., and Raphael Sassower. *Narrative Experiments: The Discursive Authority of Science and Technology.* U. of Minn. Pr. 1989 $39.95. ISBN 0-8166-1820-8. Argues that science and technology should not be viewed as privileged ways of knowing, but must be continually open to cultural and linguistic interpretation.

Pacey, Arnold. *The Culture of Technology.* MIT Pr. 1983 $11.95. ISBN 0-262-66056-3. Presents a general investigation of the links between technology and social, cultural, political, and scientific values; includes such examples as nuclear weapons proliferation, automation, medicine, and Third World development.

Paepke, C. Owen. *The Evolution of Progress: The End of Economic Growth and the Beginning of Human Transformation.* Random 1993 $25.00. ISBN 0-679-41582-3. Featuring a mainly deterministic view, concludes that economic expansion through traditional technological change in the United States is effectively over; predicts, however, that biotechnology and genetic engineering will play a major role in reshaping contemporary society.

Perrow, Charles. *Normal Accidents: Living with High-Risk Technologies.* Basic 1985 $17.50. ISBN 0-465-05142-1. Argues that the systems characteristics of modern technologies are so complex that potentially catastrophic accidents must now be considered normal; claims that better management of high-risk technologies should be possible through improved design of organizations that respond to malfunctions.

Pickering, Andrew, ed. *Science as Practice and Culture.* U. Ch. Pr. 1992 $65.00. ISBN 0-226-66800-2. Presents 15 original essays that examine current perspectives and debates contributing to the sociology of scientific knowledge; covers the twin perspectives of scientific practice and the culture in which it operates.

Piller, Charles. *The Fail-Safe Society: Community Defiance and the End of American Technological Optimism*. Basic 1991 $20.00. ISBN 0-465-02274-X. Analyzes the Not In My Backyard (NIMBY) phenomenon; suggests how to control political conditions conducive to meaningful public involvement in scientific and technological decision making.

Pirsig, Robert M. *Zen and the Art of Motorcycle Maintenance: An Inquiry into Values*. Morrow 1974 $22.95. ISBN 0-688-00230-7. Relates an accordant relationship with technology, revealed by the peace Pirsig achieves through methodical tuning of his motorcycle and the logical solving of mechanical problems; includes a lengthy consideration of the relationship of quality and technology.

Postman, Neil. *Technopoly: The Surrender of Culture to Technology*. Knopf 1992 $21.00. ISBN 0-685-51846-9. Argues that technology has become deified; and, in the process, has damaged traditional beliefs. Suggests that to understand and change a technological society, people must distance themselves from it.

Proctor, Robert N. *Value-Free Science? Purity and Power in Modern Knowledge*. HUP 1991 $34.95. ISBN 0-674-93170-X. Offers a philosophical and political analysis of the relationship between values and science. Discusses the reasons why scientists traditionally have approached and portrayed their fields as value-neutral; views the notion of value-neutrality as having its own societal context that changes over time.

Ravetz, J. R. *The Merger of Knowledge with Power: Essays in Critical Science*. Mansell 1990 o.p. Presents a collection of essays by one of the pioneers of viewing science as socially conditioned; includes topics such as recombinent DNA, military technology, Francis Bacon, and the Gaia Theory.

Romanyshyn, Robert D. *Technology as Symptom and Dream*. Routledge 1989 $45.00. ISBN 0-415-00786-0. Presents technology as a cultural-historical dream, which since the fifteenth century has radically transformed our understanding of the material world and our own bodies.

Rosenberg, Nathan. *Inside the Black Box: Technology and Economics*. Cambridge U. Pr. 1983 $19.95. ISBN 0-521-27367-6. Describes how individual technologies have influenced the rate of productivity, the nature of the learning process underlying technological change, the speed of technology transfer, and the effectiveness of government policies designed to influence the development of these technologies.

Rothschild, Joan, ed. *Machina Ex Dea: Feminist Perspectives on Technology*. Athene Ser. Pergamon 1983 $48.50. ISBN 0-08-029404-9. Offers 12 essays that redefine the relationship of women and technology. Covers inventions by women, contributions of women to engineering, effects of office automation, household technology, role of gender in scientific and technical occupations, significance of reproductive technology, and feminist utopias and dystopias.

Rouse, Joseph. *Knowledge and Power: Toward a Political Philosophy of Science*. Cornell Univ. Pr. 1987 $34.50. ISBN 0-8014-1959-X. Discusses the need to understand the actual practice of scientific research and its inseparability from the political-power dimensions of the sciences.

Rybczynski, Witold. *Taming the Tiger: The Struggle to Control Technology*. Viking Penguin 1985 $8.95. ISBN 0-14-007564-X. Argues that "we must learn to live with the machine" because technology is an inherent part of human culture; suggests that when people view technology in this way, they shall discover that the struggle to control technology has all along been a struggle to control themselves.

Sassower, Raphael. *Knowledge without Expertise: On the Status of Scientists*. State U. NY Pr. 1993 $44.50. ISBN 0-7914-1481-7. Examines the claims and effects of expertise in science; draws on research by the British Association for the Advancement of Science.

Schumacher, E. F. *Small Is Beautiful: Economics As If People Mattered*. 1976. HarpC 1989 $10.00. ISBN 0-06-091630-3. These essays challenge conventional socialist and capitalist economics. Instead of progress accompanied by cataclysmic change, the author advocates the use of technologies that promote decentralization, preservation, compatibility with nature, self-reliance, and provide work that is creative and nonexploitative.

Schwarz, Michiel, and Michael Thompson. *Divided We Stand: Redefining Politics, Technology, and Social Choice*. U. of Pa. Pr. 1990 $31.95. ISBN 0-8122-8233-7. Demonstrates that a substantive core providing a theoretical basis for the study of technological decision making does not exist. Describes a plurality of contending and contradictory problem assumptions, such as various contradictory views of nature as benign, ephemeral, capricious, or perverse/tolerant. Argues that a synthesis of diversity, contradiction, contention, and criticism are the best means to understand technology decisions.

Skolnikoff, Eugene B. *The Elusive Transformation: Science, Technology, and the Evolution of International Politics*. Princeton U. Pr. 1993 $39.50. ISBN 0-691-08631-1. Explores how the international political system is affected by advances in science and technology; uses such examples as the green revolution and the proliferation of new weapons systems.

Sladovich, Hedy E., ed. *Engineering as a Social Enterprise*. Natl. Acad. Pr. 1991 $19.00. ISBN 0-309-04431-6. Presents six feature essays originally delivered at a 1990 Silver Anniversary National Academy of Engineering Symposium; examines the societal forces that shape engineering as well as how engineering has affected society throughout history; also discusses how engineering may affect society in the future.

Snow, Charles P. *Two Cultures: And a Second Look*. Cambridge U. Pr. 1969 $11.95. ISBN 0-521-09576-X. Features Snow's classic plea for interdisciplinary education based on the traditional inability and unwillingness of scientists and humanists to communicate; has been a catalyst for many interdisciplinary programs in science, technology, and society.

Street, John. *Politics and Technology. The Conduct of Science Ser.* Guilford Pr. 1992 $40.00. ISBN 0-089862-087-2. Shows the interconnections between technology and politics especially related to the democratic control of technology, which Street prefers over the extremes of either the Green Movement or those who believe wholeheartedly in the "technological fix."

Teich, Albert H., ed. *Technology and the Future*. St. Martin 1993 $21.35. ISBN 0-312-06747-X. Presents a useful anthology designed to stimulate student thinking about purpose and direction in technological development; features a diversity of perspectives that include Leo Marx, Lester Brown, Emanuel Mesthene, Samuel Florman, Robert Weinberg, William Lowrance, E. F. Schumacher, and Langdon Winner.

Toffler, Alvin. *Future Shock*. Random 1970 $18.95. ISBN 0-394-42586-3. Theorizes that moral and technological change is accelerating beyond the adaptive skills of human beings; claims that the result is future shock, a peculiar amalgam of stress, mental illness, family problems, and information overload.

———. *The Third Wave*. Bantam 1984 $5.95. ISBN 0-553-24698-4. Presents an assemblage of anecdotes, studies, and mass-media clippings to support Toffler's contention that society is on the brink of a new age of individuality and decentralization in entertainment, information, technology, education, and other cultural forms.

Tuana, Nancy, ed. *Feminism and Science. Race, Gender, and Science Ser.* Ind. U. Pr. 1989 $35.00. ISBN 0-253-36045-5. Fourteen essays originally published in two special issues of *Hypatia: A Journal of Feminist Philosophy*; arranged into two categories: feminist theories of science and feminist critiques of the practice of science.

Turkle, Sherry. *The Second Self: Computers and the Human Spirit*. S&S Trade 1985 $12.95. ISBN 0-671-60602-6. Investigates the changes in modes of thinking experienced by individuals, especially children, as a result of their exposure to computers. Suggests that because the impact is primarily mental and personal, the computer may dissolve the traditionally sharp division between physics and psychology.

Wajcman, Judy. *Feminism Confronts Technology*. Pa. St. U. Pr. 1991 $28.50. ISBN 0-271-00801-6. Argues that the gendered character of technology need not engender pessimism but instead offer "fresh possibilities for feminist scholarship and action." Reviews feminist theories of science and technology and then examines specific areas of technology such as sexual divisions in paid work, reproductive technologies, housework, domestic architecture, urban systems, and transportation.

Weil, Vivian, and John Snapper, eds. *Owning Scientific and Technological Information: Value and Ethical Issues.* Rutgers U. Pr. 1989 $40.00. ISBN 0-8135-1454-1. Features 15 essays that examine the ethical and values questions related to knowledge as intellectual property.

Weizenbaum, Joseph. *Computer Power and Human Reason: From Judgment to Calculation.* W. H. Freeman 1976 $14.95. ISBN 0-7167-0463-3. Argues against the ultimate quest of computer researchers: to create an electronic version of the human mind. Claims that this goal is a misuse of computer technology as well as a delusion. Weizenbaum considers especially misguided and dangerous the substitution of computers for humans in situations requiring judgment, interpersonal interaction, and respect, as well as understanding.

Wenk, Edward, Jr. *Tradeoffs: Imperatives of Choice in a High-Tech World.* 1986. Johns Hopkins 1989 $13.95. ISBN 0-8018-3942-4. Argues that the conflict between the tangible fruits of technology, the quality of life that technology can achieve, and the threats to life and liberty have created a strong polarity in our culture. Covers topics such as technological risk, politics, and industry, then discusses how decisions are made, and the roles for citizens; includes a set of principles to analyze technological initiatives.

Wiener, Norbert. *The Human Use of Human Beings: Cybernetics and Society.* 1967. Da Capo 1988 $9.95. ISBN 0-306-80320-8. Features a collection of essays using the concept of cybernetics as a starting point for more general discussions of communication processes in society, scientific discovery, technology and religion, and militarism.

Woolgar, Steve. *Knowledge and Reflexivity: New Frontiers in the Sociology of Knowledge.* Sage 1988 $39.95. ISBN 0-8039-8120-1. Offers nine essays with editorial "reflexions" that examine the position of scholars who claim that both natural scientific knowledge and knowledge generated by the social sciences is socially constructed by reflexivity.

——. *Science: The Very Idea. Key Idea Ser.* Routledge Chapman & Hall 1989 $19.95. ISBN 0-7458-0041-6. Presents an overview of the sociology of science, argues that sociologists' interpretations are not worthy of special authority because they are constructed as the knowledge claims of science they explain.

Yearley, Steven. *Science, Technology, and Social Change.* Unwin Hyman 1988 o.p. Examines how science and technology relate to change in both developed and underdeveloped nations. Yearley draws on the insights of political economy and the sociology of scientific knowledge to adopt a stance of "moderate constructionism."

Zimmerman, Jan, ed. *The Technological Woman: Interfacing with Tomorrow.* Greenwood 1983 $42.95. ISBN 0-275-91730-4. Presents a collection of 31 essays that address current technologies that still reflect values of sexism, racism, and classism; examines how women's lives are affected by household, workplace, and medical technologies.

CHRONOLOGY OF AUTHORS

Mumford, Lewis. 1895–1990
Bronowski, Jacob. 1908–1974
Ellul, Jacques. 1912–
Barbour, Ian. 1923–
Roy, Rustum. 1924–
Florman, Samuel C(harles). 1925–

Meadows, Donella H. 1931–
Nelkin, Dorothy. 1933–
Roszak, Theodore. 1933–
Petroski, Henry. 1942–
Latour, Bruno. 1947–

BARBOUR, IAN. 1923–

Throughout his career, Ian Barbour has been at the forefront of the dialogue between scientists and theologians. Trained as a physicist, with a Ph.D. from the University of Chicago (1950), and as a theologian, with a B.D. from Yale University (1956), Barbour has drawn on the philosophical insights of both disciplines to transcend their boundaries. As a professor of both physics and religion, Barbour's initial books depict the relationships between physical science and religion. For example, his broad-ranging overview *Issues in Science and Religion* (1966) and his classic *Myths, Models and Paradigms* (1974) focused on the language parallels between these disciplines.

During the 1970s and 1980s, Barbour began to expand his focus to include technological and environmental themes; at that time, the field of STS emerged in response to increased concern over technology's societal impacts, especially regarding energy and the environment. During this period he published *Technology, Environment, and Human Values* (1980) and *Energy and American Values* (1982), as well as several edited collections of essays, including *Earth Might Be Fair: Reflections on Ethics, Religion and Ecology* (1971) and *Western Man and Environmental Ethics* (1972). All of these books focus on the need for an enhanced technological and environmental ethic.

Recently, Barbour has continued to pursue these intertwined themes in his 1989–91 Gifford Lectures at the University of Aberdeen, published as *Religion in an Age of Science* (1990) and *Ethics in an Age of Technology* (1993). Barbour serves as Winifred and Atherton Bean Professor Emeritus of Science, Technology, and Society at Carlton College.

BOOKS BY BARBOUR

Christianity and the Scientist. Association Pr. 1960 o.p. Offers insights and suggestions concerning how scientists seek meaning in their work in respect to the Christian notion of "vocation."

Earth Might Be Fair: Reflections on Ethics, Religion and Ecology. P-H 1972 o.p. Articulates an ecological theology and ecological ethic; includes themes such as the unity of human beings with nature, responsible stewardship, the intrinsic worth of all living things, social justice, resource-usage constraints, and pollution control.

Energy and American Values. (coauthored with Harvey Brooks, Sanford Lakoff, and John Opie). Greenwood 1982 $39.95. ISBN 0-275-90758-9. A multidisciplinary team of authors with expertise in history, technology, political science, religion, and physics examine the relationship of American values and energy alternatives. Argues that energy continues to be an important issue because of its centrality to society; advocates a strong program of energy conservation, and a diverse mix of supply options within a democratic context.

Ethics in an Age of Technology. The Gifford Lectures. Vol. 2 HarpC 1993 $19.00. ISBN 0-06-060935-4. Examines the ethical issues posed by technology and applied science. Extends Barbour's earlier analysis of environment and values and incorporates additional case studies on agriculture and genetic engineering, energy, and computers; suggests that constructive change can be realized through education, political action, response to crises, and alternative visions of a more just, participatory, and sustainable society.

Issues in Science and Religion. P-H 1971 $12.95. ISBN 0-06-13566-1. Elucidates scientific parallels in the methods of science and religion in a historical investigation. Defends the necessity for integration rather than the conceptualization of science and religion as separate modes of knowledge; suggests that science and religion are actually "complementary languages."

Myths, Models and Paradigms: A Comparative Study in Science and Religion. 1974. HarpC 1976 $10.95. ISBN 0-06-060388-7. Considers symbolic models in science meaningful in understanding religious reality and suggests that even in science, metaphors or models should be symbolically apprehended. Believes that an enhanced appreciation of the plurality of religious experiences can occur when absolute claims are not made in science.

Religion in the Age of Science. The Gifford Lectures. Vol. 1 HarpC 1990 $16.95. ISBN 0-06-060383-6. Examines five scientific challenges to religion: the successes of the methods of science; new views of nature (e.g., the "big bang" evolution and DNA research); a new context for theology, especially the doctrines of human nature and creation; religious pluralism in a technical age of global communication and interdependence; and the ambiguous power of technology.

Science and Secularity: The Ethics of Technology. HarpC 1970 o.p. Broadens earlier analyses of science to include the challenges that technology poses for modern society. Among the challenges discussed are the technological mentality, developments in molecular biology, cybernetics, and the political control of technology.

Technology, Environment and Human Values. Greenwood 1980 $27.95. ISBN 0-275-90448-2. Offers an excellent survey of the relationship of values and technology in relation to environmental concerns; includes a general discussion of values as well as environmental policies, cost-benefit analysis and technology assessment, scarce resources, population growth, and food production.

Western Man and Environmental Ethics: Attitudes toward Nature and Technology. Addison-Wesley 1972 o.p. Presents 16 essays that focus on the way people perceive and interact with nature; written by notable proponents of STS with the goal of developing a new environmental ethic.

BRONOWSKI, JACOB. 1908–1974

Born in Poland, Jacob Bronowski moved to England at the age of 12. He received a scholarship to study mathematics at Cambridge University, where he earned a Ph.D. in 1933. At Cambridge, Bronowski also edited a literary magazine and wrote verse. He served as lecturer at University College in Hull before joining the government service in 1942.

Bronowski's participation in military research during World War II was critical to his career as an author; he pioneered developments in operations research, which enhanced the effectiveness of Allied bombing raids. In 1945 Bronowski wrote a report on the devastating effects of the atomic bomb, which eventually was incorporated in his book *Science and Human Values* (1965). After viewing the ruins of Hiroshima and Nagasaki, Bronowski refused to continue military research and became involved with the ethical and technological issues related to science. After World War II Bronowski joined the Ministry of Works, assuming several government posts concerned with research in power resources.

In 1964 Bronowski came to the United States, serving as senior fellow (1964–70) and then director (1970–74) of the Council for Biology in Human Affairs at the Salk Institute for Biological Studies in La Jolla, California. He also taught and lectured at several American universities, including MIT, Columbia University, and Yale. Until his death, Bronowski remained a resident fellow at the Salk Institute.

Bronowski's writing career can be divided into two periods. Prior to World War II, he wrote mathematical papers, poetry, and literary criticism. After the war, Bronowski mainly wrote about scientific values, science as a humanistic enterprise, language, and creativity.

In 1973 Bronowski's acclaimed 13-part BBC television series, "The Ascent of Man," chronicled attempts to "understand and control nature" from antiquity to the present. The series called for a democracy of intellect in which "knowledge sits in the homes and heads of people with no ambition to control others, and not up in the isolated seats of power."

In an issue of the journal *Leonardo*, David R. Topper identifies five major themes developed in Bronowski's writings: (1) fundamental concepts of science are intelligible to lay people; (2) science involves values; (3) scientific development is open ended; (4) like art, science is creative; and (5) human beings are unique because of their imagination.

Neither naive nor utopian, Bronowski remained a consistent optimist and defender of science. In *A Sense of the Future* (1977), Bronowski states that, as science becomes increasingly preoccupied with relations and arrangement, it too becomes engaged in the search for structure that typifies modern art. He believed that "knowledge is our destiny. Self-knowledge, at last bringing together the experience of the arts and the explanations of science, waits ahead of us." To date, a full-length biography of Bronowski has not been written. However, a 1985 issue of *Leonardo* was devoted to a retrospective; in addition to a lengthy and thorough biography and bibliography, there were essays on Bronowski's life and work and excerpts from his publications.

BOOKS BY BRONOWSKI

The Ascent of Man. Little 1976 $29.95. ISBN 0-316-10933-9. Offers 13 well-illustrated essays derived from Bronowski's acclaimed television series about the progressive attempts of human beings to understand and control nature—from agriculture to relativity. In his optimistic conclusion, Bronowski states: "The ascent of man is always teetering in the balance. There is always a sense of uncertainty. . . . And what is ahead for us? At last the bringing together of all that we have learned, in physics and in biology, towards an understanding of where we have come: what man is."

Biography of an Atom. (coauthored with Millicent E. Selsam). HarpC 1965 $12.89. ISBN 0-06-020641-1. Explains atomic theory for children; traces the journey of a carbon atom from the earth's origins to its incorporation into a steak dinner.

The Common Sense of Science. HUP 1953 $7.95. ISBN 0-674-14651-4. Presents essays on science and sensibility; the scientific revolution and the machine; Isaac Newton; the eighteenth century and the idea of order; the nineteenth century and the idea of causes; the idea of chance; the common sense of science, truth, and value; science as destroyer or creator.

The Identity of Man. Natural His. 1965 o.p. A series of essays, first presented as lectures at the American Museum of Natural History, that discuss the nature of a person as either a machine or as a self; interpretations are based on two modes of knowledge: the knowledge of the physical world and the knowledge of experience.

Science and Human Values. 1965. HarpC 1990 $7.95. ISBN 0-06-097281-5. Explores the relationship between science and art, discussing the origins of knowledge, perception, language, scientific discourse, and method.

A Sense of the Future: Essays in Natural Philosophy. Ed. by Piero Ariotti and Rita Bronowski. MIT Pr. 1977 $12.95. ISBN 0-262-52050-8. Features a collection of previously published essays spanning 20 years in which Bronowski calls for a union between science and everyday living and thinking. Claims that science, like art, employs creativity and imagination but must be faithful to facts.

Technology: Man Remakes His World. (coauthored with others). Macdonald 1964 o.p. An encyclopedic, well-illustrated survey of technology that includes transportation and energy technologies as well as the manufacture and use of textiles, metals, ceramics, and other products and materials.

The Western Intellectual Tradition: From Leonardo to Hegel. (coauthored with Bruce Mazlish). Ayer repr. of 1960 ed. $37.00. ISBN 0-8369-2448-7. Features an intellectual history from the Renaissance to the nineteenth century; each chapter focuses on the outlook of a representative or group of individuals from each period.

ELLUL, JACQUES. 1912–

Jacques Ellul, historian, theologian, and sociologist, is one of the foremost and widely known contemporary critics of modern technological society. Born in Bordeaux, France, Ellul received a doctorate in the history of law and social science in 1936 from the University of Bordeaux. In 1947 he was appointed professor of social history at the University of Bordeaux, remaining there until his retirement in 1980. Although influenced strongly by his early reading of the Bible and MARX (see Vols. 3 and 4), Ellul has been unable to synthesize Marxist doctrine with Christianity. These readings and experiences have influenced his later philosophy and writing.

Ellul has taught and written extensively in his areas of specialization—Roman law, the history and sociology of institutions, Marxism, propaganda, and technique in society. He also served in the French Resistance during World War II, worked as a lay pastor, and has been active with various theological organizations, including the World Council of Churches. In addition, Ellul has been active in the environmental movement and has worked to prevent juvenile delinquency and violence. Since 1969, he has been editor of *Foi et Vie (Faith and Life)*. Although retired as a teacher, Ellul has continued writing. One of his writing projects is an autobiography to be published after his death.

Ellul has provided a sociopolitical as well as a theological analysis of contemporary society in more than 40 books and 800 articles. *The Technological Society*, written in 1954, but not translated into English for another decade, established Ellul as a social critic. The book has had a major impact on the collective consciousness of a society just beginning to recognize the central role and force of technology. Here Ellul develops the notion of "technique," a concept much broader than technology: "Technique is the totality of methods rationally arrived at." In Ellul's view, technology in this sense tends to become all-encompassing. His subsequent books, especially *The Political Illusion* (1965) and *Propaganda* (1962), further develop and refine elements of this central theme. This "trilogy" of books reflects Ellul's desire to alert readers to the dangers of technological determinism and thereby help them transcend it.

Because of a dialectical approach separating his sociopolitical and theological studies, Ellul has often been criticized as overly pessimistic in his sociologically based writings. His theological works, however, provide a more positive perspective and counterpoint to his sociological work. Most notable are *The Politics of God and the Politics of Man* (1966), *The Meaning of the City* (1970), and especially *The Ethics of Freedom* (1973).

The main body of Ellul's sociopolitical critique of technical society is reflected by *The Technological Society*, *The Political Illusion*, *Propaganda*, and *The Technological System*. Among his other works are *Autopsy of Revolution* (1969), which questions what kind of revolution is realistically possible; *The Humiliation of the Word* (1981), which expands upon the concept of "human techniques"; and *The Technological Bluff* (1990), which discusses the state of contemporary society, especially in regard to such technologies as computers and genetic engineering and the progressive "discourse" that surrounds their societal incorporation.

An in-depth understanding of Ellul requires reading major portions of his extensive published work. The reader, however, can facilitate the process by reading *In Season, Out of Season* (1981), an extended interview with Ellul; Darrell Fasching's systematic introduction, *The Thought of Jacques Ellul* (1982);

and David Lovekin's excellent philosophical study, *Technique, Discourse, and Consciousness: An Introduction to the Philosophy of Jacques Ellul* (1991).

Whether the reader finds Ellul overly pessimistic or insightfully revealing, an individual interested in the societal context of contemporary technology should understand the two central themes of his work—"technology as a threat to human freedom and hope as the foundation of a Christian ethic of freedom" (Fasching, *The Thought of Jacques Ellul*).

BOOKS BY ELLUL

Autopsy of Revolution. 1969. Trans. by Patricia Wolf. Knopf 1971 o.p. Ponders whether people are actually aware of the revolution that will be necessary to transform modern technological society.

The Ethics of Freedom. 1973. Ed. and trans. by Geoffrey W. Bromiley. Eerdmans 1976 o.p. Ellul states that he "planned that *The Ethics of Freedom* would be the dialectical counterpoint to my studies of Technique."

The Humiliation of the Word. 1981. Trans. by Joyce Main Hanks. Eerdmans 1985 $17.95. ISBN 0-8028-0069-6. Presents an expansion of the chapter called "Human Techniques" in *The Technological Society.*

In Season, Out of Season: An Introduction to the Thought of Jacques Ellul, Based on Interviews by Madelaine Garrigou-Lagrange. 1981. Trans. by Lani K. Niles. Peter Smith 1983 o.p. Offers an excellent introduction to Ellul's philosophy; many of the questions in this autobiographical interview were originally formulated by Ellul.

The Meaning of the City. 1970. Trans. by Dennis Pardee. Eerdmans o.p. Views the modern city as symbolizing the ultimate secular world of humankind and hence the rejection of God; views the heavenly city of Jerusalem as a place of communication between God and humankind. According to John Wilkinson's introduction, this book is the theological counterpoint to *The Technological Society.*

Perspectives on Our Age: Jacques Ellul Speaks on His Life and Work. 1981. Ed. by William H. Vanderburg. Trans. by Joachim Neugroschel. Harper SF forthcoming. Features Ellul's response to questions posed by the editor. Focuses more on his thought than *In Season, Out of Season*, which is more personal and theologically oriented.

The Political Illusion. 1965. Trans. by Konrad Kellen. Knopf 1967 o.p. Pointing to the increasing centralization of the technological state, Ellul claims that political action in response to the crisis of contemporary society is an illusion and that the greatest pitfall is the concept of political solutions. Suggests that genuine political problems consist of contradictory facts that are not amenable to political solutions, only to equitable settlements; argues that politics should be demythologized, placing it in its proper place and focusing on productive "tensions" based on legitimate interests and concerns. (The theological counterpoint is *The Politics of God and the Politics of Man.*)

The Politics of God and the Politics of Man. 1966. Trans. by Geoffrey W. Bromiley. Eerdmans 1972 o.p. According to Joyce Hanks and John Wilkinson, well-known scholars of Ellul and translators of some of his works, this book is "the theological counterpart of *The Political Illusion.*"

Propaganda: The Formation of Men's Attitudes. 1962. Trans. by Konrad Kellen and Jean Lerner. Random 1973 $9.00. ISBN 0-394-71874-7. Analyzes the sociological character and the psychological and sociopolitical effects of propaganda. Suggests that the technological society promotes propaganda and, at the same time, depends on its "integration" capacity to make people follow desired patterns. "Propaganda is called upon to solve problems created by technology, to play on maladjustments, and to integrate the individual into a technological world" (Preface).

The Technological Bluff. Trans. by Geoffrey W. Bromiley. Eerdmans 1990 $24.95. ISBN 0-8028-3678-X. Defines and discusses "technological bluff" as the all-engulfing discourse that promises salvation from societal problems through the progressive application of technology.

The Technological Society. 1954. Trans. by John Wilkinson. Random 1967 $7.95. ISBN 0-394-70390-1. A critical, mainly pessimistic sociological analysis of contemporary society that analyzes the significant shaping and controlling role of technology, which is defined as "technique." According to Ellul, technique is not an isolated fact in society but is related to every factor in the life of modern man, affecting social facts as well as all others. This book represents Ellul's central sociological work and the starting point for a serious review of this major scholar.

The Technological System. 1977. Trans. by Joachim Neugroschel. Continuum 1980 o.p. Argues that technology is all-encompassing and has become the determining factor in culture and that people are integrated in a technological milieu in which choice is not possible. Focuses attention on the increasing use of computers.

What I Believe. Trans. by Geoffrey W. Bromiley. Eerdmans 1989 $19.95. ISBN 0-8028-3658-5. Summarizes Ellul's current theological thinking.

BOOKS ABOUT ELLUL

Christians, Clifford G., and Jay M. Van Hook, eds. *Jacques Ellul: Interpretive Essays*. U. of Ill. Pr. 1981 $29.95. ISBN 0-252-00812-X. Presents essays on ideas Ellul adopted from Marx, Barth, and Kierkegaard; his sociopolitical perspective; and his theological thought.

Fasching, Darrell J. *The Thought of Jacques Ellul: A Systematic Exposition. Toronto Studies in Theology*. E. Mellen 1982 $89.95. ISBN 0-88946-961-X. According to the publisher, Ellul calls this book "the best introduction that I know for understanding my work."

Gill, David W. *The Word of God in the Ethics of Jacques Ellul*. Scarecrow 1984 $25.00. ISBN 0-8108-1667-9. Presents an overview of Ellul's work and analyzes the place of Christ and scripture in contemporary Protestant ethics.

Hanks, Joyce Main, and Asal Rolf. *Jacques Ellul: A Comprehensive Bibliography*. Supp. 1 to *Research in Philosophy and Technology*. Jai Pr. 1984 $63.50. ISBN 0-89232-478-3. Offers an extremely comprehensive, annotated bibliography of Ellul's lifework that covers books, articles, interviews, reviews, dissertations, and a valuable section of works, mostly articles, about Ellul and his philosophy; also includes helpful author, title, and subject indexes. (Updates included in *Research in Philosophy and Technology*, 1986 Vol. 9).

Holloway, James Y., ed. *Introducing Jacques Ellul*. Eerdmans 1970 o.p. This was the first book about Ellul originally published in 1970 as a special issue of *Katallagete: Be Reconciled*.

Lovekin, David. *Technique, Discourse, and Consciousness: An Introduction to the Philosophy of Jacques Ellul*. Lehigh Univ. Pr. 1991 $38.50. ISBN 0-934223-01-07. Features the most current and complete philosophical analysis of Ellul's work, in which technology is understood and treated as "a symbol construction."

FLORMAN, SAMUEL C(HARLES). 1925–

An American civil engineer and vice-president of Kreisler Borg Florman Construction Company, Samuel Florman was influenced personally and professionally by his liberal undergraduate education at Dartmouth College as well as by his graduate studies at Columbia University, where he received an M.A. Florman's first book, *Engineering and the Liberal Arts* (1968), highlights the importance of a liberal arts education for engineers. As a result of the book's popularity, Florman was invited to speak at universities about the role of technology and engineering in society. During the emergence of science/technology/society studies as an academic field of study in the mid-1970s, Lewis Lapham invited Florman to write a series of articles for *Harper's*. Between 1976 and 1980, Florman wrote dozens of articles and eventually became a contributing editor at *Harper's*. He also regularly contributes to *Technology Review*.

In his subsequent books, *The Existential Pleasures of Engineering* (1977) and *Blaming Technology* (1982), Florman expresses his concern about a growing antitechnological backlash and a decline in the status of engineers. Florman's style eschews bitterness and delightfully conveys his belief that "technological creativity is a wondrous manifestation of the human spirit."

BOOKS BY FLORMAN

Blaming Technology: The Irrational Search for Scapegoats. St. Martin 1982 $6.95. ISBN 0-312-08363-7. Presents a rebuttal to anti-technological writing; rejects technological determinism and dismisses the "technocratic elite" as a myth. Florman also argues that engineers are politically important, denies that small is beautiful, and explains why few women become engineers.

The Civilized Engineer. St. Martin 1987 $15.95. ISBN 0-312-00114-2. Florman's fourth book covers his wide range of concerns, from dual attraction to engineering and the humanities, to engineering ethics, especially his encouragement of engineers to be introspective; includes several articles that originally appeared in *Technology Review* and comments on the loss of the space shuttle *Challenger* as a case study of the tensions between engineers and managers.

Engineering and the Liberal Arts: A Technologist's Guide to History, Literature, Philosophy, Art, and Music. McGraw 1968 o.p. Florman's first book advocates a liberal arts education for engineers and explores relationships between engineering and the liberal arts. He provides guides for engineers, students, or practitioners, to explore the five subject areas mentioned in the title.

The Existential Pleasures of Engineering. St. Martin 1977 $7.95. ISBN 0-312-27546-3. Describes the intellectual and spiritual rewards of engineering by vigorously confronting critics of technology, notably Ellul, Dubos, Mumford, and Roszak. States that engineers cannot be held responsible for damages done by technology because they have not been granted the politician's power nor the historian's hindsight.

HOLTON, GERALD. 1922–

[SEE Chapter 2 in this volume.]

KRANZBERG, MELVIN. 1917–

[SEE Chapter 3 in this volume.]

LATOUR, BRUNO. 1947–

A native of Burgundy, France, Bruno Latour serves as professor at the Centre de Sociologie de l'Innovation at the École Nationale Supérieure des Mines, Paris. During the past 15 years, he has emerged as one of the leading and most discussed scholars associated with the social studies of science. Latour is generally viewed as a sociologist, but his expertise transcends several disciplines. Trained as a philosopher with anthropological field experience, his research to date has focused on understanding science and scientists "in action," or before the knowledge gained becomes "black-boxed," or so widely accepted, that one can no longer understand how it evolved. Latour wrote the first significant, detailed laboratory study in the field, *Laboratory Life* (1979), which was expanded upon and generalized in his extremely important work *Science in Action* (1987). Latour argues that scientific reality is not discovered in nature. Instead it is "constructed" as more "actors" are "enrolled" in support of a statement or artifact until scientific reality becomes too costly to challenge or modify in favor of an alternative. At this point, the construction is "blackboxed" and no longer controversial; it has become "fact." Latour's recent publications, especially *We Have Never Been Modern*, takes a more philosophical approach, discussing the broader implications of science. Although often viewed (even in his own words) as "idiosyncratic," Latour currently is a significant figure in the social studies of science.

BOOKS BY LATOUR

Aramis, or the Love of Technology. HUP forthcoming. Analyzes the subway system of Paris, France.

Laboratory Life: The Construction of Scientific Facts. (coauthored with Steve Woolgar). 1979. Princeton U. Pr. 1986 $45.00. ISBN 0-691-09418-7. Presents the first detailed ethnographic study of the generation of knowledge or "construction of facts" within a scientific laboratory; based on participant observation research conducted at the Salk Institute for Biological Studies in La Jolla, California. (The second edition contains a postscript response to criticisms made of the original 1979 study.)

The Pasteurization of France. Trans. by Alan Sheridan and John Law. 1984 HUP 1988 $32.50. ISBN 0-674-65760-8. Analyzes historical texts related to Pasteur and the field of bacteriology; makes conclusions about the medical network of Pasteurian France.

Science in Action: How to Follow Scientists and Engineers through Society. HUP 1987 $12.95. ISBN 0-674-79291-2. Argues that "technoscience" can be understood only by examination of its practice in action; delineates a set of rules of method and principles to understand the social construction of science and technology.

We Have Never Been Modern. HUP ISBN 0-674-94838-6. Argues that society has never functioned according to a great divide between society on one side and nature on the other. Questions the fundamental paradigm of modernity for understanding the world.

MEADOWS, DONELLA H. 1931–

Trained as a biophysicist, American scientist Donella H. Meadows earned a Ph.D. from Harvard University. Early in her career, Meadows was a member of a joint Harvard-MIT research group that developed a computer simulation model clarifying relationships between growth and finite resources on the earth. Using this model, the Club of Rome sponsored extensive research that resulted in the best-selling book, *The Limits to Growth* (1972), coauthored by Meadows and others. Attention was focused on a doomsday prognosis if growth continued unchecked. Meadows and her associates, however, presented options for achieving a sustainable society if there were a movement away from dependence on growth, equity in wealth, and if technologies were used to enhance efficiency of natural-resource use. *Toward Global Equilibrium* (1973) and *Dynamics of Growth in a Finite World* (1974) are companion technical volumes to *The Limits to Growth.* They present reports on the simulation models, examinations of economic, political, and ethical implications of the findings, and a detailed description of the computer model, World3.

In addition to her research sponsored by the Club of Rome, Meadows, as one of the editors of *Groping in the Dark* (1982), fully articulates that basic human needs can be met in the future if social and political structures, as well as values, do not hinder efforts for sustainability and equity. Meadows states that equity, rather than individual and national-wealth aggrandizement, is increasingly recognized as a major factor in planetary survival. Twenty years after *The Limits to Growth*, Meadows and others in *Beyond the Limits* (1992) find that some options for a sustainable future have narrowed. However, they claim that new technologies can, if employed wisely, contribute to sustainability. The book emphasizes social-policy options rather than models.

After working for two years on the Club of Rome research project, Meadows became a member of the faculty at Dartmouth College, where she is systems analyst and adjunct professor in the Environmental Studies Program. Meadows has a lifestyle that reflects her views about sustaining finite resources and valuing equity rather than personal economic gain. Although she remains an academic, her interests have shifted from biophysics toward philosophy. She has lived in a commune, studies Zen Buddhism, and believes that people today are ultimately responsible for a future that holds "unspeakable horrors or undreamed-of wonders."

Books by Meadows

Beyond the Limits: Confronting Global Collapse, Envisioning a Sustainable Future. (coauthored with Dennis L. Meadows, and Jorgen Randers). Chelsea Green 1992 $19.95. ISBN 0-930031-55-5. In the 20 years since publication of *The Limits of Growth*, the authors find that some options for sustainable future development have narrowed while new technologies and institutions present possibilities for reducing the consumption of resources and eliminating poverty. Describes how the use of some essential resources and pollution indicate uncontrollable decline, but argues that a sustainable society is possible if there is an emphasis on equity in wealth, quality of life rather than quantity, and efficiency in resource use.

Dynamics of Growth in a Finite World. (coauthored with Dennis L. Meadows and others). Prod. Press 1974 $60.00. ISBN 0-262-13142-0. Explores *The Limits to Growth* and presents a detailed description of the computer model, World3. The model provides a dynamic theory of the complex changes and interrelationships generated by physical growth, environmental pollution, technological advances, and the depletion of finite resources; the third volume in the series sponsored by the Club of Rome.

The Electronic Oracle: Computer Models and Social Decisions. (coauthored with J. M. Robinson). Wiley 1985 $165.00. ISBN 0-471-90558-5. Reviews modeling, particularly computer modeling. Discusses models that simulate the process of industrialization and technological change as well as the use of these models in social-policy decision making.

Groping in the Dark: The First Decade of Global Modelling. (coedited with John Richardson and Gerhart Bruckmann). Wiley 1982 $71.50. ISBN 0-471-10027-7. Explains global models, introduces the major models in use, and discusses their value and what we have learned from them. Concludes that there are no physical or technical reasons why basic needs cannot be met for the world's people in the future, but social and political structures, values, norms, and world views prevent achievement of global sustainability and equity; based on the proceedings of a symposium on computer modeling.

The Limits to Growth: A Report for the Club of Rome's Project on the Predicament of Mankind. (coauthored with others). NAL-Dutton 1972 o.p. Concludes that the persistence of growth trends would culminate in limits reached within a decade. Focuses on population levels and material consumption that could be sustained on the earth as well as the relations of technological advances to physical constraints; developed from projections generated by a computer-based world model.

Toward Global Equilibrium: Collected Papers. (coedited with Dennis L. Meadows). Prod. Press 1973 $44.95. ISBN 0-262-13143-9. This companion volume to *The Limits to Growth* contains technical reports that present simulation models constructed to determine the dynamics of relationships within one or more subsectors of the project's global model: population, pollution, agriculture, nonrenewable resources, and capital equipment; also includes papers that examine the economic, political, and ethical implications of the project findings to determine how society might move from dependence on growth toward stable accommodation.

MUMFORD, LEWIS. 1895–1990

Lewis Mumford has been referred to as one of the twentieth century's most influential "public intellectuals." A thinker and writer who denied the narrowness of academic speciality, Mumford embraced a cultural analysis that integrated technology, the natural environment, the urban environment, the individual, and the community. Although he lacked a formal university degree, Mumford wrote more than 30 books and 1,000 essays and reviews, which established his "organic" analysis of modern culture. His work defined the interdisciplinary studies movement, especially American studies; urban studies and city planning; architectural history; history of technology; and, most important in the present context, the interaction of science, technology, and society.

Mumford studied at the City College of New York, Columbia University, and the New School for Social Research, where he was motivated by THORSTEIN VEBLEN (see Vol. 3). He worked briefly in the textile industry and as a laboratory assistant but was drawn to journalism and cultural commentary. Mumford eventually became editor of *Dial*, the most distinguished literary magazine of its era. In 1920 he served as editor of *Sociological Review* in London and was strongly influenced by Sir Patrick Geddes, the Scottish botanist, sociologist, and town planner. In 1923, Mumford became a charter member of the Regional Planning Association of America, an experimental group that studied city problems from a regional as well as an ecological point of view. Mumford's well-known principle of "organicism" (the exploration of a cultural complex, where values, technology, individual personality, and the objective environment complement each other and together could build a world of fulfillment and beauty) was discussed in all of his work, spanning a career of nearly 70 years.

Mumford's first book, *The Story of Utopias* (1922), introduces reliance on history to understand the present as well as to plan for the future. His books on architectural history, *Sticks and Stones* (1924) and *The Brown Decades* (1931), as well as his works in urban studies, *The Culture of Cities* (1938) and *The City in History* (1961), established Mumford's reputation as the leading American critic of architecture and city planning. Each book views and analyzes the city, or built environment, in the context of form, function, and purpose within the larger culture. Mumford's books are focused on technology's role in civilization, especially "the machine" and "megatechnics." As a result, they have provided formative direction and structure to science, technology, and society studies and have established Mumford's stature as one of the foremost social critics of the twentieth century.

Technics and Civilization (1934) was Mumford's first extensive treatment of technology as a factor in contemporary society. The book contains a schema that organizes the history of technology into three phases: eotechnic (wind and water power, wood materials), paleotechnic (coal, steam, iron), and neotechnic (electricity and alloys). Still reflecting a generally positive attitude toward the possibilities of technologies, Mumford begins to question the directions of technological change, emphasizing the need for technologies that are supportive of human beings. Eighteen years later, in *Art and Technics* (1952), Mumford explores the merger of art and technology in the hope of restoring the human personality, especially its autonomy and spontaneity, to the machine culture.

Mumford's most profound and important analysis of technology (and the work that most directly influenced interdisciplinary technology-society studies) is the two-volume *The Myth of the Machine*: Volume 1, *Technics and Human Development* (1967), and Volume 2, *The Pentagon of Power* (1970). It was written following World War II (during which Mumford lost his son) after the deployment of atomic weapons by Russia and the United States, and during the arms race. This major work reflects a noticeable reinterpretation of the role of technology and a deep pessimism regarding "megatechnics," a metaphor Mumford uses for intrusive, all-encompassing systems of control and oppressive order. He views the military-industrial complex (the most horrendous "mega-machine") as destroyer of the emotive and organic aspects of life. Mumford argues against the loss of personal autonomy and the organic world by electricity-based computer systems.

Despite deepening pessimism, Mumford continued to write and to lecture in order to foster the values that could reshape technologies for creative and constructive purposes. He always retained the hope of realizing his vision of the "good life" in which objective and personal worlds complement each other through integration of tools, machines, knowledge, values, skills, and arts. Although Mumford refused to define himself narrowly as a historian, sociologist, urbanist, or architectural critic, he became the ideal interdisciplinary observer to inspire and articulate the contextual study of science, technology, and society.

BOOKS BY MUMFORD

Architecture as a Home for Man: Essays for Architectural Record. Ed. by Jeanne M. Davern. McGraw 1975 o.p. Presents a collection of 24 essays, originally published from 1928 to 1968, that evaluate architectural principles and concepts related to human and moral goals; discusses the future of the city, urban transportation, domestic architecture, and building for the aged.

Art and Technics. Bampton Lectures. 1952. Col. U. Pr. 1972 $34.00. ISBN 0-231-01903-3. ISBN 0-231-08509-5. Features a series of lectures that discuss the merging of art and technics into a working relationship; suggests that the machine should be readapted to conform with the human personality by integrating the autonomy and spontaneity of art.

The Brown Decades: A Study of the Arts in America, 1865–1895. 1931. Dover 1955 $4.95. ISBN 0-486-20200-3. Demonstrates that art and architecture in this 30-year period generally mirrored the sooty browns and the functionalism of industralization; includes the works of Eakins, Howells, Dickinson, the Roeblings, Sullivan, Wright, and others.

The City in History: Its Origins, Its Transformations and Its Prospects. 1961. HarBraceJ 1968 $21.95. ISBN 0-15-618035-9. Examines the city, from ancient agricultural village to modern megalopolis and suburbia, in regard to form, function, and purpose within its culture. Argues for organic unity between human beings and the urban environment; includes comprehensive and useful bibliography.

The Culture of Cities. 1938. HarBraceJ 1970. $19.95. ISBN 0-15-623301-0. Views cities from medieval times to the contemporary urban centers of the 1930s. Examines the roles of protection, ceremony, politics, industrial production, regional development, the megalopolis, and the social basis of the new urban order.

Findings and Keepings: Analects for an Autobiography. HarBraceJ 1975 o.p. Features idiosyncratic, but charming, collection of writings mainly from Mumford's early career. Contains letters, articles, a short story, a play about the building of the Brooklyn Bridge, and "Prologue to Our Time, 1895–1975," which is a summary of Mumford's thought; also discusses the process of writing *Technics and Civilization.*

The Highway and the City. 1963. Greenwood 1981 $38.50. ISBN 0-313-22747-0. Presents a collection of previously published essays that discuss the problems and goals of the contemporary city. Topics include the UNESCO house, skyscrapers and traffic congestion in London, Wright and the Guddenheim Museum, the interior design of Pennsylvania Station, and the automobile and highway systems.

Interpretations and Forecasts, 1922–1972: Studies in Literature, History, Biography, Technics, and Contemporary Society. 1973. HarBraceJ 1979 $5.95. ISBN 0-15-644903-X. A selection of 42 essays and reviews that provide a stimulating overview of Mumford's thought and style. Drawing examples from Leonardo and Kepler as well as philosophers and inventors, Mumford demonstrates that new technologies become part of a complex, interdependent, totalitarian system. Views mechanical devices as symptoms of our failure to appreciate essential human values.

The Lewis Mumford Reader. Ed. by Donald Miller. Pantheon 1986 $23.95. ISBN 0-394-55526-0. Presents the scope of Mumford's thought and contributions in a fine selection of his writings; arranged under five primary themes: architecture, urban history, the future of the city, American culture, and technology.

The Myth of the Machine. 1967–70. 2 vols. HarBraceJ 1971–74 $19.95 ea. Vol. 1 *Technics and Human Development.* ISBN 0-15-662341-2. Vol. 2 *The Pentagon of Power.* ISBN 0-15-671610-0. Questions the present commitment to technical and scientific progress as an end in itself. By tracing the course of human development, doubt is cast on theories that present Homo Sapiens as essentially a toolmaker; Volume 2 deals with "megatechnics" and the misdirection of human energies that has not allowed people to experience satisfying lives.

My Works and Days: A Personal Chronicle, 1895–1975. HarBraceJ 1979 o.p. Presents biographical narratives of life, adolescence, marriage, and children in combination with concerns about the technological society, nuclear war, and the place of art in society. Mumford's evolving thought is evident in these selected writings spanning from 1914 to 1977.

Sketches from Life: The Autobiography of Lewis Mumford—the Early Years. 1982. Beacon Pr. 1983 o.p. Chronicles the events and the personalities that shaped Mumford's career and thought, such as New York City, members of his family, a lover, Patrick Geddes, and Frank Lloyd Wright. Although it has been described by a reviewer as reflecting the "tone of an urban Thoreau," the volume suffers from nostalgia.

Sticks and Stones: A Study of American Architecture and Civilization. 1924. Dover rev. ed. 1955 $4.95. ISBN 0-486-20202-X. A groudbreaking study in the history of American architecture that views architecture within cultural and social contexts. Demonstrates that civilization and architecture develop simultaneously by discussing the influences, including industrialization, that shaped buildings of such various periods and locales as a New England village, the estate of Monticello and a pioneer settlement.

The Story of Utopias. 1922. Peter Smith 1959 $23.50. ISBN 0-8446-1319-3. From Plato to H. G. Wells, utopias are viewed as attempts to make reality over in a more humane way; focusing attention on the mechanical utopias of the industrial age; final chapter surveys how science, technology, and art have escaped from the service of humankind and suggests how they can become more humane to form a foundation for utopia, or the good place.

Technics and Civilization. 1934 HarBraceJ 1963 $10.95. ISBN 0-15-688254-X. Presents a historical study of the machine, covering 1,000 years; presents the first extensive examination of the reciprocal nature of the relationship between technical forces and the social milieu.

The Urban Prospect. HarBraceJ 1969 o.p. A collection of articles, from the 1950s and 1960s, in which Mumford criticizes many of the urban planners of this century. Claims that innovators such as Wright, LeCorbusier, and Doxiadis have perpetuated dispersal, suburban sprawl, and inefficient transportation systems.

BOOKS ABOUT MUMFORD

Blake, Casey Nelson. *Beloved Community: The Cultural Criticism of Randolph Bourne, Van Wyck Brooks, Waldo Frank, and Lewis Mumford.* U. of NC Pr. 1990 $34.95. ISBN 0-8078-1935-2. Describes how four young intellectuals, among the first generation to adopt an "Americanist" view of cultural criticism, confronted industrial society and its reflections in art, literature, politics, and social studies; traces their thought and influence from 1900 to 1940.

Carrithers, Gale H., Jr. *Mumford, Tate, Eiseley: Watchers in the Night.* La. State U. Pr. 1991 $29.95. ISBN 0-807-1650-5. Considers Lewis Mumford, Alan Tate, and Loren Eiseley as forming an "intellectual confluence," expressing their understanding of nature, science, and self as an integration of cultural ideas; describes how these three writers explored the use of authority imposed by intellectuals, institutions, and establishments.

Conrad, David R. *Education for Transformation: Implications in Lewis Mumford's Ecohumanism.* ETC Pubns. 1976 $19.95. ISBN 0-88280-030-2. Examines Mumford's ideas of organic technology and architecture as well as his devotion to the creation of life-affirming urban and suburban environments; includes a consideration of the implications of Mumford's concepts of wholeness and interrelatedness for education.

Hughes, Thomas P., and Agatha C. Hughes, eds. *Lewis Mumford: Public Intellectual.* OUP 1990 $39.95. ISBN 0-19-506173-X. Features a collection of 15 papers from the Lewis Mumford Conference at the University of Pennsylvania in 1989. Individual sections discuss technology and regional development, the megamachine and organicism, values and community, peril and hope; contributors include STS scholars Howard Segal, Leo Marx, Donald Miller, and Rosalind Williams.

Miller, Donald L. *Lewis Mumford, A Life.* Grove Pr. 1989 $24.95. ISBN 1-55584-244-5. Presents the authorized and authoritative biography of Mumford; focuses on his philosophy, writings, and his personal life reflected in his work.

Morley, Jane, comp. *On Lewis Mumford: An Annotated Bibliography. Program for Assessing and Revitalizing the Social Sciences.* U. of Pa. Pr. 1985 o.p. An introductory compendium of secondary works that provides the reader with a helpful guide to the major Anglo-American sources on Mumford. Most of the well-annotated entries focus on humanities and social-science books and articles published since 1950, which analyze Mumford and his work; includes several bibliographies and a list of scholarly reviews of Mumford's books.

NELKIN, DOROTHY. 1933–

A sociologist, science policy researcher, and teacher, Dorothy Nelkin has been a faculty member of Cornell University for most of her career. Born in Boston, Massachusetts, she worked as a senior research associate in the Science, Technology, and Society Program at Cornell University from 1969 to 1972. At Cornell she met and married Mark Nelkin, a physicist and professor of physics. Her first book, *Migrant: Farm Workers in America's Northwest* (1971), reflects her interest in the process of social and science policy making. Nelkin's subsequent books present case studies of the various factors that affect governmental decision making and policy development. She has focused on the dynamics of controversy, the role of citizen's groups, the press, and governmental or legal authorities in most of her studies. Nelkin was involved personally in a science-related social controversy, when a power company proposed building a nuclear power plant on Cayuga Lake. She has moved on to wider-ranging controversies related to governmental housing, weapons research at MIT, methadone maintenance, textbooks and the creation-evolution debate, use of biological tests, the antinuclear movement in France and Germany, and AIDS. Two of her books, *Science as Intellectual Property* (1983) and *Selling Science* (1988), examine scientific information—who owns it, who controls it, and how it is presented to the public. Perhaps her most well-known book, *Controversy: Politics of Technical Decisions*, presents a diverse collection of case studies, especially valuable for classroom use. In 1992 the book appeared in its third revised edition.

Nelkin's prolific writing career has been supported by grants, as well as by visiting scholar and consultant positions. She has been awarded fellowships by the Guggenheim Foundation, National Science Foundation, and the Russell Sage Foundation. She has held visiting scholar appointments at Resources for the Future, Hastings Institute, and at research institutes in Berlin and Paris. Nelkin was an adviser for the Office of Technology Assessment and is a member of the National Advisory Council to the National Institutes of Health Human Genome Project. She also is a member and serves on the boards of directors of the Council for the Advancement of Science Writing, Medicine in the Public Interest, and Society for the Social Studies of Science. After her initial appointment in Cornell's Science, Technology, Society Program, Nelkin became professor of sociology at Cornell from 1972 to 1989 and is now professor of sociology and affiliate professor of law at New York University. Nelkin is best known for establishing the case study method in interdisciplinary science/technology/society studies.

BOOKS BY NELKIN

The Atom Beseiged: Extraparliamentary Dissent in France and Germany. Ed. by Dorothy Nelkin and Michael Pollak. MIT Pr. 1981 $9.95. ISBN 0-262-64021-X. Notes that, in France, the antinuclear movement has not affected policy, while in Germany the movement has resulted in a nuclear moratorium. This comparative study reveals factors that shaped these social conflicts and the outcomes including institutional factors, administrative procedures, historical experiences, ideologies; appendices provide information on nuclear installations and major court cases in France and Germany.

Controversy: Politics of Technical Decisions. Sage 1992 $46.00. ISBN 0-8039-4466-7. Documents decision making when technology and politics conflict over values by examining 12 original case studies. Cases cover issues such as moral versus scientific values (fetal research, animal rights, surrogacy), technological catastrophy and the environment (ozone layer, Exxon Valdez, nuclear power), economics and health (cancer-diet debate, occupational health, genetic testing), and individual rights and social goals (creation-evolution debate, testing for AIDS, recombinant DNA).

The Creation Controversy: Science or Scripture in the Schools. Norton 1982 $16.95. ISBN 0-393-01635-8. Views the motives and perceptions surrounding the conflict over the teaching of evolutionary theory and creationism as criticism of contemporary science and its values as well as a rejection of the role of expertise. Traces the historical context of the dispute, analyzes the social and political base of the textbook watchers, details several disputes in different states, and discusses the impact of this controversy between science and individual religious beliefs.

Dangerous Diagnostics: The Social Power of Biological Information. (coauthored with Laurence Tancredi). 1989 Basic 1991 $10.95. ISBN 0-465-01572-7. Investigates the potential uses and abuses of biological tests resulting from research in genetics and the neurosciences. Discusses the use of tests, not only for health diagnosis but also in the workplace, to predict performance and health and in the schools to diagnose learning problems; also examines the "cultural appeal" of testing and reliability of tests.

A Disease of Society: Cultural and Institutional Responses to AIDS. (coedited with David P. Willis and Scott V. Parris). Cambridge U. Pr. 1991 $44.95. ISBN 0-521-40411-8. This collection of essays considers the effects of AIDS on specific aspects of our culture, including personal relationships and social institutions. Describes how AIDS has changed cultural images, the concept of family, the prison system, the regulatory process for new drugs, the culture and politics of medicine, sexual freedom, guilt, and discrimination.

Methadone Maintenance: A Technological Fix. Braziller 1973 o.p. Analyzes the use of methadone as a substitute for heroine addiction in terms of the prevailing tendency to apply quick technological solutions to major problems. Considers not only society's willingness to embrace the available technological "fix" but also the implications, such as control over individuals and the deliberate establishment of addiction to a drug.

The University and Military Research; Moral Politics at M.I.T. Cornell Univ. Pr. 1972 o.p. Chronicles events leading to the decision by MIT in 1970 to divest itself of the Instrumentation Laboratory, which conducted military-sponsored research in inertial guidance systems. Issues discussed in connection with this year-long controversy include the responsibility of scientists and technologists for use or misuse of their research, the reallocation of research to remedy social problems, and the relationship between the university and national political institutions.

PETROSKI, HENRY. 1942–

Henry Petroski is an American engineer with wide-ranging historical and sociocultural interests. He earned a Ph.D. in theoretical and applied mechanics from the University of Illinois at Urbana-Champaign in 1968, and became Aleksandar S. Vesic professor and chair of the Department of Civil and Environmental Engineering at Duke University. Petroski teaches traditional engineering subjects, as well as courses for nonengineering students, that place the field in a broad social context. One of the major themes that transcends his technical and nontechnical publications is the role of failure and its contribution to successful design. This is the central theme in his study *To Engineer Is Human: The Role of Failure in Successful Design*, which is accessible to both engineers and general readers. This theme is also incorporated into Petroski's *The Pencil: A History of Design and Circumstance* (1990), which relates the history of the pencil to broader sociocultural themes. The theme is expanded further, illustrating the relationship of engineering to our everyday life in *The Evolution of Useful Things* (1992). Petroski's most recent book, *Design Paradigms: Case Histories of Error and Judgment in Engineering*, is planned for publication in 1994. After that, he will begin a study of the complex interrelationships between engineering and culture. Widely recognized and supported by both the technical and humanities communities, Petroski's work has effectively conveyed the richness and essence of engineering in its societal context for the general reader.

BOOKS BY PETROSKI

Beyond Engineering: Essays and Other Attempts to Figure without Equations. St. Martin 1986 $17.95. ISBN 0-312-07785-8. Presents 31 nontechnical essays that include views on the ideas of C. P. Snow, and computers, balancing the budget, and converting baseball and football scoring into the metric system; features a delightfully revealing portrait of the non-stereotypical engineer.

The Evolution of Useful Things. Knopf 1992 $24.00. ISBN 0-679-41226-3. Reveals the relationship of engineering and design to such artifacts of everyday life as forks and spoons, paper clips, "stick-on" notes, "tin" cans, and zippers, among many others; represents Petroski's most sophisticated and broad-ranging book to date.

The Pencil: A History of Design and Circumstance. Knopf 1990 $25.00. ISBN 0-394-57422-2. Chronicles the history of the pencil from early Greek and Roman origins through the sixteenth-century discovery of graphite in England to its present yellow standard form; illustrates how technical-engineering design is related to the broader societal and economic contexts in which it is embedded.

To Engineer Is Human: The Role of Failure in Successful Design. St. Martin 1985 $17.95. ISBN 0-312-80680-9. Offers a popular explanation of why failure and risk are a necessary aspect of modern engineering practice.

ROSZAK, THEODORE. 1933–

Born in Chicago, Illinois, the son of a cabinetmaker, Theodore Roszak received a Ph.D. from Princeton University and then taught at Stanford University. Since the mid-1960s, Roszak has been teaching at California State University, Hayward. His only lengthy departure from academia was when he served as editor of *Peace News* in London during 1964 and 1965. Roszak's writings and social philosophy have been controversial since the publication of

The Making of a Counter Culture in 1968. In his classic work, Roszak views the youthful dissident culture of the 1960s as an alternative to the dominant technocratic environment. To transform society from "technological totalitarianism" and the depersonalized methodology of science, Roszak gracefully suggests a merger of subjectivity, individualism, mysticism, a symbiotic relationship with nature, and an ethical concern for the well-being of others.

A major criticism of Roszak's emphasis on spiritual transformation and his faith in youthful dissidents is his "apolitical" philosophy. Reliance on expanded consciousness and personal fulfillment is not viewed as a viable force for change. In his subsequent books, especially *Where the Wasteland Ends* (1972) and *Person/Planet* (1978), Roszak articulates an "intercommunion between man and nature," which recognizes that a synthesis of human needs and the well-being of the planet can be a force to displace the ideologies of industrial society. Unfortunately, these works often have been simplistically read as paeans to individual expanded consciousness. Roszak analyzes the influences on the radical movement of the 1960s, seeking a union between scientific thinking and other modes of consciousness: mystic, aesthetic, and ethical. In *The Voice of the Earth* (1992), Roszak bridges the scientific and the subjective mind to stimulate a culture that nourishes both personal fulfillment and the well-being of the earth. Roszak departs from his general thesis in *The Cult of Information* (1986) to challenge the folklore surrounding the computer revolution and to address the distinction between the processing of information and thinking. He opposes technological-industrial development and the preeminence of science but continues to support changes in attitudes, consciousness, and values in order to transform technological and scientific achievements into engines for the well-being of human beings.

BOOKS BY ROSZAK

The Cult of Information: The Folklore of Computers and the True Art of Thinking. Pantheon 1986 $17.45. ISBN 0-394-54622-9. Critiques the use of computers in education and society, challenging the claims in support of the computer by elements in our society who make "morally questionable uses of computer power." Discusses the folklore that has been created around the computer: "images of power, illusions of well-being, the fantasies and wishful thinking, . . ." and *information* has been given a global definition of "all good things to all people;" insists there is a vital distinction between a machine processing information and a mind thinking.

The Making of a Counter Culture: Reflections on the Technocratic Society and Its Youthful Opposition. Doubleday 1968 o.p. Considers the counterculture movement evolving in the late 1960s a cultural movement that rejects the values and assumptions held by mainstream society since the seventeenth century. Discusses how the counterculture rejects technocratic politics in search of a new reality principle. Views this youthful rebellion as our hope to fight "technocratic totalitarianism;" examines people and phenomena that include Marcuse, Ginsberg, Paul Goodman, psychedelic experience, oriental and American Indian mysticism, the psychology of alienation, and communitarianism.

Person/Planet: The Creative Disintegration of Industrial Society. Doubleday 1978 o.p. Suggests that a sensibility for the needs of the individual is merging with environmental awareness of a global scale, which is beginning to affect central institutions in our society. Sketches the cultural transformation in which the interrelationships between these two drives have enough political force to displace the ideologies of industrial society.

Sources: An Anthology of Contemporary Materials Useful for Preserving Personal Sanity While Braving the Great Technological Wilderness. Ed. by Theodore Roszak. HarpC 1972 o.p. Features a large anthology of classic and lesser-known essays by generally contemporary writers; views personal liberation in expanding arenas including the person, body, community, whole earth, and transcendence; designed as a survival kit in a technology dominated world.

The Voice of the Earth. Summit Bks. 1992 $23.00. ISBN 0-671-72968-3. Presents an essay in "ecopsychology" that bridges the artificial separation between pure science and the subjective mind. Roszak claims that the gap between the personal and the planetary must be closed to create a quality of life that nurtures the complete person; examines psychology, mysticism, self-awareness, social environments, products of technology, narcissism, and ecological consciousness.

Where the Wasteland Ends: Politics and Transcendence in Postindustrial Society. Doubleday 1973 $4.95. ISBN 0-385-02738-9. Views the renewal of religious spirit as a signal that society has reached a vantage point where we can visualize "where the wasteland ends and where a culture of human wholeness and fulfillment begins." States that the wasteland has evolved from urban-industrial development, technocracy, the preeminence of science, and the secularization of consciousness.

ROY, RUSTUM. 1924–

Born and educated in India, Rustum Roy received an M.S. degree in chemistry in 1948 and a Ph.D. in ceramics from Pennsylvania State University. With brief exception, he has taught and has conducted research at Pennsylvania State until the present. Roy has been a major figure in the emerging field of STS for more than two decades. During this period, he has combined a scientific-technical background in materials science with interests in science policy and education. He was the founding director of the Materials Research Laboratory at Penn State and is currently Evan Pugh Professor of the Solid State, Professor of Geochemistry, and Professor of Science, Technology, and Society. Roy's extensive research has focused on the synthesis of new ceramic materials. One of his most important publications is *Radioactive Waste Disposal* (1982), in which he covers the technical issues of radioactive-waste encapsulation.

Among the vanguard of the scientists and engineers who increasingly came to recognize the societal implications of science and technology, Roy helped to establish the Penn State Science, Technology, and Society Program in 1969 and served for many years as its director. His experiences with this particular STS program and his concerns regarding science and technology have focused Roy's interests in three areas: science and technology policy, science education, and the science-religion interface. Roy has published widely in each of these areas and has been actively involved in science policy making and analysis at the state and federal levels, as well as having served on numerous advisory committees and boards. His *Lost at the Frontier: U. S. Science and Technology Policy Adrift* (1985), written with Deborah Shapley, critiques the pure science orientation of postwar policy. Some of the alternative national science policy proposals in this volume have exercised considerable influence. In addition, Roy has become an outspoken critic of the scientific peer-review system.

Roy's experiences with the STS program at Penn State led to his involvement with major efforts to enhance the scientific and technological "literacy" of American students and future citizens. This was to be achieved by promoting an understanding of the social context of science and technology rather than by merely enhancing the training of professional scientists. To accomplish this end, Roy established an annual series of national Technology Literacy Conferences, which have evolved into the National Association of STS (NASTS). Roy serves as founder, corporate chair, and editor of the NASTS affiliated *Bulletin of Science, Technology, and Society.*

In his personal life, Roy's interest in the interface between science and religion have resulted in his appointment as first chair of the National Council of Churches Committee on Science, Technology, and the Church. He also has presented the prestigious Hibbert Lectures on Theology in London, which subsequently were published as *Experimenting with Truth: The Fusion of Religion with Technological Need for Humanity's Survival* (1981).

Roy has successfully combined the attributes of established scientific research with scholarship and strong leadership in the science policy and science education arenas, and has readily transcended traditional disciplinary boundaries, which is a hallmark of STS proponents.

Books by Roy

Experimenting with Truth: The Fusion of Religion with Technology Needed for Humanity's Survival. Hibbert Lecture Ser. Pergamon 1981 $80.00. ISBN 0-08-025820-4. Illustrates "the coupling of the worldview of the modern enterprise of science *and technology* with the worldview of the 'radical' 'avant-garde' Christian community."

Lost at the Frontier: U.S. Science and Technology Policy Adrift. (coauthored with Deborah Shapley). ISI Pr. 1985 $19.95. ISBN 0-89495-041-X. Features "an experiment in science criticism," in which Shapley and Roy argue for a science policy that emphasizes directed basic research, applied science, engineering, and technology in contrast to the current excessive emphasis on undirected basic research.

The Major Ternary Structural Families. (coauthored with Olaf Muller). Presents a partial series of technical volumes on the crystal chemistry of non-metallurgic materials; written for practicing non-specialist materials researchers and graduate students in related fields.

Radioactive Waste Disposal. Vol. 1 *The Waste Package.* Pergamon 1982 o.p. A technical but easy-to-read book; argues that radioactive waste disposal is not solely a technical issue, but one that is also socio-political and regulatory in nature.

WINNER, LANGDON. 1944–

[See Chapter 5 in this volume.]

ZIMAN, JOHN M. 1925–

[See Chapter 2 in this volume.]

CHAPTER 7

Special Issues in Science, Technology, and Society

Carl Mitcham, Joyce Williams, and Richard A. Deitrich

> Science and technology are not just our society—but our politics, art, even religion. Until we understand this, we will not understand anything. . . . And while we're at it, we ought to note the very gendered character of our supposedly neutral science and technology.
> —WILHELM E. FUDPUCKER, *In Conversation*

The general literature of science, technology, and society encompasses primarily the fields of history, philosophy, and ethics of science, technology, and medicine. In addition, this literature is enhanced by studies in several closely allied specialized areas. These special areas include science and technology policy; feminist and gender studies; science, technology, and art; and science, technology, and religion.

In three of these specialized areas, the literature focuses on a certain institution or a particular aspect of society—for example, on politics and management, on art, or on religion—and considers the relationship of these areas to science and technology. This relationship might center on the influence of politics, art, and religion on science and technology; on the influence of science and technology on politics, art, and religion; or on their interactions. In each case, however, these areas of study typically shed light on special aspects of science and technology themselves.

For example, politics and management policy relating to science and technology readily addresses practical issues. Science and technology policy views science more as a resource for technological invention and economic progress than as a pure intellectual or cognitive activity. By contrast, religious debates about science often have emphasized their theoretical and cognitive aspects and how they might be at odds with religious doctrine; for example, GALILEO's (see also Vol. 4) idea that the earth revolves around the sun, or DARWIN's theory of evolution. In each case, certain aspects of science and technology are viewed as engaging different aspects of society.

It is important to note that the analysis of each of the three special areas presented here also can be supplemented by the surveys in Volumes 1–4 of *The Reader's Adviser*. The chapter on political science and the chapters on the arts in Volume 3, the science fiction literature in Volumes 1 and 2, and the chapter on contemporary issues in religious thought in Volume 4 are among the obvious examples.

The fourth special issue discussed in this chapter, feminist and gender studies, does not focus on any one institution or aspect of society. Rather, the gender aspects of science and technology are addressed in the context of societal institutions. Clearly, such gender studies deserve to be integrated into STS analyses and are highlighted here, in part to remedy their neglect in much of the STS general literature.

SCIENCE AND TECHNOLOGY POLICY

Science and technology policy issues can be traced back to Classical political philosophy. ARISTOTLE (see Vols. 3 and 4), for instance, argues that politics rightly decides what sciences and technologies are to be pursued in a state. Later, Renaissance and Enlightenment proposals for the creation of an autonomous, technologically oriented science with state support first raised these policy issues in their modern form. However, only since World War II, when governmental funding of science and technology began on a historically unprecedented scale (unprecedented both in the amount of money involved and the size of scientific-technological projects undertaken) have science and technology policy studies taken on their present, distinct character. This powerful postwar role of science also prompted public concern, as expressed by President Eisenhower in his "Farewell Address" in 1961: "[I]n holding scientific research and discovery in respect, as we should, we must also be alert to the equal and opposite danger that public policy could itself become the captive of a scientific-technological elite."

The terms "science policy" and "technology policy" are sometimes defined in distinct ways. "Science policy" usually is used to refer to the management of scientific research, while "technology policy" refers to the public or governmental promotion of industrial development. In this sense, technology policy is often the equivalent of industrial policy. However, given the increasing interpenetration of science and technology, such distinctions carry less and less import. Indeed, many scientists today often argue for governmental funding because of the secondary economic benefits claimed for pure research.

Another commonly voiced distinction amplifies an ambiguity in the term "science and technology policy." The label can refer, on the one hand, to politics or policy engaged in the management of science and technology, that is, how government functions to support, regulate, or control science and technology. On the other hand, it also can refer to science and technology in politics, that is, the incorporation of scientific-technical knowledge and practice in government decision making, often by means of scientific research and advice. However, the two definitions are closely related, since management of the technical community often proceeds on the basis of advice from scientific and technical experts.

Since World War II and the Manhattan Project that had been established to produce the atomic bomb, and the worldwide unprecedented expansion in scientific-technological development, science has come to be seen as central to the economic growth and national self-definition of many countries. This has led to widespread debate in many countries about their scientific-technological progress compared with that of other nations, as well as the most effective means of achieving this development, given their own unique social and cultural traditions. As a result, science and technology policy has been subject to extensive analysis and assessment by the policy sciences. Such analysis typically has focused on one or more of the following issues: the adequacy of problem definition; clarification of the policy process; and evaluation research, that is, efforts to determine whether the policy was effective in realizing some projected goal and whether it was cost effective.

In the United States, for instance, concern grew in the late 1980s that this country had fallen behind other industrialized nations in formulating a coherent science policy agenda. This alleged failure was attributed by some to the decentralization of scientific research, since government, industries, and universities all attempt to maintain their autonomy and to conduct research in their own way. At the same time, the need for public review and direction of science in a democracy began to be more widely recognized. Although science has spent centuries trying to overcome political controls, some direction and guidelines by government increasingly are being called for. What is behind this development? Today, advances in science have enormous consequences, not only for U.S. industrialization and economic growth but also for the attendant environmental impact and population patterns and pressures. Moreover, policy on industrial and agricultural science and technology in the developing nations may well determine the future of life on this planet. Yet, as policy analysts themselves admit, effective science and technology policy analysis requires far more research.

The studies listed here attempt in various ways to illuminate the problems and possibilities of science policy. Some are the writings of scientists, some are by social scientists; yet all are the work of concerned citizens. Their writings focus on the mechanics of policy making, the history of science advising, and the public character of science.

Averch, Harvey A. *A Strategic Analysis of Science and Public Policy.* Johns Hopkins 1985 $34.00. ISBN 0-8018-2467-2. Examines the strategies used by actors in the science and technology arena. Averch's useful instruction in cutting through the language of policy makers to the substance of underlying motivation of their studies helps make policy more rational and explicit.

Brooks, Harvey. *The Government of Science.* MIT Pr. 1968 o.p. A collection of papers from the 1960s by this influential science policy participant and scholar emphasizes the importance of flexibility and multiple competing centers of decision making in science; he thus argues for the unique strengths of decentralized science policy in the United States.

Brooks, Harvey, and Chester L. Cooper, eds. *Science for Public Policy.* Pergamon 1987 $67.00. ISBN 0-08-034770-3. Proceedings of an international conference (1984) focusing on "the use of scientific evidence, data, and insights to illuminate public policy issues that are not primarily scientific but are strongly dependent on scientific and technological information."

Burns, Tom R., and Reinhard Ueberhorst. *Creative Democracy: Systematic Conflict Resolution and Policymaking in a World of High Science and Technology.* Greenwood 1988 $37.95. ISBN 0-275-92957-4. This study is concerned with "the forms and quality of exchange among experts, politicians, and citizens in a democratic society." It advocates "systematic democratic discourse" in which political representatives work with scientists to produce a variety of approaches on a given issue. Decisions then will be made by informed public debate.

Clark, Norman. *The Political Economy of Science and Technology.* Blackwell Pubs. 1985 $55.00. ISBN 0-631-14293-2. Focuses specifically on science and technology policy and demonstrates how economic analysis, broadly defined, can inform this process. Macroeconomic theory and analysis are applied to technical innovation in industry and to technology transfer to less developed countries.

Cole, Leonard A. *Politics and the Restraint of Science.* Rowman 1983 $29.50. ISBN 0-86598-125-6. Based on a 1979 survey of American scientists, this book sheds light on their views of the restraint and control of science by government authority; recommends a "Science Hearings Panel" to balance free inquiry and public interest.

Dickson, David. *The New Politics of Science*. U. Ch. Pr. 1988 $14.95. ISBN 0-226-14763-0. According to the author, "In the mid-1970s, concerns . . . focused primarily on the undesirable consequences of the social applications of science through technology. . . . Today, the political agenda of the scientific community is filled by a very different set of topics, those raised by the implications of efforts to maximize the contribution of science to commercial and military ends."

Goggin, Malcolm L., ed. *Governing Science and Technology in a Democracy*. U. of Tenn. Pr. 1986 $36.95. ISBN 0-87049-506-2. A collection of essays, centered on four questions: Who should govern science and technology? When should they act? Where should authority be located? To what ends should science and technology be directed? The author advocates a more democratic approach.

Golden, William T., ed. *Worldwide Science and Technology Advice to the Highest Levels of Governments*. AAAS 1981 $29.95. ISBN 0-08-040406-5. Four broad overview essays in this field are followed by 35 essays describing science and technology advising organizations and their effectiveness in individual countries.

_____. *Science Advice to the President*. AAAS 1992 repr. of 1980 ed. $28.95. ISBN 0-87168-509-4. First published as a special issue of *Technology in Society*, vol. 2, nos. 1-2 (1988). Eight of the 10 presidential science advisers from 1957 to 1979 discuss their experiences. Other policy experts also offer critical histories of the Office of Science Adviser, the President's Science Advisory Committee, and federal science policy.

_____. *Science and Technology Advice to the President, Congress, and Judiciary*. AAAS 1992 repr. of 1988 ed. $28.95. ISBN 0-87168-510-8. A comprehensive collection of essays by politicians, policy participants, and scholars, written with an eye to the future of science and technology advising in all branches of government.

Goldhaber, Michael. *Reinventing Technology: Policies for Democratic Values*. Routledge 1986 $35.00. ISBN 0-7102-0906-1. Proposes a "social goals-directed technology and science program." "The premise of [such a program] is that there are many socially valuable technologies which only the government has the capacity to develop. Not attempting to do so amounts to an injustice."

Goldsmith, M., ed. *Strategies for Europe: Proposals for Science and Technology Policies*. Franklin 1978 $78.00. ISBN 0-08-022992-1. A transcription of the proceedings of a 1978 symposium organized by the Science Policy Foundation in collaboration with the Commission of the European Community; includes recommendations for the organization of European science policymaking, as well as for industrial social innovations.

Greenberg, Dan. *The Politics of Pure Science*. Berkeley Pub. 1967 o.p. A classic in the science-technology policy field by an author who edits the newsletter *Science and Government*.

Haberer, Joseph, ed. *Science and Technology Policy*. Policy Studies 1976 $12.00. ISBN 0-918592-17-8. A collection of 17 studies, most of which first appeared as a special issue of the *Policy Studies Journal*, vol. 5, no. 2 (Winter 1976). Influential scholars define issues that remain relevant.

Hass, Ernst B., and others. *Scientists and World Order: The Uses of Technical Knowledge in International Organizations*. U. CA Pr. 1978 $50.00. ISBN 0-520-03341-8. How do scientists and scientific knowledge shape the world order? How can scientific institutions improve life on the planet? "[M]an and society are part of nature and are increasingly dependent on it for the fulfillment of political goals *even if that fulfillment calls for the manipulation and control of nature*. . . . The scientific culture has become coterminous with political life."

Herken, Gregg. *Cardinal Choices: Presidential Science Advising, from the Atomic Bomb to SDI*. OUP 1992 $24.95. ISBN 0-19-507210-3. Chronicles science advising from FDR to Bush in all its institutional forms, as well as the conflicts between the interests of scientists and politicians; focuses heavily on science and technology policy as driven by military concerns.

Hiskes, Anne L., and Richard P. Hiskes. *Science, Technology, and Policy Decisions*. Westview 1986 $20.95. ISBN 0-86531-632-5. Stresses the normative aspects of policymaking, as well as the mechanics of decision making. The main argument set

forth: "[T]hose who make and those who study science and technology policy need
to be aware of the . . . philosophical, institutional, participatory, economic, and
ethical dimensions of science and technology decisions."

James, Jeffery, and Susuma Watanabe, eds. *Technology, Institutions, and Government
Policies*. St. Martin 1985 $29.95. ISBN 0-312-79006-6. Essays on the theme of
industrial development in the Third World; includes macroeconomic, political-
economic, and game-theoretic models, as well as empirical studies.

Jasanoff, Sheila. *The Fifth Branch: Science Advisers as Policymakers*. HUP 1990 $30.00.
ISBN 0-674-30061-0. Focusing on various advisory committees of the EPA and FDA,
argues that the technocratic and democratic models of science policy making are
inadequate, given political realities; concludes that there is no objectively verifiable
truth in either science or regulation.

Kistiakowsky, George B. *A Scientist at the White House*. HUP 1976 $37.50. ISBN 0-674-
79496-6. The private diary of President Eisenhower's Special Assistant for Science
and Technology reveals his observations during the depths of the cold war.

Kuehn, Thomas J., and Alan L. Porter. eds. *Science, Technology, and National Policy*.
Cornell Univ. Pr. 1981 $49.50. ISBN 0-8014-1343-5. Ten essays on the social context
of technology and science, 15 on the confused attempts of the U.S. government to
regulate technology and science. This collection of writings by important authors is
well organized and includes an annotated bibliography.

Lambright, W. Henry. *Governing Science and Technology*. OUP 1976 $15.95. ISBN 0-19-
501980-6. A study of the "science and technology intensive agencies, such as the
Department of Defense, NASA, the Energy Research and Development Administration, the National Science Foundation, and the National Institutes of Health, that
points toward the need for a broader understanding of the interactions of
government, politics, and research and development.

McIntyre, John R., and Daniel S. Papp. *The Political Economy of International Technology
Transfer*. Greenwood 1986 $55.00. ISBN 0-89930-128-2. Technology transfer in three
directions (North-South, West-West, and East-West) is analyzed in terms of economics and politics from two major perspectives: power politics and transnationalism.
Examines multinational corporations, international law, development, and world
trade.

Meredith, Margaret O., and others, eds. *AAAS Science and Technology Policy Yearbook
1991*. AAAS 1991 $19.95. ISBN 0-8716-8427-6. The first of an important new series of
annual collections.

Morin, Alexander J. *Science Policy and Politics*. P-H 1992. ISBN 0-13-795246-5. A
concise, data-filled textbook that covers the complex development of science policy
in the United States, the institutions of government and science, and the allocation of
federal resources; perhaps the best general introduction to science policy in the
United States.

Pillar, Charles. *The Fail-Safe Society: Community Defiance and the End of American
Technological Optimism*. Basic 1991 $20.00. ISBN 0-465-02274-X. Chronicles the
backlash against science and industry in the wake of disasters like Love Canal and
Three Mile Island; suggests "a framework for creating the political conditions that
could allow meaningful public involvement in scientific and technological decision
making."

Sachs, Wolfgang, ed. *The Development Dictionary: A Guide to Knowledge as Power*.
Humanities 1992 $25.00. ISBN 1-85649-044-0. Nineteen trenchant criticisms of
Third World economic development policies in science and technology.

Salomon, Jean-Jacques. *Science and Politics*. Trans. by Noël Lindsay. MIT Pr. 1973
$32.50. ISBN 0-262-19111-3. A classic analysis of the distinction between politics in
science and science in politics; written by an influential French science policy
adviser and former head of the Science Policy Division of the Organization for
Economic Cooperation and Development.

Shapley, Deborah, and Rustum Roy. *Lost at the Frontier: U.S. Science and Technology
Policy Adrift*. ISI Pr. 1985 $19.95. ISBN 0-89495-041-X. Pointed critiques of U.S.
science policy that are insightful and frequently provocative; suggests that basic

research is overfunded, while engineering and applied science are outpaced by foreign competition. Scientific knowledge cannot be efficiently turned into beneficial and needed technology and products without reforms in government, industry, education, and professional ethics.

Smith, Bruce L. R. *The Advisers: Scientists in the Policy Process.* Brookings 1992 $36.95. ISBN 0-8157-7990-9. Whereas the author's *American Science Policy Since World War II* stresses the political governance of science and technology, this study examines how scientists themselves have participated in and influenced government.

————. *American Science Policy Since World War II.* Brookings 1990 $34.95. ISBN 0-8157-7998-4. Divides American science policy into three eras: postwar consensus, 1945-1965; policy disarray, 1966-1980; and Reagan era developments. A well-documented, authoritative history.

Snow, C. P. *Science and Government.* HUP 1961 o.p. A classic analysis by the British scientist and intellectual who probed the two-culture dichotomy between scientists and humanists.

Street, John. *Politics and Technology. The Conduct of Science Ser.* Guilford Pr. 1992 $40.00. ISBN 0-0898-6087-2. Maintains that technological disasters, such as Chernobyl and Bhopal, and stratospheric ozone depletion have political and technological causes. He considers ways in which telecommunications, biotechnology, and other technologies can be used to serve or subvert political goals.

Wad, Atul, ed. *Science, Technology, and Development.* Westview 1988 o.p. Fourteen papers arguing for an interdisciplinary appreciation of the complexities of development as a requisite to achieving more balanced, successful outcomes; topics range from the philosophical and epistemological presuppositions of science and technology to their practical management in developing countries dealing with questions of high tech versus appropriate technology, technology transfer, and diffusion.

Wenk, Edward, Jr. *Tradeoffs: Imperatives of Choice in a High-Tech World.* Johns Hopkins 1989 repr. of 1986 ed. $13.95. ISBN 0-8018-3942-4. A valuable and often cited guide for both professionals and concerned citizens. Provides insights on how science affects our lives and how we can affect the conduct of science; argues that public attention must turn to issues of long-range technology management because politics has not yet established an adequate policy here.

Research Institutions

Science and technology policy studies are often the product of research institutions. Three such organizations are the Brookings Institution, the U.S. Congressional Office of Technology Assessment, and the Organization for Economic Cooperation and Development—one private, one national, and one multinational. Brief profiles of these organizations, with listings of some of their relevant publications, follow.

BROOKINGS INSTITUTION

Growing out of a 1916 initiative by reformers who wanted to bring a scientific approach to federal government management, the Brookings Institution, originally called the Institute for Government Research (IGR), is now the oldest "think tank" in Washington, D. C. In 1927 two other initiatives by Robert S. Brookings, a wealthy self-made philanthropist, were merged with IGR to form Brookings as a private nonprofit organization devoted to research, education, and the publication of studies on important domestic and foreign policy issues. Today, Brookings boasts 100 resident and visiting scholars, a support staff of 200, and an extensive library.

Its research projects normally result in published studies that analyze strengths and weaknesses in governmental management and explore policy alternatives. However, Brookings does not take public policy positions. From the beginning, nevertheless, by virtue of its commitment to scientific management in government, its orientation has been progressive. Even so, during the early years of Franklin D. Roosevelt's presidency, many Brookings studies criticized New Deal programs and policies. Since World War II, Brookings once again has emerged as a primary source of policy studies drawn upon by Democratic leaders and other liberal politicians.

Although not devoted solely to science and technology policy research in any narrow sense, Brookings publications commonly address the scientific evaluation of government actions and public policies. Moreover, given the major role played by science and technology in contemporary American society, many Brookings publications bear directly on the management of science and technology. Some were listed in the previous bibliography above. Here are additional Brookings studies, running a gamut from domestic economic policies to military strategy. Their titles are largely self-explanatory.

Baily, Martin Neil, and Alok K. Charkrabarti. *Innovation and the Productivity Crisis.* Brookings 1988 $26.95. ISBN 0-8157-0759-2

Betts, Richard K. *Nuclear Blackmail and Nuclear Balance.* Brookings 1987 $31.95. ISBN 0-8157-0936-6

Carter, Ashton, B., and others, eds. *Managing Nuclear Operations.* Brookings 1987 $48.95. ISBN 0-8157-1314-2

Church, Thomas W., and Robert T. Nakamura. *Cleaning Up the Mess: Implementation Strategies in the Superfund Program.* Brookings 1993 $34.95. ISBN 0-8157-1414-9

Cohen, Linda R., and others. *The Technology Pork Barrel.* Brookings 1991 $36.95. ISBN 0-8157-1508-0. Examines federal support for the development of private-sector technologies, with case histories of the supersonic transport, communications satellites, the space shuttle, the breeder reactor, photovoltaics, and synthetic fuels.

Crandall, Robert W., and Kenneth Flamm, eds. *Changing the Rules: Technological Change, International Competition, and Regulation in Communications.* Brookings 1989 $39.95. ISBN 0-8157-1596-X

Flamm, Kenneth. *Creating the Computer: Government, Industry, and High Technology.* Brookings 1988 $34.95. ISBN 0-8157-2850-6

———. *Targeting the Computer: Government Support and International Competition.* Brookings 1987 $34.95. ISBN 0-8157-2852-2

Huber, Peter W., and Robert E. Litan, eds. *The Liability Maze: The Impact of Liability Law on Safety and Innovation.* Brookings 1991 $39.95. ISBN 0-8157-3760-2

Melnick, R. Shep. *Regulation and the Courts: The Case of the Clean Air Act.* Brookings 1983 $36.95. ISBN 0-8157-5662-3

Nolan, Janne E. *Trappings of Power: Ballistic Missiles in the Third World.* Brookings 1991 $29.95. ISBN 0-8157-6069-5

Smith, James Allen. *Brookings at Seventy-Five.* Brookings 1991 $22.95. ISBN 0-8157-8008-7. A volume on the Brookings Institution itself.

THE U.S. CONGRESSIONAL OFFICE OF TECHNOLOGY ASSESSMENT (OTA)

The Office of Technology Assessment was established to assist Congress in "the legislative assessment of matters" pertaining to technology, because "it is essential that, to the fullest extent possible, the consequences of technological applications be anticipated, understood, and considered." The basic function of the OTA is "to provide early indications of the probable beneficial and adverse impacts of the applications of technology" (Technology Assessment Act of 1972). The OTA is governed by a bipartisan board of six senators, six representatives, and the nonvoting OTA director. The OTA works in 27 subject areas, from aging to waste management, which are grouped into three major divisions: Energy, Materials, and International Security; Health and Life Sciences; and Science, Information, and Natural Resources.

The OTA provides briefings, testimony, and major reports to Congress, which relies on this information to identify policy options and new developments of importance. Studies not only are done in-house by the approximately 150-member OTA staff but also are contracted out to specialists. Sample OTA publications include the following.

Biotechnology in a Global Economy. OTA 1992 $95.00. ISBN 0-941375-60-9. Examines the impact of new biological technologies on national economies as well as the international economy.

Critical Connections: Communications for the Future. OTA 1990 $17.00. ISBN 0-16-018464-9. Discusses the development of integrated communication networks and the prospects for the future.

Development Assistance, Export Promotion, and Environmental Technology. OTA 1993 $6.50. ISBN 2-003-01332-1

Fueling Development: Providing Energy Technologies for Developing Countries. OTA 1992 $247.45. ISBN 0-8490-5618-0. Examines the importance of improving energy technology in developing nations and analyzes the potential impact of providing assistance in helping those nations meet their current and future energy needs.

Global Standards: Building Blocks for the Future. OTA 1992 $29.95. ISBN 0-912702-70-2

Green Products by Design: Choices for a Cleaner Environment. OTA 1992 $6.50. ISBN 2-003-01303-7. Examines the scope and future of environmentally-safe products.

New Technological Era for American Agriculture. OTA 1992 $23.00. ISBN 2-003-01290-1. Analyzes the role of new technology in agriculture and assesses the potential for the future.

Science and Technology Issues in Coastal Ecotourism. OTA 1992 $2.00. ISBN 2-003-01312-6. Looks at the potential role of science technology in providing ecologically-friendly tourism.

THE ORGANIZATION FOR ECONOMIC COOPERATION AND DEVELOPMENT (OECD)

The Organization for Economic Cooperation and Development was founded in 1960 as an outgrowth of the Organization for European Economic Co-operation (OEEC), which was established in 1948 in connection with the Marshall Plan. The OECD now includes the 24 industrialized market economy countries of Europe, North America, and Asia. Its goals are "to achieve the highest sustainable economic growth . . . in member countries, . . . to contribute to sound economic expansion in member as well as nonmember countries in the process of economic development, . . . [and] to contribute to the expansion of world trade."

Its approximately 200 specialized bodies (committees, working parties, etc.) are organized into a series of nine directorates, one of which is the Directorate for Science, Technology, and Industry. Especially important in this directorate is the Committee for Scientific and Technological Policy, which facilitates cooperation in major science projects and analyzes issues arising from science and technology policies related to research, innovation, and specialized technologies (computers, biotechnology, etc.) as well as the interaction of such policies with industry, trade, and the economy. The Committee for Scientific and Technological Policy has published book-length analyses of the science and technology policies of all member and many nonmember countries. Its annual *Science and Technology Policy Outlook* provides regular updates and overviews of key issues.

The Committee for Information, Computer, and Communications Policy, which monitors changes in telecommunications and information technology and analyzes their impacts on competitiveness and productivity, and the Industry Committee, which attends to industry-related policies in member countries and their impact on competitiveness, while analyzing national industrial subsidies and their economic implications, are also part of the Directorate for Sciences, Technology, and Industry.

The Environmental Directorate and such semiautonomous bodies as the Energy Agency, the Nuclear Energy Agency, and the Development Center also undertake research and publication closely related to science and technology policy. Indeed, the annual catalog of OECD publications lists approximately 300 titles, of which at least one-quarter have some direct bearing on science and technology policy.

Climate Change: Policy Initiatives. OECD 1992 $37.00. ISBN 92-64-13754-8. Authoritative source on energy policies of OECD Member countries related to climate change. Describes national commitments to reduce emissions of greenhouse gases and the policies governments will employ to meet them.

Energy and the Environment: Policy Overview. OECD 1990 $40.00. ISBN 92-64-13306-2. Analyzes the way energy policies can be adapted to environmental concerns. Considers the effectiveness of measures such as fuel substitution, improved energy efficiency, add-on pollution control devices, cleaner energy technologies, taxation, and regulation.

Megascience and Its Background. OECD 1993 $17.00. ISBN 92-64-13926-5. Presents an introduction to the problems associated with undertaking and funding large-scale scientific projects. Describes the evolution of megascience and sets out issues, definitions, and the present state of affairs.

Science Responds to Environmental Threats: Country Studies. OECD 1992 $58.00. ISBN 92-64-03688-1. The country studies accompanying the report listed below. Austria, Finland, Germany, Italy, Netherlands, Norway, Sweden, and the United Kingdom are the countries included.

Science Responds to Environmental Threats: Synthesis Report. OECD 1992 $18.00. ISBN 92-64-03687-3. Environmental threats have been increasingly taken into account in scientific and technological policy formulation. But research and development efforts have been uneven among countries and there have been different institutional developments. What place should environmental research have? Results from an exploratory exercise undertaken in selected OECD countries.

Use of Efficiency Standards in Energy Policy. OECD 1992 $48.00. ISBN 92-64-13785-8. Highlights the related experiences of Japan, several countries in North America and Europe, and of international organizations, in designing and applying energy efficiency standards.

World Energy Outlook. OECD 1993 $28.00. ISBN 92-64-13904-4. Contains projections for world energy markets through 2010. Also examines the potential impact of carbon taxes in the OECD area.

FEMINIST AND GENDER STUDIES

JOAN ROTHSCHILD has said that "Creating a gender framework for incorporating feminist materials into technology means showing how and why gender is a necessary category of analysis for thinking and studying about technology." This call for feminist and gender studies by a leading writer in the field highlights the growing interest and concern in this aspect of science, technology, and society. Rothschild and Judy Wajcman, in effect, have distinguished three feminist approaches in STS: (1) studies of women and science-technology, that is, examinations of how technological-scientific changes affect women; (2) studies of women in science and technology, that is, the roles and contributions of women in these fields; and (3) studies of how women can alter or transform science and technology by introducing new perspectives and attitudes.

It should be emphasized, however, that feminist studies not only introduce an important, new perspective into understanding science and technology in society but also reflect diverse viewpoints. Feminism is not some oversimplified ideology but a rich source of new interpretation and analysis. The heightened awareness of the role of gender in science and technology that is at the core of feminist research has given rise to different areas of research and new fields of interest while stimulating divergent ideas about the appropriateness and desirability of a variety of societal distinctions.

Although these new concerns deserve to be integrated into the field of science, technology, and society (some are cited in Chapter 6) they also are highlighted here because of the major importance of this developing body of work.

Bertsch, Sharon M. *Nobel Prize Women in Science: Their Lives, Struggles, and Momentous Discoveries.* Carol Pub. Group 1992 $24.00. ISBN 1-55972-146-4. Biographies of 14 women Nobel laureates.

Bleier, Ruth, ed. *Feminist Approaches to Science.* Pergamon 1986 $36.50. ISBN 0-08-032787-7. These nine essays explore "the nature of contemporary science and [attempt] to extend our visions toward a science that is different, better, feminist, and emancipating."

Cockburn, Cynthia. *Machinery of Dominance: Women, Men, and Technical Know-How.* NE U. Pr. 1988 $32.50. ISBN 1-5555-3041-9. A British-based study of how women are faring as the workplace is altered by computers.

Cowan, Ruth Schwartz. *More Work for Mother: The Ironies of Household Technology, from the Open Hearth to the Microwave.* Basic 1983 $17.95. ISBN 0-465-04731-9. A now classic study of how labor-saving household appliances, in fact, did not reduce housework, for women but only intensified it.

De Lauretis, Teresa. *Technologies of Gender.* Ind. U. Pr. 1987 $7.95. ISBN 0-253-20441-0. Views the social constructs of gender, especially in film and fiction, as a form of technology.

Duden, Barbara. *The Women beneath the Skin: A Doctor's Patients in Eighteenth-Century Germany.* Trans. by Thomas Dunlap. HUP 1991 $24.95. ISBN 0-674-95403-3. A study of "how people of another time experienced the body" mediated by a medical technology quite different from that which exists today.

Harding, Sandra. *Disembodying Women: Perspectives on Pregnancy and the Unborn.* HUP 1993 $17.95. ISBN 0-674-21267-3. A study of fetal imaging techniques and their influence on women's experience of their own bodies.

———. *The Science Question in Feminism.* Cornell Univ. Pr. 1986 $12.95. ISBN 0-8014-9363-3. Examines major trends in feminist critiques of science and its culture; then identifies inadequacies, tensions, obstacles, and gaps in these critiques in order to transform them into "more powerful tools for the construction of emancipatory meanings and practices."

———. *Whose Science? Whose Knowledge? Thinking from Women's Lives.* Cornell Univ. Pr. 1991 $13.95. ISBN 0-8014-2513-1. Sets forth feminist theories about the methodology and epistemology of the natural and social sciences; emphasizes that scientists must be aware of biases that shape ways of seeking knowledge and that new processes should be developed using the perspectives and insights of dominated groups.

Kass-Simon, G., and Patricia Farnes, eds. *Women of Science: Righting the Record.* Ind. U. Pr. 1993 $14.95. ISBN 0-253-3364-8. Contains chapters on women in archeology, geology, astronomy, mathematics, engineering, physics, biology, medicine, chemistry, and crystallography.

Keller, Evelyn Fox. *Reflections on Gender and Science.* Yale U. Pr. 1986 $11.00. ISBN 0-300-03636-1. Argues that both gender and science are social constructs.

———. *Secrets of Life, Secrets of Death: Essays on Language, Gender, and Science.* Routledge 1992 $42.95. ISBN 0-4159-0524-9. Essays on the role of language in science and its use in integrating feminist theory, historical insight, and the accomplishments of women scientists.

Kramarae, Cheris, ed. *Technology and Women's Voices Keeping in Touch.* Routledge 1988 $13.95. ISBN 0-7102-0679-8. A British collection stressing the impacts of various technologies on women's lives.

Longino, Helen E. *Science as Social Knowledge: Values and Objectivity in Scientific Inquiry.* Princeton U. Pr. 1990 $37.00. ISBN 0-691-07342-2. Challenges the supposed value-free nature of scientific inquiry; uses feminist theory to develop a view that reconciles the objectivity of science with its social construction. Emphasizes research on human biological evolution and sex differences.

McIlwee, Judith S., and J. Gregg Robinson. *Women in Engineering: Women, Power, and Workplace Culture.* SUNY Pr. 1992 $19.95. ISBN 0-7914-0870-1. An empirical study of the experience of women in the engineering profession.

Merchant, Carolyn. *The Death of Nature.* HarpC 1990 $12.00. ISBN 0-06-250595-5. A classic study in the history of ideas, suggesting that with the rise of modern science "the image of an organic cosmos with a living female earth and its center gave way to a mechanistic worldview in which nature was reconstructed as dead and passive, to be dominated and controlled by humans."

Reinharz, Shulamit. *Feminist Methods: Social Research.* OUP 1992 $21.00. ISBN 0-19-507386-X. Argues that there is no "politically correct" feminist method, or approach, but instead a variety of perspectives.

Rodda, Annabel. *Women and the Environment.* Humanities 1991 $15.95. ISBN 0-86232-985-X. On women as users, producers, and managers of Earth's resources, showing how environmental degradation affects women's health and lives. It also focuses on how women can bring about environmental change.

Rosser, Sue V. *Biology and Feminism: A Dynamic Interaction.* Twayne 1992 $14.95. ISBN 0-8057-9755-6. This study details contributions of women biologists and also critiques the presumed gender neutrality of modern biology.

Rothschild, Joan, ed. *Machina ex Dea: Feminist Perspectives on Technology.* Tchrs. Coll. 1993 repr. of 1983 ed. $48.50. ISBN 0-8077-6222-9. Twelve provocative essays on the place, role, and relationship of women and technology in Western culture.

Schiebinger, Londa. *The Mind Has No Sex? Women in the Origins of Modern Science.* HUP 1989 $12.95. ISBN 0-674-57625-X. An intellectual archeology of the relation between women and science, focused especially on "the site of modern science in Europe in the 17th and 18th centuries [and] on the circumstances that led to the exclusion of women."

——. *Nature's Body: Gender in the Making of Modern Science.* Beacon Pr. 1993 $25.00. ISBN 0-8070-8900-1. Includes an argument that mammals were named "mammals" more because of male ideas about femininity than for any objective biological reason.

Shiva, Vandana. *Staying Alive: Women, Ecology and Development.* Humanities 1989 $17.50. ISBN 0-86232-823-3. On the relation of women to the forests, food chain, and water supplies, and how the violation of nature is linked to the violation of women in developing countries.

Spallone, Patricia, and Deborah Lynn Steinberg, eds. *Made to Order: The Myth of Reproductive and Genetic Progress.* Pergamon 1987 $50.00. ISBN 0-08-034954-4. Proceedings of the Feminist International Network of Resistance to Reproductive and Genetic Engineering Conference, Sweden, 1985. Conference resolution: "We, women of [16 countries] declare that the female body, with its unique capacity for creating life, is being expropriated and dissected as raw material for the technological production of human beings."

Stamp, Patricia. *Technology, Gender, and Power in Africa.* UNIPUB 1989 $15.00. ISBN 0-88936-538-5. Argues that the social empowerment of women, especially at the grassroots level, is crucial to African technological development.

Stanworth, Michelle, ed. *Reproductive Technologies: Gender, Motherhood and Medicine.* U. of Minn. Pr. 1988 $14.95. ISBN 0-8166-1646-9. Nine original essays on the political, legal, and economic contexts and consequences of test-tube babies, in-vitro fertilization, etc.

Strasser, Susan. *Never Done: A History of American Housework*. Pantheon 1982 $13.56. ISBN 0-394-70841-5. Stresses the impact of technology on the transformation of housework.

Tuana, Nancy, ed. *Feminism and Science. Race, Gender, and Science Ser.* Ind. U. Pr. 1989 $35.00. ISBN 0-253-36045-5. Fourteen essays originally published in two special issues of *Hypatia: A Journal of Feminist Philosophy*, here arranged under two categories: feminist theories of science and feminist critiques of the practice of science.

Wajcman, Judy. *Feminism Confronts Technology*. Pa. St. U. Pr. 1991 $28.50. ISBN 0-271-00801-6. Reviews feminist theories of science and technology and then looks at specific areas of technology: sexual divisions in paid work, reproductive technologies, housework, domestic architecture, and urban systems of transportation.

Zimmerman, Jan, ed. *The Technological Woman: Interfacing with Tomorrow*. Greenwood 1983 $57.95. ISBN 0-275-91730-4. Contributors examine how various technologies affect women's lives, including household, workplace, and medical technologies.

Zuckermann, Harriet, and others, eds. *The Outer Circle: Women in the Scientific Community*. Yale U. Pr. 1992 $18.00. ISBN 0-300-05439-4. Proceedings from a series of symposia on sociological, legal, and other constraints that cause women to continue to be excluded from the "inner circle" of science.

SCIENCE, TECHNOLOGY, AND ART

For nearly three decades, scholars have been drawing attention to the dichotomy between the science-based disciplines and the arts, stemming from years of increasing specialization during the past century. Nowhere has this fragmentation of knowledge been felt more keenly than in the relationship among the visual arts and science and technology.

However, such a gulf has not always existed. Historically, technology has been much more closely related to art than to science. During the Renaissance, for example, such artists as Nicola Pisano, Lorenzo Ghiberti, Filippo Brunelleschi, LEONARDO DA VINCI (see Vol. 3), and ALBRECHT DÜRER (see Vol. 3) executed major works in painting, sculpture, architecture, furniture, jewelry design, and civil and military engineering, and in Leonardo's case, effortlessly combined the invention of mechanical devices with the illustration of human and animal anatomy. The architect and writer Leon Battista Alberti in *Della pittura* (1436) emphasized the technical and scientific basis of the visual arts and the necessity for all artists to have a thorough grounding in the sciences and mathematics. He explained to artists how they could understand motion in human beings by considering the body as a system of weights and levers, of balances and counterbalances. These generalist artists brought together what are today more often viewed as separate disciplines. Renaissance artists were polymaths. They combined the talents of artist, artisan, scientist, technologist, and scholar. Until recently, the same also was true in other societies, times, and places.

As a countermovement to overspecialization during the last two centuries (largely a consequence of the scientific and industrial revolutions), a series of syntheticizing, integrating efforts were attempted. Examples include the arts and crafts movement in England during the nineteenth century and the early twentieth-century industrial design activities of the Bauhaus in Germany. There have, of course, been similar movements in literature, drama, music, and other fields, but here the focus is on the visual arts, that is, those arts in which meaning has been imbued within the appearance of the object, especially in painting, sculpture, architecture, and design.

The present review of science and technology in the visual arts circumscribes the subject based on the following seven categories.

1. *Seeing and knowing.* These books examine the phenomenon of sight and uncover many of the problems that all people confront whether they are artists, scientists, or technologists. This is a difficult area, covering the psychology and philosophy of perception, and is one that poses awkward questions about how entrenched beliefs can alter observations. Is it possible to be absolutely objective in artistic or laboratory observations, or do societal and personal experiences influence what is seen?

2. *Perspective, light, and color.* These are important aspects of seeing that concern artists, designers, scientists, and technologists. Many methods have been used to depict pictorial space in drawing: overlapping objects diminishing in size as they recede up the paper (into the distance), color and texture gradients, modeling and foreshortening. All of these visual cues are part of perspective, a scientific method of equating what the eye sees in nature with what similar objects should look like when they are represented graphically on a flat surface. Other intriguing questions that continue to engage the artist and scientist are: What is light? What is color? What is the spectrum? How do light and the eye interact? How do colors mix, additively and subtractively?

3. *Creativity.* Books in this category look at different ways in which creativity has been defined through the ages and ask what, if any, similarities exist in scientific, technological, and artistic creativity? Are we all creative to some extent? If so, how can we improve on this ability?

4. *Historical and historiographical considerations.* Most books on the history of ancient Egypt, Greece, or Rome will reveal the connections between art, science, and technology. For the period from the Renaissance to the nineteenth century, MARTIN KEMP's *The Science of Art* (1989) breaks new ground. During those centuries, he suggests, "[T]here were special kinds of affinity between the central intellectual and observational concerns in the visual arts and the sciences." Another interesting society to study is Paris during the era of the Impressionist painters, when many new scientific and technological developments emerged as Western Europe underwent rapid mechanization and industrialization. Photography, synthetic pigments, metal tubes to hold paint, new support materials, the changing facade of gaslighted city streets, all were developments that influenced the way Impressionist painters saw and recorded their world.

Reflection on specific periods in history leads to important questions about the different interpretations historians have placed on the relationship between art, science, and technology in various periods in history, sometimes emphasizing certain aspects while neglecting or ignoring others. Historiography is the study of the history of history writing in different periods and places, noting how contemporary societal imperatives helped dictate one interpretation rather than another. Historians are not neutral observers of events; they bring their biases and selectivity, as well as their value systems, to their narratives.

5. *Scientific and technological illustration.* This is a long-standing and fruitful area of collaboration. Leonardo and Dürer as anatomists, Audubon as documenter of wildlife, medical artists as recorders of surgical operations, draftsmen-artists as those who define architectural detail or the design of a railway engine—all are part of a rich legacy of work that has contributed to the

understanding and advancement of science and technology. Today, computers are being used to great effect to further this same work.

6. *Scientific attributes and detection of forgery in art.* How do we know by whom, when, and where a particular work was produced? How do we distinguish between a genuine work and a fake? Science and technology help answer such questions through an expanding armory of techniques, including carbon dating, dendrochronology, thermoluminescence, and so forth. With these developments have come advances in the related fields of art conservation and restoration.

7. *Photography and filmmaking.* This is another important art form in which art, science, and technology converge.

Adams, James I. *Conceptual Blockbusting: A Guide to Better Ideas.* Addison-Wesley 1990 $7.64. ISBN 0-201-55086-5. A practical book by a design engineer interested in the interplay between aesthetic and technical considerations in design. Helpful to those concerned with the development of conceptual and problem-solving abilities. Suggests techniques to identify and overcome thinking blocks.

Arnheim, Rudolf. *Art and Visual Perception: Psychology of the Creative Eye, The New Version.* U. CA Pr. 1974 $14.95. ISBN 0-520-02613-6. Deals with the visual image from the standpoint of Gestalt psychology: that is, analyses from the structure of the whole to the constituent parts, as contrasted to building knowledge from particular components. First published in 1954, this work has become a classic, but it is important to consult the new 1974 version.

Barber, Peter, and Christopher Board. *Tales from the Map Room: Fact and Fiction about Maps and Their Makers.* BBC Bks. 1993 o.p. A beautifully illustrated book of historical maps, but one with a serious theme. The map-maker's art is one of selection. Thus maps have always told us as much about the maker's perceptions, intentions, needs, beliefs, and vision as about the land they represented. A fascinating survey.

Barlow, Horace, Colin Blakemore, and Miranda Weston-Smith, eds. *Images and Understanding.* Cambridge U. Pr. 1990 $89.95. ISBN 0-521-34177-9. A collection of essays by distinguished writers in various fields of the sciences and the arts imparting their ideas about communicating through images. The subject is explored by examining drawings and paintings, color, diagrams, pictorial instructions, body movements and gestures, sign language, dance, and computer graphics, as well as by considering how images are created by oral and written narratives and music.

Baxandall, Michael. *Patterns of Intention: On the Historical Explanation of Pictures.* Yale U. Pr. 1987 $12.95. ISBN 0-300-03763-5. Examines the Forth Bridge in Scotland as a historical artifact made to solve a problem at a certain time under specific circumstances; also compares cultural objects, thus showing similar imperatives that govern the production of all man-made objects. An excellent book that unites technological and artistic products through the intentions of their production.

Baynes, Ken, and Francis Pugh. *The Art of the Engineer.* Seven Hills Bk. Dists. 1981 o.p. Reproductions and discussions of engineering drawings in the transport industry, from the late sixteenth century to the present. Each drawing is placed in its historical, social, and technical context, examining why and where it was done, who executed it, for whom, and how it was used. Contains elegant drawings of high visual quality.

Bevlin, Marjorie Elliott. *Design Through Discovery: The Elements and Principles.* HB Coll. Pubs. 1989 $38.00. ISBN 0-03-026303-4. Using practical terminology, identifies the principles of design in nature and shows how they have been applied throughout history and how they can be used in specific fields today.

Billington, David P. *The Tower and the Bridge: The New Art of Structural Engineering.* Princeton U. Pr. 1985 $14.95. ISBN 0-691-02393-X. A well-reasoned thesis that engineering structures in steel and concrete are a new art form in the realm of architecture. The author looks back two centuries to Telford's iron bridge (1779) at

Coalbrookdale, England, and discusses subsequent major pioneering works. His object is to initiate a course in structural art with its own history and principles of form.

Broude, Norma. *Impressionism: A Feminist Reading: The Gendering of Art, Science, and Nature in the Nineteenth Century.* Rizzoli Intl. 1991 $40.00. ISBN 0-8478-1397-5. A new alternative interpretation of landscape painting in the late nineteenth century. Broude believes Impressionism has been miscast as an art of rational scientific objectivity; that it was, in fact, associated with positivism and the sciences in order to gender it. An intelligent, informative study of the philosophical connections between art and science.

Christian, James L. *Philosophy: An Introduction to the Art of Wondering.* HR&W Sch. Div. 1990 $31.50. ISBN 0-03-030414-8. Emphasizes the view that philosophy, like science, technology, and art, does not take place in a vacuum. Covers diverse material on science and the arts; contains a useful glossary.

de Noblet, Jocelyn, ed. *Industrial Design: Reflections of a Century.* Flammarion/APCI. 1993. ISBN 2-08013-539-2. Contains 30 beautifully illustrated essays investigating major themes and issues in industrial design in the twentieth century. Looks at inventions, such as the Singer sewing machine, the Remington typewriter, the Coca-Cola bottle, the Model-T Ford, the Walkman, and the Apple MacIntosh computer, in the context of cultural, political, and artistic trends in their period.

Ferguson, Eugene S. *Engineering and the Mind's Eye.* MIT Pr. 1992 $24.95. ISBN 0-262-06147-3. Argues for more training of engineers in a physical, "hands-and-eyes-on" method rather than retaining the traditional theoretical and mathematical approach.

Fleming, Stuart J. *Authenticity in Art: The Scientific Detection of Forgery.* Inst. of Physics. 1975 $14.50. ISBN 0-8448-0752-4. Describes the development of scientific authentication methods; surveys the shift in the detection of forgery from aesthetic stylistic criteria to the techniques of the forensic scientist. Includes sections on paintings, ceramics, and metals, each with numerous references to citations in the text; written by a physicist specializing in thermoluminescence.

Ford, Brian J. *Images of Science: A History of Scientific Illustration.* OUP 1993 $45.00. ISBN 0-19-520983-4. Shows how the natural world has been depicted at different periods in history; including cave art, ancient Egyptian wall paintings, Roman mosaics, medieval maps, Leonardo's human anatomy, Dürer's rhinoceros, Audubon's flamingo, and many more. Views scientific illustration as humans' efforts through the ages to understand the world about them, beautifully illustrated.

Forty, Adrian. *Objects of Desire: Design and Society Since 1750.* Thames Hudson 1986 $17.95. ISBN 0-500-27412-6. Looks at the appearance of consumer goods from penknives to computers and asks how consumers make their choices—on aesthetic grounds, on new features offered, or in response to marketing campaigns.

Goldsworthy, Andy. *Andy Goldsworthy: Collaboration with Nature.* Abrams 1990 $45.00. ISBN 0-8109-3351-9. Unlike some ecological artists who try to dominate and control nature, Goldsworthy leaves only footprints and brings away only photographic memories. He works in the environment through the seasons, for example, doing ice sculpture that melts in the spring sunshine and leaf and twig constructions that come to pieces and blow away in the wind.

Gombrich, Ernst H. *Art and Illusion: A Study in the Psychology of Pictorial Representation.* Pantheon 1977 o.p. An analysis of the psychology of vision in art by a renowned art historian who claims that the process of representation in the visual arts is governed by schema and correction, from the indefinite to the definite; not easy reading but well worthwhile.

———. *The Sense of Order: A Study in the Psychology of Decorative Art.* Cornell Univ. Pr. 1979 $57.50. ISBN 0-8014-1143-2. The history and theory of humankind's impulse to seek order and harmony in space and time. Asks: Why do we decorate? What is style? What is the connection between patterns in nature and human-made geometric or serpentine shapes? An excellent book that explains the visual visually, with extensive diagrams and pictures throughout the text.

Gregory, Richard L. *Eye and Brain: the Psychology of Seeing.* Princeton U. Pr. 1990 $12.95. ISBN 0-691-02456-1. Written for the general reader by a well-known neuropsychologist of the brain and perception. Should be read before the Gombrich book because it leads the reader through the basics step by step; contains an annotated bibliography.

Gregory, Richard L., and E. H. Gombrich, eds. *Illusion in Nature and Art.* Focus Info. Gr. 1973 o.p. Excellent articles by the two editors. Other contributors include Colin Blakemore, psychologist, on the baffled brain; Jan B. Deregowski, psychologist, on illusion and culture; H. E. Hinton, zoologist, on natural deception; and Roland Penrose, art theorist, on the merits of illusion in art.

Hart, Ivor B. *The Mechanical Investigations of Leonardo da Vinci.* Greenwood 1982 repr. of 1963 ed. $48.50. ISBN 0-313-23489-2. This, like Hart's work on Leonardo, is valuable reading.

Herbert, Robert I., and others. *George Seurat (1859-1891): The Metro.* Metro Mus. Art. 1991 $60.00. ISBN 0-87099-618-5. The *catalogue raisonné* (Musée d'Orsay, Paris) that accompanied the major retrospective exhibition commemorating the centenary of the artist's death. Places Seurat in the scientific and sociocultural context of the late nineteenth century. The appendixes explain the nineteenth-century theories of light and color that Seurat applied; good color plates are included.

Jones, Mark, ed. *Fake? The Art of Deception.* U. CA Pr. 1990 $55.00. ISBN 0-520-07086-0. Discusses well-known art and artifact fakes in history; also describes the role of the art market in confusing monetary and aesthetic values. The scientific methods of detection discussed include visual examination by microscopy, ultraviolet- and X-radiography; radiocarbon dating; dendrochronology; and thermoluminescence.

Kemp, Martin. *The Science of Art: Optical Themes in Western Art from Brunelleschi to Seurat.* Yale U. Pr. 1989 $10.00. ISBN 0-300-04337-6. This major study of linear perspective demonstrates the impact of optics and the science of color on the development of European art.

Koestler, Arthur. *The Act of Creation.* Viking Penguin 1990 $10.95. ISBN 0-14-019191-7. A quite readable classic that examines parallels between scientific inventions and artistic creation. Koestler believed all creative activities have a common basic pattern: "bisociation," or the association of two self-consistent but usually incompatible frames of reference.

Locher, J. L., ed. *Escher: His Life and Complete Graphic Works.* Abrams 1982 $65.00. ISBN 0-8109-0558-1. The definitive study of the Dutch graphic artist's life and works, with 600 illustrations (36 in color) and articles by the artist himself. His visual illusions, exploiting the ambiguity between figure and ground and between flat pattern and apparent three-dimensional recession, have recently attracted the interest of mathematicians.

Macaulay, David. *The Way Things Work.* HM 1988 $29.45. ISBN 0-395-42857-2. A wonderful book for both children and adults, illustrating the principles of mechanics, power, waves, transport, communications, electricity, automation, and the computer; explains everything from the zipper to the TV. Demonstrates the effectiveness of the drawing medium and its status as an art form in its own right.

Matilsky, Barbara C. *Fragile Ecologies: Contemporary Artists' Interpretation and Solutions.* Rizzoli Intl. 1992. ISBN 0-8478-1592-7. Presents challenging art works, Smithson's "Spiral Jetty" and Christo's "Running Fence," that upset many ecologists in areas where they were erected. Author asks readers to consider: Are such works too invasive ecologically to be held up as examples of art?

Meikle, Jeffrey L. *Twentieth Century Limited: Industrial Design in America, 1925–1939.* Temple U. Pr. 1981 $19.95. ISBN 0-87722-246-0. Critically traces how the marriage of art and industry, helped by modern advertising, created American consumer desires. Also shows how competing industries produced more goods than buyers could afford.

Oddy, Andrew, ed. *The Art of the Conservator.* Smithsonian 1992 $39.95. ISBN 1-56098-229-2. Contains 12 chapters by specialists in different fields; each explains his or her viewpoint on preservation and describes his or her work and methods.

Ring, Melvin L. *Dentistry: An Illustrated History*. Abrams 1985 $75.00. ISBN 0-8109-1100-0. Pictorial survey of past cures for bad and decaying teeth, including folk remedies from the Middle Ages; an interesting and amusing book. Contains a delightful Thomas Rowlandson cartoon of 1787 that shows a tooth implant and nineteenth-century posters, one advertising Mrs. Winslow's soothing syrup for teething problems.

Robbins, Judd. *Fun with Fractals*. Sybex 1993 $29.95. ISBN 0-7821-1126-2. Interesting discussion on fractals as a method of generating art. A book/disk combination with installation information and complete instructions to create 22 different fractal generating programs to use with a PC; compatible with DOS, Windows, and OS/2.

Roberts, K. B., and J.D.W. Tomlinson. *The Fabric of the Body: European Traditions of Anatomical Illustration*. OUP 1992 $125.00. ISBN 0-19-261198-4. Anatomical illustrations in the European tradition, from the pre-scientific medieval period to the beginning of the scientific anatomical thought of the present day. A beautifully produced, very readable book, with a good bibliography.

Rock, Irvin, ed. *The Perceptual World: Readings from Scientific American Magazine*. W. H. Freeman 1989 $12.95. ISBN 0-7167-2068-X. Contains 12 up-to-date articles by experts in the field of visual perception. Although the Introduction provides a useful background, it would be even more useful first to have read Gregory's *Eye and Brain* or Rock's earlier book, *Perception* 1984.

Rothenberg, Albert, and Carl R. Hausman, eds. *The Creativity Question*. Duke 1976 $39.95. ISBN 0-8223-0353-1. Readings by a psychiatrist and a philosopher, covering a variety of approaches and points of view on the creative process and the creative person; includes both subjective and literary accounts, experimental and clinical studies, and future trends and alternative approaches.

Rudwick, Martin J. S. *Scenes from Deep Time: Pictorial Representations of the Prehistoric World*. U. Ch. Pr. 1992 $45.00. ISBN 0-226-73104-9. A beautifully produced book exploring the ideas and the visual constructions underlying our thinking about the eons before human existence on Earth. The author believes too many of our ideas are based on very fragmentary evidence, such as fossil skeletons, and are inadequate. This important book increases our awareness of how images can be manipulated.

Scharf, Aaron. *Art and Photography*. Viking Penguin 1991 $16.00. ISBN 0-14-013132-9. An informative book on the history and development of photography in England and France. Reveals how artists clandestinely used the photograph in its early days. The many illustrations of paintings and photographs take the reader up to the time (and beyond) when photography asserted itself as an art form.

Shluim, Leonard. *Art and Physics: Experiments in Space, Time and Light*. Morrow 1991 $25.00. ISBN 0-688-09752-9. The author's thesis is that art informs science; thus, revolutionary art anticipates visionary physics. Citing examples from Classical Greece to the early twentieth century, he then demonstrates how modern art anticipated scientific thought on space, time, and light before Einstein's theory of relativity. Well-written, illustrating the theory of the visionary artist.

Stephenson, Jonathan. *The Materials and Techniques of Painting*. Thames Hudson 1993 repr. of 1989 ed. $18.95. ISBN 0-500-27704-4. A well-produced, informative, and practical manual providing contemporary artists with technical knowledge and advice about the materials of their craft. Fills a gap in the artist's disappearing tried-and-tested heritage, now seldom taught in workshops and art schools: how to stretch and ground a canvas with gesso and how to prepare paper to accept water colors.

Todd, Stephen, and William Latham. *Evolutionary Art and Computers*. Acad. Pr. 1992 $59.95. ISBN 0-12-437185-X. Mathematician/computer graphics expert (Todd) and artist (Latham) explain why and how computers are used to create art. The main art theme here is natural evolution and artificial life. Each step in the process is traced, from the initial hand-drawn sketches, to the three-dimensional graphic stage, to the process of selective mutation where forms breed forms, to the final gallery article or animation.

Tufte, Edward E. *Envisioning Information*. Graphics Pr. 1990 $48.00. ISBN 0-9013921-1-8. A catalog showing good, clear visual displays of information; charts, diagrams, graphs, tables, guides, instructions, directories, and maps are used to exemplify a high standard of visual presentation.

Vasari, Giorgio. *Vasari on Technique: Being the Introduction to the Three Arts of Design, Architecture, Sculpture and Painting.* Ed. by G. Baldwin Brown. Trans. by Louisa S. Maclchose. Dover 1960 $9.95. ISBN 0-486-20717-X. Although these chapters were written as an intrinsic part of Vasari's *Lives*, they were not translated with the main work; this valuable sourcebook remained unknown for many years because of modernist notions about the separation between science and technology and the arts. Shows how versatile and practical artists of his day had to be.

Wade, Nicholas. *The Art and Science of Visual Illusions.* Routledge 1982 $59.95. ISBN 0-7100-0868-6. Aims to span the gap between the artist's and the scientist's approach to visual illusions. May be seen as a primer on Op Art, though the illustrations were collected and presented with theoretical issues in mind: The author always asks why the particular phenomena under study occur.

White, John. *The Birth and Rebirth of Pictorial Space.* HUP 1987 $15.95. ISBN 0-674-07475-0. A classic, first published in 1957, that tells the story of the origins of perspective in antiquity and its rediscovery in Italy during the Renaissance. The 1987 edition has a substantial new appendix on "Leonardo, Brunelleschi and the View Distance."

Whiting, Roger. *Leonardo: A Portrait of the Renaissance Man.* Bk. Sales Inc. 1992 $29.98. ISBN 1-55521-716-6. Beautifully produced book, full of Leonardo's drawings, describing their purpose in his stylish script; portrays the man and his achievements as a Renaissance polymath—painter, sculptor, anatomist, scientist, naturalist, civil and military engineer, inventor, and architect.

SCIENCE, TECHNOLOGY, AND RELIGION

Beginning with GALILEO's (see also Vol. 4) work in astronomy in the sixteenth century, through CHARLES DARWIN's biological theories in the nineteenth century, conflicts have arisen in the Christian West between the theories of modern science and traditional religious doctrines. Such conflicts often characterized earlier historical and cultural periods as well, for example, the tensions between Aristotelian science and first, Islamic, then Christian revelation in the tenth and thirteenth centuries.

Such theoretical and doctrinal conflicts usually have elicited three basic responses. First, it is argued that scientific knowledge is completely true, and religion is true only to the degree that religion is confirmed by science. Second, it is argued that religious knowledge is completely true, and science is true only insofar as it does not contradict religion. Third, it is argued that both science and religion possess some truth, each in its own ways or in its own spheres of competence.

Today, the conflict between science and technology and religion is slightly different, more uniquely modern. Now problems are not so much concerned with knowledge or truth as with practical behavior and ethics. Although science seems to have won out in the long contest with religion, both sides now clearly admit the limits of this victory. As IAN BARBOUR has written, "What is the place of religion in an age of science? How can one believe in God today? . . . Much of humanity has turned to science-based technology as a source of fulfillment and hope. . . . However, for all its benefits, technology has not brought the personal fulfillment or social well-being it promised." At the same time, modern science and technology make possible, indeed tend to encourage, practices and behavior that can be opposed to traditional religious moral codes, or at the very least, that present challenges to their adaptation. Among such problems are chemical and nuclear weapons, artificial conception and contraception, the changing forms of industrial labor, environmental pollution, biomedical prolongation of life, genetic engineering, and others.

In the practical realm, there are basically two responses to the conflict between religion and science and technology. Some argue that strictly secular moral reflection is sufficient to deal with these problems; others insist that it is not. In the latter case, an opportunity, or a need, arises for bringing religious tradition and reflection to bear on the varied, perplexing challenges associated with modern technological development. The ways in which religious reflection addresses these challenges are, however, as diverse as the religious traditions and communities that exist in our advanced technological world. The works cited here illustrate this diversity.

Barbour, Ian G. *Ethics in an Age of Technology*. Harper SF 1992 $35.00. ISBN 0-06-060934-6. Includes some discussion of religious values but tends to downplay the relevance of religion.

————. *Religion in an Age of Science*. Harper SF 1990 $17.00. ISBN 0-06-060383-6. Analyzes relations between religion and the methods and theories of science; concludes by attempting to bring both religion and science to bear on understanding human nature, the natural world, and God.

Barrow, John D., and Frank J. Tipler. *The Anthropic Cosmological Principle*. OUP 1988 $17.95. ISBN 0-19-282147-4. The anthropic principle points out how the observed values of many physical and cosmological quantities are not equally probable and postulates that only the relatively improbable set that actually exists could have made carbon-based life possible. This is a new form of the "argument from design" for the existence of God.

Barry, Robert. *A Theory of Almost Everything: A Scientific and Religious Quest for Ultimate Answers*. OUP 1993 $18.95. ISBN 1-85168-045-4. Addresses complex issues, such as the nature of reality and the meaning of life; links scientific and religious worldviews using insights from psychological theory and quantum physics.

Bartholomew, Fletcher. *Iconoclasm: The Way Out of the High Technology Dark Age*. Info. Inst. 1989. ISBN 0-939823-01-2

Birch, Charles, and John B. Cobb. *The Liberation of Life: From the Cell to the Community*. Environ. Ethics Bks. 1990 repr. of 1981 ed. $14.95. ISBN 0-9626807-0-2. An "ecological model of life" that brings together science, philosophy, religion, sociology, and politics more effectively than the reigning model of biological mechanism or materialism. A collaborative work by a biologist and a philosopher; first published in 1981.

Birch, Charles, and others, eds. *Liberating Life: Contemporary Approaches to Ecological Theory*. Orbis 1990 $16.95. ISBN 0-88344-689-8. Fifteen essays by scholars and activists that include Latin American and non-Christian perspectives.

Birtel, Frank, ed. *Religion, Science, and Public Policy*. Crossroad NY 1987 $16.95. ISBN 0-8245-0833-5. Eight lectures by A. R. Peacocke, Langdon Gilkey, Stephen Toulmin, Richard S. Westfall, Karl E. Peters, Philip Hefner, and John T. Noonan, Jr., pursuing the "critical realist" thesis that science and theology are engaged in a joint effort to render reality intelligible.

Bradley, Ian. *God Is Green*. Doubleday 1990 $8.00. ISBN 0-385-42279-2. An apology/defense against charges that the Christian religion has caused environmental destruction. Calls for a "Christian environmentalism"; the author views the problem as not the Christian message but rather its perversion.

Budhamanda, Swami. *Can One Be Scientific and Yet Spiritual?* Vedanta Pr. 1973 $1.95. ISBN 0-87481-145-7. An attempt to promote reciprocity between religion and science from the Hindu perspective.

Capra, Fritjof, and others. *Belonging to the Universe: Explorations on the Frontiers of Science and Spirituality*. Harper SF 1992 repr. of 1991 ed. $10.00. ISBN 0-06-250195-X. New-paradigm thinking in theology parallels that in science; this parallel is explored, arguments are set forth, and social implications are laid out in dialogue form.

Davies, Paul. *God and the New Physics*. S&S Trade 1984 $11.00. ISBN 0-671-52806-8. An extended argument by a theoretical physicist that science, especially the physics and cosmology of the last half century, "offer a surer position than religion" in the search of God. "Science does have something to say about religious matters. In topics such as the nature of time, the origin of matter and life or causality and determinism, the very conceptual framework in which the religious questions are posed can be altered by scientific advances."

Eastham, Scott Thomas. *Nucleus: Reconnecting Science and Religion in the Nuclear Age*. Bear and Co. 1986 $9.95. ISBN 0-939680-31-9. Asserts that without the reconnection of science and religion the stark possibility of a nuclear holocaust exists. The three worlds involved in this reconnection are the biosphere, humanity, and the divine.

Ferré, Frederick, ed. *Hellfire and Lightning Rods: Liberating Science, Technology, and Religion*. Orbis Bks. 1993 $24.95. ISBN 0-88344-856-4. The author believes that the human and environmental crises in industrial societies call for new forms of science, technology, and religion to guide a more humane global society in acting in harmony with nature.

————. *Technology and Religion*. JAI Pr. 1990 o.p. Of these 14 papers, the taxonomy of technology-religion relations by William B. Jones and A. Warren Matthews is especially useful.

Hawkin, David J. *Christ and Modernity: Christian Self-Understanding in a Technological Age*. Humanities 1985 o.p. Following an exploration of the modern interpretation of Christianity and theories of modernity, Hawkin argues that "the Christian in the technological society must be discriminating in the approach to modernity; simple acceptance or rejection is [not the answer.]"

Hopper, David H. *Technology, Theology, and the Idea of Progress*. Westminster/John Knox 1991. ISBN 0-664-25203-6. The author asserts that the idea of progress through technology is a secularized version of the traditional Christian hope of salvation that creates special problems.

Hunt-Badiner, Allan, ed. *Dharma Gaia*. Parralax Pr. 1990 $15.00. ISBN 0-938077-30-9. Green Buddhism is the theme of these 31 essays on Buddhism and ecology.

Mangum, John M., ed. *The New Faith-Science Debate: Probing Cosmology, Technology, and Theology*. Augsburg Fortress 1989 $12.00. ISBN 0-8006-2390-8. Eleven essays by such scholars as Arthur Peacocke, Harold Nebelsick, Ted Peters, Robert John Russell, and others presented at an ecumenical conference. This general argument promotes the compatibility of science, technology, and religion, though it recognizes real problems, especially those between technology and religion.

McDonagh, Sean. *The Greening of the Church*. Orbis Bks. 1990 $16.95. ISBN 0-88344-694-4. Part 1, based on McDonagh's experience as a missionary to the T'boti people of the Philippines, which he sees as a "microcosm of the problems facing other Third World people, the rest of humanity and the earth itself," argues an interrelation among international debt, overpopulation, and rain forest destruction. Part 2 examines Hebrew and Christian scriptures for ways to approach these problems.

Mitcham, Carl, and Jim Grote, eds. *Theology and Technology: Essays in Christian Analysis and Exegesis*. U. Pr. of Amer. 1984 $61.25. ISBN 0-8191-3808-8. Structured around five possible relations between Christian theology and technology derived from H. Richard Niebuhr's classic *Christ and Culture* (1956). Includes 20 original essays, with a 200-page annotated bibliography.

Monsma, Stephen V., ed. *Responsible Technology*. Eerdmans 1986 $12.95. ISBN 0-8028-0175-7. Six scholars at the Calvin Center for Christian Scholarship collaborated on this distinctly Christian perspective on the nature and responsible use of technology. To them, technology is a problem because of the intentions that inform it.

Nebelsick, Harold. *Theology and Science in Mutual Modification*. OUP 1981 $15.00. ISBN 0-19-520213-2. To the author, science and Western philosophy-theology influence each other to the benefit of both. The modern tension between the two is investigated from the seventeenth century on, and tensions are seen as narrowing with the emergence of twentieth-century physics.

Patel, Ishwarbhi, ed. *Sciences and the Vedas.* S. Asia 1986 $12.50. ISBN 0-8364-1663-4

Rahner, Karl. *Modern Science and Christian Faith.* Crossroad NY 1988 $29.50. ISBN 0-8245-0888-2. A prominent Catholic theologian examines how modern science has influenced theology; provides reflections on faith and Christianity from the perspective of modern theology.

Ratzsch, Del. *Philosophy of Science: The Natural Sciences in Christian Perspective.* 1986 o.p. Aims to give Christians an initial understanding of what natural science is, what it can do, how and why it works, and what it cannot do.

Ravindra, Ravi, ed. *Science and Spirit.* Paragon Hse. 1990 $14.95. ISBN 0-89226-082-3

Rohr, Janelle, ed. *Science and Religion: Opposing Viewpoints.* Greenhaven 1988 $9.95. ISBN 0-89908-406-0. A collection of articles on historical debates between science and religion.

Roy, Rustum. *Experimenting with Truth: The Fusion of Religion with Technology, Needed for Humanity's Survival.* Franklin 1981 $88.00. ISBN 0-08-025820-4. An effort by this materials scientist and lay "pantheist" theologian "to single out the most important parts on which modern science and contemporary Christian thought agree." He concludes by showing how "a life-policy is achieved in practice, in doing theology, by experimenting with truth" in holistic ways.

Ruse, Michael. *The Darwinian Paradigm: Essays on Its History, Philosophy and Religious Implications.* Routledge 1989 $25.00. ISBN 0-415-00300-8. Having previously considered Darwinian theory in history (*The Darwinian Revelation,* 1979), as science (*Darwinism Defended,* 1982), and in relation to philosophy (*Taking Darwin Seriously,* 1986), the author considers why Darwin's paradigm of organic evolution remains a continuing source of debate. Of particular relevance is the final essay on the tension between "the foundational moral nihilism of Darwinism" and moral theology.

Russell, Colin A. *Crosscurrents: Interactions between Science and Faith.* Bks. Demand repr. of 1985 ed. $70.80. ISBN 0-685-23460-6. A sensitive and knowledgeable overview of the history of science and technology in the West. Especially good on the tension between science and "biblical ideology" during the Scientific Revolution and on contemporary problems of environmental pollution and nuclear weapons.

Russell, Robert J., William R. Stoeger, George V. Coyne, and S. J. Coyne, eds. *Physics, Philosophy, and Theology: A Common Quest for Understanding.* U. of Notre Dame Pr. 1988 $30.00. ISBN 0-268-01576-7. Eighteen papers presented at a 1987 Vatican conference. Scholars such as Ian Barbour, Ernan McMullin, W. Norris Clark, Mary Hesse, Ted Peters, and John Polkinghorne argue the compatibility of physics and theology; this conference contributed to the Vatican's revoking the condemnation of Galileo.

Sheldrake, Rupert. *The Rebirth of Nature.* Bantam 1992 $12.50. ISBN 0-553-35157-5. Asserts that science, especially biology, has begun to transcend a mechanistic worldview. "The uncreative world machine has turned into a creative, evolutionary cosmos." Gives this an animistic or pantheistic theological interpretation.

Shinn, Roger. *Forced Options: Social Decisions for the Twenty-First Century.* Pilgrim Pr. 1991 $8.95. ISBN 0-8298-0934-1. "Forced options" are those about which we cannot refuse to make a choice; to try to do so is itself a choice. Such options or choices include energy use, world hunger, population growth, genetic engineering, etc., all intimately involved with technology.

Slocum, Robert E. *Ordinary Christians in a High-Tech World.* Word Bks. 1986 o.p. A "where-the-rubber-meets-the-road" call to the laity. Vigorously written, this book is a call to maintain effective Christian living in witness to our socio-technical civilization; representative of a large number of such evangelical publications.

Stanesby, Derek. *Science, Reason, and Religion.* Routledge 1988 $12.95. ISBN 0-415-02657-1. On the relations between the philosophy of science and the philosophy of religion; defends Karl Popper's realist philosophy of science as beneficial for a realist philosophy of religion.

Steward, Ian, and Martin Golubitsky. *Fearful Symmetry: Is God a Geometer?* Viking Penguin 1992 $12.50. ISBN 0-14-013047-0. Explores the concept of symmetry. Also discusses symmetry-breaking, in which symmetric causes can have asymmetric effects. Clearly written, it delves into the symmetry of nature and what this implies concerning a creator-god.

White, Lynn, Jr. *Medieval Religion and Technology: Collected Essays.* U. CA Pr. 1978 $15.00. ISBN 0-520-05896-8. These pioneering scholarly studies analyze how Western European Christian ideas and practices promoted the development of modern technology.

Wilkinson, Loren, ed. *Earthkeeping in the Nineties: Stewardship and Creation.* Eerdmans 1991. ISBN 0-8028-0534-5. Updates a book first published in 1980.

World Religions and Ecology. Cassel 1992 o.p. This five-volume series sponsored by the World Wide Fund for Nature is aimed at the general reader; draws its materials not only from theologians and church officials but also from mystics, social activists, poets, and artists of the major religious traditions, stressing the ways each tradition presents the sacredness of the earth. The titles of the volumes are *Christianity and Ecology, Islam and Ecology, Hinduism and Ecology, Buddhism and Ecology,* and *Judaism and Ecology.*

CHRONOLOGY OF AUTHORS

Bush, Vannevar. 1880–1974
Tillich, Paul. 1886–1965
Gilkey, Langdon B. 1919–
Jaki, Stanley L. 1924–
Rothschild, Joan. 1928–

Kemp, Martin. 1942–
Tichi, Cecilia. 1942–
Haraway, Donna. 1944–
Rothman, Barbara Katz. 1948–

BARBOUR, IAN. 1923–

[SEE Chapter 6 in this volume.]

BUSH, VANNEVAR. 1880–1974

Educated as an electrical engineer, Vannevar Bush had a distinguished career that included electrical engineering and a number of contributions to the development of the computer. He is best known, however, as an administrator of government science, for Bush, more than anyone else, was responsible for shaping governmental support for science after World War II. His work here included the creation of the National Science Foundation, the premier funding agency of scientific research in the United States.

Bush was professor and then dean of engineering of the Massachusetts Institute of Technology. He also served as president of the Carnegie Institution of Scientific Research. His most important post, however, was as director of the U.S. Office of Scientific Research and Development during World War II. This job gave him direct access to Presidents Roosevelt and Truman, enabling him, almost single-handledly, to shape postwar U.S. science and technology policy. His writings, although not numerous, also were singularly influential in conveying to government leaders and to the world at large his vision of science as the progressive influence in the modern world.

BOOKS BY BUSH

Endless Horizons. Ayer 1975 $19.00. ISBN 0-405-06581-7. A collection of papers that includes *Science the Endless Frontier.*

Modern Arms and Free Men: A Discussion of the Role of Science in Preserving Democracy.
Greenwood 1985 repr. of 1949 ed. $55.00. ISBN 0-313-24985-7. An overview of
technological developments in warfare during the first half of the twentieth century,
concluding with an argument for weapons development to defend democracy
through strategic deterrence.

Pieces of the Action. Morrow 1970 o.p. An autobiographical account.

Principles of Electrical Engineering. (coauthored with William Henry Timbie). Wiley
1953 o.p. A standard textbook.

Science Is Not Enough. Morrow 1967 o.p. A collection of occasional essays.

Science the Endless Frontier: A Report to the President. Ayer 1980 repr. of 1945 ed. $16.00.
ISBN 0-405-12534-8. Bush's report to Truman that was to define the values and
imperatives of American science from the viewpoint of the scientific community in
the postwar era. Just as the federal government supported the conquest of the
Western frontier, Bush argued, it should fund research on the scientific frontier to
ensure that America reaped similar, if not greater, economic and cultural benefits.

BOOK ABOUT BUSH

Nyce, James M., and Paul Kahn, eds. *From Memex to Hypertext: Vannevar Bush and the
Mind's Machine.* Acad. Pr. 1991 $44.95. ISBN 0-12-523270-5. A collection of Bush's
writings about Memex, interspersed with essays by historians and computer
researchers.

ELLUL, JACQUES. 1912–

[SEE Chapter 6 in this volume.]

GILKEY, LANGDON B. 1919–

Born in Chicago, Langdon Gilkey received his B.A. at Harvard University
(1940) and earned a Ph.D. at Columbia University (1954). He has been a
Fulbright scholar at Cambridge University (1950–51) and has been awarded two
Guggenheim fellowships, the first to Germany in 1960–61, and then to Rome in
1965. Gilkey is currently a professor of theology emeritus at the University of
Chicago Divinity School.

As a teacher in China in the 1940s, Gilkey became interned by the Japanese
during the war, first at Yenching University and later at a prison camp near
Weihsien in Shantung Province. At the camp, he served as a helper to the
camp's mason, cook, and kitchen administrator. He returned to China while a
Fulbright visiting professor at Kyoto University in 1975.

Gilkey's pedagogical concern is in examining the place of religion within a
secular culture. With the prevailing appearance of religious sentiments such as
fundamentalism, cult practices, meditation, and private ideology, he notes
religion to be very much an aspect of our scientific and technological age. The
question for our age, Gilkey says, will be *"not* will religion survive, as much as
will *we* survive and with what *sort* of religion, a creative or demonic one?"

BOOKS BY GILKEY

Creationism on Trial: Evolution and God at Little Rock. HarpC 1985 $8.50. ISBN 0-86683-
780-9. A fascinating, blow-by-blow account of the author's experiences as a
theological witness for the American Civil Liberties Union at the 1981 Creationism
trial in Little Rock. Gilkey comes out more a critic of scientism than of creationism.

How the Church Can Minister to the World without Losing Itself. HarpC 1964 o.p. How is
the practice of the church related to the scientific-technological culture in which we
all live?

Maker of Heaven and Earth: The Christian Doctrine of Creation in Light of Modern Knowledge. U. Pr. of Amer. 1986 repr. of 1959 ed. $23.25. ISBN 0-8191-4976-4. Deals with how to think about creation under the influence of modern science.

Message and Existence: An Introduction to Christian Theology. Harper SF 1984 $20.00. ISBN 0-8164-0450-X. Attempts a short, contemporary statement of Christian faith for a scientific-technological culture.

Naming the Whirlwind: The Renewal of God-language. Bobbs-Merrill 1969 o.p. Big-book defense of new ways to speak about God in a scientific and secular culture.

Religion and the Scientific Future: Reflections on Myth, Science, and Theology. Mercer Univ. Pr. repr. of 1970 ed. $13.95. ISBN 0-86554-030-6. Argues the mutual influence and dependence of science and theology. Includes chapters on religious dimensions in science and myth in scientific culture.

Shantung Compound: The Story of Men and Women under Pressure. Harper SF 1975 $11.00. ISBN 0-06-063112-0. Memoir of Gilkey's time spent in a Japanese prison camp in China during World War II. Recounts a growing recognition of the shallowness of technology as a solution to human problems. He notes that "Crises occurred that involved not a breakdown in character, showing the need for more moral integrity and self-sacrifice."

HARAWAY, DONNA. 1944–

Born in Denver, Colorado, Donna Haraway is currently a professor of the History of Consciousness Board, a special program at the University of California at Santa Cruz. She received a B.A. from Colorado College in 1966 and an M.A. (1969) and a Ph.D. (1972) from Yale University.

A theorist in the fields of anthropology and women's studies, Haraway focuses on the political and social dimensions of science and emphasizes the idea that society's concepts of nature and of experience are socially and culturally constructed. Her most recent book, *Simians, Cyborgs, and Women: The Reinvention of Nature* (1991), expresses her belief in the pervasive influence of cultural categories, such as gender, race, and class, on the content and structure of science. Haraway ultimately focuses on the questions of what historical and political context constructs our scientific knowledge and what role feminists should play in creating this knowledge. Her intent is to promote a socialist-feminist society.

BOOKS BY HARAWAY

Crystals, Fabrics, and Fields: Metaphors of Organicism in Twentieth-Century Developmental Biology. Yale U. Pr. 1976 $37.00. ISBN 0-300-01864-9. A study of the organicist theories of Ross G. Harrison, Joseph Needham, and Paul Weiss. Argues that these authors introduce a new way of viewing the organism, replacing the old vitalism-mechanism debate with one between organicism and reductionism.

Primate Visions: Gender, Race, and Nature in the World of Modern Science. Routledge 1989 $19.95. ISBN 0-415-90114-6. Discusses post-World War II primatology: "Monkeys and apes—and the people who construct scientific and popular knowledge about them—are part of cultures in contention. Never innocent, the visualizing 'technology' of this book draws from contemporary theories of cultural production, historical and social studies of science and technology, and feminist and anti-racist movements and theories to craft a view of nature as it is constructed and reconstructed in the bodies and lives of 'third world' animals serving as surrogates for 'man.'"

Simians, Cyborgs, and Women: The Reinvention of Nature. Routledge 1991 $16.95. ISBN 0-415-90387-4. Essays that extend Haraway's interpretations, reflecting a development of critical analysis from Marx to the post-modern.

HARDING, SANDRA G. 1935–
[SEE Volume 4.]

JAKI, STANLEY L. 1924–

Born in Györ, Hungary, Stanley Jaki was ordained a Benedictine priest in the Catholic Church in 1948 and earned his doctorate in theology at the Pontifical Institute of San Anselmo in Rome in 1950. Seven years later he earned a second doctorate in physics from Fordham University in New York. In the years since, the primary focus of his historical, philosophical, and theological research and writing has been the relationship between theology and modern science.

Exiled from his native country, Jaki has been visiting fellow at Princeton University, the Institute for Advanced Study in Princeton, and the Center for Theological Inquiry in Princeton. He gave the Gifford Lectures at the University of Edinburgh, 1974–76, and was awarded the Templeton Prize for Progress in Religion in 1987. Jaki is currently distinguished university professor of theology at Seton Hall University.

BOOKS BY JAKI

The Absolute beneath the Relative and Other Essays. U. Pr. of Amer. 1989 $39.75. ISBN 0-8191-7182-4. Fourteen essays suggesting that a proper understanding of science can help reverse contemporary social trends toward disorder, which are actually abetted by misinterpretations of modern science.

Angels, Apes and Man. Sugden 1983 $7.95. ISBN 0-89385-017-9. Chapter Two addresses the issue of the conflict between Darwinism and Christianity.

Brain, Mind, and Computers. Herder 1969 o.p. A critique of the idea of artificial intelligence.

Chance or Reality and Other Essays. U. Pr. of Amer. 1986 o.p. Thirteen collected essays unified by a concern for the fate of humanistic values under the "ever more pervasive presence of the sciences in every facet of human life."

Chesterton: A Seer of Science. U. of Ill. Pr. 1986 $19.95. ISBN 0-252-01283-6. Unusual interpretation of Chesterton as an antagonist of scientism and critic of evolutionism, but a defender of a very realistic science.

Cosmos and Creator. Regnery Gateway 1980 o.p. A somewhat popularized summary statement of Jaki's arguments about creation "both as an article of Christian faith and as a foundation of natural science."

The Only Chaos and Other Essays. U. Pr. of Amer. 1990 $42.25. ISBN 0-8191-7895-0. Seventeen essays critical of scientific humanism and antiscientific or bucolic humanism, and in defense of genuine humanism.

The Road of Science and the Ways to God. U. Ch. Pr. 1978 o.p. The Gifford Lectures of 1974–76. Part I is an extended interpretation of the history of science from the Greeks to the nineteenth century. Part II focuses on twentieth-century physics.

Science and Creation: From Eternal Cycles to an Oscillating Universe. U. Pr. of Amer. 1990 $32.25. ISBN 0-8191-7839-X. Argues that modern science could only have arisen within the Christian philosophical and cosmological framework. Documents numerous stillbirths of science. The same thesis is advanced with different emphases in *The Origin of Science and the Science of Its Origin* (1979) and *The Savior of Science* (1988), both of which also affirm a fundamental harmony between Christian revelation and physics.

Scientist and Catholic: Pierre Duhem. Christendom Pr. 1991 $9.95. ISBN 0-931888-44-1. A study of the work of the French Catholic physicist and philosopher of science. Defends Duhem's arguments about the beneficial influence of Christian faith on science.

KEMP, MARTIN. 1942–

Martin Kemp is Professor of Fine Art at the University of St. Andrews in Scotland. His publications make an impressive contribution to the understanding of the Renaissance, and his latest work, *The Science of Art: Optical Themes in Western Art from Brunelleschi to Seurat* (1989), is representative of his outlook and influence.

Trained initially as a physicist, Kemp brings his scientist's eye to the study of art and the history of art. This dual vision shines through his writings and, by bringing to bear both his expertise as a scientist and as an art analyst and historian, he illumines the field in a revealing way. *The Science of Art*, because it is so representative of Kemp and his work, reveals much about his approach to art. The first part of the book examines artists' use of linear perspective, covering artists from Filippo Brunelleschi to JOSEPH MALLARD WILLIAM TURNER (see Vol. 3). According to Kemp, whatever the apparent diversities in theory and practice of these artists, they all share one important assumption: that the science of geometrical optics corresponds to the central facts of the visual process, so that we see a three-dimensional object drawn on a flat surface as having the same visual arrangements as presented to our eyes by the original object. Kemp also examines optical devices, such as the camera obscura, that have been invented to help artists achieve an imitation of nature, and he analyzes the contributions of scientists, such as ARISTOTLE (see also Vol. 4) and NEWTON on art. Kemp shows, for example, how Aristotelian pigment-mixing theory gave rise to the painter's tradition of the color circle of the three primaries (red, blue, and yellow) and their secondaries (purple, green, and orange), which are made from mixing two adjacent primaries. These pigments act in this way because they absorb bands of color from the spectrum of white light that strikes them, thus coloring the reflected light. Newton showed that by passing light through a triangular glass prism, sunlight (white light) could be separated into seven colors, which he believed, at first, were the primaries because they could not be broken down any further. Later, however, Newton accepted the idea that white light could be reconstituted from three primaries. This approach of connecting artistic principles to scientific ones is typical of Kemp's work.

BOOKS BY KEMP

The Altarpiece in the Renaissance. Cambridge U. Pr. 1991 $69.95. ISBN 0-521-36061-7. Interesting examination of Renaissance altarpieces—their design, symbolism, and function.

Dr. William Hunter at the Royal Academy of Arts. U. of Glasgow Pr. 1978 o.p.

Leonardo da Vinci: Artist, Scientist, Inventor. Yale U. Pr. 1992 repr. of 1989 ed. $42.00. ISBN 0-300-04563-8 The catalog for the Hayward Gallery, London, 1989 exhibition on Leonardo.

Leonardo da Vinci: The Marvelous Works of Nature and Man. HUP 1981 o.p. Awarded the Mitchell Prize in 1981.

Leonardo on Painting. (coedited with Peter Humfrey) Yale U. Pr. 1989 $13.00. ISBN 0-300-04509-3. Translation and compendium of Da Vinci's writings.

The Science of Art: Optical Themes in Western Art from Brunelleschi to Seurat. Yale U. Pr. 1992 repr. of 1990 ed. $35.00. ISBN 0-300-05241-3. Kemp's most important book. Filled with some 570 illustrations.

ROTHMAN, BARBARA KATZ. 1948–

A professor of sociology at Baruch College of the City University of New York, Barbara Katz Rothman specializes in the fields of reproductive health and childbirth. In particular, she seeks to describe the experience of motherhood within our contemporary, highly technologized, and fixed medical structure. Rothman's more recent books develop this theme while examining specific new procreative technologies and how these technologies act to alter the occasion of childbirth.

Rothman is a strong critic of market-based assumptions that define babies as "products of conception." She argues that to treat fetuses simply as objects encased in a woman's uterus does not adequately describe the relationship between mother and child; it only leads to illogical arguments regarding reproductive policy and legal actions against pregnant women who do not follow doctors' orders. Furthermore, Rothman points out that parent's mistakes in childrearing are idiosyncratic, while those of professionals are more dangerous because they are systematic and based on such motivations as ideology, self-interest, or bureaucratic efficiency.

Rothman received her B.A. from Brooklyn College of the City University of New York (1969), and an M.A. (1972) and Ph.D. (1979) from New York University. Long associated with the City University of New York and also with the state university, Rothman favors a feminist-centered view of parental rights and responsibilities.

BOOKS BY ROTHMAN

Encyclopedia of Childbearing: Critical Perspectives. (ed.) Oryx Pr. 1993 $74.50. ISBN 0-89774-648-1. Useful work includes bibliographical references and an index.

In Labor: Women and Power in the Birthplace. Norton 1991 $10.95. ISBN 0-393-30798-0. This work examines how modern medicine turns pregnancy into a pathological condition requiring the ministrations of a technological complex.

Recreating Motherhood: Ideology of Technology in a Patriarchal Society. Norton 1990 $10.95. ISBN 0-393-30712-3. Takes a feminist approach toward reproduction and identifies three aspects, within a historical context, that lead to reproductive conflicts and interfere with sound public policy—patriarchy, capitalism, and technology. Also argues that a better acknowledgment of parental rights and responsibilities rest on the bonds of relationship and caring in childrearing, rather than the determination of genetics.

The Tentative Pregnancy: How Amniocentesis Changes the Experience of Motherhood. Norton 1993 $9.95. ISBN 0-393-30998-3. Examines how a simple technological procedure alters the way we think about childbirth and parenthood, forcing us to ask questions such as: What do we do if there is a "problem" fetus?

ROTHSCHILD, JOAN. 1928–

Joan Rothschild was born in New York City and was educated first at Cornell University, where she received a B.A. degree in 1948, and then at New York University, where she earned both M.A. and Ph.D. degrees in 1966 and 1970 respectively. She has done postdoctoral research at the Harvard Program on Technology and Society, the City University of New York, and Brooklyn Polytechnic University. Rothschild has worked as a writer for the (now defunct) *New York Herald Tribune* and taught at a number of universities, including the City University of New York, the University of Cincinnati, and the University of Massachusetts at Lowell. At the latter she directed the Technology, Society and Human Values Program and served as coordinator of Women's Studies for the university. In these positions, and as a founding member of the National Women's Studies Association, Rothschild has exercised a formative influence on the development of feminist scholarship and has worked to bring to feminist studies special attention to those issues related to science and technology.

BOOKS BY ROTHSCHILD

Machina Ex Dea: Feminist Perspectives on Technology. Tchrs. Coll. 1993 repr. of 1983 ed. $48.50. ISBN 0-8077-6222-9. A classic collection with contributions by Autumn Stanley, Martha Moore Trescott, Sally L. Hacker, Rosyln L. Feldberg and Evelyn Nakano Glenn, Rothschild, Carolyn Merchant, Ynestra King, Evelyn Fox Keller, Corlann Gee Bush, Sally M. Gearheart, Jalna Hanmer, and Patrocinio Shweickart.

Teaching Technology from a Feminist Perspective: A Practical Guide. Tchrs. Coll. 1988 $36.50. ISBN 0-8077-6236-6. Very helpful overview of approaches. Includes a collection of university course syllabi.

Technology and the City. HUP 1970 o.p. Part of a series issued by the Harvard University Program on Technology and Society, this book deals with the impact of technological change on the American city. While it excludes such issues as pollution, architecture and design, and city problems that are not directly related to technology, it seeks to give lengthy reviews of a number of relevant books and articles on the subject.

Turing's Man, Turing's Woman, or Turing's Person? Gender, Language, and Computers. Wellesley College Center for Research on Women 1986 o.p. Alluding to Alan Turing, the mathematician whose work in artificial intelligence Rothschild invokes, this book examines the meaning of gender in the uses of computers and technology in general. A good feminist critique of the fundamental differences language reveals of perceptions in human understanding.

Women, Technology and Innovation. Franklin 1981 $92.00. ISBN 0-08-028943-6. Examines the role women have played in technological innovations through the centuries.

ROY, RUSTUM. 1924–

[SEE Chapter 6 in this volume.]

TICHI, CECILIA. 1942–

Cecilia Tichi was born in Pittsburgh, Pennsylvania, and earned her B.A. degree from Pennsylvania State University (1964), an M.A. degree from Johns Hopkins University (1965), and a Ph.D. from the University of California at Davis (1968). Following an extended appointment at Boston University, she is currently professor of English at Vanderbilt University. Tichi's research has focused on the literary appropriation of and response to modern technology in ways that give particular attention to the visual. Her book *Shifting Gears* (1987), for instance, explores how, between the late 1800s and early 1900s, the images of gear-and-girder technology informed and influenced not only literature but also the visual arts of painting and photography and an increasingly visual popular culture. Tichi's latest publication is a revised edition of *The Harper American Literature*, which she coedited with Donald McQuade and others.

BOOKS BY TICHI

Electronic Hearth: Creating an American Television Culture. OUP 1991 $29.95. ISBN 0-19-506549-7. Offers an examination of the "television environment" beyond the context of its programming.

New World, New Earth: Environmental Reform in American Literature from the Puritans through Whitman. Yale U. Pr. 1979 $35.00. ISBN 0-300-02287-5. A pioneering study of American environmentalism.

Shifting Gears: Technology, Literature, Culture in Modernist America. U. of NC Pr. 1987 $39.95. ISBN 0-8078-1715-5. A richly illustrated study of the popular acceptance of and literary fascination with gear-and-grind technology from the 1890s to the 1920s; focuses on both literature and the visual arts.

TILLICH, PAUL. 1886–1965

Born in Germany, but longtime resident and teacher in the United States, Paul Tillich was one of the most influential philosopher-theologians of the twentieth century. His writings and lectures on culture, including art, science, technology, psychotherapy, medicine, politics, and social history, attempted a synthetic interpretation of the entire scope of human existence.

Tillich early represented a union of traditional Lutheran piety and liberal German idealistic culture. As a chaplain in the German army during the First World War, Tillich experienced both the reality of battle and death and the destruction of an inherited cultural unity. During his subsequent career as a German university professor, he tried to create a new unity around "religious socialism." When the National Socialists came to power in 1933, however, Tillich's opposition led to his dismissal from the University of Frankfurt and his emigration to the United States.

In the United States, Tillich taught first at Union Theological Seminary (1933–55) in New York, then at Harvard University (1955–62), and finally at the University of Chicago Divinity School (1962–65). Tillich's teaching in such works as *The Courage to Be* (1952), *Theology of Culture* (1959), and *The Eternal Now* (1963), during the latter decades of his life, fostered a new recognition and understanding of the tragic, as well as a new confidence in an ultimate, meaningful unity in life.

BOOKS BY TILLICH

Christianity and the Encounter of the World Religions. Col. U. Pr. 1961 $7.15. ISBN 0-231-08555-9. Fascism and Communism as quasi-religions, as well as Eastern religions, are examined vis à vis Christianity. The victory of secularism in Western scientific culture in this encounter is discussed.

The Courage to Be. Yale U. Pr. 1952 $11.00. ISBN 0-300-00241-6. Religion in the light of science and philosophy is Tillich's theme here. The three types of existential anxieties that plague humanity are set forth: anxieties of guilt, of nonbeing, and of meaning. The power of Tillich's original mind is evident.

The Spiritual Situation in Our Technical Society. Ed. by J. Mark Thomas. Mercer U. Pr. 1988 $30.00. ISBN 0-8655-4292-9. A posthumous collection of writings on the spiritual implications of modern technological society, documenting Tillich as perhaps the foremost theologian of technical culture.

Systematic Theology: Life and the Spirit, Vol. 3. U. Ch. Pr. 1963 $11.00. ISBN 0-226-80339-2. Tillich's thinking on science, technology, and religion. An encompassing schema, his "multi-dimensional unit of life" is set forth, as well as the source of science and technology in human beings. Ambiguities, dangers, dilemmas, and the power created by modern technology are incisively examined.

Theology of Culture. OUP 1959 $8.95. ISBN 0-19-500711-5. The richness of Tillich's understanding of modern techno-scientific culture is seen here; a section entitled "Science and Theology" features a discussion of Albert Einstein's rejection of a personal god for modernity. Existentialism and ethics, time and space, and an evaluation of Martin Buber's influence on Protestant and Jewish thought are also discussed.

BOOKS ABOUT TILLICH

Adam, James Luther. *Paul Tillich's Philosophy of Culture, Science, and Religion.* Schocken 1970 o.p. Probably the best introduction to Tillich's thought; argues the failure and inability of science to provide adequate guidance in the modern world.

——, and others, eds. *The Thought of Paul Tillich.* HarpC 1985 o.p. An anthology of 18 essays examining Tillich's view of contemporary civilization; contributors include Langdon Gilkey and Roger Shinn.

Carey, John O., ed. *Theology and Autonomy: Studies in Tillich's Engagement with Modern Culture*. Mercer Univ. Pr. 1984 o.p. A collection of 13 scholarly appraisals, nearly half of which deal with Tillich's thought concerning modern science and technology; lends substance to his reputation as the leading theologian of modern culture.

Nuovo, Victor. *Visionary Science*. Wayne St. U. Pr. 1987 $29.95. ISBN 0-8143-1940-8. A translation of Tillich's 1919 German lecture (and his first published speech), "On the Idea of a Theology Culture." Examines this lecture for Tillich's insights into the relationship of scientific and religious cultures.

PART TWO

TECHNOLOGY

CHAPTER 8

Engineering and Technology

William Frederick Williams

Mathematics and Science education must not simply become more widely available and technically enriched. They must also be embedded in a broader education about the ethical, moral, and social implications of technology. In some ways our technological expertise already exceeds our capacity to deal with its moral implications. To create a new generation of scientists ill-prepared to make morally complex social decisions would not be in the best interest of the country.
—WILLIAM JEFFERSON CLINTON, *The Next Educational Reform*

In the thirteenth edition of this volume, this chapter was prefaced by quotations from CHARLES KINGSLEY's (see Vol. 1) *Yeast* (1848) and J. ROBERT OPPENHEIMER's *Science and the Common Understanding* (1953). Both Kingsley and Oppenheimer were champions of science and technology during the mid-nineteenth century and mid-twentieth century respectively. Viewed from a current perspective, more than 40 years after Oppenheimer and nearly 150 years after Kingsley, three things were remarkable about their statements: (1) they did not specify what "engineering" is, (2) they did not mention the word *technology*, and (3) they implied that engineering always was beneficial.

The *Oxford English Dictionary* does not provide a useful definition of either *engineering* or *technology*; the definitions are either circular or limited. For example, engineering is defined as "the art and science of the engineer's profession," and technology as "the scientific study of the practical or industrial arts." Because they cannot keep pace with change in professional practices and change in popular usage, dictionary definitions of terms such as "engineering" and "technology" are inevitably outdated. In fact, both terms have expanded and subdivided significantly during the latter part of the twentieth century. Today technology is widely understood to embrace the various divisions of engineering such as biotechnology (which includes genetic engineering), food technology, information technology, and others. Several authors have attempted to provide detailed descriptions of technology. For example, Kline considers technology to have four dimensions: (1) hardware or artifacts—nonnatural objects (of all kinds) manufactured by humans; (2) the sociotechnical systems of manufacture—the complete working system: people, machinery, resources, processes, and the legal, economic, political, and physical environment; (3) knowledge, technique, know-how, and methodology—the information, skills, processes, and procedures for accomplishing tasks; and (4) sociotechnical systems of use—what people do with the hardware and software after it has been manufactured.

In the introductory quote to this chapter, U.S. President Bill Clinton does not mention engineering, but it seems implicit in his approach. Both he and Patricia Maugham (the author of this chapter in the thirteenth edition) acknowledge the necessary role of technology but are conscious that it can have adverse effects. They insist that people must manage technology to maximize its benefits and minimize its drawbacks, not only in the interest of human beings but in the interest of the entire biosphere. For example, Maugham wrote: "As a result of the ever-increasing uses of engineering and technology, people and their environment have been affected in a variety of ways, some good and some bad. The quickening development of the ability to alter the environment has added new responsibilities to the job of the engineer and the technologist."

Discussion on this issue has tended to polarize people. Unquestionably, technology is essential to human survival. In fact, human beings are unique in their reliance on tools—from primitive flint and wooden digging tools to microprocessors and bioengineering tools. It is difficult to imagine any human society without technology. But, is technology always necessary? Should technology be limited or controlled? JOHN KENNETH GALBRAITH (see Vol. 3) argues that the advance of technology is inexorable and that if it can be done, it will be done—a sort of free market approach. In contrast, Perrow and Schumacher maintain that technology is a human activity subject to social control. They claim that there are technologies with drawbacks so great that the technologies should either be severely limited or abandoned altogether.

This chapter introduces a wide range of general and popular works describing current engineering and technological developments, and explores the debate on the effects of technological advances.

GENERAL WORKS

Baynes, Ken, and Francis Pugh. *The Art of the Engineer*. Overlook Pr. 1981 $85.00. ISBN 0-87951-128-1. "This book reproduces and discusses a selection of mechanical engineering drawings made for the transport industries between the late sixteenth century and the present day. It contains many superb examples of draughtsmanship, a number of which are equal in quality to the finest drawings of any kind" (Introduction).

Borgmann, Albert. *Technology and the Character of Contemporary Life: A Philosophical Inquiry*. U. Ch. Pr. 1987 $14.95. ISBN 0-226-06629-0. Expresses the opinion that technology and the new products resulting from it constitute a major influence on the quality of modern life, causing people to become distanced from production and susceptible to technological distractions. Borgmann maintains, however, that technology is not a neutral tool and that it constitutes only a limited component of a rewarding life in our day and age.

Boyle, G., D. Elliot Roy, and R. Roy, eds. *The Politics of Technology*. Longman 1977 o.p. Comprises 28 essays by American and British authors as a reader for an Open University (UK) course; includes a wide coverage of the field and concludes with a guide to the literature.

Burke, John G., and Marshall C. Eakin, eds. *Technology and Change*. Boyd & Fraser 1979 o.p. Presents readings from 72 nineteenth- and twentieth-century authors, including such notables as Engels, Einstein, Sakharov, Nader, and McLuhan. The readings are carefully selected to be readable and interesting, as well as to raise different points of view on many of the issues surrounding engineering and technology. The readings are classified in five groups: technology on trial, technology's effects, conditions of technological development, sources of technological change, and retrospect and prospect.

Collingridge, David. *The Social Control of Technology*. St. Martin 1980 $27.50. ISBN 0-312-73168-X. "Considers one of the most pressing problems of our time—can we control our technology—can we get it to do what we want and can we avoid its unwelcome consequences?" (Preface). Written by a philosopher who has considerable experience with technology policy; examines several case studies to highlight the dimensions of the problem and then describes general principles.

Congdon, R. J., ed. *Introduction to Appropriate Technology: Toward a Simpler Life-Style.* Rodale Pr. Inc. 1977 o.p. A book by technical revolutionaries who think that appropriate technology offers a humanistic counterweight to the mechanistic view of the world that has prevailed for the past three centuries; presents a lively critique of Western technology and explores the spirit of appropriate technology in revolutionary societies such as China, Cuba, and North Vietnam.

Cotterill, Rodney. *The Cambridge Guide to the Material World.* Cambridge U. Pr. $29.95. ISBN 0-521-37932-6. Covers the physical, chemical, and biological properties of many materials including glass, plastics, ceramics, metals, minerals, and crystals in a large-format and beautifully illustrated text. Useful in exploring materials science and mineral and chemical engineering.

Cross, Hardy. *Engineers and Ivory Towers. Essays Index Repr. Ser.* Ayer 1980 repr. of 1952 ed. $17.00. ISBN 0-8369-1404-X. A collection of technical and nontechnical articles, transcribed speeches, classroom notes, society papers, and graduate lectures on the philosophy of engineering; edited by a former student of Cross at Yale University.

Davidson, Frank Paul. *Macro: Reindustrializing America and the World.* Morrow 1983 o.p. Davidson argues that "particular projects, such as a transcontinental supersonic subway . . ., are quite feasible, not science-fiction dreams; that they are necessary; that planning for them must begin now, even if the groundbreaking is decades away" (*N.Y. Times Book Review*).

DeGregori, Thomas R. *A Theory of Technology: Continuity and Change in Human Development.* Iowa St. U. Pr. 1985 $14.95. ISBN 0-8138-1778-1. Generates a clear, coherent, consistent definition of technology; argues that the impact of technology on human life is a primary and continuing cause of positive change in society.

Dorf, Richard C. *Technology, Society, and Man.* Boyd & Fraser 1974 o.p. Provides an introduction to engineering as a discipline; examines its influence in areas such as history, trade, agriculture, human safety, ecology, technology assessment, the state, and the military; concludes with an examination of technology and the future.

Dorf, Richard C., and Yvonne L. Hunter, eds. *Appropriate Visions, Technology, the Environment and the Individual.* Boyd & Fraser 1978 o.p. Documents a series of programs held in late 1977 devoted to the problems of growing technology, the need for energy conservation, and the maintenance of human values. Records the presentations made at the conference featuring well-known speakers E. F. Schumacher (*Small Is Beautiful*) and Barry Commoner (*The Closing Circle*).

Farvar, M. Taghi, and John P. Milton, eds. *The Careless Technology: Ecology and International Development.* Doubleday 1972 o.p. Described as "of vital importance to those concerned with large-scale (and supposedly beneficial) government-backed schemes. Each of the fifty case histories . . . records a long roster of well-documented ecological mistakes, and in so doing it raises profound scientific, social and ethical issues." Supports responsible technology in areas such as pest control, the Aswan High Dam, and nuclear waste disposal.

Feibleman, James. *Technology and Reality.* Kluwer Ac. 1982 $25.00. ISBN 90-247-2519-4. Explores the historical impact of technology on philosophy and suggests what positive effects on philosophy recent advances in the physical sciences might produce.

Goulet, Denis. *The Uncertain Promise.* Apex Pr. 1989 $17.50. ISBN 0-945257-04-X. Examines whether modern technology is the key to successful development; if technology will deliver on it its promise to bring development to the developing nations; whether technology can be transferred from one cultural setting to another with beneficial rather than deleterious effects; and how policies for modernizing relate to broader national goals and concerns.

Greenhill, Ralph. *Engineer's Witness: A Photographic Panorama of Nineteenth Century Engineering Triumphs.* Godine 1985 $35.00. ISBN 0-317-65898-0. "Visually, the 90-plus photographic plates are a worthy complement [to nineteenth-century engineering] . . . the steel and stone memorials spread across the continent, attest to the ingenuity and vision of the American engineer, and Mr. Greenhill's dramatic pictorials and informative texts celebrate the imagination, industry, and sheer exuberance of 19th-century America" (*Christian Science Monitor*).

Krohn, Wolfgang, and others, eds. *The Dynamics of Science and Technology*. Kluwer Ac. 1978 o.p. Examines science and technology in their social context; the "scientification" of technology; and the conceptual distinctions between science and technology.

Kursunoglu, Behram, and Arnold Perlmutter, eds. *Impact of Basic Research on Technology. Studies in the Natural Sciences*. Plenum Pub. 1973 o.p. Presents seven essays on scientific and technical developments by contributors such as Vladimir Zworykin, Edward Teller, John Bardeen, and P.A.M. Dirac.

Lawless, Edward W. *Technology and Social Shock*. Rutgers U. Pr. 1977 $15.00. ISBN 0-8135-0781-2. Presents the results of a study funded by the National Science Foundation concerning episodes of public alarm over technology that have inspired major news stories.

Layton, Edwin T. *The Revolt of the Engineers: Social Responsibility and the American Engineering Profession*. Johns Hopkins 1986 repr. of 1971 ed. $37.50. ISBN 0-8018-3286-1. Traces the development of a sense of professional identity and social responsibility among American engineers and describes the conflict between progressive and conservative factions within the profession; focuses on engineering professionalism and ethics.

Mazur, Allan. *The Dynamics of Technical Controversy*. Broadcasting Pubns. 1981 o.p. Describes the controversies concerning a variety of scientific and technological products and suggests how they might be used as effective means for technology assessment. Mazur suggests regularities in behavior that occur across classes of technological controversies and indicates the kinds of data needed to enhance our understanding of them.

Merkel, James A. *Basic Engineering Principles*. Van Nos. Reinhold 1983 o.p. A basic introduction to the principles of engineering for nonengineers interested in developing an appreciation for and understanding of engineering knowledge. Covers topics such as fluid mechanics, heat transfer, air conditioning, and basic electricity.

Nevers, Noel de, ed. *Technology and Society*. Addison-Wesley 1972 o.p. Presents a selection of essays from authors, past and present, including Malthus, Lord Kelvin, Admiral Rickover, and Garrett Hardin. Features annotated bibliographies and discussion questions on each essay as well as discussion sessions on other relevant, separately published essays, such as Marshall McLuhan's interview in *Playboy* and two of C. P. Snow's famous works, *The Two Cultures* and a *Second Look at Science and Government*. Considered by some as a classic, the book is informative, wide-ranging, readable, and thoughtprovoking.

Nussbaum, Bruce. *The World after Oil: The Shifting Axis of Power and Wealth*. S&S Trade 1984 o.p. "Nussbaum argues that 'the world is poised to take a quantum leap to a higher technological plateau.' He outlines the possible efforts on the world of three burgeoning technologies: robotics, bioengineering, and telecommunications. . . . With stakes so high, Nussbaum argues, these high-techs will encourage international spying, industrial crime . . . and a shift in world power" (*Library Journal*).

O'Neill, Gerard K. *The Technology Edge: Opportunities for America in World Competition*. S&S Trade 1984 o.p. Discusses microengineering, robotics, genetic engineering, magnetic flight, private aircraft, and space science. Describes each area from a business and science perspective and compares progress made in the United States with other countries. The author's goal is to determine which of the six technologies offer real promise for the next decade.

Petroski, Henry. *Beyond Engineering: Essays and Other Attempts to Figure without Equations*. Prima Pub. 1986 o.p. A collection of essays and articles (many of which have appeared elsewhere) on the nature of engineering and technology. Describes some of Petroski's experiences at the Argonne National Laboratory; includes his observations on engineering education, the effects of technology on family life, and several whimsical pieces with a technological bent.

Rybczynski, Witold. *Paper Heroes: A Review of Appropriate Technology.* Doubleday 1991 $8.95. ISBN 0-14-015375-6. Critical examination of the Appropriate Technology movement, which attempts to grapple with, among other issues, the relationship between technology and development, ideology and industrialization, and people and machines.

———. *Taming the Tiger: The Struggle to Control Technology.* Viking Penguin 1985 $8.95. ISBN 0-14-007564-X. A worldwide treatment illustrating the sociological and environmental impact of technology. Presents historical as well as current perspectives with anecdotes that support Rybczynski's central theme: If we are to control technology, we must first control ourselves.

Seurat, Silvere. *Technology Transfer: A Realistic Approach.* Bks. Demand repr. of 1979 ed. $47.90. ISBN 0-685-23783-4. Explores fully and conveys the complexity of technology transfer, which the author defines as the capacity to store and transmit to people both industrial know-how and the accumulated experience and understanding of others.

Sladovich, Hedy E., ed. *Engineering as a Social Enterprise.* Natl Acad. Pr. 1991 $19.00. ISBN 0-309-04431-6. Presents six essays that examine how social and political influences affect engineering and, conversely, examine engineering's social consequences. The essays address (1) the technological and social aspects of technical change and how they interact, as well as the need for engineering education to include such matters; (2) the impact of cultural values on engineering, with particular emphasis on risk, uncertainty, and public trust; (3) the conflicting demands in the auto industry for economic growth, jobs, and safer, less polluting cars; (4) the declining public confidence in science and technology; (5) how engineering can respond to society's needs as well as influence them; and (6) lessons to be learned from the failure of some inventions and the success of others.

Susskind, Charles. *Understanding Technology.* Bks. Demand repr. of 1985 ed. $10.00. ISBN 0-911302-53-0. "It discusses how technology developed, how inventions like electronic equipment and the computer ushered in a new era, and the relationship of society to the technologist. Many modern inventions and processes are described in terms the reader with little technical background could easily grasp" (*Library Journal*).

The Techno/Peasant Survival Manual: The Book That Demystifies the Technology of the 80's. Bantam 1980 o.p. A consciousness-raising book that describes selected major new technological advances and explains, in simple language, how they work. Discusses the potential for liberation and potential harmful effects; also examines the cogent political and social issues associated with each technological advance.

Wenk, Edward, Jr. *Tradeoffs: Imperatives of Choice in a High-Tech World.* Johns Hopkins 1986 $32.00. ISBN 0-8018-3378-7. A scholarly treatment of the costs and benefits of technological progress, as well as the influence of government in fostering technological developments. Case studies include the invention of the steam engine and the disposal of nuclear wastes.

GENERAL REFERENCE WORKS AND GUIDES

Abbott, David, ed. *The Biographical Dictionary of Scientists: Engineers and Inventors.* P. Bedrick Bks. 1986 $28.00. ISBN 0-87226-009-7. Provides a collection of short biographical sketches, which follow a brief introduction to the chronology of technology—from prehistory to the age of the microchip; includes an 8-page subject index and a 14-page glossary of engineering terminology.

Anthony, L. J., ed. *Information Sources in Engineering.* K. G. Saur 1988 $105.00. ISBN 0-408-03050-X. Presents a perspective on the international scene in engineering by bringing together in one volume both published information sources and the known channels of access to these sources. Provides an introduction to the structure of engineering information; covers primary and secondary sources; includes 18 chapters on specialized subject fields; and concludes with 16 pages of indexes to subjects, information services, and organizations.

Bell, S. P., comp. *A Biographical Index of British Engineers in the 19th Century.* Garland 1975 o.p. Provides access to the obituary notices of about 3,500 British engineers who died prior to 1900; lists many of those responsible for major developments in British engineering in the second quarter of the nineteenth century and for its influence worldwide in the second half of the nineteenth century.

Brown, John F. *A Student Guide to Engineering Report Writing.* United Western Pr. 1989 o.p. "It provides information regarding the reasons why technical writing is important, report format, presentation of technical data . . . photography, and writing style and grammar" (*Automotive Engineering*).

Ernst, Richard. *Comprehensive Dictionary of Engineering and Technology.* 2 vols. Cambridge U. Pr. 1985 Vol. 1 *French/English.* $135.00. ISBN 0-521-30377-X. Vol. 2 *English/French.* $131.00. ISBN 0-521-30378-8. "Entries are alphabetical. The author has placed each term within its own specialized field. All branches of modern industry are covered. These range from raw materials and their extraction to the processing industries with their products, research, development, and manufacture" (*Mining Engineering*).

Gieck, Kurt. *Engineering Formulas.* McGraw 1986 o.p. Organized in a classified arrangement with an eight-page subject index. Provides a brief, clear, and handy guide to the more important technical and mathematical formulae.

Grogan, Denis. *Science and Technology: An Introduction to the Literature.* Shoe String 1982 o.p. Intended for the would-be practitioner who is familiar with the general sources of information and wishes to learn about the literature of science and technology; emphasis is on the general structure and pattern of this literature. Each of 22 chapters is devoted to specific sources, e.g., guides to the literature, encyclopedias. Criteria for selecting items in these lists was accessibility and value to students.

Hellemans, Alexander, and Bryan Bunch. *The Timetables of Science: A Chronology of the Most Important People and Events in the History of Science.* S&S Trade 1988 $29.95. ISBN 0-671-62130-0. Despite its title, a useful reference work. Each two-page spread shows contemporary notable events, people, and technology in general and in anthropology and archeology, astronomy and space, biology, chemistry, earth science, mathematics, medicine, and physics—from two and a half million years ago to the present.

Hicks, Tyler, G., and S. D. Hicks. *Standard Handbook of Engineering Calculations.* McGraw 1985 $84.50. ISBN 0-07-028735-X. "Revised, updated, and considerably expanded, this edition provides step-by-step calculation procedures for solving the kinds of engineering problems encountered most frequently. It contains more than 1,100 comprehensive, numbered, procedures—each with a typical worked-out practical design problem, plus more than 4,000 related procedures" (*Automative Engineering*).

Lesko, Matthew. *Lesko's New Tech Sourcebook: A Directory to Finding Answers in Today's Technology Oriented World.* HarpC 1986 o.p. Covers more than 170 high-tech topics and lists government, commercial, and not-for-profit organizations that do research in these fields. Also lists available, relevant databases and journals. Provides a helpful list of people who respond to mail and telephone request for information.

McGraw-Hill Dictionary of Science and Engineering. McGraw 1984 $46.95. ISBN 0-07-045483-3. Covers more than 35,000 terms spanning 100 subject disciplines. Like other McGraw-Hill reference sources, includes an indication of the general discipline from which the term is derived in advance of providing a definition; written for the general reader.

McGraw-Hill Dictionary of Scientific and Technical Terms. McGraw 1989 $95.00. ISBN 0-07-045252-0. More than 115,000 definitions are provided in this reference source, which is among the best scientific and technical dictionaries currently available. Identifies each term by general discipline before providing its definition. Provides many illustrations of definitions and several useful appendixes; includes a listing of biographical entries, periodic chart of the elements, and metric system units.

Malinowsky, H. Robert, and Jeanne M. Richardson. *Science and Engineering Literature: A Guide to Reference Sources*. Libs Unl. 1980 o.p. Lists and describes 1,273 reference sources in science and engineering; emphasizes current, in-print titles, major bibliographies, and abstracting and indexing services. Each annotation includes information on the work's scope, intended audience, and special features. Covers primary and secondary sources in the scientific and technical literature and includes separate chapters on a variety of scientific and technical subject disciplines.

Matschoss, Conrad. *Great Engineers. Essay Index Repr. Ser.* Trans. by H. S. Hatfield. Ayer repr. of 1939 ed. $27.50. ISBN 0-8369-1837-1. An illustrated biography of engineers from antiquity to the twentieth century. "This book is addressed to lovers of technical achievement, and of the men responsible for it, who show by their lives that great deeds are brought about by ideals which are far beyond the mere material valuation of technical work" (Preface).

Morris, Christopher, ed. *Dictionary of Science and Technology*. Acad. Press 1992 o.p. A more compact (2,432 pp.) and less costly alternative to the same publisher's monumental tome of similar title (see entry under Myers). Well-produced and illustrated, but written for those with a solid background in science and technology.

Mount, Ellis. *Serving End-Users in Science-Technology Libraries*. Haworth Pr. 1984 $26.95. ISBN 0-86656-327-X. A reference that should be used in conjunction with the reference desk and card and computer catalogs to get the most out of engineering and technology libraries.

Myers, Robert A., ed. *Encyclopedia of Physical Science and Technology*. 15 vols. Acad. Pr. 1987 o.p. A monumental work covering all major aspects of the physical sciences and technology. Contains more than 400 original articles written by experts. Each article contains a table of contents, a glossary of unusual terms, and a concise definition of the subject, followed by an in-depth presentation. All articles are juried by peer groups of the authors. Well illustrated, the set includes more than 3,300 bibliographic entries and 45,000 subject index entries.

Parker, Sybil P., ed. *Concise Encyclopedia of Science and Technology*. McGraw 1989 $110.00. ISBN 0-07-045512-0. Covers more than 7,000 topics in a single volume, many of which are extracted from the larger 15-volume set of the *McGraw-Hill Encyclopedia of Science and Technology*; includes a useful index comprising 30,000 entries.

_____. *McGraw-Hill Dictionary of Engineering*. McGraw 1985 $46.95. ISBN 0-07-045412-4. Gathered from the vocabularies of 10 major engineering disciplines: aerospace engineering, civil engineering, design engineering, industrial engineering, materials science, mechanical engineering, metallurgical engineering, mining engineering, petroleum engineering, and systems engineering; each of the 16,000 terms is identified by its field of primary use.

_____. *Modern Scientists and Engineers*. 3 vols. McGraw 1980 o.p. Presents "extended biographical data on contemporary leaders of science and engineering around the world in a form possessing reference value for the librarian and educational value for the students" (Preface).

Rolt, L. T. *Great Engineers*. G. Bell 1962 o.p. Covers some of the famous engineers whose work influenced the course of engineering history. Describes, through 10 biographies of British engineers, the history of the Industrial Revolution in England.

Roysdon, Christine M., and Linda A. Khatri. *American Engineers of the Nineteenth Century: A Biographical Index*. Garland 1978 o.p. Provides for the first time in a single source, personal-name indexing to brief biographies of several thousand American engineers and technologists that appeared in the technical and trade press of the nineteenth century. Indexed engineers and technologists were engaged in activities that characterized the middle and late nineteenth century, especially the development of railroads and canals and the beginning of industrialization.

Schenk, Margaret T., and James K. Webster. *What Every Engineer Should Know about Engineering Information Sources*. Dekker 1984 o.p. A selective, noncomprehensive review of a variety of engineering information formats; includes periodicals, nonbibliographic databases, standards and specifications, patents, trade literature, audiovisual materials, statistical sources, software, and technical reports.

Smiles, Samuel. *Lives of the Engineers.* 3 vols. Kelley 1968 repr. of 1861 ed. $125.00. ISBN 0-678-05632-3. Presents a collection of biographies that traces the influence and contributions of foreign engineers as well as the development of indigenous engineering in Great Britain. With an introduction by L. T. Roh.

Subramanyam, Krishna. *Scientific and Technical Information Resources.* Dekker 1981 o.p. Examines the various phases of scientific information, including its generation through research and development, its recording, surrogation, synthesis, and dissemination. Provides an overview of the structure and characteristics of scientific and technical literature; includes more than 1,500 sources arranged in a classified system.

Turner, Roland, and Steven L. Goulden, eds. *Great Engineers and Pioneers in Technology.* Vol. 1 St. Martin 1982 $69.50. ISBN 0-312-34574-7. A projected three-volume series that will bring together information on many engineers from all fields of engineering. Covers a variety of cultures and time periods, from antiquity to the present. Volume 1 begins with builders mentioned in the earliest records of civilization through the Industrial Revolution.

Who's Who in Technology Today. 5 vols. Res. Pubns. CT 1981–82 o.p. Presents biographical summaries subdivided by specific areas within a volume; also includes an index of principal expertise and an index of names.

Young, Margaret Labash, ed. *Scientific and Technical Organizations and Agencies Directory.* 2 vols. Gale 1987 $195.00. ISBN 0-8105-2103-3. "More than 12,000 entries are divided into 13 broad categories such as R&D centers, federal and state agencies and programs, patent and standard organizations, [etc.]. . . A master name and keyword index to all thirteen chapters is provided . . . the orientation of STOAD is national, although some foreign organizations are listed" (Preface).

AERONAUTICS AND AVIATION

Dreams of being able to imitate birds and fly go back a long time, from the myth of Icarus, to LEONARDO DA VINCI'S (see Vol. 3) flying machines, to ballooning in the eighteenth and nineteenth centuries, to Jules Verne's rocket to the moon. Realization of these dreams has occurred only in the present century, however, beginning with the early tentative flights of Bill Frost and the Wright brothers and culminating in wide-bodied jets, supersonic transports, and the U.S. space shuttle.

Originally a branch of mechanical engineering, the field of aeronautics expanded dramatically after World War II. For example, flight propulsion developed from simple propellers to such technologies as turboprops, ramjets, turbojets, and rockets. Air speeds have correspondingly increased from hundreds of miles per hour to the blistering speeds of space vehicles and satellites. In recent years, much of the early trial-and-error method of aeronautics has been replaced by a vast and complicated research, design, and production industry that deals with such things as fluid mechanics, wind tunnel testing, flight control, navigational aids, control engineering, flight simulation, and much more. Current aeronautics design techniques also rely on a variety of fields, including mathematical analysis, metallurgy, and computing.

Apostolo, Giorgio. *The Illustrated Encyclopedia of Helicopters.* Bonanza Pub. 1984 o.p. Provides data on engines, size, weight, and maximum speed for military and civilian helicopters worldwide. Color drawings are supplied for most models; includes indexes by country of origin, designer, and model number.

Bergman, Jules, and David Bergman. *Anyone Can Fly.* Doubleday 3rd rev. ed. 1986 $19.95. ISBN 0-385-19298-3. Provides instructions on how to fly and describes the experience of piloting a plane. Covers the basics of flight, takeoff, landing, soaring, cross-country flight, solo flying, and weather conditions. Well illustrated, includes a glossary of flight terminology.

Boyne, Walter J. *The Smithsonian Book of Flight.* Crown Pub. Group 1988 $35.00. ISBN 0-517-56614-1. Illustrated chronicle of the history of flight. Produced by Smithsonian Books and the National Air and Space Museum.

Etkin, Bernard. *Dynamics of Atmospheric Flight.* Wiley 1972 $74.95. ISBN 0-471-08936-2. "This work has excited great interest and appreciation among leaders in the field" (*Choice*).

Gollin, Alfred. *No Longer an Island: Britain and the Wright Brothers, 1902–1909.* Stanford U. Pr. 1984 $49.50. ISBN 0-8047-1265-4. "Gollin has provided a fascinating survey of British reactions to the advent of aviation. As an essay of weapons procurement, it is, however . . . inconclusive" (*American Historical Review*).

Hart, Clive. *The Prehistory of Flight.* U. CA Pr. 1985 $52.50. ISBN 0-520-05213-7. Examines the concept of flight beginning with Classical Greek culture. Describes design and construction of heavier-than-air flying machines from the ninth century B.C. through the eighteenth century. The well-illustrated text includes a listing of more than 50 historical attempts at flight.

Irving, Clive. *Wide-Body: The Triumph of the 747.* Morrow 1993 $25.00. ISBN 0-688-09902-5. . . . [T]old in full and in a most readable way. . . . [Irving] has understood the achievement of Boeing structural engineers and aerodynamicists in exploiting the swept wing to allow high flight speeds . . . and extending the expertise to new generations of airlines. He also shows the power politics and rivalries that are the natural result when talented and justifiably self-confident engineers clash in the design and production of a new machine" (*New Scientist*).

Jackson, Robert. *Flying Modern Jet Fighters.* Sterling 1989 $27.00. ISBN 0-8095-7082-3. Describes the experience of flying a modern combat plane and discusses training and air-superiority tactics. Examines the F-111, Hawk, F-14 Tomcat, F-15, F16, F-104, and Harrier, among other aircraft. Concludes with a discussion of the future of manned combat aircraft.

Lomax, Judy. *Women in the Air.* Ivy Books 1988 $3.95. ISBN 0-8041-03311-9. Presents a complete, colorful, and detailed history of women's involvement in aviation from Mme Thible's balloon flight in 1784 to Jeana Yeager's 1987 flight aboard the Voyager. The lives of early pioneers such as Amelia Earhart are chronicled in separate biographical chapters.

Millspaugh, Ben P. *Ultralight Airman's Manual.* TAB Bks. 1987 $14.95. ISBN 0-8306-2391-4. Modern composite materials have permitted the construction of the new ultralight airplane, a frail-looking experimental aircraft weighing only a few hundred pounds complete with engine. The book introduces the basics of ultralight engines and aerodynamics, basic chart reading, meteorology, and significant legal and operational restrictions. It also contrasts the operation of conventional planes with ultralight craft.

Montgomery, M. R., and Gerald L. Foster. *A Field Guide to Airplanes.* HM 1992 $14.45. ISBN 0-395-62888-1. Provides descriptions and illustrations for more than 300 civilian and military airplanes in an easy-to-handle, pocket-size volume.

Pace, Steve. *North American XB-70 Valkyrie.* Vol. 3. Aero Ser. TAB Bks. 1989 $11.95. ISBN 0-8306-8620-7. A new edition of an historical account describing the concept, design, research, and development that produced two flying prototypes.

Serling, Robert J. *Legend and Legacy: The Story of Boeing and Its People.* St. Martin 1992 $24.95. ISBN 0-312-05890-X. A celebratory historical account of Boeing's growth. Recommended for corporate history collections.

Simonson, G. R., ed. *The History of the American Aircraft Industry.* MIT Pr. 1968 o.p. "This collection brings together some of the important 'classic selections' on the industry, many [of which] are out of print or available in scattered copies only" (*Library Journal*).

Sweetman, Bill. *High Speed Flight*. Janes Info. Pub. 1983 o.p. Supplements aviation literature by providing a thorough and well-illustrated review of international high-speed aircraft, emphasizing the years following World War II. Provides extensive statistical information on each plane and examines the importance of various aviation developments to the history of aviation.

Welch, John F. *Van Sickle's Modern Airmanship*. TAB Bks. 1990 $39.95. ISBN 0-8306-7451-9. Source book on flight principles, techniques, and performance standards. Updated to reflect advances in technology and flying procedures.

Wescott, Lynanne, and Paula Degen. *Wind and Sand: The Story of the Wright Brothers at Kitty Hawk Told through Their Own Words and Photographs*. Abrams 1984 o.p. "An enthralling addition to the accounts of what the Wright Brothers wrought at Kitty Hawk. . . . [Wescott and Degen] have balanced words that are mostly those of the sensitive geniuses from Dayton, Ohio, with photographs that are as much works of art as they are historic documents" (*N.Y. Times Book Review*).

Yeager, Chuck, and Leo Janos. *Yeager: An Autobiography*. Bantam 1985 $17.95. ISBN 0-553-05093-1. Chronicles Yeager's many aviation achievements, such as breaking the sound barrier. Describes both the private and public life of this well-known supersonic aviator. Includes anecdotes about fellow pilots.

Yeager, Jeana, and Phil Patton. *Voyager*. Knopf 1987 $19.95. ISBN 0-394-55266-0. Yeager (no relation to Chuck) and Dick Rhutan flew their craft nonstop around the world without refueling. The book reveals the human side of this great technological feat.

AGRICULTURAL FOOD ENGINEERING

The change from a nomadic hunting and gathering lifestyle to a more settled existence was based on the domestication of plants and animals; this became the earliest origins of today's biggest worldwide industry—agriculture. The agricultural industry, primarily the production of food, has dramatically changed the face of the planet and has had a major impact on its ecology. Humans have cleared forests, controlled rivers, reclaimed land, created countless new hybrid plants and animals, spread certain species beyond their original habitats, and eliminated other species completely. People have tilled the land and harvested its produce, at first by hand and increasingly by larger and more sophisticated machines. The use of fertilizers, herbicides, and pesticides has enabled agricultural production to increase, while at the same time altering the natural environment.

The effects of the reorganization of the environment to meet the needs of the agricultural industry are most apparent in the United States, the source of much of the world's food. In this country, agriculture and its peripheral industries account for a large portion of the gross national product (GNP), and the agricultural labor force, although decreasing, is still significant. The United States has also been one of the leaders in agricultural food engineering, which is concerned with the design and implementation of improved methods of providing food and fibers. Although significant progress has been made in increasing the production and harvesting of crops, the demand is still great for newer and better equipment and techniques to further increase efficiency and reduce costs.

Brady, N. C., ed. *Advances in Agronomy*. Vol. 45 Acad. Pr. 1991 $75.00. ISBN 0-12-000745-2. Contains eight articles by 17 contributors on worldwide agricultural issues. Includes material on nitrogen in wetlands, genetic resources in agriculture, crop management, and soil productivity.

Francis, Charles, Cornelia Flora, and Larry King, eds. *Sustainable Agriculture in Temperate Zones*. Wiley $74.95. ISBN 0-471-62227-3. Contains 16 chapters by 23 contributors on newly developing alternatives to energy-intensive monoculture practices used in most farming today. Intended for students and professionals in agronomy as well as farmers.

Harlander, Susan K., and Theodore P. Labuza, eds. *Biotechnology in Food Processing.* Noyes 1986 $48.00. ISBN 0-8155-1073-X. "This volume presents the proceedings of a 1985 symposium. . . . this symposium explored the current status of the economic, technological, and regulatory impact of evolving areas of high technology on food and food-related industries. The references are current and extensive. . . . this volume provides an excellent current reference source in a rapidly developing field" (*Choice*).

Powledge, Fred. *The Fat of the Land: What's Behind Your Shrinking Food Dollar and What You Can Do about It.* S&S Trade 1984 o.p. "This book examines the food system from farm to grocery store, concentrating on the economic additives that increase the cost of food. Powledge discusses the effects of agricultural practices and marketing on food quality and quantity, points out the costs that highly processed and fabricated foods add, and describes the roles played by the distributors. . . . Concluding chapters focus on food and nutrition organizations that perform watchdog or consumer education functions" (*Library Journal*).

Sangwan, R. S., and B. S. Sangwan-Norreel. *The Impact of Biotechnology on Agriculture.* Kluwer Ac. 1990 $148.00. ISBN 0-7923-0741-0. Papers written for a conference on fundamental and applied in vitro culture research. Addresses a variety of plant science and biotechnology issues pertaining to agriculture.

AUTOMOTIVE ENGINEERING

[SEE under Transportation and Automotive Engineering in this chapter.]

BIOTECHNOLOGY

The origin of biotechnology goes back thousands of years; the use of fermented foods and the development of food preservation techniques are associated with the early Neolithic Age. Microbial activity was not discovered until much later, however, during the nineteenth century when scientists such as Theodor Schwann, LOUIS PASTEUR, and Eduard Buchner pioneered the fields of alcohol bioconversion, microbial fermentation, and cell-free metabolism.

Further advances in industrial fermentation were made as a result of food shortages during World War I and World War II. Since World War II, fermentation processes have been used to produce penicillin and other pharmaceuticals. Industrial microbiology and fermentation have also expanded to include exploration into enzymes, pesticides, vitamins, and solvents. In recent years, molecular biology and genetics have shifted the emphasis of biotechnology towards analysis and manipulation of the genetic structure—the genetic engineering of plants, animals, and even humans. It is now possible, for example, to produce new disease- and pest-resistant crops, to increase milk yields in cows, and to identify (and perhaps in time, eliminate) genes that cause disease in plants, animals, and even humans. Biotechnology is also concerned today with areas of study such as waste treatment, sterilization, textile microbiology, and petroleum processes. Many of the changes wrought by biotechnology bring benefits, but many also pose potential dangers as well as management and ethical problems.

Antébi, Elizabeth, and David Fishlock. *Biotechnology: Strategies for Life.* MIT Pr. 1986 $47.50. ISBN 0-262-01089-5. Presents a collection of 24 chapters that feature original essays by scientists and technologists in the field addressing topics, problems, and noted names in biotechnology. Much of the original fieldwork is described, as well as current and potential future applications. A separate chapter reviews the machinery currently used to run the new technology. The text is well illustrated and includes a complete glossary, bibliography, and chronology of important landmarks in biotechnology.

Bills, Donald D., and Shain-dow Kung. *Biotechnology and Nutrition: Proceedings of the Third International Symposium*. Buttrwrth-Heinemann 1992 $59.95. ISBN 0-7506-9259-6. Contributors discuss the use of biotechnology to alter the composition of plants and animals to improve the nutritional value of food obtained from them.

Calder, Nigel. *The Green Machines*. Putnam Pub. Group 1986 o.p. "Calder's awesome command of information covering all aspects of current biotechnology makes this prophetic and visionary book an instructive delight to read. The major portion of it constitutes a late-20th century review of what has been and is on the brink of being achieved . . . from the point of view of the early 21st century. What is embedded . . . is the capability of avoiding a nuclear winter, chaos, and much worse by the advent of an enlightened king of social revolution . . . an exemplary, practical blueprint for an optimistic future" (*Choice*).

Cheremisinoff, Paul N., and R. P. Ouellette, eds. *Applications of Biotechnology*. Technomic 1985 $29.50. ISBN 0-87762-438-0. "In 49 chapters written by people who really know their fields, the reader is treated to a very broad survey of biotechnology . . . as it stands today, as well as a glimpse of what one futurist is thinking. . . . The chapters are very readable and understandable by persons with an average background in biology and biochemistry" (*Food Technology*).

Chet, Llan. *Biotechnological Control of Plant Pathogens*. Wiley 1993. ISBN 0-471-56084-7. Discusses such issues as "The Impact of Biotechnology on Plant Breeding" (chapter 1), molecular genetic research in disease control, and various aspects of the impact and applications of biotechnology in agriculture.

Fiechter, A., ed. *Advances in Biochemical Engineering—Biotechnology, Vol. 46: Modern Biochemical Engineering*. Spr.-Verlag 1992 $129.00. ISBN 0-387-55276-6. Describes some of the most recent advances in biochemical engineering. Most useful for biochemical engineers and biotechnologists.

Higgins, I. J., and Jennifer Jones, eds. *Biotechnology: Principles and Applications*. Blackwell Pubs. 1990 $60.00. ISBN 0-632-01029-0. Discusses materials, chemical engineering, food, genetics, medicine, agriculture, and energy, as well as a wide range of other topics and their relationship to biotechnology. Organized into nine chapters; an index and suggested further readings are included; requires a general background in biology, chemistry, and enzymology.

Olson, Steve. *Biotechnology: An Industry Comes of Age*. Bks. Demand repr. of 1986 ed. $33.30. ISBN 0-8357-4214-8. A compact synthesis of the state-of-the-art thinking on biotechnology's accomplishments and future; from proceedings of the 1985 Symposium on Biotechnology sponsored by the National Academies of Science and Engineering, Institute of Medicine, and Academy Industry Program.

CHEMICAL ENGINEERING

Chemical engineering is a very broad field, embracing the development and production of industrial and consumer products from a variety of raw materials, such as ores, salt, natural gas, petroleum, water, air, sulfur, and coal. The origins of the field lie in the manufacturing of chemical bleaches and alkalis for the textile industry. Now, however, the field extends to the development and production of plastics, polymers, synthetic fibers, foods, paper, pharmaceuticals, nuclear fuel, metals, petrochemicals, and fertilizers. The chemical engineer deals with problems of mass transfer, heat transfer, fluid flow, reaction kinetics, thermodynamics, computer design and control, environmental considerations, and safety. The profession is interdisciplinary, and chemical engineers touch on a number of different fields.

Grayson, Martin, ed. *Kirk-Othmer Concise Encyclopedia of Chemical Technology.* Wiley 1985 o.p. "A one volume summary of the monumental 26-volume third edition of *Kirk-Othmer* . . . . A handy, compact reference which is extracted from the 'bible' of chemical technology incorporating over 1,100 entries" (*Metal Finishing*).

Hollard, Charles D., and Rayford G. Anthony. *Fundamentals of Chemical Reaction Engineering.* P-H 1989 $74.00. ISBN 0-13-335639-6. Text/reference includes 12 chapters arranged in order of difficulty. Explains fundamentals as well as the design of thermal and catalytic reactions.

Miles, Wyndham D., ed. *American Chemists and Chemical Engineers.* Am. Chemical 1976 $32.95. ISBN 0-8412-0278-8. "Contains both informative and evaluative biographical material for more than 500 men and women who have made prominent contributions in one or more fields of chemistry. . . . The time span is more than 300 years— from early colonial alchemists to truly contemporary individuals" (*Choice*).

Ray, M. S., and D. W. Johnson. *Chemical Engineering Design Project.* Gordon & Breach 1989 $65.00. ISBN 2-88124-712-1. A practical guide for final-year undergraduates providing instruction for the completion of a design project. Covers stages from the technical and economic feasibility study to the design stage.

Tabor. *Genetic Engineering Technology: Principles and Applications..* Dekker 1988 $125.00. ISBN 0-8247-8011-6. For students and practitioners. A review of the field including gene-cloning techniques, current expression systems, fermentation bioreactors, novel applications, and present and future trends in gene therapy.

Wei, James, and others, eds. *Advances in Chemical Engineering.* Vol. 15 *Serial Publication Ser.* Acad. Pr. 1990 $99.00. ISBN 0-12-008515-1. Contains one paper of use to biologists, "Rheological Models of Suspensions," which discusses the theoretical results of rheological properties of multiparticle suspensions.

CIVIL ENGINEERING

Civil engineering is one of the original branches of engineering. Civil engineers were the first to call themselves engineers in order to distinguish themselves from military engineers and to establish themselves as a professional group. The first person to call himself a civil engineer was the Englishman JOHN SMEATON, who did so in 1782. The work of the early civil engineers was confined primarily to the building of roads, canals, and railways. That range has been extended as the demands of industry and society have developed. Today civil engineers are involved in urban and regional planning; in building airports; in the development of water resources; in the design of sewage and sanitation systems; in building dams, bridges, harbors, and power stations; and in dealing with a variety of environmental problems. Because civil engineering is such a broad field, its subdisciplines, such as construction and sanitary and transportation engineering, are covered elsewhere in this chapter.

Bracegirdle, Brian, and Patricia H. Miles. *Thomas Telford.* David & Charles 1973 o.p. "It presents, in 112 superb photographs and a minimum of explanatory text, a fascinating selection of Telford's achievements. The well-known items are all there—St. Mary's Bridgnorth, Chirk and Pontycysyllte aqueducts, Ellesmere Port warehouses, the Caledonian and Göta canals, the Menai, Conway and Waterloo bridges and St. Katharine's Dock. . . . This is a book to appeal to the artist as much as to the engineer or industrial archaeologist" (*Times Literary Supplement*).

Chang, Luh-Maan. *Preparing for Construction in the 21st Century.* Am. Soc. Civil Eng. 1991 $63.00. ISBN 0-87262-801-9. Papers presented at the April 1991 Specialty Conference Construction Congress; address topics of construction.

Haswell, Charles K., and Douglas S. De Silva. *Civil Engineering Contracts: Practice and Procedure*. Buttrwrth-Heinemann 1989 $75.00. ISBN 0-408-03201-4. A guide for engineers and students preparing for qualification, based on British practice and law. Pays special attention to arbitration and covers overseas projects.

Kannappan, Sam. *Introduction to Pipe Stress Analysis*. Wiley 1986 $54.95. ISBN 0-471-81509-6. "Kannappan has written a clear and useful guide or handbook for the designer and stress analyst of industrial piping systems. . . . it is a reference volume . . . . the book will be useful to engineering or engineering technology students who are designed or building piping systems as part of design of laboratory projects as well as to graduate engineers and technologists in design offices" (*Choice*).

Kissam, Philip. *Surveying for Civil Engineers*. McGraw 1981 $43.96. ISBN 0-07-034882-0. "An in-depth work that works well as an instructional guide or as a reference. The five major sections of the book cover instruments and methods for large surveys, operations, procedures for precise control, photogrammetry for construction and land surveys, and the appendix. . . . there are numerous drawings, diagrams, tables, charts, and other illustrations" (*Public Works*).

Schodek, Daniel L. *Landmarks in American Civil Engineering*. MIT Pr. 1987 $55.00. ISBN 0-262-19256-X. "This handsome volume traces the history of a number of projects—bridges, dams, roads, tunnels, railroad cuts and the like—formally designated as significant landmarks by the American Society of Civil Engineers. The list includes some of the most beautiful built objects in the American environment. . . . by bringing to his chronicle the same balance of precision and passion one would hope for in a fine engineer, Mr. Schodek comes close to persuading his reader to invest heavily in bridge bonds and municipal sewer systems" (*N.Y. Times Book Review*).

Schultz, Marilyn Spigel, and Vivian Loeb Kasen. *Encyclopedia of Community Planning and Environmental Management*. Bks. Demand $126.00. ISBN 0-8357-4255-5. "Basic, short definitions are provided here for nonspecialists in the fields of land use, transportation, housing, planning, urban design, census, and social surveys. The entries are concise, and a complex system of cross-references is included. . . . Schultz and Kasen's book is useful . . . for public, high school, and beginning college collections" (*Choice*).

Schuyler, Hamilton. *The Roeblings: A Century of Engineers, Bridge-Builders and Industrialists*. AMS Pr. 1972 repr. of 1931 ed. $29.50. ISBN 0-404-05625-3. "A century ago, John A. Roebling, a native of Muhlhausen, Germany, immigrated to this country, and founded a line of Roeblings who have ever since been important figures as engineers, bridge-builders, and industrialists. Founders of a great wire cable industry, three generations of the family have been connected with the building of suspension bridges, from the famous Brooklyn Bridge projected in 1867, to the 'George Washington Bridge' over the Hudson, opened in 1931" (*Journal of American History*).

Scott, John S. *Dictionary of Civil Engineering*. Halsted Pr. 1981 o.p. Published originally in Great Britain, this book contains more than 300 pages of definitions of terms commonly used in civil engineering. Excludes terminology related to building and construction, but provides cross-references to a companion volume, *The Penguin Dictionary of Building* (Viking Penguin 1986 $8.95); includes a units and conversion factors chart and list of abbreviations.

Shaw, Ronald E. *Erie Water West: A History of the Erie Canal 1792–1854*. U. Pr. of Ky. 1990 $30.00. ISBN 0-8131-1711-9. Fascinating and thoroughly researched account of the political battles over 30 years that led to the building of the Erie Canal, which opened up the West and established the primacy of New York City. Covers the canal's design and engineering and its impact from a commercial, agricultural, industrial, environmental, social, and cultural perspective.

CONSTRUCTION AND MAINTENANCE

Construction and maintenance is a branch of civil engineering that specializes in various aspects of the building process: structure, construction materials, building methods, prefabrication, cost estimating, equipment selection and scheduling, building maintenance, and the dismantling of structures.

Bianchina, Paul. *Illustrated Dictionary of Building Materials and Techniques*. TAB Bks. 1986 o.p. "A complete listing of some 4,000 terms dealing with building materials and techniques is the backbone of this fine book. Areas covered include electrical, tools, plumbing, solar, moldings, finishes, stairs, roofs, and heating. Methods, products, materials, applications, and equipment are enhanced by 800 clear line drawings. . . . More than 60 pages of appendixes provide additional helpful information: abbreviations, conversions/tables/weights; sections about building, framing, lumber, plywood, hardware, electrical, and plumbing" (*Choice*).

Boyer, Lester L., and Walter T. Grondzik. *Earth Shelter Technology*. Texas A&M Univ. Pr. 1987 $32.50. ISBN 0-89096-273-1. Discusses the fundamental variables that determine successful earth-sheltered designs. Not a "how-to" manual, the text still presents many examples of interesting and thought-provoking earth-sheltered designs; includes a complete and recent list of additional readings on the subject.

Brumbaugh, James E. *Complete Roofing Handbook: Installation, Maintenance, Repair*. Macmillan 1986 $29.95. ISBN 0-02-517850-4. Reviews the major types of roofs and their methods of construction, roofing materials, and techniques for application. Also discusses minor structural repairs needed to complete re-roofing projects. Special problems are also treated, including ventilation, dormers, and skylights; includes a listing of trade and professional organizations and roofing manufacturers, as well as a large number of drawings and photographs.

Lenchek, Tom, and Chris Mattock. *Superinsulated Design and Construction: A Guide for Building Energy-Efficient Homes*. Van Nos. Reinhold 1986 $30.95. ISBN 0-442-26051-2. Using information from Canadian and U.S. government programs, the text presents four approaches to building energy-efficient housing and discusses the pros and cons of each method. Covers insulation, sealing, controlling interior humidity, blocking air infiltration, and air/vapor barrier systems. Useful to both homebuilders and contractors.

Lewis, Bernard T. *Building Maintenance Engineering Price Book: 1985–1986*. Routledge Chapman & Hall 1986 $39.95. ISBN 0-412-01071-2. A basic authoritative reference for maintenance costs, estimation of costs, and standard time data. A fully validated compilation of information, it gives accurate cost or standard time data for performing a variety of maintenance jobs. Intended for use by building maintenance staff to help them estimate time and cost data in a timely manner.

Frantz, Douglas. *From the Ground Up: The Business of Building in an Age of Money*. H. Holt & Co. 1991 $27.50. ISBN 0-8050-0996-5. A study of entrepreneurship and construction as exemplified by San Francisco's Rincon Center. While praising the architect of the project, Scott Johnson, for his use of public space, the author notes the failure to meet the needs of low-income people.

Sodhi, Devinder S., ed. *Cold Regions Engineering: Proceedings of a Conference, 1991*. Am. Soc. Civil Eng. 1991 $70.00. ISBN 0-87262-798-5. Proceedings of the Sixth International Cold Regions Engineering Specialty Conference, Feb. 1991. Papers cover a range of subject areas such as frozen-soil mechanics and ice mechanics.

Stein, J. Stewart. *Construction Glossary: An Encyclopedic Reference and Manual*. Wiley 1993 $95.00. ISBN 0-471-56933-X. Revised and expanded version including the definitions of 30,000 words and terms essential for construction professionals.

DESIGN, INVENTORS, AND INVENTING

It is impossible to think about engineering and technology without exploring how inventions are incorporated and how best to use existing knowledge, processes, and materials to deal with a particular task (i.e., to design). Inventions extend the range of materials, processes, and devices available to the designer, who employs them to find ways of designing and producing. The invention-production process, which was first tackled systematically by THOMAS A. EDISON, is now employed regularly by government and industry laboratories and is the rationale of science parks. The inventor looks for some novel solution to a particular problem; the designer uses accepted knowledge, materials, processes, and devices to deal with a task that has been set; and the result is often the development or invention of a new material, process, or device and, perhaps, an advancement of existing knowledge.

Arnold, Tom. *Patent Alternative Dispute Resolution Handbook*. Clark Boardman Callaghan 1991 $85.00. ISBN 0-87632-775-7

Botkin, James, and others. *The Innovators: Rediscovering America's Creative Energy*. U. of Pa. Pr. 1986 $16.95. ISBN 0-8122-1224-X. Presents a collection of case studies illustrating technological and educational issues affecting innovation in American and international businesses. Explores high-tech developments and the incorporation of new technologies into basic industries.

Copp, Newton H., and Andrew W. Zanella. *Discovery, Innovation and Risk*. MIT Pr. 1993 $39.50. ISBN 0-262-03199-X. "Written as a textbook for U.S. sixth-form colleges and universities, and funded by the Alfred P. Sloan foundation, a body set up to foster 'an understanding of technology and quantitative reasoning' among students. . . . a series of case studies: telegraphy, hydroelectric power, powered flight, electricity generation, oil refining, prestressed concrete, vaccines, the greenhouse effect and atomic power. It looks at the history and development of each one, and at the science and technology behind it" (*New Scientist*).

Jewkes, John, and others. *Sources of Invention*. Norton 1971 o.p. Part 1 of the text presents modern views on invention, reviews inventors and inventions of the nineteenth century, and traces industrial research developments. Parts 2 and 3 feature a variety of case studies covering technological inventions such as diesel-electric railways, the cyclotron, freon refrigerants, and the long-playing record.

Josephson, Matthew. *Edison: A Biography*. Wiley 1992 $15.95. ISBN 0-471-54806-5. Gathered from original sources, this biography is interesting not only for its coverage of Edison but also for the material on Jay Gould, George Westinghouse, J. P. Morgan, and several other of Edison's entrepreneurial and financial associates.

Lasson, Kenneth. *Mouse Traps and Muffling Cups: One Hundred Brilliant and Bizarre United States Patents*. Morrow 1986 $9.95. ISBN 0-87795-786-X. Offers a catalog of inventions compiled from the records of the U.S. Patent and Trademarks Office; includes major accomplishments such as the airplane, sewing machine, and parking meter, as well as unsuccessful patents for items such as luminous hats and tapeworm traps.

Leslie, Stuart W. *Boss Kettering*. Col. U. Pr. 1986 $17.00. ISBN 0-231-05601-X. Presents a biography of Charles F. Kettering, acknowledged in his lifetime as America's greatest living engineer and inventor. He made significant contributions to the development of inventory control systems, nontoxic refrigerants, high-speed diesel engines, solar energy, four-wheel brakes, and leaded gasoline.

MacCracken, Calvin D. *A Handbook for Inventors: How to Protect, Patent, Finance, Develop, Manufacture, and Market Your Ideas*. Macmillan 1983 $19.95. ISBN 0-684-17906-7. Describes the steps required to get a patent and methods for protecting your invention. MacCracken, who is a professional inventor, also discusses financing and manufacturing methods. The book is written for the general reader.

Petroski, Henry. *Pencil*. Knopf 1990 $25.00. ISBN 0-394-57422-2. A unique history of the pencil and tracing its use from the time of Leonardo da Vinci to the present.

_____. *The Evolution of Useful Things*. Knopf 1992 $25.00. ISBN 0-679-41226-3. The history of a multitude of everyday objects. Explores the relationship between increased specialization of tasks and the evolution of everyday tools.

_____. *To Engineer Is Human: The Role of Failure in Successful Design*. St. Martin 1985 $17.95. ISBN 0-312-80680-9. Suggests that failures have been instrumental in improving engineering designs and projects throughout history. ("We learn by our mistakes.") The lively text includes many unexpected literary references and cites examples of many well-known incidents and newsworthy disasters.

Runes, Dagobert D., ed. *The Diary and Sundry Observations of Thomas Alva Edison.* Greenwood repr. of 1968 ed. $39.75. ISBN 0-8371-0067-4. Includes excerpts from Edison's personal diary and Edison's observations on motion pictures and the arts, war and peace, education and work, people and machines, "a better world," life after death, and spiritualism.

EDUCATION AND CAREERS

Throughout the history of the profession, engineers have been concerned with educating future engineers and continuing their education as new developments occur. Part of this concern is based on the need to equip engineers to cope responsibly with the claims made upon them; part is the urge to enhance the engineer's status. In recent years there has been an increased interest in introducing social as well as technical components in the professional training of engineers. There has also been an increased interest in recruiting women to the field, and professional institutions have advertised the great range of engineering careers available, stressing how suitable and attractive these prospects are to women.

Beakley, George C., and Deloss H. Bowers. *Careers in Engineering and Technology.* Macmillan 1987 $32.25. ISBN 0-02-307620-8. An introductory text that reviews career fields and employment opportunities in engineering and technology. Begins with a short history of engineering, and then discusses the professional responsibilities of engineers, oral and written technical communication, computers and engineering, modeling and the design process, and the technical work team.

Ferguson, Eugene S. *Engineering and the Mind's Eye.* MIT Pr. 1992 $24.95. ISBN 0-262-06147-3. Supports the need for more emphasis on design skills, nonverbal feel for physical behaviour, and common sense judgment; argues that the traditional theoretical and mathematical approach in the education and training of engineers should be deemphasized.

Kemper, John D. *Engineers and Their Profession.* H. Holt & Co. 1982 o.p. A comprehensive review of the profession covering the environment; public responsibility; energy issues; engineers in private practice, industry, and government; engineering management; creativity; salaries; professional registration; unions; engineering societies; and the various branches of engineering.

Laithwaite, Eric. *Invitation to Engineering. Invitation Ser.* Blackwell Pubs. 1985 $29.95. ISBN 0-85520-661-6. "Written to give as good an insight as possible into what the daily life of a practicing engineer is really like, whether it be in industry . . . or as an academic" (Preface).

Pletta, Dan H. *The Engineering Profession: Its Heritage and Its Emerging Public Purpose.* U. Pr. of Amer. 1984 o.p. Covers the history and organization of the engineering profession and reviews the purpose and obligations of professions, economic and political constraints on the field, engineering education, the law of public interest, and engineering management and societal leadership. Pletta is an emeritus professor at the Virginia Polytechnic Institute.

Pytlik, Edward C., Donald P. Lauda, and David L. Johnson. *Technology, Change and Society.* Delmar 1985 $15.95. ISBN 0-87192-084-0. An adult-level text, in two parts, designed for a course of the same title. Part 1 discusses subjects such as technology and society and technology and the individual; includes several case studies. Part 2 describes several important issues such as population growth, energy, and the environment. Bibliographies and discussion questions are included in each chapter. Part 2 begins with the debatable assumption that "by its nature, technology is neutral."

Red, W. Edward. *Engineering: The Career and the Profession*. Brooks-Cole 1982 o.p.
Designed to help students determine if their interests and talents are compatible
with an engineering career and to help them decide what branches of engineering to
specialize in. Also assists students in understanding the distinctions between
educational and professional engineering careers; includes selective bibliography of
introductory readings.

Winkler, Connie. *Careers in High Tech: Exciting Jobs in Today's Fastest-Growing Fields*.
P-H 1987 $9.95. ISBN 0-668-06537-0. "A useful guide to the types of jobs available in
the high-tech industry . . . describes the kind of training and education usually
deemed suitable for successful careers. . . . chapters outline specific types of
positions in various disciplines such as data processing, personal computers,
artificial intelligence, biotechnology and publishing" (*Booklist*).

ELECTRICAL ENGINEERING AND ELECTRONICS

The history-making advances in electrical engineering closely parallel the
landmark discoveries and inventions of the past. Several notable examples
include the development of the electric battery by Alessandro Volta in 1800, the
demonstration of electrolysis a few weeks later by William Nicholson and Sir
Anthony Carlisle, the discovery of electromagnetic induction by MICHAEL
FARADAY, Samuel Morse's patenting of the telegraph, the prediction of electromagnetic waves by JAMES CLERK MAXWELL and their subsequent demonstration
and application by HEINRICH HERTZ and Guglielmo Marconi, and the development of the high-resistance filament lamp by THOMAS A. EDISON in 1880.

The early emphasis on the generation and distribution of electricity, and on
electric machinery, has expanded steadily. Today electrical and electronic
engineering and technology—the heavy and light current sides of the industry
now being inseparable both practically and institutionally—embrace many
diverse but related activities. A check on the publications of the institutions
reveals the following headings: science; measurement and technology; electric
power applications; generation, transmission, and distribution; control theory
and applications; computers and digital techniques; radar and signal processing; circuits, devices, and systems; microwaves, antennas, and propagation;
communications; speech and vision; and optoelectronics. Moreover, each of
these headings in turn covers a wide range. For example, hidden within those
cryptic headings are subjects such as intelligence systems, software engineering, medical and biological engineering, instruments, sonar, direction finding
and navigation, avionics, satellites, and information technology. And, last but
not least, radio and television.

The field is constantly changing and will continue to change. Solid-state
devices are replacing thermionic valves; microwaves are providing long-dis-
tance communication links; linear motors are entering manufacturing processes and transport systems; and optical fibers are replacing telephone wires.

Aitken, Hugh G. J. *The Continuous Wave: Technology and American Radio, 1900–1932*.
Princeton U. Pr. 1985 $67.50. ISBN 0-7837-4330-0. "Aitken's accounting . . . provides
an unprecedented cohesiveness, many new details, and a few challenges to older
interpretations. During the period covered, business and government were learning
which organizational forms and managerial techniques worked best for technological innovation. Because radio makes a revealing case study in this process, this book
is important for a wide range of readers" (*Science*).

Baylin, Frank. *Satellites Today: The Complete Guide to Satellite Television*. Baylin Pubns.
1987 $11.95. ISBN 0-318-41083-4. Discusses the nature, design, history, and cost of
communication satellites and earth stations. Also includes a detailed examination of

operating problems, available programs, legal issues, and the future of satellite television.

Clifford, Martin. *Your Telephone: Operation, Selection and Installation.* Howard Sams 1983 o.p. Well-illustrated text that explains the parts of the telephone, different types of phones, telephone security issues, mobile telephones, and the use of new technologies. Particularly useful to home consumers, since so many people now own or are considering purchase of their phones.

Cogdell, John R. *Foundations of Electrical Engineering.* P-H 1990 $57.67. ISBN 0-13-329525-7. Text for use in a sophomore-level course for E. E. majors. Assumes a year of calculus and a good grounding in mechanics and electrical physics.

Decareau, Robert V., and R. A. Peterson. *Microwave Processing and Engineering.* VCH Pubs. 1986 $90.00. ISBN 0-89573-407-9. "The authors begin with a general discussion of microwave applications and design philosophies, then follow with chapters on microwave power sources; power supplies and microwave plumbing; typical applicators; materials of construction; design measurements and equipment; control systems; and microwave leakage and its measurement and control. Material for this volume is drawn from the author's extensive knowledge and experience as well as from the substantial patent and technical literature" (*Choice*).

Eargle, John. *Handbook of Recording Engineering.* Van Nos. Reinhold 1991 $44.95. ISBN 0-442-00553-9. A logical review of the elements required for successful recording, including microphones, audio transmission, loudspeakers, signal processing devices, and monitoring systems. Discusses analog magnetic, disc, and digital recording.

Faber, Rodney B. *Essentials of Solid-State Electronics.* Wiley 1985 o.p. "A traditional and conventional 'bottom up' approach to solid-state electronics . . . summaries provide a compact statement of the main equations and definitions which have been developed . . . a very supportive text minimizing the level of mathematical skill required" (*IEEE Proceedings*).

Friedel, Robert, and others. *Edison's Electric Light: Biography of an Invention.* Rutgers U. Pr. 1987 $16.95. ISBN 0-8135-1254-9. Examines the invention of the electric light, which the authors characterize as a complex human achievement and one of the most important agents for change in the last two centuries; based on a careful study of the Edison archives.

Grayson, Martin, ed. *Encyclopedia of Semiconductor Technology.* Wiley 1984 $140.00. ISBN 0-471-88102-3. Presents well-illustrated articles authored by industrial and academic experts on nearly every aspect of semiconductors, including their manufacture and use, integrated circuits, magnetic materials, and super-conductors. Reprinted from the well-known *Kirk-Othmer Encyclopedia of Chemical Technology.* Full texts, tables, figures, and reference materials from the original are reproduced unchanged.

Guide to Electronics in the Home. Consumer Reports Bks. 2nd ed. 1986 o.p. Provides product descriptions, ratings, and recommendations for a variety of home electronic products; includes stereo systems, cassette recorders, calculators, smoke detectors, video cameras, and VCRs. Most of the material has been extracted from previously published issues of *Consumer Reports.*

Holzman, Harvey N. *Modern Residential Wiring.* Goodheart 1991 $23.80. ISBN 0-87006-902-0. Covers introductory concepts of electricity and explains complicated wiring tasks. Contains a wealth of information and many illustrations for the homeowner.

Hughes, Thomas Parke. *Elmer Sperry: Inventor and Engineer.* Johns Hopkins 1971 $39.50. ISBN 0-8018-1133-3. A readable account of Sperry's life. In addition to the gyroscopic work that made his fame and fortune, Sperry invented a variety of other devices and founded the American Institute of Electrical Engineers.

Isailovic, Jordan. *Videodisc Systems: Theory and Applications.* P-H 1987 $51.00. ISBN 0-13941-865-2. "A most-welcome addition to a seriously limited group of books on videodisc systems. This field is obviously in an expansive mode and will become an integral part of everyone's life in a very short time. Isailovic treats both theoretical and practical aspects of videodisc systems . . . detailing the principles and descriptions of optical and capacitive playback systems . . . discuss[ing] recording and production . . . programmable optical videodisc systems . . . signal processing and frequency modulation techniques" (*Choice*).

Kybett, Harry, and Delton T. Horn. *The Complete Handbook of Videocassette Recorders.* TAB Bks. 1986 $14.95. ISBN 0-8306-2731-6. The text explains how to use VCRs and how they work, and discusses portable VCRs and camcorders. Suitable for the professional and layperson; includes many diagrams.

Linggard, Robert. *Electronic Synthesis of Speech.* Cambridge U. Pr. 1985 $34.50. ISBN 0-5212-4469-2. "Describes how speech can be generated artificially using computers and special electronic circuits" (*Mechanical Engineering*).

McGraw-Hill Dictionary of Electrical and Electronic Engineering. McGraw 1985 $23.95. ISBN 0-07-045413-2. Contains almost 500 pages of concise definitions of terms used in the fields of electrical and electronic engineering.

McMahon, M. *The Making of a Profession: A Century of Electrical Engineering in America.* Inst. Electrical 1984 $39.95. ISBN 0-87942-173-8. A history of the electrical engineering profession as seen through the actions of several greats in the field.

Pehl, Erich. *Microwave Technology.* Bks. Demand repr. of 1985 ed. $59.80. ISBN 0-685-20803-6. "Deals with wave propagation in various media, including coaxial cable, waveguide, and transmission lines, and the circuit elements that can be formed of these media. . . . Pehl's style is straightforward. He introduces a concept, presents the mathematical background for the idea, and then offers a practical example to illustrate the concept" (*Microwaves & RF*).

Rains, Darell L. *Major Home Appliances: A Common Sense Repair Manual.* TAB Bks. 1987 $15.95. ISBN 0-8306-2747-2. Clearly written and well illustrated, the text provides extensive diagnostic and repair procedures for washers, dryers, refrigerators, and dishwashers. Also covered are methods to prolong the life of major home appliances, safety factors, warranties, and parts suppliers.

Read, Oliver, and Walter L. Welch. *From Tin Foil to Stereo.* Howard Sams 1976 o.p. Presents the most comprehensive and best-illustrated story of the phonograph from 1877 up to the complex mechanical, acoustical, and electronic inventions that culminated in the stereophonic disk process of the late 1950s.

Reid, T. R. *The Chip: How Two Americans Invented the Microchip and Launched a Revolution.* S&S Trade 1985 o.p. Provides a detailed history of the development of the integrated circuit. Discusses its two inventors, Robert Noyce and Jack Kilby, showing how each independently came up with the same idea; includes selected illustrations and a reading list.

Roberts, R. S. *Dictionary of Audio, Radio and Video.* Buttrwrth-Heinemann 1981 $54.95. ISBN 0-408-00339-1. Provides 240 pages of illustrated definitions and explains the meanings and applications of terms common to audio, radio, and video engineering. Appendices cover classifications of radio frequencies and emissions, a list of common acronyms and abbreviations, and European and American television system standards.

Roberts, Steven, ed. *International Directory of Telecommunications.* Longman 1986 o.p. "Fulfills well the object of its compiler: to produce a reference companion for use by managers and researchers who want a general overview of the international telecommunication and broadcasting organisations and industries . . . will serve well those who have an interest in the international telecommunication scene" (*British Telecommunications Engineering*).

Ryder, John Douglas. *Engineers and Electrons: A Century of Electrical Progress.* IEEE Pr. 1983 o.p. This book is "not intended as a scholarly history, but it does provide, in an informal and readable way, the story of how electrical engineering began and grew over the decades to provide the technology that is a part of our daily lives. . . . The illustrations are excellent, and each chapter provides a list for further reading" (*Science Books & Films*).

Singleton, Loy. *A Global Impact: The New Telecommunication Technologies.* Harper Busn. 1989 $26.95. ISBN 0-88730-259-9. Presents an update of his previous work explaining the new technologies for the general reader.

Truxal, John G. *The Age of Electronic Messages*. MIT Pr. 1990 $35.00. ISBN 0-262-20074-0. Presents an introduction to the technology of electronics. Describes its effects on individuals and on society. Clearly written, the book is intended for the nontechnology student and general reader.

Twiss, B. C., ed. *Forecasting for Technologists and Engineers: A Practical Guide for Better Decisions. IEE Management of Technology Ser: No. 5*. Inst. Elect. Engr. 1992 $69.00. ISBN 0-86341-265-3. A practical guide to using forecasting of technological advances and market changes as part of making technical decisions.

Ward, Stephen A., and Robert H. Halstead. *Computation Structures. Electrical Engineering and Computer Science Ser*. MIT Pr. 1989 $55.00. ISBN 0-262-23139-5. Textbook designed for electrical engineering and computer science majors at MIT. Approaches digital systems architecture from simple electronics into representative computer systems.

Watson, John. *Mastering Electronics*. McGraw 1990 $34.95. ISBN 0-07-068482-0. Explains the operation of devices such as digital circuits, television, radio, and amplifiers for the general reader. Suggests and describes home projects for each of these devices, with particular emphasis on understanding the ABCs of how they work.

ENGINEERING GEOLOGY

[SEE under Petroleum Engineering and Engineering Geology in this chapter.]

ENGINEERING HISTORY

To understand engineering and technology, it is essential to study the history of these fields—the buildings and the water management projects of the ancient Egyptians; the city layouts and temples of the ancient Greeks; the road-building efforts and use of the arch by the ancient Romans; the huge cathedrals of the Middle Ages; and, nearer to our own time, the Erie Canal; the great dams of North America; the development and use of electricity; and electronics. Some knowledge of these developments is important in order to put the current field of engineering in perspective, to provide readers with a clearer view of these subjects as historical processes, and to show how engineering and technological knowledge advances.

Clark, Ronald W. *Works of Man*. Viking Penguin 1985 o.p. Surveys the history of engineering and technology, focusing on developments in Western civilization since the invention of the steam engine; includes a detailed index, many colored photographs, and a short list of suggested readings.

Corn, Joseph J., ed. *Imagining Tomorrow: History, Technology and the American Future*. MIT Pr. 1988 $30.00. ISBN 0-262-03115-9. An extensive examination of technology that assesses innovations against changing times. Covers a variety of inventions, such as radio and plastics, technological events including world's fairs, and the impact of technology on commercialism.

De Camp. L. Sprague. *The Ancient Engineers*. Ballantine 1988 $4.95. ISBN 0-345-00876-6. A most readable popular history of technology. "Mr. de Camp has written a detailed but anecdotal history of how mechanical things got done in the ancient civilizations—how the pyramids were built, and the Great Wall of China, what ancient siege engines were like and how they operated, and much more. For all history buffs as well as modern technicians" (*Publisher's Weekly*).

Ferguson, Eugene S. *Oliver Evans: Inventive Genius of the Industrial Revolution*. Hagley Museum 1980 $4.95. ISBN 0-914650-18-1

Flaxman, Edward, ed. *Great Feats of Modern Engineering. Essays Index Repr. Ser*. Ayer repr. of 1938 ed. $20.00. ISBN 0-8369-0446-X

Landes, David S. *The Unbound Prometheus: Technological Change and Industrial Development in Western Europe from 1750 to the Present*. Cambridge U. Pr. 1969 $18.95. ISBN 0-521-09418-6. Presents a comprehensive, scholarly treatment of the topic; includes occasional references to the United States, Japan, and China.

Morison, Elting E. *Men, Machines, and Modern Times*. MIT Pr. 1966 $9.95. ISBN 0-262-63018-4. "A series of essays and lectures giving historical perspective on technological change" (*Library Journal*).

Pacey, Arnold. *The Culture of Technology*. MIT Pr. 1983 $11.95. ISBN 0-262-66056-3. Provides a thought-provoking analysis of technology, examining its various cultural dimensions such as practice, progress, expertise, resources, imperatives, values, and innovation; includes a brief, but useful bibliography.

———. *The Maze of Ingenuity: Ideas and Idealism in the Development of Technology*. Holmes & Meier 1975 $32.50. ISBN 0-8419-0181-3. Presents the changes in outlook that accompanied the development of technology in Europe between 1100 and 1870. Also discusses the humanitarian, social, and intellectual ideals and objectives of technology in the 1970s.

———. *Technology in World Civilization*. MIT Pr. 1990 $25.00. ISBN 0-262-16117-6. Presents a historical approach to the subject, beginning with "Asian technology A.D. 700–1100" and concluding with "Survival technology in the twentieth century." Covers hydrology, windmills, metallurgy, gunpowder, weaving, steam engines, railways, and much more; includes a useful bibliography that is more extensive than that in *The Culture of Technology*.

Parsons, William Barclay. *Engineers and Engineering in the Renaissance*. MIT Pr. 1968 o.p. "The topics include Da Vinci, machines and mechanism (not clocks), mining, the engineering of cities, of rivers, canals and harbors, of bridges and domes. Here is the famous account of how Domenico Fontana moved the obelisk to St. Peter's, and the story of the design and construction of the Rialto Bridge in Venice, the Pont Neuf over the Seine, the Santa Trinità across the Arno, the great domes of Florence and of Rome" (*Scientific American*).

Robinson, Eric H., and A. E. Musson. *James Watt and the Steam Revolution: A Documentary History*. Kelley 1969 $29.50. ISBN 0-238-78937-3. Presents a selection of reprinted documents, produced on the bicentenary of Watt's first patent; includes previously unpublished material on Watt's research.

Rothenberg, Marc, ed. *The Papers of Joseph Henry*. Vol. 6 *January 1844–December 1846, The Princeton Years*. Smithsonian 1992 $55.00. ISBN 1-56098-112-1. Covers the life and work of one of the pioneers of electromagnetism; discusses Henry's role in the development of industrial equipment.

Susskind, Charles. *Twenty-Five Engineers and Inventors*. San Francisco Pr. 1977 $10.00. ISBN 0-911302-29-8

Turner, Roland, and Steven L. Goulden, eds. *Great Engineers and Pioneers in Technology: From Antiquity through the Industrial Revolution*. Vol. 1 St. Martin 1982 $69.50. ISBN 0-312-34574-7. "Entries for individual engineers are arranged in chronological order by actual or presumed date of birth and include a brief biographical sketch, a discussion of outstanding engineering achievements, and suggestions for further reading. . . . Reference and research use is enhanced by inclusion of an alphabetical index of biographical entries, a brief glossary of technical terms, a chronological table of significant engineering events, a bibliography of major historical studies on engineering, a list of illustrations, and a general index" (*Choice*).

Wasserman, Neil H. *From Invention to Innovation: Long Distance Telephone Transmission at the Turn of the Century*. Johns Hopkins 1985 $24.00. ISBN 0-8018-2715-9. Presents a twofold study in technological innovation—one examines a particularly significant innovation in telephone transmission; the second explores how large enterprise in the United States developed the capability of using modern science and engineering.

Weitzman, David. *Windmills, Bridges and Old Machines: Discovering Our Industrial Past*. Macmillan Child Grp. 1982 o.p. Presents a well-illustrated industrial history for all readers, young and old.

York, Neil Longley. *Mechanical Metamorphosis: Technological Change in Revolutionary America.* Greenwood 1985 $42.95. ISBN 0-313-24475-8. "York's investigation covers the era of the American revolution, roughly from 1760 to 1790. . . . The book's sixth chapter 'Limits to innovation: the Pennsylvania rifle,' presents a superb account of an instance when institutional resistance to an invention . . . frustrated its adoption . . . . York is at his best when discussing the work and vision of specific inventors in the context of a largely indifferent and occasionally hostile society" (*Science*).

FLIGHT

[SEE under Aeronautics and Aviation in this chapter.]

HOLOGRAPHY

[SEE under Lasers and Holography in this chapter.]

INDUSTRIAL ENGINEERING
AND ENGINEERING MANAGEMENT

Once engineering moves out of the workshop and into the factory, it becomes a subject of study in itself: how to make the best of something on a large scale after it has been conceived on a small scale. For example, the production of Ford automobiles on a worldwide scale, with factories on every continent, is altogether different from Henry Ford's small, early workshop, where his first models were built virtually on demand. Businesses today must address a host of concerns: how to work efficiently and become cost effective, how to envisage and develop models years ahead of actual production, how to appeal to a mass market, and how to maintain an efficient (and often multinational) labor force. These concerns are within the purview of industrial engineering and engineering management.

The first person to study such issues in a serious and systematic way was Frederick Taylor (1856–1915), who is often referred to as the father of scientific management. Industrial engineering as a field of study began in the nineteenth century, when factory production replaced household or cottage industries. Taylor's work at that time formed the basis on which the field was conceptualized and grew. From Taylor's initial studies in work design, measurement, planning, and scheduling grew later research efforts in cost reduction, inventory control, assembly line balancing, workplace design, and productivity improvement. Modern industrial engineering concerns, such as computer analysis, management information systems, human factors engineering, and biomechanics, are also outgrowths of Taylor's initial efforts, and present-day methods owe a great deal to his pioneering efforts in the field.

Bain, David L. *The Productivity Prescription: The Manager's Guide to Improving Productivity and Profits.* McGraw 1986 $12.95. ISBN 0-07-003236-X. "A timely work on a topic that currently is generating a great deal of interest. . . . What sets this 'how to' book apart . . . is the author's emphasis on increasing productivity without increasing capital investment. . . . He suggests that by making use of contemporary behavioral theory productivity can be increased. . . . The case studies Bain includes are a particularly valuable feature" (*Library Journal*).

Clark, Forrest D., and A. B. Lorenzoni. *Applied Cost Engineering*. Bks. Demand repr. of 1985 ed. $80.40. ISBN 0-8357-6022-7. "A very well written textbook that ranges from the bare basics in cost engineering to the latest techniques in cost engineering and project controls . . . very easy to follow. . . . there are 10 'case studies' at the end of the 25 formal chapters" (*Chemical Engineering*).

Grove, Andrew S. *High Output Management*. Random 1985 $3.95. ISBN 0-285-62659-0. "The author deals with basic management techniques rather than with a new management method. . . . by means of . . . simple analogies he [seeks to] enable the reader to comprehend the complexities of managing both small and large organizations" (*Library Journal*).

Kendrick, John W. *Improving Company Productivity: Handbook with Case Studies*. Johns Hopkins 1986 $15.95. ISBN 0-8018-2993-3. A summary of the current state of the art with respect to the measurement of company productivity, the various practical uses to which productivity measures may be put, and the development of productivity improvement programs.

Melman, Seymour. *Profits without Production*. U. of Pa. Pr. 1987 $19.95. ISBN 0-8122-1258-4. "The thesis of this book strikes at the heart of a much debated current issue, the relative decline in U.S. productivity compared with that of Japan, West Germany, and other developed countries. . . . [Melman] carefully reevaluates much of the territory addressed by . . . others . . . who contend American managers have been overly preoccupied with short-term profits at the expense of long-run product quality . . . [a] well documented, scholarly work" (*Library Journal*).

Meredith, Dale D., and others. *Design and Planning of Engineering Systems*. P-H 1985 $34.95. ISBN 0-1320-0189-6. "Presents techniques for problem solving and discusses such items as systems modeling, optimization concepts, evaluations, linear graph analysis, calculus methods, linear programming, decision analysis, network planning, and others" (*Public Works*).

Rosenberg, Nathan. *Inside the Black Box: Technology and Economics*. Cambridge U. Pr. 1983 $17.95. ISBN 0-521-27367-6

——. *Perspectives on Technology*. M. E. Sharpe 1984 $15.95. ISBN 0-87332-303-3

——. *Technology and American Economic Growth*. M. E. Sharpe 1972 $15.95. ISBN 0-87332-104-9

Rosenberg, Nathan, Ralph Landau, and David C. Mowery, eds. *Technology and the Wealth of Nations*. Stanford U. Pr. 1992 $49.50. ISBN 0-8047-2083-5. Proceedings of a conference at Stanford University that addresses the reasons why English-speaking countries have not always converted science and technology into industrial wealth. No formula for success emerges, but the problem is analyzed and several useful ideas are presented.

Schonberger, Richard. *Japanese Manufacturing Techniques: Nine Hidden Lessons in Simplicity*. Free Pr. 1982 $32.95. ISBN 0-02-929100-3. Schonberger's book is "eminently readable and clearly organized into nine chapters, each containing a lesson from Japanese experience, especially Just-In-Time production and Total Quality Control, the implications of which are well explained. . . . The stress is on production management . . . the author . . . enriches the book by interesting case-study examples" (*Choice*).

LASERS AND HOLOGRAPHY

The light we receive every day, whether from the sun or from electric lights, originates in many billions of atoms. These atoms travel through space as light waves arranged in a random fashion; that is, the peaks and troughs of the "waves" vary, and there is a broad range of wavelengths. A laser (which stands for Light Amplification by Simulated Emission of Radiation) is a device that generates a narrow and intense beam of light of (usually) only a single wavelength, with the all the peaks and troughs of the "waves" in synch.

Holography is a technique for utilizing this special property of laser light. It compares the direct light from a laser and that same light as it is reflected off an object. The difference between these two measurements produces a three-dimensional outline of the object's shape. The photographic record of this outline is called a hologram.

Since the introduction of lasers in 1960, the scope of their application has increased steadily. High-intensity lasers are used in delicate surgery and in various types of military technology. Low-intensity lasers are used as scanners to read bar codes on products at supermarket checkouts, to keep track of books in libraries, and to read videodiscs. Laser-surveying instruments are in use accurately measuring distances between points on the earth. Holography is widely employed as a means of optical image formation, and the use of holograms includes microscopy, state-of-the-art advertising techniques, and artistic expression. Of great importance in engineering and technology, holography is also used to study surface irregularities, stresses in components and structures, rotating and vibrating objects, and chemical reactions.

Broad, William J. *Teller's War: Behind the Star Wars Deception.* S & S Trade 1992 $25.00. ISBN 0-671-70106-1

Hecht, Jeff. *Laser Guidebook.* McGraw 1992 $44.95. ISBN 0-07-027737-0. An important reference for laser users. The first few chapters describe basic ideas while the following chapters deal with the technology and usage of individual laser types.

Laurence, Clifford L. *The Laser Book: A New Technology of Light.* P-H 1986 o.p. Reviews the history of laser technology and discusses the common types of laser. Chronicles the increasing fields in which the laser is used currently, such as optics, holography, medicine, the military, and communications. Provides basic definitions for terms such as the index of refraction, frequency, wavelength, and coherence. Includes information about careers in laser technology.

Orayevskiy, A. N., ed. *Research on Chemical Lasers. Proceeding of Lebedev Physics Institute Ser.* Vol. 193. Nova Sci. Pubs. 1992 $87.00. ISBN 1-56072-053-0. Discusses specific topics related to chemical lasers including problems of setting up experiments and a mathematical model for chemical lasers with nontoxic products.

Vasilenko, G. I., and L. M. Tsibul'Kiu. *Image Recognition by Holography.* Plenum Pub. 1989 $89.50. ISBN 0-306-11017-2. An account of current holographic recognition systems, including their theory, principles of construction, and applications.

Wenyon, Michael. *Understanding Holography.* P-H Gen. Ref. & Trav. 1985 $14.95. ISBN 0-668-6414-5. Provides a basic introduction to the holograph, a device that produces a three-dimensional image of an object by using lasers. Discusses principles and applications of holography and the future of holography and describes how to make holograms.

MECHANICAL ENGINEERING

One of the first disciplines to break away from civil engineering, mechanical engineering is concerned with the design and production of machinery and its components. The field borrows heavily from the study of mathematics, material mechanics, statics, dynamics, thermodynamics, and fluid dynamics. Today mechanical engineering also encompasses such areas as tribology, which is concerned with lubrication and surfaces; orthopedic biomechanics, which, among other things, develops artificial knee and hip joints; manufacturing engineering; computer-aided engineering; and automotive engineering.

Del Vecchio, Alfred. *Dictionary of Mechanical Engineering.* Naturegraph 1961 o.p. Provides more than 300 pages of definitions of terms used in the fields of architecture, automatic controls, engineering mechanics, combustion, and power plants. Selective definitions also given in the related fields of electricity, heat treatment of metals, mathematics, and welding; includes 20 pages of conversion factors following the main text.

Hine, Charles R. *Machines Tools and Processes for Engineers.* Kreiger 1982 repr. of 1971 ed. o.p. "The author covers all the important tools with a descriptive and analytical treatment that shows how they should be used, what they can and cannot be expected to do" (*Library Journal*).

Nayler, G. H. *Dictionary of Mechanical Engineering.* Buttrwrth-Heinemann 1986 $65.00. ISBN 0-408-01505-5. Provides more than 400 pages of partially illustrated definitions for terms commonly used in the fields of mechanical power in engines, transport, and mechanisms. Excludes definitions that pertain to hand tools and fields allied to mechanical engineering such as welding and metallurgy; appendices include definitions of units.

Reader, G. T., and C. Hooper. *Stirling Engines.* Routledge Chapman & Hall 1982 o.p. A coherent and easy-to-read account of the Stirling engine, which is experiencing renewed popularity because of its potential for reducing fuel consumption.

Rothbart, Harold A. *Mechanical Design and Systems Handbook.* McGraw 1985 $129.50. ISBN 0-07-054020-9. Includes five sections: Mechanical Engineering Fundamentals, System Analysis and Synthesis, Mechanical Design Fundamentals, Mechanical Fastener Component, and Power-Control Components and Subsystems. Recommended for engineering collections serving upper-division undergraduate and beginning graduate students, as well as for designers.

Stein, Benjamin, and John S. Reynolds. *Mechanical and Electrical Equipment for Buildings.* Wiley 1991 $69.95. ISBN 0-471-52502-2. Provides theory and design guidelines for systems and equipment in all areas. An excellent resource for all technical college and engineering libraries.

Walker, Graham. *Stirling Engines.* OUP 1980 $105.00. ISBN 0-1985-6209-8. Offers a comprehensive treatise on the Stirling engine, which operates on a closed regenerative thermodynamic cycle and embraces a large family of machines with different functions, characteristics, and configurations.

Whitt, Frank Rowland, and David Gordon Wilson. *Bicycling Science: Ergonomics and Mechanics.* MIT Pr. 1982 $13.50. ISBN 0-262-73060-X. Written for mechanically inquisitive bicyclists, teachers of introductory mechanics and physiology, engineers, and others interested in exploring approaches to reduce dependence on high-energy-consumption transportation. Includes a short chapter on the history of bicycles and tricycles. The subtitle reflects engineering's recent awareness of ergonomics, or designing machines that consider how the human body will interact with them. With a foreword by James McCullagh.

MILITARY ENGINEERING

The field of military engineering goes back a long way: It was used by the ancient Romans in constructing catapults and other machines of war, and other ancient civilizations employed military engineering for similar purposes. In more recent times, military engineering has been used in the design of submarines, tanks, radar, nuclear weapons, and intercontinental ballistic missiles. In fact, since World War II, the majority of scientists and engineers in the world have been employed in serving the military. With the end of the cold war, military engineering may have to refocus its energies; yet, the field is likely to remain substantial and important for the foreseeable future.

Brodie, Bernard, and Fawn M. Brodie. *From Crossbow to H-Bomb.* Ind. U. Pr. 1973 $29.95. ISBN 0-253-32490-4. Chronicles the contributions of science to warfare; includes a wealth of information written in a easy-to-read style.

Chako, George K. *Technology Management: Applications for Corporate Markets and Military Missions.* Greenwood 1988 $45.00. ISBN 0-275-92941-8. Fifteen applications of "concomitant coalition" (CONCOL), an approach incorporating competitive cooperation as a technology management strategy applicable to both markets and the military.

Clary, David A. *Fortress America: The Corps of Engineers, Hampton Roads, and United States Coastal Defense*. U. Pr. of Va. 1990 $35.00. ISBN 0-8139-1238-5. Uses the strategic Hampton Roads area of the American coast as a case study for a discussion of U.S. Army engineers and national defense policies.

Diamant, Lincoln. *Bernard Romans: Forgotten Patriot of the American Revolution, Military Engineer and Cartographer of West Point and the Hudson Valley*. Harbor Hill Bks. 1985 $15.95. ISBN 0-916346-56-0. Treats the life and accomplishments of a relatively obscure figure of the revolutionary war.

Macksey, Kenneth. *Technology in War: The Impact on Science of Weapon Development and Modern Battle*. P-H Gen. Ref. & Trav. 1986 o.p. "Traces the influence of scientific and technical developments on weapons over several centuries up to the present. Ranges from the design of forts to missiles. It is a handsome book with many photographs and drawings . . . but it is also a sobering book in considering the effects of modern weapons, including firearms, submarines, and aircraft" (*Library Journal*).

MINING AND METALLURGY

Mining, the extraction of minerals from the earth, is an activity that dates back to early human history. Gold, silver, copper, and other metals have been mined and used for ornaments or tools for thousands of years. In more recent times, the demand for minerals has increased and mineral exploration has assumed greater importance, becoming highly technical and costly as a result. With increasing demand for minerals, systematic exploration has replaced accidental discovery, and the size of mining sites has increased correspondingly. This, in turn, has both depleted resources and caused pollution, resulting in growing concern for the effects on the environment and increasing pressure for better conservation and recycling.

Metallurgy, the study and technology of the production and use of metals, also has a long history. Copper was first smelted (separated from its ore through melting) in about 4000 B.C., iron was first smelted about a thousand years later, and the production of the first alloy, bronze, occurred about 3500 B.C. Although metallurgy was originally used primarily for fine art and decoration, it soon evolved to include more pragmatic applications as well. Today metallurgy has widened considerably in scope to include physics, chemistry, mechanical engineering, and chemical engineering. Metallurgical plants now supply metals and alloys to the construction and manufacturing industries in a variety of forms. Moreover, such technologies as nuclear power generation, space exploration, and telecommunications have all required new techniques of metal production and processing. Equally important to the field of modern metallurgy are the areas of energy and materials conservation, recycling of secondary metals, and environmental pollution.

Metals Handbook Desk Edition. American Society for Metals. ASM 1985 $136.00. ISBN 0-87170-188-X. "A new addition to the *Metals Handbook* series in a format which complements rather than replaces the current ninth edition . . . its publication represents a response to the demand for a single-volume, readily accessible, practical first reference to metals technology" (*International Journal of Production Research*).

Moore, John J. *Chemical Metallurgy*. Buttrwrth-Heinemann 1990 $70.00. ISBN 0-408-05369-0. A basic introduction to materials science. Assumes college sophomore chemistry and physics and related mathematics.

Orrego, Vicuna F. *Antarctic Mineral Exploitation: The Emerging Legal Framework.* Cambridge U. Pr. 1988 $120.00. ISBN 0-521-32383-5. Examines issues of international cooperation in managing Antarctic resources including discussions of the Antarctic Treaty, sovereignty, and jurisdiction as they relate to exploitation of the area's mineral supply.

Peters, William C. *Exploration and Mining Geology.* Wiley 1987 $64.95. ISBN 0-471-83864-0. Discusses issues of mining, minerals, the environment, and the bridge between the work of geologists and the field of mining. Recommended for exploration and mining geologists, geological engineers, and upper-level students in geology and mining programs.

Sawkins, Frederick J., ed. *Metal Deposits in Relation to Plate Tectonics.* Spr.-Verlag 1983 $65.00. ISBN 0-387-12752-6. "The author . . . was one of the first to realize the potential impact of the theory of plate tectonics on our understanding of how mineral deposits are formed and how we can find more. He has written a book that is clear and terse. . . . there is something for everyone, whether general reader or specialist" (*Science*). Covers well-known mines and mining districts.

Smallman, R. E. *Modern Physical Metallurgy.* Buttrwrth-Heinemann 1985 o.p. "The flavour of the new edition has remained unaltered. The original aims were to bring together, to illustrate, and to make comprehensible at undergraduate students' level the ways in which physical metallurgy has developed" (*British Corrosion Journal*).

NAVAL ENGINEERING

Naval engineering involves the design of hulls, structures, and cargo-handling systems, as well as propulsion, electrical, and hydrodynamic systems. The field evolved gradually, eventually becoming a combination of both science and art. Its origins, like those of military engineering, are to be found thousands of years ago with the ancient Greek triremes that plied the Aegean and Mediterranean seas and the ancient Egyptian feluccas that sailed up and down the Nile River. These early vessels are dwarfed, however, by the hugh ocean liners, monstrous oil tankers, and nuclear submarines of today. Vessels have changed in other ways as well. Construction materials have evolved from reeds or wood to steel, plastics, and aluminum alloys. Power has changed from manpower to sail, steam, electrical, and nuclear power. And the vessels of today are also designed for a greater variety of purposes: military use, the transportation of materials, the carrying of passengers, and leisure activity. The naval engineering of today is based on an amalgam of experience, trial and error, and computer-aided design, and it relies on sophisticated mathematical theory supported by the testing of models in tanks. Among the major concerns of naval engineers today are the increasing costs of ship construction and the availability of fuels.

Beaver, Paul. *Nuclear-Powered Submarines.* Sterling 1986 o.p. Offers a collection of well-chosen, captioned photographs of nuclear submarines. Some of the photographs illustrate rare views of everyday life for shipboard personnel.

Jordan, John. *An Illustrated Guide to Modern Destroyers.* P-H 1986 $10.95. ISBN 0-13-450776-2. Presents a readable, good overview in less than 200 pages; includes narratives, technical data, and profuse color illustrations for 54 classes of postwar destroyers from 19 countries worldwide.

Marshall, Roger, and Paul Larsen. *A Sailor's Guide to Production Sailboats.* Morrow 1986 $17.95. ISBN 0-688-05842-6. Initially, reviews the principles for selecting and inspecting sailboats and then provides manufacturer-supplied data on topics such as engines, propellers, fuel capacity, steering, safety, rigging, beam width, displacement, ballast, draft, and interior fittings. Covers more than 400 production sailboats and provides interior diagrams, photographs, and sketches along with the text; designed as a buyer's guide.

Preston, Antony. *Atlas of Maritime History.* Facts on File 1986 $29.95. ISBN 0-8160-1132-X. An excellent atlas containing 200 maps, 75 charts and graphs, and a concise text, which provides a full description of maritime and naval history.

Taylor, David A. *Introduction to Marine Engineering.* Buttrwrth-Heinemann 1990 $34.95. ISBN 0-408-05706-8. Explains the operation of all ship machinery from propulsion and steering to deck machinery and electrical equipment.

Tsinker, Gregory P. *Floating Ports—Design and Construction Practices.* Gulf Pub. 1986 $49.00. ISBN 0-87201-723-0. An excellent guide to the construction of large floating marine terminals. Useful to the marine, civil, and ocean engineer. Also provides a general introduction and background for anyone involved in port construction.

Vego, Milan. *Soviet Navy Tactics.* Naval Inst. Pr. 1986 $7.95. ISBN 0-87021-675-9. Provides about 70 pages of photographs illustrating destroyers, submarines, minesweepers, aircraft carriers, and other ocean-going military vessels of the former Soviet Union; accompanied by a limited text.

Verney, Michael. *The Compleat Book of Yacht Care.* Sheridan 1986 $45.00. ISBN 0-911378-62-6. Presents a comprehensive review of boat maintenance, which includes the tools and materials needed to do good work. The text covers general mechanics, engines, deck work, sails, painting and varnishing, rigging and ropes; includes a separate chapter on dinghies and trailers.

NUCLEAR ENGINEERING

Nuclear engineering is a large, complex, and controversial field concerned with the design, development, construction, and operation of facilities that produce heat and electricity from the fission and fusion processes. The existence of nuclear fission was confirmed in 1939, when scientists found that the division of the nucleus of an atom resulted in the release of a vast amount of energy—vast compared with the equivalent chemical reaction by which energy is derived from conventional fossil fuels. Today there are hundreds of nuclear power plants making a significant contribution to the world's energy resources. Nuclear engineers are responsible for the design, construction, and maintenance of these installations and for the newly emerging task of decommissioning them. One of the most difficult problems facing nuclear engineers is the disposal of nuclear waste, much of which is dangerously radioactive. Issues involving the safe storage and disposal of this waste are still to be resolved. In recent years, public anxieties about the safety of nuclear power plants and the problems of nuclear waste are such that some plants have been forced to close, and few new plants are now under construction.

Adato, Michelle, and others. *Safety Second: The NRC and America's Nuclear Power Plants.* Ind. U. Pr. 1987 $22.50. ISBN 0-2533-5034-4. The text answers four basic questions about the Nuclear Regulatory Commission (NRC), the federal agency that is commonly the nation's nuclear watchdog: (1) Has the Nuclear Regulatory Commission tackled the most difficult and wide-ranging safety issues? (2) Does the NRC enforce its rules consistently and to the letter of the law? (3) Is the public allowed to influence NRC decision making? (4) Has the NRC maintained objectivity and distance from the industry in its regulatory functions?

Almenas, K., and R. Lee. *Nuclear Engineering: An Introduction.* Spr.-Verlag 1992 $89.50. ISBN 0-387-53960-3. Basic text covering core subjects for engineering students and nuclear power plant operators. Special attention paid to subjects relevant to safe operation.

Craig, Paul P., and John A. Jungerman. *The Nuclear Arms Race: Technology and Society.* McGraw 1985 $23.95. ISBN 0-07-013345-X. Reviews the history of the arms race, civil defense, the effects of nuclear weapons, and verification. Covers most technical aspects of nuclear arms and their control.

Empty Promise: The Growing Case against Star Wars. Union of Concerned Scientists. Beacon Pr. 1986 o.p. Offers 10 chapters covering various issues related to the Strategic Defense Initiative, or "Star Wars." Explores the political ramifications of the program as well as unusual technical problems.

Green, Jonathon. *A-Z of Nuclear Jargon.* Routledge 1986 $37.50. ISBN 0-7102-0641-0. Clarifies and demystifies the technology behind nuclear jargon. Covers all aspects of nuclear warfare: arms control, personnel and weapons systems, tactics and strategies, and disarmament talks. Provides background, context, and implications of nuclear technology so that the underlying meaning of the words and abbreviations becomes understandable.

Jastrow, Robert. *How to Make Nuclear Weapons Obsolete.* Little 1985 o.p. Jastrow, formerly affiliated with the National Aeronautics and Space Administration (NASA), describes the fundamental components of "Star Wars." Represents an unpopular perspective opposed by many respected scientists. Portions of the text appeared in *The New York Times.*

Knief, Ronald A. *Nuclear Engineering: Theory and Technology of Commercial Nuclear Power.* Hemisphere Pub. 1992 $149.50. ISBN 1-56032-089-3. An introductory text useful to a wide audience. Incorporates new data and reflects increased emphasis on safety as well as changes in the world energy situation and the availability of oil.

Leclercq, Jacques. *The Nuclear Age.* Le Chene 1986 o.p. Describes nuclear reactor design, fabrication, and installation; the fuel cycle; the history of nuclear engineering; and nuclear safety issues. About half of the book is comprised of colored maps, diagrams, photographs, and drawings; translated from the French.

Lewins, Jeffery D., and M. Becker, eds. *Advances in Nuclear Science and Technology.* Vol. 21 Plenum Pub. 1990 $85.00. ISBN 0-306-43614-0. A technical assessment of new approaches and techniques necessary for the U.S. nuclear power program.

Nitske, W. Robert. *The Life of Wilhelm Conrad Röntgen: Discoverer of the X-Ray.* U. of Ariz. Pr. 1971 o.p. "The book can be appreciated by the general reader, as well as by scientists and scholars. It contains an extensive bibliography and several appendixes providing a chronology, a genealogy, and English translations of Röntgen's three original publications on x-rays" (*Library Journal*).

The Nuclear Waste Primer: A Handbook for Citizens. League of Women Voters Education Fund. Lyns & Burford 1993 $10.95. ISBN 1-55821-226-4. Provides a concise, balanced introduction to the nuclear waste issue. Defines the forms, sources, and dangers of radiation and reviews history, key legislation, and current status of high- and low-level waste management. Identifies sources for further information and shows citizens how they can influence the decision-making process.

Patterson, Walter C. *Nuclear Power.* Viking Penguin 1983 $7.95. ISBN 0-14-022499-8. Presents an updated version of the standard layperson's reference; written by a well-informed, technically knowledgeable critic of nuclear energy. Describes the different types of nuclear reactors and the history of reactor development. Details problems related to various nuclear accidents, analyzes the risks and the potential benefits of nuclear power, discusses the possible future of nuclear industry.

Tirman, John, ed. *The Fallacy of Star Wars: Based on Studies Conducted by the Union of Concerned Scientists.* Random 1984 $4.95. ISBN 0-685-09693-9. Discusses the technical difficulties inherent in "Star Wars," the likely ease with which offensive measures to counteract American weapons might be undertaken, and the probability of an escalation of the weapons race; appendix includes a model treaty drafted by the Union of Concerned Scientists, a public interest group concerned with nuclear arms control and nuclear power safety.

Walker, Charles A., and Edward J. Woodhouse, eds. *Too Hot to Handle? Social and Policy Issues in the Management of Radioactive Wastes.* Yale U. Pr. 1983 $60.30. ISBN 0-7837-5310-1. Examines the technical and political ramifications of handling nuclear wastes. Reviews the nature of radioactive waste, current disposal methods, and those under consideration for future use; includes public views on the topic for readers' consideration.

Warf, James C. *All Things Nuclear*. SC Fed. Scientists 1989 $25.00. ISBN 0-9626706-0-X. "The topics are chosen so as to cover the most important subjects in a pithy manner. Persons who are not specialists in the nuclear field can gain general proficiency, but it will require a modest effort." (Preface). Covers basic theory and peaceful and military uses of nuclear power, and includes a discussion of nuclear policy and diplomacy.

PATENTS

[SEE under Design, Inventors, and Inventing in this chapter.]

PETROLEUM ENGINEERING AND ENGINEERING GEOLOGY

Petroleum engineering has recently received greater attention as increasing demands are made on crude oil and natural gas supplies to meet our growing energy needs. The field is concerned primarily with the discovery of new oil and natural gas deposits and with the extraction of these resources and their subsequent processing. Petroleum engineers are also involved in analyzing existing reservoirs of oil and natural gas and in assessing production rates of both existing and newly discovered reserves. Current efforts are focused on more economic retrieval methods and on developing new and more sophisticated recovery techniques necessitated by exploration in such difficult areas as polar and offshore ocean regions.

Gibson, N., ed. *Major Hazards Onshore and Offshore. Chemical Engineers Symposium Ser: No. 13*. Hemisphere Pub. 1992 $175.00. ISBN 1-56032-259-4. Proceedings of 1992 Conference of Engineers, which was held to review what has been learned about major hazards and to consider present and future applications of that information.

Giuliano, Francis A. *Introduction to Oil and Gas Technology*. P-H 1989 $48.00. ISBN 0-13-474354-7. Concentrates on "upstream" functions of the industry: exploration, land work, drilling, production, recovery, and transportation. Includes discussions on related topics such as geology, economics, and government.

Klein, George de Vries. *Sandstone Depositional Models for Exploration for Fossil Fuels*. Intl. Human Res. 1985 $48.00. ISBN 0-934634-82-3. "While the basic principles of depositional systems described in the 1980 second edition are still valid, the revision includes new sedimentological concepts and newly released information on the application of sandstone models to exploration for oil, coal, uranium, and mineral deposits" (*Journal of Petroleum Technology*).

Lapeyrouse, Norton J. *Formulas and Calculations for Drilling, Production and Workover*. Gulf Pub. 1992 $45.00. ISBN 0-88415-011-9. A quick reference for drilling operations.

Shaffer, Ed. *The United States and the Control of World Oil*. St. Martin 1983 o.p. Presents a mass of information regarding American control of oil. Demonstrates the relationship between the rise of oil as a world commodity and the growth of the United States as a world power. Also discusses problems the United States faces since it is no longer the dominant force in the world oil market.

Sherrill, Robert. *The Oil Follies of 1970–1980: How the Petroleum Industry Stole the Show (and Much More Besides)*. Doubleday 1983 o.p. "Sherrill offers one chapter on the energy development of each year from 1970 to 1980—and then includes an appendix . . . that consists of background essays on the history of Standard Oil, the industry's consistent pattern of underestimating supply, the Government's efforts to regulate natural gas, etc." (*N.Y. Times Book Review*).

Whittaker, Alan, ed. *Field Geologist's Training Guide*. Intl. Human Res. Development 1985 $34.00. ISBN 9-0277-1932-2. "Designed for oil industry people who are interested in petroleum geology, drilling procedures, formation evaluation, but at an introductory level . . . a basic book that conveniently assembles . . . a lot of well-established facts" (*Geophysics*).

ROBOTICS AND CONTROL ENGINEERING

Many visionaries have dreamed of robots taking over all of the jobs that humans find boring, laborious, and dangerous. While that may occur sometime in the future, robots have already made a significant impact on some industrial processes, most notably in automobile production. This has been made possible by linking computers with mechanical devices and then programming these devices to perform a variety of functions. The increased use of robots in industry is motivated partly by the desire of managers to replace human labor, which is seen as costly, unreliable, and occasionally rebellious, with nonhuman workers. Whether for that reason or others, robotics is a rapidly growing field. For some operations, such as handling highly radioactive or toxic materials, it is essential. Control engineering, an older discipline, has close links with robotics. It is concerned with methods of controlling—by electrical, electronic, computational, or pneumatic devices—the vast and complex systems on which much modern engineering depends, from the thermostatic control of a heating system to the control of a nuclear power plant.

Asimov, Isaac, and Karen A. Frenkel. *Robots: Machines in Man's Image*. Robot Inst. Am. 1985 $21.95. ISBN 0-317-39396-0. A well-illustrated, easy-to-understand overview of robotics that discusses the origins of robots, pioneers in the field of robotics, uses of industrial robots, how robots work, personal and hobby robots, jobs and the economy; includes an example of research and development and the influence of robots on society.

Caudill, Maureen. *In Our Own Image: Building an Artificial Person*. OUP 1992 $23.00. ISBN 0-19-507338-X. A glimpse into the current state of robotic research and fantasy speculation on the future positions of robots in society.

Deken, Joseph. *Silico Sapiens: The Fundamentals and Future of Robots*. Bantam 1986 o.p. An easy-to-understand answer book about robots and their effects on human beings. Includes answers to such questions as, What are robots? How will they evolve in the near and distant future? How will they coexist with people? Does robot intelligence endanger or enhance the human species?

Dorf, Richard C. *Modern Control Systems*. Addison-Wesley 1992 $61.25. ISBN 0-201-51713-2

Dorf, Richard C., and Shymon Y. Nof. *International Encyclopaedia of Robotics*. Wiley 1990 $109.00. ISBN 0-471-87868-5

Hanafusa, Hideo, and Hirochika Inoue, eds. *Robotics Research*. MIT Pr. 1985 $70.00. ISBN 0-262-08151-2. "Sixty-two contributions . . . provide a unique opportunity to view the future shape of robotics in such areas as arm and hand design, dynamics, image understanding, locomotion, touch and compliance, systems, kinematics, visual inspection, control, assembly, and sensing" (*Automotive Engineering*).

Kelly, Derek. *A Layman's Introduction to Robotics*. Petrocelli 1986 $27.95. ISBN 0-89433-265-1. Describes several main features of robotics for the general reader. Addresses topics such as the history of robotics, robotic concepts, hardware and software, implications of robotics, careers in robotics, and the future of robotics.

Logsdon, Tom. *The Robot Revolution*. S&S Trade 1984 o.p. Presents a well-illustrated historical description of the development and future of robots. Describes the factory of the future and discusses the civilian and military applications of robotics.

Miller, Richard K. *Industrial Robot Handbook*. Van Nos. Reinhold 1986 $99.00. ISBN 0-442-23733-2. Presents a collection of 79 easy-to-read articles that describe the use of robots in a wide range of industrial settings; includes a list of robot manufacturers and many useful illustrations.

Miller, Richard K., and Terri C. Walker. *Robotics in Non-Industrial Environments*. SEAI Tech. Pubns. 1991 o.p.

Nof, Shimon Y., ed. *Handbook of Industrial Robotics*. Wiley 1985 $110.00. ISBN 0-471-89684-5. "In 77 highly illustrated, informative chapters, this volume presents the most current relevant information on the research, development, design, and application of industrial robots. . . . should serve as a guidebook for courses in mechanical, electrical, and industrial engineering, and production/operations management" (*Automotive Engineering*).

Parsegian, V. L. *This Cybernetic World: Of Men, Machines, and Earth Systems*. Doubleday 1972 o.p. A volume in the *Science Study Series* that examines the similarities in the systems of computers, humans, and ecologies.

Sheridan, Thomas B. *Telerobotics, Automation, and Human Supervisory Control*. MIT Pr. 1992 $39.95. ISBN 0-262-19316-7. A broad-based study of robotics with emphasis on the human-robot interface and how it can best evolve. Intended for undergraduate and graduate-level engineering and computer science students.

Todd, D. J. *Fundamentals of Robot Technology: An Introduction to Industrial Robots, Teleoperators and Robot Vehicles*. Halsted Pr. 1986 $37.95. ISBN 0-470-20301-3. Covers most types of robots in operation in the world today as well as those in early-, mid-, and late-developmental stages. Written by a mechanical engineer, this is one of the most comprehensive and best-presented books on the subject currently available.

Tzafestas, Spyros G., ed. *Intelligent Robotic Systems*. Dekker 1991 $190.00. ISBN 0-8247-8135-X. Eighteen contributions describe recent developments of industrial robots capable of performing intelligent action and decision making.

Valavanis, Kimon P., and George N. Saridis. *Intelligent Robotic Systems: Theory, Design, and Applications*. Kluwer Ac. 1992 $105.00. ISBN 0-7923-9250-7. Melds the disciplines of artificial intelligence, operations research, and systems theory into the discipline of machine intelligence.

Waldman, Harry. *Dictionary of Robotics*. Macmillan 1985 o.p. Presents one of the most comprehensive international dictionaries on robotics, defining more than 2,000 terms and featuring more than 100 illustrations. Covers major manufacturers, publications, and individuals in the field. The preface includes a brief review of highlights in the development of industrial robots from 1939 to the present.

SAFETY ENGINEERING

Traditionally, the most important criteria related to designing and building a machine were reliability and economics. Safety related to operation of machines meant little more than putting a guard around the most dangerous parts and assuming that users would be careful. Today the demands of consumers and industrial unions have changed this position regarding the safe operation of machines. A host of federal, state, and local laws, such as the Federal Occupational Safety and Health Act, have created standards of performance and safety for most workplaces and machines in our society. These laws, coupled with an increasing willingness on the part of the public to sue corporations, has made safety a prime design consideration. Although there has been considerable progress made in recent years, the tragedies of Bhopal, Chernobyl, and the *Challenger* demonstrate that much more needs to be done.

De Grazia, Alfred. *A Cloud over Bhopal: Causes, Consequences and Constructive Solutions*. S. Asia 1985 $12.00. ISBN 0-685-12345-6. Explores all aspects of the Union

Carbide accident in Bhopal, India, and examines the impact of multinational corporations on developing countries, responsibility and negligence in relation to corporate and government involvement, and to what extent people can reasonably expect technology to save the world.

Ferry, Ted S., ed. *New Directions in Safety*. ASSE 1985 $45.00. ISBN 0-939874-9. "Twenty-seven articles . . . have been compiled in this book to represent the best readings in safety over the past two years" (*Occupational Hazards*).

Hunter, Thomas A. *Engineering Design for Safety*. McGraw 1992 $54.95. ISBN 0-07-031337-7. Emphasizing the mechanical and structural aspects, explains how to identify and avoid potential hazards of consumer, industrial, and commercial products early in the design process. For design and safety engineers.

Kletz, Trevor A. *Learning from Accidents in Industry*. Buttrwrth-Heinemann 1988 $42.95. ISBN 0-408-02696-0

———. *Lessons from Disaster: How Organizations Have No Memory and Accidents Recur*. Gulf Pub. 1993 $49.00. ISBN 0-88415-154-9. "Draws upon the wealth of experience of its author, formerly safety adviser to the petro-chemical division of ICI. His thesis is that it is not lack of knowledge that causes industrial accidents but mainly our failure to use the knowledge that is already available" (*New Scientist*).

———. *What Went Wrong: Case Histories of Process Plant Disasters*. Gulf Pub. 1985 $45.00. ISBN 0-87201-919-5. "A much more informative book than its title would imply. The author has collected hundreds of case records of accidents or near-accidents in process and chemical plants. . . . cause and effect are described. The book then examines many tragedies and provides details of remedial actions that could have prevented most, if not all, of these events" (*Chemical Engineering*).

Kumar, Shrawan, ed. *Advances in Industrial Ergonomics and Safety, No. 4*. Taylor & Francis 1992 $220.00. ISBN 0-7484-0031-1. Proceedings from 1991 conference comprising 23 sections on various techniques and issues related to safety.

Morone, Joseph G., and Edward J. Woodhouse. *Averting Catastrophe: Strategies for Regulating Risky Technologies*. U. CA Pr. 1986 $34.95. ISBN 0-520-05723-6. Discusses the potential of risky technologies for producing major catastrophes in the United States. Explores current strategies and questions whether safeguards could be improved.

Perrow, Charles. *Normal Accidents: Living with High-Risk Technologies*. Basic 1984 $21.95. ISBN 0-465-05143-X. Reviews the phenomenon that, as technology expands, we create systems that increase risks to ourselves and to future generations. Explores several of these systems such as nuclear power plants, space missions, and genetic engineering with the hope that better understanding of their risky nature can reduce their attendant dangers.

Roland, Harold E., and Brian Moriarity. *System Safety Engineering Management*. Wiley 1990 $69.95. ISBN 0-471-61816-0

SANITARY ENGINEERING

Sanitary engineering, a sub-branch of civil engineering, is concerned primarily with water treatment; distribution and supply; sewage handling; water pollution prevention and control; air and water quality; and environmental factors affecting public comfort, safety, and health. It is an area of increasing interest and concern and one in which there is growing consumer interest. In recent years there has been a particular concern with sanitary engineering in developing nations, where sanitation and health problems abound. Yet sanitation concerns are also pressing in industrial nations, and both Europe and North America have considerable problems with environmental pollution that sanitary engineers are trying to address.

Franceys, R., J. Pickford, and R. Reed. *A Guide to the Development of On-Site Sanitation.* Vol. 7 World Health 1992 $42.30. ISBN 92-4-154443-0. Provides a detailed technical guide to the design, construction, operation, and maintenance of all the main options for on-site sanitation.

Salvato, Joseph A. *Environmental Engineering and Sanitation.* Wiley 1992 $125.00. ISBN 0-471-52377-1. A practical reference which details the use of formulas, rules of thumb, and guidelines for good practice and illustrates solutions to specific problems.

Sheaffer, John R., and Leonard A. Stevens. *Future Water: An Exciting Solution to America's Resource Crisis.* Morrow 1983 o.p. Examines the problems associated with current procedures for purifying sewage and describes their effects, such as the tainting of ground and surface water supplies. Proposes purifying these water supplies rather than "dumping" waste into existing bodies of water.

Tedder, D. William, and Frederick G. Pohland. eds. *Emerging Technologies in Hazardous Waste Management III. Symposium Ser.* Am. Chemical 1993 $119.95. ISBN 0-8412-2530-3. Based on a symposium held in 1991, this volume is both an introduction to hazardous waste treatment and a specific reference for experts.

Twort, A. C., and F. M. Law. *Water Supply.* Arnold 1985 o.p. "Introduces new approaches and techniques while reemphasizing the old tried and true methods and processes and continuing to deal with those aspects of supply that are of concern to the water engineer: ensuring an adequate supply and safeguarding its quality" (*Journal of the American Water Works Association*).

Walski, Thomas M. *Analysis of Water Distribution Systems.* Krieger 1992 repr. of 1984 ed. $53.95. ISBN 0-89464-624-9. "Provides field-tested, practical advice for examining and solving problems with water distribution systems. . . . Well illustrated with photographs, diagrams, drawings, charts, graphs, and is suitable as a reference or textbook" (*Public Works*).

Yegulalp, Tuncel M., and Kim Kunsoo, eds. *Environmental Issues and Management of Waste in Energy and Materials Production.* Battelle 1992 $87.50. ISBN 0-935470-64-6. Discussion of the environmental issues facing the world energy and minerals production industry and identification of future courses of action.

STRUCTURAL ENGINEERING

Structural engineering is concerned with the design of various structures, such as bridges, viaducts, pylons, and frame buildings. These structures require careful and tested design if they are to fulfill their function reliably and safely. When designing a structure, structural engineers must consider four basic areas: functional requirements, structural scheme, stress analysis, and internal forces. They use both theoretical and experimental methods in creating their designs and in testing them (at both the model and completed stages). Structural engineers must also take into account the appearance, safety, cost, and maintenance of the finished structure. Computers and holography have greatly improved the ability of structural engineers to analyze and optimize their structural designs. These technologies have allowed them to devote more time to creative planning for aesthetics, function, and structural layout, and to consider more complex structures than was possible before the advent of powerful computer programs.

Cowan, Henry J. *The Master Builders: A History of Structural and Environmental Design from Ancient Egypt to the Nineteenth Century.* Krieger 1985 repr. of 1977 ed. $40.00. ISBN 0-89874-804-6. Thoroughly examines the history of building science.

————. *Science and Building: Structural and Environmental Design in the Nineteenth and Twentieth Centuries.* Wiley 1978 o.p. A companion to the preceding book that updates the history of building science.

Epstein, Samuel, and Beryl Epstein. *Tunnels.* Little 1985 $14.95. ISBN 0-316-24573-9. Covers the history and methods of tunnel construction; discusses aqueducts, railway tunnels, subway tunnels, sewers, and underwater tunnels for use by automobiles. One of the few books about tunnels for the general reader.

Loyrette, Henri. *Gustave Eiffel.* Rizzoli 1985 o.p. "This is a biography of the French structural engineer. Eiffel's family background is described, as is his education and training, and his role in advancing the state of the art in . . . engineering throughout his life. . . . [Among the works described are] the Budapest Station, the Douro Bridge . . . the Garabit Viaduct . . . the iron framework of the Statute of Liberty, and . . . the Eiffel Tower" (*Choice*).

Plowden, David. *Bridges: The Spans of North America.* Norton 1988 $40.00. ISBN 0-393-01936-5. "This book is not about the social or environmental consequences that attend any form of construction; it is simply about bridges—how, when, where, and by whom some of the most important ones have been built in North America, and what they look like" (Preface).

Thornton, Charles H. *Exposed Structure in Building Design.* McGraw 1992 $42.00. ISBN 0-07-064538-8. Conversations on the use of exposed architecture with top architects and engineers. Covers a variety of topics.

Trachtenberg, Alan. *Brooklyn Bridge Fact and Symbol.* U. Ch. Pr. 1979 $9.95. ISBN 0-226-81115-8. Reviews the facts and symbolism associated with the Brooklyn Bridge, a major construction in New York City. Describes how the Brooklyn Bridge became a vehicle for ideas and feelings associated with conditions found in industrialized America; well illustrated.

Tzou, H. S., and G. L. Anderson, eds. *Intelligent Structural Systems. Solid Mechanics and Its Applications Ser.* Vol. 13 Kluwer Ac. 1992 $169.00. ISBN 0-7923-1920-6. Summary of research results on the evolution of intelligent (smart) structures and systems.

Xanthakos, Petros P. *Ground Anchors and Anchored Structures.* Wiley 1991 $84.95. ISBN 0-471-52520-0. Focusing on designs that are safe and economical, this book deals with the planning, use, and maintenance of anchors as they pertain to the laws of statics and theories governing the transfer of load.

TRANSPORTATION AND AUTOMOTIVE ENGINEERING

There are roughly 200 million automobiles in the United States, and throughout the country large areas of land are taken up with some aspect of automobiles: roads, freeways, parking lots, garages, car washes, service stations, and automotive showrooms. The automobile has revolutionized life in the twentieth century, and it is a major concern of transportation and automotive engineering. Transportation engineering is a dynamic field concerned with the movement of goods and people. In addition to the automobile and highway systems, the field also encompasses water, rail, air, and subway transport systems, and it is concerned with issues related to each area—airports, air traffic control, flight booking systems (and their railway equivalents), harbor design, freight shipping, road network planning, road traffic engineering, and many more. Automotive engineering also covers the research, design, and production of automobiles. In recent years, transportation engineering has seen some marked changes. Water transportation systems increasingly have relied on larger equipment, necessitating larger waterways. Air transportation systems have grown dramatically, necessitating larger airports and better air traffic control. The railroad industry, though less dynamic than other transportation industries, continued to develop faster and safer methods of operating trains and moving cargo. In addition, population growth and urbanization-suburbanization have had a major impact on transportation engineering. More and more, transportation engineers see the need to develop integrated transport systems for cities, regions, and even nations to deal with growing populations, to provide economic viability to large interconnected areas, and also to deal with growing pollution problems and health and safety problems brought on largely by the automobile.

Allen, G. Freeman. *Railways: Past, Present and Future.* Morrow 1982 o.p. Presents a worldwide study of the evolution of modern railways; beautifully illustrated.

Altshuler, Alan, and James Womack. *The Future of the Automobile: The Report of MIT's International Automobile Program.* MIT Pr. 1986 o.p. The book, originally published in 1984, "is a study of the world automotive industry. An international team of 130 authors spent four years looking into . . . industrial efficiency, labor relations, international competition, organizational trends . . . as well as into technological innovations and . . . the question of the automobile's future status" (*Choice*).

Bobrick, Benson. *Labyrinths of Iron: A History of the Subways.* Ed. by Danielle Bobrick. Newsweek 1981 o.p. Combines aspects of a sociological study and an engineering history to provide a comprehensive understanding of the development of subway transport worldwide; written for the layperson.

Brady, Robert N. *Automotive and Small Truck Fuel Injection Systems: Gas and Diesel.* P-H 1985 $51.00. ISBN 0-8359-0315-X. Describes most of the current fuel injection systems and discusses combustion chamber designs, fuel characteristics, and system components. Compares current systems, reviews their design and operation, but excludes coverage of problem diagnosis, service, and repairs; concludes with a description of turbocharging.

Gabbard, Alex. *Vintage and Historic Racing Cars.* Ed. by Dean Batchelor. Gabbard Writing & Photo. 1986 $25.00. ISBN 0-89586-405-3. Provides detailed descriptions and photographs of Ferraris, Bugattis, Porsches, Jaguars, and other racing cars built during the last 60 years; written for the general reader and car buff.

Ingram, Arthur, and Martin Phippard. *Highway Heavy Metal: The World's Trucks at Work.* Sterling 1986 o.p. Thoroughly documents the features of an international selection of trucks of different types and sizes. Contains numerous photographs, many in color, and fills the gap in the literature on this topic; includes discussions on trends in future truck design and information on truckline ownership.

Itzkoff, Donald M. *Off the Track: The Decline of the Intercity Passenger Train in the United States.* Greenwood 1985 $42.95. ISBN 0-313-24331-5. "The classic passenger trains are gone, and this book is the first to analyze their demise in clear and penetrating detail. . . . although short, it gives comprehensive coverage, including an impressive list of sources" (*Choice*).

Lacey, Robert. *Ford: The Men and the Machine.* Little 1986 $24.95. ISBN 0-316-51166-8. The first half of the book presents an excellent history of Henry Ford, his company, and the development of the American automobile industry. The second half chronicles the fortunes of the company as control passed to Ford's descendants.

Logsdom, Tom. *The Navstar Global Positioning System.* Van Nos. Reinhold 1992 $44.95. ISBN 0-442-01040-0. "An up-to-date guide on what the system can do and how it works . . . not some esoteric piece of knowledge for a specialist profession. For the first time in history, individuals expect . . . to known their exact positions on the earth's surface. Even those who choose to stray from the beaten tracks for fun are under pressure to carry the latest technology, rather than put rescuers' lives at risk. Satellite navigation has liberated the navigator from sextant and charttable, and saved thousands of lives" (*New Scientist*).

Lud, Ned. *Automagic: The Secret Life of Machines.* Golemacher 1985 o.p. "A book for everyone who ever gave a motor car a personal name, coaxed a new one into reluctant life on a cold morning, or nursed an ageing one through its umpteenth nervous breakdown. . . . [the reviewer] heartily endorse[s] Martin Gardner's enthusiastic review in the *Skeptical Inquirer*, where he describes *Automagic* as 'absolutely metal bending'" (*New Scientist*).

Miller, William H. *The Last Atlantic Liners.* St. Martin 1985 o.p. Provides detailed descriptions of more than half of the approximately 200 ocean liners that regularly sail or have sailed across the Atlantic Ocean. Arranged by nationality of the liners, the text provides stories about voyages as well as many photographs. Appendices include information on length, tonnage, and notable events.

Nelkin, Dorothy. *Jetport: The Boston Airport Controversy.* Transaction Pubs. 1974 $24.95. ISBN 0-87855-111-5. Describes the controversy over the plan to expand Boston's Logan Airport in the early seventies. One of the busiest airports in the world (handling about 10 million passengers each year), Logan is situated only two miles from downtown Boston and immediately adjacent to the 40,000 working-class people of East Boston. The issue raised questions of social justice and minority rights—important factors in many other technological projects.

Philip, Cynthia Owen. *Robert Fulton: A Biography.* Watts 1985 o.p. The "best current biography of Fulton. There are 32 high quality plates that illustrate the man, his machines, friends, and foes. American landscape, he argued, required transportation for goods, services, and defense. . . . Fulton's imagination pulsed with steam engine-like enthusiasm that he hoped would be contagious throughout his country" (*Choice*).

Potter, Stephen. *On the Right Lines: The Limits of Technological Innovation.* St. Martin 1987 $35.00. ISBN 0-312-00488-5. An easy-to-read account of factors that shaped the railroad's growth and subsequent decline. Examines the technical aspects of potential methods to improve railroad performance.

Reynolds, J. F. *Brakes.* P-H 1986 o.p. Describes the basics of automotive and truck brakes, including how they are made, how they work, and how to repair them. Chapters are devoted to brake diagnosis, electric brakes, and antiskid brakes; includes principles of shop safety and equipment for servicing brakes.

Sikorsky, Robert. *Drive It Forever: Your Key to Long Automobile Life.* McGraw 1989 $7.95. ISBN 0-07-057522-3. Discusses the preservation, maintenance, and repair of cars to extend their life and improve gas mileage; written for all car owners.

Williams, Jed. *From Sails to Satellite: The Origin and Development of Navigational Science.* OUP 1993 $35.00. ISBN 0-19-856387-6. "How do you fix a position-line from the heavens onto a line of longitude when that line moves 15 degrees east every hour? . . . Williams covers this and much more in a well-written and exhaustive history of navigation from the Phoenicians onward [and] takes us forward into his own speciality, air navigation" (*New Scientist*).

CHRONOLOGY OF AUTHORS

Brindley, James. 1716–1772
Smeaton, John. 1724–1792
Telford, Thomas. 1757–1834
Rennie, John. 1761–1821
Rennie, Sir John. 1794–1874

Brunel, Sir Isambard Kingdom. 1806–1859
Edison, Thomas A(lva). 1847–1931
Vincenti, Walter Guido. 1917–
Florman, Samuel C(harles). 1925–
Bugliarello, George. 1927–

BRINDLEY, JAMES. 1716–1772

James Brindley is best remembered for his pioneering work in conceiving, designing, and building the canals of England. Yet that only partly describes this extraordinary man. His biographer, Samuel Smiles, calls Brindley a mechanical genius, but that, too, misleads.

Brindley had no formal schooling; he taught himself to read and write while serving a seven-year apprenticeship to a millwright between 1789 and 1796. After completing his apprenticeship, he set up his own business as a millwright and wheelwright. He also used water power and later steam power to pump out mines and tunnels and devised means of doing various types of work required by the growing industries of England.

Brindley earned his fame by designing and building the first canal in England, the Bridgewater, which connected mines at Worsley with the factories at Manchester. As his reputation grew, Brindley was commissioned to build even bigger canals and canal systems, displaying great ingenuity in the process and never becoming daunted by the difficulties encountered. With most of his work, he rarely put pen to paper, instead carrying his designs in his head. For years he saw himself as a journeyman, charging only 2 shillings a day (perhaps the equivalent of $20 today), plus an additional stipend if he had to travel.

The network of canals that Brindley initiated quickly spread throughout the north of England and the midlands, providing a transport system that dramatically reduced both the time and cost of carrying materials and goods. In doing so, it also provided an essential basis for the Industrial Revolution, altering the nature of labor and capital, and changing the face of England.

While canals were Brindley's principal legacy, he also made other important contributions to the mechanization of industry, lending his designs to silk mills, cotton mills, coal mines, and potteries. Being only semiliterate, Brindley's only writings were some very minimal notebooks. However, he wrote eloquently on the map of England with wood and iron and stone and water. THOMAS CARLYLE (see Vol. 1) wrote of him: "The ineloquent Brindley, behold he has chained seas together; his ships do visibly float over valleys, invisibly through the heart of mountains; and the Mersey and the Thames, the Humber and the Severn have shaken hands."

BOOKS ABOUT BRINDLEY

Rolt, L.T.C. *Great Engineers*. G. Bell 1962 o.p. Covers various engineers, including Brindley, whose work influenced the course of engineering history.

_____. *The Inland Waterways of England*. Allen & Unwin 1966 o.p. Devotes much of the two chapters on canals, locks, aqueducts, tunnels, and other works to Brindley's engineering feats and to his influence on later transport engineers.

Smiles, Samuel. *James Brindley and the Early Engineers*. J. Murray 1864 o.p. This abridged version of Volume 1 of Smiles's *Lives of the Engineers* is an eloquent and detailed tribute to the work of an enormously productive man; written 90 years after Brindley's death, when his full impact was evident.

BRUNEL, SIR ISAMBARD KINGDOM. 1806–1859

Isambard Kingdom Brunel began his working life assisting his father, Sir Marc Isambard Brunel, in building the first tunnel under the River Thames, the Thames Tunnel (now known as the Rotherhithe Tunnel). Injured during the project when the tunnel was flooded, he spent his convalescence designing a suspension bridge for the Avon Gorge. Known as the Clifton Suspension Bridge, it is still in use today. Brunel also built docks at Monkwearmouth, Bristol, Brentford, Milford Haven, and Plymouth, and bridges at Maidenhead, Chepstow, and Saltash. He was the first to use compressed air caissons to sink pier foundations.

Brunel also built three ships, each one the largest in the world at the time of its launching. The *Great Western*, built in 1837, was a wooden paddle steamship and became the first regular transatlantic liner. The iron-hulled *Great Britain* was the first large vessel driven by a screw propeller. (Today, it is a museum in the dry dock in which it was built.) The *Great Eastern*, which remained the largest passenger ship for 40 years, has gone down in history as the ship that laid the first successful transatlantic cable. In addition to his work with ships, tunnels, and bridges, Brunel improved the design of large guns, built a floating armored barge for the Crimean War in 1854, and designed a prefabricated hospital for the Crimean War in 1855.

Despite his many and varied achievements, Brunel is best remembered for his work as a pioneer railway engineer. More than any other person, he was responsible for construction of the Great Western Railway, which served the southwest of England. He used a broad 7-foot gauge for the tracks to give greater stability and allow higher speeds. He built tunnels, viaducts, and bridges to carry the railway bed. And he established high standards of service and reliability. To this day, the Great Western Railway, although absorbed into the British national railway system, symbolizes the best in railways.

BOOK BY BRUNEL

The Life of Isambard Kingdom Brunel: Civil Engineer. Fairleigh Dickinson 1972 repr. of 1870 ed. $60.00. ISBN 0-8386-1201-6

BOOKS ABOUT BRUNEL

Beckett, Derrick. *Brunel's Britain.* Trafalgar 1980 o.p. Concentrates primarily on Brunel's railway work, plus a fascinating chapter on steamships. Includes a gazetter of Brunel's sites and technical appendixes.

Pugsley, Alfred, ed. *The Works of Isambard Kingdom Brunel: An Engineering Appreciation.* Inst. of Civil Engineers 1976 o.p. Essays by nine eminent twentieth-century engineers assessing many of Brunel's achievements. Contains much detailed information as well as reproductions of some of Brunel's own drawings, which are fascinating for their meticulous precision and their ingenious designs.

Rolt, L.T.C. *Isambard Kingdom Brunel: A Biography.* Gale 1958 o.p. Good account of Brunel's life and works; in three parts—his early life, railways, and steamships.

Smiles, Samuel. *Lives of the Engineers.* Vol. 3. Kelley 1968 repr. of 1861 ed. $125.00. ISBN 0-678-05632-3. Provides a detailed look at Brunel and his work. Particularly interesting because it was written by a contemporary writer and journalist with 21 years experience as a railway administrator.

Tames, R. *Isambard Brunel.* Heinle & Heinle 1973 o.p.

Vaughan, Adrian. *Isambard Kingdom Brunel: Engineering Knight-Errant.* Trafalgar 1992 $45.00. ISBN 0-7195-4636-2. A very fine biography that focuses on Brunel's engineering works, while at the same time providing an intimate, personal portrait of the man; includes interesting photographs.

BUGLIARELLO, GEORGE. 1927–

George Bugliarello was born and received his early education in Italy. He was a Fulbright scholar at the University of Minnesota from 1952 to 1954 (M.S. civil engineering) and received a Ph.D. from the Massachusetts Institute of Technology in 1959. In his distinguished academic career, Bugliarello has taught and done research at Carnegie-Mellon University, the Technical University of Berlin, and the University of Illinois at Chicago. Moreover, since 1973, he has been president of the Polytechnic University of New York. Bugliarello has published in fields as diverse as civil engineering, computer languages, biomedical engineering, and fluid mechanics. In addition, he has always shown a deep concern for the role of the engineer and the social implications of technology. This is reflected in particular by his founding the journal *Technology in Society* in 1978. Bugliarello has been influential as a member of the National Academy of Engineering and the American Association for the Advancement of Science, as well as serving as editor of *Technology in Society.* He chaired a commission and edited its report, *Science and Technology in New York City for the 21st Century: Report by the Mayor's Commission for Science and Technology*

(Polytechnic Pr. 1989). Engineers and technologists usually do not reflect about their work; Bugliarello is, and has been for many years, an honorable exception. A quotation of his from *The History and Philosophy of Technology* admirably portrays one aspect of his thinking: "Unfortunately the dimension of time, both past and future, is almost totally lacking today in our engineering curricula." Here and in other publications, Bugliarello urges more cooperation between the historian and the engineer.

BOOKS BY BUGLIARELLO

Bioengineering: An Engineering View. San Francisco Pr. 1968 $15.00. ISBN 0-911302-03-4

Computer Systems and Water Resources. (coauthored with Fred Gunther). Elsevier 1974 o.p. "Not a study of water resource systems or methodologies for the planning, design, and operation of such systems. . . . Rather, the book addresses itself to an area in water resource technology that has received practically no attention in the literature: the description and assessment of the pervasive role that computer systems have come to exert in this field, and are likely to exert in the future" (Preface).

The History and Philosophy of Technology. (coedited with Dean B. Bonner). U. of Ill. Pr. 1973 o.p. Presents 23 chapters in three parts. "For the human race to survive and thrive, it is absolutely essential that we understand the nature of the process called technology" (Preface). Provides much thought-provoking material for the general reader; concludes with a discussion of the future of technology. Includes an introduction by Melvin Kranzberg.

The Impact of Noise Pollution: A Socio-Technological Introduction. (coauthored with Ariel Alexandre and others). Franklin 1976 $196.00. ISBN 0-08-018166-X

The Intelligent Layman's Guide to Technology. Polytechnic Pr. 1987. ISBN 0-918902-27-4

Science and Technology in New York City for the 21st Century: Report by the Mayor's Commission for Science and Technology. Polytechnic Pr. 1989. ISBN 0-918902-26-6.

Technology, the University, and the Community. Franklin 1976 $214.00. ISBN 0-08-017872-3

EDISON, THOMAS A(LVA). 1847–1931

Thomas Alva Edison was the stereotypical all-American hero of the industrial system—a rags-to riches entrepreneur and holder of over 1,000 patents who brought enormous improvements to the lives of millions of people.

At an early age, Edison became interested in telegraphy and worked as a freelance traveling telegraphist. By the time he was 22, he had made improvements to telegraphs for Western Union and to the stock ticker and stock printer for the New York Stock Exchange. From that point on, Edison had a very active career spanning more than 60 years. Among the highlights of his career were the invention of the incandescent electric light bulb, which led to widespread domestic lighting; the invention and development of the phonograph; improvements to motion picture equipment and the telephone; and the discovery of the Edison effect—thermionic emission—the foundation of the electronics industry. To exploit his many inventions, Edison founded several companies, including the Edison Telephone Company and the Edison General Electric Company (which later merged to form General Electric). Edison also contributed both directly and indirectly to the growth of many other companies.

While he was perhaps best known for his inventions, Edison's most significant innovation was the industrial science laboratory, the forerunner of today's science parks. His first small laboratory was set up in Newark, New Jersey, to develop his improvements in telegraphy and stock tickers and printers. In 1876 he moved to a new site at Menlo Park, New Jersey, where he established a much larger laboratory. From his Menlo Park laboratory came a stream of inventions, developments, and patents. Eventually, Edison moved to an even larger facility at West Orange, New Jersey; this laboratory is now a museum and contains the Edison archives.

Idolized during his lifetime, Edison never took this adulation too seriously. He regarded himself as just a hard-working man, informed by a good understanding of scientific principles and possessed with a great determination to solve scientific and technical problems and to develop ways in which to apply his findings commercially. In this last he did not always succeed. Edison backed some remarkable flops, but the number of his profitable ventures far exceeded his failures. Profit was not his primary consideration, however. Edison's main goal was to explore the things that interested him and to turn his findings into something useful.

BOOKS BY EDISON

Diary and Sundry Observations of Thomas Alva Edison. Ed. by Dagobert D. Runes. Greenwood 1968 $39.75. ISBN 0-8371-0067-4

The Papers of Thomas Alva Edison: Vol. 1, The Making of the Inventor, February 1847–June 1873. Ed. by Reese V. Jenkins and others. 1989 $65.00. ISBN 0-8018-3100-8. Includes journal entries, sketches, and drawings.

BOOKS ABOUT EDISON

Clark, Ronald W. *Edison: The Man Who Made the Future.* Putnam Pub. Group 1977 o.p. Illustrated biography that describes Edison's early untutored upbringing, his first inventions, and his struggles with industry and big business.

Conot, Robert. *Thomas Alva Edison: A Streak of Luck.* Da Capo 1986 $13.95. ISBN 0-306-8-261-9

Egan, Louise. *Thomas Alva Edison.* Barron 1987 $4.95. ISBN 0-8120-3922-X

Hughes, Thomas P. *Thomas Edison: Professional Inventor.* HM 1976 o.p. Succinct account of Edison's life and works. Despite its brevity, the book fills out encyclopedic entries remarkably well.

Jones, Nancy C., and Douglas C. Jones. *Edison and his Invention Factory.* Eastern Acorn 1987 $3.95. ISBN 0-915992-35-3

Josephson, Matthew. *Edison.* McGraw 1959 $10.95. ISBN 0-07-033046-8. Comprehensive biography focusing on Edison's genius and individuality as an inventor.

Mintz, Penny. *Thomas Edison: Inventing the Future.* Fawcett 1989 $3.95. ISBN 0-449-90378-8. Examines Edison's importance and his role in ushering in the modern technological society.

Vanderbilt, Byron M. *Thomas Edison, Chemist.* Am. Chemical 1971 $14.95. ISBN 0-8412-0129-3. Records Edison's many explorations of the chemistry essential to his inventions: materials for electric light and the phonograph, experiments in iron ore concentration and in cement and concrete, development of the alkaline storage battery, and ways of producing rubber from locally available plants.

FLORMAN, SAMUEL C(HARLES). 1925–

Samuel Charles Florman holds degrees in civil engineering from Dartmouth University and in English from Columbia University, where he studied under Krilling and JOSEPH WOOD KRUTCH. He also holds honorary degrees from Manhattan and Clarkson Colleges. Florman served with the Seabees in the Philippines and Truk toward the end of World War II, worked as a field engineer in Venezuela, and then worked as a construction engineer with several New York firms. He has been the vice-president and general manager of Kreiger, Borg, and Florman Construction Company since 1955. He has been described as the "defender of the faith," because of his support for the value and importance of engineers and engineering against unfair criticism and sniping.

Florman views the achievements of engineering as testimonials to human aspirations and abilities, while also advocating concern for social and environmental considerations. According to Florman, "the compleat engineer/technologist" should be a well-rounded person, sensitive to the needs of society and the ecosystem, fulfilling an important and rewarding role in our culture. Florman is critical of engineering schools, which concentrate on purely technical education and fail to encourage imagination, social concern, or cultural interest.

BOOKS BY FLORMAN

Blaming Technology: The Irrational Search for Scapegoats. St. Martin 1982 $6.95. ISBN 0-312-08363-7. Presents a compendium of anecdotes gathered during the author's lecture tour of college campuses, which followed the publication of his *The Existential Pleasures of Engineering*, and a series of articles written for *Harper's* featuring issues that are concerned with the public debate on technology.

The Civilized Engineer. St. Martin 1988 $8.95. ISBN 0-312-02559-9. A collection of essays on a wide range of topics of interest to technologists and humanists alike; includes the contribution of women to engineering, the *Challenger* disaster, and emerging technologies of the twenty-first century.

Engineering and the Liberal Arts. Wiley 1968 o.p.

The Existential Pleasures of Engineering. St. Martin 1977 $7.95. ISBN 0-312-27546-3. "Valuable reading for engineers given to self-scrutiny" (*Time*).

PETROSKI, HENRY. 1942–

[SEE Chapter 6 in this volume.]

RENNIE, JOHN. 1761–1821

A Scottish civil engineer who helped develop Britain's transportation system during the Industrial Revolution, John Rennie was born at Phantassie in Haddingtonshire. Born into a farm family, he had an early keen mechanical aptitude, which led him to work with a local millwright who was an inventor of an early threshing machine. In 1780 Rennie attended Edinburgh University and, for the next three years, combined his study and a millwright business that he began to operate.

In 1784 Rennie worked with James Watt in his shop near Birmingham and later that same year joined Watt and Matthew Boulton in London, where he helped design and build the steam engine and machinery for the new Albion Flour Mill at Blackfriars. His success prompted Rennie to set up his own business in 1791 as a mechanical and civil engineer.

During the Industrial Revolution, Rennie became one of the leading builders and creators of England's new transportation infrastructure. Indeed, his achievements rivaled those of his more famous contemporary, Thomas Telford. Rennie designed the London Docks and the docks at Liverpool, Hull, Dublin, Leith, Blackwall, and Greenock. He modernized the harbor and dockyards at Portsmouth, Plymouth, Chatham, and Sheerness. The Lancaster Canal, the Rochdale Canal, and the Royal Canal of Ireland, as well as numerous aqueducts, tunnels, and viaducts, were among his many other civil engineering feats. Throughout his remarkable career, Rennie combined practical mathematics and civil engineering. His understanding of structural theory and practice made possible the famous canals, docks, harbors, and breakwaters that he constructed throughout Britain.

Rennie was perhaps best known for his remarkable series of bridges, notably Waterloo Bridge and the Old Southwark Bridge in London, as well as the Kelso and Musselburgh bridges in Scotland, and the bridges at Leeds, New Galloway, and Newton-Stewart. These, and his plans for London Bridge (executed by his son SIR JOHN RENNIE), attested to his mastery of design and use of cast iron in structural systems. Rennie's most celebrated project was his gigantic mile-long breakwater at Plymouth (also completed by his son John).

BOOK ABOUT RENNIE

Boucher, Cyril T. G. *John Rennie, The Life and Work of a Great Engineer.* St. Martin 1963 o.p.

RENNIE, SIR JOHN. 1794–1874

Born in London, the Scottish engineer John Rennie followed in the footsteps of his father, the prominent civil engineer JOHN RENNIE. Educated by private tutors, he learned engineering at his father's Blackfriars establishment, under the guidance of the engineer responsible for building the Waterloo Bridge. Rennie then worked closely with his father in building the Southwark Bridge in 1815. Before his death in 1821, the senior Rennie acknowledged his son's ability by designating him as his heir to carry on the major engineering enterprises that his company was planning or had already launched.

The younger Rennie's greatest achievement was the construction of London Bridge, faithfully implementing his father's design and plan. When this structure, with its impressive multiple masonry arches, was completed in 1831, Rennie was knighted by King William IV. His subsequent career was marked by continued success, including construction of the huge breakwater at Plymouth, as well as several other harbor and dredging projects planned by his father. He also entered the new field of railroad engineering, and worked for the governments of Sweden and Portugal in planning railroads there. During his later career, Rennie served as engineer to the Admiralty, was president of the Institution of Civil Engineers, and wrote several works on harbors systems.

BOOK BY JOHN RENNIE

Autobiography. Routledge 1875 o.p.

SMEATON, JOHN. 1724–1792

"John Smeaton was the earliest of the great British civil engineers and the first to achieve distinction as an engineering scientist. It is also to him, more than any other person, that credit is due for laying the foundations of the civil engineering profession in this country; foundations on which his successors, very notably THOMAS TELFORD, built the superstructure." This is how Professor A. W. Skempton of Imperial College, London, opens his book of essays on Smeaton (published in 1981, by a strange coincidence, by Thomas Telford Limited). Skempton's description aptly sums up Smeaton's importance. The achievement for which he is best remembered is the rebuilding of the Eddystone Lighthouse, two previous structures (built on an exposed rock in the open sea) having been destroyed by storm and fire. Smeaton's lighthouse (1756–59) posed great problems of design, organization, and execution; solving these problems demanded a great deal of ingenuity and planning. That his Eddystone endured for over 120 years is testimony to Smeaton's abilities. A symbolic representation of the lighthouse was adopted by the Institution of Civil Engineers on its crest and armorial bearings and is still so used today.

Smeaton's earliest work was as a scientific instrument maker, and he continued this work as well as investigations into the science of mechanics throughout his life. Others recognized his talents early on, and in 1753, at the very young age of 28, he was elected a Fellow of the Royal Society. Writing was not his forte; the book in which he described his undertaking of the Eddystone lighthouse "cost him more labour than did the building of the lighthouse itself." Nevertheless, in addition to his *Diary*, he published a total of 18 papers. These include three notable ones given to the Royal Society: "Experimental Enquiry concerning the Natural Powers of Water and Wind" (1759); "An Experimental Examination of the Quantity and Proportion of Mechanic Power" (1776), in which he unravels for the first time the relationship between work, momentum, and kinetic energy; and "New Fundamental Experiments upon the Collision of Bodies" (1782). These three papers (reproduced in *Tracts on Hydraulics*, 1837) laid the foundations of the science of mechanics.

While conducting his scientific explorations, Smeaton established civil engineering as a respected profession. He is credited with more than a hundred major works, including 59 water-, 3 wind- and 6 steam-powered mills; 13 steam engines; and 36 civil engineering works. Among these latter were lighthouses, navigations, bridges, drainages, harbors, canals, and dams, some of which still function today.

Smeaton was one of the founding members, in 1771, of the Society of Civil Engineers, a dining club at which engineers could meet socially and exchange experiences. Still in existence today, the society is more frequently known as the Smeatonian Society, or the Smeatonians.

BOOKS BY SMEATON

John Smeaton's Diary. Ed. by A. Titley. Newcomer Society 1938 o.p. A record of Smeaton's journeys through Belgium and Holland in 1755, during which he gathered information about engineering work to aid his own subsequent activities. "His *Reports*, written in direct and homely language, are outstanding examples of the lucidity that might well be followed today" (A. Titley).

Tracts on Hydraulics. Ed. by Thomas Tredgold. M. Taylor 1837 o.p. Part I of this book comprises three important papers delivered to the Royal Society.

BOOKS ABOUT SMEATON

Penrose, C. *Two Men and Their Contributions in Two Countries*. Newcomen Society 1951 o.p. The 1951 commencement address delivered at the Whitman College in the State of Washington; includes a eulogy of Smeaton and Patrick Henry and their works.

Skempton, A. W. *John Smeaton FRS*. Thomas Telford Ltd. 1981 $30.00. ISBN 0-7277-0088-X. Essays by several distinguished modern engineers covering various aspects of Smeaton's work: the Eddystone Lighthouse, mills, rivers and canals, fen drainage, bridges, steam engines, harbours, and so forth. An eloquent tribute to Smeaton's contribution to his profession and to his abiding influence.

TELFORD, THOMAS. 1757–1834

Thomas Telford was the son of a Scottish shepherd who died three months after he was born. Telford's early training was as a stonemason, and within a few years, he began work as an architect. His early formative experiences stood him in good stead throughout his life and influenced his work as one of the foremost engineers of his day. Formal recognition as an engineer came with Telford's appointment as agent and engineer to the Ellesmere Canal Company in 1793.

Telford's achievements were many, varied, and huge. They include some of the earliest suspension bridges, hundreds of miles of roads and canals, docks and harbors, many road bridges, and two notable aqueducts. Since there were no steel cables at the time, Telford used wrought iron links to support his bridges. His Menai Straits bridge is still in use, although the wrought iron links were replaced by steel cables in 1939. His Conway suspension bridge still stands, but a modern bridge beside it now carries the greatly increased traffic.

In 1820 Telford was elected the first president of the Institution of Civil Engineers. Despite some suspicion and reluctance from his fellow engineers, he was "determined that [the Institution] should succeed and become neither a social mutual admiration society nor a marketplace for engineering talent, but a common pool of knowledge and experience which would promote the advancement and recognition of the new profession." He was elected Fellow of the Royal Society in 1827.

In 1829 Telford undertook the building of the Liverpool and Birmingham Canal Junction, which was not finished until six months after his death six years later. One reason for the delay was that Lord Anson would not allow the construction of a section through his pheasant shoot, Shelmore Wood, as originally planned and authorized. The resulting one-mile detour required the building of Shelmore Bank, a 60-foot high embankment that collapsed repeatedly, causing delays and more and more expense. During this trying period, at which time Telford was becoming very deaf and isolated, he resumed work that had engaged his interest years earlier—testing model barges to determine the relationship between the velocity and resistance. After his death, he was interred in Westminster Abbey where there is a monument to his memory, a suitable tribute to a great engineer.

BOOKS BY TELFORD

Atlas to the Life of Thomas Telford. Ed. by J. Rickman. 1838 o.p.

The Life of Thomas Telford Written by Himself. Ed. by J. Rickman. 1839 o.p. This book and *Atlas to the Life* are invaluable because they reveal, in his own words, what Telford thought about his works. Copies may be hard to find.

BOOKS ABOUT TELFORD

American Society of Civil Engineers. *Thomas Telford: Civil Engineer.* Thomas Telford UK 1980 $23.75. ISBN 0-7277-0084-7

Bracegirdle, Brian, and Patricia M. Miles. *Thomas Telford.* David and Charles 1973 o.p. Lavishly illustrated account of several of Telford's major works.

Gibb, Alexander. *The Story of Telford.* Alexander Maclehose 1935 o.p. Written by the great-grandson of John Gibb, Telford's colleague and great friend for the last 25 years of his life and himself a distinguished engineer. Provides a good overview with much interesting detail. Lists Telford's achievements in 30 pages of items, briefly annotated.

Pearce, R. M. *Thomas Telford.* Newbury Bks. 1973 $3.50. ISBN 0-912728-78-7

Rolt, L.T.C. *Thomas Telford.* Viking Penguin 1986 $15.95. ISBN 0-14-008125-9. "Mr. Rolt writes faithfully and thoroughly of Telford's work and achievements. He brings to their interpretation the outlook of an engineer, something from which his book benefits greatly" (*Sunday Times*).

Smiles, Samuel. *Lives of the Engineers, Vol. 2.* David and Charles 1968 o.p. Standard reference work, although the romantic accounts are not always reliable.

VINCENTI, WALTER GUIDO. 1917–

Walter Vincenti is professor emeritus of aeronautics and astronautics at Stanford University and a member of the U.S. National Academy of Engineering. He is an acknowledged authority on transonic, supersonic, and high-temperature gas flows, and on the history of technology, particularly the epistemology of engineering. Vincenti was instrumental in establishing an interdisciplinary program for engineering and nonengineering students at Stanford University.

This program is devoted to historical, ethical, and social studies of technology and engineering. He is regarded by his colleagues as one of the wise men of engineering, a constant source of inspiration and support, and he is held in similar high regard by his peers around the world. His outlook on engineering and engineers is admirably demonstrated in his book, *What Engineers Know and How They Know It* (1990), "now the starting point for anyone trying to understand engineering, especially the character of engineering knowledge." (Jane Morley) For Vincenti, engineering design knowledge is generated through a varying process, sometimes scientific and theoretical in character, other times independent of science and rooted in experience and craft. Engineering knowledge and methods are thus partly indigenous, and their influence on society is enormous and must be exerted responsibly. In recent years, Vincenti has worked to further the history of engineering as an important subfield of the history of technology. Vincenti's awards include a Gold Medalist Pi-Tau-Sigma (1948), a Rockefeller Public Service Award (1956), a Guggenheim Fellowship (1963), and an Usher Prize (1984).

Books by Vincenti

Annual Review of Fluid Mechanics. (Coauthored with M. Van Dyke). 18 vols. Annual Reviews 1970–present. $40.00 ea. An annual publication that surveys developments in the field of fluid mechanics.

The Britannia Bridge. (coauthored with Nathan Rosenberg). Wiley 1978 o.p.

Introduction to Physical Gas Dynamics. (coauthored with Charles H. Kruger, Jr.). Wiley 1975 repr. of 1965 ed. $48.50. ISBN 0-88275-309-6. Contains chapters on basic kinetic theory, chemical thermodynamics, equilibrium flow, and nonequilibrium cases. Geared toward the specialist.

Proceedings of the International Congress of Applied Mechanics, 12th, Stanford University 1968. Spr.-Verlag 1969 $126.00. ISBN 0-387-04420-5

Proceedings of the 1960 Heat Transfer and Fluid Mechanics Institute. (coauthored with D. M. Mason and W. C. Reynolds). Stanford U. Pr. 1960 o.p. Based on the thirteenth in a series of meetings devoted to the presentation of the results of fundamental research of current interest in heat transfer, fluid mechanics, and related fields.

What Engineers Know and How They Know It: Analytical Studies from Aeronautical History. Johns Hopkins 1990 $45.00. ISBN 0-8018-3974-2. A series of essays examining why and how scientific knowledge is obtained, the structure of the knowledge, and what it suggests about engineering knowledge both specifically and generally. Clarifies the role of design—especially of normal design at the lower levels of the hierarchy.

CHAPTER 9

Agriculture and Food Technology

Peter J. Bohn

And he gave it for his opinion, that whoever could make two ears of corn or
two blades of grass to grow upon a spot of ground where only one grew
before, would deserve better of mankind, and do more essential service to his
country than the whole race of politicians put together.
—JONATHAN SWIFT, *Gulliver's Travels*

In 1900 the average yield of corn (*Zea mays*) in the United States was 25 bushels
per acre. Today, average corn yields exceed that amount by 5 or even 10 times.
This stunning increase has not been confined to corn production. Dramatic
increases in average yields have been duplicated by most food and fiber crops,
providing evidence that JONATHAN SWIFT's (see Vol. 1) injunction (quoted in the
epigraph to this chapter), has been realized by agriculturists in the past century.

Five agriculture-related fields have played a significant role in this success.
Pedologists have conducted research on soil that has resulted in the discovery of
the nutritional requirements of crop plants and the development of specific
fertilizers to provide the correct nutrients to satisfy them. Plant breeders have
made advances in genetics that have produced uniformly superior crop lines.
Entomologists have helped increase crop yields by developing chemical
pesticides that protect crops from insect predation. Agricultural engineers have
contributed superior machinery that has facilitated more efficient planting and
harvesting techniques, thus increasing yields. And agricultural educators have
disseminated scientific literature and provided demonstrations to farmers that
achieved acceptance of the many agricultural innovations that have been made
in the past century. Therefore, it has been an ensemble of discoveries and
technologies that have resulted in substantial increases in crop yield.

At the end of the eighteenth century, agricultural yields in Europe and
America were similar to those of antiquity, and classical agricultural writers,
such as Cato, Varro, and COLUMELLA, often were quoted as authorities on
agricultural matters. The agricultural innovations between antiquity and the
nineteenth century were largely changes in tools that allowed cultivation of
dense or rocky soils and increased the power of draft animals. The settlement of
the Americas, however, presented several agricultural problems to the European colonists. For example, newly cleared land (without the benefit of centuries
of manuring, which had been practiced in Europe) quickly lost its fertility. Many
early agriculturists searched for means to maintain or to improve soil fertility,
experimenting with various substances and reporting their results in widely
circulated books and pamphlets. These experiments, however, largely anecdotal, lacked sufficient rigor to transform agriculture radically. The investigations
of the nineteenth century formally set agricultural research on a sound

scientific basis, and the technological innovations of the twentieth century radically increased agricultural productivity.

The scientific revolution, which followed FRANCIS BACON's (see Vol. 4) urging to use experimentation in order to discover underlying principles of nature, led to significant advances in agriculture. By the middle of the nineteenth century, scientists were searching for the underlying principles that determined agricultural yields, focusing especially on soil fertility. The investigations of German agricultural chemists, particularly JUSTUS VON LIEBIG, were crucial to the advancement of agricultural science. Aided by newly developed techniques for identifying the elemental composition of substances, experimenters were able to identify the specific elements required for plant growth. Once agricultural researchers had determined the elemental composition of plants, they began to search for substances that would stimulate crop growth when applied to soils. Although agriculturists had long been familiar with the beneficial effects of manuring, they had little basis for the scientific improvement of soils until the advances of the nineteenth century. The discovery of the Haber process in 1914 enabled inexpensive fertilizer production and fertilizer use, which caused agricultural yields to expand rapidly.

Throughout history, agricultural societies have selected crops for the characteristics that make them useful or adaptable to a specific environment. The use of systematic plant breeding has made the process for developing new varieties more efficient and has been aided significantly by advances in plant physiology, plant pathology, genetics, and statistics. Two notable achievements in plant breeding that have contributed greatly to the increase in agricultural yields in this century are hybridization and the methodologies associated with the "green revolution." Hybridization is a breeding technique in which two inbred lines are combined to produce an offspring of superior vigor. Begun in the 1920s, hybridization now is the preferred breeding method for many crops. "Green revolution" is the term used to describe the sustained breeding effort begun in the 1940s to increase crop yields in developing nations. It relies on developing crop varieties that are adapted to local conditions but are capable of responding to high levels of fertilizer inputs. By providing high crop yields and disease- and insect-resistant crop varieties, plant breeding has played an important role in increasing agricultural productivity.

Crops always have been vulnerable to insect predations and losses caused by fungal, bacterial, and viral diseases. When plant breeding has been unable to create resistance in crop plants, the application of pesticides has been highly successful. The early pesticides developed during the late nineteenth century were mostly arsenic compounds, which soon were recognized as potentially harmful to domestic animals and to the farmers who applied them. In 1942 workers in a Swiss chemical laboratory discovered dichloro-diphenyl-trichloroethane (DDT), which had a tremendous impact on agriculture, as well as public health. Initially heralded as a safe and effective alternative to arsenic pesticides, DDT was used widely for the control of insects. Although later withdrawn from use in some countries because of its toxic effects, the use of DDT paved the way for the standard use of chemical pesticides in agriculture.

Mechanization also has played a role in increasing agricultural productivity. The innovations of the nineteenth century largely centered around harnessing the power of draft animals for such tasks as sowing, mowing, reaping, and threshing. Nineteenth-century innovations, including Cyrus McCormick's reaper, Eli Whitney's cotton gin, and George Brown's corn planter, greatly reduced the amount of manual labor required in agriculture. The introduction of the tractor in the twentieth century dramatically increased the speed and reduced the number of laborers required to perform agricultural tasks. Increased speed permitted more timely planting, cultivating, and harvesting of crops. Agricultural mechanization also facilitated the uniform placement and arrangement of seed and the application of fertilizers and pesticides. The influence of the rational allocation of land, labor, and capital resources is illustrated clearly by agricultural mechanization.

The revolutions in agricultural science and technology required innovations in the way people farmed the land. In traditional agriculture, knowledge resides with the practitioners. In contrast, modern agriculture, spurred on by development of the natural sciences, created new repositories for agricultural information in the form of books, journals, and highly trained agricultural specialists. Efforts to achieve greater democracy by making education available to farmers and laborers led to establishment of the Land Grant Colleges in the United States (Morrill Act of 1862). The curricula of these colleges were designed to widen the horizons of students in arts and letters, as well as to provide instruction in the natural sciences for application to agriculture and the mechanic arts. In addition to training their students, the Land Grant Colleges offered instruction and demonstration of new farming techniques at "farmers' schools." Subsequent establishment of Agricultural Experiment Stations (Hatch Act of 1887) resulted in a publicly funded research corps to address problems of agriculture and rural life. In the United States, the education of farmers became formalized in 1912, with establishment of the Extension Service, which disseminated the current advances in agricultural science and technology to farmers. In fact, agricultural education has played a significant role in integrating into agricultural production the scientific advances and technology in soil fertility, plant breeding, mechanization, and pest control and thereby has contributed to increased agricultural productivity.

Technological innovations in such areas as transportation and communications have affected agriculture significantly. The distance from farm to dinner table has increased, with agricultural commodities now traded and marketed worldwide. For example, the North American consumer might have the opportunity to purchase grapes from Chile, orange juice from Brazil, chocolate from Switzerland (made from African cocoa), lamb from New Zealand, hydroponically produced tomatoes from the Netherlands, breakfast cereal from the United States, and so on. The worldwide distribution of agricultural commodities has been influenced heavily by progress in food processing. The intercontinental marketing of agricultural commodities has been made possible by a greater understanding of food preservation, food processing inventions, and the availability of refrigeration.

A highly productive form of agriculture has emerged from the integration of the innovations discussed above. The books listed in this chapter provide the reader with an introduction to the science and technology of agriculture and food production. Research and technological innovation continue in agriculture. Although the methods of modern agricultural research differ widely from their predecessors in the nineteenth and early twentieth century, their goal remains to "make two blades of grass where only one grew before."

GENERAL REFERENCE

Adrian, J., ed. *Parat Dictionary of Food and Nutrition*. VCH Pubs. 1988 $60.00. ISBN 0-89573-404-4. Covers the nature, structural biochemistry, and physical chemistry of food components and their nutritional values. Contains some 2,000 entries with cross-references.

Agricultural Statistics: A Reference Book on Agricultural Production, Supplies, Facilities, Consumption. Gordon Pr. 1991 $79.95. ISBN 0-8490-5060-X. A basic and useful reference work.

Bender, Arnold E. *Dictionary of Nutrition and Food Technology.* Butterworth-Heinemann 1990 $59.95. ISBN 0-408-03753-9. Contains some 4,000 entries defining technical terms, equipment and techniques, abbreviations, proprietary names, and the composition of common foods.

Cedra, C. *Illustrated Lexicon of Agricultural Machines and Equipment.* Fr. & Eur. 1991 $85.00. ISBN 0-8288-7258-9

Fenton, Thomas P., and Mary J. Heffron, eds. *Food, Hunger, Agribusiness: A Directory of Resources.* Orbis Bks. 1987 $12.95. ISBN 0-88344-531-X. Information on organizations and materials; includes annotated entries, supplementary entries, and sources of additional information.

Goreham, Gary A., David L. Watt, and Roy M. Jacobsen. *The Socioeconomics of Sustainable Agriculture: An Annotated Bibliography.* Garland Pub. 1992 $53.00. ISBN 0-8240-7127-1. Key references to some 1,000 books, journal articles, government publications, conference papers, and technical bulletins.

Heldman and Lund, eds. *Handbook of Food Engineering.* Dekker 1992 $195.00. ISBN 0-8247-8463-4. Includes essential information on research, development, and operations in the food industry.

Herren, Ray V. *The Agriculture Dictionary.* Delmar 1991 $9.00. ISBN 0-8273-4096-6

Hui, Y. H. *Data Sourcebook for Food Scientists and Technologists* VCH Pubs. 1991 $125.00. ISBN 1-56081-009-2. Provides access to a wide range of useful scientific, technical, and legal information.

————. *Encyclopedia of Food Science and Technology.* 4 vols. Wiley 1991 $495.00. ISBN 0-471-50541-2. Comprehensive reference detailing the properties, analysis, and processing of foodstuffs. Includes 550 alphabetical articles covering every major food-related subject in the basic and applied sciences.

Jensen, Richard D., and Nathan M. Smith. *Agricultural and Animal Sciences Journals and Serials: An Analytical Guide.* Greenwood 1986 $59.95. ISBN 6-313-24331-X. Well-organized guide to over 362 research-oriented English-language serials.

Lewis, Richard J. *Food Additives Handbook.* Van Nos. Reinhold 1989 $84.95. ISBN 0-442-20508-2. Up-to-date, but quite technical, guide to over 1,350 direct and indirect additives, pesticides, packaging materials, and selected animal drugs.

Lilley, George P., ed. *Information Sources in Agriculture and Horticulture.* K. G. Saur 1992 $110.00. ISBN 0-408-30101-5

Macrae, Robert, R. K. Robinson, and M. J. Sadler, eds. *Encyclopedia of Food Science, Food Technology, and Nutrition.* 8 vols. Acad. Pr. 1993 $1795.00. ISBN 0-12-226850-4

Morris, Scott, ed. *Agriculture and Vegetation of the World. Using and Understanding Maps Ser.* Chelsea Hse. 1993 $15.95. ISBN 0-7910-1804-0. Series of maps showing the major agricultural and vegetation regions of the world.

Rumney, Thomas A., *The Geography of Agriculture: A Selected Bibliography.* Vance Biblios. 1990 $14.50. ISBN 0-7920-0650-X

Saulson, Donald S., and Elizabeth M. Saulson. *A Pocket Guide to Food Additives.* VPS Pub. 1991 $1.95. ISBN 0-9629606-0-8. Handy, concise pocket guide to over 500 food additives.

Schapsmeier, Frederick H., and Edward L. Schapsmeier. *Encyclopedia of American Agricultural History.* Greenwood 1976 $55.00. ISBN 0-8371-7958-0. Useful and interesting; entries trace the history of agriculture in the United States and of the important people, inventions, technological developments, and major issues on the subject.

Smith, J. *Food Additive User's Handbook.* Van Nos Reinhold 1991 $125.95. ISBN 0-442-31431-0. Presents technical information on the sources, characteristics, intended and unintended effects, and regulation of a wide range of chemical additives.

The State of Food and Agriculture, 1987–1988. UNIPUB 1988 $45.00. ISBN 92-5-102660-2. Current information on world food and agriculture; includes a glossary of acronyms and definitions. An essential reference.

Whitby, M., and others. *The Agricultural Handbook.* Sheridan 1988 $24.50. ISBN 0-00-383128-0

Stephans, A. *Dictionary of Agriculture.* IBD Ltd. 1990 $20.50. ISBN 0-948549-13-0

World Agricultural Statistics. UNIPUB 1990 $9.00. ISBN 92-5-002896-2. Compilation on world statistics on agricultural production, agricultural workforce, and farm-based income.

PRODUCTION AGRICULTURE

Production agriculture refers to the dominant form of agriculture today, that which is highly dependent on advanced agricultural and related technologies (tractors, large-scale crop storage and transportation facilities, etc.). The following references survey the great strengths and achievements, as well as some of the special problems, of this mode of agricultural production.

Audrey, Robert L. *American Agricultural Implements, a Review of Invention and Development in the Agricultural Implement Industry of the United States: Part 1 General History of Invention and Improvement. Part 2 Pioneer Manufacturing Centers.* Ayer 1972 repr. of 1894 ed. $20.00. ISBN 0-405-04681-2. Overview of the innovations in agricultural mechanization in the United States until the end of the nineteenth century.

Bayliss-Smith, T. P. *The Ecology of Agricultural Systems.* Cambridge U. Pr. 1982 $19.95. ISBN 0-521-29829-6. Analyzes pre-industrial, semi-industrial and fully industrialized agricultural production systems.

Benton, Neville. *Pigs, a Guide to Management.* Trafalgar 1990. Handbook of swine management covering nutrition, reproduction, management, housing, and animal health.

Birch, Gordon G. *Food Science.* Pergamon 1986 $37.00. ISBN 0-08-031980-7. Excellent introductory text concerning food and its role in the nutrition of the body, as well as methods used in food processing to prevent spoilage.

Blakely, James, and David H. Bade. *The Science of Animal Husbandry.* P-H 1989 $43.00. ISBN 0-685-44714-6. Useful introduction to the most common farm animals; a guide to identifying various breeds of animals; offers practical information on nutritional rations and aids in the identification and treatment of animal diseases.

Brown, Dave, and Sam Meadowcroft. *The Modern Shepherd.* Diamond Farm Bk. 1989 $27.95. ISBN 0-85236-188-2. A guide to the care, feeding, and handling of sheep.

Buol, S. W., F. D. Hole, and R. J. McCracken. *Soil Genesis and Classification.* Iowa St. U. Pr. 1989 $46.95. ISBN 0-8138-1462-6. Useful introduction to the science of pedology, a subdiscipline of soil science that studies the description and classification of the soil.

Calbally, E. I., and J. R. Freney, eds. *Cycling of Carbon, Nitrogen, Sulfur and Phosphorus in Terrestrial and Aquatic Ecosystems.* Spr.-Verlag 1982 $44.00. ISBN 0-387-11272-3. Useful introduction to the cycling of major chemical elements in agriculture, a key to understanding soil fertility.

Daniel, Pete. *Breaking the Land: The Transformation of Cotton, Tobacco and Rice Cultures since 1880.* U. of Ill. Pr. 1986 $14.95. ISBN 0-252-01391-3. Describes the revolution in production techniques of these important cash crops.

Dempsey, J. M. *Fiber Crops.* U. Press Fla. 1975 $27.95. ISBN 0-8130-0449-7. Useful introduction to the origin, biology, and management of such important fiber crops as jute, kenaf, cotton, hemp, and flax; somewhat dated.

Edmond, J. B. *Fundamentals of Horticulture.* McGraw 1975 o.p. Botanical descriptions, cultural practices, and market use of common fruit, vegetable, and ornamental crops.

Ensminger, M. Eugene. *Animal Science*. Interstate 1991 $73.25. ISBN 0-675-47574-3. Comprehensive reference on animal care, feeding, nutrition, and production.

Gideon, Siegfrid. *Mechanization Takes Command*. Norton 1969 $16.95. ISBN 0-393-00489-9. Covers the relationship between machines and the organic world, discussing such topics as farm machinery, meat packing, and bread making.

Giller, Ken E. *Nitrogen Fixation in Tropical Cropping Systems*. C. A. B. Intl. 1991 $57.00. ISBN 0-85198-671-4. The biology of nitrogen fixation by tropical crop plants, its potential to increase the productivity of crops in tropical environments without the expense of costly nitrogen fertilizers, and its limitations in tropical regions of the world.

Gutschick, Vincent P. *A Functional Biology of Crop Plants*. Timber 1987 $39.95. ISBN 0-88192-046-0. Sophisticated description of the ecophysiology of crop plants.

Harper, F. *Principles of Arable Crop Production*. Sheridan 1983 $22.50. ISBN 0-246-11741-9. Covers all major aspects of crop production; emphasizes integration of scientific principles with agricultural practice.

Hurt, R. Douglas. *American Farm Tools: From Hand Power to Steam Power*. Sunflower U. Pr. 1989 repr. of 1982 ed. $15.00. ISBN 0-89745-026-4. Illustrated history of farm tools and equipment.

Johnson, Stanley. *The Green Revolution*. HarpC 1972 o.p. Examples of the "success" of the introduction of industrialized agriculture to developing countries in Africa, Latin America, and Asia; written when the benefits of the green revolution were highly extolled.

Jones, J.G.W., and P. R. Street. *Systems Theory Applied to Agriculture and the Food Chain*. Elsevier 1990 $109.75. ISBN 1-85166-510-2. Wide-ranging discussion of systems theory applied to agricultural research, modeling, and education.

Lockhart, J.A.R., and A.J.L. Wiseman. *Introduction to Crop Husbandry, Including Grasslands*. Pergamon 1988 $62.00. ISBN 0-08-034201-9. Well-illustrated introduction to the science and technology of crop production.

Marcus, Alan I. *Agricultural Science and the Quest for Legitimacy: Farmers, Agricultural Colleges, and Experiment Stations 1870–1890*. Iowa St. U. Pr. 1985 $26.95. ISBN 0-8138-0083-8. Lively history of the cultural setting of late-nineteenth-century rural America and the beginnings of the Agricultural Experiment Stations, which were dedicated to improvement of agriculture through the application of scientific principles.

McLarsen, J. S. *Chemical Manipulation of Crop Growth and Development*. Buttrwrth-Heinemann 1982 $120.00. ISBN 0-408-10767-7. Detailed discussion of plant growth regulators and their use in agriculture and ornamental horticulture.

Miller, Darrell. *Forage Crops*. McGraw. Useful reference for many pasture and meadow species. Covers their establishment, management, diseases, and insect pests.

Nonnecke, Ib Libner. *Vegetable Production*. Van Nos. Reinhold 1989 $72.95. ISBN 0-442-26721-5. Detailed and comprehensive description of commercial vegetable production.

Parnes, Robert. *Fertile Soil: A Grower's Guide to Organic and Inorganic Fertilizer*. 1990 $39.95. ISBN 0-932857-03-5. Guide to various amendments that increase or maintain the productive capacity of the soil.

Pierce, J. T. *The Food Resource*. Halsted Pr. 1990 $45.95. ISBN 0-052-30537-3. Comprehensive analysis of the resource base of agricultural production based on conceptualization of food supply and demand relations. Discusses climate change, energy use, and constraints to production.

Roberts, D. A. *Fundamentals of Plant Pest Control*. W. H. Freeman 1978 o.p. The conceptual basis for pest control strategies to prevent encroachment of weeds, insects, diseases, nematodes, and herbivorous animals.

Smith, Page, and Charles Daniel. *The Chicken Book*. N. Point Pr. 1982 o.p. Comprehensive guide to the management of chickens for meat and egg production.

United States Soil Conservation Service 1975. *Soil Taxonomy*. Krieger 1988 repr. of 1983 ed. $76.00. ISBN 0-89464-286-3. The taxonomic system for soil used within the

United States, covering soil color, texture, depth, and its ability to support crops or various building structures.

Spedding, C.R. *Biological Efficiency in Agriculture*. Acad. Pr. 1981 $106.00. ISBN 0-12-656560-0. The concept of efficiency of biological processes, using specific examples of crops and farm animals.

Sposito, Garrison. *The Chemistry of Soils*. OUP 1989 $42.50. ISBN 0-19-504615-3. Numerous models describing the composition and the behavior of soil elements.

Tan, Kim. *Principles of Soil Chemistry*. Dekker 1992 $6.95. ISBN 0-8247-8989-X. Concerning the complex web of chemical reactions and equilibria that characterize soils.

Toussaint-Samat, Maguelonne. *A History of Food*. Blackwell Pubs. 1992 $39.95. ISBN 0-631-17741-8. Comprehensive history of food, treating the origin and history of such foodstuffs as bread, wine, and cheese.

Ture, Alfred C. *History of Agricultural Education in the United States 1785–1925. American Education: Its Men, Institutions and Ideas, Series 1*. Ayer 1969 repr. of 1929 ed. $19.00. ISBN 0-405-01485-6. Provides a basis for understanding the important role that agricultural education has played in the development of increased agricultural production.

Voisin, André. *Grass Productivity*. 1959. Island Pr. 1988 $29.95. ISBN 0-933280-63-7. Influential book on the management of pastures for optimal animal productivity.

Webster, John. *Understanding the Dairy Cow*. Blackwell Sci. 1993. ISBN 0-632-03438-6. Guide to the management of cows for milk production.

TRADITIONAL AGRICULTURE

Traditional agriculture has remained stable for centuries, accepting innovations slowly and with great discrimination. In contrast to those of production agriculture (described above), the tools and implements of traditional agriculture are made by farmers rather than by engineers and scientists. Crops and animals are not the result of systematic breeding by professional scientists; they are determined by countless generations of selection by farmers. In general, traditional agriculture is characterized by the wide diversity of tools, customs, plants, and animals reflecting the adaptations by various societies to obtain food from the land.

The introduction to agriculture of industrial methods of production has, in many instances, greatly disturbed or destroyed societies rooted in traditional agriculture. For example, the peasant societies of Europe have all but disappeared, either through collectivization of agriculture or by assimilation into the market economy. In the United States—although one might argue that agriculture always has been a commercial enterprise—technical innovation and market economics have radically transformed the traditional agriculture and agricultural communities of the eighteenth and nineteenth centuries.

During the period of great technological innovation in agriculture, traditional agriculture often was regarded as a collection of superstitions, with little value for the scientist or technologist. However, the recent emphasis on sustainability in agriculture has forced a reexamination of traditional methods of production and of the societies that have used them successfully for centuries.

Allan, William. *The African Husbandman*. Greenwood 1977 repr. of 1965 ed. $55.00. ISBN 0-8371-8287-5. Describes the tools and methods of traditional African agriculture.

Berger, John. *Pig Earth*. Random 1992 $11.00. ISBN 0-679-73715-4. Insight into the practices and sensibilities of the peasant world of Alpine France, an agricultural society threatened by the encroachment of the industrialized world.

Cato and Varro. *On Agriculture. Loeb Classical Library.* HUP $15.50. ISBN 0-674-91313-6.
  The agricultural practices of antiquity.
Chayanov, Alexander. *The Theory of Peasant Cooperatives.* Ohio St. U. Pr. 1991 $63.50.
  ISBN 0-8142-0566-6. An examination of Russian peasantry.
Columella. *De Re Rustica.* 3 vols. *Loeb Classical Library.* HUP Vol. 1 ISBN 0-674-99398-5.
  Vol. 2 ISBN 0-674-99448-5. Vol. 3 ISBN 0-674-99449-3. A classical author's
  observations and recommendations on agricultural husbandry.
Heitland, William E. *Agricola: A Study of Agriculture and Rustic Life in the Greco-Roman
  World from the Point of View of Labor.* Greenwood 1970 $6.50. ISBN 0-8371-4088-9
Jefferson, Thomas. *The Garden and Farm Books of Thomas Jefferson.* Ed. by Robert C.
  Baron. Fulcrum Pub. 1987 o.p. Observations by the founder of American agrarian-
  ism provide an insight into the practices of early American agriculture and its efforts
  toward scientific improvement.
Shanin, Theador. *Peasant and Peasant Societies.* Blackwell Pubs. 1987 $55.00. ISBN 0-
  631-15212-1
Vasey, Daniel E. *An Ecological History of Agriculture, 10,000 B.C.–A.D. 10,000.* Iowa St. U.
  Pr. 1992 $34.95. ISBN 0-8138-0909-6.

ALTERNATIVE AGRICULTURE

Unquestionably, production agriculture has achieved enormous success in
increasing the food supply. Yet some have not been impressed by the well-
stocked shelves of supermarkets and the bursting granaries; they argue that
many of the techniques of production agriculture harm the environment,
exploit labor, and disrupt, if not often destroy, traditional culture. However, the
criticism of production agriculture and the remedies proposed have not been
unified, because various authors have focused their attention only on their
specific areas of concern. Nevertheless, a body of literature is beginning to
emerge that has examined some of the detrimental side effects of production
agriculture in both the industrialized and the developing worlds and proposed
alternative methods of production. The techniques proposed for alternative
agriculture are less dependent on chemical inputs, are more aware of soil
conservation, and are more attentive to existing social structures in developing
countries. The future and continued sucess of alternative methods remains
unclear.

Addiscott, T. M., A. P. Whitmore, and D. S. Powlson. *Farming, Fertilizers and the Nitrate
  Problem.* C. A. B. Intl. 1991 $25.50. ISBN 0-85198-658-7. Discusses the potential
  aquatic pollution from overapplication of nitrogenous fertilizers and manures to
  cropland.
Berry, Wendell. *The Unsettling of America: Culture and Agriculture.* Sierra 1986 $9.00.
  ISBN 0-87156-772-5. Observations on the relations between culture and the highly
  mechanized techniques of production agriculture in the United States; written by
  one of the foremost essayists in the United States.
Brown, Lester R., and Edward C. Wolf. *Global Perspectives on Causes and Remedies of
  Soil Erosion.* World Watch Institute 1984 o.p. Argues that soil erosion must be
  reduced if sufficient food is to be available for future generations.
Committee on the Role of Alternative Farming Methods in Modern Production
  Agriculture, Board of Agriculture. *Alternative Agriculture.* Natl. Acad. Pr. 1989
  $24.95. ISBN 0-309-03985-1. Comprehensive study emphasizing the scientific
  validity of many alternative agricultural techniques.
Dover, Michael J. *A Better Mousetrap: Improving Pest Management for Agriculture.* World
  Resources Inst. 1985 $10.00. ISBN 0-915825-04-0. Suggestions for improving
  prevailing methods of chemical pest control through more efficient application
  technologies, as well as the use of biological control of insects.

Edwards, Clive, ed. *Sustainable Agricultural Systems*. The Soil and Water Conserv. 1990 $40.00. ISBN 0-935-73421-X. Examines the concept of sustainability by referring to special agricultural practices in temperate and tropical environments.

George, Susan. *Food Strategies for Tomorrow*. Global Hunger Project 1987 o.p. Examines alternative agricultural development strategies.

_____. *Ill Fares the Land: Essays on Food, Hunger and Power*. Inst. Policy Stud. 1984 $5.95. ISBN 0-89758-039-7. Excellent collection of essays arguing against uncritical exportation of industrialized agricultural techniques to developing nations.

Hightower, Jim. *Hard Tomatoes, Hard Times*. Transaction Pubs. 1978 $18.95. ISBN 0-8467-0516-8. Thought-provoking study of the agricultural research and business complex in the United States.

Koeph, Herbert H., B.O.D. Petterson, and Wolfgang Schaumann. *Biodynamic Agriculture*. Trans. by Biologishe Landwirtschaft. Anthroposophic Press, Inc. 1976 o.p. Discusses the history and practices of agriculture based on the teachings of the philosopher Rudolf Steiner.

Schwenke, Karl. *Successful Small-Scale Farming: An Organic Approach*. Storey Comm. Inc. 1991 repr. of 1979 ed. $19.95. ISBN 0-685-47450-X. Excellent, well-illustrated how-to text for alternative agriculture.

Widdowson, R. W. *Towards Holistic Agriculture: A Scientific Approach*. Pergamon 1987 $30.00. ISBN 0-08-034211-6. Integrative text describing the application of various principles of agroecology to commonly encountered farm management decisions.

FOOD TECHNOLOGY

The production of food and the technology associated with it have had a dramatic effect on the planet. To produce enough food to sustain populations, humans have cleared forests, controlled rivers, reclaimed land, created new hybrid plants and animals, and spread some species beyond their original habitats or eliminated some species completely. Sophisticated machinery has enabled humans to cultivate more land, and the use of fertilizers and pesticides has led to increased food production while altering the natural environment. While the successes of food production technologies have led to food sufficiency and better diets throughout much of the world, they have also contributed to a growing population problem that threatens to overwhelm our ability to produce enough food.

The effects of food technology are most apparent in the United States. As one of the leaders in food technology, the United States has been very concerned with designing and implementing improved methods of producing food. Significant progress has been made, but there is still a great demand for newer and better techniques to further increase the efficiency of food production and reduce costs.

Blaxter, Kenneth, and Leslie Fowden, eds. *Technology in the Nineteen Nineties— Agriculture and Food*. Scholium Intl. 1985 $73.00. ISBN 0-85403-253-3. Contains a series of papers discussing future prospects in the field of agriculture and food technology, including the use of pesticides, fertilizers, and genetic engineering.

Brady, N. C., ed. *Advances in Agronomy*. Vol. 45 Acad. Pr. 1991 $75.00. ISBN 0-12-000745-2. Contains eight articles by seventeen contributors on worldwide agricultural issues. Includes material on nitrogen in wetlands, genetic resources in agriculture, crop management, and soil productivity.

Francis, Charles, Cornelia Flora, and Larry King, eds. *Sustainable Agriculture in Temperate Zones*. Wiley $74.95. ISBN 0-471-62227-3. Contains 16 chapters by 23 contributors on newly developing alternatives to energy-intensive monoculture practices used in most farming today. Intended for students and professionals in agronomy as well as farmers.

Harlander, Susan K., and Theodore P. Labuza, eds. *Biotechnology in Food Processing.* Noyes 1986 $48.00. ISBN 0-8155-1073-X. "This volume presents the proceedings of a 1985 symposium . . . this symposium explored the current status of the economic, technological, and regulatory impact of evolving areas of high technology on food and food-related industries. The references are current and extensive . . . this volume provides an excellent current reference source in a rapidly developing field" (*Choice*).

Henyon, Debra K., ed. *Food Packaging Technology.* ASTM 1991 $46.00. ISBN 0-8031-1417-6. Eight articles discussing aspects of food packaging, including the extending of shelf life and flavor management.

Lambert, Mark. *Food Technology. Technology in Action Ser.* Watts 1992 $12.90. ISBN 0-531-18400-5. Brief, general discussions on various types of food technologies. Includes a glossary and index.

Penfield, Marjorie P., and Ada M. Campbell. *Experimental Food Science.* Acad. Pr. 1990 $50.00. ISBN 0-12-157920-4. Discusses topics such as alternative sweeteners, synthetic fats, extruded foods, and water activity during microwave heating.

Powledge, Fred. *The Fat of the Land: What's Behind Your Shrinking Food Dollar and What You Can Do about It.* S&S Trade 1984 o.p. "This book examines the food system from farm to grocery store, concentrating on the economic additives that increase the cost of food. Powledge discusses the effects of agricultural practices and marketing on food quality and quantity, points out the costs that highly processed and fabricated foods add, and describes the roles played by the distributors. . . . Concluding chapters focus on food and nutrition organizations that perform watchdog or consumer education functions" (*Library Journal*).

Rhodes, Martha E. *Food Protection Technology.* Lewis Pubs. 1990 $72.95. ISBN 0-87371-377-X. Focuses on recent advances in the food industry and techniques needed by food professionals to ensure food safety.

Sangwan, R. S., and B. S. Sangwan-Norreel. *The Impact of Biotechnology on Agriculture.* Kluwer Ac. 1990 $148.00. ISBN 0-7923-0741-0. Papers written for a conference on Fundamental and Applied in vitro culture Research. Addresses a variety of plant science and biotechnology issues pertaining to agriculture.

Shewfelt, Robert L., and Stanley E. Prussia, eds. *Postharvest Handling: A Systems Approach.* Acad. Pr. 1992 $79.00. ISBN 0-12-639990-5. Discusses new techniques of food handling, marketing techniques and systems, and food safety technologies.

Urbain, Walter M. *Food Irradiation.* Acad. Pr. 1986 $96.00. ISBN 0-12-709370-2. Well-organized presentation of the subject. Includes definitions and discussions of important terms and the author's own evaluation of the topics.

CHRONOLOGY OF AUTHORS

Columella, Lucius Junius Moderatus. fl. 1st century A.D.
Boussingault, Jean-Baptiste. 1802–1887
Liebig, Justus von. 1803–1873
Lawes, John B. 1814–1900
Gilbert, Joseph H. 1817–1901
Wallace, Henry. 1836–1916
Benson, Ezra Taft. 1899–
Borlaug, Norman. 1914–
Rodale, Robert D. 1930–1990
Berry, Wendell. 1934–
Jackson, Wes. 1936–

BENSON, EZRA TAFT. 1899–

An agricultural scientist and food-marketing specialist, Ezra Taft Benson was raised on his Mormon family's farm in Whitney, Idaho. From 1918 to 1921, he attended Utah State Agricultural College and then went to England on a mission for the Mormon Church. On his return to the United States, Benson and his brother Orval operated the family farm and also studied agricultural science at Brigham Young University, where Benson received his B.S. degree in 1926. In 1929 Benson joined the agricultural extension service of the University of Idaho, working as extension economist and marketing specialist. Within these years he had become an active force in the farmers cooperative movement and organized the Idaho Cooperative Counsel, for which he served as secretary from 1933 to 1938. In 1939 Benson was elected executive secretary of the National Council of Farmers Cooperatives, a post he held until 1944. During this period he also served the cooperative movement as its representative in Washington, D.C.

In Washington, D.C., Benson urged the federal government to extend agricultural cooperatives and improve the management of its surplus crop purchase programs. He became an outspoken foe of government bureaucratic farm controls and crop subsidies. In 1943 Benson was chosen as a member of the Quorum of the Twelve Apostles, the governing body of the Mormon Church, and he devoted himself fully to his religious responsibilities during the war years. After the war he supervised the church's postwar program of distributing food and supplies in Europe. From 1946 to 1950 he was director of the Farm Foundation and was greatly sought after as a farm-marketing specialist.

During the 1950s, Benson strongly urged farm cooperatives to rely less on federal subsidies and controls and more on providing service to their members. He also viewed farm cooperatives as a key component of the nation's free enterprise system, and he continued to urge cooperatives to improve both their farming methods and marketing techniques. Although his church role limited his participation in politics, Benson supported William Howard Taft over Dwight D. Eisenhower for the Republican 1952 presidential nomination. Nevertheless, after Eisenhower's victory, the new president chose Benson as his secretary of agriculture, a move endorsed by both the American Farm Bureau Federation and the National Farmers Union. Accepting this cabinet post on leave of absence from his church, Benson tackled the serious problem of huge crop surpluses by ending fixed farm price supports and adopting a flexible scale to curb production. He also launched a soil bank program in 1956 to encourage farmers to withdraw more land from crop production. During Eisenhower's two terms in office, Benson's policies enjoyed some success and reflected the administration's conservative farm policy.

BOOKS BY BENSON

Cross Fire: The Eight Years with Eisenhower. Greenwood 1976 repr. of 1962 ed. $41.50. ISBN 0-8371-8422-3. Personal reminiscences of his experiences as secretary of agriculture in the Eisenhower administration.

Farmers at the Crossroads. Greenwood 1982 repr. of 1956 ed. $55.00. ISBN 0-313-23484-1. Urges American farmers to improve farm methods and adopt more competitive farming techniques.

Missionaries to Match Our Message. Bookcraft Inc. 1991 $4.95. ISBN 0-88494-779-3

The Proper Role of Government. Hawkes Pub. Inc. 1975 repr. 1968 ed. $2.50. ISBN 0-89036-122-3. Presents his views on the role of government in American agriculture and his thinking on such issues as federal subsidies and price supports.

BERRY, WENDELL. 1934–

Wendell Berry was born in Henry County, Kentucky, where he now lives with his wife Tanya on a small farm alongside the Kentucky River. Berry received his B.A. and M.A. degrees from the University of Kentucky and was a Wallace Stegner Writing Fellow at Stanford University from 1958 to 1959. He has taught at Stanford University, New York University, and the University of Kentucky, where he has continued teaching on and off since 1964. The recipient of fellowships from the Guggenheim and Rockefeller foundations, Berry has also been awarded the Vachel Lindsay Prize by *Poetry* magazine and the National Institute of Arts and Letters Literary Award.

Berry's writing includes fiction, poetry, essays, and criticism. He has also served as a contributing editor for *New Farm* and *Organic Gardening and Farming*, both published by Rodale Press. In such works as *Farming: A Handbook* (1970), *The Unsettling of America* (1977), and *The Gift of Good Land* (1981) Berry has argued for the importance of agriculture not simply as an economic activity, but as a way of life and culture. By words and through example, he has sought to reaffirm the American tradition of agricultural stability and a life in harmony with the land.

BOOKS BY BERRY

A Continuous Harmony. Peter Smith 1972 $19.00. ISBN 0-8446-6704-8. Berry's first book of essays.

Harlan Hubbard: Life and Work. U. Pr. of Ky. 1990 $23.00. ISBN 0-8131-1725-9. Beautifully illustrated with drawings, photographs, and 20 color reproductions.

Home Economics. FS&G 1987 $9.95. ISBN 0-86547-275-0. Fourteen essays on themes related to homestead farming and living on the land.

Meeting the Expectations of the Land. FS&G 1984 $22.50. ISBN 0-86547-172-X

Sex, Economy, Freedom, and Community: Eight Essays. Pantheon 1993 $20.00. ISBN 0-679-42394-X. Carves out a unique position in American social debate. A powerful emetic.

The Unforeseen Wilderness. FS&G 1991 repr. of 1971 ed. $19.95. ISBN 0-86547-462-1. With photographs by Gene Meatyard.

The Unsettling of America: Culture and Agriculture. Sierra 1986 repr. of 1977 ed. ISBN 0-87156-772-5. Berry's most sustained critique of modern, high-tech production agriculture in the United States.

What Are People For? FS&G 1990 $10.95. ISBN 0-86547-437-0. Two prose poems and a series of essays on writers with whom Berry is sympathetic (Harry Caudill, Edward Abbey, Wallace Stegner, and others), and on themes such as waste, food, local culture, feminism, and nature.

BOOK ABOUT BERRY

Merchant, Paul, ed. *Wendell Berry*. *American Authors Ser*. Confluence Pr. 1991 $24.95. ISBN 0-917652-88-6. Collection of 18 appreciation essays by colleagues and critics, with a selected bibliography of Berry's publications.

BORLAUG, NORMAN. 1914– (NOBEL PRIZE 1970)

Norman Borlaug is a prominent plant pathologist and geneticist who helped pioneer the Green Revolution to increase crop yields worldwide. Born on a farm near Cresco, Iowa, Borlaug studied forestry at the University of Minnesota, earning his B.S. in 1937. He then undertook graduate work there in plant pathology, earning his M.S. in 1939 and his Ph.D. in 1942. After a year of teaching at the university, he left to accept a job as a biochemist for the E. I. duPont de Nemours Company.

The turning point in Borlaug's career came in 1944, when he became a member of a team of scientists who founded the International Maize and Wheat Improvement Center in Mexico. Under the auspices of the Rockefeller Foundation, the center's goal was to introduce the elements of the modern agricultural revolution into Mexican agriculture. In addition to mechanization, improved irrigation, and the use of new chemical fertilizers, Borlaug and his colleagues at the center emphasized the development of new varieties and hybrids of wheat. Their efforts were directed at finding a variety of wheat for Mexican farmers that was disease resistant, responsive to fertilizers, and produced increased crop yields. Their research was soon successful, and the so-called Green Revolution—the great expansion in food production worldwide—was underway. Borlaug and most agricultural scientists believed the new high-yielding varieties of rice, corn, wheat, and other cereal crops—the staple foods in developing countries—would end hunger there and enable the governments of those countries to feed their rapidly growing populations.

During the decades after World War II, Borlaug lent his expertise to the governments of Morocco, India, Pakistan, Afghanistan, and other developing nations. He also continued his work in Mexico and became associate director of the Rockefeller Foundation Inter-American Food Program in 1964. In 1970 he received the Nobel Peace Prize for his humanitarian work in combating world hunger. It is notable that Borlaug is one of the few scientists to have won this honor.

For the rest of his career, Borlaug continued his work in developing hybrid cereal crops, finally achieving success in introducing a variety of corn that greatly increased the food supply in developing nations dependent on that crop. During the 1980s, however, Borlaug's success seemed challenged by declines in yields of hybrid crops due to their dependence on expensive fertilizers. The reliance of hybrid cereal crops on large-scale mechanized agriculture also was viewed by some critics as a growing threat to small farmers in developing nations. Since 1984 Borlaug has been Distinguished Professor of International Agriculture at Texas A&M University.

BOOKS BY BORLAUG

The Green Revolution: Peace and Humanity. U. Ch. Pr. 1971 o.p. Presents Borlaug's views on the importance of increased worldwide agricultural production.

Land Use, Food, Energy and Recreation. (coauthored with Paul F. Bente, Jr.). U. Pr. of Amer. 1983 $7.75. ISBN 0-8191-5877-2

The World Food Problem: Present and Future. U. Ch. Pr. 1972 o.p. Analyzes the issue of food productivity and what can be done to improve crop yields.

BOOK ABOUT BORLAUG

Bickel, Leonard. *Facing Starvation: Norman Borlaug and the Fight against Hunger*. 1974 o.p.

BOUSSINGAULT, JEAN-BAPTISTE. 1802–1887

For the scientific agricultural researcher, as well as for the twentieth-century farmer, it is often difficult to imagine the importance of the contributions to knowledge and technique made by the pioneering agricultural researchers of the nineteenth century. Although limited by crude and often inaccurate instruments, those nineteenth-century researchers laid the foundations for the agricultural research that would follow in the late nineteenth and early twentieth century. Jean-Baptiste Boussingault, although his reputation is not as large as or as grand as JUSTUS VON LIEBIG's, must be considered as a leading contributor to agriculture for his discoveries in the area of nitrogen metabolism and nitrogen cycling. He is also remembered for his pioneering work with field plot experimentation and his work in improving animal feed rations.

Born in Paris in 1802, Boussingault traveled widely in South America, and his work presents a keen interpretation of the agricultural practices of South American Indians, from which he gleaned insights for practical application to

European agriculture. Later, as a professor of chemistry at Lyons and then at the Conservatory of Arts and Crafts in Paris, he carried out experiments proving that plants absorb carbon dioxide from the atmosphere as well as elucidating the function of plant leaves. He also conducted experiments on the fertilizing value of manure and proved that plants absorb nitrogen from nitrates in soil and not from the atmosphere.

BOOK BY BOUSSINGAULT

Chemistry Applied to Agriculture. Appleton-Century-Crofts 1845 o.p. Sometimes titled *Rural Economy and its Relations to Chemistry, Physics, and Meteorology.* Although written in the nineteenth century, this work reveals the detailed and painstaking research of this pioneer of agricultural science. In addition to descriptions of his experiments with animal feed rations and manures, Boussingault provides vivid and insightful observations of the traditional agriculture of the South American Indians. The work reveals Boussingault's thorough understanding of the principles of chemistry, physics, and meteorology, as they were known at the time, and his unique ability to apply these principles to practical questions of agriculture.

CARSON, RACHEL LOUISE. 1907–1964

[SEE Chapter 23 in this volume.]

COLUMELLA, LUCIAS JUNIUS MODERATUS. fl. 1st century A.D.

Lucias Junius Moderatus Columella, the author of the most detailed and comprehensive writing on agriculture produced by the Roman world, was a native of the province of Cadiz (Gades) in southern Spain. From various references in his writings, it has been deduced that Columella was born early in the first century A.D. and died in the same century while serving with the Roman legion at Tarentum (in what is now Syria).

Columella took up agriculture in the vicinity of Rome, and through his writing attempted to reawaken in the Roman world a dedication to proper husbandry of the soil. He argued that soils, when properly tended, could be restored to their fruitfulness through the application of animal manures and the use of legumes. His writings provided advice on the choice of land; the enrichment of soils; the grafting and pruning of vines and trees; the management of horses, mules, cattle, sheep, goats, and dogs; and the preparation and preservation of food. He also developed a calendar for the performance of various agricultural tasks in accordance with astronomical events.

The scope and detail of Columella's writings contributed to his reputation as the leading authority in antiquity on agricultural topics. His work has been cited by a variety of authors throughout history, and agriculturalists continued to consult his work for advice on practical matters well into the nineteenth century. The adoption of the scientific method as the basis of agricultural research caused his works to become increasingly neglected, however. Nevertheless, the modern reader will be impressed with the depth of Columella's knowledge, which he obtained through observation and experience without recourse to either the techniques or intellectual methods of modern science.

BOOK BY COLUMELLA

De Re Rustica. 3 vols. HUP (Loeb Classical Library: No. 361, 407, 408.) $15.50 ea. ISBNs 0-674-99398-5, 0-674-99448-5, 0-674-99449-3. Contains his observations and recommendations on agricultural husbandry.

JACKSON, WES. 1936–

Wes Jackson, the president of the Land Institute in Salinas, Kansas, has become an influential voice in arguing for an agriculture that is more conservative of land and water resources. Born in 1936 on a farm in Topeka, Kansas, Jackson was subsequently trained as a biologist and botanist at Kansas Wesleyan and the University of Kansas, respectively. He was awarded a Doctor of Philosophy for his work in genetics by North Carolina State University in 1967. After completing his education, Jackson established an Environmental Studies program at California State University in Sacramento, where he served as a professor until 1976. In that year, he resigned from his professorship to establish the Land Institute, where he has since applied his scientific training to the breeding of a perennial wheat and to developing sustainable agricultural techniques. Through his writing, Jackson has articulated a vision of agriculture that is not only environmentally sound, but also provides a basis for the reinvigoration of rural communities.

BOOKS BY JACKSON

Altars of Unhewn Stone. FS&G 1987 $9.95. ISBN 0-86547-287-4. Collection of 18 essays, none originally intended for publication. The title refers to a passage from biblical scripture that invokes the altar as a reminder to man to be more mindful of the original materials of the universe than of themselves. Eloquently recounts that directive in asserting that science is to be pursued as though its original material is more important than the work of scientists who are shaping it, thereby lessening the chances of disrupting nature's patterns upon which all humans are inextricably dependent.

Man and the Environment. Wm. C. Brown Co. 1971 o.p. A thorough source of information on population and food concerns, as well as problems of environmental destruction. Seeks to show that behavior that was formerly adaptive to humankind is now practiced at the peril of the species. Argues that the only rational course of action is for humankind to change its behavior, not as a self-seeking manipulator of the land but as a finite cohabitor of nature.

Meeting the Expectations of the Land FS&G 1984 $12.50. ISBN 0-86547-172-X. Criticizing the commercial, market-oriented agricultural practices of our time, this book describes a new agriculture that is sustainable, delivers a healthful diet, and conforms to Wendell Berry's definition of an agriculture that "does not deplete soils or people." Focused group of essays shows Amish practice to be a model for meeting the expectations of the land.

New Roots for Agriculture. U. of Nebr. Pr. 1985 repr. of 1980 ed. $7.95. ISBN 0-8032-7562-5. Optimistic vision of the possibilities of a new method of agriculture. Intriguing discussion of agriculture itself as a problem and threat to our biosphere, leading to the steady erosion of the land and causing destruction as it has traditionally been practiced throughout most of history. Jackson advocates a bio-technical fix practiced within the bounds of sustainable agriculture.

LAWES, JOHN B., 1814–1900 and GILBERT, JOSEPH H. 1817–1901

John Lawes and Joseph Gilbert were British scientists whose collaboration in the commercial production of crop fertilizers helped spur the agricultural revolution in England. Born near Harpenden, Hertfordshire, Lawes attended Eton and Oxford University, where he became interested in chemistry. In 1834 he inherited a large estate known as Rothamsted, where he began the agricultural experiments that were to bring him wealth and scientific fame. Working with mineral phosphates (ground bones), he discovered a method of treating them with acids that greatly increased their reliability and effectiveness as a fertilizer. In 1843 he opened a factory to manufacture his "superphosphate," and he hired Joseph Gilbert to help him, especially in laboratory work and chemical analyses.

Joseph Gilbert was a neighbor who had also been born at Harpenden, near the Rothamsted estate. Gilbert had attended Glasgow University and University College, London, where he studied chemistry. The collaboration of Lawes and Gilbert, which lasted nearly half a century, made Rothamsted renowned in agricultural science. The two men ideally complemented each other. Lawes was a pragmatic businessman who enjoyed dealing in large-scale schemes and disliked details. Gilbert was a dedicated laboratory chemist, meticulous and methodical, who retested every step of his research.

Lawes and Gilbert's phosphate fertilizer helped to increase greatly the output of wheat (called corn in England). Even JUSTIS VON LIEBIG's assertion that nitrogenous and humus-forming manures were ineffective fertilizers had, by 1851, been proven incorrect by Lawes and Gilbert in a series of field experiments. During the 1850s the financial basis of Rothamsted was threatened by the widespread pirating of the superphosphate patent. Eventually, Gilbert was successful in a long legal battle to end infringements on his patent, and that victory enabled Rothamsted to expand its agricultural laboratories and to conduct extensive research in grassland economy, animal feeding, and water balance.

As is often inevitable in collaborative partnerships, the Rothamsted project eventually began to stagnate. Gilbert's innate conservatism led to an intolerance of young chemists and new ideas at the same time that Lawes felt innovations were needed. When Lawes took on a new personal assistant, Gilbert took it as a personal affront, and personal relations soured between the two men. In 1872 Lawes sold his phosphate business, but he continued to manufacture other agricultural products like citric and tartaric acids. In 1889 he turned over Rothamsted to the Lawes Agricultural Trust, which he set up with a generous endowment to assure the continuation of his work. Both Lawes and Gilbert were elected to the Royal Society, and Gilbert was knighted in 1893.

BOOK BY LAWES AND GILBERT

Rothamsted Memoirs on Agricultural Chemistry and Physiology. Routledge 1893–99 o.p.

LIEBIG, JUSTUS VON. 1803–1873

Born in Darmstadt, Germany, Justus von Liebig was widely acknowledged as the founder of agricultural chemistry. He initially studied pharmacy but eventually turned to chemistry and pursued his studies at the University of Bonn and the University of Erlangen, where he received a doctorate in 1822. That same year he went to Paris, where he worked with the French chemist JOSEPH GAY-LUSSAC. In 1824 he became professor of chemistry at Giessen and in 1852 at Munich.

At the beginning of the nineteenth century, the mechanisms of plant growth had not yet been identified. Thus, there was considerable confusion and controversy about the source of the elements found in plants. Scientists did not know whether the elements found in plants came from the air or from the soil. Liebig's research in agriculture began in 1838 and led to the publication in 1840 of his *Organic Chemistry in Its Application to Agriculture and Physiology.* His research showed that carbon in plants was obtained from atmospheric carbon dioxide rather than from the humic substances in the soil. He also demonstrated that alkaline metals, phosphorus, and nitrogen (essential nutrient elements of plants) were supplied by the soil. Liebig claimed that the proper amount of fertilizer for optimum crop growth could be determined by analyzing the elemental composition of plants. Thus, he provided the first rational framework for improving soil fertility. Liebig's Law of the Minimum, which states that plant growth is limited by the element available in the smallest amount, exerted great influence on subsequent agricultural research in soil fertility.

Although Liebig's theories were incomplete and sometimes flawed, his work provided the foundation for systematic investigations into soil fertility. During his lifetime, Liebig's recommendations and methods for improving soil fertility were accepted and promoted in agriculture. Yet, perhaps his greatest legacy was the rigorous training he gave young chemists who eventually discovered the natural laws of husbandry.

BOOK BY LIEBIG

The Natural Laws of Husbandry. Use and Abuse of America's Natural Resources Ser. Ayer 1972 repr. of 1863 ed. $25.50. ISBN 0-405-04541-7. The observations, experiments, and theories of Liebig applied to crop yields and animal production.

BOOK ABOUT LIEBIG

Moulton, F. P., ed. *Liebig and After Liebig.* Dover 1942 o.p. Discusses Liebig's work and its influence on chemistry and agriculture.

PASTEUR, LOUIS. 1822–1895

[SEE Chapters 13 and 22 in this volume.]

RODALE, ROBERT DAVID. 1930–1990

The Rodale Press of Emmaus, Pennsylvania, has been a major proponent of alternative agricultural systems in the United States. Founded by Jerome Irving Rodale in 1942, the Rodale Press has carried the message that environmental quality and human health depend on the adoption of "organic" agricultural techniques that do not rely on the use of synthetic chemicals for pest control or heavy use of fertilizers for increasing crop yields.

Robert David Rodale, the son of J. I. Rodale, became head of Rodale Press in 1971 and campaigned vigorously for the adoption of organic agricultural techniques. Under Robert Rodale's guidance, research conducted by the Rodale Research Center has been widely disseminated in *Organic Gardening* and *The New Farmer*, two publications of the Rodale Press. Publication of this research not only has spread the practice of organic agriculture but also has helped build a political consensus for changing the course of public policy and research priorities in agriculture. Robert Rodale died from injuries sustained in an automobile accident while visiting Moscow in September 1990. He was in Russia to promote a Russian-language edition of *The New Farmer*.

BOOKS BY RODALE

Our Next Frontier: A Personal Guide for Tomorrow's Lifestyle. Ed. by Carol Stoner. Rodale Pr. Inc. 1981 $14.95. ISBN 0-87857-365-8
Save Three Lives, a Plan for Famine Prevention. Sierra 1991 $20.00. ISBN 0-87156-621-4. Examination of alternative strategies for alleviating hunger and famine in developing countries.

WALLACE, HENRY. 1836–1916

American agricultural writer and publicist Henry Wallace was born to a Scotch-Irish farm family in West Newton, Pennsylvania. After graduating from Jefferson College in Pennsylvania in 1859, Wallace taught briefly at Columbia

College in Kentucky. He then went on to study theology at Allegheny Seminary in Pennsylvania and at Monmouth College in Illinois, and served as a Union chaplain in the Civil War. After the war he was a minister in Illinois and Iowa until forced to retire because of health reasons.

After his retirement from the ministry, Wallace's career took a new turn into writing about agriculture. Earlier in his life he had been interested in journalism and had written a few articles advocating the abolition of slavery, temperance, and other reforms. Writing now became the central focus of his life, and his interests shifted back to his roots in farming. In 1877 he moved his family to Winterset, Iowa, where he bought a farm and became involved in editorial work on local farm papers. His journalistic interest and success eventually led to part ownership of the *Iowa Homestead*. In 1895 he and his two sons founded a new agrarian newspaper known as *Wallaces' Farmer*.

During the turbulent years of the Populist movement and depressed farm prices, *Wallaces' Farmer* gave voice to farmers' deep discontents. It advocated regulating railroad rates to end rebates and other pricing practices that discriminated against small farmers. It urged expanded training and education in state agricultural colleges. During its existence from 1895 to 1916, *Wallaces' Farmer* became a vital source of information and aid for the nation's farmers and a leading organ for their interests.

Interestingly, Wallace's family carried on this heritage. One of Wallace's sons, Henry Cantrell Wallace, served as secretary of agriculture in the 1920s. His grandson, Henry Agard Wallace, studied scientific agronomy at Iowa State University, pursuing plant research and agricultural economics. Young Wallace also developed a new species of hybrid corn and calculated detailed studies of midwestern weather cycles and their effects on crops. Fittingly enough, Henry Agard Wallace also served in the same cabinet post as his father, appointed secretary of agriculture by President Franklin D. Roosevelt in the 1930s. In this position, he was instrumental in implementing the New Deal strategy of paying farmers to cut back on crop production. As Roosevelt's vice-presidential running mate in 1940, Henry Agard Wallace's strength in farm states contributed significantly to Roosevelt's reelection.

BOOK BY WALLACE

Our Debt and Duty to the Farmer. Ayer 1975 repr. of 1925 ed. $23.50. ISBN 0-405-06838-7.
    A facsimile edition of Wallace's thoughts on the importance of America's farmers.

BOOK ABOUT WALLACE

Lord, Russell. *The Henry Wallaces of Iowa*. DaCapo 1971 repr. of 1947 ed. $69.50. ISBN 0-306-70325-4. Looks at the life and contributions of the Wallace family.

CHAPTER 10

Energy

Edward S. Cassedy

> Civilization is not running out of energy resources in absolute sense, nor is it running out of technological options for transforming these resources into the particular forms that our patterns of energy use require. We are, however, running out of the cheap oil and natural gas that powered much of the growth of modern industrialized societies, out of environmental capacity to absorb the impacts of burning coal, and out of public tolerance for the risks of nuclear fission.
>
> —JOHN P. HOLDREN, *Energy Agenda for the 1990s*

Energy in the modern world has several varied meanings: scientific, technological, economic, and behavioral. The physical laws governing the production, storage, conversion, and conservation of energy are based on scientific knowledge. However, this body of scientific knowledge (*thermodynamics*) was developed in the nineteenth century, concurrent with the evolving technology of the steam engine, which greatly influenced the Industrial Revolution. Industrial economies were built and the living patterns of people were changed irreversibly by these heat-driven engines for manufacturing, transportation, and (later) electricity generation.

The industrial economies have been based on fossil fuel resoures, such as coal, oil, and natural gas. Initially, these fossil fuels supplied heat energy so inexpensively that waste was of little consequence to corporations or individuals. The pervasive acceptance of low-cost fuels was based on the erroneous belief that these natural resources were limitless. Only a few people cautioned that fossil fuel resources might be finite. The oil crises of the 1970s, however, illustrated to most people that such resources are not inexhaustible.

In 1980 the energy situation of the United States, and the Western world in general, appeared bleak. In the space of a decade, oil prices had risen from $2 per barrel to more than $30, and the members of the Organization of Petroleum Exporting Countries (OPEC) were amassing great wealth at our expense. Many of the economic problems of the late 1970s, such as high interest rates and high inflation, were blamed on the sharp increase in oil prices. Motorists spent hours at gas stations waiting in line. Natural gas shortages forced industries and schools to close in the Northeast, causing widespread disruptions. President Carter had addressed the nation wearing a sweater, talking of shortage and sacrifice, and Congress spent years bickering over the president's proposals.

A decade later, the situation changed dramatically. Oil prices fell as low as $9 per barrel, OPEC was in disarray, and the media spoke of the "oil glut." Natural gas in the United States became apparently abundant, and the worldwide coal supply surplus favored consumers.

But even today all is not as rosy as it might seem. Some of the developing countries that had looked to oil exports as a path to economic development—

such as Nigeria, Indonesia, and Mexico—suffered devastating blows as oil prices collapsed. The question of nuclear safety remains far from resolved, as demonstrated by the accident at Chernobyl. Indeed, nuclear plants have become so expensive to build that the economic feasibility of nuclear power, which President Eisenhower once thought would produce "electricity too cheap to meter," remains in grave doubt. After the collapse of the Texas oil and gas industry, oil imports to the United States are again on the rise, and many knowledgeable observers predict a resurgence of OPEC in the 1990s when world oil demand begins to grow again. The Middle East remains in chaos, with various forces threatening the conservative regimes in the region.

How can an individual become informed on a topic so beset with controversy, subject to so many uncertainties, and yet so important to our lives? For each expert opinion, there is likely to exist a contrary view, espoused by an equally eminent expert. Even "facts" are hard to establish. The actual quantities of oil, coal, and natural gas still remaining are difficult to establish for three main reasons: (1) most of these resources are underground and therefore subject to the uncertainties of geology; (2) there exists an intrinsic relationship between price and availability; and (3) even if the information were known with reasonable certainty, those who possess the data might have political or economic reasons for hiding, distorting, or even falsifying published data.

Moreover, another energy concern that has arisen in recent years is pollution of the *environment*. This is not the first time in history that fossil-fuel burning has polluted the environment. Centuries ago, for example, coal burning in England was causing significant air pollution, and it reached an acute stage for public health in the mid-1950s. By the mid-1970s, clean-air legislation had been enacted in the Western industrial countries, and it has been upgraded in the decades following. Unfortunately, the legislation and enforcement have been weakened at every stage by compromises with the energy industry as well as with state and local governments. Today, millions of Americans live in localities that are not in compliance with national air quality standards. The Los Angeles air basin regularly suffers from pollution caused by fossil-fuel energy users, such as automobiles, power plants, and factories.

Although local air quality has been a matter of increasing concern, even broader issues, such as acid rain, have arisen during the past decade. Acid rain is a problem that has interregional and international ramifications. The most recent amendment (1990) to the Clean Air Act was designed primarily to reduce acid precipitation in the northeastern United States and Canada originating from coal-burning industries and power plants in the American Midwest. Again, the legislation and its enforcement have been subject to conflicting pressures from industrial and municipal interests that have resulted in compromises.

Recently, long-term dilemmas regarding possible *climate change* due to gaseous emissions from fossil-fuel combustion have been hotly debated. Although global warming from the "greenhouse effect" of such gases as carbon dioxide is unproven, an international consensus has been reached (see the IPCC Reports 1991 in the bibliographies below) to limit these emissions. Consequently, there has been a new impetus toward developing renewable and sustainable alternative energy sources, such as solar, wind, and biomass technologies.

GENERAL BIBLIOGRAPHY

The following references will provide the reader with a good overview of the major issues and illustrate important aspects of the problems society faces in dealing with energy questions.

Brower, Michael. *Cool Energy—Renewable Solutions to Environmental Problems*. MIT Pr. rev. ed. 1992 $12.95. ISBN 0-262-52175-X. Advocates renewable energy technologies, such as solar, wind, biomass, and geothermal, to meet the challenge of rising costs, security risks, and environmental degradation from fossil fuel and nuclear sources. Easy-to-read, useful introduction to these issues.

Cassedy, Edward S., and Peter Z. Grossman. *Introduction to Energy—Resources, Technology, and Society*. Cambridge U. Pr. 1990 $64.95. ISBN 0-521-35091-3. Textbook promoting *technological literacy* and critical thinking about modern technology. Covers energy resources and conventional technology, electric power generation and its impacts, and energy technologies for the future. Contains appendices on scientific principles (including basic thermodynamics), a review of ethical theories and synopses of prospective new technologies, including solar cells, alcohol fuels, nuclear fusion, electric vehicles, and wind generation. Discusses energy economics and the criteria for public health and safety; designed for liberal arts students and laypersons.

Debeir, Jean-Claude, Jean-Paul Deleage, and Daniel Hemery. *In the Servitude of Power— Energy and Civilization through the Ages*. Humanities 1991 $55.00. ISBN 0-86232-942-6. Comprehensive survey of the role of energy resources in shipping history, from antiquity to the late nineteenth century.

Howes, Ruth, and Anthony Fainberg. *The Energy Source Book—A Guide to Technology, Resources and Policy*. Am. Inst. Physics 1990 $75.00. ISBN 0-88318-705-1. Comprehensive collection of papers covering most known energy resources and technologies, including fossil fuels, nuclear (fission and fusion) power, solar (electric and thermal), hydroelectricity, geothermal, biomass, and wind. Also analyzes end-use technologies, such as transportation, agriculture, manufacturing, and commercial buildings. Somewhat technical, but a useful reference for the general reader.

Jevons, W. S. *The Coal Question*. Kelley 1965 repr. of 1906 ed. $45.00. ISBN 0-678-00107-3. Historic reference on energy by a nineteenth-century English economist who was one of the first to comment on the depletion of coal.

Markun, Patricia M. *Witnesses for Oil*. Am. Petroleum 1976 o.p. The oil industry's perspective, presented in excerpts from testimony presented at Congressional hearings.

Mills, Russell, and Arun N. Toké. *Energy, Economics and the Environment*. P-H 1985 $55.00. ISBN 0-13-277468-2. Elementary textbook for undergraduates in "energy and society." Linear organization covers history, (physical) fundamentals, and resources, as well as economics, environmental, social, and political analysis; includes useful figures and photographs.

Morris, David. *Be Your Own Power Company*. Rodale Pr. Inc. 1983 o.p. "An understandable account of the technical and legal aspects of producing one's own electricity and selling it. Includes wind, hydroelectric, and photovoltaic generating devices, cogeneration (producing both heat and electricity at once), and solar power" (*Library Journal*).

Pimentel, David, and Marcia Pimentel. *Food, Energy, and Society*. Halsted Pr. 1979 o.p. Excellent, nontechnical presentation of the interdependencies between food and energy and their impacts on society. Compares the energy inputs for grain versus livestock production and examines the role of energy in fisheries, food packaging, and food preparation.

Wells, Malcolm, ed. *Notes from the Energy Underground*. Krieger 1980 o.p. Series of essays that challenge some cherished cultural beliefs with wit and originality; includes contributions by Isaac Asimov and Russell Baker.

Yergin, Daniel. *The Prize—The Epic Quest for Oil, Money, and Power.* S&S Trade 1992 $16.00. ISBN 0-671-75705-9. Pulitzer prize-winning narrative of the world oil industry since its inception in the late nineteenth century, showing the profound influence of oil exploration on modern world history.

THE GEOPOLITICS OF OIL

During the 1970s, the inherent insecurity of the industrial world's most important energy source—oil—became dramatically clear. Actually, the profound influences of the uneven distribution of petroleum resources worldwide had been apparent to the international oil companies and Western governments since the early part of the twentieth century (see Yergin's *The Prize*, cited above). For example, the granting of oil rights, and even the establishment of nations (e.g., Iraq), can be traced to that period, influencing the regional antagonism that led to the Persian Gulf War (1991). The willingness of the industrial nations to wage war in the Persian Gulf was, according to many commentators, merely the latest incident in the geopolitics of oil.

The problem created by the concentration of oil resources in certain regions, such as the Persian Gulf, did not become clear to most people in the United States and other industrial countries until the early 1970s, when the OPEC cartel, by placing embargoes on shipments, raised the price of crude oil nearly five times. By the end of the decade, when OPEC controlled nearly 50 percent of world oil production, the price of oil had more than doubled from its previous high level. The dramatic increase in oil prices had a serious impact worldwide, contributing significantly to global economic recession in the early 1980s. The developing nations suffered as well, finding themselves on a treadmill of international debt that hindered their economic advancement.

However, OPEC could not sustain these high world prices, because the economic law of supply and demand began to take over. High oil prices, accompanied by price increases in other fuels, stimulated energy conservation. Moreover, high-efficiency appliances and higher gasoline mileage cars became popular, causing the consumption of all energy resources to decrease. In addition, other sources of oil, such as the North Sea, had begun to contribute significantly to world production. The combined effects of falling demand and rising production of oil caused a so-called oil glut on the world market. By 1983, oil had dropped to about half of its 1980 price. There even was a brief period in the mid-1980s when world oil prices dropped to about one-third of the 1980 peak levels. Following these fluctuations, world oil prices have varied between $15 and $20 per barrel, equivalent in current dollars (accounting for inflation) to the 1983 levels, or about double the 1974 level.

Currently, the world market is supplied less than 50 percent by OPEC—about 60 million barrels daily. From a strategic standpoint, this situation is less precarious than the 1970s oil-crisis period. For example, the loss of about two million barrels daily from Kuwait and Iraq during the Persian Gulf War did not cause a major disruption. But major economic chaos would have occurred worldwide if the production of all the southern Gulf states, including Saudi Arabia, the United Arab Emirates, Bahrain, and Qatar, had been affected.

The breakup of the Soviet Union begins another chapter in oil geopolitics. Czarist Russia was one of the first countries that the oil companies tapped (see Yergin, 1991), exporting oil as early as 1888. After the Bolshevik Revolution, most of Russian oil production was used domestically and later was confined mostly to the East European trading bloc. However, by the 1980s, the Soviet Union had become a major world exporter of natural gas, through a huge pipeline to Western Europe.

The economic dislocations accompanying the dissolution of the Soviet Union have caused a severe drop in Russian oil production. In fact, the former Soviet Union currently is having difficulty in supplying domestic oil demand. The potential for greatly increased oil production remains, however, with a demonstrated output capacity (more than 12 million barrels daily) that rivals that of Saudi Arabia. Consequently, Western oil companies again are considering leasing arrangements, which conceivably could make Russia the world counterbalance to OPEC and the oil-rich countries of the Persian Gulf.

For the next several decades, oil will continue to play a major role in the world's economy and geopolitics. Other countries, including China and several other developing nations, have the potential to play a significant role in the world oil game. Readers interested in following developments in this area should review such periodicals as *Foreign Affairs* (published by the Council on Foreign Relations, New York), *The Energy Journal* (published by the International Association of Energy Economists, Washington, D.C.), and *The Oil and Gas Journal* (published by PennWell, Tulsa, OK).

Blair, John. *The Control of Oil.* Pantheon 1976 o.p. Describes the beginning of the oil crisis period to the mid-1970s. Reviews establishment of the Middle East oil ventures in the early twentieth century, focusing on the international oil companies. Covers the history of United States domestic oil policies, starting with the discovery of oil in the Southwest during the 1920s and continuing to the first international oil crisis, in 1973.

Dienes, Leslie, and Theodore Shabad. *The Soviet Energy System: Resource Use and Policies.* Halsted Pr. 1979 o.p. Excellent overview of the energy resources of the Soviet Union.

Dorian, James P., and F. Fesharaki, eds. *International Issues in Energy Policy, Development and Economics.* Westview 1992 $49.50. ISBN 0-8133-8621-7. Updates analysis of the world oil market to the post-Gulf War and post-Soviet Union era. Discusses medium-term prospects beyond the Gulf crisis and long-term prospects for oil production in Russia; includes consideration of global environment.

MacAvoy, Paul W. *Crude Oil Prices—As Determined by OPEC and Market Fundamentals.* Harper Busn. 1982 $34.95. ISBN 0-88410-870-8. Data on production, reserves, and prices through the oil-crisis period, focusing on OPEC; somewhat dated and designed for economists.

Mohammad, Yousuf H., and Walter H. Mead. *World Oil Prices: Demand, Supply and Substitutes.* Intl. Res. Ctr. Energy 1990 $24.00. ISBN 0-918714-16-8. Excellent, succinct discussion of prices, production, and demand of the world oil market from 1973 to 1988. Reviews alternative fuels and demand responses in the industrial countries, by fuel and by economic sector; accessible to the general reader, with most industry terms self-explanatory or explained in footnotes.

Pachauri, R. K. *The Political Economy of Global Energy.* Johns Hopkins 1985 $12.95. ISBN 0-8018-2469-9. Historical analysis of the world oil market through the oil-crisis period, with economic projections over the next several decades with OPEC. Covers influences of oil revenues on the world economy and on developing countries; requires some knowledge of economic theory but accessible to the general reader.

Sampson, Anthony. *The Seven Sisters.* Bantam 1976 o.p. Refers to the major multinational oil companies—Exxon, Mobil, Shell, BP, Texaco, Standard, and Gulf. A bestseller written by a British journalist.

Shojai, Siamack, and Bernard S. Katz, eds. *The Oil Markets in the 1980s: A Decade of Decline.* Greenwood 1992 $55.00. ISBN 0-275-93380-6. Collection of economic essays covering the oil-crisis/oil-glut period, describing the dynamics of OPEC and other oil-exporting countries. Examines inflationary and depression pressures on the general economics and fiscal pressures on governments of oil-exporting and oil-importing groups. Discusses the inevitable political tensions that accompany such economic forces; somewhat detailed for the general reader but includes useful economic concepts and a wealth of information.

Turner, Louis. *Oil Companies in the International System.* Allen & Unwin 1983 o.p. Similar in scope to Anthony Sampson's book but comes to a different conclusion: despite their size and notoriety, the multinational oil companies have been relatively unimportant players in international politics.

Valencia, Mark J. *South East Asian Seas: Oil under Troubled Waters.* OUP 1986 $24.95. ISBN 0-19-582645-0. Excellent brief history of oil resources and international relations in such disputed areas as the Gulf of Tonkin, the South China Sea, and the Gulf of Thailand.

Van der Linde, Coby. *Dynamic International Oil Markets: Oil Market Developments and Structure, 1860–1990.* Kluwer Ac. 1991 $94.00. ISBN 0-7923-1478-6. Valuable perspective of dynamic phases or cycles to describe evolving markets. Designed for economists and market analysts, but general readers will find the statistics and trends informative.

Woodward, Kim. *The International Energy Relations of China.* Stanford U. Pr. 1980 $77.50. ISBN 0-8047-1008-2. Despite its considerable length, strongly recommended as a starting point for studying energy issues in China. Examines energy problems in the context of China's relationships with the former Soviet Union, Japan, and the West and discusses the ongoing modernization process; includes nearly 100 tables in a comprehensive statistical profile.

World Bank Staff. *Energy Transition in Developing Countries.* World Bank 1983 o.p. The two oil price increases of the 1970s were particularly hard on developing countries, many of which had to borrow from American and European banks to finance the additional costs of oil. Thus the already widespread problems of developing country debt were intensified. An excellent overview of the energy problems of developing countries and how the international financial institutions can remedy these problems.

THE ENERGY POLICY OF THE UNITED STATES

Energy policy as a national concern has existed only since the oil crisis of the 1970s. Policy directions have shifted widely from interventionist to laissez faire and back again. The debate on energy policy has focused almost exclusively on the fossil fuels (oil, natural gas, and coal), because they are the major fuel sources for industrial society and are finite. During the oil crisis period of the 1970s, energy conservation and energy efficiency entered the debate. Recently, concerns about environment and climate change have arisen, along with the large-scale use of alternatives to fossil fuels.

The following references cover the last two decades, illustrating shifts of energy policy. The reader will find proceedings of congressional hearings and *The Congressional Quarterly* (both available from the U.S. Government Printing Office) a useful way to keep informed of current issues. The publications or advertisements of the various interest groups (e.g., industry representatives or environmental/public interest groups) also are good indicators of current energy issues. One notable such publication is *State of the World*, an annual review of environmental, climate, and related issues published by the World Watch Institute, an advocacy group.

Byrne, John, and Daniel Rich, eds. *The Politics of Energy Research and Development.* Transaction Pubs. 1986 $18.95. ISBN 0-88738-653-9. Collection of papers that describe how decisions are made to fund research and development in particular energy technologies and the impact of this process on the energy system.

Energy Policy Project Staff. *A Time to Choose: America's Energy Future*. Harper Busn. 1974 $12.95. ISBN 0-88410-024-3. Published soon after the first oil embargo, this well-known and widely cited study argues the need for an energy policy. Examines the choices that must be made, particularly with respect to changing the rate of growth of overall energy consumption through energy efficiency measures.

Gever, John, Robert Kaufmann, and David Skole. *Beyond Oil: The Threat to Food and Fuel in the Coming Decades*. Harper Busn. 1986 $34.95. ISBN 0-88730-074-X. Examines the prospects of finite natural resources if current patterns of consumption, population growth, and resource policies continue. Shows possible variations on the classic (bell-shaped) production curves for finite resources, such as fossil fuels, using a computer model of the United States economy. Discusses policy choices in plain, stark terms.

Goldenberg, José. *Energy for a Sustainable World*. World Resources Inst. 1987 $10.00. ISBN 0-915825-21-X. Brief analysis of the world energy situation in the late 1980s, including the insecurity of the world oil market, the dangers of nuclear weapons proliferation, and the future of world energy consumption. Emphasizes the role of structure shifts in the various economic sectors, impacts on energy consumption and energy efficiency in consumption.

Grubb, Michael. *Emerging Energy Technologies: Impacts and Policy Implications*. Ashgate Pub. Co. 1992 $54.95. ISBN 1-85521-180-7. Reviews historic patterns of energy production and use, as well as prospective alternatives; demand-side technologies, such as automobile efficiency, electrical appliance and lighting efficiencies, and energy management in buildings; supply-side technologies, including new gas turbines, "clean coal" techniques, wind-power generation, and solar cells; future impacts and energy policy questions.

Intergovernmental Panel on Climate Change. *Climate Change: The IPCC Response Strategies*. Island Pr. 1991 $60.00. ISBN 1-55963-103-1. The uncertain prospects for climate change caused by the effects of "greenhouse" gases, such as carbon dioxide, sulfur dioxide, and various nitrogen oxides. Based on scientific data collected in a companion report; accessible to the general reader.

Landsberg, Hans, ed. *Energy: The Next Twenty Years*. Harper Busn. 1979 $16.95. ISBN 0-88410-094-4. Thorough discussion of future energy resources and technologies from a late-1970s perspective; emphasizes oil and other fossil fuels.

Lee, Thomas H. *Energy Aftermath: How We Can Learn from the Past to Create a Hopeful Energy Future*. Harvard Business Sch. 1990 o.p. Critical review of energy choices made (beginning in the 1970s) by government and industry regarding resources, supply, usage, and consumption; concise review of energy markets (mostly oil) over the past two decades and the alternatives to conventional fuels. Describes ideal "integrated" energy systems, which are clean, secure, reliable, safe, economical, and "robust."

National Academy of Sciences. *Policy Implications of Greenhouse Warming*. Natl. Acad. Pr. 1991 $14.95. ISBN 0-309-04440-5. The Academy's recommendation for mitigation of greenhouse gas emissions, achieved through energy management in the industrial, transportation, residential, and commercial sectors of the national economy; includes appendix defining scientific terms and phenomena related to greenhouse warming.

Rosen, Louis, and Robert Glasser, eds. *Climate Change and Energy Policy*. Am. Inst. Physics 1992 $55.00. ISBN 1-56396-017-6. Proceedings of a conference sponsored by the United States Department of Energy (National Laboratories) in which various authors and panels of scientists discuss the variables that might be associated with climate change; includes technological prospects for mitigation of potential climate change.

Schmidheiny, Stephan. *Changing Course: A Global Business Perspective on Development and Environment*. MIT 1992 $35.00. ISBN 0-262-69153-1. Proposals for sustainable and environmentally sound energy policies from a business perspective. Discusses markets, regulation, investments, international debt, and new technologies.

Schurr, Sam, and others. *Energy in America's Future: The Choices before Us. Resources for the Future Ser.* Johns Hopkins 1979 $20.00. ISBN 0-8018-2281-5. Outstanding analysis of the economic and political ramifications of using finite, insecure, and increasingly expensive energy resources; written from a late-1970s perspective.

Stern, Paul C., Daniel Druckman, and Oran R. Young, eds. *Global Environmental Change: The Human Dimensions.* Natl. Acad. Pr. 1991 $29.95. ISBN 0-309-04494-4. Introduces inquiry into the human causes and human consequences of global environmental change. Cites behavioral causes, including population growth, economic growth, and technological change; possible human responses, based on individual perceptions and group reactions related to market, social, and political systems.

Stobaugh, Robert, and Daniel Yergin, eds. *Energy Future.* Random 1983 $6.95. ISBN 0-394-71063-0. Widely publicized report of the Energy Project at the Harvard Business School. Argues for greater emphasis on conservation and low-technology solar power.

ENERGY ECONOMICS

Energy economics is tied inextricably to the availability of energy resources, as illustrated by the geopolitics of oil. Today, fossil-fuel (oil, coal, and natural gas) energy accounts for more than 85 percent of primary energy usage in the United States. Because these fuels are economic commodities, their prices obey the classic laws of supply and demand. Unlike other commodities, such as food and clothing, fossil-fuel prices are governed by special economic pressures because they are *exhaustible*, or finite, resources. Consequently, their depletion ultimately will make them more costly. The scarcity-induced energy price rises of the 1970s have induced a reduction in consumption (at least for a period). Reduced consumption, however, was achieved not simply by "doing without" (e.g., turning down the thermostat), but mainly through "technical efficiency" improvements (e.g., improved auto gas mileage), as advocated in the seminal *Time to Choose.* Energy conservation has been achieved also by supplementing fossil fuels or electricity with solar heat or solar-cell electricity.

The energy sector of the industrial and developing countries has been the subject of extensive study by economists since the 1970s. An impressive literature in energy economics has developed, including the work of eminent economists, such as MORRIS A. ADELMAN, and the *Energy Journal* (published by the International Association of Energy Economists).

Because of rising energy costs, the consumption of fuels and electricity growth declined dramatically in the United States during the oil-crisis period. From 1972 to 1981, industrial energy use fell by about 6 percent, whereas production in paper, aluminum, steel, and cement increased by 13 percent, implying that the energy intensity of these basic materials fell by more than 15 percent. Similar reductions were made in transportation fuels (as evidenced by the increasing fleet average miles per gallon) and in the household sector. Yet the United States still has a long way to go: for example, estimates suggest that homes in Sweden have, on average, twice the insulation values of homes in northern Minnesota.

Adelman, M. A. *The World Petroleum Market. Resources for the Future Ser.* Johns Hopkins 1973 $37.00. ISBN 0-8018-1422-7. Classic exposition of the industry written before the subject became a public issue. Contains excellent analyses of the evolution of the world market since World War II.

Adelman, M. A., G. A. Kaufman, and Martin B. Zimmerman. *Energy Resources in an Uncertain Future: Coal, Gas, Oil and Uranium Forecasting.* Harper Busn. 1983 $45.00. ISBN 0-88410-644-6. Economic theory of the exploration of exhaustible resources; estimation of fossil and mineral reserves; models of discovery of resources; examples from the United States and world resources; also discusses uncertainties related to estimation of fossil fuels and uranium.

Beckman, William A., S. A. Klein, and J. A. Duffie. *Solar Heating Design: By the f-Chart Method.* Wiley 1977 o.p. A classic for the solar enthusiast: a step-by-step guide to determine the size of home hot-water or space-heating solar collector systems of the flat-plate type; based on sophisticated thermal-engineering calculations described in another book by Duffie and Beckman. Discusses heat load, regional location, and local siting for determining the collector size, collector orientation, hot-water storage capacity, back-up heater, and optimum capacity to serve the daily hot-water or space-heating needs of a home.

Davidson, A., and others. *Natural Gas: Governments and Oil Companies in the Third World.* PennWell Bks. 1988 $59.95. ISBN 0-19-730008-1. Economic analysis of natural gas resources in developing countries. Covers planning and coordination with host governments and relationships to the world oil markets.

Dick-Larkham, Richard. *Cutting Energy Costs.* Beekman Pubs. 1977 $24.95. ISBN 0-8464-0309-9. Describes how to save energy and reduce energy costs in agriculture; includes energy-saving ideas for berry growers and/or the manufacturer of farm alcohol and gas from grain.

Kohl, Wilfrid L. *After the Oil Price Collapse: OPEC, the United States and the World Oil Market.* Johns Hopkins 1991 $39.95. ISBN 0-8018-4097-X. Collection of economic essays focusing on the market economics of oil as an exhaustible resource. Discusses price and supply dynamics within OPEC and other oil-exporting countries; the economics of oil exploration and well production, as well as the refining, marketing, and transportation "downstream." Written mainly for economists, but not theoretical or mathematical. Also examines national policy related to security, foreign policy, and economic impacts.

MacAvoy, Paul W. *Energy Policy: An Economic Analysis.* Norton 1983 $4.95. ISBN 0-393-95321-1. Excellent objective presentation of pricing, taxation, and regulation of oil, gas, and electricity.

Merklein, Helmut A., and W. Carey Hardy. *Energy Economics.* Gulf Pub. 1977 o.p. Excellent introduction to the subject; accessible to the general reader.

Munasinghe, Mohan. *Energy Analysis and Policy.* Buttrwrth-Heinemann 1990 $105.00. ISBN 0-408-05634-7. Treatise on energy economics and planning for developing countries and in-depth analysis of the particular difficulties of oil-importing developing countries. Although written primarily for economists and planners, the book enables general readers to understand planning in developing countries, especially as it relates to the demand for energy.

Nivola, Pietro S. *The Politics of Energy Conservation.* Brookings 1986 $32.95. ISBN 0-8157-6088-4. Examines the role of Washington politics, special interest groups, and public opinion in shaping Congressional voting patterns that led to compromises delaying an effective conservation response to the oil price shocks of the 1970s.

Office of Technology Assessment. *Residential Energy Conservation.* Rowman 1980 o.p. Comprehensive discussion of energy conservation options in the household sector; by a technically well-respected office of the government.

Reay, David A. *Industrial Energy Conservation: A Handbook for Engineers and Managers.* Pergamon 1979 o.p. Technically advanced book that examines the conservation potential in specific industry groups that are especially energy intensive—iron and steel, aluminum, chemicals, pulp and paper, glass, food processing, and textiles.

Strong, Steven J., with W. G. Scheller. *The Solar Electric House: A Design Manual for Home-Scale Photovoltaic Power Systems.* Rodale Pr. Inc. 1987 o.p. Discusses the steps required to supply and conserve electricity in the home. Describes necessary equipment and steps to determine the number of solar cells needed to supplement utility electricity or for "stand-alone" operation; includes a brief history and operating principles for semiconductor photovoltaic cells.

Thumann, Albert. *Plant Engineers' and Managers' Guide to Energy Conservation: The Role of the Energy Manager.* P-H 1982 $89.33. ISBN 0-13-689639-1. Comprehensive, easy-to-read guide to reducing energy costs in existing facilities and new plants. Designed for a technical audience, but accessible to lay persons with a knowledge of freshman physics and math.

Tussing, Arlon R., and Connie Barlow. *The Natural Gas Industry: Evolution, Structure, and Economics*. Harper Busn. 1984 $34.95. ISBN 0-88410-975-5. Good presentation of the history of the natural gas industry in the United States. Describes the role of federal government regulation of interstate pipelines.

Verleger, Phillip K., Jr. *Oil Markets in Turmoil: An Economic Analysis*. Harper Busn. 1982 $35.00. ISBN 0-88410-867-8. Analyzes the international oil market in the 1970s and makes an excellent companion to Adelman's book.

Webb, Michael G., and Martin J. Ricketts. *The Economics of Energy*. Halsted Pr. 1981 o.p. A more advanced text than Merklein and Hardy; includes a particularly good discussion of energy tax policy.

COAL, OIL, AND GAS

The development of modern industrial nations and the rapid growth in prosperity of the Western nations in the first half of the twentieth century resulted from the availability of apparently limitless amounts of cheap oil. Even after the 1970s, it has remained clear that the energy needs of industrialized and developing economies will depend on fossil fuels for several decades to come. Indeed, until the oil embargo of 1973 and 1974, the finite nature of the world's oil resources had attracted little attention outside the oil industry. This section includes titles that focus on the physical and technical issues: where and how to find oil, the transformation of crude oil to useful products (petroleum refining), and the operation of world oil markets.

For geological reasons, natural gas usually is found in the same places as oil, and most oil fields produce so-called associated gas; yet, until recently, very little exploration effort was directed explicitly to natural gas fields. Moreover, for many of the oil-producing developing countries, finding a use for indigenous natural gas is a problem because these countries lack the large residential and commercial markets that account for most natural gas consumption in the United States and Europe. Consequently, much natural gas in Nigeria and the Middle East simply is flared (i.e., burned off at the well site) because the development of industries that can use gas (fertilizers, steel manufacture, and so forth) has lagged. Algeria and Russia have benefited from the proximity of markets in Europe that can be reached by pipeline, and Indonesia exports gas in liquefied form to Japan.

Two leading periodicals that cover natural gas are *The Petroleum Economist*, published in the United Kingdom (Box 105, 107 Charterhouse St., London EC1M 6AY), with good coverage of oil and gas economics and policy issues, and *The Oil and Gas Journal*, published by PennWell (Tulsa, Oklahoma), with coverage of policy issues, drilling/production, exploration, transportation, and refining.

Gary, James H., and Glenn E. Handwerk. *Petroleum Refining: Technology and Economics*. Dekker 1975 o.p. Useful for those who have mastered the material in Leffler's book and who require greater engineering detail.

Herbert, John H. *Clean Cheap Heat: The Development of Residential Markets for Natural Gas in the United States*. Greenwood 1992 $42.95. ISBN 0-275-94204-X. The history of natural gas use in United States markets, regulation, and resource dynamics from the early twentieth century to the present. The early relationship to manufactured gas is especially interesting in view of the revived interest in "synthetic" gas (derived from coal or biomass).

Leffler, William L. *Petroleum Refining for the Nontechnical Person.* PennWell Bks. 1985 $54.95. ISBN 0-87814-280-0. Petroleum refining, in which crude oil is converted into such familiar products as gasoline and jet fuel, is a highly complex technology. Most books on the subject are filled with technical jargon familiar only to experts and petroleum engineers, but this book is highly recommended as an introduction.

Link, Peter K. *Basic Petroleum Geology.* Oil & Gas 1987 $40.00. ISBN 0-930972-10-4. More comprehensive treatment of oil exploration than Welker (1985), covering basic geology, oil basin and reservoir formations, engineering aspects of exploration, and recovery; includes fundamentals for laypersons and nonspecialists.

Megill, Robert E. *An Introduction to Exploration Economics.* PennWell Bks. 1988 $64.95. ISBN 0-87814-331-9. Written for those "who know little about the subject and have forgotten most of their college math." An excellent introduction to the methods used in the industry to evaluate potential oil fields.

Welker, Anthony J. *The Oil and Gas Book.* PennWell Bks. 1985 $32.95. ISBN 0-87814-279-7. Describes the exploration, drilling, and production of natural gas and oil, which "provides three-fourths of the energy consumed in the U.S." Contains many illustrative and often amusing figures about deposits and wells; accessible to the general reader.

Wijetilleke, Lakdasa, and Anthony J. Ody. *The World Refinery Industry: Need for Restructuring.* World Bank 1985 o.p. Review of world petroleum supply and demand and the consequences of the worldwide refining industry. Requires only a basic knowledge of economics and science.

Wilson, Carroll L., ed. *Coal-Bridge to the Future.* Harper Busn. 1980 $29.95. ISBN 0-88410-099-5. Report of the World Coal Study, an international project involving 16 major coal-producing and consuming countries; concludes that coal will have to supply between one-half and two-thirds of the additional energy needed by the world through the year 2000. Controversial, reflecting the bias of coal proponents.

ELECTRIC POWER INDUSTRY

A dramatic transformation has occurred in the electric power industry over the past decade. There has been a drop in the rate of growth of electricity consumption; cancellation of new nuclear plants; and a rise of independent (nonutility) power producers, all of which has changed the structure of the once glacially staid electric power industry. The slowing of growth resulted from higher prices for electricity and other forms of energy. Nuclear power plant construction ceased in the United States over a decade ago and slowed elsewhere, because of cost escalation and safety concerns. The shocking aftermath of the Chernobyl accident and the current uncertainties regarding radioactive waste disposal have dimmed prospects for implementing nuclear (fission) technology in the foreseeable future.

Meanwhile, new electric-generation plants have been constructed throughout the United States and other industrial countries, operated by independent power producers. These enterprises were aided in the United States by the Public Utilities Regulatory Policies Act (PURPA) of 1978, which required utilities to purchase electric power from independent producers at "avoided" costs. The electric-generation business has prospered with co-generation (see references below) and mini hydro but now seems ready to expand into wind and solar generation (see the section on renewables). Recent unrest in the industry has developed over the rights of independent power producers to use the transmission lines of the utilities, so that their sales can be made to remote customer loads. To keep informed of these changes, the reader should consult the *IEEE Power Engineering Review*, which reprints articles from its parent

IEEE (Institute of Electrical and Electronic Engineers), as well as from a variety of other soures.

Burns, Grant. *The Atomic Papers: A Citizen's Guide to Selected Books and Articles.* Scarecrow 1984 $27.50. ISBN 0-8108-1692-X. Mainly covers nuclear weapons but also examines nuclear power during its peak years (1950–80). Provides a well-balanced perspective on the issue of nuclear power.

Butler, Charles H. *Cogeneration: Engineering, Design, Financing and Regulatory Compliance.* McGraw 1984 o.p. Comprehensive survey of cogeneration. Written for the engineer and entrepreneur, but the general reader will find the photographs, cutaway drawings, and diagrams informative.

Collier, J. G., and G. F. Hewitt. *Introduction to Nuclear Power.* Hemisphere Pub. 1987 $65.00. ISBN 0-89116-269-0. Nuclear fission technology for the nonspecialist; includes physical principles, workings of nuclear reactors, emergency safety systems, and high-level waste disposal.

Devine, Michael D. *Cogeneration and Decentralized Electricity Production: Technology Economics and Policy.* Westview 1987 o.p. Reviews nonutility power production, using a variety of technologies, including cogeneration, waste to energy, small hydropower, and wind power. Generally emphasizes policies that promote decentralized (dispersed, small power plants) electric generation; accessible to the general reader.

International Atomic Energy Agency Publications Catalog. UNIPUB 1985 o.p. Annotated catalog of hundreds of reports on nuclear power; prepared for and by this agency of the United Nations.

Katz, James E., and Onkar S. Marwah. *Nuclear Power in Developing Countries: An Analysis of Decision Making.* Lexington Bks. 1982 o.p. Examines the increasingly controversial subject of nuclear power commercialization in developing countries and the possible relationship to weapons proliferation. Describes the nuclear programs of 15 countries, including China, India, Pakistan, Iran, and Egypt.

Keeny, Spurgeon M., Jr. *Nuclear Power Issues and Choices.* Harper Busn. 1977 $19.95. ISBN 0-88410-065-0. Report of a major and well-known study sponsored by the Ford Foundation identifies and discusses the issues underlying the debate on nuclear power at home and abroad.

Medvedev, Grigori. *The Truth about Chernobyl.* Basic 1992 $12.00. ISBN 0-465-08776-0. Describes the nuclear accident at Chernobyl in 1986 and its aftermath; includes an extensive collection of graphic photographs.

Morone, Joseph G., and Edward J. Woodhouse. *The Demise of American Nuclear Power: Learning from the Failure of a Politically Unsafe Technology.* Yale U. Pr. 1989 $25.00. ISBN 0-300-04448-8. Treats the problems of nuclear power as a failure of institutions—the industry, the technologists, and the government; interesting and thought-provoking reading.

Mould, Richaiel. *Chernobyl: The Real Story.* Franklin 1988. ISBN 0-08-035718-0. Detailed description of the 1986 Chernobyl nuclear accident. Written by a former member of the Soviet nuclear establishment with a thorough knowledge of nuclear technology and administration in the former Soviet Union.

New Electric Power Technologies: Problems and Prospects for the 1990's. Gordon Pr. 1991 $79.95. ISBN 0-8490-4975-X. Comprehensive presentation of the financial problems of electric utilities, the forces that are leading them to explore new technologies, and specific prospects for the new technologies; strongly recommended as a starting point for research on the future of the electric power industry.

Nuclear Power: Technical and Institutional Options for Health, Safety, and the Environment. Natl. Acad. Pr. 1992 $27.00. ISBN 0-309-04395-6. Examines the status of nuclear power in the United States, as required by Congress in 1989. Covers construction costs, plant performances, public attitudes, operational safety, and institutional aspects of the nuclear industry. Also reviews trends in electricity demand nationwide and prospects for meeting rising demand, in view of a slower rate of demand growth and the contribution of nonutility generation. Discusses the prospects for safe nuclear reactors and for the safe disposal of nuclear waste.

Nuclear Power in an Age of Uncertainty. Gordon Pr. 1984 o.p. The dramatic decline in electricity growth is a main reason for the many cancellations of nuclear power plants in the last 10 years. For example, in 1974 the projected peak power demand for 1984 (estimated by the North American Reliability Council) was over 750 gigawatts: the actual demand was 425 gigawatts. Examines this and other uncertainties facing the nuclear power industry in the United States.

Payne, F. William. *Cogeneration Sourcebook.* Fairmount Pr. 1985 o.p. Comprehensive introduction to cogeneration. Updates the industry and its benefits; evaluates the regulatory benefits; provides a nontechnical view of the operation of commercial and light-industrial systems. Intended for individuals seriously interested in the cogeneration industry.

RENEWABLE ENERGY TECHNOLOGIES

Over the past decade a new perspective has evolved regarding the renewable technologies. Throughout the oil crisis period the rationale for using solar, wind, or hydro energy was to replace the finite and insecure petroleum fuels. Cost also was a major factor. During the peak of the oil-crisis period, oil prices affected the prices of other fossil fuels, including natural gas and coal, that can be substituted for oil in many applications. In order for renewable energy to become competitive with fossil-fuel energy in the energy market, the cost had to be reduced. This did not happen during the 1970s or 1980s, except for a revival of local hydrogeneration. Solar and wind power remains expensive compared to fossil fuel. In the early 1980s the sharp drop in oil prices undercut any prospects for these renewable technologies to compete with oil in the energy marketplace.

Another rationale for using renewable technologies is to protect environmental quality and preserve the global climate. In the United States, local air pollution has reached the acute stage in southern California and in many other metropolitan areas in the Midwest and Northeast. Global climate change now is deemed, by consensus of many scientists, to be a possibility. Thus, there is an even greater need to substitute for fossil fuels today. Society might find itself willing to pay for clean energy technologies that do not emit greenhouse gases, such as carbon dioxide. This evolving perspective, combined with technological gains in renewable energy, might revive alternatives to fossil fuels, including solar cells, solar heat collection, wind generation, and biomass-based fuels (e.g., methane and alcohols). Biomass resources include wood, energy crops, and organic wastes, which complete the carbon cycle by fixing as much carbon dioxide in growth as is emitted from combustion.

The following represent merely a selection of many books that have been published recently on renewable or "sustainable" energy technologies.

Anderson, Bruce, ed. *Solar Building Architecture.* MIT Pr. 1990 $45.00. ISBN 0-262-01111-5. Argues for "passive-solar" design, which does not require "active" systems to control, transport, or distribute the collected energy. An excellent review of the evolution and architectural concepts of solar design, plus social and political influences. Also covers the necessary architectural features for solar enhancement (e.g., exteriors, interiors, thermal storage, and heat distribution); includes designs for commercial buildings and homes.

Blackburn, John O. *The Renewable Energy Alternative: How the United States and the World Can Prosper without Nuclear Energy or Coal.* Duke 1987 $37.50. ISBN 0-8223-0687-5. Advocates a switch of energy sources for the United States from fossil and nuclear to renewable energy, such as solar, wind, and biomass. Describes the problems related to fossil and nuclear fuels and anticipates much of the criticism directed against renewables; presentation is entertaining but general.

Gordon, Deborah. *Steering a New Course: Transportation, Energy and the Environment.* Island Pr. 1991 $19.95. ISBN 1-55963-134-1. Advocates major changes in the use of energy by motor vehicles. Reviews the transportation sector in the United States and Europe, summarizing environmental impacts in a compact, comprehensive manner. Proposes alternatives to petroleum-based combustive fuels, including natural gas, alcohols, and hydrogen. Discusses alternative automotive technologies, such as electric vehicles powered by batteries or fuel cells. Identifies advantages and disadvantages of these alternatives, as well as barriers to widespread adoption.

Hollander, Jack M., ed. *The Energy-Environment Connection.* Island Pr. 1992 $48.00. ISBN 1-55963-119-8. Collection of essays assessing the many connections between energy production/consumption and the environment. Focuses on emission of greenhouse gases, such as carbon dioxide, which have the potential to cause worldwide climate changes. Also discusses air pollution and acid rain in light of the various Clean Air Act amendments since 1969. Covers benefits of energy efficiency and speculates about the future, with a vision of a "sustainable world" by William D. Ruckelshaus.

Intergovernmental Panel on Climate Change. *Climate Change: The IPCC Scientific Assessment.* AGPS 1991 $24.95. ISBN 0-644-13497-6. Collection of scientific conclusions reached by international scientists on the history of global temperature changes, the effects of carbon dioxide and other greenhouse gases, climate responses to gases, results of climate models for prediction of changes, and an analysis of global temperatures and atmospheric composition. The companion volume to the IPCC Response Strategies listed in the Energy Policy section.

Johansson, Thomas B., and others, eds. *Renewable Energy: Sources for Fuels and Electricity.* Island Pr. 1992 $85.00. ISBN 1-55963-139-2. Major collection of papers by experts in the renewable energy technologies, including hydropower, wind energy, solar-thermal power, solar photovoltaic electricity, geothermal power, biomass fuels, and solar hydrogen. Compiled for the United Nations Conference on Environment and Development (UNCED) held in Rio de Janeiro (1992), which promoted the theme of "sustainable development." Provides a wealth of information on the feasibility of these new technologies and how long it will take for them to become competitive with fossil fuel-based technologies; some of the detailed data might be meaningful only to specialists.

Keisling, Bill. *The Homeowner's Handbook of Solar Water Heating Systems.* Rodale Pr. Inc. 1983 $16.95. "Covers systems over a broad range of complexity, from the most simple to those [that] require professional handling. Includes tables and formulas for determining system requirements as well as plans for different types of heaters" (*Library Journal*).

Kreider, Jan F., and Frank Kreith, eds. *Solar Energy Handbook.* McGraw 1981 o.p. Authoritative compendium for the assessment and design of solar systems.

Lovins, Amory B. *Soft Energy Paths: Toward a Durable Peace.* HarpC 1979 repr. of 1977 ed. $4.95. ISBN 0-06-090653-7. Argues for a so-called soft energy strategy that emphasizes conservation and small-scale decentralized technology rather than one based on large-scale, centralized technology, especially nuclear power. Dismissed by some as an amateur, Lovins had a profound influence on the energy policy of the Carter administration.

MacKenzie, James J., and Mohamed T. El-Ashry. *Air Pollution's Toll on Forests and Crops.* Yale U. Pr. 1992 repr. of 1989 ed. $21.00. ISBN 0-300-05232-4. Documents forest decline and crop damage resulting from acid rain, ozone, and other air pollutants in Europe and North America. Reviews health effects and assesses economic impacts of air pollution; somewhat detailed, but accessible to the general reader.

Maycock, Paul D., and Edward N. Stirewalt. *A Guide to the Photovoltaic Revolution: Sunlight to Electricity in One Step.* Rodale Pr. Inc. 1985 o.p. Promotes the concept of converting sunlight to electricity directly in solar (photovoltaic) cells in an easy-to-read introduction for the general reader; includes a historical perspective and photographs of PV installations.

Ogden, J. M., and R. H. Williams. *Solar Hydrogen: Moving beyond Fossil Fuels*. World Resources Inst. 1989 $10.00. ISBN 0-915825-38-4. Argues for the use of ultraclean fuel: solar-generated hydrogen. Describes solar cell conversion and electrolytic separation of hydrogen from water. Optimistic forecasts of costs and feasibility.

Ross, D. *Energy from the Waves*. Pergamon 1981 o.p. The first book entirely devoted to wave energy; written for the general reader.

Sperling, Daniel. *New Transportation Fuels: A Strategic Approach to Technological Change*. U. CA Pr. 1988 $19.00. ISBN 0-520-06977-3. Proposes alternative transportation fuels (mostly liquids), such as biomass-derived alcohols and methane, and alternative fossil resources, including natural gas, methanol, and solar-derived hydrogen. Analyzes costs (processing and feedstocks) and describes automotive technologies (e.g., fuel cell and battery electric vehicles). Also covers fuel markets, impacts on air quality, and energy policy options.

White, L. P., and L. G. Plaskett. *Biomass as Fuel*. Acad. Pr. 1982 $86.50. ISBN 0-12-746980-X. Examines the technical and economic considerations of using crop, animal, wood, and municipal wastes as energy sources and the prospects for tree farming, aquaculture, and marine harvesting; includes an excellent bibliography.

CHRONOLOGY OF AUTHORS

Adelman, Morris A. 1917–
Rose, David J. 1922–1985
Duffie, John A. 1925–
Boer, Karl W. 1926–

Holdren, John P. 1944–
Munasinghe, Mohan. 1945–
Yergin, Daniel. 1947–

ADELMAN, MORRIS A. 1917–

Born in New York City, Morris A. Adelman is a renowned energy economist. He earned a B.S. degree from the City College of New York and a Ph.D. in economics from Harvard University in 1948. Since 1948, Adelman has been affiliated with the Massachusetts Institute of Technology as a professor of economics, now emeritus. He was a cofounder of the International Association of Energy Economists (IAEE) and became the organization's third president in 1981. In 1982 he received the IAEE award for outstanding contributions to the profession. His research publications on the political economy of oil date from 1970, covering exploration economics, oil import quotas, the OPEC cartel, international oil agreements, world oil prices, and oil supply modeling.

Books by Adelman

The Supply and Price of Natural Gas. Rothman 1962 o.p. Interesting look at the economics of the natural gas market.

The World Petroleum Market. Bks. Demand repr. of 1972 ed. $123.70. ISBN 0-7837-2179-X. Analysis of the world oil market, focusing on OPEC and other major producers.

BOER, KARL W. 1926–

Karl Boer was born and educated in Germany, where he was a member of the faculty at Humboldt University in Berlin. He left Germany in 1961, when the Berlin Wall was being erected. Since 1962, he has been at the University of Delaware, where he is professor of physics and engineering. He founded the Institute of Energy Conversion there in 1971. From 1972 until 1979, he was chairman of the board of SES, Inc., a subsidiary of Shell Oil Company, and he is a fellow of the American Physical Society. In his honor, the University of Delaware created the Karl W. Boer Solar Energy Award. The first recipient was former President Jimmy Carter, who accepted the award in February 1993.

Boer has made significant contributions to energy research on solar (photovoltaic) cells. Since 1970 he has published more than 290 research articles on solid state physics, including 80 on photovoltaic cells. He is a cofounder of *Physics Status Solidi* (a journal on solid state physics research) and is currently editor-in-chief of the authoritative series *Advances in Solar Energy*.

Boer's articles on solar energy cover the semiconductor physics of solar cells, the solar spectrum, and demonstrations of solar-system operation. He holds 28 patents in solid state and solar devices.

BOOK BY BOER

Survey of Semiconductor Physics. Van Nos. Reinhold 1992 $79.95. ISBN 0-442-00672-1

DUFFIE, JOHN A. 1925–

A leading authority on solar-heat collector technology, John A. Duffie is professor emeritus in the Chemical Engineering Department at the University of Wisconsin and is a fellow of the American Institute of Chemical Engineers. He has published more than 60 research papers, contributed to many symposia on solar systems, and is a former president of the International Solar Energy Society (ISES). He is coauthor of several widely used books on solar heat systems and thermal engineering and has been editor-in-chief of the respected *Journal of Solar Energy* since 1985.

In 1948, Duffie received an M.A. in chemical engineering from Rensselaer Polytechnic Institute and a Ph.D. in chemical engineering from the University of Wisconsin in 1951. In 1977, he visited Australia as a Fulbright-Hayes Scholar.

In 1983, Duffie's Solar Energy Laboratory, at the University of Wisconsin, received the first Achievement through Action Award from ISES, and in 1987, ISES awarded Duffie the Farrington Daniels Award.

BOOKS BY DUFFIE

Solar Energy Research. (coedited with F. Daniels). Bks. Demand repr. of 1961 ed. $76.50. ISBN 0-317-10982-0
Solar Energy Thermal Processes. (coauthored with W. A. Beckman). Wiley 1974 o.p.
Solar Engineering of Thermal Processes. (coauthored with W. A. Beckman). Wiley 1991 $64.95. ISBN 0-471-51056-4
Solar Heat in Design by the f-Chart Method. (coauthored with W. A. Beckman and S. A. Klein). Wiley 1977 o.p.

HOLDREN, JOHN P. 1944–

A leading energy-policy scholar, John P. Holdren is professor of energy and resources at the University of California, Berkeley, and chair of the technical division of the energy and resources research group. In 1970, Holdren received a Ph.D. in aeronautics/astronautics and plasma physics from Stanford University. He has written nearly 200 research publications on plasma physics, fusion-reactor technology, energy options for developing countries, population growth, and international security. He has made significant contributions in safe nuclear fusion reactor design, assessment of nuclear fission technology, environmental risk assessment, and the interrelations between environment, economic development, and international security. Holdren is a member of the

National Academy of Sciences, American Academy of Arts and Sciences, American Physical Society, and the American Association for the Advancement of Science.

BOOKS BY HOLDREN

Building of Global Security through Cooperation. (coedited with Joseph Rotblat). Spr.-Verlag 1991 $83.00. ISBN 0-387-52813-X. Examines the issue of arms and global security relationships and considers the importance of multinational cooperation.
Earth and the Human Future: Essays in Honour of Harrison Brown. Westview Pr. 1986 o.p. Series of essays assessing the effects of science on the world's future.
Ecoscience, Population, Resources, Environment. (coauthoried with Paul Ehrlich and Anne Ehrlich). W. H. Freeman 1977 o.p.
Global Ecology: Readings Towards a Rational Strategy for Man. (coauthored with Paul Ehrlich). HarBraceJ 1971 o.p. Analyzes environmental risks and poses solutions for ecological problems.
Human Ecology: Problems and Solutions. W. H. Freeman 1973 o.p.
Strategic Defense and the Future of the Arms Race: A Pugwash Symposium. St. Martin 1987 $37.50. ISBN 0-312-00789-2

MUNASINGHE, MOHAN. 1945–

An outstanding authority and author in energy economics and international development, Mohan Munasinghe received his undergraduate education in engineering at Cambridge University and went on to McGill University, receiving a Ph.D. in electrical engineering in 1973. He then turned his attention to economics, receiving an M.A. at Concordia College (Montreal) in 1975. Since that year, he has been division chief for environmental policy at the World Bank in Washington, D.C. His work at the World Bank has related to projects in developing countries concerning energy, electricity, transportation, water, urban infrastructures, and telecommunications. He has been a prolific author, writing nearly 200 technical papers and numerous books and monographs.

In addition, Munasinghe has been active in the affairs of his native country, Sri Lanka, where he has served as senior energy advisor to the president, a board member of the Natural Resources, Energy, and Science Authority, governor of the Arthur Clarke Center for Modern Technologies, and founder of the Energy Managers Association. He is a fellow of the National Academy of Sciences of Sri Lanka, the Institution of Electrical Engineers (UK), and the Institute of Engineers of Sri Lanka. Munasinghe's honors include the Surha Gold Medal, 1985 (Lions International); International Award, 1987 (International Association of Energy Economists); and the Prize for Outstanding Contribution, 1988 (Fifth Latin American and Caribbean Conference on Power and Energy).

BOOKS BY MUNASINGHE

Economics of Power System Reliability and Planning: Theory and Case Study. Johns Hopkins 1980 $14.95. ISBN 0-8018-2277-7
Electricity Pricing. (coauthored with J. J. Warford). Johns Hopkins 1982 $108.00. ISBN 0-7837-4405-6
Energy Analysis and Policy. Buttrwrth-Heinemann 1990 $105.00. ISBN 0-408-05634-7
Energy Economics, Demand Management. Westview 1985 o.p.
Energy Efficiency: Optimization of Electric Power Distribution Losses. (coauthored with W. G. Scott). World Bank 1982 o.p.
Environmental Economics and Sustainable Development. World Bank 1992 $7.95. ISBN 0-8213-2352-0
Rural Electrification for Development: Analysis and Policy Applications. Westview 1987 o.p.

ROSE, DAVID J. 1922–1985

A pioneer researcher in the area of controlled thermonuclear fusion and nuclear waste management, David Rose was a researcher at Bell Laboratories and professor of nuclear engineering at the Massachusetts Institute of Technology.

In 1969 Rose founded and became the first director of the Office of Long Range Planning at the Oak Ridge National Laboratory. Before returning to MIT in 1971, he established the Laboratory's energy division and promoted research in energy conservation and various environmental quality programs. At MIT in the 1970s, Rose conducted research that illuminated the complex relationships between world energy use and global climate. In 1980 MIT rewarded his achievements and distinguished career by presenting him with the James R. Killian, Jr., Faculty Achievement Award. From 1981 until his death, Rose was a senior research fellow at the East-West Center in Honolulu, Hawaii.

BOOKS BY ROSE

Learning about Energy. Plenum Pub. 1986 $75.00. ISBN 0-306-42124-0. Interesting look at various energy sources and their use.

Plasmas and Controlled Fusion. (coauthored with Melville Clarke). MIT Pr. 1961 o.p.

YERGIN, DANIEL. 1947–

Born in Los Angeles, California, Daniel Yergin attended Yale University as an undergraduate and received a Ph.D. in international relations from Cambridge University in England. Regarded as an authority on energy, international politics, and economics, Yergin also is recognized as an outstanding analyst of history, especially related to international strategic politics.

Yergin has written and edited influential books on the past oil-crisis period of the 1970s, and he won the 1992 Pulitzer Prize for general nonfiction with *The Prize* (see below). Yergin founded and is president of Cambridge Energy Research Associates, an international energy consultant firm. He also lectures at Harvard University's School of Business and the Kennedy School of Government.

BOOKS BY YERGIN

The Cold War from Yalta to Peking. Macmillan 1977 o.p.

Energy Future. (coedited with Robert Stobaugh). Random 1983 $6.95. ISBN 0-394-71063-0. Outstanding examination of the oil-crisis period of the 1970s. Discusses fossil fuels and nuclear power and proposes comprehensive energy conservation programs that cover manufacturing, commercial, and transportation sectors of the economy. Also focuses on the political aspects of energy policy; includes a chapter on energy alternatives for the future, focusing on solar and wind power, hydro-power, and biomass fuels.

Global Insecurity: A Strategy for Energy and Economic Renewal. HM 1982 o.p. Interesting look at the effect energy supplies and the search for energy sources have on geopolitics and economics.

The Prize: The Epic Quest For Oil, Money, and Power. S & S Trade 1991 $16.00. ISBN 0-671-79932-0. Examines the history of oil during the twentieth century and the significant influence that the quest for oil has had on world economics and politics; received the 1992 Pulitzer Prize and was made into an eight-hour documentary aired on PBS television.

Shattered Peace: Origins of the Cold War and the National Security State. Viking Penguin 1990 $10.95. ISBN 0-14-012177-3. Traces the history and development of the Cold War and its effects on national economic and political systems.

CHAPTER 11

Communications Technology

William F. Williams and Harold Groff

> A new psychological feature has been introduced into social relationships by the invention of electrical communication.
> —LANCELOT HOGBEN, *Science for the Citizen*

> Speech and writing are . . . systems of communication . . . But life in the modern world is coming to depend more and more upon technical means of communication, telephone and telegraph, radio . . . . Commnications have enabled social units to grow, from village to town . . . until today we are organized systems of mutual dependence grown to cover whole hemispheres. Communications engineers have altered the size and the shape of the world.
> —COLIN CHERRY, *On Human Communication*

When Alexander Graham Bell said in 1878, "I believe in the future . . . [when] a man in one part of the country may communicate with another distant place," he was clearly emphasizing his belief in the importance of the telephone as the focus of communications. In a little over a hundred years, the telephone has become ubiquitous: It is an essential tool in homes, offices, and cars, at sea, on rail, and in the air. Moreover, telephone connections are now made not only by landlines, but also by satellite, radio link, and fiber optics. No technological innovation comes from nowhere, of course. The telephone owed its origin to the telegraph, itself only fifty years older and, giving credit where it is due, the foundation upon which modern electronic communications has been built.

The science of communications (closely allied to the idea of information), which developed from the invention of the telegraph and telephone and originally was directed at perfecting those devices, covers a very broad field and is surveyed in Chapter 17. In this chapter the focus is on communications technology itself.

During the centuries before the telephone and other electronic devices came to occupy their position of importance in the world, many other means of communication were vital to human society. A partial, selective list would include speech and writing; messages carried by runners, riders on animals, and on modes of transportation (boats, trains, cars, planes); hilltop beacons; smoke signals; tom-tom drums; semaphore flags; written messages transmitted by the printing press; and many more. All these methods of communication were put to varied uses, from military and political to commercial and scientific, in addition to their role in social exchange.

As first outlined by CLAUDE SHANNON and Warren Weaver (1948), the technical analysis of the process of communication, by whatever means, includes five elements: (1) an information source of any form (written, verbal, visual, aural); (2) the transmitter or sender; (3) a means of transmission (light, sound, radio waves, etc.); (4) some type of receiver; and (5) a destination. In nontechnologically mediated communication, the first two elements merge into the person communicating, and the last two merge into the person with whom one is communicating. For example, a person speaks through the medium of sound waves in air to another person; both voice box and ear are integral parts of the information source, as well as its destination.

What distinguishes technological, especially electronic, communication, is a separation between the first and last pair of elements. For example, (1) a person speaks into (2) the mouthpiece of a telephone, which converts sound into (3) an electronic signal that travels along a wire to (4) the headpiece of another phone that converts the signal back into sound to be heard by (5) another person. Invention and development in communications technology primarily involves technological transformation in elements (3) through (4).

This transformation has made electronic communications technology the primary focus of modern communications. There is no longer any serious attempt to communicate by means of smoke signals or semaphor and the letter-carrying Postal Service is largely a tradition-bound bureaucratic institution, improved only insofar as it adopts new technologies in transportation and transmission. Any changes in the means of transporting written letters do not, of themselves, affect the communication itself. In electronic communication, however, technological developments, such as the change from telegraph and telephone to radio, TV, and satellite relays (not to mention phonographs, motion pictures, and faxes), are integral to and are themselves influenced by the communication process.

In terms of electronic technologies, the means of transmission can be further divided into two distinct functions: the transmission from one point to another; and the distribution, routing, or switching of the information transmitted. Today's electronic equivalent to the carrying of messages by runners and their distribution by town criers is the transmission of information by microwave relay and its distribution by (electronic) telephone switchboard or TV station. These two functions, transmission and switching, are the focus of major sections of this chapter. Because of the growing importance of using modulated light signals as a means of transmission, fiber optics is the focus of another section. A fourth major section focuses on data communication and the problem of transmitting and switching extremely large volumes of electronic signals, or messages.

During the last fifty years, there has been an enormous expansion and improvement in communications, particularly in the industrialized world. To some extent this has occurred as a result of spin-offs from developments in military communications during and since World War II. For example, telephone, radio, and television have all benefitted from advances in military technology, and they continue to do so. The next generation promises equally phenomenal growth in the developed countries (with the hope that less developed countries will also benefit). Moreover, newer technologies, such as computers, faxes, cellular communications, wireless and fiber optic networks, high-definition television (HDTV), integrated service digital networks (ISDNs), and others yet to be discovered and developed, promise to have a major impact on communications throughout the world. It is precisely the literature on such communications technologies that is given special treatment here.

GENERAL WORKS

The books cited here provide general introductions to communications theory and practice and bridge the more specific categories that follow. These books are of two general types. Some offer the reader a basic understanding of the overall field of communications, its principles, methods, and equipment, past and present. Others provide a more future-oriented survey of the field, although usually with a technical emphasis. Works in the first category are readily understandable by the non-specialist reader; those in the second often require more advanced knowledge or prior familiarity with the field. Among the latter are works that describe the future toward which many present-day communications organizations are striving: an integrated communications system that will give the user access to information from many sources by a variety of means. The proposed merger in 1993 of Bell Atlantic and the cable company TCI (Tele-Communications Incorporated) may be the first step toward that future.

Chorafas, Dimitris N. *Telephony: Today and Tomorrow.* P-H 1984 $33.95. ISBN 0-13-902700-9. A clear, comprehensive introduction to telecommunications, from a general social overview and policy decisions to technical components of contemporary and advanced systems; covers Telcos, voice systems, PBXs, optical fibers, satellite systems, and local and long-haul networks. Excellent introductory text.

Forester, Tom, ed. *The Information Technology Revolution.* MIT Pr. 1985 $42.00. ISBN 0-262-06095-7. Although focused primarily on the computer, this collection of nearly fifty articles with numerous suggestions for further reading provides a helpful introduction to social issues, especially the chapters, "The Telecommunications Explosion," "Banks, Shops, Hospitals," and "Global Issues."

Gurrie, Michael L. *Voice-Data Telecommunications Systems: An Introduction to Technology.* P-H 1986 $52.00. ISBN 0-13-943283-3. General overview of the telecommunications industry, with emphasis on the systems and methods used by business; technicians, communications managers, and other professionals will find this book useful for its real-world applications.

Hambley, Allan R. *An Introduction to Communication Systems.* W. H. Freeman 1990 $54.95. ISBN 0-7167-8184-0. A complete introduction to the major concerns of communications systems engineering suitable for the junior or senior student in electrical engineering. Covers traditional analog communication systems, error control coding, spread-spectrum techniques, and optical fiber systems, but (appropriately enough, given contemporary developments) is concerned chiefly with digital systems.

Hiltz, Starr Roxanne, and Murray Turoff. *The Network Nation: Human Communication Via Computer.* MIT Pr. rev. ed. 1993 $45.00. ISBN 0-262-58120-5. First published in the 1970s, this book is the classic document and reference in the field of computer-mediated communications. Includes selected bibligraphy.

Kamen, Edward W. *Introduction to Signals and Systems.* Macmillan 1989 $59.00. ISBN 0-02-361681-4. An introductory, comprehensive treatment of signals and systems, with a strong emphasis on computers using programs written in BASIC; requires a background in calculus, physics, and elementary differential equations, as well as electrical circuits.

Kuc, Roman. *Introduction to Digital Signal Processing.* McGraw 1988 $48.50. ISBN 0-07-035570-3. Presents the material in a clear and concise manner; richly illustrated with examples and graphic out-puts.

Ludeman, Lonnie C. *Fundamentals of Digital Signal Processing.* Wiley 1986 $61.95. ISBN 0-471-60363-5. Background and fundamental material on discrete-time systems, basic digital processing techniques, design procedures for digital filters, and the discrete Fourier transform; for electrical and computer engineers.

McChesney, Robert W. *Telecommunications, Mass Media, and Democracy.* OUP 1993 $45.00. ISBN 0-19-507174-3. Powerful and controversial work examining the emergence and consolidation of U.S. commercial broadcasting economically, politically, and ideologically. Employs an unprecedented amount of primary documentation.

Marvin, Carolyn. *When Old Technologies Were New: Thinking about Electric Communication in the Late Nineteenth Century.* OUP 1988 $42.50. ISBN 0-19-504468-1. Enlightening introduction to the historical context in which electronic communications technology first developed.

Mirabito, Michael M. *The New Communications Technologies.* Focal Pr. 1989 $28.95. ISBN 0-240-80012-5

Murphy, R. J. *Telecommunications Networks: A Technical Introduction.* Sams 1987 o.p.

O'Reilly, John J. *Telecommunication Principles.* Van Nos. Reinhold 1989 o.p. An introduction to telecommunications suitable for first- and second-year undergraduates pursuing degree or similar courses in electronic engineering; requires few prerequisites other than a general background in electrical circuit principles and a level of mathematical maturity consistent with entry engineering courses in British universities.

Oslin, George P. *The Story of Telecommunications.* Mercer 1993 $35.00. ISBN 0-86554-418-2. A history of the human quest for simpler, faster, and more efficient means of communication. From smoke signals to satellites, from line-of-sight semaphore to lightspeed lasers, and from the cumbersome encoding of words for longline transmission to digital microcomputers, Oslin tells a story not just of machines, but of dreamers and schemers, inventive geniuses and pragmatic planners, and the famous and the not-so-famous. This book is the lifework of Oslin, who for 34 years was director of public relations for Western Union.

Rogers, Everett M. *Communication Technology.* Free Pr. 1986 $29.95. ISBN 0-02-927120-7. A nontechnical introduction; first book in the new series *Communication Technology and Society.*

Schatt, Stanley, and Steven Fox. *Voice/Data Telecommunications for Business.* P-H 1990 $52.00. ISBN 0-13-107889-5. Solid foundation in the basics of voice transmission and data communications that shows how these principles have been incorporated in integrated voice/data products found in many Fortune 500 offices; no technical background necessary.

Singleton, Loy A. *Telecommunications in the Information Age: A Nontechnical Primer on the New Technologies.* Ballinger 1986 $24.95. ISBN 0-8873-0098-7. Describes in plain language the basic features of the most-asked-about new telecommunication technologies; technical jargon is explained. Contents of each chapter are concisely organized into four headings: background, how it works, applications, and forecast.

Sklar, Bernard. *Digital Communications: Fundamentals and Applications.* P-H 1988 $58.00. ISBN 0-13-211939-0. Comprehensive coverage for undergraduates, first-year graduate students, and practicing engineers. Emphasizes digital communications and includes analog fundamentals.

Truxal, John G. *The Age of Electronic Messages: Primer on the New Technologies.* MIT Pr. 1990 $37.50. ISBN 0-262-20074-0. Explains the scientific principles on which current communications technology is based and explores its capabilities, limitations, risks, and benefits; describes how communications technology has become an integral part of work and leisure. Written in straightforward language, accompanied by numerous illustrations; the best general introduction available.

Westerway, Peter. *Electronic Highways: An Introduction to Telecommunications in the 1990's.* Allen and Unwin 1990 o.p. Provides "a framework which enables the student to understand how the unfolding revolution in telecommunications shapes the world today." Includes a glossary and a chronology of significant events.

Williams, Frederick. *The New Telecommunications: Infrastructure for the Information Age.* Free Pr. 1991 $39.95. ISBN 0-02-935281-9. Identifies "innovative applications in a wide range of business, public service, and residential environments" and discusses how new telecommunications services are "an important infrastructure component in city, state, and national planning."

Wired Cities: Shaping the Future of Communications. Macmillan 1987 $29.95. ISBN 0-8161-1853-1. An examination of "the driving forces and social implications of new communications technologies through the study of wired cities." A country-by-country presentation of national policy and wired city projects in the United States, Japan, France, West Germany, and Great Britain, with a final summary chapter.

TRANSMISSION SYSTEMS AND METHODS

The works in this section focus on three central issues. First is the basic theory of transmitting information. Essentially, this theory states that the more sophisticated the information to be sent, the bigger the channel necessary to carry it. For example, color television needs a wider band width than black and white. Second is the distinction between analog and digital transmission. An analog signal conveys information by the size or amplitude of a signal. Digital methods convert information into numbers (usually on a binary scale), send a series of numbers, and convert the numbers back into information at the receiver. The bar code on products scanned at the supermarket checkout is a digital signal. Third are explanations and discussions of communications networks and integration systems, including teleconferencing and what promises to be the integrated system of the future, integrated service digital networks, or ISDNs.

Barker, Forrest L. *Communications Electronics: Systems, Circuits, and Devices.* P-H 1987 $52.00. ISBN 0-13-153883-7. Intended for readers with "the knowledge and skills associated with installing and maintaining communications equipment," as well as the "generalist electronic technician student" and those who want to do "hands-on work with electronic equipment."

Brierley, H. G. *Telecommunications Engineering.* Arnold 1986 o.p. For the advanced electrical engineering student.

Coates, R.F.W. *Modern Communication Systems.* Scolium Intl. 1983 $30.00. ISBN 0-333-35832-5. Covers a "two-year course on communications system engineering at the B. Sc. level."

Couch, Leon W. *Digital and Analog Communication Systems.* Macmillan 1992. ISBN 0-02-325281-2. Compares the strengths and weaknesses of these two competing communications technologies.

Das, J. *Review of Digital Communication: State of the Art in Digital Signalling, Digital Switching and Data Networks.* Wiley 1988 $47.95. ISBN 0-470-20221-1. Discusses nearly all aspects of digital signalling including: principles of digital modulation; source encoding; data transmission through cables and optical fibers; digital radio, including satellite communication, data networks and digital switching; information theory and coding; survival of communication, including spread-spectrum techniques; and future trends, including ISDNs. Contains information otherwise available only in specialized journals; includes state-of-the-art information and a bibliography.

Davenport, Wilbur B. *An Introduction to the Theory of Random Signals and Noise.* Inst. Electrical 1987 $49.95. ISBN 0-87942-235-1

Dayton, Robert L. *Integrating Digital Services: T1, DDS, and Voice Integrated Network Architecture.* McGraw 1989 $44.95. ISBN 0-0701-6188-7. Provides a solid understanding of all the parts in an integrated digital services world, with discussion of telephone company digital services and the integration of end-user equipment; written for the telecommunications end-user as a practical technical book about integrating digital services.

———. *Telecommunications.* McGraw 1991 $34.95. ISBN 0-07-016189-5. Although a technical book in premise, technical terms are not used in this discussion of transmission principles and other topics in telecommunications; written in easy-to-understand language for the non-technical reader.

Dunlop, J. *Telecommunications Engineering.* Routledge Chapman & Hall 1990 $39.50. ISBN 0-412-38190-7. A complete discussion of telecommunications engineering, requiring familiarity with electronic engineering, electromagnetic theory, probability theory, and differential calculus.

Gagliardi, Robert M. *Introduction to Communications Engineering*. Wiley 1988 $69.95. ISBN 0-4718-5644-4. An introduction to modern communications engineering through examples and diagrams. Suitable for advanced undergraduates or first-year graduate students with a background in electronics, electromagnetic theory, and linear system theory.

Gibson, Jerry D. *Principles of Digital and Analog Communications*. Macmillan 1992. ISBN 0-0234-1860-5. Explains the differences between analog and digital systems.

Goldstein, Fred R. *ISDN in Perspective*. Addison-Wesley 1992 $32.25. ISBN 0-2015-0016-7. Witty account of major changes in telecommunications today; illustrates applications that potential ISDN users are likely to find valuable and describes various services ISDN can offer.

Griffiths, J. M., ed. *ISDN Explained: Worldwide Network and Applications Technology*. Wiley 1992 $42.95. ISBN 0-4719-3480-1. Discusses the technology for integrating worldwide communications networks.

Hardwick, Steve. *ISDN Design: A Practical Approach*. Acad. Pr. 1989 $39.00. ISBN 0-1232-4970-8. An easy-to-understand reference for ISDN, including topics "relating to both theoretical and practical issues concerning ISDN." It is not, however, designed to be "a definitive technical reference," since technical information is used only to clarify specific examples for both "the newcomer and experienced design engineer."

Haykin, Simon S. *An Introduction to Analog and Digital Communications*. Wiley 1989 $64.95. ISBN 0-4718-5978-8. Examines communication theory as applied to the transmission of information. Treatment is self-contained, with worked out examples to support the theory. Recommended for upper level undergraduate students.

———. *Communication Systems*. Wiley 1983 $61.95. ISBN 0-4710-9691-1

Helgert, Hermann J. *Integrated Services Digital Networks*. Addison-Wesley 1991 $59.25. ISBN 0-201-52501-1

Kanefsky, Morton. *Communication Techniques for Digital and Analog Signals*. HarpC 1985 o.p. Designed as a text on modern communication theory for the undergraduate; a good introduction to the "basic concepts in terms of discrete communication techniques."

Keiser, Bernhard. *Broadband Coding, Modulation, and Transmission Engineering*. P-H 1989 $61.00. ISBN 0-1308-3387-8. "Provides an engineering description of the methods used to process and transmit broadband signals." Includes "both the analog and digital transmission of data and graphic information, as well as multiplexed voice transmission"; suitable for the practicing engineer and as a supplement to "more theoretical texts used in telecommunications engineering courses" at the senior and graduate level.

Kennedy, George. *Electronic Communication Systems*. McGraw 1985 $40.95. ISBN 0-07-034054-4

Kessler, Gary C. *ISDN*. McGraw 1990 $47.95. ISBN 0-0703-4242-3. A good first introduction to various aspects of ISDN. Defines important terms, concepts, standards and protocols, issues, services, trials, and products current in ISDN; uses little technical jargon.

Killen, Harold B. *Modern Electronic Communication Techniques*. Macmillan 1985 o.p.

Kwakernaak, Huibert, and Raphael Sivan. *Modern Signals and Systems*. P-H 1990 $56.00. ISBN 0-1380-9252-4. An exploration of the basics of signal theory, and of both the time-and-frequency domain analysis of systems.

Lathi, B. P. *Modern Digital and Analog Communication Systems*. HR&W Sch. Div. 1989 $68.00. ISBN 0-0302-7933-X. Good introduction to "communication systems and the broad principles of modern communication theory at an early stage in the undergraduate curriculum"; concepts and results are interpreted with little technical language.

Olgren, Christine H. *Teleconferencing Technology and Applications*. Artech Hse. 1983 o.p. Complete assessment of the major trends in teleconferencing. Discusses future trends in teleconferencing; reader is assumed to have little background.

Pierce, John Robinson. *Signals: The Telephone and Beyond*. W. H. Freeman 1981 o.p. A light account of the science and technology of communication. Interspersed with biographical profiles; suitable for any audience.

————. *Signals: The Science of Telecommunications*. W. H. Freeman 1990 $32.95. ISBN 0-7167-5026-0. A major revision of *Signals: The Telephone and Beyond*, reflecting recent trends in telecommunications such as digital and fiber optic transmission systems; More technical than the previous edition.

Pooch, Udo W. *Telecommunications and Networking*. CRC Pr. 1990 $59.95. ISBN 0-8493-7172-4. Discusses the current state of communications technolgy and its use in networking.

Roddy, D. *Electronic Communications*. P-H 1984 $52.00. ISBN 0-8359-1598-0

Ronayne, John, ed. *Integrated Services Digital Networks: From Concept to Application*. Wiley 1987 $200.00. ISBN 0-273-02677-1

Schwartz, Mischa. *Information Transmission, Modulation, and Noise*. McGraw 1990 $50.22. ISBN 0-07-055909-0. A complete treatment of modern communications systems; assumes no prior knowledge. "Takes reader to up-to-date developments in digital communications and communication theory"; explains theoretical concepts by applications to telephony, space, and satellite communications fields.

Schweber, William L. *Electronic Communications Systems: A Complete Course*. P-H 1991 $50.00. ISBN 0-13-590092-1. A college-level textbook that analyzes new technology and shows how these systems build on the fundamentals made possible by digital signals, microprocessors, and ICS.

Skaug, R., and others, eds. *Spread Spectrum in Communication*. Inst. Elect. Eng. 1985 $79.00. ISBN 0-86341-034-0

Stallings, William. *ISDN and Broadband ISDN*. Macmillan 1992. ISBN 0-02-415475-X. Looks at the current status and future of different types of integrated service digital networks.

Stanley, William D. *Electronic Communication Systems*. P-H 1992 $52.00. ISBN 0-8359-1666-9. Presentation of "the general principles of electronic communications at a systems level . . . with an emphasis on the signal processing functions of various modulation and demodulation operations." Discusses mathematical "models for communications systems analysis and design," with emphasis on "applied design and operational approach" rather than theory; less mathematical in nature than many other books on communications theory, although some knowledge of calculus and probability theory is helpful.

Stark, Henry. *Modern Electrical Communications: Analog, Digital, and Optical Systems*. P-H 1988 $59.00. ISBN 0-13-593112-6. New edition of a textbook at senior/graduate level.

Taub, Herbert. *Principles of Communication Systems*. McGraw 1986 $49.33. ISBN 0-07-062955-2

Thomas, John Bowman. *An Introduction to Communication Theory and Systems*. Spr.-Verlag 1987 $65.00. ISBN 0-387-96672-2. A good first treatment of statistical communication theory and communication systems at the senior-graduate level. The only formal prerequisite is knowledge of elementary calculus; familiarity with linear systems and transform theory is also helpful. Contains many examples.

Weber, Charles L. *Elements of Detection and Signal Design*. Spr.-Verlag 1987 $54.00. ISBN 0-387-96529-7. A comprehensive study of the theory of transmitter optimization for coherent and noncoherent digital communication systems.

Williams, Richard A. *Communication Systems Analysis and Design: A Systems Approach*. P-H 1987 o.p.

Wilson, Edward A. *Electronic Communications Technology*. P-H 1989 $52.00. ISBN 0-13-250333-6

Winder, Alan A. *Space-Time Information Processing*. Peninsula CA 1981 $31.95. ISBN 0-932146-04-X. A fine reference work, discussing theory of the Fourier transform, statistical analysis, correlation and spectra, as well as measuring functions, orthogonality and integral transformations, optimal filtering procedure, and acoustical interpretations of results. Very mathematical in nature; for the advanced student, with many references.

SWITCHING SYSTEMS

In our advanced technological world the most obvious importance of the switching system is its use in telephony: One person picks up the telephone, dials the number of the person to whom he or she wishes to speak. The phone network then has to switch connections at several points between the caller and the person called to correctly route the call. But, as everyone knows, this does not always happen. Connections occasionally go astray, so that one is connected to the wrong party or even listening in on someone else's conversation. In fact, what was once done manually by telephone operators, with a rather high error rate, is now done electronically by specially designed electronic switching systems.

Bellamy, John. *Digital Telephony*. Wiley 1991 $69.95. ISBN 0-4716-2056-4. Revised and updated reference for specialists. Bridges gap between theory and practice.

Coughlin, Vince. *Telecommunications: Equipment Fundamentals and Network Structures*. Van Nos. Reinhold 1984 o.p. Sets "in perspective the operating principles that underlie the various telecommunications equipment and network structures used to grow" effective telecommunications networks. Serves as a user guide to set up these networks; written for many audiences in non-technical language.

Hills, Michael Turner. *Telecommunications Switching Principles*. MIT Pr. 1979 $40.00. ISBN 0-2620-8092-3. "Shows the unified set of principles behind the centre designs"; also gives application of these principles using modern technology and describes the "implementation of the design principles in some of the switching centre types in use today." Requires basic knowledge of computers; written for the university student.

Pearce, J. Gordon. *Telecommunications Switching*. Plenum Pub. 1981 $69.50. ISBN 0-3064-0584-9. Good discussion of the application of telecommunications switching principles without immersion in mathematical jargon. Sacrifices proofs and derivations of results for creative design and application; written for the university student.

Purser, Michael. *Computers and Telecommunications Networks*. Alfred Waller Ltd. 1987 o.p. "Addresses the topic of the 'covergence' between data processing and telecommunications." Emphasis is on the computer person who is involved with telecommunications systems as the means of linking computers and terminals as control subjects by management; a familiarity with synchronous transmission and line procedures is assumed.

DATA COMMUNICATIONS

The very title of Schwaderer's *Modems and Communication on the IBM PCs* listed below conveys the essence of this section. The growth of computers in our society has brought with it a need to communicate with each other, that is, for users to send and receive information by means of a computer. Data is transmitted by some communication link. This can be something as simple as two PC users sending messages by electronic mail (e-mail) or two mainframe computers on different continents sharing programs.

Banks, Michael A. *Modem Reference*. Brady Compu Bks. 1991 $24.95. ISBN 0-1358-9862-5. Covers hardware, software, on-line services, and applications. Includes telecomputing, safe computing, and modem/FAX services.

Bingham, John A. C. *The Theory and Practice of Modem Design.* Wiley 1988 $74.95. ISBN 0-471-85108-6. "Intended mainly for practicing and aspiring modem designers," but also useful "as an ancillary book for a graduate course in data (digital) communications; it shows many ways in which all that theory can be put to use." Familiarity with undergraduate level of mathematics and Fourier, LaPlace, and z transforms, as well as matrix and probability theory is required.

Blahut, Richard E. *Digital Transmission of Information.* Addison-Wesley 1990 $64.50. ISBN 0-2010-6880-X

Guy, C. G. *Data Communications for Engineers.* McGraw 1992 $29.95. ISBN 0-0702-5354-4. "Sets a study of the engineering mechanisms for data transfer in the context of data communications." Serves as an excellent support for an introductory course in digital communications at the second or third level of an engineering degree course, and for practicing engineers; accessible to nearly any student or practicing engineer.

Haykin, Simon S. *Digital Communications.* Wiley 1988 $69.95. ISBN 0-4716-2947-2. Provides a good overview of the principles of digital communications, with a focus on basic issues "relating theory to practice." Written at a level "suitable for a one-semester course in digital communications"; requires a familiarity with Fourier techniques and probability theory.

Karl, John H. *An Introduction to Digital Signal Processing.* Acad. Pr. 1989 $55.00. ISBN 0-12-398420-3

Killen, Harold B. *Digital Communications with Fiber Optics and Satellite Applications.* P-H 1988 $51.00. ISBN 0-13-213018-1. Excellent introductory text to digital communications. Introduces basic principles and discusses system theory with more emphasis on application than theory. Requires little background by the student; also suitable for general audiences.

Komo, John J. *Random Signal Analysis in Engineering Systems.* Acad. Pr. 1987 $63.00. ISBN 0-12-418660-2

Korn, I. *Digital Communications.* Van Nos. Reinhold 1985 o.p. Intended for those with some background in communications; directed at students of electrical engineering and computer science specializing in digital communications, as well as practical engineers who apply digital communications techniques to telecommunications systems, digital radio, digital satellites, fiber optics, and the physical layer of computer networks. Requires basic knowledge of calculus.

Kunt, M. *Digital Signal Processing.* Artech Hse. 1988 $29.00. ISBN 0-89006-187-4. Contains a good "presentation of the different basic methods of digital signal processing," as well as their application. Transformation theory also is introduced; basic knowledge of mathematics is required.

Lee, Edward A. *Digital Communication.* Kluwer Acad. 1988 $79.50. ISBN 0-8983-8274-2. Provides a comprehensive guide to the signal processing techniques necessary for transmitting a data stream from one point to another.

Martin, James. *Systems Analysis for Data Transmission.* P-H 1972 $71.80. ISBN 0-13-881300-0

Morris, David Joseph. *Communication for Command and Control Systems.* Pergamon 1983 $40.00. ISBN 0-08-027596-6. "Provides a sound exposition of the basic theoretical and practical features involved in the design of communication networks for command and control systems"; useful for anyone involved in "planning, designing, and implementing communication systems" as both a text and reference book at the postgraduate level.

Peebles, Peyton Z. *Digital Communication Systems.* P-H 1986 $58.00. ISBN 0-13-211970-6

Proakis, John G. *Digital Communications.* McGraw 1989 $51.12. ISBN 0-0705-0937-9

Schwaderer, W. David. *Modems and Communications on IBM PCs. IBM PC Series.* Wiley 1986 $21.95. ISBN 0-4718-4459-4

Ziemer, Rodger E. *Introduction to Digital Communication.* Macmillan 1992. ISBN 0-02-431681-4. Good introduction to the "transmission of information by electrical means using digital communication techniques." Serves as a useful college textbook requiring no special background other than junior-level probability and linear systems courses; provides "in-depth treatment of the theory and design of digital communications systems for undergraduates and first-year graduate students.

FIBER OPTICS

Light signals have a long history as a means of carrying signals. Examples include smoke signals, the Aldiss lamp (which uses Morse-code-like breaks in a beam of light aimed from sender to receiver), semaphore, beacons, etc. Of course, such signals are limited to transmitting one message at a time, rather clumsily, and only over a direct line of sight. In recent years, however, two developments have opened up enormous new possibilities in signal transmission: the laser and optic fibers. Lasers provide intense light sources, and fibers made of transparent materials with very low absorption channel light signals by means of internal reflection. The marriage of the two constitutes fiber optic communications.

Adams, Michael J. *Optical Fibres and Sources for Communications*. Plenum Pub. 1990 $59.50. ISBN 0-306-43711-2. Introduces basic principles and key areas of research in the literature of fibers and sources.

Agrawal, G. P. *Fiber-Optic Communication Systems*. Wiley 1992 $59.95. ISBN 0-471-54286-5. Focuses on a physical understanding of the subject. Graduate textbook and reference.

Chaffee, C. David. *The Rewiring of America: The Fiber Optics Revolution*. Acad. Pr. 1987 $49.00. ISBN 0-12-166360-4. Historical account of the birth and rise of fiber optics, with insightful comments and observations. No technical knowledge presupposed; suitable for general audiences.

Geisler, J. *Optical Fibers*. Franklin 1986 $260.00. ISBN 0-08-030577-6. Complete discussion of the advantages, disadvantages, applications, and the present and likely future progress of fiber-optic link systems. In-depth yet assumes no previous knowledge; useful for interested audiences.

Green, Paul Eliot. *Fiber Optic Networks*. P-H 1992 $59.00. ISBN 0-13-319492-2. "A comprehensive text and reference volume that can be used in education, research, and development in the combined field of communication theory and computer networks"; is both an instructive and encyclopedic text suitable for any interested audience and requires little background.

Halley, Pierre. *Fibre-Optic Systems*. Wiley 1987 $49.95. ISBN 0-4719-1410-X. Introduction to the important aspects of optical fiber systems, emphasizing communications, particularly over long distances.

Jones, William B. *Introduction to Optical Fiber Communication Systems*. SCP 1988 $62.75. ISBN 0-03-009544-1

Keiser, Gerd. *Optical Fiber Communications*. McGraw 1991 $44.94. ISBN 0-0703-3617-2. "Provides the basic material for an introductory senior of first-year graduate course in the theory and application of optical-fiber communication technology." Also serves as a reference for practicing engineers dealing with modern optical fiber communication system designs. Contains many examples that require background in electromagnetic theory, calculus, elementary differential equations, optics, and electronics; a solutions manual is available from the publisher.

Killen, Harold B. *Fiber Optic Communications*. P-H 1991 $45.00. ISBN 0-13-313578-0. Provides basic information on fiber optics technology as well as specialized technical sub-topics.

Lacy, Edward A. *Fiber Optics*. P-H 1982 $55.00. ISBN 0-13-314278-7. Gives the average electronics technician the practical foundation for the operation and maintenance of fiber-optic systems, as well as the basics of fiber-optic components and systems. Arranged logically with appendixes; no prior knowledge necessary.

Marcuse, Dietrich. *Principles of Optical Fiber Measurements*. Acad. Pr. 1981 $71.00. ISBN 0-12-470980-X. Covers the "principles of most optical fiber measurements." Acts as a guide for "those who would like to establish or improve a fiber measurement capability, as well as those who desire a better understanding of fiber specifications"; for specialists and aspiring specialists in the field.

Midwinter, John E. *Optical Fibers for Transmission*. Krieger 1992 $62.50. ISBN 0-89464-595-1. Provides a good introduction on fiber communications systems and properties of optical fibers, with basic knowledge in physics, chemistry, or engineering; relatively modest mathematical knowledge is required. Provides the basis for a M. S. course on fiber communications.

_____. *Optoelectronics and Lightwave Technology*. Wiley 1992 $64.95. ISBN 0-471-92934-4. Provides complete coverage of optoelectronics at the junior-senior or graduate-level, addressing many features of this fast-moving field; extensive knowledge of mathematical and engineering techniques is required.

Palais, Joseph C. *Fiber Optics Communications*. P-H 1992 $44.00. ISBN 0-13-473554-4

Personick, Stewart D. *Optical Fiber Transmission Systems*. Plenum Pub. 1981 $49.50. ISBN 0-306-40580-6. Gives a systems-engineering view of fiber optics for transmission, emphasizing research, exploratory development, and application of fiber transmission systems, rather than the derivation of mathematical results. Heuristic arguments motivate results, and references are used on the details of derivations.

Senior, John. *Optical Fiber Communications: Principles and Practice*. P-H 1984 $59.60. ISBN 0-13-638248-7

Sibley, M.J.N. *Optical Communications*. McGraw 1991 $34.95. ISBN 0-07-057216-X. Surveys current optical communications technology and systems and discusses its potential for the future.

TECHNICAL REFERENCES

Works included here are useful technical handbooks on communications technology design, installation, and utilization.

Freeman, Roger L. *Telecommunication Transmission Handbook*. Wiley 1991 $84.95. ISBN 0-471-51816-6. Multi-purpose book that is useful as a reference. Learning aid for the electrical engineer who wishes to know more about transmission and for the graduate engineer who wishes to implement such a system; also helpful to the nonengineer as an introduction to transmission engineering.

_____. *Telecommunication System Engineering: Analog and Digital Network Design*. Wiley 1980 o.p. Presents the general engineering considerations necessary for the design of practical telecommunications networks; provides a practical understanding of both tradition and revolution in telecommunications.

_____. *Telecommunication System Engineering*. Wiley 1989 $84.95. ISBN 0-471-63423-9

Green, James H. *The Business One Irwin Handbook of Telecommunications*. Busn. One Irwin 1991 $90.00. ISBN 1-55623-333-7. Discusses information needed to manage outside experts; knowledge of building blocks and how they work in a successful telecommunications system is necessary. Technologies are not discussed in depth, instead the focus is on understanding technologies in order that they may be applied intelligently.

Held, Gilbert. *The Complete Modem Reference*. Wiley 1991 $26.95. ISBN 0-471-52911-7. Written for technically oriented modem owners and purchasers; provides answers to every conceivable modem question. Presents clear information that demystifies modems and their operation; an indispensable reference.

Lenk, John D. *Handbook of Data Communications*. P-H 1984 $47.00. ISBN 0-13-377317-5. Offers a "mini course" in data or digital communications and is written for readers with many different interests: the engineer, the technician, the programmer/analyst, and students and hobbyists. Differences among this diverse audience are bridged by efforts to bring all readers to the same level of understanding; useful both as an introduction and for applications.

Lindberg, Bertil C. *Troubleshooting Communications Facilities: Measurements and Tests on Data and Telecommunications Circuits, Equipment, and Systems.* Wiley 1990 $59.95. ISBN 0-471-61286-3. Intended for engineers and others who are concerned with measurements and tests on data and telecommunications circuits, equipment, and systems, with an emphasis on troubleshooting and fault locating in communications facilities; the first comprehensive book on these subjects.

McKay, L. R. *WEESKA Electronic Communication Systems.* Dekker 1989 $45.00. ISBN 0-8247-8008-6. This book notes common pitfalls, relevant regulatory data, and offers guidelines for selecting and operating short-, medium-, and long-distance communication technologies.

Maynard, Jeff. *The Computer and Telecommunications Handbook.* Granada 1984 o.p.

Minoli, Daniel. *Telecommunications Technology Handbook.* Artech Hse. 1991 $89.00. ISBN 0-89006-425-3. Provides a exposition of contemporary communication fields to managers, addressing both technical and managerial aspects. "A comprehensive guide to the telecommunications field, with emphasis on issues affecting the industry in the 1990s."

Silveria, Terry. *Buyer's Guide to Modems and Communications Software.* Petrocelli 1985 o.p. Invaluable for those considering the purchase of a modem or communications software for any personal computer. Discusses background on modems for those completely new to the field and provides a quick reference glossary of all technical terms; emphasis is on information on the products themselves.

Townsend, A.A.R. *Digital Line-of-Sight Radio Links: A Handbook.* P-H 1988 $65.60. ISBN 0-13-212622-2

Using New Communications Technologies; A Guide for Organizations. Media Inst. 1986 $12.95. ISBN 0-937790-30-3. "Acquaints the reader with a number of new technologies that are being used with growing frequency to enhance business communication. . . . It shows how even groups with modest budgets can communicate more effectively by using the new technologies, and offers helpful lists of suppliers and contact persons." Includes a glossary and is reader-friendly.

Widner, Doug. *Teleguide: A Handbook on Video-Teleconferencing.* Public Service Satellite Consortium 1986 o.p. Provides basic information on video-teleconferencing and its use. Looks at the future of this technology.

CHRONOLOGY OF AUTHORS

Cherry, Colin. 1914–1979
Freeman, Roger L. 1928–
Keiser, Bernhard E(dward). 1928–

Hiltz, Starr Roxanne. 1942–
Tomasi, Wayne. 1946–

CHERRY, COLIN. 1914–1979.

A native of England, Colin Cherry was educated at the University of London, where he received his B.Sc. (1936), M.Sc. (1940), and D.Sc. (1958). After working in the research laboratories of General Electric London (1936–1945), Cherry spent the remainder of his professional life with the Department of Electrical Engineering at the Imperial College of Science and Technology, where from 1958 until his death he was the Henry Mark Pease Professor of Telecommunications.

During his professional career, Cherry also served on the board of the Open University, and was a member of the United Kingdom National Commission for UNESCO. In 1978 he was awarded the Fourth Marconi International Fellowship in recognition of scientific achievement for the benefit of humanity in the field of communications science and technology. Cherry's book *On Human Communication*, which was first published in 1957, has remained in print ever since and is often considered the single most important general analysis of communication technology.

BOOKS BY CHERRY

The Age of Access: Information Technology and Social Revolution: Posthumous Papers of Colin Cherry. Routledge Chapman & Hall 1985 o.p. Cherry was working on this book at his death in 1979. Although incomplete, it comprises a substantial postscript to *On Human Communication*.

Information Theory: Fourth London Symposium. (ed.) Butterworths 1961 o.p. Thirty-six papers from an influential international conference.

On Human Communication: A Review, a Survey, and a Criticism. MIT Pr. 1978 $30.00. ISBN 0-262-03065-9. covers linguistics, phonetics, statistical communication theory, semantics, and psychology, all in relation to communications technology.

Pragmatic Aspects of Human Communication. (ed.) Kluwer Ac. 1974 $75.00. ISBN 90-277-0432-5. Eight original papers approaching the subject from diverse perspectives.

World Communication: Threat or Promise?: A Socio-technical Approach. Bks. Demand repr. of 1978 ed. $60.80. ISBN 0-317-55718-1. The themes of this book reflect Cherry's socialist political sympathies and his involvement with the education of technical professions from the Third World.

FREEMAN, ROGER L. 1928–

Born in New York City, Roger Freeman is a widely known telecommunications engineer, educator, and author of several handbooks and manuals for students and telecommunications engineers. From 1948 until 1951, Freeman attended Northeastern University. He dropped out to work as a radio officer with the Military Sea Transportation Service and was stationed in Brooklyn, New York (1952–59). In 1959 he went to work as an engineer for Bendix Radio in Spain, where he remained until 1962. He spent the next 16 years as a research engineer and technical director for International Telephone and Telegraph Communications Systems (ITT). While working for ITT, Freeman earned a B.A. (1966) and an M.A. (1973) in electrical engineering from New York University. Since 1978 he has been senior principal engineer and program manager of the equipment division at the Raytheon Company of Sudbury, Massachusetts, as well as faculty member of Northeastern University.

BOOKS BY FREEMAN

Radio System Design for Telecommunications (1–100 GHz). Wiley $64.95. ISBN 0-471-81236-6. The purpose of this book is to provide essential design techniques for radiolinks in the point-to-point service operating in the range of 1-100 GHz. Prepared with both the student and working engineer in mind.

Reference Manual for Telecommunications. Wiley 1985 $125.00. ISBN 0-471-86753-5. Provides basic information for repeated application by telecommunications engineers. Covers basic disciplines of transmission and switching in 26 subject areas; includes an index.

Telecommunication Transmission Handbook. Wiley 1981 $79.95. ISBN 0-471-27789-4. Provides practical information used in telecommunication design for single links or complete networks; designed for practicing telecommunications engineers and advanced students.

HILTZ, STARR ROXANNE, 1942–

Starr Roxanne Hiltz was born in Little Rock, Arkansas, and educated at Vassar College and Columbia University, where she received an M.A. (1964) and Ph.D.

(1969) in sociology. She has taught at Upsala College and Rutgers University, and is currently at the New Jersey Institute of Technology, where she holds the title of Distinguished Professor in the Departmentof Computer and Information Science. Hiltz has also served as director of the Collaborative Systems Laboratory and associate director of the Computerized Conferencing and Communications Center, both at New Jersey Institute of Technology.

Hiltz's book *Network Nation* (1978), which was co-authored with Murray Turoff, received the "TSM Award" of the Association of American Publishers for the Best Technical Publication, and quickly became the standard reference in the field of computer-mediated communications (CMC). The first part of this work covered the nature of computerized conferencing; the second part dealt with its potential applications and impacts; and the third part discussed the future of computerized conferencing and its regulation. The second edition of *Network Nation* (1993) contains new material on superconnectivity developments during the last fifteen years, and updates on the future.

Hiltz is a member of the Association for Computing Machinery (ACM) and has received major grants from the National Science Foundation, the National Institutes of Mental Health, the Annenberg Foundation and Corporation for Public Broadcasting, and the Sloan Foundation. In 1990 she was recipient of the Electronic Networking Association's Rodale Award for Creative Achievement. Her current research focuses on video and the virtual classroom.

BOOKS BY HILTZ

Computer-Mediated Communication Systems: Status and Evaluation (coauthored with Elaine B. Kerr). Acad. Pr. 1982 $50.00. ISBN 0-12-404980-X
Network Nation: Human Communication via Computer (coauthored with Murray Turoff). MIT Pr. 1993 $24.95. ISBN 0-262-58120-5. Includes new discussions of ehtical issues. Contains a bibliography of key literature.
Online Communities: A Case Study of the Office of the Future. Ed. by Ben Shneiderman. Ablex Pub. 1984 $55.00. ISBN 0-89391-145-3. Looks at online communication networks and their potential role in the future.
The Virtual Classroom: A New Option for Learning. Ablex Pub. 1993 ISBN 0-89391-928-4

KEISER, BERNHARD E(DWARD). 1928–

Born in Richmond Heights, Missouri, and educated at Washington University, Bernhard Keiser is among the leading telecommunications and electrical engineers in the United States. After receiving a D.Sc. in electrical engineering (1953), Keiser became a project engineer at White-Rodgers Electric Company. During the late 1950s and early 1960s, he worked for the RCA Corporation as a group leader of new communication systems. From 1964 until 1969, he managed RCA's Communication Project at the Kennedy Space Center in Florida and then supervised the RCA Missile and Surface Radar Division in New Jersey. Keiser became director of analysis for Fairchild Space and Electronics Company in the early 1970s before founding Keiser Engineering, Inc. in 1975. He is a fellow of the Institute for Electrical and Electronics Engineers and currently lives in Vienna, Virginia, with his wife and five children.

BOOKS BY KEISER

Broadband Coding, Modulation and Transmission Engineering. P-H 1989 $61.00. ISBN 0-13-083387-8. Treats both the analog and digital transmission of data and graphic information, as well as multiplexed voice transmission.
Principles of Electromagnetic Compatibility. Bks. Demand repr. of 1979 ed. $89.20. ISBN 0-8357-5583-5

TOMASI, WAYNE. 1946–

After serving in the U.S. Army, Wayne Tomasi studied at Arizona State University, where he earned a degree in engineering. He continued with graduate work at that same institution. During his career, Tomasi has worked for six years as a communications engineer with AT&T, three years as a design engineer of biological test equipment, one year as a TV broadcast engineer, and one year as supervisor of the electronic communications department at Arizona State University. His background of practical experience is evident in the very accessible texts he has produced during 17 years as professor of electronics, first at the DeVry Institute of Technology in Phoenix and later at Mesa Community College. In addition to the books he has authored, he has also written five laboratory manuals. Tomasi is a man committed to his subject and to cultivating that same commitment in his students.

BOOKS BY TOMASI

Advanced Electronic Communications Systems. P-H 1987 $50.00. ISBN 0-13-011214-3. A good text on data communications, digital transmission, multiplexing, microwave, satellite, and fiber communications. Not recommended for beginners.

Digital and Data Communications (coauthored with Vincent F. Alisouskas). P-H 1985 $44.00. ISBN 0-13-212424-6. "This book is written so that a reader with a background in basic communications (AM and FM theory), basic digital theory, and mathematics through trigonometry can easily become better acquainted with this area. Numerous examples are provided for a better understanding of the theory." (Preface). Deals with voice and data transmission over telephone lines, both analog and digital.

Electronic Communications Systems: Fundamentals through Advanced. P-H 1988 $55.00. ISBN 0-13-250804-4. A good introduction to basic electronic communications fundamentals and modern digital and data communications systems. Requires an understanding of mathematics through trigonometry; knowledge of calculus is also helpful but not necessary. Important concepts are illustrated by numerous examples.

Fundamentals of Electronic Communications Systems. P-H 1988 $47.00. ISBN 0-13-336579-4. Assumes a basic group of electronics principles and math up through trigonometry.

Telecommunications: Voice/Data with Fiber Optic Applications. P-H 1988 $52.00. ISBN 0-1390-2602-9. Written so that the reader with a background in basic communications, basic digital theory, and math through trigonometry can become acquainted with this rapidly advancing field.

CHAPTER 12

Medicine and Health

Daniel T. Richards

The progress of medicine . . . is something wonderful. Any lover of humanity who looks back on the achievements of medical science must feel his heart glow and his right ventricle expand with the pericardiac stimulus of a permissible pride. Just think of it. A hundred years ago there were no bacilli, no ptomaine poisoning, no diphtheria, and no appendicitis. Rabies was but little known, and only imperfectly developed. All of these we owe to medical science!

—STEPHEN B. LEACOCK, *Literary Lapses*

There have been many new books on wellness, health professional education, national health care reform, and homeopathy in recent years. Moreover, wilderness and environmental medicine, mind/body purification, the path to medical discoveries, quackery, the health risks of working with computers, medical technology, herbalism, choosing the best doctor, and the rise of for-profit hospital "chains" also have been the topics of recent new books. Medical center-sponsored family health guides—some specialized, others general—are now available in libraries and bookstores together with standards sponsored by major health associations. The human body continues to fascinate people as reflected by new titles describing organs and systems that have appeared. There also is substantial interest in the aging process, family planning, birth techniques, child development, and the social aspects of health care. Additionally, the established high level of publication of books on nutrition, diet therapy, fitness and exercise, and parenting and child care has been maintained. All of these observations indicate that the audience for books on medical subjects remains strong, which further illustrates the enduring demand for authoritative and readily available information about the practice of medicine.

The heightened involvement of the consumer in determining health care choices is predicated on access to comprehensible discussions of complex medical subjects and issues. Television specials on health issues and specific diseases have created a demand for supplementary readings that are accessible to general readers. Based on the large number of new publications on medical topics, there are many authors who have valuable insights and viewpoints on health care and a substantial number of publishers that are willing to package and market these works.

As a result, there has been a virtual flood of new books on many facets of health care. In fact, medical publishing is second only to the social sciences in the number of titles produced annually. Within medical publishing, however, there are different growth rates among the specialties, affected mainly by the currents in medical research. Although the general rate of advance in medicine is rapid, much of the published literature is standard, and the newest or most recent book may not necessarily be the best. This chapter is designed to introduce the many health-related books available. The following books concentrate on the functioning of the healthy body and its organs, the physiological aspects of human development, and the maintenance of health. This chapter also includes books that describe the various health care professions, education for those professions, and some historical treatments of medical subjects. Finally, there are books on the continuing debate over health care costs and the organization, management, and economics of various health care delivery systems. The recent White House initiative in this area suggests that interest in such books will increase during the next several years.

The following list represents a selection of authoritative and informative titles, as well as introductory reference works. All books were selected on the basis of clarity and accessibility of the information presented, the significance and validity of the content, expertise of the author(s), and its scope in treating the subject. The opinions of critics, reviewers, colleagues, and physicians also have been used.

Each category is introduced with a brief definition and, where possible, a statement about the extent of the publishing activity in that particular area. The factors that have been considered in selecting subjects are their use in organizing bookstore and library collections, the general availability of books on the subject, and how readers might approach the literature of the health sciences. Consequently, the subjects vary somewhat in their level of specificity. Unless otherwise indicated, the opinions expressed in the annotations are those of the compiler.

REFERENCE BOOKS

The following list includes only representative titles of the many dictionaries, guides, and directories available. Most are written specifically for the medical consumer.

Advice for the Patient. USPC 1990 $39.00. ISBN 0-913595-48-9. Provides information for the patient on about 3,000 prescription drugs, including allergic reactions, contraindications, and interactions with other drugs. Price includes update service; easy to understand.

American Society of Hospital Pharmacists. *Consumer Drug Digest.* Facts on File 1992 $27.95. ISBN 0-8160-1254-7. Provides descriptions of the ailment, as well as names of drugs appropriate for the problem; includes information about side effects and possible allergic reactions.

The American Medical Association Family Medical Guide. Random rev. ed. 1987 $35.00. ISBN 0-394-55582-1. A useful guide for home use that provides reliable health advice and includes understandable explanations of anatomy, diseases, and surgical operation; divided into four sections (health maintenance, self-diagnosis, diseases, and caring for the sick).

Bosco, Dominick. *The People's Guide to Vitamins and Minerals from A to Zinc.* Contempo. Bks. 1989 $13.95. ISBN 0-8092-4582-5. Lists individual vitamins and minerals, their specific functions in the body, problems of insufficiency and overdose, toxic qualities, and effectiveness in disease prevention.

Brace, Edward R. *A Popular Guide to Medical Language.* Van Nos. Reinhold 1983 o.p. Provides information on more than 1,000 medical terms, tests, procedures, and diseases; easy to understand.

Bricklin, Mark. *Rodale's Encyclopedia of Natural Home Remedies.* Rodale Pr. 1982 $23.95. ISBN 0-87857-396-8. Compilation of advice from *Prevention* magazine on everything from acne to warts; does not include questionable or potentially hazardous remedies.

The Columbia University College of Physicians and Surgeons Complete Home Medical Guide. Crown Pub. Group 1989 $39.95. ISBN 0-517-57216-8. A comprehensive and encyclopedic approach to health care advice from medical experts on the diagnosis, prevention, treatment, and cure of many common diseases and ailments; also includes information on health and wellness, drugs, and medical emergencies.

Dial 800 for Health. People's Med. Soc. 1993 $5.95. ISBN 0-9627334-9-0. A useful directory featuring information on more than 300 health-related organizations that can be reached by toll-free telephone numbers.

Dox, Ida, John Melloni Biagio, and Gilbert M. Eisner. *Melloni's Illustrated Medical Dictionary.* Parthenon 1993 $28.95. ISBN 0-85070-479-1. Features clear illustrations and comprehensible definitions.

Dulbecco, Renato, ed. *Encyclopedia of Human Biology.* 8 vols. Acad. Pr. $1950.00. ISBN 0-685-48179-4. "Intended as a comprehensive overview of current knowledge of human biology, this easy-to-use set is written for both the layperson and the scholar. Signed articles have been prepared by specialists. Detailed subject index brings together information on a topic throughout the set" (*Library Journal*).

The Good Health Fact Book. Reader's Digest 1992 $26.50. ISBN 0-89577-416-X. Offers a commonsense approach to self-help, utilizing a question-and-answer technique to promote good health.

Health, United States 1991. U.S. Gov. Printing Office 1992 o.p. From the Department of Health and Human Services; a superb annual source for basic statistics and information on health topics of current interest.

Karlin, Leonard. *Medical Secretary's and Assistant's Encyclopedic Dictionary.* P-H 1984 $19.95. ISBN 0-13-572909-2. Presents brief definitions of many medical procedures, disease states, terms, and drugs (generic and proprietary); accessible to the general reader.

Lampe, Kenneth F., and Mary Ann McCann. *American Medical Association Handbook of Poisonous and Injurious Plants.* AMA 1985 $28.00. ISBN 0-89970-183-3. Descriptions are accurate and brief. Among the best books available for information on plants that are toxic to human beings; arranged alphabetically by botanical name.

Larson, David E., ed. *Mayo Clinic Family Health Book: The Ultimate Home Medical Reference.* Morrow 1990 $40.00. ISBN 0-688-07819-2. Provides a wealth of authoritative information on a wide range of health topics; easy to understand.

The Marshall Cavendish Encyclopedia of Family Health. 12 vols. Marshall Cavendish 1991 $449.95. ISBN 1-85435-420-5. "A revision of their 1986 24 volume *Illustrated Encyclopedia of Family Health*, this set includes over 900 alphabetical entries covering the basics of human anatomy, physiology, medicine, health and disease in clearly written and profusely illustrated articles" (*Library Journal*).

The Mosby Medical Encyclopedia. Viking Penguin 1992 $18.00. ISBN 0-452-26672-6. An authoritative and handy medical reference for the general reader, containing more than 22,000 entries, drug information, and numerous tables and charts.

Napoli, Maryann. *Health Facts: A Critical Evaluation of the Major Problems, Treatments, and Alternatives Facing Medical Consumers.* Overlook Pr. 1984 $22.95. ISBN 0-87951-132-X. A directory that helps consumers take responsibility for and to make their health care decisions; includes historical and current viewpoints, statistics, suggestions, and recommended readings.

The PDR Family Guide to Prescription Drugs. Med Econ Data 1993 $24.95. ISBN 1-56363-020-6. Provides drug-specific information in readable, extensively indexed form; based on the familiar and more comprehensive *Physicians Desk Reference*.

Rees, Alan. *Personal Health Reporter.* Gale 1992 $95.00. ISBN 0-8103-8392-6. A compilation of interesting material culled from standard lay and clinical sources. Presents information on 148 topics, including AIDS, HMOs, quackery, organ transplants, and others.

Rothenberg, Robert E. *The New American Medical Dictionary and Health Manual.* Viking Penguin 1992 $14.00. ISBN 0-452-01102-7. An excellent, easy-to-use medical dictionary with basic explanations of medical terms, diseases, and disorders.

The Wellness Encyclopedia: The Comprehensive Resource to Safeguarding Health and Preventing Illness. HM 1991 $29.45. ISBN 0-395-53363-5. "An excellent family health guide that is derived from articles that appeared in *Wellness Letter*, a publication of the School of Public Health at the University of California, Berkeley. Arranged under five broad divisions, information is presented on making intelligent choices for healthier living" (*Library Journal*).

Zimmerman, David R. *Zimmerman's Complete Guide to Nonprescription Drugs.* Gale 1992 $42.95. ISBN 0-8103-8874-X. An extensively revised and updated edition of his *Essential Guide to Nonprescription Drugs.* Using the FDA's Over-the-Counter Drug Review database, rates the safety and efficacy of the active ingredients in nonprescription medications; more useful than the *PDR* because Zimmerman compares and evaluates various products used for the same illness.

BIOGRAPHY AND HISTORY OF MEDICINE

Books on the history of medicine usually are erudite treatments directed at other scholars. There has been, however, a significant growth in the number of titles published for the general reader, as reflected by the following list. Autobiographies that describe training experiences are included with the "Health Professions" section that appears later in this chapter. (See also Chapters 3 and 13.)

Anderson, Odin W. *Health Services in the United States: A Growth Enterprise Since 1875.* Health Admin. Pr. 1985 $29.00. ISBN 0-910701-02-4. An excellent study of an extraordinary period in the history of health care in the United States, showing the evolution of health services from a predominantly private enterprise to one involving the federal and state governments on a large scale.

Armstrong, David, and Elizabeth Metzger Armstrong. *The Great American Medicine Show.* P-H 1991 $18.00. ISBN 0-13-364027-2. A whimsical compendium of unusual facts, fads, oddities, and charlatans that characterize the progress of American medicine; also includes some good overviews of medicine shows and diets.

Bean, William N. *Walter Reed: A Biography.* Bks. Demand 1988 $54.10. ISBN 0-685-44473-2. The first full-length biography of the discoverer of the transmission mechanism for yellow fever; also an important piece of U.S. Army history.

Bell, Whitfield J. *The Colonial Physician and Other Essays.* Watson Pub. Intl. 1975 $16.00. ISBN 0-88202-024-2. Examines the education, demeanor, and attitudes of the American physician, during the colonial and revolutionary periods.

Brieger, Gert H., ed. *Theory and Practice in American Medicine.* Science History 1976 o.p. A collection of historical studies arranged in five categories—medical education, medical theory and research, medical practice, surgery, and medical care; most studies cover nineteenth-century developments.

Caplan, Arthur L., ed. *When Medicine Went Mad: Bioethics and the Holocaust. Contemporary Issues in Biomedicine, Ethics, and Society Ser.* Humana 1992 $22.50. ISBN 0-89603-235-3. A sober and scholarly analysis of the Nazi physicians who carried out experiments on unwilling victims during World War II.

Cassedy, James H. *American Medicine and Statistical Thinking, 1800–1860.* HUP 1984 $32.50. ISBN 0-674-02560-1. Well-written account of the medical use of statistics and the social development of medicine in the United States.

Cournand, Andre F. *From Roots . . . to Late Budding: The Intellectual Adventures of a Medical Scientist.* Gardner Pr. 1986 $21.95. ISBN 0-89876-108-5. Autobiography of the 1956 Nobel Prize-winner in physiology.

Dally, Ann. *Women under the Knife: A History of Surgery.* Routledge 1992 $27.50. ISBN 0-415-90554-0. A rational and scholarly historical work that illuminates the conflict between the medical establishment, especially between the male doctor and the female patient.

Dobkin, Bruce H. *Brain Matters*. 1988 o.p. An autobiographical description of clinical neurology.

Drachman, Virginia G. *Hospital with a Heart: Women Doctors and the Paradox of Separatism at the New England Hospital, 1862–1969*. Cornell Univ. Pr. 1984 $34.00. ISBN 0-8014-1624-8. A detailed description of the evolution of a hospital from an institution of medical charity to one of medical science.

Franklin, Jon, and John Sutherland. *Guinea Pig Doctors: The Drama of Medical Research Through Self-Experimentation*. Morrow 1984 $17.95. ISBN 0-688-02666-4. A physician (John Sutherland) and a Pulitzer Prize-winning journalist (Jon Franklin) describe physicians in history and their autoexperimentation.

Gifford, George E., ed. *Physicians Signers of the Declaration of Independence*. Watson Pub. Intl. 1976 $14.95. ISBN 0-88202-159-1. Biographical essays on the five physicians who signed the Declaration of Independence—Josiah Bartlett, Matthew Thornton, Oliver Wolcott, Lyman Hall, and Benjamin Rush.

Hamburger, Jean. *Diary of William Harvey: The Imaginary Journal of the Physician Who Revolutionized Medicine*. Trans. by Barbara Wright. Rutgers U. Pr. 1992 $35.00. ISBN 0-8135-1825-3. An absorbing translation of a fictionalized diary written by Harvey.

Harden, Victoria A. *Inventing the NIH: Federal Biomedical Research Policy, 1887–1937*. Johns Hopkins 1986 $40.00. ISBN 0-8018-3071-0. The story of the long legislative effort to implement a program of federal biomedical research.

Harvey, A. McGhee. *Science at the Bedside: Clinical Research in American Medicine, 1905–1945*. Johns Hopkins 1981 $48.00. ISBN 0-8018-2562-8. A scholarly examination of the various contributors to clinical research efforts in the United States during the first half of the twentieth century.

Helman, Ethel. *An Autumn Life: How a Surgeon Faced His Fatal Illness*. Faber & Faber 1986 $6.95. ISBN 0-571-13704-0. A loving biography by the surviving widow of a South African surgeon.

Hudson, Robert P. *Disease and Its Control: The Shaping of Modern Thought*. Greenwood 1983 $55.00. ISBN 0-313-23806-5. Reviews the major concepts leading to the present theories of disease and its control in the West; follows a conceptual rather than a chronological organization.

Huston, Perdita. *Motherhood by Choice: Pioneers in Women's Health and Family Planning*. Feminist Pr. 1992 $35.00. ISBN 1-55861-068-5. A collection of oral history interviews with 12 previously uncelebrated family planning pioneers from industrialized and developing countries.

Kanigel, Robert. *Apprentice to Genius: The Making of a Scientific Dynasty*. Macmillan 1986 $19.18. ISBN 0-02-560650-6. Clearly describes research in the fields of neuroscience and neuropharmacology and the way in which leaders in the field were mentors for each other.

Kaufman, Martin. *American Medical Education: The Formative Years, 1765–1910*. Greenwood 1976 $45.00. ISBN 0-8371-8590-4. Traces the evolution of American medical education from colonial times to the period immediately following publication of the influential Flexner Report.

Kaufman, Sharon R. *The Healer's Tale: Transforming Medicine and Culture Life Course Studies*. U. of Wis. Pr. 1993 $27.50. ISBN 0-299-13550-0. A collective biography of seven distinguished physicians (all in their eighties) who experienced the exciting years of the development of penicillin and antibiotics, also provides an intelligent critique of twentieth-century medical practice.

King, Lester S. *Medical Thinking: A Historical Preface*. Bks. Demand 1982 $90.30. ISBN 0-8357-4197-4. Presents a wide-ranging account of the problems faced by physicians and the development of the critical skills needed to solve them; analyzes changing and constant elements of the definitions of important medical concepts, such as signs and symptoms, syndromes, fact and theory, disease entity, and clinical entity.

_____. *The Philosophy of Medicine: The Early Eighteenth Century*. Bks. Demand 1978 $80.80. ISBN 0-7837-4161-8. Places eighteenth-century medicine in the setting from which it emerged and examines assumptions on which the physicians worked.

Koop, C. Everett. *Koop: The Memoirs of America's Family Doctor.* Random 1991 $22.50. ISBN 0-394-57626-8. A fascinating and well-written autobiography of a controversial pediatrician who was appointed Surgeon General of the United States by Ronald Reagan; covers his formative years, education and family life, as well as his professional and public career.

Kramer, Mark. *Invasive Procedures: A Year in the World of Two Surgeons.* Viking Penguin 1984 $6.95. ISBN 0-14-007411-2. Presents an intelligent view of dedication to task, obsession with technical perfection, peer relationships, and ambivalent involvement with patients of two successful surgeons; written for the general reader.

Leavitt, Judith W. *The Healthiest City: Milwaukee and the Politics of Health Reform.* Princeton U. Pr. 1982 $45.00. ISBN 0-691-08298-7. A social history documenting Milwaukee's transformation from a typically unhealthy city to one acclaimed as the healthiest in the United States.

Levenson, Dorothy. *Montefiore: The Hospital as Social Instrument, 1884–1984.* FS&G 1984 $19.95. ISBN 0-374-21228-7. A fascinating study of a hospital, social change, and philanthropy in New York City.

Levin, Beatrice S. *Women and Medicine.* Scarecrow Pr. 1980 $16.00. ISBN 0-8108-1296-7. A light, humorous approach to the topic; includes a historical overview of the challenges, cultural attitudes, riots, and discrimination that women have faced in the medical profession.

McLaughlin, Loretta. *The Pill, John Rock, and the Church: The Biography of a Revolution.* Little 1983 o.p. A biography of the man who discovered the birth control pill.

Marks, Geoffrey, and William K. Beatty. *The Story of Medicine in America.* Macmillan 1972 o.p. A succinct and highly organized literature review of medicine in the United States from the founding of Jamestown through medical advances of the twentieth century.

Medawar, Peter. *Memoir of a Thinking Radish: An Autobiography.* OUP 1986 $19.95. ISBN 0-19-217737-0. The 1960 Nobel Prize-winner for physiology and medicine provides a witty and discerning view of biological research through his career in immunology.

Miller, G. Wayne. *The Work of Human Hands: Hardy Hendren and Surgical Wonder at Children's Hospital.* Random 1993 $23.00. ISBN 0-679-40264-0. Easy-to-read biography of a pediatric surgeon called by former Surgeon General Koop "a surgeon's surgeon"; especially moving testimonial to the importance and strength of a positive physician-patient relationship.

Morantz, Regina M., Cynthia Pomerleau, and Carol H. Fenichel. *In Her Own Words: Oral Histories of Women Physicians.* Greenwood 1982 $55.00. ISBN 0-313-22686-5. Features interviews with nine female physicians, over three generations from the 1920s to the 1970s, coupled with extensive editorial commentary. Covers their obstacles, triumphs, and disappointments; includes an especially revealing analysis of the reconciliation of career and family.

Morantz-Sanchez, Regina M. *Sympathy and Science: Women Physicians in American Medicine.* OUP 1987 $24.95. ISBN 0-19-503627-1. A major intellectual achievement that examines the role of women in American medicine from the colonial period through the early decades of the twentieth century.

Morse, Thomas S. *A Gift of Courage.* Doubleday 1982 o.p. Narrates the experiences of a pediatric surgeon.

Pappas, Charles N. *The Life and Times of G. V. Black.* Quintessence 1983 $38.00. ISBN 0-931386-55-1. A biography of the founder of scientific dentistry.

Patterson, Jane, and Lynda Madaras. *Woman Doctor: The Education of Jane Patterson, M.D.* Avon 1983 o.p. A vivid portrayal of the stresses of medical training in obstetrics and gynecology and of one woman's journey to self-acceptance.

Post, Jerrold M., and Robert S. Robins. *When Illness Strikes the Leader: The Dilemma of the Captive King.* Yale U. Pr. 1993 $30.00. ISBN 0-300-05683-4. A fascinating account of what occurs when a head of state becomes mentally or physically ill; includes numerous examples of leaders who have become dangerous to their countries.

Radetsky, Peter. *Invisible Invaders: The Story of the Emerging Age of Viruses.* Little 1991 $22.95. ISBN 0-316-73216-8. "With a novelist's flair and a scientist's clarity" (*Library*

Journal), relates the frustrating story of humankind's experiences with the elusive, mutable, and complex enemies of contemporary biomedicine.

Sacks, Oliver. *A Leg to Stand On*. Summit Bks. 1984 $14.70. ISBN 0-671-46780-8. Describes the experience of the author (a neurologist) when he lost the use of his leg as the result of a mountain-climbing accident.

Selzer, Richard. *Letters to a Young Doctor*. S&S Trade 1983 $9.95. ISBN 0-671-44299-6. In combination with his earlier *Confessions of a Knife* (1979), constitutes a collection of essays and vignettes on medical topics.

Sheehan, John C. *The Enchanted Ring: The Untold Story of Penicillin*. MIT Pr. 1982 $24.00. ISBN 0-262-19204-7. Describes the American production of the drug during World War II.

Shorter, Edward. *From Paralysis to Fatigue: A History of Psychosomatic Illness in the Modern Era*. Free Pr. 1991 $24.95. ISBN 0-02-928665-4. Describes how culture and society affect the diagnosis and treatment of psychosomatic diseases; easy-to-read history.

Sidel, Victor W., and Ruth Sidel. *Reforming Medicine: Lessons of the Last Quarter Century*. Pantheon 1984 $19.45. ISBN 0-394-50213-2. A collection of essays documenting postwar reform in the health care system of the United States.

Silverstein, Arthur M. *Pure Politics and Impure Science: The Swine Flu Affair*. Johns Hopkins 1981 $28.00. ISBN 0-8018-2632-2. The application of Murphy's first law to the nation's preparation for the 1976 swine flu epidemic that never materialized.

Smith, T. Burton, with Carter Henderson. *White House Doctor*. Madison 1992 $24.95. ISBN 0-8191-8625-2. Represents the latest in the line of autobiographies of physicians to the president.

Smolan, Rick. *Medicine's Great Journey: One Hundred Years of Healing*. Bulfinch Pr. 1992 $50.00. ISBN 0-8212-1987-1. A historical chronicle of medical progress during the last century; an excellent reference for those who want a brief history of medicine or for those who need photographic documentation.

Starr, Paul. *The Social Transformation of American Medicine: The Rise of a Sovereign Profession and the Making of a Vast Industry*. Basic 1984 $18.00. ISBN 0-465-07935-0. A landmark work tracing the evolution of the U.S. health care system over two centuries.

Thomas, Lewis. *The Youngest Science: Notes of a Medicine-Watcher*. Bantam 1984 $6.95. ISBN 0-553-34066-2. The memoir of a distinguished scientist and educator.

Weisse, Allen B. *Conversations in Medicine*. NYU Pr. 1984 $50.00. ISBN 0-8147-9200-6. A collection of interviews with 16 physicians involved in major medical advances of the twentieth century.

———. *Medical Odysseys: The Different and Sometimes Unexpected Pathways to Twentieth-Century Medical Discoveries*. Rutgers U. Pr. 1991 $36.00. ISBN 0-8135-1616-1. Traces the role of serendipity and how it has led to many recent landmark medical discoveries; well-documented.

Whorton, James. *Crusaders for Fitness: A History of American Health Reformers*. Princeton U. Pr. 1982 $47.50. ISBN 0-691-04694-8. A chronicle of the health reform movements in the United States from the early 1800s to the present.

Young, James H. *American Health Quackery: Collected Essays*. Princeton U. Pr. 1992 $24.95. ISBN 0-691-04782-0. Young continues his historical forays into quackery with this collection of new and previously unpublished essays.

———. *The Medical Messiahs: A Social History of Health Quackery in 20th Century America*. Princeton U. Pr. 1992 repr. of 1968 ed. $16.95. ISBN 0-691-00579-6. A definitive historical study of a fascinating subject; entertaining and easy-to-read.

AGING

Although there is extensive literature on aging as a social phenomenon, the following list emphasizes the clinical and psychological aspects of the aging

process and health services for the aged. Books on nutrition and aging are
included under section "Nutrition and Diet" in this chapter.

Arie, Tom, ed. *Health Care of the Elderly.* Bks. Demand 1981 $60.00. ISBN 0-317-39703-6.
Essays by distinguished experts that present a critical evaluation of the current status
of several aspects of aging as a social issue; thought-provoking and easy-to-read.

Berghorn, Forrest J. *The Dynamics of Aging: Original Essays on the Processes and
Experience of Growing Old.* Westview Pr. 1981 o.p. An up-to-date, multidisciplinary
survey of the field of aging; addresses the biology of aging, social roles, public policy,
service delivery, and other topics.

Bortz, Walter M. *We Live Too Short and Die Too Long: How to Achieve and Enjoy Your
Natural 100-Year-Life Span.* Bantam 1991 $19.95. ISBN 0-553-07227-7. Recommends
moderation, sensible diet, and continued physical and mental activity to reach a ripe
old age; written in an entertaining and authoritative style.

Bosse, Raymond, and Charles L. Rose. *Smoking and Aging.* Free Pr. 1983 $37.00. ISBN 0-
669-05230-2. An excellent reference that emphasizes the relationship between
smoking, aging, and disease in the elderly.

Breitung, Joan. *Care of the Older Adult.* Tiresias Pr. 1981 $11.95. ISBN 0-913292-2. A
useful, idea-packed text for families of aging individuals, as well as for home health
care workers.

Brody, Elaine M. *Mental and Physical Health Practices of Older People: A Guide for Health
Professionals.* Springer Pub. 1985 $28.95. ISBN 0-8261-4870-0. Despite its subtitle, a
useful book for the general reader as well as the health professional.

Burdman, Geri Marr. *Healthful Aging.* P-H 1986. ISBN 0-13-385543-0. Discusses factors
that prevent aging people from realizing their wellness potential; also includes a
"Resources" section that lists organizations, periodicals, and more.

Busse, Ewald W., and George L. Maddox. *The Duke Longitudinal Studies of Normal Aging,
1955–1980: Overview of History, Design, and Findings.* Springer Pub. 1985 $26.95.
ISBN 0-8261-4150-1. Readable, well-written and clearly organized. Describes the
classic Duke research on aging; easy-to-read.

Duncan, Theodore G. *Over 55: A Handbook on Aging.* Erlbaum 1982 $89.95. ISBN 0-
89859-726-9. A comprehensive manual that examines the medical, emotional,
financial, and social interests of the elderly.

Edelman, Deborah S. *Sex in the Golden Years: What's Ahead May Be Worth Aging For.*
Fine 1992 $21.95. ISBN 1-55611-207-6. Presents sex in later life as a significant
challenge that awaits the aging couple; covers the various impediments to sexual
function that accompanies aging.

Futrell, May, ed. *Primary Health Care of the Older Adult.* Duxbury Pr. 1980 o.p. Presents
detailed information about the health care of persons 65 and older; useful for
professionals and for caregivers but less so for general readers.

Hall, David A. *The Biomedical Basis of Gerontology.* PSG Pubns. 1984 o.p. A compact and
integrated study of all aspects of the aging process from a scientific viewpoint.

Hallowell, Christopher. *Growing Old, Staying Young.* Morrow 1985 o.p. A report on the
aging process as it affects the individual and society; emphasizes the effect that a
large aged population will have on the United States.

Haug, Marie R., ed. *Elderly Patients and Their Doctors.* Springer Pub. 1981 $24.95. ISBN
0-8261-3570-6. An interesting compilation of articles on the physician-patient
interaction in gerontology.

Health in an Older Society. Bks. Demand 1985 $65.30. ISBN 0-8357-4269-5. Features
landmark papers from the 1983 symposium on societal health; covers specific topics,
such as cardiovascular aging, depressive illnesses, dementias, as well as the life-style
and care of the elderly as determinants of health status.

Henig, Robin M. *The Myth of Senility: Misconceptions about the Brain and Aging.* Am.
Assn. Retire 1985 $14.95. ISBN 0-673-24831-3. A timely reexamination and redefini-
tion of senility that identifies the differences between the normal effects of aging and
the abnormal signs and effects of cerebral illness or damage.

Horne, Jo. *Caregiving: Helping an Aged Loved One.* Amer. Assn. Retire 1987 $13.95. ISBN 0-673-24822-4. Provides valuable home health care information for the caregiver.

Hogstel, Mildred O. *Nursing Care of the Older Adult: In the Hospital, Nursing Home, and Community.* Delmar 1988 $42.95. ISBN 0-8273-4259-4. A blend of clinical experience and scientific fact that is useful for caregivers in all settings.

Kastenbaum, Robert. *Old, Sick, and Helpless: Where Therapy Begins.* Ballinger 1981 o.p. A holistic approach to geriatric care that encompasses the history of care of the aging, the therapeutic relationship, and a series of case histories.

Koch, Tom. *A Place in Time: Caregivers for Their Elderly.* Greenwood 1993 $19.95. ISBN 0-275-94483-2. Explores why families continue to provide care to the elderly despite great personal loss and hardship to themselves; from a series of interviews with 12 caregivers.

Lammers, William W. *Public Policy and the Aging.* Congr. Quarterly 1983 o.p. Describes the political agenda for the aging, the history of the three White House Conferences on Aging, and discusses at length the health, long-term care, social services, and housing policy for the elderly.

Leutz, Walter N., and others. *Changing Health Care for an Aging Society: Planning for the Social Health Maintenance Organization.* Free Pr. 1985 $37.95. ISBN 0-669-10139-7. Discusses the evolution of a SHMO for the elderly; offers a solid foundation for those interested in improving the delivery of health care services to the elderly.

Margolis, Simeon, ed. *The Johns Hopkins Medical Handbook: The 100 Major Medical Disorders of People over the Age of 50.* Rebus 1993 $39.95. ISBN 0-929661-04-4. A useful compendium of symptoms, diagnostic procedures, treatments, causes, and preventive measures that affect people over 50.

Morgan, Robert F., with Jane Wilson. *Growing Younger: Adding Years to Your Life by Measuring and Controlling Your Body Age.* Stein & Day 1983 o.p. Suggests that hypnosis, yoga, graphotherapy, diet, and so on, can promote longevity; written by a psychologist.

Murray, Ruth B., M.M.W. Huelskoetter, and Dorothy L. O'Driscoll. *The Nursing Process in Later Maturity.* Appleton & Lange 1980 o.p. A comprehensive survey of the needs and problems of senior citizens; an excellent reference for individuals involved in geriatric care.

Oberleder, Muriel. *The Aging Trap.* Acropolis 1982 $11.95. ISBN 0-87491-496-5. A thoughtful examination of the aging process designed to dispel many of its associated myths.

Ogle, Jane. *Ageproofing.* NAL-Dutton 1984 o.p. Refutes the notion that degenerative processes associated with aging are inevitable; advocates that proper nutrition and exercise can delay the aging process.

Pegels, C. Carl. *Health Care and the Elderly.* Aspen 1981 o.p. A good introductory reference and overview of health care policymaking and its financing for the aged.

Palmore, Erdman. *International Handbook on Aging: Contemporary Developments and Research.* Greenwood 1980 $55.00. ISBN 0-313-20890-5. A substantial sourcebook for the field of aging.

Phillips, Harry T., and Susan A. Gaylord, eds. *Aging and Public Health.* Springer Pub. 1985 $30.95. ISBN 0-8261-4380-6. A comprehensive treatment that stresses the important role of the public health movement and practitioner in improving the well-being of the elderly.

Pizer, Hank. *Over Fifty-Five, Healthy, and Alive: A Health Resource for the Coming of Age.* Van Nos. Reinhold 1983 o.p. A manual focusing on the health concerns of people over the age of 55; includes chapters written by a variety of health professionals.

Rob, Caroline, and Janet Reynolds. *The Caregiver's Guide: Helping Older Friends and Relatives with Health and Safety Concerns.* HM 1992 $22.45. ISBN 0-395-50086-9. In-depth information about the changes that accompany aging and how to make life easier both for the caregiver and the aged individual.

Roy, F. Hampton, and Charles Russell. *The Encyclopedia of Aging and the Elderly.* Facts on File 1992 $45.00. ISBN 0-8160-1869-3. "This encyclopedic reference responds to

the need for a limited, authoritative work on aging from a strictly medi-
cal/sociological perspective" (*Library Journal*).

Smith, Kerri S. *Caring for Your Aging Parents: A Sourcebook of Timesaving Techniques
and Tips. Working Caregiver Ser.* Amer. Source Bks. 1992 $8.95. ISBN 0-9621333-8-8.
A compact guidebook on ways to recognize and resolve health, financial, and legal
problems faced by aging parents.

Walford, Roy L. *Maximum Life Span.* Avon 1984 $4.50. ISBN 0-380-65524-1. A timely
book that focuses on the historical and the current implications of longer life spans.

Williamson, John B., Judith Shindul, and Linda Evans. *Aging and Public Policy: Social
Control or Social Justice?* C. C. Thomas 1985 $51.25. ISBN 0-398-0504-6. A review of
health delivery in the United States and an examination of the profits and cost
containment of long-term care with limited funds.

ALTERNATIVE HEALTH CARE
AND OTHER SPECIAL SYSTEMS

This section is highly selective, featuring books that discuss alternatives to
traditional clinical medicine. In particular, the holistic health movement has
spawned a great many publications. Moreover, the opening of China in the
1970s has triggered a renewed emphasis on oriental therapies. Inclusion of
titles here does not constitute endorsement of the techniques but rather, an
effort to include nontraditional approaches to health care.

Achterberg, Jeanne. *Imagery in Healing: Shamanism and Modern Medicine.* Shambhala
1985 $9.95. Explores the meaning of shamanism in worldwide cultures past and
present.

Albright, Peter, and Beth Parker Albright. *Body, Mind, and Spirit: The Journey Toward
Health and Wholeness.* Stephen Greene Pr. 1980 o.p. "A collaborative work on
holistic health, which testifies for the triune wholeness of the person in whom the
components are unified into a matrix of love and naturalistic health practices"
(*Choice*).

Becker, Robert O., and Gary Selden. *The Body Electric: Electromagnetism and the
Foundation of Life.* Morrow 1987 $10.95. ISBN 0-688-06971-1. A description of
Becker's more than 30 years of research, the insights derived from it, and the
personal and political experiences of a working scientist who challenged accepted
views.

Bird, Christopher. *Persecution and Trial of Gaston Naessens.* Kramer 1991 $12.95. ISBN
0-915811-30-8. Naessans developed a controversial substance called 714-X, which
some say is effective against cancer and immune system disorders; describes
Naessens's ostracism by the medical establishment.

Bliss, Shepherd, ed. *The New Holistic Health Handbook: Living Well in a New Age.* Viking
Penguin 1985 $14.95. ISBN 0-8289-0561-4. A wide-ranging compilation of articles on
all aspects of the holistic health movement.

Castleman, Michael. *The Healing Herbs.* Rodale Pr. 1991 $27.95. ISBN 0-87857-934-6. A
compendium of information about the use of herbs to treat a wide range of ailments.

Castro, Miranda. *The Complete Homeopathy Handbook: Safe and Effective Ways to Treat
Fevers, Coughs, Colds and Sore Throats, Childhood Ailments, Food Poisoning, Flu,
and a Wide Range of Everyday Complaints.* St. Martin 1991 $14.95. ISBN 0-312-
06320-2. A clear, well-organized manual from a London homeopath that provides
advice on common ailments, such as headache, flu, and indigestion.

Chin, Richard M. *The Energy Within: The Science Behind Every Oriental Therapy from
Acupuncture to Yoga.* Paragon Hse. 1992 $12.95. ISBN 1-55778-349-7. A comprehen-
sive explanation of the basics of Oriental treatment; includes a 30-day exercise
program and lists of energy-related foods.

Chinese Massage Therapy: A Handbook of Therapeutic Massage. Shambhala 1984 o.p.
Explains Chinese massage therapy principles and describes 24 commonly used

techniques; illustrates important acupoints in a text that is detailed but clear; accompanied by line drawings.

Chopra, Deepak. *Ageless Body, Timeless Mind: The Quantum Alternative to Growing Old.* Crown Pub. Group 1993 $22.00. ISBN 0-517-59257-6. Combines philosophy, biology, and modern health research to convince the reader that the effects of aging are largely preventable.

Deliman, Tracy, and John S. Smolowe. *Holistic Medicine: Harmony of Body, Mind, Spirit.* Reston 1982 o.p. Sixteen contributors discuss a holistic helping process designed to increase the harmony of mind, body, and spirit.

Dever, G. E. Alan. *Community Health Analysis: A Holistic Approach.* Aspen 1980 o.p. A comprehensive, well-documented text that provides a philosophical approach to holistic health; well-written.

Eisenberg, David. *Encounters with Qi: Exploring Chinese Medicine.* Viking Penguin 1987 $10.00. ISBN 0-14-009427-X. Balanced account that presents many Chinese ideas and practices worthy of careful examination for their therapeutic value; written from the viewpoint of a Western physician.

Family Guide to Natural Medicine: How to Stay Healthy the Natural Way. Reader's Digest 1993 $30.00. ISBN 0-89577-433-X. "An excellent and enjoyable overview of holistic medicine" (*Library Journal*).

Freund, Peter E. S., and Miriam Fisher. *The Civilized Body: Social Domination, Control, and Health.* Temple U. Pr. 1983 o.p. Describes the relationship between social structure and disease; represents the first attempt to carefully integrate the individualistic literature of the holistic health movement with sociological concepts of social control and stratification.

Griggs, Barbara. *Green Pharmacy: A History of Herbal Medicine.* Viking Penguin 1982 o.p. Provides a history of botanical medicine, or herbalism, from Galen to the present.

Hand, Wayland D., ed. *American Folk Medicine: A Symposium.* U. CA Pr. 1976 o.p. A classic and fascinating work that features the papers from a landmark symposium held at the University of California at Los Angeles; includes folk practices among various ethnic groups.

Hastings, Arthur C., James Fadiman, and James S. Gordon. *Health for the Whole Person: The Complete Guide to Holistic Medicine.* Westview Pr. 1980 o.p. A comprehensive summary of world health practices related to holistic health; covers the diverse field of holistic health practices with clarity and excellent documentation.

Hittleman, Richard. *Yoga for Health: The Total Program.* Ballantine 1985 $12.95. ISBN 0-345-32798-5. A manual of Hatha yoga exercises, vegetarian nutrition, and meditation.

The Holistic Health Lifebook: A Guide to Personal and Planetary Well-Being. And/Or Pr. 1981 $12.95. ISBN 0-915904-53-5. An extension of *Holistic Health Handbook* (1979) that extends the concept of holism beyond health to one's entire lifestyle.

Inglis, Brian, and Ruth West. *The Alternative Health Guide.* Knopf 1983 $19.95. ISBN 0-394-52789-5. Examines historical backgrounds, procedures, research findings, and typical applications for 66 physical, psychological, and paranormal therapies, ranging from osteopathy to spiritualism.

Kaptchuk, Ted J. *The Web That Has No Weaver: Understanding Chinese Medicine.* Congdon & Weed 1992 $19.95. ISBN 0-312-92932-3. Emphasizes the basic differences of approach to recognizing and treating disharmony in the human body; comprehensive and easy-to-read.

Lawrence, D. Baloti, and Lewis Harrison. *Massageworks: A Practical Encyclopedia of Massage Techniques.* Putnam Pub. Group 1983 $9.95. ISBN 0-399-50748-5. A beginner's guide to massage self-care for a variety of complaints.

LeShan, Lawrence. *The Mechanic and the Gardener: Making the Most of the Holistic Revolution in Medicine.* H. Holt & Co. 1982 o.p. Asserts that both allopathy and holistic treatment are necessary to the healing process; designed for the health care consumer.

Lillyquist, Michael J. *Sunlight and Health.* Dodd 1985 $15.95. ISBN 0-396-08482-6. Describes how sunlight is necessary for good health and is a health hazard; a well-documented summary of current knowledge.

Lowe, Carl, and Jim Nechas. *Body Healing.* Rodale Pr. 1983 o.p. A guide to selected alternative therapies, exercise, and self-care; notable for its clear, straightforward instructions.

Mindell, Earl, *Earl Mindell's Herb Bible.* S&S Trade 1992 $25.00. ISBN 0-671-76113-7. Covers more than 100 common and useful herbs, giving preparation and dosage, benefits, and cautions; written by a pharmacist and professor of nutrition.

Otto, Herbert A., and James W. Knight. *Dimensions in Wholistic Healing: New Frontiers in the Treatment of the Whole Person.* Nelson-Hall 1979 $39.95. ISBN 0-88229-513-6. An important collection of writings focusing on the various aspects of holistic health care. Covers its development in the United States and its early historic framework.

Pizer, Hank. *Guide to the New Medicine: What Works, What Doesn't.* Morrow 1982 o.p. A consumer's guide to alternative health care. Evaluates various techniques, including homeopathy, acupuncture, meditation, and biofeedback; based on a review of scientific findings.

Ryman, Daniele. *Aromatherapy: The Encyclopedia of Plants and Oils and How They Help You.* Bantam 1993 $10.95. ISBN 0-553-37166-5. Provides a detailed history of aromatherapy, explains how essential oils are extracted and applied, and offers do-it-yourself instructions for those so inclined; clearly written.

Salmon, J. Warren, ed. *Alternative Medicines: Popular and Policy Perspectives.* Routledge Chapman & Hall 1984 o.p. Essential for those interested in the future direction of health care and delivery; represents the first straightforward treatment of several alternative medicines in one volume.

Sinclair, Brett J. *Alternative Health Care Resources: A Directory and Guide.* P-H 1992 $24.95. ISBN 0-13-030073-X. A timely, useful compilation of almost 400 self-help groups, organizations, and institutions; also offers information on alternative health care.

Sofowora, Abayomi. *Medicinal Plants and Traditional Medicine in Africa.* Bks. Demand 1982 $68.50. ISBN 0-685-23592-0. Covers the fundamental procedures of traditional African healing methods and compares their advantages and disadvantages to methods used in modern medicine.

Stalker, Douglas, and Clark Glymour. *Examining Holistic Medicine.* Prometheus Bks. 1986 $29.95. ISBN 0-87975-303-X. A collection of 20 essays that critically analyze the philosophy, methodology, and practice of holistic medicine.

Steiner, Richard P., ed. *Folk Medicine: The Art and the Science.* Am. Chemical 1986 $24.95. ISBN 0-8412-0939-1. Examines the folk medicine traditions of nine countries, encompassing nine cultures, to establish the scientific basis for remedial actions of treatment.

Tierra, Lesley. *The Herbs of Life: Health and Healing Using Western and Chinese Techniques.* Crossing Pr. 1992 $28.95. ISBN 0-89594-499-5. An American acupuncturist/herbalist's guide to the use of Eastern and Western herbal preparations.

Tierra, Michael, ed. *American Herbalism: Essays on Herbs and Herbalism by Members of the American Herbalist Guild.* Crossing Pr. 1992 $28.95. ISBN 0-89594-541-X. A compendium of articles on several varieties of herbal medicine, such as Native American, traditional Chinese, and Ayurvedic, many of which are well documented; also includes appendices of herbal training classes and suggested readings.

Trotter, Robert T., and Juan A. Chavira. *Curanderismo: Mexican American Folk Healing.* U. of Ga. Pr. 1981 o.p. A comprehensive work on the theory and practice of curanderismo; also covers its characteristics and social nexus.

Weil, Andrew. *Health and Healing: Understanding Conventional and Alternative Medicine.* HM 1988 $9.70. ISBN 0-395-36200-8. This thoughtful and stimulating book challenges Western ideas of orthodox medicine and considers homeopathy, osteopathy, naturopathy, chiropractic, Chinese medicine, and so on; represents the most important book available in English on the subject.

Weiss, Gaea, and Shandor Weiss. *Growing and Using the Healing Herbs*. Outlet Bk. Co. 1992 $12.99. ISBN 0-517-06650-5. Presents the history of herbal healing in many cultures; includes practical hints for growing and manufacturing your own herbs.

West, Ruth, and Joanna E. Trevelyan. *Alternative Medicine: A Bibliography of Books in English*. Cassell 1985 $80.00. ISBN 0-7201-1721-6. A quality work of its kind that brings together English-language books on therapies outside the mainstream of medicine.

Wilen, Joan, and Lydia Wilen. *Live and Be Well: New Age and Old Folk Remedies*. HarpC 1992 $10.00. ISBN 0-06-096563-0. Offers an assortment of old folk remedies, New Age methods, and nutritional recommendations for common health problems; written by the authors of the immensely popular *Chicken Soup and Other Folk Remedies*.

Worwood, Valerie Ann. *The Complete Book of Essential Oils and Aromatherapy*. New Wrld Lib. 1991 $16.95. ISBN 0-031432-82-0. A comprehensive book drawn from research on aromatherapy and features advice on everything from first aid to cooking with essential oils; based on the premise that the most effective way to use herbs medicinally is by external application or inhalation.

ANATOMY

[SEE the section on The Healthy Body in this chapter.]

CARDIOLOGY

[SEE Chapter 13 under Cardiovascular Diseases, in this volume.]

CHILD CARE AND DEVELOPMENT

The reader will find in many bookstores and libraries a separate section on the topic of child care, one that produces many new titles each year. The following list represents a sample of the important books in this area.

Anastasiow, Nicholas J., and others. *The Adolescent Parent*. P. H. Brooks 1982 o.p. Offers a concise review of the worldwide problems of adolescent pregnancy and a thorough summary of knowledge about physical and intellectual development in adolescents.

Arnold, L. Eugene, and Donna Esteicher. *Parent-Child Group Therapy: Building Self-Esteem in a Cognitive-Behavioral Group*. Free Pr. 1985 $32.95. ISBN 0-669-09934-1. Describes a successful method to build self-esteem and improve the functioning of learning- and behavior-disordered children.

Auckett, Amelia D. *Baby Massage: Parent-Child Bonding Through Touching*. Newmarket 1988 $8.95. ISBN 1-55704-022-2. Presents massage as a positive experience for parents and children that results in improved communication.

Batshaw, Mark L., and Yvonne M. Perret. *Children with Handicaps: A Medical Primer*. P. H. Brookes 1986 $26.00. ISBN 0-933716-64-8. An important book about the medical aspects of handicaps in children; easy to read, clear, and sensitive.

Baum, Andrew, and Jerome E. Singer. *Issues in Child Health and Adolescent Health*. Erlbaum 1982 $55.95. ISBN 0-85859-184-8. A collection of works on the study of behavioral disorders, including reviews of the literature and relevant research findings.

Brazelton, T. Berry. *Touchpoints: Your Child's Emotional and Behavioral Development, the Essential Reference*. Addison-Wesley 1992 $22.95. ISBN 0-201-09380-4. An important new guidebook that can be used to assess the emotional development of the child.

————. *Working and Caring*. Addison-Wesley 1992 $10.95. ISBN 0-201-63271-3. An excellent book by the renowned Harvard pediatrician, focusing on working parents and the issues they confront.

Brown, Jeffrey L. *The Complete Parents' Guide to Telephone Medicine, How, When, and Why to Call Your Child's Doctor: A Ready Reference for Childhood Illnesses, Common Emergencies, Newborn Infant Care, Psychological and Behavior Problems*. Berkeley Pub. 1983 $3.50. ISBN 0-425-05496-9. Presents advice similar to that of major child development physicians, such as Spock, Brazelton, and Dodson.

Cuthbertson, Joanne, and Susie Schevill. *Helping Your Child Sleep Through the Night*. Doubleday 1985 $10.00. ISBN 0-385-19250-9. A useful book arranged in chapters by age and positive in tone in which the authors describe specific day-by-day plans of action.

DeLorenzo, Lorisa, and Robert DeLorenzo. *Total Child Care: From Birth to Age Five*. Doubleday 1982 o.p. A comprehensive book on childrearing by a physician and a psychologist.

Dickens, Monica. *Miracles of Courage: How Families Meet the Challenge of a Child's Critical Illness*. Dodd 1985 $14.95. ISBN 0-396-08554-7. Relates the experiences of people who have faced critical illness in their children; written in a style that is vivid, compassionate, and emotionally wracking.

Dodson, Fitzhugh, and Ann Alexander. *How to Parent*. NAL-Dutton 1973 $5.99. ISBN 0-451-15625-0. A commonsense combination of love and discipline that offers a creative, complete, and mutually enjoyable program for guiding the child from birth to 5 years of age; an alternative to Spock.

Ferber, Richard. *Solve Your Child's Sleep Problems*. S&S Trade 1986 $10.00. ISBN 0-671-62099-1. Discusses the physiology of sleep and uncommon sleep problems and presents systematic approaches to these problems; written by a medical expert.

Flating, Sonja. *Child Care: A Parent's Guide*. Facts on File 1991 $24.95. ISBN 0-8160-2232-1. A useful compendium of issues to consider and criteria to apply when selecting child-care settings.

Goldberg, Susan, and Barbara Divitto. *Born Too Soon; Preterm Birth and Early Development*. W. H. Freeman 1983 o.p. A useful summary of information about premature babies; cites numerous studies from medical and academic sources.

Haessler, Herbert A. *How to Make Sure Your Baby Is Well—And Stays That Way: The First Guide to Over 400 Medical Tests and Treatments You Can Do at Home to Check Your Baby's Daily Health and Growth*. Macmillan 1984 $17.95. ISBN 0-89256-260-9. An understandable guide to routine tests and treatments that parents can perform to assess and maintain the health of their child.

Harrison, Helen, and Ann Kositsky. *The Premature Baby Book: A Parents' Guide to Coping and Caring in the First Years*. St. Martin 1983 $18.95. ISBN 0-312-63649-0. Presents clinical and technical information exhaustively but succinctly.

Henig, Robin M., and Anne B. Fletcher. *Your Premature Baby: The Complete Guide to Caring for Your Premie During That Crucial First Year*. Ballantine 1984 $7.95. ISBN 0-345-31365-8. Offers clear, practical, and comforting advice for parents on a wide range of topics associated with premature children; written by a medical writer and a physician.

Hillman, Sheilah, and others. *The Baby Checkup Book: A Parents' Guide to Well Baby Care*. Bantam 1984 $3.95. ISBN 0-553-23659-8. An excellent book on baby checkups, with particular emphasis on the physical examinations.

Jones, Monica Loose. *Home Care for the Chronically Ill or Disabled Child: A Manual and Sourcebook for Parents and Professionals*. HarpC 1985 o.p. Well-researched book that emphasizes the care of ill children.

Kagan, Jerome. *The Nature of the Child*. Basic 1986 $17.00. ISBN 0-465-04851-X. An eloquent examination of child development, which suggests that many popular notions about parenting are askew.

Kelly, Paula. *First Year Baby Care: An Illustrated Step-by-Step Guide for New Parents*. Meadowbrook Pr. 1989 $7.00. ISBN 0-671-69206-2. A concise how-to-do-it and what-to-use manual of baby care; also includes a symptoms index of health problems and emergencies.

Leach, Penelope. *Your Baby and Child.* Knopf 1989 $29.95. ISBN 0-394-57951-8. "A detailed and authoritative account of the development stages between birth and 5 years of age and how development accomplishments are expressed in a child's behavior" (*Library Journal*).

Lieberman, Adrienne, and Thomas Sheagren. *The Premie Parents' Handbook: A Lifeline for the New Parents of a Premature Baby.* NAL-Dutton 1984 o.p. Thoroughly covers causes of premature birth and treatments for premature infants; discusses what parents can contribute to the well-being of the hospitalized infant and considerations for subsequent pregnancies.

Nance, Sherri, and others. *Premature Babies: A Handbook for Parents.* Berkeley Pub. 1984 $3.50. ISBN 0-425-07256-8. An account by parents of premature babies, hospital staff who deal with premies and parents, grandparents, and friends; topical arrangement.

Novick, Nelson Lee. *Baby Skin: A Leading Dermatologist's Guide to Infant and Childhood Skin Care.* Potter Pubns. 1991 $13.00. ISBN 0-517-58422-0. Offers useful advice for baby skin care and explanations of skin diseases, rashes, and other abnormalities.

Restak, Richard M. *The Infant Mind.* Doubleday 1986 $18.95. ISBN 0-385-19531-1. Describes the normal development of the brain in infants and children.

Rosemond, John. *Parent Power: A Common-Sense Approach to Parenting in the '90s and Beyond.* Andrews & McMeel 1991 $9.95. ISBN 0-8362-2808-1. A practical common-sense approach to parenting, including discipline; written by the parenting columnist for *Better Homes and Gardens*.

Samuels, Mike, and Nancy Samuels. *The Well Child Book.* Summit Bks. 1983 $10.75. ISBN 0-671-43893-X. Clearly written, well-illustrated medical self-care manual for parents and children.

Shelov, Steven P. *Caring for Your Baby and Young Child: Birth to Age 5.* Bantam 1993 $15.95. ISBN 0-553-37184-3. "A substantive handbook, issued under the auspices of the American Academy of Pediatrics, providing detailed information on specific health problems of young children" (*Library Journal*).

Spock, Benjamin, and Michael B. Rothenberg. *Dr. Spock's Baby and Child Care.* NAL-Dutton 1992 $25.00. ISBN 0-525-93400-6. The classic baby book.

Worth, Cecilia, with Anna Marie Brooks. *New Parenthood: The First Six Weeks.* McGraw 1985 o.p. A concise, positive, and well-designed source of basic information about normal infant care.

DEATH AND DYING

[SEE Chapter 13 in this volume.]

DENTAL CARE

[SEE the section on The Healthy Body in this chapter.]

DENTISTRY

[SEE the section on Health Professions, Dentistry in this chapter.]

DERMATOLOGY

[SEE the section on The Healthy Body in this chapter; for skin diseases, see Chapter 13 in this volume.]

DIAGNOSTIC TESTING

The medical consumer of the 1990s is subjected to a diversity of tests as part of routine physical examinations or office visits for a particular illness. Medical tests and technologies are becoming increasingly more sophisticated. In light of this, the following section will introduce the reader to many common techniques and tests.

Byrne, C. Judith, and others. *Laboratory Tests: Implications for Nurses and Allied Health Professionals*. Addison-Wesley 1986 $25.75. ISBN 0-201-12670-2. Provides, in a clear and concise format, information on many current laboratory tests; an excellent book for allied health practitioners and the students of these disciplines.

Culyer, A. K., and B. Horisberger, eds. *Economic and Medical Evaluation of Health Care Technologies*. Spr.-Verlag 1983 o.p. Illustrates the necessity for the public to become better informed on the technological bases of health care; accessible to the general reader.

DeMarre, Dean A., and David Michaels. *Bioelectric Measurements*. P-H 1983 o.p. Concise overview of the present status of bioelectronic measurement, useful to individuals interested in learning about some of the instrumentational aspects of medical care.

Gofman, John W. *Radiation and Human Health*. Sierra 1981 $29.95. ISBN 0-87156-275-8. A sourcebook featuring practical information for individuals to make personal and family decisions about voluntary exposures to medical and dental radiation, as well as occupational exposures.

Lenburg, Carrie B. *The Clinical Performance Examination: Development and Implementation*. Appleton & Lange 1979 o.p. This well-written, well-indexed book is the first volume on clinical performance examinations based on comprehensive research rather than on trial and error.

Lutz, Harald, and R. Meudt. *Manual of Ultrasound*. Spr.-Verlag 1984 $60.00. ISBN 0-387-12377-6. The conciseness of style, the diagrams, and the extensiveness of the topics covered make this an excellent book for the technologist, health care personnel, and student interested in the fundamentals of ultrasound.

McFarland, Mary B., and Marcia M. Grant. *Nursing Implications of Laboratory Tests*. Delmar 1988 $26.95. ISBN 0-8273-4307-8. Covers physiological functions rather than test types/groups, as most other "test guides." Consequently, descriptions of single laboratory tests that test multiple functions are frequently repeated under each function.

McNeil, Barbara J., and Ernest G. Cravalho, eds. *Critical Issues in Medical Technology*. Greenwood 1981 $28.00. ISBN 0-86569-070-7. The record of an interesting and thought-provoking conference of known experts in the field who carefully address social and ethical implications of technological advances and applications in medicine.

Pinckney, Cathy, and Edward R. Pinckney. *Do-It-Yourself Medical Testing*. Facts on File 1989 $14.95. ISBN 0-8160-2085-X. Offers valuable information for persons interested in taking an active role in their health care; describes medical tests thoroughly.

Reiser, Stanley M. *Medicine and the Reign of Technology*. Cambridge U. Pr. 1981 $19.95. ISBN 0-521-28223-3. Examines the influence that technology has had on physicians' ability to diagnose disease more precisely.

Tresler, Kathleen M. *Clinical Laboratory Tests: Significance and Implications for Nursing*. P-H 1982 o.p. An outstanding book for individuals studying and practicing health care delivery.

Williams, A. Roy. *Ultrasound: Biological Effects and Potential Hazards*. Acad. Pr. 1983 $104.00. ISBN 0-12-756960-X. A useful and informative presentation of physical, biological, and epidemiological aspects of ultrasound exposure and its potential risk.

DIET

[SEE the section on Nutrition and Diet in this chapter.]

DRUGS AND PHARMACEUTICAL PREPARATIONS

[SEE the section on Pharmacology and Toxicology in this chapter.]

ENDOCRINOLOGY

[For endocrine diseases, SEE Chapter 13 in this volume.]

EPIDEMIOLOGY

[SEE Chapter 13 in this volume.]

EXERCISE AND PHYSICAL FITNESS

The current fitness boom has been accompanied by many new titles on specific kinds of exercise for children, the aged, and other populations. The following section includes representative titles of each type.

Alter, Judy. *Surviving Exercise*. HM 1990 $7.70. ISBN 0-395-50073-7. Claims that the goal of exercise should be to tone muscles, not to stress ligaments, grind joints, or fray tendons; provides well-illustrated, recommended exercises, and sound advice on what exercises to avoid.

Bland, Jeffrey. *Nutraerobics: The Complete Individualized Nutrition and Fitness Program for Life after 30*. HarpC 1983 o.p. Offers a good general discussion and guide to the benefits of an improved lifestyle and better nutrition; written by a physician.

Bove, Alfred A., and David T. Lowenthal. *Exercise Medicine: Physiological Principles and Clinical Applications*. Acad. Pr. 1983 $90.00. ISBN 0-12-119720-4. Provides an excellent reference for physicians and individuals involved in exercise programs.

Bricklin, Mark, and Maggie Spilner. *The Practical Encyclopedia of Walking for Health: From Age Reversal to Weight Loss, the Most Complete Guide Ever Written*. Rodale 1992 $22.95. ISBN 0-87596-110-X. A comprehensive walking guidebook that offers advice on foot care, socks, nutrition, exercises, techniques, and terrain therapy; also includes a detailed walking plan for an entire year.

Brown, Millie. *Low-Stress Fitness*. HP Bks. 1985 o.p. A book with many useful tips to help the sedentary person develop a sensible fitness program.

Cannon, Geoffrey, and Hetty Einzig. *Dieting Makes You Fat: A Guide to Energy, Food, Fitness and Health*. PB 1987 $3.95. ISBN 0-671-62530-6. Advocates a food regimen that increases metabolic rate combined with aerobic exercise; cites numerous studies and reports.

Cooper, Kenneth H. *The Aerobics Program for Total Well-Being*. Bantam 1983 $11.95. ISBN 0-553-34422-6. Provides a program for balancing nutrition, exercise, and emotional health; includes a directory of sports medicine clinics and descriptions of medical examinations.

————. *Kid Fitness: A Complete Shape-up Program from Birth Through High School*. Bantam 1991 $19.50. ISBN 0-553-07332-X. Offers wise advice on how to motivate children and to test their fitness, keyed to age and development levels; designed for parents who want to teach their children the basics of good exercise and proper nutrition.

Craig, Jenny. *Jenny Craig's What Have You Got to Lose?* Prima Pub. 1993 $12.95. ISBN 1-55958-301-0. Outline of the weight management system based on food exchanges that Craig developed and currently markets across the country.

DeVries, Herbert, with Dianne Hales. *Fitness after 50*. Macmillan 1982 $12.95. ISBN 0-684-17485-5. Explains the relationship between continued fitness and aging.

Dietrich, John, and Susan Waggoner. *The Complete Health Club Handbook*. S&S Trade 1983 o.p. A comprehensive manual that describes how to determine what type of health club best suits one's needs; includes (with candid reviews) a directory of facilities in ten major U.S. cities.

Dusek, Dorothy. *Thin and Fit: Your Personal Lifestyle*. Wadsworth Pub. 1982 o.p. A clear and concise introduction to a holistic plan to promote thinness; presents a readiness/self-responsibility profile to help readers assess their independence, spontaneity, assertiveness, and emotions.

Edwards, Diana, and Kathy Nash. *Prime Moves: Low-Impact Exercises for the Mature Adult*. Avery Pub. 1993 $12.95. ISBN 0-89529-394-3. A comprehensive selection of exercises, including moves that can be done from both sitting and standing positions; features recommended combinations to improve joint flexibility and breathing capacity.

Hales, Dianne, and Robert E. Hales. *Be All You Can Be! The U.S. Army Total Fitness Program*. Crown Pub. Group 1985 o.p. An eight-week exercise regimen based on the U.S. Army's Fit to Win program. The program can be individually tailored using the self-assessment test provided.

Huey, Lynda, and Robert Forster. *The Complete Waterpower Workout Book: Programs for Fitness, Injury Prevention, and Healing*. Random 1993 $13.95. ISBN 0-679-74554-8. Guide to water fitness and training that advocates water training as a versatile exercise for most people.

Jamieson, Robert H. *Exercise for the Elderly*. Taplinger 1985 $6.95. ISBN 0-8008-2564-0. Large-print book that describes and demonstrates simple limbering, stretching, and strengthening exercises; includes exercises for bedridden or wheelchair-bound individuals.

Katz, Jane. *The W.E.T. Workout: Water Exercise Techniques to Help You Tone Up and Slim Down, Aerobically*. Facts on File 1985 $18.95. ISBN 0-8160-1159-1. A progressive three-month, illustrated program of stretching and toning exercises for use in water.

McArdle, William D., and others. *Exercise Physiology: Energy, Nutrition, and Human Performance*. Lea & Febiger 1991 $52.50. ISBN 0-8121-1351-9. Emphasizes the interrelationships of body composition, obesity, weight control, and the role of exercise in these areas. Appendixes include useful data on the nutritive value of foods, the amount of energy used in various forms of exercise, and more; written for the general reader.

Meyers, Casey. *Walking: A Complete Guide to the Complete Exercise*. Random 1992 $12.00. ISBN 0-679-73777-4. Argues that walking is the best method of weight loss and cardiovascular fitness.

National Board of YMCAs. *The Official YMCA Fitness Program*. Warner Bks. 1986 $4.50. ISBN 0-446-32875-8. A good all-around illustrated program that promotes individual fitness through calisthenics, proper nutrition, and good mental health.

Peters, Jane S. *The Indoor Bicycling Fitness Program: A Complete Guide to Equipment and Exercise*. McGraw 1985 o.p. Provides a consumer's checklist of available equipment, exercise programs for cardiovascular fitness, muscle tone, and more; includes useful appendixes of books, periodicals, catalogs, manufacturers, and so on.

Reiman, Reuben. *Combating Your Child's Cholesterol: A Pediatrician Shows You How*. Plenum Pub. 1993 $24.95. ISBN 0-306-44468-2. An encyclopedia approach to the topic that features extensive background information about cholesterol in children, including "diet-for-life," food tables, and calorie charts.

Ronsard, Nicole. *Beyond Cellulite: Nicole Ronsard's Ultimate Strategy to Slim, Firm and Reshape Your Lower Body*. Random $12.00. ISBN 0-679-73936-X. An update of her best-selling 1973 book, *Cellulite: Those Lumps, Bumps and Bulges You Couldn't Lose Before*; recommends a holistic approach to total body health that also will eliminate cellulite.

Simon, Harvey B. *Staying Well: Your Complete Guide to Preventive Medicine*. HM 1992 $22.45. ISBN 0-395-53762-2. "A superior single author health guide for the lay reader" (*Library Journal*).

Simopoulos, Artemis P., Victor Herbert, and Beverly Jacobson. *Genetic Nutrition: Designing a Diet Based on Your Family Medical History.* Macmillan 1993 $22.00. ISBN 0-02-611295-7. Explains how to plot a family tree and determine a genetic predisposition based on the assumption that genetic factors may determine one's susceptibility to disease.

Van Orden, Naola, and S. Paul Steed. *The Bio-Plan for Lifelong Weight Control.* Dial 1983 o.p. Combines nutritional advice with a vigorous program of exercise; includes nutritional information on the composition of foods and recommended daily allowances of protein, carbohydrates, and fats.

FORENSIC MEDICINE

[SEE the section on Medicine and the Law in this chapter.]

GERONTOLOGY/GERIATRICS

[SEE the section on Aging in this chapter.]

GYNECOLOGY

[SEE the section on Women's Health in this chapter.]

HEALTH CARE

General

This section includes books on the philosophy and organization of health care. The books examine past, present, and future organization, financing, and management of health care delivery. The following list also includes works on Health Maintenance Organizations (HMOs) and Preferred Provider Organizations (PPOs).

Aaron, Henry J., and William B. Schwartz. *The Painful Prescription: Rationing Hospital Care.* Brookings 1984 $28.95. ISBN 0-8157-0034-2. "Attempts to predict the consequences of financial barriers to medical care that will result from the budgetary limitations being imposed, at the state and federal levels, in an attempt to restrict the heretofore unlimited increase in the costs of hospital care. Highlights issues of concern to patients and physicians alike" (*Choice*).

Beasley, Joseph D. *Betrayal of Health: The Impact of Nutrition, Environment, and Lifestyle on Illness in America.* Random 1991 $22.50. ISBN 0-8129-1897-5. A stinging indictment of the American health care system which, in the author's opinion is fixated on treatment of disease rather than prevention.

Bell, Roger, ed. *Assessing Health and Human Service Needs: Concepts, Methods and Applications. Community Psychology Ser.* Human Sci. Pr. 1983 $45.95. ISBN 0-89885-057-6. "After a brief introduction to the concepts of needs assessment comes discussion of conceptual issues, methodological techniques, the use of these methodologies in actual program planning, and a summary that includes a very useful annotated bibliography" (*Choice*).

Boland, Peter. *New Healthcare Market: A Guide to PPOs for Purchases, Payors and Providers.* Aspen 1985 $90.00. ISBN 0-87094-534-3. "A comprehensive treatment of the phenomena of competitive marketing in health care known as preferred provider arrangements or preferred provider organization (the PPO in the title).

Presents 16 case studies of operational PPO's sponsored by physician groups, hospitals, insurance companies, and private investor groups" (*Choice*).

Brickner, Philip, and Linda Scharer. *Health Care of Homeless People*. Springer Pub. 1985 $36.95. ISBN 0-8261-4990-1. "Defines the homeless population, introduces historical background of experiences, discusses medical disorders, explains that consideration of homeless populations is based on impressions rather than on types of illness, deals with access to care, [and] health care teams and hospital experiences" (*Choice*).

Brown, Lawrence D. *Politics and Health Care Organization: HMO's as Federal Policy*. Brookings 1983 $36.95. ISBN 0-8157-1158-1. "The complexity and, on occasion, the incomprehensibility of the American health care system are nowhere better shown than in this detailed study. This is an analysis of the origins of health maintenance organizations (HMOs) in the dual context of progressive federal involvement through Medicare and Medicaid" (*Choice*).

Dowling, Harry F. *The City Hospitals: The Undercare of the Underprivileged*. HUP 1982 $30.00. ISBN 0-674-13197-5. "Traces the development of city hospitals through four periods: the almshouse period, lasting until approximately 1860 in the larger eastern cities; the practitioner period, from 1860 to 1910; the academic period, from about 1910 to 1965; and the present community period" (*Choice*).

Duffy, John. *The Healers: Rise of American Medicine*. U. of Ill. Pr. 1979 repr. of 1976 ed. $12.95. ISBN 0-252-00743-3. "Deals, often very briefly, with the whole range of medical and public health. Rich in insights about the social aspects of medicine" (*American Scientist*).

Feder, J., and T. Marmor, eds. *National Health Insurance: Conflicting Goals and Policy Choices*. Urban Inst. 1980 $50.50. ISBN 0-87766-035-2. "Considers the choices that policymakers (legislators and administrators) must make in enacting and implementing any national health insurance program" (*Choice*).

Foltz, Anne-Marie. *An Ounce of Prevention: Child Health Politics under Medicaid*. Health and Public Policy Ser. MIT Pr. 1982 o.p. "A highly critical and at times cynical case study of the Early and Periodic Screening, Diagnosis, and Treatment (EPSDT) Program under Medicaid from its first inauspicious beginning in 1968 to the present day [1982]" (*Choice*).

Ginzberg, Eli, and Edith M. Davis. *Local Health Policy in Action: The Municipal Health Services Program*. Rowman 1985 $50.00. ISBN 0-8476-7425-8. "The book represents the findings and recommendations based on the Municipal Health Services Program, which remained in existence from 1978 to 1984, as a demonstration of primary health care delivery to urban populations in Baltimore, Cincinnati, Milwaukee, St. Louis, and San Jose" (*Choice*).

Haddad, Amy Marie. *High Tech Home Care: A Practical Guide*. Aspen 1987 o.p. A significant contribution to home care, covering the broad scope of home care management, delivery, and services; provides the consumer with a wealth of useful facts and sound advice about frequently bewildering medical technology.

Hassinger, Edward W. *Rural Heath Organization: Social Networks and Regionalization*. Iowa St. U. Pr. 1982 $12.95. ISBN 0-8138-1589-4. "Basic thesis is that, in order to understand the delivery of medical services in rural areas, one must consider both the cultural aspects of rural life and the organizational aspects of the health system" (*Choice*).

Havighurst, Clark C. *Deregulating the Health Care Industry: Planning for Competition*. Ballinger 1982 o.p. "Basic premise is that shortsighted, if not stupid, regulatory controls have led to excessive costs, monopolistic practices, and reduced quality. Examines the condition necessary for a greater reliance on market forces to correct these problems" (*Choice*).

Health Planning in the United States: Selected Policy Issues. Natl. Acad. Pr. 2 vols. 1981 o.p. "The final report of a two-year study commissioned by the Health Resources Administration" (*Choice*).

Kark, Sidney L. *The Practice of Community-Oriented Primary Health Care*. Appleton & Lange 1980 o.p. "A thorough treatment of all that community health encompasses;

identifies problems and needs for programming; describes successful programs in detail" (*Choice*).

Miller, Irwin. *The Health Care Survival Curve: Competition and Cooperation in the Marketplace*. Irwin 1984 o.p. "Analyzes current health policies, innovative community strategies, and industrialization of health delivery and the benefits of voluntarism. Contends there must be a balance between competition and operation if institutions are to succeed and communities are to be well served" (*Choice*).

Milner, Murray, Jr. *Unequal Care: A Case Study of Interorganizational Relations*. Col. U. Pr. 1980 $49.00. ISBN 0-231-05006-2. "A sociologist examines the source of inequality in the delivery of health care in the U.S." (*Choice*).

Morris, Jonas. *Searching for a Cure*. Universe Pub. Co. 1984 o.p. "Provides a detailed account of the battle over national health insurance during the last 20 years. Good exploration of the legislative process" (*Choice*).

Numbers, Ronald L., ed. *Compulsory Health Insurance: The Continuing American Debate*. *Contributions in Medical History Ser*. Greenwood 1982 $38.50. ISBN 0-313-23436-1. "Papers by historians and social scientists originally presented at a 1979 symposium at the University of Wisconsin" (*Choice*).

Sidel, Victor, and Ruth Sidel, eds. *Reforming Medicine: Lessons from the Last Quarter Century*. Pantheon 1984 $7.96. ISBN 0-394-71259-4. "Experts in social medicine describe reforms in the health care delivery system—Medicare, Medicaid, women's health care, medical education, occupational health and safety" (*Library Journal*).

Thompson, John D., and Grace Goldin. *The Hospital: A Social and Architectural History*. Yale U. Pr. 1975 o.p. "A handy source for information about hospitals and how they have functioned" (*American Scientist*).

U.S. Dept. of Health and Human Services, Task Force on Health Risk Assessment. *Determining Risks to Health: Federal Policy and Practice*. Greenwood 1986 $42.95. ISBN 0-85659-139-X. "One of the first accounts to promote general public understanding of the role of the U.S. Department of Health and Human Services in the assessment of health risks. Discusses various approaches used in studying risk assessments, results found through surveys and analysis, and recommendations for improving the present policies and practices" (*Choice*).

Vogel, Morris J. *The Invention of the Modern Hospital: Boston, 1870–1930*. U. Ch. Pr. 1985 $6.95. ISBN 0-226-86241-0. "Explores the evolution of the hospital from a voluntary organization assisting charity patients into a primary supplier of health care for all social classes" (*Library Journal*).

Waitzkin, Howard B. *The Second Sickness: Contradictions of Capitalist Health Care*. Free Pr. 1986 $11.95. ISBN 0-02-933750-X. "A frustrating, nettlesome, and in parts, significant critique of health care organization in capitalist countries, most specifically the [United States]. First part establishes the author's Marxist perspective; second explores specific problems with capitalist health care; third covers policies for social change" (*Choice*).

Williams, Stephen J., ed. *Issues in Health Services*. Wiley 1980 o.p. "Introduces the concept of health services; raises questions about the effects of medicine on health and mortality; deals with the utilization of services and meeting the demand for services; discusses how to assess and affect performance of health service systems; and explores different organizational forms for health services delivery" (*Choice*).

Williams, Stephen J., and Paul R. Torrens, ed. *Introduction to Health Services*. Delmar 1992 $37.95. ISBN 0-8273-5010-4. A comprehensive introduction to health service structures in the United States; written for the college undergraduate.

Wohl, Stanley M. *The Medical Industrial Complex*. Crown Pub. Group 1984 $14.95. ISBN 0-517-55351-1. "A lucid, thoughtful, balanced, and erudite exposition of the background, history, evolution, virtues, and dangers of the almost total monetarization of the health care system" (*Choice*).

Work in America Institute. *Improving Health-Care Management in the Workplace*. Pergamon 1985 o.p. "Intended to help both employers and unions select health plan options that are cost effective, not just inexpensive" (*Choice*).

Zawadski, Rick T., ed. *Community-Based Systems of Long-Term Care*. Haworth Pr. 1984 $37.95. ISBN 0-86656-255-9. "Reports of eight federally funded community-based projects that offered elderly persons an alternative to nursing home care. A critical review of past successes and errors" (*Choice*).

Comparative Studies

The following includes books on the organization and economics of national and international health care delivery systems. The books feature analysis and comparisons of health care delivery systems worldwide.

Akin, John S., and David K. Guilkey. *The Demand for Primary Health Services in the Third World*. Rowman 1985 $61.50. ISBN 0-8476-7355-3. "Combines economic variables with data from medical anthropology, sociology, and geography, and organizes them within an economic framework. Selected simple and complex theoretical models of demand for medical care are critically reviewed, and the authors also formulate their own model. The book's joining of economic and noneconomic variables and its questioning of widespread assumptions about Third World primary health care constitute significant contributions to international health work" (*Choice*).

Bennett, Arnold, and others, eds. *Looking North for Health: What We Can Learn from Canada's Health Care System*. Jossey-Bass 1993 $25.95. ISBN 1-55542-516-X. A collection of essays by Canadian and U.S. health care officials; provides valuable insight into the Canadian health care system in contrast with that in the United States.

Braithwaite, Ronald L., and Sandra E. Taylor, eds. *Health Issues in the Black Community*. Jossey-Bass 1992 $39.95. ISBN 1-55542-477-5. Reviews African American health care concerns as expressed in essays from 25 leading experts in the field.

Ehrlich, Isaac, ed. *National Health Policy: What Role for Government?* Hoover Inst. Pr. 1982 o.p. "Includes economic theorizing about government and health care; descriptions of national health insurance proposals and health insurance in Germany and Australia; an analysis of access to medical care in the U.S.; a statement of a business perspective on health costs; an agenda for increasing the role of competition in health services; and an after-dinner speech" (*Choice*).

Fox, Daniel M. *Health Policies, Health Politics: The British and American Experience, 1911–1965*. Princeton U. Pr. 1986 $34.00. ISBN 0-691-04733-2. "Although specialists may want more evidence than the author provides, the book is valuable as the first comparative study of 20th-century health policy" (*Choice*).

Goodman, John C. *National Health Care in Great Britain: Lessons for the U.S.A.* Fisher Inst. 1980 o.p. "A conservative polemic on all that ails the British National Health Service. The book provides a brief historical background of developments leading to the creation of the NHS in 1946, and then takes a sector-by-sector view of the Service, its administration, financing, and delivery of care. Although it is subtitled 'Lessons for the U.S.A.,' the volume spends just 4 ½ pages on this important topic" (*Choice*).

Heidenheimer, Arnold J., and Nile Elvander, eds. *The Shaping of the Swedish Health System*. St. Martin 1980 $27.50. ISBN 0-312-71627-3. "Covers the historical roots of the Swedish health care system. Uses cross-national comparisons to bring a sense of perspective and to explain the organization of the Swedish system" (*Choice*).

Lanza, Robert, ed. *Medical Science and the Advancement of World Health*. Greenwood 1985 $47.95. ISBN 0-275-91317-1. "Argues that physicians and health professionals have the tools and obligation to arouse world powers from their apathy and to organize a concerted international effort in the areas of individual and public health. A well-balanced, intelligent, unbiased overview of the problem" (*Choice*).

Maxwell, Robert. *Health and Wealth: An International Study of Health-Care Spending*. Free Pr. 1982 $27.50. ISBN 0-669-04109-2. "Studies the health-spending habits of ten developed countries: Australia, Canada, France, West Germany, Italy, Netherlands, Sweden, Switzerland, Britain, and the U.S." (*Choice*).

Mirzahi, Andree, and others. *Medical Care, Morbidity and Costs: Graphic Presentation of Health Statistics.* Pergamon 1983 $35.00. ISBN 0-08-031295-0. "Provides graphic and pictorial representation of a wide range of health-related statistics: 81 annotated charts cover historical trends and current data for France in the areas of mortality and morbidity, medical expenditures, health service utilization, and supply of health care providers. A limited number of French/U.S. charts give the volume an international flavor" (*Choice*).

Morgan, Kathleen O., ed. *Health Care State Rankings, 1993: Health Care in the 50 United States.* Quinto $43.95. ISBN 0-9625531-4-X. Compares and ranks state health care organizations, structures, and communication.

Raffel, Marshall, ed. *Comparative Health Systems: Descriptive Analyses of Fourteen National Health Systems.* Pa. St. U. Pr. 1984 $45.00. ISBN 0-271-00363-4. "Reviewed in considerable detail are the systems of Australia, Belgium, Canada, China, Denmark, England, France, Germany, Japan, Netherlands, New Zealand, Sweden, USSR, and U.S." (*Choice*).

Snow, Loudell F. *Walkin' over Medicine: Traditional Health Practices in African-American Life.* Westview 1993 $55.00. ISBN 0-8133-1074-1. Documents how the health care system in the United States has shortchanged African Americans; written by an anthropologist who has spent many years working with black patients.

Stone, Deborah A. *The Limits of Professional Power: National Health Care in the Federal Republic of Germany.* U. Ch. Pr. 1981 $21.00. ISBN 0-226-77553-4. "Focuses on the power of physicians' organizations, governmental and consumer groups, and the limits of each. Deals with some policy questions and answers" (*Choice*).

Consumerism and Health Promotion

The following brief list of books examines the increasing role of consumers in the medical marketplace, as well as the organization and implementation of patient and consumer health education programs.

Arnot, Robert. *The Best Medicine: How to Choose the Top Doctors, the Top Hospitals, and the Top Treatments.* Addison-Wesley 1992 $22.95. ISBN 0-201-57792-5. Discusses 14 operations or procedures and 11 chronic illnesses. Describes the process by which physicians find excellent health care for themselves and their families; written by a television newscaster.

Corry, James M. *Consumer Health: Facts, Skills, and Decisions.* Wadsworth Pub. 1983 o.p. "Beginning with major concerns of the medical marketplace and those psychosocial factors relating to consumerism, the author considers all phases of consumer health practices, including individual and societal responsibilities" (*Choice*).

Haug, Marie, and Bebe Lavin. *Consumerism in Medicine: Challenging Physician Authority.* Bks. Demand 1983 $62.20. ISBN 0-8357-8428-2. "Two medical sociologists discuss how patients have grown more skeptical about the ability of the physician to 'cure' and use sampling techniques to determine attitudes of both physician and patient" (*Choice*).

Huttman, Barbara. *The Patient's Advocate.* Viking Penguin 1981 o.p. "Hints on how to cope with hospitalization as well as insight into what to expect and demand as a patient" (*Library Journal*).

Lesko, Matthew. *What to Do When You Can't Afford Health Care: An A–Z Sourcebook for the Entire Family.* Info USA 1993 $24.95. ISBN 1-878346-16-4. A directory of resources to assist patients, care givers, and students who cannot afford to pay for health care.

Mailick, Mildred, and Helen Rehr, eds. *In the Patient's Interest: Access to Hospital Care.* Watson Pub. Intl. 1982 $17.50. ISBN 0-88202-136-2. "An excellent book dealing with the needs of the consumer of hospital-based services. Organized in four parts: access to hospital-based services; community-based programs; patient adversary; and conclusions and recommendations needed to deal with obstacles to services needed by consumers" (*Choice*).

Oppenheim, Michael. *A Doctor's Guide to the Best Medical Care.* Rodale Pr. 1992 $24.95.
ISBN 0-87857-982-6. A somewhat uneven and occasionally dated guide that
describes treatment options for many common ailments.

Rosenfeld, Isadore. *The Best Treatment.* S&S Trade 1993 $22.95. ISBN 0-8161-5657-3.
Provides advice on therapies for a wide range of illnesses and injuries; easy to read.

Shulman, Neil, and Letitia Sweitzer. *Better Health Care for Less.* Hippocrene Bks. 1993
$14.95. ISBN 0-7818-0122-2. A consumer guide to medical procedures; includes
specific tips for assuring high quality care at the best price.

Squyres, Wendy. *Patient Education and Health Promotion in Medical Care.* Mayfield Pub.
1985 $41.95. ISBN 0-87484-553-X. "A resource in matters of program implementa-
tion, beginning with establishing a department in a medical setting. Includes needs
assessment, educational methods and evaluation, and recognizing that information
alone seldom changes behavior" (*Choice*).

Sutherland, Ian, ed. *Health Education: Perspectives and Choices.* Allen & Unwin 1980
o.p. "An excellent and wide-ranging consideration of health education, its values,
uses, and practical applications in many settings and situations. . . . Though written
in terms of problems, services, and agencies in the United Kingdom, the basic tenets
would be quite applicable to their counterparts here in the U.S." (*Choice*).

Economics

Traditionally, funding of health care systems has been accompanied by
controversy and debate. The books in this section examine economic, philosophical, and organizational considerations, and the roles played by the medical
profession, the hospital industry, as well as government and private insurance
agencies.

Altman, Stuart H., and others, eds. *Ambulatory Care: Problems of Cost and Access.* Free
Pr. 1983 $30.00. ISBN 0-669-06401-7. "An analytical look at ambulatory care, its
successes and shortcomings. Contains analyses and reports on the problems of
access and cost. Areas addressed include access to care, payer's perspective,
organizational considerations, choice of ambulatory-care settings, and research
findings" (*Choice*).

Bogdanich, Walt. *The Great White Lie: How America's Hospitals Betray Our Trust and
Endanger Our Lives.* S&S Trade 1991 $23.00. ISBN 0-671-68452-3. A collection of
stories of hospital malpractice and malfeasance; concludes that the hospital system
has a systemic disease that undermines the type and level of care it can provide.

Brown, Jack H. U. *The High Cost of Healing: Physicians and the Health Care System.*
Human Sci. Pr. 1985 $35.95. ISBN 0-89885-222-6. "Provides an overview of the costs
of the health care system and then examines the factors that influence the costs of
medical care with particular attention to the role of the physician in private practice,
in the hospital, in the technological scene, and in medical education. Ancillary
factors that affect the practice and cost of medicine (e.g., ethics and insurance) are
also examined" (*Choice*).

Califano, Joseph A., Jr. *America's Health Care Revolution: Who Lives? Who Dies? Who
Pays?* S&S Trade 1989 $9.95. ISBN 0-671-68371-3. "Filled with up-to-date statistics
on the costs of the health care system and information on efforts to control these
costs. Individual chapters detail the current status of what Califano describes as an
incredibly inefficient and wasteful system and explore the medical profession, the
hospital industry, medical supplies industries, long-term care, government, and
other third-party payment systems" (*Choice*).

Christianson, Jon B., and Kenneth R. Smith. *Current Strategies for Containing Health
Care Expenditure: A Summary of Their Potential, Performance and Prevalence.* Luce
1985 $24.95. ISBN 0-88331-130-5. "One of the most comprehensive overviews of
health cost-containment issues available in print" (*Choice*).

Fuchs, Victor. *The Health Economy.* HUP 1986 $14.95. ISBN 0-674-38341-9. "Compila-
tion of previously published articles and essays on a wide range of health-related

topics such as national health insurance, health promotion, cigarette smoking, time preferences, market competition, physician control, and other economic aspects of health and medical care" (*Choice*).

Ginzberg, Eli, ed. *From Health Dollars to Health Services: New York City, 1965–1985.* Rowman 1986 $45.50. ISBN 0-8476-7440-1. "Codifies, organizes and elucidates data into an eminently readable and comprehensible account. The principal actor in the tale is Medicare, with strong support from Medicaid, private insurance, and the ever increasing and expensive medical technology" (*Choice*).

Lindorff, Dave. *Marketplace Medicine: The Rise of the For-Profit Hospital Chains.* Bantam 1992 $22.50. ISBN 0-553-07552-7. A cynical and irreverent, but well-documented examination of the effects of "for-profit" hospitals on physicians, patients, and on poor and middle-class health care consumers.

Sloan, Frank A., and James M. Perrin, eds. *Uncompensated Health Care: Rights and Responsibilities. Contemporary Medicine and Public Health Ser.* Bks. Demand 1986 $57.80. ISBN 0-8357-8358-8. "Raises questions about individual rights to health care and how to finance services provided to those who cannot afford to pay for them. Recommends that a way must be found to relieve the health care providers of the financial burden of the nation's uninsured indigents" (*Choice*).

Sorkin, Alan. *Health Care and the Changing Economic Environment.* Free Pr. $25.00. ISBN 0-669-09016-6. "Evaluates the impact of the changing economic environment upon our health care system, including the effects of federal expenditures, inflation, alterations in manpower, malpractice costs, and the growth of for-profit organization. Discusses in detail the increased competition from the increased numbers of physicians, nurses, and physician extenders. The problems and future directions of the Medicare and Medicaid programs are given careful consideration" (*Choice*).

Straub, LaVonne A., and Norman Walzer, eds. *Rural Health Care: Innovation in a Changing Environment.* Greenwood 1992 $55.00. ISBN 0-275-94315-1. A collection of 17 essays on how to alleviate the rural health care crisis.

Legislation/Governmental Role

This section includes books that describe the responses of state and federal government to the challenge of providing and funding health care. The debate over health care precipitated by President Bill Clinton's national health care proposals in 1993 will no doubt lead to a number of new books on this issue in coming years.

Bovbjerg, Randall R., and John Holahan. *Medicaid in the Reagan Era: Federal Policy and State Choices.* Urban Inst. Pr. 1982 $12.00. ISBN 0-87766-319-X. "Two events occurred in 1981 that shook Medicaid to its foundations: the onset of the deepest recession since the Great Depression and passage of the Omnibus Budget Reconciliation Act. Chronicles these events in concise, nontechnical prose and then goes on to analyze how the states have coped in a time of rising demands and declining resources" (*Choice*).

Health Policy: The Legislative Agenda. Congr. Quarterly 1980 o.p. "A concise historical description of the problems, the issues, the executive and legislative proposals introduced to control health care costs, to provide a more effective delivery system and to promote personal and environmental health" (*Choice*).

Kronenfeld, Jennie J., and Marcia L. Whicker. *U.S. National Health Policy: An Analysis of the Federal Role.* Greenwood 1984 $59.95. ISBN 0-275-91207-8. "Describes the American health care system, with an emphasis on increased use of technology, rising costs, and the difficulty of evaluating the benefits. Focuses on national health policy" (*Choice*).

Wasley, Terree P. *What Has Government Done to Our Health Care?* Cato Inst. 1992 $19.95. ISBN 0-932790-88-7. Argues that the main problem with the current health care "mess" lies with the federal government.

Home Health Care and Nursing Homes

Books in this section offer a brief survey of the past, present, and future of home health care services and nursing homes.

Buckingham, Robert W. *Complete Book of Home Health Care*. Continuum 1984 o.p. "Outlines the history and economics of home health care, criteria and marketing for home health care agencies and the kinds of services home care should provide" (*Library Journal*).

Diamond, Timothy. *Making Gray Gold: Narratives of Nursing Home Care*. Women in Culture and Society Ser. U. Ch. Pr. 1992 $24.95. ISBN 0-226-14473-9. A sympathetic account of nursing home residents and their caregivers; concludes with recommendations for sweeping change in the way this country handles its elderly population.

Ginzberg, Eli, and Miriam Ostow. *Home Heath Care: Its Role in the Changing Health Services Market*. Rowman 1984 $45.00. ISBN 0-916672-65-4. "[This] final report of a study conducted on home health care by the Conservation of Human Resources, Columbia University, includes a review of the literature, results of patient and agency studies, and a discussion of short- and long-range futures of home health care. Its particular strength is in describing detailed patient needs and services rendered" (*Choice*).

Vladeck, Bruce C. *Unloving Care: The Nursing Home Tragedy*. Basic 1980 o.p. "Details the history of nursing home policies, touching upon such things as reimbursement systems, real estate loopholes, and regulatory legislation" (*Library Journal*).

Trends

This section includes books that provide an overview of the present and future structure and organization of health care delivery.

Fisher, Jeffrey A. *Our Medical Future: Breakthroughs in Health and Longevity by the Year 2000 and Beyond*. PB 1993 repr. of 1992 ed. $10.00. ISBN 0-671-73845-3. Originally issued as *RX 2000: Breakthroughs in Health, Medicine and Longevity for the Next Five to Forty Years*. Explores medical trends for the next several decades; comprehensive and well-written.

Ginzberg, Eli. *American Medicine: The Power Shift*. Rowman 1985 $56.00. ISBN 0-8476-7439-8. "Ginzberg's historical perspective lends rationale for the current monetarized status of health care; his visionary approach affords ideas for preventing further erosion of the eleemosynary purpose in meeting the health care needs of people in all socioeconomic sectors" (*Choice*).

——. *The Medical Triangle: Physicians, Politicians, and the Public*. HUP 1990 $30.00. ISBN 0-674-56325-5. An excellent discussion of the conflict between government, consumers, and the medical establishment.

——, ed. *The U.S. Health Care System: A Look at the 1990s*. Rowman 1985 $24.50. ISBN 0-8476-7468-1. "Five papers presented at a 1985 conference, provide a range of perspectives, and focus on policy choices for the 1990s, organizational innovations in health care, the changing role of the hospital, the impact of new technology, and health care financing in the 1990s" (*Choice*).

Konner, Melvin. *Medicine at the Crossroads*. Pantheon 1993 $23.00. ISBN 0-679-41545-9. A polemic that blames the American culture and social system for the crisis in U.S. health care, which provides the best and most to those who can afford it and the poorest and the least to those who cannot.

Koop, C. Everett, and Timothy Johnson. *Let's Talk*. Random 1992 $3.99. ISBN 0-8129-2063-5. A spirited but friendly dialogue between the former Surgeon General and a television reporter; covers abortion, euthanasia, AIDS, and health care reform.

Leyerle, Betty. *Moving and Shaking American Medicine: The Structure of a Socioeconomic Transformation*. Contributions in Economics and Economic History Ser. Greenwood 1984 $45.00. ISBN 0-313-24020-5. "Traces changes within the structure of the American health care system that have been both a cause and a consequence of a transformation in the occupational authority enjoyed by physicians" (*Library Journal*).

Mechanic, David. *From Advocacy to Allocation: The Evolving American Health Care System.* Free Pr. 1986 $27.95. ISBN 0-02-920830-0. "Exceptionally useful to anyone interested in the present and future state of the U.S. health care system. Divided into four major areas: issues in health policy, promotion of health and management of illness, the health profession, and the health of special populations (the elderly, the mentally ill, etc.)" (*Choice*).

Meltzer, Judith, Frank Farrow, and Harold Richman, eds. *Policy Options in Long-Term Care.* U. Ch. Pr. 1982 $28.00. ISBN 0-226-51973-2. "Emphasizes that although personal support systems often exist for some disabled persons, their resources for long-term care are unpredictable and largely unsupported financially" (*Choice*). Papers from a National symposium on Long-Term Care Policy Options held in Williamsburg, Virginia, June 1980.

Miller, Alfred E. *Options in Health and Health Care: The Coming of Post-Industrial Medicine. Health, Medicine, and Society Ser.* Wiley 1981 o.p. "Describes some of the pertinent trends in the history of medicine and then thoroughly examines the free-market, public-service, and regulated-utility aspects of our current system" (*Library Journal*).

HEALTH PROFESSIONS

The following section features books about health and allied health occupations, as well as professional issues related to those occupations, such as licensing and education. The section also includes some representative autobiographies.

General

Gross, Stanley. *Of Foxes and Hen Houses: Licensing and the Health Professions.* Greenwood 1984 $42.95. ISBN 0-89930-059-6. Examines a very complex and important public issue (i.e., does self-regulation in the health care field protect the public?).

McGuire, Christopher H., and others. *Handbook of Health Professions Education.* Jossey-Bass 1983 o.p. Presents a comprehensive critical review (by leading scholars) of where we have been and where we are going in health professions education in the United States; easy-to-read.

Mechanic, David, ed. *Handbook of Health, Health Care, and the Health Professions.* Free Pr. 1983 $75.00. ISBN 0-02-920690-1. An impressive compilation of essays that features a wealth of information on determinants of health and illness in the United States and on the organization and provision of health care.

U.S. Directory Service. *150 Careers in the Health Care Field.* Reed Ref. Pub. 1993 $59.95. ISBN 0-87228-054-3. A significantly expanded and updated directory that includes valuable introductory information on potential careers in health care for students whose interests and capacities are in areas other than professional preparation in medicine, dentistry, nursing, and pharmacy; represents a useful reference for concise information and further exploration.

Dentistry

Davis, Peter. *The Social Context of Dentistry.* Routledge Chapman & Hall 1980 o.p. An excellent examination of the major institutional features of contemporary dentistry within a broad social and historical context.

Peterson, Haller Alvarey. *Preparing to Enter Dental School.* P-H 1979 $13.95. ISBN 0-13-697326-4. A complete guide for applying to dental school and being accepted.

Explains selection of schools and provides information about the Dental Admissions
Test (DAT); includes tables and appendixes.

Wiles, Cheryl B., and William J. Ryan. *Communication for Dental Auxiliaries.* P-H 1982
o.p. A thorough presentation of communication applicable to dentistry.

Medicine

Broadhead, Robert S. *The Private Lives and Professional Identity of Medical Students.*
Transaction Pubs. 1983 $28.95. ISBN 0-87855-478-5. An interesting study (by a
sociologist) of the effects of medical school on the private lives and functioning of
medical students.

Colombotos, John, and *Corinne Kirchner. Physicians and Social Change.* OUP 1986
$39.95. ISBN 0-19-503685-9. Examination of how physician attitudes vary according
to social background, professional profile, and medical specialty; easy to read.

Hoffman, Stephen A. *Under the Ether Dome: A Physician's Apprenticeship at Massachusetts General Hospital.* Carroll Pub. 1990 $9.95. ISBN 0-8065-1204-5. The sensitive,
literate, and compelling story of a medical internship at one of the greatest teaching
hospitals in the United States.

Illich, Ivan. *Medical Nemesis: The Expropriation of Health.* Pantheon 1982 $11.95. ISBN
0-394-71245-5. A classic and controversial call for reform in the delivery of health
care.

Israel, Lucien. *Decision-Making: The Modern Doctor's Dilemma—Reflections on the Art of
Medicine.* Random 1982 o.p. A brief, but important, commentary on the use of
decision-making techniques for the optimization of medical performance.

Johnson, David G. *Physicians in the Making.* Jossey-Bass 1983 o.p. A report on the
personal, social, economic, and educational characteristics of contemporary medical students; suggests guidelines for reforms in the admission and training of
America's future physicians.

Kelman, Steven. *Improving Doctor Performance: A Study in the Use of Information and
Organizational Change.* Human Sci. Pr. 1980 $45.95. ISBN 0-87785-444-4. An
analysis of how various administrative and data systems can improve physician
performance in hospital practice.

Klass, Perri. *Baby Doctor.* Random 1992 $21.50. ISBN 0-679-40957-2. A personal account
of the author's year of residency in a major pediatric hospital.

Konner, Melvin. *Becoming a Doctor: A Journey of Initiation in Medical School.* Viking
Penguin 1988 $11.00. ISBN 0-14-011116-6. A self-critical account of the clinical
experiences of medical school and how those experiences mold the practitioner.

Kra, Siegfried J. *Examine Your Doctor: A Patient's Guide to Avoiding Medical Mishaps.*
Ticknor & Fields 1982 o.p. Discusses appropriate pre- and postsurgical care and
covers major medical problems.

LeBaron, Charles. *Gentle Vengeance: An Account of the First Year at Harvard Medical
School.* Viking Penguin 1982 o.p. Offers a somewhat condemning but realistic
description of medical education at Harvard Medical School.

Ludmerer, Kenneth M. *Learning to Heal: The Development of American Medical
Education.* Basic 1985 o.p. An engrossing narrative history of the rise of the modern
medical college and teaching hospital.

Morgan, Elizabeth. *The Making of a Woman Surgeon.* Berkeley Pub. 1988 $3.95. ISBN 0-
425-10037-5. A gripping first-person account of one woman's medical school
experience and residency in surgery at Yale University.

Rosen, George. *The Structure of American Medical Practice, 1875–1941.* U. of Pa. Pr. 1983
$17.95. ISBN 0-8122-1153-7. Examines the changes in doctors' attitudes and actions
and discusses the reasons for the transfer of the doctor's activity from the patient's
home to the office or the hospital.

Sarason, Seymour B. *Caring and Compassion in Clinical Practice.* Jossey-Bass 1985 o.p.
A wise and important book by the dean of clinical psychologists; examines the lack of
care and compassion that often characterizes clinical professional services.

Nursing

Aiken, Linda H., and Susan R. Gortner, eds. *Nursing in the 1980s: Crises, Opportunities, Challenges.* Lippincott 1982 o.p. An interdisciplinary work of excellent quality that examines issues, dilemmas, and challenges facing the nursing profession.

Archer, Sarah E., and Patricia A. Goebner. *Nurses: A Political Force.* Wadsworth Pub. 1982 o.p. A specific, well-written overview of nursing and politics.

Armstrong, Penny. *A Midwife's Story.* Ivy Books 1988 $3.95. ISBN 0-8041-0178-7. The autobiography of a twentieth-century midwife in Lancaster County, Pennsylvania.

Brown, Michael. *Nurses: The Human Touch.* Ivy Books 1992 $4.99. ISBN 0-8041-0800-2. Features stories of life as a nurse, its frustrations, and satisfactions in a variety of hospital departments.

Bullough, Vern L., and Bonnie Bullough. *The Care of the Sick: The Emergence of Modern Nursing.* Watson Pub. Intl. 1978 o.p. "Nursing has included a diverse collectivity, from priests and attendants in the temples of ancient Greece to maids and servants in wealthy households" (*American Scientist*).

Carpineto, Jane F. *R.N.: The Commitment, the Heartache and the Courage of Three Dedicated Nurses.* St. Martin 1992 $18.95. ISBN 0-312-07095-0. An engaging account of life as a nurse from the perspectives of an administrator, a recent graduate, and an experienced nurse.

Chaska, Norma L., ed. *The Nursing Profession: A Time to Speak.* McGraw 1983 $33.95. ISBN 0-07-010696-7. A comprehensive view of the state of the nursing profession—its research, education, practice, theory, and administration; includes predictions about the future of the nursing profession.

Davitz, Joel R., and Lois L. Davitz. *Inferences of Patients' Pain and Psychological Distress: Studies of Nursing Behaviors.* Springer Pub. 1981 o.p. A comprehensive, well-written, well-documented text on nursing behavior related to patient pain and psychological distress.

DelBueno, Dorothy J., and Cynthia M. Freund. *Power and Politics in Nursing Administration: A Casebook.* Rynd Comm. 1986 o.p. A creative, practical reference work for nursing administrators in organizational settings, as well as for students in health care settings.

DeVries, Raymond G. *Regulating Birth: Midwives, Medicine and the Law.* Temple U. Pr. 1985 o.p. A sociological examination of laws regulating midwives and the impact of those laws on the practice of midwifery.

Gino, Carol. *The Nurse's Story.* Bantam 1983 $3.95. ISBN 0-553-23667-9. An autobiography based on 16 years' experience in several hospitals.

Gow, Kathleen M. *How Nurses' Emotions Affect Patient Care: Self-Studies by Nurses.* Springer Pub. 1982 o.p. An analysis of the nurse-patient relationship.

Having Your Baby with a Nurse Midwife: Everything You Need to Know to Make an Informed Decision. American College of Nurse-Midwives Staff and Sandra Jacobs. Hyperion 1993 $9.95. ISBN 1-56282-860-6. Describes the nurse-midwife at work and discusses safety factors, costs, and insurance, as well as accurate information on benefits and limits to nurse-midwife assisted births.

Heron, Echo. *Intensive Care: The Story of a Nurse.* Macmillan 1987 $18.95. ISBN 0-687-11808-2. A moving and personal account of a nurse's life from training to practice to burnout.

Huttman, Barbara. *Code Blue: A Nurse's True-Life Story.* Berkley Pub. 1984 o.p. Presents the story of a 40-year-old corporate wife and mother who decides to become a nurse.

Janosik, Ellen H., and Lenore B. Phipps. *Life Cycle Group Work in Nursing.* Jones & Bartlett 1983 repr. of 1982 ed. $33.75. ISBN 0-86720-388-9. An important contribution to the field of nursing and one of the few works written by and for nurses on the subject of group process and treatment.

Kalisch, Beatrice J., and Philip A. Kalisch. *Politics of Nursing.* Lippincott 1982 o.p. An excellent handbook for the nursing profession; advocates that nurses should be politically active.

Litoff, Judy B. *The American Midwife Debate: A Sourcebook on Its Modern Origins.* Greenwood 1986 $49.95. ISBN 0-313-24919-0. Identifies the origins of the ongoing debate about the value of midwife management as opposed to medical management of normal labor and delivery.

Melosh, Barbara. *The Physician's Hand: Work Culture and Conflict in American Nursing.* Temple U. Pr. 1982 $16.95. ISBN 0-87722-290-8. Analyzes one of nursing's most persistent controversies; the schism between professionalization and apprenticeship culture that began with the founding of nursing schools in the late nineteenth century.

Petrowski, Dorothy D. *Handbook of Community Health Nursing: Essentials for Clinical Practice.* Springer Pub. 1984 o.p. A comprehensive, easy-to-read basic text for community health nursing students and others interested in the profession.

Yedidia, Michael J. *Delivering Primary Health Care: Nurse Practitioners at Work.* Greenwood 1981 $35.00. ISBN 0-86569-075-8. A brief historical summary of the evolution of primary health care precedes an in-depth differentiation between the "cure" concept of medicine and the "care" concept of nursing; recommended for nurses, but also relevant for other allied health professions.

Other Health Professions

Colen, B. D. *O.R.: The True Story of Twenty Four Hours in a Hospital Operating Room.* NAL-Dutton 1993 $20.00. ISBN 0-525-93518-5. In the words of the author, this book is "an album of snapshots that together form a mosaic of life in the operating room."

Cromwell, Florence S. *The Changing Roles of Occupational Therapists in the 1980s.* Haworth Pr. 1984 $32.95. ISBN 0-86656-294-X. Examines the emerging roles that are being undertaken by a significant health care profession. Important reading not only for occupational therapists, but also for health care administrators, vocational sociologists, and others working in collaboration with occupational therapists.

Cummings, Stephen, and Dana Ullman. *Everybody's Guide to Homeopathic Medicines.* J. P. Tarcher 1991 $10.95. ISBN 0-87477-641-4. An introduction to the rudiments of homeopathic practice in which the authors point out symptoms that contraindicate the home remedy approach; includes a list of the most important medicines and their corresponding physiological and psychological symptoms.

Gevitz, Norman. *The D.O.'s: Osteopathic Medicine in America.* Johns Hopkins 1991 repr. of 1982 ed. $16.95. ISBN 0-8018-4321-9. Examines osteopathy from its founding in the late nineteenth century to the present; includes principles of current practice and a good summary of the relationship between the American Medical Association and the American Osteopathic Association.

Kaufman, Martin. *Homeopathy in America: The Rise and Fall of a Medical Heresy.* Bks. Demand 1971 $41.30. ISBN 0-8357-9273-0. The best history of homeopathy; describes how the nineteenth-century medical establishment attempted to stop the homeopathy movement.

Langone, John. *Chiropractors: A Consumers' Guide.* Addison-Wesley 1982 o.p. An objective, well-organized guide to chiropractic. Covers the history, principles, educational requirements, most common treatments, fees, and other characteristics of the specialty; also includes an appendix of state laws, schools, and associations.

Serrett, Karen D. *Philosophical and Historical Roots of Occupational Therapy.* Haworth Pr. 1985 $26.95. ISBN 0-86656-456-X. A compact volume tracing the development of occupational therapy, especially in mental health. Useful for historical purposes and for a perspective on current practice.

Sexton, Patricia Cayo. *The New Nightingales: Hospital Workers, Unions, New Women's Issues.* Enquiry Pr. 1982 o.p. Examines the nature of nonprofessional work in a hospital from a feminist perspective. Written in a journalistic style; recommended for general readers.

Shapiro, Paul D., with Mary B. Shapiro. *Paramedic.* A well-written, fast-paced, and informative quasi-autobiography of life as a New York City emergency medical technician.

Weston, Alan J. *Survey of Allied Health Professions.* College-Hill 1980 o.p. Discusses the various allied health professions, regarding employment trends and professional publications.

Zarbock, Sarah F., and Kenneth Harbert. *Physician Assistants: Present and Future Models of Utilization.* Greenwood 1986 $47.95. ISBN 0-275-92065-8. A useful summary of the education, role, and utilization of physician assistants in modern medical practice.

THE HEALTHY BODY

There are many books that provide basic, authoritative, and reliable information about the body, its organs, and systems. The following list includes representative books in most areas. Chapter 13, "Illness and Disease," provides titles on specific diseases and groups of diseases.

Allport, Susan. *Explorers of the Black Box: The Search for the Cellular Basis of Memory.* Norton 1986 o.p. An interesting account of the inroads made by neurobiologists to explain the mechanisms of memory.

Amsterdam, Ezra A., and Ann M. Holmes. *Take Care of Your Heart.* Facts on File 1984 o.p. Discusses the major risk factors for coronary heart disease and features guidelines for changing one's life-style accordingly; includes sections on anatomy, physiology, diagnostic tests, and treatments.

Baldwin, Dorothy. *Understanding Male Sexual Health.* Hippocrene 1993 $11.95. ISBN 0-7818-0128-1. An updated version of *Male Sexual Health* (published in 1991). Provides reliable information about men's sexual organs, covering functional, preventive, and disease issues.

Barnard, Christiaan, and John Illman, eds. *The Body Machine: Your Health in Perspective.* Crown Pub. Group 1981 o.p. An important, wide-ranging, thought-provoking report on body systems and how they function together as a "machine."

Baum, Andrew, Robert Gatchel, and David Krantz. *An Introduction to Health Psychology.* Random 1988 $23.95. ISBN 0-394-37921-7. A good overview of the psychological aspects of health and the interrelationship between mind and body.

Berkley, George. *On Being Black and Healthy: How Black Americans Can Lead Longer and Healthier Lives.* P-H 1982 o.p. Dispenses good advice for healthy living, regardless of skin color. Describes symptoms of diseases that affect black Americans more than whites and discusses treatment through diet rather than drugs; easy to read.

Blakeslee, Thomas R. *The Right Brain: A New Understanding of Our Unconscious Mind and Its Creative Power.* Berkley Pub. 1984 $3.95. ISBN 0-425-09163-5. Offers some unusual theories on brain function laterality and sex differences; advances in a cogent style the position that left brain functions may no longer play the critical, dominant role they have historically assumed.

Bloom, Floyd E., and others. *Brain, Mind, and Behavior.* W. H. Freeman 1988 $33.95. ISBN 0-7167-1863-4. Presents information about brain organization and its role in body function, emotions, learning, and so on; designed for readers with little or no scientific background.

Brody, Jane E. *Jane Brody's The New York Times Guide to Personal Health.* Random 1982 $19.95. ISBN 0-686-95972-8. Based on Brody's popular columns. A useful compilation of information on some of the most popular topics in health and medicine; includes recommended readings and organizations for further information.

Bursztajn, Harold. *Medical Choices, Medical Chances: How Patients, Families, and Physicians Can Cope with Uncertainty.* Routledge 1990 $14.95. ISBN 0-415-90292-4. Presents in clear-cut terms the uncertainty of life with particular reference to disease states, medical care, and choices for patients; well-written and of interest to professionals and the general public.

Changeux, Jean-Pierre. *Neuronal Man: The Biology of Mind.* Pantheon 1985 $19.95. ISBN 0-394-53692-4. Describes the human nervous system from a multidisciplinary stance encompassing anatomy, physiology, biology, and chemistry; an award-winning book by a molecular neurobiologist.

Coleman, Richard M. *Wide Awake at 3:00 A.M.: By Choice or By Chance.* W. H. Freeman 1986 $12.95. ISBN 0-7167-1796-4. Describes circadian rhythms and their relationship to normal body function.

Conwell, Russell. *Acres of Diamonds.* R. H. Sommer 1987 $7.95. ISBN 0-933062-23-0. A substantial book that describes the fundamentals of dental care for the entire family.

Creager, Joan G. *Human Anatomy and Physiology.* W. C. Brown 1992 $34.95. ISBN 0-697-12134-8. Valuable as a quick reference for accurate information on the structure and function of the human body.

Davis, Goode P., and Edwards Park. *The Heart: The Living Pump.* U.S. News 1981 o.p. Excellent blend of historical and current information in a series of well-illustrated essays.

Denholz, Melvin, and Elaine Denholz. *How to Save Your Teeth and Your Money: A Consumer's Guide to Better, Less Costly, Dental Care.* Van Nos. Reinhold 1980 o.p. A nontechnical and practical book, describing techniques and procedures one can employ to minimize the expense of dental care.

Desowitz, Robert S. *The Thorn in the Starfish: The Immune System and How It Works.* Norton 1988 $8.95. ISBN 0-393-30556-2. Unravels the mysteries of the body's immune system; written by a parasitologist and World Health Organization researcher.

Diagram Group. *The Brain: A User's Manual.* Berkley Pub. 1983 $5.50. ISBN 0-425-06053-5. Concise but thorough introduction to the anatomy and functions of the various regions of the human brain.

Donovan, Bernard T. *Hormones and Human Behaviour.* Cambridge U. Pr. 1985 $59.95. ISBN 0-521-25881-2. Introduction to the complex interactions among the fields of neuroendocrinology, physical psychology, and psychiatry; easy-to-read, but not overly simplified.

Dvorine, William. *A Dermatologist's Guide to Home Skin Care.* Macmillan 1984 $12.95. ISBN 0-684-17875-3. An easy-to-read guide to the prevention and treatment of simple skin disorders; features information about skin physiology, as well as advice about creams, aging skin, common diseases, when to see a doctor, and so on.

Edelman, Gerald M. *Bright Air, Brilliant Fire: On the Matter of the Mind.* Basic 1992 $25.00. ISBN 0-465-05245-2. Edelman has written several books on the biology of the brain. Expounds his theory that the mind has arisen through evolutionary morphology, i.e., a product of biological forms that have developed through natural selection.

Ehrlich, David, with George Wolf. *The Bowel Book.* Schocken 1987 $9.95. ISBN 0-8052-0673-6. Using authoritative information from medical experts, presents the medical physiology and psychology of the gastrointestinal system.

Fasciana, Guy S. *Are Your Dental Fillings Poisoning You?* Keats 1986 $12.95. ISBN 0-87983-391-2. The hazards of the mercury controversy; written by a dentist who was forced out of practice by the toxic effects of dental mercury.

Fields, Willa L., and Karen M. McGinn-Campbell. *Introduction to Health Assessment.* P-H 1982 o.p. Arranged by systems and body regions, provides basic information on standard assessment procedures (inspection, palpation, and percussion); valuable for both beginning and advanced students.

Foster, M. S. *Protecting Our Children's Teeth: A Guide to Quality Dental Care from Infancy Through Age Twelve.* Plenum Pub. 1992 $23.95. ISBN 0-306-44122-5. Provides clear concise descriptions of the development of the teeth of children, as well as advice about tooth brushing, baby teeth, and other related topics; written by a pediatric dentist.

Freymann, Robert, with Leslie Holzer. *What's So Bad about Feeling Good?* Jove Pubns. 1983 $2.95. ISBN 0-87216-997-9. Uses doctor-patient dialogues to illustrate common health problems and the way they can be treated; advocates the position that the doctor-patient relationship can be used to motivate patients to change poor health habits.

Galton, Lawrence. *1,001 Health Tips.* S&S Trade 1984 o.p. A useful collection of remedies, hints, and guidelines on a variety of medical subjects; presented in nontechnical language.

Gilbaugh, James H. *Men's Private Parts: An Owner's Manual.* Crown Pub. Group 1993 $12.00. ISBN 0-517-88064-4. Provides useful information about the anatomy and physiology of men's sexual organs. Discusses circumcision, sexual dysfunction, sexually transmitted diseases, and other related topics.

Goldberg, Kathy E. *The Skeleton: Fantastic Framework.* U.S. News 1982 o.p. A comprehensive, easily understood introduction to historical and current advances in science involving the skeleton, bone growth, and healing.

Goldman, A. Richard, with Virginia McCullough. *TMJ Syndrome: The Overlooked Diagnosis.* Congdon & Weed 1987 o.p. Presented in a clear, nontechnical style, this first book written for the general reader does an excellent job of covering the manifestations and clinical problems associated with this common disorder— temporomandibular joint pain dysfunction syndrome; written by the Director of the Institute for the Treatment and Study of Headaches in Chicago.

Goldstein, Marc, and Michael Feldberg. *The Vasectomy Book: A Complete Guide to Decision Making.* HM 1982 o.p. A highly recommended and long overdue book that provides useful and objective information on the benefits and risks of vasectomies.

Goleman, Daniel, and Joel Gurin, eds. *Mind, Body Medicine: How to Use Your Mind for Better Health.* Consumer Reports 1993 $24.95. ISBN 0-89043-580-4. Collection of essays takes a calm and serious view of alternative medicine without endorsing it. The style is objective, practical and comprehensive; written almost exclusively by MDs and PhDs.

Hamburg, David A., Glen R. Elliott, and Delores L. Parron. *Health and Behavior: Frontiers of Research in the Biobehavioral Sciences.* Bks. Demand 1982 $101.30. ISBN 0-8357-3118-9. A one-of-a-kind book providing broad coverage of present knowledge of how human behavior influences health; accessible to the general reader.

Harth, Erich. *Windows on the Mind: Reflections on the Physical Basis of Consciousness.* Morrow 1982 o.p. A synthesis of facts, theories, and paradoxes from several disciplines. Provides a valuable overview of the nature of human consciousness; written for the general reader.

Hausman, Patricia. *The Calcium Bible: How to Have Better Bones All Your Life.* Warner Bks. 1986 $3.95. ISBN 0-446-34173-8. Offers a convincing and easy-to-read discussion of the role calcium plays in general health.

Haymes, Emily M., and Christine L. Wells. *Environment and Human Performance.* Human Kinetics 1986 $34.00. ISBN 0-83722-039-0. An excellent resource offering practical and theoretical information on how the environment affects the cardiovascular, respiratory, renal, muscular, and neural systems.

Jensen, Karen. *Reproduction: The Cycle of Life.* U.S. News 1982 o.p. An extremely informative, well-illustrated, historical, and current perspective on human reproduction.

Johnson, G. Timothy, and Stephen E. Goldfinger. *The Harvard Medical School Health Letter Book.* Warner Bks. 1982 $3.95. ISBN 0-446-30104-3. An excellent resource for the general reader on a wide array of important health topics.

Kals, W. S. *Your Health, Your Moods, and the Weather.* Doubleday 1982 o.p. Written from the viewpoint that one-third of the population is weather sensitive; describes the common components of the weather (temperature, wind, and so on) that can affect human comfort and shows practical ways to avoid or ameliorate unfavorable conditions.

Klatell, Jack, Andrew Kaplan, and Gray Williams. *The Mount Sinai Medical Center Family Guide to Dental Health.* Macmillan 1992 $29.95. ISBN 0-02-563675-8. Discusses the recent revolution in dental technology and treatment; presents much scientifically sound information in a clear, easy-to-read fashion.

Lillyquist, Michael J. *Sunlight and Health: The Positive and Negative Effects of the Sun on You.* Dodd 1987 $7.95. ISBN 0-396-08957-7. A handy compilation of scientific information concerning the sun, skin types, and the physiology of the skin.

Louria, Donald B. *Stay Well*. Macmillan 1982 o.p. Proposes that a sensible program of preventive health care can save lives, reduce medical expenses, and prevent illness. Describes a series of simple but effective strategies for minimizing risk factors and detecting early symptoms of major disease; straightforward, practical, and well researched.

Lynch, James J. *The Language of the Heart: The Body's Response to Human Dialogue*. Basic 1985 o.p. An excellent example of serious science made interesting. Discusses the heart and how its health is affected by emotions and social interactions; scholarly but easy to read.

Marshall, Daniel P., and others. *Staying Healthy Without Medicine: A Manual of Home Prevention and Treatment*. Nelson-Hall 1983 $34.95. ISBN 0-88229-639-3. A manual of preventive medicine that is divided into two sections: general principles of healthy living and common health problems.

Masiak, Mary J., and Mary D. Naylor. *Fluids and Electrolytes Through the Life Cycle*. Appleton 1985 o.p. Provides fundamental information on fluid, electrolyte, and acid-balance homeostasis in health and disease; designed for nurses but accessible to the general reader.

Moyers, Bill. *Healing and the Mind*. Doubleday 1993 $29.95. ISBN 0-385-46870-9. An entertaining analysis of the ways our thoughts and feelings affect our health; traces historical antecedents and reports on recent research on the brain.

Ottoson, David. *Physiology of the Nervous System*. OUP 1983 o.p. A highly recommended sourcebook on the complex subject of the functional organization of the nervous system; easy to read.

Page, Jake. *Blood: The River of Life*. U.S. News 1981 o.p. A blend of introductory historical and current information on blood; well illustrated.

Perkins, D. N. *The Mind's Best Work*. HUP 1981 $12.95. ISBN 0-674-57624-1. Describes how the mind works for the general reader.

Questions Patients Most Often Ask Their Doctors. Medical Tribune Editors. Bantam 1983 o.p. An especially well-written question-and-answer book combining the skills of medical writers with the expertise of medical specialists; emphasizes preventive maintenance and major health problems of body systems.

Restak, Richard M. *The Brain*. Bantam 1991 $17.50. ISBN 0-553-35307-1. An outgrowth and expanded version of the popular eight-part public television series on the brain.

Samuels, Mike, and Hal Z. Bennett. *Well Body, Well Earth: The Sierra Club Environmental Health Sourcebook*. Sierra 1983 o.p. Based on the premise that the earth is a living entity and that its functions are closely interconnected to human health, well-illustrated and includes appendixes of toxic substances, political action groups, and recommended readings.

Sorochan, Walter D. *Promoting Your Health*. Wiley 1981 o.p. A stimulating presentation on health promotion, awareness of lifestyle behaviors, and self-assessment of health.

Sydney, Sheldon B. *Ignore Your Teeth and They'll Go Away: The Patient's Complete Guide to the Prevention and Treatment of Periodontal (Gum) Disease*. Devida 1982 $19.95. ISBN 0-9607498-0-2. A clear and well-illustrated description of warning signs, clinical examinations, and treatment methods for most common gum diseases; written by a practicing periodontist.

Vickery, Donald M. *Take Care of Yourself: The Consumer's Guide to Medical Care*. Addison-Wesley 1993 $24.95. ISBN 0-201-63292-6. A popular and well-written compendium.

Vogel, Steven. *Vital Circuits: On Pumps, Pipes and the Workings of the Circulatory System*. OUP 1992 $24.95. ISBN 0-19-507155-7. Discussion and description of the heart, blood vessels, and cardiovascular physiology; easy to read and well illustrated.

Wertenbaker, Lael T. *The Eye: The Window of the World*. U.S. News 1981 o.p. An introduction to the human eye and its functions; well illustrated.

Wood, Norman. *The Complete Book of Dental Care*. Hart Pubns. 1979 o.p. A highly recommended informative guide to dentistry from the consumer's point of view; includes information on how to choose and evaluate a dentist and when to seek a dental specialist.

Xenakis, Alan P. *Why Doesn't My Funny Bone Make Me Laugh? Sneezes, Hiccups, Butterflies, and Other Funny Feelings Explained.* Random 1993 $18.00. ISBN 0-394-58715-4. An informative and entertaining book about yawning, belching, and other normal body functions.

HEMATOLOGY

[SEE the section on The Healthy Body in this chapter; for blood (hematologic) diseases, see Chapter 13 in this volume.]

HISTOLOGY

[SEE the section on The Healthy Body in this chapter.]

HISTORY OF THE HEALTH SCIENCES

[SEE the section on Biography and History of Medicine in this chapter.]

MEDICINE AND THE LAW

The relationship between medical knowledge and the law has received greater attention during the past two decades. Consequently, the number of books that have been published in the area continues to increase. The following titles include collections of pathological case studies, as well as introductions to malpractice law.

Annas, George J. *The Rights of Patients: the Basic ACLU Guide to Patient Rights.* Humana 1992 $29.50. ISBN 0-89603-182-9. A thorough, reliable, and comprehensive treatment of patient rights; covers living wills, hospital ethics committees, and includes bibliographic references and an index.

Annas, George J., Leonard H. Glantz, and Barbara F. Katz. *The Rights of Doctors, Nurses and Allied Health Professionals: A Health Law Primer.* Ballinger 1983 o.p. An American Civil Liberties Union (ACLU) handbook that offers a wealth of information on medico-legal issues not found in such a convenient form elsewhere; includes a useful glossary of legal terms.

Belkin, Lisa. *First, Do No Harm.* S&S Trade 1993 $23.00. ISBN 0-671-68538-4. Offers a gripping and personal look at medical ethics in a Texas hospital.

Browne, Douglas, and Thomm Tullett. *Bernard Spilsbury: Famous Murder Cases of the Great Pathologist.* Academy Ch. 1983 o.p. A fascinating collection of actual murder cases, and the role of pathology in their solution.

Champagne, Anthony, and Rosemary N. Dawes. *Courts and Modern Medicine.* C. C. Thomas 1983 o.p. Analysis of the interplay between the American legal and health care systems; somewhat scholarly.

Christoffel, Tom. *Health and the Law: A Handbook for Health Professionals.* Free Pr. 1985 $17.95. ISBN 0-02-905960-7. An excellent resource and guide for persons interested in the law and health care; provides an overview, historical perspective, and issues analysis on a wide range of topics.

Corea, Gena. *The Hidden Malpractice: How American Medicine Mistreats Women.* HarpC 1985 o.p. The definitive book on malpractice against women and racial minorities. Provides a historical overview of sex discrimination and its results in medical care for the general reader.

Eisenberg, John F. *Medical Malpractice Litigation*. Mason 1982 o.p. A compendium that discusses the applicable laws and the resolution of landmark cases in medical malpractice.

King, Joseph H. *The Law of Medical Malpractice in a Nutshell*. West Pub. 1986 $13.95. ISBN 0-314-98200-0. A succinct exposition of laws relating to liability-producing conduct arising from the delivery of professional medical services in the United States; includes sections on standards of care, proof of negligence, mental distress, and so on.

Kwitny, Jonathan. *Acceptable Risks*. Poseidon Pr. 1992 $24.00. ISBN 0-671-73244-7. A thoughtful discussion of the legal and ethical issues involved in balancing the possibility of harmful side effects of new drugs with denying desperately ill patients promising but unproved treatment options.

Smyth, Frank. *Cause of Death: The Story of Forensic Medicine*. Van Nos. Reinhold 1980 o.p. A history of the topic that includes useful summaries of different categories of the causes of death.

Weiler, Paul C., and others. *A Measure of Malpractice: Medical Injury, Malpractice, Litigation, and Patient Compensation*. HUP 1993 $29.95. ISBN 0-674-55880-4. A scholarly, well-referenced monograph on physician liability, the economic aspects of malpractice, and the malpractice insurance industry; accessible to the general reader.

Zobel, Hiller B., and Stephen N. Rous. *The Doctor and the Court: The Physician's Guide to Surviving*. Norton 1993 $22.95. ISBN 0-393-03450-X. Provides information about medical malpractice and insurance claims; written mainly for medical professionals.

NEUROLOGY

[SEE the section on The Healthy Body in this chapter; for the diagnosis and treatment of nervous system diseases, SEE Chapter 13 in this volume.]

NURSING

[SEE the section on Health Professions, Nursing in this chapter.]

NUTRITION AND DIET

This section includes books on food science, including nutrients, their assimilation, utilization, action, interaction, and balance in relation to health and disease. This aspect of health care has a very active publishing history with several new titles on diet being published regularly. This list therefore is extremely selective, featuring subsections on childhood nutrition and nutrition and aging.

Aubert, Claude, and Pierre Frapa. *Hunger and Health*. Rodale Pr. Inc. 1985 o.p. Discusses the problems caused by modern techniques of food production and processing, as well as by the Western diet emulated in other parts of the world.

Bennett, William, and Joel Gurin. *The Dieter's Dilemma: Eating Less and Weighing More*. Basic 1982 o.p. A valuable compendium of diet information and guidelines that challenges the professional and lay communities to reevaluate basic assumptions about the biological basis of obesity.

Berger, Stuart M. *Dr. Berger's Immune Power Diet*. NAL-Dutton 1989 o.p. A convincing multipart program to strengthen the body's immune system so that it functions properly.

Bourre, Jean-Marie. *Brainfood: A Provocative Exploration of the Connection Between What You Eat and How You Think*. Little 1993 $22.95. ISBN 0-316-10362-4. A survey of the basics of dietary biochemistry from proteins through trace elements and discusses how they affect the brain and senses.

Brisson, Germain J. *Lipids in Human Nutrition: An Appraisal of Some Dietary Concepts*. Burgess 1981 o.p. Addresses the role of fats in the diet and the advisability of dietary intervention to lower the blood cholesterol level in the mass population; concise and well written.

Brody, Jane E. *Jane Brody's Good Food Book: Living the High Carbohydrate Way*. Bantam 1987 $15.00. ISBN 0-553-34618-0. A useful and practical guide to carbohydrates and healthy eating.

Calabrese, Edward J., and Michael W. Dorsey. *Healthy Living in an Unhealthy World: Food for Survival in a Polluted World*. S&S Trade 1984 o.p. A balanced selection of information from the scientific literature on environmental health hazards due to substances introduced by modern technology.

Carroll, David. *The Complete Book of Natural Foods*. Summit Bks. 1985 o.p. A sensible text focusing on avoiding unhealthy foods.

Cataldo, Corinne B. *Nutrition and Diet Therapy: Principles and Practice*. West Pub. 1992 $49.75. ISBN 0-314-93359-X. A textbook on the role of diet therapy in proper nutritional practice.

Cheraskin, Emanuel, and others. *The Vitamin C Connection*. Bantam 1984 $3.95. ISBN 0-553-24434-5. A well-documented book that updates earlier works on the therapeutic role of vitamin C and that reviews the research literature in popular language.

Colgan, Michael. *Your Personal Vitamin Profile*. Morrow 1982 $8.95. ISBN 0-688-01506-9. A controversial book that suggests nutrients in much higher amounts than Recommended Daily Allowances (RDAs) are necessary to prevent disease and to maintain optimum health; written in a clear and interesting style.

DeBakey, Michael E., and others. *The Living Heart Diet*. S&S Trade 1986 $13.00. ISBN 0-671-61998-4. An excellent guide designed to promote a healthy heart; information is technical but easy to understand.

Finn, Susan, and Linda Stern Kass. *The Real Life Nutrition Book*. Viking Penguin 1992 $15.00. ISBN 0-14-013174-4. An excellent evaluation of fast foods, prepared supermarket foods, and advice on how to fit good nutritional practices into hectic lifestyles.

Fried, John. *Vitamin Politics*. Prometheus Bks. 1984 $18.95. ISBN 0-87975-222-X. Essentially an update of his earlier *The Vitamin Conspiracy*. Details the controversy between vitamin enthusiasts and medical researchers over the testing, use, and hazards of vitamin and megavitamin therapies; well-written and informative.

Gaby, Alan. *B-6: The Natural Healer*. Keats 1987 $3.95. ISBN 0-87983-434-X. Originally published as *The Doctor's Guide to Vitamin B-6*, an updated review (in nontechnical language) of the research on the efficacy of vitamin B6 in disease treatment; exceptionally well-documented.

Garrison, Robert H., and Elizabeth Somer. *The Nutrition Desk Reference*. Keats 1990 $16.95. ISBN 0-87983-488-9. A clear and easy-to-understand book that presents information on the fundamentals of human nutrition and highlights topics of current interest and/or controversy.

Gebo, Sue. *What's Left To Eat?* McGraw 1992 $24.95. ISBN 0-07-023476-0. Includes an analysis of food research, as well as other helpful information on food contamination, food handling, and the links between food consumption and a variety of diseases, such as hypertension, cancer, and heart disease; well researched and referenced.

Gibney, Michael J. *Nutrition, Diet, and Health*. Cambridge U. Pr. 1986 o.p. A technical treatment that is accessible to the educated reader.

Gurr, Michael I. *Role of Fats in Food and Nutrition*. Elsevier 1984 $63.00. ISBN 0-85334-298-9. An unbiased approach to a controversial topic. Discusses the nature, occurrence, and characteristics of biologically important fats and their metabolic and nutritional roles; written for the undergraduate.

Haas, Robert. *Eat to Win: The Sports Nutrition Bible.* NAL-Dutton 1985 $5.99. ISBN 0-451-15509-2. The goal of this book is to improve performance, reduce the effects of aging, and promote faster and stronger healing of athletic injuries.

Hamilton, Eva M. N. *Nutrition: Concepts and Controversies.* West Pub. 1991 $49.25. ISBN 0-314-81091-9. The latest edition of a standard textbook that presents in a balanced way a comprehensive view of the field of nutrition; easy to read.

Hausman, Patricia. *Jack Sprat's Legacy: The Science and Politics of Fat and Cholesterol.* Richard Marek Pubs. 1981 o.p. A well-written, well-documented book that discusses nutrition research and the controversies among nutritionists, medical researchers, farmers, milk producers, politicians, and the government.

Herbert, Victor, and Stephen Barrett. *Vitamins and Health Foods: The Great American Hustle.* G. F. Stickley 1981 o.p. A cogent discussion of how the American public has been victimized by health hucksters who exploit the insecurities of individuals.

Hunter, Beatrice T. *Food Additives and Federal Policy: The Mirage of Safety.* Macmillan 1975 o.p. Presents the toxicological hazards of food additives. Valuable to those interested in the regulatory process and the interplay of the regulatory agencies, industry, and the consumer.

————. *The Sugar Trap and How to Avoid It.* HM 1982 o.p. A carefully documented book on the discovery and processing of refined (cane sugar), traditional (honey), artificial (saccharin), and rare natural (sorbitol) sweeteners.

Jacobson, Michael, and others. *Safe Food.* Berkley Pub. 1993 $4.99. ISBN 0-425-131621-3. An excellent compilation of information about selecting, handling, and preparing safe and healthy food, including naturally occurring toxins.

Jelliffe, E. F. Patrice, and Derrick B. Jelliffe, eds. *Adverse Effects of Foods.* Plenum Pub. 1982 $115.00. ISBN 0-306-40870-8. Useful to food scientists, nutritionists, and persons concerned with public health; presents an overview of the subject followed by detailed topical chapters prepared by recognized authorities.

Katahn, Martin. *Beyond Diet: The 28-Day Metabolic Breakthrough Plan.* Berkley Pub. 1987 $4.50. ISBN 0-425-09915-6. Proposes that dieters can break the low-calorie diet cycle by reprogramming the body's metabolic processes and making a commitment to daily physical activity.

LeRiche, W. Harding. *A Chemical Feast.* Facts on File 1982 $22.95. ISBN 0-87196-643-3. Well-documented discussion of microbiological infection, poor nutrition, and accidental environmental contamination.

Liebman, Bonnie, Michael Jacobson, and Greg Moyer. *Salt: The Brand Name Guide to Sodium Content.* Warner Bks. 1988 $4.95. ISBN 0-446-35513-5. A well-researched guide to the dietary effects of sodium; includes substantial information on low- or reduced-sodium foods.

Lindberg, Gladys, and Judy L. McFarland. *Take Charge of Your Health: The Complete Nutrition Book.* HarpC 1982 o.p. Presents a comprehensive nutritional program to overcome poor health resulting from a vitamin, mineral, protein, or fiber deficient diet; written by the founder and owner of Lindberg's health food store chain.

Long, Patricia J., and Barbara Shannon. *Nutrition: An Inquiry into the Issues.* P-H 1983 $26.95. ISBN 0-13-627802-7. Discusses the principles of nutrition and presents information on current issues and controversies; written for college students interested in nutrition.

Marshall, Charles W. *Vitamins and Minerals: Help or Harm?* Lippincott 1985 $11.95. ISBN 0-397-53060-4. A discussion of each vitamin and mineral, its usefulness, the quantity needed, and symptoms of overdosage.

Michael, Jane W. *Breakfast, Lunch, and Dinner of Champions: Star Athletes' Diet Programs for Maximum Energy and Performance.* Morrow 1984 o.p. Accurate and informative about sports and nutrition; covers the dietary regimens of famous people in many athletic activities.

Mindell, Earl. *Earl Mindell's Vitamin Bible.* Warner Bks. 1989 $5.99. ISBN 0-446-36184-4. A handy reference guide that presents concise, up-to-date, and reliable information about vitamins and their role in human nutrition.

Mirkin, Gabe. *Getting Thin: All About Fat—How You Get It, How You Lose It, How You Keep It Off for Good.* Little 1986 $11.95. ISBN 0-316-57439-2. A highly recommended and interesting book about theories that explain why people get fat, why exercise is a key factor in maintaining ideal weight, and why certain popular diet plans are faulty or dangerous.

Morgan, Brian L. G. *The Lifelong Nutrition Guide: How to Eat for Health at Every Age and Stage of Life.* P-H 1983 o.p. A clearly written overview of the typical American diet; discusses vitamin and mineral requirements and specialized nutrition information for vegetarians and pregnant women.

Natow, Annette B., and JoAnn Heslin. *Nutrition for the Prime of Your Life.* McGraw 1984 $8.95. ISBN 0-07-028418-0. In a question-and-answer format, covers basic facts about essential nutrients, caffeine, alcohol, and so on; quotes recent scientific research.

Novin, Donald, Wanda Wyrwicka, and George A. Bray. *Hunger: Basic Mechanisms and Clinical Implications.* Raven 1976 $89.00. ISBN 0-89004-059-1. Extensive coverage of the factors related to the control of food intake.

Null, Gary. *Gary Null's Complete Guide to Health.* Outlet Bk. Co. 1993 $11.99. ISBN 0-517-09301-4. A comprehensive handbook for the general reader.

Passwater, Richard A., and Elmer M. Cranton. *Trace Elements, Hair Analysis, and Nutrition.* Keats 1983 $18.95. ISBN 0-87983-348-3. An authoritative book that describes each trace element, its role in nutrition, diagnostic techniques for establishing levels in the body, and specific case studies of ill health relating to undesirable levels of trace elements in the system.

Polivy, Janet, and C. Peter Herman. *Breaking the Diet Habit: The Natural Weight Alternative.* Basic 1983 o.p. Interesting and well-documented, proposes that overweight people should not diet but should remain at their "natural" weight by eating only when hungry.

Pritikin, Nathan. *The Diet for Runners.* S&S Trade $8.95. ISBN 0-671-55623-1. The health and diet theories that Pritikin presented in his earlier work have been expanded to cover the needs of runners, who need to be especially aware of cholesterol levels during exercise.

_____. *The Pritikin Promise: 28 Days to a Longer, Healthier Life.* PB 1991 $5.99. ISBN 0-671-73267-6. A basic plan for a controlled regimen of diet and exercise.

Rippe, James M., with Patricia Amend. *The Exercise Exchange Program: The Unique System That Allows You to Design Your Own Diet and Workout Every Day for a Lifetime of Good Health.* S&S Trade $12.00. ISBN 0-671-79453-1. A commonsense approach to weight loss that avoids quick fixes and gimmicks; developed and tested at the Exercise Physiology and Nutrition Laboratory at University of Massachusetts Medical School.

Simonson, Maria, and Joan R. Heilman. *The Complete University Medical Diet.* Warner Bks. 1985 $3.50. ISBN 0-446-32338-1. Describes a safe, sensible diet and exercise regimen.

Smith, Lendon. *Feed Yourself Right.* Dell 1988 $5.95. ISBN 0-440-20066-0. Describes the effects of diet and life-style on behavior, personality, and physical well-being; written by a respected expert on nutrition.

Somer, Elizabeth. *The Essential Guide to Vitamins and Minerals.* HarpC 1992 $30.00. ISBN 0-06-271516-0. A broad and extensively researched guide to vitamins and minerals that also includes information about deficiency symptoms, supplements, and the role of vitamins and minerals in illness and disease.

Tobias, Alice L., and Patricia J. Thompson. *Issues in Nutrition for the 1980s: An Ecological Perspective.* Wadsworth Pub. 1980 o.p. An excellent reference for anyone concerned with balanced nutrition on a world scale; presents 55 selections by various authors.

Tracy, Lisa. *The Gradual Vegetarian.* Dell 1993 $5.99. ISBN 0-440-21585-4. Helps readers avoid eating refined, overprocessed foods.

Wright, Jonathan V. *Dr. Wright's Guide to Healing with Nutrition.* Keats 1990 $14.95. ISBN 0-87983-530-3. Offers a persuasive argument that many common ailments are caused by digestive disorders, food allergies, or dietary deficiencies.

Yetiv, Jack Z. *Popular Nutritional Practices: A Scientific Appraisal*. Popular Medicine Pr. 1986 $23.95. ISBN 0-936575-30-1. An authoritative text that provides a clear understanding of information in a critical and often neglected area of human health.

Childhood Nutrition

Atwood, Stephen J. *A Doctor's Guide to Feeding Your Child*. Macmillan 1982 o.p. A guide to children's nutrition from the prenatal stage of development through adolescence.

Baggett, Nancy, and others. *Don't Tell 'Em It's Good for 'Em*. Random 1984 o.p. Offers a reasonable, commonsense approach to a serious problem; fills a gap in diet-book literature because it is suited for all members of the family.

Cohen, Mindy, and Louis Abramson. *Thin Kids*. Beaufort Bks. 1985 o.p. A successful outline for a balanced nutritionally sound diet for children similar to those offered by some of the national weight loss programs for adults.

Cohen, Stanley A. *Healthy Babies, Happy Kids*. Putnam Pub. Group 1982 o.p. A comprehensive and practical guide to nourishing babies and children, including more than the usual information on early childhood digestive disorders.

Goulart, Frances S. *Beyond Baby Fat: Weight-Loss Plans for Children and Teenagers*. Berkley Pub. 1991 $3.95. ISBN 0-425-11616-6. A compilation of several different diets aimed at specific weight problems; also offers solid information on childhood nutrition.

Hirschmann, Jane R., and Lela Zaphiropoulos. *Are You Hungry? A Completely New Approach to Raising Children Free of Weight and Food Problems*. Fawcett 1990 $6.95. ISBN 0-449-90512-8. An innovative book in which the authors set forth a plan for self-demand feeding that they feel will allow children to develop a comfortable relationship with food.

Kamen, Betty, and Si Kamen. *Kids Are What They Eat: What Every Parent Needs to Know about Nutrition*. P-H Gen. Ref. & Trav. 1983 o.p. A warmly written, well-documented book that suggests a childhood diet rich in whole grains, sprouts, fresh fruits, and vegetables.

Lambert-Legace, Louise. *Feeding Your Baby From Conception to Age Two*. Surrey Bks. 1991 $10.95. ISBN 0-940625-37-7. A revised and scaled down practical guide based on the premise that if parents teach their children to eat and enjoy healthful food, the youngsters will do so into adulthood and thus avoid junk food, obesity, and illness.

Mahan, L. Kathleen, and Jane M. Rees. *Nutrition in Adolescence*. Mosby Yr. Bk. 1984 o.p. A comprehensive book that combines not only nutritional facts but also knowledge of the physical and social needs of the adolescent.

Ritchey, S. J., and L. Janette Taper. *Maternal and Child Nutrition*. HarpC 1983 o.p. A sound sequencing of the relationship of nutrition to the health of the child at various developmental stages.

Weiner, Michael E., and Kathleen Goss. *The Art of Feeding Children Well*. Warner Bks. 1982 $6.95. ISBN 0-446-97890-6. This work promotes the maintenance and recovery of children's health through good nutrition with practical information on balancing diets and incorporating a variety of nonprocessed foods into the diet.

Winick, Myron. *Feeding the Mother and Infant*. Wiley 1985 o.p. An excellent reference source for practitioners and students in the health sciences; a comprehensive state-of-the-art review of nutrition and child development.

Wunderlich, Ray, and Dwight Kalita. *Nourishing Your Child*. Keats 1986 o.p. Advocates a bioecologic approach to child nutrition; emphasizes the use of appropriate vitamins, minerals, amino acids, and enzymes, as well as a healthful diet for children.

Nutrition and Aging

Armbrecht, H. James, John M. Prendergast, and Rodney M. Coe. *Nutritional Intervention in the Aging Process*. Spring.-Verlag 1984 $87.00. ISBN 0-387-96025-2. Compiles current knowledge of the field and proposes applications of the knowledge to the care of the elderly; a significant contribution to the field.

Feldman, Elaine B. *Nutrition in the Middle and Later Years.* Warner Bks. 1986 $3.95. ISBN 0-446-34081-2. Various aspects of nutrition as they pertain to the aging individual are covered by investigators working in this area.

Hendler, Sheldon P. *The Complete Guide to Anti-Aging Nutrients.* S&S Trade 1986 $8.95. ISBN 0-685-11924-6. A balanced and moderate, though somewhat uneven, attempt to sort out the conflicting claims for and against many vitamins and amino acids.

Kart, Gary S., and Seamus P. Metress. *Nutrition, the Aged, and Society.* P-H 1984 $16.95. ISBN 0-13-627521-4. A comprehensive book on aging and nutrition with appeal to a wide spectrum of professional and lay interests.

Kenton, Leslie. *Ageless Aging: The Natural Way to Stay Young.* Grove Pr. 1986 o.p. Provides a useful summary of information on the nutritional aspects of longevity; advocates a low-calorie diet.

Mollen, Art. *Dr. Mollen's Anti-Aging Diet: The Breakthrough Program of Easy Weight-Loss and Longevity.* NAL-Dutton 1992 $21.00. ISBN 0-525-93450-2. Emphasizes fruits, vegetables, grains, and legumes with small amounts of animal and vegetable protein, moderate exercise, and a positive mental outlook; written by a physician and founder of the Southwest Health Institute.

Watkin, Donald M. *Handbook of Nutrition, Health, and Aging.* Noyes 1983 o.p. An excellent multidisciplinary review of geriatric nutrition.

OBSTETRICS

[SEE the section on Women's Health, Pregnancy and Childbirth in this chapter.]

OCCUPATIONAL MEDICINE AND HEALTH

[SEE the section on Public, Environmental, and Occupational Health in this chapter.]

OPHTHALMOLOGY

[SEE the section on The Healthy Body in this chapter; for books on the medical and surgical treatment of its defects and diseases, and blindness (eye disorders), see Chapter 13 in this volume.]

OTOLARYNGOLOGY

[SEE Ear and Throat Disorders in Chapter 13 in this volume.]

PEDIATRICS

[SEE the section on Child Care and Development in this chapter.]

PHARMACOLOGY AND TOXICOLOGY

Pharmacology is the study of the origin, nature, properties, and actions of drugs, as well as their effects on living organisms. Toxicology is concerned with the detection and action of chemicals and poisons. There has been increasing public interest in toxic chemicals in the environment and also on the development of new drugs to combat disease and to maintain health. This section contains representative books for each discipline.

Altschul, Siri von Reis. *Drugs and Foods from Little-Known Plants: Notes in Harvard University Herbaria.* HUP 1973 $42.50. ISBN 0-674-21676-8. A scholarly but readable compendium of folklore on food, drug, and aromatic plants, culled from the field notes on 2,500,000 specimens.

Apfel, Roberta J., and Susan M. Fisher. *To Do No Harm: DES and the Dilemmas of Modern Medicine.* Yale U. Pr. 1984 $27.00. ISBN 0-300-03192-0. A well-researched and probing work that examines the events attending the use of DES without either muckraking or denying their seriousness.

Beyer, Karl H. *Discovery, Development, and Delivery of New Drugs.* Spectrum Bks. 1978 o.p. A historically important work; a statement of how things were done at Merck, Sharp & Dohme and a chronicle of the development of several new drugs.

Blum, Kenneth. *Handbook of Abusable Drugs.* Gardner Pr. 1993 $49.95. ISBN 0-89876-196-4. A compilation of information on the spectrum of abused substances, including their histories, biochemistry, pharmacology, toxicity, and behavioral and psychological aspects.

Burger, Alfred. *Drugs and People: Medications, Their History and Origins, and the Way They Act.* U. Pr. of Va. 1988 $10.95. ISBN 0-8139-1101-X. An explanation, in readable terms, of medications and their backgrounds; a wealth of interesting facts.

Carlton, Peter L. *A Primer of Behavioral Pharmacology: Concepts and Principles in the Behavioral Analysis of Drug Action.* W. H. Freeman 1983 $18.95. ISBN 0-7167-1451-5. Destined to become a standard guide for students of behavioral pharmacology; provides a comprehensive analysis of the general principles of the science of drug-behavior interactions.

Carson, Bonnie L., Harry V. Ellis, and Joy L. McCann. *Toxicology and Biological Monitoring of Metals in Humans: Including Feasibility and Need.* Lewis Pubs. 1986 $72.95. ISBN 0-87371-072-X. A one-stop source in a brief, uniform format for information on the toxicity of the 52 elements and rare earths.

Castleman, Michael. *An Aspirin a Day: What You Can Do to Prevent Heart Attack, Stroke, and Cancer.* Hyperion 1993 $7.95. ISBN 1-56282-880-0. A well-documented discussion of aspirin use as a preventive therapy for a wide range of common diseases.

Drake, Donald, and Marian Uhlman. *Making Medicine, Making Money.* Andrews & McMeel 1993 $5.95. ISBN 0-8362-8023-7. A well-documented attack on the pharmaceutical industry in the United States.

Dreyfus, Jack. *A Remarkable Medicine Has Been Overlooked.* PB 1983 $4.95. ISBN 0-671-47673-4. Claims that DPH (diphenylhydantoin usually marketed under the trade name Dilantin), an anticonvulsant drug, is also efficacious in treating disorders of the nervous system.

Folb, Peter I. *The Safety of Medicines: Evaluation and Prediction.* Spring.-Verlag 1980 o.p. A comprehensive approach to a difficult subject, the book outlines the general principles of evaluation and prediction that are available for the developers of new medicines, the pharmaceutical industry, drug regulatory agencies, medical practitioners, and the general public.

Friedman, Robert M. *Interferons: A Primer.* Acad. Pr. 1981 o.p. A useful addition to the literature that provides basic, easy-to-understand information about this new therapy; appropriate for the student, scientist, or educated layperson.

Gabe, Jonathan, and Paul Williams. *Tranquillisers: Social, Psychological and Clinical Perspectives.* Routledge 1986 $57.50. ISBN 0-422-79930-0. An extremely valuable book that effectively deals with a topic of current concern.

Graedon, Joe. *Aspirin Handbook: A User's Guide to the Breakthrough Drug of the 90s.* Bantam 1993 $4.99. ISBN 0-553-56119-7. Describes the use of moderate amounts of aspirin to help prevent heart attacks, strokes, colon cancer, diabetic eye problems, and insomnia; derived from newspaper columns and from an information survey.

Green, Nancy S. *Poisoning Our Children: Surviving in a Toxic World.* Noble Pr. 1991 $12.95. ISBN 0-9622683-7-2. A convincing case for parents to change from a toxic to a non-toxic lifestyle; includes advice on how to accomplish this change.

Griggs, Barbara. *Green Pharmacy: A History of Herbal Medicine.* Inner Tradit. 1991 repr. of 1982 ed. $14.95. ISBN 0-89281-427-6. A useful, well-written introduction to the history of herbal medicines from the early Greeks to modern pharmacology and current chemical derivatives from plants.

Hallenbeck, William H., and Kathleen M. Cunningham-Burns. *Pesticides and Human Health.* Spring.-Verlag $50.00. ISBN 0-387-96050-3. A brief digest of human health effects and the toxicology of human exposure to pesticides.

Halstead, Bruce W., and Sylvia A. Youngberg. *The DMSO Handbook: A Complete Guide to the History and Use of DMSO.* Golden Quill 1981 $10.95. ISBN 0-993904-08-8. A clearly written introduction to the diversified pharmacological effects of the controversial agent dimethyl sulfoxide.

Harkness, Richard. *Drug Interactions Guide Book.* P-H 1991 $24.95. ISBN 0-13-219601-8. A well-organized and easy-to-read compendium that provides information on how drugs, particularly prescriptions, may affect one another.

Harte, John, and others. *Toxics A to Z: A Guide to Everyday Pollution Hazards.* U. CA Pr. 1991 $75.00. ISBN 0-520-07223-5. "An eminently readable guide to the toxins we live with" (*Library Journal*); provides a general overview of toxic issues and a detailed discussion of more than 100 toxic substances common in daily life.

Kaufman, Joel, and others. *Over-the-Counter Pills That Don't Work.* Pantheon 1983 o.p. Identifies various over-the-counter drugs and discusses their use and alternatives to their use.

Kehrer, James P., and Daniel M. Kehrer. *Pills and Potions: New Discoveries about Prescription and Over-the-Counter Drugs.* P-H Gen. Ref. & Trav. 1983 o.p. Details developments in drugs and pharmaceuticals; covers not only new drugs and new uses for old drugs, but also the technological, economic, and social changes regarding drugs.

Lappe, Marc. *Germs That Won't Die: Medical Consequences of the Misuse of Antibiotics.* Doubleday 1982 o.p. Traces the use and misuse of penicillin and other antibiotics and the development of antibiotic-resistant strains of organisms.

Leber, Max. *The Corner Drugstore.* Warner Bks. 1983 $6.95. ISBN 0-446-97989-9. A handy well-written book with first-aid information and drug interaction precautions for 17 categories of drugs.

Lewis, Walter H., and P. F. Elvin-Lewis. *Medical Botany: Plants Affecting Man's Health.* Wiley 1982 $28.95. ISBN 0-471-86134-0. A carefully prepared review of injurious, healing, nourishing, and psychoactive plants.

Long, James W. *The Essential Guide to Prescription Drugs.* HarpC 1992 $35.00. ISBN 0-06-271534-8. A comprehensive reference on the 225 most commonly prescribed drugs.

Melville, Arabella. *Cured to Death: The Effects of Prescription Drugs.* Ed. by Colin Johnson. Madison Bks. 1983 $16.95. ISBN 0-8128-2889-5. A convincing argument that Western medicine has allowed itself to become too reliant on the use of drug therapy.

Meyers, Robert. *D.E.S.: The Bitter Pill.* Putnam Pub. Group 1983 o.p. A less evenhanded, though still important, contribution to the literature on DES; focus is on its use to control miscarriage.

Parascandola, John. *The Development of American Pharmacology: John J. Abel and the Shaping of a Discipline.* Johns Hopkins 1992 $32.50. ISBN 0-8018-4416-9. A scholarly history of the rise of pharmacology in the United States; accessible to the general reader.

Roffman, Roger A. *Marijuana as Medicine.* Madrona Pubs. 1982 o.p. A well-written, carefully documented discussion of the use of marijuana in treatment, especially to counter side effects resulting from cancer therapies.

Schoemaker, Joyce M., and Charity Y. Vitale. *Healthy Homes, Healthy Kids: Protecting Your Children from Everyday Environmental Hazards.* Island Pr. 1991 $19.95. ISBN

1-55963-057-4. Provides sound advice to parents about potential environmental dangers in the home; well-referenced and accessible to the general reader.

Silverman, Milton M., Philip R. Lee, and Mia Lydecker. *Prescriptions for Death: The Drugging of the Third World.* U. CA Pr. 1982 $40.00. ISBN 0-520-04721-4. An important little book documenting how international drug manufacturers operate in developing nations as compared to the way they are forced to operate under federal regulations in the United States.

Smith, John E., and M. O. Moss. *Mycotoxins: Formation, Analysis, and Significance.* Wiley 1985 $57.95. ISBN 0-471-90671-9. Mycotoxins are substances formed by molds that cause illness and sometimes death; a technical (less so than others available on the topic) book about this important medical and biological topic.

Smith, Richard B. *The Development of a Medicine.* Groves Dict. Music 1985 o.p. A brief synopsis of the process by which medicines are developed, from the discovery of a substance to its evaluation, approval, marketing, and ultimate prescription.

Sneader, Walter. *Drug Discovery: The Evolution of Modern Medicines.* Wiley 1985 $99.95. ISBN 0-471-90471-6. Provides substantial information, in an easy-to-read format, on the evolution of chemical substances in the therapeutic agents used in clinical biomedicine.

Wedeen, Richard P. *Poison in the Pot: The Legacy of Lead.* S. Ill. U. Pr. 1984 $29.95. ISBN 0-8093-1156-9. A fascinating history of lead poisoning, including a discussion of the economic importance of lead and how that importance has reinforced resistance to wide recognition of lead's dangers.

Witters, Weldon L., Peter Venturelli, and Glen Hanson. *Drugs and Society: A Biological Perspective.* Jones & Bartlett 1992 $40.00. ISBN 0-86720-317-X. An interesting treatment of drug abuse from the biological standpoint rather than the psychological or sociological view.

PHYSIOLOGY

[SEE the section on The Healthy Body in this chapter.]

POISONS

[SEE the section on Pharmacology and Toxicology in this chapter.]

PUBLIC, ENVIRONMENTAL, AND OCCUPATIONAL HEALTH

Public health is the branch of medicine concerned with the prevention and control of disease and disability, and the promotion of physical and mental health on the international, national, state, or municipal level. Consequently, it encompasses a wide variety of concerns. This section primarily includes books on environmental and occupational issues. Epidemiological titles, which demonstrate disease patterns and transmission, are included in Chapter 13 in this volume.

Burgess, William A. *Recognition of Health Hazards in Industry: A Review of Materials and Processes.* Wiley 1981 $74.95. ISBN 0-471-06339-8. Provides an understanding of industrial operations and the physical contaminants and stresses present in such operations.

Cairncross, Sandy, and Richard G. Feachem. *Environmental Health Engineering in the Tropics: An Introductory Text.* Wiley 1993 $36.95. ISBN 0-471-93885-8. An interesting book for those seeking information about public and environmental health in the tropics, especially in developing countries.

Doyle, Rodger Pirnie. *The Medical Wars*. Morrow 1983 o.p. The status of 16 of today's most publicized medical controversies, from megavitamin therapy and dietary fiber to Masters and Johnson and the Love Canal; assesses these controversies through the application of "good" research criteria.

Drake, Alvin W., and others. *The American Blood Supply: Issues and Policies of Blood Donation*. MIT Pr. 1982 $32.50. ISBN 0-262-04070-0. A description of the history, development, structure, and problems of the American blood banking system.

Environment and Health. Editorial Research Reports. Congr. Quarterly 1981 o.p. A distillation of a vast quantity of materials on environmental health issues into a slim manageable report; accessible to the general reader.

Feshbach, Murray, and Alfred Friendly. *Ecocide in the USSR: Health and Nature under Siege*. Basic 1992 $24.00. ISBN 0-465-01664-2. A historical review that demonstrates how 70 years of unregulated industrial pollution has devastated the Russian environment and created a host of insurmountable medical problems for the Russian health service.

Fisher, Albert L. *Health and Prevention of Disease in a Free Society*. Schildge Pub. 1980 o.p. Some very interesting and provocative views on health and disease prevention and their relationship to political, economic, and social forces.

Gersuny, Carl. *Work Hazards and Industrial Conflict*. Kerr 1992 repr. of 1981 ed. $12.00. ISBN 0-88286-174-3. A study of the ongoing conflict over issues of occupational health and safety within the context of a changing legal framework.

Harwin, Ronald, and Colin Hayes. *Healthy Computing: Risks and Remedies Every Computer User Needs to Know*. AMACOM 1991 $17.95. ISBN 0-8144-7766-6. Provides a useful summary of current knowledge and evaluates safeguards for individuals working with or around office computers; written by a chiropractor and a business writer.

Henderson, George, and Martha Primeaux. *Transcultural Health Care*. Addison-Wesley 1981 $24.50. ISBN 0-201-03237-6. A knowledgeable discussion of the cultural factors that have an impact on the behavior of providers as well as consumers of health care.

Hinds, William C. *Aerosol Technology: Properties, Behavior, and Measurement of Airborne Particles*. Wiley 1982 $84.95. ISBN 0-471-08726-2. A practical book with a public health orientation; implicates aerosols in public health concerns.

Kunitz, Stephen J. *Disease Change and the Role of Medicine: The Navajo Experience*. U. CA Pr. 1983 $42.50. ISBN 0-520-04926-8. Examines the Navaho experience with modern medicine and the impact that medicine has had on Navaho morbidity and mortality rates since the late nineteenth century.

Moeller, Dade. *Environmental Health*. HUP 1992 $39.95. ISBN 0-674-25858-4. Discusses how the environment affects the lives and future of all living things; written by the dean of Harvard's School of Public Health.

Ng, Lorenz K. Y., and Devra Lee Davis, eds. *Strategies for Public Health: Promoting Health and Preventing Disease*. Van Nos. Reinhold 1981 o.p. A compilation of a variety of offerings that address the theme of health promotion through a better understanding of the nature of health and the way in which it is affected by individual attitudes, the health care industry, and the environment.

Norris, Ruth, ed. *Pills, Pesticides, and Profits: The International Trade in Toxic Substances*. North River 1982 $15.00. ISBN 0-88427-050-5. A well-documented examination of the sale and distribution of drugs, pesticides, and other chemicals in developing nations by multinational corporations and the problems such activities pose for the inhabitants.

Pelletier, Kenneth R. *Healthy People in Unhealthy Places: Stress and Fitness at Work*. Delacorte 1985 $16.95. ISBN 0-385-29275-9. A thorough documentation of health hazards in the workplace with a discussion of stress reactions and management.

Russell, Louise B. *Is Prevention Better Than Cure?* Brookings 1986 $26.95. ISBN 0-8157-7632-2. In this review of the policy debates that surround several preventive health measures, Russell demonstrates by cost-effective analysis the complexities involved in evaluating these attempts to improve health.

Stellman, Jeanne, and Mary Sue Henifin. *Office Work Can Be Dangerous to Your Health: A Handbook of Office Health and Safety Hazards and What You Can Do about Them.* Fawcett 1989 $4.95. ISBN 0-449-21676-4. A thorough review of the available literature, this useful work explores various aspects of known and suspected office hazards.

Sugarman, Ellen. *Warning: The Electricity Around You May Be Hazardous to Your Health: How to Protect Yourself from Electromagnetic Fields.* S&S Trade 1992 $11.00. ISBN 0-671-75875-6. An excellent nontechnical introduction to EMFs in the home, the community, and the workplace; includes significantly more information on this topic than other books.

Trieff, Norman M., ed. *Environment and Health.* Technomic 1980 $29.50. ISBN 0-254-40275-0. Deals with the adverse effects on health of toxic environments, the adverse effects themselves, and the solutions; a good book for the uninitiated.

Turiel, Isaac. *Indoor Air Quality and Human Health.* Stanford U. Pr. 1985 $27.50. ISBN 0-8045-1255-7. A rather good book on indoor air quality that provides general information on indoor air pollution sources and pollutants, with potential health effects arising from exposure.

Upton, Arthur C., and Eden Graber, eds. *The New York University Medical Center Family Guide to Staying Healthy in a Risky Environment.* S&S Trade 1993 $32.50. ISBN 0-671-76815-8. Provides information on health hazards, risk assessment, effects on the body, and sources of environmental hazards; a timely but basic environmental health reference for the general reader.

Urquhart, John, and Klaus Heilmann. *Risk Watch: The Odds of Life.* Facts on File 1984 $24.95. ISBN 0-87916-984-X. A readable, commonsense discussion of the many variables that have the potential for limiting both the length and quality of our lives.

RADIOLOGY

[SEE the section on Diagnostic Testing in this chapter.]

TOXICOLOGY

[SEE the section on Pharmacology and Toxicology in this chapter.]

UROLOGY

[SEE Chapter 13 in this volume.]

WOMEN'S HEALTH

Gynecology and obstetrics are distinct medical specialties with separate but related literatures. This section contains representative books from each of these specialties, with Pregnancy and Childbirth included as a separate subsection.

Anderson, Mary M. *An A-Z Gynecology: With Comments on Aspects of Management and Nursing.* HarpC 1986 o.p. A compact introductory manual/handbook on the topic.

Asso, Doreen. *The Real Menstrual Cycle.* Wiley 1983 o.p. Discusses the origin and operation of biological cycles and hormone interplay during the menstrual cycle. Because of the depth of subject matter and comprehensive format, the book is recommended for use at the undergraduate level rather than at the senior high school level.

Boston Women's Health Book Collective. *The New Our Bodies, Ourselves*. S&S Trade 1992 $20.00. ISBN 0-671-79176-1. Provides an update to their earlier volume of current and useful information on the physiology and psychology of women.

Bruning, Nancy. *Breast Implants: Everything You Need to Know*. Hunter Hse. 1992 $7.95. ISBN 0-89793-119-X. An excellent book that answers questions in a straightforward style accessible to the general reader. Describes the types of implants that have been used, the complications; includes a bibliography, as well as a source list.

Buchsbaum, Herbert J., ed. *The Menopause*. Spr.-Verlag 1983 $81.00. ISBN 0-387-90825-0. An edited volume of articles by authorities, describing various facets of menopause and postmenopause; well written and well researched.

Budoff, Penny Wise. *No More Hot Flashes and Other Good News*. Warner Bks. 1989 $5.99. ISBN 0-446-35879-7. Aimed at mature women over 40, Budoff details the hormonal changes that occur as women age and the effect of these changes on health; informative, well-documented, and readable.

Cutler, Winnifred Berg, and others. *Menopause: A Guide for Women and the Men Who Love Them*. Norton 1993 $13.95. ISBN 0-393-30995-9. A basic and useful guide to information about menopause written for the general public.

Fuchs, Nan Kathryn. *The Nutrition Detective: A Woman's Guide to Treating Your Health Problems Through the Foods You Eat*. HM 1985 o.p. A good book written for women suffering from symptoms that can be eliminated through diet and diet supplements.

Gluckin, Doreen, with Michael Edelhart. *The Body at Thirty: A Woman Doctor Talks to Women*. Berkley Pub. 1983 $3.50. ISBN 0-425-08504-X. Gluckin believes that women in their thirties are experiencing a rich and stimulating period of their life, but it is also a time when women begin to confront great change. This theory is explored in depth.

Greenwood, Sadja. *Menopause, Naturally: Preparing for the Second Half of Life*. Volcano Pr. 1992 $13.95. ISBN 0-912078-95-2. Provides extensive information on how to promote good health; discusses interesting and controversial questions on all aspects of menopause, osteoporosis, estrogen therapy, exercise, and more.

Greer, Germaine. *The Change: Women, Aging and the Menopause*. Knopf 1992 $23.50. ISBN 0-394-58269-1. An impressive synthesis of available information about menopause. Also highlights important information that has yet to be discovered about menopause.

Harrison, Michelle. *Self-Help for Premenstrual Syndrome*. Random 1985 $12.00. ISBN 0-394-73502-1. Harrison describes self-help strategies including diet modification, exercise, and stress reduction, and discusses medical treatment.

Henkel, Gretchen. *Making the Estrogen Decision*. Lowell Hse. 1992 $21.95. ISBN 1-56565-005-0. An unbiased, well-researched investigation of the Hormone Replacement Test; interviews with physicians explore the test's advantages and disadvantages.

Hongladarom, Gail G., Ruth McCorkle, and Nancy F. Woods, eds. *The Complete Book of Women's Health*. P-H 1982 o.p. Comprehensive and accurate sourcebook that serves equally well as a primary instructional aid to teenagers and as a resource for mature women.

Keyser, Herbert H. *Women Under the Knife: A Gynecologist's Report on Hazardous Medicine*. Warner Bks. 1986 $3.95. ISBN 0-446-32911-8. Educated, interesting, and wholesomely opinionated.

Lauersen, Niels H., Steven Whitney, and Eileen Stukane. *It's Your Body: A Woman's Guide to Gynecology*. Putnam Pub. Group 1993 $17.95. ISBN 0-399-51830-4. A delightfully informative book using excerpts from letters as a means to present factual data; easy to read and well-illustrated.

_____. *PMS: Premenstrual Syndrome and You: Next Month Can Be Different*. S&S Trade 1984 $3.95. ISBN 0-523-42260-1. Includes an overview of female physiology and case histories, along with information on the causes, physical and emotional symptoms, and diagnosis of PMS.

Lewin, Ellen, ed. *Women, Health, and Healing: Toward a New Perspective*. Routledge Chapman & Hall 1985 o.p. The focus of this collection of original essays by North

American and British feminist scholars is women's health in a comprehensive sociocultural context.

Lichtendorf, Susan S. *Eve's Journey: The Physical Experience of Being Female*. Berkley Pub. 1983 $3.95. ISBN 0-425-05868-9. Brings together medical authorities and ordinary women who discuss the physical aspects of womanhood with personal comments and histories.

McCain, Marian Van Eyk. *Transformation Through Menopause*. Greenwood 1991 $39.95. ISBN 0-89789-268-2. A well-documented discussion of menopause from a holistic perspective; also provides exercises and other coping techniques.

Morgan, Susanne. *Coping with a Hysterectomy: Your Own Choice, Your Own Solutions*. NAL-Dutton 1985 o.p. Morgan is a medical sociologist who carefully examines the current status of hysterectomy in Western medical practice.

Nachtigall, Lila. *Estrogen: The Facts Can Change Your Life*. HarpC 1986 o.p. A useful book on the therapeutic use of estrogen.

Norris, Ronald V., with Colleen Sullivan. *PMS: Premenstrual Syndrome*. Berkley Pub. 1987 $4.95. ISBN 0-425-10332-3. Describes the physical and psychological symptoms, possible causes, therapies, and the social and legal implications of PMS.

Notelovitz, Morris, and Diana Tonnessen. *Menopause and Midlife Health*. St. Martin 1993 $24.95. ISBN 0-312-09337-3. An encyclopedia of general health for mid-life women that covers the basics of choosing and dealing with a physician; written for the physician doing research in this area.

Older, Julia. *Endometriosis: A Women's Guide to a Common but Often Undetected Disease That Can Cause Infertility and Other Major Medical Problems*. Macmillan 1985 $10.95. ISBN 0-684-18505-9. Using information from popular and scholarly publications and interviews with experts, provides a good overview of the subject, including surgical options and drug therapies.

Schrotenboer, Kathryn, and Genell J. Subak-Sharpe. *Freedom from Menstrual Cramps*. PB 1981 $2.95. ISBN 0-671-43714-3. Up-to-date, medically accurate information on the etiology, diagnosis, and treatment of menstrual abnormalities; concise and well organized.

Sheehy, Gail. *The Silent Passage: Menopause*. Random 1992 $16.00. ISBN 0-679-41388-X. Examines the medical, psychological, and social aspects of what the author calls the "silent passage"; based on interviews with more than 100 women in various stages of menopause and with more than 75 experts on menopause.

Shephard, Bruce D., and Carroll A. Shepard. *The Complete Guide to Women's Health*. NAL-Dutton 1990 $18.00. ISBN 0-452-26439-1. A comprehensive, well-organized problem-oriented guide to health strategies, birth control methods, pregnancy, and childbirth, as well as information on diseases of the female reproductive tract. One of the best general female health references available.

Sollie, Eddie C. *Straight Talk with Your Gynecologist: How to Get Answers That Will Save Your Life*. Beyond Words Pub. 1993 $12.95. ISBN 0-685-61700-9. An excellent introduction to women's health issues; written by a gynecologist and lecturer on women's health care issues.

Strausz, Ivan K. *You Don't Need a Hysterectomy: New and Effective Ways of Avoiding Surgery*. Addison-Wesley 1993 $24.95. ISBN 0-201-60827-8. An introductory work that offers sophisticated details on options to hysterectomy.

Valins, Linda. *When a Woman's Body Says No To Sex: Understanding and Overcoming Vaginismus*. Viking Penguin 1992 $22.00. ISBN 0-670-84355-5. A valuable, well-researched book on a poorly understood condition; includes a list of organizations, practitioners, and other resources for women who think they may suffer from vaginismus.

Winick, Myron. *For Mothers and Daughters: A Guide to Good Nutrition for Women*. Berkley Pub. 1985 $3.50. ISBN 0-425-07681-4. A comprehensive, easy-to-read discussion of the specific nutritional requirements of women during adolescence, the reproductive years, pregnancy, lactation, menopause, and aging.

Witt, Reni L. *PMS: What Every Woman Should Know about Premenstrual Syndrome.*
Stein & Day 1983 o.p. A readable description of the causes, symptoms, and diagnosis
of PMS; includes a useful glossary of terms.

Pregnancy and Childbirth

[SEE ALSO the related section, Child Care and Development, in this
chapter; for books on abortion, SEE Chapter 5, Ethics in Science,
Technology, and Medicine, in this volume.]

Andrews, Lori B. *New Conceptions: A Consumer's Guide to the Medical, Emotional and
Legal Aspects of Genetic Counseling, New Infertility Treatments, Artificial Insemina-
tion, In Vitro Fertilization, and Surrogate Motherhood.* Ballantine 1985 $3.95. ISBN 0-
345-32307-6. Covers the more traditional treatments for infertility, as well as the
newer possibilities.

Ashford, Janet Isaacs, ed. *Birth Stories: The Experience Remembered.* Crossing Pr. 1984
$8.95. ISBN 0-89594-149-X. Ashford solicited birth stories from three generations of
women.

_____. *The Whole Birth Catalog: A Sourcebook for Choices in Childbirth.* Crossing Pr.
1983 o.p. An impressive collection of material on pregnancy, childbirth, and the
postpartum period; emphasis is on exploring alternatives to the medical model of
pregnancy and childbirth.

Bellina, Joseph H., and Josleen Wilson. *You Can Have a Baby: Everything You Need to
Know about Fertility.* Bantam 1986 $12.95. ISBN 0-553-34255-X. Provides compre-
hensive information on causes, diagnosis, and treatments for infertility. Special
topics include selection of professionals for treatment; miscarriage; pregnancy after
35; contraceptives; and religious, moral, and legal issues.

Blackstone, Margaret, with Tahira Homayun. *Recovering from a C Section.* Longmeadow
Pr. 1991 $6.95. ISBN 0-681-41154-6. "A well-written and much-needed guide for
pregnant women who might face a C section" (*Library Journal*).

Brown, Judith E. *Nutrition for Your Pregnancy: The University of Minnesota Guide.* U. of
Minn. Pr. 1983 o.p. A highly recommended and well-respected guide to good
nutrition during pregnancy and the postpartum period.

Caplan, Ronald. *Pregnant Is Beautiful.* PB 1985 $3.95. ISBN 0-671-53259-6. Explains how
to keep in shape during pregnancy for a more comfortable pregnancy, as well as a
quick return to pre-pregnancy fitness; concise and easy to read.

Cohen, Nancy Wainer. *Open Season: A Survival Guide for Natural Childbirth and VBAC
in the 1990s.* Greenwood 1991 $29.95. ISBN 0-89789-252-6. A somewhat emotional
diatribe that focuses on serious questions associated with childbirth practices in the
medical health care systems of the United States.

Corea, Gena. *The Mother Machine: Reproductive Technologies from Artificial Insemina-
tion to Artificial Wombs.* HarpC 1986 $9.95. ISBN 0-06-091325-8. An in-depth look at
historical, social, legal, and medical trends combined with descriptions of the state
of the art in eugenics, cloning, surrogate motherhood, and so forth.

Edwards, Margot, and Mary Waldorf. *Reclaiming Birth: History and Heroines of American
Childbirth Reform.* Crossing Pr. 1984 o.p. An impressive contribution to women's
history.

Eheart, Brenda, and Susan Martel. *The Fourth Trimester: On Becoming a Mother.*
Ballantine 1984 $3.50. ISBN 0-345-31751-3. This book treats the changes caused
during the first three months of motherhood; an exceptionally thorough book.

Eisenberg, Arlene. *What to Eat When You're Expecting.* Workman Pub. 1986 $8.95. ISBN
0-89480-015-9. A well-balanced guide to the nutritional aspects of pregnancy and
how to adjust the diet accordingly.

Fay, Francesca C., and Kelly S. Smith. *Childbearing After 35: The Risks and the Rewards.*
Balsam 1985 $24.95. ISBN 0-917439-08-2. A thorough, comprehensive guide for
older pregnant women. In addition to the basic topics found in most pregnancy

guides, this book covers the concerns specific to women over the age of 35 and the many advantages of becoming an older parent.

Feinbloom, Richard I., and Betty Y. Forman. *Pregnancy, Birth, and the Early Months: A Complete Guide.* Addison-Wesley 1992 $19.95. ISBN 0-201-58149-3. A complete and well-balanced guide that covers every medical and emotional aspect of childbirth and the first few months of life.

Freeman, Roger K., and Susan Pescar. *Safe Delivery: Protecting Your Baby During High Risk Pregnancy.* Facts on File 1982 o.p. A comprehensive, well-written guide to high-risk obstetrics and neonatology; reassuring and sensitive presentation.

Fried, Peter. *Pregnancy and Life-Style Habits.* Beaufort SC 1983 o.p. A carefully researched study of the effects of exogenous substances on the developing fetus. Detailed sections on the effects of various substances, for example, alcohol and prescription and nonprescription drugs.

Glass, Robert H., and Ronald J. Ericsson. *Getting Pregnant in the 1980s: New Advances in Infertility Treatment and Sex Preselection.* U. CA Pr. 1982 $24.95. ISBN 0-520-04828-8. An infertility specialist and a research biologist present clear, concise chapters on infertility and the infertility workup, as well as detailed sections on new reproductive technology. A skillful combination of clinical medicine and basic research for the general reader.

Goldberg, Larry H., and Joann M. Leahy. *The Doctor's Guide to Medication During Pregnancy and Lactation.* Morrow 1984 o.p. Answers many of the questions women ask during pregnancy; easy to read and not oversimplified.

Graham, Janis, and Claire Zion, eds. *Breastfeeding Secrets and Solutions.* PB 1993 $10.00. ISBN 0-671-74963-3. Focuses on the how-to's of breastfeeding. Also provides lists of support groups and mail-order companies from which to purchase fashions, breast pumps, etc.; written in a personal, anecdotal style.

Hales, Dianne, and Robert K. Creasy. *New Hope for Problem Pregnancies: Saving Babies Before They're Born.* Berkley Pub. 1984 $3.95. ISBN 0-425-06847-1. Contains superior sections on nutrition and drugs during pregnancy; includes excellent tables on food additives and drugs. Complete, up-to-date, and medically accurate.

Harkness, Carla. *The Infertility Book: A Comprehensive Medical and Emotional Guide.* Celestial Arts 1992 $14.95. ISBN 0-89087-664-9. Features helpful information on procedures during the standard infertility work-up. Also covers adoption, surrogate parenting, and child-free living.

Harper, Michael J. K. *Birth Control Technologies: Prospects by the Year 2000.* U. of Tex. Pr. 1985 $10.95. ISBN 0-292-70757-6. Details proposed improvements in existing methods of contraception, as well as a number of proposed new techniques; derived from extensive high-level research.

Hess, Mary Abbott, and Anne Elise Hunt. *Eating for Two: The Complete Guide to Nutrition During Pregnancy.* Macmillan 1992 $12.95. ISBN 0-02-065441-3. This revised and updated version of *Pickles and Ice Cream* (1982) provides a thorough review of current research on prenatal nutrition.

Katz, Jane. *Swimming through Your Pregnancy.* Doubleday 1984 $10.95. ISBN 0-385-18059-4. A complete swimming program for pregnant women; an enthusiastic and logical presentation that provides an inspirational approach to exercise for some pregnant women.

Kitzinger, Sheila. *Homebirth: the Essential Guide to Giving Birth Outside of the Hospital.* Kindersley 1991 $18.95. ISBN 1-879431-01-7. A well-referenced guide for expectant parents who wish to make a choice between hospital and home birth; includes a well-balanced presentation of both options.

Klaus, Marshall H., and Phyllis H. Klaus. *The Amazing Newborn.* Addison-Wesley 1985 $12.95. ISBN 0-201-11672-3. A product of the new interest in research on infancy, this book focuses on the characteristics and abilities of newborns. Well illustrated, this book also translates clinical research into useful observations for parents.

Kohn, Ingrid, Perry-Lynn Moffitt, and Isabelle A. Wilkins. *A Silent Sorrow: Pregnancy Loss: Guidance and Support for You and Your Family.* Delacorte 1993 $22.50. ISBN 0-385-30828-0. Provides useful information on how to cope with miscarriage.

Korte, Diana, and Roberta Scaer. *A Good Birth, A Safe Birth*. Bantam 1984 $7.95. ISBN 0-553-34068-9. A summary of current medical research on childbirth and mothers' preferences for birthing.

Lauersen, Niels H. *Childbirth with Love: A Complete Guide to Fertility, Pregnancy, and Childbirth for Caring Couples*. Berkley Pub. 1991 $9.95. ISBN 0-425-07390-4. This highly recommended book presents detailed information on all aspects of pregnancy and childbirth, including choosing an obstetrician.

McCutcheon-Rosegg, Susan, with Peter Rosegg. *Natural Childbirth: The Bradley Way*. NAL-Dutton 1984 $14.95. ISBN 0-452-26754-2. Provides comprehensive information on preparing for childbirth, the three stages in delivery, and controversies in childbirth.

Mitford, Jessica. *The American Way of Birth*. NAL-Dutton 1992 $23.00. ISBN 0-525-93523-1. Examines American obstetrics, as well as hospitals, clinics, and welfare agencies that supervise the prenatal care and birth of American babies. Concludes with an indictment of the medical practices surrounding the birth process.

Noble, Elizabeth. *Childbirth with Insight*. HM 1983 $8.95. ISBN 0-395-33962-6. Well-written, thought-provoking, and controversial book; argues "that the value and appropriateness of mechanical practice of classroom techniques designed for a reflex voluntary experience such as labor needs to be examined" (*Library Journal*).

_____. *Having Twins: A Parent's Guide to Pregnancy, Birth and Early Childhood*. HM 1991 $24.45. ISBN 0-395-51088-0. A significantly revised and expanded edition of this indispensable book on the history and physiology of twinning; includes new material on prenatal care, birthing, bonding, and an expanded section on nutrition.

Norwood, Christopher. *How to Avoid a Caesarean Section*. S&S Trade 1984 o.p. Summarizes the current research and documents that over half of C-section deliveries are not necessary.

Robinson, Susan, and H. F. Pizer. *Having a Baby Without a Man: Single Woman's Guide to Alternative Fertilization*. S&S Trade 1985 o.p. A clear explanation of the various methods of alternative fertilization, their history, and their success rates.

Rothman, Barbara K. *In Labor: Women and Power in the Workplace*. Norton 1991 $10.95. ISBN 0-393-30798-0. Examines the current status of Western obstetrics in this well-written, well-researched study.

Sandelowski, Margarete. *Pain, Pleasure, and American Childbirth: From the Twilight Sleep to the Read Method*. Greenwood 1984 $37.50. ISBN 0-313-24076-4. An erudite work that traces the history of childbirth in the United States from 1914 through 1960; a very readable and excellent history.

Scher, Jonathan, and Carol Dix. *Will My Baby Be Normal? Everything You Need to Know about Pregnancy*. Dial 1983 o.p. A general up-to-date compendium of information about each stage of pregnancy and delivery.

Schrotenboer, Kathryn, and Solomon Weiss. *Dr. Kathryn Schrotenboer's Guide to Pregnancy over 35*. Ballantine 1985 o.p. A guide that addresses the issues and problems faced by pregnant women over the age of 35; an inspiring book.

Shapiro, Howard I. *The Pregnancy Book for Today's Woman: An Obstetrician Answers All Your Questions about Pregnancy and Childbirth and Some You May Not Have Considered*. HarpC 1983 $12.95. ISBN 0-318-36208-1. A unique, refreshing guide for pregnant women

Sidenbladh, Erik. *Water Babies: The Igor Tjarkovsky Method for Delivering in Water*. St. Martin 1983 $12.95. ISBN 0-312-85688-1. A narrative description of the beliefs of Tjarkovsky (i.e., that if infants are born and fed underwater their potential for physical and mental development is greatly enhanced).

Simkin, Penny, and others. *Pregnancy, Childbirth, and the Newborn*. Ed. by Tom Grady. Meadowbrook 1991 $12.00. ISBN 0-88166-177-5. An excellent, clearly written book, covering all aspects of pregnancy.

Sirota, Adair. *Preparing for Childbirth: A Couple's Manual*. Contempo. Bks. 1983 o.p. A basic outline of typical hospital childbirth procedures; focuses on the Lamaze breathing method.

Stoppard, Miriam. *Conception, Pregnancy, and Birth*. Dorling Kindersley 1993 $29.95.
ISBN 1-56458-182-9. Presents information about preparing for pregnancy, conceiving, fitness, prenatal care, nutrition, birthing choices and many other related topics;
well written, well documented, and well illustrated.
Wood, Carl, and Ann Westmore. *Test-Tube Conception*. P-H 1984 $6.95. ISBN 0-685-
07921-X. A guide for prospective parents, doctors, and anyone interested in this
exciting new method of treating infertility.

CHRONOLOGY OF AUTHORS

Vesalius, Andreas. 1514–1564   Gray, Henry. 1825–1861
Harvey, William. 1578–1657   Osler, William. 1849–1919
Nightingale, Florence. 1820–1910   Pavlov, Ivan Petrovich. 1849–1936

GRAY, HENRY. 1825–1861

Henry Gray was a British physician who wrote a general anatomy textbook at
the age of 33; his work is still regarded as a standard after more than 100 years.
Considering the fame of his modest textbook, relatively little is known about
Gray. He was trained at St. George's Hospital, London, where he demonstrated
an early interest in anatomical studies, by writing a prize-winning essay
comparing the structure of the human eye to the eyes of other vertebrates. Gray
maintained his connection to St. George's and taught anatomy to medical
students until his death from smallpox. In his short career, he wrote a book on
the spleen, *The Structure and Use of the Spleen* (London, 1854) and published
Anatomy, Descriptive and Surgical (1858), which assured him a place in medical
history.

Although there were other anatomy textbooks available at the time, Gray's
approach was much clearer than all of the others. He was described by a
contemporary as a "lucid teacher of anatomy" because of his organization of
materials and the effective use of illustrations, drawn by Henry Vandyke Carter.
Gray also hired a professional editor to work with his prose to make it less
technical and more comprehensible to the student. "This accessibility has been
one of the great factors in the *Anatomy*'s success and has influenced other
writers of anatomy textbooks" (*Dictionary of Scientific Biography*).

BOOK BY GRAY

Anatomy of the Human Body. Ed. by Carmine D. Clemente. Lea & Febiger 1985 $89.50.
ISBN 0-8121-0644-X. For many years, there have been American and British
editions. This is the most current American edition.

BOOK ABOUT GRAY

Goss, Charles Mayo. *A Brief Account of Henry Gray, F.R.S., and His Anatomy, Descriptive,
and Surgical, During a Century of Its Publication in America*. Lea & Febiger 1959 o.p.
Goss edited Gray's textbook through three editions and prepared this brief history of
the American publication process. Features the most thorough biography of Gray to
date, a photograph of him in the anatomy lecture hall, a detailed chronology of the
American and British editions, and brief biographies of the several editors who
developed the American edition.

HARVEY, WILLIAM. 1578–1657

Born in Folkestone, Kent, England, Harvey was a British physiologist whose
discovery of the circulation of the blood drastically changed medicine. In fact,

Harvey is generally regarded as the founder of modern physiology. The publication of his *Exercitatio Anatomica de Motu Cordis et Sanguinis in Animalibus* (1628) was a landmark event, widely considered the most important medical book ever published. His observations of the heart's functions and blood flow were based on anatomical studies on cadavers, animals, and himself.

The son of a wealthy businessman, Harvey was a student at Cambridge University, where he studied medicine. He completed his medical training at the leading European medical school of the period, Padua, where he was a student of the famous anatomist Girolamo Fabricius. When he completed his doctorate in medicine in 1602 he returned to London and was appointed physician to St. Bartholomew's Hospital. His reputation grew, and he was elected to the Royal College of Physicians, with which he was associated for the rest of his career. Ten years prior to the publication of his great work, he was appointed as a physician to James I. After the Scottish civil war and the demise of James I, Harvey returned to London and resumed his medical practice. He continued to observe animal life wherever he traveled and wrote two additional works on animal locomotion and comparative and pathological anatomy. However, it was the publication of his book on the circulation of the blood that assured him "a place of first importance in the history of science and medicine. By this discovery he revolutionized physiological thought" (*Dictionary of Scientific Biography*). His work also encouraged others to study anatomy. Harvey's personal library, which he donated to the London College of Physicians, was unfortunately destroyed in the Great Fire of 1666.

BOOKS BY HARVEY

The Anatomical Lectures of William Harvey: Prelectiones anatomie universalis, De musculis. Ed. and trans. by Gweneth Whitteridge. Livingstone 1964 o.p. Presents an annotated facsimile reproduction of two extant Harvey lectures from manuscripts in the British Museum. Features extensive commentary and bibliography of works about Harvey; text is in English and Latin.

The Circulation of the Blood and Other Writings. Ed. by Andrew Wear. C. E. Tuttle 1993 $9.95. ISBN 0-460-87362-8. Classic work on the circulatory system.

De Motu Cordis: Anatomical Studies on the Motion of the Heart and Blood. Trans. by Chauncey D. Leake. Thomas 1978 $28.25. ISBN 0-398-00793-4. A scholarly, heavily annotated edition of Harvey's most important work.

On the Motion of the Heart and Blood in Animals. Prometheus Bks. 1993 $9.95. ISBN 0-87975-854-6

Works. Trans. by Robert Willis. Johnson Repr. 1965 repr. of 1847 ed. $45.00. ISBN 0-384-21710-9. The standard English translation of Harvey's complete works.

BOOKS ABOUT HARVEY

Bylebyl, Jerome, ed. *William Harvey and His Age: The Professional and Social Context of the Discovery of Circulation*. Johns Hopkins 1979 o.p. A scholarly collection of essays that discuss the extraordinary impact of Harvey's discovery on science and society; easy to read.

Cohen, I. Bernard, ed. *Studies on William Harvey*. Ayer 1981 $65.00. ISBN 0-405-13866-0. Series of articles on Harvey's work.

Frank, Robert G., Jr. *Harvey and the Oxford Physiologists: A Study of Scientific Ideas and Social Interaction*. U. CA Pr. 1980 $55.00. ISBN 0-520-03906-8

Keele, Kenneth D. *William Harvey: The Man, The Physician, and the Scientist*. Nelson 1965 o.p. An excellent survey of Harvey's work that features abundant biographical detail. The author attempts "to see Harvey in the larger perspective of the history of medicine and science."

Keynes, Geoffrey, and G. Whitteridge. *Bibliography of Dr. William Harvey.* Ashgate Pub.
   Co. 1987 o.p. A scholarly and definitive bibliography and discussion of the many
   editions of Harvey's published works.
Keynes, Geoffrey, Sir. *The Life of William Harvey.* Clarendon Pr. 1966 o.p. The definitive
   biography, extensively annotated and well illustrated; inclusive appendixes feature
   contemporary and subsequent analyses of the reception of Harvey's discovery, its
   debate in the Royal Society, as well as a reproduction of his Will.
Marcus, Rebecca B. *William Harvey: Trailblazer of Medicine. Immortals of Science Ser.*
   Modan/Adama Bks. 1962 o.p. Provides a useful introduction to the life of a great
   figure in medical history; well-illustrated and written for the adolescent.
Pagel, Walter. *William Harvey's Biological Ideas: Selected Aspects and Historical
   Background.* Hafner 1967 o.p. Discusses selective parts of Harvey's theories and
   discoveries and their impact on the biological sciences.
Whitteridge, G. *William Harvey and the Circulation of the Blood.* Elsevier 1971 o.p.
   A scholarly study of how Harvey arrived at his discovery of the circulation of the
   blood as well as the scientific debate it stirred in the seventeenth century.

NIGHTINGALE, FLORENCE. 1820–1910

   Born in Florence, Italy, of wealthy parents, Florence Nightingale was a
British nurse who is regarded as the founder of modern nursing practice. She
was a strong proponent of hospital reform and has been the subject of more
than 100 biographies and many magazine pieces. As a young woman in the early
nineteenth century, she had limited opportunity for a career. But Nightingale
was very intelligent, and had extraordinary organizational capacities. She
probably chose to become a nurse because of her great need to serve humanity.
She was trained in Germany at the Institute of Protestant Deaconesses in
Kaiserswerth, which had a program for patient care training and for hospital
administration. Nightingale excelled at both. As a nurse and then administrator
of a barracks hospital during the Crimean War, she introduced sweeping
changes in sanitary methods and discipline that dramatically reduced mortality
rates. Her efforts changed British military nursing during the late nineteenth
century.
   Following her military career, she was asked to form a training program for
nurses at King's College and St. Thomas Hospital in London. The remainder of
her career was devoted to nurse education and to the documentation of the first
code for nursing. Her 1859 book *Notes on Nursing: What It Is and What It Is Not*
has been described as "one of the seminal works of the modern world." The
work went through many editions and remains in print today. Using a
commonsense approach and a clear basic writing style, she proposed a
thorough regimen for nursing care in hospitals and homes. She also provided
advice on foods for various illnesses, cleanliness, personal grooming, ventilation, and special notes about the care of children and pregnant women.

BOOK BY NIGHTINGALE

Notes on Nursing: What It Is and What It Is Not. Ed. by Barbara S. Barnum. Lippincott
   1992 $24.95. ISBN 0-397-55007-3. An annotated American edition of Nightingale's
   famous book.

BOOKS ABOUT NIGHTINGALE

Baly, Monica E. *Florence Nightingale and the Nursing Legacy.* Routledge 1986 $49.95.
   ISBN 0-7099-3941-8. A scholarly study of how Nightingale changed nursing from a
   highly personalized caring service to a well-organized and principled profession.
Cook, Edward Tyas. *The Life of Florence Nightingale.* 2 vols. Macmillan 1913 o.p. The
   standard biography of Nightingale, based on extensive research of her letters.

Volume 1 is devoted to the period 1820–1861 and Volume 2 from 1862 to her death; includes appendixes for works by Nightingale, works about her, and a list of portraits.

Cope, Zachary. *Florence Nightingale and the Doctors.* Museum Pr. 1958 o.p. A documentary study of Nightingale's relationship with physicians.

Dengler, Sandy. *Florence Nightingale: Nurse to Soldiers.* Moody 1988 $4.50. ISBN 0-8024-2627-1. Covers her career in the military nursing service and how she influenced reform.

Gordon, Richard. *The Private Life of Florence Nightingale.* Macmillan 1979 $9.95. ISBN 0-689-10929-6. Focuses more on Nightingale's personal life than on her professional accomplishments.

Hebert, Raymond G. *Florence Nightingale: Saint, Reformer, or Rebel?* Krieger 1981 $10.50. ISBN 0-89874-127-0. A historical analysis that views Nightingale's position in history from three perspectives.

Smith, F. B. *Florence Nightingale: Reputation and Power.* St. Martin 1982 $26.00. ISBN 0-312-29649-5. A historical study of Nightingale that analyzes her lasting influence.

Woodham-Smith, Cecil. *Florence Nightingale.* Macmillan 1983 repr. of 1950 ed. $11.95. ISBN 0-689-70652-9. A comprehensive biography that features information from many manuscripts not available to Cook's work; includes an extensive list of quoted sources and a detailed index.

OSLER, WILLIAM. 1849–1919

Born in Bond Head, Ontario, William Osler was a physician whose influence on medical education in the United States and the United Kingdom was profound and lasting. He began his medical training at the University of Toronto but received his medical degree from McGill University in 1872. After a few years at medical clinics in Europe, he became a professor at McGill in the Institute of Medicine, where his reputation grew rapidly. In 1884 he left McGill and was named chair of the Department of Medicine at the University of Pennsylvania and then joined the faculty at Johns Hopkins University in 1889. There, Osler wrote a comprehensive textbook, *The Principles and Practice of Medicine*, a work that received immediate acclaim for both its clarity of presentation and its erudition. The work became a model for later textbooks and remains in print.

During his 15 years at Johns Hopkins, Osler became a major force in medical education, combining the bedside methods of the English medical school with the laboratory and clinical practices of many of the major European medical schools. His efforts laid the groundwork for the 1910 Carnegie Foundation study that changed the shape of medical education to its current approach, a combination of classroom and clinical study. In 1904 he was enticed to move to Oxford University, where he spent the remainder of his career. He influenced British medicine to the degree that his *Lancet* obituary unapologetically called him "the greatest personality in the medical world."

BOOKS BY OSLER

Acquanimitas: With Other Addresses to Medical Students, Nurses, and Practitioners of Medicine. McGraw 1932 $50.00. ISBN 0-07-047915-1. A collection of philosophical essays designed for health professionals.

Modern Medicine, Its Theory and Practice, in Original Contributions by American and Foreign Authors. 7 vols. Lea & Febiger 1907–1910. o.p. A monumental set that includes individually authored chapters and articles on virtually all medical topics.

William Osler: The Continuing Education. Ed. by John P. McGovern and Charles G. Roland. C. C. Thomas 1969 $41.25. ISBN 0-398-01256-3. A collection of Osler's

essays on medical education not published elsewhere; each essay is accompanied by
critical commentary by prominent medical educators.

The Principles and Practice of Medicine. Ed. by A. McGehee Harvey and others. Appleton
& Lange 1988 $65.00. ISBN 0-8385-7944-2. The most recent edition of Osler's
famous textbook.

Science and Immortality. Ayer 1977 repr. of 1904 ed. $14.00. ISBN 0-405-09581-3. An
incisive essay on fame and how its achievement influences scientific endeavor.

Student Life, and Other Essays. Ayer 1931 $15.00. ISBN 0-8369-0756-6. A collection of
essays on medical student life outside the classroom and its important role in
shaping the practicing professional.

BOOKS ABOUT OSLER

Barondess, Jeremiah, and others. *The Persisting Osler.* U. Park Pr. 1985 o.p. Demonstrates Osler's enduring influence on the practice of medicine.

Cushing, Harvey. *Life of Sir William Osler.* 2 vols. OUP 1940 $75.00. ISBN 0-19-500524-4.
The definitive biography, described by some as one of the finest biographies ever
written.

Noble, Iris. *The Doctor Who Dared, William Osler.* S&S Trade 1959 o.p. A biography
written for the general reader.

Wagner, Frederick B. *The Twilight Years of Lady Osler: Letters of a Doctor's Wife.* Watson
Pub. Intl. 1985 $20.00. ISBN 0-88135-002-8. A biography based mainly on excerpts
from letters to friends, relatives, and acquaintances in which Mrs. Osler describes
her husband.

PAVLOV, IVAN PETROVICH. 1849–1936 (NOBEL PRIZE 1904)

Born in Ryazan, Russia, originally trained to be a priest, Ivan Pavlov was a
physiologist and pharmacologist whose experiments on digestion added significantly to the knowledge of this life process. His studies in digestion also led to
the discovery of the conditioned reflex, a contribution of extraordinary
significance to the field of neurophysiology.

Under the mentorship of MENDELEEV, Pavlov received his medical training at
the University of St. Petersburg, earning a Ph.D. in 1883. He then studied for a
brief period in Germany before he became director of physiology at the St.
Petersburg Institute for Experimental Medicine. He held this position for 45
years—from 1890 until 1935. At the St. Petersburg laboratory, Pavlov began his
famous experiments with dogs. These experiments led to the discovery of the
secretory nerves, the explication of the role of the vagus nerve in gastric
secretion, and ultimately the identification of the three phases of digestion:
nervous, pyloric, and intestinal. He also confirmed that digestion is controlled
by hormones and published his conclusions in Russian in *O nervakh, zavedyva-
yushchikh rabotoy v podzheludochnoy zheleze* (1897). The importance of this
work was recognized immediately and was translated into German the
following year, appearing as *Die Arbeit der Verdauungsdrüsen.*

BOOKS BY PAVLOV

Conditioned Reflexes: An Investigation of the Physiological Activity of the Cerebral Cortex.
Trans. by G. V. Anrep. Peter Smith 1979 $14.50. ISBN 0-8446-5839-1. A fine
translation that features incisive commentary.

The Work of the Digestive Glands. Trans. by W. H. Thompson. 1902. Lippincott 1910 o.p.
An important English translation of Pavlov's Nobel Prize-winning discoveries of the
physiology of digestion.

BOOKS ABOUT PAVLOV

Babkin, Boris P. *Pavlov: A Biography.* U. Ch. Pr. 1975 $4.25. ISBN 0-226-03373-2.
A concise, well-illustrated biography.

Frolov, Yuril P. *Pavlov and His School.* Trans. by C. P. Dutt. Johnson Repr. 1970 repr. of 1938 ed. $23.00. ISBN 0-384-17060-9. A scholarly treatment that elucidates Pavlov's influence in the history of medicine.

VESALIUS, ANDREAS. 1514–1564

Born in Brussels, Belgium, Andreas Vesalius was a Flemish anatomist whose sixteenth-century work, *De humani corporis fabrica*, is widely considered one of the most influential medical books. Educated at the University of Louvain, Vesalius chose the University of Paris for his medical training, where he became interested in anatomy and acquired his skills at dissection, both in the tradition of Galen. He left Paris and completed his education in 1537 at the University of Padua, then the most famous college in Europe. In Padua, Vesalius published a dissection manual for his students and continued to refine his dissection techniques and to expand his knowledge of human anatomy, mainly by dissecting cadavers. He also began to note discrepancies between his observations and what was then published about human anatomy, based on Galen's work in the second century. In 1540 Vesalius began developing the *Fabrica*, as it is called, which took nearly three years. He supervised all aspects of the making of the book and its publication in 1543, giving the world the finest elucidation of anatomy to that date. It proved that much of Galenic anatomy was based on inaccurate assumptions, thus altering the study of medicine profoundly. The exquisite illustrations, drawn by artists in TITIAN's Venetian studio, are so outstanding that they are important as art and as science. Several supplements to the original and a second edition of this great anatomical treatise were published in Vesalius's lifetime. Surprisingly, he gave up his anatomical studies and became a court physician to Emperor Charles V and later to Philip II of Spain, at whose court he remained until his death.

BOOK BY VESALIUS

The Illustrations from the Works of Andreas Vesalius of Brussels. Trans. by J. B. de C. M. Saunders and Charles D. O'Malley. Peter Smith 1979 repr. of 1950 ed. $18.00. ISBN 0-8446-4830-2. A scholarly edition of the *Fabrica*, includes an interesting discussion of the process by which the anatomical plates were made, the authorship, and a biographical sketch of Vesalius.

BOOKS ABOUT VESALIUS

Cushing, Harvey W. *A Bio-Bibliography of Andrea Vesalius.* Shoe String 1962 repr. of 1943 ed. o.p. A scholarly review of the significance and importance of the works of Vesalius. Emphasizes the two editions of the *Fabrica*; includes a census of copies.

O'Malley, Charles D. *Andreas Vesalius of Brussels, 1514–1564.* U. CA Pr. 1964 o.p. Scholarly biography and study of the influence of Vesalius on medicine; includes extensive bibliographical references and a detailed subject index.

CHAPTER 13

Illness and Disease

Daniel T. Richards

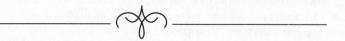

> There is such a thing as sober conjecture, as well as sober certainty. And diseases are treated, and cures are achieved, and lives are saved, as often under the guidance of one as the other.
> —PETER MERE LATHAM, *Diseases of the Heart*

The surging level of interest in public health, which characterized the late 1980s, has continued apace into the 1990s, and there is no reason to expect it to abate in the near future. With the cost of health care continuing to escalate, reform has been undertaken by President Bill Clinton. Thus, it is safe to predict that developments in the health care field will affect the American public for years to come. People are learning more about their own ailments and those of their families; research results routinely are front page news, and most major newspapers have a regular column or feature on health topics. Patients now are demanding and receiving greater power in the decision-making process on proposed treatment, and consumer advocacy groups continue to increase in number and in influence. A new and rapidly growing field of scientific endeavor called outcomes research is using advanced computer technology to analyze chronologically and geographically disparate case reports of the same disorder or disease. This research ultimately will lead to practical guidelines so that routine medical procedures can be carried out in the most efficient and effective manner possible.

There continues to be a steady stream of new books on "hot" ailments and self-treatment. The AIDS epidemic is more than a decade old without a cure. As a result, the ongoing search for a cure and for palliative approaches to ease the suffering of those afflicted has become a regular topic in the popular press. Indeed, the amount of literature focused on AIDS is overwhelming, a sad indicator of the extent to which this disease has affected our society. Nevertheless, the literature on cancer, heart disease and diabetes still finds an eager audience. Books on the latter diseases are being joined by several others on the exciting and controversial potential of gene therapy and fetal tissue research.

Progress has been made in the fight against many diseases, as reflected by the shelves of local bookstores and libraries. The following compilation of books is a guide to some of that literature and is not intended to be an exhaustive review. Rather, it indicates the range and variety of information available. Many of the books included are recent, but there are also some older works that continue to be useful compilations on diagnosis and treatment modalities. Publishing trends and public interest often dictate the kinds of books published on some diseases or conditions. Consequently, there is a welter of literature on some; yet for others, the offerings are relatively sparse. The length of the bibliographies in

366

some of the following sections reveal some of these "peaks and valleys." The goal has been to list resources on diagnosis, treatment, prognosis, incidence, and rehabilitation for most of the disorders and diseases that affect human beings. For the most part, only those books that discuss current orthodox therapy have been included.

In addition to commercially available books, there are many associations and organizations that publish booklets and pamphlets. These publications, which provide a succinct and clearly written explanation of the medical background and treatment for a particular disease, often are distributed free or at a minimal charge. Lists of these organizations can be found in several of the general reference books listed at the beginning of Chapter 12, "Medicine and Health," in this volume. Finally, physicians sometimes suggest to their patients publications that they have found helpful.

REFERENCE WORKS

Dictionaries

Altman, Roberta, and Michael Sarg. *The Cancer Dictionary*. Facts on File 1992 $35.00. ISBN 0-8160-2608-4. Extensive cross-references and appendices of support groups, clinical trials cooperative groups, and care centers; accessible to the general reader.

Diseases: Causes, and Diagnosis, Current Therapy, Nursing Management, Patient Education. Springhouse 1984 o.p. Provides simpler explanations than major medical texts of the signs and symptoms of most diseases and disorders. Covers expected clinical courses, diagnostic tests, treatment, possible complications, and nursing interventions.

Dorland's Illustrated Medical Dictionary. Saunders 1988 $51.25. ISBN 0-7216-3154-1. The best-known medical dictionary. Excellent illustrations.

Firkin, B. G., and J. A. Whitworth. *Dictionary of Medical Eponyms*. Prthnon Pub. 1987 $48.00. ISBN 1-85070-138-5. Description of the disease and background notes on the person who identified it.

Mágalini, Sergio I., and Euclide Scrascia. *Dictionary of Medical Syndromes*. Lippincott 1981 o.p. Concise descriptions (including synonyms), symptoms, diagnostic procedures, treatment, and prognosis of more than 2,700 syndromes.

Smith, Doris C., ed. *Physicians' Guide to Rare Diseases*. Dowden Pub. 1992 $69.50. ISBN 0-9628716-0-5. Handbook of basic information on more than 700 rare diseases, defined as those that affect fewer than 200,000 Americans. Index provides access by symptom and includes information about so-called orphan drugs developed to treat rare diseases; designed for the primary care physician.

Webster's Medical Desk Dictionary. Merriam-Webster Inc. 1993 $27.95. ISBN 0-87779-026-4. All entries are in a single alphabetical list, with a part-of-speech; places British spellings in their own alphabetical place; includes more than 1,300 brief biographies.

Directories

American Hospital Association Guide to the Health Care Field. Amer. Hospital 1992. $70 members. $195 nonmembers. ISBN 0-87528-577-8. Revised yearly. Statistics on numbers of beds, facilities and services, type of ownership (government, nonfederal or federal, nongovernment, not-for-profit, investor-owned, osteopathic), length of stay, and occupancy rates; listings are alphabetical by state and city.

American Medical Association Directory of Physicians in the United States. 4 vols. AMA 33rd ed. 1992 $545.00. ISBN 0-89970-523-5. Current information on more than 640,000 physicians; includes name, address, type of practice, medical school and year of graduation, and primary specialty.

The Complete Directory for People with Disabilities. Grey Hse. Pub. 1992 $125.00. ISBN 0-939300-12-5. Links disabled persons with specialized products, resources, books and services. Lists nearly 6,000 assistive devices; well indexed.

The Official American Board of Medical Specialties (ABMS) Directory of Board Certified Medical Specialists, 1994. 4 vols. Marquis Who's Who 1994. ISBNs Vol. 1 0-8379-0530-3. Vol. 2 0-8379-0531-1. Vol. 3 0-8379-0532-X. Vol. 4 0-8379-0533-8. Revised biennially. The only biographical directory authorized by the ABMS. Lists more than 435,000 specialists certified by the 25 U.S. specialty boards. Includes information on internship, residency, training, fellowships, and professional associations. This is the 26th edition.

Shrout, Richard N. *Resource Directory for the Disabled.* Facts on File 1992 $45.00. ISBN 0-8160-2216-X. Arranged by impairment, i.e., mobility, visual, and so on; easier to use than *The Complete Directory for People with Disabilities* but not as comprehensive.

Encyclopedias

Galton, Lawrence. *Medical Technician: The Layperson's Guide to Today's Medical Miracles.* HarpC 1985 $19.95. ISBN 0-06-015372-5. Information on state-of-the-art procedures and techniques—from adoptive pregnancy to zona-free hamster egg test; includes potential problems and history of development.

Kiple, Kenneth F., ed. *The Cambridge World History of Human Disease.* Cambridge U. Pr. 1993 $150.00. ISBN 0-521-33286-9. Outstanding compilation of information that brings together articles from more than 150 authors.

Walton, John, and Ronald B. Scott, eds. *The Oxford Companion to Medicine.* 2 vols. OUP 1986 $150.00. ISBN 0-19-261191-7. Collection of definitions, short essays, and biographies. "Covering topics such as diagnosis, experimental method, health insurance in the United States, law and medicine in the United Kingdom, medical microbiology, physiology, rehabilitation, and veterinary medicine, these often include short bibliographies and illustrations. The one-paragraph biographies of more than 1,000 physicians and other contributors to medical knowledge provide, albeit diffusely, historical background beyond that provided in some of the long articles" (*Wilson Library Bulletin*).

BIOGRAPHIES

These titles represent a selection from the many titles dealing with illness and disease from a professional or a personal point of view. (See also Chapters 3 and 12 in this volume.)

Astor, Gerald. *The Disease Detectives: Deadly Medical Mysteries and the People Who Solved Them.* NAL-Dutton 1984 o.p. "Tells about the feelings, thoughts, and procedures of the men and women from the Centers for Disease Control who are responsible for investigating and studying outbreaks of cholera, bubonic plague, toxic shock syndrome and other medical problems" (*Library Journal*).

Austrian, Robert. *Life with the Pneumococcus: Notes from the Bedside, Laboratory and Library.* U. of Pa. Pr. 1985 $47.95. ISBN 0-8122-7977-8. "The history of this fascinating bacterial pathogen and of the gradual recognition of its great diversity and disease-producing capacity is recounted lucidly. Woven into the fabric of the book, without much in the way of emphasis, is the story of Austrian's own considerable contribution to the modern developments in the control of pneumococcal disease" (*American Scientist*).

Beckler, Alfred W. *A Gift of Life: The Powerful True Story of How Family Love and One Man's Indomitable Spirit Brought Him Back from Death to a Joyous Life.* Macmillan 1983 o.p. "Gives hope that a diabetic can face the absolute worst and eventually conquer. Beckler is special because he is walking around with a new kidney and a new pancreas—both medical wonder operations" (*Library Journal*).

Cahan, William G. *No Stranger to Tears: A Surgeon's Story*. Random 1992 $24.50. ISBN 0-394-56518-5. Autobiography of a surgeon at New York's Memorial Sloan-Kettering Cancer Center; reveals the emotional struggle endured by doctor and patient when facing death in the battle against cancer.

Dossey, Larry. *Meaning and Medicine: A Doctor's Tales of Breakthrough and Healing*. Bantam 1991 $20.00. ISBN 0-553-07869-0. Autobiographical chronicle of incidents in which beliefs, hopes, and faith have resulted in unexpected recoveries from serious illness.

Henig, Robin A. *A Dancing Matrix: Voyages along the Viral Frontier*. Knopf 1993 $23.50. ISBN 0-394-58878-9. "Instructive, well-researched reading that provides a cutting edge account of research in virology" (*Library Journal*).

Kendall, Edward C. *Cortisone: Memoirs of a Hormone Hunter*. Macmillan 1971 $7.95. ISBN 0-684-31062-7. "[Much] more than an exciting autobiography of the scientist Edward C. Kendall, [rather an] account of happenings in the medical sciences in the United States. Most of Kendall's book is concerned with research on the adrenal cortex. The most dramatic part of Kendall's story pertains to his collaboration with the rheumatologist Phillip S. Hench and the administration of cortisone to a patient severely afflicted with rheumatoid arthritis" (*American Scientist*).

McGill, Frances. *Go Not Gently: Letters from a Patient with Amyotrophic Lateral Sclerosis*. Ed. by Lillian G. Kutscher. Ayer 1980 $18.00. ISBN 0-405-12643-3. Letters to a group of friends dealing with the author's perceptions of her terminal illness; written between July 1974 and June 1979.

Paul, Olgesby. *Take Heart: The Life and Prescription for Living of Dr. Paul Dudley White*. HUP 1986 $19.95. ISBN 0-317-04059-6. Captivating biography about a preeminent physician whose outspoken views against the unnecessary invalidism of patients with heart disease bettered the lives of millions of persons worldwide during his 60-plus years of medical practice" (*Library Journal*).

Springarn, Natalie Davis. *Hanging in There: Living Well on Borrowed Time*. Stein & Day 1982 o.p. "Encouragement for people living with the knowledge that they have a serious illness, typically cancer, who because of the protracted course of the illness are neither well nor completely disabled for an undefined period" (*Library Journal*).

Zola, Irving Kenneth, ed. *Ordinary Lives: Voices of Disability and Disease*. Applewood 1982 o.p. "This anthology brings together powerful and touching stories expressing individuals' feelings about chronic disease and disability" (*Choice*).

AIDS

[SEE the section on Immunology in this chapter.]

ALLERGY

[SEE the section on Immunology in this chapter.]

ANESTHESIOLOGY

Anesthesiology is the science concerned with the pharmacological, physiological, and clinical basis of anesthesia. Few titles on this topic are written for general readers.

Brown, Robert C. *Perchance to Dream: The Patient's Guide to Anesthesia*. Nelson-Hall 1981 o.p. Outlines the history of anesthesia. Discusses types of anesthetic agents, their actions, and possible complications.

Pernick, Martin S. *A Calculus of Suffering: Pain, Professionalism and Anesthesia in Nineteenth-Century America.* Col. U. Pr. 1985 $17.00. ISBN 0-231-05187-5. "This book can be recommended to a reader seeking to learn more about the social and professional aspects of pain relief in the half-century following the discovery of anesthesia" (*American Scientist*).

ARTHRITIS

[SEE the section on Rheumatic Diseases in this chapter.]

ARTIFICIAL AND TRANSPLANTED ORGANS, PROSTHESES, AND IMPLANTS

The following books describe biotechnological advances in medicine, including implants, transplants, artificial hearts and joints, as well as the ethical, social, and economic impact of this technology.

Bigelow, W. G. *Cold Hearts: The Story of Hypothermia and the Pacemaker in Heart Surgery.* Firefly Bks. 1984 o.p. "Dr. Bigelow's story makes research look just plain fun and gives credit where credit is due" (*Anesthesiology*).

Cauwels, Janice M. *The Body Shop: Bionic Revolutions in Medicine.* Mosby 1986 o.p. "Skillfully interweaves human interest vignettes, technical explanations, and in-depth interviews with researchers in such fields as artificial joints; artificial hearts; post-surgery prostheses for faces, breasts, and limbs; and rehabilitation of patients devastated by neuromuscular disease" (*Library Journal*).

Cook, Albert M., and John G. Webster, eds. *Therapeutic Medical Devices: Application and Design.* P-H 1981 $72.00. ISBN 0-13-194796-9. "Reviews in some detail the medical devices that are [currently] available" (*Choice*).

Davis, Audrey B. *Medicine and Its Technology: An Introduction to the History of Medical Instrumentation.* Greenwood 1981 $59.95. ISBN 0-313-22007-8. "Emphasis is placed on the major pioneering areas of medical technology: thermometry, stethoscopy, and the more varied instrumentation used to measure pulse rate, blood pressure, and other specialized cardiovascular functions" (*Choice*).

Lynch, Wilfred. *Implants: Reconstructing the Human Body.* T. C. Pub. 1982 $35.00. ISBN 0-686-48258-1. "Provides a review and explanation of many types of surgical-implant devices and biomaterials" (*American Scientist*).

Marget, Madeline. *Life's Blood: A Story of Medical Science and Human Courage.* S&S Trade 1992 $23.00. ISBN 0-671-69488-X. Well-written book that combines descriptions of marrow transplants with a sensitive discussion of the emotional aspects of this experience.

Organ Transplants: A Patient's Guide. Massachusetts General Hospital Organ Transplant Team. Ed. by H. F. Pizer. HUP 1991 $24.95. ISBN 0-674-64235-6. Useful guide for a specialized but growing audience. Describes transplants of the heart, lung, kidney, pancreas, liver, and bone marrow and explains immunosuppression for the general reader.

Pekkanen, John. *Donor.* Little 1986 $16.95. ISBN 0-316-69792-3. "An absorbing and moving book that follows the donation of organs from a young woman after her death in an automobile accident" (*Library Journal*).

Plough, Alonzo L. *Borrowed Time: Artificial Organs and the Politics of Extending Lives. Health, Society, and Policy* Temple U. Pr. 1986 $34.95. ISBN 0-87222-415-3. "Examines federal programs for the treatment of kidney failures as well as the problem of chronic and catastrophic illness and the cultural and political forces that have come to shape policies concerning new technologies" (*Choice*).

Reiser, Stanley J., and Michael Anbar, eds. *The Machine at the Bedside: Strategies for Using Technology in Patient Care.* Cambridge U. Pr. 1984 $74.95. ISBN 0-521-

26718-8. "Examines the social, ethical, and economic impact of the diagnostic, therapeutic, palliative, and rehabilitative technologies that constitute the armamentarium of modern health care" (*American Scientist*).

BLINDNESS

[SEE the section on Eye Disorders in this chapter.]

BLOOD DISEASES

[SEE the section on Hematologic Diseases in this chapter.]

BONE DISEASES

[SEE the section on Orthopedics in this chapter.]

CANCER

Cancer is a term used commonly to indicate various malignant neoplasms, most of which invade surrounding tissues, can spread (metastasize) to other sites, and are likely to recur after attempted removal. Cancer invariably results in death unless it is adequately treated. The following represents a selection of the many books on cancer. They describe specific cancers, their detection, treatment, prognosis, and incidence, as well as the personal and psychosocial impact of this disease.

Berger, Karen, and John Bostwick, III. *A Woman's Decision: Breast Care, Treatment and Reconstruction.* Quality Med. Pub. 1993 $17.00. ISBN 0-942219-04-X. "Compiled with the aid of Reach to Recovery and the American Cancer Society. Couples personal accounts with information on this special surgery" (*Library Journal*).

Bracken, Jeanne M. *Children with Cancer: A Comprehensive Reference Guide for Parents.* OUP 1988. $10.95. ISBN 0-19-505659-0. "Includes chapters on specific cancers; standard treatments; coping; and lists of international, national, and regional organizations and clinics" (*Library Journal*).

Bruning, Nancy. *Coping with Chemotherapy.* Ballantine 1993 $5.95. ISBN 0-34537409-6. "Gives possible causes of cancer, the therapies, side effects, emotional impact of chemotherapy and ways to cope with the treatment. In-depth and understanding coverage of all aspects of the physiological and emotional aspects of chemotherapy" (*Library Journal*).

Creasey, William A. *Diet and Cancer.* Lea & Febiger 1985 $16.50. ISBN 0-8121-0975-6. "Covers nutrition and cancer patients, protein and caloric intake, fibers, fats, vitamins, minerals, alcohol, and coffee" (*Library Journal*).

Cukier, Daniel, and Virginia McCullough. *A Ray of Hope: Coping with Radiation Therapy.* Lowell Hse 1993 $21.95. ISBN 1-56565-000-X. Overview of radiation therapy followed by chapters on side effects, diet, emotional issues, and a discussion of therapies for specific types of cancer; good source of information for the cancer patient facing radiation therapy.

Eades, Mary Dan. *Breast Cancer: Reducing Your Risk.* Bantam 1993 $12.95. ISBN 0-553-37203-3. Useful discussion of risk factors and how to avoid them; written for the general reader.

Edelhart, Michael, and Jean Lindenmann. *Interferon: The New Hope for Cancer.* Ballantine 1982 $3.50. ISBN 0-345-30298-2. "What interferon is and how it works" (*Choice*).

Fjermedal, Grant. *Magic Bullets: A Revolution in Cancer Treatment.* Macmillan 1984 $15.95. ISBN 0-02-538550-X. "The inside story of major cancer research funded by the NIH" (*Library Journal*).

Goldberg, Richard T., and Robert M. Tull. *The Psychosocial Dimensions of Cancer.* Free Pr. 1983 $23.95. ISBN 0-02-911980-4. "Includes discussion of children's comprehension of disease and death at various ages; special problems of adolescent patients; drug-related issues; physical and psychological causes of nausea; issues in pain control and drugs used for this purpose" (*Choice*).

Graham, Jory. *In the Company of Others.* HarBraceJ 1987 $4.95. ISBN 0-15-64496-9. A syndicated columnist describes her unsuccessful struggle against metastasized cancer.

Greenwald, Howard P. *Who Survives Cancer?* U. CA Pr. 1992 $25.00. ISBN 0-520-07725-3. Thought-provoking epidemiological study of the likelihood of surviving cancer. Contends that funding for research would be better spent on providing health care for cancer victims who cannot afford treatment.

Hirshaut, Yashar, and Peter Pressman. *Breast Cancer, the Complete Guide.* Bantam 1992 $24.50. ISBN 0-553-08960-9. Comprehensive, up-to-date information on all aspects of the disease; written by an oncologist and a surgeon.

Holleb, Arthur I., and others, eds. *The American Cancer Society's Complete Book of Cancer: Prevention, Diagnosis, Treatment, Rehabilitation, Cure.* Doubleday 1986 $24.95. ISBN 0-385-17847-6. Excellent compilation covers such topics as smoking and cancer, monoclonal antibodies, genetic factors, specific cancers and their treatment, aids to early detection, and decision making on treatment and aftercare.

Hummell, Sherilynn J. with Marie Lindquist. *Ovarian and Uterine Cancer: Reducing Your Risk.* Bantam 1992 $9.00. ISBN 0-553-35425-6. Useful advice about risk factors associated with these two common types of cancer; an addition to Bantam's *If It Runs in Your Family* series.

Kessler, I. *Cancer Control: Contemporary Views on Screening, Diagnosis, and Therapy, Including a Colloquy on the Delaney Clause.* Univ. Park Pr. 1980 $32.00. ISBN 0-8391-1539-3. "Specific chapters cover immunodiagnosis, chemotherapy, and cytohistopathy (the study of cancer mechanisms in cells as individuals and groups). The practical as well as the theoretical aspects of control are discussed" (*Choice*).

Levenson, Frederick B. *Causes and Prevention of Cancer.* Madison Bks. UPA 1986 $8.95. ISBN 0-8128-6255-4. "Understanding both the genetic and psychoanalytic bases of the disease is necessary to formulate an effective therapy, the author states" (*Library Journal*).

Livingston-Wheeler, Virginia, and Edmond G. Addeo. *The Conquest of Cancer; Vaccines and Diet.* Waterside Prodns. 1993 $9.95. ISBN 0-9627145-1-8. "A personal narrative chronicling the author's research and continuing struggle for recognition. Also a description of the regimen prescribed by her San Diego cancer clinic, complete with recipes and food lists" (*Library Journal*).

McAllister, Robert M., and others. *Cancer.* Basic 1993 $20.00. ISBN 0-465-00845-3. User-friendly, nontechnical, and accurate picture of the latest advances in cancer research, diagnoses, and therapy.

Margolies, Cynthia P., and Kenneth B. McCredie. *Understanding Leukemia.* Macmillan 1990 $9.95. ISBN 0-684-18725-6. "A rigorous discussion of possible causes and treatment protocols (chemotherapy, radiotherapy, bone marrow transplants, etc.)" (*Library Journal*).

Morra, Marion, and Eve Potts. *Choices: Realistic Alternatives in Cancer Treatment.* Avon 1987 $12.95. ISBN 0-380-753008-1. Supplements the information provided by physicians on the nature of cancer, diagnostic tests, treatment modalities, experimental investigation, unproven treatments, and more; includes advice on selecting a physician.

One in Three: Women with Cancer Confront an Epidemic. Cleis Pr. 1991 $24.95. ISBN 0-939416-50-6. Anthology by women who have experienced cancer. Discusses the impact of government, polluters, and the medical establishment; includes a resource guide.

Petrek, Jeanne A. *A Woman's Guide to the Prevention, Detection and Treatment of Cancer.*
Macmillan 1985 $16.30. ISBN 0-02-595940-9. "Provides an overview of cancer, with
sections on diagnosis, treatment, and a discussion of risk factors" (*Library Journal*).

Prescott, David M., and Abraham S. Flexer. *Cancer: The Misguided Cell.* Sinauer Assocs.
1986 $26.95. ISBN 0-87893-708-0. "A well-documented review of the basic ap-
proaches to cancer research conducted over the past decade" (*Library Journal*).

Rosenberg, Steven A., and John M. Barry. *The Transformed Cell: Unlocking the Mysteries
of Cancer.* Putnam Pub. Group 1992 $24.95. ISBN 0-399-13749-1. Fascinating story
of scientific research involving large corporations, the federal government, scientific
pride and money.

Rosenblum, Daniel. *A Time to Hear, a Time to Help: Listening to People with Cancer.* Free
Pr. 1993 $22.95. ISBN 0-02-927105-3. The importance of communication among the
physician, the patient, and the patient's family.

Shamberger, Raymond J. *Nutrition and Cancer.* Plenum Pub. 1984 o.p. "Reviews the role
of nutrition in carcinogenesis, notes certain mutagens formed during processing or
cooking or naturally occurring carcinogens in relation to causation. Also covered
are additives, artificial sweeteners, antioxidants, and food contaminants. Reviews
unproven cancer diet claims" (*American Scientist*).

Siegel, Mary-Ellen. *The Cancer Patient's Handbook: Everything You Need to Know about
Today's Care and Treatment.* Walker 1986 $24.95. ISBN 0-8027-0898-6. "Provides a
clear description of each of the therapeutic approaches to treating cancer, including
immunologic therapies with biologic-response modifiers. Discusses 'unproved'
cancer treatment. Defines tests and examinations" (*New England Journal of
Medicine*).

Simone, Charles. *Cancer & Nutrition: A Ten-Point Plan to Reduce Your Risk of Getting
Cancer.* Avery 1982 $12.95. ISBN 0-89529-491-5. Positive, prevention-oriented
program to assess and reduce cancer risk; well documented and updated.

Spletter, Mary. *A Woman's Choice: New Options in the Treatment of Breast Cancer.*
Beacon Pr. 1981 o.p. "Provides descriptions of treatments, explanations of medical
terminology, survival statistics, and other information that will enable a woman to
know her own cancer risk, ask questions of physicians, and make informed choices
(*Library Journal*).

Wadler, Joyce. *My Breast: One Woman's Cancer Story.* Addison-Wesley 1992 $15.00.
ISBN 0-201-63283-7. Personal narrative of the experience.

CARDIOVASCULAR DISEASES

This section features information on the anatomy and actions of the heart,
symptoms, diagnosis, treatment (including the role of diet and exercise), and
prevention of stroke, heart attack, and hypertension. The following is a selection
of books that provide historical and current information on the normal and
abnormal functions of the heart and cardiovascular system.

The American Heart Association. *Heartbook: A Guide to the Prevention and Treatment of
Cardiovascular Diseases.* Dutton 1980 o.p. Comprehensive manual on the causes,
prevention, and treatment of heart attack, stroke, hypertension, and cardiac
emergencies; written for the general reader.

The American Medical Association. *Straight-Talk No-Nonsense Guide to Heart Care.*
Random 1984 $8.95. ISBN 0-394-73545-5. "Details how the individual can prevent
heart disease. Emphasizes preventive care, problems and symptoms" (*Library
Journal*).

Caris, Timothy N. *Essential Hypertension: A Strategy for Individualized Treatment.* JBK
Pubs. 1990 $11.95. ISBN 0-945892-01-2. User-friendly discussion of warning signs for
hypertension and of a wide variety of treatment modalities.

Cranton, Elmer, and Arline Brecher. *Bypassing Bypass: The New Technique of Chelation
Therapy.* Hampton Roads Pub. Co. 1990 $9.95. ISBN 0-9624375-1-4. "Explains the

controversial form of therapy in which EDTA (ethylene-diamine-tetra-acetic acid) is
given intravenously" (*Library Journal*).

Diethrich, Edward B. *Women and Heart Disease: What You Can Do to Stop the Number
One Killer of Women*. Random 1992 $21.50. ISBN 0-8129-1974-2. The special hazards
heart disease poses for women.

Eisenberg, Mickey, and Judy Pierce, eds. *Sudden Cardiac Death in the Community*.
Greenwood 1984 $37.95. ISBN 0-275-91428-3. "The authors argue that quick
treatment delivered by skilled people who have the training and equipment to
stabilize the victim of a cardiac arrhythmia/arrest in the field is currently the
principle around which prehospital cardiac care is/should be organized" (*Choice*).

Garrett, R. C., and U. G. Waldmeyer. *The Pill Book of High Blood Pressure*. Bantam 1985
o.p. "Provides information on specific illness and the drugs commonly prescribed to
treat them" (*Library Journal*).

Halperin, Jonathan L., and Richard Levine. *Bypass: A Cardiologist Reveals What Every
Patient Needs to Know*. Random 1987 $8.95. ISBN 0-89586-509-2. "Traces [the]
historical development of cardiology, provides an interesting behind-the-scenes
glimpse into the world of medicine—the actual bypass operation, postoperative care
in the intensive care unit, and cardiac rehabilitation" (*Library Journal*).

Hoffman, Nancy Y. *Change of Heart: The Bypass Experience*. HarBraceJ 1985 $17.95.
ISBN 0-15-116641-2. "Drawn from the experiences of 800 questionnaire respondents
and 200 interviewees, all of whom have undergone coronary bypasses" (*Journal of
the American Medical Association*).

Johnson, Stephen L. *The History of Cardiac Surgery 1896–1955*. Johns Hopkins 1970 o.p.
"Trace[s] the crucial technological breakthroughs [such as] the first successful
suture of a human heart wound, by Ludwig Rehn in 1896; extracardiac surgery,
pioneered in the 1930s by Robert Gross and others; and in the late 1940s and 1950s,
the attack of valvular heart disease" (*American Scientist*).

Kaplan, Norman M. *Prevent Your Heart Attack*. Tor Bks. 1984 o.p. "A practical
commonsense guide to help decrease the chances of having cardiovascular disease"
(*Library Journal*).

Kerman D. Ariel, with Richard Trubo. *The HART Program: A Comprehensive Guide to
Lowering Your Blood Pressure without Drugs*. HarpC 1991 $20.00. ISBN 0-06-
016575-8. Describes the use of several techniques to reduce hypertension without
the use of drugs; HART is an acronym for Hypertensive Autonomic Relaxation
Treatment.

Klieman, Charles, and Kevin Osborn. *Heart Disease: Reducing Your Risk*. Bantam 1991
o.p. Review genetic indicators for a predisposition to cardiovascular disease and
provides useful information about how to identify and avoid other risk factors
associated with heart ailments; easy to read.

Kowalski, Robert E. *8 Steps to a Healthy Heart*. Warner Bks. 1992 $21.95. ISBN 0-446-
51664-3. Concise, well-documented comprehensive program covering lifestyle and
emotional changes needed for recovery from heart surgery and return to optimum
health.

Kra, Siegfried. *Coronary Bypass Surgery: Who Needs It?* Norton 1986 o.p. "Discusses
alternatives to surgery that he feels are better, in some cases, than surgery" (*Library
Journal*).

Richardson, Robert G. *The Scalpel and the Heart*. Macmillan 1970 o.p. "Includes a
historic review of the circulation; operations for the relief of patients with angina
pectoris; and the pioneering efforts of Drs. Hufnagel, Harken, and Starr in
developing the valvular prostheses" (*American Scientist*).

Sonnenberg, David, and others. *Understanding Pacemakers*. PB 1986 $4.50. ISBN 0-671-
55674-6. "Deals simply with cardiac physiology and pacing technology and addresses
many of the problems and anxieties faced by pacemaker patients" (*Library Journal*).

Sorrentino, Sandy, and Carl Hausman. *Coping with High Blood Pressure*. Barricade Bks.
1990 $9.95. ISBN 0-942637-25-9. "Stresses personal responsibility for managing high
blood pressure. An excellent guide to the medications prescribed for hypertension"
(*Library Journal*).

Trowbridge, John P., and Morton Walker. *Chelation Therapy: The Key to Unclogging Your Arteries* . . . Devin 1990 $3.95. ISBN 0-685-45581-5. "An argument for the value of a controversial treatment (infusion of a manmade amino acid, EDTA, into the body to rid it of calcium and other minerals)" (*Library Journal*).

Warren, James, and Genell Subak-Sharpe. *Managing Hypertension: The Complete Program Developed by the Cleveland Clinic*. Doubleday 1986 $14.95. ISBN 0-385-18768-8. "Presents sound advice regarding hypertension therapy, extensive information on diagnosis, nondrug therapy, weight control, stress, and cigarette among other topics" (*Library Journal*).

Wilson, Philip K. *Policies and Procedures of a Cardiac Rehabilitation Program: Immediate to Long-Term Care*. Lea & Febiger 1978 o.p. "Divided into five areas: scientific foundations, organizational procedures, evaluation process, exercise prescription, and future directions" (*Choice*).

Yalof, Ina L. *Open Heart Surgery: A Guidebook for Patients and Families*. Random 1983 $12.95. ISBN 0-394-71513-6. "Describes the anatomy and actions of the heart and various heart diseases and conditions. Outlines diagnostic tests and exams, basic types of surgery, pre- and postoperative care, the recovery and convalescent periods, and possible complications" (*Library Journal*).

Zaret, Barry L., and others, eds. *Yale University School of Medicine Heart Book*. Morrow 1992 $30.00. ISBN 0-688-09719-7. Comprehensive, easy-to-read discussion of the basics of the cardiovascular system as well as extensive information about heart disease (in a section called "Encyclopedia of Common Heart Disorders").

CHILDHOOD DISEASES

This section covers several specialized childhood disorders, including fetal alcohol syndrome, sudden infant death syndrome (SIDS), and the psychosocial impact of birth defects or critical illness on families and children. (See also Chapter 12 in this volume.)

Abel, Ernest L. *Fetal Alcohol Syndrome*. Blackwell Pubs. 1990 $79.95. ISBN 0-86542-160-9. Comprehensive scholarly discussion of the causes, treatment, and social consequence of this disease.

Batshaw, Mark L. *Your Child Has a Disability: A Complete Sourcebook of Daily and Medical Care*. Little 1991 $27.95. ISBN 0-316-08369-0. Discusses the diagnosis of childhood disabilities and provides practical information on treatment; written by a pediatrician.

Bergman, Abraham B. *The "Discovery" of Sudden Infant Death Syndrome: Lessons in the Practice of Political Medicine*. U. of Wash. Pr. 1988 $12.50. ISBN 0-295-96601-7. "SIDS kills approximately 10,000 infants a year. Its cause is still unknown, but suspected causes, such as viruses, have been ruled out. Rarely does a book offer so much insight into human need and into political medicine" (*Choice*).

Colen, B. D. *Born at Risk*. PB 1982 $2.95. ISBN 0-671-43781-X. "The fictionalized account of sick newborn infants and how their struggle for life affects the parents who hope for their survival and the physicians and nurses who treat them" (*Library Journal*).

Dorris, Michael. *The Broken Cord*. HarpC 1989 $11.00. ISBN 0-06-092287-7. Intense and eloquent memoir of a family's struggle with fetal alcohol syndrome.

Golding, Jean, and others. *Sudden Infant Death: Patterns, Puzzles, and Problems*. U. of Wash. Pr. 1985 o.p. "Two British epidemiologists and a research pediatrician sum up clearly what is known in a fascinating and human account, a fine case study in epidemiology and its problems" (*Scientific American*).

Goodman, Richard M., and Robert J. Gorlin. *The Malformed Infant and Child: An Illustrated Guide*. OUP 1983 $39.50. ISBN 0-19-503254-4. "Presents 200 malformation syndromes grouped according to fetal environment syndromes, developmental defects, or genetic syndromes. Each syndrome is discussed in terms of clinical features, prenatal diagnosis, differential diagnosis, postnatal basic defects, genetics, prognosis, and age-related progress, prevention, and treatment" (*Choice*).

Haerle, Tracy, ed. *Children with Tourette Syndrome: A Parents' Guide*. Woodbine House 1992 $14.95. ISBN 0-933149-44-1. The medical, social, educational, and legal issues associated with TS addressed in clear, comprehensive essays by specialists and parents.

Hilgard, Josephine R. *Hypnotherapy of Pain in Children with Cancer*. Brunner-Mazel. 1991 repr. of 1989 ed. $19.95. ISBN 0-86576-074-8. "Innovative clinical study of hypnotherapy for children in pain from cancer. Describes limitations and techniques utilized" (*Choice*).

Levin, Toby. *Rainbow of Hope: A Guide for the Special Needs Child*. Starlight FL 1992 $12.95. ISBN 0-9624680-1-0. "This guide will empower parents who are devastated by a diagnosis of disability to regain control over their children's destinies" (*Library Journal*).

Neill, Catherine A., Edward B. Clark, and Carleen Clark. *The Heart of a Child: What Families Need to Know about Heart Disorders in Children*. Johns Hopkins 1993 $24.95. ISBN 0-8018-4234-4. Authoritative source of information about heart disorders in children, risk factors, heart defects, treatment options, and transplantation.

Schopmeyer, Betty B., and Fonda Lowe, eds. *The Fragile X Child*. Singular Publishing 1992 $39.95. ISBN 1-879105-83-7. Superb treatment of the most common form of genetically inherited mental retardation; written by researchers and practitioners.

Shanks, Susan J., ed. *Nursing and the Management of Pediatric Communication Disorders*. College-Hill 1983 o.p. "Concerned with children having speech, language, and hearing disorders. Basic information, definitions, examples, practical approaches, and references" (*Choice*).

Stevens, Maryann. *Breathing Easy: A Parent's Guide to Dealing with Your Child's Asthma*. P-H 1991 $9.95. ISBN 0-13-083692-3. Useful information about the causes, treatment, and term prognosis for asthma.

CHRONIC DISEASES AND LONG-TERM CARE

This section addresses the psychological, physiological, and practical aspects of providing care for those with chronic or long-term illness. The books are written for health care professionals and general readers.

Buckingham, Robert W. *Among Friends: Hospice Care for the Person with AIDS*. Prometheus Bks. 1992 $19.95. ISBN 0-87975-720-5. Sensitive treatment of the history and philosophy of hospice care; special emphasis on benefits for AIDS patients.

Burish, Thomas G., and Laurence A. Bradley. *Coping with Chronic Disease: Research and Applications*. Acad. Pr. 1983 $81.00. ISBN 0-12-144450-3. "Covers the general issues in chronic disease care and research. Specific diseases discussed include obesity, epilepsy, spinal cord injuries, cancer, respiratory disorders, heart disease, and stroke" (*Choice*).

Cailliet, Rene. *Head and Face Pain Syndromes*. Davis Co. 1992 $18.95. ISBN 0-8036-1625-2. Excellent guide to diagnosing and treating chronic pain.

Coombs, Jan. *Living with the Disabled: You Can Help—A Family Guide*. Sterling 1984 o.p. "Includes selection of medical and rehabilitation care, finances, accepting a disability, dealing with stress, and adaption of the environment" (*Library Journal*).

Covell, Mara B., and Eileen Hanley. *The Home Alternative to Hospitals and Nursing Homes: Creating Your Own Home Health Care Center*. Macmillan 1983 $15.95. ISBN 0-89256-236-6. "A thoughtful, compassionate, and detailed treatment of home health care, this runs the gamut from how to set up an appropriate health care environment for different age groups to dealing with a wide variety of health problems" (*Library Journal*).

Friedman, Jo Ann. *Home Health Care: A Guide for Patients and Their Families*. Nat'l League Nurse 1987 $10.95. ISBN 0-449-90230-7. "Complete and readable handbook for anyone involved in, planning for, or contemplating home care. Succinct yet inclusive information of the practical and psychological aspects, specific advice on disease and type of care needed, daily living tips, and insurances and equipment guidelines" (*Library Journal*).

Gohlke, Mary. *I'll Take Tomorrow: The Story of a Courageous Woman Who Dared to Subject Herself to a Medical Experiment; The First Successful Heart-Lung Transplant*. Ed. by Maureen Heffernen. M. Evans 1985 o.p. "Although typical of inspirational success stories, realistically recounts the pain and psychological pressure of chronic disease as well as the consequences of transplantation for the human body" (*Library Journal*).

Hastings, Diana. *A Complete Guide to Home Nursing*. Ed. by Helen L. Maule. Barron 1986 $16.95. ISBN 0-8120-5754-6. "Basic nursing observation techniques and procedures such as lifting the patient, taking vitals, changing bedclothes, and giving bed baths" (*Library Journal*).

Heath, Angela. *Long Distance Caregiving: A Survival Guide for Far Away Caregivers*. The Working Caregiver Ser. Amer. Source Bks. 1993 $9.95. ISBN 0-9621333-9-6. Introductory guide for those facing the prospect of caring for loved ones over long distances. Useful information on planning, dealing with relatives, support groups, legal, and financial issues.

Holzman, Arnold D., ed. *Pain Management: A Handbook of Psychological Treatment Approaches*. Allyn 1986 $56.95. ISBN 0-205-14370-9. "A review of contemporary psychological approaches to treating pain. Presents the state of the art in regard to theory, treatment rationale, and data" (*Choice*).

Horowitz, Karen, and Douglas M. Lanes. *Witness to Illness: Strategies for Caregiving and Coping*. Addison-Wesley 1992 $9.95. ISBN 0-201-63229-2. Practical advice on caring for someone with chronic or acute illness.

Kerson, Toba S., and Lawrence A. Kerson. *Understanding Chronic Illness: The Medical and Psychosocial Dimensions of Nine Diseases*. Free Pr. 1985 $32.95. ISBN 0-02-918200-X. "Discusses financial and other sources of assistance for the chronically ill, describes the medical, social, and psychological aspects of cancer, dementia, diabetes, epilepsy, heart diseases, respiratory diseases, stroke, and substance abuse" (*Choice*).

Lang, Denise, and Derrick M.. *Coping with Lyme Disease: A Practical Guide to Dealing with Diagnosis and Treatment*. H. Holt & Co. 1993 $12.95. ISBN 0-8050-2650-9. Illustrates the financial, physical, and emotional toll of this chronic disease; written by the mother of a teen-age Lyme Disease victim.

Locker, David. *Disability and Disadvantage: The Consequences of Chronic Illness*. Routledge 1984 $15.95. ISBN 0-422-78740-X. "Presents data obtained from interviews with 24 persons severely disabled by rheumatoid arthritis in Great Britain" (*Choice*).

Milunsky, Aubrey, ed. *Coping with Crisis and Handicap*. Plenum Pub. 1981 o.p. "Vivid and cogent writing about the coping efforts of children and families faced with serious crisis, death, and/or handicap; the impact on professionals working with them; and the rich range of creative helping approaches and strategies" (*Choice*).

Nassif, Janet Z. *The Home Health Care Solution: A Complete Consumer Guide*. HarpC 1985 o.p. "A thorough handbook for anyone looking for home care services, resources, alternatives, equipment, personnel, financial advice, and all the nitty-gritty practical aspects of arranging for someone's care" (*Library Journal*).

Slaby, Andrew Edmund, and Arvin Sigmund Glicksman. *Adapting to Life-Threatening Illness*. Greenwood 1985 $55.00. ISBN 0-275-91324-4. "Demonstrates how biological, psychological, and social factors combine to create certain styles of adaptation in three life-threatening conditions: cancer, heart attack, and trauma" (*Choice*).

Steinberg, Franz U. *The Immobilized Patient*. Plenum Pub. 1980 o.p. "A concise and well-written review of the effects of immobilization in patient care. Provides chapters on the general effects of immobilization, as well as specific effects related to circulation, respiration, bone, skeletal muscles, joints, skin, and psychological health" (*Choice*).

Tallmer, Margot, ed. *Sexuality and Life-Threatening Illness*. C. C. Thomas 1984 o.p. "A thought-provoking discussion of the sexual needs of individuals who have been disabled, have a debilitating illness, or are dying" (*Choice*).

COMMUNICABLE DISEASES

[SEE the section on Infectious Diseases in this chapter.]

COSMETIC SURGERY

[SEE the section on Plastic Surgery in this chapter.]

DEAFNESS

[SEE the section on Ear and Throat Disorders in this chapter.]

DEATH AND DYING

Most of the titles in this section examine the philosophy and evolution of the hospice concept of care in the United States. Some books cover the controversial issue of euthanasia. (See also Chapter 5 in this volume.)

Anderson, Patricia. *Affairs in Order: A Complete Resource Guide to Death and Dying*. Macmillan 1993 repr. of 1991 ed. $12.00. ISBN 0-02-030280-0. Comprehensive guide on how to prepare for one's death or the death of a loved one. Divided into three parts: before, during, and after death. The last section is directed at survivors.

Beresford, Larry. *The Hospice Handbook: A Complete Guide*. Little 1993 $12.95. ISBN 0-316-09138-3. Outlines the practical aspects of hospice care and the kinds of services it provides; written by an expert on health policy.

Corr, Charles A., and Donna M. Corr, eds. *Hospice Care: Principles and Practice. Death and Suicide Ser*. Springer Pub. 1983 $34.95. ISBN 0-8261-3540-4. "A comprehensive collection of 26 essays regarding the hospice concept of care. An excellent resource with extensive bibliographic references" (*Choice*).

Dubois, Paul. *The Hospice Way of Death*. Human Sci. Pr. 1980 $35.95. ISBN 0-87705-415-0. Case studies of three hospices—two successful and one unsuccessful. Good description of the state of the hospice movement in the late 1970s.

Hamilton, Michael P. *A Hospice Handbook*. Eerdmans 1980 o.p. Excellent resource, especially for planners of hospice care within the community. Reviews hospice care, fundamentals of the patient's family, and the care-team role in decision making as equals. Introduction by Edward M. Kennedy.

Humphry, Derek, and Ann Wickett. *The Right to Die: Understanding Euthanasia*. Hemlock Soc. 1990 $10.00. ISBN 0-9606030-9-3. "Cofounders of the Hemlock Society in Los Angeles argue for the right of terminally ill people to be delivered from their condition. May help to sway public opinion on an emotional level, but is of limited value as a philosophical and moral approach" (*New York Times Book Review*).

Kevorkian, Jack. *Prescription Medicide: The Goodness of Planned Death*. Prometheus Bks. 1991 $26.95. ISBN 0-87975-677-2. Thought-provoking and controversial discussion of the issues associated with, and the benefits of, planned death; written by one of its leading proponents.

Kübler-Ross, Elisabeth. *Living with Death and Dying*. Macmillan 1982 $9.00. ISBN 0-020-08649-6. "Advocates open expression of feelings about death—denial, anger, fear, and guilt—as an important step in achieving acceptance" (*Publishers Weekly*).

———, ed. *Death: The Final Stage of Growth. Human Development Ser.* S&S Trade 1986 $9.00. ISBN 0-671-62238-2. Essays by various contributors on the philosophical, religious, and sociological approaches to death; a landmark in the field.

Kübler-Ross, Elisabeth, and M. Warshaw. *To Live Until We Say Good-Bye*. P-H 1980 $12.95. ISBN 0-13-922955-8. Beautiful, sensitive book that portrays how Beth, Jamie, Louise, and Jack cope with terminal illness; includes outstanding photographs.

Kutscher, Austin, and Margot Tallmer, eds. *Hospice U.S.A.*. Col. U. Pr. 1983 o.p. "A joint effort of 45 authorities who have had various experiences in establishing hospice alternatives. Topics include the hospice movement; ethical and human issues; helping the dying; alternatives to in-hospice care; and a look to the future" (*Choice*).

Mannon, James M. *Caring for the Burned: Life and Death in a Hospital Burn Center*. C. C. Thomas 1985 $42.50. ISBN 0-398-05089-9. "Provides a rich description and analysis of the setting and of burn patients and their families as well as such issues as pain, work among the burned, patient compliance, the dying patient, recovery, and improving the care of the burned" (*Choice*).

Mumley, Annie. *The Hospice Alternative: A New Context for Death and Dying*. Basic 1983 o.p. "A well-organized and comprehensive report on the hospice concept of care and support for the dying" (*Library Journal*).

Quill, Timothy E. *Death and Dignity: Making Choices and Taking Charge*. Norton 1993 $21.95. ISBN 0-393-03448-8. How the medical profession's emphasis on technology and "life at all costs" ignores the suffering that accompanies terminal illness.

Sankar, Andrea. *Dying at Home: A Family Guide for Caregiving*. Johns Hopkins 1991 $19.95. ISBN 0-8018-4230-1. Explores the physical, social, and emotional impact; written for those already caring for a terminally ill loved one or those considering it.

Siebold, Cathy. *The Hospice Movement: Easing Death's Pains. Social Movements of Past and Present Ser.* Macmillan 1992 $26.95. ISBN 0-8057-3867-3. Examines the accomplishments and failures of the hospice movement using social movement theory.

Wentzel, Kenneth B. *To Those Who Need It Most, Hospice Means Hope*. Charles River Bks. 1980 $20.00. ISBN 0-89182-020-5. Excellent explanation of hospice philosophy and practice.

DIABETES

[SEE the section on Endocrine Diseases in this chapter.]

DIET

[SEE the section on Nutritional Disorders in this chapter
and SEE ALSO Chapter 12 in this volume.]

EAR AND THROAT DISORDERS

The following books provide information on anatomy, physiology, treatment, and preventive measures, as well as the social and psychological aspects of speech and hearing problems.

Benderly, Beryl L. *Dancing without Music: Deafness in America*. Gallaudet U. Pr. 1990 $12.95. ISBN 0-930323-59-9. "Covers deafness as a social role but adds discussions of language acquisition and learning by deaf people, the adventitiously deaf, and mainstreaming, and gives a detailed history of attitudes toward the deaf" (*Library Journal*).

Freese, Arthur S. *You and Your Hearing: How to Protect It, Preserve It, and Restore It.* Macmillan 1980 $3.95. ISBN 0-684-16240-7. "Describes the hearing process and the complex physiological system [that] makes it possible; causes, cures, and preventive measures for some of the most common forms of hearing loss" (*Library Journal*).

Higgins, Paul C. *Outsiders in a Hearing World: A Sociology of Deafness.* Sage 1980 $19.95. ISBN 0-8039-1421-0. "Discusses the identity deviance and stigma associated with members of the deaf community. A major work concerning the sociological aspects of deaf individuals living in a deaf community interacting with a hearing world" (*Choice*).

Lane, Harlan. *When the Mind Hears: A History of the Deaf.* Random 1989 $16.95 ISBN 0-685-27139-0. "Traces the controversy [that] developed between advocates of signing and advocates of oral speech and takes the position that the signing community constitutes a linguistic minority. This book reveals ways in which the deaf have been denied their rights to bear children, to educate themselves, to support themselves" (*Library Journal*).

Rezen, Susan V. *Coping with Hearing Loss: A Guide for Adults and Their Families.* Barricade Bks. 1993 $17.95. ISBN 0-942637-83-6. "A good balance between the social, psychological, physical, and practical aspects of hearing loss" (*Library Journal*).

Schubert, E. D. *Hearing: Its Function and Dysfunction.* Spring-Verlag 1980 $39.00. ISBN 0-387-81579-1. "Concerns normal and abnormal aspects of hearing. Covers anatomy and physiology of the auditory system, psychoacoustics, and hearing loss" (*Choice*).

Sommers, Ronald K. *Articulation Disorders.* P-H 1983 $39.00. ISBN 0-13-049080-6. "A succinct and complete discussion of articulation disorders and related issues. Presents a framework for understanding and treating aberrant articulatory behavior in children and adults" (*Choice*).

Thomsett, Kay, and Eve Nickerson. *Missing Words: The Family Handbook on Adult Hearing Loss.* Gallaudet U. Pr. 1993 $21.95. ISBN 1-56368-023-8. Easy-to-read book that provides insight and in-depth information about progressive adult hearing loss; written by a mother-daughter team.

Turkington, Carol, and Allen Sussman. *Encyclopedia of Deafness and Hearing Disorders.* Facts on File 1992 $45.00. ISBN 0-8160-2267-4. Comprehensive overview of deafness and hearing disorders organized in an A-Z format; includes biographical information, suggested readings, and a range of appendices covering organizations and support services.

EMERGENCY MEDICINE

The following books provide information on deciding whether or not injured or acutely ill patients need immediate medical treatment. Some books cover basic first aid and the organization and management of emergency medical services.

American Medical Association. *American Medical Association Pocket Guide to Emergency First Aid.* Random 1993 $3.99. ISBN 0-679-74672-2. Authoritative advice on numerous common emergency medical situations. Describes how to distinguish between true emergencies and problems that are alarming to the victim but do not require immediate emergency help and when and how to call the doctor, emergency room, and ambulance.

American Red Cross. *Standard First Aid.* Mosby Yr. Bk. 1993 $6.00. ISBN 0-685-61103-5. Concise directions on wounds and severe bleeding; treating specific injuries, such as head injuries; managing choking, shock, and poisoning. Also covers bandages and dressing and emergency rescue.

Auerbach, Paul S. *Medicine for the Outdoors: A Guide to Emergency Medical Procedures and First Aid for Wilderness Travelers*. Little 1991 $27.95. ISBN 0-316-05932-3. Concise explanations of a wide range of medical problems. General information precedes sections on specific procedures.

Franklin, Jon, and Alan Doelp. *Shock-Trauma*. Fawcett 1981 $4.95. ISBN 0-449-24387-7. "Chronicles the establishment of the Maryland Institute of Emergency Services and the obstacles, both political and financial, that threatened it" (*Library Journal*).

Heimlich, Henry J., and Lawrence Galton. *Dr. Heimlich's Guide to Emergency Medical Situations*. S&S Trade 1984 $5.95. ISBN 0-671-53075-5. Information on more than 250 emergency situations. Describes how to recognize what is wrong, how to cope, and when to seek medical help; written by the inventor of the Heimlich maneuver.

Lefevre, M. J., ed. *First Aid Manual for Chemical Accidents: For Use with Nonpharmaceutical Chemicals*. Trans. by Ernest I. Becker. Van Nos. Reinhold 1989 $34.95. ISBN 0-442-20490-6. "A ready reference for emergency treatment of chemical accidents. The procedures given are based on those developed by recognized authorities and a major chemical producer" (*Choice*).

Newkirk, William, and William Linden. *Managing in the Emergency Medical Services: Principles and Practice*. P-H 1984 $41.00. ISBN 0-8359-4198-1. "Divided into five sections: techniques for management by objectives, project evaluation, and review; organization of personnel and finances; effective communication, negotiating, delegation, and handling of change; quality control; and survival as an EMS manager in terms of coping with stress" (*Choice*).

Waller, Julian A. *Injury Control: A Guide to the Causes and Prevention of Trauma*. Lexington Bks. 1984 o.p. "Presents an overview of concepts, methods, and problems of injury control and discusses models for analyzing injury events, contributing factors, and guidelines for evaluating countermeasures" (*Choice*).

Wilkerson, James A., and others. *Hypothermia, Frostbite and Other Cold Injuries: Prevention, Recognition, and Pre-Hospital Treatment*. Mountaineers 1986 $11.95. ISBN 0-89886-024-5. "Written for outdoor enthusiasts and attendant emergency medical personnel. Explains the stages of physiological deterioration of the human body as its core temperature decreases. Discusses recognizing hypothermia and procedures for rewarming" (*Library Journal*).

Williams, Susan, and Barbara McVan, eds. *Giving Emergency Care Competently*. Springhouse Pub. 1983 o.p. "Deals with all types of emergency situations from triage to cardiovascular, neuro, respiratory, and psychiatric emergencies" (*Choice*).

ENDOCRINE DISEASES

Endocrine diseases result from abnormal functioning of the endocrine glands (e.g., thyroid, pituitary, pancreas). Books about endocrine diseases are written by and for health care professionals. However, many books have been published for the general reader on diabetes, a condition caused by a malfunction of the pancreas. A representative selection of these books are described below.

Anderson, James W. *Diabetes*. Warner Bks. 1987 $4.95. ISBN 0-446-34399-4. "A comprehensive guide to the treatment of diabetes through the High Carbohydrate High Fiber diet. Also discusses insulin, obesity, and complications of diabetes" (*Library Journal*).

Bayliss, R. I. S. *Thyroid Disease: The Facts*. OUP 1991 $19.95. ISBN 0-19-26104-1. Describes the functioning of the thyroid gland, how it manufactures hormones, and the complex interaction of the thyroid and pituitary gland. Discusses diagnosis, treatment, and prognosis for thyroid disorders such as hyperthyroidism, Hashimoto's (autoimmune) thyroiditis, goiter, hypothyroidism, and cancer of the thyroid gland.

Bliss, Michael. *The Discovery of Insulin*. U. Ch. Pr. 1982 $25.00. ISBN 0-226-05897-2. "Re-creates the complex and dramatic series of events at the University of Toronto in

1921–22. Describes the treatment of diabetes before insulin and the research of earlier scientists and concludes by outlining the treatment of diabetes with insulin and the current production of human insulin through the development of genetic engineering" (*Library Journal*).

Brisco, Paula. *Diabetes: Questions You Have—Answers You Need*. People's Med. Soc. 1993 $9.95. ISBN 1-882606-02-7. In-depth coverage of the various types of diabetes and extensive discussion of complications.

Diabetes Education Center. *Diabetes: The Comprehensive Self-Management Handbook*. Ed. by John R. Aloia. Doubleday 1984 o.p. "A reference text for people who have diabetes: self-testing, control of insulin, meal preparation, exercise . . . everyone can learn a great deal from it in the general areas of nutrition, weight control, stress, food labeling, how the body works, and more" (*Library Journal*).

Edelwich, Jerry, and Archie Brodsky. *Diabetes: Caring for Your Emotions as Well as Your Health*. Addison-Wesley 1987 $17.95. ISBN 0-201-10609-4. "Covered extensively are diet, exercise, work, medications, sexuality, and new technology. Emphasis is on changes in lifestyle and family relations resulting from the disease" (*Library Journal*).

Hamilton, Helen, and Minnie B. Rose, eds. *Endocrine Disorders*. Springhouse Pub. 1984 o.p. "Reviews the anatomy and physiology of the endocrine system and the pathophysiology of endocrine imbalance; nursing assessment and guidelines for developing a nursing diagnosis; diagnostic tests; and specific disorders" (*Choice*).

Raymond, Mike. *The Human Side of Diabetes: Beyond Doctors, Diets and Drugs*. Noble Pr. 1991 $13.95. ISBN 1-879360-09-8. "A personable, well-written and welcome addition to the small library of first-hand accounts of the psychological aspects of living with diabetes" (*Library Journal*).

Subak-Sharpe, Genell. *Living with Diabetes: The Revolutionary Self-Care Diabetes Program Developed by Rockefeller and Cornell University Researchers*. Doubleday 1985 o.p. "Intended to provide a better understanding of the disease and the manner in which the treatment can be adjusted to fit one's lifestyle" (*Library Journal*).

Wood, Lawrence C., David S. Cooper, and Chester E. Ridgway. *Your Thyroid: A Home Reference*. Ballantine 1986 $4.95. ISBN 0-345-33447-7. "Devotes individual chapters to such problems as goiter, disorders associated with hyper- and hypothyroidism, thyroid cancer in adults and children, and the effects of drugs, food, stress, and radiation on the thyroid" (*Library Journal*).

EPIDEMIOLOGY

Epidemiology is concerned with the determination of causes, frequency, and characteristic behavior of diseases affecting human populations; it also covers the interrelationships of host, agent, and environment in relation to the distribution and control of disease. (See also Chapter 12 in this volume.)

Brilliant, Lawrence B. *The Management of Smallpox Eradication in India*. U. of Mich. Pr. 1985 o.p. "Using a case study approach, the author documents the chronology of smallpox eradication in India, analyzes aspects of program management, and summarizes management lessons learned from this program" (*Choice*).

Cipolla, Carlo M. *Cristofano and the Plague: A Study in the History of Public Health in the Age of Galileo*. U. CA Pr. 1973 o.p. "Information from Tuscan archives enabled the author to analyze the demographic and economic consequences of the epidemic of plague [that] ravaged northern Italy around 1630. He speculates that all the epidemics of plague [that] occurred during the entire period 1613–66 belonged to one single pandemic cycle [that] swept across the subcontinent [and] concludes that besides medical ignorance and the absence of cooperation from the mass of the people, the lack of adequate economic resources was perhaps the most important factor in frustrating the work of the public health officers" (*American Scientist*).

Culyer, A. J., ed. *Health Indicators: An International Study for the European Science Foundation*. St. Martin 1983 $32.50. ISBN 0-312-36530-6. Papers from three workshops held at the University of York from 1979 to 1981, established by the British Social Science Research Council. "An attempt to find more subtle ways of measuring health than by death or obvious disability, so that such measures can be used affirmatively for the health of the nation" (*Choice*).

Goodfield, June. *Quest for the Killers*. Hill & Wang 1987 $9.95. ISBN 0-8090-1532-3. "Links medical progress over epidemic disease with social philosophy. Brings a sense of personal immediacy to the story of the triumphs over smallpox, leprosy, and schistosomiasis" (*Library Journal*).

Greenberg, Michael R. *Urbanization and Cancer Mortality: The United States Experience, 1950–1975*. OUP 1983 $45.00. ISBN 0-19-530173-3. "Analyzing cancer mortality data by age, race, and sex for each of the five-year periods extending from 1950 to 1975, this book provides information showing that whereas 25 years ago central U.S. cities had much higher rates of many types of cancer than the rest of the country, the difference between urban and rural areas has diminished considerably over the period examined" (*Choice*).

Gruenberg, Ernest M., and others, eds. *Vaccinating against Brain Dysfunction Syndromes: The Campaign against Measles and Rubella*. OUP 1986 $29.95. ISBN 0-19-503631-X. "Thirty well-recognized authorities in the fields of epidemiology, public health, immunology, bacteriology, pediatrics, and psychiatry tell the success story of the near eradication of rubella and measles in the U.S." (*Choice*).

Rothschild, Henry R., ed. *Biocultural Aspects of Disease*. Acad. Pr. 1981 $134.00. ISBN 0-12-598720-X. "Excellent reviews of how prevalent worldwide diseases, such as malaria, trypanosomiasis, leishmaniasis, schistosomiasis, amebiasis, cholera, diarrhea, and thalassemia (to name only a few), interact with the culture, habitat, and genotypes of people around the globe. . . . Chapters on disease susceptibility, prevalence of disease, rare hereditary diseases, cultural beliefs associated with disease and health care, and social impacts of diseases" (*Choice*).

Rouechè, Berton. *The Medical Detectives*. NAL-Dutton 1991 $10.95. ISBN 0-457-26588-6. The 45 essays in these collections originally appeared in *The New Yorker* between 1947 and 1990. The detectives of these tales are epidemiologists, public health officers, hospital staff members, and family doctors. The case histories include organic mercury in a hog farmer's family and the man who turned orange from eating too many carrots and tomatoes; other case histories involve strange illnesses, rare diseases, and the threat of plague.

Ryan, Frank. *The Forgotten Plague: How the Battle against Tuberculosis Was Won—and Lost*. Little 1993 $24.95. ISBN 0-316-76380-2. "A compelling picture of the process of scientific research as well as a troubling look at an emerging public health crisis" (*Library Journal*).

Thomas, Gordon, and Max Morgan-Witts. *Anatomy of an Epidemic*. Doubleday 1982 o.p. "Effectively interweaves the tragic human story of some of the victims of the epidemic of Legionnaire's Disease that occurred in the summer of 1976 in Pennsylvania, with the hard work and good science that eventually solved the mystery" (*Library Journal*).

Vogt, Thomas M. *Making Health Decisions: An Epidemiologic Perspective on Staying Well*. Nelson-Hall 1983 o.p. "Readable, entertaining, and thoughtful examination of personal health decisions based on a careful review of epidemiological data. Begins with a brief and entertaining survey of what epidemiology has done and can (cannot) do" (*Choice*).

EYE DISORDERS

Because most monographs on eye disorders are written for a professional audience, there are a limited number of entries in this section.

Dobree, John H., and Eric Boulter. *Blindness and Visual Handicap: The Facts*. OUP 1982 $13.95. ISBN 0-19-261328-6. "Deals primarily with diseases causing blindness, the effects of blindness, and how the blind and partially sighted can be helped. Relates primarily to practices and programming in England, with a few international components" (*Choice*).

Hine, Robert V. *Second Sight*. U. CA Pr. 1993 $20.00. ISBN 0-520-08195-1. Sensitive story of a man who slowly lost his vision in graduate school and underwent a risky operation that restored partial sight to one eye.

Kelman, Charles D. *Cataracts: What You Must Know about Them*. Crown Pub. Group 1982 $14.00. ISBN 0-517-54850-X. "Lucid descriptions of surgical techniques. What to expect after surgery and methods for achieving visual correction after surgery" (*Library Journal*).

Resources for Rehabilitation Staff. *Living with Low Vision: A Resource Guide for People with Sight Loss*. Resc. Rehab. 1993 $35.00. ISBN 0-929718-09-7. Comprehensive reference describing resources for individuals with low vision.

Rosenbloom, Alfred A., and Meredith Morgan. *Vision and Aging*. Buttrwrth-Heinemann 1993 $69.95. ISBN 0-7506-9311-8. "A comprehensive treatment of the relationship between aging and vision changes. Explores the assessment and correction of visual problems in the elderly, also looks at the psychosocial environment as it pertains to visual function" (*Choice*).

Shulman, Julius. *Cataracts: The Complete Guide from Diagnosis to Recovery for Patients and Families*. Am. Assn. Retire. 1987 $7.95. ISBN 0-673-24824-0. "Reviews the fundamentals of cataracts, the parts of the eye and probable causes of cataracts. Details cataract surgery, with an in-depth discussion of the three major types: intracapsular, extracapsular, and phaecoemulsification" (*Library Journal*).

FIRST AID

[SEE the section on Emergency Medicine in this chapter.]

GASTROINTESTINAL DISEASES

Most books on diseases of the digestive system are written for professionals who provide patient care. Therefore, there are few entries in the following section.

Ehrlich, David, and George Wolf. *The Bowel Book: A Practical Guide to Good Health*. Schocken 1987 $9.95. ISBN 0-8052-0673-6. "Addresses such subject areas as the way the gastrointestinal system works, the effects of emotion on it, methods of improving bowel function, and bowel disorders" (*Library Journal*).

Janowitz, Henry. *Indigestion: Living Better with Upper Intestinal Problems from Heartburn to Ulcers and Gallstones*. OUP 1992 $18.00. ISBN 0-19-506308-2. Answers questions about the causes and prevention of common gastrointestinal disorders; companion to earlier *Your Gut Feelings*, by the same author.

Jeter, Katherine. *These Special Children: The Ostomy Book for Parents of Children with Colostomies, Ileostomies, and Urostomies*. Bull Pub. 1982 o.p. Excellent, insightful text.

Mullen, Barbara D., and Kerry A. McGinn. *The Ostomy Book: Living Comfortably with Colostomies, Ileostomies, and Urostomies*. Bull Pub. 1991 $14.95. ISBN 0-923521-12-7. "A wealth of information concerning the psychological as well as medical aspects of ostomy surgery, care of the body after the procedure, equipment, diet and exercise" (*Library Journal*).

Mylander, Maureen. *The Great American Stomach Book*. Ticknor & Fields 1982 o.p. "Explores the range of digestive diseases from such common problems as indigestion and hiccups to such serious afflictions as hepatitis and gastrointestinal cancer" (*Library Journal*).

National Foundation for Ileitis and Colitis. *The Crohn's Disease and Ulcerative Colitis Fact Book*. Ed. by Peter A. Banks, Daniel H. Present, and Penny Steiner. Macmillan 1983 $18.95. ISBN 0-684-17967-9. "Traces the causes, symptoms, and diagnosis of the diseases, discusses the various treatment options from medication to surgery, and concludes with advice on coping with the illnesses" (*Library Journal*).

Phillips, Robert. *Coping with an Ostomy: A Guide to Living with an Ostomy*. Avery 1986 $9.95. ISBN 0-89529-277-7. "Explains ostomy surgery and care of the ostomy. Greatest value lies in its coverage of the emotional and lifestyle changes caused by an ostomy" (*Library Journal*).

Plaut, Martin E. *The Doctor's Guide to You and Your Colon: A Candid, Helpful Guide to Our Number One Hidden Health Complaint*. HarpC 1982 o.p. "In this highly readable guide, Plaut explains how the bowel works, the process of digestion, and how stool is formed" (*Library Journal*).

Thompson, W. G. *The Angry Gut: Coping with Colitis and Crohn's Disease*. Plenum Pub. 1993 $26.95. ISBN 0-306-44470-4. Especially useful resource for understanding and coping with digestive-tract disease and disorders.

HEARING DISORDERS

[SEE the section on Ear and Throat Disorders in this chapter.]

HEART DISEASES

[SEE the section on Cardiovascular Diseases in this chapter.]

HEMATOLOGIC DISEASES

Hematologic diseases are diseases of the blood and blood-forming tissues. Most books on diseases affecting the blood are very technical; therefore, the paucity of entries.

Callender, Sheila T. *Blood Disorders: The Facts*. OUP 1986 $18.50. ISBN 0-19-261473-8. Discusses the various blood abnormalities and disorders resulting from variances in normal function; disease mechanisms, diagnosis, relevant blood tests, and the rationale behind the treatment" (*Choice*).

Johnson, Mohamed Ismail. *The World and the Sickle-Cell Gene: A Study in Health Education*. Trado-Medic 1984 o.p. "Brings together essential information related to sickle-cell disease. Covers the relationship of sickle-cell disease and malaria, the inheritance process and geographic distribution of the disease, personal and community health and education problems associated with sickle-cell disease, and diagnostic and management approaches" (*Choice*).

IMMUNOLOGY

Immunology is the study of how the body's immune system responds to pathogenic (disease-causing) organisms and other foreign bodies. Because the immune system recognizes self from nonself, it must be suppressed if a transplanted organ (kidney, heart, or lung) is to be accepted successfully by the body. Immunization is the process by which human beings are rendered immune to disease (e.g., whooping cough, diphtheria, tetanus) by injection of a weakened or dead culture of a specific microbe. Allergies are an acquired sensitivity in persons susceptible to allergens, such as a specific drug, chemical, or pollen. Asthma is a condition in which there is widespread narrowing of the airways in the lungs in the course of an allergic reaction. The first half of this section mainly covers allergies and asthma; the second section is devoted to Acquired Immune Deficiency Syndrome (AIDS).

Allergies and Asthma

Berland, Theodore, and Lucia Fischer-Pap. *Living with Your Allergies and Asthma*. St. Martin 1983 $5.95. ISBN 0-312-49249-9. "Meant to help the allergy sufferer understand the affliction and be able to find solutions and proper methods of treatment" (*Library Journal*).

Dadd, Debra Lynn. *Nontoxic, Natural & Earthwise*. J. P. Tarcher 1990 $12.95. ISBN 0-87477-584-1. Promotes the use of nontoxic products that are safe for humans and the environment; also includes source lists of companies in the United States from which allergy sufferers can purchase nontoxic products.

Faelton, Sharon. *The Allergy Self-Help Book: A Complete Guide to Detection and Natural Treatment of Allergies*. Rodale Pr. Inc. 1983 $21.95. ISBN 0-87857-458-1. "An exhaustive treatment of the controversial subject of allergy identification and treatment" (*Library Journal*).

Frazier, Claude A. *Coping with Food Allergy: Symptoms and Treatment*. Random 1985 $8.95. ISBN 0-8129-1149-0. "Includes the RAST test; new medications such as cromolyn sodium; allergies to the food preservatives and additives BHA, BHT, MSG and sulfites; and the efforts to get all food ingredients labeled" (*Library Journal*).

Levin, Alan Scott, and Merla Zellerbach. *The Type 1/Type 2 Allergy Relief Program*. Berkley Pub. 1985 $3.50. ISBN 0-425-09044-2. "Defines each type, explains the symptoms, allergens, and treatment, and presents case histories" (*Library Journal*).

Reisman, Barry. *Jared's Story: A Boy in a Bubble and How His Family Saved His Life*. Crown Pub. Group 1984 $10.95. ISBN 0-517-55423-2. "About a baby who after 18 months of normal behavior became incapacitated by a mysterious ailment" (*Library Journal*).

Rothera, Ellen. *Encyclopedia of Allergy and Environmental Illness: A Self-Help Approach*. Sterling 1991 $19.95. ISBN 0-7153-9954-3. Excellent synthesis from a variety of sources on environmental allergies. Discusses medical conditions that can be caused by household cleaners, air pollution, cooking gas, and other agents.

Stevens, Laura J. *The Complete Book of Allergy Control*. Macmillan 1983 $14.95. ISBN 0-02-614450-6. "Informs sufferers of the environmental causes of allergies, helps them identify allergens, and teaches them how to manage these problems" (*Library Journal*).

Young, Stuart H. *The Asthma Handbook: A Complete Guide for Patients and Their Families*. Bantam 1989 $9.95. ISBN 0-553-34712-8. "An excellent guide which covers environmental and dietary factors that contribute to the disease, drug and physical therapies and the role of stress in attacks" (*Library Journal*).

AIDS

Bartlett, John G. *The Johns Hopkins Guide to the Medical Care of Patients with HIV Infection*. Williams & Wilkins 1992 $10.00. ISBN 0-683-00447-6. Comprehensive caregiver's guide; includes well-illustrated procedures and cautions.

Bartlett, John G., and Ann K. Finkbeiner. *The Guide to Living with HIV Infection: Developed at the Johns Hopkins AIDS Clinic*. Johns Hopkins 1993 $40.00. ISBN 0-8018-4663-3. Comprehensive resource that addresses the medical, legal, and emotional aspects of living with AIDS.

Brown, Marie A., and Gail M. Powell-Cope. *Caring for a Loved One with AIDS: The Experiences of Families, Lovers, and Friends*. U. of Wash. Pr. 1992 $4.95. ISBN 0-295-97183-5. Conversational guide to meeting the needs of caregivers and AIDS patients.

Callen, Michael. *Surviving AIDS*. HarpC 1991 repr. of 1990 ed. $10.00. ISBN 0-06-092125-0. Excellent narrative by an individual who has been HIV-positive for more than 10 years.

Cantwell, Alan, Jr. *AIDS: The Mystery and the Solution*. Ed. by Jim Highland. Aries Rising 1986 $14.95. ISBN 0-917211-08-1. "One more example of the effort to explain AIDS. Asks some fundamental questions about the assumptions used by the medical and scientific community in evaluating the nature and cause of the illness" (*Choice*).

Corea, Gena. *The Invisible Epidemic: The Story of Women and AIDS*. HarpC 1992 $23.00. ISBN 0-06-016648-7. "Using in-depth interviews and sources in the popular and scientific literature, Corea offers a chronology of the impact of this epidemic on the female population" (*Library Journal*).

Corless, Inge, and Mary Pittman-Lindeman. *AIDS: Principles, Practices, and Politics*. Hemisphere Pub. 1989 $95.00. ISBN 0-89116-716-1. Collection of essays, including one by former Surgeon General C. Everett Koop, on many aspects of AIDS, such as education, alternatives to hospital care, and legal considerations.

Dane, Barbara O., and Samuel O. Miller. *AIDS: Intervening with Hidden Grievers*. Greenwood 1992 $45.00. ISBN 0-86569-028-6. Explores how caregivers, lovers, family members, and members of the health care team respond to death; drawn from interviews, support groups, and clinical experiences with survivors of persons who have died from AIDS.

Fee, Elizabeth, and Daniel M. Fox, eds. *AIDS: The Burden of History*. U. CA Pr. 1988 $35.00. ISBN 0-520-06395-3. Erudite analysis of the place of AIDS in history; series of contributions from historians and social scientists that are accessible to the general reader.

———. *AIDS: The Making of a Chronic Disease*. U. CA Pr. 1992 $45.00. ISBN 0-520-07569-2. Important collection of historiographic essays describing the change in perception of AIDS from a classic plague to a chronic infection.

Feldman, William H., and others, eds. *The AIDS Directory: An Essential Guide to the 1500 Leaders in Research, Services, Policy, Advocacy and Funding*. Buraff Pubns. 1993 $250.00. ISBN 1-882594-00-2. Profiles more than 1,500 AIDS-related organizations, agencies, support groups, and service providers, supplemented by 10 indexes.

Fettner, Ann Giudici, and William A. Check. *The Truth about AIDS: Evolution of an Epidemic*. H. Holt & Co. 1985 o.p. Narrative of the discovery of AIDS by physicians from the Centers of Disease Control and other leading medical centers.

Froman, Paul K. *After You Say Goodbye: When Someone You Love Dies of AIDS*. Chronicle Bks. 1992 $10.95. ISBN 0-8118-0088-1. Empathetic personal guide to the emotional, practical, spiritual, and political aspects of AIDS-related death.

Gallo, Robert. *Virus Hunting: AIDS, Cancer and the Human Retrovirus; A Story of Scientific Discovery*. Basic 1993 $15.00. ISBN 0-465-09815-0. Easy-to-read account of political intrigue and scientific accomplishment in which the author defends his stake in the discovery of the AIDS virus.

Glaser, Elizabeth, and Laura Palmer. *In the Absence of Angels: A Hollywood Family's Courageous Story*. Putnam 1991 $21.95. ISBN 0-399-13577-4. The emotional story of the impact of AIDS on a well-known family. Describes how Glaser turned her anguish into political activism.

Gong, Victor, and Norman Rudnick, eds. *AIDS: Facts and Issues*. Rutgers U. Pr. 1986 o.p. Twenty-five essays, contributed by experts in the fields of health care, social welfare, education, and law, provide current information about AIDS" (*Library Journal*).

Huber, Jeffrey T., ed. *Dictionary of AIDS-Related Terminology*. Neal-Schuman 1993 $39.95. ISBN 1-55570-117-5. Useful compendium of definitions of technical terms associated with AIDS and HIV.

———. *How to Find Information About AIDS*. Haworth Pr. 1991 $32.95. ISBN 1-56024-140-3. Easy-to-use directory offering comprehensive listings for service organizations, federal agencies, education centers, among others.

Jacobs, George, and Joseph Kerrins. *The AIDS File*. Cromlech Bks. 1987 $7.95. ISBN 0-9618059-0-0. Focuses on techniques for prevention of AIDS transmission and provides answers to frequently asked questions about AIDS.

Jarvis, Debra. *The Journey through AIDS: A Guide for Loved Ones and Caregivers*. Lion USA 1992 $9.99. ISBN 0-7459-2220-1. Practical but compassionate guide for caregivers offering detailed information on daily care.

Jarvis, Robert M., and others. *AIDS Law in a Nutshell*. West Pub. 1992 repr. of 1990 ed. $15.95. ISBN 0-314-80908-2. Compendium of laws related to AIDS.

Joseph, Stephen. *Dragon within the Gates: The Once and Future AIDS Epidemic*. Carroll & Graf 1992 $20.95. ISBN 0-88184-905-7. Cogent argument for quarantine, contact tracking, mandatory reporting, voluntary testing, needle exchange programs, and condom distribution programs.

Kayal, Philip M. *Bearing Witness: Gay Men's Health Crisis and the Politics of AIDS*. Westview 1993 $55.00. ISBN 0-8133-1728-2. Fascinating biography of one of the largest and most influential independent agencies committed to AIDS education, research and assistance.

Kittredge, Mary. *Teens with Aids Speak Out*. Thorndike Pr. 1993 $15.95. ISBN 1-56054-691-3. Emotional and informative text in which teenagers tell how they contracted AIDS, what it is like to live with, and what information is necessary to prevent HIV infection.

Mann, Jonathan, Daniel J. Tarantola, and Thomas Netter, eds. *AIDS in the World, 1992*. HUP 1992 $45.00. ISBN 0-674-01265-8. Well-documented assessment of the impact of AIDS worldwide, the global response, key policy issues, and future ramifications.

Martelli, Leonard, and others. *When Someone You Know Has AIDS: A Practical Guide*. Crown Pub. Group 1993 $16.00. ISBN 0-517-88039-3. Useful and substantive guide to providing assistance to AIDS patients; includes sections on insurance, health maintenance, wills, and grieving.

National Commission on Acquired Immune Deficiency Syndrome. *America Living with AIDS: Transforming Anger, Fear, and Indifference into Action; Report of the National Commission on Acquired Immune Deficiency Syndrome*. Diane Pub. 1992 $124.95. ISBN 1-56806-106-4. Recommendation for a national policy on AIDS in the United States; from a controversial commission established by former President Reagan.

Nixon, Bebe, and Nichola Nixon. *People with AIDS*. Godine 1991 $45.00. ISBN 0-87923-908-5. Extraordinary juxtaposition of photographs and testimony from persons suffering with the disease.

Pogash, Carol. *As Real As It Gets: The Life of a Hospital at the Center of the AIDS Epidemic*. Carol Pub. Group 1992 $18.95. ISBN 1-55972-127-8. Remarkable tale of life on the wards of San Francisco General Hospital during the AIDS epidemic.

Sergios, Paul. *One Boy at War: A Life in the AIDS Underground*. Knopf 1993 $23.00. ISBN 0-679-41839-3. Personal narrative of a young California man that relates his efforts to cope with an HIV-positive diagnosis and then full-blown AIDS.

Shilts, Randy. *And the Band Played On: Politics, People and the AIDS Epidemic*. St. Martin 1987 $24.95. ISBN 0-312-00994-1. Comprehensive chronicle of the AIDS epidemic from 1981 to 1986. Scientific but disjointed chronologies trace the clinical and epidemiological story of AIDS, scientific research, and the impact of the disease on both individuals and society at large; accessible to the general reader.

Siegal, Frederick P., and Marta Siegal. *AIDS: The Medical Mystery*. Grove Pr. 1983 $12.50. ISBN 0-394-62496-3. "Provides an authoritative description of the disease, its physical manifestations, social dilemmas, possible causes, available but as yet unsuccessful forms of therapy" (*Choice*).

Wilton, Tamsin. *Antibody Politic: AIDS and Society*. New Clarion Pr. 1993 $44.50. ISBN 1-873797-05-2. Introduction to AIDS as a social phenomenon; written by a British professor of health and women's studies.

Women, AIDS, and Activism. ACT-UP–New York Women and AIDS Book Group Staff. South End Pr. 1990 $25.00. ISBN 0-89608-394-2. Comprehensive analysis of recent issues concerning women and AIDS.

INFECTIOUS DISEASES

Infectious diseases are caused by organisms ranging in size from microscopic viruses to large parasitic worms. They might be contagious in origin, result from nosocomial (hospital-acquired) infection or they might result from endogenous microflora inhabiting the nose and throat, skin, or bowel. Communicable diseases are transmitted from one human to another or from an animal or insect to a human, either directly or indirectly. The following books cover the history, epidemiology, treatment, and prevention of infectious and communicable diseases.

Balfour, Henry H. Jr., and Ralph C. Heussner. *Herpes Diseases and Your Health.* U. of Minn. Pr. 1984 o.p. "Describes the transmission, clinical course, treatment and aftereffects of genital herpes, chicken pox, shingles, mononucleosis, and cytomegalovirus infection" (*Library Journal*).

Beveridge, W. I. *Influenza, the Last Great Plague: An Unfinished Story of Discovery.* Watson Pub. Intl. 1977 $12.50. ISBN 0-88202-125-7. "Develops the reasons why influenza differs from other major worldwide infectious diseases. Notes how evidence has gradually shown the mechanism by which major waves of infection spread across the countries of the world" (*Choice*).

Brandt, Allan M. *"No Magic Bullet": A Social History of Venereal Disease in the United States since 1880.* OUP 1987 $37.00. ISBN 0-19-503469-4. "More a study of social attitudes and medicine than a social history, this book shows how attitudes affect attempts to control disease" (*Library Journal*).

Brettle, R. P., and M. Thomson. *Infection and Communicable Diseases.* Heyden 1984 o.p. "Gives up-to-date accounts of management and control including specific therapy and nursing care involved with the common bacterial and viral infections as well as rarer conditions such as those acquired by travellers" (*Choice*).

Chase, Allan. *The Truth about STD: The Old Ones—Herpes and Other New Ones—The Primary Causes—The Available Cures.* Morrow 1983 o.p. "An overview of the sexually transmitted disease problem in the U.S. today. Of particular interest is the historic perspective on the sexually transmitted disease problem" (*Choice*).

Desowitz, Robert S. *The Malaria Capers: More Tales of Parasites and People, Research and Reality.* Norton 1991 $21.95. ISBN 0-393-03013-X. Engaging narrative about how malaria and leishmaniasis have reappeared worldwide after nearly being eradicated.

Donaldson, R. J. *Parasites and Western Man.* Univ. Park Pr. 1979 $32.00. ISBN 0-8391-1432-X. "Deals mainly with parasites in the Western, developed countries. Covers all aspects of both internal and external parasites as well as the interrelations of man and other animals" (*Choice*).

Freudberg, Frank. *Herpes: A Complete Guide to Relief and Reassurance.* Running Pr. 1982 o.p. "A comprehensive and easy-to-understand summary of what is known about the diagnosis and management of herpes virus infections" (*Choice*).

Gregg, Charles T. *A Virus of Love and Other Tales of Medical Detection.* U. of NM Pr. 1985 o.p. "An introduction to the likes of swine flu, Legionnaire's disease, Reye syndrome, and herpes. A fascinating account as seen by epidemiologists, researchers, physicians, and the afflicted" (*Choice*).

Gurevich, Inge, and Burke A. Cunha. *The Theory and Practice of Infection Control.* Greenwood 1984 o.p. "An excellent compilation of information on the most commonly encountered infectious diseases. Comprehensive and in sufficient detail to serve as a valuable reference" (*Choice*).

Hamilton, Richard. *The Herpes Book.* St. Martin 1980 o.p. Essential facts on how herpes is contracted and prevented, symptoms, and the course of the disease. Reviews the history, evolution, and knowledge about herpes virus infections in people.

Hopkins, Donald R. *Princes and Peasants: Smallpox in History.* U. Ch. Pr. 1983 $25.00. ISBN 0-226-35176-9. "Proceeding civilization by civilization, European, African, Asian, and New World, Hopkins has made extensive literary and documentary searches to discover when smallpox was first noted and how it affected the impacted culture. Traces the history of inoculation and then the development of vaccination" (*Choice*).

Jones, James H. *Bad Blood: The Tuskegee Syphilis Experiment.* Free Pr. 1993 $22.95. ISBN 0-02-916675-6. The Tuskegee study (by the Public Health Service from 1932 to 1972) was conducted to follow the course of syphilis. Most of the subjects thought they were being helped by the various tests they underwent. Strongly critical of participating physicians and health personnel for withholding information and treatment from patients.

Langston, Deborah P. *Living with Herpes: The Comprehensive and Authoritative Guide to the Causes, Symptoms, and Treatments of Herpes Viruses.* Doubleday 1983 o.p. "Describes the various viruses, the types and methods of infection, and the varieties of treatment. Discusses the relation between herpes and cancer and pregnancy, birth, and the postnatal period" (*Library Journal*).

Meltzer, Alan S. *Sexually Transmitted Disease: Guidelines for Physicians and Health Workers.* Eden Press 1971 o.p. "Highlights some practical aspects of the problem of the increasing incidence of sexually transmitted diseases" (*Choice*).

Neustadt, Richard E., and Harvey V. Fineberg. *The Epidemic That Never Was: Policy-Making and the Swine Flu Scare (The Swine Flu Affair).* Random rev. ed. 1983 o.p. "The 1976 swine flu crisis prompted a massive federal immunization program, which had questionable benefits and serious side effects in a small number of cases. Well written, indeed it is more like a novel than a complex government document" (*Choice*).

Ostrow, David G., and Yehudi M. Felman, eds. *Sexually Transmitted Diseases in Homosexual Men: Diagnosis, Treatment, and Research.* Plenum Pub. 1983 $55.00. ISBN 0-306-41337-X. "Material ranges from general considerations to discussions of specific types of sexually transmitted diseases" (*Choice*).

Paul, John Rodman. *A History of Poliomyelitis.* Yale U. Pr. 1971 o.p. Paul, who headed the Yale Poliomyelitis Study unit for almost 40 years after its foundation in 1931, here tells "the history [of the disease], starting with ancient records in Egypt and Greece, to the observations of Dr. Caufield on an epidemic of 'lame distemper' in New England in 1771–72; the tragic premature vaccine trials in 1935; the futile attempts to control epidemics with convalescent serum; and finally the various contributions of virology and statistical epidemiology that led to the triumphant success of the inactivated and attenuated live virus vaccines" (*American Scientist*).

Saunders, Paul L. *Edward Jenner—The Cheltenham Years, 1795–1823: Being a Chronicle of the Vaccination Campaign.* U. Pr. of New Eng. 1982 o.p. "A first-rate account of the final years of the man responsible for vaccination against smallpox" (*Library Journal*).

Semmelweis, Ignaz. *The Etiology, Concept and Prophylaxis of Childbed Fever.* Trans. by K. Codell Carter. *History of Science and Medicine Ser. No. 2.* U. of Wis. Pr. 1983 $35.00. ISBN 0-299-09360-3. "The painstaking attention to empirical detail and the persuasive urgent tone were the products of a man frustrated by his inability to convince his peers and administrative superiors that they were allowing the deaths of thousands of mothers" (*Choice*).

Van der Heyningen, W. E., and John Seal. *Cholera: The American Scientific Encounter, 1947–1980.* Westview 1982 o.p. "Chronicles a 30-year war against the spread of 'Vibrio Cholerae.' A war waged by a shifting international team of men and women, largely Americans who knew little of cholera but much of physiology and biochemistry, allied with the experienced doctors of the cholera countries" (*Scientific American*).

Zinner, Stephen H. *STD: Sexually Transmitted Diseases.* Summit 1985 o.p. "Discusses 18 diseases, includes background material, symptoms, treatment, and preventive measures. Handy quick reference for the layperson" (*Library Journal*).

MUSCULOSKELETAL DISORDERS

[SEE the sections on Orthopedics and Sports Medicine in this chapter.]

NEUROLOGICAL DISEASES

Some neurological diseases and disorders can be caused by infection, whereas others can be of uncertain origin. Whatever their cause, they affect the functioning of nerves and muscles. Alzheimer's Disease is a degenerative brain disorder of uncertain pathogenesis that does not manifest itself until middle age. It received much media attention beginning in 1984 and 1985. A selection of the numerous books for nonspecialists on this subject are listed. The causes, prognosis, etiology, and treatment of this and other equally destructive neurological diseases are described. The following section also lists practical manuals for professionals and families, and personal narratives that describe the psychological impact of these diseases.

Baier, Sue, and Mary Zimmeth. *Bed Number Ten*. CRC Press 1989 $14.95. ISBN 0-8493-4270-8. "Baier chronicles her severe bout with Guillain-Barre syndrome, a puzzling illness that can occur after a viral infection, causing degeneration of nerve sheaths and resulting in temporary paralysis" (*Library Journal*).

Bair, Frank E. *Alzheimer's, Stroke, and Twenty-Nine Other Neurological Disorders: A Sourcebook Containing Basic Information on Types, Symptoms, Causes, Diagnostic Methods, and Treatments*. Vol. 2 Health Reference Ser. Omnigraphics Inc. 1993 $80.00. ISBN 1-55888-748-2. Reliable information but much of it is available from associations devoted to these diseases; value diminished by limited scope.

Carroll, David L., and Jon Dorman. *Living Well with Multiple Sclerosis: A Guide for Patient, Caregiver, and Family*. HarpC 1993 $10.00. ISBN 0-06-055345-6. "A compact, highly readable guide, which includes information on diagnosis, psychological coping, exercise, and nutrition, and practical tips for everyday living" (*Library Journal*).

Cohen, Donna, and Carl Eisdorfer. *The Loss of Self: A Family Resource for the Care of Alzheimer's Disease and Related Disorders*. Norton 1986 $19.95. ISBN 0-393-02263-3. "Discussions of practical information include criteria for recognizing serious memory problems, obtaining a thorough diagnosis, working effectively with a patient, dealing with financial and legal problems in institutionalizing a patient. Case-study accounts tie theory to reality" (*Choice*).

Critchley, Macdonald. *The Citadel of the Senses and Other Essays*. Raven 1986 $45.00. ISBN 0-88167-105-3. "Subjects include aphasia, migraine, neurosyphilis, Samuel Johnson, John Hughlings Jackson, and Alphonse Daudet" (*Journal of the American Medical Association*).

Cytowic, Richard E. *The Man Who Tasted Shapes: A Bizarre Medical Mystery Offers Revolutionary Insights into Emotions, Reasoning, and Consciousness*. J. P. Tarcher 1993 $21.95. ISBN 0-87477-738-0. "In a series of thought-provoking essays, this neurologist expounds upon the issue of subjective experience" (*Library Journal*).

Dement, William C. *The Sleepwatchers*. Stanford Alumni Assn. 1992 $12.95. ISBN 0-916318-48-6. Anecdotal autobiography of the director of Stanford University's Sleep Disorders Clinic. Discusses insomnia, narcolepsy, sleep apnea, jet-lag and many other sleep-related disorders and their remedies.

_____. *Some Must Watch while Some Must Sleep: Exploring the World of Sleep*. Norton 1978 $5.95. ISBN 0-393-09001-9. "A balanced account of the basic landmarks in the realm of human sleep. An overview of the behavioral and physiological correlates of sleep and sleep loss is followed by discussions of dream content, sleep disorders and their treatment, sleep disturbance and mental illness, and creativity during sleep" (*American Scientist*).

Doernberg, Myrna. *Stolen Mind: The Slow Disappearance of Ray Doernberg*. Algonquin Bks. 1989 $8.95. ISBN 0-945575-11-4. "Ray Doernberg suffered from a form of dementia known as 'Binswanger's disease.' Subcortical arteriosclerotic encephalopathy, as it is officially known, results in progressive degeneration of the subcortical region of the brain, leading to diminished intellectual capacity, loss of judgment, and problems with memory, orientation, language, and other essential skills" (*Library Journal*).

Dorros, Sidney. *Parkinson's: A Patient's View*. Seven Locks Pr. 1989 $12.95. ISBN 0-932020-74-7. A personal narrative of a patient's experience with Parkinsonism over a period of 30 years.

Dreifuss, Fritz E., and others. *Pediatric Epileptology: Classification and Management of Seizures in the Child*. PSG Pubns. 1983 o.p. "An up-to-date classification of and guide to, the management of seizures in children. Describes various types of seizures, their prognosis, management, and psychosocial implications" (*Choice*).

Dryer, Bernard, and Ellen S. Kaplan. *Inside Insomnia: How to Get a Good Night's Sleep*. Random 1986 o.p. "Coverage of numerous perspectives including sleep physiology, biorhythms, effects and interactions of drugs and alcohol on sleep, sleeping problems, and the role of relaxation therapies and other nondrug techniques" (*Library Journal*).

Dudley, Rosemary, and Wade Rowland. *How to Find Relief from Migraines*. Bantam 1984 $3.50. ISBN 0-553-23589-0. "An in-depth guide to the causes, treatment, and prevention of migraine headache in adults and children" (*Library Journal*).

Fletcher, Sally. *The Challenge of Epilepsy*. Aura Pub. Co. 1986 $9.95. ISBN 0-9615513-9-9. "Serves the dual purpose of educating the general public about the nature of epilepsy and of helping the epilepsy sufferer and family members cope with the disorder" (*Library Journal*).

Franklin, Jon, and Alan Doelp. *Not Quite a Miracle: Brain Surgeons and Their Patients on the Frontier of Medicine*. Doubleday 1983 o.p. "The main events in this fascinating book are the operations to reconnect a nerve and to remove various tumors" (*Library Journal*).

Gino, Carol. *Rusty's Story*. Bantam 1986 $3.95. ISBN 0-553-25351-4. "Rusty was a teenager when she was stricken with epilepsy. Misdiagnosed as a paranoid schizophrenic, for years she suffered more from inappropriate medical treatment than her condition" (*Library Journal*).

Hales, Dianne. *The Complete Book of Sleep: How Your Nights Affect Your Days*. Addison-Wesley 1987 o.p. "Describes normal and abnormal sleep patterns and the effect on sleep of factors such as lifestyle and health" (*Library Journal*).

Hayden, M. R. *Huntington's Chorea*. Spring-Verlag 1984 $66.00. ISBN 0-387-10588-3. "Describes the history, geographical distribution, and epidemiology of the disease, and analyzes its genetic implications. Covers the major problem of diagnosis and describes the management of the disease through medication" (*Choice*).

Josephs, Arthur. *Stroke: An Owner's Manual: The Invaluable Guide to Life after Stroke*. Amadeus CA 1992 $14.95. ISBN 0-9631493-9-3. Practical book offering hope for the stroke victim as well as the caregiver.

Lance, James W. *Migraine and Other Headaches: A Renowned Physician's Guide to Diagnosis and Effective Treatment*. Macmillan 1986 $14.00. ISBN 0-684-18654-3. "Briefly describes the various types of headache, then proceeds with further explanation of migraine, cluster, and tension headaches and other headache-causing conditions including tic douloureux, brain tumor, and sinusitis" (*Library Journal*).

LaPlante, Eve. *Seized: Temporal Lobe Epilepsy as a Medical, Historical, and Artistic Phenomenon*. HarpC 1993 $20.00. ISBN 0-06-016673-8. Incorporates the stories of three contemporary TLE sufferers with accounts of famous people who probably suffered from the disease.

Mace, Nancy L., and Peter V. Rabins. *The Thirty-Six Hour Day: A Family Guide to Caring for Persons with Alzheimer's Disease, Related Dementing Illness and Memory Loss in Later Life*. Johns Hopkins 1991 $38.95. ISBN 0-8018-4033-3. "An excellent practical manual for families and professionals involved in the care of persons with progressive dementing illness" (*Library Journal*).

Martin, Russell. *Matters Gray and White: A Neurologist, His Patients, and the Mysteries of the Brain*. Fawcett 1988 $4.95. ISBN 0-449-21606-3. "Medical terminology and explanations are skillfully intertwined with patient vignettes and heartfelt conversations over the approach to the patient with a chronic disabling neurological disease" (*Library Journal*).

Meinhart, Noreen T., and Margo McCaffrey. *Pain: A Nursing Approach to Assessment and Analysis*. Appleton 1983 o.p. "Includes discussion of the neurophysiology of pain, the cultural and psychological factors that influence pain perception, and the various pain syndromes" (*Choice*).

Melzack, Ronald, and Patrick D. Wall. *The Challenge of Pain*. Basic 1989 $10.00. ISBN 0-14-015660-3. "Incorporates findings on pain in sensory physiology, neurochemistry, and behavioral medicine and serves to remind us of our ignorance regarding certain kinds of pain and treatments used to alter pain" (*Choice*).

Middleton, Allen H., and Gregory Walsh. *Epilepsy*. Little 1982 $16.45. ISBN 0-316-56952-6. "An attempt to demystify the diagnosis and management of epilepsy, particularly for parents of epileptic children" (*Library Journal*).

Neurological Disorders. Springhouse Pub. 1984 o.p. "Complex anatomical information and pathophysiological processes are described with thoroughness and clarity" (*Choice*).

Powell, Lenore, and Katie Courtice. *Alzheimer's Disease: A Guide for Families*. Addison-Wesley 1993 $12.95. ISBN 0-201-63201-2. "Discusses knowledge of the disease, the practical and psychological challenges of caring for and understanding the patient, and the emotional and other problems of caregivers themselves" (*Library Journal*).

Rabin, Roni. *Six Parts Love: A Family's Battle with Lou Gehrig's Disease (ALS)*. Macmillan 1985 o.p. "Dr. David Rabin was a successful scientist working in the area of male contraception when in 1979 he learned he had ALS (amyotrophic lateral sclerosis). His daughter chronicles his progressive disease and the family's resolve to fight back" (*Library Journal*).

Sacks, Oliver. *The Man Who Mistook His Wife for a Hat: And Other Clinical Tales*. Peter Smith 1992 $21.50. ISBN 0-8446-6529-0. "One man who could not recognize common objects at a glance, another who suddenly developed an acute sense of smell, and retarded brothers who could juggle huge prime numbers are among the subjects of these essays" (*New York Times Book Review*).

———. *Migraine: The Evolution of a Common Disorder*. U. CA Pr. 1992 $30.00. ISBN 0-520-08101-3. "Anyone having any interest in migraine will profit from and enjoy reading this book" (*American Scientist*).

Selby, George. *Migraine and Its Variants*. PSG Pubns. 1983 o.p. "Covers the historical aspects with discussion of the etiology, trigger factors, [and] pathology related to the changes in vessel caliber, differential diagnosis of the various types of the disorder, treatment by drug and nondrug remedies and prognosis" (*Choice*).

Severo, Richard. *Lisa H: The True Story of an Extraordinary and Courageous Woman*. HarpC 1985 o.p. The story of a 21-year-old woman suffering from neurofibromatosis who underwent a radical life-threatening operation to remove the tumors and reconstruct her face.

Smoller, Bruce, and Brian Schulman. *Pain Control: The Bethesda Program*. Zebra 1983 $3.95. ISBN 0-8217-1289-6. "[Describes] in detail the causes and effects of pain (being careful to balance physical and psychological considerations) and the process of learning to cope with it" (*Library Journal*).

Soll, Robert W., and Penelope B. Genoble. *MS—Something Can Be Done and You Can Do It*. Contemp. Bks. 1984 o.p. "Soll believes that multiple sclerosis may involve a hypersensitivity to one's own myelin, exacerbated by infections and hidden food allergies. He claims remarkable success in rehabilitating MS patients through a program of diet, motivation, behavioral self-management, and physical therapy" (*Library Journal*).

Tarlov, Edward, and David D'Costa. *Back Attack: A Neurosurgeon's Advice on the Best and Latest Methods for Diagnosis and Treatment.* Little 1987 $9.95. ISBN 0-316-83189-1. Includes "a brief but necessary anatomy course of back and neck, explains diagnostic tests, [and] touches on many surgical and nonsurgical therapies" (*Library Journal*).

Temkin, Owsei. *The Falling Sickness: A History of Epilepsy from the Greeks to the Beginnings of Modern Neurology.* Johns Hopkins 1971 o.p. "(The) definitive account of the varying concepts of epilepsy, 'the falling sickness,' from the brave Hippocratic rejection of the disease as 'sacred' to the study of the syndrome inaugurated chiefly by John Hughlings Jackson (1835–1911). Temkin considers the broad spectrum of epileptic disorder, from severe convulsions to mild transitory amnesias, as it has been debated from ancient times. [An] informative introduction to our knowledge of epilepsy in the Western world from antiquity to the early twentieth century" (*American Scientist*).

Trieschmann, Roberta B. *Spinal Cord Injuries: Psychological Social and Vocational Adjustment.* Demos Pubns. 1988 $54.95. ISBN 0-939957-08-6. "Myths are laid to rest on emotional and grief processes following disability, and attention is turned to environmental and personnel influences on rehabilitation" (*Choice*).

White, Augustus A., III. *Your Aching Back: A Doctor's Guide to Relief.* S&S Trade 1990 $9.95. ISBN 0-671-71000-1. Provides a wealth of information on the causes, prevention, and treatment of back pain.

Zarit, Steven H., and others. *The Hidden Victims of Alzheimer's Disease: Families under Stress.* NYU Pr. 1985 $35.00. ISBN 0-8147-9662-1. Covers causes and symptoms, guidelines for assessment, possible interventions, and useful strategies to help the patient and family.

NUTRITIONAL DISORDERS

This section includes books on adverse reactions to foods and the role of nutrition in disease and health. The wide cross section of titles encompasses professional publications, some of which require an understanding of biology and chemistry; orthodox and unorthodox views on links between physical disorders and diet; and personal narratives about anorexia nervosa, a disorder mainly affecting young women that began to receive much media attention only a decade ago.

Adverse Reactions to Foods. USGPO 1984 $9.50. ISBN 0-16-002624-5. "Discusses history and prevalence of adverse reactions to foods, the chemistry of selected food antigens, the fate of ingested antigens in the intestinal tract; reviews reported adverse reactions both to foods that [either] involve or are suspected of involving immune mechanisms, diagnosis and treatment. Includes recommendations for future studies" (*Choice*).

Bland, Jeffrey, ed. *Medical Applications of Clinical Nutrition.* Keats 1983 $25.00. ISBN 0-87983-327-0. "Emphasizes the preventive and management role of nutrition for degenerative diseases such as cardiovascular disease, diabetes, and gastrointestinal dysfunction" (*Choice*).

Bruch, Hilde. *The Golden Cage: The Enigma of Anorexia Nervosa.* HUP 1978 $18.50. ISBN 0-674-35650-0. Case histories of patients treated by the author/psychiatrist are recounted. Possible causes and treatments are explored. A landmark book.

Carpenter, Kenneth J. *The History of Scurvy and Vitamin C.* Cambridge U. Pr. 1988 $54.95. ISBN 0-521-32029-1. "About two thirds of this book is devoted to scurvy and early medical attempts to understand its etiology. The other third chronicles the discovery of vitamin C" (*Choice*).

Diet, Nutrition, and Cancer. Nat. Acad. Pr. 1982 $22.95. ISBN 0-309-03280-6. Prepared by the National Research Council Committee on Diet, Nutrition, and Cancer. "A comprehensive study of the scientific information concerning the relationship of diet and nutrition to cancer. Summarizes the most relevant scientific information on diet and cancer and recommends several interim dietary guidelines" (*Choice*).

Emmett, Steven Wiley, ed. *Theory and Treatment of Anorexia Nervosa and Bulimia: Biomedical, Sociocultural, and Psychological Perspectives*. Brunner-Mazel 1985 $43.95. ISBN 0-87630-384-X. "Includes a great deal of historical, empirical, and demographic data. Highly technical medical language, frequent statistical data in tables, graphs, or illustrations" (*Choice*).

Fredericks, Carlton. *Carlton Fredericks' Nutrition Guide for the Prevention and Cure of Common Ailments and Diseases*. S&S Trade 1982 $9.95. ISBN 0-671-44509-X. "States [that] many physical disorders and diseases may be prevented, cured, or improved by the use of vitamins, minerals and other nutrients, and correct diet" (*Library Journal*).

Garfinkel, Paul E., and David M. Garner. *Anorexia Nervosa: A Multidimensional Perspective*. Brunner-Mazel 1982 $39.95. ISBN 0-87630-297-5. "A most comprehensive yet cautious treatment of the topic of anorexia nervosa. A source of valuable information" (*Choice*).

Hui, Yiu H. *Essentials of Nutrition and Diet Therapy*. Jones & Bartlett 1985 $31.25. ISBN 0-534-04380-1. Clear and understandable basic information about normal and therapeutic nutrition in humans; written for nurses and allied health workers.

Mitchell, James E. *Anorexia Nervosa and Bulimia: Diagnosis and Treatment. Continuing Medical Education Ser.* U. of Minn. Pr. 1985 $29.95. ISBN 0-8166-1388-5. "Detailed coverage from past research and treatments, to current diagnostic methodologies and care, to future research possibilities. Minimal use of technical language" (*Choice*).

Palmer, R. L. *Anorexia Nervosa: A Guide for Sufferers and Their Families*. Viking Penguin 1989 $7.95. ISBN 0-14-010034-2. "Palmer's hypothesis is that anorexia nervosa is a psychobiological regression disorder" (*Library Journal*).

Romeo, Felicia F. *Understanding Anorexia Nervosa*. C. C. Thomas 1986 $26.50. ISBN 0-398-05191-7. "Clearly points out the major symptoms. A concise and accessible treatment" (*Choice*).

Rose, John, ed. *Nutrition and Killer Diseases: The Effects of Dietary Factors on Fatal Chronic Diseases*. Noyes 1982 $25.00. ISBN 0-8155-0902-2. Focuses on the effects of dietary factors on atherosclerosis, cancer, and diabetes.

Rumney, Avis. *Dying to Please: Anorexia Nervosa and Its Cure*. McFarland & Co. 1983 $15.95. ISBN 0-89950-083-8. "Written from personal experience. Discusses a variety of therapeutic approaches used for anorexia (psychoanalysis, behavior modification, drug therapy, hypnotherapy, and family therapy)" (*Choice*).

Sours, John A. *Starving to Death in a Sea of Objects*. Aronson 1992 $25.00. ISBN 0-87668-435-5. "An unusual device is a novella that occupies 192 pages of the book. Analyzes the condition from a variety of historical, psychodynamic and developmental aspects" (*Choice*).

Trowell, H. C., and others, eds. *Dietary Fibre, Fibre-Depleted Foods and Disease*. Acad. Pr. 1985 $121.00. ISBN 0-12-701160-9. "A comprehensive perspective on the relationship of food fiber, or the lack of it, in the diet to various disease processes. Ranges from the basic chemistry and physiology of fiber to risk factors and symptoms of disease to the diseases themselves" (*Choice*).

Winick, Myron. *Nutrition in Health and Disease*. Wiley 1987 $47.50. ISBN 0-471-83040-2. Comprehensive compilation of nutrition knowledge related to healthy and diseased individuals.

ONCOLOGY

[SEE the section on Cancer in this chapter.]

ORTHOPEDICS

Orthopedics is a medical specialty that utilizes surgical and physical methods to treat and correct deformities, diseases, and injuries to the musculoskeletal system. Most books on the treatment of bone and joint diseases are written for physicians, physical therapists, and other health care personnel. Other than for osteoporosis, there are few books for the general reader on any bone disorders. The following books on osteoporosis are a representative selection from the many published. (See also the section on Sports Medicine in this chapter.)

Berquist, Thomas A., ed. *Radiology of the Foot and Ankle*. Raven 1989 $157.50. ISBN 0-88167-445-1. A comprehensive text/reference, unifying the clinical-imaging approach to foot and ankle disorders.

Cantu, Robert C. *Exercise Injuries: Prevention and Treatment*. Stone Wall Pr. 1983 $14.95. ISBN 0-913276-45-6. Recommends fitness as a desirable and obtainable goal, and deals with sports injuries" (*Choice*).

Fardon, David F. *Osteoporosis: Your Head Start to the Prevention of Fractures*. Macmillan 1985 $15.34. ISBN 0-02-537120-7. "Coverage of all pertinent aspects: causes; the role of nutrition, exercise and lifestyle; detection methods; and how osteoporosis and fractured bones are treated" (*Library Journal*).

Harkless, Lawrence B., and Steven M. Krych, eds. *Handbook of Common Foot Problems*. Churchill 1990 $20.95. ISBN 0-443-08622-2

Notelovitz, Morris, and Marsha Ware. *Stand Tall!. Every Woman's Guide to Preventing Osteoporosis*. Bantam 1985 $7.95. ISBN 0-553-34143-X. "Well-documented scientific information on prevention, diet, exercise, hormone therapy and diagnostic screening techniques" (*Library Journal*).

Pritt, Donald S., and Morton Walker. *The Complete Foot Book: First Aid for Your Feet*. Avery Pub. 1992 $12.95. ISBN 0-89529-434-6. Comprehensive discussion of common foot ailments, such as corns, calluses, and flat feet; includes a useful description of foot anatomy.

Schneider, Myles J., and Mark D. Sussman. *The Family Foot Care Book: Prevent Foot Problems for Your Children and Yourself*. Acropolis 1986 $9.95. ISBN 0-87491-808-1

Steinmann, Marion. *The American Medical Association's Book of Back Care*. Random 1982 o.p. "Well-illustrated description of the anatomy of the back and the changes that occur during the aging process. Discusses diseases and treatment regimens of back problems" (*Library Journal*).

OSTEOPOROSIS

[SEE the section on Orthopedics in this chapter.]

PLASTIC SURGERY

Most books on plastic surgery are either designed for specialists or written for general readers. The following are four examples of the latter type.

Cirillo, Dennis P., and Mark Rubinstein. *The Complete Book of Cosmetic Facial Surgery: A Step-by-Step Guide to the Physical and Psychological Process*. S&S Trade 1984 o.p. "Gives commonsense guidelines for choosing a surgeon. Discusses types of surgery and nonsurgical treatment" (*Library Journal*).

Goldwyn, Robert M. *Beyond Appearance: Reflections of a Plastic Surgeon*. Dodd 1986 $16.95. ISBN 0-396-08669-1. Goldwyn comments in the introduction that "this book is about the process of plastic surgery, about some of my patients and myself, and about our relationship."

Reardon, James J., and Judi McMahon. *Plastic Surgery for Men: The Complete Illustrated Guide*. Dodd 1981 o.p. "Explains complicated techniques in easy-to-understand language" (*Library Journal*).

Snyder, Marilyn. *An Informed Decision: Understanding Breast Reconstruction*. M. Evans 1984 o.p. "A very personal account of her own double mastectomy and subsequent chemotherapy and breast reconstruction. A manual on how to explore the options of this special surgery" (*Library Journal*).

Wilson, Josleen. *The American Society of Plastic and Reconstructive Surgeons' Guide to Cosmetic Surgery*. S&S Trade 1992 $25.00. ISBN 0-671-76105-6. Balanced and reliable view of what plastic surgery can and cannot do; written for the general reader.

PSORIASIS

[SEE the section on Skin Diseases in this chapter.]

PROSTHESES

[SEE the section on Artificial and Transplanted Organs, Prostheses, and Implants in this chapter.]

RADIOLOGY

Radiology is the use of X-rays for diagnostic or therapeutic purposes. Thus, there are few books on radiological examination and therapy accessible to the nonspecialist.

Gofman, John W., and Egan O'Connor. *X-Rays: Health Effects of Common Exams*. P-H 1985 $25.00. ISBN 0-87156-838-1. Useful and authoritative book detailing exposure levels for various types of radiological imaging; includes information about effects and treatment for overexposure.

Laws, Priscilla W., and The Public Citizen Health Research Group. *The X-Ray Information Book: A Consumers' Guide to Avoiding Unnecessary Medical and Dental X-Rays*. FS&G 1983 o.p. Explains X-rays, how they harm living tissue, and major sources of unnecessary exposure. Helps consumers to minimize risks associated with unneeded exposure without reducing the benefits of diagnostic X-ray examination.

Steeves, Richard. *A Cancer Patient's Guide to Radiation Therapy: A Cancer Patient's Primer. Focus on Health Ser*. Med. Physics Pub. 1992 $9.00. ISBN 0-944838-26-X. Simple, easy-to-understand approach to the basics of radiation therapy.

RESPIRATORY DISEASES

Any disease that does not allow the lungs to function properly is a respiratory disease. The following list includes lung anatomy and function in health and disease, a discussion of how airborne particles affect human lungs, and care and treatment of patients with respiratory diseases.

Hamilton, Helen, and Minnie B. Rose, eds. *Respiratory Disorders*. Springhouse Pub. 1984 o.p. "Provides a general overview of the care of the patient with pulmonary dysfunctions. Reviews pulmonary anatomy and physiology" (*Choice*).

Harrington, Geri. *The Asthma Self-Care Book: How to Take Control of Your Asthma*. HarpC 1991 $19.95. ISBN 0-06-016584-7. Basic information about asthma and its treatment; written for the general reader.

Perera, Frederica P., and A. Karim Ahmed. *Respirable Particles: Impact of Airborne Fine Particulates on Health and the Environment.* Harper Busn. 1979 o.p. "A useful, compact reference book about tiny airborne particles of all sorts" (*Choice*).

Shayevitz, Myra, and Berton Shayevitz. *Living Well with Emphysema and Bronchitis: A Cardiopulmonary Fitness Program for a Healthier More Active Life.* Doubleday 1985 $17.95. ISBN 0-385-19438-2. "A step-by-step program for the COPD patient to follow daily; everything from diet, exercise, and medication charts to recreation, sex, and cooking tips" (*Library Journal*).

Williams, Chris. *Lung Cancer: The Facts.* OUP The Facts Ser. 1992 $21.95. ISBN 0-19-262251-X. "A basic overview of lung cancer—epidemiology, diagnostic and staging procedures, and treatment modalities" (*Choice*).

Youtsey, John W., and Kanute P. Rarey. *Respiratory Patient Care.* P-H 1981 o.p. "Presents respiratory care information in a well-organized form. The various pieces of equipment and their uses are described concisely and clearly" (*Choice*).

RHEUMATIC DISEASES

Rheumatic diseases are various conditions that produce pain and/or other symptoms to the joints or musculoskeletal system. The following books for the general reader provide current information on the different types of rheumatic disease and their treatment.

Arthritis Foundation. *Understanding Arthritis: What It Is, How It's Treated, How to Cope with It.* Macmillan 1986 $18.95. ISBN 0-684-18199-1. "An overview of diagnosis, accepted treatments, and emotional and financial strains of arthritis. Details the 16 most common rheumatic diseases" (*Library Journal*).

Davidson, Paul. *Are You Sure It's Arthritis: A Guide to Soft-Tissue Rheumatism.* Macmillan 1985 o.p. "Soft-tissue rheumatism, which includes bursitis, tendonitis, carpal tunnel syndrome, tennis elbow, and a host of other frequently treatable conditions, often is confused by the layperson with arthritis" (*Library Journal*).

Eades, Mary Dan. *Arthritis: Reducing Your Risk.* Bantam 1992 o.p. Explores how additional risk factors can be avoided; based on the premise that arthritis might be a genetically transmitted disease.

Gadd, Irna, and Laurence Gadd. *Arthritis Alternatives.* Bks. Demand repr. of 1985 ed. $45.50. ISBN 0-8357-5769-2. "An excellent sourcebook, with emphasis on self-help groups and physicians that provide nontraditional therapies" (*Library Journal*).

Jetter, Judy, Nancy Kadlec, and Herbert Rubinstein. *The Arthritis Book of Water Exercise.* H. Holt & Co. 1985 o.p. "An Arthritis Foundation-approved program of aquatic exercise suitable for those with joint or limb impairment, whether from arthritis, stroke, surgery or accident" (*Library Journal*).

Keough, Carol. *Natural Relief for Arthritis.* Rodale Pr. Inc. 1987 o.p. "Discusses the different kinds of arthritis and related disorders and summarizes in popular form the many treatments available, including arthritis diets, exercise, folk remedies, acupuncture, drugs, and surgery" (*Library Journal*).

Riggs, Gail Kershner, and Eric P. Gall, eds. *Rheumatic Diseases: Rehabilitation and Management.* Buttrwrth-Heinemann 1984 o.p. "Covers the interdisciplinary team approach, techniques in the care of patients with rheumatic diseases, and rehabilitation techniques for regional disorders and specific diseases" (*Choice*).

Trien, Susan F., and David Pisetsky. *The Duke University Medical Center Book of Arthritis.* Fawcett $22.00. ISBN 0-449-90254-4. Basic facts about arthritis, major forms and treatments for the disease, and a description of the Duke Basic Arthritis Program (a comprehensive approach to symptom relief and prevention of complications); accessible to the general reader.

SKIN DISEASES

Books that discuss skin problems usually fall into one of two categories—texts written for physicians and books covering patient care and self-help—many of which offer advice on facial skin care. The books listed below illustrate these types.

Aldhizer, T. Gerard, and others. *The Doctor's Book on Hair Loss.* P-H 1983 $14.95. ISBN 0-13-216580-5. "Discusses what it means to be bald, how hair grows and the types and causes of hair loss, and the use of 'cover-ups,' treatments (medical, surgical, and quack), and hairpieces" (*Library Journal*).

Bruning, Nancy. *What You Can Do about Chronic Hair Loss.* Dell 1993 $3.99. ISBN 0-440-21364-9

Carson, L. H. *The Irreverent, but Indispensable, Guide to Hair Loss Solutions: A Myth-Exploding Survey of the 37 Alternatives to Baldness.* EADS Pub. 1993 $19.95. ISBN 0-9634667-0-4

Goodman, Thomas. *The Skin Doctor's Skin Doctoring Book.* Sterling 1984 $9.95. ISBN 0-8069-5574-0. "Focuses on the most common skin problems, clearly identifies signs and symptoms, and then gives advice on how to treat these problems with over-the-counter products. Cautions that not all skin problems can be cured at home—some will need the attention of the physician" (*Library Journal*).

Litt, Jerome Z. *Your Skin and How to Live In It.* Ballantine 1984 $2.95. ISBN 0-345-31308-9. Easy-to-understand descriptions of the most common dermatological conditions, as well as the physiology of the skin.

Marks, Ronald. *Acne: Advice on Clearing Your Skin.* Arco 1984 o.p. Useful book providing practical advice on the most effective over-the-counter remedies for skin problems and the use and application of these products. Also describes symptoms that indicate a physician should be consulted and discusses specific treatments that might be prescribed.

Pervan, Anthony S. *Natural Hair Growth: Abnormal Hair Loss Prevention, Scalp Hair Restoration; A Self-Administered Therapy.* Lifetime 1988 $9.95. ISBN 0-8119-0715-5

Stegman, S. J. *Cosmetic Dermatologic Surgery.* Mosby Yr. Bk. 1989 $79.00. ISBN 0-8151-7920-0. Useful information about skin grafts and skin surgery; somewhat technical for the general reader.

SPORTS MEDICINE

This section provides information on the importance of conditioning and training in sports, the physiological and psychological effects of anabolic steroids (used by athletes to increase muscle bulk), and the care and treatment of sports injuries. (See also the section on Orthopedics in this chapter.)

Benjamin, Ben, and Gale Borden. *Listen to Your Pain: The Active Person's Guide to Understanding, Identifying and Treating Pain and Injury.* Viking Penguin 1984 $16.00. ISBN 0-14-006687-X. "Helps weekend athletes understand the physiology of injury and will assist them in making informed decisions regarding treatment" (*Library Journal*).

Goldman, Bob. *Death in the Locker Room: Steroids and Sports.* Price Stern 1987 o.p. "Marshals an abundance of evidence that the use of anabolic steroids has severe, long-lasting physiological and psychological effects, which vitiate any immediate benefit to the athlete" (*Library Journal*).

Griffith, H. Winter. *Complete Guide to Sports Injuries.* Price Stern 1986 o.p. "Discussions of injuries help the athlete and/or coach understand the anatomy involved as well as appropriate care, possible complications, and outcomes of treatment. Injuries are arranged alphabetically by body part, ailments by common name" (*Library Journal*).

Halpern, Alan A. *The Runner's World Knee Book: What Every Athlete Needs to Know about the Prevention and Treatment of Knee Problems.* Macmillan 1984 $13.95. ISBN 0-02-547500-2. "Covers all types of knee problems, with detailed evaluations and therapies" (*Library Journal*).

Hoffman, Marshall, and William Southmayd. *Sports Health: The Complete Book of Athletic Injuries.* Putnam Pub. Group 1981 $17.95. ISBN 0-399-51107-5. "A comprehensive study of the injuries that can plague all athletes, professional and amateur. Concentrates on the care and treatment rather than the prevention of sports-related injuries" (*Library Journal*).

Jackson, Douglas W., and Susan C. Pescar. *The Young Athlete's Health Handbook: A Guide to Sports Medicine and Sports Psychology for Parents, Teachers, Coaches, and Players.* Dodd 1981 o.p. "Conditioning, training, physical and psychological traits, alcohol and drugs, nutrition, aggressiveness, the female athlete, levels of competition, the physically and mentally handicapped, orthopedic considerations, predicting injuries, diagnostic procedures, medications, general safety, and first aid are thoroughly covered" (*Library Journal*).

Sandweiss, Jack H., and Steven J. Wolf, eds. *Biofeedback and Sports Science.* Plenum Pub. 1985 $35.00. ISBN 0-306-41995-5. "Offers several ideas and applications about biofeedback techniques used in the psychological and rehabilitative aspects of athletics as well as in enhancing athletic performance" (*Choice*).

Shangold, Mona, and Gabe Mirkin. *The Complete Sports Medicine Book for Women: Revised for the '90s.* S&S Trade 1992 $13.00. ISBN 0-671-74427-5. Primer on exercise physiology precedes sections on diving, nutrition, drugs, injuries, menstrual cycles, menopause, pregnancy, and birth control as they are affected by exercise; updates information on steroids and birth control implants.

Taylor, William N. *Anabolic Steroids and the Athlete: With a Chapter on Human Growth Hormone.* McFarland & Co. 1982 $18.95. ISBN 0-89950-055-2. Factual and straightforward account of this controversial issue.

STRESS AND DISEASE

Stress long has been recognized as an exacerbating factor in many disease states. In the 1950s Hans Selye developed the hypothesis that animals react to stress or injury by a certain sequence of physiological reactions, called the "general adaptation syndrome." He later applied this concept to human beings in his book *Stress Without Distress* (see below) and in other works. Selye now advocates a constructive management approach to stress.

Twenty years after Selye, Herbert Benson advocated meditation to relieve the harmful effects of stress on health. More recently, Meyer Friedman has recommended behavior modification of "Type A" personalities to prevent their early death from stress-related diseases. Current research in this area focuses on the effects of stress in specific systems and as an underlying cause of some disease states.

Antonovsky, Aaron. *Health, Stress, and Coping: New Perspectives on Mental and Physical Well-Being. Social and Behavioral Sciences Ser.* Jossey-Bass 1979 $32.95. ISBN 0-87589-412-7. Argues that researchers should ask why people stay healthy, not why they get sick.

Benson, Herbert, and Eileen M. Stuart, eds. *The Wellness Book: The Comprehensive Guide to Maintaining Health and Treating Stress-Related Illness.* S&S Trade 1993 $13.00. ISBN 0-671-79750-6. Using a workbook format, the editors and their colleagues at the New England Deaconess Hospital and Harvard Medical School Mind-Body Medical Institute describe their experience in treating chronic and stress-related symptoms. Provides basic information about the essentials of a healthy lifestyle.

Benson, Herbert, and Miriam Z. Klipper. *The Relaxation Response*. Avon 1976 $5.50. ISBN 0-380-00676-6. Advocates the use of meditation to guard against the destructive effects of stress; a landmark work.

Brown, Barbara B. *Between Health and Illness: New Notions on Stress and the Nature of Well-Being*. Bantam 1985 $3.95. ISBN 0-553-24798-0. Analyzes the structure of the psyche; describes the stress of life in terms of psychic hurts and bruises and how various techniques can relieve discomfort of mind and body.

Friedman, Meyer, and Diane Ulmer. *Treating Type A Behavior—and Your Heart*. Knopf 1984 $15.95. ISBN 0-394-52286-9. "Uses information obtained through a major study project as the basis for a program of behavioral modification" (*Library Journal*).

Matarazzo, Joseph D., and Sharlene M. Weiss. *Behavioral Health: A Handbook of Health Enhancement and Disease Prevention*. Wiley 1984 o.p. "A collection of significant behavioral and medical insights in health promotion and disease prevention strategies written by noted experts in their respective fields" (*Choice*).

Milsum, John H. *Health, Stress and Illness: A Systems Approach*. Greenwood 1984 $38.95. ISBN 0-275-91443-7. "Uses a systems approach to clarify existing knowledge and to present a broad perspective on health-stress relationships" (*Choice*).

Pelletier, Kenneth R. *Mind as Healer, Mind as Slayer: A Holistic Approach to Preventing Stress Disorders*. Peter Smith 1984 $21.00. ISBN 0-8446-6093-0. Well-documented exploration of the relationship between heart disease, respiratory disease, and stress. Describes techniques for stress reduction, such as meditation, biofeedback, autogenic training, and visualization; a holistic milestone.

Selye, Hans. *Stress without Distress*. NAL-Dutton 1975 $4.99. ISBN 0-451-16192-0. Classic guide to the constructive management of stress.

SUBSTANCE ABUSE

Substance abuse is a major problem of contemporary society because of its effects on the quality of life and individual health. Many books are available for the general reader describing the causes, effects, and possible treatments for substance abuse.

Blum, Kenneth. *Handbook of Abusable Drugs*. Gardner Pr. 1984 $85.00. ISBN 0-89876-036-4. Information on the spectrum of abused substances, including narcotics, sedatives, hallucinogens, psychotropics, alcohol, tobacco, and over-the-counter drugs; includes an overview of the history, biochemistry, pharmacology, toxicity, and behavioral and psychological aspects of each group of abused drugs.

Milkman, Harvey B., and Howard J. Shaffer. *The Addictions: Multidisciplinary Perspectives and Treatments*. Free Pr. 1984 $37.95. ISBN 0-669-08739-4. Proceedings of a 1983 conference offering readers an opportunity to consolidate often conflicting theoretical information regarding the etiology and treatment of addictions; includes etiology of addictive behavior and therapeutic approaches.

Alcoholism

Beauchamp, Dan E. *Beyond Alcoholism: Alcohol and Public Health*. Temple U. Pr. 1982 $16.95. ISBN 0-87722-286-X. Reviews the history of alcoholism; Prohibition, America's failure to legislate temperance; contemporary ideas and myths of disease causation; and the emerging trends in international alcohol consumption.

Deutsch, Charles. *Broken Bottles, Broken Dreams: Understanding and Helping the Children of Alcoholics*. Tchrs. Coll. 1982 $17.95. ISBN 0-8077-2663-X. Part 1 defines alcoholism and considers its effect on members of the family; Part 2 covers the helping process for the children of alcoholic parents.

Elkin, Michael. *Families under the Influence: Changing Alcoholic Patterns*. Norton 1990 $9.95. ISBN 0-393-30670-4. Theoretical explanation of alcoholism.

Galanter, Marc, ed. *Recent Developments in Alcoholism.* Plenum Pub. Vol. 2 1984 $85.00. ISBN 0-306-41534-8. Vol. 4 1986 $85.00. ISBN 0-306-42170-4. Volume 2 covers learning and social models, alcohol and the liver, aging and alcoholism, and anthropology. Organized under five main headings: Experimental Social and Learning Models of Drinking Alcohol; Alcohol and the Liver; Recent Developments in Preclinical and Clinical Research; Aging and Alcoholism; and Contributions from Anthropology to the Study of Alcoholism. Volume 4 covers combined alcohol and drug abuse, typologies of alcoholics, the withdrawal syndrome, and renal and electrolyte consequences; includes a useful 7-to-10-page overview chapter that introduces each section.

Heather, Nick, and others, eds. *The Misuse of Alcohol: Crucial Issues in Dependence, Treatment and Prevention.* NYU Pr. 1985 $50.00. ISBN 0-8147-3432-4. Considers the designation of alcoholism as a syndrome and discusses treatment and prevention of alcoholism.

Light, William J. Haugen. *Neurobiology of Alcohol Abuse.* C. C. Thomas 1986 $39.50. ISBN 0-398-05197-6. Introduces neurobiology and the chemistry of human consciousness. Addresses depression, antidepressant drugs, alcohol, and the relation of depression to alcohol and brain function.

Marlin, Emily. *Hope: New Choices and Recovery Strategies for Adult Children of Alcoholics.* HarpC 1988 $8.95. ISBN 0-06-091511-0. "A thorough, sympathetic psychotherapeutic guide to recovering from the trauma of having an alcoholic parent. . . . [Marlin] speaks from a knowledgeable point of view, experimental and scholarly, and is able to pass on both theoretical information and practical help" (*Kirkus Reviews*).

Mendelson, Jack H., and Nancy K. Mello. *Alcohol: Its Use and Abuse in America.* Little 1985 $25.00. ISBN 0-316-56663-2. Overview of alcoholism, problems arising from its use and abuse, and its impact on the quality of life.

Meryman, Richard. *Broken Promises, Mended Dreams: An Alcoholic Woman Fights for Her Life.* Little 1984 o.p. The process of residential treatment for one alcoholic woman; based on the experiences of several individuals.

Moran, Megan. *Lost Years: Confessions of a Woman Alcoholic.* Doubleday 1985 o.p. Vivid portrayal of life as an alcoholic.

Mumey, Jack. *Sitting in the Bay Window: A Book for Parents of Young Alcoholics.* Contempo. Bks. 1984 o.p. Brief, easy-to-read guide offering specific suggestions for effective limit-setting; makes clear recommendations.

Olson, Steve, and Dean R. Gerstein. *Alcohol in America: Taking Action to Prevent Abuse.* Natl. Acad. Pr. 1985 $14.95. ISBN 0-309-03449-3. Distillation of a 1981 report initiated by the National Research Council and papers from a 1984 National Institute of Alcohol Abuse and Alcoholism conference.

Pace, Nicholas, and Wilbur Cross. *Guidelines to Safe Drinking.* 1985 Fawcett $3.50. ISBN 0-449-20918-0. Guide for drinking safely. Discusses locations, times, and types of drink; encourages alcoholics to abstain.

Plant, Moira L. *Women, Drinking, and Pregnancy.* Routledge Chapman & Hall 1987 $16.95. ISBN 0-422-61750-4. Presents historical and current information about alcohol consumption and its effects on pregnancy.

Rachel V. *Family Secrets: Life Stories of Adult Children of Alcoholics.* Routledge Chapman & Hall 1987 $16.95. ISBN 0-422-61750-4. Fifteen stories of people who have experienced trauma or abuse as children of alcoholics. Stories provide tools for recovery and suggest ways of forgiving the alcoholic parent and giving up self-destructive behavior patterns.

———. *A Woman Like You: Life Stories of Women Recovering from Alcoholism and Addiction.* HarpC 1985 o.p. Women tell of their drinking and its effects on their lives and of how they attained sobriety.

Rosett, Henry L., and Lyu Weinder. *Alcohol and the Fetus: A Clinical Perspective.* OUP 1984 $37.50. ISBN 0-19-503458-9. Reviews the literature on fetal alcohol syndrome and examines the clinical, experimental, and epidemiologic experience at the Boston City Hospital prenatal clinic.

Seixas, Judith S., and Geraldine Youcha. *Children of Alcoholism: A Survivor's Manual.*
HarpC 1986 $11.00. ISBN 0-06-097020-0. Sympathetic exploration of the psychological and physical scars that can result from growing up in an alcoholic home.
Provides advice on how to come to terms with the past and where to seek
professional help.

Wholey, Denis. *The Courage to Change: Personal Conversations about Alcoholism with
Denis Wholey.* G. K. Hall 1985 o.p. Celebrity accounts of struggles with alcohol and
other drugs are grouped by theme: the beginning of alcoholism, the progression,
quitting, a new life, the woman alcoholic, and alcoholism and homosexuality.

Drug Abuse

Baron, Jason D. *Kids and Drugs: A Parent's Handbook of Drug Abuse Prevention and
Treatment.* Putnam Pub. Group 1984 o.p. Covers drugs and their dangers, the factors
leading to drug use, and preventive techniques and treatment.

Barth, Richard B., Jeanne Pietrzak, and Malia Ramler. *Families Living with Drugs and
HIV: Intervention and Treatment Strategies.* Guilford Pr. 1993 $45.00. ISBN 0-89862-
888-1. Brings together information about drug abuse and HIV infection, with in-
depth coverage of such topics as addiction, affected infants, and prevention of
substance abuse; scholarly treatment but accessible to the general reader.

Courtwright, David T. *Dark Paradise: Opiate Addiction in America Before 1940.* HUP 1982
$27.50. ISBN 0-674-19261-3. Meticulous account of the demography of American
opiate addiction before 1940.

Ettorre, Elizabeth. *Women and Substance Use.* Rutgers U. Pr. 1992 $37.00. ISBN 0-8135-
1863-6. Argues convincingly that most research in the substance abuse field is
insensitive to the needs of women.

Gold, Mark S. *800-Cocaine.* Bantam 1984 $3.95. ISBN 0-553-34388-2. Taken primarily
from Dr. Gold's experience with the callers to the toll-free cocaine hotline he
founded in May 1983. Contains case reports demonstrating the problems relating to
cocaine abuse and Gold's recommended solutions.

Goulart, Frances Sheridan. *The Caffeine Book.* Dodd 1984 o.p. Provides references to
medical studies and reports concerning caffeine addiction and its effects on the
body.

Green, Bernard. *Getting Over Getting High: How to Overcome Dependency on Cocaine,
Caffeine, Hallucinogens, Marijuana, Speed, and Stimulants the Natural and Permanent Way.* Morrow 1984 $7.95. ISBN 0-688-03949-9. Identifies why people become
addicts, how patterns of abuse develop, and the nature of psychological dependency.
Recommends proper nutrition, megavitamins, minerals, relaxation, meditation, and
mind expansion to replace psychological and physiological cravings for drugs of
abuse.

Jones, Helen C., and Paul W. Lovinger. *The Marijuana Question and Science's Search for
an Answer.* Dodd 1985 $25.95. ISBN 0-396-08399-4. Comprehensive examination of
the potential physiological and psychological effects of marijuana; thoroughly
referenced.

Maddux, James F., and David P. Desmond. *Careers of Opioid Users.* Greenwood 1981
$42.95. ISBN 0-275-90675-2. Wealth of data on the life history of opioid addicts,
including family background, social adjustment, initial drug and polydrug use, and
mortality and morbidity.

Mann, Peggy, and Nancy Reagan. *Marijuana Alert.* McGraw 1984 o.p. Comprehensive
well-documented book about the use, abuse, and harmful effects of marijuana.

Platt, Jerome J. *Heroin Addiction: Theory, Research and Treatment.* Krieger 1993. ISBN 0-
89464-267-7. Begins with a detailed review of changes in the legal status of narcotic
use in the United States. Describes the physiology and associated medical complications of heroin addiction, theories of addiction, an addict profile, and various
treatments.

Reilly, Patrick. *A Private Practice.* Macmillan 1984 $15.95. ISBN 0-02-604410-2. More
than just another personal account of overcoming drug addiction. Not only

describes the intense physical and psychological struggle to master addiction to tranquilizers and sleeping pills but also puts into perspective how Reilly's profession—medicine—contributed to the problem.

Rolling Stone Editors. *How to Get off Drugs.* S&S Trade 1984 o.p. Guide for drug users who are thinking about kicking their habit and for the friends and families who plan to assist them; includes illicit psychoactive drugs, alcohol, prescription drugs, and other substances.

Weil, Andrew, and Winifred Rosen. *From Chocolate to Morphine: Everything You Need to Know about Mind-Altering Drugs.* HM 1993 $13.45. ISBN 0-395-66079-3. Reliable information about a variety of drugs. Declares that education is the only solution to the nation's drug problem.

Smoking

The federal office of the U.S. Department of Health and Human Services, Public Health Service, Office on Smoking and Health issues useful periodic reports on smoking and related topics. They include *The Health Consequences of Smoking: A Report of the Surgeon General*, which is issued annually and focuses on specific aspects of smoking (1982, Cancer; 1984, Lung Disease; 1986, Involuntary Smoking; 1988, Nicotine Addiction; 1990, Benefits of Cessation; 1992, Smoking in the Americas) and *Smoking Tobacco and Health: A Fact Book* (1987). Another useful title is *Review and Evaluation of Smoking Cessation Methods: United States and Canada, 1978–1985*, published in 1987. These reports are found in most public libraries, or they can be purchased from the Superintendent of Documents, U.S. Government Printing Office, Washington, D.C. The following are additional titles on smoking.

Ashton, Heather, and Rob Stepney. *Smoking: Psychology and Pharmacology.* Routledge Chapman & Hall 1982 $14.95. ISBN 0-422-77710-2. Summarizes the psychological, sociological, pharmacological, commercial, and medical aspects of smoking.

Cocores, J. A., ed. *The Clinical Management of Nicotine Dependence.* Spr.-Verlag. 1991 $89.00. ISBN 0-387-97464-4. Reference for psychologists, social workers, nurses, counselors, and physicians.

Eyserck, H. J. *Smoking, Personality, and Stress.* Spr.-Verlag 1991 $29.00. ISBN 0-387-97493-8. Argues that psychosocial factors contribute to cancer and other diseases traditionally attributed to smoking.

Fried, Peter, and Harry Oxorn, *Smoking for Two: Cigarettes and Pregnancy.* Free Pr. 1980 $14.95. ISBN 0-02-910720-2. An especially useful book on the effects of smoking on the unborn child, including "passive smoking," in which the pregnant woman inhales secondhand smoke.

Krogh, David. *Smoking: The Artificial Passion.* W. H. Freeman 1991 $17.95. ISBN 0-7167-2246-1. Explores the motivations of smokers and the difficulties of quitting.

Tollison, Robert D., eds. *Smoking and Society: Toward a More Balanced Assessment.* Free Pr. 1985 $45.00. ISBN 0-669-11602-3. Up-to-date compilation of essays on the social, economic, physiological, and political aspects of smoking.

Viscusi, W. Kip. *Smoking: Making the Choice under Uncertainty.* OUP 1992 $24.95. ISBN 0-19-507486-6. Explores personal choices and government regulation of smoking behavior; emphasizes smoking as individual risk-taking activity.

Winter, Ruth. *The Scientific Case against Smoking.* Crown Pub. Group 1980 o.p. Compilation and discussion of scientific data derived from the 1979 *Surgeon General's Report on Smoking and Health*.

SURGERY

Surgery is a medical specialty in which operative or chiropractic procedures are used to treat diseases, injuries, or deformities. There are a limited number of entries in this section because most books about surgery are written by and for physicians.

Christian, Rebecca, and others. *The Prevention Guide to Surgery and Its Alternatives.* Rodale Pr. Inc. 1980 o.p. "Covers seeking a second opinion, hospital choice, preoperative care, and operating and recovery room procedures as well as descriptions of common operations, such as gallbladder removal, hysterectomy and surgery for ulcers" (*Library Journal*).

Eiseman, Ben. *What Are My Chances?* Saunders 1980 o.p. Statistics on the probabilities of cures and the compilations of diseases, arranged in a flowchart with explanatory annotations.

Inlander, Charles B., and People's Medical Society Staff. *Good Operations—Bad Operations: The People's Medical Society's Guide to Surgery.* Viking Penguin 1992 $25.00. ISBN 0-670-83778-4. Covers the 100 most commonly performed diagnostic and surgical procedures. The advice is referenced, reliable and authoritative; includes a glossary with technical terms highlighted and explained.

Kra, Siegfried J., and Robert S. Boltax. *Is Surgery Necessary.* Macmillan 1981 o.p. "Covers choices available to patients for whom surgery has been recommended" (*Library Journal*).

Schneider, Robert G. *When to Say No to Surgery: How to Decide If You Need the Most Often Performed Operations.* P-H 1982 o.p. "Examines 21 of the most commonly performed operations in America, discusses when they are or are not indicated, and the risks, complications, alternatives, financial guidelines, and other information not generally publicly available" (*Library Journal*).

Sylvester, Edward J. *The Healing Blade: Neurosurgery on the Edge of Life and Death.* S&S Trade 1993 $22.00. ISBN 0-671-76054-8. Fine scholarly treatise, accessible to the general reader.

THERAPEUTICS

Therapeutics is a plan of treatment for a disease or defect based on a correct interpretation of the symptoms and a knowledge of the physiological action of the remedy used. Because most of the books on therapeutics are extremely technical, there are few entries in this section.

Berkow, Robert, ed. *The Merck Manual of Diagnosis and Therapy.* Merck 1992 $26.00. ISBN 0-911910-16-6. Organized by organ system primarily affected or by discipline; includes symptoms, complications, diagnosis, treatment, and prognosis.

Grinspoon, Lester, and James B. Bakalar. *Marihuana, the Forbidden Medicine.* Yale U. Pr. 1993 $22.50. ISBN 0-300-05435-1. Outstanding compilation of essays documenting positive effects of marijuana as a therapeutic agent. Compelling argument to decriminalize marijuana for therapeutic purposes.

Mangel, Charles, and Allen Weisse. *Medicine: The State of the Art.* Doubleday 1984 o.p. "Describes advances in cardiology, orthopedics, organ transplants, burn treatment, and cancer" (*Library Journal*).

Napoli, Maryann. *Health Facts: A Critical Evaluation of the Major Problems, Treatments and Alternatives Facing Medical Consumers.* Overlook Pr. 1984 $23.95. ISBN 0-87951-132-X. "A critical but relatively fair evaluation of some of the major health problems and treatments. Will help readers to choose more intelligently from the available alternatives" (*Choice*).

Robin, Eugene. *Matters of Life and Death: Risks vs. Benefits of Medical Care.* W. H. Freeman 1984 o.p. "Analyzes the risk versus benefit of various diagnostic or therapeutic tests (procedures), the interrelationship between patient and physician, the factors affecting the decision to accept risky procedures or heroic therapy, and finally, basic principles for the care of the terminally ill patient" (*Choice*).

UROLOGIC DISEASES

Most books on diseases of the urinary system affecting such organs as the kidneys and bladder are extremely technical. However, the following books are accessible to the general reader.

Gillespie, Larrian, and Sandra Blakeslee. *You Don't Have to Live with Cystitis! A Woman Urologist Tells How to Avoid It—What to Do about It.* Avon 1988 $9.00. ISBN 0-380-70486-2. "Discusses causes, diagnosis, treatment and prevention. Covers childhood, pregnancy, and menopause as they relate to cystitis" (*Library Journal*).

The Human Body. The Kidneys: Balancing the Fluids. Torstar Bks. 1985 o.p. Describes the role of the kidneys in maintaining health; includes physiology, anatomy, disease and disorders, transplantation, and dialysis.

Managing Incontinence: A Guide to Living with the Loss of Urinary Control. Ed. by Cheryle Gartley. Green Hill 1985 o.p. "Personal recollections, revealing and often humorous, of men and women with continence problems stemming from a variety of causes. Deals with anatomy and physiology of the urinary tract, medical treatments frequently used, devices and products, and coping strategies" (*Library Journal*).

Scharf, Martin. *Waking Up Dry: How to End Bedwetting Forever.* Writers Digest 1986 o.p. Based on the successful program Scharf developed as a specialist at the Sleep Disorders Laboratory of Mercy Hospital in Cincinnati.

Seidick, Kathryn. *Or You Can Let Him Go.* 1984 $15.95. ISBN 0-385-29276-7. "The compelling valiant struggle of the [Seidick] family when faced with the sudden onset of end-stage renal disease in their eight-year-old son" (*Library Journal*).

CHRONOLOGY OF AUTHORS

Fauchard, Pierre. 1678–1761
Virchow, Rudolf Karl. 1821–1902
Pasteur, Louis. 1822–1895
Lister, Joseph. 1827–1912

Fleming, Sir Alexander. 1881–1955
Banting, Sir Frederick Grant.
1891–1941

BANTING, SIR FREDERICK GRANT. 1891–1941 (NOBEL PRIZE 1923)

Born in Alliston, Ontario, Frederick Banting, the son of a farmer, trained as an orthopedic surgeon at the University of Toronto, and later became a professor there. His fame, however, was related to endocrinology, because he helped discover insulin, the hormone the body uses to regulate the synthesis of glucose. His discovery has allowed millions of people to lead normal lives. Banting reviewed and analyzed a number of existing theories about pancreatic function to form a theory regarding the potential antidiabetic possibilities of that organ. He joined the physiology laboratory of J.J.R. Macleod at the University of Toronto, and, working with a graduate student, Charles H. Best, produced a pancreatic extract that controlled diabetes in a dog whose pancreas had been removed. Further research produced an extract from a cow's pancreas, which was used with inconsistent success on human subjects, probably the consequence of impurities in the extract. Macleod turned to J. B. Collip, a biochemist, for assistance with purification of the cow extract. In a short time, insulin injections had proved to be reliable and efficacious in human beings. In 1923, Banting and Macleod shared the Nobel Prize for their efforts. They, in turn, shared the prize with Best and Collip. In 1924, Banting established the Banting Research Foundation in Toronto, followed by the

Banting Institute (1930). He was knighted in 1934. Banting was killed in a plane crash off Newfoundland while on a mission during World War II.

BOOK BY BANTING

The Antidiabetic Functions of the Pancreas and the Successful Isolation of the Antidiabetic Hormone, Insulin. (coauthored with J.J.R. Macleod). London 1923 o.p. The early documentation of this remarkable medical milestone appeared in scientific journals in 1922. Series of three Beaumont lectures that Macleod and Banting presented, providing a historical background as well as a description of the laboratory research culminating in the discovery of insulin.

BOOK ABOUT BANTING

Bliss, Michael. *Banting: A Biography.* U. of Toronto Pr. 1992 repr. of 1984 ed. $19.95. ISBN 0-8020-7386-7. Comprehensive, well-researched and illustrated biography; easy to read.

FAUCHARD, PIERRE. 1678–1761

Born in Brittany, Pierre Fauchard was a French surgeon who is known as the founder of modern dentistry. He is credited with elevating dental surgery, as it was termed then, from a trade to a profession by developing systematic improvements to dental operations, such as the fastening of crowns and the extraction of diseased teeth. He also improved the design of removable dentures by customizing them to conform with the shape of the mouth. Perhaps his most enduring achievement, however, was the publication in 1728 of his two-volume treatise, *Le chirugien dentiste, ou Traité des Dents*, in which he attempted to synthesize and record all of the knowledge to date on the practice of dentistry. This landmark work appeared in a significantly revised and enlarged second edition in 1746 and continues to be historically important. It was the first dental textbook and it also contains some of the earliest and most detailed descriptions of dental clinical cases and instruments as well as the first description of pyorrhea, or "bad breath." Fauchard's contributions formed the basis for dental practice and training for many decades. His accomplishments are even more remarkable because he was self-taught.

BOOK ABOUT FAUCHARD

Weinberger, Bernhard W. *Pierre Fauchard, Surgeon-Dentist.* Pierre Fauchard Academy. 1941 o.p. Comprehensive biography that encompasses the history of modern dentistry, development of the first dental textbook, and information about dental professional life in eighteenth-century Europe.

FLEMING, SIR ALEXANDER. 1881–1955 (NOBEL PRIZE 1945)

Born in Ayrshire, Sir Alexander Fleming was a Scottish bacteriologist credited with the discovery of penicillin in 1928. His accolades came relatively late in life; he spent much of his career working as an assistant to another eminent bacteriologist, Sir Almroth Wright, at St. Mary's Hospital, London. Fleming authored more than 100 scientific papers, most of which appeared in prominent British journals. Fleming also was a professor of medicine at the University of London for many years. Although his laboratory research resulted in the discovery of penicillin, he was unable to stabilize and purify it for testing. He admitted that his knowledge of chemistry was insufficient to the task, but even the work of chemists failed to produce a substance that could be employed in a clinical trial. Fleming continued to believe in the enormous potential of his "mold juice" but he turned his attention to the sulfonamides. In 1940 Ernst

Chain, Howard Florey, and colleagues achieved the stabilization and purification that had eluded Fleming and applied penicillin as a therapeutic agent for the first time. Penicillin was used widely as an antibiotic for the first time on the battlefields of World War II and became generally available to the medical community soon thereafter. In 1945 Fleming shared the Nobel Prize in physiology or medicine with Florey and Chain. Discovery of the therapeutic value of penicillin ushered in a new research focus for medicine—antibiotics.

BOOK BY FLEMING

Penicillin, Its Practical Application. Intl. Med. Pub. 1946 o.p. Describes the scientific background of his discovery and provides important information about Chain and Florey's work to stabilize the compound for commercial production.

BOOKS ABOUT FLEMING

Ludovici, L. J. *Fleming: Discoverer of Penicillin.* Norwood Edns. 1979 repr. of 1952 ed. o.p. Brief biography that appeared three years before Fleming died.

Macfarlane, Gwyn. *Alexander Fleming, the Man and the Myth.* HUP 1984 $27.50. ISBN 0-674-01490-1. Reviews Fleming's life and contributions as a scientific drama rather than as the human drama of standard biography. Concludes that Fleming's fame for discovering the bacteriological properties and effects of penicillin actually was dependent on Chain and Florey, who discovered the therapeutic value.

Maurois, André. *The Life of Sir Alexander Fleming: Discoverer of Penicillin.* Trans. by Gerard Manley Hopkins. NAL-Dutton 1959 o.p. An "official" biography (written at the request of Mrs. Fleming) that contains personal photographs and reproductions from manuscripts, including a page from the notebooks in which Fleming drew the original mold growth and made his first observations of penicillin.

LISTER, JOSEPH. 1827–1912

Born in Upton, Essex, England, Joseph Lister was a British surgeon and the founder of antiseptic surgery, one of the most profound advances in medical care. He also was the first physician to be made an English lord. Lister's discoveries and the resulting doctrines and practices "transformed the ancient craft of surgery into an enlightened art governed by scientific disciplines" (*Dictionary of Scientific Biography*). He received his medical training at University College, London, graduating in 1852, about the time that anesthesia was being perfected. After graduating he became house surgeon to James Syme (whose daughter he married in 1856) at Edinburgh Royal Infirmary. Lister recognized the extraordinary promise of anesthesia but was troubled by the septic conditions under which surgical operations were being performed. With the advent of anesthesia, the number of operations rose dramatically, as did the problem with sepsis. In the 1860s, Lister became aware of the work of LOUIS PASTEUR, who had demonstrated that tissue putrefaction actually is fermentation. Lister experimented with a variety of substances before attempting to "cleanse" a wound with crude carbolic acid. His early efforts were so promising that he then spent a year perfecting a carbolic acid dressing for surgical wounds. His work was reported in the scientific press and at scientific meetings, notably those of the Royal Society, of which he was president from 1895 until 1900. By the late 1860s, his "antiseptic principle" had been widely adopted. Lister did not write any books but published widely in prominent medical and scientific journals.

BOOK BY LISTER

The Collected Papers of Joseph, Baron Lister. Ed. by Hector Cameron and others. 2 vols. OUP 1909 o.p. Lister's published contributions to medicine, compiled by a committee to commemorate Lister's 80th birthday; Lister helped select articles to include, choosing those that possessed permanent and historical interest and importance.

BOOKS ABOUT LISTER

Cheyne, William Watson. *Lister and His Achievement*. Longman 1925 o.p. Easy-to-read, brief, personal memoir written by one of Lister's lab assistants; based on his Listerian lectures of 1925.

Fisher, Richard B. *Joseph Lister, 1827–1912*. Stein & Day 1977 o.p. Scholarly biography, with extensive references, that sheds new light on Lister's role in the history of aseptic surgery.

Godlee, Rickman J. *Lord Lister*. Macmillan 3rd ed. 1924 o.p. Monumental biography that shows the benefits (access to records, evidence of Lister's impressions of events) and the difficulties (Lister's hand is apparent in some of the editing) of direct access to and influence by the subject; written by his nephew.

Guthrie, Douglas. *Lord Lister, His Life And Doctrine*. Livingstone 1949 o.p. Brief biography that uses extensive quotations from Lister's letters to trace the major events of his life.

Truax, Rhoda. *Joseph Lister, Father of Modern Surgery*. Bobbs 1944 o.p. Well researched, illustrated biography that is written for the general reader.

PASTEUR, LOUIS. 1822–1895

The son of a tanner, Louis Pasteur, whose name is immortalized in the household word "pasteurization," was a French microbiologist who discovered and developed the concept of vaccination. The product of a classical education, he spent his university years at the École Normale Supérieure in Paris, where he specialized in chemistry. His first university appointment was to the science faculty of Université de Strasbourg. He also served at other universities before the creation of the Institute Pasteur in Paris, which he directed until his death. Pasteur's life was dedicated to medical research, and he achieved phenomenal success in attracting the finances required to support those efforts. He was among the earliest physicians to patent his discoveries and to demonstrate their value to society, both avenues producing additional revenue for his diverse research projects.

Pasteur made major contributions to fields as diverse as crystallography, structural chemistry, fermentation, and silkworm diseases. He discredited the concept of spontaneous generation, proving it erroneous. His overall contribution to science was substantial largely because of his passionate commitment to the principle of application of research results. Pasteur's accomplishments demonstrated the vast medical and economic potential of experimental biology and led to improvements in industry as well as in medicine. Although he discovered and refined only a single treatment (for rabies) that had direct application, "his widely publicized and highly successful efforts on behalf of the germ theory were immediately credited with saving much money and many lives. It is for this reason above all that his name remains a household word" (*Dictionary of Scientific Biography*).

BOOKS ABOUT PASTEUR

Dubos, René. *Pasteur and Modern Science*. Sci. Tech. Pubs. 1988 repr. of 1960 ed. $22.00. ISBN 0-910239-18-5. Important analysis and review of the scope and significance of Pasteur's achievement, from the perspective of a science historian.

Koprowski, Hilary, and Stanley A. Plotkin, eds. *World's Debt to Pasteur*. Wiley 1985 o.p. Proceedings of a centennial symposium commemorating the first rabies vaccination; includes papers that reflect on Pasteur's significant contributions to society.

Vallery-Radot, René. *The Life of Pasteur*. Trans. by R. L. Devonshire. 1923 repr. of 1908
    ed. R. West o.p. The standard biography, arranged in brief chronological segments.

VIRCHOW, RUDOLF KARL. 1821–1902

Born at Schivelbein, Pomerania, Rudolf Virchow was a German physician
generally regarded as the greatest pathologist of all time and frequently referred
to as the founder of cellular pathology. He also was a distinguished statesman,
serving nearly 50 years on the Berlin City Council. Further, he made
contributions to the field of physical anthropology by founding the Berlin
Society of Anthropology, which was among the most influential professional
groups in the discipline for much of the late nineteenth century. Virchow's
observations and definitions of pathological phenomena at the cellular level still
form the foundation for much of current diagnosis and treatment of disease.

His most influential work, *Die Cellularpathologie in ihrer Begründung auf
physiologische und pathologische Gewebelehre*, was derived from a series of
lectures that he delivered in Berlin (1858). The work contains an historical
survey of the development of cell theory, a fundamental concept in the
biological and medical sciences. Although others had suggested that cells arise
only from cells, Virchow was the first to apply the principle to pathology, which
had an immediate and profound positive effect. Virchow also made important
contributions to the study of cancer, as well as the function of animal parasites;
his methods for post-mortem examinations altered profoundly the study of
morbid anatomy. In 1847 he founded the *Archiv für pathologische Anatomie und
Physiologie, und für die klinische Medizin*, which became one of the most
influential medical periodicals of the nineteenth century and still is published.

BOOKS BY VIRCHOW

Cellular Pathology, As Based upon Physiological and Pathological Histology. Trans. by F.
    Chance. R. M. De Witt 1860 o.p. Second updated edition, of Virchow's famous
    treatise, revised and translated.
Collected Essays on Public Health and Epidemiology. 2 vols. Watson Pub. Intl. 1985
    $50.00. ISBN 0-317-38928-9. Important collection of Virchow's essays on medical
    reform; originally published in German in 1879.
Disease, Life, and Man, Selected Essays. Stanford U. Pr. 1958 $37.50. ISBN 0-8047-0557-7.
    Virchow's translated speeches on the philosophy of medicine, some reprinted from
    periodicals.

BOOKS ABOUT VIRCHOW

Ackerknecht, Erwin Heinz. *Rudolf Virchow: Doctor, Statesman, Anthropologist*. Ayer
    1981 repr. of 1901 ed. $45.00. ISBN 0-405-13832-6. The most important work on
    Virchow, because it includes not only a superb biography but also an analysis of his
    ideas and how his accomplishments affected society.
Byers, James M. *From Hippocrates to Virchow: Reflections on Human Disease*. Am. Soc.
    Clinical 1987 $35.00. ISBN 0-89189-257-5. Fine, brief history of the development of
    pathology as a discipline; written for the scholar but accessible to the general reader.

CHAPTER 14

Clinical Psychology and Psychiatry

Amedeo Giorgi

> The psychiatric patient stands apart from the rest of the world. . . . Loneliness is the central core of his illness, no matter what his illness may be. Thus, loneliness is the nucleus of psychiatry. If loneliness did not exist, we could reasonably assume that psychiatric illness could not occur either, with the exception of the few disturbances caused by anatomical or physiological disorders of the brain.
>
> —J. H. VAN DEN BERG, *A Different Existence*

It has been said that psychology has a long past but a short history. It has a long past because the subject matter of psychology—how individuals experience, behave in, and make sense of the world—was studied and written about by ARISTOTLE (see Vol. 3) and other ancient Greeks. During the Middle Ages, questions about the mind and the behavior of individuals were left to the religious scholars and philosophers, so one can say that the history of psychology has been short in the sense that only in modern times have psychology and psychiatry been able to access these questions from a scientific point of view. Thus, in the modern sense, psychology and psychiatry began with their institutionalization within the framework of science, which itself undergoes evolution as it grows and expands to meet the pressures of concrete problems.

The modern era of psychology began in 1875 with the experimental work of the American philosopher WILLIAM JAMES (see also Vols. 3 and 4) and the establishment of a psychology laboratory at the University of Leipzig in Germany by WILHELM WUNDT (see Vol. 3) in 1879. Early experimental psychologists studied the phenomenon of consciousness—trying to determine its individual elements and how these elements were synthesized. Essentially, this type of psychology consisted of many introspective studies and experiments in sensation and perception. However, psychology in its scientific phase did not remain within the limits of this definition for very long. Around 1915, three important differentiations took place. What today is known as Gestalt psychology, reacting to the elementism of the Wundtian study of consciousness, emphasized that the experience of the world was organized and structured into patterns and that the task of psychology was to study these experiential patterns. At the same time, JOHN B. WATSON (see Vol. 3), an American psychologist, thought that the study of consciousness was too narrow and elusive, and declared that psychology should study the behavior of organisms because it was more tangible, more robust, and practically speaking, workable. Finally, SIGMUND FREUD's (see also Vol. 3) influence began to infiltrate academic circles. Because of his studies of hysterics and dreams, Freud emphasized a psychology based on the unconscious, not consciousness. These three basic perspectives and their offshoots competed for dominance within scientific psychology for about 40 years.

In the mid-1950s, two more differentiations took place. One was the return to the mind and its characteristics in the form of cognitive psychology, currently the dominant perspective of mainstream psychology. This perspective emphasizes the study of how the mind gets, processes, and responds to information about the world. The other was the emergence of humanistic psychology, founded to fill a perceived gap in mainstream psychology, namely, the study of the human person as a unique individual and of the human species as possessing unique characteristics.

This brief overview is meant to show that psychology is not all of one piece. Given the complexity of human existence and the brief time that modern psychology and psychiatry have had to discover their niches and accomplish their tasks, this should not be surprising. Nevertheless, the subject is even more complicated if clinical psychology and the professional dimensions of the fields are considered, because they pressure psychology in a wholly different way: How helpful is psychology to people suffering various experiential and behavioral maladies and conflicts?

Clinical psychology developed from the need to help people who were functioning poorly in their everyday world but were not primarily physically ill. Two major developments resulted: the establishment of clinics for dealing initially with retarded or handicapped individuals and later with purely psychological disturbances; and the invention and refinement of measuring and testing instruments, first for sensory and motor capacities, then for assessing intelligence and personality. Thus, clinical psychology was always concerned both with practical issues and the amelioration of either social or personal problems. Today, clinical psychologists still follow in this tradition, but in a highly expanded way. They are interested in theoretical issues of personality development, such as normal and abnormal functioning, personal capacities, skills and interests, and in such practical work as psychotherapy, diagnostic testing, educational and vocational evaluation of individuals and groups, and, in general, the use of techniques and practical strategies to help people help themselves. Of all these interests, testing and psychotherapy seem to be the major ones. There are many types of tests and many competing forms of psychotherapy—behavioral therapy, Gestalt therapy, psychoanalysis, cognitive therapeutic approaches, and humanistic orientations—which more or less parallel the academic differentiations discussed below.

Psychiatry, like medical psychology, goes back to the ancient Greeks, with whom the discipline reached a high level of sophistication. It declined, however, after the fall of Rome and continued to do so through the Middle Ages. Resurrected during the Renaissance by the work of JUAN LUIS VIVES (see Vol. 4), PHILIPPUS AUREOLUS PARACELSUS (see also Vol. 4), Weyer, and others, it finally became a specialty in its own right in the nineteenth century, especially with the classificatory system of Emil Kraepelin.

Psychiatry has its roots in and continues to be involved with "abnormal psychology," that is, with behavior or experience that is in some way or other bizarre or inappropriate to the circumstances. Everything else in psychiatry revolves around this primitive but concrete fact. Given this inappropriate or ineffective manifestation, one can look for the causes in the body, such as in the nervous or endocrine systems; in the depths of the unconscious psyche or preconscious infantile experiences; or in the individual's relation to significant others or to culture as a whole. Once these abnormalities are discovered, one can describe, typify, and rank them. One can then also develop a therapy to address the assumed cause: shock therapy for neurological causes, drugs for chemical malfunctions, psychoanalysis for unconscious causes, and other forms of psychotherapy to deal with cultural deprivations.

Thus, psychiatry is not all of one piece either. Indeed, conflict has long been the norm in psychiatry, and today the disunity is compounded by the presence of "antipsychiatrists," that is, those wishing to break away from the medical model altogether. Whether this movement is the beginning of a true answer to the perennial quest of psychiatry or just another element in the conflict, only time will tell. Having found itself in the nineteenth century, perhaps psychiatry can find a way of interpreting its various dimensions in the remaining years of the twentieth century.

GENERAL PSYCHOLOGY

Abramson, Paul. *Personality*. H. Holt & Co. 1980 o.p. "Interesting, readable, and thereby appealing to both the nonmajor and major in psychology" (*Contemporary Psychology*).

Atwater, W. Eastwood. *Psychology of Adjustment: Personal Growth in a Changing World*. P-H 4th ed. 1990. ISBN 0-13-732157-0. Excellent introductory text; employs a humanistic, growth-oriented approach.

Averill, James R. *Anger and Aggression: An Essay on Emotion*. Spr.-Verlag 1982 $66.00. ISBN 0-387-90719-X. "Ought to be read by anyone who is seriously interested in theories of emotion" (*Contemporary Psychology*).

Bandura, Albert, ed. *Psychological Modeling: Conflicting Theories. Controversy Ser.* Lieber-Atherton 1971 o.p. Consists of nine chapters written by expert scientists; exceptionally good reference features.

Beigel, Hugo G. *Dictionary of Psychology and Related Fields*. Ungar 1971 o.p. "Indispensable for those doing research based on original works of Freud, Jung, Adler, Binswanger, Bleuler, et al." (*Choice*).

Boring, E. G. *A History of Experimental Psychology*. P-H 1950 $60.00. ISBN 0-13-390039-8. Classic text of the field, with plenty of biographical information and good discussions of substantive issues.

Coon, Dennis. *Introduction to Psychology: Exploration and Application*. West Pub. 6th ed. 1992 $53.25. ISBN 0-314-92211-3. "'Instructionally engineered' should be emblazoned on the cover of this introductory book, whose design includes as many features intended to facilitate learning the contents as any nonprogrammed text I have seen" (*Contemporary Psychology*).

Corsini, Raymond J., ed. *Encyclopedia of Psychology*. 4 vols. Wiley 1984 $400.00. ISBN 0-471-86594-X. Up-to-date summary of psychological terms.

Freedheim, Donald K., and others, eds. *History of Psychotherapy: A Century of Change*. Am. Psychol. 1992 $69.95. ISBN 1-55798-149-3. Offers a retrospective investigation of the roots and the development of psychotherapy from four basic perspectives: theory, research, practice, and training.

Gelso, Charles J., and Bruce R. Fretz. *Counseling Psychology. William James Centennial Ser.* HarBraceJ 1992 $42.75. ISBN 0-03-027858-9. Broad overview of the specialty of counseling psychology—its professional practices and issues, its interventions, its science and research, and its basic concept; especially suited for the beginning student.

Gilligan, Carol. *In a Different Voice: Psychological Theory and Women's Development*. HUP 1993 $8.95. $20.00. ISBN 0-674-44544-1. "Gilligan treats her subject clearly and concisely" (*Book Review Digest*).

Goldenberg, Herbert. *Contemporary Clinical Psychology. Psychology Ser.* Brooks-Cole 1982 o.p. Good introduction for nonclinical professionals.

Harriman, Philip L. *Dictionary of Psychology*. Citadel Pr. 1971 repr. of 1960 ed. o.p.
_____. *Handbook of Psychological Terms. Quality Pap. Ser.* Littlefield 1977 repr. of 1965 ed. $6.95. Guidebook to the technical vocabulary of scientific psychology.

The Harvard List of Books in Psychology. HUP 1971 $4.95. ISBN 0-674-37601-3. Contains 744 entries arranged by basic subject areas and selected by 40 specialists in their respective fields.

Haynes, Stephen N., ed. *Psychosomatic Disorders: A Psychological Approach to Etiology and Treatment.* Greenwood $52.95. ISBN 0-275-90640-X. "A scholarly, readable volume on an array of disorders (*Contemporary Psychology*).

Hersen, Michel, and others. *The Clinical Psychology Handbook.* Allyn 1991 $130.95. ISBN 0-205-14362-8. Extensive overview of theory, research, clinical methods, and perspectives.

Hillman, James. *Revisioning Psychology.* HarpC 1992 $11.00. ISBN 0-685-52543-0. "As an explorer of the imaginal realm of the psyche, faithful to the reality of the archetypes rather than to one theory about them, Hillman has no living peer" (*Library Journal*).

Lifton, Robert J. *Boundaries: Psychological Man in Revolution.* S&S Trade 1976 o.p. Contains reflections on man's changing sense of self in relation to the complex themes of life, such as death, destruction, and revolution.

Miller, Jean B. *Toward a New Psychology of Women.* Beacon Pr. 1986 $20.00. ISBN 0-8070-2910-6. Social psychological analysis of the role and status of women.

Nordby, Vernon J., and Calvin S. Hall. *A Guide to Psychologists and Their Concepts. Psychology Ser.* W. H. Freeman 1974 $13.95. ISBN 0-7167-0759-4. "Each concept is individually treated, in a logical order, and then explained . . . in laymen's terms" (*Book Review Digest*).

Rutan, J. Scott, ed. *Psychotherapy for the 1990s.* Guilford Pr. 1992 $35.00. ISBN 0-89862-798-2. Covers the broad array of contemporary psychotherapies, the issues in practice today, and new conceptualizations and modalities.

Sanford, Nevitt. *Issues in Personality Theory. Social and Behavioral Sciences Ser.* Bks. Demand repr. of 1970 ed. $48.30. ISBN 0-317-08243-4. "Organized in terms of issues ordered according . . . 'to a broad, theoretically neutral conceptual scheme' " (*Contemporary Psychology*).

Shaffer, John B. *Humanistic Psychology. Foundations of Modern Psychology Ser.* P-H 1978 $19.00. ISBN 0-13-447680-8. Good supplementary reader.

Tarczan, Constance. *An Educator's Guide to Psychological Tests: Descriptions and Classroom Implications.* C. C. Thomas 1975 o.p. Makes psychological testing and its implications of use to the teacher or school counselor.

Van der Zanden, James W. *Human Development.* McGraw 1989 $37.30. ISBN 0-07-066997-X. "A good introductory developmental text, well written, carefully documented, and broad in its approach" (*Contemporary Psychology*).

Watson, Robert I. *The Great Psychologists.* HarpC 1990 $53.50. ISBN 0-06-041919-9. Covers important figures and historical problems in the development of psychology.

Wheelis, Allen. *How People Change.* HarpC 1975 $9.00. ISBN 0-06-090447-X. "This is a well-written, even poetic book that defines in direct human terms the meaning of freedom and the importance of the exercise of free choice in the creative growth and fulfillment of the individual" (*Library Journal*).

————. *Quest for Identity.* Norton 1966 $7.95. ISBN 0-393-00745-6. Essay on modern man and his quest for identity as well as a critique of the role of psychoanalysis in this quest.

Wolman, Benjamin B. *Dictionary of Behavioral Science.* Acad. Pr. 1989 $59.00. ISBN 0-12-762455-4. Contains 1,200 short entries on terms, persons, and tests in psychology, psychiatry, and neurology.

Zusne, Leonard. *Names in the History of Psychology: A Biographical Sourcebook.* Wiley 1975 o.p. "Biographical information about the most eminent psychologists" (*Library Journal*).

PSYCHIATRY

American Psychiatric Association. *Biographical Directory of the American Psychiatric Association.* Bowker 1977 o.p. Authoritative biographical record of psychiatrists in the United States and Canada. Guide to the 20,000 members of the American Psychiatric Association as of 1977; members listed alphabetically with a geographical index for convenient cross-reference. Excellent sourcebook and an essential for all libraries.

Arieti, Silvano, and others, eds. *American Handbook of Psychiatry*. 8 vols. Basic 2nd rev. ed. $132.00. ISBN 0-465-00153-X. Complete encyclopedia of psychiatric forms and concepts.

Brown, Terrance. *The Diversity of Normal Behavior: Further Contributions to Normatology*. Ed. by D. Offer and M. Sabshin. Basic 1992 $45.00. ISBN 0-465-01685-5. Critical analysis that addresses contemporary controversies within psychiatry.

Brussel, James A. *The Layman's Guide to Psychiatry*. B&N Imports 1971 o.p.

Brussel, James A., and George L. Cantzlaar. *The Layman's Dictionary of Psychiatry*. HarpC 1967 o.p. "The approximately 1,500 descriptive psychiatric terms (including names of famous psychoanalysts and psychiatrists) found in this dictionary are defined in an understandable, jargon-free style" (*Choice*).

Fink, Paul Jay, and Allan Tasman, eds. *Stigma and Mental Illness*. Am. Psychiatric 1992 $35.00. ISBN 0-88048-405-5. Collection of papers dealing with all aspects of stigma related to mental illness, offering an understanding of its impact and importance.

Grinker, Roy R., Sr. *Psychiatry in Broad Perspective*. Human Sci. Pr. 1975 $42.95. ISBN 0-87705-231-X. "This book is largely a personalized, multidisciplinary overview of aspects of psychiatric research by a psychiatrist who has spent 40 years in the field. It considers topics such as the qualities of a researcher, designing a research program [and] aspects of biological, psychoanalytic and clinical research" (*Library Journal*).

Grob, Gerald, ed. *The Inner World of American Psychiatry, 1890 to 1940: Selected Correspondence*. Rutgers U. Pr. 1985 $40.00. ISBN 0-8135-1081-3. Correspondence from those who helped shape American psychiatry. Organized in light of many contemporary issues and problems of psychiatry" (*Contemporary Psychology*).

Hinsie, Leland E., and Robert Campbell. *Psychiatric Dictionary*. OUP 1970 $26.50. ISBN 0-19-501132-5. ". . . a continuing version of the Dictionary by Leland E. Hinsie and Jacob Shatzky, first published in 1940. . . . About five hundred entries have been deleted and some fourteen hundred new listings included" (*Contemporary Review*).

Horton, Paul C. *Solace: The Missing Dimension in Psychiatry*. U. Ch. Pr. 1983 $7.95. ISBN 0-226-35387-7. "Useful introduction to the concept of transitional phenomena" (*Contemporary Psychology*).

Melges, Frederick T. *Time and the Inner Future: A Temporal Approach to Psychiatric Disorders*. Wiley 1982 o.p. Well organized and enjoyable; includes bibliography and index.

Miller, Milton H. *If the Patient Is You (Or Someone You Love): Psychiatry Inside Out*. Scribner 1977 o.p. Popular work written for the layperson; includes bibliographical references and index.

Strecker, Edward Adam. *Basic Psychiatry*. Random 1952 o.p. Excellent survey for the general reader.

Tseng, Wen-Shing, and John McDermott, Jr. *Culture, Mind and Therapy: An Introduction to Cultural Psychiatry*. Brunner-Mazel 1981 o.p. Well-written pioneer work in the discipline of cultural psychiatry.

Wing, John K., and Brenda Morris, eds. *Handbook of Psychiatric Rehabilitation Practice*. OUP 1981 $15.95. ISBN 0-19-261276-X. Practical manual for professionals and their staffs who currently provide rehabilitative services for the mentally ill.

Zilboorg, Gregory, and George W. Henry. *A History of Medical Psychology*. Norton 1967 o.p. Fascinating account of the development of psychiatry from the ancient Greeks to the twentieth century; good reading for anyone interested in cultural history, not just psychiatry.

SPECIAL READING LISTS

Children

Aichhorn, August. *Wayward Youth.* Northwestern U. Pr. 1983 repr. of 1936 ed. o.p. Important early interpretation of the application of psychoanalytic theory to problems of children.

Cattanach, Ann. *Play Therapy with Abused Children.* Taylor & Francis 1992 $60.00. ISBN 1-85302-120-2. Describes ways of starting play therapy and explains how the abused child can use the process for healing; valuable book for professionals who work with abused children.

Chess, Stella. *An Introduction to Child Psychiatry.* Saunders 1969 o.p.

Coles, Robert. *Children of Crisis.* 5 vols. Little Vol. 1 1968 $19.95. ISBN 0-316-15154-8. Vol. 2 1973 $24.95. ISBN 0-316-15176-9. Vol. 3 1973 $19.95. ISBN 0-316-15177-7. Vol. 4 1977 o.p. Vol. 5 1980 $24.95. ISBN 0-316-15150-5. Classic studies on children's perspectives on life by a respected psychiatrist; engaging and insightful.

Conners, C. Keith. *Food Additives for Hyperactive Children.* Plenum 1980 o.p. Written for a well-informed adult.

Copeland, Donna R., and others, eds. *The Mind of the Child Who Is Said to Be Sick.* C. C. Thomas 1983 o.p. Broadly informative book dealing with the situation of the chronically ill, cancer-stricken child or adolescent.

Corsini, Raymond J., and Genevieve Painter. *The Practical Parent: The ABC's of Child Discipline.* HarpC 1975 o.p. Presents "the Dreikurs/Adlerian method of family living and child rearing" (*Library Journal*).

Finkelhor, David. *Sexually Victimized Children.* Free Pr. 1981 $14.95. ISBN 0-02-910210-3. "For anyone interested in the child sexual abuse/incest question" (*Contemporary Psychology*).

Frude, Neil, ed. *Psychological Approaches to Child Abuse.* Rowman 1981 o.p. Good selection of papers giving an overview of diverse approaches to understanding the etiology and effects of abusive care-taking.

Hodges, William F. *Interventions for Children of Divorce: Custody, Access, and Psychotherapy.* Wiley 1991 $49.95. ISBN 0-471-52255-4. Clear, consistent, conceptual understanding of the effects of separation and divorce on children at different stages of development.

Jenkins, Richard L., and Ernest Harms, eds. *Understanding Disturbed Children: Professional Insights into Their Psychiatric and Developmental Problems.* Spec. Child 1976 o.p. Excellent presentation of the subspecialty for students of child psychiatry.

Josephson, Martin M., and Robert T. Porter. *Clinician's Handbook of Childhood Psychopathology.* Aronson 1979 $40.00. ISBN 0-87668-357-6. "Pediatricians, teachers, and other professionals who work with children and require only a broad, but shallow, exposure to child psychopathology will find the book helpful" (*Contemporary Psychology*).

Kagan, Jerome, and Robert Coles, eds. *Twelve to Sixteen: Early Adolescence.* Norton 1972 $11.95. ISBN 0-393-09621-1. "In this very uncommon collection of essays, a group of experts from a variety of social science disciplines talk about the young adolescent (*Contemporary Psychology*).

Kanner, Leo. *Child Psychiatry.* C. C. Thomas 1979 $90.50. ISBN 0-398-02199-6

———. *Childhood Psychosis: Initial Studies and New Insights.* Halsted Pr. 1973 o.p.

Lahey, Benjamin B., Alan E. Kazdin, and others, eds. *Advances in Clinical Child Psychology.* 15 vols. Plenum Pubs. 1980–93 $45.00–$69.50. Up-to-date readable reviews.

Moustakas, Clark E. *The Child's Discovery of Himself.* Aronson 1974 o.p.

Poussaint, Alvin, and *James Comer. Black Child Care.* S&S Trade 1975 o.p. Studies the development of the black child from infancy through adolescence; written in a question-and-answer format.

Starr, R. H., Jr., ed. *Child Abuse Prediction: Policy Implications.* Harper Busn. 1982 $34.95. ISBN 0-88410-378-1. Readable and well researched.

Walker, Sydney, III. *Help for the Hyperactive Child.* HM 1979 o.p. "His examples, for the most part, are drawn from cases that clearly demonstrate medical or emotional problems other than what has been called 'minimal brain dysfunction' or the 'hyperkinetic-learning disability syndrome' " (*Library Journal*).

Whiting, Beatrice B., and John Whiting. *Children of Six Cultures: A Psycho-Cultural Analysis.* HUP 1974 o.p. "A study of the observed social behavior of 134 children from the ages of three to eleven in Okinawa, Kenya, India, Mexico, and the United States" (*Library Journal*).

Willis, Diane J., and others, eds. *Prevention of Child Maltreatment: Developmental and Ecological Perspective.* Wiley 1991 $42.95. ISBN 0-471-63419-0. Includes an extensive review of the literature on child abuse prevention and concrete ideas for implementing prevention programs in a wide variety of clinical settings.

Zimbardo, Philip G., and Shirley Radl. *The Shy Child: A Parent's Guide to Preventing and Overcoming Shyness from Infancy to Adulthood.* McGraw 1981 o.p. "Presents a conceptualization of shyness based primarily on survey data, anecdotal case material and clinical experience and intuition" (*Contemporary Psychology*).

Methods and Approaches in Counseling and Therapy

Bellack, Alan S., Michael Hersen, and Alan E. Kuzdin, eds. *International Handbook of Behavior Modification and Therapy.* Plenum Pubs. 1982 $95.00. ISBN 0-306-43348-6. Indispensable book for libraries and reference collections.

Bellak, Leopold, David M. Abrams, and Ruby Ackermann-Engel. *Handbook of Intensive Brief and Emergency Psychotherapy.* C.P.S. Inc. 1987 repr. of 1983 ed. $14.95. ISBN 0-918863-00-7. Systematic, pragmatic handbook for dealing with emergency and crisis situations.

Binder, Virginia, Arnold Binder, and Bernard Rimland, eds. *Modern Therapies.* P-H 1976 o.p. General panorama of therapies including the innovations of the 1970s; prepared for the lay reader.

Blocher, Donald H., and Donald A. Biggs. *Counseling Psychology in Community Settings.* Springer Pub. 1983 o.p. "A treatise that offers a reservoir of clear ideas that will help students understand and prepare for the challenges of this profession" (*Contemporary Psychology*).

Bockus, Frank. *Couple Therapy.* Aronson 1980 $40.00. ISBN 0-87668-412-6. "Leaves the reader with an excellent understanding of what the experimental approach has to offer" (*Contemporary Psychology*).

Burks, Herbert M., Jr., and Buford Stefflre, eds. *Theories of Counseling.* McGraw 1979 o.p. Basic information on theories of counseling for beginning counselors and personnel workers.

Chertok, Leon. *Sense and Nonsense in Psychology: The Challenge of Hypnosis.* Pergamon 1981 o.p. "The reader will learn much that is of value about hypnosis and its ability as a therapeutic and research tool" (*Contemporary Psychology*).

Chirban, John T., ed. *Health and Faith: Medical, Psychological and Religious Dimensions.* U. Pr. of Amer. 1991 $38.00. ISBN 0-8191-8284-2. Offers interdisciplinary sensitivity to matters of health (including AIDS and cancer) from the perspectives of medicine, psychology, and religion.

Collier, Helen V. *Counseling Women: A Guide for Therapists.* Free Pr. 1982 $32.95. ISBN 0-02-905840-6. "Addressed to mental health workers, psychiatrists, psychologists, and social workers, but also will be useful to others who serve or are interested in women's needs" (*Library Journal*).

Crits-Cristoph, P., and J. P. Barber, eds. *Handbook of Short-Term Dynamic Psychotherapy.* Basic 1991 $35.00. ISBN 0-465-02875-6. Invaluable reference for students, teachers, clinicians, and researchers.

De Schill, Stefan, ed. *The Challenge for Group Psychotherapy: Present and Future.* Intl. Univs. Pr. 1974 o.p. Eleven different authors provide several interesting glimpses of analytic therapy.

Dinkmeyer, Don C., and James J. Muro. *Group Counseling: Theory and Practice*. Peacock Pubs. 1979 o.p. Useful introduction for anyone interested in learning about group work.

Doyle, Robert E. *Essential Skills and Strategies in the Helping Process*. Brooks-Cole 1992 $36.50. Provides students who are studying the counseling process with a comprehensive understanding of the skills and strategies that are of critical importance in this process (*Preface*).

Engelkes, James R. *Introduction to Counseling*. HM 1982 o.p. "Simple, but useful introduction to difficult concepts of counseling" (*Contemporary Psychology*).

Feder, Bud, and R. Ronall, eds. *Beyond the Hot Seat: Gestalt Approaches to Group*. Brunner-Mazel 1980 o.p. "A reflection of the current mental health gestalt, with all its promise of great benefits, its multidirectional development, and its ambiguities" (*Contemporary Psychology*).

Forsyth, Donelson R. *Group Dynamics*. Psychology Ser. Brooks-Cole 1990 $54.75. ISBN 0-534-08010-3. Good introduction to the field.

Frank, Jerome D. *Persuasion and Healing: A Comparative Study of Psychotherapy*. Johns Hopkins 1993 repr. of 1991 ed. $16.95. ISBN 0-8018-4636-6. Attempt to sort out what is common to many forms of psychotherapy; very comprehensive.

Freeman, Dorothy R. *Marital Crisis and Short-term Counseling: A Casebook*. Free Pr. 1982 o.p. "Recommended to the novice, the general reader, and the experienced clinician alike" (*Contemporary Psychology*).

Freeman, Harrop A. *Counseling in the United States*. Oceana 1967 $12.00. ISBN 0-379-00308-2. "A very detailed study on the most elementary aspects of counseling as a distinct profession" (*Library Journal*).

Geller, Janet A. *Breaking Destructive Patterns: Multiple Strategies for Treating Partner Abuse*. Free Pr. 1992 $27.95. ISBN 0-02-911605-8. This book describes an intervention model that uses multiple methods in the treatment of domestic violence . . . using case examples extensively (*Preface*).

Getz, William L., and others. *Brief Counseling with Suicidal Persons*. Free Pr. 1982 $29.95. ISBN 0-669-04090-8. Logical and clear exposition presenting concrete examples and concepts.

Gibson, H. B. *Hypnosis: Its Nature and Therapeutic Uses*. Taplinger 1980 repr. of 1978 ed. o.p. "For the person who is reading about hypnosis for the first time, this book immediately captures the interest and holds the attention of the reader" (*Choice*).

Greenhill, Maurice H., and Alexander Gralnick, eds. *Psychopharmacology and Psychotherapy*. Free Pr. 1982 o.p. Readers with clinical interests will find this book especially appealing.

Guerin, Philip J., Jr., ed. *Family Therapy: Theory and Practice*. Gardner Pr. 1976 $37.50. ISBN 0-89876-070-8. "Covers a rich variety of clinical and theoretical issues in 31 articles on technique, approaches, and significant clinical issues in family therapy" (*Contemporary Psychology*).

Gustafson, James Paul. *The Complex Secret of Brief Psychotherapy*. Norton 1986 o.p. Notes the profound differences separating therapies and how some of these differences can be reconciled; marvelously readable.

Haley, Jay. *Ordeal Therapy: Unusual Ways to Change Behavior*. Social and Behavioral Sciences Ser. Jossey-Bass 1984 $28.95. ISBN 0-87589-595-6. Thirteen case histories demonstrating the approach of ordeal therapy.

———. *Problem-Solving Therapy: New Strategies for Effective Family Therapy*. HarpC 1984 $6.95. ISBN 0-06-131991-0. Designed to teach therapists specific techniques for dealing with family relationships" (*Contemporary Psychology*).

Harper, R. *The New Psychotherapies*. P-H 1975 o.p. Survey of treatment methods that have developed since 1959. ". . . a helpful map for the existing psychotherapy maze" (*Contemporary Psychology*).

Horewitz, James S. *Transactional Analysis and Family Therapy*. Aronson 1979 o.p. For the paraprofessional who does not have extensive training in psychiatry.

Kahn, Marvin W. *Basic Methods for Mental Health Practitioners*. Little 1981 o.p. "Directly helpful to workers in community mental health programs and those involved in training, supervising, and working with paraprofessionals" (*Contemporary Psychology*).

Keeney, Bradford P. *Improvisational Therapy: A Practical Guide For Creative Clinical Strategies*. Guilford Pr. 1991 $14.95. ISBN 0-89862-486-X. Depicts psychotherapy as a performing art, emphasizing the advantages of improvising one's own therapeutic style.

Kelly, Edward J., and Gary J. Vitali, ed. *Conduct Problem/Emotional Problem Interventions: A Holistic Perspective*. Slosson Educational Pubs. 1992 o.p. Emphasizes the importance of personal, experiential, qualitative, subjective self-perceptual, and purposive-voluntary considerations in understanding human motivation and action (*Preface*).

Korchin, Sheldon. *Modern Clinical Psychology*. Basic 1976 $24.95. ISBN 0-465-04638-X. Broad overview of modern techniques and approaches to clinical psychology.

Kovel, Joel. *A Complete Guide to Therapy: From Psychotherapy to Behavior Modification*. Pantheon 1977 o.p. "Recommended to the ordinary consumer of therapeutic services" (*Contemporary Psychology*).

Krippner, Stanley, and Alberto Villoldo. *The Realms of Healing*. Celestial Arts 1986 $9.95. ISBN 0-89087-474-3. Survey of types of therapies and healings, including those of other cultures and primitive societies.

Kroger, William S. *Clinical and Experimental Hypnosis: In Medicine, Dentistry and Psychology*. Lippincott 1977 $57.50. ISBN 397-50377-6. "A convenient beginning library for anyone becoming intrigued by hypnosis" (*Contemporary Psychology*).

Lanyon, Richard I., and Barbara P. Lanyon. *Behavior Therapy: A Clinical Introduction*. Topics in Clinical Psychology Ser. Addison-Wesley 1978 $11.95. ISBN 0-201-04100-6. Excellent introduction to the subject.

Marlatt, G. Alan, and Peter E. Nathan. eds. *Behavioral Approaches to Alcoholism*. Rutgers Center of Alcohol Studies Pubns. 1978 $6.00. Good, stimulating introduction.

Mendelsohn, Roy M. *Leaps: Facing Risks in Offering a Constructive Therapeutic Response When Unusual Measures Are Necessary*. Aronson 1992 $40.00. ISBN 0-87668-566-1. Presents some unconventional ways in which therapists can deal with an impasse in therapy; argues that because each treatment venture is unique, psychotherapists must always be open to new learning.

Morse, Stephen J. *Psychotherapies: A Comparative Casebook*. H. Holt & Co. 1977 o.p. Good reference book including 24 case studies.

Naar, Ray. *A Primer of Group Psychotherapy*. Human Sciences Pr. 1982 $35.95. ISBN 0-89885-289-7. "Presents marvelous case material that illustrates his approach to group treatment . . . should be of particular interest to beginning group psychotherapists interested in the practical aspects of group leadership" (*Contemporary Psychology*).

Okun, Barbara F., and Louis J. Rappaport. *Working with Families: An Introduction to Family Therapy*. Dunbury Pr. 1980 o.p. Good introduction to systems and developmental theory; a solid survey of different approaches to family systems therapy.

O'Leary, K. Daniel, and G. Terence Wilson. *Behavior Therapy: Application and Outcome*. P-H 1975. ISBN 0-13-073890-5. Suitable for use by undergraduates.

Patterson, C. H. *Theories of Counseling and Psychotherapy*. HarpC 1980 $53.50. ISBN 0-06-045053-3. Thorough overview of different counseling and therapy theories.

Paul, Norman L., and Betty Paul. *A Marital Puzzle: Trans-generational Analysis in Marriage Counseling*. Gardner Pr. 1986 repr. of 1975 ed. o.p. Includes transcripts of eight therapy sessions.

Perez, Joseph F. *Family Counseling*. Van Nos. Reinhold 1979 o.p. Should be read by anyone interested in social injustice.

Peszke, Michael A. *Involuntary Treatment of the Mentally Ill: The Problem of Autonomy*. C. C. Thomas 1975 o.p. "Valuable for those uninformed about the basis of traditional worlds of mental disorders" (*Contemporary Psychology*).

Rossi, Ernest Lawrence. *The Psychobiology of Mind-Body Healing: New Concepts of Therapeutic Hypnosis*. Norton 1986 $25.95. ISBN 0-393-70034-8. An excellent review of the neurophysiological dimensions of body-mind reactions and an elaboration of how hypnosis may help normal functioning.

Segraves, R. Taylor. *Marital Therapy: A Combined Psychodynamic-Behavioral Approach.* Plenum 1982 $45.00. " 'Must' reading for students of marital therapy. . . . [The] author presents volumes of information on the topic in a well-organized style" (*Contemporary Psychology*).

Seligman, Milton. *Group Counseling and Group Psychotherapy with Rehabilitation Clients.* C. C. Thomas 1977 o.p. "Effective combination of scholarly work and practical methods that results in a very readable book" (*Contemporary Psychology*).

Shear, Howard J. *Understanding Psychotherapy: A Paradox of Being.* Dabor Science Pubns. 1977 o.p. Good for the undergraduate or general reader.

Stephenson, F. Douglas, ed. *Gestalt Therapy Primer: Introductory Readings in Gestalt Therapy.* Aronson 1978 o.p. Collection of articles about the history, philosophy, methods, and practice of Gestalt therapy written by 11 first- and second-generation practicing Gestalt therapists.

Tjosvold, Dean, and *Mary Tjosvold. Working with Mentally Handicapped Persons in Their Residences.* Free Pr. 1981 o.p. Useful resource for professionals.

Usdin, Gene, ed. *Overview of the Psychotherapies.* Brunner-Mazel 1975 o.p. Recognized experts in the field of psychiatry write about different approaches to therapy, including the use of drugs in the treatment of mental illness.

Watkins, Mary. *Invisible Guests: The Development of Imaginal Dialogues.* Analytic Pr. 1986 $16.95. ISBN 0-938434-81-0. Shows the value that imaginal dialogues—dialogues with imaginary others—have for individuals throughout their lives; an important contribution to the life of the imagination.

Watzlawick, Paul. *The Language of Change: Elements of Therapeutic Communication.* Basic 1978 $16.95. ISBN 0-465-03792-5. "Psychotherapists and those interested in interpersonal influence will appreciate and benefit from this work" (*Contemporary Psychology*).

———. *The Situation Is Hopeless, But Not Serious: The Pursuit of Unhappiness.* Norton 1983 $16.95. ISBN 0-393-01821-0. Lay readers will find Watzlawick's writing engaging, intriguing, thought-provoking, accessible, and encouraging.

Wedding, Dan, and Raymond J. Corsini, eds. *Great Cases in Psychotherapy.* Peacock Pubs. 1979 o.p. Intended for the student with little background in the field.

Weiner, Irving B., ed. *Clinical Methods in Psychology.* Wiley 1983 o.p. "Surveys assessment and intervention methods in a way that addresses the needs of both beginning and experienced clinicians" (*Contemporary Psychology*).

Weiner, Myron F. *Therapist Disclosure: The Use of Self in Psychotherapy.* U. Park Pr. 1983 o.p. Recommended for therapists and readers interested in psychotherapy.

Wolberg, Lewis R. *The Technique of Psychotherapy.* Saunders 1988 $180.00. ISBN 0-8089-1877-X. Valuable compendium for students and professionals.

Yablonsky, Lewis. *Psychodrama: Resolving Emotional Problems through Role-playing.* Gardner Pr. 1981 repr. of 1976 ed. $14.95. ISBN 0-87630-698-9. A practicing psychodramatist writes about his profession in a clear and readable way.

Yalom, Irvin D. *Existential Psychotherapy.* Basic 1980 $33.00. ISBN 0-465-02147-6. Students, teachers, and practitioners will benefit from Yalom's presentation of concepts and lucid explanations.

Miscellaneous

Arieti, Silvano. *The Will to Be Human.* Dell 1975 o.p. "[This] humanistic examination of the capacity of man to grow by conscious willing places Arieti—despite some specific disagreements with their theories—in the same school with Fromm and Erikson" (*Publishers Weekly*).

Askenasy, Alexander. *Attitudes Toward Mental Patients.* Mouton 1974 $38.75. ISBN 90-2797-891-3. Ideally suited for public officials who have the influence to bring about necessary changes.

Axline, Virginia M. *Dibs: In Search of Self.* Ballantine 1986 $4.95. ISBN 0-345-33925-8. Story of the transformation of a disturbed child into a healthy personality.

Back, Kurt W. *Beyond Words: The Story of Sensitivity Training and the Encounter Movement.* Russell Sage 1972 $45.00. ISBN 0-87154-077-0. An "excellent attempt at appraising sensitivity training as a social movement without uncritically accepting it or irrationally denouncing it. Back puts sensitivity training into historical perspective" (*Choice*).

Baruch, Dorothy W. *One Little Boy.* Dell 1983 o.p. Describes the world of a typical boy with insight.

Bellak, Leopold. *Overload: The New Human Condition.* Human Sciences Pr. 1975 $35.95. ISBN 0-87705-245-X. "Bellak attempts to integrate clinical and research psychiatry into a method by which the crises faced by contemporary society may be treated, in much the same manner as a psychiatrist treats a patient" (*Library Journal*).

Bloom, Bernard L., and Shirley J. Asher, eds. *Psychiatric Patient Rights and Patient Advocacy: Issues and Evidence.* Community Psychology Ser. Human Sciences Pr. 1982 $42.95. ISBN 0-89885-056-8. Chapters deal with major issues in mental health law, such as stigma, involuntary treatment, the insanity defense, prediction of dangerousness, and confidentiality and informed consent. Useful resource for anyone interested in law and psychiatry policies.

Blum, Richard H. *The Dream Sellers: Perspectives on Drug Dealers.* Social and Behavioral Sciences Ser. Jossey-Bass 1972 o.p. Highly detailed look at drugs and the world of the drug dealer.

Bowlby, John. *Maternal Care and Mental Health.* Monograph Ser. World Health 1952 $7.20. ISBN 92-4-140002-1. Constitutes the most comprehensive and integrated summary of the literature.

———. *Separation: Anxiety and Anger. Attachment and Loss Ser.* Basic 1973 $20.00. ISBN 0-465-09716-2. "Written in clear, well-organized style . . . an authoritative contribution to the field" (*Book Review Digest*).

Burton, Arthur. *Twelve Therapists: How They Live and Actualize Themselves.* Social and Behavioral Sciences Ser. Jossey-Bass 1973 o.p. Biographical material providing important insights into those who practice the art of mental healing.

Caplan, Gerald. *Support Systems and Community Mental Health.* Human Sciences Pr. 1974 o.p. ". . . a welcome addition to the literature on volunteerism that is illustrating the need and readiness of most of us to respond to opportunities to be helpers in areas where we have resources from which others can benefit" (*Contemporary Psychology*).

Cohen, Raquel E., and Frederick L. Ahearn, Jr. *Handbook for Mental Health Care of Disaster Victims.* Johns Hopkins 1980 $28.00. ISBN 0-8018-2427-3. "Organization is direct and strong, style is brisk . . . language is clear" (*Contemporary Psychology*).

Coles, Robert. *The Mind's Fate: Ways of Seeing Psychiatry and Psychoanalysis.* Little 1976 o.p. Collection of book reviews, articles, and other writings.

De Beauvoir, Simone. *A Very Easy Death.* Warner Bks. 1985 $11.00. ISBN 0-394-72899-8. Includes elements of De Beauvoir's autobiography and her own philosophical interpretation of death's meaning.

Deutsch, Helene. *Confrontations with Myself.* Norton 1973 o.p. "A psychiatrist who received her training from Freud and then went on to become the first director of the Vienna Training Institute, Deutsch reminisces about her experiences and insights over a long career in analysis" (*Library Journal*).

Deutsch, Morton. *The Resolution of Conflict: Constructive and Destructive Processes.* Yale U. Pr. 1973 $18.00. ISBN 0-300-02186-0. "This approach is clearly written and argued" (*Book Review Digest*).

Diamond, Edwin. *The Science of Dreams.* Doubleday 1962 o.p. Informative, readable material about dreams, ranging from the beliefs of primitive man to the theories of psychoanalysis.

Fingarette, Herbert. *On Responsibility.* Basic 1967 o.p. "A brave work, a brilliant analysis, an exciting experience" (*Book Review Digest*).

———. *Self-Deception*. Humanities 1969 o.p. Brief philosophical analysis of rationalization and repression, drawn from the literature of clinical psychopathology and a variety of other sources.

Fisher, Seymour, and Rhoda L. Fisher. *Pretend the World Is Funny and Forever: A Psychological Analysis of Comedians, Clowns, and Actors*. Erlbaum 1981 $39.95. ISBN 0-89859-073-6. "Presentation is simple, straightforward, and aimed at the general reader" (*Contemporary Psychology*).

Fromm, Erich, and Michael Maccoby. *Social Character in a Mexican Village*. P-H 1970 o.p. Empirical study of Mexican peasants.

Gedo, Mary M. *Picasso: Art as Autobiography*. U. Ch. Pr. 1980 $20.00. ISBN 0-226-28482-4. Gedo "examines the role played by personal experience in . . . Picasso's stylistic innovations" (*Book Review Digest*).

Gibson, H. B. *Pain and Its Conquest*. Dufour 1982 $30.00. ISBN 0-7206-0595-4. "Clear and psychologically comprehensible book; intended as a practical manual for those who suffer pain" (*Contemporary Psychology*).

Gilkey, Langdon. *Shantung Compound*. HarpC 1975 $8.95. ISBN 0-06-063112-0. Daily observations recorded by the well-known American theologian while imprisoned in a Japanese internment camp during World War II.

Goethals, George R., and Stephen Worchel. *Adjustment and Human Relations*. Knopf 1981 o.p. Nontechnical and effective introduction for students to the rudiments of personality, developmental, and social psychology.

Goldenson, Robert M. *The Encyclopedia of Human Behavior: Psychology, Psychiatry, and Mental Health*. 2 vols. Doubleday 1970 o.p. More than 1,000 articles on such topics as dream interpretations, phobia, and Parkinson's disease; arranged alphabetically.

Haight, M. R. *A Study of Self-Deception*. Humanities 1980 o.p. "Readable and makes good use of a variety of methods and considerations" (*Contemporary Psychology*).

Hall, Calvin S., and Gardner Lindzey. *Theories of Personality*. Wiley 1978 $54.95. ISBN 0-471-34227-0. Excellent, readable overview of several approaches to personality theory.

Halleck, Seymour. *The Politics of Therapy*. Aronson 1971 o.p. "Of particular importance to mental health professionals and teachers as well" (*Choice*).

Harding, M. Esther. *I and the "Not-I."* Bollingen Ser. Princeton U. Pr. 1965 $9.95. ISBN 0-691-01796-4. "Harding is usually lucid enough for any reader who has followed the better popular psychological works" (*Library Journal*).

Herr, Stanley S., Stephen Arons, and Richard E. Wallace. *Legal Rights and Mental Health Care*. Lexington Bks. 1983 $32.95. ISBN 0-669-04910-7. A "fine book for the beginner in the area of patients' rights with respect to the law and mental health sciences" (*Contemporary Psychology*).

Jacoby, Russell. *Social Amnesia: A Critique of Contemporary Psychology from Adler to Laing*. Beacon 1976 repr. of 1975 ed. o.p. Commentary on contemporary psychology.

Kastenbaum, Robert, and Ruth Aisenberg. *The Psychology of Death*. Springer Pub. 1976 $29.95. ISBN 0-8261-1920-4. Stimulating and comprehensible.

Kiell, Norman, ed. *Psychoanalysis, Psychology and Literature: A Bibliography*. Scarecrow 1982 $85.00. ISBN 0-8108-1421-8. "The first attempt at a bibliography of works approaching literature from a psychoanalytic or psychological point of view" (*Book Review Digest*).

Kubler-Ross, E. *On Death and Dying*. Macmillan 1979 $17.95. ISBN 0-02-089130-X. The book that broke the taboo. A necessity for the lay reader who is interested.

Lane, Harlan, and Richard Pillard. *The Wild Boy of Burundi*. Random 1978 o.p. "Main purpose is to convey to the scientifically untrained reader an appreciation of scientific method within this extraordinary context" (*Contemporary Psychology*).

Lee, Courtland D., and Bernard L. Richardson. eds. *Multicultural Issues in Counseling: New Approaches to Diversity*. Am. Coun. Assn. 1991 $32.95. ISBN 1-55620-082-X. Focuses on cultural experiences related to racial or ethnic factors in counseling.

Levinson, Daniel. *The Seasons of a Man's Life*. Ballantine 1978 $24.95. ISBN 0-394-40699-X. Study of the phases of the adult male development.

Lifton, Robert J. *Death in Life: Survivors of Hiroshima.* Basic 1982 $19.95. ISBN 0-465-01581-6. Winner of the 1969 National Book Award in the Sciences. Lifton's citation reads in part: "This perceptive analysis in depth by a psychiatrist of the survivors of the first atomic bomb serves to remind us of an event too easily forgotten."

Lingeman, Richard R. *Drugs from A to Z: A Dictionary.* McGraw 1974 o.p. "The whole history of drugs and addicts . . . from amphetamines to zonked, from Miltown to STP" (*Choice*).

Lomas, Peter. *The Case for a Personal Psychotherapy.* OUP 1981 $22.95. ISBN 0-19-217680-3. Its "greatest strength is the book's way of bringing to life, via clinical vignettes, ideas that have become stale through repetition, such as the openness and trust in the clinical relationship" (*Contemporary Psychology*).

Luber, Raymond F., ed. *Partial Hospitalization: A Current Perspective.* Plenum 1979 $39.50. ISBN 0-306-40201-7. "Succeeds as both a primer for the uninitiated and as a beacon for those interested in making partial hospitalization a viable treatment" (*Contemporary Psychology*).

Lundberg, Margaret J. *The Incomplete Adult.* Greenwood 1974 $49.95. ISBN 0-8371-7362-0. "Lundberg argues that degree of personality development is directly related to social class membership" (*Contemporary Psychology*).

Lynd, Helen M. *On Shame and the Search for Identity.* HarBraceJ 1970 repr. of 1958 ed. o.p. Brings expertise to the relationship between shame and identity.

Moore, Dwight, and Fred Leafgren, eds. *Problem Solving Strategies for Men in Conflict.* Am. Coun. Assn. 1990 $28.95. ISBN 1-55620-067-6. Practical and challenging book addressing the special issues that concern men today.

Moustakas, Clark E. *Loneliness and Love.* P-H 1990 $7.95. ISBN 0-13-540386-3. "This book will reaffirm those who have been through loneliness and will hopefully reawaken those out of step with their inner selves who flee loneliness because they feel 'safer' in the herd. Highly recommended" (*Library Journal*).

Neisser, Edith G. *Mothers and Daughters: A Lifelong Relationship.* HarpC 1973 o.p. Well-documented, carefully researched, and enjoyable work.

Quinnett, Paul G. *The Troubled People Book: A Comprehensive Guide to Getting Help.* Continuum 1982 o.p. Useful guide for the lay reader.

Rachman, Stanley J. *Fear and Courage.* Psychology Ser. W. H. Freeman 1989 $33.95. ISBN 0-7167-2061-2. "Clear and graceful prose; presents a diversity of source material" (*Contemporary Psychology*).

Reason, James, and Klara Mycielska. *Absent Minded?: The Psychology of Mental Lapses and Everyday Errors.* P-H 1982 o.p. Of interest to both the general reader and the psychologist.

Reisman, John M. *A History of Clinical Psychology.* Irvington 1982 repr. of 1976 ed. $32.50. ISBN 0-89874-487-3. Easy to read and very informative.

Rennie, Ysabel. *The Search for Criminal Man: A Conceptual History of the Dangerous Offender.* Lexington Bks. 1978 o.p. Good for lay readers interested in the history of criminology.

Reynolds, David K., and Norman Farberon. *Endangered Hope: Experiences in Psychiatric Aftercare Facilities.* U. CA Pr. 1978 $30.00. ISBN 0-520-03457-0. "Should be read by persons interested in helping former patients make a successful transition back to society" (*Contemporary Psychology*).

Ricks, David, Alexander Thomas, and Merrill Roff, eds. *Life History Research in Psychopathology.* U. of Minn. Pr. 1970 o.p. Collection of papers presented at Columbia University Teachers College; includes verbatim transcripts of questions, answers, and discussions of each paper.

Roback, Abraham A. *History of Psychology and Psychiatry.* Greenwood 1969 repr. of 1961 ed. $49.75. ISBN 0-8371-2104-3. An excellent survey.

Sadoff, Robert L. *Violence and Responsibility: The Individual, the Family and Society.* Halsted Pr. 1978 o.p. "Overview of relatively current thinking on topics such as family violence, child abuse, juvenile violence, etc." (*Contemporary Psychology*).

Seabrook, Jeremy. *Loneliness.* Universe Bks. 1975 o.p. "Conveys more about the nature of loneliness than many studies full of statistics and case histories" (*Library Journal*).

Seeley, John. *The Americanization of the Unconscious*. Intl. Sci. Pub. 1967 o.p. Presents Seeley's thesis that revolutionary changes in American psychiatry and sociology are producing a "distinctly American Unconscious."

Shostrom, Everett. *Man, the Manipulator*. Bantam 1968 o.p. Discusses the differences between "manipulation," or the exploitation involved in relationships to which one does not give oneself, and "actualization," its opposite. Also discusses the application of these concepts to various forms of psychotherapy.

Singer, Kenneth S., and J. L. Pope, eds. *The Power of Human Imagination: New Methods in Psychotherapy*. Plenum 1978 o.p. "An eye-opener for people relatively uninformed about this vantage point" (*Contemporary Psychology*).

Stein, Leonard, and Mary Ann Test, eds. *Alternatives to Mental Hospital Treatment*. Plenum 1978 o.p. Readable overview.

Straus, Murray A., and Richard J. Gilles. *Behind Closed Doors: Violence in the American Family*. Doubleday 1981 o.p. Highly readable; designed for the lay reader.

Vonnegut, Mark. *The Eden Express*. Bantam 1976 o.p. Engaging descriptions of his schizophrenic experiences.

Walker, Lenore. *The Battered Woman Syndrome. Focus on Women Ser.* Spring Pub. 1984 o.p. Good reading for anyone concerned with social injustice.

Watts, Alan W. *The Book: On the Taboo Against Knowing Who You Are*. Random 1989 $8.00. ISBN 0-679-72300-5. This authority on comparative religions brings "insights from the Eastern religions . . . to bear upon the problems of Western man's misuse of his technological knowledge to the point of his imminent destruction. A timely, thoughtful, relevant book" (*Library Journal*).

———. *Psychotherapy East and West*. Random 1975 $7.00. ISBN 0-394-71609-4. A search for common ground between Western psychotherapy and Eastern philosophy.

World Health Organization. *Advances in the Drug Therapy of Mental Illness: Proceedings*. World Health 1976 $12.00. ISBN 92-4-156051-7. A collection of 21 papers.

Zimbardo, Philip G., and *Shirley Radl. Shyness: What It Is, What to Do about It*. Addison-Wesley 1977 $9.95. ISBN 0-201-08793-6. Aimed at the general reader.

Psychoanalysis

Alexander, Franz. *Fundamentals of Psychoanalysis*. Norton 1968 o.p. Well-organized, readable, and compact outline.

Alexander, Franz, Samuel Einstein, and Martin Grotjahn, eds. *Psychoanalytic Pioneers*. Basic 1966 o.p. Includes Ferenczi, Rank, Jung, Federn, Briehl, W. Reich, M. Klein, K. Horney, H. Hartmann, E. Kris, Anna Freud, and others.

Berne, Eric. *A Layman's Guide to Psychiatry and Psychoanalysis (The Mind in Action)*. Ballantine 1982 o.p. "One of the fine things about this book is the skillful use of anecdote; the examples are always informative as well as intriguing, and most of the people in them seem like characters in search of a novelist" (*Publishers Weekly*).

Console, William A., Richard C. Simmons, and Mark Rubinstein. *The First Encounter: The Beginnings in Psychotherapy*. Aronson 1977 o.p. Discusses psychoanalytic psychotherapy.

Eidelberg, Ludwig, ed. *Encyclopedia of Psychoanalysis*. Free Pr. 1968 o.p. "A fairly comprehensive compendium of the more important concepts of the classical or orthodox Freudian school. There are 643 entries . . . a bibliography of 1,500 titles, and an index of 6,000 items. The material is clearly and concisely written" (*Library Journal*).

English, Horace B., and Ava C. English. *A Comprehensive Dictionary of Psychological and Psychoanalytical Terms*. Longman 1958 o.p. Useful for medical, academic, and many categories of special libraries.

Fingarette, Herbert. *The Self on Transformation: Psychoanalysis, Philosophy and the Life of the Spirit*. HarpC 1965 o.p. Enlightened description of the phases of a self being transformed.

Frosch, John, and Nathaniel Ross, eds. *The Annual Survey of Psychoanalysis: A Comprehensive Survey of Current Psychoanalytic Practice and Theory*. 10 vols. 1965.

Intl. Univs. Pr. o.p. Summaries of studies on the history, theory, and applications of psychoanalytic psychiatry, therapy, and training; best single source of information about psychoanalytic literature.

Greenson, Ralph R. *Explorations in Psychoanalysis.* Intl. Univs. Pr. 1978 $70.00. ISBN 0-8236-1810-2. A work that "provides convenient access to Greenson's abundant, authoritative, clinical wisdom" (*Contemporary Psychology*).

Grinstein, Alexander, ed. *The Index of Psychoanalytic Writings.* Intl. Univs. Pr. Vols. 1–5 1956–60 $150.00. ISBN 0-8236-8400-8. Vols. 6–9 1963–66 $150.00. ISBN 0-8236-8401-6. Vols. 10–14 1973 $150.00. ISBN 0-8236-8402-4. Revision and update of John Richmann's *Index Psychoanalyticus* (1893–1926).

Guntrip, Harry. *Psychoanalytic Theory, Therapy, and the Self.* Basic 1973 $17.00. ISBN 0-465-09511-9. "The basic philosophy of Guntrip, who is a world leader in psychological theorizing, is that 'to care for people is more important than to care for ideas'. . . . An important contribution to a human rather than mechanistic view in personality growth and treatment" (*Choice*).

Hedges, Lawrence E. *Interpreting the Countertransference.* Aronson 1992 $47.50. ISBN 0-87668-532-7. Varieties of therapist responses are organized along a developmental axis of human relatedness possibilities; offers alternative considerations to therapists' emotional reaction toward clients.

Kris, Ernst. *Psychoanalytic Explorations in Art.* Intl. Univs. Pr. 1962 $47.50. ISBN 0-8236-4440-5. The study of art and creative processes from a psychoanalytic perspective.

Liebert, Robert S. *Michelangelo: A Psychoanalytic Study of His Life and Images.* Yale U. Pr. 1983 o.p. "Recommended as a humane and informed meditation on the complex personality of a great artist" (*Contemporary Psychology*).

Malcolm, Janet. *Psychoanalysis: The Impossible Profession.* Random 1982 $9.00. ISBN 0-394-71034-7. "An excellent essay on personality . . . which transcends reportage" (*N.Y. Times Bk. Review*).

Muensterberger, Werner, ed. *The Psychoanalytic Study of Society.* Vol. 17 Analytic Pr. 1992 $36.00. ISBN 0-88163-151-5. "The wide area of applicability of psychoanalytic concepts and the vitality of contemporary psychoanalytic thinking are well documented in this volume" (*Contemporary Psychology*).

Neumann, Erich. *Depth Psychology and a New Ethic.* Shambhala Pubns. 1990 repr. of 1969 ed. $19.95. ISBN 0-87773-571-9. "Neumann has dealt very effectively with the ethical implications of the unconscious, noting the old and new ethic, the stages of ethical development, and the aims and values of the new ethic" (*Choice*).

Scharff, Jill Savege. *Projective and Introjective Identification and the Use of the Therapist's Self.* Aronson 1992 $40.00. ISBN 0-87668-530-0. Landmark work on object relations integrating theory and practice, with particular coverage of countertransference; written in a vivid, personally candid style.

Wyss, Dieter. *Psychoanalytic Schools from the Beginning to the Present.* Trans. by Gerald Onn. Aronson 1973 $30.00. ISBN 0-87668-099-6. Good historical survey.

Psychological Disorders

Alvarez, Alfred. *The Savage God: A Study of Suicide.* Norton 1990 $8.95. ISBN 0-393-30657-7. A reflection on the meaning of suicide with references to classical literature and some case histories.

Alvarez, Walter C. *Minds That Came Back.* Lippincott 1961 o.p. A prominent writer and emeritus professor of medicine at the University of Wisconsin offers his own reviews of outstanding autobiographies of about 75 abnormal personages . . . . who successfully returned from the strange limbo of insanity, alcoholism, neurosis, epilepsy, phobia, or psychoanalysis" (*Library Journal*).

Angyal, Andras. *Neurosis and Treatment: A Holistic Theory. Psychoanalysis Examined and Re-examined Ser.* Da Capo 1982 $35.00. ISBN 0-306-79709-7. A jewel of a book, presenting Angyal's formulations about the origins of neuroses and psychological health.

Arieti, Silvano. *Interpretation of Schizophrenia*. Basic 1974 o.p. Awarded a 1975 National Book Award "for its scientific content and profound humanism."

———. *Understanding and Helping the Schizophrenic: A Guide for Family and Friends*. S&S Trade 1981 o.p. "An excellent portrait of the world of the schizophrenic . . . in language directed toward the lay reader" (*Book Review Digest*).

Barnes, Mary, and J. Berke. *Mary Barnes: Two Accounts of a Journey through Madness*. Ballantine 1978 o.p. "The book will provide absorbing reading" (*Book Digest*).

Beyond Symptom Suppression: Improving Long-Term Outcomes of Schizophrenia. Group for the Advancement of Psychiatry, Committee on Psychopathology. Am. Psychiatric 1992 $25.00. ISBN 0-87318-202-2. Multidimensional, longitudinal treatment approach, focusing on stage-specific disabilities and needs from a developmental perspective.

Blatt, Sidney J., and Cynthia M. Wild. *Schizophrenia: A Developmental Analysis*. Acad. Pr. 1976 o.p. Covers the concept of boundary disturbances.

Brenner, Charles. *The Mind in Conflict*. Intl. Univs. Pr. 1982 $35.00. ISBN 0-8236-3365-9. "Extraordinarily well-suited as a teaching text for students at any level of academic or clinical training" (*Contemporary Psychology*).

Brown, George W., and Tirril Harris. *Social Origins of Depression: A Study of Psychiatric Disorder in Women*. Free Pr. 1978 o.p. 'Massive data presented for those interested in social and psychological aspects of depression" (*Contemporary Psychology*).

Bruch, Hilde. *The Golden Cage: The Enigma of Anorexia Nervosa*. Random 1979 $8.00. ISBN 0-394-72688-X. "Based on clinical observations from the author's own extensive casework" (*Contemporary Psychology*).

Cegelka, Patricia T., and Herbert J. Prehm. *Mental Retardation: From Categories to People*. Merrill 1982 o.p. Descriptive accounts of casework provide a solid framework of basic and applied facts about retardation for students of special education.

Clarke, Ann M., and Alan D. Clarke, eds. *Mental Deficiency: The Changing Outlook*. Free Pr. 1986 $49.95. ISBN 0-317-40304-4. Definitive work.

Duke, Marshall, and Stephen Nowicki, Jr. *Abnormal Psychology*. HarBraceJ 1986 $52.95. ISBN 0-03-004404-9. Good introduction for students without a strong background in the subject.

Eysenck, H. J., ed. *You and Neurosis*. Sage 1979 o.p. "Highly readable and lucid pioneer on the theory, practice, and results of behavioral therapy" (*Contemporary Psychology*).

Fadiman, James, and D. Kawman. *Exploring Madness: Experience, Theory, and Research*. Psychology Ser. Brooks-Cole 1979 o.p.

Fann, W. E., and others, eds. *Phenomenology and Treatment of Depression*. Spectrum 1977 o.p. Interesting book with something for everyone.

———, eds. *Phenomenology and Treatment of Schizophrenia*. Spectrum 1978 o.p. Offers a good deal of information to anyone with an interest in schizophrenia.

Fingarette, Herbert. *The Meaning of Criminal Insanity*. U. CA Pr. 1972 o.p. "An excellent book—well written and well argued" (*Book Review Digest*).

Forrest, Gary G. *How to Live with a Problem Drinker and Survive*. Macmillan 1986 $8.95. ISBN 0-689-70706-1. Self-help book written for the families of people with drinking problems.

Friedrich, Otto. *Going Crazy*. S&S Trade 1976 o.p. "Dozens of stories told efficiently by the author. . . . Conveys that we are all at the mercy of various forces" (*Contemporary Psychology*).

Gottesfeld, Harry. *Abnormal Psychology: A Community Health Perspective*. Science Research Associates 1979 o.p. Well written.

Grant, Brian W. *Schizophrenia: A Source of Social Insight*. Westminster John Knox 1975 o.p. A "scholarly work, written with an exceptional understanding" (*Library Journal*).

Ingalls, Robert P. *Mental Retardation: The Changing Outlook*. Macmillan 1978 o.p. The best introductory level text.

Kaplan, Berton H., eds. *The Inner World of Mental Illness: A Series of First Person Accounts of What It Was Like.* HarpC 1964 o.p. Collection of 31 personal statements, describing the experience of patients under the influence of psychoses and neuroses.

Kisker, George W. *The Disorganized Personality.* McGraw 1977 $42.90. ISBN 0-07-034878-2. Undergraduate text.

Kuiper, Pieter C. *The Neuroses.* Intl. Univs. Pr. 1972 o.p.

Levitt, Eugene E. *The Psychology of Anxiety.* Erlbaum 1980 $19.50. ISBN "An almost excellent first undergraduate reference for a course in which anxiety is the central issue" (*Contemporary Psychology*).

Lidz, Theodore. *Origin and Treatment of Schizophrenic Disorders.* Basic 1990 repr. of 1973 ed. $24.95. ISBN 0-8236-828-9. Analysis of the world of schizophrenia.

McCall, Raymond J. *The Varieties of Abnormality: A Phenomenological Analysis.* C. C. Thomas 1975 $59.50. ISBN Intended for undergraduates; relies completely on clinical description.

McKeller, Peter. *Mindsplit: The Psychology of Multiple Personality and the Dissociated Self.* Biblo 1979 o.p. Well written, scholarly, and entertaining.

Mathew, Andrew M., Michael G. Gelder, and Derek W. Johnston. *Agoraphobia: Nature and Treatment.* NYU Pr. 1986 $22.50. ISBN 0-8147-5426-0. Of interest to lay readers, students, and mental health professionals.

Matson, Johnny L., and James A. Mulick. eds. *Handbook of Mental Retardation. General Psychology Ser.* Allyn 1991 $100.95. ISBN 0-205-14413-6. "Valuable service for the serious student or professional who needs exposure to the wide range of current knowledge in a burgeoning field" (*Contemporary Psychology*).

Meyer, Robert G., and Yvonne Hardaway Osborne. *Case Studies in Abnormal Behavior.* Allyn 1982 $27.00. ISBN 0-205-10472-X. "Presents cases and the therapist's perspective of pathology, diagnosis, and treatment in a way that is understandable to the student or novice" (*Contemporary Psychology*).

Nathan, Peter E., and Sandra L. Harris. *Psychopathology and Society.* McGraw 1980 o.p. "Social learning perspective appropriate to integrate etiology, treatment, and description" (*Contemporary Psychology*).

Neale, John M., and Thomas F. Oltmanns. *Schizophrenia.* Wiley 1980 o.p. Excellent survey of the field.

Neale, John M., Thomas F. Oltmanns, and G. C. Davidson. *Case Studies in Abnormal Psychology.* Wiley 1982 $24.95. ISBN 0-471-53106-5. Case studies containing important clinical descriptions.

Page, James D. *Psychopathology: The Science of Understanding Deviance.* OUP 1975 $18.95. ISBN 0-19-502293-9. Excellent text with a good introduction to abnormal psychology.

Perlin, Seymour, ed. *A Handbook for the Study of Suicide.* OUP 1975 $19.95. ISBN 0-19-501856-7. Eleven contributions examining suicidal behavior in the contexts of history, literature, philosophy, anthropology, sociology, biology, psychiatry, and epidemiology.

Polich, J. Michael, and David J. Armor. *The Course of Alcoholism: Four Years after Treatment.* Ed. by Harriet B. Braiker. Wiley 1981 o.p. "Recommended that everyone interested in alcoholism read the study with an open mind. It is thorough and well-written" (*Contemporary Psychology*).

Price, Richard H., and S. J. Lynn. *Abnormal Psychology.* Dorsey 1986 o.p. Excellent volume, bringing the realm of the "abnormal" into the realm of understanding.

Reid, William H., ed. *The Psychopath: A Comprehensive Study of Antisocial Disorders and Behaviors.* Brunner-Mazel 1978 o.p. Comprehensive presentation of both the clinical and experimental perspectives.

Reynolds, David K., and Norman Farberon. *The Family Shadow: Sources of Suicide and Schizophrenia.* U. CA Pr. 1981 $32.50. ISBN 0-520-04213-1. "Should be compulsory reading" (*Contemporary Psychology*).

Rowe, Dorothy, ed. *The Experience of Depression.* Wiley 1978 o.p. A large portion of the text is devoted to transcripts of therapy sessions with depressed patients.

Sacks, Oliver. *The Man Who Mistook His Wife for a Hat and Other Clinical Tales.* HarpC 1987 repr. of 1986 ed. $12.00. ISBN 0-06-097079-0. Highly readable and informative series of stories, revealing the mysterious depths of human existence and the concrete problems that psychiatry and clinical psychology must face; good literature and good science. Can be recommended for all readers.

Salzman, Leon. *Treatment of the Obsessive Personality.* Aronson 1992 repr. of 1985 ed. $45.00. ISBN 0-87668-881-4. "... merits a prize for this jargon-free discussion of the obsessive-compulsive personality, 'today's most prevalent neurotic character structure' " (*Library Journal*).

Scharfetter, Christian. *General Psychopathology: An Introduction.* Trans. by Helen Marshall. Cambridge U. Pr. o.p. "Provides a detailed descriptive, phenomenological survey of mental disorders. . . . The clinical examples provide an unusually rich and varied source of descriptive case material" (*Contemporary Psychology*).

Scheper-Hughes, Nancy. *Saints, Scholars, and Schizophrenics: Mental Illness in Rural Ireland.* U. CA Pr. 1979 $13.95. ISBN 0-520-09786-9. Very readable study.

Shean, Glenn. *Schizophrenia: An Introduction to Research and Theory.* U. Pr. of Amer. 1987 $22.00. ISBN 0-8191-6476-3. Introductory text.

Shneidman, Edwin S. *Definition of Suicide.* Wiley 1985 o.p. Series of ideas about suicide, put forward in order to help forge a new understanding of this tragic phenomenon.

Silver, Daniel, and Michael Rosenbluth, eds. *Handbook of Borderline Disorders.* Intl. Univs. Pr. 1992 $75.00. ISBN 0-8236-2290-8. Handbook seeking to present the most contemporary views, questions, and methods on the topic.

Smith, Robert J. *The Psychopath in Society.* Acad. Pr. 1978 $30.00. ISBN 0-12-652550-1. "Offers fluid writing, penetrating thinking, and sound scholarship" (*Contemporary Psychology*).

Snyder, Solomon H. *Biological Aspects of Mental Disorder.* OUP 1980 $12.95. ISBN 0-19-502715-9. Good for the undergraduate reader.

Spitzer, Robert L. *Psychopathology: A Case Book.* McGraw 1983 $26.10. ISBN 0-07-060350-2. Includes 54 case descriptions, most of which are accompanied by discussion of the psychopathology and diagnosis, etiology, treatment, and prognosis.

Stein, Laszlo, Eugene D. Mindel, and Theresa Jabaley, eds. *Deafness and Mental Health.* Am. Deaf & Rehab. 1985 $5.00. ISBN 0-914494-13-9. Good for training teachers and professionals.

Sutherland, N. S. *Breakdown.* Stein & Day 1977 o.p. "Case study of author's own experience and layperson's guide to the mental health disciplines" (*Contemporary Psychology*).

Thorman, George. *Incestuous Families.* C. C. Thomas 1983 $34.25. ISBN 0-398-04808-8. Highly readable work for the general concerned public.

Thornberry, Terence P., and Joseph E. Jacoby. *The Criminally Insane: A Community Follow-Up of Mentally Ill Offenders.* U. Ch. Pr. 1979 $24.00. ISBN 0-226-79818-6. A book that will "appeal to a wide variety of audiences concerned with related policy, scientific, and theoretical issues" (*Contemporary Psychology*).

Torrey, E. Fuller. *Surviving Schizophrenia: A Family Manual.* HarpC 1988 $22.95. ISBN 0-06-015112-9. "Valuable resource for families of schizophrenics. Has the aim of educating the layperson and providing tools for coping" (*Contemporary Psychology*).

Val, Edwardo R., Moises Gaviria, and Joseph Flaherty. *Affective Disorders, Psychopathology and Treatment.* Bks. Demand repr. of 1982 ed. $132.10. ISBN 0-8357-7634-4. The audience for this book should be students.

Westermeyer, Joseph. *A Primer on Chemical Dependency.* Williams & Wilkins 1976 o.p. "Rigorous and elegant research; an excellent primer" (*Contemporary Psychology*).

White, Robert W., and Norman F. Watt. *The Abnormal Personality.* Wiley 1981 o.p. Good textbook on abnormality.

Williams, Robert L., and Ismet Karacan. *Sleep Disorders: Diagnosis and Treatment.* Wiley 1978 $70.00. ISBN 0-471-83721-0. Essential reading.

Yochelson, Samuel, and Stanton Samenow. *The Criminal Personality: The Drug User.* 3 vols. Aronson 1976–86 $40.00 ea. ISBN 0-87668-901-2. Unique interpretation of the criminal personality with plenty of supporting data.

Zarit, Steven H. *Aging and Mental Disorders: Psychological Approaches to Assessment and Treatment.* Free Pr. 1983 $16.95. ISBN 0-02-935980-5. Provides useful information for the general reader.

Sexuality

Adelson, Edward T., ed. *Sexuality and Psychoanalysis.* Brunner-Mazel 1975 o.p. "This collection of essays presents . . . physiological, anatomical, biochemical, and psychological research in sexuality and relates it to classical and modern psychoanalytic thinking" (*Library Journal*).

Bootzin, Richard R., and Joan Acocella. *Abnormal Psychology: Current Perspectives.* Random 1992 $34.36. ISBN 0-07-911168-8. Clearly slanted toward undergraduates and nonpsychology majors.

Brecher, Edward M. *The Sex Researchers.* Specific Pr. 1979 $9.50. ISBN 0-317-34150-2. "This account combines a readable, non-technical style with scientific accuracy. Quotations from the original works are used extensively to illustrate accurately the sex-researchers' position. Brecher's major theme is the gradual convalescence of our culture from the debilitating sexual disease of Victorianism" (*Contemporary Psychology*).

Brierly, Harry. *Transvestism: A Handbook with Case Studies for Psychologists, Psychiatrists, and Counselors.* Pergamon 1979 o.p. "A good beginning for the comprehension of a complex issue" (*Contemporary Psychology*).

Bullough, Vern L., and Bonnie Bullough. *Sin, Sickness, and Sanity: A History of Sexual Attitudes.* New Amer. Lib. 1977 o.p. For the general reader.

Carlton, Eric. *Sexual Anxiety: A Study of Male Importance.* B & N Imports 1980 o.p. For the intelligent lay reader.

Ellis, Albert, and Albert Abarbanel, eds. *The Encyclopedia of Sexual Behavior.* Hawthorn Bks. 1961 o.p. More than 100 articles by international authorities on the biology, physiology, and anatomy of sex. Excellent reference work.

Gillan, Patricia, and Richard Gillan. *Sex Therapy Today.* Grove 1977 o.p. "Excellent and highly readable introduction to current sex therapy practices" (*Contemporary Psychology*).

Masters, William H., and others. *The Pleasure Bond: A New Look At Sexuality and Commitment.* Bantam 1976 o.p. "Considers in a more personal way, the values of sexual relations" (*Contemporary Psychology*).

Moore, Donna M., ed. *Battered Women.* Sage 1979 o.p. "Useful guide for workers in shelters for battered women" (*Contemporary Psychology*).

Sanderson, Christiane. *Counseling Adult Survivors of Child Sexual Abuse.* Taylor & Francis 1990 $57.00. ISBN 1-85302-045-1. Examines theories that attempt to account for the occurrence of child sexual abuse, explains the traumatic impact, and looks at ways in which these effects can be ameliorated.

Szasz, Thomas S. *Manufacture of Madness: A Comparative Study of the Inquisition and the Mental Health Movement.* HarpC 1977 $7.95. ISBN 0-06-131984-8. "This book is addressed to a less technical reading audience" (*Choice*).

CHRONOLOGY OF AUTHORS

James, William. 1842–1910
Freud, Sigmund. 1856–1939
Ellis, Havelock. 1859–1939
Adler, Alfred. 1870–1937
Brill, A(braham) A(rden). 1874–1948
Jung, C(arl) G(ustav). 1875–1961
Binswanger, Ludwig. 1881–1966
Klein, Melanie. 1882–1960

Rank, Otto. 1884–1937
Horney, Karen. 1885–1952
Reik, Theodor. 1888–1969
Straus, Erwin. 1891–1975
Sullivan, Harry Stack. 1892–1949
Menninger, Karl Augustus. 1893–1990
Perls, Frederick. 1893–1970
Freud, Anna. 1895–1982

Winnicott, Donald Woods. 1896–1971
Allport, Gordon W(illard). 1897–1967
Fromm, Erich. 1900–1980
Erickson, Milton H. 1901–1980
Lacan, Jacques. 1901–1981
Erikson, Erik H. 1902–
Rogers, Carl Ransom. 1902–1987
Bettelheim, Bruno. 1903–1990
Boss, Medard. 1903–
Frankl, Viktor. 1905–
Maslow, Abraham H(arold). 1908–1970
May, Rollo. 1909–

Berne, Eric Lennard. 1910–1970
Ellis, Albert. 1913–
Kohut, Heinz. 1913–1981
Van den Berg, J. H. 1914–
Bugental, James F. T. 1915–
Wolpe, Joseph. 1915–
Beck, Aaron T. 1921–
Schafer, Roy. 1922–
Glasser, William. 1925–
Foucault, Michel. 1926–1984
Laing, R(onald) D(avid). 1927–1989
Lazarus, Arnold A. 1932–

ADLER, ALFRED. 1870–1937

This Austrian psychiatrist, who was born near Vienna and received his M.D. from the University of Vienna in 1895, founded the school of individual psychology. He first practiced as an ophthalmologist but later turned to mental disease about 1900. He was associated with the early group of SIGMUND FREUD's (see also Vol. 3) followers, but he later left it, rejecting Freud's emphasis on (biological) sexual drives as the chief psychological determinants of personality. Adler saw personality disorders as arising from feelings of inferiority or inadequacy in the ability to reach one's life goals. For Adler the processes of socialization within one's culture are the important factors in determining a character style.

After his break with Freud in 1911, Adler founded his own school. In 1919 he set up the first child guidance clinic within the Vienna school system. A few years before he died, Adler moved to the United States, where he spent the rest of his life in psychiatric practice and in lecturing. Adler and CARL JUNG were two of the most important contemporary dissenters from Freud.

BOOKS BY ADLER

The Education of Children. 1930. Trans. by E. F. Jensen. Regnery-Gateway 1978 $3.95. ISBN 0-89526-981-3. "Many a child will be better understood by those who acquaint themselves with Dr. Adler's wise counsel" (*Boston Transcript*).

Education of the Individual. Greenwood 1970 repr. of 1958 ed. $35.00. ISBN 0-8371-2134-5. Deals with four major problems every individual has to face: his/her relationship with others, his/her sense of equality, the escape of the ephemeral, and the meaning of his/her actions.

The Individual Psychology of Alfred Adler: A Systematic Presentation in Selections from His Writings. Ed. by Heinz L. Ansbacher and Rowena R. Ansbacher. HarpC 1964 $14.00. ISBN 0-06-131154-5. Systematic and authentic presentation of Adler's thought selected by his foremost disciples.

The Neurotic Constitution. Select Bibliographies Ser. Ayer 1972 repr. of 1926 ed. $31.00. ISBN 0-836-9925-8

The Practice and Theory of Individual Psychology. 1923. *Quality Pap. Ser.* Littlefield 1973 repr. of 1929 ed. $14.25. ISBN 0-8226-0209-1. Adler's presentation of individual psychology as a separate science.

The Problem Child. Capricorn Bks. 1963 o.p. Treats the problem child through the use of specific cases.

The Problems of Neurosis: A Book of Case Histories. 1929. HarpC 1964 o.p. Running comments on case material briefly presented to illustrate special points.

The Science of Living. 1929. Ed. by Heinz L. Ansbacher. Doubleday 1969 o.p. "A surprisingly clear and simple statement of the fundamental principles of psychology" (*N.Y. Times*).

Superiority and Social Interest: A Collection of Later Writings. Ed. by Heinz L. Ansbacher and Rowena R. Ansbacher. Norton repr. of 1979 ed. $12.95. ISBN 0-393-00910-6. Continuation of the systematic presentation of Adler's own thought collected by his disciples.

Understanding Human Nature. 1927. Trans. by W. B. Wolfe. Fawcett 1978 $13.95. ISBN 1-85168-021-7. Presentation of the fundamentals of individual psychology and demonstrations of its practical applications for the layperson.

What Life Should Mean to You. 1931. Ed. by Alan Porter. Little 1992 $13.95. ISBN 1-85168-022-5. Consistent application of the principles of individual psychology to all aspects of life.

BOOKS ABOUT ADLER

Brachfeld, F. Oliver. *Inferiority Feelings in the Individual and the Group.* Trans. by Marjorie Gabain. Greenwood 1973 repr. of 1951 ed. $49.75. ISBN 0-8371-6245-9. Exhaustive survey of the literature pertaining to unorganized inferiority (inferiority of the individual) and organized inferiority (inferiority of the group) arranged around such topics as inferiority in relation to the newborn, crime, sex, and racial inferiority.

Mosak, Harold H., ed. *Alfred Adler: His Influence on Psychology Today.* Noyes Pr. 1973 o.p. Evaluation of Adler's work and influence by his disciples and followers.

Sperber, Manes. *Masks of Loneliness: Alfred Adler in Perspective.* Macmillan 1974 o.p. "The reader will gain insight into the conflict between Adler and Freud, the influence of Marxist ideas on Adler, the flavor of Austria and Vienna in the early days of psychoanalysis and the personalities of Adler and Freud" (*Choice*).

Stepansky, Paul E. *In Freud's Shadow: Adler in Context.* Analytic Pr. 1983 $29.95. ISBN 0-88163-007-1. Critical, historical study of Adler, the historical development of his theory, and the impact and social repercussions of his thought (Introduction).

ALLPORT, GORDON W(ILLARD). 1897–1967

Gordon Allport was born in Montezuma, Indiana, and received his undergraduate and doctoral degrees from Harvard University. He served as teacher and later professor of psychology at Harvard from 1930 until his death. He is known for his important work in the study of social attitudes and in the study of personality and its measurement. As a youth he visited SIGMUND FREUD (see also Vol. 3) in Vienna and, according to the *N.Y. Times,* though impressed by Freud, he nevertheless felt there was "room for one more behavioral scientist in the world." Allport believed that the Freudian personality theories were fitted for only a small minority of individuals. He once called his own ideas a form of empiricism restrained by reason.

Allport was especially concerned with, and outspoken against, religious and racial prejudice. He shared "with William James and John Dewey the resolute capacity to see man as human regardless of whatever particular scientific trends may hold sway at any given moment. Allport helps fulfill his own prediction, that 'soon . . . psychology will offer an image of man more in accord with the democratic ideals by which psychologists as individuals live' " (ROLLO MAY, *Saturday Review*). He served as president of the American Psychological Association in 1937, receiving its Gold Medal Award in 1963. He was editor of the *Journal of Abnormal and Social Psychology* for 12 years.

BOOKS BY ALLPORT

Becoming: Basic Considerations for a Psychology of Personality. Terry Lectures Ser. Yale U. Pr. 1955 $8.00. ISBN 0-300-00002-2. Instructive comparison of two very different approaches to the field of psychology.

The Individual and His Religion: A Psychological Interpretation. 1950. Macmillan 1967 o.p. "An interpretation of the significance of religion from a psychological standpoint" (*Annals of the American Academy of Political and Social Science*).

Letters from Jenny. (ed.). HarBraceJ 1965 $6.95. ISBN 0-15-650700-5. "Mr. Allport shows us how existentialist philosophers and therapists would see Jenny's daily life and explain it" (*New York Times Book Review*).

The Nature of Prejudice. 1954. Addison-Wesley 1979 $12.45. ISBN 0-201-00179-9. "The book can be used as a text, but it will almost surely find its way into discussion groups and eventually to the general reader" (*Social Forces*).

Pattern and Growth in Personality. Holt 1961 o.p. Presents his theory of personality from a structured and articulated perspective.

Personality and the Social Encounter: Selected Essays. U. Ch. Pr. 1981 o.p. "Twenty-one reprints, covering the period 1931 to 1960 . . . range from the open system of personality theory to the problems of war and peace, from ethics to ego-psychology, from metaphysics to metapsychology" (*Contemporary Psychology*).

The Person in Psychology. Beacon Pr. 1968 o.p. Selected essays "dealing with the applications of varieties of psychological theories, the influence and relationship between personality development and social institutions, prejudice as a personality trait, and finally a biographical section which provides a biographical approach to the psychological theories of individual psychologists" (*Library Journal*).

Psychology of Radio. (coauthored with Handley Cantril). Ayer 1971 repr. of 1935 ed. $24.95. ISBN 0-405-03574-8

The Psychology of Rumor. (coauthored with Leo Postman). Russell 1965 repr. of 1947 ed. o.p. Scholarly, but interesting reading.

Studies in Expressive Movement. (coauthored with Philip E. Vernon). 1933. Hafner repr. of 1966 ed. o.p. "The authors believe that their work demonstrates that gesture and handwriting both reflect an essentially stable and constant individual style, and that the theories of specificity and identical elements are wholly inadequate to account for the consistency obtained" (*Psychological Abstracts*).

The Use of Personal Documents in Psychological Science. 1942. Kraus repr. of 1942 ed. $4.50. o.p. "The book seeks to improve the appraisal of the self-revealing records of personal experience through an analysis of the form and content value of examples illustrating the various types of personal documents" (*Social Forces*).

BOOKS ABOUT ALLPORT

Evans, Richard I. *Gordon Allport: The Man and His Ideas.* Dutton 1971 o.p. Transcript of a lengthy interview filmed with Allport shortly before his death.

Ghougassian, Joseph P. *Gordon W. Allport's Ontopsychology of the Person.* Philos Document 1972 o.p. "It is contended that Allport's humanistic psychology with its emphasis on the uniqueness of the individual personality and on the principle of functional autonomy is a revolutionary force in American psychology" (*Psychological Abstracts*).

BECK, AARON T. 1921–

A native of Rhode Island, Aaron Beck had an early interest in psychology. A graduate of Brown University, he embarked on a career in medicine at Yale University with the intention of specializing in psychiatry. Dissatisfied with classical psychoanalysis, he turned to modified psychoanalytic approaches and was particularly influenced by Rapaport's ego psychology. This spawned his interest in cognition, and over time Beck abandoned the psychoanalytic framework and formulated his own cognitive theory—behavior therapy for patients of depression and other psychiatric disorders. Beck also developed numerous measurement scales, including the Beck Depression Inventory, the Beck Hopelessness Scale, and the Self-Concept Test, which are widely used as diagnostic and research tools in the field. He continues to teach, consult, and write about the use of cognitive therapy in treating emotional disorders and other problems.

BOOKS BY BECK

Anxiety Disorders and Phobias, a Cognitive Perspective. Basic 1990 $16.00. ISBN 0-465-00385-0. "Case illustrations and a review of cognitive approaches to therapy" (*Contemporary Psychology*).

Cognitive Therapy in Clinical Practice: An Illustrative Casebook. Ed. by J. Jan Scott, Mark G. Williams, and Aaron T. Beck. Routledge 1991 $16.95. ISBN 0-415-06242-X. Collection of papers by various authors, each dealing with distinctive disorders and specific problems, such as panic disorders, drug abusers, eating disorders, and offenders.

Cognitive Therapy of Depression. Gilford Pr. 1987 $45.00. ISBN 0-89862-000-7. Outline of the theoretical basis and the mechanics of cognitive behavior therapy as applied to depressed patients.

Cognitive Therapy of Personality Disorders. (coauthored with Freeman Arthur). Guilford Pr. 1990 $35.95. ISBN 0-89862-434-7. Broad overview of historical, theoretical, and therapeutic aspects; includes clinical chapters that detail treatment of specific personality disorders.

Love Is Never Enough. How Couples Can Overcome Misunderstandings, Resolve Conflicts and Solve Relationship Problems through Cognitive Therapy. HarpC 1989 $11.00. ISBN 0-06-091604-4. Popular presentation of Beck's ideas suitable for the layperson.

BERNE, ERIC LENNARD. 1910–1970

A native of Montreal and the son of a physician and a professional writer and editor, Eric Berne received a medical degree from McGill University, where he earned money by writing humor under the pen name Ramsbottom Horseley. He later studied at the Yale Psychiatric Clinic and the New York Psychoanalytic Institute before settling and studying in California after World War II.

Berne was a practicing psychiatrist and the author of the best-selling work *Games People Play* (1964), which remained on bestseller lists until 1967. In it Berne argued that people tend to play games with each other in their interpersonal relationships for a number of reasons, namely, to escape from reality, to hide ulterior motives, and to avoid actual participation in real life. A few of these games are destructive, but most are desirable and necessary. Berne demonstrated to his readers how to recognize these games and how to play the most socially useful roles.

The founder of Transactional Analysis (TA), Berne once said, "I could have spent the rest of my life disproving psychoanalysis, but I decided to invent TA instead." At the time of his fatal heart attack in 1970, Berne was a lecturer in group therapy at the Langley Porter Neuropsychiatric Institute and a consultant at the McAuley Clinic in San Francisco.

BOOKS BY BERNE

Beyond Games and Scripts. (coauthored with C. Steiner). Ballantine 1981 $5.95. ISBN 0-345-30053-X. "Selections range from the by now familiar 'games' and 'scripts' that influence behavior to telltale words and gestures, group dynamics, sex and TA, and games psychotherapists (and their patients) play. Useful to people actively involved with TA" (*Publishers Weekly*).

Games People Play: The Psychology of Human Relationships. 1964. Ballantine 1978 $4.95. ISBN 0-345-32719-5. "A compendium of unconscious maneuvers nearly everyone makes in his relationships with other people, and its forthright language and somewhat acid style understandably appeal to laymen who may easily recognize themselves as adept life-game players" (*Newsweek*).

Happy Valley. Grove 1968 o.p. A python named Shardlu rolls down the hill one day into a
flowery valley and has many adventures with the strange animals and people who
live there.

Intuition and Ego States: The Origins of Transactional Analysis. Ed. by Paul McCormick.
HarpC 1977 o.p. Series of papers discussing intuition, diagnosis, communication,
ego states, etc., from a transactional perspective.

Layman's Guide to Psychiatry and Psychoanalysis (The Mind in Action). 1957. Ballantine
1982 o.p. Introduction to psychoanalysis for laypersons by a "young Freudian."

Principles of Group Treatment. OUP 1966 o.p. "Meets a need by sharpening some of the
basic issues involved in group methods of treatment. The author makes conceptual
comparisons among different methods and schools and presents his views of a
variety of related topics" (*Contemporary Psychology*).

Sex in Human Loving. S&S Trade 1970 o.p. "Delves amusingly into the male-female
relationship in many aspects, from the coy euphemisms most of us employ as a
'sexual vocabulary' to the sex act itself, its biology, its psychology, its deviations, and
the guises and disguises under which the old Adam-and-Eve game is played in our
time" (*Publishers Weekly*).

Structure and Dynamics of Organizations and Groups. Grove 1966 o.p. "Berne's
approach to a theory of group structure and function is bold and creative" (*Amer.
Journal of Public Health*).

Transactional Analysis in Psychotherapy: A Systematic Individual and Social Psychiatry.
Ballantine 1986 $3.95. ISBN 0-345-33836-7. Outlines Berne's unified system of
individual and social psychiatry, in which he sees structural analysis as a more
general theory than orthodox psychoanalysis.

What Do You Say after You Say Hello: The Psychology of Human Destiny. 1972. Bantam
1984 $4.95. ISBN 0-553-25822-2. "As a psychiatrist, Dr. Berne found that each
person—under the powerful influences of his parents—writes in early childhood his
own script that will determine the general course of his life. . . . [Dr. Berne]
demonstrates how each life script gets written, how it works, and how each of us can
break free of it to help us attain real autonomy and true fulfillment" (Publisher's
note).

BOOK ABOUT BERNE

Jorgenson, Elizabeth Watkins, and Henry Irvin Jorgenson. *Eric Berne: Master Games-
man—A Transactional Biography.* Grove 1984 o.p. Sympathetic biography of the
founder of transactional analysis.

BETTELHEIM, BRUNO. 1903–1990

Bruno Bettelheim had remarkable success in treating very deeply emotionally disturbed children. A pupil of SIGMUND FREUD's (see also Vol. 3), he was a
vehement opponent of the "operant conditioning" methods of B. F. SKINNER
(see Vol. 3) and other behaviorists. Austrian-born, Bettelheim came to America
in 1939. Profoundly influenced by the year he spent in a German concentration
camp during World War II, much of his writings reflect his sensitivity and
knowledge of the fear and anxiety induced under such conditions. His famous
Individual and Mass Behavior (1943), first published in a scientific periodical
and then in pamphlet form, is a study of the human personality under the stress
of totalitarian terror and concentration camp living. Bettelheim sees a
relationship between the disturbances of the concentration camp survivors and
those of the autistic (rigidly withdrawn) children whom he describes in *The
Empty Fortress* (1967), because both have lived through "extreme situations."

The Children of the Dream (1969) describes with considerable enthusiasm the
absence of neurosis in children brought up on kibbutzim in Israel in groups of
other children and cared for by adults who are not their parents. Bettelheim

believes that American ghetto children would benefit from this kind of experience in preference to the at best partial help of present programs designed to accelerate educational progress for the deprived.

In 1941 Bettelheim married Gertrud Weinfeld; the couple had three children. From 1944 to 1973, Bettelheim served as the principal of the Sonia Shankman Orthogenic School, a residential laboratory for the treatment of disturbed children at the University of Chicago. Up until his death, Bettelheim remained active in his scholarly pursuits, continuing to write about the nurturing of healthy children and devoting himself to improving the human condition.

BOOKS BY BETTELHEIM

The Children of the Dream. 1969. Avon 1970 o.p. An appraisal of childrearing in the Israeli kibbutz.

Dialogues with Mothers. 1972. Avon 1971 o.p. "Consisting of reports of group discussions with parents, this book is basically concerned with 'getting them [parents] to analyze a particular situation in their own words, on the basis of their own anxieties, notions and ideas'" (*Psychological Abstracts*).

The Empty Fortress: Infantile Autism and the Birth of the Self. 1967. Free Pr. 1972 $23.95. ISBN 0-02-903130-3. "Striking combination of casebook, plea for charity, and medical polemic, . . . analyzes the nature of infantile autism with exhaustive care, describes (only to dismiss) rival theories of its origins, explodes some myths that have arisen about this form of psychosis, charts courses of treatment, and offers some tentative theories of his own" (Peter Gay, *The New Yorker*).

Freud and Man's Soul. Random 1984 $7.95. ISBN 0-394-71036-3. "The main thrust of his analysis of Freud's mistranslation is a critique of American psychoanalysis and the American approach to psychology in general" (*Nation*).

A Home for the Heart. 1973. U. Ch. Pr. 1985 o.p. "At once a summation and a further expansion of both his basic psychological concepts and his practical application of his ideas about institutional care. It may be Bettelheim's most lucid exposition of his notion of the 'therapeutic community,' and as such is indispensable to professionals, students and concerned lay readers" (*Publishers Weekly*).

The Informed Heart: Autonomy in a Mass Age. 1960. Free Pr. $27.95. ISBN 0-02-903200-8. Describes how people can achieve self-realization in spite of present barriers.

Love Is Not Enough. Free Pr. 1950 $27.95. ISBN 0-02-903280-6. Study in which Bettelheim points out that parents, besides loving their children, should "create a setting in which both their own legitimate needs and the needs of their children can be satisfied with relative ease"; he describes the methods of his own school in this light.

Paul and Mary: Two Case Histories of Truants from Life. Free Pr. 1961 o.p.

Recollections and Reflections. Thames Hudson 1990 o.p. Autobiography presented via a collection of papers by the author, permitting the reader to arrive at his or her own ideas.

Social Change and Prejudice. (coauthored with Morris Janowitz). Free Pr. 1964 $27.95. ISBN 0-02-904380-9. "Represents a highly creative and systematic attempt at synthesis of psychoanalytic and sociological method and interpretations" (*Saturday Review*).

Surviving and Other Essays. 1979. Random 1980 $14.95. ISBN 0-394-74264-8. "Superbly written essays—penetrating and incisive. . . . Highly recommended for general collections" (*Library Journal*).

Symbolic Wounds: Puberty Rites and the Envious Male. Free Pr. 1954 o.p. Points out the need for a revision of Freudian theories in light of more recent knowledge.

Truants from Life: The Rehabilitation of Emotionally Disturbed Children. Free Pr. 1964 $21.95. ISBN 0-02-903440-X. Case studies of four psychotics successfully treated at Bettelheim's school.

The Uses of Enchantment: The Meaning and Importance of Fairy Tales. Random 1989
    $11.00. ISBN 0-679-72393-5. Thoughtful, humane, and sensitive approach to the fairy
    tale.

BINSWANGER, LUDWIG. 1881–1966

Ludwig Binswanger was born in Kreuzlingen, Switzerland, to a family of
physicians and psychiatrists. He studied medicine in Lausanne, Heidelberg, and
Zurich, receiving his medical degree in 1907. While at Zurich Binswanger
studied with CARL JUNG and was a psychiatric intern under Eugene Bleuler. His
father, Robert Binswanger, was the director of the sanatorium Bellevue at
Kreuzlingen, and Ludwig served as his associate from 1908 to 1910. Binswanger
succeeded his father in 1921 and remained as medical director until his
retirement in 1936.

Binswanger was friends not only with SIGMUND FREUD (see also Vol. 3) but
also with MARTIN HEIDEGGER (see also Vol. 4), the existential philosopher, who
visited Bellevue and discussed Binswanger's concept of "existential analysis"
with him. Unfortunately, Binswanger's work is largely untranslated, and the
books that are in translation are mostly technical. However, his small book of
reminiscences reveals a great deal about both Binswanger and Freud.

BOOKS BY BINSWANGER

Dream and Existence. (coauthored with Michel Foucault). Ed. by Keith Hoeller. Trans. by
    Forrest Williams and Jacob Needleman. Humanities 1986 $12.50. ISBN 0-914857-03-
    7. Early text by Binswanger foreshadowing his development of existential analysis.
Sigmund Freud: Reminiscences of a Friendship. Grune & Stratton 1957 o.p.

BOSS, MEDARD. 1903–

Born in St. Gallen, Switzerland, Medard Boss was educated at the University
of Zurich and served in many capacities, ranging from staff psychiatrist to head
psychiatrist at many hospitals and clinics in the Zurich area. He was appointed
professor of psychotherapy at the University of Zurich's medical faculty in 1954
(he is currently emeritus) and has been in private practice since 1935.

During his career, he has been closely associated with SIGMUND FREUD (see
also Vol. 3), CARL JUNG, Eugene Bleuler, H. W. Maier, LUDWIG BINSWANGER, and
MARTIN HEIDEGGER (see also Vol. 4). In addition, he has taught and has been
therapist for numerous psychotherapists throughout the world. He founded the
Institute for Daseinanalytic Psychotherapy and Psychosomatics in Zurich in
1971, which is based on his own synthesis of Heidegger's concept of being and
Freud's psychoanalysis.

BOOKS BY BOSS

The Analysis of Dreams. Philos Document 1958 o.p. "A large part of the book is devoted
    to a critical analysis of other dream theories, notably those of Freud and Jung"
    (*Contemporary Psychology*).
Existential Foundation of Medicine and Psychology. (ed.). 1977. Aronson 1983 $30.00.
    ISBN 0-87668-667-6. "If one is willing to persevere and follow Boss's perspectives,
    the effort will be a rewarding one" (*Contemporary Psychology*).
I Dreamt Last Night. Gardner Pr. 1977 $23.95. o.p. "A casebook . . . the theory is presented
    painlessly and piecemeal in the discussion of specimen dreams" (*Contemporary
    Psychology*).
A Psychiatrist Discovers India. Dufour 1965 o.p. Puts forth the results of Boss's
    investigation into the relevance of eastern psychological assumptions to western
    psychiatric practice.

Psychoanalysis and Daseinanalysis. Da Capo 1982 repr. of 1963 ed. $32.50. ISBN 0-306-79708-9. "Represents necessary reading for all American psychologists because of its searching inquiry into philosophic issues created by what Boss perceives as the invasion of Man's inner sanctum by science-based concepts and techniques, i.e., psychotherapy and/or psychoanalysis" (*Contemporary Psychology*).

BOOK ABOUT BOSS

Scott, Charles, ed. *On Dreaming: An Encounter with Medard Boss.* Scholars Pr. GA 1982 $15.95. ISBN 0-89130-603-X. "Contains seven papers by two philosophers, two theologians, two psychologists, and Medard Boss. . . . Boss's paper utilizes some other theorists' published dreams to illustrate his disagreements with their interpretations and to explain his own daseins-analytical, phenomenological dream theory" (*Religious Studies Review*).

BRILL, A(BRAHAM) A(RDEN). 1874–1948

A. A. Brill was the first psychoanalyst in America. He was also the first to bring SIGMUND FREUD's (see also Vol. 4) teaching to this country and translate his works into English. He also translated many works of CARL JUNG.

Brill was born in Austria and came to the United States as a teenager. Alone and penniless, he worked at menial jobs while learning to speak English. It took Brill only three years to complete his American elementary and high school education, and he graduated from New York City College in 1898. He went on to earn a B.A. in philosophy from New York University on a scholarship and received his medical degree from Columbia University College of Physicians and Surgeons in 1903. As a medical student, Brill was interested in neurology and psychiatry, but it was his later meeting with Freud in Vienna that had the greatest impact on his life and work. Learning the essentials of psychoanalysis from "the source" and continuing to correspond with his teacher and friend until Freud's death, Brill returned to the United States in 1908 and set up the first psychoanalytic practice in the United States in New York City. Brill's *Psychoanalysis: Its Theory and Application* (1912) was the first American book on the subject of psychoanalysis, and his *Basic Principles of Psychoanalysis* (1949) is the classic handbook of psychoanalysis for lay readers.

BOOKS BY BRILL

Basic Principles of Psychoanalysis. 1949. U. Pr. of Amer. 1985 repr. of 1949 ed. $19.50. ISBN 0-8191-4665-X
Freud's Contribution to Psychiatry. 1944. Peter Smith 1972 $11.25. ISBN 0-8446-1738-5. "An excellent set of lectures by an American pioneer in the field of psychoanalysis" (*The New Yorker*).
Fundamental Conceptions of Psychoanalysis. Ayer 1973 repr. of 1921 ed. $22.00. ISBN 0-405-05198-0.
Psychoanalysis, Its Theories and Practical Application. Medicine and Society in America Ser. Ayer 1972 repr. of 1913 ed. $20.00. ISBN 0-405-03939-5

BUGENTAL, JAMES F. T. 1915–

James Bugental was born in Fort Wayne, Indiana, the son of a contractor and a music teacher. He received his Ph.D. in psychology from Ohio State University in 1948. Initially he taught at the University of California at Los Angeles, but gradually his interest shifted to intensive individual psychotherapy, thereby leading him to found a group practice, the Psychological Service Association, in 1953. Dissatisfied with psychology as he found it, Bugental became active in the creation of the humanistic psychology movement. He helped found the Association for Humanistic Psychology in 1962. Subsequently he has developed an existential-humanistic intensive psychotherapy that emphasizes the client's perceptions and feelings. Bugental is the author of, and contributor to, numerous books and articles. According to *Contemporary Authors*, he tries "to challenge the boundaries between textbooks and popular literature, between factual reporting and using fiction to portray deeper truths, between the objective and the subjective, and between the personal-emotional and the shared-overly rational."

BOOKS BY BUGENTAL

Challenges of Humanistic Psychology. Ed. by J. F. T. Bugental. McGraw 1967 o.p. Edited collection of essays, surveying the field of humanistic psychology and delineating some of the early research findings of the humanistic orientation.

Intimate Journeys: Stories from Life-Changing Therapy. Jossey-Bass 1990 $27.50. ISBN 1-55542-274-8. "In simplest terms this is the story of my journey. It is a movement from seeing human lives chiefly in terms of their outward manifestations to the explosive recognition that life is truly invisible to our usual ways of seeing" (*Preface*).

Psychotherapy and Process: The Fundamentals of an Existential-Humanistic Approach. Addison-Wesley 1978 $17.70. ISBN 0-07-554827-5. Introduction to intensive psychotherapy with a coherent sketch of the psychological features, main procedures, and the hoped-for outcomes.

The Search for Authenticity: An Existential-Analytic Approach to Psychotherapy. Irvington 1989 $19.95. ISBN 0-8290-1298-2. Provides clarification of sometimes difficult concepts by using case material and by sharing his experiences practicing psychotherapy.

The Search for Existential Identity: Patient-Therapist Dialogues in Humanistic Psychology. Jossey-Bass 1976 $30.95. ISBN 0-87589-273-6. Six detailed patient-therapist dialogues provide a rare and instructive look at the day-to-day exchanges of intensive psychotherapy.

DEWEY, JOHN. 1859–1952

[SEE Volumes 3 and 4.]

ELLIS, ALBERT. 1913–

Albert Ellis is a clinical psychologist and a marriage counselor. "I usually work with psychotherapy and marriage counseling," he told the editors of *Contemporary Authors*, "from 9:45 A.M. to 11 P.M., including the holding of eight different psychotherapy groups every week." Ellis originated the rational-emotive therapy movement, which ignores Freudian theories and advocates the belief that emotions come from conscious thought "as well as internalized ideas of which the individual may be unaware." At first Ellis's books on marital romance and sexuality were criticized by some as being radical and sensational; however, few realized that Ellis was merely laying the groundwork for modern sex education.

Ellis was born in Pittsburgh, Pennsylvania, and was educated at the City College of New York and at Columbia University, where he received a Ph.D. in psychology in 1943. He taught for a number of years at Rutgers University, New Jersey, and the Union Graduate School. Presently, he is executive director of the Institute for Rational Living, Inc., in New York City.

BOOKS BY ALBERT ELLIS

Anger: How to Live with and without It. 1977. Citadel Pr. 1987 repr. of 1977 ed. $12.95. ISBN 0-318-36381-X. Provides a step-by-step technique to help you explore and understand the roots and nature of your own anger.

The Art and Science of Love. Carol Pub. Group 1960 $7.95. ISBN 0-8184-0009-9

The Art of Erotic Seduction. (coauthored with Roger O. Conway). Lyle Stuart 1968 o.p.
Guide to seducing an initially reluctant or unwilling female; includes an excellent
chapter on how to establish a long relationship.

Brief Psychotherapy in Medical and Health Practice. (coauthored with Eliot R. Abrahms).
Springer Pub. 1978 o.p. "Provides brief RET techniques for helping patients deal
with their health-related anxiety, anger, and depression" (Publisher's catalog).

Clinical Applications of Rational-Emotive Therapy. (with Michael E. Bernard, eds.).
Plenum 1985 $52.50. ISBN 0-306-41971-8. "Leading RET therapists deal with love,
sexuality, athletic performance, midlife problems, dying, marriage and divorce, and
other topics.

Death Jag. (coauthored with Jeff Slaton). Woodhill 1980 o.p.

The Encyclopedia of Sexual Behavior. (with Albert Abarbanel, eds.). Hawthorn Bks. 1961
o.p. "An authoritative encyclopedia, written with clarity and good taste . . . still a
standard in the field and . . . frequently cited" (*Wilson Library Bulletin*).

Executive Leadership: A Rational Approach. 1972. Inst. Rational-Emotive 1978 repr. of
1972 ed. o.p. "In this book he outlines the applications of his growth-through-reason
principles for the normal executive" (*Library Journal*).

A Garland of Rational Songs. Inst. Rational-Emotive 1977 $3.50. ISBN 0-917476-09-3.
"Songs satirizing people's irrational philosophies are set to popular tunes with lyrics
by Albert Ellis" (Publisher's catalog).

Growth through Reason. Wilshire 1980 $7.00. ISBN 0-87980-264-2. Consists of actual
dialogues between patient and therapist; fascinating experience for professionals
and others interested in personal growth.

A Guide to Personal Happiness. (coauthored with Irving Becker). Wilshire 1982 $7.00.
ISBN 0-87980-395-9. Specifically demonstrates how to use RET and other methods
to undo the main blocks to personal happiness and achieve self-acceptance"
(Publisher's catalog).

A Guide to Successful Marriage. (coauthored with Robert Harper). Wilshire 1977 $7.00.
ISBN 0-87980-044-5. "Practical handbook for improving communication, resolving
disagreements, handling anger and frustration, coping with kids, and enhancing sex
and love feelings" (Publisher's catalog).

Handbook of Rational-Emotive Therapy. (coauthored with Russell Grieger). Springer
1977 $39.95. ISBN 0-8261-2202-7. "Geared for the novice in the cognitive-behavioral
world" (*Contemporary Psychology*).

How to Live with a Neurotic. 1969. Wilshire 1985 $7.00. ISBN 0-87980-404-1. "Shows how
to ease the strain of living, working or associating with neurotics or psychotics; also
useful as a treatment adjunct for therapists" (Publisher's catalog).

How to Master Your Fear of Flying. 1972. Inst. Rational-Emotive 1977 $3.95. ISBN 0-
917476-10-7. "Deals both with specific fears about flying, and general fears about
dying" (Publisher's catalog).

How to Raise an Emotionally Healthy, Happy Child. Wilshire 1966 $7.00. ISBN 0-87980-
208-1. Shows parents how to help their offspring develop self-acceptance and
frustration tolerance" (Publisher's catalog).

Humanistic Psychotherapy: The Rational-Emotive Approach. 1973. Ed. by Edward
Sagarin. McGraw 1974 $6.95. ISBN 0-07-019237-5. Shows how rational-emotive
therapy differs from psychoanalytic, behavioral, and other therapies in theory,
method, and effectiveness.

Is Objectivism a Religion? Lyle Stuart 1968 o.p. Thorough and scholarly analysis of the
philosophy of objectivism as espoused by Ayn Rand and Nathaniel Branden.

Murder and Assassination. (coauthored with John M. Gullo). Carol Pub. 1971 $10.00.
ISBN 0-8184-0057-9. "In a popular and graphic style, the authors trace case histories
of a number of vivid murders from Nero to Stalin and Hitler" (*Choice*).

A New Guide to Rational Living. (coauthored with Robert Harper). Wilshire 1961 o.p.
"Presents the basics of Ellis' Rational-Emotive Therapy (RET) which is directed
toward helping people change their emotions and actions by changing their attitudes
and their thinking. . . . This is one of the most useful books in the self-help genre"
(*Library Journal*).

Overcoming Procrastination. (coauthored with William J. Knaus). New Amer. Lib. 1979
$4.50. ISBN 0-451-15931-4. "Provides specific, practical techniques for changing old
delay tactics into more self-disciplined, creative living" (Publisher's catalog).

Overcoming Resistance: Rational-Emotive Therapy with Difficult Clients. Springer Pub.
1985 $27.95. ISBN 0-8261-4910-3. "Cognitive, emotive, and behavioral techniques
for helping turn around negative client patterns" (Publisher's catalog).

Rational-Emotive Approaches to Problems of Childhood. (with Michael E. Bernard, eds.).
Plenum 1983 $75.00. ISBN 0-306-41331-0. Twenty-four authorities show how to
apply RET to the problems of childhood.

Reason and Emotion in Psychotherapy. 1962. Citadel Pr. 1984 $7.95. ISBN 0-8065-0909-0.
"Describes its [rational-emotive therapy] origins, differences from other major
psychotherapeutic methods, and explains how this kind of holistic approach can
achieve good results in a wide range of disturbances" (Publisher's catalog).

The Sensuous Person: Critique and Corrections. Carol Pub. 1973 $6.00. ISBN 0-8184-
00773. "With some wit leavening his blunt language, Ellis not only points out the
follies of the sex-book writers but makes an earnest pitch for full sexual self-
acceptance 'with whatever actual or potential weaknesses you have' " (*Publishers
Weekly*).

Sex and the Liberated Man. Lyle Stuart 1976 $12.95. ISBN 0-8184-0222-9. Covers the art
of sexual persuasion, including how to relate to, arouse, and satisfy your partner and
yourself on a physical and emotional level.

Sex without Guilt. 1966. Lyle Stuart 1966 $4.95. ISBN 0-8184-0121-4. A classic, covering
every phase of human sex relations.

ELLIS, HAVELOCK. 1859–1939

The son of a British ship's captain, Havelock Ellis spent much of his
childhood in the Pacific. He became a teacher in New South Wales, then studied
medicine in London, eventually devoting himself to research and writing in
England. Ellis's works fall under many heads: science, art, travel, poetry, and
essays. He has achieved distinction in many different fields. His most important
work was *Studies in the Psychology of Sex* (1898), which, when first published in
England, was the subject of legal battles as to its "obscenity." However, the
book helped to change public attitudes toward sex and greatly contributed to
the study of sexual problems. Ellis interpreted his data from a biological rather
than a clinical viewpoint. SIGMUND FREUD (see also Vol. 3), who drew from his
material, regarded Ellis's conclusions as "happy anticipations of our own
deductions." Ellis's most popular philosophical work is *The Dance of Life*
(1923), a survey of modern civilization giving the author's own outlook on life.
Many of his earlier books are out of print.

BOOKS BY HAVELOCK ELLIS

The Dance of Life. 1923. Richard West 1978 repr. of 1923 ed. $35.00. ISBN 0-8371-6572-5

From Rousseau to Proust. 1935. *Essay Index Repr. Ser.* Ayer 1968 repr. of 1935 ed. $18.00.
ISBN 0-8369-0412-5. Collection of biographical and critical essays and introductions
dating from 1904 to 1934.

The Psychology of Sex: A Manual for Students. 1933. HarBraceJ 1978 o.p. "Makes appeal
to the lay reader and renders common property many details and instances which
had better be reserved for the professional office" (*Booklist*).

Studies in the Psychology of Sex. 1898. 2 vols. Random 1936 o.p.

The World of Dreams. 1922. Omnigraphics Inc. 1976 repr. of 1922 ed. $42.00. ISBN 1-
55888-241-3. Psychoanalytic study of Ellis's own dreams.

BOOK ABOUT HAVELOCK ELLIS

Robinson, Paul. *The Modernization of Sex: Havelock Ellis, Alfred Kinsey, William Masters
and Virginia Johnson.* Cornell U. Pr. 1988 repr. of 1976 ed. $14.95. ISBN 0-8014-
9539-3

ERICKSON, MILTON H. 1901–1980

Born in Nevada in 1901, Milton Erickson grew up on a farm in Wisconsin. As a pioneer in the use of hypnosis, he established hypnosis as a valid and effective therapeutic technique. His books on hypnotherapy, although geared toward health professionals in medicine, dentistry, and psychotherapy, are written in an original and personal style. Both a psychiatrist and a psychologist, he was a member of many national and international professional organizations. At the time of his death, he was the world's leading practitioner of medical and therapeutic hypnosis.

BOOKS BY ERICKSON

Advanced Techniques of Hypnosis and Therapy: Selected Papers of Milton H. Erickson, M.D. Ed. by Jay Haley. Grune 1967 o.p.

Experiencing Hypnosis: Therapeutic Approaches to Altered States. (coauthored with Ernest L. Rossi). Irvington 1981 $39.50. ISBN 8290-0246-4. Includes two audio cassettes.

The Nature of Hypnosis and Suggestion. Irvington 1980 $39.95. ISBN 0-8290-0542-0

Teaching Seminar with Milton H. Erickson, M.D. Ed. by Jeffrey K. Zeig. Brunner-Mazel 1980 $30.95. ISBN 0-87630-247-9

BOOKS ABOUT ERICKSON

Bandler, Richard, and John Grinder. *Patterns of Hypnotic Techniques of Milton H. Erickson, M.D.* META Pubns. 1975 $8.95. ISBN 0-91699001-X

Haley, Jay. *Uncommon Therapy: The Psychiatric Techniques of Milton H. Erickson, M.D.* Norton 1986 $19.95. ISBN 0-393-01100-3. "Valuable reading for both graduate and undergraduate students who are interested in the outcomes of hypnotic training . . ." (*Choice*).

Lankton, Stephen R., and Jeffrey K. Zeig, eds. *Extrapolations: Demonstrations of Ericksonian Therapy.* Brunner-Mazel 1989 $26.95. ISBN 0-87630-567-2. Six video-taped demonstrations are described and commented upon by faculty members of the Milton H. Erickson Center for Hypnosis and Psychotherapy.

Zeig, Jeffrey K. *Experiencing Erickson: An Introduction to the Man and His Work.* Brunner-Mazel 1985 $25.00. ISBN 0-87630-409-9. Personal record of working with Milton Erickson and his ideas; close-up report.

ERIKSON, ERIK H. 1902–

American youth by the thousands have taken up Erik Erikson's concern with their "identity" and "identity crisis." He is a practicing psychoanalyst whose theory of human development views the ego as evolving through the classical Freudian stages, which are each affected by cultural, social, and biological factors. According to Erikson, the search for an "identity" during adolescence becomes crucial. The conflicts between the self and its new view of parents as well as the world at large cause an "identity crisis"—that Erikson finds a phenomenon affecting whole peoples in ways analogous to its effect on single individuals. Similarly, Erikson theorized that in the formative years we go through stages of development and also that passing through developmental stages, each of which contains some "crisis," is a lifelong process.

Born in Germany, Erikson graduated from the Vienna Psychoanalytic Institute and came to the United States in 1933. He holds an honorary degree from Harvard University, where he was professor emeritus of human development and lecturer on psychiatry. He has done extensive research at various American universities and was for a decade a senior staff member at the Austen

Riggs Center, an institute in Stockbridge, Massachusetts, for the study and treatment of neuroses. He now lives in southern California.

BOOKS BY ERIKSON

Childhood and Society. 1950. Norton 1986 $22.50. ISBN 0-393-02295-1. "Erikson's approach is basically that of psychoanalysis, but of psychoanalytic theory sophisticated with the insight of cultural anthropology and with a keen sense for history" (Clyde Kluckhohn).

Dimensions of a New Identity. Norton 1979 $3.95. ISBN 0-393-00923-8. "Provocative and readable . . . should be in libraries where Jefferson scholars and those concerned with the interaction of the individual psyche history are likely to seek it" (*Library Journal*).

Identity: Youth and Crisis. Norton 1968 $5.95. ISBN 0-393-09786-2. An adaptation of major essays over the period 1958 to 1968.

Identity and the Life Cycle. 1967. *Psychological Issues Monograph Ser.* Norton 1980 $4.95. ISBN 0-393-00949-1. "Three influential articles . . . detail the progress of the author's thinking as he advanced from clinical evidence to theoretical outline to therapeutical applications via the employment of his psycho-history technique" (*Booklist*).

In Search of Common Ground. (coauthored with Huey P. Newton). Ed. by Kai T. Erikson. Norton 1973 $12.95. ISBN 0-393-05483-7

Insight and Responsibility. Norton 1964 $8.95. ISBN 0-393-09451-0. Six lectures dealing with the ethical implications of psychoanalytic insight and people's responsibility to succeeding generations.

The Life Cycle Completed: A Review. Norton 1985 $7.95. ISBN 0-393-30229-6. "There is a freshness and vitality in the presentation of the life cycle that would lead one to feel the insights were being discovered for the first time" (*Choice*).

Life History and the Historical Moment. Norton 1975 o.p. Collection of previously published essays from the late 1960s and early 1970s, covering a wide range of Erikson's interests.

Vital Involvement in Old Age: The Experience of Old Age In Our Time. Norton 1986 $19.95. ISBN 0-393-02359-1. Presentation of Erikson's thought in his later years, when the outline of his developmental schema continues into old age.

Young Man Luther: A Study in Psychoanalysis and History. 1958. Norton 1962 $5.95. ISBN 0-393-00170-9. "A unique integration of psychoanalysis, history, and the problem of the Great Man" (Margaret Mead).

BOOKS ABOUT ERIKSON

Coles, Robert. *Erik H. Erikson: The Growth of His Work.* Little 1970 o.p. ". . . examines the intellectual thrust of Erikson's work in a lively, systematic fashion; [Coles] is free enough to be both sympathetic and critical; and he is scholarly without being pedantic" (*Choice*).

Evans, Richard I. *Dialogue with Erik Erikson: And Reactions from Ernest Jones.* Praeger 1981 $38.50. ISBN 0-275-90613-2. "A psychologist and teacher of psychology at the University of Houston has attempted to extract [Erikson's] underlying philosophies and conceptualizations by utilizing the Socratic method—that is, teaching his audience through questioning his subjects" (*New York Times*).

Maier, Henry W. *Three Theories of Child Development.* Longman 1978 o.p. Covers the theories of Piaget, Erikson, and Sears. Compelling and somewhat simpler approach for individuals beginning to study child development.

FOUCAULT, MICHEL. 1926–1984

One of the most prominent French thinkers of his generation, Michel Foucault was educated at the École Normale Superieure and the Sorbonne, obtaining his diploma in 1952. He later held a chair as professor of the history of systems of thought at the Collège de France in Paris. Foucault wrote on a wide variety of topics, including madness, its historical determinants, and its forms of treatment. Only four volumes of his last work, a proposed six-volume series entitled *The History of Sexuality* (1976, 1984), were completed at the time of his death.

BOOKS BY FOUCAULT

The Birth of the Clinic: An Archaeology of Medical Perception. Random 1974 $9.00. ISBN 0-394-71097-5. "There is so much in this book . . . that it is impossible to do more than hint at its interest or at the counter arguments that it stimulates" (*New Statesman*).

Madness and Civilization: A History of Insanity in the Age of Reason. 1965. Random 1973 $11.00. ISBN 0-679-72110-X. "Rather than to review historically the concept of madness, the author has chosen to recreate, mostly from original documents, mental illness, folly, and unreason as they must have existed in their time, place, and proper social perspective" (*Christian Century*).

Mental Illness and Psychology. U. CA Pr. 1986 $8.95. ISBN 0-520-05919-0

The Order of Things: An Archaeology of the Human Sciences. 1970. Random 1973 $10.00. ISBN 0-394-71935-2. Distinguishes among the styles of thought and expression in the late Renaissance, the classical period, and the modern period.

BOOKS ABOUT FOUCAULT

Hoy, David. *Foucault: A Critical Reader.* Blackwell Pubs. 1986 $14.95. ISBN 0-631-14043-3

Rajchman, John. *Michel Foucault: The Freedom of Philosophy.* Col. U. Pr. 1986 $15.50. ISBN 0-231-06071-8

FRANKL, VIKTOR. 1905–

Viktor Frankl was born in Austria, where he subsequently studied medicine and became a psychiatrist. Under the Nazis, Frankl and most of his immediate family were placed in concentration camps; only Frankl himself survived. Having observed that the prisoners who were able to survive the suffering and humiliation of the concentration camps were those who could find some spiritual meaning in their suffering, Frankl was led to posit the "will-to-meaning" as the basic struggle of human existence, and he built his concept of logotherapy around this idea. Frankl states that "logotherapy . . . makes the concept of man into a whole . . . and focuses its attention upon mankind's groping for a higher meaning in life."

Frankl was, for many years, professor of neurology and psychiatry at the University of Vienna Medical School and distinguished professor of logotherapy at U.S. International University.

BOOKS BY FRANKL

The Doctor and the Soul: From Psychotherapy to Logotherapy. 1965. Random 1986 $6.95. ISBN 0-394-74317-2. "Set[s] forth his theory of Logotherapy, a concept of the existential form of life as the goal of psychotherapy. An important contribution to psychoanalysis, and, as well, to the fields of religion and philosophy" (*Publishers Weekly*).

Man's Search for Meaning: An Introduction to Logotherapy. 1962. Beacon Pr. 1992 $15.00. ISBN 0-8070-2918-1. "Today we hear a great deal about disaffiliation, alienation, existential emptiness and identity crises. All these seem to include the problem of a self that finds no reason for being, and it is precisely to this problem that Frankl, in simplicity and eloquence, addresses his quest and directs his therapeutic answer" (*Contemporary Psychology*).

Psychotherapy and Existentialism: Selected Papers on Logotherapy. WSP 1967 o.p. "The concepts of 'life purpose,' 'noögenic neurosis,' and 'paradoxical intention' are well described and illustrated by impressive case studies" (*Choice*).

The Unheard Cry for Meaning: Psychotherapy and Humanism. S&S Trade 1979 $8.95.
   Extends the discussion of logotherapy to its philosophical bases and talks about the
   light it sheds on ordinary life.
The Will to Meaning: Foundations and Applications of Logotherapy. 1969. NAL-Dutton
   1988 $7.94. ISBN 0-452-00946-4. "Presents little new for the professional, but in
   combination with *Man's Search for Meaning,* it may be a very good introduction to
   logotherapy for the undergraduate or interested layman" (*Choice*).

BOOK ABOUT FRANKL

Fabry, Joseph B. *The Pursuit of Meaning: Viktor Frankl, Logotherapy, and Life.* Inst. Logo.
   1987 $7.95. ISBN 0-917867-04-1

FREUD, ANNA. 1895–1982

Anna Freud, daughter of SIGMUND FREUD (see also Vol. 3), was instrumental in
carrying on the work and studies of her famous father. Born in Vienna, Austria,
she later immigrated to England and became a British citizen in 1938. An
exponent of orthodox Freudian theory, she wrote *Psychoanalysis for Teachers
and Parents* (1935) in order to explain her father's basic theory to the general
public. It is a charming exposition and reminds us of the fact that we recognize
so much of it as familiar and of the tremendous impact that Freud has had on
the general culture of the twentieth-century Western world as well as the
understanding and healing his work made possible for troubled human beings.
Deeply interested in the problems of children, Freud organized a residential war
nursery for homeless youngsters during World War II and for many years
directed the Hampstead Child Therapy Clinic in London, where she made her
home. Freud made significant contributions in the field of child psychoanalysis.
Some of her important work was on the functioning of the ego in normal and
disturbed children. Although she lacked medical training, her vast experience
and lucid writing earned her the respect of many physicians and medical
institutions.

BOOKS BY ANNA FREUD

Children in the Hospital. (coauthored with Thesi Bergmann). Intl. Univs. Pr. 1966 $27.50.
   ISBN 0-8236-0800-X. "A number of brief sketches of children with various kinds of
   difficulties provide a basis for insightful commentary" (*Contemporary Psychology*).
Difficulties in the Path of Psychoanalysis: A Confrontation of Past with Present Viewpoints.
   Intl. Univs. Pr. 1969 o.p.
Introduction to Psychoanalysis: Lectures for Child Analysts and Teachers. Intl. Univs. Pr.
   1974 $30.00. ISBN 0-8236-6870-3
Introduction to the Technic of Child Analysis. Classics in Child Development Ser. Ayer
   1975 $17.00. ISBN 0-405-06460-8
Psychoanalysis for Teachers and Parents. 1935. Trans. by Barbara Low. Norton 1979
   $6.95. ISBN 0-393-00918-1. Explains the basic principles and terminology of
   analysis.
The Psycho-Analytical Treatment of Children: Lectures and Essays. 1946. Intl. Univs. Pr.
   1965 $25.00. ISBN 0-8236-5080-4. "Anna Freud deals in detail with the differences in
   analytic work with child as opposed to adult. . . . Combines sophistication with clear
   explanation, and is readable and valuable" (*Contemporary Psychology*).
Psychoanalytic Psychology of Normal Development (1970–1980). Intl. Univs. Pr. 1981
   $49.50. ISBN 0-8236-6877-0. "Throughout this volume, the language is clear, the
   style is informal and almost conversational" (*Science Books and Films*).
War and Children. (coauthored with Dorothy T. Burlingham). Greenwood 1973 repr. of
   1943 ed. $40.00. ISBN 0-8371-6942-9. "It is the most gripping and moving volume
   this reviewer has read in the vast literature of WWII" (*Boston Globe*).

Writings. 7 vols. Intl. Univs. Pr. 1937–74 o.p. "[The author's] range of knowledge is topped off by a fine literary style which makes the articles a very real pleasure to read" (*Choice*).

BOOK ABOUT ANNA FREUD

Peters, Uwe H. *Anna Freud: A Life Dedicated to Children.* Schocken 1984 $24.95. ISBN 0-8052-3910-3. Straightforward, chronological account of the life and work of Anna Freud. Fine historical account of the development of psychoanalysis.

FREUD, SIGMUND. 1856–1939

Few men can claim a wider or deeper influence on their age than Sigmund Freud. His was the revolutionary theory of the unconscious, that strange submerged part of the human mind. His was the new method of treating mental and emotional illness, which he called psychoanalysis—the beginning of modern psychiatry. His theories and concepts have influenced anthropology, education, art, and literature.

Born in Freiburg, Moravia, of a middle-class Jewish family, Freud lived most of his life in Vienna, graduating from the University of Vienna in 1881. Later he decided to specialize in neurology and studied under Jean-Martin Charcot in Paris. With his collaborator Josef Breuer, Freud worked originally toward curing patients of hysteria by uncovering their "unconscious" through hypnosis. He later substituted his own method of free association for the same end. His theories of personality were not well received by the medical profession or the general public until about 1909, when he first explained himself in the United States. Although many of Freud's contemporaries, such as ALFRED ADLER, CARL JUNG, and later KAREN HORNEY and ERICH FROMM, disagreed with his emphasis on the infantile sexual instinct and the Oedipus complex, his work will remain basic.

BOOKS BY SIGMUND FREUD

The Basic Writings of Sigmund Freud. Trans. by A. A. Brill. Modern Lib. 1977 $19.95. ISBN 0-394-60400-8. "The introduction is offensively egotistic. Otherwise, a fine job" (*The New Yorker*).

Beyond the Pleasure Principle. 1920. Norton 1990 $5.95. ISBN 0-393-00769-3

Cocaine Papers. Ed. by Robert Byck. New Amer. Lib. 1975 o.p. "Provides access to some psycho-pharmacologic notes of 19th century authors who first studied cocaine" (*Library Journal*).

The Collected Papers of Sigmund Freud. 5 vols. Trans. by Joan Riviere and others. Ed. by Ernest Jones. Basic 1959 $55.00 ea. $250.00 set. ISBN 0-465-01248-5. "This is a great service to American students of human behavior. It may result in a large number of them reading much of Freud himself" (*American Journal of Sociology*).

The Complete Psychological Works: Standard Edition. 24 vols. Ed. and trans. by James Strachey. Norton 1976 $895.00. ISBN 0-393-01128-3

Delusion and Dream and Other Essays. Beacon 1966 o.p.

The Ego and the Id. 1923. Trans. by James Strachey. Ed. by Joan Riviere. Norton 1990 $4.95. ISBN 0-393-00142-3. "The serious student of Freud will appreciate Strachey's lengthy introduction to the book, which sets the historical context, discusses the issues that led Freud to write it and traces the development of some of the significant ideas that are elaborated in it" (*Contemporary Psychology*).

Freud: A Dictionary of Psychoanalysis. Ed. by Nandor Fodor and Frank Gaynor. Greenwood 1969 repr. of 1950 ed. $35.00. ISBN 0-8371-2135-3. "Basic terms of psychoanalysis defined for psychologists, psychiatrists, and psychoanalysts" (*Christian Century*).

The Freud-Jung Letters: The Correspondence between Sigmund Freud and C. G. Jung. 1974. Ed. by William McGuire. Trans. by Ralph Manheim and R. F. C. Hull. *Bollingen*

Ser. Princeton U. Pr. 1988 $16.95. ISBN 0-674-32330-0. "Read sequentially, the letters convey the inexorable quality of tragic drama: two honest and devoted men gripped by a revolutionary insight into the human mind struggle to be true to that insight while grappling with their own unconscious reactions to each other" (*Library Journal*).

The Future of an Illusion. 1927. Trans. by W. D. Robson-Scott. Norton 1975 $10.95. ISBN 0-393-00831-2

General Selections from the Works of Sigmund Freud. Doubleday 1989 $9.00. ISBN 0-385-09325-X

Group Psychology and the Analysis of the Ego. 1922. Trans. by James Strachey. Norton repr. 1975 $6.95. o.p.

The History of the Psychoanalytic Movement. 1917. Trans. by A. A. Brill. Norton 1990 o.p.

Infantile Cerebral Paralysis. Trans. by Lester A. Russin. U. of Miami Pr. 1968 $19.95. ISBN 0-87024-044-3. ". . . one of the most thorough and complete expositions of a subject which even today is replete with controversy, disagreement, and uncertainty; and which remains refractory to any generally successful treatment" (*Choice*).

Inhibitions, Symptoms, and Anxiety (Problem of Anxiety). 1936. Norton 1990 $6.95. ISBN 0-393-01166-6. Detailed account of Freud's thinking about the role of anxiety on the neurosis.

The Interpretation of Dreams. 1900. Avon 1965 $4.95. ISBN 0-380-01000-3. The variorum edition, "incorporating all the alterations, additions, and deletions made by the author in the German text over a 30-year period, copiously annotated by the translator, with complete recast bibliographies, new appendixes, indexes of dreams, and a massive general index" (*Library Journal*).

Introductory Lectures on Psychoanalysis: A General Introduction to Psychoanalysis. 1910. Liveright 1990 repr. of 1966 ed. $5.95. ISBN 0-393-00743-X. Covers all Freud's major theories.

Leonardo da Vinci: A Study in Psychosexuality. 1932. Random 1955 $6.00. ISBN 0-394-70132-1. "An interesting study of one genius by another" (*New York Review of Books*).

Letters of Sigmund Freud. Trans. by James Stern and Tania Stern. Ed. by Ernst L. Freud. Dover 1992 repr. of 1960 ed. $12.95. ISBN 0-486-27105-6. More than 300 letters selected by Freud's youngest son to present a portrait of the man. Arranged chronologically from June 1873 to September 1939. Recipients include friends and disciples, members of Freud's family, and such noted persons as Einstein, Thomas Mann, Rolland, Schnitzler, H. G. Wells, and Arnold Zweig and Stefan Zweig.

The Letters of Sigmund Freud and Arnold Zweig. Ed. by Ernst L. Freud. HarBraceJ 1971 o.p. "This correspondence, which includes 42 letters by Freud and 77 by Zweig, and covers the fateful years from 1927 to 1939, presents an interesting human document of the last and tragic period of Freud's life" (*Library Journal*).

Moses and Monotheism. 1939. Ed. by Katherine Jones. Random 1955 $8.00. ISBN 0-394-70014-7. "An epoch-making work. Professor Freud here ventures into fields hitherto unexpected" (*Living Age*).

On Aphasia. Trans. by E. Stengel. Intl. Univs. Pr. 1953 o.p.

Origin and Development of Psychoanalysis. Regnery-Gateway 1960 $7.95. ISBN 0-89526-919-8

The Origins of Psychoanalysis: Letters to Wilhelm Fliess, Drafts and Notes, 1887–1902. Ed. by Marie Bonaparte, Anna Freud, and Ernst Kris. Basic 1977 $22.95. ISBN 0-465-09711-1. "Students and scholars will be grateful for the publication in this book of the material on which Jones based his study" [*The Collected Papers of Sigmund Freud*] (*Library Journal*).

Psychoanalysis and Faith: The Letters of Sigmund Freud and Oskar Pfister. Trans. by Eric Mosbacher. Basic 1963 o.p. Correspondence between Freud, the "unrepentant heretic," and a Protestant clergyman.

A Psycho-Analytic Dialogue: The Letters of Sigmund Freud and Karl Abraham, 1907–1926. Trans. by Bernard Marsh and Hilda C. Abraham. Ed. by Hilda C. Abraham and Ernst L. Freud. Basic 1966 o.p. "In their letters—which Dr. Glover points out read 'like the index to a textbook of abnormal (and normal) psychology'—the two analysts traded ideas about many of the principal ideas and subjects Freud was investigating. . . . Richly rewarding" (*Library Journal*).

The Psychopathology of Everyday Life. 1904. Norton 1990 $5.95. ISBN 0-393-00611-5

Selected Papers on Hysteria and Other Psychoneuroses. 1909. Trans. by A. A. Brill. Johnson Repr. repr. of 1912 ed. o.p.

Selections from Three Works by Freud. Ed. by John Richman. Hogarth Pr. 1939 o.p.

Sigmund Freud and Lou Andreas-Salomé: Letters. Ed. by Ernst Pfeiffer. HarBraceJ 1985 $6.95. ISBN 0-393-30261-X. Collection of letters covering the years from 1911 to 1936.

Three Essays on the Theory of Sexuality. 1905. Trans. and ed. by James Strachey. Basic 1982 $12.00. ISBN 0-465-08606-3. "The annotations . . . are indispensable. In addition, Strachey has provided a concordance, a system of cross-references reminding the reader when a point, a theme, or an incident has been mentioned before" (*Contemporary Psychology*).

Totem and Taboo. Buccaneer Bks. 1913. 1989 $26.95. ISBN 0-89966-634-5. Freud attempts to trace the origins of religion and morality.

A Young Girl's Diary. Gordon Pr. 1972 $300.00. ISBN 0-87968-040-7

BOOKS ABOUT SIGMUND FREUD

Abramson, Jeffrey A. *Liberation and Its Limits: The Moral and Political Thought of Freud*. U. Pr. of Amer. 1993 $38.50. ISBN 0-8191-9018-7. "Offering a fresh interpretation of the nature of Freud's work, he contends that our contemporary view of liberation represents a radical and dangerous departure from Freud's original conception of what constitutes healthy freedom" (*Booklist*).

Anzieu, D. *Freud's Self-Analysis*. Intl. Univs. Pr. 1986 $72.50. ISBN 0-8236-2045-X

Appignanesi, Richard, and Oscar Zarate. *Freud for Beginners*. Pantheon 1979 $5.95. ISBN 0-394-7380-0. Intellectual/biographical cartoon introduction to Freud. Combines "refreshing slapstick with a remarkable amount of fairly sophisticated and tightly compacted—but lucid—information" (*Village Voice*).

Berliner, Arthur K. *Psychoanalysis and Society: The Social Thought of Sigmund Freud*. U. Pr. of Amer. 1983 o.p.

Bersani, Leo. *Baudelaire and Freud*. Quantum Ser. U. CA Pr. 1984 $32.50. ISBN 0-520-03402-3

Brandell, Gunnar. *Freud: A Man of His Century*. Trans. by Iain White. Humanities 1979 o.p.

Brill, A. A. *Freud's Contribution to Psychiatry*. Peter Smith 1972 $11.25. ISBN 0-8446-1738-5. Set of lectures by the pioneer in the field of psychoanalysis in the United States.

Brome, Vincent. *Freud and His Disciples: The Struggle for Supremacy*. Longwood 1984 o.p.

————. *Freud and His Early Circle*. Apollo 1969 o.p. "Mr. Brome's book concentrates not on the theoretical divergences between rival schools, though he handles them competently enough, but on the tangle of motives, temperaments, and misunderstandings of which this complex story is composed" (J. W. Burrow, *Saturday Review*).

Chabot, C. Barry. *Freud on Schreber: Psychoanalytic Theory and the Critical Act*. U. of Mass. Pr. 1982 $22.50. ISBN 0-87023-348-3. "No mere reading of Freud's case study on paranoia, this significant work cogently argues the necessity of a psychological theory to the interpretive processes of literary criticism" (*Choice*).

Dilman, Ilham. *Freud and the Mind*. Blackwell Pubs. 1985 o.p. "In addition to philosophic readers, [many] will find Dilman's book an excellent and thoughtful guide" (*Contemporary Psychology*).

Fancher, Raymond E. *Psychoanalytic Psychology: The Development of Freud's Thought*. Norton 1973 $9.95. ISBN 0-393-09356-5. "Fancher has indeed made Freudian psychology clear, with more grace and less dogmatism than Calvin Hall. But he has also achieved a mix of biography and exegesis that constitutes first-rate history of science" (*Choice*).

Fine, Reuben. *Development of Freud's Thought: From the Beginnings (1886–1899) through Id Psychology (1900–1914) to Ego Psychology (1914–1939)*. Aronson 1987 $40.00. ISBN 0-87668-085-6

Freeman, Lucy, and Herbert S. Strean. *Freud and Women*. Continuum Pr. 1987 $10.95. ISBN 0-8264-0385-9. "Freud emerges from this examination as a well-intentioned investigator of the female psyche. . . . General readers will enjoy reading about Freud's studies in this fast-moving, jargon-free narrative peopled with fascinating characters, chief of whom is Freud" (*Library Journal*).

Freud, Martin. *Sigmund Freud: Man and Father*. Aronson 1983 $25.00. ISBN 0-87668-722-2. Freud's eldest son recalls events of his childhood in a refreshing series of episodes.

Fromm, Erich. *Sigmund Freud's Mission: An Analysis of His Personality and Influence*. Peter Smith 1978 $19.25. ISBN 0-8446-4544-3. "Brilliantly written" (*New York Times*).

Grinstein, Alexander. *Sigmund Freud's Dreams*. Intl. Univs. Pr. 1980 $55.00. ISBN 0-8236-6074-5. "[The author] has limited himself to 19 dreams Freud had from 1895 to 1900 when Freud analyzed himself and made some of his greatest discoveries. . . . An important contribution to both Freudiana and the science of dream interpretation" (*Library Journal*).

Grosskurth, Phyllis. *The Secret Ring: Freud's Inner Circle and the Politics of Psychoanalysis*. Addison-Welsley 1992 $12.95. ISBN 0-201-63220-9. Describes how Freud exerted his control over the founding men of psychoanalysis, how they fought with one another and competed for his favor, and how through the activities of this committee the foundations of psychoanalysis were laid down.

Hale, Nathan G., Jr. *Freud and the Americans: The Origin and Foundation of the Psychoanalytic Movement in America, 1876–1918*. OUP 1971 $27.50. ISBN 0-19-501427-8. In dealing with Freud's impact on America, Hale "proposes to deal with . . . the state of psychiatry, neurology and sexual morality in this country before Freud's appearance at the Clark University Conference in September 1909" (*America*).

Hall, Calvin S. *A Primer of Freudian Psychology: Twenty-Fifth Anniversary Edition*. NAL-Dutton 1955 $4.99. ISBN 0-451-62625-7

Isbister, J. N. *Freud: An Introduction to His Life and Work*. Blackwell Pubs. 1985 o.p.

Jones, Ernest. *The Life and Works of Sigmund Freud*. 3 vols. Ed. and abr. by Lionel Trilling and Steven Marcus. Basic 1974 $15.95. ISBN 0-465-09700-6. Detailed, lucid, informed study of Freud's personal history and his work.

Kanzer, Mark, and Jules Glenn, eds. *Freud and His Patients*. Aronson 1979 $40.00. ISBN 0-87668-367-7

Kline, Paul. *Fact and Fantasy in Freudian Theory. Methuen's Manuals of Modern Psychology Ser.* Methuen 1981 o.p. ". . . the most interesting part of [the book] consists of tape-recorded interviews which Dr. Kurt Eissler conducted in 1952 on behalf of the Freud archives [with] the surviving early analysts about their contact with Freud" (*Nation*).

Krull, Marianne. *Freud and His Father*. Norton 1986 $18.95. ISBN 0-393-01854-7

McCaffrey, Phillip. *Freud and Dora: The Artful Dream*. Rutgers U. Pr. 1984 $35.00. ISBN 0-8135-1056-2

Miller, Jonathan, ed. *Freud: The Man, His World, His Influence*. Little 1972 o.p. "Portrayed are Freud's Vienna—sensual, anti-Semitic, a crucible of intellect and art; as well as Freud's relationship to Marx, philosophy, child rearing, anthropology, aesthetics, morality, and surrealist art" (*Library Journal*).

Oring, Elliott. *The Jokes of Sigmund Freud: A Study in Humor and Jewish Identity*. U. of Pa. Pr. 1984 o.p. Interesting investigation into an aspect of Freud's life not often studied.

Roazen, Paul. *Freud and His Followers*. NYU Pr. 1992 $17.95. ISBN 0-306-80472-7. "[Roazen's] book is scholarly but not forbidding, well-written, of importance to specialists, but also fascinating for anyone interested in the history of psychology or in the personalities of Freud's circle" (*Library Journal*).

———. *Freud: Political and Social Thought. Psychoanalysis Examined and Re-examined Ser.* Da Capo 1986 repr. of 1968 ed. $35.00. ISBN 0-306-76294-3. A political scientist, in "an endeavor to develop the relationship between psychoanalysis and political science [examines] Freud's own application of his concepts and their political and social implications" (*Library Journal*).

———. *Sigmund Freud.* P-H 1973 $6.95. ISBN Collection of ten papers discussing Freud as a pioneer in psychoanalysis and the effect of psychoanalysis on the social sciences. Contributors include Fromm, Riesman, Marcuse, Parsons.

Ruitenbeek, Hendrik, ed. *Freud As We Knew Him.* Da Capo 1987 $39.95. ISBN 0-306-80292-9. "A selection of 60 pieces . . . which bring alive a vivid picture of Freud the man as he appeared to a remarkable set of individuals, including James Putnam, Thomas Mann, Stefan Zweig, Roy Grinker, Sr., and Hilda Doolittle (H.D.)" (*Contemporary Psychology*).

Salome, Lou A. *Freud. Austrian-German Culture Ser.* Black Swan 1989 $20.00. ISBN 0-933806-32-9

Shepherd, Michael. *Sherlock Holmes and the Case of Doctor Freud.* Methuen 1985 o.p.

Stewart, Walter. *Psychoanalysis: The First Ten Years, 1888–1898.* Macmillan 1967 o.p. "A delineation of Freud's theories which led to his blind alleys and an outlining of how Freud resolved his difficulties. Dr. Stewart is scholarly, detached, and dedicated to the task he has assigned himself" (*Library Journal*).

Wittels, Fritz. *Freud and His Time.* Liveright 1956 repr. of 1939 ed. o.p. One of the best statements of the Freudian theories yet to appear in English.

———. *Sigmund Freud: His Personality, His Teaching and His School.* Trans. by Eden Paul and Cedar Paul. *Select Bibliographies Repr. Ser.* Ayer 1977 repr. of 1924 ed. $20.00. ISBN 0-8369-5869-1

FROMM, ERICH. 1900–1980

Born in Frankfurt, Germany, Erich Fromm studied sociology and psychology at the universities of Heidelberg, Frankfurt, and Munich, and received a Ph.D. from Heidelberg in 1922. After training in psychoanalysis in Munich and Berlin, he devoted himself to consultant psychology and theoretical investigation. He first visited the United States in 1933 and later became an American citizen. His *Man for Himself* (1947) brought a "new trend in the study of man." *Escape from Freedom* (1941) studies the causes of totalitarianism. In *The Art of Loving* (1956), he discussed love generally and came to the conclusion that, although the "principle underlying capitalistic society and the principle of love are incompatible . . . love is the only sane and satisfactory answer to the problem of human existence." In *May Man Prevail?* (1961), he wrote that what is required above all is a drastic change in the U.S. attitude: "What can save us and what can help mankind is a renaissance of the spirit of humanism, of individualism, and of America's anticolonist tradition." Fromm was a humanist and a socialist in the pure sense. In *Beyond the Chains of Illusion* (1962), he shows that socialism had been badly distorted from its Marxian ideals. He believed that bureaucratic capitalism, toward which the West seemed to be heading, offered the best probability for the avoidance of nuclear war. In his later years, Fromm was no longer a practicing analyst but taught at New York University as well as at the National University of Mexico.

BOOKS BY FROMM

The Anatomy of Human Destructiveness. H. Holt & Co. 1992 $16.95. ISBN 0-8050-1604-X. "Writes with brilliant insight in attempting to break the deadlock in the struggle between the instinctivism of Konrad Lorenz, who affirms man's 'innate' aggressiveness, and behaviorist B. F. Skinner's 'social engineering' stance" (*Publishers Weekly*).

The Art of Loving. 1956. HarpC 1989 $10.00. ISBN 0-06-091594-3. Discusses all aspects of love.

Beyond the Chains of Illusion. 1962. S&S Trade 1985 $7.95. ISBN 0-317-16272-1. "Fromm bares his own battle to come to terms with Marx and Freud, both of whom, he writes, 'have given us the intellectual tools to break through the sham of rationalization and ideologies, and to penetrate to the core of individual and social reality' (*Saturday Review*).

The Crisis of Psychoanalysis. H. Holt & Co. 1991 $10.95. ISBN 0-8050-1607-4. Collection of essays presenting his views on the development of Freud's theories and the ineffective use of them by many psychoanalysts.

The Dogma of Christ, and Other Essays on Religion, Psychology, and Culture. H. Holt & Co. 1992 $11.95. ISBN 0-8050-1606-6. Projection of the concept of fatherhood found in psychoanalysis to the experience of early Christianity; emphasizes the role of the Son and the doctrine of a God-made man.

Escape from Freedom. 1941. Avon 1976 $5.99. ISBN 0-380-01167-0. Important and challenging book bridges the gap between economics and psychology.

The Forgotten Language: An Introduction to the Understanding of Dreams, Fairytales and Myths. Grove 1987 $10.95. ISBN 0-8021-3050-X. "Fromm develops the theme of symbolism as 'the only universal language the human race ever developed.' . . . Freud's views on dreams are broadened to include 'the significant expression of any kind of mental activity under the condition of sleep' " (*Psychological Abstracts*).

The Greatness and Limitations of Freud's Thought. NAL-Dutton 1980 $4.95. ISBN 0-06-011389-8. Easily readable material, enhanced with historical, anthropological, and mythological references.

The Heart of Man: Its Genius for Good and Evil. HarpC 1980 $5.95. ISBN 0-06-090795-9. "This book is in some respects a counterpart to 'The Art of Loving.' While the main topic there was man's capacity to love, the main topic here is his capacity to destroy, his narcissism and his incestuous fixation" (Erich Fromm).

Man for Himself: An Inquiry into the Psychology of Ethics. 1947. H. Holt & Co. 1990 $10.95. ISBN 0-8050-1403-9. "The thesis is developed that the clinician must reject modern ethical relativism (values are matters of culturally-determined preferences) and accept humanistic ethics in the study of personality whether viewed theoretically or therapeutically" (*Psychological Abstracts*).

Marx's Concept of Man. Milestones of Thought Ser. Ungar 1982 $9.95. ISBN 0-8044-6161-9. "The texts made available here are extremely interesting to anyone who wants to arrive at his own image of Marx's system" (*Library Journal*).

May Man Prevail? Doubleday 1961 o.p. "An intelligent and masterful analysis of the problem, assuredly controversial" (*Kirkus*).

Nature of Man: A Reader. (with Ramón Xirau, eds.) *Problems of Philosophy Ser.* Macmillan 1968 o.p. Some 70 selections ranging from the Upanishads to David Riesman.

On Disobedience and Other Essays. Winston Pr. 1981 o.p. "A collection of nine essays . . . [that] elaborates in various ways on his well-known humane socialism and socially responsible neo-Freudian ideas" (*Choice*).

The Revolution of Hope: Toward a Humanized Technology. HarpC 1968 o.p. "[This] will undoubtedly become another classic" (*Library Journal*).

The Sane Society. 1955. H. Holt & Co. 1990 $11.95. ISBN 0-8050-1402-0

Social Character in a Mexican Village. (coauthored with Michael Maccoby). P-H 1970 o.p. "An empirical study of Mexican peasants by two distinguished psychoanalysts" (*Choice*).

To Have or To Be? Bantam 1983 $4.95. ISBN 0-553-27485-6. "Fromm's richly coherent discourse beautifully seeks out the meaning of 'being' as it illuminates or underlies Biblical writings, the thought or lives of Master Eckhart, the Buddha and later figures like Spinoza, Schweitzer and others—including Marx and Lenin, about whom his insights are remarkably acute" (*Publishers Weekly*).

You Shall Be as Gods: A Radical Interpretation of the Old Testament and Its Traditions. H. Holt & Co. 1991 $10.95. ISBN 0-8050-1605-8. "The legitimacy of this method is extremely questionable, but his conclusion and clear presentation [are of] . . . interest" (*Library Journal*).

Books about Fromm

Evans, Richard I. *Dialogue with Erich Fromm.* Praeger 1981 $41.95. ISBN 0-275-90614-0. His ideas as elicited by a professor from the University of Houston "in an eminently readable manner" (*Library Journal*).

Funk, Rainer. *Erich Fromm: The Courage to Be Human.* Continuum 1982 o.p. "The most comprehensive and detailed exposition of Fromm's thought to appear in any language" (*Choice*).

Gotesky, Rubin. *Personality: The Need for Liberty and Rights.* Libra 1967 $10.00. ISBN 0-87212-0

Hammond, Guyton B. *Man in Estrangement: Paul Tillich and Erich Fromm Compared.* Vanderbilt U. Pr. 1965 $55.70. ISBN 0-8357-3256-8. Historical approach, highlighting the fundamental differences between Fromm and Tillich.

Hausdorff, Don. *Erich Fromm.* Twayne 1972 o.p. "Brief but very informative. Provides an evaluation of Fromm's work in a spirit of 'critical sympathy and intellectual curiosity' " (*Choice*).

Knapp, Gerhard Peter. *The Art of Living: Erich Fromm's Life and Works.* P. Lang Pubs. 1989 $49.95. ISBN 0-8204-1034-9. Critical appraisal of Fromm's work as teacher and analyst, as well as of all his writings; intended for both the uninitiated reader and the specialist.

GLASSER, WILLIAM. 1925–

William Glasser, who was born in Cleveland, Ohio, first earned a degree in chemical engineering from the then Case Institute of Technology and later became a psychiatrist. He found himself doubting much of the conventional psychoanalysis, in which often the patient is seen as the helpless victim of past traumas, and insisted that the cobwebs of the past be brushed aside and that the patient develop a plan of action for the future. Glasser's conviction that success breeds success and that failure breeds failure led him to develop his reality therapy, a remedy for people for whom conventional psychotherapy does not work and a prescription of use to people regardless of their circumstances. Glasser has also done much for and within the school system, dealing with the issues of motivation, quality in the school, and problems of delinquency.

Glasser, whose books have been translated into many languages, has wide experience as a psychiatrist in Los Angeles and is a consultant to the school system.

Books by Glasser

The Identity Society. HarpC 1975 $11.00. ISBN 0-06-090446-1. The search for identity is seen as the cause of many social problems.

The Quality School: Managing Students without Coercion. HarpC 1990 $11.00. ISBN 0-06-096955-5. Constructive guide to problematic issues in the school setting for educators as well as parents.

Reality Therapy: A New Approach to Psychiatry. HarpC 1975 $7.00. ISBN 0-06-080348-7. Glasser's attack on the Freudian method of concentrating on the past in therapy; explains how his new therapy is based on showing patients how to manage their present and future lives.

Book about Glasser

Bassin, A., T. E. Bratter, and R. L. Rachin, eds. *The Reality Therapy Reader: A Survey of the Work of William Glasser M.D.* HarpC 1976 o.p. Extensive collection of papers covering Glasser's life, theory, and practice.

HORNEY, KAREN. 1885–1952

Karen Horney was born in Hamburg, Germany, the daughter of a Norwegian father and a Dutch mother. While attending medical school at the University of Berlin, she became interested in psychoanalysis. She came to the United States in 1932 to be assistant director of the Chicago Institute of Psychoanalysis. She then became a practicing analyst and lecturer at the New School for Social Research in New York. In 1941 she helped found the American Institute of Psychoanalysis and held the post of dean until her death.

Like that of other analysts, much of Horney's work involved a restatement of Freudian theory. "I believe," she wrote in her first book, "that deference for Freud's gigantic achievements should show itself in building on the foundations that he has laid, and that in this way we can help to fulfill the possibilities which psychoanalysis has for the future, as a theory as well as a therapy." The *New York Times* has said of her, however: "Much of Karen Horney's psychological theorizing has passed into common currency. . . . During the thirties and forties, [she] was a revolutionary thinker, pitting her culturally embedded, female-accented psychology against what she considered SIGMUND FREUD's (see also Vol. 3) excessively male, materialistic and biologically determined theories."

BOOKS BY HORNEY

Feminine Psychology. Ed. by Harold Kelman. Norton 1973 $4.95. ISBN 0-393-00686-7. An interesting collection revealing Horney's gradually evolving ideas about feminine psychology, including ideas for solutions to the problems created by distrust between the sexes.

Neurosis and Human Growth: A Study of Self-Realization. 1950. Norton 1991 $9.95. ISBN 0-393-30775-1. "Karen Horney's book is an important and constructive document in the growing controversy" (*New York Times*).

The Neurotic Personality of Our Time. 1937. Norton 1965 $4.95. ISBN 0-393-00742-1. "Clearly written; for intelligent laymen, social workers, teachers, and psychiatrists" (*Booklist*).

New Ways in Psychoanalysis. 1939. Norton 1964 $4.95. ISBN 0-393-00133-4. "The material is presented with lucidity and, if read in conjunction with *The Neurotic Personality*, should present no difficulties to the lay mind" (*Churchmen*).

Our Inner Conflicts: A Constructive Theory of Neurosis. 1945. Norton 1993 $7.95. ISBN 0-393-30940-1. "I know of no other writer today in the field of psychoanalysis with a directness, a clarity, a reasonableness devoid of professional jargon and technical trim which equals that of Karen Horney, whose *New Ways in Psychoanalysis* was an important modern contribution" (*Kirkus*).

Self-Analysis. 1942. Norton 1968 $5.95. ISBN 0-393-00134-2. Dr. Horney's book contains a great deal of interesting new material" (*Survey Graphic*).

BOOKS ABOUT HORNEY

Kelman, Harold. *Helping People: Karen Horney's Psychoanalytic Approach.* Aronson 1971 o.p. "An extensive presentation of Kelman's modification of Horney's theory of neurosis, psychoanalytic concepts and techniques, and stages of the treatment process" (*Library Journal*).

Westkott, Marcia. *The Feminist Legacy of Karen Horney.* Yale U. Pr. 1986 $13.00. ISBN 0-300-03706-6. Insightful, fresh look at Horney's relevance to contemporary issues.

JAMES, WILLIAM. 1842–1910

William James, the brilliant and readable Harvard University "pragmatic" philosopher and the first Harvard professor of psychology (1889–97), is one of the pioneers of American psychology. After brief personal investigation of the work of HERMANN HELMHOLTZ, Ewald Hering, and WILHELM WUNDT (see Vol. 3) in Germany, he introduced experiments in psychology in a Harvard graduate course on "The Relations between Physiology and Psychology" in 1875. His *Principles of Psychology* (1890) became a standard textbook. James saw human psychology as a biological adjustment to the changing environment—with the state of consciousness as a "selecting agency." His student G. STANLEY HALL (see Vol. 3), later himself a pioneer of distinction in the field, recalled (says Gay Wilson Allen) how in the early days James kept "in a tiny room under the staircase of the Agassiz museum . . . a metronome, a device for whirling a frog," and other novel research tools for the period. His philosophical and psychological studies each had an effect on the other, but in 1897 he took the Harvard chair in philosophy and devoted the rest of his life to that discipline.

BOOKS BY JAMES

The Principles of Psychology. 1890. HUP 1983 $25.00. $22.50. ISBN 0-674-70625-0. Authorized unabridged edition. "This critical text of the preeminent classic of American psychology incorporates the results of the highest standards of textual scholarship to present James's intentions in a definitive edition" (*Choice*).

Psychology: The Briefer Course. 1892. HUP 1984 $40.00. ISBN 0-674-72102-0

Talks to Teachers on Psychology: And to Students on Some of Life's Ideals. 1899. HUP 1983 $33.00. ISBN 0-674-86785-8. Consists of fifteen lectures and three addresses including preliminary notes and drafts, descriptions of source documents and editing procedures, and a historical account of the original lectures and their publication.

The Varieties of Religious Experience: A Study in Human Nature. Gleneida Pub. 1991 $8.95. ISBN 0-8007-3011-9. "For James *The Varieties of Religious Experience* was an occasion to summarize many of his ethical and philosophical views, but also an opportunity to show what he believed the human mind is all about, and not least, how psychologists and psychiatrists ought to think about their work" (*The New Republic*).

William James on Psychical Research. Ed. by Gardner Murphy and Robert Ballou. HUP 1986 $45.00. ISBN 0-674-26708-7. "James' writings on psychic phenomena are presented under the following headings: 'Early Impressions'; 'General Statements'; 'Clairvoyance, Levitation and the Astral Body'; 'William James and Mrs. Piper'; 'William James and Frederic Meyers'; 'Religion and the Problems of the Soul and Immortality'; and 'The Last Report' " (*Psychological Abstracts*).

The Writings of William James: A Comprehensive Edition. Ed. by John J. McDermott. U. Ch. Pr. 1978 $19.95. ISBN 0-226-39188-4. Drawn from classic James as well as unpublished papers and newspaper interviews; comprehensive portrait of a great American philosopher.

BOOKS ABOUT JAMES

Eisendrath, Craig R. *The Unifying Moment: The Psychological Philosophy of William James and Alfred North Whitehead.* HUP 1971 $22.50. ISBN 0-674-92100-3. "Fulfills a real need for a comparison of the thought of James and Whitehead. . . . A very good book for those interested in epistemological issues arising in process philosophy" (*Choice*).

Johnson, Michael G., and Tracy B. Henley, eds. *Reflections on the Principles of Psychology: William James after a Century.* L. Erlbaum Assocs. 1990 $49.95. ISBN 0-8058-0205-3. Contributions by contemporary psychologists on the lasting influence of James's classic, *The Principles of Psychology*; the continuing relevance of James's thought for contemporary psychology can be seen in the broad range of topics covered.

Linschoten, Hans, ed. *On the Way Toward a Phenomenological Psychology: The Psychology of William James.* Trans. by Amedeo Giorgi. *Philosophical Ser.* Duquesne

U. Pr. 1968 o.p. Points out the greatness of James's philosophy despite its internal contradictions; written by a noted psychologist for psychologists.

Wilshire, Bruce. *William James and Phenomenology: A Study of "The Principles of Psychology."* AMS Pr. 1979 repr. of 1968 ed. $24.00. ISBN 0-404-15226-0

JUNG, C(ARL) G(USTAV). 1875–1961

The Swiss-born Carl Jung was one of the most famous of modern psychologists and psychiatrists. The son of a minister, Jung originally set out to study archaeology. He switched to medicine and began practicing psychiatry in Basel after receiving his degree in 1902. Jung first met SIGMUND FREUD (see also Vol. 3) in 1907 when he became his foremost associate and disciple. The break came with the publication of Jung's *Psychology of the Unconscious* (1912), which did not follow Freud's theories of the libido and the unconscious. Jung eventually rejected Freud's system of psychoanalysis for his own "analytic psychology." This emphasizes present conflicts rather than those from childhood; it also takes into account the conflict arising from what Jung called the "collective unconscious"—evolutionary and cultural factors determining individual development. Considered as a "deserter" and a "mystic" by Freud's followers, Jung's theories have continued to be the topic of heated discussions.

Jung invented the association word test and contributed the word *complex* to psychology, and first described the "introvert" and "extrovert" types. Jung's interest in the human psyche, past and present, led him to study mythology, alchemy, oriental religions and philosophies, and traditional peoples. Later he became interested in parapsychology and the occult. He thought that unidentified flying objects (UFOs) might be a psychological projection of modern people's anxieties.

Jung was elected a fellow of the Royal Society of Medicine and received an honorary D.Sc. by Oxford University, the first psychologist to receive such an honor in England. He also received honorary degrees from Harvard University, the University of Calcutta, the Banaras Hindu University, the University of Allahabad in India, and the University of Geneva.

BOOKS BY JUNG

Analytical Psychology, Its Theory and Practice: The Tavistock Lectures. 1935. Random 1970 o.p. "This book of five lectures by Jung is a summary of his views, delivered to a London professional audience in 1935" (*Library Journal*).

The Basic Writings of C. G. Jung. Ed. by Violet de Laszlo. *Bollingen Ser.* Modern Lib. 1990 $12.95. ISBN 0-691-01902-9. "A representative selection from Jung's writings . . . covering the entire period of his production." (*Psychological Abstracts*).

C. G. Jung: Letters, 1906–1950. Ed. by Gerhard Adler and Aniela Jaffe. Trans. by R. F. C. Hull. *Bollingen Ser.* Princeton U. Pr. 1973 o.p. More than 900 letters selected from over 1,600 written between 1906 and 1950 to different persons of prominence.

The Collected Works of C. G. Jung. 20 vols. Ed. by G. Adler and others. Trans by R. F. Hull. Princeton U. Pr. Vol. 1 *Psychiatric Studies.* 1970 $47.50. ISBN 0-691-09768-2. Vol. 2 *Experimental Researches.* 1973 $59.00. ISBN 0-691-09764-X. Vol. 3 *The Psychogenesis of Mental Disease.* 1960 $45.00. ISBN 0-691-09769-0. Vol. 4 *Freud and Psychoanalysis.* 1985 $45.00. ISBN 0-691-09765-8. Vol. 5 *Symbols of Transformation.* 1967 $65.00. ISBN 0-691-09775-5. Vol. 6 *Psychological Types.* 1971 $65.00. ISBN 0-691-09770-4. Vol. 7 *Two Essays on Analytical Psychology.* 1966 $42.50. ISBN 0-691-09776-3. Vol. 8 *The Structure and Dynamics of the Psyche.* 1969 $65.00. ISBN 0-691-09774-7. Vol. 9 Pt. 1 *The Archetypes and the Collective Unconscious.* 1968 $60.00. ISBN 0-691-09761-5. Vol. 9 Pt. 2 *Aion—Researches into the Phenomenology of the Self.* 1968 $39.50. ISBN 0-691-09759-3. Vol. 10 *Civilization in Transition.* 1970 $65.00. ISBN 0-691-09762-3. Vol. 11 *Psychology and Religion—West and East.* 1969 $67.50. ISBN 0-

691-09772-0. Vol. 12 *Psychology and Alchemy.* 1968 $65.00. ISBN 0-691-09771-2. Vol. 13 *Alchemical Studies.* 1968 $49.50. ISBN 0-691-09760-7. Vol. 14 *Mysterium Coniunctionis.* 1970 $65.00. ISBN 0-691-09766-6. Vol. 15 *The Spirit of Man, Art, and Literature.* 1966 $27.50. ISBN 0-691-09773-9. Vol. 16 *The Practice of Psychotherapy.* 1966 $49.50. ISBN 0-691-09767-4. Vol. 17 *The Development of Personality.* 1985 $39.50. ISBN 0-691-09763-1. Vol. 18 *The Symbolic Life.* 1976 $80.00. ISBN 0-691-09892-1. Vol. 19 *Bibliography of Jung's Writings.* 1979 $29.50. ISBN 0-691-09893-X. Vol. 20 *General Index.* 1979 $75.00. ISBN 0-691-09867-0

Essays on a Science of Mythology: The Myths of the Divine Child and the Mysteries of Eleusis. (coauthored with Carl Kerenyi). 1949. *Bollingen Ser.* Princeton U. Pr. 1969 $8.95. ISBN 0-691-01756-5. Presents and relates two myths to psychological experience.

The Freud-Jung Letters: The Correspondence between Sigmund Freud and C. G. Jung. Ed. by William McGuire. Trans. by Ralph Manheim and R. F. C. Hull. *Bollingen Ser.* Princeton U. Pr. 1988 repr. of 1974 ed. $16.95. ISBN 0-674-32330-0. "The reader of these letters will find in them, or read out of them, whatever his personal inclinations dictate. They are, of course, a gold mine for the historian" (*Contemporary Psychology*).

Memories, Dreams, Reflections. Random 1989 $12.00. ISBN 0-679-72395-1. Profound and absorbing autobiographical book, accessible in its language and its thought to the lay reader as well as to psychologists; mostly written from interviews, but four chapter, including those on his childhood and his skepticism about theology, were written by Jung himself.

Modern Man in Search of a Soul. 1933. HarBraceJ 1955 $6.95. ISBN 0-15-661206-2. "Involved as the book is, it will repay a careful reading on the part of those who have some knowledge of what has been done in analytical psychology" (*Churchmen*).

The Portable Jung. Ed. by Joseph Campbell. Viking Penguin 1976 $9.95. ISBN 0-14-015070-6. Collection of Jung's major writings, spanning his entire career.

Psyche and Symbol: A Selection from the Writings of C. G. Jung. Ed. by Violet de Laszlo. Princeton U. Pr. 1990 $12.95. ISBN 0-691-01903-7

Psychological Reflections: A New Anthology of His Writings, 1905–1961. Ed. by Jolande Jacobi and R. F. C. Hull. *Bollingen Ser.* Princeton U. Pr. 1970 $14.95. ISBN 0-691-01786-7. "This new edition of the 1953 book draws on over 30 additional sources, including interviews and posthumously published works" (*Library Journal*).

The Psychology of Dementia Praecox. Johnson repr. of 1909 ed. $19.00. ISBN 0-384-28229-6. Retranslation by A. A. Brill of the study originally published in 1906 and translated by him into English in 1909.

The Theory of Psychoanalysis. Johnson Repr. repr. of 1915 ed. o.p.

The Undiscovered Self. NAL-Dutton 1974 $3.95. ISBN 0-451-62539-0. "Wise, witty, and forthright counsel for the reflective reader" (*Booklist*).

BOOKS ABOUT JUNG

Aziz, Robert. *C. G. Jung's Psychology of Religion and Synchronicity.* State U. NY Pr. 1990 $59.50. ISBN 0-7914-0167-7. Comprehensive study of synchronicity for the initiated Jungian reader.

Bennett, E. A. *What Jung Really Said.* Schocken 1983 $12.00. ISBN 0-8052-0753-8. "Bennett, a psychotherapist and friend of the late Dr. Jung, reviews Jung's work as it developed: first with Bleuler and Janet; then with Freud, who had the most influence on him; and finally, his own independent work, as creator and leader of a new influential school of thought and therapy" (*Library Journal*).

Brome, Vincent. *Jung: Man and Myth.* Atheneum 1981 $11.95. ISBN 0-689-10853-2. "The best biography of C. G. Jung ever written. . . . This British author has done a good job of presenting a balanced portrait of a complicated man; he has neither oversimplified nor become lost in trivial psychological analysis" (*Choice*).

Cohen, Edmund D. *C. G. Jung and the Scientific Attitude. Quality Pap. Ser.* Littlefield 1976 o.p. "A standard review of Jungian principles, never seriously criticizing Jungian concepts" (*Choice*).

Cowan, Lyn. *Masochism: A Jungian View*. Spring Pub. 1982 $13.50. ISBN 0-88214-320-4

Cox, David. *Modern Psychology: The Teachings of Carl Gustav Jung*. B & N Imports 1958 o.p. Good overview and in-depth perspective into the nature of Jung's psychological approach to life.

Hall, Calvin S., and Vernon J. Nordby. *A Primer of Jungian Psychology*. NAL-Dutton 1973 $3.99. ISBN 0-451-62578-1. "The aim of this little book is 'to present Jung's concepts and theories clearly, simply, and accurately.' This the authors have done—and very competently" (*Library Journal*).

Homans, Peter. *Jung in Context: Modernity and the Making of a Psychology*. U. Ch. Pr. 1982 o.p. "The analysis of the psychological influences that shaped Jung's work is given the most attention" (*Contemporary Psychology*).

Jacobi, Jolande F. *The Psychology of C. G. Jung*. Trans. by Ralph Manheim. Yale U. Pr. 1973 $16.50 ISBN 0-300-01673-5

_____. *The Way of Individuation*. NAL-Dutton 1983 o.p. Nontechnical discussion of Jung's concept of individuation, the innate tendency of an individual to realize himself as a unique, whole person.

Jaffe, Aniela. *The Myth of Meaning*. Trans. by R. F. C. Hull. Humanities 1984 $14.00. ISBN 0-85630-500-9. "The author, an analytical psychologist and personal secretary to Carl Jung during his last years, devotes herself to the problem of explaining Jung's main interest—the meaning and aim of human existence" (*Library Journal*).

Matton, Mary Ann. *Jungian Psychology in Perspective*. Free Pr. 1985 $10.95. ISBN 0-02-920650-2

Neumann, Erich. *The Great Mother: An Analysis of the Archetype*. Trans. by Ralph Manheim. *Bollingen Ser*. Princeton U. Pr. 1964 $16.95. ISBN 0-0691-0178-8. "A major study of the way women have been regarded since prehistory" (*Publishers Weekly*).

Nichols, Sallie. *Jung and Tarot: An Archetypal Journey*. Weiser 1984 $14.95. ISBN 0-87728-515-2

Samuels, Andrew. *Jung and Post-Jungians*. Routledge 1984 $24.95. ISBN 0-7102-0864-2

Staude, John-Raphael. *The Adult Development of C. G. Jung*. Routledge 1981 $17.95. ISBN 0-7100-0749-3. "Staude's book puts Jung's adult development into the framework of 'life-span developmental psychology.' It thus makes valuable contrasts between academic and Jungian psychology: the former concentrates on the ego and the latter revitalizes it and relates it to the Jungian self" (*Choice*).

Stein, Murray, ed. *Jungian Analysis*. Shambhala 1984 $10.95. ISBN 0-87548-350-X. "This book, with its distinguished roster of contributors, its clinical orientation, and its useful list of references at the end of each chapter, will certainly be important to those who are actively involved with Jungian practice" (*Contemporary Psychology*).

Storr, Anthony. *C. G. Jung. Modern Masters Ser*. Viking Penguin 1973 o.p. Clear and simple explanation of Jung's complex theories of analytical psychology.

Ulanov, Ann Belford. *The Feminine in Jungian Psychology and in Christian Theology*. Northwestern U. Pr. 1971 o.p. The author's work "revolves around Jung's approach to and the structure of the psyche, his concept of the feminine in both male and female, and the concept of the feminine as it relates to the religious function and the doctrine of man, God and Christ, and the Spirit" (*Choice*).

Van der Post, Laurens. *Jung: And the Story of Our Time*. Random 1976 $10.95. ISBN 0-394-72175-6. "Loaded with rich perceptions. . . . A most stimulating book" (*Publishers Weekly*).

KLEIN, MELANIE. 1882–1960

Melanie Klein was born in Vienna, the fourth and youngest child of Jewish parents. Her childhood setting was a highly intellectual one, and, at the age of 14, she knew she wanted to study medicine. Her prospects came to an end when she married at an early age and became the mother of three children. Klein was a wife and mother when she entered psychoanalysis in 1912. Using insights that she gained from her psychoanalysis and applying them to disturbed children, she became the first major child psychologist. In 1919 she presented her first paper, "The Development of a Child," at a meeting of the Budapest Psychoanalytic Society. In 1921 she moved to Berlin and began developing her theory of mental functioning in young children and her analytic *play technique*. She moved permanently to London in 1926, where her theoretical framework created bitter controversy in the British Psychoanalytic Society. She nonetheless persisted in her work, and her writings are still widely read long after her death. Klein's work with children remains influential, and her theoretical framework still enjoys considerable respect.

BOOK BY KLEIN

The Writing of Melanie Klein. 4 vols. Free Pr. 1984 $150.00. ISBN 0-02-918460-6. A new edition of her complete works with editorial notes clarifying the main themes of her life's work (*Preface*).

BOOKS ABOUT KLEIN

Hughes, Judith M. *Reshaping the Psychoanalytic Domain: The Work of Melanie Klein, W. R. D. Fairbairn and D. W. Winnicott.* U. CA Pr. 1989 $37.50. ISBN 0-520-06480-1. Intended to provide coherent appreciation for object relations theory and how it differs from classical psychoanalytic theory.

Segal, Hanna. *Introduction to the Work of Melanie Klein.* Basic 1980 $13.00. ISBN 0-465-03584-1. Collection of lecture notes aimed at the psychoanalytic student as an introduction but not a substitute for her work.

Weininger, Otto. *The Clinical Psychology of Melanie Klein.* C. C. Thomas 1984 o.p. Detailed presentation of theory and practice as understood and practiced by Klein; intended for the experienced reader.

KOHUT, HEINZ. 1913–1981

Heinz Kohut was an Austrian-born psychoanalyst who studied at the University of Vienna and later moved to the United States to escape the Nazis in 1940. He is the founder of a branch of psychoanalysis called self-psychology. His foundation is psychoanalytic but modified in such a way that the self in relation to others is emphasized. Kohut devoted more than 20 years to the subject of narcissism. He believed that the narcissistic struggle was central to human development, downplaying the significance of psychoanalytical concepts such as the Oedipal complex, intrapsychic conflict, and the libido. An essential part of Kohut's approach is the notion of empathy on the part of the therapist. He viewed empathetic understanding as critical for the client in order to resolve emotional and developmental problems in relation to the self. He saw this particular relationship as being helpful in resolving certain types of mental problems.

BOOKS BY KOHUT

The Analysis of the Self: A Systematic Approach to the Psychoanalytic Treatment of Narcissistic Personality Disorders. Intl. Univs. Pr. 1971 $47.50. ISBN 0-8236-0145-5. In-depth, scholarly treatment of the topic, suitable for the initiated reader.

How Does Analysis Cure? Contributions to the Psychology of the Self. Ed. by A. Goldberg and P. E. Stepansky. U. Ch. Pr. 1984 $27.50. ISBN 0-226-45034-1

The Restoration of Self. Intl. Univs. Pr. 1977 $45.00. ISBN 0-8236-5810-4. Presents a psychology of the self that puts the self at the center and examines its genesis, development, and constituents in health and disease.

BOOKS ABOUT KOHUT

Goldberg, A., ed. *The Future of Psychoanalysis: Essays in Honor of Heinz Kohut.* Intl.
Univs. Pr. 1983 o.p. Collection of papers focusing on present controversial or
problematic issues with a view toward the future rather than a presentation of
current theory and historical background.

Jacoby, M. *Individuation and Narcissism: The Psychology of the Self in Jung and Kohut.*
Trans. by Myron Gubitz. Routledge 1990 $35.00. ISBN 0-415-00827-1. Attempts to
clearly present some complex concepts and bring together and review different sets
of observations, theories, and therapeutic systems.

Stepansky, Paul E., and Arnold Goldberg, eds. *Kohut's Legacy: Contributions to Self
Psychology.* Bks. Demand 1984 $72.30. ISBN 0-8357-4385-3. Collection of papers by
Kohut's students and those who worked closely with him; each paper presents a
different aspect of Kohut's contribution.

LACAN, JACQUES. 1901–1981

Jacques Lacan was born into an upper-middle-class Parisian family. He
received psychiatric and psychoanalytic training, and his clinical training began
in 1927. His doctoral thesis, "On Paranoia and Its Relation to Personality,"
already indicated an original thinker; in it he tried to show that no physiological
phenomenon could be adequately understood without taking into account the
entire personality, including its engagement with a social milieu.

Practicing in France, Lacan led a "back to Freud" movement in the most
literal sense, at a time when others were trying to interpret SIGMUND FREUD (see
also Vol. 3) broadly. He emphasized the role of the image and the role of milieu
in personality organization. Seeking to reinterpret Freud's theories in terms of
structural linguistics, Lacan believed that Freud's greatest insight was his
understanding of the "talking cure" as revelatory of the unconscious. By taking
Freud literally, Lacan led a psychoanalytic movement that evolved into a very
specific school of interpretation. Often embroiled in controversy, in the 1950s
he opposed the standardization of training techniques, the classification of
psychoanalysis as a medical treatment, and the then emerging school of ego
psychology. Although general readers may find Lacan difficult to read, his works
are provocative and rewarding.

BOOKS BY LACAN

Ecrits: A Selection. Trans. by Alan Sheridan. Norton 1982 $12.95. ISBN 0-393-30047.
"These nine essays, chosen by Lacan himself, are the first sizable chunk of Lacan's
work to be available in English. . . . Readers with the necessary background and
energy will find in *Ecrits* important insights into structuralism and Freud's theories"
(*Library Journal*).

Feminine Sexuality. Ed. by Juliet Mitchell and Jacqueline Rose. Norton 1985 $9.95. ISBN
0-393-30211-3. "Lacan sees sexuality as a psychic rather than a biological construct,
which is why many feminists have been attracted to his work" (*The New Republic*).

The Four Fundamental Concepts of Psycho-Analysis. Trans. by Alan Sheridan. Norton
1981 $14.95. ISBN 0-393-00079-6. "Enigmatic, provocative, at times too cute, but in
the end very rewarding to read" (*Choice*).

The Language of the Self: The Function of Language in Psychoanalysis. Dell 1975 o.p.

Speech and Language in Psychoanalysis. Trans. by Anthony Wilden. Johns Hopkins 1981
$13.95. ISBN 0-8018-2617-9

BOOK ABOUT LACAN

Mueller, J. P., and W. J. Richardson. *Lacan and Language: A Reader's Guide to Ecrits.*
Intl. Univs. Pr. 1982 $50.00. ISBN 0-8236-2945-7. Useful guide in which the authors
render Lacan accessible to the novice.

LAING, R(ONALD) D(AVID). 1927–1989

R. D. Laing, a prominent British psychoanalyst, won wide attention in the United States, especially among young people, for his questioning of many of the old concepts of what is "normal" and what is "insane" in a world that he sees as infinitely dangerous in the hands of "normal" people. Born and educated in Glasgow, Scotland, Laing questioned many of the basic assumptions of Western culture. Taking the role of social critic, he wrote in *The Politics of Experience* (1967): "A little girl of seventeen in a mental hospital told me she was terrified because the Atom Bomb was inside her. That is a delusion. The statesmen of the world who boast and threaten that they have Doomsday weapons are far more dangerous, and far more estranged from 'reality' than many of the people on whom the label 'psychotic' is affixed."

Much of Laing's work was in the field of schizophrenia. Philosophical and humanist in approach, he questioned many of the cut-and-dried classifications for the mentally ill, whom he regarded with great compassion; he looked beyond the "case" to the man or woman trying to come to grips with life in the broadest human context. He was a compelling writer of great literary skill who brought to his studies a worldview that reached far beyond the confines of his profession. Until his death, Laing continued to expand on his early themes, which are also evident in his poetry, interviews, and conversations with children.

BOOKS BY LAING

Conversations with Adam and Natasha. Pantheon 1984 o.p. "The short dialogues recorded here actually took place among Laing, his wife and their two children. . . . The conversations reflect the emotional development of fairly healthy children within the context of a secure, reciprocal relationship with their parents" (*Publishers Weekly*).

The Divided Self. 1960. Viking Penguin 1965 o.p. "Any therapist who wants to deepen his feeling for man will profit from the hours in Laing's stimulating company" (*Critic*).

The Facts of Life: An Essay in Feelings, Facts and Fantasy. Ballantine 1984 o.p. "His metaphoric, cryptic and elliptic style leaves much to the reader but is appropriate for the complex discussion of psyche-soma interrelations" (*Library Journal*).

Interpersonal Perception. (coauthored with Herbert Phillipson and A. Russell Lee). Springer Pub. 1966 o.p. Presents a theory and a method for studying how two persons perceive each other.

Knots. Random 1972 $9.00. ISBN 0-345-29815-2. "Of interest to followers of Laing, therapy group members, and students of behavior in general" (*Library Journal*).

The Politics of Experience. 1967. Ballantine 1981 $2.50. ISBN 0-345-29815-2. Interesting discussion of Laing's psychological theories—for lay people—in the context of the modern world. Brief and beautifully written.

The Politics of the Family and Other Essays. Random 1972 $8.00. ISBN 0-394-71809-7. "Laing, a psychoanalyst . . . here questions assumptions about the family" (*Canadian Forum*).

Reason and Violence: A Decade of Sartre's Philosophy, 1950–1960. (coauthored with David G. Cooper). 1964. Random 1971 o.p. With a foreword by Jean-Paul Sartre. "The publication of *Reason and Violence* does . . . convey some sense of the contemporary relevance of Sartre's *Critique*" (*Journal of Philosophy*).

The Self and Others. 1961. Viking Penguin 1972 $5.95. ISBN 0-14-021376-7. Essay on human relationships.

The Voice of Experience. Pantheon 1982 o.p. Coherent examination of the nature of experience.

Wisdom, Madness and Folly: The Making of a Psychiatrist, 1927–1957. McGraw 1986 $4.95. ISBN 0-07-035850-8. Memoir of the first 30 years of his life.

BOOKS ABOUT LAING

Boyers, Robert, and Robert Orrill, eds. *R. D. Laing and Anti-Psychiatry*. Hippocrene Bks.
1974 repr. of 1971 ed. o.p. "[A] collection of critical essays and transcripts of
interviews and symposiums by psychiatrists, sociologists, literature professors and
psychologists . . . many-faceted, well-rounded treatment" (*Publishers Weekly*).

Friedenberg, Edgar Z. *R. D. Laing. Modern Masters Ser.* Viking Penguin 1974 o.p.
"Friedenberg discusses the limitations of Laing's research, the ambiguity of much of
his writing, the rejection of scientifically controlled observation, and the influences
of Eastern philosophy" (*Library Journal*).

LAZARUS, ARNOLD A. 1932–

Arnold Lazarus was born in Johannesburg, South Africa. His intention was to
become a journalist, but he became intrigued by psychology instead. After
receiving his clinical training in behavior modification with phobic patients,
Lazarus became one of the leaders in promoting behavior therapy in South
Africa. Increasingly unhappy with the political situation in South Africa, he
brought his family to the United States in 1967 to settle in Philadelphia,
Pennsylvania. Lazarus's major contribution, "multimodal assessment," evolved
out of his view that conventional therapy was too limited. He advocated
technical eclecticism, claiming that assessment and therapy must include our
interactive **B**ehavior, **A**ffective processes, **S**ensations, **I**mages, **C**ognitions,
Interpersonal relationships, and biological functions, which in therapy often
means the use of **D**rugs. In essence, Lazarus's multimodal assessment is the
thorough assessment of a person's BASIC I.D.

BOOKS BY LAZARUS

The Essential Arnold Lazarus. Counseling and Psychotherapy Ser. Ed. by W. Dryden.
Whurr 1991 o.p. Draws together twenty of his pieces, covering a broad range of
topics; illustrates how his "multimodal" position developed into the orientation that
has earned him an international reputation.

The Practice of Multimodal Therapy: Systematic, Comprehensive and Effective Psychother-
apy. Johns Hopkins 1989 $14.95. ISBN 0-8018-3811-8. Overview of the theoretical
and clinical foundations of multimodal therapy along with some case studies and
clinical reports.

BOOK ABOUT LAZARUS

Dryden, W. *A Dialogue with Arnold Lazarus: "It depends." Therapeutically Speaking Ser.*
Open U. Pr. 1991 $80.00. ISBN 0-335-09280-2. In-depth discussion between Arnold
Lazarus and Windy Dryden, providing an overview of Lazarus's perspective.

LEWIN, KURT. 1890–1947

[SEE Volume 3.]

MASLOW, ABRAHAM H(AROLD). 1908–1970

In its first edition, Abraham Maslow's *Toward a Psychology of Being* (1962)
sold more than 100,000 copies. Like R. D. LAING, Maslow questioned the old
psychoanalytic notions of being well or ill "adjusted" to the world and spoke
from a broadly human base. Human nature—the inner nature of every
individual which is uniquely his or her own—"seems not to be . . . necessarily
evil; . . . the basic human capacities are on their face either neutral, premoral or
positively 'good.' What we call evil behavior appears most often to be a
secondary reaction to frustration of this intrinsic nature." On this foundation
Maslow built an affirmation of people and people's potentialities for self-

fulfillment and psychological health. He considered his "humanistic" or "Eupsychian" approach to be part of the revolution then taking place in psychology, as in other fields, toward a new view of people as sociable, creative, and loving beings whose welfare is not in the cure of "neurosis" or other ills but on the development of their most socially and personally constructive potentials.

Maslow was born in New York City and received his B.A., M.A., and Ph.D. from the University of Wisconsin. He was chairman of the psychology department at Brandeis University, Waltham, Massachusetts, taught for 14 years at Brooklyn College, and was the president of the American Psychological Association from 1967 to 1968. His wife Bertha helped edit his journals and last papers after his death and assisted with a memorial volume about him.

BOOKS BY MASLOW

Dominance, Self-Esteem, Self-Actualization: Germinal Papers of A. H. Maslow. Ed. by Richard J. Lowry. Brooks-Cole 1973 o.p. "The editor has expertly woven into a coherent text eight of the important early papers spanning the years from 1936 to 1950 by A. H. Maslow, one of the founders of the third force or humanistic psychology" (*Choice*).

Eupsychian Management: A Journal. Irwin 1965 o.p. "Throughout the reader is confronted with Maslow's unique blend of values and science as he sketches the possibility of moving toward Utopia (or Eupsychia) through improved management" (*Contemporary Psychology*).

The Farther Reaches of Human Nature. Viking Penguin 1976 $9.95. ISBN 0-14004-265-2. "A collection of papers from the leading spokesman of humanistic psychology . . . a source book for ideas, concepts, hypotheses, and theories that will probably occupy psychologists, other social scientists, and laymen for many years to come" (*Choice*).

The Journals of A. H. Maslow. 1973. Ed. by Bertha G. Maslow and others. Brooks-Cole 1979 o.p. Entries from his personal journals provide an understanding of the man and his ideas.

Motivation and Personality. (ed.). 1954. HarpC 1970 o.p. "In this book Maslow presents a systematic theory and application of motivation and personality which he has derived from a synthesis of 3 approaches: holistic, dynamic, and cultural" (*Psychological Abstracts*).

New Knowledge in Human Values. (ed.). 1959. Regnery-Gateway repr. 1970 $6.95. ISBN 0-89526-987-3. "The reader will be well advised to read and judge these papers on their individual merits and to disregard the dubious attempt to glean from them a 'scientific' indication of 'creative altruism' " (*Annals of the American Academy of Political and Social Science*).

The Psychology of Science: A Reconnaissance. 1966. Regnery-Gateway 1966 repr. $3.95. ISBN 0-89526-972-4. Criticism of Western science, including psychology.

Religions, Values and Peak-Experiences. 1964. Peter Smith 1983 $17.50. ISBN 0-8446-6070-1. "[A] small but powerful book. . . . His observations and reflections lead him not so much to deny once and for all that any two-dimensional world and experience exist, as to assert that this formulation of reality is obscurantist" (*Contemporary Psychology*).

Toward a Psychology of Being. 1962. Krieger 1968 o.p.

BOOKS ABOUT MASLOW

Lowry, Richard J. *A. H. Maslow: An Intellectual Portrait.* Brooks-Cole 1973 o.p. Sympathetic and scholarly treatment of Maslow as a theorist.

Maslow, Bertha G., and others, eds. *Abraham H. Maslow: A Memorial Volume.* Brooks-Cole 1972 o.p.

MAY, ROLLO. 1909–

"The development of an existential psychology in America is in good part the work of Rollo May. He helped bring existentialism to psychology some fifteen years ago, and since then his impact has increased each year. As he says here, he isn't an existentialist in a 'cultist' sense. In American psychology the existential approach is part of a wider trend which includes many views" (Eugene T. Gendlin, *Psychology Today*). May's psychology is sometimes referred to as humanistic—he is one of the affirmative, "third force" American psychologists who are also critical of the society in which we live. Gendlin writes further: "In . . . *Psychology and the Human Dilemma* [1966], May offers a wealth of valid and stimulating ideas in a totally engaging and readable fashion. [The human dilemma is that] man is always both an active subject and a passive object . . . May [says]: 'Only in knowing ourselves as the determined ones are we free.' This last sentence and his many similar discussions seem to mean that we can't help what happens, but only what attitude we take toward what happens. In fact, he means more than this—in taking an attitude toward what happens we change what happens." In late 1968, May was the subject of an article in the *New York Times* in which he was said to feel that "one sign that the modern age is dying is that its myths are dying." We are at present in a "limbo" between myths—the situation in which people become disoriented and "alienated." "In the new myths," he said, "I would think that racial variation will be seen as a positive value, that emphasis on one world will replace fragmented nationalism, and that things will be valued more for their intrinsic worth rather than in use— what they can be banked for."

As a young man, May taught for a period at the American College in Saloniki, Greece. An ordained Congregational minister, May received his Ph.D. at Columbia University in 1949. He worked as supervisory and training analyst at the William Alanson White Institute in New York City and adjunct professor of clinical psychology at the New York University Graduate School of Arts and Sciences for many years. Currently May lives in the San Francisco area, writes, still sees clients, and was instrumental in establishing the Rollo May Center for Humanistic Studies at Saybrook Institute in San Francisco.

BOOKS BY MAY

The Art of Counseling. Abingdon 1978 o.p.

The Courage to Create. Bantam 1984 $4.95. ISBN 0-553-26361-7. "[The author] provides a lucid and highly concentrated analysis of the creative process in the course of covering a good deal of familiar territory" (*Saturday Review*).

The Discovery of Being. Norton 1986 $7.95. ISBN 0-393-30315-2. "May . . . provides the reader with principles of his existential psychotherapy; delineates his view of the cultural-historical context that gave rise to both psychoanalysis and existentialism; and sets forth what he considers to be the contributions to therapy of an existential approach" (*Choice*).

Dreams and Symbols: Man's Unconscious Language. (coauthored with Leopold Caligor). Basic 1969 o.p.

Existence: A New Dimension in Psychiatry and Psychology. (with others, eds.). 1958. Gardner Pr. 1990 $21.95. ISBN 0-89876-156-5. "This is a book which gives a compelling hint of what is coming in psychological therapy and psychological science" (*Contemporary Psychology*).

Existential Psychology. (ed.). Random 1961 o.p. "This is a book which undergraduates and professional psychologists of varying persuasions can pick up, read readily, and use to satisfy curiosity about the concept 'existentialism' as it is related to psychology" (*Contemporary Psychology*).

Freedom and Destiny. Norton 1981 $14.95. ISBN 0-393-01477-0. "He insists that freedom is intertwined with the idea of destiny, or a pattern of limits and potentials that make up the givens of one's life. . . . May picks lively arguments with Gay Talese, Christopher Lasch, Fromm and B. F. Skinner in a wise, courageous and inspiring essay that offers fresh hope for individuals and society" (*Publishers Weekly*).

Love and Will. Doubleday 1989 $11.00. ISBN 0-385-28590-6. The "focus is man vis-a-vis his contemporary world. And he finds that man is a very troubled soul, not because of his world but because of himself" (*Choice*).

Man's Search for Himself. Dell 1973 $10.95. ISBN 0-440-55069-6. "This volume was written for laymen, and it is altogether successfully adapted to a lay audience" (*Chicago Sunday Tribune*).

The Meaning of Anxiety. 1950. WSP 1979 o.p. Compendium of the modern theories of anxiety.

My Quest for Beauty. Saybrook 1987 $9.95. ISBN 0-933071-13-2. Weaves art and clinical insight together to demonstrate a more humane psychotherapy.

Paulus. Saybrook Pub. Co. 1988 $6.95. ISBN 0-933071-18-3. "The well-known author and psychotherapist has written a striking personal portrait of Paul Tillich in which he combines his personal respect and love for his friend with psychological and theological insight" (*Choice*).

Power and Innocence: A Search for the Sources of Violence. Norton 1972 $14.95. ISBN 0-393-01065-1. Inquiry into the human need for dignity, significance, and self-assertion.

Psychology and the Human Dilemma. 1966. Norton 1980 repr. of 1978 ed. $8.76. ISBN 0-393-00978-5. An "existential discussion of the dichotomy between reason and emotion and the resulting isolation of the individual" (*Library Journal*).

Symbolism in Religion and Literature. (ed.). Braziller 1960 o.p.

MENNINGER, KARL AUGUSTUS. 1893–1990

The Menninger Clinic was founded in Topeka, Kansas, in 1920 by Karl Menninger and his father, Charles Frederick Menninger, and in 1926 they were joined by Karl's brother William. The Menninger Foundation, started in 1941, was established for the purpose of research, training, and public education in psychiatry. Karl Menninger was instrumental in founding the Winter Veterans' Administration Hospital, also in Topeka, at the close of World War II. It functioned not only as a hospital but also as the center of the largest psychiatric training program in the world. *The Crime of Punishment* attracted much attention (and some controversy) when it was published in 1968. A former professor of criminology and an officer of the American League to Abolish Capital Punishment, Menninger believed that there may be less violence today than there was 100 years ago but that it is now better reported. "We need criminals to identify ourselves with," he said, "to secretly envy and to stoutly punish." The "controlling" of crime by "deterrence," he said, makes "getting caught the unthinkable thing" for offenders (quoted in the *New York Times*). His plea is for humane, constructive treatment in place of vengeance and an end to public apathy.

Menninger was born in Topeka and received his medical degree from Harvard University in 1917. He became interested in neurology and psychology while interning at Kansas City General Hospital. As one of the first physicians to complete psychoanalytic training in the United States and be aware of the critical need for psychiatrically trained personnel, he became administratively involved in various associations over the course of his lifetime. Internationally known as a pioneer in the treatment of mental illness, Menninger wrote with great clarity and human sympathy. His work has done much to dispel misunderstandings about mental illness and its treatment.

BOOKS BY MENNINGER

The Crime of Punishment. Viking Penguin 1968 o.p. "This, an expansion and rewriting of the Isaac Ray Award lectures given by Dr. Menninger at Columbia University in 1963 and 1964, and at the University of Kansas in 1966, indicts the U.S. penal system and presents proposals for its reform" (*Library Journal*).

The Human Mind. 1930. Knopf 1945 o.p. "An absorbing book, which is easy to read, profusely illustrated with illuminating examples of the cases cited, and one well calculated to appeal both to the casual reader and to the person who would have a more serious purpose" (*Annals of the American Academy of Political and Social Sciences*).

Love against Hate. (coauthored with Jeanetta Lyle Menninger). 1942. HarBraceJ 1959 $10.95. ISBN 0-15-653892-X. In this analysis of the war of emotions within each of us, the authors show how the power of love can shape our aggressiveness.

Man against Himself. 1938. HarBraceJ 1956 $10.95. ISBN 0-15-656514-5. "It is valuable because it presents in readable and complete form the psychoanalytic theory of suicide, heretofore buried piecemeal in psychoanalytic journals and books" (*American Sociological Review*).

The Vital Balance: The Life Process in Mental Health and Illness. (coauthored with Martin Mayman and Paul Pruyser). 1963. Peter Smith 1983 $21.25. ISBN 0-8446-6077-9. With two psychologists at the Menninger Clinic, Menninger presents to the lay reader his hopeful new unitary concept of mental illness, which treats all mental health problems as aspects of the same basic disorder.

BOOKS ABOUT MENNINGER

Faulkner, Howard J., and Virginia Pruitt. *The Selected Correspondence of Dr. Karl A. Menninger.* Yale U. Pr. 1989 $40.00. ISBN 0-300-03978-6. These articulate, outspoken, and witty letters include correspondence with Freud, Norman Cousins, Joseph Wood Krutch, and H. L. Mencken.

Friedman, Lawrence J. *Menninger: The Family and the Clinic.* Knopf 1990 $29.95. ISBN 0-394-53569-3. Focuses on the famous Menninger Clinic and its innovative founding family. Covers family dynamics, the clinic's beginnings, and Karl Menninger's writing and research.

PAVLOV, IVAN PETROVICH. 1849–1936

[SEE Volume 3.]

PERLS, FREDERICK (FRITZ). 1893–1970

Frederick Perls was born in Berlin, Germany, and received his medical degree there. In 1933, with the arrival of Hitler, Perls left Germany for Holland. He subsequently went to the United States in 1946, where he founded the New York Institute for Gestalt Therapy, based on his own method of psychotherapy. Perls's major contribution to psychology was the method he called Gestalt therapy. To some degree, Gestalt therapy is based upon psychoanalytic concepts, such as the importance of inner unresolved conflicts that must be worked through, but Perls added a strong emphasis on the "here and now." His more humanistic orientation stressed freedom, responsibility, and the client's power to make choices.

BOOKS BY PERLS

Ego, Hunger, and Aggression: A Revision of Freud's Theory and Method. Vin. 1992 $20.00. ISBN 0-939266-18-0. Details the transition from orthodox psychoanalysis to the development of the Gestalt approach.

The Gestalt Approach and Eyewitness to Therapy. Sc. & Behavior 1973 $12.95. ISBN 0-8314-0034-X. Theoretical background is provided in Part One and examples of therapy in Part Two.

Gestalt Therapy: Excitement and Growth in the Human Personality. Bantam 1977 $5.95. ISBN 0-553-25445-6. Helpful in understanding the attitude of Gestalt therapy; requires the reader to assume a "Gestaltist" mentality in order to understand its content fully.

Gestalt Therapy Verbatim. Ed. by J. Wysong. Real People Pr. 1992 $20.00. ISBN 0-939266-17-2. "The book is essential for understanding recent development in this school of existentialist therapy" (*Book Review Digest*).

In and Out of the Garbage Pail. Ed. by J. Wysong. Real People Pr. 1992 $20.00. ISBN 0-939266-17-2. An autobiography in which Fritz Perls applies his theory of focusing on awareness, and writes "whatever wants to be written." Partly in poetic form, sometimes theoretical, the book is a many-faceted mosaic of memories and reflections on his life (*Cover*).

BOOKS ABOUT PERLS

Latner, Joel. *The Gestalt Therapy Book.* Gestalt Journal 1984 repr. of 1974 ed. $18.50. ISBN 0-939266-04-0. Clear, thorough explanation of the theoretical foundations of Gestalt Therapy; provides a context and background for understanding Gestalt writings and therapy.

Shepard, Martin. *Fritz.* Second Chance. $15.95. ISBN 0-933256-15-9. Personal account of the life and work of Perls.

PIAGET, JEAN. 1896–1980

[SEE Volume 3.]

RANK, OTTO. 1884–1937

Considered to be one of the most gifted psychotherapists of his time, Otto Rank investigated matters "beyond psychology" and became known for his energy, intellectual curiosity, and self-awareness.

Born in Vienna, Rank had a very deprived childhood. Despite troubled feelings and suicidal thoughts during his adolescence, he read a great deal and became interested in the psychology of creativity. He first formulated his theories about art and neuroses in the series of remarkable daybooks (1903–1904). In 1912 he helped to found *Imago*, the first European journal of psychoanalysis. In the years of his association with SIGMUND FREUD (see also Vol. 3) from 1905 to 1925, he served as secretary to the psychoanalytic movement, and it was generally assumed that Freud regarded him as his successor. Rank, however, eventually came to see the roots of all psychoneuroses in the experience of birth. This theory he described in *The Trauma of Birth* (1924). Such differences caused his break with Freud in the middle 1920s, after which he lived in Paris and then New York.

BOOKS BY RANK

Art and the Artist: The Creative Urge and Personality Development. 1907. Peter Smith 1992 $19.75. ISBN 0-8446-6489-8. "The author presents a more matured consideration of a problem which engaged him about twenty-five years ago, viz., that of the psychological bases for the production of artistic works" (*Psychological Abstracts*).

Beyond Psychology. 1941. Dover 1959 $6.95. ISBN 0-486-20485-5. 'He argues for an acceptance of 'the fundamental irrationality of the human being and life in general with allowance for its dynamic functioning in human behavior' and for a more balanced evaluation of the irrational as against the rational" (*Psychological Abstracts*).

The Don Juan Legend. Trans. and ed. by David G. Winter. Princeton U. Pr. 1975 o.p. "An *interpretation* of the theme, drawing on psychoanalysis (before and after his break with Freud), literature, history, and anthropology to examine some of the psychological processes that operate within the legend" (*Choice*).

Double: A Psychoanalytical Study. Ed. by Harry Tucker, Jr. Brunner-Mazel 1990 $20.95. ISBN 0-946439-58-3. Pioneer psychoanalytic study on the double in literature.

Modern Education: A Critique of Its Fundamental Ideas. 1932. Knopf 1932 o.p. "Presents a sociological and metaphysical consideration of the relations of education to psychology, the nature and needs of the child, the place of sex in development and education, leadership, the influence of current ideology, vocational choice and fitness, family relationships, and self guidance" (*Psychological Abstracts*).

The Myth of the Birth of the Hero: A Psychological Interpretation of Mythology. 1909. Johnson Repr. 1971 repr. of 1914 ed.

Psychology and the Soul. 1950. 2 vols. Cath Art Soc. 1992 $187.00. ISBN 0-685-57256-0. Rank's views of the origin, development, and nature of mental life. Based on 30 years of experience and field studies.

The Significance of Psychoanalysis for the Mental Sciences. (coauthored with Hans Sachs). 1916. Johnson Repr. 1971 repr. of 1916 ed. o.p.

The Trauma of Birth. 1924. Brunner-Mazel 1952 o.p. Rank's approach to mental development, based on separation anxiety at birth.

Will Therapy and Truth and Reality. 1936. Norton 1978 o.p. "Fundamentally a philosophical treatise, dealing with the problems of the mind from a psychoanalytical point of view" (*Psychological Abstracts*).

Books about Rank

Lieberman, E. James. *Acts of Will: The Life and Work of Otto Rank.* Free Pr. 1985 $32.95. ISBN 0-02-919020-7. "Affords an excellent introduction—for both scholars and informed lay readers—to the work of a brilliant psychoanalytic innovator whose seminal theories on birth trauma, separation anxiety, and time-limited therapy (to name just a few) are still central issues today" (*Library Journal*).

Menaker, Esther. *Otto Rank: A Rediscovered Legacy.* Col. U. Pr. 1982 o.p. "Dr. Menaker is right in her contention that Rank anticipates all the 'separation anxiety theories,' ranging from Klein to Bowlby, Mahler, and Kohut. . . . [She] has done a splendid service in resuscitating the work of a man unjustly neglected for so many years, and to read her book is to share some of the excitement of Rank's agile mind" (*Times Literary Supplement*).

REIK, THEODOR. 1888–1969

Viennese-born psychoanalyst Theodor Reik became Sigmund Freud's (see also Vol. 3) pupil in 1910, completed the first doctor's dissertation on psychoanalysis in 1911, and received his Ph.D. in psychology from the University of Vienna in 1912. He lectured at the Vienna Psychoanalytic Institute in Berlin and at The Hague. He came to the United States in 1938 and became an American citizen. Reik's lack of medical training led him to found the National Psychological Association for Psychoanalysis in 1948, which accepts lay analysts for membership and has programs for their training. His *Listening with the Third Ear* (1948) is a stimulating discussion of Freud's development of psychoanalysis and describes in great detail his own cases during 37 years of active practice. Reik's books show great erudition and are written with literary skill; they sparkle "with insights and with witty profundities." He may properly be regarded as "the founding father of *archaeological psychoanalysis*," a branch of depth psychology dedicated to the probing of archaeological data from psychoanalytic viewpoints.

BOOKS BY REIK

Compulsions to Confess: On the Psychoanalysis of Crime and Punishment. Essay Index Repr. Ser. Ayer repr. of 1959 ed. $33.00. ISBN 0-8369-2856-3. "[The book] is distinguished by Reik's ability to convey his recondite concepts with such charm and humor as to make them not only informative, but vastly entertaining" (*Kirkus*).

The Creation of Woman: A Psychoanalytic Inquiry into the Myth of Eve. 1960. McGraw 1973 o.p. "Insights and literary skill make the reading of this new book an exciting experience" (*Library Journal*).

Dogma and Compulsion. Greenwood 1973 repr. of 1951 ed. $55.00. ISBN 0-8371-6577-6. "Reik gives a detailed account of the development of the dogma of the godhead of Christ in order to show that dogma is the most important expression of the people's obsessional thinking, with the same mechanisms as the obsessional neurosis of individuals" (*Psychological Abstracts*).

Fragment of a Great Confession. Greenwood 1973 repr. of 1965 ed. o.p.

Jewish Wit. Gamut Pr. 1962 o.p. Reik "has written . . . a kind of analytic joke book to illustrate a comparative social psychology of [the Jewish] people. . . . The book is fascinating reading and at the very least gives some unusual insights into the psychological aspects of the cultural heritage of a people" (*Library Journal*).

Listening with the Third Ear: The Inner Experience of a Psychoanalyst. 1948. FS&G 1983 $14.95. ISBN 0-374-51800-9. Provides the answers to the layman's question: "What is psychoanalysis?"

Myth and Guilt. Braziller 1957 o.p. "Collective human guilt may be traced back to the prehistoric killing and eating of a father whose rule was experienced as divine" (*Psychological Abstracts*).

The Need to Be Loved. FS&G 1963 o.p. Examination of the many aspects of the problems from infancy to old age.

Of Love and Lust: On the Psychoanalysis of Romantic and Sexual Emotions. Jove Pubns. 1976 o.p. "The freshest, most charming pages are those discussing the emotional differences between the sexes. You must read these for yourself. *Love and Lust* is thoughtful and profound; and these final pages, on the differences between men and women, are pure gold" (*Contemporary Psychology*).

The Search Within: Inner Experiences of a Psychoanalyst. 1968. Aronson 1974 o.p. "This, the first of a series of volumes of selections from Theodor Reik's works, is a synthesis of his frank reminiscences of his personal life, his training, practice and the development of his philosophy" (*Psychological Abstracts*).

The Secret Self: Psychoanalytic Experiences in Life and Literature. Greenwood 1973 repr. of 1953 ed. o.p. "It is probably the most mature and sophisticated book of this prolific psychoanalytic author" (*Saturday Review*).

The Unknown Murderer. Intl. Univs. Pr. 1978 $24.95. ISBN 0-685-02648-5. "A psychoanalytic study of some aspects of murder and the judicial process. The author shows that what passes for logical evidence in the investigation of murder crimes is oftentimes psychological evidence" (*Psychological Abstracts*).

ROGERS, CARL RANSOM. 1902–1987

Educated at the University of Wisconsin, Carl Rogers intended to become a Protestant minister, entering the Union Theological Seminary in 1924. When he realized that he was more interested in spirituality than religion, he left the seminary. While working on his Ph.D. at Columbia University, he began to question some of the accepted techniques of psychotherapy, especially in the area of therapist-patient relationships. According to *Current Biography*, "he is best known as the originator of the nondirective 'client centered' theory of psychotherapy. This prescribes a person-to-person, rather than a doctor-patient relationship between therapist and client, and allows the client to control the course, pace, and length of his own treatment." Rogers incorporated many of the elements of this theory into the basic structure of encounter groups.

The author of many books and articles, Rogers taught at several large universities for many years and conducted a private practice as a counseling psychologist. He received many professional awards in official recognition of his high achievements, most notably the presidency of the American Psychological Association (1946–47).

BOOKS BY ROGERS

Becoming Partners: Marriage and Its Alternatives. 1972. Dell 1973 $9.95. ISBN 0-385-28070-X. "Rogers' summary of the qualities of a lasting relationship—commitment, communication, dissolution of roles, becoming a separate self—is not new, but what is significant is his idea that modern couples should think of themselves as pioneers free to explore all possibilities" (*Library Journal*).

Carl Rogers on Encounter Groups. HarpC 1970 o.p. Highly readable, informative presentation about what goes on within encounter groups; includes many examples.

Carl Rogers on Personal Power. Dell 1978 $4.95. ISBN 0-385-28169-2. Rogers extends his therapeutic views to education, business, politics, and international affairs, always affirming the inherent goodness of human nature.

Client-Centered Therapy. HM 1951 $32.36. ISBN 0-395-05322-6. "The recent development of the techniques of client-centered counseling is interpreted, the attitude and orientation of the counselor, the relationship as experienced by the client, and the process of therapy are discussed" (*Psychological Abstracts*).

Counseling and Psychotherapy. HM 1942 o.p.

Freedom to Learn for the Eighties. Merrill 1983 $16.95. ISBN 0-675-20012-1. "A powerful statement on behalf of the kind of enlightened teaching that many prominent educators have been urging for some time" (*Contemporary Psychology*).

Measuring Personality Adjustment in Children Nine to Thirteen Years of Age. 1931. AMS Pr. 1982 repr. of 1931 ed. $22.50. ISBN 0-404-53458-X. "The development of a 40-minute pencil and paper group test—yielding '4 diagnostic scores, indicating the degree of the child's Personal Inferiority, Social Maladjustment, Family Maladjustment, and Daydreaming'—and its application to 52 problem children and to a larger group of normal children" (*Psychological Abstracts*).

On Becoming a Person. HM 1961 $8.95. ISBN 0-395-08409-1. Presents Rogers's general view of personality problems.

Person to Person: The Problem of Being Human. (coauthored with Barry Stevens). Real People Pr. 1967 $7.50. ISBN 0-911226-01-X. "An excellent job of presenting the Rogerian philosophy. For those who would like data or science, this book will be disappointing; for those who prefer humanism this book will be exciting" (*Choice*).

Psychotherapy and Personality Change. (with Rosalind F. Dymond, eds.). U. Ch. Pr. 1954 o.p. "Describes and explains a large-scale research program in client-centered psychotherapy, carried out at the Counseling Center of the University of Chicago" (*Psychological Abstracts*).

Therapist's View of Personal Goals. Pendle Hill 1960 $3.00. ISBN 0-87574-108-8. "In his therapeutic work Rogers sees clients take such directions as: away from facades; away from 'oughts'; away from meeting expectations; away from pleasing others; toward being a process; toward being a complexity; toward openness to experience; toward acceptance of others; toward trust of self" (*Psychological Abstracts*).

A Way of Being. HM 1980 $8.95. ISBN 0-395-30067-3. "This is a book rich in theoretical insights and experiential sharing, and full of invigorating optimism. . . . The reader has a vivid sense of a man reviewing his life and taking stock" (*Library Journal*).

BOOK ABOUT ROGERS

Evans, Richard I. *Carl Rogers: The Man and His Ideas.* Dutton 1975 o.p. "This volume may be seen as a valuable asset to a general understanding of Rogers' thought. . . . The book's primary contribution, besides an insight into Rogers the man, will probably be the whetting of academic appetites for further study in Rogerian thought" (*Choice*).

ROYCE, JOSIAH. 1855–1916
[SEE Volume 4.]

SCHAFER, ROY. 1922–

Born in the Bronx, New York, Roy Schafer received a B.S. degree from the City College of New York, an M.A. from the University of Kansas, and a Ph.D. from Clark University. He is currently an adjunct professor of psychology and psychiatry at Cornell University Medical College, a training analyst at Columbia University Center for Psychoanalytic Training and Research, and he also maintains a private practice. He received the American Psychological Association's Award for Distinguished Professional Contribution to Knowledge in 1983.

Much of Schafer's work has concentrated on the analysis and comparison of psychoanalytic theories. In addition, in recent years he has focused his attention on such topics as the effects of narration and dialogue on psychoanalysis.

BOOKS BY SCHAFER

The Analytic Attitude. Basic 1983 $30.00. ISBN 0-465-00268-4. "Readers of various degrees of philosophic and psychological sophistication may be stimulated by reading this book" (*Contemporary Psychology*).

The Clinical Application of Psychological Tests. 1948. *Menninger Foundation Monograph Ser.* Intl. Univs. Pr. 1967 $42.50. ISBN 0-8236-0900-6. A sequel to *Diagnostic Psychological Testing*; mainly a collection of concrete, individual case records.

Diagnostic Psychological Testing. (coauthored with David Rapaport). 1944. Intl. Univs. Pr. 1968 $62.50. ISBN 0-8236-1260-0. "Designed to be a 'focused and theoretically oriented handbook of diagnostic psychological testing' " (*Contemporary Psychology*).

Language and Insight: The Sigmund Freud Lectures at University College London. Bks. Demand 1978 $58.30. ISBN 0-8357-8202-6. "The book is always provocative and thoughtful, often brilliant" (*Contemporary Psychology*).

A New Language for Psychoanalysis. Yale U. Pr. 1976 $17.00. ISBN 0-300-02761-3. "Should be of considerable interest to a wider public since it proposes a radical reformulation of psychoanalytic theory" (*New York Review of Books*).

Projective Testing and Psychoanalysis. Intl. Univs. Pr. 1967 $30.00. ISBN 0-8236-4380-8. Collection of nine articles originally published between 1953 and 1960.

Psychoanalytic Interpretation in Rorschach Testing: Theory and Application. Grune 1954 o.p. "Brief summary statements of defenses, each followed by a review of expected Rorschach test indicators and illustrative case protocols. Differences and similarities between Rorschach responses and dreams are discussed. Individual differences in defense style are emphasized" (*Psychological Abstracts*).

SKINNER, B. F. 1904–
[SEE Volume 3.]

STRAUS, ERWIN. 1891–1975

Erwin Straus was born in Frankfurt, Germany. He received a comprehensive classical education and in 1910 began to study medicine and philosophy. His studies were interrupted by World War I, during which he served as a field doctor on the Polish front.

Straus's teachers and acquaintances form a veritable list of notables of twentieth-century German intellectual life. Among the former were JUNG, HUSSERL (see Vol. 4), Reinach, SCHELER (see Vol. 4), Pfander, Kraepelin, and Geiger, and his friends included CASSIRER (see Vol. 4), von Gebsattel, BINSWANGER, Zutt, and Minkowski.

Straus first lectured at the University of Berlin in 1927, but, because of his partial Jewish background, he had to cease teaching in 1934 after the Nazis came to power. He fled the Nazis in 1938 and taught at the experimental community of Black Mountain College in North Carolina. In 1946 Straus went to the Veterans Administration Hospital in Lexington, Kentucky, as director of research and education, and remained there for the rest of his life. In addition to authoring many creative and original articles, Straus played a formative role in introducing the anthropological and phenomenological orientation to psychiatry in this country.

BOOKS BY STRAUS

Man, Time and World: The Anthropological Psychology of Erwin Straus. Duquesne U. Pr. 1982 o.p. "English translation of *Event and Experience* (1930) and *The Archimedian Point* (1957). . . . The works point out inadequacies in reductionist psychological theories, and propose a holistic, anthropological account of psychological phenomena based on the individual's experience of time and becoming" (*Contemporary Psychology*).

Phenomenological Psychology. Trans. in part by E. Eng. Basic 1966 o.p. Series of essays on phenomenological psychology, written with erudition and style; makes sense of many common experiences.

The Primary World of the Senses. Trans. by J. Needleman. Free Pr. 1963 o.p. Critique of Pavlov's views in order to restore the value of sensory experience for the interpretation of human existence.

SULLIVAN, HARRY STACK. 1892–1949

Harry Stack Sullivan was born in Norwich, New York, and grew up on a farm in Smyrna. Originally interested in physics, he turned to medicine and psychiatry, entering the Chicago College of Medicine and Surgery in 1913 and receiving his degree in 1917. Following World War I, Sullivan dealt with war veterans disabled by neuropsychiatric conditions and was a psychiatrist in the Public Health Institute from 1921 to 1922. In 1925 he became director of clinical research at Sheppard-Pratt hospitals in Baltimore and associate professor of psychiatry at the University of Maryland. Throughout his career he pursued his interest in schizophrenia. He left Sheppard-Pratt in 1930 and went into private practice, treating obsessionals and schizophrenics and supervising other analysts.

Conceptions of Modern Psychiatry (1940) was originally published as articles in the periodical *Psychiatry*, of which Sullivan was an editor. He contributed greatly to the understanding of schizophrenia and obsessional states. As head of both the William Alanson White Foundation (1934–43) and of the Washington School of Psychiatry (1936–47), he brought to public and professional attention his view that psychoanalysis needed to be supplemented by a thoroughgoing study of the impact of cultural forces on the personality.

BOOKS BY SULLIVAN

Clinical Studies in Psychiatry. Norton 1973 repr. of 1956 ed. $12.95. ISBN 0-393-00740-5. "A representative selection from the clinical lectures given at Chestnut Lodge" (*Preface*).

Conceptions of Modern Psychiatry. 1940. Norton 1966 $9.95. ISBN 0-393-00740-5. "This series of five lectures constitutes a comprehensive survey of modern psychiatric thought" (*Psychological Abstracts*).

The Fusion of Psychiatry and Social Science. Norton 1971 repr. of 1964 ed. o.p. Attempts to tie his psychoanalytic theories into the workings of society.

The Interpersonal Theory of Psychiatry. Norton 1968 repr. of 1953 ed. $5.95. ISBN 0-393-00138-5. "This may well turn out to be the most seminal look in its field in this decade" (*Saturday Review*).

Personal Psychopathology: Early Formulations. Norton 1984 repr. of 1972 ed. $9.95. ISBN 0-393-30184-2. "An unsystematic and somewhat fragmented presentation of the Sullivanian approach to mental illness and treatment. However, the . . . student and layman will profit from the many valuable clinical insights offered here" (*Choice*).

Psychiatric Interview. Norton 1970 repr. of 1954 ed. $4.95. ISBN 0-393-00506-2. "Although the lectures were directed primarily towards psychiatrists, Sullivan also meant them for all those who engage in dynamic interviewing" (Preface).

Schizophrenia as a Human Process. Norton 1974 repr. of 1962 ed. $10.95. ISBN 0-393-00721-9. This posthumously gathered volume consists of the early work of Sullivan when he was associated with the Sheppard-Pratt hospital.

BOOKS ABOUT SULLIVAN

Mullahy, Patrick, ed. *Psychoanalysis and Interpersonal Psychiatry: The Contributions of Harry Stack Sullivan.* Aronson 1967 o.p.

Pearce, Jane, and Saul Newton. *Conditions of Human Growth.* Citadel Pr. 1969 repr. of 1963 ed. $6.95. ISBN 0-685-08130-3. "The volume suffers from the lack of an index, a curious omission from an otherwise careful and thoughtful piece of work. It is recommended for all collections in the psychiatric and clinical psychological fields, as well as general collections for the informed layman who wants an overview of the interpersonal theory of the Sullivan school" (*Library Journal*).

THORNDIKE, EDWARD LEE. 1874–1949

[SEE Volume 3.]

VAN DEN BERG, J. H. 1914–

Born in Deventer, The Netherlands, J. H. van den Berg began his career as a high school teacher of mathematics and then studied medicine and decided to specialize in psychiatry at the University of Utrecht. He did his doctoral dissertation under H. C. Rumke and was introduced to phenomenology and trained as a psychotherapist. In 1947 he began private practice and was appointed head of the Psychiatric Clinic at the University of Utrecht. In 1954 he was appointed professor of conflict psychology at the University of Leiden and later became professor emeritus there. In the course of his own research, he found it necessary to develop a "metabletic" method that investigates the meaning of cultural and human changes that occur within the same time period.

BOOKS BY VAN DEN BERG

The Changing Nature of Man: Introduction to a Historical Psychology. Norton 1983 repr. of 1961 ed. $5.50. ISBN 0-393-3011-X. "Dealing with such issues as child-rearing practices, belief in God, the status of women, the kinds of neurotic symptoms people show, and the delaying of maturity, he makes a case for his thesis which is well worth attention" (*Contemporary Psychology*).

A Different Existence: Principles of Phenomenological Psychopathology. Duquesne U. Pr. 1972 $14.50. ISBN 0-8207-0244-7. Excellent introduction, written in a lively style; shows the differences between psychoanalytic and existential-phenomenological interpretations of a client.

Divided Existence and Complex Society: An Historical Approach. Duquesne U. Pr. 1974 o.p. "Discusses the relationship of 'divided existence' (i.e., multiple personality) to culture" (*Psychological Abstracts*).

Dubious Maternal Affection. Duquesne U. Pr. 1972 o.p.

The Psychology of the Sickbed. Humanities 1967 o.p. "Presents 'an existential approach to the meaning of illness . . .' with a discussion of lying and its various forms, recommendations to visitors, the sickbed recovery of the patient, and the patient and his physician" (*Psychological Abstracts*).

WINNICOTT, DONALD WOODS. 1896–1971

Donald W. Winnicott was born into a well-to-do nonconformist family in Plymouth, England. He started his career as a pediatrician at the Paddington Green Children's Hospital in London. While working there, he developed an increasing interest in, and concern for, the emotional problems of his parents, as well as some of his patients. Hence, he later became a psychoanalyst and child psychiatrist. Twice president of the British Psycho-Analytical Society and the author of many books, Winnicott took the theory of emotional development back into earliest infancy, even before birth. His ideas, along with those of his contemporaries, led to the development of the British "object relations" school within psychoanalysis. This focused on familiar, inanimate objects that children use to counter anxiety during times of stress.

BOOKS BY WINNICOTT

Babies and Their Mothers. Addison-Welsley 1992 $10.95. ISBN 0-201-63269-1. Novel collection that makes Winnicott's basic ideas about babies and mothers available to the lay reader.

Home Is Where We Start From: Essays in Psychoanalysis. Norton 1990 $12.95. ISBN 0-393-30667-4. Collection of mostly previously unpublished papers, now posthumously published.

Human Nature. Brunner-Mazel repr. of 1988 ed. $19.95. ISBN 0-7630-6202-2. Outline of Winnicott's views on this vast topic; suitable for postgraduate students with some background in dynamic psychology.

The Maturational Processes and the Facilitating Environment: Studies in the Theory of Emotional Development. Intl. Univs. Pr. 1965 $37.50. ISBN 0-8236-3200-8. Collection of papers from the period 1957 to 1963, centered around theme of carrying back Freud's theories to infancy.

Playing and Reality. Routledge 1982 $10.95. ISBN 0-422-78310-2. Winnicott's thought and theory presented clearly with case examples.

BOOKS ABOUT WINNICOTT

Davis, Madeleine, and David Wallbridge. *Boundary and Space: An Introduction to the Work of D. W. Winnicott.* Brunner-Mazel 1981 o.p. General introduction and appraisal of Winnicott's main concepts; intended for the beginning student.

Rudnytsky, Peter L. *The Psychoanalytic Vocation: Rank, Winnicott, and the Legacy of Freud.* Yale U. Pr. 1991 $30.00. ISBN 0-300-05067-4. A history of psychoanalysis after Freud.

WOLPE, JOSEPH. 1915–

Joseph Wolpe received his medical degree from the University of Witwatersrand, South Africa. After medical and surgical internships, he went into private practice and then in 1946 decided to enter psychiatric training and research. During this time, he did the research on which his behavioral therapy is based.

Wolpe was professor of psychiatry at the University of Virginia School of Medicine from 1960 to 1965. Since then, he has been director of the Behavior Therapy Unit at Temple University Medical School and a senior research psychiatrist at Eastern Pennsylvania Psychiatric Institute in Philadelphia.

BOOKS BY WOLPE

The Practice of Behavior Therapy. Pergamon 1982 $96.00. ISBN 0-08-027165-3. "Wolpe's significance, and our enduring respect for him as an interpreter of behavior therapy, come less from the rightness of his particular theories . . . than from regard for his values: that psychological principles derived from the laboratory can be adroitly adapted to clinical concerns and that the performance, though always improvisational, can be evaluated by the standards of scientific method" (*Contemporary Psychology*).

Psychotherapy by Reciprocal Inhibition. Stanford U. Pr. 1958 $30.00. ISBN 0-78373947-8. "Taking a reductionist position, Wolpe begins his argument with a description of 'the making and unmaking of functional neural connections,' from which he moves to a behavioral learning theory, presumably after having established a neural basis for such a theory" (*Contemporary Psychology*).

PART THREE

THE SCIENCES

CHAPTER 15

Mathematics

Joseph W. Dauben

"The essence of mathematics is its freedom."
—GEORG CANTOR, *Mathematische Annalen*

Mathematics always has been regarded as the supreme example of the rational power of the mind. Along with the ability to speak and develop languages and alphabets, the creation of numbers, counting, and the invention of the most rudimentary arithmetic is associated with all human civilizations. From antiquity, people have recognized the need to measure distances and areas that led to geometry, or to count things that led to arithmetic.

It was the Greeks, however, who discovered in mathematics the great power of abstract reasoning based on axiomatic and deductive proof. The fact that one could apparently establish for all time the necessary truth of mathematical propositions was extraordinary. For example, the Pythagorean theorem states that, for all right triangles, no matter what their dimensions, the sum of the squares on the two sides of a right-angled triangle is equal to the area of the square on the hypotenuse: $a^2 + b^2 = c^2$.

Beginning with the ancient Greeks, mathematical argument has been regarded as the unique form of knowledge that, once rigorously established, could never be challenged. Consequently, some have argued that mathematics is the one branch of human knowledge that is truly cumulative. Unlike astronomy, physics, chemistry, or biology, mathematics rarely rejects its past. Mathematical "truth"—the positive results of arithmetic, geometry, and algebra that the ancients had established—remains true and is still used today.

For example, EUCLID has never been rejected or "replaced" the way Ptolemy, Galen, and even NEWTON (see also Vol. 4) were replaced by COPERNICUS, Harvey, and EINSTEIN (respectively). Even when something so startling as non-Euclidean geometry was discovered in the nineteenth century, it neither nullified nor replaced the other Euclidean geometry. Instead, it supplemented the results of traditional geometry and shed light on the nature and meaning of mathematics. Whenever mathematics seems to undergo dramatic transformations, it does so through new discoveries or innovative theories that greatly enlarge its scope, generality, and power.

Apart from the purely intellectual interest it provides for many theoreticians, mathematics has always been valued by primitive and advanced civilizations alike for its practical applications. *Geometry*, for example, literally means "earth measurement," and was developed by the Egyptians to aid in the surveying of land. In fact, the oldest mathematical document that still exists is the Rhind Papyrus that dates to about 1800 B.C. It is derived from a still earlier prototype probably written around 2000 B.C. The Rhind Papyrus is replete with practical problems of everyday life solved by simple arithmetic, geometry, and even some rudimentary algebra.

Today the applications of mathematics are more complex, sophisticated, and varied. Everything from the precise measurement of time by atomic clocks to the synchronization of traffic lights or the simple tallying of a shopkeeper's bill involves some form of mathematics.

For mathematicians, however, what matters most is the highly abstract character of the concepts they use and the austere rigor of the results they achieve. When asked to define mathematics—what it is and what it does—mathematicians give a variety of answers. Mathematics has been defined by some as the science of quantity, now a rather old-fashioned view. It has also been equated with logic. Others regard mathematics as a highly abstract enterprise, the study of "significant form." This may range from the familiar figures of geometry or the forms of numbers to various forms of logic itself. Rather than expect any one comprehensive definition to suffice, mathematics is readily defined by the various branches that comprise it. A brief list of some major specialties includes number theory, real and complex analysis, differential topology, group theory, algebraic geometry, operations research, computer science, combinatorics, and mathematical programming.

The following bibliography focuses on elementary algebra, geometry, number theory, and calculus. The encyclopedia and handbooks described below will introduce readers to many of the other, more specialized branches of mathematics. The guides listed may also be used to provide helpful suggestions for further reading. The needs and abilities of general readers have been considered in the selection of books for this bibliography. Mathematicians will find other guides to more advanced and specialized literature, especially in *Mathematical Reviews*, published monthly by the American Mathematical Society.

All of the books listed here are in English. Most are in print, and have been selected for their readability without requiring detailed knowledge of technical mathematics, unless otherwise noted. Anyone who has taken high school geometry and algebra should be able to read and understand most of the books described below without unreasonable difficulty.

HANDBOOKS AND REFERENCE BOOKS

The books listed below represent readily available guides for readers interested in learning more about mathematics. Handbooks include compact introductions to the subject. Reference books comprise bibliographic aids and other resources of interest to mathematicians, or to those who wish to learn more about the subject.

Bronshtein, I. N., and K. A. Semendyayev, eds. *Handbook of Mathematics*. Trans. by K. A. Hirsch. Van Nos. Reinhold 1985 $52.95. ISBN 0-442-21171-6. This work, originally in Russian, has gone through more than 20 editions in Russian and German. Many mathematicians have contributed new material (as old sections were revised or new sections were added to the original *Handbook*) to keep pace with advances in contemporary mathematics. Topics covered include tables and graphs, elementary mathematics, algebra, geometry, analysis (including calculus, calculus of variations, differential equations, and functions of complex variables), probability and statistics, linear optimization, numerical analysis and computation techniques (including computers), advanced analysis (including functional analysis, measure theory, tensor calculus, and integral equations), operations research, and data processing.

Throughout, definitions are clearly labeled; examples and diagrams are frequently given to clarify explanations. An extensive bibliography of works in English also is included.

Fang, J. A. *Guide to the Literature of Mathematics Today*. Paideia MA 1972 o.p. This book provides a comprehensive guide to international congresses of mathematicians and mathematical societies. It also includes a comparison of major topics in mathematics in 1900 versus 1970, and provides lists of major series (colloquiums, memoirs, proceedings, translations). A section is also devoted to the collected works of mathematicians. This is an excellent reference work for a reader wishing a concise overview of the most important sources used by mathematicians.

Gaffney, M. P., and L. A. Steen. *Annotated Bibliography of Expository Writing in the Mathematical Sciences*. Math. Assn. 1976 o.p. This reference work covers all major areas of mathematics, but limits itself almost exclusively to expository sources. It is written mostly for readers with little knowledge of mathematics. Only a small portion of the works listed are annotated, leaving readers to judge the appropriateness of selections based on titles alone; includes articles as well as books.

Gillispie, Charles C. *Dictionary of Scientific Biography*. 8 vols. Macmillan 1970–80 1981 $1,080.00. ISBN 0-684-16962-2. Probably the most important reference work in the history of science today. It includes signed biobibliographical articles on nonliving scientists and mathematicians who were deemed to have made an "identifiable difference to the profession or community of knowledge." The eighth volume contains a name and subject index and a list of scientists by field.

James, Glenn, and Robert C. James, eds. *Mathematics Dictionary*. Van Nos. Reinhold 1976 $44.95. ISBN 0-442-24091-0. This dictionary presents "a correlated condensation of mathematical concepts designed for time-saving reference work. Nevertheless, the general reader can come to an understanding of concepts in which he has not been schooled by looking up the unfamiliar terms in the definitions at hand and following this procedure for familiar concepts" (Preface). The multilingual index provides English equivalents for mathematical terms in French, German, Russian, and Spanish. The appendix provides many useful tables and an extensive list of mathematical symbols, each with a brief explanation.

Kenschaft, Patricia C., and Sandra Keith, eds. *Winning Women into Mathematics*. Math. Assn. 1991 $11.00. ISBN 0-88385-453-8. The goal of this handbook (compiled by the Committee on the Participation of Women of the Mathematical Association of America) is to increase the number and effectiveness of women in mathematics. Identifies fifty-five cultural customs that discourage women from entering mathematics as a profession with prescriptions about how these attitudes can be changed and how women can best be recruited into the field; includes a bibliography of more than 100 works devoted to women in mathematics, descriptions of programs that have proven especially successful in training women as mathematicians, and more than 50 photographs of prominent women in mathematics.

McGraw-Hill Encyclopedia of Science and Technology. 20 vols. McGraw 1992 $2,639.00. ISBN 0-07-909206-3. See especially the article of "Mathematics" by Solomon Bochner (Vol. 10, pp. 537–42). Copious illustrations, line drawings, and halftones contribute to the utility, clarity, and interest of the text. Most of the longer articles include bibliographies. Volume 20 contains both an analytical and topical index. It also provides a glossary of scientific notation that clarifies usage of symbols, abbreviations, and technical nomenclature. This encyclopedia is supplemented by an annual *McGraw-Hill Yearbook of Science and Technology*.

Millington, T. Alaric, and William Millington, eds. *Dictionary of Mathematics*. HarpC 1971 $8.95. ISBN 0-06-463311-X. This dictionary seeks to convey *concepts*, as its compilers say, not just overly simplified definitions. Ample cross-references guide readers to related topics and areas of interest. Historical references also are given when appropriate. The language of sets, groups, rings, fields, vectors, logic, and modern geometry are all explained, as well as standard terminology in the traditional branches of mathematics. Illustrations and diagrams supplied throughout, where suitable, enhance the intelligibility of the explanations given.

Steen, Lynn A., ed. *Library Recommendations for Undergraduate Mathematics*. Math. Assn. 1992 $15.00. ISBN 0-88385-076-1. Updates previously published "Basic Library Lists" issued in the late 1970s. Classifies works as "Essential" and "Highly Recommended," and identifies 25 major subject areas (with subclassifications). Also covers journals and periodicals.

Van Nostrand's Scientific Encyclopedia. 2 vols. Van Nos. Reinhold 1988 $195.00. ISBN 0-442-21750-1. This concise reference work offers definitions and descriptions for scores of topics pertaining to mathematics and related topics. A list of mathematical symbols with brief definitions is given on pp. 1802–03.

Watters, Carolyn. *Dictionary of Information Science and Technology*. Acad. Pr. 1992 $29.95. ISBN 0-12-738510-X. Entries define each term and include references to additional literature, includes a subject outline at the end of the book that is a useful means of identifying the context for terms defined in the entries.

GENERAL MATHEMATICS

The following books represent a highly selective sample of the hundreds of books currently available that give broad summaries of all aspects of mathematics. In most cases they are designed for the general reader who has no substantial background or familiarity with mathematics. Several works included here, however, (such as the series of books by A. D. Aleksandrov and his colleagues) give readers familiar with mathematics an idea of what more advanced mathematics at the college level and beyond has to offer.

Aleksandrov, A. D., A. N. Kolmogrorov, and M. A. Lavrent'ev, eds. *Mathematics—Its Contents, Methods and Meanings*. 3 vols. MIT Pr. $39.95. ISBN 0-262-51014-6. This notable series of books is translated from the original work compiled by a group of Russian mathematicians. Viewing abstraction, proof, and applications as the most essential characteristics of mathematics, this series begins with a general overview of mathematics, including arithmetic, geometry, and elementary and contemporary mathematics. Other chapters cover analysis, analytical geometry, algebra, ordinary and partial differential equations, calculus of variations, functions of real and complex variables, prime numbers, theory of probability, linear algebra, abstract spaces, topology, functional analysis, groups, and other algebraic systems. Suggestions for further reading are supplied at the end of each chapter.

Bernice, Daniel D. *Precalculus Mathematics*. P-H 1985 $57.00. ISBN 0-13-695503-7. This book presents standard introductions to algebra, trigonometry, geometry, and elementary functions with calculus-oriented examples. Thus the mathematics goes beyond basic high school material to prepare the student for the kind of problems, methods, and thinking needed for a later course in calculus.

Courant, Richard, and Herbet Robbins. *What Is Mathematics? An Elementary Approach to Ideas and Methods*. OUP 1979 $17.95. ISBN 0-19-502517-2. Originally published in 1941, this book remains one of the best expository introductions to a wide range of selected mathematical topics. The authors look beyond mathematical formalism and manipulation to grasp "the real essence of mathematics." They believe actual contact with the *content* of living mathematics is necessary to convey any real understanding of it. Beginning with a historical and philosophical introduction, the book progresses to consideration of natural numbers, the number system in general of rational and irrational numbers, geometrical constructions, the algebra of number fields, projective geometry, axiomatics, non-Euclidean geometries, topology, functions and limits, maxima and minima, the calculus, and so on. This book requires only a good high school knowledge of basic mathematics. Excellent suggestions are offered for further reading.

Davis, Martin. *Lectures on Modern Mathematics*. 3 vols. Gordon & Breach 1967 $94.00. ISBN 0-677-00200-9. Davis explores a variety of topics in modern mathematics that he believes should be incorporated into the teaching of high school mathematics.

The topics are also well developed to give readers an idea of the serious content of contemporary mathematics. Major topics covered include algebra, geometry, calculus, sets, and computers.

Davis, Martin, and Reuben Hersh. *The Mathematical Experience*. Spr.-Verlag 1981 o.p. This book gives an idea (in nontechnical terms) of exactly what professional mathematicians do and why they do it. It also explains why the results of modern mathematics are so important. Rather than being a comprehensive introduction to mathematics, this work displays the extraordinary variety—and vitality—of modern mathematics. Both history and philosophy are used to demonstrate how mathematical knowledge develops and grows. As its authors say, the book should be regarded as an "impression" of what mathematics is. Although parts of the book were contributed by a variety of authors, Davis and Hersh are responsible for the bulk of material presented. Topics covered include general aspects of "the mathematical landscape" and "varieties of mathematical experience," as well as specific discussions of group theory, non-Euclidean geometry, nonstandard analysis, pedagogical issues, and aspects of "mathematical reality."

Dunham, William. *Journey Through Genius: The Great Theorems of Mathematics*. Wiley 1990 $19.95. ISBN 0-471-50030-5. Presents an anthology of 12 classics from the history of mathematics that include Hippocrates' quadrature of lunes in antiquity and Georg Cantor's revolutionary discovery of the nondenumerability of the real numbers at the end of the nineteenth century. Provides biographical details, historical contexts, and technical explanations in easy-to-understand terms; emphasizes mathematical conceptualization and ingenious, but clear methods of proof.

Kline, Morris. *Mathematics for the Non-Mathematician*. *Popular Science Ser*. Dover 1985 $11.95. ISBN 0-486-24823-2. This book presents a basic understanding of what mathematics is for the general reader.

———, ed. *Mathematics: An Introduction to Its Spirit and Use*. W. H. Freeman 1979 o.p. Selected readings from articles on mathematics that appeared in *Scientific American*.

———. *Mathematics in Western Culture*. OUP 1964 $14.95. ISBN 0-19-500714-X. Demonstrates the myriad ways in which mathematics has contributed to Western civilization, from art and architecture to applications in science (especially physics) and technology. Provides impressive evidence of the significance of mathematical thought in Western culture from antiquity to the present; well illustrated.

Kramer, E. E. *The Nature and Growth of Modern Mathematics*. Princeton U. Pr. 1982 $18.95. ISBN 0-691-02372-7. This book provides a comprehensive overview of mathematics from the Babylonians to Bourbaki (the group of mathematicians who worked together in the twentieth century). Emphasis is placed on "mathematical content, history, lore and biography," integrated to offer "an overall, unified picture of the mother science" (Preface). Although Kramer surveys all of mathematics, he emphasizes aspects of primary importance in the twentieth century. Written for nonspecialists, the book conveys a sense of the manifold aspects of modern mathematics, including connections with other branches of science.

Lang, Serge. *The Beauty of Doing Mathematics: Three Public Dialogues*. Spr.-Verlag 1985 $25.00. ISBN 0-387-96149-6. This brief work presents three lectures in English given in Paris at the *Palais de la Découverte* (the old Museum of Science and Technology). The challenge to communicate what mathematics is to a general audience is admirably met. At times, however, the level of mathematical detail strays beyond the grasp of nonmathematicians. Even so, by using examples of prime numbers, diophantine equations, geometry, and space, Lang explores the general question, "What does a mathematician do and why?"

Miller, Charles D., Vern E. Heeren, and E. John Hornsby, Jr. *Mathematical Ideas*. Scott F. 1990 $29.00. ISBN 0-673-38829-8. Designed as an introduction to mathematics for liberal arts students. An explanation of how to use calculators in mathematical problem solving facilitates student interaction with the text; includes many examples and exercises that provide direct applications of the topics covered.

Neuman, James R. *The World of Mathematics.* 4 vols. S&S Trade 1956 o.p. "A small library of the literature of mathematics from Aᶜh-mosé the scribe to Albert Einstein, presented with commentaries and notes" (Title Page). Volume 1 reprints articles and extracts from books of a general survey nature. Historical and biographical materials are presented, as well as articles about arithmetic and the mathematics of space and motion. Volume 2 contains excerpts related to mathematics and the physical world, including probability, laws of chance, and aspects of mathematics applied to the social sciences. Volume 3 covers statistics and the design of experiments, group theory, infinity, mathematics, and logic. Volume 4 is a potpourri of articles on mathematics in warfare, literature, and music. To give a sense of how eclectic this is, it includes Oswald Spengler on "the meaning of numbers" as well as an article on mathematics as a "culture clue." Another section covers "amusements, puzzles, and fancies." Each selection is preceded by an introduction (usually of several pages) setting the context of the article or excerpt. This is followed by the reading in question, with notes as necessary. There are also short asides—on the vocabulary of mathematics, for example, or the "unreasonableness" of mathematics, or still another on mathematics as art. All volumes are well illustrated.

Sawyer, W. W. *Prelude to Mathematics.* Dover 1983 $4.95. ISBN 0-486-24401-6. This book presents aspects of mathematics that are of intrinsic interest in themselves—mathematics that is unusual, out-of-the-ordinary, or seemingly impossible. Beginning with a discussion of the beauty and power of mathematics, Sawyer goes on to describe the qualities of a mathematician. He then presents ten chapters covering subjects such as pattern and generalization in mathematics, non-Euclidean geometry, matrix algebra, projective geometry, apparent impossibilities in mathematics, transformations, finite arithmetics and geometries, and group theory.

Steen, Lynn A. ed. *Mathematics Today: Twelve Informal Essays.* Spr.-Verlag 1984 $42.00. ISBN 0-387-9035-4. This collection of essays by prominent mathematicians is another survey of contemporary mathematics, both pure and applied, in order to give nonspecialists a sense of how mathematicians work. It includes not only their methods, but also the different ways in which mathematicians go about their work. Interviews and expository articles cover topics including the psychology of mathematical creativity and the relevance of mathematics to contemporary society.

——. *Mathematics Tomorrow.* Spr.-Verlag 1981 $29.80. ISBN 0-387-90564-2. A collection of articles written by mathematicians reflecting their opinions and predictions about the immediate future of mathematics research and education and the directions they should take. The volume begins with six essays that discuss what mathematics is and what it is not. A second substantial section covers the teaching and learning of mathematics. This is followed by a shorter section, "Issues of Equality," which treats the special problems and challenges women face in mathematics. The final section, "Mathematics for Tomorrow," examines mathematics that concern curricula and applications, including issues that concern the increasing use of computers by mathematicians and scientists.

Whitehead, Alfred N. *An Introduction to Mathematics.* OUP rev. ed. 1959 $9.95. ISBN 0-19-500211-3. Worried that mathematics is viewed by the general public as too difficult or even impossible to understand, Whitehead blames this on the fact that "its fundamental ideas are not explained to the student disentangled from the technical procedure which has been invented to facilitate their exact presentation in particular instances." Thus, his approach is to offer general ideas first, without a massive amount of technical jargon or intimidating notation. The book does not profess to teach mathematics, but it does seek to explain what mathematics is about and why it is an exemplar of exact thought as well as essential for studying natural phenomena.

ALGEBRA

Algebra began as the branch of mathematics that studied the general properties of numbers and number systems. Above all, it was concerned with methods for solving polynomial equations with one or more unknown quantities. Modern algebra, largely a product of the twentieth century, is highly abstract. It is primarily concerned with relations and properties of systems in general, and not necessarily systems of numbers.

The word *algebra* is Arabic, appearing in a ninth-century work *Al-jabr wa'l-mugābala* (c.830) by the Islamic mathematician Abū Ja'far Muhammad ibn Mūsā al-Khwārizmī. *Algebra* actually means "restoration" or "completion," and is a reference to the way in which simple equations may be solved by moving elements from one side of an equation to another. For example, the equation $x - 2 = 5$ is solved by "restoring" 2 to the right side of the equation: $x = 5 + 2 = 7$. This method of "restoring" numbers shows algebra, in its earliest form, developed from the study of numbers and number systems. In time, it grew into a body of knowledge that was especially successful in facilitating the solution of equations.

The history of algebra is, in large measure, the story of how mathematicians have invented methods for solving increasingly complex and general forms of equations, establishing general forms of solutions for some and demonstrating the impossibility of general solutions under specified conditions for others. As a result of the increasing sophistication of algebra, negative, irrational, and complex numbers were eventually introduced to "solve" such equations in the most general forms possible. Equations may contain any number of unknowns, and the coefficients may be integers, rational, real, or complex numbers. Prior to the modern period, the Arabs developed most of the ideas that we associate with algebra today. Moreover, they were responsible for transmitting the Indian (or Hindu) decimal, place-valued number system to the West. China had its own independent and highly successful development of algebra, closely related to counting rods and later, the abacus. Numerical solutions of equations, and even simultaneous equations with a number of different unknowns, were handled by a variety of algorithmic methods.

During the European Renaissance, mathematicians such as Chuquet, Pacioli, Recorde, Tartaglia, Cardano, Viète, DESCARTES, and FERMAT made new and significant contributions to algebra. The most far-reaching discovery, however, was made by Descartes. He connected the discrete and general character of algebra with the continuous nature of geometry, thereby inventing analytic geometry. Descartes published this discovery as part of his general treatise on method, issuing *La Géométrie* in 1637. By referring points on a geometric curve to numerical scales on axes drawn perpendicularly (usually) to one another, Descarte found that it was possible to describe a curve in terms of an equation relating the horizontal and vertical elements of the curve, usually denoted by x and y, respectively. Thus, the geometric curve, known as a simple parabola, could be written in the algebraic form $y = x^2$. Curves, as well as surfaces, and even solids or objects of higher dimension could be represented by algebraic equations. These in turn could be analyzed algebraically (or, later, by even more powerful means). Such methods were helpful in revealing properties of geometric curves not immediately obvious from examination of the actual curves themselves.

By the end of the nineteenth century, algebra began its transformation to increasingly higher levels of generality. No longer was algebra simply concerned with the study of numbers and their properties, or even with the increasingly sophisticated problem-solving equations or systems of equations. For example, the French mathematician Galois, in trying to find a general solution to the quintic equation (equations of degree 5), initiated research leading very quickly to a powerful (but very abstract) branch of modern mathematics called group theory. Other mathematicians made equally far-reaching contributions during the nineteenth century. By the end of the century, quaternions, vectors, determinants, and matrices had all been introduced as parts of the new algebra.

During the twentieth century, however, algebra has been studied both axiomatically and more abstractly than ever before. Today, modern algebra includes the study of abstract structures such as groups, rings, fields, lattices, and vector spaces, to name a few of the most prominent special areas of interest.

The following books cover a wide range of material related to algebra and represent available material at various levels of difficulty and sophistication. Most are general surveys and relatively simple introductions. But, several works also have been included that will provide interested readers with an idea of where current research is making some of its most important contributions.

Artin, Michael. *Algebra*. P-H 1991 $57.00. ISBN 0-13-004763-5. Provides in the author's words, "some concrete topics such as symmetry, linear groups, and quadratic number fields, and to shift the emphasis in group theory from permutation groups to matrix groups." Written by one of the masters of modern algebra for advanced undergraduates; combines the presentation of linear algebra with groups, rings, and fields.

Asimov, Isaac. *The Realm of Algebra*. Fawcett 1982 $3.50. ISBN 0-449-24398-2.

Birkhoff, Garrett, and Saunders Maclane. *Survey of Modern Algebra*. Macmillan 1977 o.p. A classic introduction to college algebra, the authors have revised and reworked the material presented for more than 40 years. Throughout, the authors "have tried to express the conceptual background of the various definitions used. We have done this by illustrating each new term by as many familiar examples as possible. This seems especially important in an elementary text because it seems to emphasize the fact that the abstract concepts all arise from the analysis of concrete situations." Numerous exercises are included that encourage readers to think for themselves with new concepts as they are introduced. Applications to other fields, including analysis, geometry, physics, and philosophy, are also stressed. The book also covers integers, real and complex numbers, groups, vector spaces, matrices, linear groups, determinants, Boolean algebra, lattices, transfinite arithmetic, rings, ideals, algebraic number fields, and Galois theory.

Falstein, Linda D. *Basic Mathematics: You Can Count on Yourself*. Addison-Wesley 1986 $45.25. ISBN 0-201-13363-6. This textbook begins with a rudimentary introduction to quantitative skills before covering the basics of high school algebra. Quantitative skills are developed by introducing concepts, with concrete examples illustrating what is happening at every step. Topics include integers, fractions, decimals, percents, polynomials, linear equations and inequalities, word problems, radicals, exponents, quadratic equations, and graphs. This is a useful book for those who have little or no previous knowledge of algebra.

Greub, W. H. *Linear Algebra*. Spr.-Verlag 1975 $51.00. ISBN 0-387-90110-8. An advanced textbook providing a detailed presentation of linear algebra based on an axiomatic treatment of linear spaces. Topics include vector spaces, linear mappings, matrices, determinants, algebras, gradations and homology, inner product spaces, symmetric bilinear functions, quadratics, unitary spaces, and polynomial algebra.

Herstein, I. N. *Abstract Algebra*. Macmillan 1989 $39.75. ISBN 0-02-353822-8. This widely used textbook provides a standard introduction to the fundamental concepts and methods of abstract algebra. Designed for college mathematics majors, it provides a solid foundation for the further study of modern algebra.

Hestenes, Marshal D., and Richard O. Hill, Jr. *Algebra and Trigonometry*. P-H 1986 $46.67. ISBN 0-13-021866-9. Originally written as a text for an undergraduate linear algebra course at the Massachusetts Institute of Technology, this book is designed for mathematics majors at the junior level. Abstract ideas are avoided at the beginning. Examples and graded exercises, from routine applications to those requiring considerable ingenuity, cover the basics of college algebra. They include linear equations, vector spaces, linear transformations, polynomials, determinants, inner product spaces, and bilinear forms.

Keedy, Mervin L., and Marvin L. Bittinger. *Intermediate Algebra with Problem Solving.* Addison-Wesley 1986 $32.76. ISBN 0-201-52928-9. For those who have had a year of algebra and need to prepare for college-level mathematics. Margin exercises, readiness checks, tests, and reviews help readers learn the basics of algebra.

Kohlman, Bernard, and Arnold Shapiro. *Algebra for College Students.* HarBraceJ 1990 $32.00. ISBN 0-15-502162-1. A precalculus text that takes an informal, intuitive approach. Exercises with answers help students check their progress. Calculator applications are also included.

Van der Waerden, B. L. *Algebra.* 2 vols. Spr.-Verlag 1990 $29.95 ea. ISBNs 0-387-97424-5, 0-387-97425-3. When Van der Waerdan's *Algebra* first appeared in the 1930s, it inspired a new generation of mathematicians to utilize and explore further the many rich possibilities of mathematical abstraction it presented. This is an advanced introduction, suitable for college mathematics majors. Volume 1 covers the basics, introducing groups, rings, fields, vector spaces and tensors, polynomials, Galois theory, infinite field extensions, and real fields. Volume 2 develops valuation theory.

GEOMETRY

The meaning of the word *geometry* reflects the practical, applied origins of this branch of mathematics. *Geometry* is derived from the Latin words *geo*, meaning "earth" and *metria*, meaning "measure." Thus, it literally means "earth measurement." According to the ancient Greek historian HERODOTUS (see Vols. 3 and 4), mathematics began in Egypt because of the need to survey land quickly after the annual flooding of the Nile River. Other ancient writers (including Heron of Alexandria, DIODORUS SICULUS [see Vol. 3], and STRABO [see Vol. 4]) agree. Because of the annual flooding of the Nile, which would have obscured or even shifted property boundaries, the Egyptians may have found it necessary to measure parcels of land regularly in order to levy accurate taxes. The measuring was done by so-called harpedonaptai—the "rope stretchers" or royal surveyors of Egypt, who used their measuring ropes to survey the land. The Chinese also developed similar geometric understanding, especially of the properties of right triangles, and also established their version of the so-called Pythagorean theorem—the *Gou-Gu* theorem—in such ancient works (and commentaries on them) as the *Zhou Bi Suan Jing* and the *Jiu Zhang Suan Shu*.

From such simple origins, however, the study of geometric figures in general—not just of those that could be marked on the ground—quickly developed. Eventually this was compiled into a single work by the great Greek geometer EUCLID, whose *Elements of Geometry* remains a classic of mathematical exposition.

One important branch of geometry is analytic geometry, which was a product of the seventeenth-century mathematicians, especially the insights of FERMAT and DESCARTES (see also Vol. 4). Both of these mathematicians found that, by appealing to coordinate systems of perpendicular axes, it was possible to draw the "curve" of many equations. Likewise, it was possible to represent many "curves" (like the parabola) in terms of a corresponding algebraic equation, in this case $f(x) = y = x^2$ (see the introduction to the section on "Algebra").

During the eighteenth century, both plane and solid geometry (two- and three-dimensional geometry) were developed, and mathematics began to explore the potential of projective geometry as well. Mathematicians in the nineteenth century, especially Arthur Cayley, Hermann Grassmann, and Julius Pücker, generalized analytic geometry to spaces of even higher dimension.

Among the most significant discoveries of the nineteenth century was the existence of what are today known as "non-Euclidean geometries." As the name implies, such geometrics were not included in the traditional Euclidean geometry. This is because they violate Euclid's fifth postulate—that through any point only one line can be drawn parallel to a given line. In the nineteenth century, CARL FRIEDRICH GAUSS, János Bolyai, Georg Reimann, and N. I. Lobachevsky all discovered that perfectly consistent geometries could be developed in which this postulate was given up.

The possibility of non-Euclidean geometries was first realized when attempts to "prove" the parallel postulate (as Euclid's fifth postulate is called) from the other axioms of geometry proved impossible. One elementary non-Euclidean geometry is the surface of a sphere. In Euclidean geometry, the sum of the angles of any triangle is 180°. On the surface of a sphere, however, the sum of the angles of a spherical triangle is greater than 180°. Such geometries were called "hyperbolic" by CHRISTIAN FELIX KLEIN. Another form of non-Euclidean geometry is called "elliptic." In such geometries, the sums of the angles of a triangle are *less* than 180°.

Another major branch of geometry is trigonometry. The Greek word *trigonon* means "triangle"; trigonometry is actually "triangle measurement." Trigonometry involves the study of ratios of the sides of a right triangle. Among the main trigonometric functions are the sine, cosine, and tangent. Other trigonometric functions include cotangents, secants, cosecants, and inverse functions. Spherical trigonometry is a further generalization of plane trigonometry, which deals with figures drawn on the surface of a sphere.

Baker, Henry F. *Introduction to Plane Geometry.* Chelsea Hse. 1971 o.p. Baker develops geometry in an axiomatic fashion, without assigning the notions of distance or congruence as axioms. The book also gives equal standing to real and complex elements. Beginning with Euclid's theory of parallel lines, this introduction then covers involutions, conic sections, and linear transformations in detail. The book is written at a level suitable for readers with a general knowledge of basic Euclidean geometry.

Coxeter, H. S. *Introduction to Geometry.* Wiley 1989 $34.95. ISBN 0-471-50458-0. The first 11 chapters provide a basic introduction to geometry and some analytic geometry. Regular polygons, Platonic solids, and the "golden section" are covered as well as more general notions of similarity and isometry. Part 3 covers ordered, affine, projective, absolute, and hyperbolic geometries. Part 4 covers advanced topics, including differential geometry, combinatorial topology, and four-dimensional Euclidean geometry.

Coxeter, H. S., and S. L. Greitzer. *Geometry Revisited.* Math. Assn. 1967 $13.95. ISBN 0-88385-619-0. This book is designed for high school and general readers. Using the central notion of "transformation," it explores many elementary and some advanced results of basic geometry, and demonstrates its many links with other branches of mathematics. Chapter 6, on conic sections, for example, develops the geometric properties of focus and eccentricity, showing their relation to the orbits of comets, planets, and satellites.

Coxford, Arthur F., ed. *Geometry from Multiple Perspectives.* NCTM 1991 $14.00. ISBN 0-87353-330-5. Offers a brief introduction to the geometry of shapes (triangles, rectangles, polygons, solids, fractals, etc.), basic geometric concepts of similarity and congruence, coordinate geometry; emphasizes the basic concept of mathematical proof.

Eves, Howard. *Survey of Geometry*. Allyn rev. ed. 1972 o.p. Eves's book offers many problems to challenge its readers, assuming that geometry is best learned by *doing*. Offering a comprehensive survey, this work examines the historical origins of geometry along with overviews of elementary college geometry, transformation theory, projective geometry, non-Euclidean geometry, analytic geometry, differential geometry, and abstract spaces. The spirit of the book is geometric rather than algebraic, with emphasis given to conveying geometric methods along with specific results. Part 1 is synthetic and relatively elementary, easily read by anyone with a good grasp of high school mathematics; analytical results and more advanced abstract approaches are found primarily in Part 2.

Holden, Alan. *Shapes, Space and Symmetry*. Col. U. Pr. 1971 $26.00. ISBN 0-231-03549-7. This richly illustrated book makes extensive use of cardboard, wire, and other models of three-dimensional geometric objects. As a result, readers are provided with a graphic, intuitive sense about geometry, space, and the properties of symmetry. Emphasis is given to the five so-called Platonic or perfect solids, namely the tetrahedron, cube, octahedron, dodecahedron, and icosahedron, as well as to more complicated regular and irregular polyhedra. The beautiful photographs reproduced here of hundreds of polyhedra impart a rich sense of the aesthetic as well as the theoretical fascination of the subject.

Middlemiss, Ross R., John L. Marks, and James R. Smart. *Analytic Geometry*. McGraw 1968 o.p. Although often regarded primarily as a tool for the study and application of the calculus, analytic geometry has developed as a subject of increasing interest on its own. As a result, the authors have prepared this text with connections between analytic geometry and both higher geometry and modern abstract algebra. Calculus still receives attention, but the text emphasizes concepts linked with a wide variety of applications. All of the basic theorems of analytic geometry are presented with proofs. Subjects covered include polynomials; rational, exponential, logarithmic, and trigonometric functions; graphs; vectors; parametric equations; polar, cylindrical, and spherical coordinates, as well as transformations of coordinates; algebraic, trigonometric, exponential, and logarithmic curves; conic sections; and analytic solid geometry.

Shafarevich, I. R. *Basic Algebraic Geometry*. Trans. by K. A. Hirsch. Spr.-Verlag 1990 $32.00. ISBN 0-387-08264-6. This book is designed for mathematicians who want an overview of basic algebraic geometry so that they can begin reading specialized literature on the subject. The first two parts of the book, dealing with algebraic varieties in a projective space, and with schemes and varieties, requires a college course in algebra and analytic geometry, with some knowledge of the theory of fields and communicative algebra. Part 3, devoted to algebraic varieties over the complex field and complex analytic manifolds, requires knowledge of topology and the theory of analytic functions.

Stevens, Peter S. *Handbook of Regular Pattern: An Introduction to Symmetry in Two Dimensions*. MIT Pr. 1981 $27.50. ISBN 0-262-69088-8

———. *Patterns in Nature*. Little 1974 o.p. This is a visually striking book, full of stunning photographs illustrating the diversity of patterns and forms found in the natural world. Particularly numerous are spirals, meanders, branching patterns, and 120° joints in nature. The book begins with brief discussions of space, curvature, mosaics, polyhedra, and effects of scale, and then goes on to investigate basic patterns, topology, things that flow, spirals, meanders, explosions, models of branching, trees, soap bubbles, and patterns that can be observed in packing and crating.

Stoker, James J. *Differential Geometry*. Wiley 1989 $29.95. ISBN 0-471-50403-3. Although this book is intended for readers with a minimum of mathematical training, it provides a comprehensive introduction to the special area of differential geometry. Only linear algebra and basic elements of analysis are required. Stoker has young students in mind, and makes a point of introducing (and applying) three important kinds of notation—vectors, tensors, and invariant differential forms.

NUMBER THEORY

Number theory is concerned with the character and properties of the natural numbers, or integers. Its history dates back to antiquity and the origins of *arithmetic*, a word derived from the Greek *arithmetike*, which means "counting." Arithmetic is the study of whole numbers (integers) and the operations of addition, subtraction, multiplication, and division. Applying these operations eventually leads to fractions and negative numbers. Number theory, however, is limited to the study of integers and their properties.

As the history of mathematics has progressed, so too has the sophistication of number theory. Today it is a highly abstract and specialized subject, still involving many unanswered questions. Among them is the famous theorem of FERMAT (i.e., there are no positive integers x, y, z, and n such that $x^n + y^n = z^n$ for $n > 2$). As the sophistication of mathematics has increased, tools drawn from diverse branches, including geometry, probability, and analysis, have been used to advance and enrich the results of number theory.

Berndt, Bruce C., ed. *Ramanujan's Notebooks*. 3 vols. Spr.-Verlag Vol. 1 1985 $76.00. ISBN 0-387-96110-0. Vol. 2 1988 $79.80. ISBN 0-387-96794-X. Vol. 3 1991 $89.90. ISBN 0-387-97503-9. Provides carefully edited versions of the famous notebooks written by the Indian mathematician Ramanujan. Proves many of Ramanujan's amazing formulas; Volume III deals primarily with theta functions. Five volumes are projected.

Cassels, J. W. S. *An Introduction to the Geometry of Numbers*. Spr.-Verlag 1971 o.p. An advanced approach to a special part of number theory. The book covers the subject from lattices and distance functions to packings, automorphs, and includes a final chapter on inhomogeneous problems related to convex sets.

Dantzig, Tobias. *Number: The Language of Science*. Free Pr. 4th rev. ed. 1967 $14.95. ISBN 0-02-906990-4. A popular, but somewhat dated historical treatment of the number concept, number systems, and their applications in diverse cultures, from antiquity to the present. Profusely illustrated; written for nonmathematicians.

Dudley, Underwood. *Elementary Number Theory*. W. H. Freeman 1978 $30.95. ISBN 0-7167-0076-X. *Instructor's Manual*. $4.95. ISBN 0-7167-1324-4. Designed as a one-semester or quarter introduction, requires some elementary algebra and a basic familiarity with properties of the real numbers. Proofs are presented clearly and all basic topics in number theory are covered. Numerical examples illustrate ideas and show how playing with numbers may lead to important insights or discoveries.

Niven, Ivan M. *Numbers: Rational and Irrational*. Math. Assn. 1961 $12.95. ISBN 0-88385-601-8. This book deals with one of the most fundamental structures in all of mathematics, the number system; requires a high school knowledge of mathematics. Beginning with a straightforward coverage of natural numbers, integers, and primes, the book goes on in a step-by-step way to introduce rational, irrational, trigonometric, logarithmic, and transcendental numbers. Answers and hints for solving many problems in the book are especially helpful.

Niven, Ivan M., and Herbert S. Zuckerman. *An Introduction to the Theory of Numbers*. Wiley 1980 o.p. This book is designed for undergraduate mathematics students wishing a comprehensive overview of basic number theory. Beginning with theorems about divisibility and congruences, the pace accelerates from quadratic reciprocity and Diophantine equations to continued fractions, algebraic numbers, the distribution of primes, and the density of sequences of integers.

Ore, Oystein. *Invitation to Number Theory*. Math. Assn. 1967 $12.95. ISBN 0-88385-620-4. This book, described as a "simple little guide," gives the general reader an idea of the basic properties of numbers and why they are so fascinating. A short historical chapter is followed by material on prime numbers, divisors, and various number systems and their special properties; includes congruences and applications of congruences to problems involving the days of the week and tournament schedules.

Rademacher, Hans. *Lectures on Elementary Number Theory*. Krieger 1977 repr. of 1964 ed. $15.50. ISBN 0-88275-499-8. Based on lectures given at Haverford College, Pennsylvania, in 1954 and 1955, the material presented here is designed for most undergraduates. Although it does not require previous knowledge of number theory, the book uses algebra and analysis as background to introducing fundamental results of number theory, the uniqueness of prime number factorization, and the reciprocity law of quadratic residues.

Smoryński, Craig. *Logical Number Theory: An Introduction*. Spr.-Verlag 1991 $49.00. ISBN 0-387-52236-0. Presents an introduction to number theory from the perspective of mathematical logic; also includes historical and philosophical material.

Weil, André. *Basic Number Theory*. Spr.-Verlag 1985 $76.00. ISBN 0-387-06935-6. The first part of this book was originally presented as a course for undergraduates at Princeton University. It includes basic theorems related to locally compact fields, adeles, algebraic number fields, the Zeta function, traces, and norms. The main features of both local and global class field theory also are given. The book incorporates important recent results in which compact groups, measure, and integration have made important contributions to traditional number theory.

_____. *Number Theory for Beginners*. Spr.-Verlag 1985 $29.50. ISBN 0-387-90381-X. This book by one of the world's authorities on the subject was written from weekly notes taken by Max Rosenlicht at a summer course offered by Weil at the University of Chicago in 1949. The notes are terse, but attentive reading with occasional guidance from someone with a knowledge of number theory makes this a useful, quick survey on the subject.

CALCULUS

Prior to the seventeenth century, mathematicians had achieved only limited success in treating physical problems of motion or of situations in which change occurred, for example, velocity, direction, and temperature. The traditionally static mathematics of Greek algebra and geometry were severely limited for applications in such situations, especially when the change was highly variable or infinitesimal. A new mathematics was needed that could handle the problems of change and motion that were increasingly of interest in physics. These problems included projectile motion, the natural acceleration of falling bodies, and the continuous elliptical motions of the planets and their satellites, which were influenced by gravitational forces.

ISAAC NEWTON (see Vol. 4) was one of two mathematicians in the seventeenth century who invented a new mathematics to deal with such situations—the calculus. LEIBNIZ (see Vol. 4), the German philosopher, also developed the idea of an infinitesimal calculus at virtually the same time as Newton. Because of the methods they derived for calculating areas of figures or for determining tangents to curves, their new mathematics came to be known as the "calculus." Using the concept of infinitely small quantities (known as infinitesimals), both mathematicians could deal with important and otherwise difficult-to-solve problems related to the lengths of curves, the areas of curved figures, rates of change, problems involving maxima and minima, as well as many other problems in physics and mathematics. The crucial realization, that finding the areas of curved figures was inversely related to the problem of finding tangents to the curve in question, represented a major advance. The latter, finding tangents to curves, is called differentiation; the former, finding the areas under curves is called integration.

In the eighteenth century, the power of the calculus was greatly enhanced. This occurred when LEONHARD EULER approached it as part of a general theory of functions, appealing to infinitely small increments, or differentials. The early development of the calculus culminated in the 1820s with major publications by the French mathematician AUGUSTIN LOUIS CAUCHY. He introduced new levels of rigor to the teaching of calculus by carefully defining the concepts of continuity and limit. This was refined by the German mathematician KARL WEIERSTRASS, who "arithmeticized" the calculus a generation later by adding a rigorous theory of real numbers as a foundation for the rest of the calculus. By the turn of the nineteenth century, research by Riemann, Lebesque, Denjoy, Stieltjes, and others further extended the concepts of the calculus (and of the integral in particular) to include wider and more general types of functions that could be handled.

Most recently, calculus has been further refined by nonstandard analysis (the creation largely of ABRAHAM ROBINSON), in which infinitesimals are rigorously defined and used. This makes it possible to develop many parts of mathematics more intuitively and with less complexity, appealing to infinitesimals directly instead of limits. This in turn provides the calculus with an alternative to the traditional use of δ—ε (delta-epsilon) methods favored by most mathematicians in the aftermath of the Cauchy-Weierstrass era as the only acceptably rigorous way to present definitions and proofs involving continuity and limits.

Apostol, Tom M. *Calculus*. 2 vols. Wiley. Vol. 1 *One-Variable Calculus with an Introduction to Linear Algebra*. 1967 $67.95. ISBN 0-471-00005-1. Vol. 2 *Multi-Variable Calculus and Linear Algebra with Applications*. 1969 $72.95. ISBN 0-471-00007-8. Volume 1 strikes a balance between introductions to calculus that regard it as a deductive theory, a branch of pure mathematics, and those that stress the physical origins and applications of calculus, making it more a part of applied mathematics. The proofs presented usually are preceded by some geometric or other intuitive background. Historical introductions precede explanation of all major concepts. Early physical intuitions are later translated into precise and rigorous formulations. This volume presents the calculus of functions of one variable, including infinite series and a brief (one chapter) introduction to differential equations and linear algebra, as well as applications to geometry and analysis. Volume 2 shares the same philosophy and format as Volume 1. Volume 2 is devoted to multivariable calculus and to more advanced topics. It is divided into three parts—linear analysis, nonlinear analysis, and special topics, such as probability and numerical analysis.

Kline, Morris. *Calculus: An Intuitive and Physical Approach*. Wiley 1967 o.p. This introduction to calculus adopts an intuitive approach. It includes many applications to real problems drawn largely from physics (although some from biology and the social sciences also appear.) A thoroughly rigorous treatment is outlined in the last chapter. No knowledge of physics is required. Anyone with a basic knowledge of high school algebra can obtain a good, intuitive understanding of such concepts as the derivative, integral, maxima and minima, trigonometric functions and their inverses, logarithmic and exponential functions, infinite series, partial differentiation, multiple integrals, and differential equations.

Lang, Serge. *A First Course in Calculus*. Spr.-Verlag 1988 $39.95. ISBN 0-387-96201-8. This book is designed to teach college-level students the basics of calculus, such as differentiation and integration, along with the most important techniques and applications related to them. Lange intends the book to provide "an immediate, and pleasant, access to the subject." Little previous knowledge is required. Beginning with a section on numbers, functions, graphs, and curves, differentiation of elementary functions precedes the subject of integration. This is followed by a section on Taylor's formula and series, and a final section on functions of several variables.

Leinbach, L. Carl, ed. *The Laboratory Approach to Teaching Calculus*. Math. Assn. 1991 $20.00. ISBN 0-88385-074-5. Uses in-class, tested examples to motivate study of the calculus through a combination of observations, problem solving, and analysis. Calculators and computers enhance the hands-on, laboratory approach that provides students with an immediate feeling for the basic concepts and applications of the calculus.

Niven, Ivan. *Calculus: An Introductory Approach.* Krieger 1968 repr. of 1966 ed. o.p. This book provides a basic introduction to the calculus, as well as the necessary background material from analytic geometry. Not as long or as comprehensive as many calculus texts, it focuses on several central concepts. The book is especially useful as a brief introduction to the subject. It may be used as a suitable course for liberal arts students in the social sciences, biological sciences, or business administration. Because of its conciseness, the book requires knowledge of basic high school algebra and trigonometry. Difficult problems are starred, and answers are provided for all odd-numbered problems.

Sawyer, W. W. *What Is Calculus About?* Math. Assn. 1961 $12.50. ISBN 0-88385-602-6. Using simple nontechnical language, this book conveys the basic elements of calculus. It proceeds intuitively, beginning with an analysis of speed, acceleration, and curvature, among other topics; use of equations and other mathematical notation is minimal. Diagrams and physical situations illustrate graphically how and why the calculus is so useful.

HISTORY OF MATHEMATICS

Two basic references will guide the reader to a wide variety of materials relevant to the history of mathematics. These in turn will alert the reader to dictionaries, encyclopedias, bibliographies, periodicals, abstracting journals, handbooks, indexes, sourcebooks, and archival collections, and also major articles and books on the history of mathematics.

Dauben, Joseph W., ed. *The History of Mathematics from Antiquity to the Present: A Selective Bibliography.* Garland 1985 o.p. This reference work was compiled by 49 experts from 5 continents. They have pooled their individual expertise in specific areas of the history of mathematics to provide a wide coverage of topics and time periods. More than 4,000 years of mathematics are covered, as well as topics such as the history of specific branches of mathematics, the philosophy and sociology of mathematics, mathematics education, institutions, and regional studies of African and Asian mathematics. A separate section is devoted to women in mathematics.

May, Kenneth. *Bibliography and Research Manual of the History of Mathematics.* U. of Toronto Pr. 1973 o.p. This book includes all secondary literature concerning the history of mathematics from 1868 to 1965. It is alphabetically arranged under the following sections: biography, mathematical topics, epimathematical topics (e.g., the abacus, women, and so on), historical classifications (time periods, countries, cities, organizations), and information retrieval (bibliographies, historiography, information systems, libraries, manuscripts, museums, monuments, exhibits).

The following general surveys of the history of mathematics provide only a small sampling of the rich and diverse resources available to readers with historical interests. These books will orient general readers to the major developments in the history of mathematics (sometimes extensive ones) of the specialized literature in many languages dealing with specific aspects of the history of mathematics.

Boyer, Carl B. *A History of Mathematics.* Wiley 1991 $24.95. ISBN 0-471-54397-7. A college-level textbook, with chapter exercises; more extensive in scope than Eves's *An Introduction to the History of Mathematics* (below), and more historically oriented than Kline's *Mathematical Thought from Ancient to Modern Times* (below); includes useful references such as an extensive bibliography and a 12-page chronological table.

Eves, Howard. *An Introduction to the History of Mathematics*. Saunders 1983 o.p. This book is designed as a "textbook for a one-semester undergraduate course, which meets three hours a week." The mathematical level adopted requires an introductory knowledge of calculus. Problems (with solutions) and bibliographies are presented in each section. An eight-page chronological table and an index are appended.

Katz, Victor J. *A History of Mathematics. An Introduction*. HarpC 1993 $56.50. ISBN 0-673-38039-4. Features a fully illustrated, comprehensive history of mathematics from antiquity to the present. The book is divided into four major sections, "Mathematics Before the Sixth Century," "Medieval Mathematics," "Early Modern Mathematics" (1400–1700), and "Modern Mathematics" (1700–2000). Presents many of the practical, applied problems that have influenced some of the remarkable theoretical results in the history of mathematics; includes full references, notes, bibliographies, as well as problems, solutions, and a wide variety of suggested topics for discussion.

Kline, Morris. *Mathematical Thought from Ancient to Modern Times*. 3 vols. OUP 1972 $75.00. ISBN 0-19-506135-7. "Emphasizes the leading mathematical themes rather than the men," and emphasizes Western mathematics. This is the most complete and most modern coverage of the general histories of mathematics currently available. In particular, it gives more attention to the first few decades of the twentieth century than Carl Boyer's history does. Chapter bibliographies and an index are provided.

———. *Mathematics in Western Culture*. OUP 1964 $15.95. ISBN 0-19-500714-X. On an elementary level this illustrated book advances the thesis "that mathematics has been a major cultural force in Western civilization." It emphasizes mathematical applications in a range of subjects including painting, music, and relativity theory.

Phillips, Esther R., ed. *Studies in the History of Mathematics*. Math. Assn. 1987 $36.50. ISBN 0-88385-128-8. A collection of recent studies in the history of mathematics that provides an excellent overview of the current "state of the profession." Covers number theory, geometry, topology, logic, and the relationship between mathematics and computer science.

Struik, Dirk J. *A Concise History of Mathematics*. Dover 4th rev. ed. 1987 $7.95. ISBN 0-486-60255-9. Though "concise," this book devotes two of its eight chapters to Oriental mathematics. It covers the history of mathematics to the end of the nineteenth century and is probably the only modern history of its size and reliability. Generously illustrated; includes index and chapter bibliographies.

Wilder, Raymond. *Evolution of Mathematical Concept*. Taylor & Francis 1978 $25.00. ISBN 0-335-00249-8. Wilder regards mathematics as a "cultural entity," subject to the laws that have directed and controlled its evolution as one of "the most important cultural components of every modern society."

PHILOSOPHY OF MATHEMATICS

Like the preceding section, "History of Mathematics," the following works on the philosophy of mathematics provide only a small sampling of the books currently in print. Nevertheless, they offer a reasonable overview of major issues, and these works, in turn, provide bibliographies and references that will lead readers to further reading. The philosophy of mathematics, as some of these books demonstrate, is closely related to logic and the philosophy of logic.

Baker, Stephen F. *Philosophy of Mathematics. Foundations in Philosophy Ser.* P-H 1981 o.p. A standard, brief introduction that surveys both general questions and those associated with Euclidean and non-Euclidean geometries and debates the interpretation of numbers (nominalist versus realist theories).

Benacerraf, P., and H. Putnam, eds. *Philosophy of Mathematics: Selected Readings*. Cambridge U. Pr. 1984 $27.95. ISBN 0-521-29648-X. Contains selections from Frege, Russell, Poincaré, Brouwer, and Hilbert. Two papers by Gödel, "Russell's Mathematical Logic" and "What Is Cantor's Continuum Problem?" are classics of mathematical realism. Bernays's "On Platonism in Mathematics" is especially useful. "Hilbert's Program" by G. Kreisel describes briefly the development of Hilbert's views and the opposition between his approach and that of Brouwer to mathematics; Kreisel then proceeds to a reconstruction of Hilbert's program. These are also influential papers by W. V. Quine and C. G. Hempel, and a large section devoted to excerpts from and critical commentaries on Wittgenstein's philosophy of mathematics.

Beth, E. W. *Mathematical Thought: An Introduction to the Philosophy of Mathematics.* Gordon & Breach 1965 $90.00. ISBN 0-677-00600-4. This book is useful to mathematicians interested in philosophy, as well as graduate students in philosophy without extensive knowledge of mathematics, logic, or foundations. It covers topics such as the foundations of arithmetic, traditional and symbolic logic, intuitionism, formalism, and the significance of logical and semantical paradoxes. A chapter on "recent developments" gives a clue to Beth's thinking on recent issues of concern to philosophers of mathematics.

Diamond, Cora, ed. *Wittgenstein's Lectures on the Foundations of Mathematics.* U. Ch. Pr. 1989 $13.95. ISBN 0-226-90426-1. Compilation of 31 reconstructed lectures given by Wittgenstein in 1939; provides a clear exposition of his philosophy of mathematics.

Eves, Howard. *Foundations and Fundamental Concepts of Mathematics.* PWS-Kent 1989 o.p. The third edition of this popular work is a revised version of the earlier classic by Eves and Carroll V. Newsom, *An Introduction to the Foundations and Fundamental Concepts of Mathematics* (1958).

Frege, Gottlob. *Collected Papers on Mathematics, Logic, and Philosophy.* Blackwell Pubs. 1985 $65.00. ISBN 0-631-12728-3. Frege's theory of mathematics is one of the most influential approaches of the twentieth century.

Kitcher, Philip. *The Nature of Mathematical Knowledge.* OUP 1983 $13.95. ISBN 0-19-503541-0. This book examines the nature of mathematics and how mathematical knowledge grows. Basically, Kitcher does not support "mathematical apriorism," which holds that mathematical truth is about an abstract realm of ideal objects or forms. Instead, Kitcher argues that mathematics is like the natural sciences. Both have a body of knowledge based on empirical evidence and an evolutionary history firmly rooted in aposteriori, rather then apriori, knowledge. Kitcher also refers to the sociology of knowledge in showing how mathematics is a social enterprise— usually passed on from one generation to another through teachers, journals, mathematical societies, and the "mathematical community."

Korner, Stephan. *The Philosophy of Mathematics: An Introductory Essay.* Dover 1986 $6.95. ISBN 0-486-25048-2. This "essay," as Korner calls it, was written as an introduction to mathematical logic or the foundations of mathematics. It is mainly about the construction and reconstruction of mathematical theories, and the relation between pure and applied mathematics. The early chapters are historical and expository, the latter ones are more critical. Finally, Korner presents a new philosophical position about the nature of pure versus applied mathematics in terms of perception, existence propositions, and other philosophical issues.

Lakatos, Imre. *Proofs and Refutations: The Logic of Mathematical Discovery.* Cambridge U. Pr. 1976 $13.95. ISBN 0-521-29038-4. Influenced by G. Polya and K. Popper, this book supports a dialectical approach to the history of proofs in mathematics. Two case studies provide evidence for the thesis that mathematics grows by a process in which proofs challenged by counterexamples lead to revised proofs. These in turn are subjected to the same process of criticism and development in an unending series leading to successive revisions and progressive refinements.

Russell, Bertrand. *The Principles of Mathematics.* Norton 1964 $12.95. ISBN 0-393-00249-7. This book gives Russell's most extensive philosophical presentation of logicism, the thesis that all mathematics can be reduced to logic, originally published in 1903. Throughout, Russell discusses the work of many of his predecessors, provides a lucid explanation of his famous antinomy, and describes attempts to deal with the paradoxes of set theory by various means. He also presents an exposition of his logic of relations, his analysis of the various number concepts, and much more. Russell opposed idealism and sought to refute the Kantian philosophy of mathematics. He vigorously opposed the Kantian doctrine that mathematics was not strictly formal, but always relied on intuitions. Russell refuted the Kantian program with his program, eventually embodied in the great book *Principia Mathematica*, on which he and his colleague Alfred N. Whitehead collaborated. It sought to reduce the major body of mathematical results achieved by the end of the nineteenth century to a system of symbolic logic.

Wilder, R. L. *Introduction to the Foundations of Mathematics*. Krieger 1980 repr. of 1965 ed. $31.50. ISBN 0-89874-170-X. This book grew out of an undergraduate course for students to get an idea of modern mathematics, its foundations, and the nature of its evolution. First, the book presents basic concepts and methods, including the axiomatic method, set theory, transfinite numbers, and group theory. Then, various views on the foundations of mathematics are presented. Logicism, intuitionism, and formalism are all covered. The final chapter presents mathematics from a cultural point of view, exploring general features of the change and growth of mathematics.

Wittgenstein, Ludwig. *Remarks on the Foundation of Mathematics*. Ed. by G. H. Von Wright and R. Rhees. MIT Pr. 1983 $16.95. ISBN 0-262-73067-7. Presents arguments and ideas by one of the most influential philosophers of the twentieth century. Grounds questions about mathematics in what became known as linguistic analysis.

OTHER TOPICS IN MATHEMATICS

The following books present a variety of different approaches to mathematics. Some of the books are by mathematicians reflecting on their careers and what being a mathematician has meant to them. Others deal with mathematical creativity and its origins and with social approaches to questions about mathematics and mathematicians.

Ascher, Marcia. *Ethnomathematics: A Multicultural View of Mathematical Ideas*. Brooks-Cole 1991 $40.25. ISBN 0-534-14880-8. Provides a comprehensive introduction to mathematics in a wide variety of cultures. Emphasizes context and the sophistication of mathematical concepts related to basic number systems, understanding kin relations, mathematical strategies used in games, the geometry of folk patterns in art, and others; includes examples from the lore of Native Americans, the Incas, many different Pacific Island societies, and several African tribes.

Grinstein, Louise S., and Paul J. Campbell, eds. *Women of Mathematics: A Bibliographic Sourcebook*. Greenwood 1987 $55.00. ISBN 0-313-24849-4. Presents 43 essays about important women mathematicians; covers all time periods.

Hadamard, Jacques. *Psychology of Invention in the Mathematical Field*. Dover 1945 $4.95. ISBN 0-486-20107-4. In this book one of France's most eminent mathematicians of the early twentieth century examines reasons for the genesis of abstract mathematical ideas. It is based on his own introspection and the reports of others who have analyzed the sources of their mathematical creativity; includes Pascal and Descartes. A letter by Albert Einstein about his own scientific creativity is included in the appendix.

Hardy, Godfrey H. *Mathematician's Apology*. Cambridge U. Pr. rev. ed. 1969 o.p. A famous apology for pure mathematics by one of England's greatest pure mathematicians. Hardy bases his defense of pure mathematics on its harmlessness, stating that unlike physics, chemistry, or biology, pure mathematics could never be used to kill anyone. He also emphasizes the permanence of its achievements and describes the pleasure of "doing" mathematics.

Olsen, Lynn M. *Women in Mathematics*. MIT Pr. 1974 $7.95. ISBN 0-262-65009-6. This book presents brief biographies of prominent women mathematicians, from Hypatia to Emmy Noether. Brief comments are also provided on contributions by contemporary women mathematicians. Also included are Agnesi, du Châtelet, Herschel, Germain, Somerville, and Kovalevskaya. The book is not a technical exposition of mathematics but is written for a nonmathematical audience. References for further reading are provided.

Rademacher, Hans, and Otto Toeplitz. *The Enjoyment of Mathematics: Selections from Mathematics for the Amateur.* Dover 1990 $5.95. ISBN 0-486-26242-1. Previous mathematical knowledge is not required.

Schattschneider, Doris. *Visions of Symmetry. Periodic Drawings, and Related Work of M. C. Escher.* W. H. Freeman 1990 $42.50. ISBN 0-7167-2126-0. Explains how the famous artist M. C. Escher (1898–1972) developed the geometric patterns and symmetries that have led to further geometric and topological research. Provides full color reproductions of 137 of Escher's periodic patterns mainly drawn from his notebooks. A visually stunning book that illustrates elementary concepts in group theory related to tilings and periodic patterns.

Steinhaus, Hugo. *Mathematical Snapshots.* OUP 1969 $8.95. ISBN 0-19-503267-5. A series of mathematical vignettes that convey the nature of various mathematical notions with a minimal use of formulas and a liberal use of diagrams.

Wiener, Norbert. *I Am a Mathematician.* MIT Pr. 1964 $10.95. ISBN 0-262-73007-3. An autobiographical account of Wiener's later years as a mathematician. This volume is a sequel to his earlier book (covering his childhood and adolescence), *Ex-Prodigy: My Childhood and Youth* (S&S Trade, 1953). Topics covered in *I Am a Mathematician* include quantum mechanics, the atomic bomb, and cybernetics. Wiener also includes recollections of many European and American mathematicians.

Zaslavsky, Claudia. *Africa Counts: Number and Pattern in African Culture.* L. Hill Bks. 1979 $11.95. ISBN 1-55652-075-1. This book is an examination of mathematics in African cultures south of the Sahara. It emphasizes mathematics and its connections with social and economic development. Drawing on both primary and secondary sources, topics covered include numeration systems, mystical attributes of numbers, time reckoning, currency, and measures. Geometric aspects of African art and architecture also are discussed, as well as a section on mathematical games. In-depth studies of southwestern Nigeria and East Africa include many photographs, diagrams, tables, and maps.

PUZZLE BOOKS AND RECREATIONAL MATHEMATICS

The following are noted classics among the books devoted to the genre of mathematical puzzles and games. The books listed here provide hundreds of hours of entertainment, as well as teaching important lessons about mathematics.

Ball, W. W. *Fun with String Figures.* Dover 1971 $2.95. ISBN 0-486-22809-6. This book examines the subject of string figures and various patterns that can be fashioned from loops of string wound between the fingers of both hands; describes dozens of examples from a variety of cultures and time periods. The "cat's cradle" is one example of string figures that are of considerable interest. Although the book does not go into mathematical detail, interesting questions about geometry and topology are raised by such figures.

De Morgan, Augustus. *A Budget of Paradoxes.* 2 vols. Ayer facsimile ed. 1915 $55.00. ISBN 0-8369-5119-0. First published 30 years ago after De Morgan's death; examines subjects such as Newtonian physics, extensions of the number concept, and the impossibility of perpetual motion machines. Also describes attempts to trisect angles or square the circle using only a straightedge and a compass. The "Budget" reflects De Morgan's interests in literary, scientific, and social matters, and still makes lively and entertaining reading.

Gardner, Martin. *Martin Gardner's New Mathematical Diversions from Scientific American.* U. Ch. Pr. 1984 o.p. A compendium of puzzles and problems drawn from Gardner's popular monthly column in *Scientific American* devoted to mathematical recreations.

————. *Mathematical Magic Show*. Math. Assn. 1990 $19.50. ISBN 0-88385-449-X. Offers a revised collection of Gardner's well-known columns on mathematical recreations from *Scientific American*. Covers mathematical card tricks, word puzzles, dice games, and various topics of mathematical interest; includes an opening article on "Nothing" and a closing article on "Everything."

————. *The Second Scientific American Book of Mathematical Puzzles and Diversions*. U. Ch. Pr. 1987 $12.95. ISBN 0-226-28253-8. More puzzles taken from Gardner's magazine column.

————. *Unexpected Hanging and Other Mathematical Diversions*. U. Ch. Pr. 1991 $10.95. ISBN 0-226-28256-2. Twenty essays on mathematical recreations that examine both historical and technical issues.

Hunter, J. A., and Joseph S. Madachy. *Mathematical Diversions*. Dover 1975 o.p. Something old, and something new!—as the authors describe their purpose in presenting recreational mathematics for the fun of doing it. Hunter and Madachy describe various problems and puzzles with interesting mathematical twists; includes friendly numbers, mystic arrays, topological delights, inferential problems, alphametrics, probabilities, and a final section appropriately titled "Story Teasers." Answers and solutions are provided for most of the problems proposed.

Lieber, Hugh G., and Lillian R. Lieber. *The Education of T. C. Mits*. Norton 1978 o.p. T. C. Mits is "the celebrated man in the street," for whom this book was written. It consists of challenging mathematical games and word problems designed to surprise the uncritical reader. The book includes situations that are not as mathematically straightforward as they may originally seem. The many illustrations throughout are by Hugh G. Lieber.

O'Beirne, T. H. *Puzzles and Paradoxes: Fascinating Excursions in Recreational Mathematics*. Dover 1984 repr. of 1965 ed. o.p. Compares and analyzes popular puzzles and novelties, as well as many historical references. River-crossing problems, jug-pouring problems, coin-weighing problems, two-party strategic games, logical conundrums, arithmetic problems, and many other subjects typical of recreational mathematics are included.

Salkind, C. T. *The Contest Problem Book: Annual High School Mathematics Exams*. 3 vols. Math. Assn. Vol. 1 1961 $10.00. ISBN 0-88385-605-0. Vol. 2 1966 $10.00. ISBN 0-88385-617-4. Vol. 3 1973 ISBN 0-88385-625-5. Volume 1 covers examinations administered between 1950 and 1960; Volume 2 covers 1961 through 1965; and Volume 3 covers 1966 to 1972.

Schaaf, William L. *A Bibliography of Recreational Mathematics*. 3 vols. NCTM 1970–73 $9.00 ea. ISBNs 0-87353-021-7, 0-87353-022-5, 0-87353-023-3. From magic squares to complex cryptanalysis, mathematical puzzles have amused and challenged people for centuries. Testament problems, ferrying problems, coin problems, problems of pursuit and of arrangements still are considered "old friends" as Schaaf puts it. Labyrinths, acrostics, tangrams, and palindromes are equally ageless. Recreational mathematics has generated an enormous literature. These volumes survey most of it. Both popular articles and erudite memories are included, offering something for everyone, from schoolchildren to scholarly mathematicians. Most entries are in English, but some French, German, and Italian titles are included. More than 50 headings cover categories such as arithmetical and algebraic recreations, geometric recreations, card tricks, chessboard problems, paper folding, and magic squares. Classical problems from antiquity are described, as well as cryptography and cryptanalysis, game strategy, and symmetry. Volumes 2 and 3 update Volume 1 and fill gaps and omissions without repeating material covered in the earlier publications. Volume 3 adds sections on classroom games and recreational activities of special interest to teachers. Two useful features included are a chronological synopsis of Martin Gardner's popular column in *Scientific American* and a glossary of terms related to recreational mathematics. An appendix to Volume 3 provides a useful list of general works of mathematical recreations.

————. *Mathematics and Science: An Adventure in Postage Stamps*. NCTM 1978 o.p. The main assumption is that "the postage stamps of the world are, in effect, a mirror of civilization and that multitudes of stamps reflect the impact of mathematics and science on society." This book covers the entire history of science from the Egyptians and Babylonians to the present age of computers and space exploration. Hundreds of postage stamps devoted to scientific subjects are reproduced (some in color). Two checklists are provided. One gives names of mathematicians and scientists who have been portrayed on stamps, the other notes applications of mathematics to science.

Schuh, Fred. *The Master Book of Mathematical Puzzles and Recreations*. Trans. by F. Göbel. Dover 1969 $7.95. ISBN 0-486-22134-2. An illustrated classic; comprehensive and scholarly.

Steinhaus, Hugo. *One Hundred Problems in Elementary Mathematics*. Dover 1979 $4.95. ISBN 0-486-23875-X. For anyone who enjoys solving puzzles, the level of mathematical creativity and novelty displayed here will be refreshing. Most problems require clear thinking and a background in high school mathematics. Detailed answers are provided for each of the 100 problems presented, which successfully convey a considerable amount of significant mathematics. Problems are grouped into several major areas, including problems with numbers, geometric figures, problems on chess and pursuit, and even a section on "problems without solution."

Stewart, Ian. *Game, Set and Math: Enigmas and Conundrums*. Viking Penguin 1989 $9.95. ISBN 0-14-013237-6. Offers English translations of popular mathematical puzzles and recreational problems originally published in the French edition of *Scientific American*; includes topics such as fractals and the probability of winning a tennis match.

Tietze, Heinrich. *Famous Problems of Mathematics*. Graylock 1965 o.p. Offers solved and unsolved problems from antiquity to modern times. The book emphasizes problems from geometry and number theory. Tietze avoids proofs that require lengthy explanations. Instead, he concentrates on a narrow selection of problems, emphasizing why at one time a problem resisted solution, and how it was eventually solved. Numerous portraits and color plates enhance the visual appeal of the book.

The following section provides the reader with brief biographical descriptions and books by or about a select group of the world's most important mathematicians. Coverage includes mathematicians from antiquity as well as from the twentieth century.

CHRONOLOGY OF AUTHORS

Pythagoras. c.580 B.C–c.500 B.C.
Euclid. fl. c.300 B.C.
Archimedes. c.287–212 B.C.
Diophantus. fl. c.250
Apollonius of Perga. fl. 247–205 B.C.
Descartes, René. 1596–1650
Fermat, Pierre de. 1601–1665
Newton, Sir Isaac. 1642–1727
Euler, Leonhard. 1707–1783
Gauss, Carl Friedrich. 1777–1855
Cauchy, Augustin Louis, Baron. 1789–1857
Boole, George. 1815–1864

Weierstrass, Karl Wilhem Theodor. 1815–1897
Cantor, Georg. 1845–1918
Klein, Christian Felix. 1849–1925
Poincaré, Jules Henri. 1854–1912
Hilbert, David. 1862–1943
Russell, Bertrand Arthur William, 3rd Earl Russell. 1872–1970
Noether, Emmy. 1882–1935
Gödell, Kurt. 1906–1978
Gardner, Martin. 1914–
Robinson, Abraham. 1918–1974
Bourbaki, Nicolas. 20th century

APOLLONIUS OF PERGA. fl. 247–205 B.C.

The French geometer Chasles once compared ARCHIMEDES to Apollonius. Chasles described the former as the master of measurements (by which he meant calculating areas and volumes, especially through the "method of exhaustion"), whereas Apollonius was adept at the "geometry of forms and situations." Consequently, Apollonius is often called "the Great Geometer." He presented the first systematic treatment of conic sections and coined the terms *parabola, ellipse,* and *hyperbola,* and explored their mathematical properties. Apollonius also made important contributions to astronomy by applying his knowledge of geometry to theories about planetary motions.

BOOK BY APOLLONIUS

Apollonius of Perga. Treatise on Conic Sections. Ed. by T. L. Heath. Dover 1971 repr. of
   1896 ed. o.p. *Edited in Modern Notation with Introductions Including an Essay on the
   Earlier History of the Subject.* This is the only English version of the seven surviving
   books of the treatise on conic sections by Apollonius. This is not, however, a direct
   translation. For example, it changes the order of propositions together and
   introduces modern (as of 1896) notation to express the theorems and proofs
   presented.

ARCHIMEDES. c.287–212 B.C.

Archimedes is famous for his law of the lever and for the ingenious catapults, burning parabolic mirrors, and other war machines that he designed to defend the city of Syracuse (his birthplace) during the Second Punic War between Rome and Carthage. One of these warmachines was a mechanical crane that capsized Roman ships by turning them over. During a siege of Syracuse by the Romans, Archimedes was killed by a Roman soldier. Archimedes made fundamental contributions to hydrostatics, mechanics, and mathematical astronomy. But his greatest contributions were to theoretical mathematics. His method of exhaustion may be compared with later theories of integration because it made possible the determination of areas, volumes, surfaces, and evolutes of curved figures. Archimedes ingeniously applied the method of exhaustion to find centers of gravity, as well as using it to provide a very exact approximation for the value of π. The exclamation "Eureka" is attributed to Archimedes when he discovered that an upward force is exerted upon all floating objects.

BOOKS BY ARCHIMEDES

Geometrical Solutions Derived from Mechanics. Ed. by J. L. Heiberg. Trans. by Lydia G.
   Robinson. Open Court 1942 o.p. A short 28-page translation; includes a 6-page
   introduction. In the form of a letter to Eratosthenes, Archimedes describes his
   methods for investigating (and demonstrating or proving) mathematical questions
   using mechanical devices. Includes an introduction by D. E. Smith.
The Works of Archimedes with the Method of Archimedes. Ed. by T. L. Heath. Dover repr.
   of 1897 ed. o.p. Based on Heiberg's edition of the Greek texts (1800-1801), this book
   includes translations of Archimedes's treatises on the sphere and cylinder, measurement of the circle, on connoids and spheroids, on spirals, on the equilibrium of
   planes, on the quadrature of the parabola, and on floating bodies. It also includes a
   book of lemmas, the cattle problem, and the "sand reckoner," in which the
   maximum number of grains of sand in the universe is calculated. A thorough
   historical introduction (140 pages) provides a biography of Archimedes, lists lost
   works, discusses his relation to earlier geometers, and investigates his use of
   arithmetics (including square roots). There is also a chapter on so-called "neusis"
   problems (involving constructions of lines needed to determine mean proportionals,
   trisection of angles, and so on). Other chapters cover Archimedes's solutions of
   cubic equations, his terminology, and to what extent Archimedes may have
   anticipated the integral calculus of the seventeenth century. Also included is a

translation by Heath of Archimedes's *Method*, presumed lost but rediscovered by Heiberg in Constantinople in 1906. This is the same book listed below by Heiberg (with variations in the English translations by Heath and Robinson).

BOOK ABOUT ARCHIMEDES

Clagett, Marshall. *Archimedes in the Middle Ages.* 5 vols. Bks. Demand Vol. 1 repr. of 1964 ed. $120.00. ISBN 0-8357-9771-6. Vol. 2 o.p. Vol. 3 1978 $90.00. ISBN 0-87169-125-6. Vol. 4 1980 $40.00. ISBN 0-87169-137-X. Vol. 5 1984 $50.00. ISBN 0-87169-157-4. A comprehensive set of volumes that analyzes medieval works; includes texts and translations. Extensive scholarly introductions, notes, and commentaries all show to what degree Archimedean and quasi-Archimedean techniques were used by medieval mathematicians and scholars. Volume 5, Part 5, contains a complete bibliography, diagrams, and indexes.

BOOLE, GEORGE. 1815–1864

Born in Lincolnshire, England, George Boole was a mathematician and logician at Queens College in Cork, Ireland, where he taught and developed his theory of logic. Well respected by his friends and associates, he had a reputation of being a kind of naive saint, who thought nothing of inviting a stranger to his home to continue a conversation that the two of them had begun on a train or in a shop.

Boole's development of symbolic logic had three major emphases. First, Boole believed that mathematicians of his day unnecessarily restricted themselves to the study of quantities and did not pay enough attention to abstract symbols. Second, he concerned himself with the relation between logic and language. Third, he studied the proper representation of mental operations. Thus, Boole moved from quantity to symbols to language and finally to the rules of the thinking mind itself. In 1847 Boole expressed his ideas in a pamphlet entitled *The Mathematical Analysis of Logic.* He is now remembered for using familiar symbols of algebra and arithmetic to help represent ideas of logic. The system he used is now known as Boolean algebra. In creating his algebra of logic, Boole followed in the footsteps of the classical algebraists. Through careful analysis and resourcefulness, he developed a practical language for representing and solving a broad class of mathematical problems. Today Boole's contributions can be seen in the design of the modern digital computer.

BOOKS BY BOOLE

Derivation of the Laws. St. Sebastian Pr. 1991 $34.95. ISBN 1-879508-08-7
Laws of Thought. 1854. Dover $9.95. ISBN 0-486-60028-9. Elaborates Boole's method of applying algebraic operations to logic.
Logical Works. 1852. 2 vols. Open Court 1952–53. Vol. 1 $29.95. ISBN 0-87548-038-1. Vol. 2 $31.95. ISBN 0-87548-039-X
Treatise on the Calculus of Finite Differences. 1860. Chelsea Pub. $23.95. ISBN 0-8284-1121-2

BOURBAKI, NICOLAS. (pseud.) 20th century

Nicolas Bourbaki is the pseudonym for a group of mathematicians that included Henri Cartan, Claude Chevalley, Jean Dieudonné, and Andres Weil. Mostly French, they emphasized an axiomatic and abstract treatment on all aspects of modern mathematics in *Elements de mathematique.* The first volume of *Elements* appeared in 1939. Subsequently, a wide variety of topics have been covered, including works on set theory, algebra, general topology, functions of a real variable, topological vector spaces, and integration. One of the goals of the Bourbaki series is to make the logical structure of mathematical concepts as transparent and intelligible as possible. The books listed below are typical of volumes written in the Bourbaki spirit and now available in English.

BOOKS BY BOURBAKI

Elements of Mathematics. Addison-Wesley 1975 o.p. This series provides English translations of some of the most important works by the Bourbaki group, all of which were originally published in French. The general philosophy of the series is to • present mathematics in an axiomatic, abstract framework, proceeding from the general to the specific. Each book starts "at the beginning" and gives complete explanations. This series provides a solid foundation for the entire body of modern mathematics. Two volumes in the series, *Theory of Sets* (1968) and *Integration* (1972), are currently out of print; another, *Spectral Theories*, is expected for future publication. To date, the following volumes have been translated and are in print.
Algebra I. Spr.–Verlag 1989 $69.00. ISBN 0-387-19373-1
Algebra II. Spr.–Verlag 1990 $98.00. ISBN 0-387-19375-8
Commutative Algebra. Spr.–Verlag 1989 $69.00. ISBN 0-387-19371-5
Functions of a Real Variable. Addison-Wesley 1982 ISBN 0-201-00640-5
General Topology. Spr.–Verlag 1989. Chps. 1-4 $69.00. ISBN 0-387-19374-X. Chps. 5-10 $59.00. ISBN 0-387-19372-3
Lie Groups and Lie Algebras. Spr.–Verlag 1989 $59.00. ISBN 0-387-50218-1
Topological Vector Spaces. Spr.–Verlag 1987 $79.00. ISBN 0-387-13627-4

BOOK ABOUT BOURBAKI

Fang, J. *Bourbaki.* Paideia 1970 o.p. This book represents Part 1 of the author's series *Towards a Philosophy of Modern Mathematics*, providing a comprehensive overview of "Bourbaki." Special emphasis is given to the philosophy of mathematics underlying the group's prodigious and influential books. First, the author provides a retrospective of the history of modern mathematics. Then, the books, authors, contents, and formats of publications issued under the Bourbaki name are analyzed. The group's methods, including the abstract, the axiomatic, and the structural aspects of Bourbaki publications, are also examined. Three closing chapters cover "anti-Bourbakians," questions about mathematical creativity, and the philosophy of modern mathematics.

CANTOR, GEORG. 1845–1918

Georg Cantor was born in St. Petersburg, Russia, but was educated and lived the rest of his life in Germany. He studied in Berlin and became a professor of mathematics in 1877. He was the creator of set theory and the founder of the theory of transfinite numbers. Cantor's most important work appeared between 1895 and 1897 (translated below by P. E. B. Jourdain). Besides developing the philosophical implications of his transfinite set theory, Cantor also studied the theological implications of his work. Cantor founded the German Mathematicians Union in 1891 and served as its first president. It has been said that Cantor became mentally unstable in later life because his work was not immediately accepted by the mathematics community.

BOOK BY CANTOR

Contributions to the Founding of the Theory of Transfinite Numbers. Trans. by P. E. B. Jourdain. Dover 1955 repr. of 1915 ed. $5.95. ISBN 0-486-60045-9. This work, originally issued in two parts, represents the culmination of Cantor's mathematical research and his most mature statement of transfinite set theory. Part 1 begins with the development of Cantor's theory of simply ordered sets; Part 2 develops the theory of well-ordered sets. The book contains a long, detailed, and informative introduction by Jourdain, with historical notes and an index, which makes this edition even more useful.

BOOK ABOUT CANTOR

Dauben, Joseph W. *Georg Cantor: His Mathematics and Philosophy of the Infinite.* Princeton U. Pr. 1990 $14.95. ISBN 0-691-02447-2. This intellectual biography of the German mathematician Georg Cantor traces the origins of set theory. From Cantor's early work on trigonometric series and his rigorous definition of real numbers, it covers the discovery of nondenumerably infinite sets and his creation of transfinite numbers, resulting in his development of transfinite arithmetic and his theory of both transfinite ordinal and cardinal numbers. This book also examines the social and academic context in which Cantor's work was done, as well as the theological and psychological aspects of Cantor's interest. It includes the significance of his periods of manic depression and his theological interpretation of transfinite set theory for the development of his mathematics. This biography draws heavily on manuscripts, correspondence, and archival sources; well documented with photographs and previously unpublished material.

CAUCHY, AUGUSTIN LOUIS, BARON. 1789–1857

Baron Augustin Cauchy was one of the great figures of French science in the early nineteenth century. Born in Paris, Cauchy originally studied to become an engineer. Although he began his career as an engineer, illness forced him into mathematics. Cauchy made contributions to a wide variety of subjects in mathematical physics and applied mathematics; his most important work was in pure mathematics. As a mathematician, Cauchy made major contributions to the theory of complex functions. His name is still attached to the Cauchy-Reimann equations, as well as to other fundamental concepts in mathematics, including the Cauchy integral theorem with residues, Cauchy sequences, and the Cauchy-Kovalevskaya existence theorem for the solution of partial differential equations.

As a professor at France's famous scientific school, the École Polytechnique, Cauchy taught mathematics to the country's most able future scientists. His interest in presenting fundamental concepts through clear definitions and proofs through detailed and careful arguments is reflected in the important textbooks he wrote. In fact, many mathematicians in the nineteenth century first learned their mathematics from these textbooks. Above all, Cauchy was responsible for the famous δ—ε (delta-epsilon) method for defining many fundamental concepts in mathematics, including limits, continuity, and convergence. As a result, he could establish rigorously basic propositions of calculus. He was also the first to give an existence proof for the solution of a differential equation, as well as for a system of partial differential equations. After the revolution of 1830 in France, Cauchy was forced to live in exile in Italy and Czechoslovakia.

BOOK BY CAUCHY

Ordinary Differential Equations. Johnson Repr. 1981 o.p. This volume reproduces a substantial part of the first 13 lectures (previously unpublished) presented by Cauchy as part of his course on ordinary differential equations presented at the École Polytechnique in the early nineteenth century. Christian Gilain's lengthy introduction discusses fully (in French) Cauchy's course at the École Polytechnique. Details also are provided about Cauchy's theory of differential equations, his method of successive approximations, his existence theorems, and his overall concept of analysis. The "Résumé des Leçons" comprises 136 pages of the rest of the book;

includes an appendix listing courses taught at the École Polytechnique between 1819 and 1824. With a preface by Jean Dieudonné.

BOOK ABOUT CAUCHY

Grabiner, Judith V. *The Origins of Cauchy's Rigorous Calculus*. MIT Pr. 1981 $42.50. ISBN 0-262-07079-0. This book emphasizes the eighteenth-century concern for rigorous demonstrations in mathematics, especially where arguments using the infinite or infinitesimals in connection with the calculus were concerned. In particular Grabiner shows how Cauchy's treatment of fundamental concepts such as limits, continuity, convergence, differentiation, and so one, using the familiar δ-ε method, arose from approximation techniques, above all from the work of Lagrange (1736–1813).

DESCARTES, RENÉ. 1596–1650

Born in a small town near Tours, France, René Descartes studied at a Jesuit college from the age of 8 to the age of 18. Because he was a sickly child, Descartes was allowed to do his studying at home, remaining in bed until about 11 A.M. every day.

Descarte is best known as a philosopher, especially for his critical method of doubt and his enunciation of the so-called mind-body problem. Descartes, however, was also one of the most prominent scientific minds of his time. In mathematics, he is remembered for his development of analytic geometry, which makes use of a coordinate system. The coordinate system makes it possible to refer geometric curves to algebraic formulas expressing relations between the points of a line, curve, surface, and solid. Descartes also worked in meteorology, optics, and mechanics. Developments since the seventeenth century, however, have greatly reduced his importance in these areas. Descartes signed his name in Latin, "Renatus Cartesius." Consequently, his system of philosophy is known as Cartesian.

In 1649, Queen Kristina of Sweden asked Descartes to give her private lessons. She requested that the lessons begin at 5 A.M. and be offered three days a week. As a result of the frigid winter temperatures and early-morning schedule, Descartes contracted pneumonia and soon died.

BOOK BY DESCARTES

The Geometry of René Descartes. Trans. by D. E. Smith and M. L. Latham. Dover 1954 repr. of 1925 ed. $6.95. ISBN 0-486-60068-8. This book provides an English translation on facing pages to the original French version of Descartes's *Geometry* (1637, published as an appendix to his famous *Discours de la Method*). The book covers problems of construction using straightedge and compass, as well as the analysis of curves. The major innovation of this book is Descartes's use of coordinates and his introduction of the basic methods of his analytic geometry. Although Descartes regarded this as an application of his general philosophical method, today it represents one of the major branches of mathematics.

BOOKS ABOUT DESCARTES

Chappell, Vere, ed. *René Descartes. Essays on Modern Philosophers Ser*. Garland 1992 $120.00. ISBN 0-8153-0574-5. Series of essays representing the best recent writings on Descartes.

Clark, Desmond M. *Descartes' Philosophy of Science*. Pa. St. U. Pr. 1982 $25.00. ISBN 0-271-00325-1. This book takes a fresh look at Descartes and concludes that he was "a practising scientist who, somewhat unfortunately, wrote a few short and relatively unimportant philosophical essays" (Introduction). Thus, it emphasizes Descartes as a working scientist. Experience, experiment, reason, metaphysics, physics, modes of explanation, theory confirmation, all support a reconsideration of Descartes's two major methodological essays, *Regulae* and *Discourse on Method*. The final chapter, "Descartes: An Innovative Aristotelian," provides a summary of Clarke's conclusions about Descartes.

Federico, P. J. *Descartes on Polyhedra: A Study of the "De Solidorum Elements."* Spr.-Verlag 1982 $66.00. ISBN 0-387-90760-2. This book photoreproduces an original manuscript version (actually a copy made by Leibniz) of a text by Descartes, transcribes this into legible Latin, and then offers a translation with comments and notes of a short work by Descartes that was unknown until 1860. The manuscript is a general treatment of polyhedra and of figurate numbers related to regular and semiregular polyhedra. Federico's book begins with a short introduction, followed by a brief history of the manuscript. Background in geometry and Greek number theory is provided, as well as a review of Euler's papers on the subject of polyhedra. A comparison of Descartes's and Euler's approaches as well as their conclusions is also provided.

Gaukroger, Stephen, ed. *Descartes' Philosophy, Mathematics and Physics*. B & N Imports 1980 o.p. This book contains ten essays whose theme is Descartes's concern with providing a philosophical foundation for mathematical physics. The book discusses Cartesian optics, geometry, algebra, Descartes's union of the latter two in analytic geometry, his *mathesis universalis*, as well as concepts of force, inertia, and comparisons of Descartes with Newton, Leibniz, and others.

Moyal, Georges J., ed. *René Descartes: Critical Assessments*. 4 vols. Routledge 1991 $610.00. ISBN 0-415-02358-0. Contains 116 thoughtfully chosen articles exploring a broad range of topics about Descartes and his work.

Scott, J. F. *The Scientific Work of René Descartes* (1596–1650). Garland 1987 $48.00. ISBN 0-8240-4672-2. This book concentrates on Descartes's major discoveries in mathematics and physics. In particular, it traces the steps Descartes followed which led to the development of analytic geometry, his most influential discovery, along with his studies in geometrical optics. Also included is a brief biographical introduction to Descartes's early life and training and a general survey of Descartes's scientific work. The book then provides detailed analyses of *Discourse on Method* and Descartes's contributions in dioptrics, meteorology, and geometry. The last three chapters analyze various aspects of Descartes's *Principia Philosophiae*. The concluding chapter provides a succinct evaluation of the importance of Descartes's work in the history of science.

DIOPHANTUS. fl. c.250

Although it is known that Diophantus was a Greek who lived in Alexandria, Egypt, nothing else is known about his personal life. Many consider Diophantus the father of algebra, largely because he developed many important methods and an accompanying symbolic notation for the solution of equations. Most important, Diophantus developed methods for solving both determinate and indeterminate equations that are illustrated in his *Arithmetica*. Because the solution of indeterminate equations represents an important branch of mathematics, it is still known as Diophantine analysis.

BOOK BY DIOPHANTUS

Diophantus of Alexandria: A Study in the History of Greek Algebra. Ed. by T. L. Heath. Dover 1964 repr. of 1885 ed. o.p. This book analyzes the nature and influence of the Greek mathematician Diophantus. A long appendix presents abstracts of both problems and solutions to six books of *Arithmetica* and another work by Diophantus, *On Polygonal Numbers*. The Dover edition reprints the second edition of 1910, which added a supplementary section on approaches by Fermat and Euler to solutions of Diophantine problems.

BOOK ABOUT DIOPHANTUS

Sesiano, J., ed. *Diophantus' Arithmetica: Books IV to VI in the Arabic Translation of Qusta Ibn Luqa*. Spr.-Verlag 1982 $129.00. ISBN 0-387-90690-8. Four of seven books presumed to be lost of *Arithmetica*, by Diophantus, were discovered in Arabic translation in the Shrine Library (Meshed, Iran). These have been edited and published here with an English translation and a mathematical commentary. This critical edition includes bibliography and indexes. For conflicting views about this work, its merits and defects, see R. Rashed in *Mathematical Reviews* 85H (August 1985).

EUCLID. fl. c.300 B.C.

Little is known about the life of this important Greek mathematician. But, Euclid's compilation of the major results of ancient geometry in a comprehensive axiomatic framework remains a classic and easily the most influential scientific work of all time. The *Elements* was first translated into English by Sir Henry Billingsley in 1570. However, the standard translation from the authoritative text of Heiberg is that of Sir T. L. Heath. Beginning with definitions, axioms, and postulates, the *Elements* deduces hundreds of general theorems about plane and solid geometry, including the famous Pythagorean theorem. It is claimed that, when asked by King Ptolemy if he could make his solutions easier to follow, Euclid said, "There is no royal road to geometry,"

BOOK BY EUCLID

The Thirteen Books of Euclid's Elements. 3 vols. Ed. by T. L. Heath. Dover 1956 repr. of 1926 ed. $9.95 ea. ISBNs 0-486-60088-2, 0-486-60089-0, 0-486-60090-4. Based on Heiberg's definitive edition (1883–88), this has long been the standard version in English of Euclid's *Elements*. Heath's introductions, notes, and commentaries remain valuable. His lengthy analysis of Euclid from the traditions about him to the commentators on him are included. Also covered are principal translations, editions (current to about 1925), and an analysis of the *Elements* as a mathematical work, including its definitions, axioms, postulates, theorems, problems, and the general nature of Euclid's methods as well as almost every aspect of scholarship pertaining to Euclid. Includes Greek and English indexes.

BOOKS ABOUT EUCLID

Greenberg, Marvin J. *Euclidean and Non-Euclidean Geometries: Development and History*. W. H. Freeman 1980 $30.95. ISBN 0-7167-1103-6. This book promotes "a rigorous, historically motivated presentation of the foundations of geometry" (Preface). The book then presents "the discovery of non-Euclidean geometry and the subsequent reformulation of the foundations of Euclidean geometry as a suspense story. The mystery of why Euclid's parallel postulate could not be proved remained unsolved for over two thousand years, until the discovery of non-Euclidean geometry and its Euclidean models revealed the impossibility of any such proof. This discovery shattered the traditional conception of geometry as the true description of physical space."

Knorr, Wilbur. *The Evolution of the Euclidean Elements: A Study of the Theory of Incommensurable Magnitudes and Its Significance for Early Greek Geometry*. Kluwer Ac. 1975 o.p. This book presents a detailed analysis of the discovery of incommensurable magnitudes and the eventual development of a sophisticated theory of proportions due to Eudoxus. It provides a satisfactory theory of irrationals. Works by the Pythagoreans, Theodoros, Theaetetos, Archytas, and Eudoxus examine the question of a "pre-Euclidean foundations crisis." This is a scholarly study and an essential work for anyone interested in the technical origins of Euclidean mathematics, especially the theory of proportions constituting Book X of the *Elements*.

Mueller, Ian. *Philosophy of Mathematics and Deductive Structure in Euclid's "Elements."* MIT Pr. 1981 $50.00. ISBN 0-262-13163-3. A comprehensive study of the *Elements* using the tools of modern logic to reveal the deductive methods as Euclid employed it. Mueller draws on a vast amount of earlier literature, from Zeuthen to the more recent works of Neugebauer and Neuenschwander, to present his views. He also refers to modern philosophies of logic and mathematics, especially Hilbert's on geometry, to elucidate Euclid's view of the approach to mathematics.

Smith, Thomas. *Euclid: His Life and His System.* Found. Class Reprints 1983 repr. of 1902 ed. $127.75. ISBN 0-89901-092-X. A discursive, chatty, nontechnical discussion of Euclid and the significance of his *Elements* through the ages. Digressions to subjects such as popular literature and evolution eventually return to the exactness and significance of Euclid's methods and the impact of his great compilation.

Thomas-Stanford, Charles. *Early Editions of Euclid's Elements.* A. Wofsy Fine Arts 1977 $40.00. ISBN 0-915346-29-X. The first edition of this book was published in 1926. It covers incunabula and books printed up to 1600. The preface provides brief information about Euclid and the publishing history (including translations) of the *Elements.* The annotated bibliography of editions lists those that included not less than the first six books with demonstrations in Greek, Greek and Latin, or Latin; editions of the Enunciations only; translations into Arabic and modern European languages; and fragmentary editions in various languages. Indexes of places, printers, and publishers also are provided with plates reproducing frontispieces and examples from noteworthy editions.

EULER, LEONHARD. 1707–1783

Leonhard Euler was one of the most prolific mathematicians of all time, amassing nearly 900 publications over the course of his lifetime. Born in Basel, Switzerland, Euler spent substantial amounts of time promoting mathematics at the courts of Berlin and St. Petersburg. Euler was adept at pure and applied mathematics. His textbooks on algebra and calculus became classics and remained standard introductions to both subjects for generations. He also made seminal advances in the theory of differential equations, number theory, mechanics, astronomy, hydraulics, and the calculus of variations.

In 1738, Euler lost vision in one eye. In time, he became totally blind but continued to write. During his life, Euler published more than 800 books, most of them in Latin.

BOOKS BY EULER

Elements of Algebra. 1770. Spr.-Verlag 1984 repr. of 1840 ed. $47.00. ISBN 0-387-96014-7. This book begins with a historical perspective of Euler's life and work by C. A. Truesdell ("Leonard Euler, Supreme Geometer"); includes an annotated bibliography of biographies, works, letters, manuscripts, and so on, either by or about Euler. This is followed by an excerpt from a "Memoir of the Life and Character of Euler" by Francis Horner and Bernoulli's preface to the French edition. The book was first published in German by the Royal Academy of Sciences in St. Petersburg. Additions to the work by Lagrange accompany this edition.

Opera Omnia. Birkhäuser 1975 o.p. This volume inaugurated the fourth series in the publication of Euler's *Opera Omnia* (a joint venture of the Swiss Society of Natural Sciences and the USSR Academy of Sciences). The volume describes and summarizes nearly 3,000 letters in the correspondence, arranged chronologically and alphabetically by correspondent. A detailed introduction makes clear the pervasive significance of Euler through his correspondence with many of the greatest scientific figures of the eighteenth century. Also included is an important table listing all of Euler's papers and their location in the *Opera Omnia.*

Books about Euler

Truesdell, C. A. *Essays in the History of Mechanics.* Spr.-Verlag 1968 o.p. This volume contains previously published and unpublished essays by C. A. Truesdell on the history of mechanics. Beginning with Leonardo da Vinci, they concentrate on the eighteenth century; includes the development of rational mechanics and topics such as stress, moment, momentum, and the early kinetic theory of gases. Two chapters examine connections between the history of mechanics and modern research, and a survey of "recent advances in rational mechanics." Name and subject indexes are included.

———. *Six Lectures on Modern Natural Philosophy.* Spr.-Verlag 1966 $28.00. ISBN 0-387-03684-9. By natural philosophy Truesdell means mechanics—especially rational mechanics. The book also includes the study of materials, polar and oriented media, thermodynamics and visco-elasticity, electrified materials, and the ergodic problem in classical statistical mechanics. The final chapter examines the questions of "method and taste" in natural philosophy.

FERMAT, PIERRE DE. 1601–1665

Fermat was a contemporary of Descartes and an equally prominent French mathematician. He also was a member of the French parliament. His best-known work is in algebra, probability, and number theory. Fermat was particularly interested in the study of prime numbers and is famous for his conjecture (known as "Fermat's Last Theorem") that, if x, y, and z are positive integers, then there are no integers $n > z$ such that $x^n + y^n = z^n$. Fermat devised a method of treating geometric problems algebraically, similar to Descartes's analytic geometry. He also made discoveries concerning problems of maxima and minima that are closely related to the methods of the calculus developed later in the seventeenth century by Newton (see also Vol. 4) and Leibniz. Most of Fermat's important work was communicated by letters to friends. For example, his letters to Pascal mark the beginnings of probability theory.

Book about Fermat

Mahoney, Michael S. *The Mathematical Career of Pierre de Fermat (1601–1665).* Bks. Demand repr. of 1973 ed. $109.80. ISBN 0-317-08307-4. This book provides a comprehensive overview of Fermat's life and works; emphasizes Fermat's development of number theory and his role in promoting the use of coordinates in dealing with geometric problems algebraically. His contributions to the early development of methods related to the infinitesimal calculus (later pursued successfully by Newton and Leibniz) are covered in detail.

GARDNER, MARTIN. 1914–

Born in Tulsa, Oklahoma, the son of a wildcat oil prospector, Martin Gardner attended the University of Chicago, where he was known as a demon chess player. He quit the game, however, for his greater love—philosophy. Interestingly, in his later writings, he continued to use chess as an abstract setting for bizarre philosophical problems.

Gardner started his career as a journalist and writer. While the serious Gardner published articles on logic and mathematics in such specialist quarterlies as *Scripta Mathematica*, the playful Gardner began in 1952 to compose games for *Humpty Dumpty's*, a children's magazine in New York. He became interested in mathematics by way of paper folding, an element that was a big part of his puzzle page at *Humpty*. A friend showed him a novel way to fold a strip of paper into a series of hexagons, which led to an article on combinatorial geometry in *Scientific American* in December 1956. He is probably best known, however, for his mathematical games column for the magazine *Scientific American*, as well as for *The Annotated Alice*, one of more than 20 books of light verse, puzzles, and essays—books inspired by Gardner's love for wordplay.

Gardner's talent for combining math, science, philosophy, literature, and a passion for magic has resulted in the publication of a great many unusual books of diverse natures. His first book, *In the Name of Science*, was reviewed by the *San Francisco Chronicle*, which noted: "Mr. Gardner has written a highly critical and at times hilariously entertaining account of cults and fad sciences in various fields."

BOOKS BY GARDNER

Aha! Gotcha: Paradoxes to Puzzle and Delight. W. H. Freeman 1982 $10.95. ISBN 0-7167-1361-6. Puzzles from *Scientific American* that involve mathematics and logic.

Aha! Insight. W. H. Freeman 1978 $11.95. ISBN 0-7167-1017-X Puzzles, paradoxes, and amusements.

The Ambidextrous Universe. Macmillan 1979 o.p.

Entertaining Mathematical Puzzles. Dover 1986 $2.95. ISBN 0-486-25211-6

Hexaflexagons and Other Mathematical Diversions. U. Ch. Pr. 1988 $10.95. ISBN 0-226-28254-6

Mathematical Carnival: A New Round-Up of Tantalizers and Puzzles from "Scientific American." Random 1977 $12.45. ISBN 0-394-72349-X

Mathematical Circus. Math. Assn. 1992 $19.50. ISBN 0-88385-506-2

Mathematical Magic Show. Math. Assn. 1990 $19.50. ISBN 0-88385-449-X. Offers a revised collection of Gardner's well-known columns on mathematical recreations from *Scientific American*. Covers mathematical card tricks, word puzzles, dice games, and various topics of mathematical interest.

Mathematics, Magic, and Mystery. Dover 1956 $3.95. ISBN 0-486-20335-2

Perplexing Puzzles and Tantalizing Teasers. Dover 1988 $3.95. ISBN 0-486-25637-5

The Second Scientific American Book of Mathematical Puzzles and Diversions. U. Ch. Pr. 1987 $12.95. ISBN 0-226-28253-8. More puzzles taken from Gardner's magazine column.

Time Travel and Other Mathematical Bewilderments. W. H. Freeman 1987 $12.95. ISBN 0-7167-1925-8

Wheels, Life, and Other Mathematical Amusements. W. H. Freeman 1983 $13.95. ISBN 0-7167-1589-9. Puzzles and amusements.

GAUSS, CARL FRIEDRICH. 1777–1855

Whereas Euler was the most prolific mathematician of the eighteenth century, Gauss was the most profound. His motto, *pauca sed matura* ("few, but ripe"), reflected his belief that one should publish only the most developed and complete expositions of results as possible. His most influential work was in number theory. *Disquisitiones Arithmeticae* was remarkable in the number and difficulty of problems it solved and still remains a useful introduction and guide to development of the number theory. In addition to his important contributions to physics and astronomy, Gauss was also an early contributor to the theory of statistics. For example, his method of least squares and results concerning the "Gaussian" or normal curve are still essential. The great genius of Gauss was noticed by the Duke of Brunswick, who paid for Gauss's education at the Collegium Carolinum and the University of Göttingen.

BOOK BY GAUSS

Disquisitiones Arithmeticae. Trans. by A. A. Clarke. Rev. by W. C. Waterhouse (with C. Greither and A. W. Grootendorst). Spr.-Verlag 1986 $87.00. ISBN 0-387-96254-9.

The Waterhouse edition is reprinted from the edition by Yale University Press of 1966. This version was translated from the second German edition of 1870. Covers topics such as congruences, residues, sections of a circle, forms, and indeterminate equations. According to W. K. Buehler, the English translation is not "everywhere reliable" (see [below] Buehler, *Gauss*).

BOOKS ABOUT GAUSS

Buehler, W. K. *Gauss: A Biographical Study.* Spr.-Verlag 1987 $49.80. ISBN 0-387-10662-6. This book examines Gauss's life from his birth, childhood, and student years in Göttingen (1795–98), until his death in 1855. It presents contemporary political and social background, his family life and several marriages. Above all the book devotes separate chapters to Gauss's major contributions to mathematics in number theory, arithmetic, the orbit of Ceres, *Disquisitiones Arithmeticae*, modular forms, elliptic and hypergeometric functions, geodesy and geometry, physics, astronomy, dioptrics, and the method of least squares. Appendixes offer a survey of Gauss's collected works, an analysis of secondary literature about Gauss, and an index of his works.

Dunnington, G. W. *Carl Friedrich Gauss: Titan of Science.* Exposition Pr. 1955 o.p. This study of Gauss's life and work is based on contemporary sources, both manuscript and printed. It emphasizes Gauss as a man and scientist in the context of the times in which he lived. This well-illustrated book is expository with little detail given to Gauss's technical achievements in pure mathematics.

Hall, T. *Carl Friedrich Gauss: A Biography.* Trans. by A. Froderbart. MIT Pr. 1970 o.p. This book does not feature mathematical technicalities. Instead, it presents "Gauss's most important results by formulating the problems, saying something about their origin, and illustrating them with concrete examples." Nevertheless, it includes some equations and derivations to give readers a sense of how Gauss worked and the major results that he obtained in pure and applied mathematics.

Merzbach, Uta, ed. *Carl Friedrich Gauss: A Bibliography.* Scholarly Res. Inc. 1984 $100.00. ISBN 0-8420-2169-8. This compilation includes a list of primary sources and translations, a guide to Gauss's correspondence, and an extensive list of secondary sources about Gauss; focuses on the history of mathematics. Annotations are provided for general works, indicating their usefulness. Key-word indexing is also provided. Letter and manuscript locations (other than Göttingen) are given; indexes include a list of names known to Gauss, as well as an index of topics covered.

GÖDEL, KURT. 1906–1978

Kurt Gödel was probably the most outstanding logician of the first half of the twentieth century. Born in Czechoslovakia, Gödel studied and taught in Vienna and then came to the United States in 1940 as a member of the Institute for Advanced Study at Princeton University. In 1953 he was made a professor at the institute, where he remained until his death in 1978. Gödel is especially well known for his studies of the completeness of logic, the incompleteness of number theory, and the consistency of the axiom of choice and the continuum hypothesis. Gödel is also known for his work on constructivity, the decision problem, and the foundations of computation theory, as well as his views on the philosophy of mathematics, especially his support of a strong form of Platonism in mathematics.

BOOKS BY GÖDEL

Collected Works of Kurt Gödel. Vol. 1 Ed. by Solomon Feferman and others. OUP 1986 $45.00. ISBN 0-19-503964-5. This is the first of a projected three volumes that present a comprehensive edition of the mathematical and philosophical works of the logician Kurt Gödel. Each article (or closely related group of articles) places Gödel's works in detailed historical contexts. English translations are provided for all works by Gödel (originally in German). A detailed and informative biographical essay by Solomon Feferman constitutes the introductory chapter of Volume 1. Numerous photographs of Gödel, his family, friends, and colleagues also enrich this volume. Volume 1 covers Gödel's works through 1936, including his dissertation.

Consistency of the Continuum Hypothesis. Princeton U. Pr. 1940 $18.00. ISBN 0-691-07927-7. This volume was compiled from notes taken by G. W. Brown of lectures Gödel gave at the Institute for Advanced Study, Princeton, during the autumn terms of 1938 and 1939. It contains the essence of Gödel's famous work related to the axiomatic consistency of Cantor's celebrated continuum hypothesis. In his lectures, Gödel claimed that the axiom of choice and Cantor's generalized continuum hypothesis were both consistent with the other axioms of set theory (assuming the axioms of set theory were consistent) within the Zermelo-Fraenkel set theory. Five pages of notes and a revised bibliography were added at the second and subsequent printings.

On Formally Undecidable Propositions of Principia Mathematica. . . . Trans. by B. Meltzer. Basic 1962 o.p. In this famous work, Gödel showed that every system of arithmetic contains arithmetical propositions (e.g., propositions concerned solely with relations between whole numbers), which can neither be proved nor disproved within the system. A brief introduction by R. B. Braithwaite includes a description of metamathematics, Gödel's method of "arithmetization," recursiveness, consistency, the unprovability-of-consistency theorem, as well as the syntactical character of Gödel's theorems.

BOOKS ABOUT GÖDEL

Gensler, Harry J. *Gödel's Theorem Simplified.* U. Pr. of Amer. 1984 $13.50. ISBN 0-8191-3869-X. This book tries to prove—in as simple and direct a way as possible—Gödel's famous proof that it is impossible to reduce basic arithmetic to an axiomatic system. This shows that no possible axiomatic system suffices to prove every truth (but no falsehood) of arithmetic. Only high school algebra is required. Symbolic logic (to the extent that Gensler uses it) is explained when necessary.

Mostowski, Andrej. *Sentences Undecidable in Formalized Arithmetic: An Exposition of the Theory of Kurt Gödel.* Greenwood 1982 repr. of 1952 ed. $35.00. ISBN 0-313-23151-6. "In the present booklet, an attempt is made to present as clearly and as rigorously as possible the famous theory of undecidable sentences created by Kurt Gödel in 1931." Highlighting Gödel's use of K-definability to develop his book, Mostowski adds that "in terms of the general theory of K-definable functions and relations it is possible to express clearly and conveniently the assumptions which are the common source of the various proofs of Gödel's incompleteness theorem formulated first by Gödel himself and then by Tarski and Rosser. It seems probable that the theory of K-definability will prove useful also in other logical researches" (Preface).

HILBERT, DAVID. 1862–1943

Born in Königsberg, Germany, David Hilbert was professor of mathematics at Göttingen from 1895 to 1930. Hilbert was among the earliest adherents of CANTOR's new transfinite set theory. Despite the controversy that arose over the subject, Hilbert maintained that "no one shall drive us from this paradise (of the infinite)" (Hilbert, "Über das Unendliche," *Mathematische Annalen* [1926]). It has been said that Hilbert was the last of the great universalist mathematicians and that he was knowledgeable in every area of mathematics, making important contributions to all of them (the same has been said of POINCARÉ). Hilbert's publications include impressive works on algebra and number theory (by applying methods of analysis he was able to solve the famous "Waring's Problem"). Hilbert also made many contributions to analysis, especially the theory of functions and integral equations, as well as mathematical physics, logic, and the foundations of mathematics. His work of 1899, *Grundlagen der*

Geometrie, brought Hilbert's name to international prominence, because it was based on an entirely new understanding of the nature of axioms. Hilbert adopted a formalist view and stressed the significance of determining the consistency and independence of the axioms in question. In 1900 he again captured the imagination of an international audience with his famous "23 unsolved problems" of mathematics, many of which became major areas of intensive research in this century. Some of the problems remain unresolved to this day. At the end of his career, Hilbert became engrossed in the problem of providing a logically satisfactory foundation for all of mathematics. As a result, he developed a comprehensive program to establish the consistency of axiomatized systems in terms of a metamathematical proof theory.

In 1925, Hilbert became ill with pernicious anemia—then an incurable disease. However, because Minot had just discovered a treatment, Hilbert lived for another 18 years.

BOOKS BY HILBERT

Foundations of Geometry. Trans. by E. J. Townsend. Open Court 1980 $9.00. ISBN 0-87548-164-7. This translation by E. J. Townsend represents a course of lectures given by Hilbert at the University of Göttingen in 1898 and 1899, incorporating some additions made by Hilbert for a subsequent French edition. The lectures analyze the intuition of space in terms of definitions, axioms, and a study of their relations; special attention is given to the logical development of Euclidean geometry. Of particular importance are questions of the independence of the axioms, consistency, and completeness. Also covered are plane areas, the theory of proportion, Desargues's theorem, Pascal's theorem, and geometric constructions. A substantive conclusion and appendix discuss the significance of non-Euclidean geometrics and the important work of S. Lie, M. Dehn, G. Cantor, and C. Jordan.

Gesammelte Abhandlungen. 3 vols. Chelsea Pub. 1981 repr. of 1932–35 ed. $19.50. ISBN 0-8284-0195-0. Vol. 2–3 o.p. Volume 1 consists of papers by Hilbert on number theory, including his lengthy report for *Jahresbericht der Deutschen Mathematikervereinigung*. A detailed analysis and "appreciation" of Hilbert's "algebraisch-zahlentheoretischen" works by Helmut Hasse appears at the end of the volume. Volume 2 covers algebra, invariant theory, and geometry, with an overview of Hilbert's accomplishments in algebra and invariant theory by B. L. van der Waerden; Arnold Schmidt wrote the analysis of Hilbert's work in geometry. Volume 3 covers analysis, foundations of mathematics, physics, and varia. There is a paper discussing Hilbert's work on integral equations by Ernst Hellinger, and another on foundations of mathematics by Paul Bernays. Volume 3 contains a biographical article by Otto Blumenthal, including a list of Hilbert's lectures at Göttingen, dissertations written under him, and a list of works not reprinted in *Gesammelte Abhandlungen*.

BOOK ABOUT HILBERT

Reid, Constance. *Hilbert*. Spr.-Verlag 1970 1986 $39.00. ISBN 0-387-96256-5. This detailed and captivating biography was written, as Reid says, "largely from memory" (Preface). It is based on extensive archival and other written and published resources. The book covers Hilbert's youth and childhood friends, interests in pure and applied mathematics, as well as Hilbert's long interest in the philosophy and foundations of mathematics, especially in axiomatic and logical foundations and in the nature and legitimacy of the infinite. The book is written in an expository, nontechnical style and includes many illustrations. An appendix reprints a shortened version of Hermann Weyl's assessment of Hilbert's career, "David Hilbert and His Mathematical Work" from the *Bulletin of the American Mathematical Society*, 1944.

KLEIN, CHRISTIAN FELIX. 1849–1925

Born in Düsseldorf, Germany, Felix Klein began his academic career as an assistant to the geometrician Julius Plücker at the University of Bonn. After

Plücker's death in 1868, Klein set his own course on a long, brilliant mathematical career, one linked to the universities of Erlangen and Göttingen. While still a young man, he made Erlangen the base for his mathematical research, which revolutionized geometry. It was at Göttingen, however, that Klein established long and fruitful relationships with colleagues such as DAVID HILBERT and students and protégés such as EMMY NOETHER.

In 1872 Klein presented his views on geometry in an address that became known as the *Erlanger Programm*. Its effect was to unify the various special geometries that had accumulated in the decades and centuries that preceded. In the scheme that Klein laid out, geometry is set forth as the study of those properties of figures that remain invariant (unchanged) under a certain group of transformations. For example, plane Euclidean geometry can be thought of as the study of properties, such as lengths and areas, that remain unchanged under the group of rigid transformations such as translations (shifts) and rotations in the plane. Klein showed that a group of transformations can also be established for more general geometries that do not preserve lengths or area but do preserve other properties. For example, in the transformation group for projective geometry, an ellipse is not necessarily preserved as an ellipse, but it is preserved as a conic section, perhaps as a hyperbola or a parabola.

As a result of Klein's vision, it became possible to create a kind of organization chart for geometry in which each existing branch of geometry fits above, below, or alongside each of the others. Klein's program also contains some surprises. It shows that Euclidean, hyperbolic, and elliptic geometries are all special cases of projective geometry. This fact in turn means that, if the non-Euclidean geometries are ever shown to be inconsistent, as some opponents of those geometries were trying to prove, then the established projective geometry would be inconsistent also.

In his *Development of Mathematics in the Nineteenth Century* (1926–27) Klein chronicles and interprets the rise of modern mathematics and its rich and many facets. This work is still regarded by some historians of mathematics as the finest such history ever written.

BOOKS BY KLEIN

Development of Mathematics in the Nineteenth Century. Math. Sci. Pr. 1979 $60.00. ISBN 0-915692-28-7
Famous Problems of Elementary Geometry and other Monographs. 1894. Chelsea Pub. 1956 $14.95. ISBN 0-8284-0108-X. Papers by Klein and others; the title paper was written by Klein for teachers.

NEWTON, SIR ISAAC. 1642–1727

Born in Colsterworth, England, Isaac Newton attended Trinity College, Cambridge, in 1661, after an unsuccessful attempt at farming. Newton is unquestionably one of the world's greatest scientists. He is best known for his theory of universal gravitation, first published in his book of 1687, *Mathematical Principles of Natural Philosophy* (often referred to as the *Principia*). As early as 1666, however, Newton had already worked out many of his most important ideas in physics and mathematics, including his discovery of the binomial theorem and invention of the infinitesimal calculus. Newton's calculus was developed in terms of fluxions and fluents—now called differentiation and integration. Newton succeeded in relating a method of finding areas under curves with another for finding tangents to curves. This enabled Newton to calculate the lengths of curves and areas of plane figures, to solve basic problems of maxima and minima, and to advance new results through numerous applications to problems of velocity, acceleration, and other problems of mathematical astronomy and physics.

Newton was very modest. Shortly before his death, he said: "I do not know what I appear to the world, but to myself I seem to have been only like a boy playing on the seashore, and diverting myself in now and then finding a smoother pebble or a prettier shell than ordinary, whilst the great ocean of truth lay all undiscovered before me."

BOOKS BY NEWTON

The Mathematical Papers of Isaac Newton. 8 vols. Ed. by D. T. Whiteside. Cambridge U. Pr. Vol. 1 o.p. Vol. 2 o.p. Vol. 3 *1670–1673.* 1969 $155.00. ISBN 0-521-07119-4. Vol. 4 *1674–1684.* 1971 $175.00. ISBN 0-521-07740-0. Vol. 5 *1683–1684.* 1972 $182.50. ISBN 0-521-08262-5. Vol. 6 *1684–1691.* 1975 $182.50. ISBN 0-521-08719-8. Vol. 7 *1691–1695.* 1977 $222.50. ISBN 0-521-08720-1. Vol. 8 *1697–1722.* 1981 $240.00. ISBN 0-521-20103-9

The Mathematical Works of Isaac Newton. 2 vols. Ed. by D. T. Whiteside. Johnson repr. 1964–67 o.p. This edition (by a dozen scholars on the subject of Newton's mathematics) reprints in facsimile several important short works by Newton on mathematics or about his methods of quadrature of curves, fluxions, and infinite series, which are all related to the calculus. Volume 2 reprints three works on algebra, finite differences, and geometry, including Newton's famous "universal arithmetic." Brief historical and analytic introductions by D. T. Whiteside accompany each volume.

BOOK ABOUT NEWTON

Westfall, Richard S. *Never at Rest: A Biography of Isaac Newton.* Cambridge U. Pr. 1983 $29.95. ISBN 0-521-27435-4. This exhaustive 908-page biography (with many illustrations) covers every facet of Newton's life from cradle to grave. It gives a detailed account of the progress, meteoric rise, influence, and eventual decline of one of the world's greatest scientific figures. It features Newton's mathematics, including invention of the calculus and the infamous priority dispute with Leibniz, without becoming overly technical. A comprehensive bibliographical essay is a useful guide to major sources of material related to Newtonian studies.

NOETHER, EMMY (AMALAIE). 1882–1935

Born in Erlangen, Germany, Amalaie (her actual name) Noether was the daughter of a mathematician, Max Noether. Noether was perhaps the most important female mathematician in the early twentieth century. She studied at Erlangen and Göttingen in Germany, and taught at Göttingen, Moscow, and Frankfurt. When Noether was invited by DAVID HILBERT to work at the University of Göttingen in 1915, she was not allowed to assume a full academic position. As a woman, Noether had to work in an "honorary" capacity. She immigrated to the United States (and Bryn Mawr College) in 1933, when Jewish professors were being dismissed from German universities by the Nazi government. Her most important work was in abstract algebra, making notable contributions such as her theory of primary ideals and finding that polynomial ideals had useful applications in algebraic geometry. Noether also made significant discoveries in the theory of noncummutative rings in linear algebra and used the idea of the cross product to resolve major questions about noncummutative algebras.

BOOK BY NOETHER

Collected Papers. Ed. by Nathan Jacobson. Spr.-Verlag 1983 $89.00. ISBN 0-387-11504-8. This volume contains 43 of Noether's papers, notes on lectures she gave at Göttingen on hypercomplex numbers in 1929 (containing her first account of crossed products), and a paper by H. Kapferer, part of which was jointly written by Noether. An address by P. S. Alexandrov, "In Memory of Emmy Noether," opens the book, followed by an introduction surveying her major accomplishments by Nathan Jacobson.

BOOKS ABOUT NOETHER

Dick, Auguste. *Emmy Noether, 1882–1935.* Trans. by H. I. Blocher. Birkhauser 1980 $17.50. ISBN 0-8176-0519-3. This English translation contains some additions by Dick to Noether's original German text of 1968. It is both a personal and professional account of Noether's life and her mathematics, presented with limited technical explanations and without full mathematical detail. Obituaries of Noether or notices of her life and work by A. Einstein, B. L. van der Waerden, H. Weyl, and P. S. Alexandrov also are included.

Srinivasan, Bhama, and Judith D. Sally, eds. *Emmy Noether in Bryn Mawr: Proceedings of a Symposium Sponsored by the Association of Women in Mathematics in Honor of Emmy Noether's 100th Birthday.* Spr.-Verlag 1983 $54.00. ISBN 0-387-90838-2. This book contains scientific lectures about mathematics related to topics on which Emmy Noether had worked, as well as a paper prepared for a panel discussion, "Emmy Noether in Erlangen, Göttingen, and Bryn Mawr." The book also includes two articles, "The Study of Linear Associative Algebras in the United States, 1870–1927" by Jeanne La Duke and "Emmy Noether: Historical Contexts" by Uta Merzbach.

POINCARÉ, JULES HENRI. 1854–1912

Jules Henri Poincaré is considered by many to be the last of the great universalist mathematicians, one who could comprehend and make significant contributions to virtually all branches of mathematics known in his day (the same has been said of HILBERT). Poincaré studied at the École Polytechnique, becoming professor of mathematics in 1881. Poincaré also did important work in mathematical physics and astronomy. Above all, he opened many new fields to mathematicians, especially algebraic topology. He also made singular discoveries in the theory of complex variables (especially his discovery of automorphic functions), differential equations, and celestial mechanics. In addition, Poincaré wrote for general audiences, making important contributions to both the philosophy and foundations of mathematics.

BOOK BY POINCARÉ

Papers on Fuchsian Functions. Trans. by J. Stillwell. Spr.-Verlag 1985 $49.00. ISBN 0-387-96215-8. This is one of the areas in which Poincaré made important and original contributions that grew out of his dissertation on existence theorems for differential equations.

BOOK ABOUT POINCARÉ

Slosson, Edwin E. *Major Prophets of Today.* Ayer repr. of 1914 ed. $20.00. ISBN 0-8369-0882-1. This work is composed of brief biographies of significant personalities at the turn of the twentieth century; each biography serves as an introduction to the writings of specific authors. The chapter on Poincaré is somewhat rambling, concentrating more on philosophy than science. The origins of scientific inspirations and creativity are discussed. A critical bibliographic essay, "How to Read Poincaré," provides a dated list of works about Poincaré.

PYTHAGORAS c.580 B.C.–c.500 B.C.

Little is known of the life of the ancient Greek mathematician Pythagoras. This may be due to the influence of the mystical society that he founded, since its reclusive and communal nature discouraged the release of any information about its doings. Nevertheless, the influence of Pythagoras on mathematics is profound because of the famous theorem that carries his name—the Pythagorean Theorem. (The theorem states that, if a and b are the lengths of the two legs of a right triangle and if c is the length of the hypotenuse, then $a^2 + b^2 = c^2$.)

It is unlikely that Pythagoras actually discovered the relationship that bears his name. But he may have been the first to prove it. The relationship was probably known and used by other ancients, such as the Egyptians and the Babylonians. The Pythagorean approach to the right-triangle relationship, however, is fundamentally different from that of the Babylonians and the Egyptians. They were interested in the relationship as a means of solving certain specific problems in measurement, while Pythagoras and his followers were interested in the fact that the theorem expressed a fundamental geometric relationship that was true for all right triangles. It is this attitude that characterized the Pythagoreans as mathematicians in the modern sense of the word.

This mathematical attitude also can be seen in the way in which Pythagoras approached arithmetic, not as a computational skill, but as the study of the properties of numbers. From the Pythagorean point of view, the proper role of arithmetic—and also of geometry, music, and astronomy—is to help a conscientious seeker of knowledge attain a better appreciation of truth and beauty. The Pythagoreans regarded numbers, especially whole, or counting, numbers, as a supreme example of abstractions that are eternal and unchanging. This point of view is reflected in their overall mystical philosophy.

Books by Pythagoras

The Golden Verses of Pythagoras (late sixth century B.C.). *Sacred Texts Ser.* Concord Grove 1983 o.p.

The Pythagorean Writings: Hellenistic Texts from the First Century B.C. to 3rd Century A.D. Ed. by Robert Naron. Trans. by Kenneth Guthrie. Selene Bks. 1986 $36.00. ISBN 0-933601-01-8.

Books about Pythagoras

Gorman, Peter. *Pythagoras: A Life.* Routledge 1978 $29.95. ISBN 0-7100-0006-5. Scholarly biography.

Hallam, Arthur F. *William Lloyd's Life of Pythagoras, with a New Thesis on the Origin of the New Testament.* Capitalist Pr. OH 1982 $8.50. ISBN 0-938770-01-2. Examination of William Lloyd's classic biography of Pythagoras.

Iamblicus *et al. The Pythagorean Sourcebook and Library: An Anthology of Ancient Writings Which Relate to Pythagoras and Pythagorean Philosophy.* Ed. by Kenneth S. Guthrie. Phanes Pr. 1987 $17.00. ISBN 0-933999-51-8. Collection of original writings from ancient Greek and Roman times that indicates the influence of Pythagoras' view of knowledge and traces the evolution of Pythagoreanism as a philosophy.

Levin, Flora R. *The Harmonics of Nicomachus and the Pythagorean Tradition.* Scholars Pr. GA 1974 $10.95. ISBN 0-89130-241-7. Scholarly work focusing on the relation between the philosopher Nicomachus' work on harmonics and the influence of the Pythagorean outlook.

Loomis, Elisha S. *Pythagorean Proposition. Classics in Mathematics Education Ser.* NCTM 1968 o.p. Discussion of the mathematics of Pythagoras.

McQuaid, Gary. *Pythagoras: The Reality of the New Computer Age.* Heridonius 1990
$24.95. ISBN 0-940539-11-X. Pythagoras' viewpoint on numbers and its relevance to
the computer age.

Oliver, George. *The Pythagorean Triangle: The Science of Numbers.* Kessinger Publ. 1993
$17.95. ISBN 1-56459-372-X. Examination of the meaning and significance of the
triangle and its relationships in Pythagorean philosophy and mathematics.

O'Meara, Dominic J. *Pythagoras Revived: Mathematics and Philosophy in Late Antiquity.*
OUP 1989 $49.95. ISBN 0-19-824485-1. Examines the process by which Pythagorean
philosophy in general and Pythagorean mathematics in particular were reestablished
in late antiquity.

Philip, James A. *Pythagoras and Early Pythagoreanism.* Phoenix Ser. Supplement. Bks.
Demand $58.00. ISBN 0-317-08752-5. Focuses on the origins and early development
of Pythagorean philosophy.

ROBINSON, ABRAHAM. 1918–1974

Abraham Robinson is best known among mathematicians for his revolutionary discovery and development of nonstandard analysis, a rigorous theory of
infinitesimals that Robinson used to unite mathematical logic with the larger
body of modern mathematics. Born in Waldenburg, Lower Silesia, in 1918,
Robinson spent much of his childhood in Breslau. In 1933, he emigrated from
Nazi Germany to Palestine, where he studied mathematics at the Hebrew
University with Abraham Fraenkel. Robinson studied briefly at the Sorbonne,
barely escaping to England when the Germans invaded France in June 1940.
During World War II, he worked at the Royal Aircraft Establishment in
Farnborough, analyzing the design of supersonic airfoils. Beginning with his
Ph.D. on model theory at the University of London in 1949, Robinson began to
eclipse his wartime aeronautical research. Robinson first taught at the Cranfield
College of Aeronautics and, beginning in 1951, in the Mathematics Department
at the University of Toronto. In 1957, he returned to pure mathematics as
Fraenkel's successor at Hebrew University and was appointed a professor of
mathematics and philosophy at the University of California, Los Angeles, in
1962. Robinson finally moved to a position at Yale University in 1967, where he
continued his research on model theory and nonstandard analysis until his
untimely death in 1974.

BOOKS BY ROBINSON

Complete Theories. Elsevier 2nd rev. ed. 1977 $56.50. ISBN 0-7204-0690-0. Offers a
revised edition of one of Robinson's most important works. Features his lasting
contributions to modern mathematics: the application of mathematical logic via
model theory to modern algebra.

Numbers and Ideals. Holden-Day 1965 $16.00. ISBN 0-8162-7234-4. Stimulates interest in
the simplicity and beauty (as well as the power) of abstract algebra applied to
familiar concepts such as the integers. Shows how basic ideas in modern algebra,
including groups, rings, primes and ideals, lead to general, but powerful results. A
related goal is to encourage students to think like mathematicians, and ultimately
reveal "some of the beauty of the subject in a concrete case" (p. 102).

Selected Papers of Abraham Robinson. 3 vols. H. J. Keisler, S. Körner, W.A.J. Luxemburg,
and A. D. Young. Yale U. Pr. 1979 o.p. Volume 1 presents a selection of Robinson's
most influential papers on model theory and algebra. Volume 2 reprints many of
Robinson's revolutionary contributions to nonstandard analysis and papers on the
philosophy of mathematics. Volume 3 is devoted to Robinson's many publications
on aerodynamics. Each volume contains a lengthy biographical study by George
Seligman, a colleague of Robinson's at Yale University, as well as individual prefaces
to the special topics in each volume; written by experts who also have made
significant contributions to areas related to Robinson's research.

RUSSELL, BERTRAND ARTHUR WILLIAM, 3rd EARL RUSSELL. 1872–1970 (NOBEL PRIZE 1950)

Born in England, Bertrand Russell was educated at Trinity College, Cambridge. After writing his dissertation at Cambridge University on the foundations of geometry (published in 1897), Russell assumed a special lectureship in logic and philosophy of mathematics at Cambridge. His primary scientific interest at the time concerned a general study of the principles of mathematics, which he believed could be reduced to a small set of fundamental principles. Eventually, he collaborated with his colleague ALFRED NORTH WHITEHEAD (see Vol. 4), to produce the monumental *Principia Mathematica*. Russell's interest in the paradoxes of set theory and logic led to his formulating a theory of types that was unsuccessful in saving mathematical logic from the proof (later given by GÖDEL, that no axiomatic system can be proved to be self-consistent—one of the goals *Principia Mathematica* had set for itself). A nontechnical exposition of the major intent and significance of *Principia Mathematica* was written by Russell in his *Introduction to Mathematical Philosophy*. In 1931, he attained the status of British nobility, becoming Lord Russell. In his later life, Russell was a staunch advocate of nuclear disarmament.

BOOKS BY RUSSELL

Essays in Analysis. Ed. by D. Lackey. Allen & Unwin 1973 o.p. This collection of essays by Russell focuses on the period from 1904 to 1913 leading up to his development of a mature theory of type, as well as publication of his monumental effort with Whitehead, *Principia Mathematica*. Includes three previously unpublished papers (from the Bertrand Russell Archives at McMaster University, Ontario, Canada) and two English translations of articles originally published in French. A brief introduction sets Russell's work against the background of influences on his approach to mathematics and logic—namely figures like Peano, Frege, Cantor, Whitehead, and later Wittgenstein. The appendix includes a useful bibliography of Russell's writings on logic (published and unpublished).

Introduction to Mathematical Philosophy. 1919 S&S Trade 1971 o.p. A nontechnical explanation of the ideas set forth in *Principia Mathematica*.

Principia Mathematica. (coauthored with Alfred North Whitehead). 1910–13. 3 vols. Cambridge U. Pr. 1925–27 $42.00. ISBN 0-231-04460-7

The Principles of Mathematics. Norton 1964 repr. of 1903 ed. $12.95. ISBN 0-393-00249-7. Russell's major exposition of his philosophy of mathematics, namely logicism. It contains detailed discussions of many important mathematicians and their contributions to mathematics and logic at the turn of the twentieth century. Russell also explains his famous paradox and draws the implications of the antinomies of set theory for the foundations of mathematics. The book contains an appendix on Russell's early ideas for a theory of types, later incorporated as a fundamental idea of *Principia Mathematica*.

BOOK ABOUT RUSSELL

Grattan-Guinness, Ivor. *Dear Russell—Dear Jourdain: A Commentary on Russell's Logic, Based on His Correspondence with Philip Jourdain.* Col. U. Pr. 1977 $42.00. ISBN 0-231-04460-7. This book provides running commentary and analysis by the author of an exchange of letters between two British philosopher-mathematicians during the early twentieth century—from March 1902 until Jourdain's early death in October 1919. Jourdain was especially concerned with attempts to resolve the paradoxes of set theory and prove the well-ordering principle. (Zermelo's Axiom of Choice). At the time, Russell was concerned with set theory and the paradoxes, and was also engaged with Whitehead in writing *Principia Mathematica*.

WEIERSTRASS, KARL WILHELM THEODOR. 1815–1897

After an unhappy period as a high school teacher, Karl Wilhelm Weierstrass was offered a position teaching in Berlin in 1856 on the strength of his publication of a paper on Abelian functions. Later, at the University of Berlin, he became the center of an important circle of younger mathematicians who carried out his approach to "arithmeticizing" mathematics, which was particularly influential in the latter part of the nineteenth century. In fact, supplying rigorous foundations to all mathematical arguments was one of his major preoccupations. Among the areas of research pursued by Weierstrass, the most important were analytic functions, elliptic and hyperelliptic functions, Abelian functions, and the calculus of variations. Although Weierstrass published few books and papers, he was well known for his lectures.

BOOK BY WEIERSTRASS

Mathematische Werke. 7 vols. 1894–1927. Johnson Repr. o.p. Prepared by Weierstrass with his remarks to many of the papers and revisions to some papers by colleagues and former students (as acknowledged at the end of each volume). Volumes 1, 2, and 3 contain mathematical papers; Volumes 4, 5, 6, and 7 contain lectures on the theory of elliptic and Abelian functions, as well as the variational calculus.

CHAPTER 16

Statistics and Probability

Jean Dickinson Gibbons

> It is remarkable that a science which began with the consideration of games of chance should have become the most important object of human knowledge. . . . The most important questions of life are, for the most part, really only problems of probability.
> — PIERRE SIMON LAPLACE, *Theorie Analytiques des Probabilités*

> Statistical thinking will one day be as necessary for efficient citizenship as the ability to read and write.
> —H. G. WELLS, *The Shape of Things to Come*

The news media often issue statements about statistics and probability. But few people understand what these terms mean, much less how to use them properly. As MARK TWAIN (see Vol. 1) once said, "Collecting data is much like collecting garbage. You must know in advance what you are going to do with the stuff before you collect it."

The likelihood that a particular event or outcome will occur is its probability. Probability is expressed as a number between zero and one. Zero indicates almost no chance of an event or outcome, and one indicates an almost certain chance of occurrence. Sometimes probabilities are stated as percentages between 0 and 100; for example, there is an 80 percent chance of rain. Probabilities are also given as odds. If the odds for an event's occurrence are given as "x to y," the probability of the event occurring is x divided by x + y. The odds against the occurrence of this same event are "y to x." For example, suppose that the odds for a football team winning its game are 4 to 1. The probability that the team will win is 4/5, or an 80 percent chance. In this example, probability is stated as a measure of degree of certainty that an event or outcome will occur.

The word *statistic* refers to a single number. A collection of numbers, or data, are frequently called statistics. However, statistics also can be defined as a singular noun. Statistics is the methodology of collecting, describing, and analyzing data, as well as using data to make estimates, inferences, and decisions. The foundation of statistics is the theory of probability.

A statistician is a person who studies data in numerical form. Statisticians are trained to determine what kind of data to collect, to collect that data, to obtain useful information from the data in a scientific manner, and to make informed decisions based on the collected data. A person who tabulates numbers is not a statistician. For example, a "baseball statistician" is not actually a statistician but merely a tabulator of statistics.

Computers have become increasingly essential to the work of statisticians. Calculations that formerly took weeks can now be done in seconds on a high-speed computer. Some statisticians use computers to analyze data; others use computers to help solve statistical problems whose mathematical complexity might otherwise be overwhelming; and still others use computers to find statistical models to represent actual situations. The computer has become as important to the modern statistician as the test tube is to the chemist.

A professional statistician usually has at least a master's degree in statistics. Although some colleges and universities offer a bachelor's degree in statistics, most academic programs in statistics begin at the graduate level. At some colleges and universities, there is a Department of Statistics. At other schools, statistics may be included as a subbranch of study under mathematics, business, or interdisciplinary studies. People who enjoy working with numbers and solving numerical problems often become interested in statistics.

The demand for professional statisticians has increased greatly in recent years. This has been in response to the increased need for the collection and interpretation of data, as well as the greater availability of high-speed computers. Today, statistical methodology is used widely in fields such as agriculture, biology, business, economics, education, engineering, insurance, medicine, political science, psychology, and quality control. State and federal governments employ many statisticians. Statisticians are used by lawyers as expert witnesses in court cases. Many statisticians have a consulting practice with clients from business, industry, and government. A brochure on careers in statistics is available free from the American Statistical Association, 1429 Duke Street, Alexandria, VA 22314-3402.

Research in statistics is conducted throughout the world. But modern statistical theory and methods have been developed primarily in England and the United States. In the United States, Columbia University, the University of North Carolina, the University of California-Berkeley, and Stanford University have been the most important academic centers on statistical development. Important advances in the development of statistical applications in agriculture have also been made at various land grant schools, including Iowa State University, North Carolina State University, Virginia Polytechnic Institute, and Texas A & M.

Thirteen members of the American Statistical Association have been awarded the Nobel Prize in economics. These Nobel Prize winners include Gary Becker (1992), Merton H. Miller (1990), Trygve Haavelmo (1989), Robert M. Solow (1987), Richard Stone (1984), George J. Stigler (1982), Sir Arthur Lewis (1979), Herbert A. Simon (1978), Tjaling Koopmans (1975), Wassily Leontief (1973), John Hicks (1972), Simon Kuznets (1971), and Jan Tinbergen (1969).

Even people who are not professional statisticians need to learn how to interpret statistical evidence. For example, news media often use quantitative measurement, evaluations, and so-called facts based on statistics. Thus, everyone who reads newspapers, listens to the radio, or watches television is a lifetime consumer of statistics, and therefore should be an informed consumer. The informed consumer should ask the following questions about any reported statistic: Who is making the claim? How unbiased is the claimant? Is any needed information missing? Has there been a verbal "bait and switch"?

For example, consider an advertisement that claims antacid tablet A dissolves on the average twice as fast as tablet Y. Who is making the claim? The manufacturer, through an advertising agency. Because the manufacturer obviously has a vested interest in making its products appear effective, the manufacturer's claim may be biased. Is any important information missing? The manufacturer claims it recently completed a series of laboratory studies. But no details are given about these studies. A definition of what is meant by "on the average" is also missing. The "average" could be the mean, the median, or the mode. Is there a verbal "bait and switch" going on? Perhaps the rapid rate of dissolution of the tablet (i.e., the "bait") may not have any correlation with fast and effective pain relief. Hence, the claim that attracts the consumer may not be relevant to the effectiveness of the advertised product. By learning to think like a statistician, a consumer cannot be fooled easily. Above all, the consumer must be given enough information to know whether or not the advertising claim is valid.

Statistics also is a main component of demography, the science that analyzes the distribution of human populations, as well as the vital statistics of a particular population. Demographic analysis involves the statistical treatment of raw data to reveal certain patterns about a population, such as where its members live, and age, sex, and income. The perceived patterns can then be used to predict potential changes that are occurring or may occur in the future. For example, the U.S. census involves the statistical analysis of data to determine its demographic characteristics.

Another familiar application of demography is the reliance of insurance companies on "life tables," the invention of a mid-seventeenth century English mathematician, John Gaunt. Actually, Gaunt was the first demographer, since he invented and applied the first life table. He calculated survivorship by determining the number of births that survived to 6 years of age and the number surviving to age 76. He then made a table that illustrated the number of survivors in each of the six intervening decades (i.e., 16, 26, 36, 46, 56, and 66).

The American Statistical Association defines statistical thinking as (1) an appreciation of uncertainty and data variability and their impact on decision making, and (2) using the scientific method in approaching issues and resolving problems. In addition to reading, writing, and mathematics everyone should add "statistical literacy" to his or her skills. Statistical literacy is the ability to understand and evaluate critically statistical analyses and the ability to appreciate the contributions that statistical thinking can make in formulating important public, professional, and personal decisions.

REFERENCE WORKS

Freund, John E., and Frank J. Williams. *Dictionary/Outline of Basic Statistics*. McGraw 1966 o.p. Defines statistical terms and gives an outline of statistical formulas.

Kendall, Maurice G., and W. R. Buckland. *A Dictionary of Statistical Terms*. Oliver & Boyd 1971 o.p. Defines commonly used statistical terms.

Kotz, Samuel, and Norman L. Johnson, eds. *Breakthroughs in Statistics*. Spr.-Verlag 1992 $89.00 ea. Vol. 1 *Foundations and Basic Theory*. Vol. 2 *Methodology and Distribution*. Presents 39 papers that reflect breakthroughs in the development of statistical theory and practice in the twentieth century to 1980. Each paper is introduced by a description of its importance and how the paper influenced the history of statistics; recent references also are included. Authors include Neyman and E. S. Pearson, K. Pearson, "Student," and Fisher.

———. *Encyclopedia of Statistical Sciences*. 9 vols. and supplement. Wiley Vol. 1 1982 $190.00. ISBN 0-471-05546-8. Vol. 2 1982 $190.00. ISBN 0-471-05547-6. Vol. 3 1983 $190.00. ISBN 0-471-05549-2. Vol. 4 1983 $190.00. ISBN 0-471-05551-4. Vol. 5 1985 $205.00. ISBN 0-471-05552-2. Vol. 6 1985 $175.00. ISBN 0-471-05553-4. Vol. 7 1986 $190.00. ISBN 0-471-05555-7. Vol. 8 1988 $225.00. ISBN 0-471-05556-5. Vol. 9 1988 $245.00. ISBN 0-471-85474-3. Supplement 1989 $110.00. ISBN 0-471-81274-9. Provides information about many topics in probability and statistical theory, as well as the application of statistical methods. The Preface states that "This information is intended primarily to be of value to readers who do not have detailed information about the topics but have encountered references . . . that they wish to understand; also includes biographies of many well-known statisticians.

Kruskal, William H., and Judith M. Tanur, eds. *International Encyclopedia of Statistics*. 2 vols. Macmillan 1978 $225.00. ISBN 0-02-917960-2. Includes more than 60 articles on statistics, some articles on social science topics associated closely with strong statistics, biographies, and bibliographies.

Lancaster, Henry O. *Bibliography of Statistical Bibliographies*. Lubrecht and Cramer 1968 $18.00. ISBN 0-934454-12-4. Lists biographies and relevant bibliographies of scientists and topics of interest to statisticians.

Marriott, F.H.C. *A Dictionary of Statistical Terms*. Wiley 1990 $59.95. ISBN 0-470-21349-3. Presents an update of the 1982 edition; includes 400 new entries for the past 10 years.

Sachs, Lothar. *A Guide to Statistics Methods and to the Pertinent Literature*. Spr.-Verlag 1986 ISBN 0-387-16835-4. Provides coverage through 1985.

Tietjen, Gary J. *A Topical Dictionary of Statistics*. Routledge Chapman & Hall 1986 $22.50. ISBN 0-412-01201-4. The work is divided into 15 topical chapters.

Vogt, W. Paul. *Dictionary of Statistics and Methodology: A Non-Technical Guide for the Social Sciences*. Sage 1993 $39.95. ISBN 0-8039-5276-7. Presents nontechnical definitions of statistical and methodological terms used in social and behavioral science research; includes abundant explanations and examples.

GENERAL BIBLIOGRAPHY

The following books can help the layperson become statistically literate and thereby make a more critical evaluation of the adequacy and accuracy of reported quantitative "facts."

Brewer, James K. *Everything You Always Wanted to Know about Statistics, but Didn't Know How to Ask*. Kendall-Hunt 1978 $12.95. ISBN 0-8403-1868-5. Uses a question-and-answer format to explain the basic concepts of statistics.

Brightman, Harvey J. *Statistics in Plain English*. SW Pub. 1986 price N/A ISBN 0-538-13210-8. An easy-to-read, self-teaching introduction to statistics.

Brook, Richard J., G. C. Arnold, R. M. Pringle, and T. H. Hassard, eds. *The Fascination of Statistics*. Dekker 1986 $49.75. ISBN 0-8247-7329-2. A collection of 30 essays with illustrations about how statistical methods help answer important questions in many areas. Written by experts but can be understood by laypersons.

Campbell, Stephen K. *Flaws and Fallacies in Statistical Thinking*. P-H 1974 $26.00. ISBN 0-13-32214-4. An entertaining book that helps consumers of information evaluate the quality of statistical evidence.

Cleveland, William S. *The Elements of Graphing Data*. Wadsworth Pub. 1985 $39.95. ISBN 0-534-03730-5. Explains methods for displaying data effectively to give a clear understanding and interpretation to the reader; a clear presentation that does not require an advanced mathematical background.

de Lange, Jan, and Heleen Verhage. *Data Visualization*. WINGS for Learning/Sunburst Communications 1992 o.p. An introduction to descriptive statistics using actual data; helps people evaluate critically statistics presented in the media.

Donnahoe, Alan S. *Basic Business Statistics for Managers*. Wiley 1988 $29.95. ISBN 0-471-62940-5. An introduction to statistical methods that are widely used in business, but often misunderstood by managers.

Dowdy, Shirley, and Stanley Wearden. *Statistics for Research*. Wiley 1991 $82.50. ISBN 0-471-85703-3. Describes widely used statistical methods for researchers who want to learn how to carry out a procedure and interpret the results, as well as understand why the procedure works.

Ehrenberg, A.S.C. *A Primer in Data Reduction: An Introductory Statistics Textbook*. Wiley 1982 $39.95. ISBN 0471-10135-4. A nonmathematical introduction that clearly describes the advantages and limitations of statistical methods; intended for nonspecialists.

Fabricand, Burton F. *The Science of Winning: A Random Walk on the Road to Riches.* Van Nos. Reinhold 1979 o.p. Describes how to develop successful strategies for betting or investing; well-written but requires an advanced knowledge of statistics.

Fairley, William B., and Frederick Mosteller, eds. *Statistics and Public Policy.* Addison-Wesley 1977 o.p. A collection of 18 essays by distinguished statisticians that illustrate the importance of data, analysis, and models for decision-making on public policy issues.

Folks, J. Leroy. *Ideas of Statistics.* Wiley 1981 o.p. ISBN 0-471-02099-0. Examines the history of statistics by describing well-known contributors and some of the famous controversies in statistics.

Friedman, Arthur, and Joel E. Cohen. *The World of Sports Statistics: How the Fans and Professionals Record, Compile and Use Information.* Atheneum 1978 o.p. Provides first-hand information about the use of statistics in baseball, hockey, football, and basketball. Explains how statistics are calculated and presents personal anecdotes of experiences with the New York Mets and Texas Rangers.

Gnanadesikan, Mrudulla, R. L. Schaeffer, and Jim Swift. *The Art and Technique of Simulation.* Seymour Pubns. 1986 o.p. Describes how to solve everyday probability problems through simple simulations.

Haack, Dennis G. *Statistical Literacy: A Guide to Interpretation.* Duxbury 1979 o.p. Emphasizes the proper interpretation of statistics so that readers can detect statistical doublespeak in the media and in their field of study.

Hollander, Myles, and Frank Proschan. *The Statistical Exorcist: Dispelling Statistics Anxiety.* Dekker 1984 $49.75. ISBN 0-8247-7225-3. An entertaining book that explains clearly through 26 vignettes how statistics is used in everyday life; clear, simple, and amusing, with many cartoons and quotations.

Hooke, Robert. *How to Tell the Liars from the Statisticians.* Dekker 1983 $49.75. ISBN 0-8247-1817-8. Uses 76 vignettes to illustrate how statistical reasoning affects our daily lives.

Huff, Darrell, and Irving Geis. *How to Lie with Statistics.* Norton 1954 $4.95. ISBN 0-393-09426-X. A classic that includes humorous examples of situations in which statistics can be misleading; helps people recognize sound data and analysis; easy to read with many illustrations.

————. *How to Take a Chance.* Norton 1965 o.p. An illustrated, easy-to-read book about probability theory; includes chapters on the control of chance, strategies for winning, and caveats to look for in reported statistics.

Jaffe, Abram J., and Herbert F. Spirer. *Misused Statistics: Straight Talk for Twisted Numbers.* Dekker 1987 $49.75. ISBN 0-8247-7631-3. Helps readers become critical evaluators of statistics by giving many examples of poor statistics and explaining why the conclusions were erroneous; also includes some examples of proper uses.

Johnson, Allan G. *Social Statistics without Tears.* McGraw 1977 o.p. ISBN 0-07-032601-0. Introduces the reader to statistical language, techniques, and principles that are widely used in the social sciences.

Kirk, Roger E. *Statistical Issues: A Reader for the Behavioral Sciences.* Brooks-Cole 1972 o.p. A collection of 55 essays about conceptual issues in statistics that affect behavioral science research.

Kotz, Samuel, and Donna F. Stroup. *Educated Guessing: How to Cope in an Uncertain World.* Dekker 1983 $53.20. ISBN 0-8247-7000-5. Presents a clear explanation of the concepts of probability and how they can be applied in everyday life.

Landwehr, James M., and Ann E. Watkins. *Exploring Data.* Seymour Pubns. 1986 $15.95. A book that encourages readers to organize and display data to detect patterns.

Landwehr, James M., Jim Swift, and Ann E. Watkins. *Exploring Surveys and Information from Samples.* Seymour Pubns. 1987 o.p. An elementary book that explains the techniques of obtaining information about a large population from a sample.

Larsen, Richard J., and Donna F. Stroup. *Statistics in the Real World: A Book of Examples.* Macmillan 1976 o.p. A workbook that includes examples of how statistical procedures can be applied in anthropology, biology, economics, psychology, medicine, geology, political science, history, and sociology.

Levinson, Horace C. *The Science of Chance: From Probability to Statistics*. R. Rinehart 1956 o.p. Examines the basic concepts of probability and statistics by analyzing problems and describing in probabilities and strategies games of chance. Also applies principles to actual problems in government and business.

Lieberman, Bernhard, ed. *Contemporary Problems in Statistics: A Book of Readings for the Behavioral Sciences*. OUP 1971 o.p. A collection of 45 articles from the behavioral science literature about controversial issues involving statistical applications and interpretations.

Light, Richard J., and David B. Pillemer. *Summing Up: The Science of Reviewing Research*. HUP 1984 $20.00. ISBN 0-674-85420-6. Provides practical, well-written guidelines and step-by-step procedures for summarizing findings in quantitative research studies.

Megeath, Joe D. *How to Use Statistics*. Canfield 1975 o.p. An intuitive introduction to statistical concepts; mainly concerned with business applications.

Mendenhall, William. *Beginning Statistics: A to Z*. Wadsworth Pub. 1993 ISBN 0-534-19122-3. Set of flash cards for memory reinforcement, and a data disk for sets listed in appendix.

Moore, David S. *Statistics: Concepts and Controversies*. W. H. Freeman 1991 o.p. Focuses on statistical concepts and their impact on public policy and everyday life.

Moroney, M. G. *Facts from Figures*. Viking Penguin 1953 o.p. Guides the reader through "the statisticians' workshop," explaining statistical jargon and tools; helps the layperson understand statistical information.

Moses, Lincoln E. *Think and Explain with Statistics*. Addison-Wesley 1986. Presents a clear discussion of the benefits and limitations of statistical concepts and techniques.

Mosteller, Frederick. *Fifty Challenging Problems in Probability with Solutions*. Dover 1987 $3.95. ISBN 0-486-65355-2. A selection of applied problems and detailed solutions that illustrate elementary probability and statistics.

Mosteller, Frederick, and others. *Statistics by Example*. 4 vols. Vol. 1 *Exploring Data*. Vol. 2 *Weighing Chances*. Vol. 3 *Detecting Patterns*. Vol. 4 *Finding Models*. Addison-Wesley 1972 o.p. A four-volume series of everyday problems and examples of statistical use prepared by the Joint Committee on the Curriculum in Statistics and Probability of the American Statistical Association.

Mosteller, Frederick, Stephen E. Fienberg, and Robert E. K. Rourke. *Beginning Statistics with Data Analysis*. Addison-Wesley 1983 o.p. ISBN 0-201-05974-6. Describes actual examples of statistics from a broad range of subjects that introduce readers to data handling and analysis, sampling, probability, and testing.

Naiman, Arnold, Robert Rosenfeld, and Gene Zirkel. *Understanding Statistics*. McGraw 1983 $39.50. ISBN 0-07-045863-4. An elementary book that helps people learn how to use statistics properly; does not require a mathematical background.

Neft, David S., R. M. Cohen, and J. A. Deutsch. *The World Book of Odds*. Grosset and Dunlap 1978 o.p. An elementary book that gives odds on many possible events.

Nemenyi, Peter, S. Dixon, N. B. White, and M. I. Hedstrom. *Statistics from Scratch*. Holden-Day 1977 o.p. A clear introduction to statistics that includes many interesting examples of everyday applications; helps the reader develop an intuitive feel for statistical methods.

Neter, John, and others. *Applied Statistics*. Allyn 1992 $61.00. ISBN 0-205-13478-5. Strictly written as a textbook.

Newman, Claire E., T. E. Obremski, and R. L. Scheaffer. *Exploring Probability*. Seymour Pubns. 1986 o.p. An elementary book that illustrates practical applications of probability by using individual experiments.

Peters, William S. *Counting for Something: Statistical Principles and Personalities*. Spr.-Verlag 1987 $39.00. ISBN 0-387-96364-2. Describes the principles of applied economic and social statistics in a historical context; provides descriptions of famous personalities and their original applications and contributions to statistics.

Phillips, John L., Jr. *How to Think about Statistics*. W. H. Freeman 1992 $14.95. ISBN 0-7167-1923-1. Helps teach how to think logically and quantitatively about statistical concepts.

Reichard, Robert. *The Figure Finaglers*. McGraw 1974 o.p. A book for consumers of data who want to learn how to separate fact from fiction, useful from useless, and how to recognize the signs of distortion.

Reichmann, W. J. *Use and Abuse of Statistics*. Viking Penguin 1964 o.p. An entertaining book that describes when statistics can be used properly; emphasizes the dangers of misinterpretation.

Rowntree, Derek. *Probability without Tears*. Macmillan 1984 ISBN 0-684-17502-9. An easy-to-read presentation of probability concepts for nonmathematicians; uses an interactive style that includes exercises and solutions.

Runyon, Richard P. *Winning with Statistics: A Painless First Look at Numbers, Ratios, Percentages, Means and Inference*. Addison-Wesley 1977. ISBN 0-201-06654-8. An entertaining and humorous introduction to statistical concepts.

Sarndal, C. E., and others. *Model Assisted Survey Sampling*. Spr-Verlag 1993 $49.00. ISBN 0-387-97528-4. Extends traditional sampling theory with the aid of a modern model-assisted outlook.

Slonim, Morris J. *Sampling: A Quick, Reliable Guide to Practical Statistics*. S&S Trade 1960 o.p. A book on sampling written for the layperson; includes amusing cartoons and many interesting examples of statistical applications.

Splaver, Sarah. *Nontraditional Careers for Women*. Julian Messner 1973 o.p. Presents statistics as a career for women.

Sprent, Peter. *Statistics in Action*. Viking Penguin 1977 o.p. Examines statistical concepts and the work of statisticians by presenting actual examples from many different fields.

Stigler, Stephen M. *The History of Statistics: The Measurement of Uncertainty before 1900*. HUP 1986 $25.00. ISBN 0-674-40340-1. Written by a science historian and statistician, presents the early history of statistics and probability from 1700 to 1900. Includes many illustrations.

Tanur, Judith M., and Frederick Mosteller, eds. *Statistics: A Guide to the Unknown*. Brooks-Cole 1989 $18.95. ISBN 0-534-09492-9. A collection of articles that illustrate clearly how statistics and probability can help solve problems in the life, physical, and social sciences.

Tashman, Leonard J., and Kathleen R. Lamborn. *The Ways and Means of Statistics*. HarBraceJ 1979 o.p. Helps the reader communicate information through statistics in a precise and intelligible manner; emphasizes the benefits and limitations of statistics by using examples from the news media.

Tufte, Edward R. *Envisioning Information*. Graphics Pr. 1990 $48.00. ISBN 0-9613921-1-8. Stresses the importance of displaying complex data succinctly; includes more than 100 colorful examples to support the author's view.

———. *The Visual Display of Quantitative Information*. Graphics Pr. 1983 $40.00. ISBN 0-9613921-0-X. An attractively designed book that presents a history of data graphics; includes a manual that helps the researcher display the maximum amount of data clearly and concisely by using illustrations.

———, ed. *The Quantitative Analysis of Social Problems*. Addison-Wesley 1970 o.p. A collection of papers that include actual examples of how statistical studies have been used to solve social problems.

Waller, Ray. *An Introduction to Numerical Reasoning*. Holden-Day 1979 $19.95. ISBN 0-8162-9314-7. An introduction to the basic concepts and fundamentals of statistics; includes simple experiments.

Wang, Chamont. *Sense and Nonsense of Statistical Inference: Controversy, Misuse and Subtlety*. Dekker 1993 Price n/a ISBN 0-8247-8798-6. Focuses on the abuse and misuse of statistical inference in scientific journals and statistical literature; includes many examples of citations.

Weissglass, Julian, and others. *Hands-On Statistics: Exploring with a Microcomputer.* Wadsworth Pub. 1986 o.p. An introduction to statistical concepts; includes accompanying computer software for "hands-on" learning.

Wheeler, Michael. *Lies, Damn Lies and Statistics: The Manipulation of Public Opinion in America.* Dell 1977 o.p. Describes how public opinion polls are carried out; what polls can and cannot do; and describes how to determine the trustworthiness of polls.

Willemson, Eleanor W. *Understanding Statistical Reasoning.* W. H. Freeman 1974 o.p. Helps people understand, interpret, and evaluate statistical reasoning related to research in the behavioral sciences.

Zawojewski, Judith S., and others. *Dealing with Data and Chance.* NCTM 1991 $15.00. ISBN 0-87353-321-6. Describes the usefulness of data gathering in everyday life for problem-solving and reasoning.

Zeisel, Hans. *Say It with Figures.* HarpC 1985 $9.00. ISBN 0-06-131994-5. Presents the practical applications of statistical analysis; includes information about the history of statistics and measurement.

HISTORY

The origins of the modern theory of probability began in the middle of the seventeenth century when Chevalier de Mere, a French nobleman, wrote a letter to the mathematician BLAISE PASCAL (see Vol. 4) about some problems relating to gambling and games of chance. Pascal, in turn, wrote to another mathematician, PIERRE DE FERMAT. The first published work on probability in games of chance was by CHRISTIAAN HUYGENS, a Dutch mathematician and physicist. This pamphlet inspired the work of JAKOB JAMES BERNOULLI who made major contributions to probability theory. Bernoulli asserted that probability theory could be successfully applied to civil, moral, and economic affairs.

The word *statistics* is derived from the Latin word *status*, which means "state." In fact, *statistics* originally was used as a means of describing the economic and demographic characteristics and activities necessary for the operation of a nation or state. Statistics were widely used for calculating taxation and military service requirements. In time, statistics was extended to a variety of fields, such as astronomy, genetics, agriculture, medicine, anthropology, and psychology.

Application of the normal distribution, fundamental to the development of statistical theory and methods, was introduced by ABRAHAM DeMOIVRE in 1733. Later, PIERRE LAPLACE and CARL FRIEDRICH GAUSS made extensive use of the normal distribution curve, laying the groundwork for the development of statistics.

The development of statistics as a formal discipline began in the late nineteenth century with studies of the laws of heredity and genetics by CHARLES DARWIN, GREGOR MENDEL, and FRANCIS GALTON. Florence Nightingale applied statistics to health and social problems. KARL PEARSON and his son EGON SHARPE PEARSON made significant contributions to the development of mathematical statistics and theory. Karl Pearson's student WILLIAM SEALY GOSSET made contributions by applying statistics to small population samples in industry and agriculture.

The most important figure in modern statistics is generally regarded to be RONALD AYLMER FISHER. That is because he significantly extended early statistical concepts and theories. Frank Yates, Jerzy Neyman, Maurice Kendall,

Samuel S. Wilks, and Abraham Wald also made significant contributions to statistical theory and methods.

When the costs of census taking became prohibitive, Prasanta C. Mahalanobis, founder of the Indian Statistical Institute, introduced probability sampling, which is now standard practice. In 1936 George Gallup developed new methods of conducting election polls. These methods, based on fewer interviews, are more accurate than the straw polls conducted previously. Quality control procedures, which are vital in industry today, were developed by Walter A. Shewhart and J. M. Juran and were popularized by W. Edwards Deming. In fact, the Deming Prize is awarded in Japan annually to commemorate Deming's significant contributions to Japanese industry, as well as his role in promoting the development of statistical quality control in Japan.

Although there is no official history of statistics, the following references examine important topics and related bibliographies, as well as biographies of leaders in the field.

Historical Surveys

David, Florence N. *Games, Gods and Gambling: The Origins and History of Probability and Statistical Ideas from the Earliest Times to the Newtonian Era.* Hafner 1962 o.p. An introduction to the origins and early history of probability and statistics; traces the die used in many games today to games played in the Middle Ages.

Hacking, Ian. *The Emergence of Probability: A Philosophical Study of Early Ideas about Probability, Induction, and Statistical Inference.* Cambridge U. Pr. 1975 $18.95. ISBN 0-521-31803-3. Examines the early history of probability and inference in a philosophical context; emphasizes ideas developed in the seventeenth century.

Hald, Anders. *A History of Probability and Statistics and Their Applications before 1750.* Wiley 1990 $109.00. ISBN 0-471-50230-8. Covers the period before 1750, but also examines important nineteenth-century developments in probability and statistical theory, especially its importance in the formulation of life insurance tables.

Kendall, Maurice G., and Robert L. Plackett. *Studies in the History of Probability and Statistics.* Vol. 2 OUP 1987 $45.00. ISBN 0-19-520576-6. Examines the history of special topics in statistics and probability; includes some biographies.

Krishnaiah, Paruchuri R., ed. *Developments in Statistics.* 4 vols. Acad. Pr. 1979–83 $93.00-94.00 ea. ISBNs 0-12-426601-0, 0-12-426602-9, 0-12-426603-7, 0-12-426604-5. A four-volume work that includes many historical references.

Pearson, Egon S., ed. *The History of Statistics in the 17th and 18th Centuries against the Changing Background of Intellectual, Scientific and Religious Thought: Lectures Given at the University College London during the Academic Session 1921–1933.* Lubrecht and Cramer 1978 $45.00. ISBN 0-85264-250-4. Examines the history of statistics from the 1600s until Laplace's death in 1827.

Pearson, Egon S., and Maurice G. Kendall, eds. *Studies in the History of Statistics and Probability.* Vol. 1 OUP 1987 $70.00. ISBN 0-19-520584-4. Includes biographies and histories of special topics in statistics and probability.

Stigler, Stephen M. *The History of Statistics: The Measurement of Uncertainty before 1900.* HUP 1986 $29.95. ISBN 0-674-40340-1. Written by a science historian and statistician, a well-illustrated examination of the early history of statistics and probability from 1700 to 1900; with many illustrations.

Tankard, J. W., Jr. *The Statistical Pioneers.* Schenkman Bks. Inc. 1984 $19.95. ISBN 0-87073-408-3. Provides comparative biographies of Galton, K. Pearson, W. S. Gosset and R. A. Fisher.

Walker, Helen M. *Studies in the History of Statistical Method: Special Reference to Certain Educational Problems.* Ayer 1975 repr. of 1929 ed. $19.00. ISBN 0-405-06628-7. A comprehensive history of probability and statistics; traces the concept of probability to 220 B.C. and the concept of average to the time of Pythagoras.

Westergaard, Harald. *Contribution to the History of Statistics*. Kelley 1969 repr. of 1932 ed. Describes the history of the economic, demographic, and actuarial aspects of statistics.

CHRONOLOGY OF AUTHORS

Bernoulli, Jakob. 1654–1705
DeMoivre, Abraham. 1667–1754
Laplace, Marquis Pierre Simon de. 1749–1827
Gauss, Carl Friedrich. 1777–1855

Galton, Francis. 1822–1911.
Pearson, Karl. 1857–1936
Gosset, William Sealy. 1876–1937
Fisher, Ronald Aylmer. 1890–1962
Pearson, Egon Sharpe. 1895–1980

BERNOULLI, JAKOB. 1654–1705

At the insistence of his father, a merchant banker, Jakob (James) Bernoulli earned a degree in theology at the University of Basel in Switzerland. However, Bernoulli secretly studied mathematics and astronomy. Jakob was the earliest member of nine distinguished mathematicians with the same family name.

His most important contribution was formulating the first limit theorem of probability, called the "law of large numbers." He applied the previously formulated theory of games of chance to matters of probability, evidence, and making practical decisions. Bernoulli developed the binomial distribution as well as some rules of combination of probabilities based on individual pieces of evidence.

Bernoulli's famous four-part treatise *Ars Conjectandi (Art of Conjecture)* was published posthumously in 1713. (It was reprinted in the original Latin in 1968 in Brussels.) The first part is a commentary and solutions to CHRISTIAAN HUYGEN's work. The second part describes the theory of combinations and a derivation of the exponential series; the third part includes 24 examples of the expected profit in various games; the fourth part presents Bernoulli's philosophy regarding probability.

BOOK BY BERNOULLI

Die Gesammelten Werke. Vol. 3 *Wahrscheinlichkeitsrechnung*. Birkhauser 1975 $105.95. ISBN 3-7643-0713-7.

BOOK ABOUT BERNOULLI

Bell, Eric T. *Men of Mathematics*. Simon 1986 $13.95. ISBN 0-671-62818-6. Contains a chapter on the origins and development of the Bernoulli family, featuring Jakob, Johann, and Daniel.

DEMOIVRE, ABRAHAM. 1667–1754

Abraham DeMoivre was a Frenchman who studied mathematics and physics at the Sorbonne. He moved to London about 1687 to avoid the religious persecution of Protestants in France at that time. In London, DeMoivre became a mathematics tutor and a close friend of SIR ISAAC NEWTON (see also Vol. 4).

DeMoivre's contributions are mainly in combinatorial and probability theory, including random walk and "gambler's ruin." In 1733 he was the first person to publish the density function of the normal distribution. Because he investigated the large sample behavior of the binomial distribution, DeMoivre is generally regarded as the discoverer of the central limit theorem, which is the basis for many procedures in modern statistical inference. Another of DeMoivre's interests was the theory of annuities. In fact, James Stirling's formula concerning the expansion of factorials can be traced back to the work of DeMoivre.

BOOKS BY DEMOIVRE

The Doctrine of Chances: Or a Method of Calculating the Probability of Events in Play. 1738 o.p. Describes definitions of probabilities and methods for combination of probabilities as applied to games of chance by presenting specific problems; essentially a gambler's manual; dedicated to Sir Isaac Newton.

A Treatise of Annuities on Lives. 1724 o.p. Greatly influenced the development of actuarial science.

FISHER, RONALD AYLMER. 1890–1962

Ronald Aylmer Fisher, an Englishman, graduated from Cambridge University with degrees in astronomy and mathematics. His interest in evolution, genetics, and eugenics led to his eventual study of statistical theory. Fisher later applied statistics to agricultural research at Rothamsted Experiment Station. Fisher is credited with much of the original research on many statistical techniques still widely used. These techniques include the method of maximum likelihood, analysis of variance, Fisher's z transformation, randomization, factorials, tests based on correlation coefficients, multivariate analysis, discriminant functions, analysis of covariance, and sample surveys.

Fisher taught at University College, London, and Cambridge University, and served as a visiting professor at Iowa State University and the Indian Statistical Institute. Fisher's contributions to the development of statistics are reflected by the many honors and awards he received from groups all over the world. In 1952, he was knighted by Queen Elizabeth.

BOOKS BY FISHER

The Design of Experiments. 1935. Oliver & Boyd 1966 o.p. Elaborates on the methods of experimental design.

Statistical Methods and Scientific Inference. 1956. Oliver & Boyd 1959 o.p. Introduces decision theory and acceptance sampling.

Statistical Methods for Research Workers. 1925. Oliver & Boyd 1958 o.p. Summarizes the methods of ANOVA and the principal of randomizations; 12 editions have been published in 7 languages.

Statistical Tables for Biological, Agricultural and Medical Research Workers (coauthored with Frank Yates). 1938. Hafner 1963 o.p. Includes many useful statistical tables.

BOOKS ABOUT FISHER

Bennett, J. H., ed. *Collected Papers of R. A. Fisher.* 5 vols. University of Australia, Adelaide, Australia 1971–74. o.p. Presents a complete bibliography of Fisher's published work; includes 291 of his papers and a biographical memoir.

——. *Statistical Inference and Analysis: Selected Correspondence of R. A. Fisher.* OUP 1990 $90.00. ISBN 0-19-85555-0. Presents selected correspondence between R. A. Fisher and his contemporaries.

Box, Joan Fisher. *R. A. Fisher: The Life of a Scientist.* Wiley 1985 $39.95. ISBN 0-471-83895. Biography written by Fisher's daughter; examines Fisher's statistical innovations in the context of his personal life.

GALTON, FRANCIS. 1822–1911

Francis Galton, an Englishman knighted in 1909, did not show extraordinary talent until relatively late in his life. He was not a good student and never completed his degree in mathematics at Cambridge University. Galton's early interests were geography and meteorology. When he was 43, he became interested in statistical methods, especially in how these methods can be applied to genetics and psychology. In 1877 Galton formulated the law of numerical regression (or reversion). Galton's development and use of a numerical measure of regression is very similar to the modern regression coefficient. To confirm his law of numerical regression as a reversion toward the norm, Galton raised sweet peas and experimented with moths to obtain data. He applied the statistical knowledge developed by mathematical astronomers to a variety of events—from brewing tea to eugenics. He also introduced and defined precisely the term "correlation" (originally "co-relation"). Galton wrote more than 300 publications, which include 17 books. He funded the Galton Chair of National Eugenics at University College, London, whose first occupant was KARL PEARSON.

Galton aptly summed up his view of statistics in his book *An Introduction to Mathematical Statistics and Its Applications*: "Some people hate the very name of statistics, but I find . . . [statistics] full of beauty and interest. Whenever they are not brutalized, but delicately handled by the higher methods, and are warily interpreted, their power of dealing with complicated phenomena is extraordinary. They are the only tools by which an opening can be cut through the formidable thicket of difficulties that bars the path of those who pursue the science of man."

BOOKS BY GALTON

Hereditary Genius: An Inquiry into Its Laws and Consequences. 1869. Peter Smith 1962 $16.50. ISBN 0-8446-2108-0. Uses the word *correlation* but does not provide a precise definition.
Memories of My Life. 1908. AMS Pr. repr. $32.00. ISBN 0-404-08128-2. An autobiography that examines Galton's childhood and later life.
Natural Inheritance. 1889. AMS Pr. repr. $27.50. ISBN 0-404-08129-0. First publication that explains the concepts of regression and correlation.
Probability: The Foundation of Eugenics. Henry Froude 1907 o.p.

BOOKS ABOUT GALTON

Forrest, D. W. *Francis Galton, The Life and Work of a Victorian Genius.* Taplinger 1974 o.p. Biography of Galton.
Pearson, Karl. *The Life, Letters and Labours of Francis Galton.* 3 vols. Cambridge U. Pr. 1914 o.p. One of the world's great biographies; written by Galton's closest friend.

GAUSS, CARL FRIEDRICH. 1777–1855

Carl Friedrich Gauss was already well known in Germany as a mathematician and astronomer by the time he reached his twenty-fifth birthday. Gauss's contributions are in statistical theory and statistical applications for analyzing observational data. The most widely used contributions of Gauss in statistical theory are related to estimation. He developed the concept of the standard deviation and the method of least squares. Gauss also developed new applications for the normal distribution curve, also known as the normal distribution of errors, the "Gaussian" curve, and the bell-shaped curve. Because of his contributions to Euclidian and non-Euclidian geometry, algebra, and the theory of numbers, Gauss has been called the greatest mathematician of the nineteenth century and is often referred to as the "prince of mathematics."

BOOK BY GAUSS

Disquisitiones Arithmeticae. Spr.-Verlag 1986 $87.00. ISBN 0-387-96254-9. Translation of the 1870 German edition. A major treatise related to the modern theory of numbers; includes solutions to many difficult problems.

BOOKS ABOUT GAUSS

Buehler, W. K. *Gauss: A Biographical Study*. Spr.-Verlag 1987 $49.80. ISBN 0-387-10662-6. Examines Gauss's personal and professional life; includes an extensive description of his major contributions to both mathematics and statistics.

Dunnington, G. W. *Carl Friedrich Gauss, Titan of Science: A Study of His Life and Work*. Hafner 1955 o.p. Describes the genius and modesty of Gauss; states that Gauss did not think that his formulation of the method of least squares was remarkable, because it was so obvious to him.

GOSSET, WILLIAM SEALY. 1876–1937

When William Sealy Gosset was faced with making decisions based on small sample sizes, he was working at the Guinness brewery in Dublin. He was subsequently sent to University College, London, to study under KARL PEARSON. Gosset's major contributions to statistics are related to sampling distributions of estimators, designing experiments, and applying statistics to agriculture. All of his publications are listed in journals under the pseudonym, "Student." Gosset derived several important distributions, including the sample variance from a normal distribution, the sample correlation coefficient from a bivariate normal distribution, and the Student's t distribution.

BOOKS ABOUT GOSSET

Pearson, Egon S., and John Wishart, eds. *"Student's" Collected Papers*. Cambridge U. Pr. 1947 o.p. A collection of papers published by Gosset under the pseudonym "Student."

Pearson, Egon S., R. L. Plackett, and G. A. Barnard. *Student: A Statistical Biography and William Sealy Gosset*. OUP 1990 $32.00. ISBN 0-19-852227-4. A biography of Gosset based on his statistical correspondence.

LAPLACE, MARQUIS PIERRE SIMON DE. 1749–1827

Laplace's scientific and mathematical interests include differential equations, celestial mechanics, theoretical astronomy, geodesy, probability, and statistics. Laplace also was active in French politics during the French Revolution. He is credited with naming July 14 as Bastille Day, a French national holiday. Laplace's major contributions include the establishment of Bayesian statistics, the Laplace transform, combinatorics, the theory of the incomplete beta function, the theory of generating functions, the theory of errors, the proof of least squares, and asymptotic theory. Laplace also was a leading French educator, helping establish the École Normale and École Polytechnique.

BOOKS BY LAPLACE

Celestial Mechanics. 1799–1825. 4 vols. Transl. by N. Bowditch. Chelsea Hse. $250.00. ISBN 0-8284-0194-2. Vol. 5 Chelsea Hse. 1969 repr. of 1832 ed. $35.00. ISBN 0-8284-0214-0. A four-volume work that includes the contributions of Laplace and his predecessors to the field of celestial mechanics.

A Philosophical Essay on Probabilities. 1814. Dover 1951 o.p. Translated from the sixth French edition. Presents 10 theorems of probability still used today, including definitions and means of combining probabilities; traces the history of probability to Chevalier de Mere.

PEARSON, EGON SHARPE. 1895-1980

Egon Pearson was the son of KARL PEARSON. Egon's work with Jerzy Neyman clarified the theory of statistical inference by giving a clear rationale for hypothesis testing, as well as describing the two types of errors, power, robustness, and the likelihood ratio test. Pearson also made contributions to estimation, quality control, operations research, and statistical education. After his father's death in 1936, Pearson became managing editor of *Biometrika*, retaining the position for 30 years. Egon Pearson is credit with developing the method of calculating percentage points for many types of distributions. He was head of the Department of Applied Statistics at University College, London.

BOOKS BY EGON PEARSON

The Application of Statistical Methods to Industrial Standardization and Quality Control. British Standards Inst. 1936 o.p. The first official British manual that describes the use of statistical methods in industrial quality control.

Biometrika Tables for Statisticians (coauthored with H. O. Hartley). 1954. Cambridge U. Pr. 1966 o.p. Reprint with corrections Vol. 2 1976 Lubrecht and Cramer $75.00. ISBN 0-704653-11-0. Includes a collection of statistical tables still used today.

PEARSON, KARL. 1857-1936

Karl Pearson helped build the foundations of modern mathematical statistics. He spent his entire professional life on the faculty at University College, London, in the department of eugenics and applied mathematics. The Pearson system of frequency distributions was developed as the result of solving a differential equation. Pearson's other major contributions include the method of moments, the maximum likelihood function, the correlation coefficient, the chi-square goodness-of-fit test, and the contingency table analysis. He was editor of the journal *Biometrika* from its inception in 1901 until his death in 1936. Because of some bitter controversies with other scientists, he was never elected a Fellow of the Royal Statistical Society. Pearson also was the founder and editor of the *Annals of Eugenics* in 1925.

BOOKS BY KARL PEARSON

The Grammar of Science. Dent 1937 o.p. Describes examples of how to move from classification of collected data to scientific theory; one example used is Darwin's theory of evolution.

On the Theory of Contingency and Its Relation to Association and Normal Correlation. Drapers Co. Research 1904 o.p. Examines measures of association for two variables with frequency data; illustrated as a contingency table.

Tables for Statisticians and Biometricians Parts I and II. 1914. Cambridge U. Pr. 1931 o.p. A collection of 55 statistical tables still used today.

BOOK ABOUT KARL PEARSON

Pearson, Egon S., ed. *Karl Pearson: An Appreciation of Some Aspects of His Life and Work.* Cambridge U. Pr. 1938 o.p. A biography of Karl Pearson by his son, Egon; includes selections from Karl Pearson's correspondence, excerpts from his publications, and an outline of his lectures on the history of statistics.

CHAPTER 17

Information Science and Computer Science

Heyward Ehrlich

> The Mechanical Educator could impress on the brain, in a matter of a few minutes, knowledge and skills which otherwise take a lifetime to acquire . . . . Impressing information directly on the brain, so that we can know things without ever learning them . . . . [It] is of such urgent need that civilization cannot continue for any more decades without it. The knowledge in the world is doubling every two years—and the rate is itself increasing. Already twenty years of schooling are inefficient; soon we will have died of old age before we have learned how to live, and our entire culture will have collapsed owing to its incomprehensive complexity.
> —ARTHUR C. CLARKE, *Profiles of the Future*

Within six months of taking office in 1993, Bill Clinton and Al Gore announced their e-mail addresses as "president@whitehouse.gov" and "vice.president@ whitehouse.gov." For the first time in American history, Washington, D.C., leaders could be reached directly by anyone using Internet or commercial services. E-mail, formerly a tool of academic research or business activity, now has become an instrument of politics. Today the previously separate realms of computer science and information science are merging. Indeed, the old domains of research, business, entertainment, shopping, personal services, and professional activity have come closer and closer together with remarkable speed. The new imperial infrastructure of bandwith is connecting everything electronic or digital, including computers, telephones, fax machines, and television. Suddenly, location no longer matters. A person could be sitting in a library, computer center, research laboratory, professional office, home office, or even at the beach and go "on-line." Then, in rapid succession, he or she could access a library, do shopping, be entertained, execute business, pursue research, or wield political influence—as long as the person had some sort of link, whether copper wire, cordless, cellular, fiber optic, cable, or satellite. Although computer science and information science specialists continue to maintain separate offices, they are beginning to look remarkably alike in significant ways.

The words *literacy* and *technology* have become the essentials in the phrases "information literacy," "information technology," and "computer literacy." Today one hears less and less of *science*, as in library science, information science, and computer science. Originally, libraries had taken the lead in automation and computerization; computer centers followed in providing access to electronic information in the new worldwide consortium called the "virtual library." Instantly, hundreds of libraries now can be accessed from thousands of computer centers and from millions of individual computers.

Therefore, every library, every electronic database, and every computer takes its place in one infinitely large information swarm in a single global beehive of all the users, all the machines, and all the information in the cosmos. In the Internet, order in the hive is provided by drones called Archie, Gopher, and WWW, each tirelessly doing the physical work of running whatever information errands are desired.

In the past, information in library catalogs was free to the public, but information in indexes and abstracts could be obtained only from commercial on-line services. As a result of the new high-capacity data CD-ROM, a hybrid of free data and commercial data materialized; commercially published databases have been sold on CD-ROM to libraries, which then make the information freely available to the public. At times, the medium of print has been not only challenged but also surpassed by its electronic rival. Scholars, businesspeople, scientists, students, and homemakers can choose between hardcopy and electronic data on the grounds of accessibility, convenience, and cost, often assuming, incorrectly, that there is no difference in coverage or content, and that whatever is easiest, fastest, or cheapest is necessarily the best. While the old clerical error became a thing of the past, what replaced it was its technological successor, the computer error.

During the last 30 years, computers rapidly have taken over the task of handling more and more of the transactional, informational, and visual data, whether in numbers, words, or pictures, of the industrialized nations of the world. The computer takes its name in English from World War II machines designed for massive military computations. But it is more appropriately named in other languages: *ordinateur* in French and *elaboratore* in Italian, which suggest its additional powers to perform nonmathematical functions, such as to store, arrange, and retrieve information; to be a supercorrecting typewriter; to handle telecommunications; to control and design devices in industry; to create visual presentations on paper, film, and tape; and to do thousands of other tasks.

In a famous miscalculation, IBM decided not to make computers in the late 1940s because of its estimate that only six computers could be sold worldwide. Today, millions of computers are in operation—submicroprocessors, micro-computers, minicomputers, mainframe computers, and supercomputers. Many of them are linked to each other or to data banks by telecommunication lines, satellites, or fiber optical cables. Moreover, military preparation, space exploration, national security, manufacturing and industry, agriculture, banking and finance, insurance, office work, service industries, advertising and publishing, education and research, and even modern cars and appliances depend on computers. (One side-effect of nuclear explosions is the total erasure of the internal instructions and memory stores of any computers nearby.) In recent years the quantity of computer data has increased so drastically that the phenomenon has been called an "information explosion." This new computer information must be handled in such radically different ways as to constitute the "information revolution." In fact, the expanded use of computers has taken us on a quantum leap into the "information society."

In *Profiles of the Future* (1962), ARTHUR C. CLARKE lists many unexpected inventions in the fields of communications and information of the last century that people now take for granted. These improbable inventions include the telephone, phonograph, office machine, vacuum tube, radio, television, radar, tape recorder, electronic computer, transistor, laser, communication satellite, pocket calculator, and video recorder. Clarke looks ahead to the next 100 years and foresees this list: pocket educators, new libraries, universal radiophones, telesensory devices, practical artificial intelligence, the detection of extrasolar intelligence, memory recording, and artifact coding. Other futurologists also foresee the paperless office, universal voice input and output instead of visual reading and manual keyboarding, automatic translation between human languages, two-way miniature televisions that connect with the libraries and databanks of the world, professional information centers with expert knowledge systems in the shop and office, and culture-creativity centers in the home. If these futurologists are right, we are in the springtime of an intellectual golden age.

It does not, however, feel like spring. Clarke's HAL in the motion picture *2001* reveals deep negative emotions about the future of intelligent computers. (Elsewhere Clarke–disagreeing with C. P. Snow (see Vol. 1)—suggests that we soon will need two distinct human languages, one for counting and one for feeling.) Everywhere Cassandras warn us that new information technology threatens the rise of a two-class society based on access to data, with sweeping unemployment and economic dislocation, painful losses of privacy and civil liberties, the trivialization of writing and speech, the loss or narrowing of perspective on Western ethical, philosophical, and intellectual traditions, and the degradation of scientific wisdom by a mass of unmanageable data. Above all, we are becoming aware that the growing technototalitarian state could base its extralegal power on the amalgamation of previously confidential information in the databanks that already contain our IRS, Social Security, Bell telephone, TRW bank and credit, FBI, police, real estate, tenant, political, educational, employment, membership, subscription, charity, mailing, and medical histories. In fact, until recently most people never imagined that some of these databases even existed.

Whichever version of the information future will arrive it will happen soon. By the mid-1950s, there already were more people employed in service industries than in factories in the United States. During the 1970s, large computers and satellite and telephone links were used to create huge information networks and databanks. In the 1980s, microcomputers and easy-to-use software (possessing increased speed and capacity and reduced size and cost) facilitated the expansion of interactive computer information systems into every office, factory, institution—and many homes. Now, in the mid-1990s and as we draw nearer to the twenty-first century, the wave of the future seems to be the "information highway," a fully integrated electronic communications network that will bring a host of services into the home. The 1993 proposed merger of Bell Atlantic and TCI (Tele-Communications Inc.) is a first step toward such a future.

At the same time as such developments were taking place, libraries abandoned the traditional card catalog, first moving to supplemental catalogs published in book form and then to selective on-line catalogs requiring the use of a computer terminal. Two familiar media were standard before 1970 in information systems: the typed 8½" × 11" page produced on an electric typewriter and the standard 3" × 5" file card. They were dethroned by the massive, rapidly produced, coded, hard to read (and sometimes harder to understand) computer printout on perforated, endless, zig-zag paper—and its electronic equivalent, an on-line, fully instantaneous, interactive, search-strategy-accessible, password-secured, video-display and keyboard-equipped, hierarchically structured electronic database.

The new Babel of information was not a tower of confused speech, but rather an underground web of branching, narrowing tunnels of specialist information

technology. However, understanding one set of proprietary hardware, computer languages, or search strategies did not guarantee the understanding of any
other. Moreover, the community of information workers, formerly a visible
natural society, became an invisible network of remote initiates held together
by expertise in documentation manuals, help and hot keys, and confidential
800-numbers that arise, change, or vanish each year.

The remedy for this Noah's flood of information might be much more
information. It is widely argued that people must become "computer literate,"
learning to write home computer applications in BASIC, replacing the medieval
trivium of grammar, logic, and rhetoric with expertise in computer programming and artificial intelligence, and, if possible, updating the medieval
quadrium of arithmetic, geometry, astronomy, and music with the latest
microcomputer software applications packages for spreadsheets, turtle graphics, astrology, and synthetic music. The current fashion dictates that nothing has
intellectual validity unless it was done on computer. Computers create seas of
information, but they do not automatically increase knowledge or wisdom.
People do not need to know everything; first we need to discover exactly what
needs to be known, and in the process, to feel comfortable with understanding
both the knowledge we need and the knowledge we do not need.

This chapter is designed to help the reader orient himself or herself in the
new world of information technology. It is divided into several parts: first,
introductions to computing and information science, then computer programming and software applications, and finally artificial intelligence and current
controversies. Although there are many works listed for the expert in business,
professional, or academic applications, the headnotes in each section are
designed to be most helpful to the novice.

Although books on the general principles of information and computer
science can remain useful for many years, the specific details concerning
hardware, software, services, and vendors can change very rapidly. In areas of
the most rapidly evolving marketing and technology—such as CD-ROM, color
printing, communications integration (telephone and FAX), graphical environments, hypertext, indexing, Internet, miniaturization, multitasking, multiuser
computing, networking (local, wide area, and global), object-oriented programming, on-line documentation, on-line services integration (research, business,
entertainment, and shopping), operating platforms, operating systems, portable
and laptop computers, recognition of voice and handwriting, remote access and
control, searching and retrieval, training, ultra high density data media, user
interfaces, and work groups—the printed tangible information may be out of
date before any book can go though its manufacturing cycle. To keep abreast of
any specific areas of interest, the reader might wish to follow various monthly
and weekly periodicals:

Academic: *Academic Computing, Chronicle of Higher Education, Electronic
Learning*

Business: *Barron's, Business Week, Economist, Forbes, Fortune, Wall Street
Journal*

Computing: *AI Expert, Byte, CD-ROM Professional, Communications of
the ACM, Compute!, Computer Shopper, Computers and the Humanities,
Computerworld, Data Based Advisor, Datamation, InCider, InfoWorld, Mac-
user, Newsbytes, PC Magazine, PC Week, Personal Computing, Technical
Communication*

General: *New Republic, New Statesman, Newsweek, New York Times, New York Times Book Review, New York Times Magazine, Psychology Today, Time, Times Literary Supplement (London), Whole Earth Review*
Library: *American Society for Information Science Bulletin, Booklist, Choice, Computers in Libraries, Database, Information Technology and Libraries, Library High-Tech Journal, Library Journal, Library Quarterly, Library Trends, Online, Publishers Weekly, Special Libraries, Wilson Library Bulletin*
Science: *American Scientist, Nature, New Scientist, Popular Science, Science News, Scientific American, Smithsonian*

In addition, the reader should not overlook two rapidly growing sources of textual and bibliographical information—on-line electronic services and CD-ROM publications—even though they lie outside the scope of this article. Three examples of on-line resources are the academic listservs and newgroups on Internet, the commercial user groups on Compuserve, and the commercial databases on Dialog. In addition, two examples of CD-ROM sources are the full text annuals on Computer Select and the annotated multi-year gatherings of general bibliographies on ProQuest.

INTRODUCTION TO COMPUTING

Beginner's Guides

The most successful beginner's guides to computing are well written, relaxed, and occasionally humorous. Many, written by authors who also are professional novelists, columnists, lecturers, or poets, avoid the off-putting effect of starting with excessively technical information or textbook approaches designed for the initiated. These books rightly treat the computer as a useful tool, not as an object of veneration, and are written for the user who is less interested in the engineering intricacies than in how to use the thing. With the rising public expectation that computing should be simple (and the discovery that it was not), a whole new class of books came into being for the disillusioned user. Many of these books were bluntly, if not vulgarly, entitled "xxx for dummies," "xxx for idiots," "I hate xxx," "voodoo xxx," or "xxx for not-nerds"—in each instance "xxx" specifying a computer platform or application package.

Even the best advice on computer books tends to date quickly. In some cases, the life of a software package is shorter than the production cycle of the book written on it. Heed this advice: Whenever possible, get something that was published this year or last year, technical software information tends to become outdated in two years. Look for recent editions of established works.

Anzovin, Steve. *The Green PC: Making Decisions That Make a Difference.* TAB Bks. 1993 $9.95. ISBN 0-8306-4311-7. Discusses citizen participation in environmental issues relating to computers in such areas as energy, ergonomics, and hardware disposal.

Barry, John A. *Technobabble.* MIT Pr. 1993 $12.50. ISBN 0-262-52182-2. A warning that the indiscriminate use of computer terms and computer concepts is corrupting our language and ways of thinking. Valuable for providing the history of such terms as *bug, glitch, kludge, nerd,* and *Winchester.*

Bear, John. *Computer Wimp.* Ten Speed Pr. 1983 $14.95. ISBN 0-89815-102-3. Humorous introduction designed to take the formality and tension out of first encounters with microcomputers; anecdotal approach.

Bernstein, Jeremy. *The Analytic Engine: Computers—Past, Present, and Future.* Morrow rev. ed. 1981 o.p. Series of highly readable articles on the history of computing, originally published in *The New Yorker* magazine; one of the best-written introductions to computers and their history for people who claim they cannot understand them.

_____. *Three Degrees above Zero: Bell Labs in the Information Age*. NAL-Dutton 1986 o.p. Splendidly written accounts of discoveries and developments at Bell Laboratories—including silicon chips, fiber optics, and a computer chess program called Belle. Originally published in *The New Yorker*.

Bradbeer, Robin. *The Beginner's Guide to Computers: Everything You Need to Know about the New Technology*. Addison-Wesley 1982 $10.95. ISBN 0-201-11209-4. The history and working of computers, with some application programs in BASIC. Originated as a text for the BBC "Computer Literacy Project."

Crichton, Michael. *Electronic Life: How to Think about Computers*. Ballantine 1984 o.p. Introduction to computers, presented as an interesting gathering of thoughts, feelings, and suggestions about encounters with a PC (personal computer). Written by a medical doctor best known as the author of several science fiction novels.

Deken, Joseph. *The Electronic Cottage: Everyday Living with Your Personal Computer in the 1980's*. Morrow 1981 o.p. Explains what computers can do and how they operate, including computer logic, computer languages, decision support, simulations, feedback, and information management.

Evans, Christopher. *The Micro Millennium*. Viking Penguin 1980 o.p. Enthusiastic and optimistic projection of the future of computers in our personal lives, homes, offices, schools, factories, and professions. Entertaining and easy to read.

Flock, Emil, and Howard Schulman. *The ShareWare Book: Using PC-Write, PC-File, and PC-Talk*. Osborne-McGraw 1986 o.p. Provides three manuals in one for these well-tested, well-received, and inexpensive shareware programs.

Forester, Tom. *The High-Tech Society: The Story of the Information Technology Revolution*. MIT Pr. 1989 $19.95. ISBN 0-262-06107-4. Significant survey of the history, dimensions, and problems of the computer revolution, including Silicon Valley, telecommunications, personal computers, factories, offices, and finance; good bibliography.

Hansen, Dirk. *The New Alchemists*. Little 1982 o.p. Informal history of Silicon Valley industries in California, the microchip manufacturing business, and the microelectronics revolution.

Herbert, Frank, and Max Barnard. *Without Me You're Nothing: The Essential Guide to Home Computers*. PB 1983 o.p. Introduction to home computing early in the era of microcomputing, by the author of the *Dune* science fiction novels; written with a technical collaborator, Max Barnard.

Jennings, Karla. *The Devouring Fungus: Tales of the Computer Age*. Norton 1990 $10.95. ISBN 0-393-02897-6. Light-hearted collection of amusing anecdotes, stories, and jokes, often at the expense of such solid monuments of computing as IBM, Marvin Minsky, Alan Turing, Norbert Weiner, and Joseph Weizenbaum.

Kidder, Tracy. *The Soul of a New Machine*. Avon 1990 $9.95. ISBN 0-380-71115-X. Pulitzer Prize-winning case history of the building of a new minicomputer at Data General, capturing the special dedication, euphoria, and work addiction of an engineering design team.

LeVitus, Bob, with Ed Tittel. *Stupid PC Tricks*. Addison-Wesley 1991 $19.95. ISBN 0-201-57759-3. An antidote to normality, productivity, and sanity from a bard of computer pranks and capers whose shelf of similar merciless tomes also embraces recipes for Windows and the Macintosh.

McCorduck, Pamela. *The Universal Machine: Confessions of a Technological Optimist*. HarBraceJ 1986 o.p. A look at computers all over the world as the machine of the century that might produce beneficial results for society and culture globally. Well-written, upbeat panorama of the future applications and significance of the personal computer.

McWilliams, Peter A. *The Personal Computer Book*. Prelude Press 1990 $19.95. ISBN 0-931580-30-7. One of a series of the author's highly popular introductions to PCs, word processing, and computing in business, written by a former bestselling poet, who is always humorous, informal, and partisan.

Martin, James. *The Telematic Society: A Challenge for Tomorrow*. P-H 1981 $35.95. ISBN 0-13-902460-3. Introduction to telecommunications in work, education, and leisure; originally entitled *The Wired Society* and used as the basis for an international television special.

Meilach, Dona Z. *Before You Buy a Used Computer: A Practical Guide to Computer Shopping*. Crown Pub. Group 1985 o.p. Questions, procedures, decisions, and alternatives for persons purchasing their first personal computer.

Norton, Peter. *Peter Norton's DOS Guide*. Brady Compu Bks. 4th ed. 1991 $24.95. ISBN 0-13-663048-0. Standard introduction without excessively technical material on the operating system of the IBM PC and compatibles, written by the well-known computer columnist, commentator, and author of various utilities software.

Raymond, Eric S., ed. *The New Hacker's Dictionary*. MIT Pr. 1991 $22.50. ISBN 0-262-18145-2. Pungent sampler of the unofficial and generally unprinted English and slang of hackers. Includes such choice specimens as "Microsloth Windows" and "spaghetti code." Also available in an on-line version. Illustrated by Guy L. Steele, Jr.

Ritchie, David. *The Computer Pioneers: The Making of the Modern Computer*. S&S Trade 1986 o.p. Readable introduction to the development of computers from their prehistory through the decades after World War II and to the immediate present, seen through the eyes of the persons who made them.

Sandberg-Diment, Erik. *They All Laughed When I Sat Down at the Computer and Other True Tales of One Man's Struggle with Personal Computing*. P-H 1986 o.p. Chronicle of the microcomputer revolution from 1982 to 1984, viewing industry events with old-fashioned wit and skepticism. Collected from the author's columns in the *New York Times*.

Shore, John. *The Sachertorte Algorithm and Other Antidotes to Computer Anxiety*. Viking Penguin 1986 $7.95. ISBN 0-14-008037-6. When is a Sachertorte recipe an algorithm? Sane and humorous introduction for beginners to the language and methods of computer programming.

Shurkin, Joel N. *Engines of the Mind: A History of the Computer*. PB 1985 $4.95. ISBN 0-671-60036-2. Introductory work for the nontechnical reader on computer inventions and innovations, their history, and the people who made them.

Sullivan, David R., and Curtis R. Cook. *Computing Today: Microcomputer Concepts and Applications*. HM 1988 $49.16. ISBN 0-395-42330-9. One of the first introductory textbooks to base itself not on programming in BASIC but rather on competence in standard PC software packages.

Understanding Computers: Input-Output. Time-Life 1986 o.p. One of a series of introductory books on computer basics, input and output, graphics, communications, artificial intelligence, and similar topics, each vertically explored in a few areas and accompanied by impressive graphics illustration.

Walter, Russ. *The Secret Guide to Computers*. Russ Walter 15th ed. 1991 $15.00. ISBN 0-939151-15-4. Do not be deceived by the homemade look, the weird jacket photo, the odd title, the "write-alike" contest, the sexual jokes, the bizarre examples, or the author's offer of his personal phone number. Expertly relaxes beginners and demystifies computers. Covers advanced BASIC, FORTRAN, Pascal, COBOL, other computer languages, and much more.

Willis, Jerry, and Merl Miller. *Computers for Everybody*. Weber Systems 3rd ed. 1983 o.p. Elementary and nontechnical introduction to computer hardware, software, purchasing, communications, and use in office and home.

Zinsser, William. *Writing with a Word Processor*. HarpC 1983 $12.95. ISBN 0-06-015055-6. The author of *On Writing Well* recounts his experiences, fears, misadventures, and new discoveries about the nature of writing while mastering word processing on an IBM PC in the early 1980s.

REFERENCE WORKS, COLLECTIONS, DICTIONARIES

This section includes general anthologies, histories, dictionaries, guides to computer books and software, and collections of trivia and humor. The anthologies edited by Tom Forester provide fine panoramas of the fields of computing and information technology. Incidentally, *Computer Select*, which is not a book but rather an expensive CD-ROM published monthly by Ziff, contains the full text of some 75,000 recent articles related to computers and computing from 170 periodicals.

Augarten, Stan. *Bit by Bit: An Illustrated History of Computers.* Ticknor & Fields 1984 o.p. Interest in reading about computers is increased by the excitement of seeing their pictures at the same time.

Bates, William. *The Computer Cookbook: How to Create Small Computer Systems That Work for You.* P-H 1983 o.p. Dictionary of hardware and software sources for small computers, with information on a good many topics. The annuals are updated on-line via NewsNet.

Birnes, William, and others. *McGraw-Hill Personal Computer Programming Encyclopedia: Languages and Operating Systems.* McGraw 2nd ed. 1989 $99.50. ISBN 0-07-005393-6. Guide to a number of standard operating systems, programming languages, and applications packages, including commands in Postscript, SNOBOL, SPSS, dBASE III, and Paradox. Good bibliography.

Bitter, Gary, ed. *Macmillan Encyclopedia of Computers.* 2 vols. Macmillan 1992 $150.00. ISBN 0-02-897045-4. Reference source aimed at students and nonspecialists. Includes 200 articles plus biographies.

Bowker's Complete Sourcebook of Personal Computing 1985. Bowker 1984 o.p. Single reference manual for software, hardware, glossary, books, magazines, user groups, and vendors.

Brand, Stewart. *Whole Earth Software Catalog 1986.* Doubleday 1985 o.p. Highly recommended introduction to what PC software can and cannot do, showing interesting differences of opinion among several expert users. Arose from and is updated in the *Whole Earth Review.*

Burton, Philip. *A Dictionary of Minicomputing and Microcomputing.* Garland 1985 o.p. Concise and comprehensive dictionary of current hardware and software usage, including appendices on structured programming, Pascal, magnetic bubble memory, printers, automatic control, multiprocessing, data communications, magnetic recording, and storage technology.

Computer Books and Serials in Print, 1985–1986. Bowker 1985 o.p. Guide to books and magazines pertaining to computing.

Cortade, James W. *Historical Dictionary of Data Processing Organizations.* Greenwood 1987 $65.00. ISBN 0-313-23303-9. Short notes on the more important or prominent companies concerned with computer hardware and data processing. Arranged alphabetically, from Amdahl to Xerox.

Dertouzos, Michael L., and Joel Moses, eds. *The Computer Age: A Twenty-Year View.* MIT Pr. 1979 $15.95. ISBN 0-262-54036-3. Future technological, economic, educational, and social issues as seen by Terry Winograd, Seymour Papert, Daniel Bell, Herbert A. Simon, Marvin Minsky, Joseph Weizenbaum, and others.

Ditlea, Steve, ed. *Digital Deli: The Lunch Group.* Workman Pub. 1984 o.p. Articles, cartoons, humor, and whatnots about their personal encounters with computing, by a group of New York writers who met monthly for lunch. Contributions by Steve Wozniak, Esther Dyson, Timothy Leary, and William F. Buckley, Jr., among others.

Downing, Douglas, and Michael Covington. *Dictionary of Computer Terms.* Barron 1992 $8.95. ISBN 0-8120-4824-5. Useful because of its practical examples and its pocketable format with durable soft covers and rounded corners.

Forester, Tom, ed. *Computers in the Human Context: Information Technology, Productivity, and People.* MIT Pr. 1989 $40.00. ISBN 0-262-06124-4. Useful collection of essays on computing and information technology in the mid- and late 1980s. Supersedes Forester's previous anthologies issued in 1980 and 1985.

_____. *The Information Technology Revolution.* MIT Pr. 1985 $42.50. ISBN 0-262-06095-7. Sequel to *The Microelectronics Revolution* (see below). Brings the record up to 1984 with new material on telecommunications; artificial intelligence; the "fifth-generation" computer; applications of information technology in schools, factories, offices, banks, and hospitals; and finally, problems that computers pose in the areas of weapons systems, crime, and women's rights.

_____. *The Microelectronics Revolution: The Complete Guide to the New Technology and Its Impact on Society.* MIT Pr. 1981 $16.95. ISBN 0-262-56021-6. Useful collection of articles published before 1980 on computing and information technology, especially on aspects of its economic impact on industry, the office, employment, industrial relations, and society.

Freedman, Alan. *The Computer Glossary: The Complete Illustrated Desk Reference.* AMACOM 5th ed. 1992 $36.95. ISBN 0-8144-5020-2. General introduction to computer literacy; easy to read and generously illustrated with photographs, diagrams, and cartoons.

Goldstine, Herman H. *The Computer from Pascal to Von Neumann.* Princeton U. Pr. 1993 $39.00. ISBN 0-691-02367-0. History of computing by a participant in many of the developments he describes.

Haynes, David, ed. *Information Sources in Information Technology.* Bowker-Saur 1990 $80.00. ISBN 0-408-03285-5. Evaluates essential sources in information technology, including on-line databases and CD-ROMs.

Helms, H. L. *The McGraw-Hill Computer Handbook.* McGraw 1983 o.p. Thirty sections by specialist contributors, written for the nonexpert. Many are adapted from textbooks issued by the same book publisher in the 1970s, with new chapters by Helms and introduction by Adam Osborne.

Hordeski, Michael. *The Illustrated Dictionary of Microcomputers.* TAB Bks. 1986 $26.95. ISBN 0-8306-0488-X. Latest edition, including some 4,000 new items, examples, and illustrations.

Isaacs, Alan, ed. *The Multilingual Computer Dictionary.* Fr. & Eur. 1981 $45.00. ISBN 0-8288-1371-X. About 1,600 computer terms in English, French, German, Italian, Portuguese, and Spanish, including British/U.S. variants, all combined in one alphabet.

Longley, Dennis, and Michael Shain, eds. *Dictionary of Information Technology.* OUP 2nd ed. 1986 $29.95. ISBN 0-19-520519-9. More than 6,000 entries on computing, communications, and microelectronics, some of them fairly long, with 100 diagrams. The first edition was commended as outstanding by the American Library Association.

McGraw-Hill Dictionary of Electronics and Computers. McGraw 1983 o.p. Ten thousand terms, including synonyms, acronyms, and abbreviations, in a compact desk volume, selected from the larger *McGraw-Hill Dictionary of Scientific and Technical Terms.*

Naiman, Arthur, ed. *Computer Dictionary for Beginners.* Ballantine 1983 o.p. Clear, often humorous, with illustrations and cartoons.

Nicita, Michael, and Ronald Petrusha. *The Reader's Guide to Microcomputer Books.* Macmillan 1984 $32.95. ISBN 0-86729-122-2. Critical evaluation of more than 1,000 computer books. Although the work stops in 1984, the cross-indexing and subject score summaries are unusually useful.

Popenoe, Chris. *Book Bytes: The User's Guide to 1200 Microcomputer Books.* Pantheon 1984 o.p. Some 1,200 books on PC software and hardware on the market by January 1984, described and evaluated by levels of difficulty and by quality. Chapters begin with useful highlights of recommended titles.

Ralston, Antony, and E. R. Reilly, eds. *Encyclopedia of Computer Science and Engineering.* Van Nos. Reinhold 3rd ed. 1992 $125.00. ISBN 0-442-27679-6. More than 700 articles, including 175 new items, with a classification guide, cross-referenced keywords, indexes to both subjects and names, and a table of computer terms in English and four foreign languages.

Rochester, Jack B., and John Gantz. *The Naked Computer: A Layperson's Almanac of Computer Lore, Wizardry, Personalities, Memorabilia, World Records, Mind Blowers, and Tomfoolery.* Morrow 1983 o.p. Compendium of anecdotes, trivia, facts, and world records about computers that is both entertaining and informative.

Rosenberg, Jerry M. *Dictionary of Computers, Information and Telecommunications.* Wiley 2nd ed. 1987 $65.00. ISBN 0-471-85558-8. Bestselling dictionary of more than 12,000 terms (usually briefly defined), symbols, acronyms, and abbreviations, plus glossaries of terms in Spanish and French. The second edition adds more than 2,000 new items.

_____. *McGraw-Hill Dictionary of Information Technology and Computer Acronyms, Initials, and Abbreviations.* McGraw 1992 $12.95. ISBN 0-07-053735-6. Compact source book for abbreviations, acronyms, and initials in the field of information technology.

The Software Encyclopedia, 1993: A Guide for Personal, Professional, and Business Users. 2 vols. Bowker 1993 $222.00. ISBN 0-8352-3329-4. Lists over 16,000 software programs, specifying operating system, compatibility, and hardware and memory requirements. Includes indexes and information on software publishers.

Van Tassel, Dennie, and Cynthia L. Van Tassel. *The Compleat Computer.* SRA 2nd ed. 1983 o.p. Compendium of computer news, art, cartoons, and poetry, from scholarly, popular, and unexpected sources, including reprints of contributions by Norman Cousins, Claude Shannon, Michael Crichton, Ray Bradbury, Art Buchwald, and Arthur C. Clarke, among others.

BIOGRAPHICAL AND HISTORICAL BIBLIOGRAPHY

The history of computing often is traced to the scientists and philosophers of the seventeenth century—to JOHN NAPIER (1550–1617), who built logarithmic "bones" in 1617, to BLAISE PASCAL (1623–62) (see Vol. 4), who built the first workable calculating machine in 1643, to GOTTFRIED WILHELM VON LEIBNIZ (see Vol. 4), who improved Pascal's design and made a multiple-purpose calculating machine in 1694. The modern computer era actually begins with CHARLES BABBAGE (1791–1871), who designed and attempted to build a difference engine and an analytic engine in the mid-nineteenth century. Babbage's associate, ADA, COUNTESS OF LOVELACE (1815–52), the daughter of LORD BYRON (see Vol. 1), sometimes is called the world's first programmer. The nineteenth-century mathematician GEORGE BOOLE (1815–64) invented a new form of logic that broke with Aristotelian syllogisms and reduced statements to true or not-true states. In 1890 HERMAN HOLLERITH (1860–1929) designed for the U.S. Census a machine that borrowed the punch-card design of the old Jacquard loom controllers; from Hollerith's company emerged the first manifestation of IBM.

In the 1930s, ALAN MATHISON TURING (1912–54) contributed a design and a concept that have come to be known, respectively, as the Turing Machine and the Turing Test; the former provides a scheme of controlling and accessing data, and the latter proposes a method to know when machines can be said to think. The need for high-speed and complex computations stimulated the growth of electronic computers in the 1940s. The mathematician JOHN VON NEUMANN (1903–57) proposed what has become to be known as "Von Neumann architecture," a computer flexibly storing its own program in memory along with its data, not merely wired to do one task alone. Von Neumann, who did some of the computations for the original atom bomb tests, also was interested in analogies (and the lack of analogies) between computers and the human brain, in game theory, and in self-reproducing automata. At the same time, NORBERT WIENER (1894–1964), developing a computer program to direct anti-aircraft fire by means of continuous feedback corrections, invented the field known as cybernetics. During the same decade, CLAUDE SHANNON (1916–), working with Boolean logic, developed information theory based on binary instead of digital values as the simplest form of guaranteed transmission along noisy lines, using the idea of individual bits with only two states, on and off, grouped into bytes. Since the 1970s, two companies have been prominent in the production of personal computers, Apple and IBM. The stories of many important figures remain to be told, but we can learn of Buck Rodgers's account of his years at IBM, of the founding of Apple in part by Steve Jobs, and of John Sculley's displacement of him as head of that company. Other tales of heroes, hackers, programmers, and investors have come to be part of the legends of computing.

Much of the history and prehistory of computing is accessible now in the publication of archival materials of such major figures as John von Neumann and Alan Turing.

General Accounts and Biographies

Aspray, William, ed. *Computing before Computers*. Iowa St. U. Pr. 1990 $27.95. ISBN 0-8138-0047-1. Articles on the historical contributions of Napier, Babbage, Hollerith, Vannevar Bush, and others before the appearance of the first electronically stored digital computer in 1945.

Carlston, Douglas G. *Software People: Inside the Computer Business*. P-H 1986 o.p. Accounts of hackers, programmers, entrepreneurs, venture capitalists, and others who made major contributions to computer software as we know it today.

Cringely, Robert X. *Accidental Empires: How the Boys of Silicon Valley Make Their Millions, Battle Foreign Competition, and Still Can't Get a Date*. Harper Busn. 1993 $11.00. ISBN 0-88730-621-7. Refreshing, readable, and informative stories, anecdotes, gossip, and exposés of successful computer executives in the inimitable manner of the author's column in *Infoworld*.

DeLamarter, Richard T. *Big Blue: IBM's Use and Abuse of Power*. Dodd 1986 o.p. Accusations that IBM displays poor management, makes inferior products, frustrates its clients, and is ruthless to its competitors, stemming from eight years of research by the Justice Department in its antitrust suit against IBM, which finally was dismissed by the Reagan administration in 1982.

Fishman, K. D. *The Computer Establishment*. McGraw 1982 o.p. Well-researched, well-documented, and well-written history, largely of IBM. Portions first appeared in the *Atlantic Monthly*. Paperback edition has a postscript on the IBM antitrust suit.

Fjermedal, Grant. *The Tomorrow Makers: A Brave New World of Living-Brain Machines*. Microsoft 1988 $8.95. ISBN 1-55615-113-6. Euphoric panorama of the near future of artificial intelligence; based on interviews with pioneers working at the frontiers of the field and on in-depth profiles of their progress and projected success.

Freiberger, Paul, and Michael Swaine. *Fire in the Valley: The Making of the Personal Computer*. Osborne-McGraw 1984 o.p. The people and the events in the personal computer revolution, told entertainingly.

Gassée, Jean-Louis. *The Third Apple: Personal Computers and the Cultural Revolution*. HarBraceJ 1987 $14.95. ISBN 0-15-189850-2. French view of the personal computer and its cultural revolution by a former European executive for Apple computers who counts Eve's and Newton's as apples one and two.

Lammers, Susan, ed. *Programmers at Work*. Microsoft 1989 $9.95. ISBN 1-55615-211-6. In interviews, 19 prominent programmers describe how they work, how well-known programs were developed, and what they see for the future.

Langley, Patrick, and Jan M. Zytkow. *Scientific Discovery: Computational Explorations of the Creative Process*. MIT Pr. 1987 $15.00. ISBN 0-262-62052-9. Remarkable synthesis of philosophy, computer science, and the history of science into a computational model for the process of scientific discovery. Data-driven models simulate the scientific discoveries of Roger Bacon, John Dalton, Johann Rudolf Glauber, and Georg Ernst Stahl.

Levy, Steven. *Hackers*. Dell 1985 $5.99. ISBN 0-440-13405-6. Highly readable account of the computer "whiz kids," hardware freaks, and games addicts, along with their adventures and misadventures with Ma Bell, Uncle Sam, and the Fortune 500.

Manes, Stephen, and Paul Andrews. *Gates*. Doubleday 1993 $25.00. ISBN 0-385-42075-7. Portrait of Bill Gates of Microsoft, perhaps both the most loved and the most loathed person in the software business; recites incidents from the mythology of his aggressive, confrontational style.

Metropolis, N., ed. *A History of Computing in the Twentieth Century*. Acad. Pr. 1980 $77.00. ISBN 0-12-491650-3. Collection of papers by 39 eminent persons in the world of computing; originally presented at an international conference at Los Alamos in 1976.

Nyce, James M., and Paul Kahn, eds. *From Memex to Hypertext: Vannevar Bush and the Mind's Machine*. Acad. Pr. 1991 $39.95. ISBN 0-12-523270-5. Traces the consequences of Vannevar Bush's suggestion in *Atlantic* magazine in the 1940s for nonlinear, automated retrieval of disparate texts from microfilms and how the suggestion eventually led to hypertext.

Rodgers, Buck, and Robert Shook. *The IBM Way: Insights into the World's Most Successful Marketing Organization*. HarpC 1987 $11.00. ISBN 0-06-091417-3. Rodgers, who was at IBM from 1950 to 1984, reveals IBM's approach to marketing theory, employee relations, and corporate attitudes in this best-selling book for company managers.

Wallace, James, and Jim Erickson. *Hard Drive: Bill Gates and the Making of the Microsoft Empire*. Wiley 1992 $22.95. ISBN 0-471-56886-4. Study of Gates's ambition and ruthlessness, written by two Seattle journalists; explores his youth, personal wealth, eccentricity, opportunism, battles with rivals, and vision of the future for personal computers.

INTRODUCTION TO INFORMATION AND LIBRARY SCIENCE

Guides and Introductions

The emphasis in bibliographical instruction (BI) is increasingly on the Internet, its methods and materials, and its tools, including Archie, Gopher, World Wide Web, and Hytelnet. It might surprise some people to realize that the interest in on-line procedures actually is increasing the demand for reference materials in printed form. Library computers seem to encourage a new form of "information illiteracy," resulting when hasty users, who do not understand the nature of the new electronic tools, regard their research as complete after a vaguely relevant screenful or two. This section contains works on library and information science, information systems, library automation, information retrieval, library-based community computer literacy, information technology, print versus electronic storage issues, and library reference guides.

Brandt, D. Scott. *Unix and Libraries*. Meckler 1991 $47.50. ISBN 0-88736-541-8. Series of useful tutorials on Unix for librarians; intended to supplement but not replace the Unix manual.

Buckland, Michael Keeble. *Information and Information Systems*. Greenwood 1991 $16.95. ISBN 0-313-27463-0. Stimulating and accessible introductory text that takes broad views of some key issues pertaining to information storage, resources, retrieval, and automation.

Burch, John G., and Felix R. Strater. *Information Systems: Theory and Practice*. Wiley 3rd ed. 1983 o.p. Revised edition of a standard textbook.

Burton, Paul F., and J. Howard Petie. *Information Management Technology: A Librarian's Guide*. Routledge Chapman & Hall 1991 $51.95. ISBN 0-442-34130-1. Introduction for librarians to microcomputers, library software applications, information services, and information retrieval.

Chen, Ching Chih, and Stacey E. Bressler. *Microcomputers in Libraries*. Neal-Schuman 1982 $35.00. ISBN 0-918212-61-8. Covers the use of microcomputers in the routine tasks of the library.

Costa, Betty, and others. *A Micro Handbook for Small Libraries and Media Centers*. Libs. Unl. 1991 $27.00. ISBN 0-87287-901-1. Guide to microcomputers, library applications, educational media programs, and printed handbooks; intended for workers in smaller libraries.

Curtis, Howard, ed. *Public Access Microcomputers in Academic Libraries: The Mann Library Model at Cornell University*. ALA 1987 $16.00. ISBN 0-8389-0464-5. Collection by nine contributors on planning, acquiring, staffing, and operating microcomputers for public use, with attention to software acquisition policies and information storage and retrieval. Policy statements, agreements, and legal notes are covered in the appendix.

Dewey, Patrick R. *Public Access Microcomputers: A Handbook for Librarians*. Professional Librarian Ser. G. K. Hall 1984 $30.50. ISBN 0-86729-085-4. Advice on making an Apple, IBM-compatible, or other personal computer freely available in a public library, with practical examples.

Encyclopedia of Library and Information Science. 40 vols. Dekker 1968–92 $115.00 ea. Large international encyclopedia with signed articles, containing bibliographies on all aspects of library and information science.

Fosdick, Howard. *Computer Basics for Librarians and Information Scientists*. Info. Resources 1981 $24.50. ISBN 0-87815-037-X. Includes chapters on hardware, personnel, storage, memory, system software, programming languages, and database systems; with introduction by F. Wilfrid Lancaster.

Hardesty, Larry L. *Faculty and the Library: The Undergraduate Experience*. Ablex Pub. 1991 $37.50. ISBN 0-89391-685-4. Surveys the place of libraries in the university; treats faculty attitudes, curriculum contents, and the disposition of undergraduate students.

Hills, Philip, ed. *The Future of the Printed Word: The Impact and the Implications of the New Communications Technology*. Greenwood 1980 $29.95. ISBN 0-313-22693-8. Valuable essays from 14 contributors on electronic versus paper publishing, new printing technologies, microforms, videodisks, graphics, scientific and technical problems in publication, and economic and social factors.

Lancaster, F. Wilfrid. *Information Retrieval Systems: Characteristics, Testing and Evaluation*. Information Sciences Ser. Wiley 2nd ed. 1979 o.p. Won the "Best Book on Information Science" award of the American Society for Information Science in 1968. Focuses on intellectual concepts, not equipment.

Lilley, Dorothy B., and Rose Marie Badough. *Library and Information Science: A Guide to Information Sources*. Gale 1981 o.p. Selective guide in four parts: recent changes in technology, models for search strategies, information sources for various forms of material, and types of information sources.

Loop, Liza, and Julie Anton. *Computer Town: Bringing Computer Literacy to Your Community*. P-H 1983 o.p. Implementation package for computer literacy at the community level, based on National Science Foundation research.

Martin, Edley Wainright, and others. *Managing Information Technology: What Managers Need to Know*. Macmillan 1991. ISBN 0-02-328231-2. Useful introduction to information technology management that draws its case studies from real-world business examples.

Mathies, Loraine. *Computer-Based Reference Service*. ALA 1973 o.p. On ERIC, MARC, and computer searching; issued by the American Library Association.

Neill, Samuel D. *Dilemmas in the Study of Information: Exploring the Boundaries of Information Science*. Greenwood 1992 $42.95. ISBN 0-313-27734-6. Reflections on recent philosophical issues posed by current assumptions and practices in information science and library science.

Pepinsky, Harold B. *People and Information*. Pergamon 1970 o.p. Writings from about a dozen contributors; old but still interesting for the variety of viewpoints reflected.

Purcell, Gary R., and Gail Ann Schlachter. *Reference Sources in Library and Information Services: A Guide to the Literature*. ABC-CLIO 1984 o.p. Comprehensive guide to 700 general reference works and 500 subject reference works, each annotated.

Reynolds, Dennis. *Library Automation: Issues and Applications*. Bowker 1985 $49.95. ISBN 0-8352-1489-3. Intended to serve librarians and administrators from beginners to experts who are interested in library automation, its history and background, planning and preparations, and practical applications.

Taylor, Robert Saxton. *Value-added Processes in Information Systems*. Ablex Pub. 1986 $55.00. ISBN 0-89391-273-5. Valuable work that looks at the design of information systems from the user's point of view.

Young, Heartsill. *ALA Glossary of Library and Information Science*. ALA 1983 o.p. Attempt to develop a standard set of terms for workers in information science; also includes terms from computer science, printing and publishing, telecommunications, and graphics and reprography.

Zorkoczy, Peter. *Information Technology: An Introduction*. Communications Lib. St. Mut. 1990 $120.00. ISBN 0-273-03238-0. Clear and concise introduction to telecommunications, optical communication systems, videotape and videodisk systems, computers, data protection, expert systems, microforms, voice communication with computers, data networks, electronic mail, information systems, and videotex/teletext.

Bibliographies, Indexes, Abstracts, Directories, and Handbooks

Several representative annuals are the *Annual Review of Information Science and Technology (ARIST)*, *Computing Information Directory*, and *Computing Reviews*, and an important bimonthly is the standard *Information Science Abstracts*. This section contains bibliographies, indexes, abstracts, directories, handbooks to computing, microcomputers, information science, information management, and information technology. Look for recent revisions of standard volumes, such as those edited by Hildebrandt, Longley, and Williams. Incidentally, general journal literature is indexed on CD-ROMs provided by commercial services, such as ProQuest and InfoTrac.

Annual Review of Information Science and Technology. Ed. by Martha E. Williams. Vol. 27. Knowledge Industry 1992 $89.00. ISBN 0-938-73466-0. Contains nine authoritative survey essays each year in three fixed domains of information science. Known as *ARIST* and issued by ASIS (American Society of Information Science).

Chicago Guide to Preparing Electronic Manuscripts. U. Ch. Pr. 1987 $25.00. ISBN 0-226-10393-5. Description of standardized procedures and style guide for electronic text production and transmission.

Cibbarelli, Pamela, and Edward J. Kazlauskas, eds. *Directory of Information Management Software for Libraries, Information Centers, Record Centers and Supplement 1984*. ALA 1985 o.p. Data on 85 specialist software packages, with 35 more listed in the appendix; represents various operating systems and software languages.

Collins COBUILD English Language Dictionary. Ed. by John Sinclair. Collins rev. ed. 1992 $40.00. ISBN 0-00-370023-2. Dictionary produced by the Collins Birmingham University International Language Database project (COBUILD), for which 20 million words were scanned to determine and classify actual practices in contemporary English.

Computer Publishers and Publications: An International Directory and Yearbook, 1992–1993. Ed. by Frederica Evan. Comm. Trends Inc. 1991 $199.00. ISBN 0-88709-024-9. Major annotated guide to computer magazines, books, newsletters, and journals, with purchase recommendations for academic and public libraries, lists of bestselling computer books, guides to evaluating books, and selected computer books indexed by author and title.

Computing Reviews. ACM 1960– o.p. Standard guide to computing literature from the Association for Computing Machinery; indexed by title, author, keyword, category, and terms.

Connors, Martin, and others, eds. *Computers and Computing Information Resources Directory.* Gale 1987 $160.00. ISBN 0-8103-2141-6. Annotated guide to 6,000 on-line and print sources of information relating to computers and data processing, including associations, on-line services, teleprocessing, networks, and newsletters.

Hildebrandt, Darlene M., ed. *Computing Information Directory (CID): A Comprehensive Guide to the Computing Literature.* Hildebrandt 5th ed. 1988 $133.95. ISBN 0-685-20288-7. Important annual guide to computer journals, computer center newsletters, books, dictionaries and glossaries, indexes and abstracts, software, reviews, hardware, directories, encyclopedias, handbooks, and computer languages. Contains information on more than 1,500 journals, 200 newsletters, and 30 indexes or abstracts.

Longley, Dennis, and Michael Shain. *Van Nostrand Reinhold Dictionary of Information Technology.* Van Nos. Reinhold 3rd ed. 1989 $34.95. ISBN 0-44-223685-9. Revised edition containing extended entries on artificial intelligence, CD-ROM, desktop publishing, and the three wings of information technology—computers, telecommunications, and video.

Micro Software Evaluations, 1986–1988. Ed. by Jeanne M. Nolan. Meckler 1987 o.p. Detailed narratives by users of various library software packages with practical evaluations and examples of each.

Public Management Institute. *Computer Resource Guide for Nonprofits.* 2 vols. Public Management 3rd ed. 1985–86 o.p. Evaluations of software packages for all systems. Unfortunately alphabetical by vendor only.

On-line Sources and Information Utilities

The falling cost of high-speed modems (9600 baud and over), often with fax capability, has brought these communications devices within the reach of many, and the medium-speed modem (2400 baud) has become quite inexpensive. Although the technical options in installing modem software can be daunting for those who don't have a successful model to emulate, the hardware is easy to connect and use. Miniature modems also are available for portable computers.

Internet access now is available from thousands of institutions to reach hundreds of university catalogs and national libraries all over the world. Some universities pay a licensing fee for controlled access to databases, such as RLIN, OCLC, or Dialog—valuable for their union book catalogs—and indexes to articles, reviews, and abstracts. Commercial research databases are available directly to individuals through such services as Compuserve, which also can provide access to Internet. Among the thousands of electronic newsgroups and mailing lists on the Internet and related links, PACS-L and LIBREF-L are concerned specifically with the interests of professional librarians.

Subjects covered in this section include on-line databases, information services, on-line search and research procedures and strategies, telecommunications with personal computers, and proprietary databases. Krol's introduction to the Internet is highly recommended. Stoll gives a fascinating account of a new kind of international hacker. The on-line resource guide by Strangelove and Kovacs is useful for its frequent updates.

Directory of Online Databases. Elsevier 1986 $95.00. ISBN 0-685-17450-6. Quarterly directory of online databases by type, subject, producer, conditions, content, coverage, and updating.

Ferrarini, Elizabeth. *Infomania: The Guide to Essential Electronic Services.* HM 1985 o.p. How to access electronic information about money, news, science, careers, jobs, learning, bulletin boards, computers, shopping, travel, electronic mail, people, and commercial services.

Glossbrenner, Alfred. *The Complete Handbook of Personal Computer Communications: Everything You Need to Know to Go Online with the World.* St. Martin rev. ed. 1989 $18.95. ISBN 0-312-03312-5. Standard work on how to use modems in telecommunications and how to use information utilities.

_____. *How to Look It Up Online: Get the Information Edge with Your Personal Computer.* St. Martin 1987 $14.95. ISBN 0-312-00132-0. How to seek information about books, magazines, newspapers, business, employment, sales, marketing, and government; clear and intelligible guide, with useful tips and graphics emphasis.

Hafner, Katie, and John Markoff. *Cyberpunk: Outlaws and Hackers on the Computer Frontier.* S&S Trade 1991 $22.95. ISBN 0-671-68322-5. Case studies of how three new-style hackers—sociopaths or criminals in international espionage—replaced the old-style hackers, formerly harmless and dedicated local technical amateurs with a love for free phone calls and reading other people's mail.

Howitt, Doran, and Marvin I. Weinberger. *Inc. Magazine's Databasics: Your Guide to Online Business Information.* Garland 1984 o.p. Covers databases, searching, electronic mail, and business databases by subject, vendor, hardware, and software. Intended for the business user.

Katz, Bill, and Anne Clifford, eds. *Reference and Online Services Handbook: Guidelines, Policies and Procedures for Libraries.* Neal-Schuman 1986 $39.95. ISBN 0-918212-74-X. Includes a collection of policy statements pertaining to on-line reference services in academic and public libraries.

Kehoe, Brendan P. *Zen and the Art of the Internet: A Beginner's Guide.* P-H 2nd ed. 1993 $22.50. ISBN 0-13-010778-6. Revision of a very accessible beginner's guide to the Internet; the first edition was available on-line.

Krol, Ed. *The Whole Internet User's Guide & Catalog.* Ed. by Mike Loukides. O'Reilly & Assocs. 1992 $24.95. ISBN 1-56592-025-2. Well-received and authoritative guide to the Internet; explains telnet, e-mail, finger, software on-line, FTP, Archie, Gopher, WAIS, WWW, Internet relay chat, and other advanced features.

Lambert, Steve. *Online: A Guide to America's Leading Information Services.* Microsoft 1985 o.p. Useful introduction to and handbook on the use of online data and information banks.

LaQuey, Tracy, with Jeanne C. Ryer. *The Internet Companion: A Beginner's Guide to Global Networking.* Addison-Wesley 1993 $10.95. ISBN 0-201-62224-6. Compact and inexpensive introduction that covers the necessary basics for beginners on the Internet; foreword by Vice-President Al Gore.

The North American Online Directory, 1987. Bowker 1987 o.p. Guide to online information services available in the United States and Canada.

Quarterman, John. *Matrix Computer Networks and Conferencing Systems.* P-H 1990 $50.00. ISBN 0-13-565607-9. One of the first standard treatments of the global consequences of computer networking and conferencing.

Rittner, Don. *Ecolinking.* Peachpit Pr. 1992 $18.95. ISBN 0-938151-35-5. Guide to environmental information for scientific research or political activism to be found via on-line services and databases; intended for those who already possess technical proficiency.

Sterling, Bruce. *The Hacker Crackdown: Law and Disorder on the Electronic Frontier.* Bantam 1992 $23.00. ISBN 0-553-08058-X. Examination of the 1990 crackdown in 14 cities by the Secret Service on computer hackers suspected of dealing in stolen credit card numbers and telephone access codes and of the unexpected rebound in support for First Amendment protection of computer bulletin boards.

Stoll, Clifford. *The Cuckoo's Egg: Inside the World of Corporate Espionage.* Doubleday 1989 $18.95. ISBN 0-385-24946-2. True-life detective story of the search—undertaken without assistance from the FBI, CIA, or NSA—to explain a mysterious 75-cent charge for computer time; the search discovered that "secured" computers at the Lawrence Berkeley Laboratory were being entered by a hacker in West Germany.

Stone, M. David. *Getting On-Line: A Guide to Assessing Computer Information Services.* P-H 1984 o.p. Straightforward information on information services, utilities, hardware, software, search strategies, free services, and future prospects.

Strangelove, Michael, and Diane Kovacs. *Directory of Electronic Journals, Newsletters and Academic Discussion Lists.* ARL 6th ed. 1993 o.p. Frequently updated published listing of on-line serial publications, directories, periodicals, information networks, and machine-readable documents; also available on-line.

Williams, Martha E., ed. *Computer Readable Databases: A Directory and Data Sourcebook.* 2 vols. ALA 1985 o.p. Describes more than 5,000 databases, including both text and numerical databases. Vol. 1 covers science, technology, and medicine; Vol. 2 includes business, law, the humanities, and the social sciences.

COMPUTER PROGRAMMING

A computer by itself (i.e., without software) is much like a car without a driver. The computer needs instructions to follow for the most trivial of tasks. Unfortunately, the type of instructions that computers can understand—"set the first, third, fourth, fifth, and sixth bits of the AH register high and the others low," "set the second bit of the AL register high and the others low," and so on—are not easy for humans to work with. Computer languages solve this problem by allowing the programmer to use special codes that are simpler for humans to follow but then are translated into instructions the machine can understand. Languages are categorized very broadly as either low-level or high-level. The former are little more than mnemonics for the very primitive machine-level instructions. Such languages, though tedious to work with and difficult to learn, are very powerful and economical on an operating level. The latter are far easier to learn and use but generally produce slower-running, less flexible programs.

Languages have been developed for a number of specific purposes: FORTRAN for scientific calculation, BASIC and Logo as teaching tools, SNOBOL and Icon for text processing, COBOL for business applications, and Pascal and C as structured languages. FORTRAN (FORmula TRANslation) was created to handle mathematical, scientific, and engineering procedures, but because it was the first language to establish itself widely on large computers, it has come to be used in all types of computing applications. BASIC (Beginner's All-purpose Symbolic Instruction Code) has been distributed with so many microcomputers and has been used in so many high school and "computer literacy" courses that it has become the language best known to the general public. Pascal (named for the French philosopher and mathematician) was intended to be only a demonstration language of strong structure and clear self-documentation but now is very widely used in colleges and by professional programmers. The language called C is especially favored by programmers who require a language that is highly compact and extremely portable from one operating system or environment to another. Logo was created by Seymour Papert to teach the principles of programming to young children through the use of a movable turtle and other graphic visualizations. There are many other special-purpose languages, such as SNOBOL4 and Icon for handling text strings, LISP and PROLOG in artificial intelligence, and Ada (named for ADA, COUNTESS OF LOVELACE) in Department of Defense programs. In addition, many programmers use proprietary software applications, such as dBase for database work or

SPSS for statistics, in lieu of working directly in a programming language. Some mainframe computers and microcomputers provide proprietary programming languages that are virtually extensions of their operating systems. Programmers being inveterate tinkerers, most languages go through a series of implementations that add new features. As a result, all of the established languages have grown increasingly general in purpose.

The face of computer programming has been changed in recent years by the growing acceptance of graphic interfaces, in which the trade-off for the simpler user interface is an astronomical increase in programming complexity. The new languages of choice for MS-Windows are Visual Basic for elementary routines and C++ for professional work, the latter being implemented sometimes as a kit intended for its particular operating environment. Thus, the line between programming languages and application software is becoming blurred.

Introductions, Surveys, and General Programming

Aho, Alfred V., and Jeffrey D. Ullman. *Principles of Compiler Design*. Addison-Wesley 1977 o.p. General principles in the design and implementation of compilers, taking up universal problems—such as finite state techniques, context-free grammar, and syntax-directed translation schemes—applicable to any programming language or computer hardware; includes exercises.

Aho, Alfred V., and John Hopcroft. *Design and Analysis of Computer Algorithms*. Addison-Wesley 1974 $52.75. ISBN 0-201-00029-6. First-course text emphasizing ease of understanding rather than advanced tips and tricks; assumes some knowledge of FORTRAN and COBOL programming and linear algebra. Includes examples.

Babich, Wayne A. *Software Configuration Management*. Addison-Wesley 1986 $26.95. ISBN 0-201-10161-0. Deals with coordinating programmers on team projects for maximizing productivity and minimizing compilations and delays. For software project leaders, senior programmers, and software managers; approach is valid for any language, but many of the examples draw on UNIX or Ada.

Bailey, T. E., and Kris Lundgaard. *Program Design with Pseudocode. Computer Science Ser.* PNS Pubs. 1989 $16.50. ISBN 0-534-09972-6. Introduction to problem-solving concepts and techniques for clearer thinking about programming. By emphasizing pseudocode, encourages clearer thinking about program structure, modular design, and flowcharting without limiting itself to specific languages.

Baron, Naomi S. *Computer Languages: A Guide for the Perplexed*. Doubleday 1986 o.p. General overview and detailed individual review of 21 standard programming languages that considers their history, syntax, purpose, functioning, and possible future. An appendix takes up additional, less-known languages.

Barstow, David R., Howard E. Shrobe, and Erik Sandewall. *Interactive Programming Environments*. McGraw 1983 o.p. Forty-two contributions on the subjects of programming methodology, interactive environments, software engineering, and artificial intelligence.

Birnes, W. J. *McGraw-Hill Personal Computer Programming Encyclopedia: Languages and Operating Systems*. McGraw 1989 $99.50. ISBN 0-07-05393-6. Signed articles on programming languages. Contains several translation tables on languages and their principle dialects.

Brooks, Frederick P., Jr. *The Mythical Man-Month: Essays on Software Engineering*. Addison-Wesley 1975 $23.75. ISBN 0-201-00650-2. Timely essays on software engineering, especially on the problems of attempting to speed up large projects.

Carberry, M. Sandra, and A. Toni Cohen. *Principles of Computer Science: Concepts, Algorithms, Data Structures, and Applications*. Computer Science Pr. 1986 o.p. Survey of computer foundations, systems and languages, Pascal programming, applications, and social and cultural perspectives.

Chang, Shi-Kuo, ed. *Visual Languages*. Plenum 1987 $95.00. ISBN 0-306-42350-2. Considers programming in visual languages, visual databases, how computer graphics can represent and process mental imagery, animation by children, cognitive aspects of processing Chinese characters, the computer-human interface, and visual information in human decision making.

Dijkstra, Edward W. *A Discipline of Programming*. P-H 1976 $59.00. ISBN 0-13-215871-X. Classic text on methods of top-down programming, including the use of modules in any programming language, ways of thinking about programming and problem solving, and the uses of logic, mathematics, theory, and design in creating algorithms.

Held, Gilbert. *Data Compression: Techniques and Applications, Hardware and Software Considerations*. Wiley 1991 $54.95. ISBN 0-471-92941-7. Discussion of rationales, utilizations, techniques, and software limitations in data compression. Includes IBM PC programs on an optional disk.

Hsu, Jeffrey. *Microcomputer Programming Languages*. Wiley 1987 $16.95. ISBN 0-471-62574-4. Survey of some 20 languages for microcomputers, including BASIC, COBOL, FORTRAN, and Pascal, plus lesser-known languages including Ada, APL, C, FORTH, LISP, Logo, Modula-2, PILOT, PL/1, and PROLOG, showing advantages and disadvantages of each; includes two statistical packages, SPSS and SAS, as programming languages.

Kernighan, Brian W., and P. J. Plauger. *The Elements of Programming Style*. McGraw 2nd ed. 1978 $31.45. ISBN 0-070-34207-5. Classic text for programmers, establishing standards of clarity and expression.

———. *Software Tools in Pascal*. Addison-Wesley 1981 $30.25. ISBN 0-201-10342-7. Mechanics of software engineering, with modules for structured programming and top-down design.

Knuth, Donald E. *The Art of Computer Programming*. 3 vols. Addison-Wesley 1973–81 $49.95 ea. ISBNs 0-201-03822-6, 0-201-03809-9, 0-201-03803-X. Systematic collection and discussion of algorithms. Vol. 1, on fundamental algorithms, contains a wealth of material on data structures and their manipulation; Vol. 2, on seminumerical algorithms, takes up issues of number representation and computer arithmetic; Vol. 3, on searching and sorting, is useful for information structures. Exercises are graded in progressive difficulty, entail mathematical knowledge, and include some unsolved research problems.

Lancaster, Don. *Hexadecimal Chronicles*. Sams 1981 o.p. Conversion tables for binary, octal, and decimal numbers as an aid to assembly language programming.

Mansuripur, Masud. *Introduction to Information Theory*. P-H 1987 $48.00. ISBN 0-13-484668-0. The basic concepts and advanced implications of information theory and their relation to probability theory, continuous channels, and ergodic sources; includes recent advances in universal source coding and rate distortion theory.

Pradhan, Dhiraj K. *Fault-Tolerant Computing: Theory and Techniques*. 2 vols. P-H 1986 Vol. 1 $59.00. ISBN 0-13-308230-X. Vol. 2 $49.00. ISBN 0-13-308230-X. Seven contributors on the subject of the much higher levels of reliability required in very critical applications, such as major telephone network operations and spacecraft missions.

Pratt, Terrence W. *Programming Languages: Design and Implementation*. P-H 2nd ed. 1984 o.p. Comprehensive introduction, survey, and discussion of standard programming languages, explaining programming concepts and problems, comparing approaches and strategies, and indicating advantages and disadvantages of each language. With bibliographical comments in each chapter.

Press, William, and others. *Numerical Recipes: The Art of Scientific Computing*. Cambridge U. Pr. 1989 $49.95. ISBN 0-521-38330-7. Contributions from four collaborators from research and industry on subjects of interest to scientists, engineers, and social scientists using quantitative methods; includes 200 routines in both FORTRAN and Pascal, usable on IBM PC compatibles.

Price, Jonathan. *How to Write a Computer Manual*. Benjamin-Cummings 1993 $33.95. ISBN 0-8053-6829-9. Comprehensive text for writers, software managers, and educators, demonstrating through real-world examples how to schedule, write, edit, and self-evaluate software documentation and manuals.

Ralston, Anthony, and Edwin D. Reilly, Jr., eds. *Encyclopedia of Computer Science and Engineering*. Van Nos. Reinhold 1992 $125.00. ISBN 0-442-27679-6. Excellent reference tool for computing and computers, with signed articles, cross-references, and bibliographies. Appendix lists abbreviations, acronyms, American universities that offer doctoral degrees in computer science, and a glossary of major programming languages.

Sedgewick, Robert. *Algorithms. Computer Science Ser.* Addison-Wesley 1983 o.p. Forty chapters on such topics as mathematical algorithms, sorting, searching, string processing, geometric algorithms, graph algorithms, and other advanced topics. Assumes prior knowledge of programming with Pascal.

Tanenbaum, Andrew S. *Modern Operating Systems*. P-H 1992. ISBN 0-13-588187-0. One of the best introductions to the many old and new operating systems now available for microcomputers, ranging from MS-DOS, DR DOS, and MS-Windows to Microsoft NT, OS/2, Solaris, and NeXTStep.

Tennent, R. *Principles of Programming Languages*. P-H 1981 o.p. Covers programming language structure, design, and implementation issues.

Tucker, Allen B., Jr. *Programming Languages. Computer Science Ser.* McGraw 2nd ed. 1987 o.p. Systematic treatment in depth of 11 programming languages: Ada, APL, C, COBOL, FORTRAN, LISP, Pascal, PL/1, PROLOG, SNOBOL, and Modula-2. Stresses prominent languages now in use with microcomputers but retains the initial emphasis on scientific data processing, text processing, artificial intelligence, and systems programming.

Voss, Greg. *Object-Oriented Programming: An Introduction*. Osborne McGraw 1991 $24.95. ISBN 0-07-881682-3. Demonstrations of encapsulation, inheritance, and polymorphism—the three building blocks of object-oriented programming—introduced through practical examples in four actual languages (C++, Turbo Pascal, SmallTalk, and Actor) and three application packages (Turbo Vision, C++ Views, and ObjectWindows).

Ward, Paul T. *Systems Development Without Pain: A User's Guide to Modeling Organizational Patterns*. P-H 1986 $40.00. ISBN 0-13-881392-2. Offers ASML (A Systems Modeling Language) for communications between data processing professionals and end users, using the principles of structured analysis and integrating data and process modeling. Introduction by Edward Yourdon. Includes 200 diagrams.

Wasserman, Anthony I. *Programming Language Design*. IEEE Computer Society Pr. 1980 o.p. Collection of papers including several critiques of the original Pascal design.

Wexelblatt, Richard L., ed. *History of Programming Languages*. Acad. Pr. 1981 $68.00. ISBN 0-12-745040-8. Includes several contributions by authors of programming languages or by participants in design teams.

Wirth, Niklaus. *Algorithms and Data Structures*. P-H 1986 $53.00. ISBN 0-13-022005-1. Collection of classical and basic problems in programming along with the solutions worked out logically.

Yourdon, Edward. *The Decline and Fall of the American Programmer*. P-H 1992 $24.95. ISBN 0-13-203670-3. A dirge for the overconfidence of American programmers who are pleased with how they are doing and refuse to face the competition of overseas programmers. Complete with a list of 87 books of required reading.

_____. *Structured Walkthroughs*. P-H 1989 $35.00. ISBN 0-13-855289-4. Standard work on using peer review as a procedure for facing the issue of clarity in programming.

Specific Programming Languages, Environments, Media

Alcock, Donald. *Illustrating FORTRAN (The Portable Variety)*. Cambridge U. Pr. 1983 $19.95. ISBN 0-521-28810-X. Relaxed work, executed and illustrated by Alcock's own calligraphy and designs, for new programmers or those who know some BASIC; includes methods of self-discipline, some introductory-level tips and tricks, and reference materials. Format is similar to the same author's *Illustrating BASIC*.

Cooper, Doug, and Michael Clancy. *Oh! Pascal!* Norton 1993 $30.95. ISBN 0-393-96398-5. Excellent introduction to problem solving in Pascal, stressing dos and don'ts and emphasizing nonmathematical operations.

Corré, Alan D. *Icon Programming for Humanists.* P-H 1990 $30.00. ISBN 0-13-450180-2. The first third-party treatment of Icon; intended for programmers with some previous experience.

Craig, John Clark. *The Microsoft Visual Basic Workshop.* Microsoft 1993 $39.95. ISBN 1-55615-04-2. Guide to the Visual Basic language; includes ready-made routines and shortcuts for advanced tasks, such as building your own help system.

Crawley, J. Winston, and Charles E. Miller. *A Structured Approach to FORTRAN.* P-H 2nd ed. 1986 $39.00. ISBN 0-13-854183-3. Introduction to programming, program design, and implementations, including the use of subprograms, pitfalls to avoid, and detailed explanations; contains exercises.

Dunteman, Jeff. *Complete Turbo Pascal.* Scott F. 1985 o.p. Clear and explicit tutorial for Pascal following principles of structured program design.

Dwyer, Thomas A., and Margot A. Critchfield. *BASIC and the Personal Computer.* Addison-Wesley 1978 o.p. Classic text, well written and profusely illustrated; recommended as an introduction to BASIC for nonprogrammers.

Etter, D. M. *Problem Solving with Structured FORTRAN 77.* Benjamin-Cummings 1984 $50.00. ISBN 0-8053-2524-7. Introductory-level textbook, covering debugging and programming style; includes key terms, glossary, and frequent examples.

——. *Structured FORTRAN 77 for Engineers and Scientists.* Benjamin-Cummings 4th ed. 1992 $40.95. ISBN 0-8053-1775-9. Top-down problem solving, with engineering and scientific applications, reference aids on syntax, FORTRAN statements, and self-testing features; includes special attention to numerical methods for engineers.

Feingold, Carl. *Fundamentals of Structured COBOL Programming.* HarpC 1991 $51.50. ISBN 0-673-52113-3. Useful textbook with flowcharts, program code, and reference appendixes; each section covers tables, files, and writing reports.

Friedman, Daniel P., and Matthias Felleisen. *The Little LISPer.* MIT Pr. 1987 $13.95. ISBN 0-262-56038-0. Elegant introduction to LISP and its recursive functions by one of its leading practitioners.

Goldberg, Adele. *Smalltalk-80: The Interactive Programming Environment.* Addison-Wesley 1984 o.p. Introduction to the Smalltalk language, with sections on interfacing the system, support to find objects and information, class descriptions, error correction, and files and housekeeping.

Goldberg, Adele, and David Robson. *Smalltalk-80: The Language.* Addison-Wesley 1989 $41.95. ISBN 0-201-11370-8. More advanced work than the preceding title.

Grauer, Robert T., and M. Crawford. *The COBOL Environment.* P-H 1979 $50.00. ISBN 0-13-139394-4. Discussion of program development, structured programming, top-down programming development and design, and COBOL implementations.

——. *Structured COBOL: A Pragmatic Approach.* P-H 1981 o.p. Teaches COBOL through a series of practical models and examples, unifying programming theory and commercial applications.

Griswold, Ralph E. *The Snobol4 Programming Language.* P-H 2nd ed. 1971 o.p. Standard reference work for the programming language used extensively in studies in literature and the humanities. A more elementary introduction is Ralph E. Griswold and Madge T. Griswold's *A Snobol4 Primer.*

Ide, Nancy. *Pascal for the Humanities.* U. of Pa. Pr. 1987 $28.95. ISBN 0-812-21242-8. Systematic explanations of computer programming in literary and textual analysis; takes the student step-by-step through examples of graduated difficulty in standard Pascal.

Jensen, K., and N. Wirth. *Pascal User Manual and Report.* Spr.-Verlag 3rd ed. 1990 $24.95. ISBN 0-387-96048-1. Authoritative basic reference manual and implementation of the language by the original author of Pascal.

Kemeny, John G., and Thomas E. Kurtz. *BASIC Programming.* Wiley 4th ed. 1991 $29.95. ISBN 0-387-97649-3. Standard introduction to BASIC by the creators of the original version of the program featuring many specialized applications.

Kernighan, Brian W., and Dennis M. Ritchie. *The C Programming Language*. P-H 2nd ed. 1989 $40.00. ISBN 0-13-116370-9. Standard tutorial on C for experienced programmers. (For answers to and discussions of problems raised in this book, see Clovis L. Tondo and Scott E. Gimpel, *The C Answer Book* [P-H 1985 $20.33].)

McCabe, C. Kevin. *FORTH Fundamentals: Language Glossary*. 2 vols. Crown Pub. Group o.p. Solid, traditional introduction to FORTH.

McCarthy, J., and others. *LISP 1.5 Programmer's Manual*. MIT Pr. 1962 o.p. The original LISP design.

Miller, Alan R. *BASIC Programs for Scientists and Engineers*. Sybex 1981 o.p. One of a series of high-quality texts that explains the use of BASIC as a programming language in science and engineering; companion volumes by the same author also treat FORTRAN or Pascal.

Seidel, Ken. *Microsoft COBOL*. Weber Systems 1983 $19.95. ISBN 0-88056-117-3. Applies the mainframe file-handling capabilities of COBOL to microcomputers.

Weiner, Richard S., and Richard Sincovec. *Programming in Ada*. Wiley 1983 o.p. Extensive examples of program listings for each concept presented; intended for those with previous knowledge of programming.

Winston, Patrick Henry, and Berthold K. Horn. *LISP*. Addison-Wesley 1989 $37.75. ISBN 0-201-08319-1. Introduction to basic elements of LISP programming, followed by a series of practical applications. Portions of the book supplement or replace Winston's previous work, *Artificial Intelligence* (2 vols. MIT 1979 $35.00 ea.).

Wirth, Niklaus. *Programming on Modula-2*. Spr.-Verlag 1989 $33.00. ISBN 0-387-50150-9. The author of Modula-2 and Pascal covers the structured approach for which this language is known.

_____. *Systematic Programming: An Introduction*. P-H 1973 o.p. Pascal applications by the author of the Pascal and Modula-2 languages.

Zaks, Rodnay. *Introduction to Pascal: Including Turbo Pascal*. Sybex 1986 o.p. Classic introduction to programming in Pascal, including material on a new version of the language.

Operating Systems and Environments: New Media

There are many proprietary operating systems used on mainframe computers and minicomputers; in addition, there are several microcomputer operating systems that are specific to one manufacturer's hardware. Over the years, however, as personal computers became more powerful, three families of operating systems obtained important manufacturer and user support: IBM endorsed the MS-DOS (PC-DOS) and OS/2 standards of the Microsoft Corporation, AT&T supported the UNIX system created by Bell Telephone Laboratories, and Apple Computers introduced its own operating system for the Macintosh. Many single-task and single-user microcomputers used MS-DOS or PC-DOS in the earlier 1980s; by mid-decade, more powerful operating systems, such as UNIX, began to be applied to multiuser local networks connecting microcomputers, and in the late 1980s, IBM shifted its focus from PC-DOS to OS/2, a new and more advanced operating system for simultaneous multitasking. Microcomputers already had eclipsed the power, speed, and capacity of the classic vacuum tube computers of the 1940s and 1950s, and they were approaching the capacity of the minicomputers and mainframe computers of the 1970s. For several years IBM and compatible personal computers used a character-based display, whereas Apple Macintosh computers used a graphics-based display. The character display was adequate for words and numbers, but the graphics display was superior for pictures and training. IBM introduced OS/2 to replace DOS and to incorporate the idea of a graphical (pictorial) interface.

Microsoft Windows, designed as a graphical interface, did not do well in its first two versions. The third version, however, was hugely successful, appearing to be an operating system of its own rather than a graphical interface and multitasking environment placed on top of DOS. There was a worldwide rush of software suppliers to write new versions of existing software for Windows. After IBM and Microsoft had a falling out, Windows and OS/2 went their separate ways, and Microsoft developed NT (new technology), intended to compete with UNIX, and pursued a better integration of Windows and DOS. Fortunately, these various operating systems were intended to be backwardly compatible, so that OS/2 could handle Windows programs and Windows could run DOS programs. Current works by Goodman, Norton, Petzvold, and Wolverton, having gone through several revised editions, are useful for specific assistance in programming for DOS, the Macintosh, or Windows.

At about the same time that graphical interfaces started to appear, compact disks (small laser disks) of enormous capacity were introduced for data storage. The CD-ROM device could read only what the manufacturer put on the disk (ROM stands for read only memory), but CD-I (compact disk–interactive) also could accept what the user created. Kodak added the Photo CD format, which permitted images to be added in separate sessions. The price of mastering a data CD-ROM fell promisingly to a few thousand dollars and the duplication cost to only a dollar or two.

Andrews, Nancy. *Windows: The Official Guide to Microsoft's Operating Environment.* Microsoft 1986 o.p. Introduction for programmers, using Windows to integrate multiple applications in MS-DOS and to create an operating environment that resembles the graphics capability of the Apple Macintosh.

AT&T Staff. *UNIX Programmer's Manual.* HarbraceJ 1986 $42.75. ISBN 0-03-04207-9. The definitive work on the subject, prepared by its developers. Vol. 1 is a reference manual and Vol. 2 contains tutorials and applications.

Duncan, Ray. *Advanced MS-DOS: The Microsoft Guide for Assembly Language and C Programmers.* Microsoft 1988 $24.95. ISBN 55615-157-8. Written for the advanced programmer using assembly language and C programs for maximum speed and compactness in MS-DOS. Duncan is a columnist for *Dr. Dobbs' Journal.*

Goodman, Danny, and Richard Saul Wurman. *Danny Goodman's Macintosh Handbook: Featuring System 7.* Bantam 1992 $29.95. ISBN 0-553-35485-X. Visually oriented book that out-Macs even the Apple Macintosh manual on hypertext links and balloon helps; nevertheless filled with the essential information needed by all Mac users. With a foreword by John Sculley.

Inside Macintosh. Addison-Wesley 1991 $39.95. ISBN 0-20157755-0. Official guide for programmers writing application programs, desk accessories, device drivers, and other projects. Follows the authorized requirements for the standard Macintosh user interface and explains the internal routines fixed in the Macintosh.

Lafore, Robert. *Assembly Language Primer for the IBM PC and XT.* NAL-Dutton 1984 o.p. Treats assembly language for its speed, flexibility, and graphics routines and covers DOS functions and programming with DEBUG and IBM Assembler ASM.

Lambert, Steve, and Suzanne Ropiequet. *CD ROM: The New Papyrus.* Microsoft 1986 o.p. Pioneering compilation of more than 40 articles on the CD-ROM system and design, publishing, and other applications. A sequel is Suzanne Ropiequet and others, *CD ROM 2: Optical Publishing* (Microsoft 1987 $22.95).

Levenson, Steven, and Eli E. Hertz. *Now That I Have OS/2 2.0 on My Computer, What Do I Do Next?* Van Nos. Reinhold 1992 $22.95. ISBN 0-442-01227-6. Tutorial introduction that simplifies the object-oriented Workplace Shell (WPS) in OS/2 2.0 and then thoroughly explains OS/2's four object types—devices, folders, data files, and programs.

Lu, Cary. *The Apple Macintosh book.* Microsoft 4th ed. 1992 $29.95. ISBN 1-55615-218-7. Knowledgeable, clear, concise, and no-nonsense update of the Macintosh handbook that was arguably, in 1984, the first Mac companion to appear.

McGilton, Henry, and Rachel Morgan. *Introducing the UNIX System*. McGraw 1983 $29.95. ISBN 0-07-045001-3. Intended for professionals who already possess the UNIX system documentation and Programmer's Manual; uses UNIX version 7 primarily but also refers to the Berkeley version of UNIX.

Naiman, Arthur, and others. *The Macintosh Bible: Thousands of Basic and Advanced Tips, Tricks, and Shortcuts Logically Organized and Fully Indexed*. Peachpit Pr. 4th ed. 1992 $32.00. ISBN 1-56609-009-1. Well-established reference handbook and collection of suggestions for Macintosh users that has benefited from several revisions.

Norton, Peter. *Inside the IBM PC*. Brady 1991 $24.95. ISBN 0-13-465634-2. A guide to the IBM PC microprocessor, DOS, ROM, programming, disk storage, and graphics.

_____. *Outside the IBM PC and PS/2: Access to New Technology*. Brady Books 1992 $29.95. ISBN 0-13-643586-6. Ed. by Scott Clark and Kevin Goldstein. "Outside" meaning peripherals, such as modems, laptops, printers, scanners, networks, and multimedia.

_____. *The Peter Norton Programmer's Guide to the IBM PC: The Ultimate Reference Guide to the Entire Family of IBM Personal Computers*. Microsoft 1985 o.p. Technical data and an explanation of the architecture of the IBM PC for intermediate and advanced programmers.

Norton, Peter, and Harley Hahn. *Peter Norton's Guide to Unix*. Bantam 1991 $26.95. ISBN 0-553-35260-1. Clear and concise introduction to the UNIX operating system for beginners, many of whom are making the transition from microcomputer operating systems to the world of big computers.

Norton, Peter, and John Socha. *Peter Norton's Assembly Language Book for the IBM PC*. Brady Books 1990 $44.95. ISBN 0-13-662979-0. Tutorial and reference guide to assembly language, optional diskette containing programs and utilities.

Petzvold, Charles. *Programming Windows 3.1*. Microsoft 3rd ed. 1992 $35.00. ISBN 1-55615-395-3. Standard reference guide for Microsoft Windows programmers, diligently updated, now using C++ as its fundamental programming language.

Waite Group. *UNIX Primer Plus*. Sams 1983 o.p. Good first reader on UNIX for the programmer who has some prior experience with other systems.

Wolverton, Van. *Running MS-DOS*. Microsoft 6th ed. 1993 $24.95. ISBN 1-556-15542-5. Clearer and better written explanation than the official DOS manual, both as a tutorial for utter beginners and as a useful reference for intermediate and advanced users who need to keep up with the most recent changes.

Wolverton, Van, and Dan Gookin. *Supercharging MS-DOS*. Microsoft 3rd ed. 1991 $19.95. ISBN 1-55615-371-6. Contains quite a few handy tricks and practical tips, as well as warnings of pitfalls to avoid in obtaining top efficiency from DOS commands and procedures.

COMPUTER APPLICATIONS

Business and Professional

This section contains books for business use of computers in accounting, auditing and security, personnel, contract negotiation, cost estimation, executive computing, forecasts of future information, free-lancing and consulting, hiring and training computer personnel, information systems philosophy, introduction to business applications, investment and finance, management, marketing data, marketing and business management, microcomputer management, on-line business information, preventing fraud and unauthorized access, project management, purchasing software and hardware, small businesses, and spreadsheet uses. In addition, there are titles of interest in the professions of medicine and law. Although bookstores are well stocked with them, titles dealing mainly with particular business and spreadsheet software programs are not included here.

Anbar, Michael, ed. *Computers in Medicine.* W. H. Freeman 1987 $40.95. ISBN 0-7167-8129-8. Twelve essays on patient records and accounts, diagnostic techniques, clinical decisions, diet planning, and the psychology of doctor-nurse-patient interaction. Intended for doctors, medical students, computer science and engineering personnel interested in medical applications, and health-care professionals concerned with the impact of automation.

Day, John. *Microcomputers in Business: Spreadsheet, Word Processing, and Database Management Systems.* Scott F. 1986 o.p. Introduction to business applications through standard applications packages for IBM PC and compatible microcomputers.

Dayton, Doug. *Computer Solutions for Business.* Microsoft 1987 o.p. Refreshing, clearly organized overview of microcomputer possibilities for the small- to medium-sized business; concentrates on a systems approach to problems and solutions, not specific software packages.

Deutsch, Dennis S. *Protect Yourself: The Guide to Understanding and Negotiating Contracts for Business Computers and Software.* Wiley 1984 o.p. Explains the nature of contracts, liability, and warranties in the area of acquiring business computer hardware and software by using concrete examples.

Frank, Judith. *Managing Business Microcomputer Systems.* Brady Books 1987 o.p. Comprehensive introduction to problems and issues in local area networks, multiuser systems, stand-alone personal computers, and the integration of computers into office automation and information technology.

Glossbrenner, Alfred. *Glossbrenner's Guide to Shareware for Small Businesses.* Windcrest 1992 $37.95. ISBN 0-8306-3377-4. Useful guide to the economies of shareware for the small businessowner on a tight budget; prefaced by a veritable handbook on hardware, software, shopping, installation, and configuration for the first-time PC user.

———. *How to Buy Software: The Master Guide to Picking the Right Program.* St. Martin 1984 $14.95. ISBN 0-312-39551-5. Comparative checklists of features of typical software packages, listing the criteria for selection in all standard areas of application packages.

Gralla, Preston. *PC/Computing Guide to Shareware.* Ziff-Davis 1992 $34.95. ISBN 1-56276-036-X. Encouragement for one of the last frontiers for the small, creative computing entrepreneur—the marketing of independent shareware; includes reviews of some 250 cost-efficient shareware programs in 13 categories.

Kanter, Jerome. *Computer Essays for Management.* P-H 1987 $28.00. ISBN 0-13-165994-4. Ten essays on aspects of information systems (IS), including IS as a strategic tool, the IS executive, senior management, practical considerations in IS computing, IS long-range planning, managing risk in application development, and future development in IS.

Kolve, Carolee N. *How to Buy (and Survive!) Your First Computer: A Guide for Small Business Success.* McGraw 1983 o.p. Advice for micro managers and for companies considering their first purchase, installation, training program, and systems integration for a micro- or minicomputer.

Kuong, Javier F. *Computer Security, Auditing, and Internal Control Manual.* Management Advisory Pubns. 1974 $25.00. ISBN 0-940706-05-9. How to plan and test an audit; evaluate weaknesses in EDP control organization, procedures, and staff; build effective control methods; handle emergency situations; provide insurance coverage; and solve special problems of networks and on-line databases.

Labelle, Charles, and others. *Finding, Selecting, Developing, and Retraining Data Professionals through Effective Human Resource Management.* Van Nos. Reinhold 1983 o.p. Human approach to EDP that considers the issue of supervising both new and long-term personnel in computer data operations, rather than the technical side of systems, hardware, and software.

Lobel, Jerome. *Foiling the System Breakers: Computer Security and Access Control.* McGraw 1986 o.p. How to spot weaknesses in data communication networks through planning, organizing, and controlling direct access to information systems, while balancing the requirements of normal operations and the need for security control; includes examples, charts, and graphs.

McCann, John M. *The Marketing Workbench: Using Computers for Better Performance.* Busn. One Irwin 1986 $27.50. ISBN 0-87094-763-X. Marketing management philosophy for the consumer goods industry, with case histories of computer use at such companies as Pillsbury, Frito-Lay, and General Foods.

McClung, Christina J., and Kenneth A. McClung, Jr. *Microcomputers for Legal Professionals.* Wiley 1984 o.p. How personal computers can be used by both lawyers and paralegals in the law office, including word processing, forms for court papers, maintaining client records, time billing, and computer-assisted legal research.

McNitt, Lawrence. *The Art of Computer Management: How Small Firms Increase Productivity and Profits with Small Computers.* S&S Trade 1984 o.p. Case studies from several representative business types are used to explain how to undertake a computer needs analysis and make hardware and software selections.

McWilliams, Peter. *Personal Computers and the Disabled.* Doubleday 1984 o.p. Unique treatment of an often-neglected subject.

Martin, James. *Computer Networks and Distributed Processing: Software, Techniques, and Architecture.* P-H 1981 $70.67. ISBN 0-13-165258-3. Comprehensive work on software, techniques, and organization of distributed processing for data processing managers.

——. *An Information Systems Manifesto.* P-H 1984 $65.33. ISBN 0-13-464769-6. Lively, readable, state-of-the-art advice to data processing managers on productivity, personnel and organization structures, decentralized computing, high-level programming languages, application and report generators, database query languages, decision-support microcomputer software, and the use of flexible corporate information centers.

Mellin, Michael, and Mia McCroskey, eds. *The Book of IBM Software.* Book Co. 3rd ed. 1985 o.p. Lists and describes current software for the IBM PC and compatibles according to application categories.

Nevison, Jack M. *The Elements of Spreadsheet Style.* Brady Comm. 1987 o.p. Twenty-two rules for effective spreadsheet design and functioning, including correct structures free of hidden values, models capable of subsequent modification, and how to keep spreadsheet structure that is clear and explicit regardless of size. Not limited to specific software.

——. *Executive Computing: How to Get It Done on Your Own.* Addison-Wesley 1981 o.p. How executives can effectively use personal computers in such areas as project scheduling and forecasting.

Oppenheimer, Max Stul. *Chips! Strategic Issues in Computer Industry Negotiations.* Busn. One Irwin 1986 o.p. How to negotiate with vendors for software products and services, plus some of the prospects and pitfalls of contract negotiations.

Osgood, William R., and James F. Molloy, Jr. *Business Decision Making for Higher Profits: A 1-2-3 Business User's Guide.* Weber Systems 1984 o.p. Outstanding series of business computer application books, with individual volumes on Apple computers, the IBM PC, and several spreadsheet applications packages.

Perry, William E. *Survival Guide to Computer Systems: A Primer for Executives.* Van Nos. Reinhold 1982 o.p. Explains computer systems for the business user by means of 50 rules for survival and success; emphasizes people and personnel.

Remer, Daniel. *Computer Power for Your Law Office.* Sybex 1983 o.p. Introduction to several aspects of computer applications for legal professionals, including word processing, databases, spreadsheets, and computer-directed printing of papers, correspondence, and legal research.

Rockhart, John F., and Christine V. Bullen. *The Rise of Managerial Computing: The Best of the Center for Information Systems Research.* Busn. One Irwin 1986 $44.00. ISBN 0-87094-757-5. Collection of 18 contributions on management information systems (MIS); originally part of the Working Papers Series of the Center for Information Systems Research of the Sloan School of Management of MIT.

Scheer, A. W. *Computer: A Challenge for Business Administration.* Spr.-Verlag 1985 $29.00. ISBN 0-387-15514-7. Opportunities for business administration through electronic data processing and information technology, including trends in information processing, databases, interactive processing, office automation, factory automation, and artificial intelligence.

Schiller, Herbert I. *Who Knows: Information in the Age of the Fortune 500.* Ablex Pub. 1981 $45.00. ISBN 0-89391-069-4. Discusses implications for business of many of the developments expected in the postindustrial era of the information society.

Schneider, J. Stewart, and Charles S. Bowen. *Microcomputers for Lawyers.* TAB Bks. 1983 o.p. Professional guide to using small computers in the law office to prepare court papers, handle correspondence, and undertake research.

Shneiderman, Ben. *Designing the User Interface: Strategies for Effective Human-Computer Interaction.* Addison-Wesley 2nd ed. 1992 $43.25. ISBN 0-201-57286-9. Standard work on human-computer interaction, user interfaces, and system design; useful for evaluating both general computer user interfaces and specialized library applications.

Simon, A. R. *How to Be a Successful Computer Consultant.* McGraw 1990 $32.95. ISBN 0-07-057554-1. Practical advice for software consultants and software designers on why people use consultants, some of the services and products offered, business negotiation, publicity, and how to update professional and technical knowledge.

Smedinghoff, Thomas J. *The Legal Guide to Developing, Protecting and Marketing Software: Dealing with Problems Raised by Consumers, Competitors and Employees.* Wiley 1986 o.p. Survey of legal concepts and issues pertaining to software marketing. Explores law pertaining to copyright, trade secrets, trademarks, software contracts, vendor liability, and tax implications of software transactions, with citations of relevant cases, statutes, and government regulations.

Stewart, R. D. *Cost Estimating with Microcomputers.* McGraw 1985 o.p. Covers use of spreadsheets, database application packages, and cost-scheduling systems for cost estimators, designers, project and consulting engineers, university administrators, and owners of small businesses.

Thomas, Terry, and Marlene G. Weinstein. *Computer-Assisted Legal and Tax Research: A Professional's Guide to Lexis, Westlaw, and Phinet.* West Pub. 1993. ISBN 0-314-02266-X. Comprehensive guide to computer-assisted legal research (CALR), with suggestions on using terminals, personal computers, query formulas, blank search forms, office use and office integration, and time charges and other costs.

Tufte, Edward R. *Envisioning Information.* Graphics Pr. 1990 $48.00. ISBN 0-9613921-1-8. Exciting and inspiring presentation of the relations between the visual presentation of information and its statistical content by a prophet of the new field of visual information design; shows the inherent differences in several types of graphs, charts, and diagrams. See also Tufte's *The Visual Display of Quantitative Information* (Graphics Pr. 1983 $40.00. ISBN 0-9613821-8).

Waxman, Robert. *Moonlighting with Your Personal Computer.* Pharos Bks. 1984 o.p. Practical ideas and suggestions for starting and maintaining small businesses and business services in your spare time by using standard microcomputer hardware and software.

Weil, Ulric. *Information Systems in the 80s: Products, Markets, and Vendors.* P-H 1982 $28.75. ISBN 0-13-464644-4. Guide to the impact of the information society on business; lists information system products, who sells them, and market targets for the information systems manager and professional.

Williams, Andrew T. *What If? A User's Guide to Spreadsheets on the IBM PC.* Wiley 1984 $16.95. ISBN 0-471-89218-1. Principles and good practices for using spreadsheets with standard microcomputer software packages; explains maintaining documentation to expand or modify structures, preventing hidden values, and using macros.

Winston, Patrick Henry, and Karen A. Prendergast, eds. *The AI Business: Commercial Uses of Artificial Intelligence.* Artificial Intelligence Ser. MIT Pr. 1984 o.p. Artificial intelligence applications for oil, medicine, electronics, factory automation, and other fields; especially relevant to project analysis, financing, and investment.

Woodwell, Donald R. *Automating Your Financial Portfolio: An Investor's Guide to Personal Computers*. Busn. One Irwin 2nd ed. 1986 o.p. How to gather data on stocks and companies, screen stocks and bonds for buying opportunities, and manage investment portfolios with a personal computer.

Zboray, R., and D. Sachs. *Programs for Profit: How to Really Make Money with a Personal Computer*. McGraw 1984 o.p. Explains using a small computer for profit with a business of your own; reviews software packages and what they offer for business applications.

Databases and Data Communications

This section contains books on connecting microcomputers and mainframe computers, data communications, database management systems (DBMS), design and structure, file management, relational databases, and telematics. Database software packages are continuing to become more powerful and more sophisticated and also easier to use. Titles on standard proprietary database programs are not cited here, although they can be found in bookstores.

Atre, Shakuntala. *Data Base: Structured Techniques for Design, Performance and Management: With Case Studies*. Business Data Processing Ser. Wiley 1988 $47.50. ISBN 0-471-85251-1. Real-world, practical information and case studies on high-quality database design and management. Covers database administration; relational, hierarchical, and network data models; DBMS, data storage and access, and performance issues.

Belitsos, Byron, and Jay Misra. *Business Telematics: Corporate Networks for the Information Age*. Busn. One Irwin 1986 $39.95. ISBN 0-87094-777-X. Discusses management issues and telematic technology and applications, with actual corporate examples; surveys the fields of office integration, high-speed data communications, voice/data integration, local area networks, electronic mail, teleconferencing, micro-to-mainframe links, and videotex.

Chih-Yang, Chao. *Relational Databases*. P-H 1986 $51.00. ISBN 0-13-771858-6. Advanced principles and practices of databases, including relational database models, relational algebra, tuple and domain relational calculus, and query languages.

Date, C. J. *Database: A Primer*. Addison-Wesley 1983 o.p. Introduction with practical exercises, detailed descriptions, and how-to-do-it information on microcomputer and mainframe databases. For more advanced treatment, see the same author's two-volume *Introduction to Database Systems* (Addison-Wesley Vol. 1 1981 $44.25. Vol. 2 1983 $37.75).

_____. *An Introduction to Database Systems*. Vol. 1 Addison-Wesley 5th ed. 1990 $37.56. ISBN 0-201-51381-1. Good starting point for advanced study in database management; written in the author's characteristically authoritative and comprehensive manner, with emphasis on the relational model.

_____. *Relational Database: Selected Writings*. Addison-Wesley 1986 $43.25. ISBN 0-201-14196-5. Papers on relational database management, relational versus nonrelational systems, the SQL language, and database design.

Goley, George F., IV. *The Dow Jones-Irwin Technical Reference Guide to Microcomputer Database Management Systems*. Busn. One Irwin 1987 o.p. Analysis of the capabilities, advantages, and disadvantages of most popular microcomputer DBMS packages; includes practical tips and discussions of debugging and subroutines for each package. Intended for application developers.

Jones, J. A. *Databases in Theory and Practice*. TAB Bks. 1987 $28.95. ISBN 0-8306-2600-X. How to maintain databases, the advantages and disadvantages of several database systems, their requirements, and sample case studies. For database administrators and systems analysts.

Kim, Won. *Introduction to Object-Oriented Databases*. MIT Pr. 1990 $35.00. ISBN 0-262-11124-1. Comprehensive, readable introduction to object-oriented databases, refreshing in its uniform terminology and style, reflecting both practical professional experience and close familiarity with the journal literature.

Kopeck, Ronald F. *Micro-to-Mainframe Links.* McGraw 1986 o.p. Survey of file servers, local area networks, gateways, and bridge technologies, intended to be read by data processing managers and communications professionals. Discusses installations, workstation/host relations, data transfer and data security, costs, and monitoring techniques.

Korth, Henry F., and Abraham Silberschatz. *Database System Concepts. Computer Science Ser.* McGraw 1986 o.p. Covers such subjects as entity/relationship; relational, network, and hierarchical models; their physical organization; indexing query processing; security; and applications of artificial intelligence. For readers with prior knowledge of programming and databases.

Kruglinski, David. *Data Base Management Systems—MS-DOS: Evaluating MS-DOS Database Software.* McGraw 1985 o.p. Update of Kruglinski's previous standard work on CP/M databases; valuable for its general discussion of database principles along with contemporary benchmarks for evaluating current database packages for business.

Laurie, Peter. *Databases: How to Manage Information on Your Micro.* Chapman & Hall 1985 $19.95. ISBN 0-412-26380-7. Well-written introduction for beginners covers the handling of computerized mailing lists, product information bases, and client data using microcomputer software packages; includes ample diagrams and charts.

Maier, David. *The Theory of Relational Databases.* W. H. Freeman 1983 $49.95. ISBN 0-7167-8076-3. Discusses relational algebra, functional considerations, multivalued and joint dependencies, representation theory, query modifications, database semantics, and query languages; assumes some prior knowledge of programming and databases.

Martin, James. *Principles of Data-Base Management.* P-H 1976 $59.00. ISBN 0-13-708917-1. Pioneering volume on the subject, along with the author's *Computer Data-Base Organization* (P-H 2nd ed. 1977 $49.95); emphasizes large computer systems. Still useful for advanced users.

Turpin, John, and Ray Sarch. *Data Communications: Beyond Basics.* McGraw 1986 o.p. Forty-three articles, originally published in *Data Communications* magazine in 1984 and 1985, on planning and design, new technology, applications, management, and future trends; supplements articles previously collected as *Basic Guide to Data Communications* (McGraw 1985 $29.95).

Ullman, Jeffrey D. *Principles of Database Systems.* W. H. Freeman 1982 $47.95. ISBN 0-7167-8069-0. Combines the treatment of actual database systems and query languages, such as ISBL, QUEL, Query-by-Example, and SEQUEL.

Text and Hypertext

The major word processing packages incorporate a full range of additional features, including the visual preview of printing, WYSIWYG (pronounced "wizzy-wig" and standing for "what you see is what you get"), page layout features rivaling desktop publishing packages, integrated spelling and grammar checking, on-line hypertext help and training tutorials, internal programming languages, and even text indexing and retrieval. Exploiting the spread of laser printers, most packages contain or can access a wide variety of typefaces and fonts for sophisticated text production and visual presentation.

The rise of hypertext presents three exciting promises. First, text can be broken down into screenfuls and linked by selected subjects, permitting nonlinear jumps in navigation, as in on-line help. Second, every word can be indexed in huge bibliographical databases so that direct, nonlinear retrieval is possible. Third, hypertext emerges as a way of looking at narrative and literary form in creative interactive fiction and poetry.

Bolter's study explores the consequences of hypertext on the nature of texts. Significant collections of shorter writings on hypertext in book form have been edited by Barrett, Delany, and Landow.

Barrett, Edward, ed. *The Society of Text: Hypertext, Hypermedia, and the Social Construction of Information.* MIT Pr. 1989 $19.95. ISBN 0-262-52161-X. Twenty-two essays on networking, on-line systems, hypermedia, and hypertext, including case studies of MIT's *Athena*, Brown University's *Intermedia*, and the University of Maryland's *Hyperties.*

_____. *Sociomedia: Multimedia, Hypermedia, and the Social Construction of Knowledge.* MIT Pr. 1992 $45.00. ISBN 0-262-02346-6. Papers from the first conference on The Social Creation of Knowledge at MIT in spring 1991.

_____. *Text, ConText, and HyperText: Writing with and for the Computer.* MIT Pr. 1988 $47.50. ISBN 0-262-02275-3. Collection of articles on technical communication, computer documentation, designing on-line help, and writer training.

Bolter, Jay David. *Writing Space: The Computer, Hypertext, and the History of Writing.* L. Erlbaum Assocs. 1991 $49.95. ISBN 0-8058-0427-7. Significant exploration of how hypertext differs from printed text, by the author of *Turing's Man.* Traces the major consequences for reading, writing, literary criticism, literary theory, and public literacy.

Bove, Tony, and others. *The Art of Desktop Publishing.* Bantam 2nd ed. 1987 $22.95. ISBN 0-553-34565-6. Introduction to typesetting, newsletters, brochures, clip and generated art, laser printers and their software, page makeup, fonts, CD-ROM, and optical disks. For both IBM PC and Macintosh microcomputers.

Cole, B. C. *Beyond Word Processing: How to Use Your Personal Computer as a Processor.* McGraw 1985 o.p. Describes information storage in textbases and wordbases, how special programs work, and how existing software can be used for these language databases. Professional writers will find the discussion of procedures useful even though some of the software has been superseded.

Delany, Paul, and George P. Landow, eds. *Hypermedia and Literary Studies.* MIT Pr. 1991 $39.95. ISBN 0-262-04119-7. Useful collection on the theory and design of literary hypermedia, studies of actual hypermedia projects in schools, and consequences for creative composition, teaching, and literary criticism.

Feldman, Paula R., and Buford Norman. *The Wordworthy Computer: Classroom and Research Applications in Language and Literature.* Random 1987 $13.00. ISBN 0-394-35623-3. Bibliography. Useful teacher's handbook to what lies beyond word processing, namely indexing, concordances, literary analysis, and text editing, using microcomputer examples.

Felici, James, and Ted Nace. *Desktop Publishing Skills.* Addison-Wesley 1987 $24.75. ISBN 0-201-11537-9. Primer for typesetting, page makeup, font selection, hardware and software, laser printers, and cost evaluation, using the Macintosh or IBM PC.

Fluegelman, Andrew, and Jeremy Hewes. *Writing in the Computer Age: Word Processing Skills and Style for Every Writer.* Doubleday 1983 o.p. Standard book of advice to practicing writers on the basic mechanics of writing with a word processor and on how to use the computer to achieve and refine a personal style.

Heim, Michael. *Electric Language: A Philosophical Study of Word Processing.* Yale U. Pr. 1989 $16.00. ISBN 0-300-04610-3. Sophisticated view of word processing using the transformative theory of language of Wittgenstein and Eric Holbrook and the ontological theory of language of Martin Heidegger.

Hobbs, Jerry R. *Literature and Cognition.* Ctr. Study Language 1990 $35.00. ISBN 0-937073-53-9. Twofold introduction to literary studies for cognitive scientists and cognitive science for literary specialists; written by a computer scientist with unexpected insights into literature, psychology, and discourse analysis.

Kleper, Michael L. *The Illustrated Handbook of Desktop Publishing and Typesetting.* TAB Bks. 1987 $49.95. ISBN 0-8306-0700-5. Comprehensive sourcebook on all current phases of personal computers, software, work stations, word processing, text formatters, telecommunications, data manipulation and conversion, typesetting hardware, typesetting software, desktop publishing, and output devices.

Knuth, Donald. *The T$_E$Xtbook*. Am. Math 1988 $35.00. ISBN 0-201-13448-9. Introduction to T$_E$X (pronounced "tek"); augmented by Knuth's *Computers and Typesetting* (5 vols. Addison-Wesley 1986 $32.25–$37.75 ea.), an advanced series including *T$_E$X: The Program* (Vol. 2), *Metafont: The Program* (Vol. 4), and *Computer Modern Typefaces* (Vol. 5).

Lancashire, Ian, ed. *The Humanities Computing Yearbook 1989–1990*. OUP 1991 $60.00. ISBN 0-19-824253-0. Second of a series of annual surveys, including a comprehensive guide to humanities software and other resources.

Lancashire, Ian, and Willard McCarty, eds. *The Humanities Computing Yearbook 1988*. OUP 1988 $69.00. ISBN 0-19-824442-8. First of a series of annual surveys of worldwide computing activity by humanities scholars.

Landow, George P. *Hypertext: The Convergence of Contemporary Critical Theory and Technology*. Johns Hopkins 1992 $45.00. ISBN 0-8018-4280-8. Bibliography. Discusses parallels between postmodern deconstruction in literary theory as practiced by Jacques Derrida and Roland Barthes and the decentered, readerly, and antihierarchical structure of recent computer hypertexts.

Landow, George, and Paul Delany, eds. *The Digital Word*. MIT Pr. 1993 $39.95. ISBN 0-262-12176-X. Collection of essays on text projects, electronic texts, text retrieval, text software, text corpora, text editing, electronic conferences, scholarly research, electronic publishing, critical analysis, and electronic reading.

McWilliams, Peter A. *The Word Processing Book*. Ballantine 1984 o.p. Probably the best book for beginners in computing and word processing for its feisty comments and no-nonsense approach.

Mitchell, Joan P. *The New Writer*. Microsoft 1987 o.p. Introduction to developments, concepts, and technologies in word processing and how to make the most of word processing as a writer.

Nelson, Ted. *Computer Lib/Dream Machines*. 1974. Microsoft rev. ed. 1987 $18.95. ISBN 0-914-84549-7. Reissue with some revisions of the classic double-decker that introduced the notion of hypertext.

Noble, David F., and Virginia D. Noble. *Improve Your Writing with Word Processing*. Que Corp. 1984 o.p. Offers parallels between block moves in word processing and how the writer can rearrange phrases, sentences, paragraphs, and sections; a more advanced work than the title suggests.

Postscript Language Reference Manual. Addison-Wesley 1990 $28.95. ISBN 0-201-18127-4

Postscript Language Tutorial and Cookbook. Addison-Wesley 1985 $18.95. ISBN 0-201-10179-3. This and the above title are official manuals from Adobe Systems for its standard page description programming language; for software programmers, consultants, and other users employing laser printers for word processing, graphics illustration, or CAD/CAM.

Seybold, John, and Fritz Dressler. *Publishing from the Desktop*. Bantam 1987 $19.95. ISBN 0-553-34401-3. View of developments in desktop publishing technology, including type design, digital imaging, electronic typesetting, electronic page makeup, and page design for professional results.

Will-Harris, Daniel. *Desktop Publishing with Style: A Complete Guide to Design Techniques and New Technology for the IBM PC and Compatibles*. And Bks. 1987 $24.95. ISBN 0-89708-162-5. Introduction to software, hardware, basic graphics, typesetting, dot matrix printers, laser printers, clip art, and drawing programs; with introduction by Peter A. McWilliams.

Computers and Fiction

The alchemy of computers, networks, and biotech in the 1980s led to the new wave of cyberpunk fiction by Gibson and Sterling. But the tradition for treating the social issues raised by developments in intelligent machines and biotechnology is much older. Readers should be aware of nineteenth-century classics by EDWARD BELLAMY (see Vol. 1) and MARY WOLLSTONECRAFT SHELLEY (see Vol. 1), as well as the twentieth-century masterpieces of ALDOUS HUXLEY (see Vol. 1) and GEORGE ORWELL (see Vol. 1). Science fiction aficionados will relish ISAAC ASIMOV (see Vol. 1), ARTHUR C. CLARKE (see Vol. 1), John Brunner, and ROBERT A. HEINLEIN (see Vol. 1). Mainstream authors not already mentioned who turned to computer-related themes include JOHN BARTH (see Vol. 1), SAMUEL BUTLER (see Vol. 1), and H. G. WELLS (see Vol. 1).

Significantly, in the 1990s, hypertext software and interactive fiction were combined in a new form of creative writing in which a story or a poem was published as a hypertext software package for the Macintosh. Three examples of this new form issued by Eastgate are Michael Joyce, *Afternoon, A Story* (1990), Jon Lanested and George P. Landow, *The In Memoriam Web* (1993), and Stuart Moulthrop, *Victory Garden* (1991).

Asimov, Isaac. *I, Robot*. 1956. Bantam 1991 $4.99. ISBN 0-553-29438-5. Perhaps the best-known cycle of tales on robots.

Barth, John. *Giles Goat-Boy*. 1966. Doubleday 1987 $11.95. ISBN 0-385-24086-4. A satire after Swift and Sterne on the alternate world of the computer as troll, mechanist universe, and author.

Bellamy, Edward. *Looking Backward: 2000–1887*. 1888. Random 1982 $3.75. ISBN 0-685-04266-9. The utopia of a thoroughly mechanized and bureaucratic world.

Brunner, John. *The Shockwave Rider*. Ballantine 1984 $4.95. ISBN 0-345-32431-5. Gives new meaning to the phrase "human-computer interface."

Butler, Samuel. *Erewhon*. 1872. Viking Penguin 1970 $8.95. ISBN 0-14-043057-1. See "The Book of the Machine," Chapters 21–23.

Clarke, Arthur C. *2001*. NAL-Dutton 1968 $3.95. ISBN 0-451-15580-7. Based on the filmscript by Clarke and Stanley Kubrick. See also Clarke's sequels, *2010* (also a film) and *2061*.

Gibson, William. *Neuromancer*. Ace Bks. 1984 $4.99. ISBN 0-441-56959-5. The novel that defined cyberpunk. Also by the same author: *Burning Chrome* (1986), *Count Zero* (1986), and *Mona Lisa Overdrive* (1988); with Bruce Sterling, *The Difference Engine* (1991).

Heinlein, Robert. *The Moon Is a Harsh Mistress*. Ace Bks. 1987 $5.50. ISBN 0-441-53699-9. A moon civilization overthrows earth exploitation led by its computer.

Huxley, Aldous. *Brave New World*. 1932. Borgo Pr. 1991 $20.00. ISBN 0-8095-9046-8. Original outcry against mechanization, genetic engineering, and mind control.

Orwell, George. *1984*. 1949. NAL-Dutton 1950 $4.95. ISBN 0-451-52493-4. The classic contemporary dystopia of the techno-totalitarian state and the tyranny of political thought and language.

Roszak, Theodore. *Bugs*. Doubleday 1981 o.p. The computer as insect, by the author of *The Cult of Information*.

Shelley, Mary. *Frankenstein*. 1818. Random 1993 $14.00. ISBN 0-679-60059-0. Serious anticipation of the main issues in biotechnology and scientific responsibility (unlike the film versions).

Sterling, Bruce, ed. *Mirrorshades:The Cyberpunk Anthology*. Morrow 1986 $16.95. ISBN 0-87795-868-8. Collection after the success of Gibson's *Neuromancer*. See also Sterling's own novels, *Islands in the Net* (1988) and *Crystal Express* (1989).

Wells, H. G. *A Modern Utopia*. 1905. U. of Nebr. Pr. 1967 $14.00. ISBN 0-8032-5213-7. A professional-technocratic utopia, spurring E. M. Forster's satiric reply, "The Machine Stops" (1909).

_____. *The Time Machine*. 1895. Lightyear 1992 $11.95. ISBN 0-89968-283-9. Unexpected Marxian and Darwinian analyses of far future changes in human work roles, classes, races, and species.

Creativity in Art, Fiction, Film, Language, and Music

Books in this section treat the use of computers in virtual reality, Musical Instrument Digital Interface (MIDI), fine art and commercial graphics, films and literature, interactive fiction and conversational games, computational stylistics, literary analysis, and linguistics.

Abercrombie, John R. *Computer Programs for Literary Analysis.* U. of Pa. Pr. 1984 $16.95. ISBN 0-8122-1177-4. Programs in BASIC, Pascal, and IBYX for text conversion, indexing utilities, KWIC concordances, and other forms of literary analysis.

Aukstakalnis, Steve, ed. *Silicon Mirage: The Art and Science of Virtual Reality.* Peachpit Pr. 1992 $19.95. ISBN 0-93815-182-7. Introduction to "real-world virtual reality," in which computer graphics, artificial intelligence, computer simulations, and computer-human interaction meet in metaphysical illusion, hacker cyberspace, and show business.

Boom, Michael. *Music Through MIDI: Using MIDI to Create Your Own Electronic Music System.* Beekman Pubs. 1987 $19.95. ISBN 0-8464-2614-5. How to use the standards and technology defined by MIDI to operate an electronic music system; includes applications for home, education, and studio.

Butler, Christopher. *Computers in Linguistics.* Blackwell Pubs. 1985 $49.95. ISBN 0-631-14266-5. Covers the use of computers in literary and linguistic research, with a long section on applications in the SNOBOL4 language. For readers interested in the quantitative analysis of literary data, see Butler's companion volume, *Statistics in Linguistics* (Blackwell Pubs. 1985 $39.95).

Chamberlain, Hal. *Musical Applications of Microprocessors.* Hayden 1983 o.p. Highly regarded text on analog, digital, and microprocessor sound and music systems.

Deken, Joseph. *Computer Images: State of the Art.* Stewart Tabori & Chang 1983 o.p. Beautifully illustrated book on graphics techniques, such as collage and transformations, input devices, visual communications, imagery construction, training simulations, fantasy, and the emulation of bioscientific processes.

Foley, James D., and A. van Dam. *Fundamentals of Interactive Computer Graphics.* Addison-Wesley 1982 $48.50. ISBN 0-201-14468-9. Standard tutorial covering hardware, interactive design, geometrical elements, and raster algorithms; employs BASIC concepts in Pascal and the new Core System of Standard Graphics of ACM-SIGGRAPH.

Harris, Mary Dee. *Introduction to Natural Language Processing.* Reston 1985 o.p. Useful work on natural language concepts and computer programming in the field of language and linguistics.

Hearn, D. Donald, and M. Pauline Baker. *Computer Graphics.* P-H 1986 $55.00. ISBN 0-13-165382-2. Discusses algorithms for graphics display, programming examples in Pascal, and the Graphical Kernel System (GKS); intended for those already adept in computer science.

Hockey, Susan. *A Guide to Computer Applications in the Humanities.* Johns Hopkins 1980 $13.95. ISBN 0-8018-2891-0. International survey of academic uses of computing programs in literature, publishing, and linguistics. Sections describe how the programs actually work and their strengths and limitations.

———. *SNOBOL Programming for the Humanities.* OUP 1985 $34.50. ISBN 0-19-824675-7. Tutorial introduction to text analysis and string processing through programming in SNOBOL; useful for students without a background in math.

Kenny, Anthony J. *The Computation of Style: An Introduction to Statistics for Students and Readers of Literature.* Pergamon 1982 o.p. Standard introduction to the concepts and techniques of computational stylistics.

Lewell, John. *A–Z Guide to Computer Graphics.* McGraw 1985 $29.95. ISBN 0-07-037464-3. Introductory survey to computer graphics, with a discussion of techniques and hardware, applications in graphics design, illustration, television and film, the sciences, architecture, and business. Includes 150 illustrations and examples in color.

Manning, Peter. *Electronic and Computer Music*. OUP rev. ed. 1987 $28.50. ISBN 0-19-311923-4. Critical perspective on the history of electronic and computer music, including studio developments, innovations in tape composition, live electronic performance, electronic rock and roll, and trends in computer composition of the last two decades; with bibliography and discography.

McLellan, Hilary. *Virtual Reality: A Selected Bibliography*. Educ. Tech. Pubns. 1992 $14.95. ISBN 0-87778-246-6. Twenty-seven short chapters covering both advanced technical matters and such general subjects as arts and entertainment, cyberspace, and science fiction.

Mowshowitz, Abbe. *Inside Information: Computers in Fiction*. Addison-Wesley 1977 o.p. Collection of some three dozen works or excerpts from works of fiction that pertain to computers or computing; with bibliography.

Newman, William M., and Robert F. Sproull. *Principles of Interactive Computer Graphics*. McGraw 2nd ed. 1979 $48.50. ISBN 0-07-046338-7. Elementary survey of aspects of graphics design using Pascal, including point plotting, clipping, segments, and geometric elements.

Nicholls, Peter, ed. *The Science Fiction Encyclopedia*. Doubleday 1979 o.p. Informative articles on science fiction that treat such subjects as computers, communications, linguistics, information, intelligence, and technology.

Peterson, Dale. *Genesis II: Creation and Recreation with Computers*. P-H 1983 o.p. Survey of creative work that has used the computer in the fields of music, painting, literature, and games. Well researched and well illustrated, with a bibliography of unusual sources. Reflects considerable critical understanding.

Pickover, Clifford A. *Computers and the Imagination: Visual Adventures beyond the Edge*. St. Martin 1991 $29.95. ISBN 0-312-06131-5. Serious mental games and mathematical and visual challenges that leapfrog Tetris, fractals, and similar familiar amusements. See also Pickover's *Computers, Pattern, Chaos, and Beauty: Graphics from an Unseen World* (St. Martin 1991 $19.95. ISBN 0-312-06179-X).

Porush, David. *The Soft Machine: Cybernetic Fiction*. Methuen 1985 o.p. Detailed discussion of fiction about cybernetics and computers by such authors as Vonnegut, Burroughs, Pynchon, Barth, Beckett, and Barthelme. Bibliography included.

Prueitt, Melvin L. *Art and the Computer*. McGraw 1984 o.p. Introduces technical methods to produce professional and scientific computer graphics; stunningly illustrated with about 300 photographs, mostly in color. Introduction by Carl Sagan.

Racter. *The Policeman's Beard Is Half Constructed*. Warner Bks. 1984 $9.95. ISBN 0-446-38051-2. The author is a computer program (written by Bill Chamberlain and Thomas Etter and available elsewhere as recreational software); an interesting and amusing experiment.

Rheingold, Howard. *Virtual Reality*. S&S Trade 1992 $12.00. ISBN 0-671-77897-8. Account of the social impact and cultural consequences of virtual reality, written by an editor of the *Whole Earth Review*.

Rivlin, Robert. *The Algorithmic Image: Graphic Visions of the Computer Age*. Microsoft 1986 o.p. Survey of professional applications of graphics by state-of-the-art producers, including NASA, the New York Institute of Technology, and Hollywood animation studios.

Roads, Curtis, and John Strawn, eds. *Foundations of Computer Music*. MIT Pr. 1987 $29.95. ISBN 0-262-68051-2. High-level articles, reprinted from *Computer Music Journal*, on sound synthesis, digital signal processing, and perception. Each section is preceded by a summary.

Scott, Joan E. *Introduction to Interactive Computer Graphics*. Wiley 1982 o.p. Help for professionals working in drafting, manufacturing, design, mapping, business reports, and scientific presentations; covers equipment, organization, techniques, and career opportunities.

Waite, Mitchell, and Christopher Morgan. *Graphics Primer for the IBM PC*. McGraw 1983 o.p. Introduction to Advanced BASIC for business, education, and entertainment graphics, including charts, maps, forms, animations, and games.

Warrick, Patricia S. *The Cybernetic Imagination in Science Fiction.* MIT Pr. 1980 $31.50.
ISBN 0-262-73061-8. Discusses types of science fiction that have supported stories
about automata, robots, computers. Includes bibliographies of studies, indexes,
fiction, and anthologies.

Education

Subjects treated in education books include authoring languages, BASIC,
computer acquisition and management in schools, computer applications from
kindergarten through higher education, computer-assisted instruction (CAI),
computer-assisted learning (CAL), guides to software and hardware, learning
activities, the Logo language, and writing instruction.

Blank, Marion, and Laura Berlin. *The Parent's Guide to Educational Software.* Microsoft
1991 $14.95. ISBN 1-556-15317-1. Review of 200 software packages intended for
parents; selected with a view to educational usefulness for children.

Bork, Alfred. *Learning with Computers.* HarpC 1986 o.p. Papers based on 10 years of
experience with the use of computers in the teaching of physics in the Educational
Technology Center at the University of California at Irvine. Includes sections on
graphics, authoring languages, and future developments in higher education.

Daiute, Colette. *Computers and Writing.* Addison-Wesley 1985 $25.75. ISBN 0-201-
10368-0. Solid advice to teachers of writing on how computers should and should
not be used at various levels of instruction. Distinguished by its fine realization that
writing is a cognitive and social process as well as a mechanical one.

Olsen, Solveig, ed. *Computer-Aided Instruction in the Humanities. Technology and the
Humanities Ser.* Modern Lang. 1985 $19.75. ISBN 0-87352-553-1. Essays on college-
level teaching in history, foreign languages, logic, and writing, with emphasis on
software and courseware selection, microcomputer-mainframe connections, video-
disks, and pitfalls in using computers. Extensive bibliography and list of personnel
and programs.

Oulton, A. J., and J. J. Foster. *The Teaching of Computer Appreciation and Library
Automation.* Longwood 1981 o.p. Informal pamphlet, drawing heavily on actual
examples and anecdotes, on how to introduce and instruct university-level students
in information and computer science. Issued by the British Library as Research and
Development Report No. 5647.

Papert, Seymour. *Mindstorms: Children, Computers, and Powerful Ideas.* Basic 1993
$13.00. ISBN 0-465-04674-6. The inventor of the Logo programming language
discusses computer-assisted instruction and graphics, math, and language applications.

Pea, Roy D. *Mirrors of Minds: Patterns of Experience in Educational Computing. Cognition
and Computing Ser.* Ablex Pub. 1987 $52.50. ISBN 0-89391-422-3. Fifteen papers
written between 1982 and 1986 at the Center for Children and Technology of Bank
Street College, covering Logo, multimedia in the classroom, teaching science, the
urban teacher, minority schools, and the cognitive demands of programming,
computers, and software design.

Salpeter, Judy, with Dan Derrick. *Kids and Computers: A Parent's Handbook.* SAMS 1992
$16.95. ISBN 0-6723-0144-X. Help for parents who wish to introduce their children
to computers, suggesting both what kids must know and what parents should do;
complete with reviews of approved software.

Schwartz, Helen J. *Interactive Writing.* H. Holt & Co. 1985 o.p. First important college
textbook for freshman composition courses to be based on the use of word
processing and computer technology.

Sloan, Douglas, ed. *The Computer in Education: A Critical Perspective.* Tchrs. Col. 1985
$14.95. ISBN 0-8077-2782-2. Standard collection of articles on several aspects of
computer applications in schools.

Tashner, John, ed. *Improving Instruction with Microcomputers: Readings and Resources for Elementary and Secondary Schools.* Oryx 1984 o.p. Useful anthology of 50 selections, originally published as articles or chapters in books.

Willis, Jerry, and Merl Miller. *Computers for Everybody.* Weber Systems 3rd ed. 1983 o.p. For teachers and school administrators interested in CAI, computer-managed instruction (CMI), computer testing, hardware, software, teacher training, and computer literacy; with tutorials in BASIC, PILOT, and Logo.

ARTIFICIAL INTELLIGENCE

Background and Introductory Works

No issue in computing has aroused as many hopes, fears, and controversies as has artificial intelligence (AI). Newcomers to the field will find the books by Jeremy Campbell, Howard Gardner, George Johnson, Pamela McCorduck, Howard Rheingold, and Oliver Sacks to be unusually well written and informative. The expectations of a decade or two ago that computers would easily be able to imitate human thought and judgment have not been fully met. Although computers have proved useful in manufacturing design, automation, and robotics, and have become standard in technical detection and diagnosis procedures in the biological and physical sciences, other areas of application, such as those in the humanities and social sciences, remain unsettled. In the case of national defense and international treaties, the use of artificial intelligence is a matter of continuing debate. Introductory books here on artificial intelligence contain such subjects as cognitive psychology, games and decision making, fifth-generation languages, information representation, information theory, machine translation, natural language analysis, pattern recognition, popular introductions and surveys, programming languages for AI, robots and automata, self-referential loops, and voice input/output.

Berry, Adrian. *The Super-Intelligent Machine: An Electronic Odyssey.* Salem Pr. 1985 o.p. Entertaining but serious introduction to computers and artificial intelligence; strong on quotable anecdotes and concrete examples. Useful bibliography.

Brand, Stewart. *The Media Lab: Inventing the Future at MIT.* Viking Penguin 1988 $12.00. ISBN 0-14-009701-5. Account of ongoing work at the Media Lab at MIT, including recent developments.

Campbell, Jeremy. *Grammatical Man: Information, Entropy, Language, and Life.* S&S Trade 1983 $10.95. ISBN 0-671-44062-4. Stimulating and wide-reaching synthesis of information theory and its implications for people who use both natural languages and computer programming languages.

Feigenbaum, Edward A., and Pamela McCorduck. *The Fifth Generation: Artificial Intelligence and Japan's Computer Challenge to the World.* Addison-Wesley 1983 $16.30. ISBN 0-201-11519-0. Considers whether the Japanese will be first in the 1990s with a practical supercomputer that combines government backing; a consortium of companies; fantastic speed, capacity, and versatility; expert knowledge systems; multiple processors; very high level programming languages; natural language operations in English and Japanese; and human voice input and output.

Frude, Neil. *The Intimate Machine: Close Encounters with Computers and Robots.* NAL-Dutton 1983 o.p. Highly readable book on the unusual thesis that people tend to grant to computers and robots those roles that make them resemble people.

Gardner, Howard. *The Mind's New Science: A History of the Cognitive Revolution.* Basic 1987 $16.50. ISBN 0-465-04635-5. Traces connections between computing, cognitive psychology, and philosophy, psychology, information theory, linguistics, anthropology, mathematics, and theories of perception and representation.

Hart, Anna. *Knowledge Acquisition for Expert Systems.* McGraw 1992 $39.95. ISBN 0-07-026911-4. Clear and coherent account of how the knowledge engineer—a new specialization—elicits information from experts and places it into an expert system. Covers project design, expert system organization, probability theory, fuzzy logic, machine induction, and some case histories.

Hartnell, Tim. *Exploring Artificial Intelligence on Your IBM PC.* Bantam 1986 $14.95. ISBN 0-553-34287-8. Introductory book on several easy-to-understand aspects of artificial intelligence that use elementary AI programs written in BASIC.

Hopcroft, John E., and Jeffrey D. Ullman. *Introduction to Automated Theory, Languages, and Computation.* Addison-Wesley 1979 $50.50. ISBN 0-201-02988-X. Advanced work on such language-theory concepts as nondeterminism and complex hierarchies.

Johnson, George. *Machinery of the Mind: Inside the New Science of Artificial Intelligence.* Microsoft 1987 $9.95. ISBN 1-55615-010-5. Unusually well-written and well-integrated survey of artificial intelligence, its movements, people, and controversies. Excellent selective bibliography.

Johnson-Laird, Philip. *The Computer and the Mind: An Introduction to Cognitive Science.* HUP 1988 $32.50. ISBN 0-674-15615-3. Highly readable book arguing that making models of the mind as a digital computer over three decades has been both useful, and at the same time, fraught with misunderstanding and disappointment.

Koestler, Arthur. *The Act of Creation.* Viking Penguin 1990 $10.95. ISBN 0-14-019191-7. Koestler's highly suggestive and stimulating theory that humor, creativity, and insight occur at the intersection or "bisociation" of two mental frames in the mind.

Levine, Howard, and Howard Rheingold. *The Cognitive Connection: Thought and Language in Man and Machine.* P-H 1987 o.p. Attempt to connect computer languages to natural languages as common linguistic efforts of people, reminding us that a computer is essentially a symbolic manipulator that can emulate whatever processor structures its inventors can design.

McCorduck, Pamela. *Machines Who Think: A Personal Inquiry into the History and Prospects of Artificial Intelligence.* W. H. Freeman 1981 $14.95. ISBN 0-7167-1135-4. Standard introduction to artificial intelligence. Delightful to read and based on personal knowledge and interviews, surveying the field from its forerunners in antiquity to its flowerings in the 1960s and 1970s. Highly recommended. Includes bibliography.

Michie, David, and Rory Johnston. *The Knowledge Machine: Artificial Intelligence and the Future of Man.* Morrow 1986 o.p. Optimistic view of AI not merely as a method of handling routine tasks but also of solving the complex and pressing problems of our times.

Minsky, Marvin. *The Society of Mind.* S&S Trade 1988 $19.95. ISBN 0-671-60740-5. Its pages a mosaic of separate and self-contained statements, the total book emerges as something larger, suggesting that the biological brain operates locally but becomes mind when it functions globally.

Minsky, Marvin, and Seymour Papert. *Perceptrons: An Introduction to Computer Geometry.* 1969. MIT Pr. rev. ed. 1987 $13.50. ISBN 0-262-63111-3. Expansion of the classic on learning machines; prints the 1972 corrections with a survey of subsequent progress and problems.

Raphael, Bertram. *The Thinking Computer: Mind inside Matter.* Psychology Ser. W. H. Freeman 1976 $16.95. ISBN 0-7167-0723-3. Introduction to current work on robots and artificial intelligence, with a brief history of the subject, emphasizing the nature and limits of the human mind.

Rheingold, Howard. *Tools for Thought: The People and Ideas behind the Next Computer Revolution.* P-H 1986 o.p. The history and prospects of mind-expanding technology, told in lively fashion by following the people who made the most significant contributions.

Ritchie, David. *The Binary Brain: Artificial Intelligence in the Age of Electronics.* Little 1984 o.p. Although much about the brain is neither binary nor digital, this treatment surveys the field of artificial intelligence.

Rose, Steven. *The Conscious Brain*. Random 1976 o.p. One of the best introductions to the study of the brain. Includes discussions of several philosophical issues pertaining to the physical brain, written from a humanistic viewpoint.

———. *Into the Heart of the Mind: An American Quest for Artificial Intelligence*. HarpC 1984 o.p. Introductory survey of the field of artificial intelligence.

Rothfelder, Jerry. *Minds over Matter: A New Look at Artificial Intelligence*. P-H 1986 $7.95. ISBN 0-13-583543-7. Useful survey of 30 years of developments in artificial intelligence.

Sacks, Oliver. *The Man Who Mistook His Wife for a Hat and Other Clinical Tales*. Peter Smith 1992 $21.50. ISBN 0-8146-6529-0. Fascinating case histories, written with warmth by a clinical psychiatrist, about persons with partly defective cognitive faculties; reminds the reader that many invisible steps, wholly assumed in normal human information processing, cannot be taken for granted in AI machine simulations.

Schank, Roger C., and Peter Childers. *The Cognitive Computer: On Language, Learning, and Artificial Intelligence*. Addison-Wesley 1985 $12.95. ISBN 0-201-06446-4. Practical introduction to the field of artificial intelligence, written in nontechnical language for the beginner.

Schutzer, Daniel. *An Applications-Oriented Approach to Artificial Intelligence*. Van Nos. Reinhold $51.95. ISBN 0-442-28034-3. Survey of the fundamental tools of AI programmers, such as LISP, the PROLOG language, and special hardware and software and their uses in expert systems, machine perception, natural language processing, vision and image processing, and robotics.

Staugaard, Andrew G. *Robotics and AI: An Introduction to Applied Machine Intelligence*. P-H 1988 $63.00. ISBN 0-08-036627-9. Discusses the technology of AI and robotics in both home and industry. Good coverage of the topics of speech synthesis and recognition, vision, navigation, and tactile sensing, with special attention to the distinction between automation and robotics.

Tanimoto, Steven L. *Elements of Artificial Intelligence: An Introduction Using LISP*. W. H. Freeman 1987 $45.95. ISBN 0-7167-8028-3. The principles of artificial intelligence, illustrated through LISP as a programming language. Applications and discussions include a conversational simulation of Rogerian therapy, a calculus problem solver, inference, fuzzy logic, natural language understanding, computer vision, and expert systems.

Waldrop, M. Mitchell. *Man-Made Minds*. Walker & Co. 1987 $22.95. ISBN 0-8027-0899-4. Informative current assessment of achievements, difficulties, promises, setbacks, and philosophical issues after several decades of development in the field of artificial intelligence, by a physicist and senior writer for *Science* magazine.

Winston, Patrick. *Artificial Intelligence*. Addison-Wesley 3rd ed. 1992 $53.75. ISBN 0-201-53377-4. Update of the classic text, first issued when the horizon for AI seemed unlimited. Still authoritative in introducing the three main wings of AI—representation and methods, learning and recognition, and vision and language.

Collections and Anthologies

Much of the original work in the AI field appeared as papers, not as books, and it is therefore very useful to have the collections and anthologies that have appeared since the 1950s. Although some of the earlier anthologies cannot be ignored for the capture of classic papers or for the study of the history of the subject, many readers will be more interested in recent publications, such as the Barr and Feigenbaum handbook, the Shapiro encyclopedia, or the Hofstadter and Dennett compendium.

Barr, Avron, and others, eds. *The Handbook of Artificial Intelligence*. 3 vols. Addison-Wesley 1986 $27.95–59.50 ea. ISBNs 0-201-11811-4, 0-201-11812-3, 0-201-11814-9. Standard reference collection. Vol. 1 covers searching, knowledge representation, understanding natural and spoken language; vol. 2 contains programming languages and applications in AI research; vol. 3 covers models of cognition, automatic deduction, vision, learning and inductive inference, and memory and problem solving.

Feigenbaum, Edward A., and Julian Feldman, eds. *Computers and Thought.* Krieger 1981 repr. of 1963 ed. o.p. Twenty reprinted articles on games, theorem proving, heuristics, baseball questions, pattern recognition, problem solving, verbal learning, decision making, and social behavior, reflecting the state of artificial intelligence in the early 1960s.

Haugeland, John C., ed. *Mind Design: Philosophy, Psychology and Artificial Intelligence.* MIT Pr. 1981 $13.50. ISBN 0-262-58052-7. Anthology of articles on some of the major conceptual issues raised by developments in artificial intelligence.

Hofstadter, Douglas R., and Daniel C. Dennett, eds. *The Mind's I: Fantasies and Reflections of Self and Soul.* Bantam 1982 $13.95. ISBN 0-553-34343-2. Collection of stimulating articles, fiction, and essays on mind, soul, and self in philosophy, literature, and artificial intelligence.

Schank, Roger C., and K. M. Colby, eds. *Computer Models of Thought and Language.* W. H. Freeman 1973 o.p. Important collection of AI articles, accessible to the general reader, on simulation of mental processes, language understanding, translation, and related issues.

Shapiro, Stuart C., ed. *The Encyclopedia of Artificial Intelligence.* 2 vols. Wiley 2nd ed. 1992 $249.00. ISBN 0-471-50307-X. Professional compendium of more than 200 contributors on all aspects of artificial intelligence; articles include their own bibliographies and thus amass more than 5,000 references overall.

Thro, Ellen. *The Artificial Intelligence Dictionary.* Microtrend 1991 $24.95. ISBN 0-915391-36-8. Some 1,300 terms in artificial intelligence presented in full dictionary fashion and not merely as a glossary.

Torrance, S. *The Mind and the Machine: Philosophical Aspects of Artificial Intelligence.* Halsted Pr. 1984 o.p. Fifteen advanced essays about structure, limits, function, language, epistemology, intentionality, linguistics, methodology, reasoning, inference, meaning, creativity, and learning in artificial intelligence machines.

Winston, Patrick Henry, ed. *The Psychology of Computer Vision. Computer Science Ser.* McGraw 1975 o.p. Six articles by Winston, Marvin Minsky, and others on artificial intelligence. Also includes several programs that attempt to simulate human vision and the organization of knowledge.

Winston, Patrick Henry, and Richard H. Brown, eds. *Artificial Intelligence: An MIT Perspective. Artificial Intelligence Ser.* 2 vols. MIT Pr. 1979 $35.00 ea. ISBNs 0-262-23096-8, 0-262-23097-6. Vol. 1 contains expert problem solving, natural language understanding, intelligent coaching, problems of representation, and learning procedures; vol. 2 contains vision and manipulation, productivity, computer design, and symbol management.

Philosophy, Background, Context

Much of the early euphoria of AI writers—and partisanship of AI critics—has disappeared in favor of a more skeptical but still positive attitude. Among the classics of the 1970s, Margaret Boden's masterful discussion and the critical attacks by Hubert L. Dreyfus and JOSEPH WEIZENBAUM remain required reading. More recent works by Dennett, Hofstadter, and Winograd are highly recommended approaches to the current horizons in artificial intelligence. This section also includes works on game theory, information theory, current laboratory research, psychology and psychiatry, semantics and natural language processing, and computer vision.

Boden, Margaret. *Artificial Intelligence and Natural Man.* Basic 2nd rev. ed. 1987 $17.00. ISBN 0-465-00456-3. Well-written and clear introduction to AI from a philosopher's point of view. Concrete details make it easy to understand the strengths and weaknesses of many programs.

Cherry, Colin. *On Human Communication: A Review, a Survey and a Criticism.* MIT Pr. 3rd ed. 1978 $13.95. ISBN 0-262-53038-4. Discusses the entire range of media from the point of view of an electrical engineer.

Davis, Morton D. *Game Theory: A Nontechnical Introduction.* Basic rev. ed. 1983 $15.00. ISBN 0-465-02628-1. Excellent overview of the main ideas and some of the unresolved issues of game theory.

Dennett, Daniel C. *Brainstorms: Philosophical Essays on Mind and Psychology.* MIT Pr. 1980 $16.95. ISBN 0-262-54037-1. Analyses of problems of mind, brain, and computer models of thought, perception, and sensation. Justly praised for clarity, grace, and freedom from jargon.

Dreyfus, Hubert L. *What Computers Can't Do: A Critique of Artificial Reason.* HarpC 1979 $8.95. ISBN 0-06-090613-8. Sustained attack on the methods and presuppositions of the AI field, especially its cognitive simulations of the late 1950s, semantic information processing in the 1960s, and automatic optimism of outlook. Written from the phenomenological viewpoint of a professional philosopher.

Dreyfus, Hubert L., and Stuart E. Dreyfus. *Mind over Machine: The Power of Human Intuition and Expertise in the Era of the Computer.* Free Pr. 1988 $12.95. ISBN 0-02-908061-4. The continuing case against AI, expert systems, and computers in education; written as a reply to "Fifth Generation" enthusiasts, such as Pamela McCorduck, whose optimistic *Machines Who Think* was in its turn an answer to Dreyfus's pessimistic *What Computers Can't Do.*

Gatlin, Lila L. *Information Theory and the Living System.* Molecular Biology Ser. Col. U. Pr. 1972 o.p. Ingenious application of Claude Shannon's information theory to DNA genetics as a living information channel. Includes fascinating discussions of the philosophical battle between mechanist reductionists and their opponents.

Hand, D. J. *Artificial Intelligence and Psychiatry.* Scientific Basis of Psychiatry Ser. Cambridge U. Pr. 1985 $59.95. ISBN 0-521-25871-5. Serious reconsideration of the issues in such AI programs as PARRY and ELIZA; reviews recent developments in artificial intelligence from unusual medical and professional perspectives.

Hofstadter, Douglas. *Gödel, Escher, Bach: An Eternal Golden Braid.* Basic 1979 $34.95. ISBN 0-465-02685-0. Stimulating and fascinating book on self-referential loops in the mathematician Gödel, the painter Escher, and the composer Johann Sebastian Bach, with implications for mathematical logic, DNA, music, art, computer programming, and artificial intelligence.

———. *Metamagical Themas: Questing for the Essence of Mind and Pattern.* Bantam 1986 $14.95. ISBN 0-553-34279-7. Described on its dust jacket as "An Interlocked Collection of Literary, Scientific, and Artistic Studies," most of this gathering of notions, puzzles, and queries, alternately profound and capricious in the author's unique manner, was published originally in the columns of *Scientific American* between 1981 and 1983. Includes an excellent annotated bibliography.

Shannon, Claude, and Warren Weaver. *The Mathematical Theory of Communication.* U. of Ill. Pr. 1963 $9.95. ISBN 0-252-72548-4. Classic work that founded information theory and introduced the terms *entropy* and *redundancy.* Nonmathematical readers will prefer to read an introduction to Shannon, such as J. R. Peirce's *Symbols, Signals, and Noise.*

Weizenbaum, Joseph. *Computer Power and Human Reason: From Judgment to Calculation.* W. H. Freeman 1976 $14.95. ISBN 0-7167-0463-3. Powerful critique on the dangers of artificial intelligence; a provocative book that is required reading for anyone serious about computers.

Winograd, Terry. *Understanding Natural Language.* Acad. Pr. 1972 $37.00. ISBN 0-12-759750-6. Important and stimulating book that insists that language and language representations cannot be separated from common-sense understandings of the ordinary world.

Winograd, Terry, and Fernando Flores. *Understanding Computers and Cognition.* Addison-Wesley 1987 $16.95. ISBN 0-201-11297-3. Highly acclaimed work arguing that the AI movement has made the error of pursuing the autonomous development of machine intelligence instead of developing artificial intelligence as an extension of natural human intelligence.

VIEWPOINTS ON SOCIAL AND CULTURAL ISSUES

Beyond the technical questions they raise, changes in computer and information technology also pose several heated cultural and social issues. The futurologists include DANIEL BELL (see Vol. 3), MARSHALL MCLUHAN (see Vol. 3), John Naisbitt, and ALVIN TOFFLER, but the party of the past enlists David Burnham, JACQUES ELLUL, LEWIS MUMFORD, and THEODORE ROSZAK. Analysts who have written significant works from the important middle ground include J. David Bolter, Siegfried Giedion, THOMAS S. KUHN (see also Vol. 4) and Sherry Turkle. For discussions of workplace issues, see Carson and Zuboff. For healthy doses of cultural skepticism, see Penrose and Wurman. Literacy issues are raised in the works by Hardison and Tuman. For broad perspectives on the nature of information, see writings by Lucky, Pagels, and Penzias. Other books in this section are on the arms race and national security, the belief in automatic technological progress, computer literacy, cottage industry, defining technologies, failures in educational and home computing, the future of computing, the information revolution, intellectual technology, the knowledge society, managerial surveillance, postindustrial society, the quality of life, the social and cultural costs of information automation, social and technological forecasting, threats of an informational "1984," threats to privacy and confidentiality, and unemployment and work issues.

Bell, Daniel. *Coming of Post-Industrial Society: A Venture in Social Forecasting.* Basic 1976 $17.00. ISBN 0-465-09713-8. A "venture in social forecasting" that sees the decline of corporate capitalism and the rise of a post-Marxist "knowledge society" where the new "intellectual technology" achieves "the codification of theoretic knowledge."

Bolter, J. David. *Turing's Man: Western Culture in the Computer Age.* U. of NC Pr. 1984 $11.95. ISBN 0-8078-4108-0. Major interpretation, by a classicist who is also a computer scientist, of the intellectual and philosophical impact of the computer on ways of thinking about basic concepts of time, memory, quantity, creativity, and intelligence.

Burnham, David. *The Rise of the Computer State.* Random 1983 o.p. An investigative reporter discusses the threats to privacy and personal liberty from the misuse and abuse of information in the data banks of telephone companies, credit checking services, the FBI, the IRS, the Social Security administration, and various police departments. With a foreword by Walter Cronkite.

Calder, Nigel. *1984 and Beyond: Into the 21st Century.* Viking Penguin 1984 o.p. Fascinating postscripts, two decades later, on computer and other technological predictions, originally made by contributors to Calder's symposium, *The World in 1984* (published in 1964). Told through an imaginary dialogue with a supercomputer named O'Brien (after George Orwell's villain in *1984*).

Ellul, Jacques. *The Technological Society.* Random 1967 $9.00. ISBN 0-394-70390-1. Starting point for much criticism of modern technology and its negative impact on human culture and society.

Friedrichs, Guenter, and Adam Schaff, eds. *Microelectronics and Society: For Better or for Worse; a Report to the Club of Rome.* Pergamon 1982 $16.75. ISBN 0-08-028955-X. One of a series of reports to the international planning and advisory body known as the Club of Rome, with 11 contributions on technology, enterprise, the environment, the Third World, and information technology.

Garson, Barbara. *The Electronic Sweatshop: How We Are Transforming the Office of the Future into the Factory of the Past.* S&S Trade 1988 $17.95. ISBN 0-671-53049-6.

Provocative exposé alleging that data clerks are dehumanized and managers are undermined in the "second industrial revolution" now taking place in the high-tech workplace.

Giedion, Siegfried. *Mechanization Takes Command: A Contribution to Anonymous History.* Norton 1969 $16.95. ISBN 0-393-00489-9. Classic work on the historical, cultural, and social impact of mechanization on the factory, farm, and household since 1800.

Gilder, George F. *Microcosm: The Quantum Revolution in Economics and Technology.* S&S Trade 1989 $10.95. ISBN 0-671-50969-1. Boldly stated view that the impact of the microchip on the mind and the realm of information amounts to "the overthrow of matter," expressed by a leading New Age futurist.

Hardison, O. B. *Disappearing through the Skylight: Culture and Technology in the Twentieth Century.* Viking Penguin 1990 $14.00. ISBN 0-14-011582-X. Profound queries concerning the arrival of modernism and technology in the twentieth century and the resulting disappearance of traditional ideas of nature, history, language, art, and human self-identity.

Kuhn, Thomas S. *Structure of Scientific Revolutions. Foundations of the Unity of Science Ser.* U. Ch. Pr. 2nd ed. 1970 $19.95. ISBN 0-226-45803-2. Landmark work demolishing the empiricist view of the history of science. Argues that science leaps from one conceptual realm to another as new paradigms replace the old.

Leebaert, Derek, ed. *Technology 2001: The Future of Computing and Communications.* MIT Pr. 1991 $29.95. ISBN 0-262-12150-6. Twelve visions of the next century. Scientists representing major companies, such as Digital, IBM, and Intel, explain what they expect from computer chips, cellular telephones, portable computers, optical storage devices, on-line information, and the new culture of information.

Lucky, Robert W. *Silicon Dreams: Information, Man, and Machine.* St. Martin 1989 $19.95. ISBN 0-312-02960-8. Serious yet readable overview of the nature of information, from Shannon's information theory to accounts of how language, data, and pictures are processed. Written by the executive director of research at Bell Labs.

McLuhan, Marshall. *Gutenberg Galaxy: The Making of Typographic Man.* U. of Toronto Pr. 1962 $19.95. ISBN 0-8020-6041-2. Technological optimism that electronic information will be open, auditory, parallel, social, and global, replacing print information that has been closed, visual, serial, individual, and restrictive. An influential book.

Meadows, Donella H., and others. *The Limits to Growth: A Report for the Club of Rome's Project on the Predicament of Mankind.* Universe 2nd ed. 1974 o.p. First of a series of important reports to the Club of Rome on the global and economic consequences of technological development and the distribution of finite resources.

Muller, Herbert J. *The Children of Frankenstein: A Primer on Modern Technology and Human Values.* Ind. U. Pr. 1970 o.p. Humanist approach to problems of technology in society and culture; acknowledges its starting point in previous works by Lewis Mumford and Jacques Ellul.

Mumford, Lewis. *Technics and Civilization.* HarBraceJ 1963 $18.95. ISBN 0-15-688254-X. The first important treatment in English of the history of machines and their impact on culture and society.

Naisbitt, John. *Megatrends: Ten New Directions Transforming Our Lives.* Warner Bks. 1988 $5.95. ISBN 0-446-35681-6. Successful corporation consultant looks at the states of California, Florida, Washington, Colorado, and Connecticut and makes sweeping forecasts about the information society, high technology, political decentralization, a multiple-option culture, self-help, and other trends.

Nora, Simon, and Alain Minc. *The Computerization of Society: A Report to the President of France.* MIT Pr. 1980 $8.95. ISBN 0-262-64020-1. Reveals the special role information technology is playing in national planning in Europe; introduction by Daniel Bell.

Pagels, Heinz R. *The Dreams of Reason: The Computer and the Rise of the Sciences of Complexity.* S&S Trade 1989 $9.95. ISBN 0-553-34710-1. The role of the computer in the philosophical problem of complexity and how we think about "the nature of physical reality, the problem of cognition, the mind-body problem, the character of scientific research, the nature of mathematics, and the role of instruments in research" (Preface).

Penrose, Roger. *The Emperor's New Mind: Concerning Computers, Minds, and the Laws of Physics.* OUP 1989 $30.00. ISBN 0-19-851973-7. A distinguished scientist opposes the "strong AI" position by taking the high ground of the philosophy of science, cosmology, and quantum mechanics to argue the natural limits of human consciousness.

Penzias, Arno. *Ideas and Information: Managing in a High-Tech World.* Norton 1989 $18.95. ISBN 0-393-02649-3. Thoughtful and nontechnical explanations and anecdotes of computation and information technology by a Nobel Prize winner; enlivened with reflections on European history, art, and recollections of three decades at Bell Labs.

Postman, Neil. *Technopoly: The Surrender of Culture to Technology.* Knopf 1992 $20.50. ISBN 0-394-58272-1. Controversial warning that our excessive trust in computers as harbingers of supposedly superior wisdom and intelligence will lead to dangerous consequences for contemporary thought and language.

Reinecke, Ian. *Electronic Illusions: A Skeptic's View of Our High-Tech Future.* Viking Penguin 1984 o.p. Warns against excessive confidence in computers and the technology of telephones, television, satellites, office work, schools, factories, and the information industry.

Roszak, Theodore. *The Cult of Information: The Folklore of Computers and the True Art of Thinking.* Pantheon 1986 $9.95. ISBN 0-394-75175-2. The author of *The Making of a Counter Culture* (Doubleday o.p.) notes that we might be facing an information glut, the menace of hidden agendas in computer literacy programs, and dangerous data banks that can curtail our civil liberties. One of the best antidotes to overly optimistic books about the future of computing.

Simons, Geoff. *Computer Bits and Pieces: A Compendium of Curiosities.* Viking Penguin 1985 o.p. Behind the humor and entertainment, a serious warning about the impact of intelligent machines on human life.

Toffler, Alvin. *The Third Wave.* Bantam 1984 $6.99. ISBN 0-553-24698-4. Sweeping forecast in the manner of Marshall McLuhan and Daniel Bell, seeing a global postindustrial information revolution and explosion, resulting in a new human personality, a new society centered around the "electronic cottage," and unique but appropriate patterns of culture.

Tuman, Myron C. *Word Perfect: Literacy in the Computer Age.* U. of Pittsburgh Pr. 1992 $49.95. ISBN 0-8229-3735-2. The place of the computer in the rivalry between print literacy and on-line literacy and the resulting consequences for college instruction in literature, reading, and writing.

———, ed. *Literacy Online: The Promise (and Peril) of Reading and Writing with Computers.* U. of Pittsburgh Pr. 1992 $34.95. ISBN 0-8229-3701-8. Outstanding collection of essays on the nature of literary texts, teaching English, and critical thought, addressing the impact of computers and computing technology upon standards of public literacy.

Turkle, Sherry. *Second Self: Computers and the Human Spirit.* S&S Trade 1984 o.p. Remarkable and original book that addresses the question of what children, adolescents, adult beginners, and professionals feel about computers—and what they feel about themselves while using computers. An important contribution to our understanding of what computer technology means to human personality and culture.

Wurman, Richard Saul. *Information Anxiety Is Produced by the Ever-Widening Gap between What We Understand and What We Think We Should Understand.* Doubleday 1989 $19.95. ISBN 0-335-24394-4. Offbeat and essential reading on the technology gap created by teachers who have forgotten the time of not knowing.

Zuboff, Shoshana. *In the Age of the Smart Machine: The Future of Work and Power.* Basic 1988 $11.95. ISBN 0-434-92486-5. As a result of five years of field work, a faculty member of the Harvard Business School shows the effect of the information revolution on knowledge in the workplace, the nature of computer-mediated work, and the structure of managerial power.

CHRONOLOGY OF AUTHORS

Napier, John. 1550–1617
Babbage, Charles. 1791–1871
Lovelace, Augusta Ada Byron,
   Countess of. 1815–1852
Hollerith, Herman. 1860–1929
Wiener, Norbert. 1894–1964

Von Neumann, John. 1903–1957
Hopper, Grace Murray. 1906–
Mauchly, John. 1907–1980
Turing, Alan Mathison. 1912–1954
Shannon, Claude. 1916–

BABBAGE, CHARLES. 1791–1871

Mathematician, inventor, and prolific writer, Charles Babbage is best known for his conception of the first automatic digital computer. Educated in mathematics at Cambridge University, Babbage helped found the British Analytical Society, which aimed at incorporating European developments into English mathematics. From the time he was a student, Babbage was drawn to the idea of mechanizing the production of values in mathematical tables. His difference engine of 1822 was to be an all-purpose calculating machine. Although he received government funding to build a large-scale working model of the difference engine, the project never was completed. By 1834 he had developed his ideas for an analytical engine, a computing device consisting of a processing area of wheels and racks, called a mill, for the calculation of decimals. Borrowing the idea of the punch card from the Jacquard mill, he proposed the use of separate card sets, one for controlling procedures and one for storing information, that would make the engine "programmable." Some programming ideas might have been contributed to him by LADY LOVELACE, LORD BYRON's (see Vol. 1) daughter. Babbage's analytic engine was never successfully built. Although his design was forgotten until his unpublished notebooks were discovered in 1937, his intellectual distinction is that he was the first person to plan a flexible modern mechanical computing device.

BOOKS BY BABBAGE

Babbage's Calculating Engines. Ed. by Henry Prevost. 1889. MIT Pr. 1983 o.p. Modern reprint of a classic collection of papers by Babbage, newly edited by E. Tomash.
Charles Babbage and His Calculating Engines. Ed. by Philip Morrison and Emily Morrison. 1961. o.p. Standard collection of writings by and about Charles Babbage and Lady Ada Lovelace, including a portion of Babbage's autobiography.
Passages from the Life of a Philosopher. 1864. Kelley 1969 $49.50. ISBN 0-678-00479-X. Facsimile materials from Babbage's notes and papers.
The Works of Charles Babbage. Ed. by M. Campbell-Kelly. 11 vols. NYU Pr. 1988 $1,350.00. ISBN 0-8147-1428-5. Collected works of Babbage.

BOOKS ABOUT BABBAGE

Buxton, H. W. *Memoir of the Life and Labours of the Late Charles Babbage Esq., F.R.S.* MIT Pr. 1987 $55.00. ISBN 0-262-02269-9. Classic biography, reprinted under the editorship of Anthony Hyman.
Collier, Bruce. *The Little Engines That Could've: The Calculating Machines of Charles Babbage*. Garland 1991 $76.00. ISBN 0-8240-0043-9. Originally a Harvard dissertation in the history of science.

Hyman, Anthony. *Charles Babbage: Pioneer of the Computer*. Princeton U. Pr. 1982
$42.00. ISBN 0-691-08303-7. Account of Babbage's life and times, with an appendix
containing Babbage's published works.

BOOLE, GEORGE. 1815–1864

[SEE Chapter 15 in this volume.]

HOLLERITH, HERMAN. 1860–1929

Born to German immigrant parents in Buffalo, New York, Herman Hollerith
graduated as an engineer from Columbia University. He went to work for the
U.S. Census Office, and later the Patent office, where he gained an understanding of the approaches that inventors were taking to equipment design. During
this time, he himself was designing new kinds of tabulation devices.

After several years with the government, Hollerith was asked to design and
carry out the first automated U.S. Census analysis for the 1890 survey. The
method chosen for the census analysis was punched cards, an idea contributed
by John Shaw Billings, a statistician and Hollerith's future father-in-law.
Hollerith devised the machines to deal with the cards. Their combined efforts
produced a new approach to tabulation equipment. What formerly had been a
seven-year analysis process was reduced to little more than two years, and the
simple population count took only six weeks. In addition, the opportunities for
errors in counting, arithmetic, and transferring subtotals were greatly reduced.

The technology used by Hollerith and Billings resembled a much older
approach to machine control, namely, Jacquard loom cards that were used to
control weaving machines. But their design added a new ingredient—electricity. The technique involved pushing an array of metal pins through corresponding holes in each card. The pins that went through came into contact with liquid
mercury underneath, completing an electric circuit. It worked incredibly well
and was reliable.

Hollerith designed other devices too, and in 1896 he founded the Tabulating
Machine Company. This enterprise supplied the 1900 census with equipment
and served such clients as the governments of Canada and Russia. Over time,
Hollerith's company evolved and eventually produced tabulator-printers and
other devices. In 1924 the company combined with three other data equipment
companies to become the IBM Company.

Within 50 years, with the advent of the electronic circuit and the stored
program, the clever but simple tabulating machine and data-handling methods
of Hollerith and his successors evolved into unbelievably fast powerhouses of
analytical and computational ability, used to solve atomic equations, trace the
dynamics of weather systems, and launch satellites into space.

BOOK ABOUT HOLLERITH

Austrian, G. D. *Herman Hollerith: Forgotten Giant of Information Processing*. Col. U. Pr.
1984 $53.50. ISBN 0-231-05146-8. Well-researched study by an IBM employee who
had access to the Hollerith family papers.

HOPPER, GRACE MURRAY. 1906–

Grace Murray Hopper has had a remarkable career in computer science
entwined with public service and professional leadership. Her story is a unique
chapter in the history of technology policy development in our country. Hopper
studied mathematics at Vassar College and Yale University before teaching at
Yale and then Barnard College during the 1930s and early 1940s. In 1944 she

enlisted in the U.S. Navy and took part in programming the Mark I large-scale electromechanical computer at Harvard University. Within five years, she redefined the meaning and practice of programming by using the computer itself to automatically translate easier (to a human) programming commands into pure machine-level language. The tools that do this are called compilers and symbolic assemblers. Initially, there was widespread skepticism among Hopper's colleagues, who thought either that her system would not work or that the automatically generated program statements would not be efficient. She succeeded, however, and this giant step in automatic programming helped launch the computer age. Although Hopper was not the first person to develop the concept of a compiler (Konrad Zuse had done so 10 years earlier in Germany), she was the first to realize fully its potential and its generality.

After the war, Hopper stayed on at Harvard as a research fellow in the computation laboratory until she joined the Eckert-Mauchly Computer Corporation in Pennsylvania as senior mathematician in 1949. At Eckert-Mauchly she worked on and directed various projects, most notably the development of the computer language COBOL in the late 1950s. Hopper managed to secure the acceptance of COBOL as the standard language for administrative data processing by persuading a variety of government executives to treat it as the standard language for their own groups. Because the government was a large buyer of computers, no computer company could afford not to provide COBOL to its customers.

Hopper's second career began in 1971, when she was invited to plan and conduct conferences for government managers to promote the awareness of new developments in computers, especially the great potential of microcomputers. She also consulted on better use of computers in the government and served on the faculty of George Washington University. This work culminated in 1977, when the U.S. Navy asked her to return to active duty to work more intensively on Navy applications of COBOL. She remained on active duty until 1986, when she retired.

BOOK BY HOPPER

Understanding Computers. (coauthored with Steven L. Mandell). West Pub. 1990 $48.25. ISBN 0-314-66590-0. Excellent description of computer literacy issues as well as profiles of people.

BOOKS ABOUT HOPPER

Amann, Dick, and Dick Smith. *Forgotten Women of Computer History.* Ed. by Dick Whitson. Prog. Studies 1978 $49.95. ISBN 0-917194-09-8. Survey of the leading roles played by women in the development of several "breakthrough" computer languages and in the growth of the industry and the profession.

Billings, Charlene W. *Grace Hopper: Navy Admiral and Computer Pioneer.* Enslow Pubs. 1989 $17.95. ISBN 0-89490-194-X. Factual biography concentrating on Hopper's contributions to computer science. Provides an inside look at early computer development.

Greene, Laura. *Computer Pioneers.* Watts 1985 o.p. Biographies of leading figures in computer science; includes a short but clear account of Hopper's contributions to computer language development and of her skillful advocacy of better use of computers by government managers and professionals.

LOVELACE, AUGUSTA ADA BYRON, COUNTESS OF. 1815–1852

Born in London in 1815, Augusta Ada Byron was a daughter of the English romantic poet LORD BYRON (see Vol. 1). She never knew her father personally, however, because her parents separated shortly after her birth. Privately educated and later self-taught, Lovelace's advanced education was aided by Augustus de Morgan, the first professor of mathematics at the University of London. Her deep interest in the sciences and mathematics was evidenced by her correspondence with contemporary scientists, such as MICHAEL FARADAY.

She became interested in CHARLES BABBAGE's difference engine in 1833 after seeing it and later wrote extensive notes on the operation of his analytical engine to accompany her translation of Menabrea's paper on Babbage's machine. Because some of her elaborate notes deal with the reuse of part of a set of control cards, anticipating subroutines, she sometimes is called the world's first computer programmer. In 1979 a new programming language, Ada, was named in her honor.

Her writings and correspondence have been collected in works about her and also with the materials about Babbage.

BOOKS ABOUT LOVELACE

Babbage, Charles. *Passages from the Life of a Philosopher*. Vol. 11 in *Works of Charles Babbage*. NYU Pr. 1989 $995.00. ISBN 0-8147-1113-8. Descriptions of Babbage's calculating engines, with an appendix of miscellaneous papers including references to Lovelace.

Baum, Joan. *The Calculating Passion of Ada Byron*. Shoe String 1986 $25.00. ISBN 0-208-02119-1. Biography of the Countess of Lovelace.

Moore, Doris L. *Ada, Countess of Lovelace: Byron's Legitimate Daughter*. HarpC 1977 o.p. One of the first biographies of the countess, drawn from family correspondence, including materials by her famous father.

Stein, Dorothy. *Ada: A Life and Legacy*. Ser. in the History of Computing. MIT Pr. 1985 $12.95. ISBN 0-262-69116-7. Account of the countess that dispels the myths attributed to her in popular biographies as an epoch-making mathematician and programmer; assigns to her a more plausible role in the light of contemporary historical evidence.

Toole, Betty A., ed. *Ada, the Enchantress of Numbers: A Selection from the Letters of Lord Byron's Daughter and Her Description of the First Computer*. Strawberry 1992 $29.95. ISBN 0-912647-09-4. General collection of materials by and concerning Ada Lovelace in narrative form.

MAUCHLY, JOHN. 1907–1980

John Mauchly and his colleague and partner, J. Presper Eckert, created the first fully developed general-purpose electronic computer. Completed in 1946, the enormous task of designing, building, operating, repairing, and improving this computer utilized the resources of the University of Pennsylvania, the U.S. Army, and talented scientists and mathematicians in nearby research centers.

Born in Cincinnati, Ohio, Mauchly experimented with radio circuits (crystal sets and vacuum tubes) as a youth. He also designed electrical wiring that would permit two different switches to control the same light, a problem requiring binary circuits as a solution. After graduating from Johns Hopkins University as a physicist with a specialty in meteorology, Mauchly became interested in long-term weather forecasting. This entailed equations that required intensive calculations, and he was struck by the need for faster and more powerful methods of machine-based calculation than could be realized with existing mechanical and electromechanical devices. Mauchly thus began experimenting with electronic approaches, which were much faster.

In 1941, during World War II, Mauchly left a secure and relatively prestigious position at Ursinus College to enroll as a student in a special course in electronic engineering at the University of Pennsylvania. He hoped this would give him the greater technical depth he needed in electronics. At the same time, he took part in special engineering projects related to the war effort, and he talked to everyone about his ideas for building an electronics-based automatic computer, but few were interested until he met J. Presper Eckert. Mauchly and Eckert were an interesting contrast. Mauchly had the broad vision and conceptual framework for the project, as well as good instincts, good temperament, and scientific grounding. Eckert was cooler and more controlled, brilliant and focused, thoroughly grounded in electronics, and unrelentingly practical in his approach to finding engineering solutions. He provided the engineering skill, the project strategy, and a great deal of energy. The relationship worked well, and by the time the project was completed, the world of computation was changed forever.

A research and development proposal for Mauchly and Eckert's ENIAC (Electronic Numerical Integrator and Calculator) was made to the U.S. Army in 1943 and accepted. The army's primary need at that time was for a rapid computation device that could handle calculations for artillery ballistics tables. ENIAC took two years to build, was tested in 1945, and became fully operational in 1946. Soon it was being used for solving numerous nonmilitary problems as well. ENIAC had become a genuine general-purpose computer, as Mauchly and Eckert had intended. It was succeeded by the EDVAC, which Mauchly and Eckert designed in the mid-1940s and completed in 1951.

Mauchly and Eckert left the University of Pennsylvania in 1946 so that they could retain the patents on their inventions, and they formed their own company. Although many people were involved in the development of one form or another of an automatic computer in the 1930s and 1940s, Mauchly and Eckert made the general-purpose, all-electronic automatic computer a reality.

BOOK ABOUT MAUCHLY

Ritchie, David. *The Computer Pioneers: The Making of the Modern Computer.* S&S Trade 1986 o.p. Introduction to the development of computers includes a detailed and very human sketch of how Mauchly's efforts and those of dozens of other computer pioneers gradually came together.

NAPIER, JOHN. 1550–1617

Scottish mathematician and cleric John Napier was born at Merchiston Castle near Edinburgh. After graduating from St. Andrews University, he studied in Paris and traveled throughout Europe. On his return to Scotland, he became a strong supporter of the Reform church in its struggle to eradicate Catholicism from the country. He was appointed to JOHN KNOX's (see Vol. 4) General Assembly and wrote Protestant tracts.

After the Reform church's position was ensured, Napier turned his efforts to mathematics. His landmark achievement was his invention of a system of logarithms based on the correspondence of a geometric and arithmetic series of numbers. Napier's method of computing logarithms, published in 1614 in his *Mirifici logarithmorum canonis descriptio*, gained immediate acceptance. His table of logarithms, which became the basis of a new table of common logarithms in 1624, simplified the complex calculations of trigonometry heretofore required in astronomy and navigation.

In 1617, the year of his death, Napier published *Rabdologiae; seu Numerationes per Virgulas libri duo*, in which he described a system of arithmetic computation involving the use of counting rods (also known as Napier's bones).

This system was to have great importance for physical science, making it possible to perform multiplication and division by mechanical means. It is now regarded as an early herald of the slide rule and the modern analog computer.

BOOK BY NAPIER

Rabdology. Trans. by William F. Richardson. MIT Pr. 1991 $40.00. ISBN 0-262-14046-2

BOOK ABOUT NAPIER

Hobson, E. W. *John Napier.* AMS Pr. repr. of 1914 ed. o.p.

SHANNON, CLAUDE. 1916–

Claude Shannon is considered the creator of information theory, a description of methods of sending messages from one place to another by the most efficient way possible. Information theory defines information in abstract terms and establishes laws that show how the terms relate to each other. The theorems of information theory were intended to be used with radio and telephone communications, but they can be extended to any system of sending messages. Information theory has been invaluable to computer design and to an understanding of the role of symbolic communication and information storage in DNA and other life systems.

The tool that Shannon used in developing information theory was Boolean logic, a form of logic in which all conditions are represented as being in one of two states: true or false, yes or no, 1 or 0. This two-state, or binary, logic allows information to be represented as a series of yes-no choices, known as *bits* (short for *bi*nary dig*its*). Shannon saw that symbols could be transmitted as binary codes. The information content of these messages (the number of simple decisions being communicated) could be measured and the efficiency of different forms of transmission compared.

In 1936 Shannon received two bachelor's degrees from the University of Michigan, one in electrical engineering and the other in mathematics. While working on a thesis for his master's degree, he fused together the most interesting ideas he had learned from each field. In his thesis he demonstrated how the tools of Boolean logic could be embodied in existing electric switching circuits, such as those used in telephone networks.

Shannon's thesis project grew out of a simpler one assigned to him by his professor, VANNEVAR BUSH, to analyze the logical structure of the Differential Analyzer, the famous analog computer that Bush had invented earlier for scientific computational work. Because the gear-based machine had many difficulties associated with intensive use, Shannon began to speculate on what kind of mechanisms could replace it. He seized on the idea of on-off circuits, which were clean, simple, quick, and flexible in combination. Out of that insight came his famous thesis. (Other researchers, at about the same time developed the same conclusion independently about the value of the Boolean approach to computers.)

Shannon joined Bell Labs in 1941 and remained there until 1956, when he moved to Massachusetts Institute of Technology. His major achievement came in 1948, when he published a paper entitled "A Mathematical Theory of Communication" in the *Bell System Technical Journal.* Shannon's ideas also were published the following year in book form, thus reaching a wider audience.

It is said that the years immediately following World War II witnessed three great developments in conceptual thinking within the broad field of information science. One was the successful ENIAC project of JOHN MAUCHLY and J. Presper Eckert. The second was NORBERT WIENER's theory of cybernetics (control and communications in machines and living systems). And the third was Shannon's mathematical theory of information.

BOOKS BY SHANNON

Claude Elwood Shannon: Collected Papers. Ed. by N. J. Sloane and A. D. Wyner. Inst. Electrical 1993 $69.95. ISBN 0-7803-0434-9. Contains all of Shannon's published works, as well as many of his unpublished works.

The Mathematical Theory of Communication. (coauthored with Warren Weaver). 1949. U. of Ill. Pr. 1963 $6.95. ISBN 0-252-72548-4

BOOKS ABOUT SHANNON

Computer Basics. Understanding Computers Ser. Time-Life 1985 $19.93. ISBN 0-8094-5654-0. Well-illustrated, well-researched introduction to basic computer concepts and history that includes a short account of Shannon's contribution to computer science.

Pierce, John R. *Introduction to Information Theory: Symbols, Signals, and Noise.* Dover 1980 $5.95. ISBN 0-486-24061-4. Excellent classic introduction to the information theory ideas of Shannon and to their various applications.

TURING, ALAN MATHISON. 1912–1954

Alan Turing showed early mathematical ability in an era in which such talents often were despised by other boys. He obtained a scholarship to King's College, Cambridge University, in 1931, followed by a fellowship in 1935. In addressing the issue of the "decidability" of mathematics raised by the great mathematician DAVID HILBERT, Turing wrote the landmark article "On Computable Numbers, with an Application to the Entscheidungsproblem," which appeared in *Proceedings of the London Mathematical Society* in 1937. To illustrate his position, he invented the "Turing machine," which is a mental conception (not hardware) requiring only three elements: a control unit, a continuous tape of discrete squares, and a read-write head, all of which keenly anticipate the modern computer CPU with a large amount of address space.

After completing his doctorate at Princeton University, Turing returned to England. In 1939 he developed the first set of formulas for computer chess, although he believed such a machine would not be made for another century. Despite his start as a mathematician, some of Turing's most famous achievements involved words rather than numbers. When World War II came, Turing was assigned to an intelligence unit that eventually cracked the "Enigma machine," an encoding device used by the Germans. By 1941 coded German radio traffic for U-boats was being deciphered regularly, a secret kept throughout the war.

Following the war, while working for the Mathematics Division of the National Physical Laboratory (NPL), Turing proposed building the ACE, an automatic computing engine. By the time it was completed, Turing's attention had turned elsewhere. The question of artificial intelligence also interested him deeply, and in his 1950 paper in *Mind*, "Computing Machinery and Intelligence," he invented the "Turing test," an imitation game to evaluate whether machine intelligence is distinguishable from human intelligence. In his later years, Turing focused on the general-purpose digital computer. Long before prototypes for such machines existed, he anticipated the nature of programming procedures and subroutines. His life came to an unfortunate end when he was convicted of homosexuality, then considered a crime, and committed suicide two years later.

The revival of interest in Turing is marked by the biography by Andrew Hodges (1983), adapted for the stage as *Breaking the Code* by Hugh Whitemore (1987), and by his prominent place in "Giant Brains," an episode in the BBC television coproduction "The Machine That Changed the World" (1992).

Books by Turing

A. M. Turing's ACE Report of 1946 and Other Papers. Ed. by B. E. Carpenter and R. W. Doran. MIT Pr. 1985 $27.50. ISBN 0-262-03114-0. Text of his lecture to the London Mathematical Society on 20 February 1947, proposing the building of ACE, an automatic computing engine.

Mechanical Intelligence. Ed. by D. C. Ince. North-Holland 1992 o.p. Vol. 3 of *Collected Works of A. M. Turing.* Definitive collection of Turing's writings on artificial intelligence.

Pure Mathematics. Ed. by J. L. Britton. North-Holland 1992 o.p. Vol. 1 of *Collected Works of A. M. Turing,* with a section on his statistical work written by I. J. Good. Scholarly collection of Turing's mathematical contributions.

Books about Turing

Aspray, William. *From Mathematical Constructivity to Computer Science: Alan Turing, John von Neumann, and the Origins of Computer Science in Mathematical Logic.* MIT Pr. 1980 o.p. The mathematical background of Turing's career.

Hodges, Andrew. *Alan Turing: The Enigma.* S&S Trade 1983 o.p. Scientific background on the state of mathematics and logic during Turing's era, written with drama in the tale of Turing's contributions to breaking the German code in World War II and with compassion for Turing's personal dilemmas.

Holt, R. C., and others. *The Turing Language: Formal and Informal Definitions.* P-H 1988 $32.00. ISBN 0-13-933136-0. Interesting account of the design and development of Turing's programming language.

Turing, Sarah. *A. M. Turing.* Heffer 1959 o.p. The first study of Turing.

Whitemore, Hugh. *Breaking the Code.* 1987. o.p. A successful stage play in New York and London, based on Hodges's biography.

VON NEUMANN, JOHN. 1903–1957

John von Neumann grew to legendary stature in twentieth-century mathematics, computing, economics, game theory, logic, and quantum physics. He was famed for his astonishing memory, mathematical ability, linguistic range, and humor. Born in Budapest, Hungary, he received his Ph.D. there in 1926. From 1927 to 1930, von Neumann served as a lecturer in mathematics at the University of Berlin. In his first year there, he published five papers on various aspects of mathematics and physics that earned him a reputation as a leading mathematician and led to his being invited to Princeton University in 1930 as one of the original professors at the Institute for Advanced Study, where he remained for the rest of his life. During World War II, he became interested in computers and automatic computation while working on the detonation device for the atomic bomb. He strongly contributed to the concept of the stored program computer, which distinguishes his work from the hardware-specific special-purpose computers of the day, such as ENIAC. (Several computing machines of the day had names ending in *niac*, and von Neumann worked on one named for him, Johnniac, as well as the humorously dubbed Maniac.)

His most significant contribution, the concept of "von Neumann architecture," was not a hardware device but rather an approach to computing in which the control program was stored with the data, the distinction between the two being made upon retrieval. A second major contribution was his notion of a program counter for specifying the location of program instructions. Von Newmann also introduced the idea of flowcharts in 1945. Cryptanalysis ranked with artillery firing tables and atomic research among early applications of primitive automata, and the modern computer received much encouragement from the crypto elite, of which both ALAN TURING and John von Neumann were members. His conception of a single sequence of processing remained unchallenged for more than a generation until advances in hardware made possible the use of multiple-track or parallel processing.

Also a significant contributor to artificial intelligence, von Neumann is one of the founding fathers of modern computing.

BOOKS BY VON NEUMANN

Computer and the Brain. Yale U. Pr. 1958 $8.00. ISBN 0-300-02415-0. Reveals his surprising awareness of the extent to which von Neumann machines and human brains are different.

Papers of John von Neumann on Computing and Computer Theory. Ed. by William Aspray and Arthur Burks. MIT Pr. 1986 o.p. Collection of von Neumann's papers on logical design, computer architecture, large-scale computing at high speed, and automata, with an explanatory essay by Donald Knuth. Excludes von Neumann's mathematical work but includes a general bibliography of writing by and about him.

The World of Mathematics. Ed. by James R. Newman. 4 vols. Microsoft 1988 $99.95. ISBN 1-55615-149-7. Contains von Neumann's "The General and Logical Theory of Automata" in Vol. 4.

BOOKS ABOUT VON NEUMANN

Aspray, William. *From Mathematical Constructivity to Computer Science: Alan Turing, John von Neumann, and the Origins of Computer Science in Mathematical Logic*. MIT Pr. 1980 o.p. The mathematical background of von Neumann's work.

_____. *John von Neumann and the Origins of Modern Computing*. MIT Pr. 1990 $37.50. ISBN 0-262-01121-2. Serious study of von Neumann's practical and theoretical contributions to computing, written by a historian of both mathematics and computing; heavily annotated with archival source material.

Goldstine, Herman H. *The Computer from Pascal to von Neumann*. Princeton U. Pr. 1993 $55.00. ISBN 0-691-08104-2. History of computing by a participant in many of the developments he describes.

Heims, Steve V. *John von Neumann and Norbert Wiener: From Mathematics to the Technologies of Life and Death*. MIT Pr. 1980 $13.50. ISBN 0-262-58056-X. Study of von Neumann, Norbert Wiener, and the cybernetic circle.

Poundstone, William. *Prisoner's Dilemma*. Doubleday 1992 $22.50. ISBN 0-385-41580-X. On von Neumann's mathematical career.

WIENER, NORBERT. 1894–1964

American mathematical logician Norbert Wiener was born in Cambridge, Massachusetts. An intellectually gifted child whose father taught at Harvard University, he graduated from Tufts University at the age of 14 and received his M.A. and his Ph.D. in mathematical logic from Harvard in 1914. The following year he studied at Cambridge University under BERTRAND RUSSELL (see also Vol. 4) and Godfrey Hardy and at Gottingen University, Europe's leading centers in mathematical and physical science. During World War I, Wiener taught at the University of Maine, worked as a writer and reporter, and served as a mathematician in Aberdeen, Maryland.

In 1919 Wiener joined the faculty of Massachusetts Institute of Technology (MIT), where he remained for the rest of his long, notable career. While at MIT, he was influenced by the research on statistical mechanics of chemist JOSIAH WILLARD GIBBS. Adapting Gibbs's findings, he produced major research contributions on the problem of Brownian motion. He also used Tauberian theorems in his work on harmonic analysis and produced simple proofs of the prime-number theorem. Wiener also began to study electrical circuits, especially the field of feedback control.

During World War II, Wiener went to work for the U.S. government on the construction of predictors and in research on guided missiles. Despite his wartime contributions, he resolutely opposed the use of weapons of mass destruction. However, a major outgrowth of his wartime research was his renewed study of the handling of information by complex machines like automatic computers, radar devices, and servomechanisms. His earlier research in feedback control in circuit instrumentation now prompted Wiener to postulate the similarity between the operation of these mechanisms and that of the human brain and nervous system. His work here led to a new field of science that he called cybernetics, which he defined as the study of control and communication in man and in the machine. His book *Cybernetics* (1948) was widely read by both scientists and the general public. The book popularized the study of the relationships between the creations of the new age of technology and their creators.

BOOKS BY WIENER

Cybernetics. MIT Pr. 1961 $11.95. ISBN 0-262-73009-X
Fourier Transforms in a Complex Domain. Am. Math. 1987 $45.00. ISBN 0-8218-1019-7
Ex Prodigy: My Childhood and Youth. 1953. MIT Pr. 1964 $9.95. ISBN 0-262-73008-1. Autobiographical.
I Am a Mathematician: The Later Life of a Prodigy. 1956. MIT Pr. 1964 $10.95. ISBN 0-262-73007-3. Autobiographical.
Invention: The Care and Feeding of Ideas. MIT Pr. 1993 $19.95. ISBN 0-262-23167-0. Posthumously published; discovered among Wiener's papers in the Institute Archives of the MIT Libraries.

BOOKS ABOUT WIENER

Heims, Steve V. *John von Neumann and Norbert Wiener: From Mathematics to the Technologies of Life and Death.* MIT Pr. 1980 $13.50. ISBN 0-262-58056-X. Study of John von Neumann, Wiener, and the cybernetic circle.
Masani, Pesi. *Norbert Wiener: Eighteen Ninety-Four to Nineteen Sixty-Four.* Birkhauser 1989 $79.50. ISBN 0-8176-2246-2. Extended survey of Wiener's intellectual work against a biographical backdrop.

CHAPTER 18

Astronomy and Space Science

Harry L. Shipman

In Nature's infinite book of secrecy
A little I can read.
—WILLIAM SHAKESPEARE, *Antony and Cleopatra*

Thus from these forces, by other propositions which are also mathematical, I
deduce the motions of the planets, the comets, the moon, and the sea.
—ISAAC NEWTON, *Principia*

Astronomy and space science involve profound questions that naturally arise as a result of gazing at the star-strewn night sky. Since antiquity, people have wondered: Where does the universe come from? Where is it going? Where is Earth in the universe? What are the stars, planets, and moons made of? Astronomers and space scientists address these questions using the methods of science as well as new technologies that allow us to place orbiting telescopes in space. The answers to these questions have revealed a magnificently varied universe. Like earth, some planets are essentially rocky masses. Other planets, like Saturn, are huge spheres of gas so rarefied that the gas could float on water. There are tiny, extremely dense neutron stars from which a cupful of star matter would weigh 100 billion tons. There are black holes, in which gravity is so strong that an object that came too close would be pulled inside and trapped forever. And there are huge, gossamer clusters of galaxies, extending hundreds of millions of light years from one end to the other. A light beam that left one end of a gossamer cluster when the first organisms evolved on earth only now would have finished its trip across the cluster.

For thousands of years, human beings simply described the universe. They carefully tracked the motions of stars and planets without any understanding of what they were made of or why they moved in such predictable ways. However, in a great intellectual movement that began half a millennium ago, astronomers have answered many questions about the universe and its contents. For example, SIR ISAAC NEWTON's (see also Vol. 4) laws of gravity and motion explain complex motions of heavenly bodies by appealing to the simple laws of motion, laws that can be expressed in only one or two typewritten lines in the language of mathematics. During the twentieth century, the pace of discovery has accelerated dramatically. A primary reason has been the development of new scientific technology. In 1990, for example, scientists launched into space the Hubble Space Telescope, which orbits high above the earth's atmosphere. The latest of a large battery of instruments that can detect gamma rays, X-rays, ultraviolet and infrared radiation, the Hubble Space Telescope is able to obtain razor-sharp pictures, and its tremendous light-gathering power permits astronomers to probe deep into the heart of distant galaxies.

585

Astronomers ask and try to answer some important questions about various types of cosmic objects. What is it? How does it move? How did it evolve? As astronomy became more sophisticated, astronomers progressed from answering the first question to answering the second and even the third. At the beginning of the twentieth century, with the exception of planetary motion, astronomers mainly were concerned with the first question, simply describing rather than understanding the cosmos. Planetary motion theories marked the beginning of modern astronomy.

During the twentieth century, astronomers used a wide variety of tools to probe the universe. For example, spectrographs allowed scientists to split white light into its component colors. Illustrating how light interacts with atoms eventually led to an understanding of astronomical spectra. Astronomers then used different kinds of radiation to probe the cosmos, beginning with radio waves. Like visible light, radio waves can penetrate earth's atmosphere. Today, orbiting telescopes and space probes to other planets have tied astronomy closely with the space program. This has resulted in an explosive growth of astronomical data since the late 1950s.

Astronomy includes a wide range of subdisciplines, many of which are closely related to other branches of science. For example, astronomers who study the sun and the effects of the solar wind on magnetized plasmas are called plasma physicists. They use the universe as a cosmic laboratory. Planetary scientists use concepts from geology, geophysics, meteorology, and atmospheric chemistry to determine the structure and physical phenomena of other planets. And, beyond the solar system, the astronomer or astrophysicist (there is no longer any distinction between these two designations) applies physical laws on a cosmic scale. Space science, too, has become increasingly diverse. Scientists in many fields now are using the unique environment, or vantage point, that an orbiting laboratory provides. Some space scientists are astronomers who monitor robot space probes to distant planets or orbiting telescopes above Earth's atmosphere to learn more about the electromagnetic spectrum. Others are oceanographers and geologists, who use orbiting artificial satellites to make large-scale studies of our planet, which are impossible from earth's surface. Still others are life scientists, who use the unique space environment and its absence of apparent gravity (weightlessness) to investigate effects on human beings and other organisms. Finally, the materials scientists use space as a laboratory to investigate how fluids flow and solidify in a weightless environment.

Astronomy appeals to most people in a way that few other sciences do, because anyone can appreciate what astronomers study simply by looking up on a clear night. Perhaps it is inherently human to explore further, to go where no person has gone before. In any event, there are many popular books available about various aspects of astronomy and space science. These provide vital supplementary information to the sensational aspects of astronomy that occasionally appear in the broadcast media. This literature is growing rapidly, and a host of new books are published each year.

Because of the nature of scientific research, many notable scientists in a particular discipline make their contributions in the form of journal articles rather than books. Because many great astronomers and space scientists did not write books, those listed below should not be regarded as a list of the most important people in these areas. Some of them are world-class scientists who wrote several accessible books or had a book written about them, (e.g., COPERNICUS, EDMOND HALLEY, and EDWIN HUBBLE). Some scientists have written more extensively for the general reader (e.g., SIR ARTHUR EDDINGTON and

GEORGE GAMOW). Several people are listed in this section because they are popularizers of astronomy or space science (e.g., TIMOTHY FERRIS and PATRICK MOORE).

To understand the nature of the following list, consider some important people who have been excluded because they did not write appropriate books. These important people include great pioneers of rocketry, such as Konstantin Tsiolkovsky (1857–1935), Robert H. Goddard (1882–1945), and Hermann Oberth (1894–1990). An astronomer who has been omitted is Jan Oort (1900–93), who discovered the source region of comets and the rotation of the Milky Way galaxy. Walter Adams (1876–1956) and Henry Norris Russell (1877–1957), who developed the use of spectroscopy to decode the temperature and composition of stars, also are excluded from the list. CECILIA PAYNE-GAPOSHKIN (1900–79), involved in the same work and of comparable stature in the field as Adams and Russell, is listed because there is an autobiography and two very accessible books by her in print.

REFERENCE AND GENERAL BOOKS

The segment of the astronomy literature that changes least rapidly is this category of books. There are several different kinds of books that can provide a general overview of astronomy. The most accessible books are those that are addressed exclusively to the general reader; these often contain beautiful pictures but might not be comprehensive. A second kind of book is the textbook. Although some textbooks feature a plethora of mathematical equations, most of the introductory texts are written for liberal arts college students. These textbooks generally do not contain many equations yet offer a comprehensive coverage of the field. A third kind of book listed below is the handbook, which mainly lists astronomical data in numerical form. Though primarily used by students of astronomy and professional astronomers, handbooks are well indexed so that they can be used by the general reader.

Abell, George. *Drama of the Universe*. SCP 1978 $42.25. ISBN 0-03-022401-2. Comprehensive but nonmathematical astronomy text addressed to the liberal arts student.

Allen, Clarence W. *Astrophysical Quantities*. Humanities 3rd ed. 1976 $80.00. ISBN 0-485-11150-0. One of three astronomical guides used by professional and amateur astronomers, including a great deal of numerical data but more concise than Lang or Zombeck; somewhat dated.

Allen, Richard H. *Star Names: Their Lore and Meaning*. Dover 1963 $8.95. ISBN 0-486-21079-0. Classic reference is a source of information about the origins of start names, which are rooted deep in history.

Annual Review of Astronomy and Astrophysics. 31 vols. Annual Reviews 1963–93 $53.00–$57.00 ea. Series provides authoritative reviews of current research, written for professional astronomers.

Asimov, Isaac. *The Universe*. Walker & Co. 3rd rev. ed. 1980 $15.95. ISBN 0-8027-0655-X. Comprehensive, easy-to-read survey; entertaining and accurate.

Audouze, Jean, and Guy Israel, ed. *The Cambridge Atlas of Astronomy*. Cambridge U. Pr. 2nd ed. 1988 $100.00. ISBN 0-521-36360-8. "Imagine an accurate and lucid introductory astronomy text having a team of at least 26 competent authors and an apparently unlimited budget for color illustrations. If this sounds appealing, in fact it is" (*Sky and Telescope*).

Culver, Roger, and Philip Ianna. *Astrology: True or False?* Prometheus Bks. rev. ed. 1988 $15.95. ISBN 0-87975-483-4. The most comprehensive of several books that demonstrate the problems associated with astrology.

Ferris, Timothy. *Spaceshots: The Beauty of Nature beyond Earth*. Pantheon 1984 o.p. Spectacular selection of beautiful photographs.

Fraknoi, Andrew. *Resource Book for the Teaching of Astronomy*. W. H. Freeman 1977 $7.95. ISBN 0-7167-0288-6. Originally written as an instructor's manual for a textbook; includes teaching strategies, practical suggestions for using audiovisual aids, and an excellent list of references.

Friedman, Herbert. *The Amazing Universe. Special Publications Ser*. Natl. Geog. 1975 $8.95. ISBN 0-87044-179-5. Brief, well-illustrated survey of astronomy; an excellent introduction, but somewhat dated.

Ginzburg, V. L. *Physics and Astrophysics: A Selection of Key Problems*. Pergamon 1985 $32.00. ISBN 0-08-026499-9. Reviews unanswered questions, summarizing each briefly, authoritatively, and mainly nonmathematically; written by a well-known Russian astrophysicist.

Hartmann, William K. *Astronomy: The Cosmic Journey*. Wadsworth Pub. 1991. ISBN 0-534-14946-4. Comprehensive and nonmathematical text for the general reader.

Hopkins, Jeanne. *Glossary of Astronomy and Astrophysics*. U. Ch. Pr. 2nd rev. ed. 1982 $10.00. ISBN 0-226-35169-6. Provides definitions of astronomical jargon.

Illingworth, Valerie. *The Facts on File Dictionary of Astronomy*. Facts on File rev. ed. 1986 $24.95. ISBN 0-8160-1357-8. Definitions of astronomical terms; addressed more to the general reader than Hopkins's *Glossary*.

Jastrow, Robert. *Red Giants and White Dwarfs*. Norton 3rd ed. 1990 $11.95. ISBN 0-393-85004-8. Brief, well-written overview of the subject.

Kaufmann, William J. *Universe*. W. H. Freeman 3rd ed. 1990 $42.95. ISBN 0-7167-2094-9. College text for liberal arts students.

Lampton, Christopher. *Space Sciences. Reference First Bk*. Watts 1983 $10.40. ISBN 0-531-04539-0. Brief summary.

Lang, Kenneth. *Astrophysical Data: Planets and Stars*. Spr.-Verlag 1991 $59.00. ISBN 0-387-97109-2. Descriptive handbook for astronomers and space scientists.

————. *Astrophysical Formulae: A Compendium for the Physicist and Astrophysicist*. Spr.-Verlag 1986 o.p. Mathematical handbook for astronomers and space scientists.

Malin, David, and Paul Murdin. *Colours of the Stars*. Cambridge U. Pr. 1984 o.p. Spectacular color photographs and an excellent discussion of star colors as well as how these colors are represented accurately.

McGraw-Hill Encyclopedia of Astronomy. McGraw 1993 $75.00. ISBN 0-07-045314-4. Many brief articles by professionals; complements the encyclopedias listed here, with a few lengthy articles.

Moche, Dinah L. *Astronomy: A Self-Teaching Guide*. Wiley 4th ed. 1993 $12.95. ISBN 0-471-53001-8. Textbook for the self-directed general reader.

Morrison, Philip. *Powers of Ten: About the Relative Sizes of Things in the Universe. Scientific American Lib*. W. H. Freeman 1985 $19.95. ISBN 0-7167-1409-4. Magnificently illustrated journey, starting with a picnic on the shores of Lake Michigan and moving farther away from Earth to reveal the scope of the entire universe, finally moving inward to show matter of the smallest magnitudes. A motion picture classic is based on this book.

Pasachoff, Jay. *Astronomy: From the Earth to the Universe*. SCP 1991 $41.25. ISBN 0-03-031329-5. College text for the liberal arts student.

Ronan, Colin A. *The Natural History of the Universe*. Macmillan 1991 $39.95. ISBN 0-02-604511-7. Effectively presents, in clear language, theories of relativity, curved space time, clusters and quasars. An excellent examination of events from "the Big Bang to the end of time."

Rowan-Robinson, Michael. *One Universe: An Armchair Guide*. W. H. Freeman 1992 $19.95. ISBN 0-7167-2359-X. Rowan-Robinson, a British astronomer, opens up the universe for the general reader. Twenty astronomical subjects; illustrated.

Sagan, Carl. *Cosmos*. Ballantine 1985 $5.95. ISBN 0-345-33135-4. Well-illustrated, easy-to-read coverage of the cosmos; based on a popular series seen on PBS television.

Schatzman, Evry. *Our Expanding Universe*. McGraw 1992 $9.95. ISBN 0-07-055174-X. Moves beyond the sun, the earth's climate, and human genetic quandaries to ponder the evolution of the concept of the universe.

Shu, Frank H. *The Physical Universe. Astronomy Ser.* Univ. Sci. Bks. 1982 $54.00. ISBN 0-935702-05-9. Comprehensive survey of astronomy that is "becoming the book of choice" (*Mercury*); designed for the reader who knows basic physics and algebra.

Snow, Theodore P. *The Cosmic Cycle*. Darwin Pr. 1984 $14.95. ISBN 0-87850-041-3. Brief overview of the universe; includes excellent photographs.

———. *The Dynamic Universe: An Introduction to Astronomy*. West Pub. 4th ed. 1991 $48.75. ISBN 0-314-77104-2. College text for liberal arts students. One of the best and wonderfully illustrated.

Wagoner, Robert, and Donald Goldsmith. *Cosmic Horizons*. W. H. Freeman 1982 $22.95. ISBN 0-7167-1418-3. Discusses how the combination of astronomical observations, laboratory experiments, and logical-mathematical reasoning has enabled astronomers to understand the origin and development of the universe.

Zeilik, Michael. *Astronomy: The Evolving Universe*. Wiley 6th ed. 1991 $44.95. ISBN 0-471-53735-7. College text for liberal arts students.

Zombeck, Martin. *A Handbook of Space Astronomy and Astrophysics*. Cambridge U. Pr. 1990 $75.00. ISBN 0-521-34550-2. Virtually all numerical data about the universe.

TELESCOPES, TECHNIQUES, ASTRONOMERS, AND HISTORY

This section includes books that describe the work of modern astronomers and what astronomers did in the past. The history of astronomy began before the time of writing. In fact, prehistoric monuments such as Stonehenge (which functioned, in part, as an observatory) are mute testimony to the long and enduring interest of human beings in heavenly bodies and phenomena. Contemporary facilities, such as the Hubble Space Telescope, are their modern counterparts. Some histories feature certain astronomers; many of these books are listed in the biographical section of this chapter. Others focus on specific tools and equipment, such as the telescope. Autobiographies, such as those by Cohen, Gehrels, and Lovell, provide someone considering a career in astronomy with an idea of what it is like to be an astronomer.

Bauer, Henry H. *Beyond Velikovsky: The History of a Public Controversy*. U. of Ill. Pr. 1984 $29.95. ISBN 0-252-01004-X. Dismisses Velikovsky's explanation of the history of the solar system as nonsense but also has unkind words for some of Velikovsky's critics. "Participants in and observers of the quarter-century-long Velikovsky controversy will find plenty to agree and disagree with here" (*The Skeptical Inquirer*).

Cohen, Martin. *In Quest of Telescopes*. Cambridge U. Pr. 1982 $13.95. ISBN 0-521-24989-9. Cohen is an observational astronomer, in contrast to Clayton, who analyzes data taken by others.

Dyson, Freeman. *From Eros to Gaia*. Pantheon 1992 $24.50. ISBN 0-679-41307-3. Focusing on astronomy, Dyson presents 36 essays exploring the whys and hows of scientific pursuits. A humanistic and responsible critique from a compassionate scientist and writer.

Edge, David O., and Michael J. Mulkay. *Astronomy Transformed: The Emergence of Radio Astronomy in Britain*. Wiley 1976 o.p. The growth of radio astronomy following World War II, by a radio astronomer (Edge) and a sociologist (Mulkay); includes fascinating sociological conclusions.

Gehrels, Tom. *On the Glassy Sea*. Am. Inst. Physics 1988 $35.00. ISBN 0-88318-598-9. Collection of stories, both personal and professional, written by an astronomer who devotes most of his time to searching for asteroids that might collide with Earth.

Gingerich, Owen, ed. *Astrophysics and Twentieth-Century Astronomy to 1950*. Pt. A. *General History of Astronomy Ser*. Cambridge U. Pr. 1984 $39.50. ISBN 0-521-24256-8. Compendium emphasizing the development of instrumentation, the construction of large observatories, and the growth of scientific ideas. "It should help the general reader understand how current discovery emerges from its recent past. . . . It may be trite to say so, but even in science we must learn from history or suffer from it" (*Sky and Telescope*).

Goldsmith, Donald, ed. *Scientists Confront Velikovsky*. Cornell Univ. Pr. 1977 $19.95. ISBN 0-393-00928-9. "Articles by leading scientists on the colliding worlds theory; the definitive reference book in this field" (*Mercury*).

Harwit, Martin. *Cosmic Discovery: The Search, Scope, and Heritage of Astronomy*. MIT Pr. 1984 $12.95. ISBN 0-262-58068-3. Provocative description of how astronomical research is conducted; uses the historical record to provide suggestions for the training of future astronomers and the selection of future facilities.

Krupp, Edwin C. *Echoes of the Ancient Skies: The Astronomy of Lost Civilizations*. NAL-Dutton 1984 $8.95. ISBN 0-452-00679-1. Examines the newly emerging field of archaeoastronomy; discusses prehistoric monuments, such as Stonehenge, that functioned as ancient observatories and other cultural artifacts.

Lang, Kenneth, and Owen Gingerich, eds. *A Source Book in Astronomy 1900–1975*. HUP 1980 $41.95. ISBN 0-318-13544-2. Reprints 132 important articles on significant achievements in astronomy.

Lovell, Sir A. C. Bernard. *Astronomer by Chance*. *Sloan Foundation Ser*. Basic 1990 $24.95. ISBN 0-465-00512-8. Well-written autobiography covering a remarkable astronomical career in which Lovell used surplus World War II equipment to help initiate a new field of science.

Osterbrock, Don. *James E. Keeler: Pioneer Astrophysicist*. Cambridge U. Pr. 1985 $49.50. ISBN 0-521-26582-7. Biography of one of the founders of astronomy and astrophysics in America.

Overbye, Dennis. *Lonely Hearts of the Cosmos*. HarpC 1992 repr. of 1990 ed. $13.00. ISBN 0-06-092271-0. Unexpected discoveries, seething rivalries, and inspired guesswork are all in a day's work for modern cosmologists, several of whom are profiled here.

Preston, Richard. *First Light*. Atlantic Monthly 1987 o.p. A journalist focuses on the Palomar Observatory to describe what astronomers do before and while looking through the telescope.

Smith, Robert W. *The Space Telescope: A Study of NASA, Science, Technology, and Politics*. Cambridge U. Pr. 1989 $39.50. ISBN 0-521-26634-3. Written before the launch of the Hubble Space Telescope, this book describes the history of this project and the struggles that took place in order for it to become a reality.

Zeilik, Michael. *Conceptual Astronomy: A Journey of Ideas*. Wiley 1992. ISBN 0-471-50996-5. Emphasizes astronomical and physical concepts; thoroughly illustrated.

ASTRONOMY WITHOUT INSTRUMENTS

What was the bright object you saw in the sky yesterday evening? A number of references can help you identify it—sky atlases, almanacs, and other books that provide a guide to objects in the night sky. The motion of the moon and the planets differs from year to year. Thus, if you want to know a precise planetary or lunar position, you will need an almanac. However, if you need to know only the general location of a planet, most of the books listed below are updated periodically for accuracy.

Brown, Peter L. *Star and Planet Spotting*. Sterling 1990 $9.95. ISBN 0-8069-7268-8. A historical perspective on stargazing; somewhat dated, but thorough coverage of what it presents.

Burnham, Robert, Jr. *Burnham's Celestial Handbook: An Observer's Guide to the Universe beyond the Solar System.* 3 vols. Dover 1979 $13.95 ea. ISBNs 0-486-23567-X, 0-486-23568-8, 0-486-23673-0. Comprehensive guide to celestial objects that can be seen in the night sky with a telescope; designed for the experienced astronomical observer.

Consolmagno, Guy, and Dan Davis. *Turn Left at Orion.* Cambridge U. Pr. 1990 $27.95. ISBN 0-521-34090-X. Clear, easy-to-understand photographs, providing a valuable guide to celestial objects that are visible with low-power telescopes or binoculars; useful for beginners.

Covington, M. A. *Astrophotography for the Amateur.* Cambridge U. Pr. 1991 $16.95. ISBN 0-521-40984-5. Practical advice for someone who wants to photograph the night sky.

Dickenson, Terence, and Alan Dyer. *The Backyard Astronomer's Guide.* Firefly Bks. Ltd. 1991 $39.95. ISBN 0-921820-11-9. Focusing on practical aspects, this guide is an essential reference tool for all sky observers.

Gibson, Bob. *The Astronomer's Sourcebook.* Woodbine Hse. 1992 $19.95. ISBN 0-933149-43-3. An excellent resource for the stargazing enthusiast. Lists clubs, written guides and atlases, planetariums, NASA projects, equipment, astronomical milestones, degree programs, summer camps, scholarships, and more. A unique reference.

Hirshfeld, Alan, and R. W. Sinnott, eds. *Sky Catalogue 2000.0.* Cambridge U. Pr. Vol. 1 1982 $39.50. ISBN 0-521-28913-0. Vol. 2 1985 $54.50. ISBN 0-521-25818-9. List of all the bright stars and their properties; includes brief explanatory notes.

Kals, W. S. *Stars and Planets: The Sierra Club Guide to Sky Watching and Direction Finding.* Sierra 1990 $15.00. ISBN 0-87156-671-0. Assuming no knowledge of astronomy and requiring no astronomical equipment, this ingenius handbook clearly shows how to locate major stars, planets, and constellations anywhere on both sides of the equator with the naked eye. Features some 80 illustrations.

MacRobert, Alan. *Backyard Astronomy.* Sky Pub. 1986 $2.00. ISBN 0-933346-44-1. Compilation of MacRobert's series of articles from *Sky and Telescope* magazine helps the reader appreciate objects in the night sky.

Moore, Patrick. *A New Guide to the Stars.* Norton 1974 o.p. Combination of several chapters on "What's in the sky?" and some chapters that include more than assigning names; discusses the basic nature of stars, galaxies, quasars, and pulsars.

———. *A Pocket Guide to Astronomy.* S&S Trade 1980 $7.95. ISBN 0-671-25309-3

Muirden, James. *Astronomy with Binoculars.* 1979. P-H 1985 $7.95. ISBN 0-668-05832-3. Describes how to enjoy celestial observation without using a telescope.

Mumford, George S. *The Cloudy Night Book.* Sky Pub. 1979 $6.95. ISBN 0-933346-00-X. Easy-to-read collection of humorous "astro-trivia."

Newton, Jack, and Philip Teece. *The Guide to Amateur Astronomy.* Cambridge U. Pr. 1989 $24.95. ISBN 0-521-34028-4. Comprehensive coverage of basic astronomy for the amateur sky watcher.

Pasachoff, Jay, and Donald H. Menzel. *A Field Guide to the Stars and Planets.* Peterson Field Guide Ser. HM 1983 $19.95. ISBN 0-395-34641-X. Good guide for the beginner, fashioned after the Peterson Field Guide Series; includes useful illustrations, with a minimum of detail.

Rey, H. A. *The Stars: A New Way to See Them.* HM 1976 $9.95. ISBN 0-395-24830-2. Lines are drawn between the stars to make most of the constellations resemble their names.

Ridpath, I., ed. *Norton's 2000.0 Star Atlas and Reference Handbook.* Halsted Pr. 18th ed. 1989 $41.95. ISBN 0-470-21460-0. Brief, compact atlas showing stars visible to the unaided eye, as well as some deep-space objects; the standard reference for visual observing, originally published by Arthur Norton in 1910.

Tirion, Wil. *Sky Atlas 2000.0: Twenty-six Star Charts Covering Both Hemispheres.* Cambridge U. Pr. 1981 $42.50. ISBN 0-521-24467-6. One of the best and most attractive sky maps available, but rather bulky as a field guide simply to identify constellations.

Whitney, Charles A. *Whitney's Star Finder.* Knopf 5th ed. 1989 $16.95. ISBN 0-679-72582-2. Little useful information about finding stars, but it does include many useful hints for determining the moon's location and how to distinguish planets from other celestial objects.

THE PLANETS AND THE SOLAR SYSTEM

One of the most dramatic expansions of the human perspective has come about as a result of our ability to send space probes to explore other planets. Prior to the exploration of space by these probes, very little was known about the planets in our solar system. The many moons of Jupiter and Saturn were just dots with names; except for Mars, the other planets were cloud-enshrouded mysteries. Now, however, spectacular visual images of other worlds exist as a result of the space programs of the United States and former Soviet Union. By the early 1990s, a series of probes had visited all the planets in the solar system except Pluto, and even this remote outpost has become the focus of a possible future NASA museum. Because many planetary scientists also are excellent writers, there are many books that can introduce the general reader to this subject.

Beatty, J. Kelly, Brian O'Leary, and Andrew Chaikin, eds. *The New Solar System*. Sky Pub. 3rd ed. 1990 $39.95. ISBN 0-933346-55-7. Twenty well-illustrated chapters on various aspects of solar system astronomy by well-known astronomers. "This is *the* book to have if you want to find out what we know about the solar system" (*Mercury*).

Brandt, John C., and Robert D. Chapman. *Rendezvous in Space: The Science of Comets*. W. H. Freeman 1992 $23.95. ISBN 0-7167-2175-9. The most up-to-date information on comets by the world's best authorities in this field; includes the results of spacecraft observations of Halley's comet.

Brown, Peter L. *Comets, Meteorites, and Men*. Taplinger 1974 o.p. Excellent source of anecdotes and comet lore.

Burgess, Eric. *Return to the Red Planet*. Col. U. Pr. 1990 $34.95. ISBN 0-231-06942-1. Comprehensive, well-illustrated, nontechnical introduction to the planet Mars.

———. *Venus: An Errant Twin*. Col. U. Pr. 1985 $41.00. ISBN 0-231-05856-X. Chronicles the exploration of Venus, focusing on the various space missions (mostly Russian) to that planet; does not include recent data from the Magellan space probes.

Calder, Nigel. *The Comet Is Coming: The Feverish Legacy of Mr. Halley*. Viking Penguin 1982 $7.95. ISBN 0-14-006069-3. The first of many books that greeted Halley's comet on its 1985 appearance; includes many historical anecdotes and remains a useful book about comets.

Carr, Michael H. *The Surface of Mars*. Planetary Exploration Ser. Yale U. Pr. 1984 $29.95. ISBN 0-300-03242-0. Summarizes in rather technical language the geology of Mars from data provided by the robot probes that have orbited and landed on the planet; includes 150 photographs.

Dodd, Robert T. *Thunderstorms and Shooting Stars: The Meaning of Meteorites*. HUP 1986 $12.95. ISBN 0-674-89138-4. "Referring to meteorites as the 'poor man's space probe' because they are the only extraterrestrial rocks that can be collected without leaving earth, Dodd explains the scientific data that can be extracted from meteorites, including what effect they have had on the earth and what they can tell us about the solar system" (*Booklist*).

Hartmann, William K. *Moons and Planets*. Wadsworth Pub. 2nd ed. 1983 $43.25. ISBN 0-534-00719-8. More than the usual descriptive treatment of other solar system bodies; includes some discussion of why they appear the way they do.

Henbest, Nigel. *The Planets: A Guided Tour of Our Solar System Through the Eyes of America's Space Probes*. Viking Penguin 1993 $35.00. ISBN 0-670-83384-3. Filled with glorious color photographs taken by Voyager, Pioneer, and Viking spacecraft.

Solid factual text. Not soon to become outdated, this is a culmination of grand explorations that will not be repeated for some time.

Littmann, Mark. *Planets Beyond: Discoveries in Our Outer Solar System*. Wiley 1988 $22.95. ISBN 0-471-61128-X. Well-written description of current knowledge about Uranus, Neptune, and Pluto; also fully examines the possibility of additional planets in our solar system.

Marsden, Brian, and Gareth Williams. *Catalog of Cometary Orbits 1993*. Minor Planet Center, Smithsonian Astrophysical Observatory 1993 $20.00. A list of numbers that can tell you all about the orbit of your favorite comet.

Moore, Patrick. *Mission to the Planets*. Norton 1990 $24.95. ISBN 0-393-02872-0. Moore prepared the early maps of the moon used by NASA and the USSR. Thorough coverage, which includes the 1986 rendezvous of five spacecraft with Halley's Comet.

Morrison, David, and Tobias Owen. *The Planetary System*. AW Physics Ser. Addison-Wesley 1988 $49.50. ISBN 0-201-10487-3. Clearly written textbook comparing planets in the solar system; descriptive treatment that also discusses the possible reasons why the planetary surfaces differ so much.

Murray, Bruce, Michael C. Malin, and Ronald Greeley. *Earthlike Planets: Surfaces of Mercury, Venus, Earth, Moon, and Mars*. W. H. Freeman 1981 $19.95. ISBN 0-7167-1149-4. Comparative treatment of the planets focusing exclusively on the inner solar system; somewhat dated, especially in regard to Venus.

Noyes, Robert W. *The Sun, Our Star*. HUP 1982 o.p. Easy-to-read survey of knowledge about the sun ranges from counting sunspots to the more recent observations obtained from orbiting telescopes and space probes.

Washburn, Mark. *Distant Encounters*. HarBraceJ 1983 o.p. A journalist's account of the Voyager missions to Jupiter and Saturn; the author's experience covering the mission is as intriguing as the mission itself.

STARS AND GALAXIES

The space age has produced a dramatic increase in our understanding of the distant universe with its millions of giant galaxies. Today, better electronic detectors and ingenious improvements in telescope design have wrought revolutionary changes in the ability of scientists to measure the weak signals emanating from these distant objects. Space observations now permit scientists to probe parts of the electromagnetic spectrum (such as X-rays) that are inaccessible to ground-based observatories. Books listed in this section focus on a few subfields of astronomy. For the most part, these works bring the reader to the frontiers of current research and convey the excitement of modern science.

Asimov, Isaac. *The Exploding Suns: Secrets of Supernovae*. NAL-Dutton 1986 $4.50. ISBN 0-317-02724-7. Beginning with fourth-century Chinese observations, Asimov moves on to modern ideas about the origin of supernovas and speculates about their possible effects on the solar system and on human beings.

Bartusiak, Marcia. *Thursday's Universe*. Microsoft 1988 $8.95. ISBN 1-55615-153-5. Brief examination of current research in astronomy, based on interviews with various astronomers.

Ferris, Timothy. *Coming of Age in the Milky Way*. Morrow 1988 $19.95. ISBN 0-688-05889-2. Poetic description of astronomers through the millennia, why they sought answers to profound astronomical questions, and the answers they formulated.

––––––. *Galaxies*. Stewart Tabon & Chang 1982 $18.95. ISBN 0-941434-02-8. Lucid exposition of what is known about galaxies; includes many illustrations.

Friedman, Herbert. *Astronomer's Universe: Stars, Galaxies and Cosmos*. Ballantine 1991 $14.00. ISBN 0-345-37248-4. Covers stellar evolution, quasars and post-Big Bang nucleosynthesis. "One of the most engaging . . . introductions to come along in memory" (*Publishers Weekly*).

Halpern, Paul. *Cosmic Wormholes: The Search for Interstellar Shortcuts.* NAL-Dutton 1992 $21.00. ISBN 0-525-93477-4. Excellent discussion of the possible existence of space warps.

Hartmann, William K., and others. *Cycles of Fire: Stars, Galaxies, and the Wonder of Deep Space.* Workman Pub. 1988 $27.50. ISBN 0-89480-510-X. Spectacular illustrations, photographs, charts, diagrams, and more than 100 full-color paintings complement and extend a brisk, informative text.

Kippenhahn, Rudolf. *One Hundred Billion Suns.* Trans. by Jean Steinberg. Princeton U. Pr. 1993 $16.95. ISBN 0-691-08781-4. "We not only get the scientific record straight but also the priceless inside story and human history of those who brought about this intellectual achievement . . . [a] little masterpiece" (*Sky and Telescope*).

Marschall, Larry. *The Supernova Story.* Plenum 1988 $22.95. ISBN 0-306-42955-1. Good discussion of the final, explosive stage of stellar life cycles.

Murdin, Paul, and Lesley Murdin. *Supernovae.* Cambridge U. Pr. 1985 $29.95. ISBN 0-521-30038-X. Historical and descriptive examination of these stellar explosions.

Shipman, Harry L. *Black Holes, Quasars, and the Universe.* HM 2nd ed. 1980 o.p. Describes some selected areas of current research; clearly separates current knowledge into fact, concrete theory, working model, and speculation. "An excellent account of the present status of astrophysical cosmology. . . . There is no nonsense in this book, and Mr. Shipman gives concise accounts of what is known and how it is known" (*The New Yorker*).

Spitzer, Lyman. *Searching Between the Stars. Silliman Lectures Ser.* Bks. Demand repr. of 1982 ed. $52.40. ISBN 0-7837-3329-1. Investigates the interstellar medium, the space between one star and another, and examines how the gas in this region condenses to form new stars and planets.

COSMOLOGY

Where did it all begin? Where will it all end? These questions, which have probably concerned human beings since the beginning of human history, define the field of cosmology, the study of the universe and its origin. A century ago, the ideas astronomers had about the origin of the universe were not much better than the myths told by storytellers of primitive tribes. Despite the knowledge at the time of how it worked, astronomers had no convincing idea of how the universe evolved. The 1920s discovery that the universe is expanding and the accidental discovery in 1965 of the echoes of the "big bang" (in the form of radio radiation that fills the universe) were two high points in cosmology. Today, astronomers have discovered a number of relevant facts that, if interpreted correctly, might reveal how the universe began and how it has evolved.

Because of the great curiosity about the evolution of the universe, cosmology has been an attractive topic for science writers. Consequently, modern cosmology probably has the richest lay literature of any subfield of astronomy.

Barrow, John D., and Joseph Silk. *This Left Hand of Creation: Origin and Evolution of the Expanding Universe.* Basic 1983 o.p. Easy-to-read account of cosmology.

Chaisson, Eric. *Cosmic Dawn: The Origins of Matter and Life.* Norton 1989 $8.95. ISBN 0-393-30587-2. Easy-to-read survey of cosmology, with good coverage of biological and cultural evolution as well as astronomy. Main drawback is a lack of details; presents our knowledge of cosmic evolution as a *fait accompli* without explaining how the knowledge has been achieved.

Cloud, Preston. *Cosmos, Earth, and Man.* Yale U. Pr. 1978 $16.00. ISBN 0-300-02594-7. Geology, astronomy, and some evolutionary biology; sections on geology and biology are particularly useful.

Davies, Paul C. W. *The Edge of Infinity*. S&S Trade 1983 $9.95. ISBN 0-671-46062-5. Davies has written numerous books on cosmology and particle physics, and there is considerable overlap among them. This one is a survey of cosmology.

Ferris, Timothy. *The Red Limit: The Search for the Edge of the Universe*. 1979. Morrow 1983 $12.95. ISBN 0-688-01836-X. Discusses twentieth-century cosmology, emphasizing the history of the field, especially the lives and achievements of pioneering astronomers and physicists.

Harrison, Edward R. *Cosmology: The Science of the Universe*. Cambridge U. Pr. 1981 $42.50. ISBN 0-521-22981-2. Standard treatment of "big bang" cosmology; examines the philosophical issues of modern cosmology: Where is the "center" of the universe? Does this term have any meaning? What are cosmic horizons?

_____. *Masks of the Universe*. Macmillan 1986 o.p. Summary of ideas about the universe held by different cultures, including our own. Emphasizes that a culture's idea of the universe affects its philosophical, anthropological, and historical outlook on life.

Heyneman, Martha. *The Breathing Cathedral: Feeling Our Way into a Living Cosmos*. Sierra 1993 $25.00. ISBN 0-87156-687-7. Searching for a new cosmology in a post-Reformation, post-Copernican world where God is no longer in his heaven, Heyneman combs through hundreds of world views and explores three-dimensional surfaces buried in four-dimensional space. Incorporates the latest in matter/energy–time/space theories.

Islam, Jumal N. *The Ultimate Fate of the Universe*. Cambridge U. Pr. 1983 $17.95. ISBN 0-521-24814-0. Suggests that if the universe expands forever, as indicated by current evidence, its general appearance will change over very long periods of time as stars die and galaxies collapse.

Jastrow, Robert. *God and the Astronomers*. Norton 1992 $18.95. ISBN 0-393-85000-5. Brief survey of cosmology; despite the title, there is little discussion of the impact of modern cosmology on religion.

Lemonick, Michael D. *The Light at the Edge of the Universe*. Random 1993 $24.00. ISBN 0-679-41304. A survey of the current state of astrophysics and cosmology. Up-to-the-minute observations, the most recent theories and profiles of the major figures in the field. Immensely informative and lots of fun.

Pagels, Heinz. *Perfect Symmetry: The Search for the Beginning of Time*. Bantam 1986 $4.95. ISBN 0-553-24000-5. Clearly written treatment of the early evolution of the universe; claims that the first few moments of creation can tell us a lot about particle physics, the study of the fundamental nature of matter.

Reeves, Hubert. *Atoms of Silence: An Exploration of Cosmic Evolution*. Trans. by Ruth Lewis and John S. Lewis. MIT Pr. 1983 $27.50. ISBN 0-262-18112-6. Poetic approach to cosmology, retaining the Gallic flavor in an excellent translation. Answers the question How does a human being who appreciates beauty as well as science react to cosmology?

Rosen, Joe. *The Capricious Cosmos: Universe Beyond Law*. Macmillan 1992 $19.95. ISBN 0-02-604931-7. In the same vein as Hawking and Gleick, Rosen, a physics professor, discusses what science can and cannot do.

Staguhn, Gerhard. *God's Laughter: Man and His Cosmos*. HarpC 1992 $23.00. ISBN 0-06-019004-3. For the ancient Babylonians and Aristotle, the medieval scholastics, and even Newton and Kepler, the cosmos and God were interrelated. What do we do now in the age of black holes, the expanding universe, and quarks and quanta? Gerhard attempts a modern reconciliation, examining Planck, Einstein, Heisenberg, and Bohr.

Trefil, James S. *The Dark Side of the Universe*. Doubleday 1989 $9.95. ISBN 0-384-26212-4. Excellent treatment of the frontier between cosmology and particle physics, which studies the mysteries of galaxy formation and the first instant of cosmic evolution.

_____. *The Moment of Creation: Big Bang Physics from Before the First Millisecond to the Present Universe*. Macmillan 1984 $10.95. ISBN 0-02-096770-5. Examines an exciting development of the 1980s—the use of elementary particle physics and our understanding of the fundamental forces of nature and the way that particles interact

at very close distances—to explain events in the very early universe; though somewhat technical, covers difficult concepts with thorough and clear explanations.
————. *Space, Time, Infinity.* Smithsonian 1985 o.p. Good overview of astronomy, providing a comprehensive understanding of the universe through text and illustrations; includes one of the best sets of illustrations of the universe.

Weinberg, Steven. *The First Three Minutes: A Modern View of the Origin of the Universe.* Basic 1993 $12.00. ISBN 0-465-024-37-8. Details of classic "big bang" cosmology focus on the scientific rationale for our current understanding. Because it was written in the mid-1970s, the book does not include an account of current speculations on the very early universe.

THE SPACE PROGRAM

The launch of the artificial satellite *Sputnik* by the Soviet Union on October 4, 1957, was one of the key events of the cold war. Since then, astronauts, orbiting telescopes, spy satellites, communications satellites, and many other devices have been rocketed into space. Humans have landed on the moon, and plans are being developed to send people to Mars. It remains to be seen whether other ambitious projects can be realized in a post-cold war world, since the cold war often manifested itself in a race to be the first in various space-related achievements.

Despite the origin of the space program in the now extinguished cold war, its impact on human culture has been pervasive: two-thirds of our financial transactions now are made via satellite, and many businesses, states (such as Alaska), and countries (such as Indonesia) rely on space for their communications. The heroism of space explorers and the adventure of humans exploring space have been compared to the Age of Discovery, when CHRISTOPHER COLUMBUS (see Vol. 3) discovered America and Magellan sailed around the world.

Burrows, William E. *Deep Black: Space Espionage and National Security.* Random 1987 $22.50. ISBN 0-394-54124-3. Comprehensive, authoritative account of the role of satellites in maintaining national security; includes an enormous amount of previously "top-secret" information.

Collins, Michael. *Carrying the Fire. An Astronaut's Journey.* FS&G 1989 $19.95. ISBN 0-374-11919-8

Cooper, Henry S. F. *Before Lift-Off: The Making of a Space Shuttle Crew.* Johns Hopkins 1987 $29.95. ISBN 0-8018-3524-0. An insider's perspective on the space program, following a crew from selection to the start of the mission; Cooper's earlier books on space are classics.

Cornell, James, and P. Gorenstein, eds. *Astronomy from Space: Sputnik to Space Telescope.* MIT Pr. 1983 $27.50. ISBN 0-262-53061-9. Collection of articles by leading experts in the field; covers planetary astronomy, space astronomy, and other topics.

Friedman, Louis. *Starsailing: Solar Sails and Interstellar Travel.* Wiley 1988 $9.95. ISBN 0-471-62593-0. Comprehensive look at a novel way of traveling through the solar system, possibly from one star to another.

Lewis, John S., and Ruth A. Lewis. *Space Resources: Breaking the Bonds of Earth.* Col. U. Pr. 1987 $50.50. ISBN 0-231-06498-5. Provocative book on such topics as asteroid mining; separates science fact from science fiction.

Mark, Hans. *The Space Station: A Personal Journey.* Duke 1987 $24.95. ISBN 0-8223-0727-8. An insider's view of the development of NASA's Space Shuttle and Space Station programs; Mark served as NASA's deputy administrator in the 1980s.

Mauldin, John H. *Prospects for Interstellar Travel.* Univelt Inc. 1992 $50.00. ISBN 0-87703-344-7. The only comprehensive treatment of the subject; mind-expanding but somewhat awkwardly written.

McCurdy, Howard E. *Inside NASA: High Technology and Organizational Change in the American Space Program.* Johns Hopkins 1993 $32.95. ISBN 0-8018-4452-5. Uses archival evidence and interviews with agency officials to investigate the conflicts between NASA, the U.S. Space Program, and the government.

McDougall, Walter A. *The Heavens and the Earth: A Political History of the Space Age.* Basic 1986 $13.95. ISBN 0-465-02888-8. "A narrative history of space activity, a political analysis of what caused Sputnik 1 and what Sputnik 1 caused, an exposition of the contradictions inherent in the Soviet socialist system and the American free enterprise system, and an essay on the eschatology of . . . the pursuit of power" (*The New York Times Book Review*).

Michener, James A. *Space.* Random 1985 $15.95. ISBN 0-394-5504-2. A work of fiction, but it includes enough factual information to merit listing here.

Oberg, James E. *Red Star in Orbit.* Random 1981 $16.95. ISBN 0-394-51429-7. Comprehensive and thoroughly researched history of the Soviet space program; goes beyond the official Soviet press releases to penetrate the fog of disinformation that often has frustrated historians and writers in the past.

Oberg, James E., and Alcestis Oberg. *Pioneering Space: Living on the Next Threshold.* McGraw 1986 $16.95. ISBN 0-07-048034-6. Series of charming vignettes describing the various human aspects of the space program.

Pogue, William R. *How Do You Go to the Bathroom in Space?* Tor Bks. 1991 $5.99. ISBN 0-812-51278-8. Provides an excellent idea of how it feels to be an astronaut; Pogue answers 221 questions about the daily life of an astronaut.

Shapland, David, and Michael Rycroft. *Spacelab: Research in Earth Orbit.* Cambridge U. Pr. 1984 $37.50. ISBN 0-52126077-9. Describes a wide range of human activities in space in the account of a joint European-American mission; because the focus is on a particular space mission, description of the space program lacks comprehensiveness.

Shipman, Harry L. *Humans in Space: 21st Century Frontiers.* Plenum 1989 $22.95. ISBN 0-306-43171-8. Describes the rationale and prospects for human settlement of planets in the inner solar system as well as the barriers to settlement.

_____. *Space 2000: Meeting the Challenge of a New Era.* Plenum 1987 $21.95. ISBN 0-306-42534-3. Describes what we do in space; examines space activities, including planetary exploration, communications satellites, manufacturing in space, and the technology associated with the "star wars" program.

Simpson, Theodore R., ed. *The Space Station: An Idea Whose Time Has Come.* Inst. Electrical 1985 $24.95. ISBN 0-87942-182-7. Collection of essays by experts providing brief overviews of the historical background, the decision-making process, the potential uses, and the long-term potential of space stations.

Stares, Paul B. *The Militarization of Space: U.S. Policy, 1945–1984.* Cornell Univ. Pr. 1985 $37.50. ISBN 0-8014-9471-0. Comprehensive, authoritative description of the military space programs of the Soviet Union and the United States; includes conclusions about past and future arms control negotiations.

Tobias, Russell R. *America in Space: An Annotated Bibliography.* Salem Pr. 1991 $40.00. ISBN 0-89356-669-1. NASA publications, first-person accounts by astronauts, popular histories, and scholarly studies.

Wolfe, Tom. *The Right Stuff.* Bantam 1984 $4.95. ISBN 0-553-25596-7. Informal, easy-to-read account of the space program, focusing on the period leading to Apollo. Wolfe brings the Apollo generation of astronauts to life, superbly describing the heroism, camaraderie, tragedy, and other human aspects of the space program.

THE SEARCH FOR EXTRATERRESTRIAL INTELLIGENCE

For a long time, philosophers have speculated about the possibilities of life beyond earth. Recently, astronomers and some biologists have reached the point at which they can make rough estimates of the abundance of extraterrestrial life. A great stimulus in this area was an article by Giuseppe Cocconi and Philip Morrison, demonstrating that it is possible to send intelligible radio signals to another civilization elsewhere in the Milky Way galaxy. Today several programs exist that use radio telescopes to listen for signals from other parts of the galaxy. One such program was inaugurated by NASA in 1992.

Another aspect related to the study of extraterrestrial intelligence is the persistence of reports of unidentified flying objects (UFOs). It is unquestionable that people see things in the sky that they cannot readily identify. But many of these UFOs are discovered to be natural phenomena rather than spacecraft piloted by intelligent aliens. Most of the accessible literature in this field is written by UFO enthusiasts who believe in aliens. The most rational book supporting the existence of extraterrestrial life is by J. Allen Hynek; other books listed below reflect a more skeptical approach to UFO reports. The field of extraterrestrial intelligence as a whole has a considerable body of literature because of the popular interest in it on the part of the general public.

Crowe, Michael J. *The Extraterrestrial Life Debate 1750–1900.* Cambridge U. Pr. 1988 $29.95. ISBN 0-521-55986-4. Examines this ageless inquiry from Kant to Lowell.

Drake, Frank, and Dava Sobel. *Is Anyone Out There? The Scientific Search for Extraterrestrial Intelligence.* Delacorte 1992 $22.00. ISBN 0-385-30532-X. Contemporary, clear account of the search for extraterrestrial life; written by one of the pioneers in the field.

Hynek, J. Allen. *The UFO Experience: A Scientific Inquiry.* Time-Life 1990 repr. of 1972 ed. ISBN 0-8094-8054-9. Supports the idea that UFO sightings are indications that aliens have visited Earth. To support his position, Hynek relies on "contactee" stories in which witnesses claim to have had close contact with aliens.

Klass, Philip J. *UFO-Abductions–A Dangerous Game.* Prometheus Bks. 1989 $17.95. ISBN 0-87975-509-1. Describes several widely publicized reports of alien abductions to refute the involvement of aliens.

———. *UFOs: The Public Deceived.* Prometheus Bks. 1986 $16.95. ISBN 0-87975-322-6. "The noted UFO investigator holds the favorite theories of the UFO believers up to the cold light of day; an excellent summary of the current evidence (and lack of it) (*Mercury*).

McDonough, Thomas R. *The Search for Extraterrestrial Life in the Cosmos.* Wiley 1988 $19.95. ISBN 0-471-84684-8. Easy-to-read, brief account of the search for extraterrestrial life with radio telescopes.

Regis, Edward, ed. *Extraterrestrials: Science and Alien Intelligence.* Cambridge U. Pr. 1987 o.p. Collection of essays that take novel approaches to the subject of extraterrestrial intelligence.

Sheaffer, Robert. *The UFO Verdict–Examining the Evidence. Science and the Paranormal Ser.* Prometheus Bks. 1986 $17.95. ISBN 0-87975-338-2. Thoroughly researched, skeptical book on UFOs.

Stiebing, William H., Jr. *Ancient Astronauts, Cosmic Collisions, and Other Popular Theories about Man's Past. Science and the Paranormal Ser.* Prometheus Bks. 1984 $15.95. ISBN 0-87975-285-8. An account of ancient astronauts, the lost continent of Atlantis, Velikovsky, pyramid power, and alleged "discoveries" of America before Columbus.

Swift, David W. *SETI Pioneers: Scientists Talk about Their Search for Extraterrestrial Intelligence.* U. of Ariz. Pr. 1990 $35.00. ISBN 0-8165-1119-5. Fascinating interviews with 11 of the scientists who led the way in searching for radio signals from extraterrestrials.

CHRONOLOGY OF AUTHORS

Copernicus, Nicolaus. 1473–1543
Brahe, Tycho. 1546–1601
Galilei, Galileo. 1564–1642
Kepler, Johannes. 1571–1630
Halley, Edmond. 1656–1742
Mitchell, Maria. 1818–1889
Lowell, Percival. 1855–1916
Hale, George Ellery. 1868–1938
Eddington, Sir Arthur Stanley. 1882–1944
Shapley, Harlow. 1885–1972

Hubble, Edwin Powell. 1889–1953
Payne-Gaposhkin, Cecilia. 1900–1979
Gamow, George. 1904–1968
Bok, Bart Jan. 1906–1983
Von Braun, Wernher. 1912–1977
Clarke, Arthur C(harles). 1917–
Moore, Patrick. 1923–
Sagan, Carl. 1934–
Hawking, Stephen William 1942–
Ferris, Timothy. 1944–
Ride, Sally. 1951–

ASIMOV, ISAAC. 1920–1992

[SEE Chapter 2 in this volume.]

BOK, BART JAN. 1906–1983

Born in northern Holland, Bart Jan Bok received his Ph.D. from the University of Gröningen. His poor performance on a Boy Scout examination covering the stellar constellations kindled a lifelong interest in astronomy. Prior to World War II, Bok emigrated to the United States, becoming a citizen in 1938. He served nearly 30 years on the faculty at Harvard University, where he taught astronomy and directed the Harvard Observatory. From 1966 to 1974, Bok was professor of astronomy at the University of Arizona. Bok is most widely known for the discovery of "Bok globules," small patches of dust that might be the sites of star and planet formation. In his later life, Bok developed astronomical enterprises in Australia and in Arizona.

BOOKS BY BOK

The Milky Way. (coauthored with Priscilla Bok). 1941. HUP 5th ed. 1981 $32.50. ISBN 0-674-57503-2. Classic work provides the general reader with a comprehensive view of the Milky Way galaxy, the collection of 100 billion stars that includes the sun; clearly describes the nature of the stars in the Milky Way, the spiral structure of this huge whirling disk, the gas between the stars, and the causes of spiral structure.

Objections to Astrology. (coauthored with Lawrence E. Jerome). *Science and the Paranormal Ser.* Prometheus Bks. 1975 $11.95. ISBN 0-87975-059-6. Brief book that contains a statement denying the scientific validity of astrology, signed by 182 scientists, and two articles by Bok and Jerome that provide a scientific basis for criticizing astrology.

BRAHE, TYCHO. 1546–1601

Tycho Brahe was born the son of a Danish nobleman but was raised from an early age by his childless uncle. Despite the wishes of his uncle, who wanted him to study law, Brahe's interest in astronomy developed when he was a student at the University of Copenhagen. He observed an eclipse in 1560 and a planetary conjunction in 1563, in which Saturn and Jupiter came close together in the sky. Although the eclipse occurred at the predicted time, the conjunction did not. These initial observations marked the beginning of Brahe's career, notable for his ability to make the most accurate astronomical predictions of the sixteenth century. Noting Brahe's extraordinary power of observation, King Frederick II of Denmark granted Brahe a lifelong pension and ownership of the island of Hveen, on which to build an observatory. And there, in 1577, he established Uraniborg, a magnificent observatory and household, where he and a retinue of assistants made measurements of planetary positions. After King Frederick II died in 1588, Brahe gradually lost favor with Danish royalty and he moved to Prague in 1599. He never accepted COPERNICUS's suggestion that the sun rather than the earth was the center of the solar system; yet, Brahe was an influential figure in the Copernican revolution as a result of his comprehensive and precise set of observations of planetary positions, which were used by his successor, JOHANNES KEPLER. Brahe was a colorful person and the subject of many remarkable historical anecdotes. For example, from the age of 19, he wore a false nose made of silver, because most of his nose had been cut off in a duel instigated by a quarrel over the accuracy of one of his astronomical observations.

BOOKS BY BRAHE

Astronomiae Instauratae Mechanica. 1598. I Kommission hos E. Munksgaard (Copenhagen) 1946. o.p. Brahe's description of his instruments and scientific work on the island of Hveen, near Copenhagen, Denmark.
Tycho Brahe: His Astronomical Conjecture of the New and Much Admired Star Which Appeared in the Year 1572. Da Capo 1969 o.p. Indicates that the heavens are not immutable and unchanging, owing to the 1572 appearance of a supernova, which Brahe's careful observations showed to be far beyond Earth's atmosphere.

BOOKS ABOUT BRAHE

Dreyer, John L. *Tycho Brahe: A Picture of Scientific Life and Work in the Sixteenth Century.* Peter Smith 1977 o.p. "The best single treatment of Tycho's life and work" (*Dictionary of Scientific Biography*).
Thoren, Victor E. *The Lord of Uraniborg: A Biography of Tycho Brahe.* Cambridge U. Pr. 1991 $59.95. ISBN 0-521-35158-8. An elegant and scholarly account of the scientific life and times of Brahe; excellent depiction of sixteenth-century life.

CLARKE, ARTHUR C(HARLES). 1917–

Arthur C. Clarke's education and career as a science writer and space pioneer began inauspiciously. Born in Somerset, England, he left Huish's Grammar School in Taunton to assume a civil service position in the audit department of the British government. But, as a hobby, Clarke wrote several articles for the *Journal of the British Interplanetary Society.* His experience as a radar instructor with the Royal Air Force during World War II led to his proposal of communication satellites. In an article published in *Wireless World* in 1945, Clarke suggested the use of communications satellites in a 24-hour orbit as a significant application of the space program. After World War II, he went to King's College, London, graduating in 1949. For two years Clarke abstracted articles for *Physics Abstracts* and then became a free-lance writer, science popularizer, and underwater explorer and photographer. His early books on space and rocketry were influential in gaining public support for the space program. He has written dozens of science fiction novels and an equal number of science popularizations; the novels (and the literary criticism based on them) are not listed here. Many of Clarke's science fiction books have either religious or philosophical overtones, and his *2001: A Space Odyssey* (written in 1968) became a highly successful film.

During the 1950s, Clarke emigrated to Sri Lanka, where he has served as chancellor of Moratuwa University.

BOOKS BY CLARKE

Ascent to Orbit: A Scientific Autobiography. Wiley 1984 o.p. Contains rarely seen pieces by Clarke, including his 1945 article that predicted the era of satellite communications.

The Exploration of Space. 1951. PB rev. ed. 1979 o.p. This early popularization of space travel launched Clarke's writing career and helped develop public support for the space program; selected for recognition by the Book of the Month Club.

How the World Was One: Beyond the Global Village. Bantam 1992 $22.50. ISBN 0-553-07440-7. Describes the story of global communications from the telegraph through worldwide networks; includes Clarke's role in the development of communications satellites (which he humorously refers to as "How I lost a billion dollars in my spare time").

BOOK ABOUT CLARKE

McAleer, Neil. *Arthur C. Clarke: The Authorized Biography.* Contemp. Bks. 1993 $12.95. ISBN 0-8092-3720-2. Well-written, accurate look at Clarke's career, life, and contributions; "authorized" in the sense that Clarke cooperated with its preparation.

COPERNICUS (KOPÉRNIK), NICOLAUS (MIKOLAJ). 1473–1543

Nicolaus Copernicus was born in Torún, Poland, the son of a German mother and Slavic father. Like TYCHO BRAHE, he was raised by his uncle—the bishop of Ermeland. Copernicus was not trained as a scientist, nor was his job an officially scientific one. He studied mathematics, optics, and medicine at the University of Kraków and canon law at the University of Bologna in Italy. Copernicus received a degree from the University of Ferrara in 1506 and returned to Poland when his uncle presented him with the canonry of the cathedral at Frauenberg, East Prussia (now part of Poland). As canon of Frauenberg, Copernicus developed a routine in which he divided his "working" day into thirds. One-third was devoted to religious duties, another third was for providing charity to the sick in need of medical attention, and the final third was devoted to his hobby—the study of astronomy and philosophical meditation.

Copernicus's life was devoted to understanding planetary motion. He became famous for proposing that the sun rather than earth was the center of the solar system. A preliminary version of this theory was circulated privately in 1514. However, the first publication of this radical idea, *De Revolutionibus Orbium Coelestium (On the Revolutions of the Heavenly Spheres)*, was not published until 1543, the year of his death. Copernicus's theory finally was accepted nearly 100 years later, when measurements and analyses by JOHANNES KEPLER, Brahe, GALILEO (see also Vol. 5), SIR ISAAC NEWTON (see also Vol. 4), and others permitted detailed, quantitative comparisons between predictions of the Copernican model and observation of planetary positions. The acceptance of a heliocentric solar system proposed by Copernicus represents the most fundamental change in our conception of the solar system. Because of Copernicus's leading role in this changing perspective, astronomers refer to this period as the Copernican Revolution.

BOOK BY COPERNICUS

On the Revolution of the Heavenly Spheres. Trans. from the Latin by A. M. Duncan. Wiley 1974 o.p. Synthesis of Copernicus's scheme whereby the sun was the center of the solar system; his major work and one of the classics of Western thought.

BOOKS ABOUT COPERNICUS

Adamczewski, Jan. *Nicolaus Copernicus and His Epoch*. Scribner 1974 o.p. "This brief scholarly volume . . . displays the context of Copernicus's lifetime in good color and velvety gravure, and in a meticulously detailed text" (*Scientific American*).

Butterfield, Herbert. *The Origins of Modern Science 1300–1800*. Free Pr. rev. ed. 1965 $14.95. ISBN 0-02-905070-7. Describes the Copernican Revolution, although not strictly "about Copernicus." One of the first books to discuss this intellectual development in a larger context and to point out that Copernicus's physics was not much different than Aristotle's physics.

Gingerich, Owen. *The Great Copernicus Chase*. Cambridge U. Pr. 1992 $29.95. ISBN 0-521-32688-5. Collection of articles by one of the leading historians of astronomy; includes Gingerich's search for all existing copies of Copernicus's great work.

Kuhn, Thomas S. *The Copernican Revolution: Planetary Astronomy in the Development of Western Thought*. HUP 1957 $10.95. ISBN 0-674-17103-9. Describes Copernicus's work and why the Copernican Revolution served as a model for scientific progress; considered one of the classics in the history of science.

Neyman, Jerzy, ed. *The Heritage of Copernicus: Theories "Pleasing to the Mind."* MIT Pr. 1974 $14.95. ISBN 0-262-64016-3. Collection of essays by leading biologists, physicists, astronomers, and others on the intellectual impact of the Copernican Revolution.

EDDINGTON, SIR ARTHUR STANLEY. 1882–1944

Born in Kendal, England, Arthur Eddington was the son of the headmaster of the Kendal school (at which the great physicist JOHN DALTON once taught). At the age of 16, Eddington won a scholarship to Owens College in Manchester, graduating with a degree in physics in 1902. Although he was very shy in public, he had an outstanding ability to convey mathematical concepts to the layperson. Eddington was widely known in the early twentieth century for his popular books, many of which remain in print. But he also was one of the pioneers of twentieth-century astrophysics, a founder of many important lines of astrophysical research. Eddington spent a few years studying stellar motions at the Royal Observatory at Greenwich. However, most of his professional career was spent at Cambridge University, where he was Plumian Professor of Astronomy and observatory director for four decades. His early work on stellar motions laid the foundations for subsequent work by HARLOW SHAPLEY and EDWIN HUBBLE, demonstrating that the Milky Way is one of billions of spiral galaxies in the universe. But Eddington's most important contribution relates to the understanding of relativity and the structure and composition of stars. He was one of the first people outside Germany to understand and appreciate ALBERT EINSTEIN's general theory of relativity. This led to his expedition to Principe (in South America) to test the theory experimentally.

Although the source of stellar energy—nuclear fusion—had not been discovered, Eddington's analysis of stellar interiors in the 1920s correctly demonstrated the composition of stars and stellar behavior. He predicted that nuclear reactions were ultimately responsible for the phenomenon of sunshine. In his later years, Eddington was preoccupied with establishing fundamental numerical relationships between various cosmic quantities. In fact, he first recognized the fundamental importance of a number called the fine structure constant, which is a measure of the strength of electrical interaction.

BOOKS BY EDDINGTON

The Internal Constitution of the Stars. 1926, 1930. *Cambridge Science Classic Ser.* Cambridge U. Pr. 1988 $22.95. ISBN 0-521-33708-9. Accurate description of the interior of stars, although a firm foundation for stellar evolution had not been proposed yet. The book is remarkable considering that the existence of nuclear fusion (the source of energy in all stars) still was speculative when it was written.

Space, Time, and Gravitation. 1920. *Cambridge Science Classic Ser.* Cambridge U. Pr. 1987 $17.50. ISBN 0-521-33709-7. One of the first (and still one of the best) introductions to relativity; useful not only to the scientist, but accessible also to the intelligent and well-versed general reader.

BOOK ABOUT EDDINGTON

Chandrasekhar, S. *Eddington: The Most Distinguished Astrophysicist of His Time.* Cambridge U. Pr. 1984 o.p. Brief account of Eddington's achievements, written by a Nobel laureate and scientific rival.

FERRIS, TIMOTHY. 1944–

Timothy Ferris is one of the most prolific and talented of a new generation of science writers who bring the excitement and fascination of astronomy to general audiences. He began his career as a newspaper writer and covered the national conventions of both parties for *Rolling Stone* in 1972. While astronomy serves as the focus of his books, they are often quite wide-ranging and thought-provoking, since he is comfortable writing in such areas as artificial intelligence and the history and philosophy of science. Ferris has also written and narrated a PBS television program, "The Creation of the Universe," which earned an award from the American Association for the Advancement of Science and an Emmy nomination. Ferris teaches science writing and astronomy at the University of California, Berkeley.

BOOKS BY FERRIS

Galaxies. Stewart Tabori & Chang 1982 repr. of 1980 ed. $18.95. ISBN 0-941434-01-X. This is not just a picture book of galaxies, though the illustrations are its main feature. Ferris provides a lucid exposition of what we know about these huge star-swarms.

The Red Limit: The Search for the Edge of the Universe. 1979. Morrow 1983 repr. of 1977 ed. $12.95. ISBN 0-688-01836-X. The emphasis in this discussion of twentieth-century cosmology is on the history of the field and on the lives and achievements of those pioneering astronomers and physicists who developed scientific cosmology.

Spaceshots: The Beauty of Nature Beyond Earth. Pantheon 1984 o.p. Contains a wonderful collection of spectacular pictures.

Coming of Age in the Milky Way. Morrow 1989 $11.95. ISBN 0-385-26326-0. A poetic, lushly written description of astronomers through the millenia; investigates what made them seek answers to questions relating to their field and what answers they discovered.

GALILEI, GALILEO. 1564–1642

Born in Pisa, Italy, Galileo Galilei was the eldest son of a Florentine musician. At the age of 17 he entered the University of Pisa as a medical student. Galileo is widely known as the first person to use a telescope to observe the sky. He constructed and used the first astronomical telescope to observe craters on the moon, sunspots, the phases of Venus, the moons of Jupiter, the oval appearance of Saturn (now known to be caused by the rings around this planet), and the myriad stars that make up the Milky Way. Originally, telescopes were used by the Dutch for military purposes; therefore, Galileo's improved telescope was militarily valuable as well as a key part of an intellectual revolution. Moreover, his research on pendulums and falling bodies was an important part of the development of modern physics, eventually synthesized by SIR ISAAC NEWTON (see also Vol. 4) in the late 1600s. Galileo was a professor of mathematics at the universities of Pisa and Padua (1589–1610) and later became chief mathematician to the Duke of Tuscany. His early works on astronomy were written in Latin and thus were read primarily by other astronomers. But his *Dialogues on the Two Chief World Systems* was written in Italian, a language ordinary people could read. Because he so widely promoted the Copernican model of the solar system, Galileo ran into problems with the ecclesiastical authorities. In 1633 he was tried in Rome by the Inquisition and forced to retract his support for the Copernican system. Even after the trial, when he was under house arrest and almost totally blind, he continued his investigations in physics. In 1638, Galileo published a less controversial book, *Dialogue Concerning the Two New Sciences.*

Although most scientists and intellectuals refer to Galileo by his first name, a number of publications, such as *Books in Print*, use "Galilei" for indexing purposes.

Books by Galileo

Dialogue Concerning the Two Chief World Systems, Ptolemaic and Copernican. 1632. Trans. by Stillman Drake. U. CA Pr. 2nd rev. ed. 1967 $15.95. ISBN 0-520-00450-7. Galileo's major work, ostensibly a discussion between a proponent of the Copernican system and a proponent of the geocentric universe, with a moderator; the slant in favor of the Copernican view is thinly veiled. Partly because the book was written in Italian, it helped promote the Copernican hypothesis beyond a narrow circle of intellectual astronomers. Foreword by Albert Einstein.

Dialogue Concerning the Two New Sciences. 1638. Dover 1914 $7.95. ISBN 0-486-60099-8. Establishes some of the physical principles underlying the modern view of motion; mainly written after Galileo's trial.

Discoveries and Opinions of Galileo. Trans. by Stillman Drake. Doubleday 1957 $7.95. ISBN 0-385-09239-3. Galileo's first communications of his astronomical discoveries were written mainly between 1610 and 1620. By explaining the context of each, Drake's essays help place Galileo's works in a historical context.

Siderius Nuncius, or the Starry Messenger. 1610. Trans. by Albert Van Helden. U. Ch. Pr. 1989 $29.95. ISBN 0-521-32688-5. The first account of Galileo's discoveries; includes his original drawings of lunar craters, the satellites of Jupiter, and the myriad stars of the Milky Way.

Books about Galileo

Brecht, Berthold. *Galileo.* Ed. by Eric Bentley. Trans. by Charles Laughton. Grove Pr. 1966 $5.95. ISBN 0-8021-3059-3. Controversial play, which Brecht rewrote after the bombing of Hiroshima. Galileo's recantation is viewed as an example of scientific irresponsibility; Brecht uses this as a metaphor for criticizing science as being irretrievably enmeshed with military affairs.

Drake, Stillman. *Galileo at Work: His Scientific Biography.* U. Ch. Pr. 1981 o.p. Like Drake's other books on Galileo, half is written by Galileo and the other half is Drake's commentary; brilliantly illuminates the significance of Galileo's accomplishments in their historical context.

Langford, Jerome J. *Galileo, Science, and the Church.* 1966. U. of Mich. Pr. rev. ed. 1971 $12.95. ISBN 0-472-06173-9. Authoritative, balanced review of the facts concerning Galileo's confrontation with the Catholic Church.

Segre, Michael. *In the Wake of Galileo.* Rutgers U. Pr. 1991 $27.95. ISBN 0-8135-1700-1. Fills in some of the gaps in existing Galileo literature. Examines the academies and universities that Galileo worked with.

GAMOW, GEORGE. 1904–1968

Born in Odessa, Russia, George Gamow, the son of a teacher, studied at the University of Leningrad, becoming professor of physics in 1931. He emigrated to the United States in 1933 and taught at George Washington University (1934–56) and at the University of Colorado (1956–68). His scientific work covered many fields, mostly related to nuclear physics. In the field of molecular biology, Gamow suggested the triplet mechanism for coding DNA. He and his associate Ralph Alpher developed a detailed model of the early stages of cosmic evolution in the "big bang" theory. Although Gamow's basic assumption that the primordial universe contained only neutrons was incorrect, this assumption stimulated a great deal of subsequent work in cosmology.

Gamow wrote 30 popular books on astronomy, physics, and related sciences. In his "Mr. Tompkins" series (one of the most famous), Gamow used the figure of a curious, interested bank clerk as a protagonist for various journeys into quantum physics and gravity. His sense of humor is evident in his books and in his scientific career. For example, one of the key papers on the "big bang" theory is called the alpha-beta-gamma paper. The original authors were Alpher and Gamow, and they added HANS BETHE's name as an author to complete the allusion. In 1956, UNESCO awarded Gamow the Kalinga Prize for science writing.

BOOKS BY GAMOW

The Creation of the Universe. 1952. Viking Penguin rev. ed. 1961 o.p. Excellent popularization of the "big bang" theory originally proposed by Gamow in the 1950s.
The Great Physicists from Galileo to Einstein. Dover 1988 $7.95. ISBN 0-486-25767-3
Mr. Tompkins in Paperback. Cambridge U. Pr. 1967 $11.95. ISBN 0-521-09355. Gamow's series of popular science books, based on *Mr. Tompkins in Wonderland* (1939) and *Mr. Tompkins Explores the Atom* (1945).
One Two Three . . . Infinity: Facts and Speculations. Dover 1988 repr. of 1961 ed. $6.95. ISBN 0-486-25664-2

BOOK ABOUT GAMOW

Reines, Frederick, ed. *Cosmology, Fusion, and Other Matters.* Univ. Pr. Colo. 1972 o.p. Unlike most ponderous collections of serious essays about some scientific field written by a major figure's students, this work captures the impish sense of humor that was so much a part of Gamow.

HALE, GEORGE ELLERY. 1868–1938

Born in Chicago and educated at the Massachusetts Institute of Technology, George Hale founded three great observatories and, in doing so, laid the cornerstones for American astronomical research in most of the twentieth century. The first of Hale's three great observatories is the Yerkes Observatory in Wisconsin, named for Charles T. Yerkes, the developer of Chicago's streetcar system. Mt. Wilson Observatory in California was developed under the auspices of the Carnegie Institution of Washington, and the Palomar Observatory (also in California) was developed in cooperation with Mt. Wilson and with the support of the Rockefeller Foundation. Each of these observatories was the greatest of its time when first constructed.

As a scientist, Hale worked mostly on the sun and gained fame from research on sunspots. He not only proposed a connection between sunspots and magnetic fields but also accumulated the evidence that persuaded the scientific community that the connection was really there. Hale is also noted as the inventor of the spectroheliograph.

BOOKS BY HALE

Beyond the Milky Way. Scribners 1926 o.p. Another reprint of articles from Scribners, with an article about telescopes and an article about heat from the stars supplementing the title article.

The Depths of the Universe. Scribners 1924 o.p. A short book containing three articles about galaxies; originally published in *Scribners* magazine.

BOOKS ABOUT HALE

Wright, Helen. *Explorer of the Universe.* E. P. Dutton 1966 o.p. A complete, admiring biography.

Wright, Helen, Joan Nelson Warnow, and Charles Weiner, eds. *The Legacy of George Ellery Hale: Evolution of Astronomical and Scientific Institutions.* MIT Pr. 1972 o.p. Includes a brief biography of Hale, some of his most important scientific papers, and nearly a dozen insightful essays by historians and sociologists of science.

HALLEY, EDMOND. 1656–1742

Born in London, England, Edmond Halley was the son of a wealthy English businessman and a lifelong friend of SIR ISAAC NEWTON (see also Vol. 4). Halley is most famous for his recognition that the periodic appearance of several bright comets was actually the same object, now called Halley's Comet. He supported his claim when he successfully predicted that the comet would reappear in 1758. (The comet reappears about every 76 years.) Halley, however, made many other significant contributions to science. For example, he played a key role in the publication of Newton's major work, the *Principia*, in 1687; he established the distance between earth and the sun through measurements of the transit of Venus; and he was the first to discover stellar motion across the sky. Halley's studies of terrestrial magnetism and his demonstration that solar heating causes the trade winds and monsoons laid the foundation for the science of geophysics. He also was a diplomat and was deputy controller of the Mint in 1696.

BOOK BY HALLEY

Correspondence and Papers of Edmond Halley. History, Philosophy, and Sociology of Science Ser. Ayer 1975 $30.00. ISBN 0-405-06596-5. Brief, old biographies of Halley, followed by Halley's letters to a host of correspondents, includes Halley's correspondence with leading scientists of the seventeenth and early eighteenth centuries.

BOOKS ABOUT HALLEY

Brown, Peter L. *Halley and His Comet.* Sterling 1985 o.p. Both an engaging biography of Halley and a chronicle of the appearances of Halley's comet in history.

Thrower, Norman J. W. *Standing on the Shoulders of Giants: A Longer View of Newton and Halley.* U. CA Pr. 1990 $39.95. ISBN 0-520-06589-1

HAWKING, STEPHEN WILLIAM 1942–

Stephen Hawking is the best known of a group of modern cosmologists who have unveiled much of the intellectual richness of the "big bang" theory of cosmology and ALBERT EINSTEIN's general theory of relativity. Hawking's investigations of general relativity during the early 1980s culminated in his discovery that black holes are not permanent features—they eventually evaporate and radiate. His recent research on the very early universe has revealed a possible connection to particle physics, the study of basic natural forces and the fundamental particles (such as protons and electrons) that they glue together.

Hawking is unique among contemporary cosmologists because of his popular book, *A Brief History of Time*, and because he has accomplished so much excellent research despite a very serious physical affliction; he was diagnosed with amyotrophic lateral sclerosis (commonly known as Lou Gehrig's disease) at the age of 21, well before any of his major discoveries. As the years have passed, Hawking has increasingly lost the use of his body; he used state-of-the-art medical technology and computer techniques to compose his popular book on cosmology, which has sold millions of copies. As did Einstein, Hawking attracts standing-room-only audiences to his lectures, and he has become one of the best-known scientists of the late twentieth century.

BOOKS BY HAWKING

Black Holes and Baby Universes and Other Essays. Bantam 1993 $21.95. ISBN 0-553-09523-4

A Brief History of Time: From the Big Bang to Black Holes. Bantam 1988 $19.95. ISBN 0-533-05340-X. This book, especially the last five chapters, might be too challenging for the general reader.

BOOKS ABOUT HAWKING

Boslough, John. *Beyond the Black Hole: Stephen Hawking's Universe.* Fontana 1985 o.p. Excellent job of clarifying Hawking's ideas for the general reader.

White, Michael, and John Gribbin. *Stephen Hawking: A Life in Science.* NAL-Dutton 1993 $11.00. ISBN 0-452-26988-1. The only biography of Hawking to date.

HUBBLE, EDWIN POWELL. 1889–1953

As an undergraduate at the University of Chicago, Edwin Hubble was an exceptional boxer. His boxing abilities attracted the attention of a promoter who wanted to train him to fight the contemporary world heavyweight champion, Jack Johnson. Hubble, however, resisted the temptations of the boxing ring and instead became a Rhodes scholar. He practiced law for a short time, and in 1914 he found his niche in astronomy, attending the Yerkes Observatory for graduate work. In 1919 Hubble became an astronomer at the Mt. Wilson Observatory, where he remained until 1948. From 1948 to 1953, he was an astronomer at Mt. Palomar Observatory. Hubble's research on galaxies led to his conclusion that galaxies are actually swarms of hundreds of billions of stars. Using his research and that of others (principally Milton Humason and Vesto M. Slipher), Hubble established the relation between redshift and distance, which showed that the universe is expanding.

BOOKS BY HUBBLE

The Hubble Atlas of Galaxies. Ed. by Allan Sandage. Carnegie Inst. 1984 repr. of 1961 ed. $29.00. ISBN 0-87279-629-9. Collection of photographs of galaxies, as well as a description of the Hubble classification scheme, which astronomers still use. Sandage (one of Hubble's students) produced this magnificent volume, working partly from Hubble's notes.

The Realm of the Nebulae. 1936. *Silliman Memorial Lectures Ser.* Yale U. Pr. 1982 $40.00. ISBN 0-300-02499-1. As astronomer James Gunn mentions in his foreword to the 1982 edition, the book's value is not merely historical; Hubble's lively prose makes this a useful introduction to the study of galaxies, although it lacks comprehensiveness and is somewhat dated.

BOOK ABOUT HUBBLE

Sharov, Alexander S., and Igor D. Novikov. *Edwin Hubble: The Discoverer of the Big Bang Universe.* Cambridge U. Pr. 1993. ISBN 0-521-41617-5

KEPLER, JOHANNES. 1571–1630

Born in Württemburg, Germany, Johannes Kepler was the son of a soldier of fortune who eventually deserted his family. Kepler is widely known for his three laws of planetary motion. But an authority on Kepler, Owen Gingerich, describes these as "only three elements in his search for cosmic harmonies and celestial physics." Kepler began to think about astronomy and planetary motion as a schoolteacher in Graz, Austria and published his first work, *Mysterium Cosmographicum*, in 1596. He became an apprentice to TYCHO BRAHE, whose collection of astronomical observations was the best of its kind. Kepler's work on Mars, in which he tried to fit a theory to the observations, led to his discovery that planetary motion is elliptical rather than circular. Kepler's life was somewhat chaotic as a result of the repeated harassment of Protestant teachers in predominantly Catholic Austria. Some of his ideas about cosmic harmonies, such as the theory that the spacing of planetary orbits is related to the five regular polyhedrons, were incorrect. Yet his basic approach of seeking a broad sense of order and harmony in the world led to the discovery of mathematical regularities involved in planetary motion, and ultimately, to the elegance of SIR ISAAC NEWTON's (see also Vol. 4) laws of motion. Kepler's *Somnium*, a fictional account of a voyage to the moon, is cited by historians of rocketry as an early work of science fiction that might have stimulated interest in space travel.

BOOKS BY KEPLER

Mysterium Cosmographicum. 1596. *Bilingual Eds. of Classics in Philosophy and Science Ser.* Trans. by A. M. Duncan. Abaris Bks. 1981 o.p. The first book Kepler wrote; includes most of the key ideas he subsequently developed as well as some treatment of mysticism and other interests that Kepler abandoned.

The New Astronomy. Ed. and trans. by William Donajue. Cambridge U. Pr. 1992 o.p.

Somnium: The Dream, or Posthumous Work on Lunar Astronomy. Trans. by Edward Rosen. Bks. Demand $72.30. ISBN 0-317-07803-8. Some of the mystical ideas of this great astronomer.

BOOKS ABOUT KEPLER

Armitage, Angus. *John Kepler*. Roy 1967 o.p. Like Armitage's other biographies of figures in the Copernican Revolution, this book is brief, general, and easy to read; valuable as an introduction.

Donahue, William H., ed. *Johannes Kepler's New Astronomy*. Cambridge U. Pr. 1993 $140.00. ISBN 0-521-30131-9. With a foreword by Owen Gingerich.

Koestler, Arthur. *The Watershed: A Biography of Johannes Kepler*. U. Pr. of Amer. 1985 repr. of 1960 ed. $19.75. ISBN 0-8191-4339-1. Provides more than a simple recitation of the facts to ask some fundamental questions about the nature of scientific creativity. Koestler's own mysticism tends to color this work about one of the most mystical of scientists. Foreword by John Durisen.

LOWELL, PERCIVAL. 1855–1916

American astronomer Percival Lowell was born in Boston of a patrician New England family. His sister was the noted poet AMY LOWELL (see Vol. 1). Educated at Harvard University, he established an observatory in Arizona in 1894 (known now as Lowell Observatory). Lowell is best known, however, for his observations of Mars. His advocacy of the presence of intelligent life on Mars had a considerable impact on astronomy during the early twentieth century. Mars is the only planet in the solar system whose surface is directly visible from earth. Lowell and others spent many long nights peering through telescopes at the planet, and they interpreted the random pattern of light and dark areas as a network of dark lines girdling the red planet. These long dark lines turned out to be optical illusions, as was shown by a number of American spacecraft that took close-up photographs of the planet during the 1960s and 1970s. Lowell, however, was a vocal proponent of the idea that these lines were a network of globe-girdling canals, and the clear implication was that the planet harbored a species of intelligent beings. Although public interest was galvanized by Lowell's discoveries and by his popular books, the astronomy community was less receptive to his ideas. Lowell was also known for his prediction of the existence of a ninth planet in the solar system. That planet, Pluto, was discovered by Clyde Tombaugh in 1930.

BOOKS BY LOWELL

Mars. HM 1895 o.p. This book describes the result of a single set of observations of Mars during a period when Mars was quite close to the earth. Any discussion of Martian inhabitants is left until the concluding chapter.

Mars as the Abode of Life. Macmillan 1910 o.p. This is the main work in which Lowell attempts to convince readers that Mars is inhabited and that humans should attempt to communicate with Martians.

BOOK ABOUT LOWELL

Hoyt, William G. *Lowell and Mars.* Bks. Demand repr. of 1976 ed. $102.00. ISBN 0-317-58769-2. More than just a biography, Hoyt's book shows the effects of the Martian controversy on the rest of astronomy and on the public at large.

MITCHELL, MARIA. 1818–1889

Maria Mitchell was a nineteenth-century woman who holds a place of distinction as being the first to accomplish a variety of things. America's first woman astronomer, she was also one of the first American astronomers of either gender to win worldwide recognition when she discovered a telescopic comet in 1847 (an accomplishment for which she won a gold medal from the king of Denmark). Mitchell was one of the founders of Vassar College, and she served as Vassar's professor of astronomy from 1868 until her death. She was also the first woman elected to the American Academy of Arts and Sciences.

Mitchell was born on the island of Nantucket off the coast of Massachusetts; it was in the island's fog-bound skies that she discovered her comet. Her cometary discoveries, her computations of Venus's orbit that she did for the Nautical Almanac Office, and her other scientific writings were generally published in contemporary journals, but she does leave one collection as a literary legacy.

BOOK BY MITCHELL

Maria Mitchell: Life, Letters, and Journals. Comp. by Phebe Mitchell Kendall. Rprt. Serv. 1991 repr. of 1896 ed. $69.00. ISBN 0-7812-8285-3. There is some biographical material here, but most of this book contains extracts from Mitchell's letters.

BOOK ABOUT MITCHELL

Wright, Helen. *Sweeper in the Sky.* Macmillan 1949 o.p. An admiring biography, not too detailed.

MOORE, PATRICK (ALFRED). 1923–

Patrick Moore is one of the most prolific authors of popular astronomy books. He began publishing astronomy books in 1950 and has been extremely active ever since. He is director of the lunar section of the British Astronomical Association and was director of the Armagh Planetarium in Northern Ireland from 1965 to 1968. Moore has been the host of a television program, "The Sky at Night," which appeared first on BBC in April 1957. He was awarded the Order of the British Empire in 1968 for his work in astronomy.

BOOKS BY MOORE

Armchair Astronomy. Norton 1986 $16.95. ISBN 0-393-02253-6. More than 100 one-page snippets that include entertaining anecdotes about stars and people who have observed them.

Jupiter. (coauthored with Garry Hunt). Rand McNally 1981 o.p. Superb collection of photos complemented by authoritative, well-written text from Moore and Hunt, who was a participant in the Voyager mission and is an authority on planetary atmospheres.

Saturn. (coauthored with Garry Hunt). Rand McNally 1982 o.p. Like the Jupiter book, this is one of the most authoritative popular texts.

Stargazing: Astronomy without a Telescope. Barron 1985 $21.95. ISBN 0-8120-5644-2. Month-by-month comprehensive guide for the sky observer; includes sky lore to leaven the presentation of star names and places.

PAYNE-GAPOSHKIN, CECILIA. 1900–1979

Born in England, Cecilia Payne-Gaposhkin earned an undergraduate degree from Cambridge University and came to the Harvard College Observatory in 1923, remaining at Harvard for the rest of her scientific career. She was one of the first to analyze the spectra of stars in a quantitative way, by precisely measuring their temperature and chemical composition. Payne-Gaposhkin's radical proposal that the stars are mostly hydrogen eventually was supported. Her attention then turned—or rather, was directed—to variable stars. Payne-Gaposhkin's gender hindered her professional progress throughout her career; Cambridge University was unwilling to grant a Ph.D. to a woman, and at Harvard, she was strictly a researcher until the university appointed her in 1956 as the first female full professor. She ultimately became chair of the astronomy department at Harvard, as well as Phillips Professor of Astronomy Emerita until her death. Although most of her published work is rather technical, Payne-Gaposhkin occasionally wrote and lectured for popular audiences.

BOOKS BY PAYNE-GAPOSHKIN

Cecilia Payne-Gaposhkin: An Autobiography and Other Recollections. Ed. by Katherine Haramundanis. Cambridge U. Pr. 1984 o.p. Payne-Gaposhkin's autobiography, preceded by three biographical essays by people who knew her personally and professionally.

The Galactic Novae. Elsevier 1957 o.p. Monograph about stars that suddenly increase in brightness; still used by astronomers.

Stars and Clusters. Bks. Demand repr. of 1979 ed. $73.50. ISBN 0-7837-3847-1. Describes thoroughly the stars of our local stellar neighborhood for readers who want more than a brief introduction. Payne-Gaposhkin reveals the celestial environment as would a tour guide showing a traveler the landmarks of a city.

RIDE, SALLY. 1951–

Sally Ride rode the space shuttle *Challenger* into space in 1983 and thus became America's first female astronaut. Born in Los Angeles, her training includes degrees in both English and physics, and a Ph.D. in physics, all from Stanford University. In 1978 Ride was selected as an astronaut candidate by NASA and trained as a mission specialist. Following her two space flights (in 1983 and again in 1984), she served as the astronaut office representative to the Rogers Commission, which investigated the explosion of the space shuttle

Challenger in 1986. She then wrote a very influential report to the NASA administration that has served to guide NASA's activities in the 1990s. In 1987 Ride left NASA to work at the Center for International Security and Arms Control at Stanford University.

BOOKS BY RIDE

Leadership and America's Future in Space. NASA 1987 o.p. One of the most influential planning documents of the 1980s, this book lays out the rationale for the Earth Observing System (EOS), one of NASA's major efforts for the 1990s.

To Space and Back. (coauthored with Susan Okie). Lothrop 1989 $16.95. ISBN 0-688-06159-1. One of the most delightful accounts of a space flight written by an astronaut.

BOOK ABOUT RIDE

Hurwitz, Jane, and Sue Hurwitz. *Sally Ride: Shooting for the Stars.* Fawcett 1989 $3.95. ISBN 0-449-90394-X. A brief biography celebrating Ride's heroism and accomplishments.

SAGAN, CARL. 1934–

Born in New York City, Carl Sagan is a respected planetary scientist who is widely known for his popularizaton of science in print and on television. He was educated at the University of Chicago, receiving his Ph.D. in 1960. In 1970 Sagan became professor of astronomy and space science at Cornell University. His research has involved planetary science and exobiology. Two of his noteworthy achievements in these fields are the experimental demonstration of the synthesis of the energy-carrying molecule ATP (adenosine triphosphate) in primitive-earth experiments and his theory that the greenhouse effect explains the very high temperature at the surface of Venus. More recently, Sagan made significant contributions to the Viking mission to the surface of Mars and has collaborated with other prominent scientists investigating the effects of nuclear war on the earth's climate (the "nuclear winter" scenario). His role in developing the "Cosmos" series (1980)—one of the most successful series (of any kind) to be broadcast on PBS Television—and his many popular books, such as *The Dragons of Eden*, which won the Pulitzer Prize, have established his reputation as an outstanding popularizer of science.

BOOKS BY SAGAN

Broca's Brain: Reflections on the Romance of Science. 1979. Ballantine 1986 $5.95. ISBN 0-345-33689-5. Collection of essays on a variety of topics, including several pseudosciences, whose faults are brilliantly illuminated.

Cosmos. 1980. Ballantine 1985 $5.95. ISBN 0-345-33135-4. Far-reaching, well-illustrated book about the universe that highlights Sagan's personality and philosophy.

The Dragons of Eden. 1977. Ballantine 1986 $4.95. ISBN 0-345-34629-7. Examines the fascinating topic of the origin of human intelligence; speculates on the past, present, and future state of our ability to think.

Intelligent Life in the Universe. (coauthored with I. S. Shklovskii). 1966. Holden Day 1978 o.p. The first modern exposition of the idea that life might exist elsewhere in the Milky Way galaxy and that extraterrestrial civilizations might use radio signals to communicate with us; has become a classic in the field.

Shadows of Forgotten Ancestors. Random 1992 $22.50. ISBN 0-394-53481-6. A chronicle of Homo Sapien's present state and the path leading there, in terms of evolution, consciousness, and nature.

UFOs—A Scientific Debate. (coedited with Thornton Page). Cornell Univ. Pr. 1974 $8.95. ISBN 0-393-00739-1. Expresses a variety of viewpoints, mostly skeptical, on the notion that UFOs are craft piloted by extraterrestrial beings; extracted from papers given at a 1969 meeting of the American Association for the Advancement of Science.

SHAPLEY, HARLOW. 1885–1972

Born on a Missouri farm, Harlow Shapley became interested in astronomy by accident. As told by Shapley, he went to the University of Missouri expecting to enroll in the journalism school. However, the school of journalism was not scheduled to open until the following year, so he decided to study astronomy. Shapley earned his Ph.D. from Princeton University and then moved to the Mt. Wilson Observatory. There he did his most celebrated work, such as demonstrating experimentally for the first time that earth is not at the center of the Milky Way galaxy but on the outskirts—once again illustrating that earth does not occupy a central location in the cosmos. Consequently, many of his colleagues and fellow astronomers began referring to Shapley as the "modern Copernicus." In 1921 he became director of the Harvard College Observatory, transforming the observatory into a world-famous institution during his 30-year tenure. Shapley also continued his research program, which included the discovery of the first small galaxies, called the Sculptor and Fornax dwarf galaxies after the constellations in whose direction they are oriented. He was also a well-known writer, lecturer, and public scientist, playing a major role in founding UNESCO.

BOOKS BY SHAPLEY

Galaxies. 1943. HUP 3rd rev. ed. 1972 $61.00. ISBN 0-317-09186-7. "The book is well apportioned among the various branches of the subject; it is clear, interesting, and very well illustrated" (*Science Progress*).

Of Stars and Men: Human Response to an Expanding Universe. Greenwood 1984 repr. of 1958 ed. $38.50. ISBN 0-313-24302-6. Shapley has thought more deeply than many scientists about the insignificant place of humanity in the universe.

VON BRAUN, WERNHER. 1912–1977

Born in Wirsitz, Germany, Wernher Von Braun studied engineering at Berlin and Zürich. In 1937 he became technical director of the Nazi rocket program at Peenemünde (on the shores of the Baltic Sea). Von Braun's engineering team pioneered the development and production of the V-2 rockets, which were launched against England during World War II. Von Braun and most of his engineering development team surrendered to the Americans in the closing days of the war, determining that the United States was more likely to continue aerospace research and development. He became a naturalized citizen in 1955 and a director of the U.S. Army's Ballistic Missile Agency at Huntsville, Alabama. Responding to congressional concern following the launch of Sputnik in October 1957, Von Braun and his engineers rapidly developed the Explorer 1 rocket, which was used to launch the first successful American satellite. Von Braun also was director of the Marshal Space Flight Center from 1960 to 1970. While there, he helped develop the Saturn rocket for the Apollo 8 moon landing in 1969.

BOOKS BY VON BRAUN

The Mars Project. 1952. U. of Ill. Pr. 1991 $9.95. ISBN 0-252-06227-2. Detailed blueprint for a trip to Mars that describes many of the projects Von Braun worked on during the 1960s and 1970s.

Space Travel: A History. (coauthored with Frederick I. Ordway III). HarpC 1985 rev. ed. $29.95. ISBN 0-06-181898-4. Authoritative and complete treatment of the space program; Ordway has updated earlier histories that he wrote with Von Braun.

BOOK ABOUT VON BRAUN

Ordway, Frederick I., III, and Mitchell R. Sharpe. *The Rocket Team.* MIT Pr. 1982 o.p. This story covers more than 50 years, starting with the fledgling German Rocket Society's involvement in Fritz Lang's film project (an unlikely source of funding for science), continuing through Von Braun's leading role in the American space program.

CHAPTER 19

Earth Sciences

John A. Ciciarelli

Amid all the revolutions of the globe, the economy of nature has been
uniform, and her laws are the only thing that has resisted the general
movement. The rivers and rocks, the seas and the continents have changed in
all their parts; but the laws which direct those changes and the rules to which
they are subject, have remained invariably the same.
—JOHN PLAYFAIR, *Illustrations of the
Huttonian Theory of the Earth*

The last few decades have changed forever our view of the earth.

In the late twentieth century, thousands of scientists were still working who
had once been taught in school that the floor of the ocean was a featureless
plain. They had learned that the continents simply could not drift, despite the
close-fitting shapes of eastern South America and western Africa; that life forms
evolved and took new forms at a pace almost infinitely slow; that the land is
shaped gradually, by weathering, slow uplift, and decay; and that all forms of life
ultimately depend on free oxygen and sunlight alone.

Now we know that things are less simple and more exciting. On the global
scale, most change is very slow and gradual, but exceptions do occur. The
nature of things as we now understand them is suggested by the likely possibility
that meteoritic or cometary impact on the earth played a role in the extinction
of some animals and plants. The preponderance of volcanoes and earthquakes
at crustal plate boundaries can be sudden, unexpected, and violent.

Our new view of the earth's crust can be traced back to World War II, when a
geologist turned navy submarine commander converted his depth-sounder's
readings into maps of the Pacific floor. After the war, large-scale mapping
revealed great mid-ocean ridges that divide the Atlantic and virtually encircle
the globe. Studies of rocks at the ocean bottom showed that molten rock was
welling up from below and spreading away from the ridges, perhaps pushing
apart the dozen or so great plates of the earth's crust. The rate was perhaps only
half an inch a year, but continents did drift after all. Thus plate tectonics was
born, and scientists everywhere began considering what Tjeerd Van Andel has
called "new views of an old planet."

Looking outward, the Apollo program took U.S. astronauts to the moon and
provided a new look at our old planet. Studying lunar rocks extended the very
meaning of the word "geology," which can never again mean only "knowledge
of the earth," and changed the names, and the subject matter, of university
departments everywhere. Space-related technology has produced many types of
earth-observing systems to examine our planet, its life, and its resources.
Meteorologists gathered much new data about air masses, and modern
computers gave them greater power to interpret the complex patterns of
weather and climate. On the ocean floor, scientists in submarines discovered

vents of hot water, apparently at boundaries of great crustal plates, and there found bacteria that seem to live without benefit of either sunlight or free oxygen. Elsewhere in the solar system, space probes have revealed vast canyons on Mars, volcanoes erupting on Jupiter's innermost moon, and lava flows on Venus.

All of this amounts to a revolution in science. None of us can look at the world around us in quite the same way as we had only a few decades ago.

Life itself is being reexamined. Ever since DARWIN, evidence had been accumulating to show that life evolved throughout much of earth's long history. If continents can move, however slowly, then such long-standing puzzles of how fossils came to be where we find them in the rocks can be solved. Now we wonder less about which animals and plants lived in former times and more about how, when, where, and why. The ultimate origin of life may always remain a mystery, but we are finding out more and more about how physical laws have operated on that life.

Reading the rocks and reconstructing ancient environments lead to surprises: some dinosaurs were surely warmblooded after all, they may have been live-bearers (rather than egg-layers), and they seem to have been quite intelligent despite the size of their brains. And even evolutionary change, apparently, now and then comes in bursts.

So upheavals in nature are acceptable, perhaps not even rare. A global catastrophe may explain an old problem, that of the extinction of the dinosaurs. A thin layer of clay, found on several continents and everywhere being of about the same age as the last of the dinosaurs, suggests that an asteroid collided with the earth like a giant meteorite. If so, it spread dust and ash throughout the atmosphere and changed the worldwide climate—an environmental hazard that dinosaurs (and many other life forms) did not survive.

So much for the geologic past. Here in our own time, we must cope with the problems of industrialization and growing populations. Most of us realize that our oil is running out. We have mined our minerals so intensively that some are getting very hard to find. In some places even building stone and road materials are scarce. We need more clean water. Pollution is growing and wastes are building up. Earth science is often a matter of practical politics. Should we vote for a bond issue to finance a dam? What about zoning laws for building along beaches? Do we want oil wells near national parks?

Even the way in which we organize science and study it is changing; for example, early in this century almost any college or university had a department of geology. But new specialties have now developed and others merged, and so we find those departments called earth science, geology and geophysics, or planetary science. There are many others. Academic classifications, like the earth itself, are restless.

Problems are also opportunities, and our new knowledge of the earth will at least add to our options. Everyone must adjust to the new worldview—perhaps the earth sciences most of all.

REFERENCE AND GENERAL BOOKS

The earth sciences cover the earth—and often the moon and the other planets, too. So for a first general view of the subject, consider the earth as a planet and find a general work on the solar system. Atlases and collections of photographs from space show us at a glance more than COLUMBUS (see Vol. 3) and Magellan ever knew.

Perhaps a good way to consider the earth science discipline is to divide the whole subject area into the following subcategories: the lithosphere (the solid earth), the hydrosphere (the earth's water), the biosphere (the living things), and the atmosphere (the air). If a very broad view is taken, then one could also include some aspects of astronomy, especially those portions dealing with the solar system.

Encyclopedias of earth science, paleontology, and the like are useful; their introductory chapters often give good overviews, and their lists of references lead to other sources. Also worth a close look are many works that at first seem forbiddingly technical. Curious readers should sample them carefully, for their early chapters may set the stage in simpler terms. Next are introductory textbooks. (This is like looking through a zoom microscope and turning the knob to increase the magnification and reduce the field of view.) Titles including "General" and "Elementary" may be misleading, but prefaces, introductions, indexes, and reference lists are usually helpful guides. Histories and biographies may tell even more about the science than about the people.

Much subject matter of the earth sciences can be seen and felt, so many authors find the topic easier to explain than, say, the physics of elementary particles. Thus we find many books—often collections of essays—on science and for nonscientists.

Long ago, JOHN DONNE (see Vol. 1) wrote that "no man is an island." Nor is any science: Oceanography can never be seawater alone, and students of marine science will often find themselves wandering into geology or paleontology.

Adriano, D. C., and M. Havas, and others, eds. *Acidic Precipitation: Case Studies.* 5 Vols. Spr.-Verlag. Vol. 1 1989 $119.00. ISBN 0-387-96929-2. Vol. 2 1989 $199.00. ISBN 0-387-97000-2. Vol. 3 1989 $129.00. ISBN 0-685-31289-5. Vol. 4 1989 $139.00. ISBN 0-387-97026-6. Vol. 5 1990 $149.00. ISBN 0-387-97111-4. Good treatment of the subject with many international references.

Baker, Larry, ed. *Encyclopedia of Environmental Information Sources.* Gale 1993 $125.00. ISBN 0-8103-8568-6. Contains more than 20,000 up-to-date citations covering the environment.

Bates, Robert L, and Julia A. Jackson, eds. *Dictionary of Geological Terms.* Doubleday 3rd rev. ed. 1984 $12.00. ISBN 0-385-18101-9. Definitions of the working vocabulary of the earth sciences for nongeologists. Based on the much more comprehensive *Glossary of Geology* (see below).

_____. *Glossary of Geology.* Am. Geol. 3rd ed. 1987 $75.00. ISBN 0-913312-89-4. Aided by approximately 150 other earth scientists, the editors here define 36,000 terms "as a bulwark against babelization." The most extensive work of its kind.

Bramwell, Martyn, ed. *Rand McNally Atlas of the Oceans.* Rand McNally 1977 o.p. Covers names, shapes, and locations of land and water bodies.

Considine, Douglas M., ed. *Van Nostrand's Scientific Encyclopedia.* 2 vols. Van Nos. Reinhold 1988 $195.00. ISBN 0-422-21750-1. Excellent thumbnail articles on nearly every topic in science.

Couper, Alastair D., ed. *The Times Atlas of the Oceans.* Van Nos. Reinhold 1983 o.p. Covers the topography of the basin floors which until recently was virtually unknown.

Cunningham, William P., and others, eds. *Environmental Encyclopedia.* Gale 1993 $195.00. ISBN 0-8103-8856-1. Excellent source of information on a very wide variety of environmental problems. Very good for librarians.

Ernst, Wallace G. *The Dynamic Planet.* Col. U. Pr. 1990 $17.00. ISBN 0-231-07230-9. Good overview of our planet and the building and destructive forces at work in it and on it.

Fairbridge, Rhodes W., ed. *The Encyclopedia of Atmospheric Sciences and Astrogeology*. *Encyclopedia of Earth Sciences Ser.* Acad. Pr. 1967 o.p. Although published before Apollo reached the moon, many of the entries are as good as ever.

_____. *The Encyclopedia of Geochemistry and Environmental Sciences*. *Encyclopedia of Earth Sciences Ser.* Van Nos. Reinhold 1972 o.p. Though somewhat dated, covers an unusually wide range of topics.

_____, ed. *Encyclopedia of Geomorphology*. *Encyclopedia of Earth Sciences Ser.* Van Nos. Reinhold 1968 o.p. Contains 410 articles, cross-indexed, on the land and the forces that shaped it.

_____, ed. *The Encyclopedia of Oceanography*. *Encyclopedia of Earth Sciences Ser.* Van Nos. Reinhold 1966 o.p. Fairbridge points out that in 1966 the ocean floor was "less well mapped than is the surface of the Moon."

_____, ed. *The Encyclopedia of World Regional Geology, Part 1: Western Hemisphere (Including Australia and Antarctica*. *Encyclopedia of Earth Sciences Ser.* Acad. Pr. 1975 o.p. Useful for overviews of the geology of large areas.

Fairbridge, Rhodes W., and Joanne Bourgeois, eds. *The Encyclopedia of Sedimentology*. *Encyclopedia of Earth Sciences Ser.* Van Nos. Reinhold 1978 o.p. More than 75 percent of the earth's surface is covered by sediments and sedimentary rocks.

Fairbridge, Rhodes W., and David Jablonski, eds. *The Encyclopedia of Paleontology*. *Encyclopedia of Earth Sciences Ser.* Van Nos. Reinhold 1979 o.p. Includes a chapter on "post-plate tectonics."

Frye, Keith, ed. *Encyclopedia of Mineralogy*. *Encyclopedia of Earth Sciences Ser.* Van Nos. Reinhold 1982 $156.95. ISBN 0-87933-184-4. Each article has references leading to advanced discussion. Mainly for nonmineralogists.

Gohau, Gabrial. *A History of Geology*. Rutgers U. Pr. 1991 $12.95. ISBN 0-8135-1665-X. Develops the history of the ideas generally accepted as mainstream geology.

Hallam, Anthony. *Atlas of Palaeobiogeography*. Elsevier 1973 $154.00. ISBN 0-444-40975-0. Shows where various fauna and flora lived in the geologic past, and when.

_____. *Planet Earth: An Encyclopedia of Geology*. St. Mut. 1977 o.p. Covers Earth and other planets, processes, landscapes, ocean floor, economic geology, rocks, earth history (of life and the planet itself), and history of geology.

Hodgkiss, Alan G., and Andrew F. Tatham. *Keyguide to Information Sources in Cartography*. McGraw 1986 $50.00. ISBN 0-7201-1768-2. Includes who mapped what, and where; what has been written about maps; where and how to find them.

Houghton, David D., ed. *Handbook in Applied Meteorology*. Wiley 1985 $130.00. ISBN 0-471-08404-2. Deals with fundamentals, measurements, applications, societal impacts, and resources. Basic, thorough, and rather too technical for most readers.

Huggett, Richard J. *Climate, Earth Processes, and Earth History*. Spr.-Verlag 1991 $89.00. ISBN 3-540-53419-9. Shows the interaction of climate, atmospheric circulation, sedimentation, landforms, biological patterns, and soils through geologic time.

Hunt, Lee M., and Donald G. Groves, eds. *A Glossary of Ocean Science and Undersea Technology Terms*. Compass Va. 1965 o.p. Includes more than 3,500 terms in underwater sound, oceanography, marine science, underwater physiology, and ocean engineering.

Hurlbut, Cornelius S., Jr., ed. *The Planet We Live On: An Illustrated Encyclopedia of the Earth Sciences*. Abrams 1976 o.p. About 1,800 entries, covering the solid, liquid, and gaseous earth, plus "space geology."

Keates, John S. *Cartographic Design and Production*. Wiley 1989 $47.95. ISBN 0-470-21071-0. Guide to map design and planning, especially important for maps of geology, which tend to be more complex than most printers will believe.

Lapedes, Daniel N., ed. *McGraw-Hill Encyclopedia of Geological Sciences*. McGraw 1988 $92.50. ISBN 0-07-045500-7. Contains about 560 alphabetically arranged articles covering the solid earth and relevant aspects of the oceans and atmosphere.

Lowman, Paul D., Jr.. *The Third Planet*. U. Pr. of Va. 1972 o.p. Large, high-altitude photos, mainly from Apollo 7 and 9, give a new perspective of our planet. A most useful starting point for studying any earth science.

Mitchell, Richard Scott. *Dictionary of Rocks*. Van Nos. Reinhold 1985 o.p. Dictionaries of minerals are common, but this may be the only one for the aggregations of minerals called rocks.

Mitton, Jacquelin. *A Concise Dictionary of Astronomy*. OUP 1991 $24.95. ISBN 0-19-853967-3. More than 2,400 terms clearly and simply defined. Includes many earth science terms.

Monkhouse, F. J. *A Dictionary of Geography*. Arnold 2nd ed. 1965 o.p. Extends "geography" into several other earth sciences. The diagrams are especially helpful.

O'Donoghue, Michael, ed. *The Encyclopedia of Minerals and Gemstones*. Putnam Pub. Group 1976 o.p. Describes 1,000 minerals, listed in alphabetical order. Separate sections cover their occurrence, geologic origin, and chemical composition.

Ozima, Minoru. *Geohistory-Global Evolution of the Earth*. Spr.-Verlag 1987 $27.00. ISBN 3-540-16595-9. Overview (with some technical details) of the earth in the solar system, ocean basins, and continents.

Parker, Sybil, and others, eds. *Encyclopedia of Science and Technology*. 20 vols. McGraw 1992 $2,639.00. ISBN 0-07-909206-3. Very good citations. Includes good illustrations on the most recent developments in general science and the earth sciences in particular.

Redfern, Ron. *The Making of a Continent*. Times Bks. 1986 o.p. This book, and the Public Broadcasting System film based on it, shows the building of North America over geologic time.

Roberts, Willard Lincoln, George Robert Rapp, Jr., and Julius Weber. *Encyclopedia of Minerals*. Van Nos. Reinhold 1989 $109.95. ISBN 0-442-27681-8. Describes approximately 2,200 species, with perhaps 1,000 color photos. Attempts to resolve conflicting data about mineral species previously described in print.

Seltzer, Leon E., ed. *The Columbia Lippincott Gazetteer of the World*. Lippincott 1962 o.p.

Sheriff, Robert E. *Encyclopedic Dictionary of Exploration Geophysics*. Soc. Expl. Geophys. 1973 o.p. Covers geophysics as used in seeking geologic structures that might hold oil and gas. Overlaps geology and earthquake studies.

Small, John, and Michael Witherick. *A Modern Dictionary of Geography*. Routledge Chapman & Hall 1989 $45.00. ISBN 0-340-49317-8. Illustrates the wide range of modern geography and its overlap with (say) geology. Perhaps the best of its kind.

Smith, David G., ed. *The Cambridge Encyclopedia of the Earth Sciences*. Cambridge U. Pr. 1982 o.p. Articles by 32 scientists, mostly British.

Times Atlas of the World. Random 9th rev. ed. 1992 $175.00. ISBN 0-8129-2077-5. Includes approximately 210,000 place names, with pinyin used for most of the Chinese.

Todd, David K., ed. *The Water Encyclopedia*. Lewis Pubs. 1989 $149.95. ISBN 0-87371-120-3. Covers climate and precipitation, and many aspects of water, including pollution and management.

Tver, David F. *Ocean and Marine Dictionary*. Cornell Maritime 1979 $18.50. ISBN 0-87033-246-5. Topics range from sailing ships to seaweeds.

Webster's New Geographical Dictionary. Merriam-Webster Inc. 1988 $24.95. ISBN 0-87779-446-4. Covers more than 200 maps and 47,000 entries. For the United States and Canada, most towns included have a minimum population of 2,500; for the United Kingdom, 10,000; the former Soviet Union, 40,000; China, 100,000.

Wood, Elizabeth A. *Science from Your Airplane Window*. Dover 2nd ed. rev. 1975 o.p. Subjects include standing water, coastlines, running water, weather, and rock structures, as viewed from a window seat.

Wyatt, Antony, ed. *Challinor's Dictionary of Geology*. OUP 1986 $35.00. ISBN 0-19-520505-7. Good and crisp entries, many of which are not too technical and are defined from a historical perspective.

GEOGRAPHY

Geography is a shifting field. Many people still think of it as consisting mainly of maps, political boundaries, and the distribution of life, land, water, and resources. It is all that, but any reader who explores the map of geography will find its boundaries vague and far away. As one example, geology and geography both concern mineral resources, and geography and meteorology both concern climates. Books on "physical geography" and "physical geology" may be much the same. The exploration may begin with one of the many books outlining the study of geography, or describing geographers at work, or asking "What is geography?"

Readers should consider tools such as atlases and geographical dictionaries. Next should be an introductory textbook, to be read for an idea of the range of modern geography. Artificial satellites, for instance, aid geographers in mapping land and sea, and in evaluating natural resources. Recently there has been a surge of development in the area referred to as Geographic Information Systems (GIS), the computerization of map data such as scales, names, geographic grids, topography, land use, soil varieties, geology, and so on. When GIS's are linked with computer-aided drafting and mapping techniques, one can generate maps very quickly, even change scales, superimpose new information, change colors, lettering, and rearrange labeling. So books on GIS, mapping, and computer-assisted cartography should be investigated to view the cutting edge of the geographer's age-old art of map making. More and more, geography's arena includes the continental shelves and the ocean bottom itself, so books on marine geology and oceanography may match the reader's needs and interests. In exploring the discipline of geography, one should be aware of the many disciplines with which it overlaps. Also one must remember that geography is very broad, ranging from the very technical work of the GIS specialist to the social science aspect of the field. (See the chapter on Geography in Volume 3.)

Alexander, John W., and L. Gibson. *Economic Geography*. P-H 3rd ed. 1988 $48.00. ISBN 0-13-225160-4. Topics range from agriculture through mining, manufacturing, transportation, and trade to services, and the theory of "the new geography."

Antenucci, John C., and others, eds. *Geographic Information Systems, a Guide to the Technology*. Van Nos. Reinhold 1991 $59.95. ISBN 0-442-00756-6. Good balance of information for novices and veteran practitioners in the field.

Bagrow, Leo. *History of Cartography*. Rev. by R. A. Skelton. Transaction Pubs. 1985 repr. of 1964 ed. o.p. Subject matter is inseparable, of course, from traditional geography, as well as geology and other fields.

Balchin, W.G.V., ed. *Geography: An Outline for the Intending Student*. Routledge 1970 o.p. Discusses how geography is now studied in the universities of the United Kingdom. Very useful.

Berry, Brian J., ed. *The Nature of Change in Geographical Ideas*. Perspectives in Geography Ser. N. Ill. U. Pr. 1978 $22.50. ISBN 0-87580-525-6. Concerns the social aspects of the field and various philosophical approaches.

Boyce, Ronald Reed. *Geographic Perspectives on Global Problems: An Introduction to Geography*. Wiley 1982 o.p. Proceeds from the general (earth as a planet) to the particular (urban areas) and goes on to the future (resources).

Brewer, J. Gordon. *The Literature of Geography: A Guide to Its Organisation and Use*. Shoe String 2nd ed. 1978 o.p. Deals with what is available, what is useful, how it is organized, and how it relates to other fields.

Buttimer, Annette. *Values in Geography*. St. Mut. 1987 $30.00. ISBN 81-85046-54-9. "Geography," once mainly physical and political, now straddles the humanities and the natural and social sciences.

Dickinson, R. E., and O.J.R. Howarth. *The Making of Geography*. Greenwood 1976 repr. of 1933 ed. o.p. A history of geography, beginning with the Greek philosophers (and a few even earlier).

Dunbar, Gary S. *The History of Modern Geography: An Annotated Bibliography of Selected Works. Reference Lib. of the Humanities* Garland 1985 o.p. Original intent aside, it helps define geography's range.

Freeman, T. W. *The Geographer's Craft.* Longwood 1967 o.p. Freeman uses the achievements of several eminent geographers as case histories.

Goddard, Stephen, ed. *A Guide to Information Sources in the Geographical Sciences.* B&N Imports 1983 $48.25. ISBN 0-389-20403-X. Includes geomorphology; historical, agricultural, and industrial geography; major regional sources; tools (roughly, maps, air photos, statistics, and archives).

Goudie, Andrew, ed. *The Encyclopedic Dictionary of Physical Geography.* Blackwell Pubs. 1985 o.p. Aimed at professionals and secondary-level teachers. Cross-references and index are useful to anyone searching the field of geography and also other earth sciences.

Gould, Peter. *The Geographer at Work.* Routledge 1985 $18.95. ISBN 0-7102-0459-0. Highly readable account of what geography has become in the last 30 years. Emphatically not a compilation of job descriptions.

Grim, Ronald E. *Historical Geography of the United States and Canada: A Guide to Information Sources. Geography and Travel Information Guide Ser.* Gale 1982 o.p. Deals with "the Europeanization of the American landscape," including cartographic sources, archives, and other historical works, and selected literature.

Hammond, Kenneth A., George Macinko, and Wilma B. Fairchild, eds. *Sourcebook on the Environment: A Guide to the Literature.* U. Ch. Pr. 1978 $27.50. ISBN 0-226-31522-3. Gives approximately 3,800 references.

Haring, L. Lloyd, and John F. Lounsbury. *Introduction to Scientific Geographic Research.* William C. Brown 1982 $12.76. ISBN 0-697-05262-1. Gives techniques for defining the problem, devising an approach, gathering data and analyzing it, and writing a report.

Harris, Chauncey D., ed. *A Geographical Bibliography for American Libraries.* Assn. Am. Geographers 1985 $25.00. ISBN 0-89291-193-X. Focuses on the years 1970 to 1984.

Hartshorne, Richard. *The Nature of Geography: A Critical Survey of Current Thought in the Light of the Past.* Greenwood 1978 repr. of 1949 ed. $41.50. ISBN 0-8371-9328-1. Historical development of the science leading up to the question: What kind of a science is geography?

James, Preston E., and Geoffrey J. Martin. *All Possible Worlds: A History of Geographical Ideas.* Wiley 1993. ISBN 0-471-63-414-X. A survey, with bibliography and biosketches of influential geographers.

Kates, Robert W., and Ian Burton. *Geography, Resources, and Environment: Selected Writings of Gilbert F. White.* U. Ch. Pr. 1986 $65.00. ISBN 0-226-4-2579-6. An eminent geographer discusses natural resources, hazards, and human environment.

King, Cuchlaine A. *Physical Geography.* B&N Imports 1980 o.p. Topics arranged according to scale: local (meteorology, hydrology, and so on), regional and continental, and global.

Kish, George, ed. *A Source Book in Geography.* HUP 1978 $40.00. ISBN 0-674-82270-6. Among the 123 selections: Socrates explains the nature of the earth, the Venerable Bede describes seventh-century Britain, and Jefferson asks Humboldt about the nature of Louisiana.

Lounsbury, John F., and Frank T. Aldrich. *Introduction to Geographic Field Methods and Techniques.* Macmillan 1986. ISBN 0-675-20509-3. Despite photos and other imagery from space, often geographers must still gather data in the field. Covers mapping, measuring, counting, and recording. Elementary but vital.

Miller, Richard K., and Marcia E. Rupnow. *Geographic Information Systems.* Future Tech. Surveys 1991 $200.00. ISBN 1-55865-176-4. Technical discussions by competent computer-oriented author.

Mitchell, William B. *Geography and Resource Analysis.* Halsted Pr. 1989 $49.95. ISBN 0-470-21190-3. Discusses how to handle geographic and natural resource information.

Monmonier, Mark S. *How to Lie with Maps.* U. Ch. Pr. 1991 $12.95. ISBN 0-226-53415-4. Excellent book outlining the elements of maps and the pitfalls of map interpretation.

Monmonier, Mark S., and George A. Schnell. *Map Appreciation*. P-H 1988 $38.00. ISBN 0-13-556052-7. Discusses fundamentals of maps and map reading.

Muriel, C. B. *Geography and Cartography: A Reference Handbook*. Linnet Bks. 1976 o.p. Covers "the main focal points of geographical study"—mainly organizations (as the Geological Society of London), sources (Library of Congress), publications (*Canada in Maps*), and subjects (maps, globes, map librarianship).

Prescott, John R. *The Maritime Political Boundaries of the World*. Routledge Chapman & Hall 1986 $55.00. ISBN 0-416-41750-7. Discusses measurement, claims, zones, continental shelves, the high seas. Of special interest because the United States and other nations extended their claims to 200 miles.

Stamp, Dudley, and Audrey N. Clark. *A Glossary of Geographical Terms*. Longman 1979 o.p. Long the standard reference, and still among the best.

Strahler, Arthur N., and Alan H. Strahler. *Modern Physical Geography*. Wiley 1991 $40.00. ISBN 0-471-53392-0. Encyclopedic in scope. Treats the earth as a globe, with major sections on the atmosphere and hydrosphere; climate, soils, and plants; and landforms.

Tomlin, Dana. *Geographic Information Systems and Cartographic Modeling*. P-H 1990 $47.00. ISBN 0-13-350927-3. Highly technical and computer oriented.

Vallet, Roxanne. *Geography Is Fun*. MAYA Pubs. 1992 $10.95. ISBN 1-895583-37-3. Good introduction for young readers.

Wheeler, Jesse, H., and others. *Regional Geography of the World*. Holt 1975 o.p. Solid traditional textbook, systematically describing the world we live in—physiography, climate, political boundaries, populations.

Whittow, John B. *The Penguin Dictionary of Physical Geography*. Viking Penguin 1984 o.p. Takes into account the "fundamental and conceptual changes" in the 1960s and 1970s.

Wilford, John Noble, Jr. *The Mapmakers*. Random 1982 $18.00. Thorough and engaging history of mappers and their work from the earliest times.

GEOLOGY

Geology is set apart from the other sciences by the concept of geologic time. Earth is about 4.5 billion years old, and that gives geology a lot of scope—the materials and shape of the earth, its natural forces, its life forms, and the history of all those things. Now plate tectonics and the accentuated view of the earth as a planet have forced reassessment of many long-held beliefs. Many findings of science have been reconfirmed, others modified, some disproved. And there are great surprises.

Geology relies heavily on the record of the past. But it does not only employ what is recorded in the rocks; it also gleans information from the landscape, shapes of the continents, and the present-day physical processes themselves. For, as the founders of the science tell us, the processes operating on and in the earth today are the same processes that operated in the past. So an understanding of today's processes is the key to unlocking and understanding the past.

Geology is a very broad science that interacts intimately with other related disciplines. This gives us many "hybrid" disciplines, such as geochemistry, geophysics, environmental geology, and astrogeology, to name but a few.

For an overview, seek an introductory text, though that may mean two books: some introductions stick to physical geology and leave historical geology to be treated separately. After that, the most obvious step is to find a book on rocks and minerals and another on fossils. Thereafter, individual interest usually sets the course.

Or, as an alternative, begin with field guides to fossils and to rocks and minerals, and then consult introductory textbooks. Use encyclopedia articles, too, if only for their lists of cross-references, which suggest new routes of study.

Adams, Frank Dawson. *Birth and Development of the Geological Sciences.* Dover 1954 repr. of 1938 ed. o.p. Outlines various concepts of the earth throughout history and tells how old ideas gave way to the new.

Ager, Derek V. *The Nature of the Stratigraphical Record.* Wiley 1993 $21.95. ISBN 0-471-93808-4. A respected geologist questions some generally accepted ideas. Provocative.

Albritton, Claude C. *Abyss of Time: Changing Conceptions of the Earth's Antiquity after the 16th Century.* Jones & Bartlett 1980 $30.00. ISBN 0-87735-341-7. Perhaps geologists' greatest contribution to science is the concept of geologic time.

————, ed. *The Fabrics of Geology.* Freeman Cooper 1963 o.p. Surveys the history of geology, examines its status, and considers future direction.

Blatt, Harvey, Gerard V. Middleton, and Raymond Murray. *Origin of Sedimentary Rock.* P-H 1980. ISBN 0-13-642710-3. Advanced text stressing the "profound ideas and new evidence" of the previous decade.

Burchfield, Joe D. *Lord Kelvin and the Age of the Earth.* Natural History Pr. 1975 o.p. Describes how Kelvin calculated that the earth could be no more than 24 million years old and how the discovery of radioactivity proved Kelvin wrong.

Calder, Nigel. *The Restless Earth: A Report on the New Geology.* Viking Penguin 1978 o.p. Explains how volcanoes, earthquakes, drifting continents, and erosion continue to transform the earth as they have throughout geologic time.

Cattermole, Peter, and Patrick Moore. *The Story of Earth.* Cambridge U. Pr. 1986 $34.95. ISBN 0-521-26292-5. Tells how the earth was formed from a cloud of dust and gas circling the primitive sun.

Cloud, Preston. *Cosmos, Earth, and Man: A Short History of the Universe.* Yale U. Pr. 1978 $17.00. ISBN 0-300-02594-7. Covers the universe from the "Big Bang," several billion years ago, down to the time of creatures capable of trying to reconstruct the history.

Craig, Gordon Y., and E. J. Jones, eds. *A Geological Miscellany.* Princeton U. Pr. 1985 $10.95. ISBN 0-691-02389-1. Snippets from the life and times of earth scientists confirm Toepfer's comment (in 1841) that "geologists are charming company—particularly for other geologists."

Erickson, Jon. *Plate Tectonics: Unraveling the Mysteries of the Earth.* Facts on File 1992 $24.95. ISBN 0-8160-2588-6. Sketch of the theory of plate tectonics. Also includes crustal activity on other planets and moons.

Fenton, Carroll Lane, and Mildred Adams Fenton. *Giants of Geology.* Doubleday 1952 o.p. Biographical sketches outline the development of geological ideas.

————. *Story of the Great Geologists.* Ayer 1974 repr. of 1945 ed. $22.00. ISBN 0-8369-1130-X. History of science through biography: Eratosthenes measures the earth (third century B.C.); James Hutton finds no need of the flood (A.D. 1795).

Geikie, Sir Archibald. *Charles Darwin as Geologist.* Gordon Pr. 1977 $59.95. ISBN 0-8490-1596-0. Nowadays Darwin's name evokes evolution, but he was among the first to recognize changes in sea level and to see that the shape of the land did not depend on catastrophic events.

————. *Founders of Geology.* Macmillan 1905 o.p. Covers geology from the ancient Greeks to the petrographic microscope. Geikie (1835–1924), a Scottish geologist and popularizer of geology, was also a historian.

————. *Types of Scenery and Their Influence on Literature.* Assoc. Faculty Pr. 1970 repr. of 1898 ed. $59.95. ISBN 0-8490-1596-0. Geikie dominated geology in his time and described it lucidly for nonscientists.

Gilluly, James, Aaron C. Waters, and A. O. Woodford. *Principles of Geology.* W. H. Freeman 1975 o.p. Long popular and widely respected, and with reason.

Hallam, Anthony. *Great Geological Controversies.* OUP 1983 $21.95. ISBN 0-19-854430-8. The age of the earth has long been disputed, as has the reading of the record in its rocks and the mechanism of geologic forces. Hallam tells tales of conflict among neptunists, volcanists, plutonists, catastrophists and uniformitarians and drifters.

———. *A Revolution in Earth Science, from Continental Drift to Plate Tectonics*. OUP 1973 o.p. Apparently the first to suggest that the New World and the Old World had drifted apart was Francis Bacon (1561–1626). Nearly three centuries passed before the idea was seriously revived, by Alfred Lothar Wegener (1880–1930), and general acceptance came only in the 1960s. Hallam sums up the story well.

Hardy, David A., and Murray John. *The Fires Within: Volcanism on the Earth and Other Planets*. Dragons's World Pub. 1991 o.p. Good treatment of the types and styles of volcanism on earth and other planets. Illustrations are excellent.

Harland, W. B., and others. *A Geologic Time Scale*. Cambridge U. Pr. 1990 $54.95. ISBN 0-521-38361-7. Discusses the ladder model usually used to depict the geologic time. Rungs at various distances correspond to the duration of eras and periods.

Leveson, David. *A Sense of the Earth*. AMS Pr. 1972 $18.00. ISBN 0-404-19149-5. A geologist as philosopher describes his work and comes to terms with the only earth we have.

Longwell, Chester L., ed. *Sedimentary Facies in Geologic History*. Geol. Soc. of Amer. 1949 o.p. Technical discussions about the relationships between sedimentation and geologic time.

McAlester, A. Lee. *The Earth: An Introduction to the Geological and Geophysical Sciences*. P-H 1973 $29.95. ISBN 0-685-03849-1. Physical aspects dominate; life of the past is left, mainly, for another book.

McCall, G. J. H., ed. *Astroblemes-Cryptoexplosion Structures*. Krieger 1979 o.p. Collection of papers concerning geologic structures of imperfectly explained origin.

———. *Meteorite Craters*. Krieger 1977 o.p. Included in the collection is the Tunguska event of 1908, in which many people observed a great fireball over Siberia and heard it explode from a thousand kilometers away—but no crater was found.

McPhee, John. *Basin and Range*. Farrar 1981 $19.95. ISBN 0-374-10914-1. First of a series from *The New Yorker*, published under the overall title "Annals of the Former World." Geologists praise McPhee's understanding of their science; nongeologists praise his writing.

———. *Encounters with the Archdruid*. FS&G 1971 $19.95. ISBN 0-374-14822-8. Invigorating interviews with extremes among exploiters and environmentalists, represented by the Sierra Club, the Bureau of Reclamation, a developer, and a geologist.

———. *In Suspect Terrain*. FS&G 1983 $19.95. ISBN 0-374-17650-7. McPhee's unifying theme is plate tectonics, but as he notes it does not fit all the geology everywhere— that insures interest for a long time to come.

———. *The Pine Barrens*. FS&G 1978 $17.95. ISBN 0-374-23360-8. McPhee reports on the interaction of people and geology.

———. *Rising from the Plains*. FS&G 1986 $19.95. ISBN 0-374-25082-0. Science of and in the northern Rockies, told mainly in terms of a man who grew up in Wyoming and became the acknowledged expert on the region's geology.

Mahaney, William C., ed. *Quaternary Dating Methods*. Elsevier 1984 $110.25. ISBN 0-444-42392-3. The Quaternary period includes our own time, including the most remote hominids, and the study of evolution requires precise ages for fossil remains. Discusses various methods used to fix those ages.

Mason, Shirley L., and Kirtley F. Mather, eds. *Source Book in Geology, 1400–1900*. Bks. Demand 1939 repr. $180.00. ISBN 0-7837-3850-1. Remarkable collection of writings on geology, many of them out of print and nearly all difficult to find.

Matthews, William H., III. *Geology Made Simple*. Doubleday 1982 $4.95. ISBN 0-385-17142-0. After the first brick comes out of a sidewalk the others seem easy. Matthews pulls out the first brick.

Matthews, William H., III, and others. *Investigating the Earth*. HM 1978 o.p. Junior high text, developed in the early years of the plate tectonics revolution, covering an unusually wide range of the various earth sciences. Geologists give copies of this work to their neighbors.

Merrill, George Perkins. *Contributions to a History of American State Geological and Natural History Surveys. History of Geology Ser.* Ayer 1978 repr. of 1920 ed. $49.50. ISBN 0-405-10450-2. In the opening of the West (and the East), exploration and surveys were mainly organized by the federal and state governments. No one else has condensed the history so well.

————. *The First One Hundred Years of American Geology.* Lubrecht & Cramer 1969 repr. of 1924 ed. $20.00. ISBN 0-02-849180-7. Depicts the development of a new science in a new land.

Miller, Hugh. *The Old Red Sandstone, or New Walks in an Old Field.* Edited by Claude C. Albritton, Jr. *History of Geology Ser.* Ayer 1978 repr. of 1851 ed. $34.50. ISBN 0-405-10451-0. In planning canals in England, Miller (1802–1856) found that each bed of rock had its own fossils, and that helped him find the same bed elsewhere. Now the technique is a fundamental principle of geology.

Moore, Ruth. *The Earth We Live On.* Knopf 1971 o.p. Tells how science changed and how some "natural philosophers" came to be called "geologists."

Niewenhuis, J. D. *The Lifetime of a Landslide: Investigations in the French Alps.* A. A. Balkema 1991 o.p. In-depth treatment of landslides in one area. The studies can be transposed to other areas.

Nininger, H. H. *Arizona's Meteorite Crater—Past—Present—Future.* Am. Meteorite 1956 $9.95. ISBN 0-910096-02-3. Describes the most famous crater of its kind.

Park, R. Graham. *Geologic Structures and Moving Plates.* Chapman and Hall 1988 $95.00. ISBN 0-412-01621-4. Relates small-scale structures to mega-earth structures and plate tectonics.

Parker, Ronald B. *Inscrutable Earth: Explorations in the Science of the Earth.* Macmillan 1984 o.p. "Geology is the root of the family tree of sciences." Not a text but essays introducing concepts, discoveries, and puzzles.

Pearl, Richard M. *Guide to Geologic Literature.* McGraw 1951 o.p. Essays on methods of research and library facilities, stressing specific kinds of literature.

Peterson, Morris S., and J. Keith Rigby. *Interpreting Earth History.* William C. Brown Pubs. 1990. ISBN 0-697-05088-2. The rocks bear evidence showing changes in land and water and their life throughout hundreds of millions of years. This book is historical geology and complements a text on physical geology.

Pettijohn, Francis J. *Memoirs of an Unrepentant Field Geologist.* U. Ch. Pr. 1984 o.p. "A candid profile of some geologists and their science, 1921–1981," by an expert on sands and sandstones.

Phillips, Owen M., Steven M. Stanley, and Darrell F. Strobel, eds. *Structural Geology of Fold and Trust Belts.* Johns Hopkins 1992 $55.00. ISBN 0-8018-4350-2. Analyses of folding and buckling of rock layers in mountain ranges.

Picard, M. Dane. *Grit and Clay.* Elsevier 1975 o.p. A geologist irreverently reviews not only works on geology but also novels and movies that depict geologists at work and play.

Press, Frank, and Raymond Siever. *Earth.* W. H. Freeman 1985 $45.95. ISBN 0-7167-1793-3. Physical geology only—no history of life. The text is one of the biggest and best around.

Raup, David M., and Steven M. Stanley. *Principles of Paleontology.* W. H. Freeman 1978 $41.95. ISBN 0-7167-0022-2. Discusses how fossils provide new clues bearing on plate tectonics and much else.

Rhodes, Frank H. T. *Geology. Golden Guide Ser.* Western Pub. 1971 o.p. Aimed at children, but not written down to them.

Rhodes, Frank H. T., and Richard O. Stone, eds. *Language of the Earth.* Pergamon 1981 $42.00. ISBN 0-08-025980-4. The language is really *about* the earth, by geologists, novelists, humorists, reporters, engineers, historians, and others. Many of the samples are very hard to find elsewhere.

Rossbacher, Lisa A. *Recent Revolutions in Geology.* Modana-Adama Bks. 1986 o.p. Describes recent developments usually missing from texts.

Sarjeant, William Antony S. *Geologists and the History of Geology: An International Bibliography from the Origins to 1978*. 5 vols. Krieger 1980 $450.00 ea. ISBN 0-405-10469-3. Huge, expensive, important, and unduplicated elsewhere.

Schneer, Cecil J., ed. *Two Hundred Years of Geology in America: Proceedings of the New Hampshire Bicentennial Conference*. Bks. Demand repr. of 1979 ed. $103.80. ISBN 0-8357-7522-4. Surveys the science on the nation's bicentennial.

Skinner, Brian J., ed. *Earth's History, Structure, and Materials*. Kaufmann 1980 o.p. Covers measurement of geological time, plate tectonics, and volcanic chains.

Snelling, N. J. *The Chronology of the Geological Record*. Blackwell Pubns. 1985 o.p. Despite any difficulties, the science of geology can hardly exist without a chronology of rocks, events, and life.

Steinbrugge, Karl V. *Earthquakes, Volcanoes, and Tsunamis: Anatomy of Hazards*. Shandia 1982 $35.00. ISBN 0-9609050-0-6. Case studies of damage from earthquakes, volcanoes, and tsunamis.

Stokes, W. Lee. *Essentials of Earth History*. P-H 1982. ISBN 0-13-285890-8. Sea floor spreading and global tectonics have been verified, forcing reinterpretation of evolutionary changes in life forms. Pairing this book with another on physical geology makes a solid basis for further study.

Ward, Dederick C., Marjorie Wheeler, and Robert A. Bier, Jr. *Geologic Reference Sources: A Subject and Regional Bibliography of Publications and Maps in the Geological Sciences*. Scarecrow 1981 $49.50. ISBN 0-8108-1428-5. More than most scientists, geologists depend on the record of the past, whether in rocks or on paper.

Warren, John K. *Evaporite Sedimentology*. P-H 1989 $59.00. ISBN 0-13-292335-1. Outlines the conditions necessary for the formation of evaporite deposits.

Weiner, Jonathan. *Planet Earth*. Bantam 1986 $27.95. ISBN 0-553-05096-6. Companion text to a respected Public Broadcasting System series by WQED, Pittsburgh.

Wyatt, Antony. *Challinor's Dictionary of Geology*. OUP 1986 $35.00. $16.95. ISBN 0-19-520506-5. Worthwhile when reading about British geology, for regional terms do exist.

Wykoff, Jerome. *The Story of Geology: Our Changing Earth through the Ages*. Western Pub. 1960 o.p. Not so rigorous as, say, an introductory textbook, but more readable than most.

LANDSCAPE

Everyone who goes outdoors and looks around soon notices the lay of the land. Walking down a hill or across a bridge makes us conscious of the landscape, and we may wonder how things came to be that way.

The study of the landscape and the natural forces that shape it is called geomorphology, and it is a field of science all its own. It must be remembered that landscapes (landforms) are the product of one or more physical, chemical, or biological processes. For example, there are landscapes formed by volcanoes, glaciers, streams, wind, waves, and so on. While some landscapes are a result of chemical weathering, there are those that are influenced by certain plant communities. Some are even determined by rock type, rock structure, and tectonic history. So readers must watch for cross-references to other fields of earth science. Whatever its academic classification, the landscape strongly affects the way we live. We enjoy the scenery of national parks, avoid building on flood plains, use estuaries as seaways, fly higher over mountain chains, and avoid active volcanoes—all this takes geomorphology into account.

The remarks above include key words for seeking out pertinent books. An introductory text may be the best starting point, although a first work on physical geology or physical geography may do. Less obvious are regional guides to geology, descriptions of national parks, and works on beaches and coastlines (which are reshaped rapidly by waves).

Anderson, M. G., and K. S. Richards, eds. *Slope Stability, Geotechnical Engineering, and Geomorphology*. Wiley 1987 $225.00. ISBN 0-471-91021-X. Collection of studies dealing with the mechanics of slope processes and their relation to landscapes.

Beven, Keith, and Paul Carling, eds. *Floods*. Wiley 1989 $95.00. ISBN 0-471-92164-5. Discusses implication of floods on landscapes.

Butzer, Karl W. *Geomorphology from the Earth*. U. Ch. Pr. 1976 $7.95. ISBN 0-226-08634-8. Describes features and processes from the point of view that the face of the earth is unique.

Daly, Reginald A. *The Changing World of the Ice Age*. Hafner 1963 repr. of 1934 ed. o.p. Readable and standard approach to glacial geology. Necessarily includes much geomorphology.

Feldman, Rodney M., and Richard A. Heimmlich. *Geology Field Guide: The Black Hills*. Kendall-Hunt 1980 o.p. Geomorphology and paleontology help decipher a popular scenic area.

Flint, Richard F. *Glacial and Quaternary Geology*. Wiley 1977 o.p. Describes the Quaternary period, sometimes called, loosely, the Ice Age.

Flint, Richard F., and Brian J. Skinner. *Physical Geology*. Wiley 1977 o.p. Excellent textbook. It is no criticism to say that the reader needs a book on historical geology, too.

Foster, Robert J. *General Geology*. Macmillan 1988 ISBN 0-675-20886-6. Concerns "the solid rock Earth," especially the processes that formed its surface features.

Frye, Keith. *Roadside Geology of Virginia*. Mountain Pr. 1986 $12.00. ISBN 0-87842-199-8. Travelers pass over and through the geologic record, and highway cuts strip away vegetation and soil, providing a clearer view.

Gilbert, Grove Karl. *Report of the Geology of the Henry Mountains: U.S. Geographical and Geological Surveys of the Rocky Mountain Region. History of Geology Ser*. Ayer 1978 repr. of 1877 ed. $21.00. ISBN 0-405-10441-3. Classic analysis of Gilbert's work.

Harris, Ann, and Esther Tuttle. *Geology of National Parks*. Kendall-Hunt 1990 $35.95. ISBN 0-8403-4619-0. Acceptance of global tectonics provoked this revision, showing that the "new geology" extends far from plate boundaries.

Harris, David V., and Eugene P. Kiver. *The Geologic Story of the National Parks and Monuments*. Wiley 1985 $41.95. ISBN 0-471-87224-5. Explains how many parks are painless and dramatic lessons in earth materials and geologic processes.

Hill, Mary. *Geology of the Sierra Nevada*. U. CA Pr. 1974 $11.00. ISBN 0-520-02698-5. The Sierra ranks among the earth's great ranges and is a key to understanding many other mountain systems.

Hole, Francis D., and J. D. Campbell. *Soil Landscape Analysis*. Rowman 1985 $61.50. ISBN 0-86598-140-X. Discusses soil classification and the role of soils in landscape development.

Hunt, Charles B. *Death Valley: Geology, Ecology, Archaeology*. U. CA Pr. 1975 $15.00. ISBN 0-520-03013-3. As the subtitle suggests, one science seldom stands alone.

————. *Natural Regions of the United States and Canada*. W. H. Freeman 1974 o.p. A "region" has characteristic geology, topography, climate, flora, and fauna.

Krutch, Joseph Wood. *Grand Canyon: Today and All Its Yesterdays*. U. of Ariz. Pr. repr. of 1958 ed. $12.95. ISBN 0-8165-1112-8. Essay on one of the great features of the earth, whose canyon walls represent nearly two billion years. Illustrated.

Lobeck, Armin K. *Geomorphology: An Introduction to the Study of Landscapes*. McGraw 1939 o.p. Permanent classic text with illustrations. Units of two or four pages show how natural forces shape the landscape. Includes many unsurpassed early photos of the American West by William H. Jackson, pioneer photographer.

McKee, Bates. *Cascadia: The Geologic Evolution of the Pacific Northwest*. McGraw 1972 o.p. Mount Rainier alone illustrates volcanology, glacial geology, the power of running water, and meteorology. *Cascadia* covers far more than one mountain and is a model for geological field guides.

Pethick, John. *An Introduction to Coastal Geomorphology.* Arnold 1984 o.p. Where land and ocean meet, nature moves beaches and usually defeats anyone who opposes it.

Redfern, Ron. *Corridors of Time: 1,700,000,000 Years of Earth at Grand Canyon.* Times Bks. 1980 $55.00. Panorama of earth history extending back to a time before the earliest known life. Redfern provides panoramic photos.

Shelton, John S. *Geology Illustrated.* W. H. Freeman 1966 $39.95. ISBN 0-7167-0229-0. Earth features are often best shown from the air, as in these photos and diagrams. The text explains the natural forces responsible.

Shimer, John A. *This Sculptured Earth: The Landscape of America.* Col. U. Pr. 1959 $53.00. ISBN 0-231-02331-6. Depicts the workings and results of natural sculptors—wind, water, waves, ice.

Sullivan, Walter. *Landprints: On the Magnificent American Landscape.* Times Bks. 1984 o.p. Pictures show the geologic record of the United States as any traveler can see. The text explains geologists' interpretation for nongeologist readers.

Thorn, Colin E. *Introduction to Theoretical Geomorphology.* Routledge Chapman & Hall 1988 $60.00. ISBN 0-04-551117-9. Uses major concepts of landform study and applies them globally. Examples from every continent.

ROCKS, MINERALS, AND GEOCHEMISTRY

In the earth sciences, chemistry usually means the chemical composition of the earth's materials—mainly rocks, minerals, and water—and is formally known as geochemistry. Most books and most academic treatments of the chemistry of earth materials are separated into mineralogy (the study of minerals) and petrology (the study of the origin, identification, and classification of rocks).

Because rocks are composed of minerals, the logical place to begin a study would be a mineralogy textbook. This would give the reader an insight into minerals: their properties, formation, and classification. Most introductory chapters in elementary mineralogy textbooks have the chemistry necessary for the understanding of mineralogy. Further study would lead the reader into the domain of how the minerals come together to form rocks. Here petrology or physical geology textbooks would be best. Cross-references and natural curiosity should then show the way.

Another approach is to use one of the big encyclopedias of mineralogy for a general view of the huge variety of minerals (several thousand are known). Then use a field guide to rocks and minerals to find out more about the much smaller number of minerals anyone can find in fields, road cuts, and the walls of downtown buildings. From there proceed to books on chemistry, geology, and mineralogy to learn how the rocks and minerals came to be that way.

Agricola, Georgius. *De Re Metallica.* Trans. by Herbert Clark Hoover and Lou Henry Hoover. Dover 1950 repr. of 1912 ed. $17.95. ISBN 0-486-60006-8. Leading guide to mining and technology for more than two centuries. Still remains a fascinating history.

Barnes, Virgil E., and Mildred A. Barnes. *Tektites.* Thousand Autumns Pr. 1989 $19.95. ISBN 1-882032-03-9. Discusses Tektites (glassy fragments) of unclear origin found in groups in widely scattered regions of the earth's surface.

Chesterman, Charles W. *The Audubon Society Field Guide to North American Rocks and Minerals.* Knopf 1979 $17.95. ISBN 0-394-50269-8. Handbook on discovery, identification, and labeling of specimens. Perhaps more important, it is an elementary introduction to geology and mapping.

Colman, Steven M., and David P. Delthier. *Rates of Chemical Weathering of Rocks and Minerals.* Acad. Pr. 1986 $135.00. ISBN 0-12-181490-4. Very technical but illustrates the importance of weathering as a powerful geologic agent.

Cooper, Henry S. F., Jr. *Moon Rocks.* Dial 1970 o.p. The story of the first geological field
    trips to the moon, which provided hand specimens for mineralogists and petrogra-
    phers whose work had always been purely theoretical.

Desautels, Paul E. *The Mineral Kingdom.* Grosset & Dunlap 1968 o.p. A coffee-table book,
    but also much more: history of mineralogy and crystallography, occurrences, and
    collecting.

Fleischer, Michael. *Glossary of Mineral Species 1983.* Mineralogical Record 1983 o.p.
    Catalogs mineral names, including synonyms, varieties, and discredited names, with
    chemical composition—and, often, reference to first descriptions.

Freedman, Jacob, ed. *Trace Element Geochemistry in Health and Disease.* Bks. Demand
    1975 $31.50. ISBN 0-685-16455-1. Provides examples of how tiny amounts of
    naturally occurring substances affect the health of people.

Frye, Keith. *Modern Mineralogy.* P-H 1974 o.p. A textbook on minerals—their formation,
    occurrence, properties, composition, and classification. Technical but useful.

Hurlbut, Cornelius, and Robert C. Kammerling. *Gemology.* Wiley 1991 $58.00. ISBN 0-
    471-52667-3. Excellent treatment of crystallography, physical properties, and uses of
    gemstones. Good illustrations.

Keller, Peter C. *Gemstones and Their Origin.* Van Nos. Reinhold 1991 $49.95. ISBN 0-
    442-31945-2. Emphasizes origin and emplacement of gemstones. Excellent color
    photographs of primitive mining camps.

Krauskopf, Konrad B. *Introduction to Geochemistry.* McGraw 1979 $52.23. ISBN 0-07-
    035447-2. More technical than some other introductory textbooks, but chemistry is
    essential to understanding the earth.

Lima-De-Faria, Jose, ed. *Historical Atlas of Crystallography.* Kluwer Ac. 1990 $36.00.
    ISBN 0-7923-0649-X. Excellent treatment of the development of crystallography.
    Includes extensive bibliography.

Mange, Maria A., and Heinz F. W. Maurer. *Heavy Minerals in Colour.* Chapman & Hall
    1992 $79.95. ISBN 0-412-43910-7. Discusses the significance of heavy minerals in
    science and environment. Gives descriptions through color photographs.

McDivitt, James F., and Gerald Manners. *Minerals and Men: An Exploration of the World
    of Minerals and Metals Including Some of the Major Problems That Are Posed.*
    Resources Future 1974 $11.95. ISBN 0-8018-1827-3. As suggested by the subtitle, the
    problems are economic and political as well as scientific. Written for nonspecialists.

Mason, Brian, and Carleton B. Moore. *Principles of Geochemistry.* Wiley 1982 o.p.
    Although principles remain, the subject matter changes as new data arrives from
    deep-sea cores and from imagery of the other planets.

Mitchell, Richard Scott. *Mineral Names: What Do They Mean?* Van Nos. Reinhold 1979
    o.p. Links minerals to persons, places, chemical composition, and a host of tribes,
    fictional characters, and so on.

Ollier, C. D. *Weathering.* Wiley 1975 $22.95. ISBN 0-582-30103-3. Discusses the
    breakdown of materials on or near the earth's surface and their alteration to suit
    more closely their new environment.

Pough, Frederick H. *A Field Guide to Rocks and Minerals.* Peterson Field Guide Ser. HM
    1976 $14.95. ISBN 0-395-24049-2. Includes photos, descriptions, classifications, and
    simple chemical and blowpipe tests.

Sorrell, Charles A. *A Field Guide and Introduction to the Geology and Chemistry of Rocks
    and Minerals.* Western Pub. 1973 o.p. The title is unwieldy but accurate.

Sutulov, Alexander. *Minerals in World Affairs.* U. of Utah Ptg. Servs. 1972 o.p. A better
    title might be "Minerals and Economics." It can be argued that minerals very nearly
    lead the list of motives for war.

Tomkeieff, S. I., and others, eds. *Dictionary of Petrology.* Wiley 1983 $275.00. ISBN 0-471-
    10159-1. Arranged alphabetically with each term cross-indexed to tables that
    regroup related items.

Wilk, Harry. *The Magic of Minerals.* Spr.-Verlag 1989 $60.00. ISBN 0-387-15730-1.
    Selectively chosen with 110 full-page photos.

Williams, Howel, and others. *Petrography: An Introduction to the Study of Rocks in Thin Sections.* W. H. Freeman 1983 $46.95. ISBN 0-7167-1376-4. Stresses the identification of sedimentary rocks by microscopic examination of thin slices of samples.

GEOPHYSICS

The science of geophysics is the physics of the earth. It encompasses a wide variety of subjects: seismology, earth magnetism, electrical properties of rocks, internal heat flow, radioactivity, and many others. Geophysics, like geology, has outgrown its earthbound origin and is now a discipline that includes the other planets and moons in our solar system.

With that range of subject matter, a first book in geophysics must be very general—perhaps one on the solar system itself. Physical geology is needed, too. Thereafter, the path lies in the direction of increasingly specialized fields, for example, toward plate dynamics, or volcanology, or seismology, or terrestrial magnetism.

Studying geophysics in detail eventually requires mathematics, chemistry, and physics. However, those tools are not needed to gain a general understanding of many fascinating phenomena. We can easily see that the Pacific Plate, grinding northward against the North American Plate, causes earthquakes along the San Andreas Fault. Further understanding may require learning to use the tools, but encyclopedia articles and bibliographies will guide the way.

Bullard, Fred M. *Volcanoes of the Earth.* U. of Texas Pr. 1984 o.p. Probably the most comprehensive of books on volcanoes. Ranks with the most readable.

Bullen, K. E., and Bruce A. Bolt. *An Introduction to the Theory of Seismology.* Cambridge U. Pr. 1985 $99.95. ISBN 0-521-23980-X. Not observation but theory, and technical; nevertheless, fundamental.

Carr, Michael H., ed. *The Geology of the Terrestrial Planets.* USGPO 1985. $16.00. ISBN 0-16-004162-7. As recently as the early 1960s, we knew nothing of the geology of the other planets, and very little about the rocks of the moon. Covers these topics.

Darden, Lloyd. *The Earth in the Looking Glass.* Anchor 1974 o.p. Describes remote sensing—the examination of the earth from space, or at least from high altitudes by means of photographs using visible light, infrared radiation, and other wavelengths.

Decker, Robert, and Barbara Decker. *Volcanoes.* W. H. Freeman 1989 $15.95. ISBN 0-7167-1851-0. Along with much else, the authors list 101 of the earth's most notorious volcanoes.

Eicher, Don L., A. Lee McAlester, and Marcia L. Rottman. *The History of the Earth's Crust.* P-H 1984. ISBN 0-13-389999-3. Earth history as determined from its crust.

Elder, John. *The Bowels of the Earth.* OUP 1976 $21.95. ISBN 0-19-854412-X. The earth is a "vast machine, insatiably consuming itself." Mathematical formulas are abundant, but Elder's way with words compensates for any difficulty.

French, Bevan M. *The Moon Book: Exploring the Mysteries of the Lunar World.* Viking Penguin 1977 o.p. Astronomy, rocketry, and mineralogy meet on earth's satellite.

Glen, William. *The Road to Jaramillo: Critical Years of the Revolution in Earth Science.* Stanford U. Pr. 1982. $57.50. ISBN 0-8047-1119-4. Widely scattered work on rock dating, geomagnetic reversals, and seafloor spreading cumulated in the plate-tectonics revolution.

Iacopi, Robert, ed. *Earthquake Country: California.* Lane Bks. 1971 o.p. To many Americans, "earthquake" means California, the San Andreas Fault, and the San Francisco Earthquake of 1906. Gives the science and facts for nonscientists.

Keary, Philip, and Michael Brooks. *Introduction to Geophysical Exploration.* Blackwell Sci. 1991 $104.95. ISBN 0-632-02921-8. Discusses seismic, magnetic, electrical, electromagnetic, radiometric, and bore hole methods and principles.

Menard, Henry W., ed. *Oceanic Islands*. W. H. Freeman 1986 $32.95. ISBN 0-7167-5017-1. From *Scientific American*, by scientists, for curious nonscientists.

Milsom, John. *Field Geophysics*. Halsted Pr. 1989 $25.95. ISBN 0-470-21156-3. Good thumbnail overview of using geophysics in the field.

Mission to Earth: Landsat Views the World. NASA 1976 o.p. Story of the Landsat satellite designed to assess the natural resources of the United States.

Piper, J. D. A. *Paleomagnetism and the Continental Crust*. Halsted Pr. 1987 $75.95. ISBN 0-470-20743-4. Technical treatment of the origins of magnetism in rocks, including field and laboratory techniques.

Redfern, Ron. *The Making of a Continent*. Random 1983 o.p. This book, and the Public Broadcasting System film based on it, shows the making of North America over geologic time.

Robinson, Edwin S., and Cahit Cohuh. *Basic Exploration Geophysics*. Wiley 1988 $62.95. ISBN 0-471-87941-X. Fundamental, introductory treatment of geophysics and how it is applied to exploration.

Simkin, Tom. *Volcanoes of the World*. Geo Science Pr. 1993 $25.00. ISBN 0-945005-12-1. The data is from the Smithsonian Institution. There is no other source like it.

Simon, Ruth B. *Earthquake Interpretations: A Manual for Reading Seismograms*. Kaufmann 1981 o.p. A primer for reading records of seismographs for clues to the internal structure of the earth.

Sullivan, Walter. *Continents in Motion: The New Earth Debate*. McGraw 1974 o.p. Sullivan, science editor for *The New York Times*, was one of the first to explain the "New Geology" to nonscientists.

Takeuchi, H., S. Uyeda, and H. Kanamori. *Debate about the Earth*. Jones & Bartlett 1970 $32.50. ISBN 0-87735-303-4. Describes how general acceptance of continental drift forced geoscientists to reappraise many aspects of geology and geophysics.

Van Andel, Tjeerd. *New Views of an Old Planet: Continental Drift and the History of the Earth*. Cambridge U. Pr. 1985 $37.95. ISBN 0-521-30084-3. Describes the earth's dynamism, with "a history of many brief intervals of dramatic change between longer times of relative quiescence" and major changes in "drifting of continents, fluctuations of climate, the precession of life."

Veverka, Joseph, and NASA's Planetary Geology Working Group. *Planetary Geology in the 1980s*. NASA 1985 o.p. Now that we can no longer consider the earth's rocks unique in their composition and history, we must review the accepted wisdom.

Wahrhaftig, Clyde. *A Streetcar to Subduction and Other Plate Tectonic Trips by Public Transport in San Francisco*. Amer. Geophysical 1984 $7.50. ISBN 0-87590-225-1. An ideal way and setting for a self-guided tour of geology you can see and touch.

Williams, Howel, and A. R. McBirney. *Volcanology*. Freeman Cooper 1982 repr. of 1979 ed. $37.00. ISBN 0-87735-321-2. The authors are less concerned with descriptions of eruptive peaks than with the physics and chemistry of the magma involved.

Windley, Brian F. *The Evolving Continents*. Wiley 1984 $49.95. ISBN 0-471-90390-6. Elucidates the geodynamics of plate tectonics.

HYDROLOGY AND OCEANOGRAPHY

Earth is known as the blue planet—mainly because of its water. The principal sciences of water are called oceanography and hydrology, the latter including surface water (on land) and ground water (under the surface). Most books about water concern one of the three: oceanography, surface water, or ground water. However, while those topics seem straightforward, subdisciplines and subtopics are very numerous and can be quite confusing. Oceanography, for example, is subdivided into physical oceanography, (the study of waves), water temperatures, currents, and salinity. Another subdivision is marine biology, which deals with the myriad of life forms in the sea. Other subdivisions are chemical oceanography, marine geology, and the meteorological interactions with the sea. Thus, a person embarking on the study of oceanography needs to be aware of the interplay of these many subdisciplines.

Whatever the name, the study of water often leads deeply into chemistry, physics, and mathematics. Even so, many introductory texts are both readable and worth reading. Informal works are numerous, too, as are books on even fairly specialized topics such as rivers and submarine geology. Somehow— perhaps because water is so familiar to all of us—the technical level of most works on water is easy to judge.

Books about physical geology always discuss water (solid, liquid, and gas) in the hydrologic cycle and as an agent of erosion and transport. No books on meteorology, geography, or natural hazards, and few on natural resources can neglect water. Water is as pervasive in books as in nature.

Anikouchine, William, and Richard Sternberg. *The World Ocean: An Introduction to Oceanography*. P-H 1981. ISBN 0-13-967778-X. Based on the important fact that on the surface of the globe there is much more water area than land.

Bascom, Willard. *Waves and Beaches: The Dynamics of the Ocean Surface*. Doubleday 1980 $11.00. ISBN 0-385-14844-5. Explains how the ocean sets the rules for humanity's use of land and water along the shore.

Black, Peter E. *Watershed Hydrology*. P-H 1990 $52.00. ISBN 0-13-946591-X. Study of hydrology from the starting point of individual drainage basin units.

Bras, Rafael L. *Hydrology: An Introduction to Hydrolic Science*. Addison-Wesley 1990 $63.50. ISBN 0-201-05922-3. Introduction to hydrology. Very technical and thorough.

Carson, Rachel. *The Edge of the Sea*. Time-Life 1983 $24.60. ISBN 0-8094-4333-3. Here Carson, most widely known for *Silent Spring*, turns to the coastal zone and its biology, geology, oceanography, and meteorology.

———. *The Sea Around Us*. Nal-Dutton 1954 $5.50. ISBN 0-451-62483-1. The oceans from the beginning: history, mystery, and facts. Deceptively easy reading.

Carter, R. W. G. *Coast Environments*. Acad. Pr. 1988 $39.95. ISBN 0-12-161855-2. Introduction to the interaction of physical, ecological, and cultural systems along coastlines.

Chow, Ven Te, and others. *Applied Hydrology*. McGraw 1988 $48.43. ISBN 0-07-010810-2. Discusses practical application of the principles of hydrology.

Clark, Robert B. *Marine Pollution*. OUP 1992 $35.00. ISBN 0-19-854686-6. In logical steps the author defines pollutants and how they get into the marine environment. Also discusses how to renovate the water and assess change.

Davis, Stanley N., and Roger J. M. DeWiest. *Hydrology*. Krieger 1991 repr. of 1966 ed. $64.95. ISBN 0-89464-638-9. Textbook on the chemistry and physics of water.

Flemming, N. C., ed. *The Undersea*. Macmillan 1977 o.p. Discussion of the ocean floor, water, fauna and flora, resources, use of oceans, underwater archaeology, submarines, and marine law. Not a text on oceanography.

Geraghty, James J., and others. *Water Atlas of the United States*. Water Info. 1973 $60.00. ISBN 0-91-2394-03-X. Charts and graphs show, more effectively than words, where the water is—in rivers, lakes, aquifers—and how much, and so on.

Gross, M. Grant. *Oceanography*. Macmillan 1990. ISBN 0-675-21278-2. Introduction to the composition of seawater, the mechanism of waves, and related subjects.

Heezen, Bruce C., and Charles D. Hollister. *The Face of the Deep*. OUP 1971 $22.95. ISBN 0-19-501277-1. Many photos and diagrams from one of the first to map large areas of the ocean floor.

Kaufman, Wallace, and Orrin H. Pilkey, Jr. *The Beaches Are Moving: The Drowning of America's Shoreline*. Duke 1983 $12.95. ISBN 0-8223-0574-7. Discusses the effects of the rising sea level and how people only increase the damage.

Kennett, James P. *Marine Geology*. P-H 1982. ISBN 0-13-556936-2. Emphasizes rocks and sediments at the expense of water.

Leopold, Luna B. *Water: A Primer.* W. H. Freeman 1974 o.p. Really a primer. Very informative. It may well be the best starting point for the innocent and interested.

Marchuk, Gurii I., and B. A. Kagan. *Dynamics of Ocean Tides.* Kluwer Ac. 1989 $124.00. ISBN 90-277-2552-7. Technical but thorough treatment of tidal dynamics.

Marx, Wesley. *The Oceans, Our Last Resource.* Sierra 1981 o.p. *Resource* means food, minerals, energy, recreation, scenery, and gene pool.

Maury, Matthew F. *The Physical Geography of the Sea, and Its Meteorology.* HUP 1963 $12.95. ISBN 0-674-66652-6. The first textbook of modern oceanography.

Menard, Henry W. *Anatomy of an Expedition.* McGraw 1969 o.p. Describes what an oceanographer does for a living; in this case, from desk to sea on the Nova Expedition.

Nordstrom, Karl F., and others. *Coastal Dunes.* Wiley 1990 $145.00. ISBN 0-471-91842-3. Explains the interaction of windblown and waterborn sand. Also discusses the form and classification of coastal dunes.

Pickering, K. T., and others. *Deep Marine Environments.* Routledge Chapman & Hall 1989 $130.00. ISBN 0-04-551122-5. Discusses sedimentation environments in ocean basins.

Powledge, Fred. *Water: The Nature, Uses, and Future of Our Most Abused Resource.* FS&G 1983 $13.95. ISBN 0-374-51798-3. Topics range from chemistry through water-resource management.

Schumm, Stanley A. *The Fluvial System.* Wiley 1977 $96.70. ISBN 0-7837-3468-9. Describes the ways and means of rivers.

———, ed. *River Morphology.* Van Nos. Reinhold 1982 $45.95. ISBN 0-87933-001-5. This wide-ranging survey includes classic papers hard to gather elsewhere.

Sheaffer, John R., and Leonard A. Stevens. *Future Water: An Exciting Solution to America's Most Serious Resource Crisis.* Morrow 1983 o.p. "Polluted waters," the authors says persuasively, "are really valuable resources out of place."

Shepard, Francis P. *Earth Beneath the Sea.* Bks. Demand repr. of 1967 ed. $66.30. ISBN 0-317-42340-1. Direct study of the ocean bottom and its sediments.

———. *Geological Oceanography: Evolution of Coasts, Continental Margins, and the Deep Sea Floor.* Taylor & Francis 1977 o.p. Explains how coastlines, continental margins, and the deep ocean floors differ markedly but are interrelated.

Seymour, Richard J., ed. *Near Shore Sediment Transport.* Plenum 1989 $85.00. ISBN 0-306-43157-2. Discusses various types of shoreline erosion and mechanisms of sediment movement.

Shaw, Elizabeth M. *Engineering Hydrology; Techniques in Practice.* Ellis Horwood 1989 o.p. Practical treatment of both surface and ground water problems.

Steinbeck, John, and Edward F. Ricketts. *Sea of Cortez: A Leisurely Journal of Travel and Research.* Appel repr. of 1941 ed. $40.00. ISBN 0-911858-08-3. Describes the expedition to the Gulf of California. Ricketts was the original for "Doc" of Steinbeck's Cannery Row novels (*Cannery Row* and *Sweet Thursday*).

Van Andel, Tjeerd. *Tales of an Old Ocean: Exploring the Deep-Sea World of the Geologist and Oceanographer.* Norton 1978 o.p. The adventures of an oceanographer at work as the science changes all around him.

Vetter, Richard C., ed. *Oceanography: The Last Frontier.* Basic 1973 o.p. The specialists represented here wrote for radio broadcast, so the technical level is low and the readability high.

White, Gilbert F. *Strategies of American Water Management.* U. of Mich. Pr. 1969 o.p. Explains how the demand for water leads to political, legal, and economic problems, particularly in the American West.

ATMOSPHERIC SCIENCE

Life on earth exists because of water and free oxygen, and because earth is a suitable distance from the sun. In the strict definition of the term, the study of the atmosphere is termed meteorology. However, as with most other disciplines, there are many subdivisions to it, and it encroaches upon and overlaps other subject areas.

Perhaps the best-known portion of meteorology is the physical aspect, which deals with movements of air masses, warm fronts, cold fronts, storms, etc. The chemical aspect of the science is becoming better known because of pollution problems. The long-term patterns and movements of air currents—climates—are also coming under greater scrutiny because of the concerns about ozone depletion and the greenhouse effect. In recent years the study of the interaction between the atmosphere and the oceans has become increasingly important.

A place to begin the study of meteorology, however, would be physical meteorology—concentrating on the general structure, movement, and composition of the atmosphere. Introductory textbooks would serve the reader well here. Titles of introductory textbooks in this field are likely to include "meteorology" or "climatology." Those books are likely to provoke interest in forecasting, satellite imagery, weather modification, or violent storms. Further specialization leads to advanced mathematics and computer-aided manipulation of data from artificial satellites.

Weather and climate touch everything around us. That means it is important to watch other earth sciences for works on atmospheric phenomena. Who would expect a book called *Volcano Weather*? (see Stommel and Stommel below).

Bair, Frank E., ed. *Weather of U.S. Cities*. 2 vols. Gale 1987 $190.00. ISBN 0-8103-2102-5. Compilation of U.S. government weather data that provides answers to questions about specific weather patterns in virtually every city in the United States.

Barry, Roger G., and Richard J. Chorley. *Atmosphere, Weather, and Climate*. Routledge 1993 $99.95. ISBN 0-415-07760-5. Wide ranging without being excessively technical.

Barth, Michael C., and James G. Titus, eds. *Greenhouse Effect and Sea Level Rise*. Van Nos. Reinhold 1984 $42.95. ISBN 0-442-20991-6. Discusses concerns about global warming.

Battan, Louis J. *Fundamentals of Meteorology*. P-H 1984. ISBN 0-13-341123-0. Introductory text, sparing of mathematics, physics, and chemistry. Stresses what we already know and what we need to know.

Calder, Nigel. *The Weather Machine: How Our Weather Works and Why It Is Changing*. Viking Penguin 1977 o.p. The easy reading disguises the amount of information.

Cole, Franklyn W. *Introduction to Meteorology*. Wiley 1980 $141.50. ISBN 0-7837-3494-8. Serious, sound, and thorough.

Collier, C. G. *Applications of Weather Radar Systems*. Ellis Horwood 1989 o.p. Discusses theory of weather radar and how to interpret what you see on the screen.

Conway, H. McKinley, and Linda L. Liston, eds. *The Weather Handbook*. Conway Data 1990 $39.95. ISBN 0-910436-29-0. "A summary of weather statistics for selected cities throughout the U.S. and around the world." A reference work to use in preparing to move or travel, or to fill in your mental picture of places in the news.

Critchfield, Howard J. *General Climatology*. P-H 1983. ISBN 0-13-349217-6. Straightforward and readable introduction. Not intimidating.

Donn, William L. *Meteorology*. McGraw 1975 $48.95. ISBN 0-07-017599-3. Donn notes that this introductory text retains its "marine flavor" even though he has cut back a chapter on the oceans.

Giles, Bill. *The Story of Weather*. Shell U.K. 1990 o.p. Fundamental treatment of climates, weather phenomena, forecasting, and how to read weather charts.

Lynott, Bob. *The Weather Tomorrow: Why Can't They Get It Right*. Gadfly Pr. 1987 $9.95. ISBN 0-9618077-0-9. Discusses problems and difficulties in weather forecasting.

Meneghini, Robert, and Toshiaka Kozu. *Spaceborne Weather Rader*. Artech Hse. 1990 $59.00. ISBN 0-89006-382-6. Discusses how to interpret satellite radar images.

Minnaert, M. *The Nature of Light and Colour in the Open Air.* Dover 1948 $7.95. ISBN 0-486-20196-1. Describes and explains hundreds of natural phenomena (rainbows, sun dogs, the green flash). Some are easily recognizable as probable explanations of reported sightings of UFOs.

Okken, P. A., and others, eds. *Climate and Energy.* Kluwer Ac. 1989 $95.50. ISBN 0-7923-0519-1. Collection of studies providing a strong technical treatment of the feasibility of controlling carbon dioxide emissions.

Oliver, John E., and John J. Hidore. *Introduction to Climatology.* Macmillan 1984 $29.95. As usual, includes physics and dynamics, regional aspects, and paleoclimates; not so usual are the applied studies.

Pearce, E. A., and C. G. Smith. *The Times Books World Weather Guide.* Random 1990 $17.95. ISBN 0-8129-1881-9. Arranged by country, region, city. Describes the climate for each region; then for each city is a chart showing monthly extremes and averages of temperature, precipitation, and humidity. Few books of charts are so easy to pick up and so hard to put down.

Riehl, Herbert. *Introduction to the Atmosphere.* McGraw 1974 o.p. This edition adds a discussion of artificial satellites as observation tools and takes into account humankind's increasing disturbance of the environmental equilibrium.

Sanderson, Marie, ed. *UNESCO Sourcebook in Climatology.* UNIPUB 1990 o.p. Outlines principles of climatology, energy balances, atmospheric circulation, and water in the atmosphere.

Schaefer, Vincent J., and John A. Day. *A Field Guide to the Atmosphere.* HM 1983 $21.45. ISBN 0-395-24080-8. Tells how to identify clouds, describe meteorological phenomena, understand storms, and (loosely) predict weather.

Scorer, Richard S. *Meteorology of Air Pollution.* Ellis Horwood 1990. o.p. Good discussion of causes and effects of ozone depletion, acid precipitation, and particulate and aerosol pollution in the atmosphere.

Sloane, Eric. *Look at the Sky . . . and Tell the Weather.* Dutton 1979 o.p. Anecdotal commonsense science.

Stommel, Henry, and Elizabeth Stommel. *Volcano Weather: The Story of 1816, the Year without a Summer.* Seven Seas Pr. 1983 o.p. Story of the greatest volcanic eruption in the last 10,000 years.

Takeuchi, Keij, and M. Yoshino, eds. *The Global Environment.* Spr.-Verlag 1991 $54.00. ISBN 0-387-54243-4. Collection of studies outlining the possible effects on climate of human activity.

Trewartha, Glenn T. *The Earth's Problem Climates.* U. of Wis. Pr. 1981 $32.50. ISBN 0-299-08230-X. Explains how some climates are stable and inhospitable while others are erratic and unpredictable.

Trewartha, Glenn T., and Lyle H. Horn. *An Introduction to Climate.* McGraw 1980 o.p. Presents archaeological and geological evidence that climates do change.

Wigley, T. M. L., M. J. Ingram, and G. Farmer. *Climate and History: Studies in Past Climates and Their Impacts on Man.* Cambridge U. Pr. 1981 o.p. How climate detectives determine that over geologic time, climates shift and change, leaving evidence in sediments, pollen (in rocks and glaciers), and tree rings.

Williams, Jack. *The Weather Book: An Easy to Understand Guide to the USA's Weather.* Random 1992 18.00. ISBN 0-679-73669-7. Great graphics and illustrations aimed at the lay reader; not for professionals.

Zim, Herbert S., and others. *Weather. Golden Guide Ser.* Western Pub. 1987 o.p. For a novice of almost any age or background. Deceptively informative.

NATURAL RESOURCES AND APPLIED SCIENCE

What is science good for? Sometimes the answer is fairly obvious. Sometimes the answer is "nothing—yet." Sometimes it is an intellectual challenge, training for the brain. Practical results may come along later. Our civilization depends on soil for agriculture, on rocks and minerals for materials, and on oil, gas, and coal for energy. For building and safety, we need knowledge of natural hazards (such as earthquakes, landslides, and tornadoes) and of the mechanical properties of rock and soil (as for bridge footings and road building).

That is applied science. It is also quite a mixture, with many of the pieces found under geography, geology, geomorphology, geochemistry, hydrology, and seismology. Natural resources and applied science almost necessarily includes engineering. For engineering in the broadest sense of the term is, in fact, applied science. For example, the science of geology, when actually applied to construction of dams, bridges, and other large structures is defined as engineering geology (or geological or geotechnical engineering). Therefore, consult reference lists for such topics as economic geography, geologic hazards, environmental geology, natural resources, mining, and rock mechanics. Look, too, for books on the practice of various professions—case histories, field mapping, career opportunities.

An old newspaper rule says, "Tell how people live." Add to that "Find how an earth science helps people live."

Abdel-Aal, H. K., and others, eds. *Petroleum Economics and Engineering.* Dekker 1992 $170.00. ISBN 0-8247-8428-6. In-depth treatment of the principles, methods, and techniques of engineering economics in the oil industry.

Basile, Robert M. *A Geography of Soils.* William C. Brown 1981 o.p. A basic introduction to a resource so common we sometimes forget that it is vital.

Bates, Robert L. *Geology of the Industrial Rocks and Minerals.* Dover 1969 repr. of 1961 ed. $9.95. ISBN 0-486-62213-4. To many, economic geology means oil and gas and the major ore minerals. Concentrates on materials that become brick, concrete, talcum powder, and other everyday artifacts.

———. *Stone, Clay, and Glass, Basics for Building.* Enslow Pubs. 1986 o.p. Everyday geology of the most practical kind.

Bates, Robert M., and Julia Jackson. *Our Modern Stone Age.* Kaufmann 1982 o.p. Covers about two dozen of the most common rocks and minerals used in everyday life— how they are formed, found, and converted to useful products.

Blyth, F. G., and M. H. DeFries. *A Geology for Engineers.* Crane-Russak 1974 o.p. Concerned primarily with immediately practical aspects of earth materials.

Bolt, Bruce A., and others. *Geological Hazards.* Spr.-Verlag 1982. ISBN 0-387-90254-6. Describes natural hazards that threaten people and property.

Bowen, Robert. *Geothermal Resources.* Elsevier 1989 $108.00. ISBN 1-85166-287-1. Explores the entire gamut of geothermal energy. Not too technical, with good references.

Boyle, Robert W. *Gold: History, and Genesis of Deposits.* Van Nos. Reinhold 1987 $64.95. ISBN 0-442-21162-7. Exhaustive treatment of the subject, with a good collection of references for each chapter.

Chong, Ken Pin, and John W. Smith, eds. *Mechanics of Oil Shale.* Elsevier 1984 $194.50. ISBN 0-85334-273-3. Thorough treatment of the usability of oil shales, including problems, properties, and yields.

Ciciarelli, John A. *A Practical Guide to Aerial Photography: With an Introduction to Surveying.* Van Nos. Reinhold 1991 $49.95. ISBN 0-442-00531-8. Shows how aerial photography can be used by field scientists. Includes a good introduction to surveying.

Clark, Edwin H., Jenniver A. Haverkamp, and William Chapman. *Eroding Soils: The Off-Farm Impacts.* World Wildlife Fund 1985 $15.00. ISBN 0-89164-086-X. Discusses how humans cause much of our annual erosion and how they can control it.

Coates, Donald R. *Environmental Geology.* Wiley 1981 o.p. Geology as applied to water, sewage, scenery, and similar concerns. A handbook for modern living.

———. *Geology and Society.* Routledge, Chapman & Hall 1985 o.p. A handbook for citizens covering minerals, fuels, water, geologic hazards (eruptions, quakes, slides, floods), engineering geology, pollution, waste, resource management, and political regulation.

Compton, Robert R. *Geology in the Field*. Wiley 1985 $37.95. ISBN 0-471-82902-1. Stresses the high cost of fieldwork and the importance of recognizing key geologic features the first time around. This handbook of techniques is an essential tool for anyone who goes out to look at the rocks in place.

Couniham, Martin. *A Dictionary of Energy*. Routledge 1981 o.p. Covers not only fuels, but also power from the sun, wind, tides, underground streams, and technology.

Crozier, Michael J. *Landslides: Causes, Consequences, and Environment*. Routledge Chapman & Hall 1986 $57.50. ISBN 0-7099-0790-7. Describes how landslides work, where they occur, when, and why. Practical geology for the engineer and for anyone living near slopes.

Eckes, Alfred E. *The United States and the Global Struggle for Minerals*. U. of Tex. Pr. 1979 $9.95. ISBN 0-292-78511-9. Covers the importing of mineral resources in U.S. domestic and foreign relations.

Epstein, Samuel S., Lester O. Brown, and Carl Pope. *Hazardous Waste in America*. Sierra 1983 $12.95. ISBN 0-87156-807-1. Discusses how waste from empty aluminum cans and spent uranium rods affects our environment—landfills, ground water, and scenery.

Frazier, Kendrick. *The Violent Face of Nature: Severe Phenomena and Natural Disasters*. Morrow 1979 o.p. Tells how thunderstorms, tornadoes, lightning, hail, floods, hurricanes, blizzards, volcanoes, and earthquakes happen and what can be done about them.

Gere, James M., and Haresh C. Shah. *Terra Non Firma: Understanding and Preparing for Earthquakes*. Stanford Alumni Assn. 1984 $12.95. ISBN 0-685-59010-0. Written by earthquake engineers at Stanford University, California, for potential victims. Given the information, mere common sense can help.

Griggs, Gary B., and John A. Gilchrist. *Geologic Hazards, Resources, and Environmental Planning*. Wadsworth Pub. 1983 o.p. Explains how industrialization and population growth increase the risk of death and destruction, as well as the demand for water, minerals, and energy; thus the necessity for environmental planning.

Jensen, Mead L., and Alan M. Bateman. *Economic Mineral Deposits*. Wiley 1981 o.p. Textbook covering the geological problems associated with the location and nature of ore bodies in relation to mining. Not overly technical.

Kiersch, George A., and others, eds. *Engineering Geology Case Histories*. Geol. Soc. of Amer. 1974 $12.50. Describes how knowledge of geologic materials and natural forces affected various construction projects—and, in some cases, their catastrophic collapse and failure.

Lahee, Frederic H. *Field Geology*. McGraw 1961 o.p. Handbook of conventions and methods of mapping rocks as they occur in the field.

Langenkamp, Robert D. *The Illustrated Petroleum Reference Dictionary*. Penn Well Bks. 1985 $69.95. ISBN 0-87814-272-X. Entries relate mainly to engineering and business.

Link, Peter K. *Basic Petroleum Geology*. Oil & Gas 1987 $40.00. ISBN 0-930972-10-4. Exceptional treatise on all aspects of petroleum geology, from exploration to production.

Menard, Henry W. *Geology, Resources, and Society: An Introduction to Earth Science*. W. H. Freeman 1974 o.p. Stresses practical applications.

Miller, Eugene Willard. *Environmental Hazards*. ABC-CLIO 1990 $39.50. ISBN 0-87436-234-2. Discusses disposal of radioactive and toxic wastes.

Moseley, Frank. *Methods in Field Geology*. W. H. Freeman 1981 o.p. Points out that the "black boxes" of computer-age technology have not entirely displaced field boots, rock hammer, and compass.

Odell, Peter R. *Oil and World Power*. Viking Penguin 1983 o.p. Discusses politics, economics, and resources, here at home and in the Middle East.

Pirajno, Franco. *Hydrothermal Mineral Deposits*. Spr.-Verlag 1992 $169.00. ISBN 0-387-52517-3. Good and complete discussion of hydrothermal mineral deposits around the world.

Pitts, John. *A Manual of Geology for Civil Engineers.* Halsted Pr. 1985 $38.00. ISBN 9971-97812-1. Stresses the mechanical properties of rocks and soil, effects of weathering and erosion, and how to read geologic maps, record drill cores, and describe rocks.

Ross, Charles A., and June R. Ross. *Geology of Coal.* Van Nos. Reinhold 1983 o.p. Many books on coal are limited to individual beds, mines, or basins. This collection ranges much more widely.

Rossbacher, Lisa A. *Career Opportunities in Geology and the Earth Sciences.* P-H Gen. Ref. & Trav. 1982 $7.95. ISBN 0-688-05220-1. Gives job descriptions, some by scientists working in government, industry, and schools.

Skinner, Brian J., ed. *Earth's Energy and Mineral Resources.* Kaufmann 1980 o.p. Papers from *American Scientist* explore the question of where, in the next few decades, we can find fuels and minerals for more than five billion people.

Weston, Rae. *Strategic Minerals: A World Survey.* Rowman 1984 $60.50. ISBN 0-86598-165-5. Survey of minerals that are essential to advanced technology but whose ore deposits are scarce and isolated.

White, Gilbert F., ed. *Natural Hazards: Local, National, Global.* OUP 1974 $11.95. ISBN 0-19-501757-9. Studies of human responses to such natural events as floods in New Zealand, volcanic eruptions in Hawaii, and the earthquake threat in California.

Whittow, John. *Disasters: The Anatomy of Environmental Hazards.* U. of GA Pr. 1980 o.p. Based on the premise that knowing how such things happen is the first step in preventing or avoiding them.

PALEONTOLOGY

Paleontology is the science of ancient life. One of the simplest and most obvious means of studying the life from the geologic past is through the study of fossils. A fossil is defined as a remnant of an ancient life form. This then brings to mind many questions, such as the following: What is the name of this shell? Here is a bone—what did the whole animal look like? Paleontologists ask much more: When did it live? Under what conditions? In water? How deep? In what salinity? With what other life? In short, paleontologists use the evidence of fossils to reconstruct former environments.

For perhaps a billion years, life forms have been immensely varied—nowadays, so are books about animals and plants of the geologic past. Some elementary guides to fossils do exist, but most describe only a limited range of fossils or those found in a limited area. Those may suffice, but a reader wanting to know much about fossils should begin with a biology book describing life in our own time and also one on general geology. Next should be an introduction to historical geology, which will outline the physical history of the earth and also describe the animals and plants that lived at various times in the geologic past.

Studies of paleontology normally go from the simple to the complex. First invertebrate animals, then vertebrates. Often forgotten when one thinks of paleontology are plant fossils. Leaves, logs, fern fronds, and tree bark can be fossilized and preserved just like shells and bone material. Also keep in mind microfossils, such as one-celled animals, and ancient spores and pollen. Beyond these are reconstructions of ancient environments, studies of assemblages (fauna and flora that lived in the same environment), and the great mysteries of earliest life and evolutionary change.

Evolution remains a provocative word, although paleontologists think of it as a mechanism following present-day physical laws rather than as an alternative to ultimate origin. Readable and informative books on the subject are plentiful.

Bakker, Robert. *The Dinosaur Heresies: New Theories Unlocking the Mystery of the Dinosaurs and Their Extinction.* Ed. by Maria Guarnaschelli. Morrow 1986 $24.95. ISBN 0-688-04287-2. Contradicts the long-held notion that all dinosaurs were coldblooded, laid eggs, and had little intelligence.

Casanova, Richard, and Ronald Ratkevich. *An Illustrated Guide to Fossil Collecting.* Naturegraph 1981 $8.95. ISBN 0-87961-113-8. Guide to fossil identification and collection. For laypeople and beginners.

Case, Gerard R. *A Pictorial Guide to Fossils.* Krieger 1992 repr. of 1982 ed. $49.50. ISBN 0-89464-678-8. Arranges fossils by their zoological classification.

Charig, Alan. *A New Look at the Dinosaurs.* Facts on File 1985 $29.25. ISBN 0-8160-1167-2. Good mix of scholarship, writing, and artwork.

Cleal, Christopher J., ed. *Plant Fossils in Geologic Investigation: The Paleozoic.* P-H 1991. ISBN 0-13-680877-8. Contributors discuss uses of plant fossils in understanding past geologic environments.

Colbert, Edwin H. *A Fossil-Hunter's Handbook: My Life with Dinosaurs and Other Friends.* Dutton 1980 o.p. Autobiography of one of the most widely known vertebrate paleontologists and former curator of the American Museum of Natural History (1930–70), New York.

Darwin, Charles. *Voyage of the Beagle.* Doubleday 1962 $9.95. ISBN 0-385-02767-2. Record of Darwin's observations during his five-year cruise. Supplied evidence that Lyell was right: the physical laws of the present sufficed to explain all geologic phenomena.

Eldredge, Niles. *Fossils.* Abrams 1991 $65.00. ISBN 0-8109-3305-5. Emphasizes the beauty of fossils in excellent color photographs of classic fossils examples.

———. *Unfinished Synthesis: Biological Hierarchies and Modern Evolutionary Thought.* OUP 1985 $29.95. ISBN 0-19-503633-6. Based on the premise that evolution is much more than merely a gradual development of species throughout geologic time. Evolution also concerns distribution and adaptation to environment and may involve episodic changes.

Fortey, Richard. *Fossils: The Key to the Past.* HUP 1991 $29.95. ISBN 0-674-31135-3. Shows how fossils can provide clues about past geologic environments.

Glut, Donald F. *The New Dinosaur Dictionary.* Carol Pub. Group 1982 $19.95. ISBN 0-8065-0782-9. An earlier version by the same author was merely adequate; this one is much improved. Many drawings are included.

Goldring, Roland. *Fossils in the Field.* Halsted Pr. 1991 $39.95. ISBN 0-470-21679-4. Discusses field strategies for sampling, collection, and identification of fossils.

Gould, Stephen Jay. *Ever Since Darwin: Reflections in Natural History.* Norton 1992 $9.95. ISBN 0-393-30818-9. An innovative thinker in evolutionary theory, Gould discourses on Darwin, recounts Cambrian history, and evicts Velikovsky (a later-day catastrophist).

———. *The Flamingo's Smile: Reflections in Natural History.* Norton 1987 repr. of 1985 ed. $10.95. ISBN 0-393-30375-6. Consists of wide-ranging essays on many topics, including the earth sciences.

———. *Hen's Teeth and Horse's Toes: Further Reflections in Natural History.* Norton 1993 $10.95. ISBN 0-393-31103-1. "Probes controversies, oddities and discoveries in modern evolutionary biology in a wonderful collection of essays, rich in ideas . . ." (*Publishers Weekly*).

———. *The Mismeasure of Man.* Norton 1993 $9.95. ISBN 0-393-31067-1. Talks about mistakes—honest and otherwise—in the practice of science.

———. *Ontogeny and Phylogeny.* HUP 1977 $35.00. ISBN 0-674-63940-5. This is Gould in the professional mode: the history of evolutionary theory revisited. Technical, but irresistible reading.

———. *The Panda's Thumb: More Reflections in Natural History.* Norton 1992 $9.95. ISBN 0-393-30819-7. Gould revisits Piltdown, describes episodic evolution, speculates on the dumbness—or otherwise—of dinosaurs.

Johanson, Donald, and Maitland Edey. *Lucy: The Beginnings of Humankind.* Warner Bks. 1982 o.p. Discovery and controversy surrounding fossils of early man in east Africa.

Kurtén, Bjorn. *On Evolution and Fossil Mammals.* Col. U. Pr. 1988 $40.00. ISBN 0-231-05068-3. Analyzes evolutionary strategies and discusses evolution and development of several mammal groups.

Laporte, Leo, ed. *The Fossil Record and Evolution.* W. H. Freeman 1982 o.p. Semitechnical articles from *Scientific American* that provide a readable overview of the evolution of life.

McFall, Russell P., and Jay C. Wollin. *Fossils for Amateurs: A Guide to Collecting and Preparing Invertebrate Fossils.* Van Nos. Reinhold 1983 $19.95. ISBN 0-442-26348-1. From conodonts to mammoths, this is a practical guide, giving advice on reading maps and on collecting and labeling specimens.

McKerrow, W. S., ed. *The Ecology of Fossils: An Illustrated Guide.* MIT Pr. 1981 o.p. Shows and discusses assemblages—animals and plants that occurred together in life—in a typical environment for every geologic system since the Precambrian.

Matthews, William H., III. *Fossils: An Introduction to Prehistoric Life.* B&N Imports 1962 o.p. Useful, reasonable handbook for the casual fossil hunter who wants to know more.

Nield, E. W. *Drawing and Understanding Fossils.* Pergamon 1987 $40.00. ISBN 0-08-033941-7. Uses sketching techniques to help the reader look at details in fossils. Drawing or artistic skills not needed.

Norman, David. *The Illustrated Encyclopedia of Dinosaurs.* Crescent Bks. 1985 o.p. In works like this, anyone can take the text or leave it alone.

Raup, David M., and Steven M. Stanley. *Principles of Paleontology.* W. H. Freeman 1978 $41.95. ISBN 0-7167-0022-0. Good introduction about how fossils provide new clues bearing on plate tectonics and much else.

Rhodes, Frank H. T., and others. *Fossils. Golden Guide Ser.* Western Pub. 1962 $2.95. ISBN 0-307-24411-3. Makes the subject intelligible to young readers and also informative to adults.

Sattler, Helen Roney. *The Illustrated Dinosaur Dictionary.* Lothrop 1983 o.p. Of the 300 or so kinds of dinosaurs described here, nearly 100 were discovered and named since about 1960.

Schopf, Thomas J. M. *Paleoceanography.* HUP 1980 $35.00. ISBN 0-674-65215-0. Devoted exclusively to the history of the oceans—their physics, chemistry, climatology, and biology.

———, ed. *Models in Paleobiology.* Freeman Cooper 1972 $14.00. ISBN 0-87735-325-5. Says paleontologists should turn from collecting and describing fossils and stress interpretation of the evolution and distribution of life.

Simpson, George Gaylord. *Fossils and the History of Life.* W. H. Freeman 1983 $32.95. ISBN 0-7167-1564-3. An eminent paleontologist cites evidence in the rocks for evolution.

———. *Horses: The Story of the Horse Family in the Modern World and through Sixty Million Years of History.* OUP 1951 o.p. Horses, like dinosaurs and trilobites, rank as favorites among fossil hunters and students of evolution.

———. *Meaning of Evolution: A Study of the History of Life and Its Significance for Man.* Yale U. Pr. 1967 $16.00. ISBN 0-300-00229-7. Readable and influential account for nonspecialists.

Skinner, Brian J., ed. *Paleontology and Paleoenvironments.* Kaufmann 1981 o.p. Experts discuss (in *American Scientist*) life in the geologic past: where the ancient animals and plants lived, how they evolved, and what became of them.

Stanley, Steven M. *The New Evolutionary Timetable: Fossils, Genes, and the Origin of Species.* Basic 1984 $8.95. ISBN 0-465-05014-X. Presents the idea that the *tempo* of evolution included changes in short rapid bursts (rapid as geologic time goes).

Stearn, Colin, and Robert L. Carroll. *Paleontology, The Record of Life.* Wiley 1989 $49.95. ISBN 0-471-84528-0. Illustrates and traces the record of life on earth via good illustrations of key fossils groups.

Steel, Rodney, and Anthony P. Harvey, eds. *The Encyclopedia of Prehistoric Life.* McGraw 1979 o.p. Largely descriptive (e.g., brachiopods) but also expository (e.g., evolution).

In depicting fossils the line drawings used here are often more informative than photographs. Includes charts and brief biographies.

Stewart, Wilson N. *Paleobotany and the Evolution of Plants*. Cambridge U. Pr. 1983 $39.95. ISBN 0-521-23315-1. Rather technical text, but references are extensive and useful.

Thompson, Ida. *The Audubon Society Field Guide to North American Fossils*. Knopf 1982 $13.50. Includes maps, descriptions, and other aids to identification.

Thulborn, Tony. *Dinosaur Tracks*. Routledge Chapman & Hall 1990 $69.95. ISBN 0-412-32890-9. Deals with the search for, preservation, analysis, and significance of dinosaur tracks.

Tiffney, Bruce H., ed. *Geologic Factors and the Evolution of Plants*. Yale U. Pr. 1985 o.p. Explains that ancient environments may have been quite different from now, even though controlled by the same physical laws.

Wilford, John Noble, Jr. *The Riddle of the Dinosaur*. Knopf 1985 $24.95. ISBN 0-394-52763-1. Presents evidence that some dinosaurs, at least, were warmblooded and that they may have died out quite rapidly after an asteroid struck the earth.

CHRONOLOGY OF AUTHORS

Hutton, James. 1726–1797
Lyell, Charles. 1797–1875
Powell, John Wesley. 1834–1902
Gilbert, Grove Karl. 1843–1918
Davis, William Morris. 1850–1934
Shaw, William Napier. 1854–1945
Tyrrell, Joseph Burr. 1858–1957

Bjerknes, Vilhelm Friman Koren. 1862–1951
Richter, Charles Francis. 1900–1985
Cousteau, Jacques-Yves. 1910-
McPhee, John. 1931–
Vine, Frederick John. 1939–
Ballard, Robert Duane. 1942–

BALLARD, ROBERT DUANE. 1942–

Robert Ballard was born in Wichita, Kansas, and educated at the University of California at Santa Barbara, the University of Hawaii, the University of Southern California, and the University of Rhode Island, where he received his Ph.D. in 1974. Part explorer, part geologist, part oceanographer, and part marine engineer, Ballard has worked at the Woods Hole Oceanographic Institute in Falmouth, Massachusetts, since 1969. He is currently director of the Center for Marine Exploration there.

Ballard is perhaps best known to the general public with regard to the luxury liner *Titanic*. Ballard organized and participated in the expedition that discovered the ship in 1985. More important, however, is his work in designing underwater survey vehicles and in participating in dives to explore the ocean floor. His work in marine design and engineering, in particular, has led to a dramatic increase in the scope of deep sea exploration. In the 1960s, Ballard helped develop the *Alvin*, a deep-sea, three-man submersible equipped with a remote controlled mechanical arm for collecting specimens from the ocean floor. *Alvin* and Ballard played an important role in mid-ocean studies, including exploration of the Mid-Atlantic Ridge and dives to the Cayman Trough, a 24,000-foot-deep gash in the ocean floor south of Cuba. Ballard also was part of the Galapagos Hydrothermal Expedition in 1977, which discovered and investigated deep-sea thermal vents spouting mineral-rich water from volcanic cracks in the Earth's crust. In the 1980s, Ballard helped develop the *Argo-Jason* unmanned submersible system, the most advanced craft of its kind. *Argo* is a 16-foot submersible vehicle and *Jason* is a self-propelled robot tethered to *Argo*. The search for the Titanic was undertaken as a test of the *Argo-Jason* system; the success of the expedition demonstrated its capabilities and, according to Ballard, "ushered in a new era of undersea exploration."

The author of several bestselling books on deep-sea exploration, Ballard also contributes regularly to *National Geographic* and other magazines and he has produced several videotapes of deep-sea expeditions. His reputation as a "science populizer" has prompted harsh criticism from some of his scientific colleagues. Ballard is married with two children. In 1985, he was one of four scientists to be awarded a Secretary of the Navy Research Chair in Oceanography, an award that carries with it an $800,000 grant for oceanographic research.

BOOKS BY BALLARD

Bright Shark. Delacorte 1992 $20.00. ISBN 0-385-29887-0. A novel about the deployment of undersea robot vehicles to find and explore the wreck of a long-lost Israeli submarine suspected of carrying nuclear materials.

Discovery of the Bismarck. Warner Bks. 1990 $35.00. ISBN 0-446-51386-5. Interweaves an account of the ship's discovery with an account of its last voyage.

Discovery of the Titanic. Warner Bks. 1989 $17.95. ISBN 0-446-38912-9. Chronicles Ballard's search for and discovery of the ship; well-illustrated.

Exploring Our Living Planet. Natl. Geog. 1983 $19.95. ISBN 0-87044-459-X. Magnificently illustrated look at Earth's natural wonders.

Exploring the Bismarck: The Real-Life Quest to Find Hitler's Greatest Battleship. Scholastic Inc. 1993 $6.95. ISBN 0-590-44269-1. Account of Ballard's search for the World War II battleship; suitable for young readers.

Exploring the Titanic. Scholastic Inc. 1991 $14.95. ISBN 0-590-41953-6. Details the construction of the ship and its maiden voyage and narrates Ballard's search for and discovery of the luxury liner. Suitable for young readers.

BJERKNES, VILHELM FRIMAN KOREN. 1862–1951

Bjerknes, a meteorologist and physicist, is considered one of the founders of the science of meteorology. Born in Norway, his work and writings laid the foundation for modern weather forecasting.

He began his career in science under the tutelege of his father, a mathematics professor, and later became an assistant to, and collaborator with, the famed German physicist HEINRICH HERTZ. This strong interest in physics and mathematics ultimately provided him with the background and understanding necessary for the formulation of his circulation theorems, which combined hydrodynamics and thermodynamics. He applied his discoveries to large-scale motions of the atmosphere and oceans, which in turn led to the understanding of air masses and their movements. It is this aspect of his work for which Bjerknes is most noted. Bjerknes's later research in weather prediction was supported by the Carnegie Foundation, which awarded him an annual stipend that began in 1905 and continued until the entry of the United States into World War II in 1941.

During his lifetime, Bjerknes held faculty positions at several major European universities and founded the Bergen Geophysical Institute in Norway. He profoundly influenced the career of his son Jacob, also a meteorologist, who discovered the origin of low-pressure areas and fronts that separate air masses.

BOOK BY BJERKNES

Dynamic Meteorology and Hydrography. 2 vols. Carnegie Inst. 1950 o.p.

BOOK ABOUT BJERKNES

Friedman, Robert M. *Appropriating the Weather: Vilhelm Bjerknes and the Construction of a Modern Meteorology.* Cornell Univ. Pr. 1993 $39.95. ISBN 0-8014-2062-8. Shows how Bjerknes "appropriated" the weather, gathering resources from the needs of aviators, fishers, and farmers for more accurate weather predictions.

COUSTEAU, JACUES-YVES. 1910–

Jacques Cousteau is well known throughout the world for his undersea explorations. Born near Bordeaux, in St. André de Cubzac, France, Cousteau attended the naval academy in Brest and then joined the French navy and entered the naval flying school. When an automobile accident cut short his plans for naval aviation, he became interested in diving instead.

During World War II, Cousteau worked with other divers in the French underground, and after the war this group formed an undersea research team in the navy. In 1951 he outfitted an old naval minesweeper, the *Calypso*, as a research laboratory and diving platfrom and began his own undersea explorations. In 1957, Cousteau was appointed director of the oceanographic museum of Monaco. A few years later, in 1963, he began a series of underwater explorations called Conshelf, in which divers spent long periods of time on the ocean floor.

Cousteau's books and especially his film documentaries can be credited with popularizing undersea exploration and discoveries. The film version of his book, *The Silent World* (1953), won an Oscar as did a film about his Conshelf explorations entitled *World Without Sun* (1965). In 1973 Cousteau founded the Cousteau Society, a nonprofit organization for the protection of the marine environment.

BOOKS BY COUSTEAU

The Living Sea. (coauthored with James Dugan). Lyons & Burford 1988 $12.95. ISBN 0-941130-73-8. A sequel to *The Silent World* that shows Cousteau's role in the latest developments in undersea exploration.
The Silent World. (coauthored with Frederick Dumas). Lyons & Burford 1987 repr. of 1953 ed. $13.95. ISBN 2-85089-227-X. Makes readers feel like eyewitnesses to undersea diving history.
Undersea Discoveries of Jacques-Yves Cousteau. 3 vols. Arrowood Pr. 1989 $49.98. ISBN 0-88486-017-5. Detailed look at many of Cousteau's discoveries.

BOOK ABOUT COUSTEAU

Madsen, Axel. *Cousteau: An Unauthorized Biography.* Beaufort SC 1986 $17.95. ISBN 0-8253-0386-9. An engaging and readable account of Cousteau's fascinating life and work.

DAVIS, WILLIAM MORRIS. 1850–1934

Davis, an American geographer, geologist, and meteorologist, began his varied career at the age of 20 as a meteorologist with the Argentine Meteorological Observatory. He later joined the faculty at Harvard University, where he taught for 36 years. In the 1870s his interest shifted from meteorology to geography, and he began the study of landforms and landform evolution. Davis is credited with introducing the ideas of cyclic erosion to landscape development, proposing that the crust of the earth in a certain area is initially uplifted and is then eroded downward, passing through a precise series of sequential stages. His most noteworthy essay, "The Rivers and Valleys of Pennsylvania," introduced these notions of cyclic landscape evolution.

Davis is known as the great synthesizer of the modern science of geomorphology and is recognized as the leader of the "America school" of physiographers. Although he was a prolific writer in all three of his fields of study, he is best remembered for his works in geography.

After his retirement from Harvard in 1912, Davis remained active, lecturing and conducting field studies until his death in 1934.

BOOKS BY DAVIS

Elementary Meteorology. Ginn & Co. 1894 o.p.

Elementary Physical Geography. Ginn & Co. 1894 o.p.

Geographical Essays. Ed. by Douglas W. Johnson. Dover 1954 o.p. An unabridged republication of the 1909 edition. Contains "The Rivers and Valleys of Pennsylvania."

BOOK ABOUT DAVIS

King, Philip B., and Stanley A. Schumm. *The Physical Geography of William Morris Davis.* Geoabstracts 1980 o.p.

GILBERT, GROVE KARL. 1843–1918

Gilbert has had a profound influence on the thinking of geologists all over the world. He set the standards for the application of the scientific method—the creation and testing of hypotheses—to the science of geology. His skill in making exemplary observations and his meticulous weighing of alternatives have become the hallmark of field geologists everywhere.

Gilbert was born near Rochester, New York, in 1843. At a very early age, he showed not only a genius for making detailed observations but also a vivid and creative imagination. As early as 5 or 6 years old, he was observing the growth of onion seedlings in his father's garden. After graduating from the University of Rochester at the age of 19, he joined several geological expeditions, starting in Ohio and continuing with trips to many western states. Although his detailed studies of the Henry Mountains in southeastern Utah and Lake Bonneville near Salt Lake City were his most noteworthy field accomplishments, his influence on geologic thought and investigative field techniques is his most important contribution.

Gilbert was the only person ever to have served twice as the president of the Geological Society of America. He was also the president of seven scientific societies and was the recipient of many awards and medals from American and foreign scientific organizations.

At the age of 75, Gilbert was still active in geology. He died en route to California to do fieldwork.

BOOK BY GILBERT

Report of the Geology of the Henry Mountains. Ayer 1978 repr. of 1877 ed. $21.00. ISBN 0-405-10441-3

BOOK ABOUT GILBERT

Pyne, Stephen J. *Grove Karl Gilbert: A Great Engine of Research.* U. of Tex. Pr. 1980 $22.50. ISBN 0-292-72719-4

GOULD, STEPHEN J. 1941–

[SEE Chapter 2 in this volume.]

HUTTON, JAMES. 1726–1797

Hutton is acknowledged as the father of the science of geology. Born and educated in Scotland, his published works laid the groundwork for others who profoundly influenced the development of geologic thought. Hutton is credited with originating perhaps the most important tenet of geology—uniformitarianism—the concept that the earth's present features and processes explain its past. Summarized succinctly by the phrase "the present is the key to the past," Hutton's work soon becomes familiar to every beginning geology student.

As a student, Hutton studied medicine but decided against a career as a physician; he chose instead to pursue scientific research. He was encouraged by friends to farm a plot of land his father had bequeathed to him with the same care and scientific knowledge that he would give a surgical procedure or a chemical experiment. In so doing, he observed that there was a relationship between the rock and mineral particles in the soil and the parent bedrock below. He noted, too, that certain crops had an affinity for certain soils and that rainwater washed soil from the fields, forming gullies.

Hutton was fond of walking and studying rocks around his native Edinburgh. He later studied and made similar observations in other parts of the British Isles and on the Continent as well. He kept detailed notes and published them in a two-volume work shortly before his death. His *Theory of the Earth* (1795) contained all of his theories and observations, and the evidence on which they were based. Hutton died in 1797 before his third volume was published. Much of Hutton's work, however, was popularized and made more readable by John Playfair (1748–1819) in a book published in 1802 entitled *Illustrations of the Huttonian Theory of the Earth*.

BOOK BY HUTTON

Theory of the Earth, with Proofs and Illustrations. 1795. 2 vols. Lubrecht & Cramer 1960 repr. of 1795 ed. $95.00. ISBN 3-7682-0025-6

BOOKS ABOUT HUTTON

Bailey, E. B. *James Hutton: Founder of Modern Geology.* Elsevier 1971 $20.50. ISBN 0-686-43854-X

Playfair, John. *Illustrations of the Huttonian Theory of the Earth.* Edinburgh 1802 o.p.

LYELL, CHARLES. 1797–1875

Lyell was born in Kinnordy, Scotland. His father was a naturalist, and Lyell grew up surrounded by books on natural history, geology, and other sciences. He entered Oxford University at the age of 19 after a boarding-school education that was periodically interrupted by poor health. There his interest in geology was heightened. Although he studied law, he gave up legal work to study rocks and fossils.

His contribution to geology is twofold. First, he showed that the earth is constantly changing, not by a series of worldwide catastrophes followed by new creations, but by slow, gradual processes. Like JAMES HUTTON, he believed and taught that present-day processes were the ones that shaped the past. It was the worldwide publication of Lyell's treatises and texts that led to the general acceptance of the principle of uniformitarianism, first put forth by Hutton. Second, Lyell contributed the principle of faunal succession and the notion of the time sequence of events. These were evidenced from spatial relationships among strata, faults, and intrusions.

The data on which Lyell's contributions are based were gathered on numerous field excursions, most notably in southern Europe, the United States, and Canada. During these trips, Lyell collected numerous samples that he and his wife meticulously categorized and labeled. His writings show that he was also interested in, and concerned about, human problems, as well as problems of science. He touches upon social reforms in England and the problems of slavery in the United States. Lyell was a prolific writer, summarizing his thoughts, contributions, and achievements in these major works: *Principles of Geology* (1830, 1831, 1833), *Antiquity of Man*, and *Travels in America*.

His health and strength declined after the death of his wife in 1873, and he died two years later. He was buried in Westminster Abbey.

BOOKS BY LYELL

The Antiquity of Man. Dent 1927 o.p.

Principles of Geology. 3 vols. Lubrecht & Cramer 1970 repr. of 1833 ed. $100.00. ISBN 3-7682-0685-8. Explores Lyell's argument for uniformitarianism, the view that processes now visibly acting in the natural world are essentially the same as those that have acted throughout the history of the earth.

Travels in North America, in the Years 1841–42, with Geological Observations on the United States, Canada, and Nova Scotia. Edinburgh 1852 o.p.

BOOKS ABOUT LYELL

Gould, Stephen Jay. *Times Arrow, Time's Cycle: Myth and Metaphor in the Discovery of Geological Time.* HUP 1987 $20.00. ISBN 0-674-89198-8. Fine work of literary and pictorial analysis as well as the history of science.

Wilson, Leonard G. *Lyell, Charles, Sir.* Yale U. Pr. 1972 o.p.

MCPHEE, JOHN. 1931–

Born in Princeton, New Jersey, the writer John McPhee was educated at Princeton University. Since 1964, he has worked as a staff writer for the *New Yorker*, and he has also published a number of nonfiction books on offbeat subjects and people. Among his interests is geology, and he has written several works on the subject. Although not a scientist, his research and precise observations of natural phenomena have given him a solid grasp of his subject matter. Moreover, his narrative style and lively presentation of detail help bring alive his diverse topics to the general audience.

BOOKS BY MCPHEE

Assembling California. FS&G 1993 $20.00. ISBN 0-374-10645-2. Summarizes 15 years of revelatory theories about the nature of the geologic process known as plate tectonics.

Basin and Range. FS&G 1981 $19.95. ISBN 0-374-10914-1. Looks at these geologic formations with the knowledge of a geologist and the style of a novelist.

In Suspect Terrain. FS& G 1983 $19.95. ISBN 0-374-51794-0. Chronicles a journey amidst great Western rock formations, in which McPhee is accompanied by an accomplished geologist.

The Pine Barrens. FS&G 1978 $17.95. ISBN 0-374-23360-8. Reports on the interaction of people and geology.

Rising from the Plains. FS&G 1986 $19.95. ISBN 0-374-25082-0. Science of the northern Rockies by a man who grew up in Wyoming and has first-hand knowledge of the region.

POWELL, JOHN WESLEY. 1834–1902

Powell was born in western New York. His family later moved to Ohio and then to Wisconsin, where he began his adult life as a teacher. For about nine years, he taught and took time to study at colleges in Ohio and Illinois.

When the Civil War began, he enlisted and quickly rose to the rank of major, laying out roads and designing bridges. Powell was wounded at the Battle of Shiloh and lost his right arm. Because of these events, for the remainder of his life he was referred to as Major Powell or One-arm Powell.

After the war, he organized several expeditions down the Colorado River, which heretofore had not come under scientific study. It was during these trips and others that he formulated the concept of base level and antecedent streams. Although his ideas and observations are noteworthy, Powell was not a prolific writer, and his writings were not scholarly in style.

Powell became the president of the U.S. Geological Survey, a position from which he lobbied congressmen and senators for funding for topographic mapping and technical reports. He was a strong proponent of developing the American West on a sound and realistic foundation. Powell died in Maine during the summer of 1902.

Book by Powell

The Exploration of the Colorado River and Its Canyons. 1895. Argosy-Antiquarian 1964 o.p.

Books about Powell

Darrah, William Culp. *Powell of the Colorado.* Princeton U. Pr. 1951 o.p.
Stegner, Wallace Earle. *Beyond the Hundredth Meridian, John Wesley Powell and the Second Opening of the West.* Viking Penguin 1992 $12.00. ISBN 0-14-015994-0
Terrell, John Upton. *The Man Who Rediscovered America, a Biography of John Wesley Powell.* Weybright 1969 o.p.

RICHTER, CHARLES FRANCIS. 1900–1985

Born near Hamilton, Ohio, Charles Richter was one of the pioneers of seismology, the study of the origin and intensity of earthquakes. Many people are familiar with his name in association with the Richter scale, an earthquake measurement regularly used in the reporting of earthquakes by newspapers, radio, and television. The Richter scale assigns numerical ratings to the energy released by an earthquake. The scale is based on the logarithm of the maximum amplitude of the earthquake waves observed on a seismograph—adjusted for the distance from the epicenter of the earthquake. On the Richter scale, an earthquake with a magnitude greater than 5.5 can cause significant damage.

In 1928, Richter received a Ph.D. in theoretical physics from the California Institute of Technology and went on to work as a seismologist with the Seismological Laboratory of the Carnegie Institute in Pasadena, California. While there, he collaborated with Beno Gutenburg to develop the scale that bears his name, which was introduced in 1935. Richter never referred to the instrument as the Richter scale. He thought it was unfair to Beno Gutenburg, his friend and colleague. Richter always called it "the magnitude scale" or just "the scale."

In 1937, Richter was appointed professor of seismology at the California Institute of Technology, where he taught and conducted research for almost 50 years. In the early 1960s, he advised the city of Los Angeles to remove cornices, parapets, and ornaments from buildings to minimize earthquake damage. In

1971, he was selected to serve as a member of the Los Angeles Earthquake Commission. Richter was widely honored for his seismological research. In 1959, he was awarded a Fulbright Research Scholarship at Tokyo University and was a fellow of several professional organizations, including the Geological Society of America, the American Geophysical Union, the Royal Astronomical Society, and the Royal Society of New Zealand.

BOOKS BY RICHTER

Internal Constitution of the Earth. McGraw 1951 o.p.
Seismicity of the Earth. (coauthored with Beno Gutenburg). Wiley 1954 o.p. Represents the standard reference in the field. Richter's classic work on earth movement and the origin and intensity of earthquakes.

SAGAN, CARL. 1934–

[SEE Chapter 18 in this volume.]

SHAW, WILLIAM NAPIER. 1854–1945

Born in Birmingham, England, William Shaw attended King Edward VI School and Emmanuel College, Cambridge. He then taught at Emmanuel College as well as at the Cavendish Laboratory of Cambridge University. In addition to his teaching responsibilities, Shaw held several positions involving meteorology, including secretary of the Meteorological Council and director of the British Meteorological Office.

Shaw conducted research on the atmosphere, including work on hygrometry, evaporation, and ventilation. He pioneered the use of kites and balloons to transport weather instruments to the upper atmosphere and wrote several books on weather.

BOOKS BY SHAW

Life History of Surface Air Currents. (coauthored with R. Lempfert). Darling & Son Ltd. 1906 o.p.
Manual of Meteorology. 4 vols. Cambridge U. Pr. 1936 $130.00. ISBN 0-404-16230-4. A comprehensive text examining all aspects of the field.
Weather Forecasting. (coauthored with R. Lempfert). Constable 1940 o.p.

TYRRELL, JOSEPH BURR. 1858–1957

A Canadian geologist and mining engineer, Joseph Tyrrell was born in Weston, Ontario, and was educated at the University of Toronto. He is known primarily for his studies of western and northwestern Canada. Tyrrell joined the Geological Survey of Canada in 1881. While on an expedition to the province of Alberta in 1884, he discovered the first dinosaur bones ever found in Canada. A short time later, he discovered one of the nation's largest coal deposits nearby.

During 1893 and 1894, Tyrrell travelled across Canada's Northwest Territories, the largest remaining unexplored area of North America. While on this expedition he mapped over 3,000 miles of wilderness and discovered important deposits of minerals that later would prove to be a great source of wealth for the nation.

In 1898, Tyrrell left the Geological Survey and became a mining engineer and manager, a career he pursued until his death. During his life, Tyrrell wrote many articles about the geology of Canada and about the exploration and early history of the country.

BOOK BY TYRRELL

Documents Relating to the Early History of Hudson Bay. Greenwood 1969 repr. of 1931
   ed. $55.00. ISBN 0-8371-5056-6

VINE, FREDERICK JOHN. 1939–

An English geologist and educator, Frederick Vine has made significant
contributions in the field of plate tectonics. In the early 1960s, his research of
the ocean floor off the coast of Iceland (with colleague Drummond Matthews)
provided conclusive field evidence for the hypothesis of seafloor spreading, an
idea first proposed by Harry Hess of Princeton University in 1960. The seafloor
spreading hypothesis states that oceanic crust forms along the mid-ocean ridges,
spreading laterally in both directions. During their research, Vine and Matthews
discovered alternating magnetic patterns in the igneous rocks on both sides of
the Mid-Atlantic ridge just south of Iceland. This discovery not only supported
the concept of continental drift, but also provided direct evidence for changes
in Earth's geomagnetic field over geologic time. Until the late 1950s, most
geologists thought that the rocks of the ocean floor represented the oldest part
of the Earth's crust. The research of Vine and Matthews, however, showed that
rocks on the ocean floor are actually a relatively newly formed part of Earth's
crust.

Vine was educated in England, receiving his B.A. and Ph.D. in geology from
St. John's College, Cambridge University. From 1965 to 1970, he taught at
Princeton University in the department of Geological and Geophysical Sciences.
He returned to England in the early 1970s and, in 1974, was appointed to his
current position as professor of Environmental Sciences at the University of
East Anglia.

BOOKS BY VINE

Extensional Tectonics Associated With Convergent Plate Boundaries. Scholium Intl. 1981
   $87.00. ISBN 0-85403-161-8
Global Tectonics. Blackwell Sci. 1990 $39.95. ISBN 0-632-02424-0. Comprehensive look
   at the science of plate tectonics and the concept of continental drift.

CHAPTER 20

Physics

Mohamad Nouri and Stephen Kcenich

> The content of physics is the concern of physicists, its effects the concern of all men.
> —FRIEDRICH DÜRRENMATT, *The Physicists*

Physics, formerly called natural philosophy, is concerned with those aspects of nature that can be understood in terms of basic principles and laws. Throughout history, specialized areas of physics broke away to form autonomous fields of science. Physics, however, has retained its original aim: understanding the structure of the natural world and explaining natural phenomena through mathematical techniques combined with observations of nature.

The two basic areas of physics are mechanics and field theory. Mechanics studies the motion of particles or bodies under the influence of internal or external forces. In contrast, field theory studies the origin, nature, and properties of gravitational, electromagnetic, nuclear, and other forces as comprising particular fields. Knowledge gained by physicists in these two areas provides a fundamental understanding of natural phenomena. The ultimate goal of physics is to understand all natural phenomena in terms of forces and fields.

Physics historically has been divided into specific general classes of natural phenomena. These areas, to which the methods of physics had been successfully applied, were classical mechanics, optics, acoustics, electricity, and electromagnetism. These classifications are still used, but they now are branches of applied physics, or technology, rather than divisions of physics. One branch, the field of mathematical analysis, was created primarily to answer questions posed by SIR ISAAC NEWTON's (see also Vol. 4) formulations of classical mechanics.

The modern divisions of physics (atomic, elementary particle, nuclear, plasma, and solid-state) study the behavior of elementary particles, the structure of the atom, and properties of matter in different states and subjected to different temperatures, charges, and forces.

Each area of physics is characterized by its precision and depth of understanding. Physics has created partial theories to describe many phenomena. Yet, the ultimate goal of physics, which many physicists think will be achieved within a century, is the formulation of a unified theory. This theory will reflect the structure and behavior of all natural phenomena in mathematical terms. Other sciences describe and relate phenomena in terms of concepts unique to their particular disciplines. In contrast, physicists always seek to understand phenomena as a special manifestation of the underlying uniform structure of nature. Consequently, the three main characteristics of physics are accurate instrumentation, precision of measurement, and results stated in mathematical terms.

GENERAL PHYSICS

Alvarez, Luis W. *Adventures of a Physicist.* Basic 1987 o.p. "Luis Alvarez's career in experimental physics reads like a scientific adventure story. . . . Science on the cutting edge where life and the laboratory meet" (*American Libraries*).

Bernstein, Jeremy. *The Life It Brings: One Physicist Remembers.* Ticknor & Fields 1987 o.p. "Thoroughly charming story of how one young man under the influence of some remarkable teachers, came to feel the powerful lure of modern physics and its manifold mysteries" (*American Libraries*).

Cadogan, Peter H. *From Quark to Quasar.* Cambridge U. Pr. 1985 o.p. Pictorial journey from the subatomic blur of elementary particles to the farthest and largest astronomical objects known.

Davies, P. C. *The Physics of Time Asymmetry.* U. CA Pr. 1977 $9.95. ISBN 0-520-03247-0. An established physicist discusses the conceptual difficulties inherent in a science that explains time-dependent experience in terms of fundamental physical laws that are time-independent.

Devine, Betsy, and Joel E. Cohen. *Absolute Zero Gravity: A Collection of Jokes, Anecdotes, Limericks and Riddles Revealing the Funny Side of Physics, Biology, Mathematics, and other Branches of Science.* S&S Trade 1992 $8.00. ISBN 0-671-74060-1. Did you know it is uncertain exactly where Heisenberg is buried? And how about the fact that Newton now tends to remain at rest? If you don't get these jokes, perhaps this isn't the book for you. A compendium of scientific and academic humor, with many true anecdotes.

Fairbank, J. D. *Near Zero: Frontiers of Physics.* W. H. Freeman 1988 $59.95. ISBN 0-7169-1831-6. Presents original papers on "near zero" physics that discuss control variables such as temperature, pressure, electric and magnetic fields, gravity, and thermal noise; somewhat technical, but provides an interesting view of physics frontiers.

Feinberg, Gerald. *Solid Clues: Quantum Physics, Molecular Biology and the Future of Science.* S&S Trade 1986 o.p. Concentrates on the rapidly advancing fields of physics and molecular biology; assesses science over the last 40 years and attempts to predict its direction in the next four decades. An authoritative account useful for considerations of public policy.

Feynman, Richard, Robert B. Layton, and Matthew L. Sands. *The Feynman Lectures on Physics: Commemorative Issue.* Vol. 1 Addison-Wesley 1989 $36.75. ISBN 0-685-31190-2

Halliday, David, and others. *Fundamentals of Physics.* Wiley 1993 $68.75. ISBN 0-471-52461-1. Revised, updated, and heuristically enhanced textbook. Forty-nine chapters that cover material through quantum physics and applied theory.

Kafalos, M., and R. Nadeau. *The Conscious Universe: Part and Whole in Modern Physical Theory.* Spr.-Verlag 1993 $19.95. ISBN 0-387-97262-5. Speculates on the "meta" physical more than actual scientific physics. Nevertheless, an interdisciplinary approach to the methodological processes of science and its necessary relation to human consciousness.

Landsberg, P. T., ed. *The Enigma of Time.* Intl. Pubs. Co. 1984 o.p. Anthology of reprinted essays on cosmology, irreversibility, quantum theory, black holes, literature, and art; includes a good introduction and a useful index.

Lederman, Leon, and Dick Teresi. *The God Particle: If the Universe Is the Answer, What Is the Question.* HM 1993 $24.45. ISBN 0-395-55849-2. Lederman, the Nobel-winning experimental physicist and former director of Fermilab, examines science's 2,000-year search for the nature of matter and discusses what grand discoveries may lie ahead.

Lerner, Rita G., and George L. Trigg. *Encyclopedia of Physics.* Addison-Wesley 1980 $111.96. ISBN 0-201-04313-0

Lindley, David. *The End of Physics: The Myth of a Unified Theory.* Basic 1993 $25.00. ISBN 0-465-01548-4. First-rate exposition of the state of science. Lindley is a senior editor of *Science* as well as a Ph.D. in astronomy.

Morrison, Philip, and Phyllis Morrison. *Powers of Ten: About the Relative Size of Things in the Universe.* W. H. Freeman 1991 $32.95. ISBN 0-7167-1409-4. Presents the familiar idea that natural phenomena range in linear dimensions across 42 orders of magnitude and that their characteristics vary accordingly; includes beautiful illustrations.

National Research Council, Physics Survey Committee. *Physics through the 1990s.* 6 vols. National Research Council 1986 o.p. An introductory volume and seven subject volumes. Presents a nontechnical but authoritative survey of recent advances and statements of current important problems in each major field of pure and applied physics. Although the names of prominent researchers and references are not furnished, each January issue of *Physics Today* is the only concise source available for this type and level of information.

Rigden, John S. *Rabi: Scientist and Citizen.* Basic 1989 $9.95. ISBN 0-465-06793-X. "This biography of one of America's leading men of science captures the adventure, the romance, and the excitement of twentieth-century physics" (*American Libraries*).

Spielberg, Nathan, and Byron D. Anderson. *Seven Ideas That Shook the Universe.* Wiley 1987 $32.95. ISBN 0-471-85974-5. Discusses seven ideas basic to modern physics: Copernican astronomy, Newtonian physics, quantum theory, conservation principles, symmetries, relativity, and entropy; written by physicists.

Trefil, James. *The Unexpected Vista: A Physicist's View of Nature.* Ed. by B. Lippmann. Macmillan 1985 o.p. Presents physical explanations for many everyday phenomena, demonstrating that they can be reduced to several general laws.

von Baeyer, Hans C. *The Fermi Solution: Essays on Science.* Random 1993 $19.00. ISBN 0-679-40031-1. Essays on Newtonian, quantum, and astrophysics, as well as new phenomena such as quasi-crystals and nondestructive, noninvasive analytic techniques.

Weisskopf, Victor F. *Knowledge and Wonder: The Natural World as Man Knows It.* MIT Pr. 1979 o.p. A stimulating presentation, illustrating the application of scientific methods by a well-known physicist. Covers many examples of scientific problem solving, while surveying knowledge about the natural world.

Wilczek, Frank, and Betsy Devine. *Longing for Harmonies: Themes and Variations from Modern Physics.* Norton 1989 o.p. "Wilczek and Devine draw compelling analogies between physics and music, both of which thrive on a simple structure based on themes and variations" (*American Libraries*).

Zee, Anthony. *Fearful Symmetry: The Search for Beauty in Modern Physics.* Macmillan 1986 o.p. Explains how symmetry forms the intellectual and aesthetic foundations of modern physics. Also presents arcane and abstract symmetries of particle physics and cosmology for the layperson; written by a well-known physicist.

Reference Works

Abbott, David, ed. *The Biographical Dictionary of Scientists: Physicists.* P. Bedrick Bks. 1984 $28.00. ISBN 0-911745-79-0. A volume of Bedrick's *Biographical Dictionary of Scientists* series that presents 200 short biographies of important physicists; does not include bibliographies but has a convenient glossary and a subject index.

Anderson, Herbert L., ed. *Physics Vade Mecum.* Am. Inst. Physics 1981 $25.00. ISBN 0-88318-289-0. Provides the professional with useful numerical data, definitions, and formulas; covers 22 fields of physics.

Beiser, Arthur. *Concepts of Modern Physics.* McGraw 1987 $45.72. ISBN 0-07-004473-2. A textbook that introduces modern physics to the reader with knowledge of calculus and elementary classical physics. Covers relativity, quantum mechanics, elementary particles, radioactivity, and solid state physics; intended for nonscience majors or the general reader.

Besancon, Robert M. *Encyclopedia of Physics.* Van Nos. Reinhold 1990 $51.95. ISBN 0-442-00522-9. Provides an excellent, recently revised, one-volume encyclopedia, incorporating articles by about 300 contributors. Articles are signed, illustrated, cross-referenced, and offer bibliographies for further reading.

Dictionary of Physics. McGraw 1985 o.p. Brief definitions and technical terms.

Directory of Physics and Astronomy Staff, 1990–1991. Am. Inst. Physics 1990 $60.00. ISBN 0-88318-809-0. Provides addresses and phone numbers of faculty at academic institutions and staff members of research organizations; also lists physics departments and research laboratories throughout the country with their faculty and research scientists.

Driscoll, Walter G., ed. *Handbook of Optics.* McGraw 1978 $129.50. ISBN 0-07-047710-8. A standard handbook.

Fluegge, S. *Encyclopedia of Physics.* Spr.-Verlag 1976 $170.00. ISBN 0-387-07512-7

Halliday, David, and Robert Resnick. *Fundamentals of Physics.* Wiley 1993. $68.75. ISBN 0-471-52461-1. A standard college text that requires knowledge of calculus; a widely used physics textbook.

Handbook of Chemistry and Physics. CRC Pr. annual o.p. The standard reference handbook of physical and chemical reference data.

International Who's Who in Energy and Nuclear Sciences. Gale 1983 o.p. Offers brief biographical entries on workers involved in the generation, storage, and efficient use of energy in 70 countries.

James, Arthur M., and M. P. Lord. *Chemical and Physical Data.* Van Nos. Reinhold 1992. ISBN 0-442-30895-7

Jesse, Andreas. *Physics Terminology.* Fr. & Eur. 1980 $49.95. ISBN 0-8288-22441

Kaye, G. W., and T. H. Laby. *Tables of Physical and Chemical Constants: And Some Mathematical Functions.* Wiley 1986 $59.95. ISBN 0-471-20662-4. Compact and useful set of tables for quick reference.

McGraw-Hill Editors. *Nuclear and Practice Physics Source Book.* McGraw 1989 $49.50. ISBN 0-07-045509-0. Contains about 125 articles. Derived from *McGraw-Hill Encyclopedia of Science and Technology,* 6th edition, 1987.

Olenick, Richard, and others. *Beyond the Mechanical Universe: From Electricity to Modern Physics.* Cambridge U. Pr. $39.95. ISBN 0-521-30430-X. Incorporates video technology into a textbook presentation. The textbook can be read independently or used in conjunction with the video series; includes much interesting historical information and a clear presentation of basic physics.

———. *The Mechanical Universe: Introduction to Mechanics and Heat.* Cambridge U. Pr. 1985 $34.95. ISBN 0-521-30429-6

Parker, Sybil. *McGraw-Hill Encyclopedia of Physics.* McGraw 1993 $95.00. ISBN 0-07-051400-3. Features selected articles from the 1982 edition of the *McGraw-Hill Encyclopedia of Science and Technology.* Articles are authoritative and illustrated; includes bibliographies.

Pasachoff, Jay M., and Marc L. Kutner. *Invitation to Physics.* Addison-Wesley 1985 o.p. A standard, introductory college text that does not require calculus.

Pitt, Valerie H., ed. *The Penguin Dictionary of Physics.* Viking Penguin 1977 $8.95. ISBN 0-14-051071-0

Radzig, A. A., and B. M. Smirnov. *Reference Data on Atoms, Molecules and Ions.* Spr.-Verlag 1985 $99.00. ISBN 0-387-12415-2

Rickard, Teresa. *Barnes and Noble Thesaurus of Physics.* HarpC 1985 $6.95. ISBN 0-06-463582-1

History

Crease, Robert P., and Charles C. Mann. *The Second Creation: Makers of the Revolution in Twentieth-Century Physics.* Macmillan 1985 o.p. Presents a well-reviewed and up-to-date history of twentieth-century physics, concentrating on personalities rather than theories; emphasizes the research in the last two decades to develop a unified theory.

Kevles, Daniel J. *The Physicists: The History of a Scientific Community in Modern America.* HUP 1987 $16.95. ISBN 0-674-66655-0. A landmark study that discusses how American professional physics matured. In the late 1800s American physics was based on institutions for the training of physicists rather than on research problems and research production practiced in Europe. In the late 1920s science became the object of public attention in America, as exemplified by the Einstein boom. The 1930s saw the infusion of Hitler's emigrés and the beginning of big science, which continues to this day. This book examines science during the 1920s and 1930s, as well as portraying the American physics community during these periods.

Motz, Lloyd, and Jefferson Weaver. *The Story of Physics.* Avon 1992 $12.50. ISBN 0-380-71725-5. A newer approach geared toward understanding concepts ranging from pre-Newtonian physics to cosmological quantum mechanics.

Moyer, Albert E. *American Physics in Transition: A History of Conceptual Change in the Late Nineteenth Century.* ISI Pr. 1983 $30.00. ISBN 0-938228-06-4. An easy-to-read account of late nineteenth-century American physics; examines the attitudes of 10 important representative American scientists, illustrating conceptual shifts occurring at this time.

Phillips, Melba, ed. *The Life and Times of Modern Physics.* Am. Inst. Physics 1992 $40.00. ISBN 0-88318-846-5. Compilation of some 60 articles from *Physics Today* including profiles, memoirs, narratives, and histories. Abundantly illustrated with photos.

Roche, J. *Physicists Look Back: Studies in the History of Physics.* IOP Pub. 1990 $99.00. ISBN 0-85274-001-8. Twenty essays pertaining to the history of physics. Full of fascinating material. Valuable contribution.

Snow, C. P. *The Physicists.* Little 1981 o.p. Offers a brief, well-illustrated history of the development of the atomic bomb; written from personal recollections by a contemporary physicist and an outspoken critic of nuclear weapons.

White, Michael S. *The Continuous and the Discreet: Ancient Physical Theories from a Contemporary Perspective.* OUP 1992 $72.00. ISBN 0-19-823952-1. Reconstructs Aristotelian, Epicurean, and Stoic concepts of continuity of space and time in relation to present quantum theoretic notions of atomic descriptions.

ASTROPHYSICS AND COSMOLOGY

Astrophysics is a field that bridges astronomy and physics and specifically studies nonterrestrial physical phenomena. Astrophysics focuses on the velocity, composition, temperature, and other physical characteristics of celestial objects. The planets, sun, and comets of our solar system, as well as distant stars, are commonly studied by astrophysicists. Research is conducted by optical, radio, X-ray, gamma-ray, and spectroscopic detection; special detectors are developed as needed for other portions of the electromagnetic spectrum, as well as for other waves and particles. For example, high-energy astrophysics studies astronomical phenomena with extremely high energy—ranging from 1,000 to 1 billion electrovolts. Because many observational and theoretical discoveries have been made in astrophysics in recent years, some scientists think this period will be known historically as the "golden age" of astrophysics.

Cosmology is the study of the entire universe as a physical system. Modern cosmology studies the form, chemical composition, and origin of the universe.

In the mid-1920s, EDWIN P. HUBBLE studied the distribution of galaxies in space. As a result, he discovered a method to estimate distances to remote galaxies. By counting galaxy images of 1,283 sample celestial regions, Hubble concluded that the distribution of galaxies is homogeneous and isotropic. Hubble's hypothesis was the first to incorporate observational evidence in support of the cosmological principle, which states that at any instant of cosmic time the universe appears the same to all hypothetical observers.

Since the discovery of the "expanding" universe in the 1920s, an important goal of cosmology has been to determine the history of the universe. Unresolved problems in particle physics have triggered the development of a new type of theory in physics, called gauge theory. Gauge theory has resulted in a greatly simplified view of the subatomic world. Recently, the overlapping area between high-energy physics and astronomy has become one of the most exciting fields of modern science. Today, scientists can hypothesize about the nature of the early universe in time to approximately 10 to 40 seconds after the "big bang."

General Works

Barrow, John D., and Joseph Silk. *The Left Hand of Creation: The Origin and Evolution of the Expanding Universe.* Basic 1986 $7.95. ISBN 0-465-03897-2. An informal, easy-to-read, discursive survey of current problems and theories in cosmology; features an essay style and speculative cast.

Barrow, John D., and Frank N. Tipler. *The Anthropic Cosmological Principle.* OUP 1986 $39.95. ISBN 0-19-851949-4. Describes the modern anthropic principle that links global properties to the universe with local structure. Explores the notion that many of the local and global properties of the universe can be derived from the fact of human existence; written for the specialist and layperson.

Bernstein, Jeremy, and Gerald Feinberg. *Cosmological Constants: Papers in Modern Cosmology.* Col. U. Pr. 1989 $53.00. ISBN 0-231-06376-8. Features a translated collection of landmark papers in cosmology; written between 1917 and 1982.

Boslough, John. *Stephen Hawking's Universe.* Morrow 1984 $12.95. ISBN 0-688-03530-2. Summarizes Hawking's biography and contributions to fundamental physics and cosmology; includes Hawking's essay "Is the End in Sight for Theoretical Physics?" as an appendix.

Cameron, A.G.W., ed. *Astrophysics Today.* Am. Inst. Physics 1984 $39.00. ISBN 0-88318-446-X. An anthology of articles originally published in *Physics Today* in the last decade. Covers frontiers of research in the field, including the physics of black holes, white dwarfs, and galactic physics; written for the interested layperson.

Contopoulous, G., and D. Kotsakis. *Cosmology.* Spr.-Verlag 1987 $44.00. ISBN 0-387-16922-9. An up-to-date undergraduate text that introduces modern cosmology. Divided into sections surveying observational data that must be explained by any theory; current theories and concepts of modern cosmology, including the impact of high-energy physics and more profound topics, such as the universality of physical laws, inflation and causation, and the anthropic principle.

Davies, P.C.W. *The Accidental Universe.* Cambridge U. Pr. 1982 $16.95. ISBN 0-521-28692-1. Explores how features of the universe are affected by the values of fundamental constants. For example, if the force of gravity were slightly greater, what would the universe look like? Features a fascinating and broad use of thought experiments.

Disney, Michael. *The Hidden Universe.* Macmillan 1985 o.p. Examines one of the great questions of cosmology: the end of the universe. The answer seems to depend on an accurate estimate of universal mass. Discusses the presence of hidden material (detected only by its gravitational effect) and techniques in astronomy and physics that may resolve this mystery.

Feinberg, Gerald, and Robert Shapiro. *Life beyond Earth: The Intelligent Earthling's Guide to Extraterrestrial Life.* Morrow 1980 o.p. Examines the possibilities of alternate chemistries and habitats for life forms in the universe. Highly speculative at times, but always interesting; written by a theoretical physicist and a biologist.

Fritzsch, Harald. *The Creation of Matter: The Universe from Beginning to End.* Basic 1988 $9.95. ISBN 0-465-01447-X. Offers a brief introduction to the history of the universe from the "big bang" to its end. Discusses major concepts from physics and astronomy that are required to understand this process, such as relativity, quantum theory, and stellar evolution. A current, concise treatment for the layperson, written by an authority on particle physics.

Golden, Frederic. *Quasars, Pulsars, and Black Holes: A Scientific Detective Story.* Scribner 1976 o.p. Discusses some of the most exciting discoveries of modern astrophysics and the scientists who made them; written by the science editor at *Time* magazine.

Harrison, Edward R. *Cosmology: The Science of the Universe.* Cambridge U. Pr. 1981 $44.95. ISBN 0-521-22981-2. Reviews the history of cosmology and the basics of stellar astronomy, space and time, and the frontiers of contemporary cosmology. The best available textbook at the elementary level.

_____. *Masks of the Universe.* Macmillan 1986 o.p. Examines modern rationalist models of the universe and their origins throughout history; argues that when a worldview fails to satisfy human needs, others fill the vacuum. About half of the book identifies and describes modern scientific cosmologies; features an extremely broad, speculative orientation.

Heller, Michael. *Encountering the Universe.* Trans. by J. Potock. Pachart 1982 $9.95. ISBN 0-912918-07-1. A historical discussion of scientific attempts to model the universe. Provides the reader with many modern cosmological models and their references.

Henbest, Nigel. *Mysteries of the Universe.* Van Nos. Reinhold 1983 o.p. Covers stellar and planetary formation, the origins of life, and high-energy phenomena, such as pulsars, quasars, and black holes; examines important unanswered problems, such as the "missing mass" of the universe.

Islam, Jumal N. *The Ultimate Fate of the Universe.* Cambridge U. Pr. 1983 $15.95. ISBN 0-521-24814-0. Discusses the long-term future of the universe and its ultimate fate. Also describes its large-scale structure and the evidence for a closed or open universe; written for the general reader.

Kaufmann, William J., III. *Black Holes and Warped Spacetime.* W. H. Freeman 1979 $14.95. ISBN 0-7167-1153-2. Describes the process which led to the prediction of black holes. Also discusses stellar evolution, general relativity, wormholes, quasars, and the fate of the universe.

_____. *The Cosmic Frontiers of General Relativity.* Little 1977 o.p. Presents an extensive discussion of black holes and related topics on the frontier of general relativity. Uses diagrams and pictures, rather than mathematics, to convey ideas.

_____. *Discovering the Universe.* W. H. Freeman 1992 $36.95. ISBN 0-7167-2296-8. An up-to-date, introductory text that makes extensive use of algebra and geometry but does not require calculus; includes brief essays by practicing astronomers and astrophysicists.

Layzer, David. *Constructing the Universe.* W. H. Freeman 1984 o.p. Discusses Newton's and Einstein's two theories of space time and gravity, as well as the theories of cosmic structure and evolution that were built around them; includes beautiful illustrations and diagrams, but somewhat technical for the average reader.

Lemonick, Michael D. *The Light at the Edge of the Universe.* Random 1993 $24.00. ISBN 0-679-41304-9. Survey of the current state of astrophysics and cosmology, weaving together up-to-the-minute observations, the most recent theories, and profiles of the major figures in the field.

Narlikar, Jayant V. *Introduction to Cosmology.* Jones & Bartlett 1983 $48.75. ISBN 0-86720-015-4. Provides an excellent advanced-level introduction to cosmology. Features a thorough presentation of the weaknesses as well as strengths of the various competing cosmological theories, notably the hot "big bang" and steady state theories.

_____. *The Structure of the Universe.* OUP 1977 $10.95. ISBN 0-19-289082-4. Offers a summary of modern astronomy and astrophysics. Emphasizes fundamental questions, such as the nature of gravity, inertia, and time; includes new observational information about the nature of the universe and makes a special effort to list all alternate explanations for phenomena.

Pagels, Heinz. *Perfect Symmetry: The Search for the Beginning of Time.* S&S Trade 1986 $4.95. ISBN 0-553-24000-5. Covers the present state of the universe, the early universe, and the frontiers of speculation in cosmology and unified field theories; also explains relations among theories.

Reeves, Hubert. *Atoms of Silence: An Exploration of Cosmic Evolution*. MIT Pr. 1985 o.p. Describes the origin and evolution of the universe and of its parallels with the development of life; written by a Canadian astrophysicist.

Ronan, Colin. *Deep Space: A Guide to the Cosmos*. Macmillan 1982 o.p. A well-known British astronomer explains the concepts of gravity and relativity, and discusses cosmological theories and the questions of extraterrestrial life. Well illustrated.

Rowan-Robinson, Michael. *The Cosmological Distance Ladder*. W. H. Freeman 1985 $39.95. ISBN 0-7167-1586-4. Clearly explains the methodology and problems of distance estimates. Somewhat technical, but will satisfy the curiosity of anyone who has wondered how extragalactic distances are determined.

———. *Cosmology*. OUP 1981 $36.50. ISBN 0-19-851857-9. Describes the visible universe and summarizes cosmological theory for the beginning student; discusses the "big bang" cosmological models in particular and their observational implications.

Schatzman, Evry. *Our Expanding Universe*. McGraw 1992 $9.95. ISBN 0-07-055174-X. International perspective of astrophysics and cosmology by a French authority. Discusses the philosophical aspects of the concept of the "universe." Examines the mind-bent of the future discoverers and giants of physics.

Silk, Joseph. *The Big Bang: The Creation and Evolution of the Universe*. W. H. Freeman 1988 $24.95. ISBN 0-7167-1997-5. Conveys the specific evidence for the "big bang" origin of the universe and describes the standard physical models of evolutionary cosmology; also offers another presentation of the development of the universe during its first seconds.

Trefil, James. *The Moment of Creation: Big Bang Physics from before the First Millisecond to the Present Universe*. Macmillan 1984 $10.95. ISBN 0-02-096770-5. Gives increasing insight into the structure and behavior of elementary particles and recent advances in unification theory that have greatly expanded our knowledge of the early universe; provides a clear account of the problems connected with conventional "big bang" theory and recent progress in understanding the universe's first millisecond.

Wagoner, R., and D. Goldsmith. *Cosmic Horizons: Understanding the Universe*. W. H. Freeman 1982 $13.95. ISBN 0-7167-1418-3. An informative and easy-to-read presentation of cosmology that emphasizes the development of concepts and the meaning of theories rather than simple exposition; presents the scientific method in action.

History

Borner, G. *The Early Universe: Facts and Fictions*. Spr.-Verlag 1988 $79.50. ISBN 0-387-16187-2. An account of the physics that has recently resulted from the fusion of elementary particle physics and astrophysics/cosmology.

Durham, Frank, and Robert D. Purrington. *Frame of the Universe*. Col. U. Pr. 1985 $17.00. ISBN 0-231-05393-2. Presents a history of Western cosmological ideas from antiquity to the present; interesting and well written for the general reader.

Gingerich, Owen, ed. *Astrophysics and Twentieth Century Astronomy to 1950. General History of Astronomy Ser*. Vol. 4 Cambridge U. Pr. 1984 $42.95. ISBN 0-521-24256-8

Gribbin, John, and Michael White. *Stephen Hawking: A Life in Science*. NAL-Dutton 1992 $23.00. ISBN 0-525-93447-2. A biography of the life and work of Stephen Hawking, inventor of a grand theory that unites all the forces of nature within a single set of equations.

Koyré, Alexandre. *From the Closed World to the Infinite Universe*. Johns Hopkins 1968 repr. of 1956 ed. $13.95. ISBN 0-8018-0347-0. Describes the sixteenth- and seventeenth-century revolution in cosmology, in which the heliocentric view of creation replaced the geocentric and the scientific worldview replaced the religious.

Lovell, Bernard. *Emerging Cosmology*. Ed. by Ruth N. Anshen. Praeger 1984 $12.95. ISBN 0-275-91790-8. Surveys cosmological beliefs in the West since opinions on this subject began to be based on mensuration; identifies important factors in the development of scientific cosmologies by highlighting examples proffered by Copernicus, Galileo, Newton, and Sir William Herschel.

National Research Council, Astronomy and Astrophysics Survey Committee Staff. *The Decade of Discovery in Astronomy and Astrophysics.* Natl. Acad. Pr. 1991 $24.95. ISBN 0-309-04381-6. A survey of the field, a summary of the scientific and technical opportunities of the 1990s, and a prioritized agenda for space and ground-based research into the next century.

Schatzman, Evry. *Our Expanding Universe.* McGraw 1992 $9.95. ISBN 0-07-055174-X. Discusses the evolution of the concept of the universe.

Sutton, Christine. *Spaceship Neutrino.* Cambridge U. Pr. 1992 $44.95. ISBN 0-521-36404-3. Offers an overview and an exploration of the discovery of the neutrino. For those working in nuclear and particle physics as well as the general reader.

Swimme, Brian, and Thomas Berry. *The Universe Story.* Harper SF 1992 $22.00. ISBN 0-06-250826-1. Offers a new creation myth that incorporates a scientific view of the universe with philosophical speculation on humanity's place within it.

ATOMIC AND NUCLEAR PHYSICS

Atomic physics is the study of the structure of the atom, its dynamic properties (including energy states), and its interactions with particles and fields. These atomic interactions are almost completely determined by the laws of quantum mechanics, with refined corrections required by quantum electrodynamics. Most atomic systems are characterized by enormous complexity in which each electron interacts with both the nucleus and all other orbiting electrons. Yet, the wavelike nature of particles, combined with WOLFGANG PAULI's exclusion principle, results in an amazingly orderly array of atomic properties, which are systematized by DMITRI MENDELEEV's periodic table. In addition to their classification by chemical activity and atomic weight, the various elements of the periodic table are characterized by a wide variety of observable properties that include electron affinity, polarizability, angular momentum, multiple electric moments, and magnetism.

In contrast, nuclear physics studies the structure of atomic nuclei and their interactions with each other, with their constituent particles, and with other elementary particles created by huge particle accelerators. The nuclear domain occupies a central position between the atomic range of forces and sizes and those of elementary-particle physics (characteristically within the nucleons themselves). As the only system in which all known natural forces can be studied simultaneously, the nuclear domain provides a natural laboratory for testing and extending many fundamental symmetries and laws of nature.

Nuclear physics has been used for both military and peaceful purposes. For example, the discovery of nuclear fission led to the development of the atomic bomb during World War II, as well as nuclear power reactors during the 1950s. Moreover, the discovery of the fusion process, which powers the stars, was used to develop the hydrogen bomb in the 1950s and for current energy research in the area of plasma physics.

Both atomic and nuclear physics are based on the famous experiments of ERNEST RUTHERFORD in 1911, in which he established the existence of a massive central core within the much larger atom. The concept of the atom as the basic building block was first proposed by the ancient Greeks and the electron was discovered by SIR JOSEPH JOHN THOMSON in 1897. The latter advances contributed greatly to the discipline of atomic physics and formed much of the underlying theory upon which Rutherford based his experiments.

General Works

Asimov, Isaac. *Understanding Physics: The Electron, Proton, and Neutron*. NAL-Dutton 1969 $5.95. ISBN 0-451-62634-6

Born, Max. *Atomic Physics*. Dover 1989 $11.95. ISBN 0-486-65984-4

Cottingham, W. M., and D. A. Greenwood. *An Introduction to Nuclear Physics*. Cambridge U. Pr. 1986 $64.95. ISBN 0-521-26580-0. An introductory undergraduate-level survey of modern nuclear physics from the viewpoint of basic physics; includes discussions of nuclear power generation and nuclear astrophysics.

Murrell, J. N., and S. D. Bosanac. *An Introduction to the Theory of Atomic and Molecular Collisions*. Wiley 1989 $115.00. ISBN 0-471-92365-6. An introduction to low-energy collisions of atoms and molecules. A reference for graduate students and research scientists.

Sutton, Christine, ed. *Building the Universe. New Scientist Guides Ser.* Blackwell Pubs. 1985 o.p. Presents articles originally published in *New Scientist* on recent developments in nuclear physics.

Turnbull, R. M. *The Structure of Matter: An Introduction to Atomic Nuclear and Particle Physics*. Trans-Atl. 1979 o.p. A concise account of atomic, nuclear, and elementary particle physics for the beginning student; emphasis is on explaining basic physics principles rather than on experimental methods.

Wong, Samuel S. *Introductory Nuclear Physics*. P-H 1990 $57.00. ISBN 0-13-491168-7. Textbook introducing students to such of the physics of the atomic nucleus as every physicist might be presumed to know.

History

Brush, Stephen G. *Statistical Physics and the Atomic Theory of Matter, from Boyle and Newton to Landau and Onsager*. Bks. Demand repr. of 1983 ed. $99.10. ISBN 0-7837-0247-7. Covers the last three centuries of attempts to understand macroscopic properties of matter in terms of microscopic constituents. Emphasizes modern developments, such as theories of superconductivity and superfluidity; requires a physics background.

Goldschmidt, Bertrand. *The Atomic Complex: A Worldwide Political History of Nuclear Energy*. Am. Nuclear Soc. 1982 $36.00. ISBN 0-89448-550-4

Groves, Leslie M. *Now It Can Be Told: The Story of the Manhattan Project*. Da Capo 1983 repr. of 1962 ed. $13.95. ISBN 0-306-80189-2. Features a personal account of involvement in the project to build the first atomic bomb; written by the administrative officer of the project.

Jungk, Robert. *Brighter Than a Thousand Suns: A Personal History of the Atomic Scientists*. HarBraceJ 1970 repr. of 1958 ed. $5.95. ISBN 0-15-614150-7

Keller, Alex. *The Infancy of Atomic Physics: Hercules in His Cradle*. OUP 1983 $29.95. ISBN 0-19-853904-5. Traces the development of theories about internal atomic structure from the mid-nineteenth century through the 1930s; delineates contemporary scientific culture, showing the flow of opposition and discussion that preceded each advance.

Pais, Abraham. *Niels Bohr's Times: In Physics, Philosophy, and Polity*. OUP 1991 $35.00. ISBN 0-19-852049-2. Preserves the social and scientific dimensions of a full epoch of physics in the depiction of Bohr's singular life.

Rhodes, Richard. *The Making of the Atomic Bomb*. S&S Trade 1988 $14.95. ISBN 0-671-65719-4. Well-written and thoroughly researched work on the making of the first atomic bomb. The first third of the book describes the scientific background of this massive effort, and the balance gives a detailed account of its execution. Emphasizes politics and personalities rather than science; National Book Award winner.

CLASSICAL AND QUANTUM MECHANICS

Classical mechanics is the study of the behavior of systems under the action of forces. Mechanics is further subdivided according to the specific types of systems and phenomena involved.

An important distinction involves the size of the system. Systems that are sufficiently large can be described by the Newtonian laws of classical mechanics. For example, in this category are celestial mechanics, or the study of the motions of planets, stars, and other heavenly bodies, and fluid mechanics, which studies the macroscopic characteristics of liquids and gases. Fluid mechanics is part of a larger field called continuum mechanics, or (by some physicists) classical field theory. Continuum mechanics involves any essentially continuous distribution of rigid, elastic, plastic, or fluid matter. In contrast, the behavior of microscopic systems, such as molecules, atoms, and nuclei, are interpreted by using the concepts and mathematical methods of quantum mechanics.

It is difficult to underestimate the tremendous influence of Newtonian mechanics on contemporary civilization. Not only did it provide a basis for the philosophical rationalism of the eighteenth- and nineteenth-century Enlightenment, but it also contributed significantly to the foundations of mathematical analysis, which solved problems posed by Newtonian mechanics.

Conversely, quantum mechanics, also called wave mechanics, is the modern theory of matter, electromagnetic radiation, and the interaction between matter and radiation. Quantum mechanics also involves the mechanics of phenomena to which this theory is applicable. Quantum mechanics generalizes and supersedes classical mechanics and JAMES CLERK MAXWELL's electromagnetic theory. Atomic and subatomic phenomena provide the most convincing evidence for the accuracy of quantum mechanics and clearly illustrate the differences between quantum mechanics and the mechanics of the classical physics theories. Quantum mechanics is used to explain many properties of matter, such as the temperature dependence of the specific heat of various solids.

The development of quantum mechanics occurred in the 1920s, advanced by the German physicists WERNER HEISENBERG and ERWIN SCHRÖDINGER. The inherent uncertainty in the quantum mathematical predictions of the quantum state (where a researcher can at most determine probabilities for the time evolution of a system) sharply contrasted with the determinism of classical mechanics (where the entire present and future state of a system can be completely specified by its position and momentum), slowed acceptance of quantum mechanics. To date, however, there is no better theory that explains the mechanics of the atom.

General Works

Arya, Atam P. *Introduction to Classical Mechanics.* P-H 1990 $53.33. ISBN 0-205-12028-8. Intended for a two-semester course at the undergraduate level. Forms the basis for future work in applied and pure sciences, especially advanced physics.

Atkins, P. W. *Quanta: A Handbook of Concepts.* OUP 1977 $32.95. ISBN 0-19-855494-X. A brief encyclopedia composed of about 200 illustrated articles with bibliographies that explain various concepts of quantum theory; useful for the specialist and general reader.

Black, T. D., and others, eds. *Foundations of Quantum Mechanics: Santa Fe, New Mexico, 27–31 May 1991.* World Scientific Pub. 1992 $68.00. ISBN 981-02-0980-0. Divided roughly equally between theoretical studies and discussions of experiments on quantum mechanics.

Brandt, Wiegmund, and Hans D. Dahmen. *The Picture Book of Quantum Mechanics.* Wiley 1985 o.p. Extensive computer-generated graphics that convey important aspects of quantum theory; intended for the reader with some knowledge of physics.

Davies, P.C.W. *The Ghost in the Atom: A Discussion of the Mysteries of Quantum Physics.* Cambridge U. Pr. 1986 $42.95. ISBN 0-521-30790-2. Developed from a BBC radio program in which the author interviewed eight well-known physicists with divergent interpretations of quantum mechanics; demonstrates that there is no consensus in the scientific community on this question.

———. *Other Worlds: Space, Superspace and the Quantum Universe.* S&S Trade 1981 o.p. Assesses the impact of quantum theory on our modern conception of the world and discusses implications for philosophical questions, such as the nature of reality, uniqueness and indeterminism of the universe, and the structure of space and time. The author contends that these implications have not been recognized by the general public.

———. *Quantum Mechanics.* Routledge 1984 $13.95. ISBN 0-7100-9962-2. A concise first survey of quantum mechanics, including many problems.

Eisberg, Robert, and Robert Resnick. *Quantum Physics of Atoms, Molecules, Solids, Nuclei and Particles.* Wiley 1985 $64.95. ISBN 0-471-80207-7. Presents the properties of important quantum systems for teaching elementary quantum mechanics to science students; requires an understanding of calculus and elementary physics.

Gutzwiller, M. C. *Chaos in Classical and Quantum Mechanics. Interdisciplinary Applied Mathematics Ser.* Spr.-Verlag 1993 $39.95. ISBN 0-387-97173-4. Focuses mainly on the connection between classical and quantum mechanics. Describes the apparent chaos in the long time-interval motions of simple mechanical systems.

Hey, A. J., and P. Walters. *The Quantum Universe.* Cambridge U. Pr. 1987 $59.95. ISBN 0-521-26744-7. Conveys to the nonscientist how quantum mechanics underlies our current understanding of chemistry, solid-state phenomena, superconductivity, lasers, stars, black holes, and cosmology.

Liboff, Richard L. *Introductory Quantum Mechanics.* Addison-Wesley 1992 $62.50. ISBN 0-201-54715-5. Reflects the progress of physics in both esoteric and pragmatic directions. A complete and detailed presentation, with modern applications, problems, and examples.

Martin, J. L. *Basic Quantum Mechanics.* OUP 1981 $45.00. ISBN 0-19-851815-3. Offers a well-written introductory book for science students; features a modern, nonhistorical approach.

Pagels, Heinz. *The Cosmic Code: Quantum Physics as the Law of Nature.* S&S Trade 1984 $15.95. ISBN 0-553-24625-9. Discusses quantum physics from the earliest ideas of nature to recent developments in particle physics; intended for general readers or beginning physics students.

Polkinghorne, J. C. *The Quantum World.* Princeton U. Pr. 1985 $8.95. ISBN 0-691-02388-3. Contends that the theory of quantum mechanics is the most important discovery of modern physics since it introduced probability into fundamental physical explanation. The theory is described with a minimum of mathematics, and long-standing problems of interpretation are explained; includes a glossary and a mathematically more demanding appendix.

Popper, Karl R. *Quantum Theory and the Schism in Physics.* Ed. by W. W. Barley III. Rowman 1984 $52.25. ISBN 0-8476-7018-X. Argues that contemporary physics is in a crisis of understanding, despite its apparent successes, because of the intrusion of subjectivism into modern physics and the pervasive notion that quantum theory is basically complicated; written by a famous philosopher of science and critic of scientific realism.

Resnick, Robert, and David Halliday. *Basic Concepts in Relativity and Early Quantum Theory.* Macmillan 1991. ISBN 0-02-399-340-5. An introductory text by two successful textbook authors.

Taylor, Thomas. *Mechanics: Classical and Quantum*. Franklin 1976 $176.00. ISBN 0-08-018063-9

History

Cline, Barbara L. *Men Who Made a New Physics: Physicists and the Quantum Theory*. U. Ch. Pr. 1987 $12.95. ISBN 0-226-11027-3. Describes the revolution in physics during the first three decades of the twentieth century. Emphasizes the personalities involved, notably Rutherford, Planck, Heisenberg, Einstein, and Bohr; highlights science as a human enterprise.

Feuer, Lewis S. *Einstein and the Generations of Science*. Transaction Pubs. 1982 $19.95. ISBN 0-87855-899-3. Examines the social roots of the burst of scientific creativity in physics during the early twentieth century. Contends that the work of Einstein, Bohr, and Heisenberg was part of a "generational rebellion," and relates the motivation for their scientific discoveries to the philosophical orientation of the period.

Hendry, John. *The History of Quantum Mechanics and the Bohr-Pauli Dialogue*. Kluwer Ac. 1984 $34.50. ISBN 0-318-00442-9

Jammer, Max. *The Conceptual Development of Quantum Mechanics*. History of Modern Physics and Astronomy Ser. Am. Inst. Physics 1989 $90.00. ISBN 0-88318-617-9

Van der Waerden, B. L., ed. *Sources of Quantum Mechanics*. Dover 1968 $8.95. ISBN 0-486-61881-1

ELEMENTARY PARTICLE PHYSICS

Throughout history, human beings have tried to identify the most elementary constituents of matter. The current effort to identify elementary particles and the laws governing their interactions is called elementary particle physics.

The elementary particles of matter were formerly thought to be the atoms of the chemical elements. In time, the atoms were found to be composed of electrons, protons, and neutrons. In turn, protons and neutrons, and all other hadrons (strongly interacting particles), were found to be composed of quarks, which are unusual particles that have one- to two-thirds the charge of electrons and protons, as well as different "colors," "flavors," and "spins." Quarks are suspected by some researchers to be a more elementary particle, from which all other particles are formed. It is convenient, however, to continue calling hadrons elementary particles as a way of distinguishing them from their compounds (atomic nuclei, for instance); this terminology is also justified because quarks cannot be isolated and therefore are not fundamental particles. The term "fundamental particle" is used to denote particles that are basic constituents of matter—not compounds.

To date, the known elementary particles are protons, leptons, mesons, baryons, quarks, and gluons. Because the gravitational force is very small in comparison with other forces (e.g., one million-millionth of the nuclear force), it is convenient to consider only three basic interactions (nuclear, electromagnetic, and weak), to understand the wide variety of interactions between these elementary particles.

Particle physicists have been trying to produce a grand unified theory, which would explain all of the elementary particle interactions that occur in nature. Most elementary particle physicists are optimistic that a grand unified theory will eventually be formulated.

General Works

Bros, Peter. *Atoms, Stars, and Minds: Synthesizing an Elementary Particle That Comprehends Itself*. Fin. Bk. Partners 1992 $14.95. ISBN 0-9627769-1-2. Uses measurable facts in physical reality to synthesize an elementary particle with two opposing properties, motion and attraction. Continues to use the particle to describe physical reality.

Close, Frank, and Christine Sutton. *The Particle Explosion*. OUP 1987 $39.95. ISBN 0-19-851965-6. Presents an illustrated tour of the subatomic world; includes hundreds of photographs of personalities, machines, and particle images.

Davies, P.C.W. *The Forces of Nature*. Cambridge U. Pr. 1979 $49.50. ISBN 0-521-22523-X. Provides a clear and well-organized introduction to fundamental particles and interactions of matter; emphasizes the conceptual basis of modern subatomic physics.

Dodd, James. *The Ideas of Particle Physics: An Introduction for Scientists*. Cambridge U. Pr. 1991 $64.95. ISBN 0-521-38506-7. Briefly presents the discoveries of recent high-energy physics for readers with a technical background; includes a bibliography of nonspecialist, technical references.

Fritsch, Harald. *Quarks: The Stuff of Matter*. Basic 1983 $19.95. ISBN 0-465-06781-6. Describes the complex and costly experiments involving particle accelerators that have illuminated the quark substructure of matter; written by a physics professor at the Max Planck Institute.

Herbert, Nick. *Quantum Reality*. Doubleday 1987 $9.95. ISBN 0-385-23569-0. Describes the nature of subatomic particles and their interactions.

Kane, Gordon. *Modern Elementary Particle Physics: Quarks, Leptons, and Their Interactions*. Addison-Wesley 1988 $43.95. ISBN 0-201-11749-5. Uses a deductive rather than historical approach to present particle physics as a successful theory of quarks, leptons, and their interactions.

Nachtmann, O. *Elementary Particle Physics*. Spr.-Verlag 1989 $98.00. ISBN 0-387-50496-6. A comprehensive work designed for students in particle physics with either a theoretical or an experimental inclination.

Perkins, Donald H. *Introduction to High Energy Physics*. Addison-Wesley 1987 $51.75. ISBN 0-201-12105-0. A clear, balanced presentation of high-energy physics; suitable for self-study and accessible to beginners.

Squires, E. *To Acknowledge the Wonder*. IOP Pub. 1985 $25.00. ISBN 0-85274-798-5. A survey of the world of atomic particle physics. Covers essential concepts, such as quantum electrodynamics, quantum chromodynamics, and the standard model. Discusses the link between particle physics and cosmology, and explores concepts, such as the inflationary and the anthropic principle.

Trefil, James S. *From Atoms to Quarks: The Strange World of Particle Physics*. Scribner 1982 o.p. A qualitative survey that covers the twentieth-century search for the ultimate building blocks of matter; includes a glossary.

Williams, D., ed. *Elementary Particle Physics of TASI Lecture '84: Proceedings, Ann Arbor, Michigan, June 4–29, 1984*. World Scientific Pub. 1986 $77.00. ISBN 9971-50-270-4. Twelve lectures presented at the Theoretical Advanced Study Institute in Elementary Particle Physics, The University of Michigan, Ann Arbor, Michigan, June 1984. Contents are divided in sections that include discussions of the standard model, supersymmetry, special topics, and experimental possibilities.

History

Achinstein, Peter. *Particles and Waves: Historical Essays in the Philosphy of Science*. OUP 1991 $49.95. ISBN 0-19-506547-6. Discusses methodological issues encountered in the development of particle theory.

Brown, Laurie M., and Lillian Hoddeson, eds. *The Birth of Particle Physics: Proceedings of the International Symposium on the History of Particle Physics, May, 1980*. Cambridge U. Pr. 1983 o.p. Chronicles the evolution of particle physics from 1930 to 1950. Paul Dirac, Victor Weisskopf, Robert Marshal, and others reflect on their contributions.

Brown, Laurie M., Max Dresden, and Lillian Hoddeson, eds. *Pions to Quarks: Particle Physics in the 1950s*. Cambridge U. Pr. 1989 $74.95. ISBN 0-521-30984-0. Covers developments in the field of particle physics up to 1963. Includes a wide range of topics.

Lederman, Leon, and Dick Teresi. *The God Particle: If the Universe Is the Answer, What Is the Question.* HM 1993 $24.95. ISBN 0-395-55849-2. Rollicking tour of mankind's two-thousand-year search for the nature of matter and the ultimate particles.

McCusker, Brian. *The Quest for Quarks.* Cambridge U. Pr. 1984 $17.95. ISBN 0-521-24850-7. Offers a historical account of the search for the fundamental material of nature. Discusses atomic theory, then subatomic particles and their constituent quarks; includes a chapter devoted to the "quest for the free quark," an enterprise in which the author is an active researcher.

Ne'eman, Yuval, and Yoram Kirsh. *The Particle Hunters.* Cambridge U. Pr. 1986 $19.95. ISBN 0-521-31780-0. Presents an interesting nontechnical history of twentieth-century particle physics by leading theorists in the field.

Pickering, Andrew. *Constructing Quarks: A Sociological History of Particle Physics.* U. Ch. Pr. 1986 $37.50. ISBN 0-226-66799-5. Examines the development of high-energy physics, beginning with a survey of "old physics" (1945–64) and then describing the rise of the "new physics of the subsequent decade." Provides the general reader with some knowledge of particle physics research; includes a 40-page bibliography.

Sutton, Christine. *The Particle Connection: The Most Exciting Scientific Chase Since DNA and the Double Helix.* S&S Trade 1984 o.p. Presents a nontechnical description of the circumstances surrounding the 1933 discovery of the W and Z particles at CERN (European Centre for Nuclear Research), which confirmed the theory of weak interactions.

Taubes, Gary. *Nobel Dreams: Power, Deceit, and the Ultimate Experiment.* Microsoft 1988 $8.95. ISBN 1-55615-112-8. Describes how Carlo Rubbia and Simon van der Meer of CERN won the 1984 Nobel Prize in physics for experimentally discovering the W and Z particles; suggests that politics, passions, and personalities play a role in "big science."

Watkins, Peter. *Story of the W and Z.* Cambridge U. Pr. 1986 o.p. Offers a personal account of the 1983 experiment at the CERN laboratory near Geneva that searched for the W and Z bosons predicted by the Weinber-Salam electroweak theory. Also presents a review of current ideas and experiments in particle physics; written for the general reader.

GRAVITATION AND RELATIVITY

The mutual attraction between all objects in the universe is known as the phenomenon of gravitation. Gravitational astronomy in the eighteenth and nineteenth centuries was based solely on SIR ISAAC NEWTON's (see also Vol. 4) laws and attracted leading mathematicians. At the time, it appeared that only numerical refinement would be needed to account accurately for the motions of all celestial objects. In the early twentieth century, however, ALBERT EINSTEIN's theory of relativity shattered the confidence of Newtonian proponents. Since then, the subject has been in a healthy state of flux.

A general theory of physics, or relativity, was primarily conceived by Albert Einstein. In contrast to the basic phenomenon of gravitation, relativity involves a profound analysis of time and space, which leads to a much broader generalization of physical laws, with far-reaching implications for physics and cosmology. Historically, the theory of relativity developed in two stages. Einstein's initial formulation in 1905 (now known as the special theory of relativity) does not cover gravitation. One of the two principles on which it is based (the principle of relativity) stipulates the form invariance of physical laws only for inertial reference systems. Einstein's general theory of relativity (1915) exploits a deep equivalence between inertial and gravitational effects. In the general theory of relativity, both restrictions were removed, leading to a successful "relativistic" generalization of Newton's theory of gravitation. The non-Newtonian consequences of the general theory of relativity have only been verified in a few instances, because of the extreme weakness of gravitation compared to other known forces. These non-Newtonian consequences mainly have been restricted to cosmology, the structure of neutron stars and black holes, and the motion of bodies in the solar system. The special theory of relativity adequately describes relativistic effects in atomic, nuclear, and high-energy physics. Its numerous confirmations render it among the most securely established theories.

Because Einstein's theories are deep-seated, his contemporaries did not readily accept them at first. In fact, not until the early 1920s did the theories gain critical acceptance. Ironically, as a result of this skepticism, Einstein won the Nobel Prize in 1921 for his theoretical explanation of the photoelectric effect rather than for his relativity theory. Today, however, the theory of relativity is an indispensable tool for most physicists.

General Works

Bergmann, Peter G. *The Riddle of Gravitation*. Dover 1993 repr. of 1968 ed. $7.95. ISBN 0-486-27378-4. Another Dover reprint of a classic science monograph—this last published by Scribner in a revised edition, 1987.

Calder, Nigel. *Einstein's Universe*. Viking Penguin 1980 $10.00. ISBN 0-14-005499-5. Describes how Einstein revolutionized scientific ideas of space, time, and motion by his theories of special and general relativity; written on the centennial of Einstein's birth by an author regarded as one of the most skillful writers of popular science today.

Cianci, R., ed. *General Relativity and Gravitational Physics: Proceedings of the Ninth Italian Conference*. World Scientific Pub. 1991 $103.00. ISBN 981-02-0765-4. About 70 papers collected from the conference, which was organized around four main themes related to relativity and gravitation.

D'Olivo, J. C., ed. *Relativity and Gravitation—Classical and Quantum*. World Scientific Pub. 1991 $82.00. ISBN 981-02-0715-8. About 60 contributions from the Seventh Latin-American Symposium on Relativity and Gravitation, Cocoyoc, Mexico, December 1990.

Geroch, Robert. *General Relativity from A to B*. U. Ch. Pr. 1981 $9.95. ISBN 0-226-288640-1. Explains what relativity is, how it works, to what physical phenomena it applies, and what it predicts in a clear and thorough way. Discusses some of the chains of arguments that justify the theory, to help the general reader understand how the theory is constructed, as well as its content; written for the nonscientist.

Howard, D., and J. Stachel. *Einstein and the History of General Relativity*. Einstein Studies Ser. Birkhauser 1989 $79.50. ISBN 0-8176-3392-8. Based on a 1986 conference on the history of general relativity. Covers a broad variety of topics relevant to the study of mathematics, relativity, unified field theory, and cosmology.

Kaufmann, William J., III. *Relativity and Cosmology*. HarpC 1977 o.p. Discusses relativity theory and its applications to astrophysics, as well as white holes, wormholes, and other physical phenomena; now somewhat dated, but still useful to the layperson.

Rindler, W. *Essential Relativity*. Spr.-Verlag 1990 $39.00. ISBN 0-387-10090-3. Presents a simplified treatment of relativity theory for the advanced undergraduate; covers cosmology and general relativity.

Schwinger, Julian. *Einstein's Legacy*. W. H. Freeman 1986 $32.95. ISBN 0-7167-5011-2. Explains the complex concepts of relativity theory to the layperson, using mathematics no higher than elementary algebra. Well illustrated; written by a Nobel Prize winner in quantum electrodynamics.

Wheeler, John A. *A Journey into Gravitation and Spacetime*. W. H. Freeman 1990 $32.95. ISBN 0-7167-5016-3

History

Davies, P.C.W. *The Search for Gravity Waves*. Cambridge U. Pr. 1980 o.p. Describes experimental efforts to detect gravity waves; abstract concepts are discussed without using mathematics to enable the general reader to understand the objective of the experiments.

Goldberg, Stanley. *Understanding Relativity: Origin and Impact of a Scientific Revolution*. Birkhauser 1989 $42.50. ISBN 0-8176-3150-X. Presents Einstein's theory of special relativity and historical uses of the term in scientific contexts.

Hawking, Steven. *A Brief History of Time*. Bantam 1990 $13.95. ISBN 0-553-34614-8

Narlikar, Jayant V. *The Lighter Side of Gravity*. W. H. Freeman 1982 $20.95. ISBN 0-7167-1343-8. A nontechnical presentation of the principles of modern theoretical physics; emphasizes the wide range of astronomical phenomena controlled by gravity.

Parker, Barry. *Einstein's Dream: The Search for a Unified Theory of the Universe*. Plenum Pub. 1986 $19.95. ISBN 0-306-42343-X. Popular account of twentieth-century attempts to produce a unified field theory.

Perjes, Z., ed. *Relativity Today*. Nova Sci. Pubs. 1991 $79.00. ISBN 1-56072-028-X

Weinberg, Steven. *Dreams of a Final Theory*. Pantheon 1992 $24.50. ISBN 0-679-41923-3. A summary of how far theory has gone toward uniting gravity, electromagnetism, and the weak and strong nuclear forces into a final theory.

———. *Gravitation and Cosmology: Principles and Applications of the General Theory of Relativity*. Wiley 1972 $74.95. ISBN 0-471-92567-5

OPTICS

Optics may be defined narrowly as the science of light and vision. However, to a specialist in the field, optics is the study of phenomena associated with the generation, transmission, and detection of electromagnetic radiation in the optical spectral range. This range extends from the long-wave edge of the X-ray region (one nanometer) to the short-wave edge of the radio region (1 millimeter).

Knowledge of optics was rudimentary in ancient times. SIR ISAAC NEWTON'S (see also Vol. 4) landmark work *Opticks* (1704) greatly broadened knowledge in this field. So great were Newton's contributions to optics that not until a century later were the next great accomplishments made. JAMES CLERK MAXWELL, using knowledge gained by Newton and MICHAEL M. FARADAY, made the crowning achievement in optics, the electromagnetic theory. This theory states that light consists of electric and magnetic fields propagated together through space as transverse waves, providing a basis for the general treatment of optical phenomena. ALBERT EINSTEIN further refined optics in the twentieth century with his explanation of the photoelectric effect in 1905.

The discovery that in a given population of atoms capable of occupying two energy states, there are more atoms in the higher state than in the lower one, made possible the invention of the maser and the laser in 1960. The invention of the laser and other new light sources, the development of new methods of spectroscopy and nonlinear optics, and the continuing discovery of scientific and practical applications for these new technologies have combined to place optics and optical physics in the forefront of contemporary physics.

The field of quantum optics has become an increasingly popular area of study in recent years because the statistical properties of light and the electrodynamics of matter and light are central to understanding the generation and propagation of light, the transmission of information, and many other physical processes.

General Works

Agrawal, Govind P., and Robert W. Boyd, eds. *Contemporary Nonlinear Optics. Quantum Electronics Ser.* Acad. Pr. 1992 $79.95. ISBN 0-12-045135-2. A survey of the current state of knowledge in 10 broad branches of nonlinear optics, excluding topics that have been well covered in recent treatments.

Falk, David S., and others. *Seeing the Light: Optics in Nature, Photography, Color, Vision and Holography.* Wiley 1985 $54.95. ISBN 0-471-60385-6. Presents the fundamental principles of light and geometric optics and uses them to discuss and explain everyday phenomena; well illustrated, informative, and intended for the nonspecialist.

Hecht, Jeff. *The Laser Guidebook.* McGraw 1992 $44.95. ISBN 0-07-027737-0. A guide to the wide variety of lasers available commercially; includes a brief overview of the history of lasers and of the basics of laser theory.

Klein, Miles V., and Thomas Furtak. *Optics.* Wiley 1986 $67.95. ISBN 0-471-87297-0. Standard introduction to the field of modern optics.

Lawrence, Clifford L. *The Laser Book: A New Technology of Light.* P-H 1986 o.p. An introduction to lasers, written essentially without mathematics. Covers types and applications of lasers; written for the layperson.

Mickelson, Alan R. *Physical Optics.* Van Nos. Reinhold 1992 $59.95. ISBN 0-442-00614-4. Presents a unified treatment of quantitative approaches to the analysis of a relevant set of problems in the general area of physical optics.

Optics Today. Readings from Physics Today Ser. Ed. by John N. Howard. Am. Inst. Physics 1987 $45.00. ISBN 0-88318-499-0. Presents reprints of more than 50 articles and news items originally published in *Physics Today.* Illustrates progress made during the last decade in this field. Covers topics such as X-rays and tomography, lightwave communications technology, and laser applications; written for the layperson.

Petykiewicz, J. *Wave Optics.* Kluwer Ac. 1992 $178.00. ISBN 0-7923-0683-X. Covers a wide variety of topics related to electromagnetics.

Shimoda, Koichi. *Introduction to Laser Physics.* Spr.-Verlag 1991 $36.95. ISBN 0-387-16713-7. A first-rate introduction for students with a mathematical background; written by a prolific contributor to the field.

Tarasov, L. V. *Laser Age in Optics.* Imported Pubns. 1985 o.p. Covers topics such as holography and nonlinear optics and the elementary theories required to explain these topics. Features a short historical survey of the development of modern optics; written for the layperson who wants a summary rather than a comprehensive treatment.

Yariv, Amnon. *Optical Electronics.* SCP 1991 $64.00. ISBN 0-03-047444-2. A standard textbook covering such topics as phase conjunction, ultra short pulses, and lasers. For seniors and graduate students in physics, electrical engineering, and applied physics.

History

Bertolotti, M. *Masers and Lasers: An Historical Approach.* IOP Pub. 1987 $39.00. ISBN 0-85274-437-4. A history of the discovery and development of the tools essential to much of modern science and technology, such as the laser and its precursor, the maser. Also provides an introduction to the statistical properties of light that are an important general feature of lasers; written for scientists.

Eastwood, Bruce S. *Astronomy and Optics from Pliny to Descartes: Texts, Diagrams, and Concept Structures. Collected Studies Ser.* Ashgate Pub. Co. 1989 $79.95. ISBN 0-86078-239-5

Hall, A. Rupert. *All Was Light: An Introduction to Newton's Opticks*. OUP 1993 $58.00.
ISBN 0-19-853985-1
Wolf, E., ed. *Progress in Optics*. Vol. 31 Elsevier 1993 $142.75. ISBN 0-444-89836-0

PLASMA PHYSICS

The field of plasma physics is the study of matter in the form of a highly ionized gas, composed of nearly equal amounts of positive and negative free charges (positive ions and electrons). This state of matter was called plasma by IRVING I. LANGMUIR, because it is composed of charged particles and exhibits many characteristics different from ordinary gases. Because atoms lose all of their electrons in a plasma state, a gas loses all of its characteristic properties. A gas must be heated to a temperature greater than one million degrees for a plasma reaction to occur. In addition to the importance of plasma in many new areas of applied science, most of the matter in the universe exists in the plasma state, both in stellar atmospheres and in interstellar space. Plasma has also been encountered in the tenuous ionized gases of Earth's outer atmosphere.

Understanding plasma phenomena, which are associated with sustained thermonuclear or fusion reactions, has a practical goal, since fusion can be used as a clean and virtually endless energy source. However, matter in the plasma state cannot be contained by an ordinary vessel. Plasma must be held by some other force, such as an electromagnetic field. At these high temperatures, quantum mechanics do not apply; it is necessary to apply classical statistical mechanics and electromagnetics. Plasma physicists study mainly the characteristics of plasmas in stars, such as motion, magnetic properties, and energy production properties.

General Works

Artsimovich, L. *A Physicist's ABC on Plasma*. St. Mut. 1985 $39.75. ISBN 0-317-46682-8. A brief survey of the elements of plasma physics.

Bittencourt, J. A. *Fundamentals of Plasma Physics*. Pergamon 1986 $155.00. ISBN 0-08-033924-7. An advanced, but up-to-date textbook.

Cairns, R. A. *Plasma Physics*. Heyden & Sons 1985 o.p. Discusses plasma diagnostics and nuclear fusion among other topics.

Kadomtsev, B. B., ed. *Reviews of Plasma Physics*. Vol. 17 Plenum 1993 $89.50. ISBN 0-306-11007-5. Two extended papers on the generation of noninductive current in a Tomak and resonance effects in oscillations of uneven flows of continuous media.

Peratt, A. L. *Physics of the Plasma Universe*. Spr.-Verlag 1991 $79.00. ISBN 0-387-97575-6. Argues that astrophysics can no longer ignore plasma physics in the study of such topics as magnetic fields, stellar atmospheres, radio galaxies, and cosmic rays.

Priest, E. R., and V. Krishan. eds. *Basic Plasma Processes on the Sun*. Kluwer Ac. $129.50. ISBN 0-7923-0879-4. Covers processes occurring in the solar interior, the solar photosphere, and the solar chromosphere.

Thompson, W. B. *An Introduction to Plasma Physics*. Pergamon 1962 o.p. Introductory text on plasma physics; includes a bibliography.

History

Bromberg, Joan L. *Fusion: Science, Politics and the Invention of a New Energy Source*. MIT Pr. 1982 $42.50. ISBN 0-262-02180-3. A history of the United States magnetic fusion energy program; examines the four largest programs—in California, Tennessee, New Mexico, and New Jersey—and explains the relationship between science and politics that helped fund these fusion programs.

SOLID-STATE PHYSICS

Solid-state physics primarily studies the electrical, dielectric, elastic, and thermal properties of solids in terms of fundamental physical laws. If all solid-state physicists had chemical training, then problems in solid-state physics might be called solid-state chemistry (and vice-versa). The major difference is that solid-state physics studies the properties common to large classes of compounds while solid-state chemistry deals with the dependence of properties upon their compositions. Solid-state physics also emphasizes quantitative relationships between properties and the underlying electronic structure, while solid-state chemistry tends to be more descriptive.

Increasingly, the term "condensed-matter" is replacing "solid-state." This new term encompasses noncrystalline solids (e.g., glass) as well as crystalline solids. Because of its many applications in computer technology, solid-state physics is perhaps the most rapidly developing field of physics. Solid-state physicists search for new metals with desirable properties, such as lightness, strength, and conductivity. In fact, solid-state physics is not a pure science area but rather an applied one. For example, physicists know a great deal about the properties of most metals at the atomic level, but solid-state physicists must still learn about fusions of these metals in various combinations.

To date, solid-state physicists have focused on surfaces, interfaces, and systems with strong fluctuation or varying degrees of disorder. Another active research area in solid-state physics is superconductivity, a phenomenon first produced in 1987. Physicists in this specialized field look for materials that are virtually resistance-free at normal temperatures.

General Works

Bernstein, Jeremy. *Three Degrees above Zero: Bell Labs in the Information Age.* NAL-Dutton 1986 o.p. Describes in detail important research at AT&T's Bell Laboratories. The areas of research include telephony and the discovery of cosmic background radiation by Robert Wilson and Arno Penzia, as well as the early history of solid-state physics, culminating in the invention of the transistor at Bell Labs. A good reference for those interested in the process and personalities of industrial science; written by a physicist and popular science writer.

Ehrenreich, Henry, and David Turnbull, eds. *Solid State Physics, Vol. 46: Advances in Research and Applications.* Acad. Pr. 1992 $79.00. ISBN 0-12-607746-0. Contains three articles by different authors, both physicists and engineers, each addressed to the physics underlying a different area of materials science and technology.

Ibach, H., and H. Luth. *Solid-State Physics: An Introduction to Theory and Experiment.* Spr.-Verlag 1991 $49.50. ISBN 0-387-52207-7. A textbook for a college-level introductory course in solid-state physics, emphasizing magnetism, superconductivity, and semiconductor physics.

Kittel, Charles. *Introduction to Solid State Physics.* Wiley 1986 $65.95. ISBN 0-471-87974-4. A standard text in the field.

Meyers, H. P. *Introductory Solid State Physics.* Taylor & Francis 1990 $79.00. ISBN 0-85066-759-3. Fine text for undergraduates. Contains numerous figures, a breadth of coverage within its 15 chapters, references, and exercises with answers.

Papacosta, Pangratios. *The Splendid Voyage: An Introduction to New Sciences and New Technologies.* Frontiers of Science Ser. P-H 1987 $10.95. ISBN 0-13-835380-8. Illustrates topics such as lasers and the invention of the transistor with many excellent diagrams and photographs.

Rudden, M. N., and J. Wilson. *Elements of Solid State Physics.* Wiley 1980 $59.95. ISBN 0-471-27749-5. A textbook designed for undergraduate college students and general readers with some physics background.

Solid-State Physics Source Book. Science Reference Ser. McGraw 1988 $49.50. ISBN 0-07-045503-1. Excerpts from the McGraw *Encyclopedia of Science and Technology*, 6th ed. (1987).

History

Braun, Ernest, and Stuart MacDonald. *Revolution in Miniature: The History and Impact of Semiconductor Electronics Re-explored.* Cambridge U. Pr. 1982 o.p. Focuses on technology and application, but also features excellent discussions of the foundations and early development of solid-state physics.

Eckert, Michael, and Helmut Schubert. *Crystals, Electrons, and Transistors.* Am. Inst. Physics 1989 $20.00. ISBN 0-88318-719-1. A chronology of the development of solid-state technologies, this book includes a wealth of interesting material about scientific practice and policy in general.

Hoddeson, Lillian, and others, eds. *The History of Solid State Physics.* OUP 1992 $75.00. ISBN 0-19-505329-X. Concentrates on the period between 1930 and 1960, when solid-state physics experienced a lot of growth and when its identity became well established.

Mott, Nevill, ed. *The Beginnings of Solid State Physics. Royal Society Ser.* Scholium Intl. 1980 o.p. Presents a collection of reminiscences by pioneers in the field, such as Bloch, Bethe, Wilson, and Mott; includes entertaining personal and historical information.

CHRONOLOGY OF AUTHORS

Galilei, Galileo. 1564–1642
Huygens, Christiaan. 1629–1695
Newton, Sir Isaac. 1642–1727
Laplace, Marquis Pierre Simon de. 1749–1827
Faraday, Michael. 1791–1867
Helmholtz, Hermann Ludwig Ferdinand von. 1821–1894
Maxwell, James Clerk. 1831–1879
Mach, Ernst. 1838–1916
Boltzmann, Ludwig. 1844–1906
Röntgen, Wilhelm. 1845–1923
Michelson, Albert A(braham). 1852–1931
Ramsay, Sir William. 1852–1916
Lorentz, Hendrik Antoon. 1853–1928
Thomson, Sir Joseph John. 1856–1940
Hertz, Heinrich. 1857–1894
Planck, Max. 1858–1947
Curie, Marie Sklodowska. 1867–1934
Millikan, Robert Andrews. 1868–1953
Rutherford, Ernest. 1871–1937
Einstein, Albert. 1879–1955
Born, Max. 1882–1970
Bridgman, Percy Williams. 1882–1961
Eddington, Sir Arthur Stanley. 1882–1944
Bohr, Niels. 1885–1962
Moseley, Henry Gwyn Jeffreys. 1887–1915

Schrödinger, Erwin. 1887–1961
Compton, Arthur H(olly). 1892–1962
Kapitza, Peter Leonidovich. 1894–1984
Pauli, Wolfgang. 1900–1958
Fermi, Enrico. 1901–1954
Heisenberg, Werner. 1901–1976
Dirac, Paul Adrien Maurice. 1902–1984
Wigner, Eugene Paul. 1902–
Gamow, George. 1904–1968
Oppenheimer, J. Robert. 1904–1967
Bloch, Felix. 1905–1983
Mott, Sir Nevill Francis. 1905–
Bethe, Hans Albrecht. 1906–
Tomonaga, Sin-Itiro. 1906–1979
Yukawa, Hideki. 1907–1981
Bardeen, John. 1908–
Chandrasekhar, Subrahmanyan. 1910–
Fowler, William A. 1911–
Wheeler, John Archibald. 1911–
Lamb, Willis Eugene, Jr. 1913–
Townes, Charles H(ard). 1915–
Feynman, Richard P(hillips). 1918–1988
Schwinger, Julian Seymour. 1918–
Yang, Chen Ning. 1922–
Anderson, Philip W. 1923–
Fitch, Val Logsdon. 1923–
Salam, Abdus. 1926–

Gell-Mann, Murray. 1929–
Mössbauer, Rudolf Ludwig. 1929–
Cronin, James W(ilson). 1931–
Penrose, Roger. 1931–
Glashow, Sheldon Lee. 1932–

Weinberg, Steven. 1933–
Josephson, Brian David. 1940–
Hawking, Steven William. 1942–
Binnig, Gerd. 1947–

ANDERSON, PHILIP W. 1923– (NOBEL PRIZE 1977)

Philip Anderson was the son and grandson of Midwestern science professors. After serving in World War II as an engineer at the Naval Research Laboratory, he received a Ph.D. in physics from Harvard University in 1949. In 1961 and 1962, as a visiting professor at Churchill College of Cambridge University, Anderson made early contributions to experimental research in superconductivity. He confirmed the theoretical predictions made by BRIAN DAVID JOSEPHSON, for which Josephson was awarded the Nobel Prize in 1973. In 1977, Anderson shared the Nobel Prize for physics with Mott and Van Vleck.

Although he is respected as an experimenter and researcher, perhaps Anderson's greatest quality, as noted by his colleagues, is his intuitive ability to formulate valuable concepts. For example, Anderson has shown by models how electrons move and interact in disordered materials that lack a uniform crystalline structure. Anderson retired from the directorship at Bell Laboratories in Murray Hill, New Jersey, in 1984 and presently teaches at Princeton University.

BOOKS BY ANDERSON

Basic Notions of Condensed Matter Physics. Benjamin-Cummings 1984 o.p.
Concepts in Solids: Lectures on the Theory of Solids. Benjamin-Cummings 1963 o.p.

BOOKS ABOUT ANDERSON

Cotterill, Rodney. *The Cambridge Guide to the Material World.* Cambridge U. Pr. 1985 o.p. Provides an accurate and well-written introduction to all aspects of solid-state physics; includes a brief but valuable summary of Anderson's 1958 work with electron localization.
Halley, J. Woods. *Theories of High Temperature Superconductivity.* Addison-Wesley 1988 $50.95. ISBN 0-201-12008-9. Offers nonspecialists an idea of the importance of Anderson's work in the rapidly changing world of superconductivity.

BARDEEN, JOHN. 1908– (NOBEL PRIZE 1956, 1972)

Born in Madison, Wisconsin, John Bardeen was the first person to be awarded two Nobel Prizes in physics. Bardeen shared the first Nobel Prize with Walter H. Brattain and William Shockley for their contributions to solid-state physics, specifically the development of the transistor, which has led to scientific advances, such as supercomputers and space travel.

However, Bardeen is more widely known for his second Nobel Prize in 1972, which he shared with Leon N. Cooper and John Robert Schrieffer. Their development of the Bardeen-Cooper-Schrieffer (BCS) theory greatly elucidated the process of superconductivity. Until Bardeen and his colleagues developed their theory, superconductivity had been considered only an interesting physical curiosity with little practical potential. The theory showed how superconductivity could be applied to improve measuring techniques in sophisticated computers and heavy engineering. Future possibilities might include superconductive power lines and ultrarapid trains running on super-conductive tracks.

A child prodigy, Bardeen graduated from high school when he was 15 and attained a master's degree from the University of Wisconsin at 21. Bardeen then worked as a geophysicist for Gulf Research and Development Corporation in Pittsburgh. He resumed his studies, receiving a Ph.D. in mathematical physics from Princeton in 1936. From 1935 to 1938, Bardeen was a Junior Fellow of the Society of Fellows at Harvard University. He then accepted a position as a professor of physics at the University of Minnesota, where he taught from 1938 to 1941.

During World War II, Bardeen was a physicist for the Naval Ordinance Laboratory in Washington, D.C., joining the Bell Telephone Laboratories in 1946 as a research physicist. Bardeen left Bell Laboratories in 1951 to become a professor of engineering and physics at the University of Illinois. During the mid-1950s, his research on superconductivity led to his second Nobel Prize in 1972. He retired from the University of Illinois in 1975.

BOOKS ABOUT BARDEEN

Pines, David. *Solid State Physics.* Acad. Pr. 1955 o.p. Describes Bardeen's contributions to solid-state physics and explains how he and others applied the theories of solid-state physics to their work in semiconduction and superconduction.

Schrieffer, John Robert. *The Theory of Superconductivity.* Addison-Wesley 1964 $31.95. ISBN 0-8053-8501-1. Describes in quite technical terms the development of the theory and Bardeen's contributions; features Bardeen's method of problem solving. Written by one of Bardeen's collaborators on the BCS theory.

Shockley, William. *Electrons and Holes in Semiconductors.* Van Nos. Reinhold 1950 o.p. Provides insights into Bardeen's contributions to transistor technology; accessible to the layperson.

BETHE, HANS ALBRECHT. 1906– (NOBEL PRIZE 1967)

Born in Germany, Hans Bethe was the son of a university professor. He received a Ph.D. in physics from the University of Munich and lectured in physics throughout various German universities until 1933, when he moved to England because of the rise to power of Hitler and the Nazi party. (His mother was Jewish.) In 1935 Bethe emigrated to the United States to join the physics faculty at Cornell University.

In 1938 Bethe determined the sequences of nuclear reactions that power the stars, a problem that had remained unsolved for 75 years since William Thomson Kelvin and HERMANN HELMHOLTZ first described it. For this research, Bethe received the Nobel Prize in 1967. In addition to these accomplishments, he has researched a wide range of other problems, such as electron densities in crystals and operational conditions in nuclear reactors. He was the director of the Theoretical Physics Division of the Los Alamos Laboratory from 1943 to 1946, working on the Manhattan Project to develop the atomic bomb.

Bethe has been active in science policy discussions for several decades. In 1958 he served as a delegate to the first International Test Ban Conference at Geneva, and was a leader in the nuclear disarmament movement. Bethe also played an active role in the national debate on the "Star Wars" defense proposal.

BOOKS BY BETHE

Basic Bethe. Am. Inst. Physics 1986 repr. of 1937 ed. $37.50. ISBN 0-88318-495-8
Intermediate Quantum Mechanics. Addison-Wesley 1986 $39.95. ISBN 0-8053-0757-5

Quantum Mechanics of One and Two Electron Atoms. Plenum Pub. 1977 $29.50. ISBN 0-306-20022-8

The Road from Los Alamos: Collected Essays of Hans A. Bethe. Am. Inst. Physics 1991 $24.95. ISBN 0-88318-707-8. Focuses on weapons research, arms control, and nuclear power.

BOOKS ABOUT BETHE

Bernstein, Jeremy. *Hans Bethe: Prophet of Energy.* Basic 1980 o.p. Based on two years of extensive interviews; originally published in the *New Yorker.*

York, Herbert F. *The Advisors: Oppenheimer, Teller, and the Superbomb.* Stanford U. Pr. 1989 repr. of 1976 ed. $35.00. ISBN 0-8047-1713-3. Examines the secret debate between the advocates and opponents of the hydrogen bomb. Introduction by Hans A. Bethe.

BINNIG, GERD. 1947– (NOBEL PRIZE 1986)

Born in Germany, Gerd Binnig shared half of the Nobel Prize in physics in 1986 for his work with Heinrich Rohrer in the field of scanning tunneling microscopy. Binnig's research has enabled scientists to probe even more deeply into the world of atomic and subatomic matter. The other half of the prize was awarded to Ernst Ruska for his work on the electron microscope.

Although interested in physics at an early age, Binnig devoted much time to developing his skills as a classical and rock musician. In 1978 Binnig's scientific career was given a major stimulus when he joined the IBM laboratories in Switzerland. Binnig's enthusiasm for practical physics was a significant factor in his success at the IBM laboratories. His research team received many international accolades for their pioneering research between 1978 and 1986. These awards and honors included the German Physics Prize, the Otto Klung Prize, the Hewlett Packard Prize, and the King Faisal Saudi Arabian Award for significant work in experimental physics.

BOOKS ABOUT BINNIG

Hansma, Paul K. *Tunneling Spectroscopy.* Plenum Pub. 1982 $125.00. ISBN 0-306-41070-2. Emphasizes the technical problems confronted and solved by Binnig; includes a subsection on scanning electron microscopy.

Wolf, E. L. *Principles of Electron Tunneling Spectroscopy.* OUP 1989 repr. of 1985 ed. $49.95. ISBN 0-19-506154-3. The most complete volume on electron tunneling research. Covers research done when Binnig and Rohrer were achieving their most advanced results; includes references to the Nobel laureates' published work and Wolf's comprehensive, 32-page bibliography.

BLOCH, FELIX. 1905–1983 (NOBEL PRIZE 1952)

A Swiss-American physicist, Bloch spent most of his career at Stanford University. He is best known for introducing the technique of nuclear magnetic resonance imaging (NMR) as an analytical tool. He has also worked extensively in solid-state physics, developing a detailed analysis of the behavior of electrons in crystals. In addition, he is a major figure in research on the X-ray phenomenon, and quantum electrodynamics.

NMR uses the fact that atomic nuclei will interact with a magnetic field in such a way that the nuclei will assume particular spatial orientations, representing slightly different energies. The technique was first used to study nuclear particles, but has become a basic tool for analyzing complex organic molecules, and now has medical imaging and industrial applications. Bloch was awarded the Nobel Prize in physics in 1952 for his work on NMR.

BOOKS ABOUT BLOCH

Gutfreund, H., ed. *Felix Bloch and Twentieth-Century Physics*. Rice Univ. 1980 $15.00. ISBN 0-89263-246-1

Little, W. A. *Conductivity and Magnetism: The Legacy of Felix Bloch*. World Scientific Pub. 1990 $58.00. ISBN 981-02-0194-X

Walecka, John D. *Fundamentals of Statistical Mechanics: Manuscript and Notes of Felix Bloch*. Stanford U. Pr. 1989 $45.00. ISBN 0-8047-1501-7. This book is the unique product of a long-standing course given at Stanford by Bloch.

BOHR, NIELS (HEINRIK DAVID). 1885–1962 (NOBEL PRIZE 1922)

A Danish physicist, Niels Bohr was a pioneer in the field of quantum mechanics and explained the process of nuclear fission. For these reasons, Bohr is considered one of the twentieth century's most important theoretical physicists.

Born into a distinguished scientific family in 1885, Bohr spent most of his life in Copenhagen. After receiving his Ph.D. in 1911, Bohr went to England to work with JOSEPH JOHN THOMSON, discoverer of the electron, and then with ERNEST RUTHERFORD, who had shown in 1911 that the atom consists of a small central nucleus surrounded by relatively distant electrons. At this time, the process involving electron orbits and energy transfer was not well understood due to the limitations of classical electrodynamics. In 1913, Bohr elucidated this process by proposing an explanation based on earlier research by MAX PLANCK, who had argued that radiation is emitted or absorbed by atoms in discrete units of quanta of energy. Bohr proposed that electrons exchange energy in quanta. By applying quantum theory to the atom, he derived a theoretical formula for the spectral lines in hydrogen, long observed but never explained. His formula matched the empirical formula, thus verifying the theory. For this accomplishment, Bohr received the Nobel Prize in physics in 1922.

Among Bohr's many contributions to the early development of quantum theory was his formulation of the "correspondence principle" in 1916 and the "complementarity principle" in 1927. The former principle requires that the quantum theoretical description of the atom correspond to classical physics at large magnitudes. The second principle states that it is impossible to distinguish between the actual behavior of atomic objects and their interaction with the measuring instrument.

In 1910, the government of Denmark created the Institute for Theoretical Physics to facilitate Bohr's research. He served as its director until his death. The institute under Bohr's leadership became a world center for the exchange of ideas and information on nuclear physics. He also was president of the Royal Danish Academy of Sciences from 1939 until his death.

When Denmark was occupied by the Germans in 1940, Bohr became active in the resistance movement. In 1943, he and his family escaped to Sweden in a fishing boat and then to the United States to assist in developing the atomic bomb at Los Alamos, New Mexico, on the Manhattan Project. After the war, he became a passionate advocate of nuclear disarmament. In 1952 Bohr helped create the European Centre for Nuclear Research (CERN) in Geneva, Switzerland. In 1955, he organized the first Atoms for Peace Conference in Geneva.

BOOKS BY BOHR

Atomic Theory and the Description of Nature. Ox Bow 1987 repr. of 1934 ed. $24.00. ISBN 0-918024-51-X. Presents four republished essays on quantum theory and the atom; features an introductory survey of quantum mechanics and discusses fundamental concepts, including quantum states, the correspondence principle, and the uncertainty principle.

Essays 1958–1962, on Atomic Physics and Human Knowledge. Ox Bow 1987 repr. of 1963 ed. $24.00. ISBN 0-918024-55-2. Discusses the philosophical implications of modern atomic physics and its relevance to other fields of knowledge.

Niels Bohr Collected Works. 9 vols. Elsevier 1973–1986 $174.50–$213.00 ea.

BOOKS ABOUT BOHR

Aaserud, Finn. *Redirecting Science: Niels Bohr, Philanthropy, and the Rise of Nuclear Physics.* Cambridge U. Pr. 1990 $54.95. ISBN 0-521-35366-1. Examines how the directions of scientific inquiry are influenced by issues outside of science, particularly that of financial support. Profusely illustrated; accompanied by nearly 100 pages of notes and index.

Blaedel, Niels. *Harmony and Unity: The Life of Niels Bohr.* Sci. Tech. Pub. 1988 $35.00. ISBN 0-910239-14-2. Anecdotes that capture a modest and kindly genius.

Feshbach, H., and others. *Niels Bohr: Physics and the World.* Gordon & Breach 1988 $24.00. ISBN 3-7186-0494-9. Proceedings of the Niels Bohr Centennial Symposium. Nineteen contributions on the philosophical issues associated with quantum theory and the qualities of a unique scientist.

French, A. P., and P. J. Kennedy, eds. *Niels Bohr: A Centenary Volume.* HUP 1985 $35.00. ISBN 0-674-62415-7. Offers a well-illustrated, stimulating collection of essays on Bohr and his work; includes some of Bohr's essays, such as his 1950 "Open Letter to the United Nations" on the future of atomic energy.

Hendry, John. *The Creation of Quantum Mechanics and the Bohr-Pauli Dialogue.* Kluwer Ac. 1984 $34.50. ISBN 0-318-00442-9. Examines the historical development of modern quantum mechanics and introduces its main ideas; does not provide an in-depth analysis of personalities, professional circumstances, or the cultural and political environment.

Moor, Ruth. *Niels Bohr: The Man, His Science, and the World They Changed.* MIT Pr. 1985 o.p. Originally published in 1966, this book remains the only full-length biography of Bohr written in English; discusses concepts of atomic and quantum physics that are necessary to understand Bohr's work throughout the text, making the work accessible to the layperson. Also covers Bohr's political life, anti-Nazi activities, and his postwar efforts to avert a nuclear arms race.

Murdoch, D. R. *Niels Bohr's Philosophy of Physics.* Cambridge U. Pr. 1989 $27.95. ISBN 0-521-37927-X. Important contribution to the clarification of the intellectual history of a central problem in twentieth-century physics.

Rozental, S., ed. *Niels Bohr: His Life and Work as Seen by His Friends and Colleagues.* Elsevier 1985 repr. of 1967 ed. $32.50. ISBN 0-444-86977-8. A "collective book" on Niels Bohr comprised of essays by friends, family, and professional colleagues that describe and evaluate his life and work.

BOLTZMANN, LUDWIG. 1844–1906

Ludwig Boltzmann, an Austrian theoretical physicist, was born and educated in Vienna. Boltzmann moved from post to post throughout Europe and visited the United States three times. Independent of the pioneering research of JAMES CLERK MAXWELL, Boltzmann developed the kinetic theory of gases. He also established a firm theoretical foundation for statistical mechanics by successfully interpreting the second law of thermodynamics in terms of order and disorder. Boltzmann's famous equation, $S = k \log W$, which relates the entropy S of a system to its probability W, is engraved on his tombstone. Using thermodynamics, he also derived the law governing the radiation rate of a black body. In the late nineteenth century, Boltzmann championed the controversial subject of the atomic theory of matter. As a result of serious depression caused by these bitter professional debates, he committed suicide in 1906. Ironically, this happened just before the last of his opponents finally accepted the atomic theory.

BOOK BY BOLTZMANN

Theoretical Physics and Philosophical Problems: Selected Writings. Kluwer Ac. 1974 $89.00. ISBN 90-277-0249-7

BORN, MAX. 1882–1970 (NOBEL PRIZE 1954)

Born in Breslau (Wroclaw), the German physicist Max Born received a Ph.D. in physics and astronomy from the University of Göttingen in 1921. He then taught at that university as well as the universities of Berlin and Frankfurt-am-Main. At Göttingen, Born helped make the university a world center for theoretical physics. During the years of World War I, Born and ALBERT EINSTEIN became good friends. In addition to physics, they shared a love of music, often playing pieces together (with Einstein on the violin and Born on the piano). With the enactment of Hitler's anti-Semitic laws in 1933, Born was forced to leave Germany for Great Britain. He taught at the University of Edinburgh from 1936 until his retirement in 1953.

Born devoted much of his life to formulating a mathematical explanation for NIELS BOHR's successful application of quantum theory to the behavior of electrons in atoms. While at Göttingen, for example, he and his student WERNER HEISENBERG introduced a theory called "matrix mechanics" to account mathematically (using matrix algebra) for the position of an electron in an atom. This theory was soon replaced, however, by ERWIN SCHRÖDINGER's theory of wave mechanics. Born also linked the wave function of a particle to the probability of finding it by using wave mechanics and statistics to interpret quantum theory. For his pioneering work and landmark discoveries in quantum physics, he was awarded the Nobel Prize in physics in 1954 (a prize he shared with Walter Bothe).

BOOKS BY BORN

Atomic Physics. Dover 1989 $11.95. ISBN 0-486-65984-4
Dynamical Theory of Crystal Lattices. OUP 1985 $38.95. ISBN 0-19-851248-1
Einstein's Theory of Relativity. Dover 1986 repr. of 1962 ed. $6.95. ISBN 0-486-60769-0. An easy-to-read, but in-depth exposition of the physical principles of the special and general theories of relativity; intended for the serious student but requires a minimum of formal mathematics.
My Life: Recollections of a Nobel Laureate. Taylor & Francis 1978 $60.00. ISBN 0-85066-174-9. Presents the personal reminiscences of a curious, timid, and self-deprecating Nobelist.
My Life and My Views. Scribner 1968 o.p. Features two brief essays on Born's education and work; emphasizes the social responsibilities of scientists.
Physics in My Generation. Spr.-Verlag 1989 $19.95. ISBN 0-387-90008-X. Offers a selection of Born's views on a wide range of subjects, including reflections on the nature of the new physics and his pessimistic view of the role of science in society.
Restless Universe. Dover 1951 o.p. Discusses concepts of atomic and molecular physics from the nineteenth century to the development of quantum mechanics; explains important concepts, such as temperature, mole, mass, energy, spectral line, and the Pauli exclusion principle.

BRIDGMAN, PERCY WILLIAMS. 1882–1961 (NOBEL PRIZE 1946)

Born in Cambridge, Massachusetts, Percy Bridgman studied solely at Harvard University. He received his B.S. in 1900 and graduated summa cum laude in physics in 1904; one year later he received his A.M. and in 1908 he earned his

Ph.D. Early in his career, Bridgman was drawn to studying the behavior of material when subjected to high pressures—an interest for which he became well known. Bridgman remained at Harvard after his student years; he was first named research fellow and then professor in physics.

During his research into high-pressure physics, he explored the properties of many liquids and solids and designed innovative experimental equipment. Bridgman proposed a process for synthesizing diamonds, which was finally successfully implemented in 1955. This technique was favorably applied to other problems of mineral synthesis, and his work became the basis for a new school of geology based on experiments conducted at high pressures and temperatures.

During the rise of totalitarianism in the 1930s, Bridgman wrote a manifesto, a personal statement, in which he denied access to his laboratory to, and refused to discuss his work with, any citizen from a totalitarian state. Also during this decade, Bridgman wrote *The Intelligent Individual and Society* (1939).

In 1946 Bridgman was awarded the Nobel Prize "for the invention of apparatus for obtaining very high pressures and for discoveries which he made by means of this apparatus in the field of high pressure physics." Bridgman developed a chamber that could withstand temperatures never before attained prior to his invention. His apparatus opened the way for other scientific developments and advances in thermodynamics, the properties of matter, crystallography, and electric conduction in metals.

Bridgman is also widely known as a philosopher of science. Realizing that many ambiguities arise in an examination of scientific methodology, he published *The Nature of Physical Theory (1936)* and *The Logic of Modern Physics* (1927), in which he argued his view that a scientific concept is really a set of operations ("operationalism"), a view that is still widely discussed. Bridgman died of bone cancer at the age of 79.

BOOKS BY BRIDGMAN

Collected Experimental Papers. 7 vols. HUP 1964 $300.00. ISBN 0-674-13750-7
The Logic of Modern Physics. Ayer 1980 repr. of 1927 ed. $21.00. ISBN 0-405-12594-1.
    Central exposition of operationalism; not suitable for the beginner. Rather, it should
    be read after works such as Born's *Restless Universe* (see above).
The Nature of Thermodynamics. Peter Smith $12.50. ISBN 0-8446-0512-3
Philosophical Writings of Percy William Bridgman: An Original Anthology. Ayer 1980
    $19.00. ISBN 0-405-12532-1
The Physics of High Pressure. Macmillan 1931 o.p.
Reflections of a Physicist. Ayer 1980 repr. of 1955 ed. 2nd ed. $48.50. ISBN 0-405-
    12595-X. Collection of Bridgman's nontechnical writings, discussing characteristics
    of the operational method, applications of this method to scientific situations,
    science in a social environment, and future possibilities for science.
Sophisticate's Primer of Relativity. U. Pr. N.E. 1982 o.p. This book is meant for the reader
    who, after assimilating an introduction to the special theory of relativity, seeks a
    more critical exposition of the subject.

BOOK ABOUT BRIDGMAN

Walter, Maila L. *Science and Cultural Crisis: An Intellectual Biography of Percy William
    Bridgman.* Stanford U. Pr. 1990 $45.00. ISBN 0-8047-1796-6. A splendid portrait of a
    man trying to preserve his integrity in an era of transition in U.S. science.

CHANDRASEKHAR, SUBRAHMANYAN. 1910– (NOBEL PRIZE 1983)

Born in Lahore, India (now part of Pakistan), the astrophysicist Subrahmanyan Chandrasekhar obtained his B.S. degree in 1930 from Presidency College in Madras, India. By the time he received his Ph.D. from Cambridge University in 1933, he had formulated a theory on white dwarf stars. Chandrasekhar's theory of white dwarf stars states that a white dwarf's mass cannot exceed about one and one-half times that of the sun. His calculations implied that more massive stars would end their lives as neutron stars or black holes. The Chandrasekhar limit has become one of the foundations of astrophysics. This discovery led to Chandrasekhar's first definitive work in 1939, *An Introduction to the Study of Stellar Structure*. This book was indicative of the pattern of his scientific career. He has moved from one physics area to another, publishing a definitive book on each (seven books in all).

As a result of an ongoing disagreement with SIR ARTHUR EDDINGTON on his theory of dwarf stars, Chandrasekhar left Cambridge for the University of Chicago in 1937. (At one point he was publicly and wrongly humiliated by Eddington.) The following year, he began to study the dynamics of star clusters, resulting in the publication of his second definitive work, *Principles of Stellar Systems*, in 1942.

During World War II, he served in the War Department as a scientific consultant. Specifically, Chandrasekhar contributed to the top-secret atomic weapons research at the University of Chicago with ENRICO FERMI and James Franck. Toward the end of World War II, Chandrasekhar's field of study was radiative transfer (how light energy moves and interacts with the material through which it travels) in the interior of stars and the effects of magnetism on galaxies. This research led to another landmark book, *Hydromagnetic Stability*, in 1961. Chandrasekhar was married in 1936 to a fellow student from Presidency College and became an American citizen in 1953.

During the 1960s, Chandrasekhar mainly studied ellipsoidal figures of equilibrium. His understanding of planetary rotation and the rotation of white dwarfs, neutron stars, black holes, galaxies, and clusters of galaxies culminated in *Ellipsoidal Figures of Equilibrium*, published in 1969.

In the mid-1970s, Chandrasekhar studied relativity and relativistic astrophysics, rethinking concepts he used when deriving upper limits for the mass of white dwarfs 40 years earlier. This led to the monumental work *The Mathematical Theory of Black Holes*, published in 1983.

BOOKS BY CHANDRASEKHAR

Classical General Relativity. OUP 1993 $45.00. ISBN 0-19-853980-0
Hydrodynamic and Hydromagnetic Stability. Dover 1960 $9.95. ISBN 0-486-60590-6
An Introduction to the Study of Stellar Structure. Dover 1939 $10.00. ISBN 0-486-60413-6
The Mathematical Theory of Black Holes. OUP 1992 repr. of 1983 ed. $49.95. ISBN 0-19-508147-1
Radiative Transfer. Dover 1960 $9.95. ISBN 0-486-60590-6

BOOKS ABOUT CHANDRASEKHAR

Hammond, Allen L., ed. *A Passion to Know: Twenty Profiles in Science.* Scribner 1984 o.p. A series of biographical and career sketches of some of the outstanding scientists of the world; suitable for the general reader.
Kevles, Daniel J. *The Physicists: The History of a Scientific Community in Modern America.* HUP 1987 $16.95. ISBN 0-674-66655-0. A historical survey of physics in modern times; covers the contributions of many physicists to various aspects of research and examines the political and economic ramifications of their research.
Wali, Kameshwar C. *Chandra: A Biography of S. Chandrasekhar.* U. Ch. Pr. 1990 $29.95. ISBN 0-226-87054-5

Weaver, Jefferson Hane. *The World of Physics: A Small Library of Literature of Physics from Antiquity to the Present*. 3 vols. S&S Trade 1987 $90.00. ISBN 0-671-64216-2. A series of articles on the status of physics research, written by the most active research physicists in the field. A short biographical sketch accompanies each contributor's article; especially useful for physics teachers.

COMPTON, ARTHUR H(OLLY). 1892–1962 (NOBEL PRIZE 1927)

Arthur Holly Compton, the son of a Presbyterian minister, was born in Wooster, Ohio, in 1892. He received his B.S. from the College of Wooster and his Ph.D. from Princeton University in 1916 and did postdoctoral research with ERNEST RUTHERFORD and JOSEPH JOHN THOMPSON from 1919 to 1920. Compton made significant advances in the study of X-radiation and optics. In 1923 he discovered and interpreted the change in the wavelength of scattered X-rays (the Compton effect). His research provided the first conclusive experimental proof of ALBERT EINSTEIN's light quantum hypothesis and led to the development of modern quantum theory physics.

Compton and other American scientists, most notably ROBERT ANDREWS MILLIKAN and Richardson, were initially skeptical of Einstein's hypothesis. A painstaking process of rethinking the fundamental principles of physics and extensive laboratory work enabled Compton finally to support Einstein's quantum hypothesis with experimental proof. This led to his sharing of the Nobel Prize with Charles Wilson in 1927 for his discovery of the effect named after him. During World War II, Compton played a significant role in the Manhattan Project, which culminated in the development of the atomic bomb. Compton was connected with the University of Chicago for a number of years; in 1945 he went to Washington University and later to the University of California, Berkeley.

BOOKS BY COMPTON

Atomic Quest: A Personal Narrative. OUP 1956 o.p. Describes his role in the Manhattan Project.
Scientific Papers of Arthur Holly Compton. U. Ch. Pr. 1974 $50.00. ISBN 0-226-11430-9
X-Rays and Electrons: An Outline of Recent X-Ray Theory. Van Nos. Reinhold 1926 o.p.

BOOKS ABOUT COMPTON

Johnston, Marjorie, ed. *The Cosmos of Arthur Holly Compton*. Knopf 1967 o.p. Offers a good introduction to Compton as a philosopher-scientist and as a public mentor. Provides a description of Compton in his own words; includes "A Life in Science," an autobiographical sketch prepared from notes left by Compton.
Stuewer, Robert H. *The Compton Effect: Turning Point in Physics*. Sci. Hist. Pubns. 1975 o.p. Contends that Compton's discovery did not spring from a sudden insight but rather was the culmination of years of research. Surveys developments in radiation that preceded Compton's work, focusing on the critical years from 1912 to 1922. Analyzes the immediate reaction to Compton's discovery and evaluates its permanent significance for modern physics; written by a person who is a recognized authority on Compton's career and contributions as well as being a physicist and historian.

CRONIN, JAMES W(ILSON). 1931– (NOBEL PRIZE 1980)

James Wilson Cronin was born in Chicago, Illinois. After studying particle physics at the University of Chicago, where he completed his Ph.D. in 1955, Cronin worked as an assistant physicist at the Brookhaven National Laboratory on the research team of Rodney Cool and Oreste Piccioni. This period significantly influenced Cronin's later research. During his tenure at Brookhaven, Cronin met VAL LOGSDON FITCH. Fitch encouraged Cronin to join the faculty of Princeton University, where Cronin taught from 1958 to 1971. During this time, Cronin and Fitch collaborated in a joint experiment on a subatomic particle called the "neutral K-meson." They discovered that radioactive decay of the particle violated basic physical principles of symmetry.

Cronin and Fitch's results raised startling new physical and philosophical questions about the role of symmetry in nature, time reflection, and the creation of matter and antimatter at the birth of the universe. In 1980, Cronin and Fitch shared the Nobel Prize in physics for their discovery.

In 1954 Cronin married a fellow student. Since 1971 he has been a professor of physics at the University of Chicago.

BOOK BY CRONIN

Differential Equations: Pure and Applied Math. Dekker 1980 $115.00. ISBN 0-8247-6819-1

CURIE, MARIE SKLODOWSKA. 1867–1934 (NOBEL PRIZE 1903, 1911)

Marie Curie, a Polish-born physicist and chemist, spent her adult life studying and working in France. The focus of her work was the study of radioactivity, a phenomenon discovered by Henri Becquerel in 1896. Married to the physicist Pierre Curie and working in his laboratory, she had demonstrated by the end of 1898 the existence of three new and radioactive elements—uranium, radium, and polonium—as well as some characteristics of their radioactivity. However, a successful explanation of radioactivity was proposed, not by the Curies, but by ERNEST RUTHERFORD and his students. In 1903 she received the Nobel Prize in physics jointly with her husband and Becquerel for the pioneering work on radioactivity. In 1911 she was awarded a second Nobel Prize, in chemistry, for her discovery of radium and polonium. Despite these and many other honors, as a foreign-born woman she had to contend throughout her life with the refusal of the French academic community to recognize her scientific eminence.

BOOKS ABOUT CURIE

Birch, Beverly. *Marie Curie: The Polish Scientist Who Discovered Radium and Its Life-Saving Properties.* Gareth Stevens Inc. 1988 $18.60. ISBN 1-55532-818-0. Positive portrait of Curie's life and contributions to science.

Curie, Eve. *Marie Curie: A Biography.* Doubleday 1939 o.p. Written by Marie Curie's daughter, who drew on family recollections and papers; contains a detailed index and lists of Madame Curie's prizes and decorations.

Dunn, Andrew. *Marie Curie.* Watts 1991 $12.50. ISBN 0-531-18375-0. Thoughtful biography of the scientist with illustrations and photos, a chronology, a glossary, an index, and a bibliography.

Giroud, Francoise. *Marie Curie: A Life.* Holmes & Meier 1987 $34.50. ISBN 0-8419-0977-6. Informal, emotive biography translated from the French *Une Femme Honorable,* for the general-interest lay reader. Emphasizes personal life and social issues.

Reid, Robert. *Marie Curie.* NAL-Dutton 1975 o.p. Solid narrative biography, based on research done in four countries.

DIRAC, PAUL ADRIEN MAURICE. 1902–1984 (NOBEL PRIZE 1933)

Paul Dirac, a British theoretical physicist, was a central figure in the development of quantum electrodynamics. For example, he introduced important concepts, such as magnetic monopole and electron spin, and predicted the existence of antiparticles.

Dirac was well known for his creativity as a graduate student in the 1920s. After reading WERNER HEISENBERG's first paper on relativity in 1925, for example, he promptly devised a more general form of the theory. The next year, he formulated WOLFGANG PAULI's exclusion principle in terms of quantum mechanics. Specifically, he formulated useful statistical rules for particles that obey the Pauli exclusion principle. He received his Ph.D. in physics from Cambridge University in 1926. Dirac's most important contribution occurred in 1928, when he joined special relativity to quantum theory. His theory of the electron permitted scientists to calculate its spin and magnetic moment and to predict the existence of positively charged electrons, or positrons. (Positrons were observed in 1932.) In 1933 Dirac shared the Nobel Prize in physics with ERWIN SCHRODINGER for his theory of the electron and prediction of the positron. Dirac's theoretical considerations in predicting the positron were sufficiently general to apply to all particles. This constituted an argument for the existence of antimatter. In later years, Dirac worked on "large-number coincidences," or relationships that appear to exist between some cosmological constants. He also taught mathematics at Cambridge University from 1932 until 1969. From 1968, when he retired from Cambridge, until his death in 1984, Dirac was a professor at the University of Florida in Tallahassee.

BOOKS BY DIRAC

The Development of Quantum Theory. Gordon & Breach 1971 $50.00. ISBN 0-677-02970-5. An anecdotal account of the development of quantum mechanics providing information about notable figures and their contributions.
General Theory of Relativity. Wiley 1975 o.p. A concise treatment of general relativity; intended for the general reader with some physics background.
The Principles of Quantum Mechanics. OUP 1958 $32.50. ISBN 0-19-851208-2. "Dirac's classic textbook . . . first appeared in 1930 but it remains incomparably the best book on the fundamentals of quantum theory" (*Nature*); somewhat technical for the layperson.

BOOK ABOUT DIRAC

Kragh, Helge S. *Dirac: A Scientific Biography.* Cambridge U. Pr. 1990 $49.95. ISBN 0-521-38089-8. This biography makes clear what Niels Bohr meant when he said that Dirac had "the purest soul."

EDDINGTON, SIR ARTHUR STANLEY. 1882–1944

Born in Kendal, England, Sir Arthur Eddington was a pioneer thinker on stellar structure and the general theory of relativity, and is considered to be one of the greatest English astronomers. After completing his education at Cambridge University in 1906, Eddington began his theoretical studies on stellar movements (especially notable for his statistical methods). In 1914, in recognition for his work, he was appointed director of the Cambridge Observatory, a highly influential position. In addition to his work on stellar movement, Eddington also made a theoretical study of the internal constitution of stars, an avenue of research that drew him into ALBERT EINSTEIN's general theory of relativity. This research led to the book *Mathematical Theory of Relativity* (1923), a work highlighted by Eddington's drawing attention to a tendency of extragalactic nebulae to recede from our own galaxy, the Milky Way. Eddington was the first to realize fully that Einstein's universe was unstable, and he did much to help establish Einstein's theories. In later work, Eddington tried to unify general relativity and quantum mechanics by hypothesizing that gravitation was a consequence of the exclusion principle. Although this particular research was criticized, Eddington's genius has been recognized and honored worldwide. A rather shy individual, Eddington nevertheless had an outstanding ability to convey complex mathematical ideas to the layperson, and he wrote several popular works from a philosophical perspective.

BOOKS BY EDDINGTON

The Expanding Universe. Cambridge U. Pr. 1988 $17.95. ISBN 0-521-34976-1. Investigates the experimental determination of one of the fundamental constants of astrophysics.
The Internal Constitution of Stars. Cambridge U. Pr. 1988 $27.95. ISBN 0-521-33708-9. A classic work on stellar structure.
The Mathematical Theory of Relativity. Chelsea Pub. 1975 $17.95. ISBN 0-8284-0278-7
The Nature of the Physical World. AMS Pr. repr. of 1928 ed. $27.50. ISBN 0-404-60478-1
New Pathways in Science. Macmillan 1935 o.p.
Relativity Theory of Protons and Electrons. Fleetway Pr. 1936 o.p.
Science and the Unseen World. Allen & Unwin 1929 o.p.
Space, Time and Gravitation: An Outline of the General Theory. Cambridge U. Pr. 1987 $19.95. ISBN 0-521-33709-7. Written orginally for the educated popular audience.
Stars and Atoms. Yale U. Pr. 1927 o.p.

BOOKS ABOUT EDDINGTON

Douglas, Allie. *The Life of Arthur Stanley Eddington.* Vibert 1956 o.p.
Jacks, Lawrence. *Sir Arthur Eddington, Man of Science and Mystic.* Cambridge U. Pr. 1949 o.p.
Kilmister, Clive William. *Eddington's Statistical Theory.* Pergamon 1962 o.p.
_____. *Sir Arthur Eddington.* Franklin 1966 $120.00. ISBN 0-08-011872-0
Ritchie, Arthur. *Reflection on the Philosophy of Sir Arthur Eddington.* Cambridge U. Pr. 1948 o.p.
Schleicher, Joan L. *The Essential Eddington.* Rob Briggs 1993 $6.95. ISBN 0-931191-14-9. Comprehensive overview of Eddington's life and work. A readable, worthwhile book.

EINSTEIN, ALBERT. 1879–1955 (NOBEL PRIZE 1921)

Albert Einstein is the dominant figure in modern physics, comparable in historic importance to ARCHIMEDES, GALILEO (see also Vol. 4), and SIR ISAAC NEWTON (see also Vol. 4). Born of Jewish parents in Ulm, Germany, he studied in Switzerland, graduating in 1909 from the Federal Institute of Technology in Zurich. Einstein was a Swiss citizen until 1914, when he became director of theoretical physics at the Kaiser Wilhelm Institute in Berlin. He then resumed his German citizenship. While Einstein was visiting professor at the California Institute of Technology (1933), Hitler became chancellor of Germany. Einstein never returned to Germany. In 1934 his property was confiscated by the Nazi government and he was deprived of his German citizenship. In 1940 Einstein became an American citizen and was associated with Princeton's Institute for Advanced Study, where he remained until his retirement in 1945. He was married twice. The first marriage (1903) ended in divorce; the second, with his wife's death (1936). He had two sons by his first wife.

Einstein proposed that light has a dual character, composed of particles as well as having the characteristics of waves. He explained Brownian motion and the photoelectric effect. He revolutionized the world's understanding of space, time, and matter by formulating theories of special and general relativity. Predictions based on his theories have been confirmed by observational evidence, leading to their acceptance as the standard model of physical phenomena. Einstein's first major contribution to theoretical physics was his solution of the photoelectric effect problem, published in 1905. Experimental physicists had observed that light shining on the surface of certain metals liberated electrons. However, the researchers observed that the reaction relied more on the color (frequency) of light than on the intensity of light. Einstein explained this by assuming that light energy travels in discrete packets, or quanta, called photons. Einstein received the 1921 Nobel Prize "especially for his discovery of the law of the photoelectric effect."

Einstein is world famous for his theories of relativity: special and general. Based on the assumption that the speed of light is constant, special relativity shows that nonaccelerated frames of reference are equivalent with respect to each other. General relativity shows the same result for accelerated frames of reference. These ideas are fully explained in his book *Relativity: The Special and the General Theory*.

After dramatically transforming physics, Einstein spent the last 30 years of his life trying, without success, to formulate a grand, unified theory. He claimed that nature is based on simplicity, evident in his famous remark "God may be subtle but He is not malicious." However, today, as in the year Einstein died, the prospect for a grand, unified theory is as elusive as ever.

BOOKS BY EINSTEIN

Autobiographical Notes: A Centennial Edition. Ed. by Paul A. Schilpp. Open Court 1991 $19.95. ISBN 0-87548-352-6. A 43-page essay that examines his life and work; includes the original text in German.

Essays in Physics. Philos. Lib. 1985 o.p.

Evolution of Physics: The Growth of Ideas from Early Concepts to Relativity and Quanta. 1938. (coauthored with Leopold Infeld). S&S Trade 1961 o.p. Presents a thorough exposition of the concepts of quantum mechanics; covers prerequisites, such as central ideas of classical physics and relativity.

Ideas and Opinions. Crown Pub. Group 1985 $8.00. ISBN 0-517-55601-4. Features selected essays from three previously published compendia, including *The World as I See It* (1934) and *Out of My Later Years* (1950). Describes his initial impressions of the United States and comments on ethics, social values, and the important political issues of his life.

Meaning of Relativity. Princeton U. Pr. 1956 o.p. A concise treatment of topics in special and general relativity; written at an advanced level, although formulas do not appear in the text.

Out of My Later Years. Outlet Bk. Co. 1990 $6.99. ISBN 0-517-69417-4. Covers the period from 1934 to 1950; includes articles, addresses, letters.

Relativity: The Special and the General Theory. Crown Pub. Group 1961 $4.95. ISBN 0-517-02530-2. Presents an outstanding introduction to the theories.

Sidelights on Relativity. Dover 1983 repr. of 1922 ed. $2.95. ISBN 0-486-24511-X. Describes ether and its relation to relativity and the relationship of geometry and experience.

The World as I See It. Carol Pub. Group 1979 $5.95. ISBN 0-8065-0711-X. Offers a collection of brief essays written between 1922 and 1934; covers topics such as politics and pacifism, Germany in 1933, Jews and Zionism, and scientific matters.

BOOKS ABOUT EINSTEIN

Barnett, Lincoln. *The Universe of Dr. Einstein*. Amereon Ltd. 1970 $16.95. ISBN 0-8488-0146-6. Offers a clear exposition of relativity accessible to a wide audience; originally published as an article in *Harper's* magazine.

Bernstein, Jeremy. *Einstein*. Viking Penguin 1975 $6.95. ISBN 0-14-004317-9. Outlines Einstein's personal and professional life; written by a theoretical physicist.

Born, Max. *Einstein's Theory of Relativity*. Dover rev. ed. 1962 $6.95. ISBN 0-486-60769-0. An easy-to-read exposition of the physical principles of the special and general theories of relativity; requires a minimum of formal mathematics.

Bucky, Peter A., and Allen Weakland. *The Private Albert Einstein*. Andrews & McMeel 1992 $18.95. ISBN 0-8362-7997-2. Intimate portrait by a personal, family friend. Includes previously unpublished photographs. Bucky's ties with Einstein go back to Germany.

Calder, Nigel. *Einstein's Universe*. Outlet Bk. Co. 1991 $6.99. ISBN 0-517-38570-8

Clark, Ronald W. *Einstein, the Life and Time: An Illustrated Biography*. Abrams 1984 o.p. Presents a wealth of material about Einstein's external life; unsuccessful in its coverage of Einstein's scientific work and motivations.

Dukas, Helen, and Banesh Hoffman, eds. *Albert Einstein, the Human Side: New Glimpses from His Archives*. Princeton U. Pr. 1979 $29.50. ISBN 0-691-02368-9. "Featuring bits of unpublished letters chosen by Einstein's secretary and his collabora-tor/biographer, this modest volume illuminates Einstein's character rather than his scientific theories." (*Library Journal*).

Pais, Abraham. *Subtle Is the Lord: The Science and Life of Albert Einstein*. OUP 1982 $35.00. ISBN 0-19-853907-X. A truly scientific biography that excludes philosophical issues. Successfully complements biographies by Frank and Dukas and Hoffman; written at an advanced level by a distinguished physicist.

Rosenthal-Schneider, Ilse. *Reality and Scientific Truth: Discussion with Einstein, von Laue, and Planck*. Ed. by Thomas Braun. Bks. Demand repr. of 1980 ed. $38.89. ISBN 0-318-34785-4. The author-editor corresponded with Einstein, Planck, and Max von Laue for many years on the nature of scientific truth and physical reality, as well as on lighter topics; includes selections of the correspondences with connecting text.

Roth, Gerhard. *The Autobiography of Albert Einstein*. Trans. by Malcom Green. Consorti-um Bk. Sales 1993 $13.99. ISBN 0-947757-47-3

Schilpp, Paul A., ed. *Albert Einstein: Philosopher-Scientist*. Open Court 1970 repr. of 1949 ed. $54.95. ISBN 0-87548-286-4. A collection of essays that examines nearly all aspects of Einstein's scientific and philosophical discoveries. Features contributions from many of the twentieth century's most distinguished physicists.

Whitrow, G. J., ed. *Einstein: The Man and His Achievement*. Dover 1973 repr. of 1967 ed. $3.95. ISBN 0-486-22934-3. Offers a perspective on Einstein's personal and profes-sional life and conveys the content of his theories in nonspecialist language; based on three BBC broadcasts on Einstein's life and work.

FARADAY, MICHAEL. 1791–1867

Michael Faraday, a British physicist and chemist, was one of the greatest experimentalists of the nineteenth century. The son of a blacksmith, Faraday received a minimal education, which did not include much training in mathematics. Nevertheless, in 1812 his innate intelligence attracted the attention of SIR HUMPHRY DAVY at the Royal Institution. Davy hired Faraday as a laboratory assistant in the institution, where he remained until his retirement in 1862. Here, he made his contributions to the study of electricity by formulating the laws of electrolysis in 1834. He also discovered that the circular lines of magnetic force produced by the flow of current through a wire deflect a nearby compass needle. By demonstrating this conversion of electrical energy into motive force, Faraday identified the basic principles governing the application of the electric motor. Simultaneously with Joseph Henry, Faraday discovered electromagnetic induction and then successfully built the first electric genera-tor, based on a suggestion from Scottish mathematician and physicist Lord William Thomson Kelvin.

After a series of experiments using polarized light, Faraday proposed an electromagnetic theory of light. This theory was later developed by JAMES CLERK MAXWELL and was fundamental to the later development of physics. Faraday was widely known as a popularizer of science, regularly lecturing to lay audiences from 1825 to 1862. Faraday, however, was an extremely modest person. For example, he declined honors bestowed in recognition of his accomplishments, such as a knighthood and the presidency of the Royal Society.

BOOKS BY FARADAY

The Chemical History of a Candle: A Course of Lectures Delivered before a Juvenile Audience at the Royal Institution. Cherokee 1978 repr. of 1861 ed. $19.95. ISBN 0-87797-209-5. Presents an example of Faraday's famous Christmas lecture series; mainly covers combustion.

Experimental Researches in Chemistry and Physics. Taylor & Francis 1990 $65.00. ISBN 0-85066-841-7. Reprint of the original volume of a collection of papers Faraday had brought together. The papers had appeared over the preceding 40 years in *Philosophical* magazine, *Philosophical Transactions of the Royal Society* and *The Journal of the Royal Institution.*

The Forces of Matter. Prometheus Bks. 1993 $5.95. ISBN 0-87975-811-2

BOOKS ABOUT FARADAY

Agassi, Joseph. *Faraday as a Natural Philosopher.* U. Ch. Pr. 1971 $23.00. ISBN 0-226-010446-5. Argues that Faraday viewed himself as a theoretician rather than a discoverer; describes how Faraday was frustrated because his theoretical constructions were not understood.

Thomas, J. M. *Michael Faraday and the Royal Institution.* IOP Pub. 1991 $25.00. ISBN 0-7503-0145-7. Story of Faraday's life, work, and legacy.

Tricker, R. A. *Contributions of Faraday and Maxwell to Electrical Science.* Franklin 1966 o.p. Thorough account of Faraday and Maxwell's work on electromagnetic induction; features historical, biographical, and anecdotal information as well as a brief overview of electromagnetic phenomena.

Tyndale, John. *Faraday as Discoverer.* Crowell 1868 o.p. Describes Faraday as a great discoverer of important facts of nature; written by a pupil and close personal friend of Faraday.

Williams, L. Pearce. *Michael Faraday: A Biography.* Basic 1965 o.p. A definitive biography of Faraday that makes extensive use of Faraday's writings and assesses Faraday's work in terms of modern science.

FERMI, ENRICO. 1901–1954 (NOBEL PRIZE 1938)

Born in Rome, Italy, Enrico Fermi was primarily self-taught. At the age of 17, he had already acquired a thorough understanding of classical physics. With his friend Enrico Persico, Fermi performed experiments, using handmade apparatus and thus obtaining an excellent grasp of experimental physics. He trained in Pisa, Göttingen, and Leiden, working with leading figures in the new quantum mechanics. He received his Ph.D. at the University of Pisa in 1922 and returned to Rome in 1926, where he spent several years working on the statistical mechanics of particles and wrote the first textbook on modern physics to be published in Italy. In 1934 he began a series of experiments producing new radioactive isotopes by neutron bombardment. This was the work for which he was awarded the Nobel Prize in 1938. After the prize ceremony, Fermi did not return to Italy, because of the Fascist regime, but emigrated with his wife and two children to the United States. As part of the atomic bomb effort, Fermi directed the design and construction of the first nuclear reactor at the University of Chicago, which began operating in December 1942. He spent the next two years with ARTHUR H. COMPTON leading the American team that constructed the first atomic bomb. Fermi died of cancer in 1954. The next year the newly discovered element with atomic number 100 was named fermium in his honor.

Fermi was one of the few modern physicists to excel in both theory and experiment. His accomplishments were foundation points for many branches of physics, including studies of the statistics of particles obeying the exclusion principle, quantum electrodynamics, beta-decay, artificial radioactivity, pion-nucleon collision, and nuclear chain reactions.

BOOKS BY FERMI

Collected Papers. 2 vols. U. Ch. Pr. $60.00. Vol. 1 *Italy, 1921–38.* 1962. ISBN 0-226-24359-1. Vol. 2 *United States, 1939–54.* 1965. ISBN 0-226-24360-5
Nuclear Physics. U. Ch. Pr. 1974 repr. of 1950 ed. $17.95. ISBN 0-226-24365-6
Thermodynamics. Dover 1937 $4.95. ISBN 0-486-60361-X

BOOKS ABOUT FERMI

Fermi, Laura. *Atoms in the Family: My Life with Enrico Fermi.* U. of NM Pr. 1988 repr. of 1954 ed. $12.95. ISBN 0-8263-1060-5. Biography and family portrait of this physicist's physicist.
Gottfried, Ted. *Enrico Fermi.* Facts on File 1992 $16.95. ISBN 0-8160-2623-8
Lichello, Robert. *Enrico Fermi: Father of the Atomic Bomb. Outstanding Personalities Ser.* SamHar Pr. 1972 $4.75. ISBN 0-87157-511-6. Brief biography.
Segre, Emilio. *Enrico Fermi: Physicist.* U. Ch. Pr. 1972 o.p. A nontechnical, professional portrait of Fermi; written by a compatriot, lifelong fried, and coworker. Four appendixes include letters from Fermi, the Nobel acceptance speech, and two addresses describing the Manhattan Project to develop the atom bomb.

FEYNMAN, RICHARD P(HILLIPS). 1918–1988 (NOBEL PRIZE 1965)

Richard Feynman, an American theoretical physicist, received his Ph.D. from Princeton University in 1942 and worked at Los Alamos, New Mexico, on the atomic bomb during World War II. From 1945 to 1950, he taught at Cornell University and became professor of theoretical physics at the California Institute of Technology in 1950.

Feynman has made important contributions to quantum electrodynamics (QED) and electromagnetic interactions, such as interactions among electrons. In Feynman's approach, interactions are considered exchanges of virtual particles. For example, Feynman explained the interaction of two electrons as an exchange of virtual photons. Feynman's theory has proved to be accurate in its predictions. In 1965 the Nobel Prize for physics was awarded to three pioneers in quantum electrodynamics: Feynman, JULIAN SCHWINGER, and SIN-ITIRO TOMONAGA.

Feynman was an outspoken critic of NASA for its failure to notice flaws in the design of the *Challenger* space shuttle, which resulted in its tragic explosion.

BOOKS BY FEYNMAN

Character of Physical Law. MIT Pr. 1967 $8.95. ISBN 0-262-56003-8. Offers an easy-to-read physics in simple English by an outstanding expositor. The notions of a physical theory, conservation laws, and quantum mechanics are discussed.
Feynman Lectures on Physics. 3 vols. Addison-Wesley 1989 $114.75 ea. ISBN 0-201-50064-7. Classic undergraduate treatment.
QED: The Strange Theory of Light and Matter. Princeton U. Pr. 1985 $29.95. ISBN 0-691-08388-6. Principles of quantum theory and in particular of quantum electrodynamics are explained simply and without mathematics. The book is the published form of a series of public lectures. It is witty and will reward readers of all levels.
"Surely You're Joking, Mr. Feynman!": Adventures of a Curious Character. (coauthored with Ralph Leighton). Norton 1984 $18.95. ISBN 0-393-01921-7. Based on tapes of

conversations over the years with his friend Ralph Leighton; displays the flamboyant and outrageous personality of this famous physicist.

Book about Feynman

Gleick, James. *Genius: The Life and Science of Richard Feynman.* Pantheon 1992 $27.50. ISBN 0-679-40836-3. Probing profile of Feynman's persona.

FITCH, VAL LOGSDON. 1923– (Nobel Prize 1980)

Born on a cattle ranch in Merriman, Nebraska, Val Logsdon Fitch made significant contributions in the area of particle physics. He is perhaps best known for his discovery (with James Cronin) that the neutral K-meson violated the physical principles of symmetry. For this work, which resulted in a reassessment of some basic laws of nature and the universe, Fitch shared the Nobel Prize in physics in 1980.

By his own admission, Fitch has lived an improbable life, born on a cattle ranch, joining the army, and winning the Nobel Prize in physics. Yet, he gives most credit for his accomplishments to the encouragement of parents, family, and colleagues and to his early work as a lab technician on the Manhattan Project at the Los Alamos Laboratory in New Mexico.

Fitch received a Ph.D. from Columbia University in 1952, and worked as a physics instructor from 1952 to 1953. After his appointment as professor at Princeton University in 1960, he met James Cronin, with whom he performed his monumental work. Since 1976 Fitch has been chairman of the physics department at Princeton.

Books about Fitch

Davies, P.C.W. *Space and Time in the Modern Universe.* Cambridge U. Pr. 1977 o.p. Examines the complex world of black holes, the "big bang" theory, and particle physics. The writing is straightforward, clear, and does not require prior knowledge of advanced mathematics or physics; includes drawings, an index, and a preface by the author.
Snow, C. P. *The Physicists: A Generation That Changed the World.* Little 1981 o.p. Draws on personal and professional friendships with Albert Einstein, Niels Bohr, and Enrico Fermi to describe the first 50 years of particle physics for the general reader; includes many historic photographs, an index, and an appendix.

FOWLER, WILLIAM A. 1911– (Nobel Prize 1983)

Born in Pittsburgh, Pennsylvania, in 1911, William Fowler grew up in Lima, Ohio, and, in 1929, graduated from Ohio State University, where he specialized in engineering physics. An outstanding college student, Fowler graduated with the highest grade point average ever achieved in that major. He received a B.S. after writing a thesis on low-voltage electron beams. He earned his Ph.D. in physics (1936) from the California Institute of Technology and while working as an assistant professor in physics became a superb experimental physicist. Fowler's contributions to the understanding of stellar evolution and creation of the elements that compose the universe have incorporated both theoretical calculations and laboratory experiments on nuclear interactions.

For his research and interpretation of energy transformations inside stellar interiors, Fowler was awarded a Nobel Prize in 1983 which he shared with Subrahmanyan Chandrasekhar. Moreover, this model contributed to the theory of complete nuclear synthesis for all chemical elements in the universe. The incorporation of Fowler's research and subsequent work on nuclear forces and nuclear spectroscopy has resulted in a complete theory of chemical formulation.

BOOKS BY FOWLER

Nuclear Astrophysics. Am. Phil. Soc. 1967 o.p.
Nucleosynthesis in Massive Stars and Supernovae. (coauthored with F. Hoyle). U. Ch. Pr. 1964 o.p.

GALILEI, GALILEO. 1564–1642

The scientific methods, observations, and conclusions of Galileo, the Italian physicist and astronomer, are generally considered the beginning of modern science. Specifically, Galileo is credited with establishing the effectiveness of mathematical laws to explain and predict experimental observations. Galileo was a courageous and revolutionary individual whose ideas were often in direct conflict with the accepted theories of his time—basically theories that combined Aristotelian philosophy and religion. For example, ARISTOTLE (see Vols. 3 and 4) claimed that more massive objects fall faster than less massive ones. Galileo, a firm proponent of the scientific method, tested Aristotle's claims with experiments.

Although Galileo never developed a comprehensive scientific theory, he showed that the formulation of a comprehensive theory must be based on a massive amount of detailed, scientific observations. In fact, Galileo provided the rules and motivation for scientists to gather data, as well as making initial contributions to nearly every area of science. By using the scientific method, he discovered the pendulum, invented the thermometer, and was the first person to use a telescope for making astronomical observations. With a telescope, Galileo observed mountains on the moon, sunspots, and the phases of Venus. He concluded that heavenly bodies were made of the same substances and were governed by the same processes as Earth. Galileo's discoveries enabled SIR ISAAC NEWTON (see also Vol. 4) to treat celestial and earthly phenomena from a unified point of view. Galileo is most widely known today for his famous experiment conducted from Pisa, demonstrating that bodies of different weights fall at the same speed. From these observations, he formulated the laws that govern the motion of falling bodies, which were published as *De Motu (On Motion)* in 1590. He also formulated the concept of inertia, later incorporated into Newton's first law of motion.

Galileo was a pugnacious and argumentative man. By publicly espousing the heliocentric theory of COPERNICUS, he aroused the wrath of the Catholic church. In 1616 Galileo was ordered by the church to abandon Copernican theory, but he remained personally convinced and dedicated to science and the scientific method. When Urban VIII became pope in 1624, Galileo obtained the pope's permission to present the rival heliocentric and geocentric theories in an impartial way. Instead, Galileo wrote a polemical dialogue called *Dialogue Concerning the Two Great World Systems*, which was immediately banned because of its obvious support of the heliocentric theory. As a result, Galileo was tried for heresy and sentenced to life imprisonment. Working under house arrest in his villa near Florence, Galileo summed up his life's work in *Discourses and Mathematical Discoveries Concerning the Two New Sciences*. The manuscript was smuggled out of Italy and was eventually published in Holland four years before Galileo's death.

Books by Galilei

Dialogue Concerning the Two Chief World Systems, Ptolemaic and Copernican. 1632. Ed.
by Stillman Drake. U. CA Pr. 1967 $12.95. ISBN 0-520-00450-7. Features a Galilean-
style dialogue (incorporating a new English translation since 1665) of Galileo's
controversial work on hydrostatics; includes contemporary documents that have
been translated and incorporated into the unusual format.

Dialogues Concerning Two New Sciences. 1638. Dover 1952 repr. of 1914 ed. $6.95. ISBN
0-486-60099-8. Continued investigation in physics.

Discoveries and Opinions of Galileo. Doubleday 1957 $5.95. ISBN 0-385-09239-3.
Presents several famous works, including "The Starry Messenger," letters on
sunspots, and others.

Books about Galilei

Brophy, James, and Henry Paolucci, eds. *The Achievement of Galileo.* NCUP 1962 o.p.
Features edited selections from the writings of Galileo and his contemporaries, such
as Bellarmine, and modern commentators.

Campanella, Thomas. *The Defense of Galileo.* U. of Notre Dame Pr. 1994 $27.95. ISBN 0-
405-06582-5. Trial of Galileo as seen through the eyes of his contemporary.

Drake, Stillman. *Galileo.* OUP 1981 $7.95. ISBN 0-19-287526-4. Proposes a new view of
Galileo's relation to his contemporary philosophers and scientists, as well as the
church. Argues that Galileo, in his search for freedom of inquiry, feuded with his
fellow philosophers, who sought a religious pretext for censuring.

_____. *Galileo at Work: His Scientific Biography.* U. Ch. Pr. 1981 o.p. Presents a year-by-
year chronological reconstruction of Galileo's scientific studies. Incorporates many
contemporary documents and newly translated passages into the text. Features many
anecdotes and an appendix of 200 capsule biographies; introduction to Galileo for
the general reader.

_____. *Telescopes, Tides and Tactics: A Galilean Dialogue about the "Starry Messenger"
and Systems of the World.* U. Ch. Pr. 1983 $22.50. ISBN 0-226-16231-1. Galileo's first
astronomical work, "The Starry Messenger," as an imaginary dialogue among three
of his friends.

Gebler, Karl von. *Galileo Galilei and the Roman Curia from Authentic Sources.* Richwood
Pub. 1977 repr. of 1897 ed. o.p. "Its general effect is to dissipate some of the popular
exaggerations . . . concerning Galileo's treatment by the Roman authorities. The
torture and the rigorous imprisonment are disproved, but the torture was certainly
threatened, and the movements of the philosopher were certainly watched with
unceasing jealousy" (*The Spectator*).

Langford, Jerome J. *Galileo, Science and the Church.* U. of Mich. Pr. 1971 $8.95. ISBN 0-
472-06173-9. Examines the condemnation of Galileo by the church in light of
contemporary theological, philosophical, and scientific issues. Describes Galileo as
an impatient defender of Copernican theory before sufficient evidence had accumulated and discusses how his opponents used the Bible as a scientific textbook.

McMullin, Erwin. *Galileo: Man of Science.* Scholars Bookshelf 1988 repr. of 1967 ed.
$50.00. ISBN 0-945726-02-3. Presents a collection of essays gathered for Galileo's
quadricentennial. Each essay examines a different aspect of Galileo's life and work,
such as astronomy, dynamics, and scientific methodology.

Poupard, Paul, ed. *Galileo Galilei: Toward a Resolution of 350 Years of Debate
1633–1983.* Duquesne 1986 o.p.

Redondi, Pietro. *Galileo Heretic.* Trans. by Raymond Rosenthal. Princeton U. Pr. 1990
$49.50. ISBN 0-691-08451-3. Enthralling account of Galileo's famous confrontation
with the Catholic church. Complete re-write of the history of the trial, in light of
newly discovered Vatican documents.

Santillana, Giorgio de. *The Crime of Galileo.* U. Ch. Pr. 1978 $18.95. ISBN 0-226-73481-1.
Focuses on Galileo's trial before the Inquisition and on events preceding the trial;
based on a detailed scrutiny of original texts and manuscripts.

Seeger, Raymond J. *Galileo Galilei: His Life and His Works.* Pergamon 1966 o.p. Features
selections from Galileo's writing, with introductions by Seeger. Emphasizes Galileo's
conclusions that remain valid today rather than the scientific process by which he
reached these conclusions.

Segre, Michael. *In the Wake of Galileo.* Rutgers U. Pr. 1991 $27.95. ISBN 0-8135-1700-7.
Explains how and why we know what we do about Galileo and how some of the
myths were started. In light of the Roman Catholic Church's reexamination of
Galileo's trial, Segre fills in some of the gaps in existing scholarship.

Shea, William R. *Galileo's Intellectual Revolution.* Science History Pubns. 1973 o.p.
Features Galileo's fruitful period (1610–1632), detailing contemporary debates,
discussions, science, and the natural philosophy that formed the context for his
work.

GAMOW, GEORGE. 1904–1968

The Soviet-American physicist George Gamow graduated from the University
of Petrograd (now St. Petersburg) in 1928. He worked at the Copenhagen
Institute of Theoretical Physics with NIELS BOHR and at the Cavendish
Laboratory at Cambridge University. He taught at Leningrad University, George
Washington University, and the University of Colorado.

Gamow worked primarily in theoretical nuclear physics and cosmology but
made substantial contributions to molecular biology as well. He was also widely
known as the author of valuable and exciting popular science books, notably the
"Mr. Tompkins" series, in which he used the figure of a curious bank clerk for a
layperson's exploration into quantum physics and gravity.

His early scientific work dealt with alpha- and beta-decay and with the liquid
drop model of nuclear structure. However, his work on the early universe is
better known. The "big bang" theory of the universe had first been proposed by
Georges Lemaitre. Gamow considered the state of the universe prior to the
postulated "big bang" and predicted that the original explosion would produce
a uniform background radiation. In 1964 this radiation was observed by Arno
Penzias and Robert Wilson, which gave considerable experimental support to
the "big bang" theory of the origin of the universe.

Gamow turned from astronomy to molecular biology. He theorized that the
sequences of four nucleic acid bases that constitute the DNA chain could
control the construction of proteins. He demonstrated that a sequence of three
bases was sufficient to act as a code for all known amino acids. In 1961 the
genetic code was solved and 64 groups of three bases were identified with the
respective amino acids.

BOOKS BY GEORGE GAMOW

Mr. Tompkins in Paperback. Cambridge U. Pr. 1993 $9.95. ISBN 0-521-4471-2. Includes
two of the most popular of Gamow's Mr. Tompkins series: *Mr. Tompkins in
Wonderland* (1939) and *Mr. Tompkins Explores the Atom*; updated to include more
information on advances in physics that occurred after their original publication.

My World Line: An Informal Autobiography. Viking Penguin 1970 o.p. A fragmentary and
charming autobiography; "a collection of short stories, all of them pertaining to me,
and all of them completely true."

One, Two, Three . . . Infinity. 1947. Bantam 1971 o.p. Facts and theories about the
universe in its microscopic and macroscopic manifestations by a skillful popularizer.

Thirty Years That Shook Physics: The Story of Quantum Theory. Dover 1985 repr. of 1966
ed. $5.95. ISBN 0-486-24895-X. Still a charming introduction to the development of
quantum theory, covering the period from 1900 to 1930; includes personal
recollections and impressions of important figures in physics to provide a popular

and anecdotal presentation that nonetheless conveys a good deal of information about physics.

GELL-MAN, MURRAY. 1929– (NOBEL PRIZE 1969)

Born in New York City of Austrian immigrant parents, physicist Murray Gell-Mann was a child prodigy who entered Yale University at age 15. He received his B.S. from there in 1948 and his Ph.D. from the Massachusetts Institute of Technology in 1951. From 1953 to 1955, he taught at the University of California and then joined the faculty at the California Institute of Technology. Although Gell-man originally wanted to study archeology, he chose physics instead, making a brilliant debut at the age of 24 with his theory of particle strangeness.

Gell-man's career as a theoretical physicist has spanned four decades. His approach to particle physics is characterized by a deep physical intuition based on his intimate knowledge of experimental facts and fundamentals.

Since the 1950s, he has been involved in every major advance in the field. This involvement is mainly the result of his enthusiastic approach toward gathering information, considering the ideas of others, rejecting dogma, and remaining open to new ideas.

Gell-Mann has made discoveries and has formulated theories regarding the behavior and classification of elementary particles—specifically, the law of conservation of strangeness, the "eight-fold way" (a classification of certain particles based on their mass and electrical charge), and the theory of quarks (subparticles postulated to be the basic components of all other particles). These discoveries have greatly enhanced the understanding of elementary particle physics. In 1969 Gell-Mann was awarded a Nobel Prize in physics.

BOOKS BY GELL-MAN

Broken Scale Variance and the Light Cone. (with K. Wilson). Gordon & Breach 1971 $96.00. ISBN 0-677-12060-5
The Eightfold Way. (coauthored with Y. Ne'eman). Benjamin-Cummings 1964 o.p.

GLASHOW, SHELDON LEE. 1932– (NOBEL PRIZE 1979)

Sheldon Lee Glashow grew up in New York City, and graduated from Bronx High School of Science, where he and STEVEN WEINBERG were classmates. Glashow received his Ph.D. in 1958 from Harvard University. While a student at Harvard, Glashow studied with JULIAN SCHWINGER, a pioneer of quantum electrodynamics who had become interested in the weak interaction and its possible connection with the electromagnetic interaction. In 1961 Glashow took the first step in unifying these interactions. It was finally accomplished in 1967 by Steven Weinberg and ABDUS SALAM, who worked independently from one another. In 1979 all three received a Nobel Prize in physics for developing a theory that mathematically and theoretically unifies the weak force and electromagnetic force of the atomic nucleus. Their theory also enabled physicists to predict a kind of nuclear interaction called "weak" currents.

In 1983 this theory was firmly confirmed when the predicted W and Z "carriers" of the weak interaction were experimentally observed at the CERN laboratory in Geneva, Switzerland. In 1970 Glashow and two collaborators proposed the existence of the charm quark; several years later, physicists discovered particles that contain charm quarks and antiquarks.

The grand unified theory that links the strong and electroweak interactions, which Glashow and Howard Georgi devised in 1974, accounts for many otherwise unexplained observations. However, its requirement that the proton be unstable (with an extremely long lifetime) remains unverified. Since 1979 Glashow has been on the Harvard faculty, where he occupies the Eugene Higgins Chair of Physics.

BOOKS BY GLASHOW

The Charm of Physics. Am. Inst. Physics 1991 $24.95. ISBN 0-88318-708-6. Twenty-seven pieces, derived from speeches, interviews, and published papers.

Interactions: A Journey through the Mind of a Particle Physicist and the Matter of This World. Warner Bks. 1989 $12.95. ISBN 0-446-38946-3. Engaging scientific autobiography.

BOOKS ABOUT GLASHOW

Crease, Robert P., and Charles C. Mann. *The Second Creation: Makers of the Revolution in Twentieth Century Physics.* Macmillan 1985 o.p. Reveals a personal saga of discovery in modern physics—from the Einsteinian revolution to the super atom smashers. Describes individuals who have made the discoveries (including Sheldon Glashow) and how they have changed history. Written for either the physics professional or for the general reader; includes an index and a complete glossary.

Ferris, Timothy. *Coming of Age in the Milky Way.* Doubleday 1989 $11.95. ISBN 0-385-26326-0. Covers astronomy and cosmology from the ancient Egyptians to the recent quest to unlock the atom's innermost secrets. Written unambiguously for the general reader, it locates the place of Glashow among his peers and against the backdrop of history; includes many illustrations, a detailed glossary, and a bibliography.

Hawking, Stephen W. *A Brief History of Time: From the Big Bang to Black Holes.* Bantam 1988 $22.50. ISBN 0-553-05340-X. Written by one of the great physicists of the twentieth century; discusses the details of space and time in terms of a physical reality that is accessible to the general reader. Covers Glashow's contribution to this field and how new ideas are unfolding from the evaluation of quantum and subatomic investigations.

Pagels, Heinz R. *The Cosmic Code: Quantum Physics as the Law of Nature.* Bantam 1984 $5.95. ISBN 0-553-24625-9. Introduces physics by featuring Albert Einstein, the founder of "modern physics," and comments on the meaning and importance of quantum physics, with coverage of Glashow's contributions to the field. The book is interesting and meaningful to the layperson; includes illustrations, an index, and a bibliography.

Zee, Anthony. *Fearful Symmetry.* Macmillan 1986 o.p. An outstanding book that defines the role of symmetry in modern physics. It is written specifically for the lay person. Profiles the discoveries of high-energy particle physics in the 1980s, featuring a full discussion of Sheldon Glashow's contributions; includes illustrations and an index.

HAWKING, STEPHEN WILLIAM. 1942–

Stephen Hawking, a British theoretical physicist, has made significant contributions to physics in describing space-time singularities. Working with ROGER PENROSE, Hawking used global techniques to show that, if general relativity was correct and if certain physically reasonable conditions were satisfied, space-time singularities must occur during the gravitational collapse of a star and at the beginning of an expanding universe. Hawking's research from 1970 to 1979 mainly involved the properties of black holes within the context of the classical theory of general relativity. This research enabled him to confirm part of the "no-hair" theorem, stating that a black hole will settle down very rapidly to a stationary state characterized by only three parameters: the mass, the angular momentum, and the electric charge. Otherwise, the black hole is independent of the nature of the star that collapsed. Hawking also showed that the surface area in the event horizon, the boundary of a black hole, could never decrease with time.

Despite suffering from amyotrophic lateral sclerosis (known as Lou Gehrig's Disease), Hawking attained a B.A. in physics in 1962 from University College, Oxford, and a Ph.D. from Cambridge University in 1966. In 1977 he was appointed to the chair of gravitational physics at Cambridge University. Hawking's book for the layperson, *A Brief History of Time* (1988), was a bestseller. He often makes public appearances and has appeared in films.

BOOKS BY HAWKING

Black Holes and Baby Universes and Other Essays. Bantam 1993 $21.95. ISBN 0-553-09523-4. Contains 11 essays covering autobiographical, scientific, and philosophical matters. Autobiographical sketches are not that revealing of Hawking's inner life, but other articles reveal much about his major scientific insights.

A Brief History of Time. Bantam 1990 $13.95. ISBN 0-553-34614-8

Illustrated Companion to a Brief History of Time. Bantam 1992 $25.00. ISBN 0-553-07772-4.

The Large Scale Structure of Space-Time. Cambridge U. Pr. 1975 $115.00. ISBN 0-521-20016-4

BOOKS ABOUT HAWKING

Gribbin, John, and Michael White. *Stephen Hawking: A Life in Science.* NAL-Dutton 1992 $23.00. ISBN 0-525-93447-2. Delves into great detail about Hawking's personality, as well as his personal tribulations. A definitive biography.

McDaniel, Melissa. *Stephen Hawking: Physicist.* Chelsea Hse. 1994 $18.95. ISBN 0-7910-2078-9

HELMHOLTZ, HERMANN LUDWIG FERDINAND VON. 1821–1894

A German physicist, physiologist, and popularizer of science, Hermann von Helmholtz made the first precise formulation of the principle of conservation of energy. During physiological studies of muscle action and animal heat, Helmholtz developed this idea as a result of studying the oxidation of food by animals. His formulation led to the first law of thermodynamics, which states that the total energy of a system and its surrounding remains constant even during a phase change. Helmholtz also contributed to the fields of hydrodynamics and electrodynamics, attempting to formulate a general unified theory.

Helmholtz also made significant discoveries in the physiology of vision and hearing. He invented the ophthalmoscope and promoted the three-color theory of vision to investigate color vision and color blindness.

By the enormous breadth of his scientific contributions and the exactness of his work, Helmholtz dominated German science during the middle of the nineteenth century. He helped make Germany the focus of attention for the world's scientific community. Helmholtz and his students took classical mechanics to its limits, helping to set the stage for the revolution in physics at the beginning of the twentieth century, represented by quantum theory and the theory of relativity. This revolution was mainly carried out by German scientists, applying the rigorous mathematical and experimental standards set by Helmholtz.

BOOKS BY HELMHOLTZ

Popular Scientific Lectures. Appleton 1900 o.p. Presents articles on medicine, physiology, and physics; includes an article on conservation of energy that is particularly important due to the influence of its author on the formulation of this fundamental law of physics.

Selected Writings of Hermann Von Helmholtz. Ed. by Russell Kahl. Wesleyan U. Pr. 1971 o.p. Offers a collection of 20 brief papers and lectures on topics such as perception, medicine, electricity, the solar system, and the origins of mathematics; well written.

HEISENBERG, WERNER. 1901–1976 (Nobel Prize 1932)

Werner Heisenberg, a German physicist, is regarded as the founder of quantum mechanics, which describes atomic structure in mathematical terms.

During the 1920s quantum theory became a controversial topic, following Niels Bohr's model proposal for the hydrogen atom. Heisenberg, dissatisfied with the prevalent mechanical models of the atom, conceived an abstract approach using matrix algebra. In 1925, Heisenberg, Max Born, and Pascual Jordan developed this approach into a theory they termed matrix mechanics. Unfortunately, the theory was difficult to understand, since it provided no means of visualizing the phenomena it explained. Erwin Schrödinger's wave formulation, proposed the following year, proved more successful. In 1944 Heisenberg's and Schrödinger's formulations were shown to be mathematically equivalent by John Von Neumann.

In 1927 Heisenberg stated the uncertainty principle, for which he is best known. According to this principle, it is impossible to specify simultaneously both the position and the momentum of a particle, such as an electron. This is caused by interference with those quantities by the radiation that is used to make the observation. The uncertainty principle was demonstrated by means of a thought experiment rather than by a physical observation. Heisenberg also explained ferromagnetism, tracing it to an atomic structure. In 1932 he was awarded the Nobel Prize.

Heisenberg was one of the few outstanding German physicists to remain in Germany during World War II. During the war he supervised atomic research in Germany, with the goal of constructing an atomic bomb, although he claimed not to be a supporter of the Nazi regime. Whether by intent or by circumstance, this effort proved to be unsuccessful, and contradictory statements by Heisenberg have not satisfactorily explained the outcome of the project. After the war, Heisenberg publicly declared that he would no longer take part in the production or testing of atomic weapons.

Books by Heisenberg

Encounters with Einstein: And Other Essays on People, Places, and Particles. Princeton U. Pr. 1989 $8.95. ISBN 1-691-02433-2. Nine essays which contemplate the state of science in our time.

Physicist's Conception of Nature. Trans. by Arnold J. Pomerans. Greenwood 1970 repr. of 1958 ed. $38.00. ISBN 0-8371-3107-3. A collection of essays, including "The Idea of Nature in Contemporary Physics" and "Atomic Physics and Casual Law," as well as observations on education and the beginnings of modern science.

Physics and Beyond. HarpC 1972 $10.95. ISBN 0-06-131622-9. A collection of 20 conversations with notable scientists of the atomic age, such as Pauli, Bohr, and Planck; conversations are reconstructed from Heisenberg's knowledge and recollections of his fellow scientists.

Physics and Philosophy: The Revolution in Modern Science. HarpC 1962 $13.00. ISBN 0-06-130549-9. A general discussion of physics, its philosophy, and its relation to other sciences. Features Heisenberg's responses to criticisms of his uncertainty principle by Einstein and others.

Tradition in Science. HarpC 1983 o.p. "These essays begin with a deceptive simplicity but move quickly into the abstractions of theoretical physics. . . . Heisenberg's metaphysics and his explorations into the intuitions of creative physicists in formulating 'closed systems' make him more akin to Plato than to Aristotle: the Really Real may be the idea, the abstraction" (*Kirkus Reviews*).

BOOKS ABOUT HEISENBERG

Cassidy, David C. *Uncertainty: The Life and Science of Werner Heisenberg.* W. H. Freeman 1991 $29.95. ISBN 0-7167-2243-7. Fascinating history of Heisenberg and Nazi Germany.

Heisenberg, Elisabeth. *Inner Exile: Recollections of a Life with Werner Heisenberg.* Birkhauser 1984 $29.50. ISBN 0-8176-3146-1. Examines Heisenberg's life and explains his decision to stay in Germany during World War II; written by his wife.

MacPherson, Malcolm. *Time Bomb: Fermi, Heisenberg, and the Race for the Atomic Bomb.* NAL-Dutton 1986 o.p. "Conveys in nontechnical terms the theories and lab experiments that brought Heisenberg to the brink of success in Germany, and in America led Fermi to the first self-sustaining chain reaction in uranium on Dec. 2, 1942" (*Publisher's Weekly*).

HERTZ, HEINRICH. 1857–1894

Born in Germany, Heinrich Hertz came from a prosperous and cultured family. After serving in the military for a year (1876–77), Hertz spent a year at the University of Munich, where he decided to embark upon an academic career. In 1880 Hertz received a Ph.D. at the University of Berlin. He then taught at the University of Kiel and in 1885 was appointed professor of physics at the University of Bonn. His untimely death from blood poisoning, which occurred after several years of poor health, cut short a brilliant career.

Hertz made significant contributions to the understanding of electrical phenomena and application of electrical equipment. In 1888 he produced electromagnetic waves using an electric circuit. These waves, originally called Hertzian waves (now known as radio waves) confirmed JAMES CLERK MAXWELL's prediction of the existence of electromagnetic waves, both as light waves and radio waves. Continuing his research and analysis of Maxwell's theory, Hertz published two papers in 1890. During this period, his experimental and theoretical research strengthened the field of electrodynamics. In 1887 Hertz inadvertently discovered the photoelectric effect whereby ultraviolet radiation releases electrons from the surface of a metal. Hertz died before Guglielmo Marconi made the use of radio waves a practical means of communication. In his honor the unit of frequency is now called the hertz.

BOOKS BY HERTZ

Electric Waves. Dover 1962 o.p. Researches on the propagation of electric action.

The Principles of Mechanics. Dover 1956 o.p. Presented in a new form.

BOOKS ABOUT HERTZ

Hertz, Johanna. *Heinrich Hertz: Memoirs, Letters, Diaries.* San Francisco Pr. 1977 $25.00. ISBN 0-911302-35-2

Lodge, Oliver Joseph. *Hertz and His Successors: Signalling across Space without Wires.* 1983 o.p. A description of the work of Hertz.

HUYGENS, CHRISTIAAN. 1629–1695

The Dutch physicist and astronomer Christiaan Huygens was educated at home by his father and private tutors until he was about 16 years old. From 1645 until 1647, Huygens studied law at the University of Leiden and mathematics at Frans van Schooten. Then, from 1647 until 1649, he studied law at the newly founded Collegium Arausiacum (College of Orange) at Breda. During the 1650s,

Huygens concentrated on mathematics, studying algebraic problems inspired by Pappus of Alexandria's work.

In 1656, Huygens invented a reliable pendulum clock, succeeding where many had failed, including GALILEO (see also Vol. 4) himself. He worked on the more general theory of harmonic oscillating systems throughout his life, finally publishing his *Horologium Oscillatorium* (1673). Huygens then began to work extensively on optics and dynamics. His greatest achievement was his development of the wave theory of light, published in 1678 in his *Traité de la Lumière (Treatise on Light)*. This was written to counter SIR ISAAC NEWTON's (see also Vol. 4) particle (or "corpuscular") theory of light. Huygens proposed that light travels in successive spherical shells from its source in space and that, when one shell hits a barrier, the point of contact becomes another source of light, in turn radiating light spheres. Using these ideas, Huygens successfully deduced Willebrod van Roijen Snell's law and explained the phenomenon of interference. His wave theory became accepted over Newton's corpuscular theory when it correctly predicted a decrease in the speed of light when refracted into a medium denser than air.

Huygens left Holland for Paris in 1681. He continued his optical studies, constructed numerous clocks, and wrote *Cosmotheoros*. However, during his last years, Huygens once again returned his attention to mathematics.

Essentially a solitary man, Huygens did not attract students and disciples. As was common in the seventeenth century, he was slow to publish. Nevertheless, in seventeenth-century science, he was second only to Newton in stature.

BOOKS BY HUYGENS

The Celestial Worlds Discovered: Or, Conjectures Concerning the Inhabitants, Plants, and Productions of the Worlds in the Planets. Cass repr. of 1698 ed. o.p. Provides insight into Huygens's thinking; short and nontechnical for the general reader.

The Pendulum Clock, or Geometrical Demonstrations Concerning the Motion of Pendula as Applied to Clocks (Horologium Oscillatorium). 1673. Iowa St. U. Pr. 1986 o.p.

BOOKS ABOUT HUYGENS

Baker, Bevan Braithwaite, and E. T. Copson. *The Mathematical Theory of Huygen's Principle*. 1950. Chelsea Pub. 1987 $17.95. ISBN 0-8284-0329-5. "Devoted almost exclusively to a *mathematical* analysis of Huygens's Principle, this text will be found of value to those physicists who wish to explore various ways of solving wave theory problems from a theoretical point of view" (*Choice*).

Bell, Arthur E. *Christiaan Huygens and the Development of Science in the Seventeenth Century*. Longmans 1947 o.p. Standard biography of Huygens; thorough and interesting account of his life, theoretical approach to science, and scientific work.

Yoder, Joella G. *Unrolling Time: Huygens and the Mathematization of Nature*. Cambridge U. Pr. 1989 $47.95. ISBN 0-521-34140-X. Describes how Huygens used mathematics to substantiate his mechanistic view of the universe.

JOSEPHSON, BRIAN DAVID. 1940– (NOBEL PRIZE 1973)

Born in Wales, Brian Josephson was educated at Cambridge University and received a Ph.D. in 1964. He remained at Cambridge, first becoming assistant director of research in physics from 1967 to 1972. In 1974 Josephson was appointed professor of physics. His name is associated with the Josephson effects, which he described in 1962 while still a graduate student. The work evolved from theoretical speculations on electrons between two superconducting regions separated by a thin insulating layer (a Josephson junction). The effects have been verified experimentally, thus supporting the BCS theory of superconductivity of JOHN BARDEEN and his colleagues. The Josephson junctions have been used in making accurate physical measurements and in measuring weak magnetic fields. Josephson junctions are also used as switching devices in computers. For this contribution, Josephson shared the 1973 Nobel Prize in physics with Leo Esaki and Ivar Giaever. More recently, Josephson has become interested in the study of the mind. He married in 1976 and has one daughter.

BOOK BY JOSEPHSON

Consciousness and the Physical World. Pergamon 1979 $56.00. ISBN 0-08-024695-8

BOOK ABOUT JOSEPHSON

Weintraub, Pamela, ed. *The Omni Interviews.* Ticknor & Fields 1984 o.p. Features interviews with several prominent scientists and a brief analysis of the scientist's contribution in his field. Josephson recalls the events that led him away from mainstream physics to psychic phenomena; illustrated.

KAPITZA, PETER LEONIDOVICH. 1894–1984 (NOBEL PRIZE 1978)

A Soviet experimental physicist, Peter Leonidovich Kapitza is best known for his work in low-temperature physics with the form of liquid helium that exists at temperatures close to absolute zero. He found that helium at this temperature exists in a "superfluid" state that conducts heat better than copper, the best conductor known at normal temperatures. His investigations showed that this form of helium is highly viscous and also displays an unusual form of internal convection.

Related to this work, he developed a process for liquefying helium. The subsequent availability of liquid helium permitted the production of electric semiconductors and much other low-temperature work. The early equipment that he designed and built was far superior to anything else of its day. As an example, in the course of an experiment in 1924, he produced a record high pressure that was not surpassed until 1956.

Like many other twentieth-century physicists, Kapitza was caught up in political turmoil. As a young man in 1919, he traveled to England to work on magnetic research under ERNEST RUTHERFORD at the Cavendish Laboratory of Cambridge University, eventually becoming deputy director of the laboratory. In 1930 he was made director of the Royal Society's Mond Laboratory at Cambridge, which was built for him. In 1934 he paid a visit to the Soviet Union for a professional meeting, as he had done previously. However, this time the Stalinist government ordered Kapitza detained and his passport seized. The next year Kapitza was made director of a new research institute in Moscow, and the Mond Laboratory was sold to the Soviet government and transported to Moscow for his use. Kapitza worked there until 1946, when he refused to work on the development of nuclear weapons and was put under house arrest, only to be released after Stalin's death in 1953. He was then restored to his old post as director of the institute. He was belatedly awarded the Nobel Prize for physics in 1978 for work in low-temperature physics, including studies of electrical properties of matter and the liquefaction of gases.

BOOKS BY KAPITZA

Collected Papers. 4 vols. Franklin 1965–1986 $205.00–$215.00 ea.
Collected Papers of P. L. Kapitza. 3 vols. Ed. by D. ter Haar. Kluwer Ac. 1980 $89.00. ISBN 90-277-4061-9. Volume 1 includes a succinct summary of Kapitza's scientific accomplishments up to 1955.

Experiment, Theory, Practice. Kluwer Ac. 1980 $89.00. ISBN 90-277-1061-9. Collection of articles and speeches on physics education, Russian physics institutions, and science and society. Also included are comments on notable scientific figures both contemporary and past, such as Rutherford, Lomonosov, Landau, and Franklin.
Society and the Environment: A Soviet View. Imported Pubns. 1977 o.p.

BOOKS ABOUT KAPITZA

Badash, Lawrence. *Kapitza, Rutherford and the Kremlin.* Yale U. Pr. 1985 $25.00. ISBN 0-300-01465-1. Recent work, drawing on Kapitza's recently released letters to his family written during the period immediately after his detention in 1934.
Boug, J. W., and others. *Kapitza in Cambridge and Moscow: Life and Letters of a Russian Physicist.* Elsevier 1990 $77.00. ISBN 0-444-98753-3. Eighty-four-page biographical sketch and letters to his mother, wife, and colleagues as well as various Soviet officials.
Trigg, George L. *Landmark Experiments in Twentieth Century Physics.* Crane 1975 o.p. Detailed discussion of research into low-temperature physics of helium from 1908 to 1939; includes extensive quotations and illustrations.

LAMB, WILLIS EUGENE, JR. 1913– (NOBEL PRIZE 1955)

Born in Los Angeles, Willis Lamb studied at the University of California, Berkeley, and received a Ph.D. in 1938 under the guidance of J. ROBERT OPPENHEIMER. That same year, Lamb became a physics instructor at Columbia University, becoming a professor in 1948. Lamb has made important contributions in the area of quantum electrodynamics.

In 1947 Lamb noticed a minute difference in energy levels between the two possible energy states of the hydrogen atom. This tiny difference (the Lamb shift) made it necessary to revise the theory of interaction of the electron with electromagnetic radiation. Discovery of the Lamb shift provided a more in-depth understanding of the structure of the hydrogen spectrum. By applying radio-frequency spectroscopy, Lamb was able to isolate an important characteristic of the hydrogen atom, contributing to the refinement of the theory of electrons and electromagnetic radiation. For this work, Lamb shared the Nobel Prize for physics in 1955 with another leader of physics research at Columbia, Ploykarp Kusch. Lamb had also collaborated with Kusch to develop microwave radar.

At Stanford University during the 1950s, Lamb devised microwave techniques for examining the hyperfine structure of the spectral lines of helium. He became a professor at Oxford University in 1956 and Yale University in 1962. Since 1974 he has been professor of physical and optical sciences in the physics department at the University of Arizona. Lamb has spent his entire career teaching physics and is such a dedicated professor that, upon hearing of his Nobel Prize, he taught his class in quantum mechanics before meeting the press for interviews.

BOOKS ABOUT LAMB

Eastham, D. A. *Atomic Physics of Lasers.* Taylor & Francis $40.00. ISBN 0-85066-343-1. Discusses the Lamb shift and Lamb dip, two basic concepts in laser physics. Offers a thorough explanation of the important contributions of Lamb to modern physics; requires an advanced knowledge of physics.
Fain, Venjamin M., and Yakov I. Khanin. *Quantum Electronics.* Pergamon 1969 o.p. A textbook of advanced theoretical physics that covers Lamb's work in the theory and practice of modern physics; fully examines Hans Bethe's theoretical explanation for the Lamb shift.

Grandy, Walter T. *Introduction to Electrodynamics and Radiation.* Acad. Pr. 1970 o.p. Features a complete chapter on Lamb's research; the text is well illustrated and easy to follow in its basic argument, but is designed for graduate-level physics students.

Haar, Dik T., and Marlan O. Scully. eds. *Willis E. Lamb Jr.: A Festschrift on the Occasion of his 65th Birthday.* Elsevier 1979 $7.50. ISBN 0-444-85253-0. A series of complex articles that examine the ideas that Lamb pioneered. Lamb's teaching and intellectual influence is acknowledged by former colleagues at the beginning of the book; includes some handwritten letters.

Svelto, Orazio. *Principle of Lasers.* Plenum 1982 o.p. A textbook that covers the theory of lasers for undergraduate and graduate students of physics. The diagrams and discussions are extremely useful, but the book requires a knowledge of advanced mathematics; highlights Lamb's considerable contributions to illustrate how physical theory can enhance the quality of human life—in this case, through the development of lasers.

Thirring, Walter E. *Principles of Quantum Electrodynamics.* Trans. by J. Bernstein. Acad. Pr. 1988 o.p. A basic textbook that fully covers Lamb's famous experiments from the late 1940s to the 1950s; explains the Lamb shift in clear, concise terms with valuable illustrations and diagrams.

LAPLACE, MARQUIS PIERRE SIMON DE. 1749–1827

Pierre Simon de Laplace, the son of a small estate owner, was educated at the University of Caen in France. By 1785 Laplace was a full member of the French Academy of Sciences. Laplace prospered during the reign of Napoleon, who had a genuine interest in mathematics. In fact, Napoleon took pleasure in rewarding eminent mathematicians. Laplace served as Napoleon's minister of the interior in 1799 and as one of his senators.

The Traité de mécanique céleste (Celestial Mechanics) was Laplace's greatest work. In this work, Laplace showed that the system of planets was basically stable, refuting SIR ISAAC NEWTON's (see also Vol. 4) acceptance of divine intervention as necessary to prevent the collapse of the solar system. In 1796 Laplace published *Exposition du système du mode (Exposition of the System of the World)*, in which he proposed his famous nebular hypothesis: The solar system had evolved from a rotating mass of gas that had condensed to form the sun, planets, and various planetary satellites. Laplace's other achievements included establishment of probability theory on a rigorous basis and his development of a "potential" and its description by the Laplace equation. Laplace actively promoted and encouraged the growth of French science. On his deathbed, Laplace said: "What we know is very slight; what we don't know is immense."

BOOKS BY LAPLACE

Celestial Mechanics. 1799–1825. Chelsea Pub. 1969 repr. of 1832 ed. $35.00. ISBN 0-8284-0214-0

Exposition of the System of the World. Dover repr. of 1796 ed. o.p.

A Philosophical Essay on Probabilities. Dover repr. of 1814 ed. o.p.

BOOKS ABOUT LAPLACE

Hahn, Roger. *Laplace as a Newtonian Scientist.* U. CA Pr. 1967 o.p. Originally a paper delivered at a seminar on the Newtonian influence held at Clark University.

Numbers, Ronald. *Creation by Natural Law.* U. Wash. Pr. 1977 o.p. Presents LaPlace's nebular hypothesis in American thought.

LORENTZ, HENDRIK ANTOON. 1853–1928 (NOBEL PRIZE 1902)

Born in Holland, Hendrik Lorentz was a graduate of the University of Leiden, receiving his Ph.D. in 1875. In 1877 Lorentz became a professor of theoretical physics there. Upon his retirement from the University of Leiden in 1912, Lorentz was appointed director of the Teyler Laboratory in Haarlem.

Lorentz had wide-ranging interests in physics and mathematics as his linguistic abilities allowed him to follow the scientific trends in Europe. His major work, however, was the development of the electromagnetic theory of JAMES CLARK MAXWELL. In fact, Lorentz refined the theory so that a radical change in the foundations of physics became necessary. This provided the inspiration for ALBERT EINSTEIN's theory of relativity. In a series of articles from 1892 to 1904, Lorentz proposed his "electron theory." The theory explained that atoms and molecules of matter contain small rigid bodies carrying a charge— now known as electrons. By 1895 Lorentz described the force (now known as the Lorentz force) on charged particles of matter in an electromagnetic field. In 1902 Lorentz and Pieter Zeeman shared the Nobel Prize in physics for their investigations of the influence of magnetic fields on radiation. Two years later, he published *Lorentz Transformations* concerning transformations of space and time coordinates with respect to a frame of reference. Lorentz Transformations were important in Einstein's special theory of relativity (1905).

In his later life, Lorentz played a major role in restoring international scientific relations after World War I.

BOOKS BY LORENTZ

H. A. Lorentz: Collected Papers, 1935–1939. M. Nijhoff 1940 o.p.
Problems of Modern Physics. Ginn 1927 o.p.

BOOK ABOUT LORENTZ

DeHaas-Lorentz, Geertrudia, ed. *H. A. Lorentz: Impressions of His Life and Work.* Elsevier 1957 o.p. Edited by Lorentz's daughter, the book commemorates the 100th anniversary of his birth. Presents assessments of Lorentz and his work by colleagues (including A. Einstein), as well as reminiscences by his daughter, which provide the most extensive information available on Lorentz's private life.

MACH, ERNST. 1838–1916

Educated by his father, who stressed the importance of carpentry and farming, Ernst Mach received his Ph.D. from the University of Vienna in 1860. Mach made many contributions to science in a variety of fields, but he is best known for his powerful influence on several generations of scientists as a critic of science and as a philosopher. His initial research in experimental psychology revealed the function of the semicircular canals of the ear.

Mach is best known in physics for his work on shock waves, which led to the mach number being introduced in 1929 as a measure of speed. The mach number is the ratio of the speed of an object in a fluid to the speed of sound in the fluid.

Mach is also known to cosmologists for his controversial statement of the principle of inertia, called Mach's principle. The Mach principle rejected the Newtonian notion of absolute space and time. Mach's elimination of absolute space was part of his more general program in which he hoped to eliminate metaphysics (all those purely "thought-things" that cannot be pointed to in experience) from science. His views influenced the important philosophical movement of logical positivism and also had some impact on scientific practice, especially EINSTEIN in formulating his theory of relativity. Despite his influence, Mach was a radical thinker who never accepted the existence of atoms or Einstein's theory of relativity.

BOOKS BY MACH

The Analysis of Sensations and the Relation of the Physical to the Psychical. 1914 o.p.
History and Root of the Principle of the Conservation of Energy. 1976 o.p.
Popular Scientific Lectures. 1943. Open Court 1986 $14.00. ISBN 0-87548-440-9
The Principles of Physical Optics, an Historical and Philosophical Treatment. 1953 o.p.
Principles of the Theory of Heat. Kluwer Ac. 1986 $176.00. ISBN 90-277-2206-4. Critical
    history of thermodynamics
The Science of Mechanics. 1942. Open Court 1966 $22.00. ISBN 0-87548-202-3
Space and Geometry. 1906. Open Court 1986 $8.00. ISBN 0-87548-177-9

BOOKS ABOUT MACH

Blackmore, John, ed. *Ernst Mach—A Deeper Look: Documents and New Perspectives.*
    Kluwer Ac. 1992 $125.00. ISBN 0-7923-1853-6
Blackmore, John T. *Ernst Mach: His Work, Life, and Influence.* U. CA. Pr. 1972 o.p.
Cohen, R. S., and R. J. Seeger. *Boston Studies in the Philosophy of Science: Ernst Mach,
    Physicist and Philosopher.* Vol. 6 Kluwer Ac. 1975 $56.00. ISBN 90-277-0016-8
McGuiness, Brian, ed. *Ernst Mach: Knowledge and Error.* Kluwer Ac. 1975 $126.50. ISBN
    90-277-0281-0
Musil, Robert. *On Mach's Theories.* Cath. U. Pr. 1982 o.p.
Ratliff, Floyd. *Mach Bands: Quantitative Studies on Neural Networks in the Retina.*
    Holden-Day 1965 $38.00. ISBN 0-8162-7045-7

MAXWELL, JAMES CLERK. 1831–1879

James Maxwell was a British physicist who developed a standard theoretical
model for the modern understanding of electricity and magnetism. He showed
that these two phenomena are two aspects of the same field and as a result he
unified and systematized a vast field of research. Maxwell took many diverse
observations and qualitative concepts developed by MICHAEL FARADAY and
others, formulating them into a unified theory between 1864 and 1873. On the
basis of this theory, Maxwell predicted that electromagnetic waves should exist
and travel with the speed of light, and he identified light as a form of
electromagnetic radiation. Both of these predictions were experimentally
confirmed.

Maxwell's other great contribution to physics was formulating a mathematical
basis for the kinetic theory of gases. Using a statistical approach, he related the
velocity of the molecules in a gas to its temperature, showing that heat results
from the motion of molecules. Maxwell's result had been conjectured for some
time, but it had never been supported experimentally. Maxwell then expanded
his research to study viscosity, diffusion, and other properties of gases. Maxwell
also provided the first satisfactory explanation of Saturn's rings. He established
on theoretical grounds that the rings are not solid but rather composed of many
small, fragmented objects that orbit Saturn.

BOOKS BY MAXWELL

Electricity and Magnetism. 2 vols. Dover repr. of 1891 ed. $9.95 ea. ISBNs 0-486-60636-8,
    0-486-60637-6
Matter and Motion. Dover repr. of 1920 ed. $6.95. ISBN 0-486-66895-9. Maxwell's
    exposition of Newtonian mechanics.
Maxwell on Molecules and Gases. Ed. by Elizabeth Garber and others. MIT Pr. 1986
    $65.00. ISBN 0-262-07094-4
The Scientific Letters and Papers, Vol. 1: 1846–1862. Ed. by P. M. Harman. Cambridge U.
    Pr. 1990 $210.00. ISBN 0-521-25625-9. An excellent tool to gain insight into
    Maxwell's thinking and intellectual progression. Includes letters to many physicists
    as well as papers and reports by Maxwell.

Theory of Heat. Greenwood 1970 repr. of 1872 ed. $55.00. ISBN 0-8371-4097-8

BOOKS ABOUT MAXWELL

Brush, Stephen G., ed. *Maxwell on Saturn's Rings: James Clerk Maxwell's Unpublished Manuscripts and Letters on the Stability of Saturn's Rings.* MIT Pr. 1983 $37.50. ISBN 0-262-13190-0

Buchwald, Jed Z. *From Maxwell to Microphysics: Aspects of Electromagnetic Theory in the Last Quarter of the Nineteenth Century.* U. Ch. Pr. 1988 $75.00. ISBN 0-226-07882-5. A study of the transition from Maxwellian electromagnetic field theories to electromagnetic theories based on assumptions about the microstructure of matter.

Campbell, Lewis, and William Garnett. *Life of James Clerk Maxwell.* Johnson Repr. 1970 repr. of 1882 ed. $50.00. ISBN 0-384-07295-X. Official biography written by a schoolmate and Maxwell's laboratory assistant.

Hendry, J. *James Clerk Maxwell and the Theory of the Electromagnetic Field.* IOP Pub. 1986 $79.90. ISBN 0-85274-563-X

Tricker, R. A. *Contributions of Faraday and Maxwell to Electrical Science.* Pergamon 1966 o.p. Thorough account of Faraday's and Maxwell's scientific work on electromagnetic induction, conveying historical, biographical, and anecdotal information; includes a brief overview of electromagnetic phenomena.

MICHELSON, ALBERT A(BRAHAM). 1852–1931 (NOBEL PRIZE 1907)

Born in Germany, Albert Michelson and his family emigrated to California when he was 2 years old. He graduated from the U.S. Naval Academy (Annapolis) in 1873; later he taught physics and chemistry there (1875–79). In 1880 he went to Europe to study optics. An experimental physicist, Michelson performed crucial experiments in optics. In 1882 he measured the velocity of light and refined this measurement 10 years later, using improved equipment. As part of this research, Michelson developed an extremely sensitive interferometer, a device that can divide a beam of light, send the two subbeams in different directions, and then reunite them. If the two subbeams travel different distances at the same speed or the same distance at different speeds, interference patterns result, because the light waves are no longer synchronized.

At this time, many physicists believed that Earth must be moving through ether, a static substance that was thought to fill space. The existence of the ether was assumed to be a necessary carrier for the propagation of light waves, since waves must have a medium or carrier in classical physics. Using his newly developed interferometer, Michelson devised an experiment to detect the ether. In the experiment, a beam of sunlight was split so that part would travel in the direction of Earth's motion and the other part in a direction perpendicular to that motion. If an ether medium existed, an interference pattern would be produced from which the existence of the ether could be assumed. In his first trials, Michelson could not detect any difference in the speed of light, whatever the direction. With the American scientist Edward Morley, Michelson built a more sensitive interferometer in 1887. But, once again, he could not detect the presence of ether.

Michelson was an expert at devising and perfecting precision instruments. Although he never earned a Ph.D., he received 11 honorary doctorates. As a result of Michelson's research, physicists finally considered the likelihood that the ether did not exist. This knowledge helped ALBERT EINSTEIN develop the theory of special relativity to explain the constant speed of light. In 1907 Michelson was the first American scientist to receive the Nobel Prize.

BOOK BY MICHELSON

Studies in Optics. 1927. U. Ch. Pr. 1962 o.p.

BOOKS ABOUT MICHELSON

Jaffe, Bernard. *Michelson and the Speed of Light.* Greenwood 1979 $35.00. ISBN 0-313-20777-1

Livingston, Dorothy Michelson. *The Master of Light: A Biography of Albert A. Michelson.* U. Ch. Pr. 1979 o.p. A well-organized scientific biography based on personal recollections, much reading, and interviews. Describes Michelson and his achievements, as well as the growth of physics in the United States from a few individuals in 1880 to a developed discipline in 1930; written by Michelson's youngest daughter.

MILLIKAN, ROBERT ANDREWS. 1868–1953 (NOBEL PRIZE 1923)

An American experimental physicist, Robert Millikan graduated from Oberlin College in 1891 and received his M.A. there in 1893. He earned his Ph.D. from Columbia University in 1895. One year later, Millikan joined the faculty at the University of Chicago and remained there until 1921, with the exception of the time he spent in government and military service during World War I. From Chicago Millikan went to the California Institute of Technology, where he spent the rest of his career.

Millikan made the first determination of the charge of the electron and of PLANCK's constant. He was awarded the 1923 Nobel Prize in physics for these contributions. The determination of the charge on the electron proved experimentally that electrons are particles of electricity. Millikan accomplished this feat by designing an experiment studying the fall of oil droplets in an electric field. He conjectured that the droplets would take up integral multiples of electrical charge. By measuring the strength of the field required to counteract the gravitational force on the droplets, he was able to compute a highly accurate unit charge for the particle.

Millikan also studied the photoelectric effect experimentally in 1916, confirming ALBERT EINSTEIN's equation relating the kinetic energy of a particle emitted by incident radiation to the frequency of that radiation. Until his retirement, Millikan studied cosmic rays and the ultraviolet spectra of many elements.

BOOKS BY MILLIKAN

The Autobiography of Robert A. Millikan. Ayer 1980 repr. of 1950 ed. $26.50. ISBN 0-405-12558-5. Autobiography, detailing events of the life of the man who was for many years the central figure in American physics.

Electron: Its Isolation and Measurement and the Determination of Some of Its Properties. Bks. Demand repr. of 1968 ed. $82.50. ISBN 0-317-08089-X

Electrons, Protons, Photons, Neutrons and Cosmic Rays. U. Ch. Pr. 1935 o.p.

Evolution in Science and Religion. 1927. Arden Lib. 1976 repr. of 1929 ed. o.p. Published version of a series of lectures on the evolution of twentieth-century physics and of religion; Millikan emphasizes the lack of dogmatism in modern physics.

Science and Life. Ayer repr. of 1924 ed. $14.00. ISBN 0-8369-1307-8. Essays on the practical value of pure science and science related to religion and society.

Science and the New Civilization. Ayer repr. of 1930 ed. $18.00. ISBN 0-8369-2418-5. "A collection of addresses previously published in various magazines, and which carry the same essential message: a defense of scientific knowledge against its detractors" (*Isis*).

BOOK ABOUT MILLIKAN

Kargon, Robert H. *The Rise of Robert Millikan: Portrait of a Life in American Science.* Cornell Univ. Pr. 1982 $35.95. ISBN 0-8014-1459-8. Study of the life and work of one of America's most prominent physicists. This is a "selective essay" on Millikan's career and modern American science, focusing on selected personalities and episodes rather than covering the entire story.

MOSELEY, HENRY GWYN JEFFREYS. 1887–1915

The brilliant career of Henry Gwyn Jeffreys Moseley, a British physicist, was brief, cut short by his death as a soldier in World War I. When war broke out, Moseley enlisted in the British Army and was commissioned in the Royal Engineers. In 1915 he was sent to Turkey on a disastrous campaign, where he was killed at the age of 27. Moseley is mainly known for his work with X-ray spectra. As X-rays are produced by an element, they emit powerful radiation at a few characteristic wavelengths. By obtaining data for consecutive elements of the periodic table, Moseley was able to infer a relationship between the X-ray wavelengths of an element and its atomic number (the number of protons in its nucleus). This permitted him to correct ambiguities in contemporary atomic number assignments and to predict the existence of several then unknown elements. Moseley soon realized that there were important links between his discovery and NIELS BOHR's atomic model. Before Moseley's research, only electrons and negatively charged particles were known to occur in discrete, or quantized, energy packets (entire atoms are neutral in charge). His research showed that the positive charge (in the nucleus) that neutralizes the negative charge of the atom's electron shell is also quantized. This research gave early insight into nuclear structure.

BOOK BY MOSELEY

Non-Ionising Radiation: Microwaves, Ultra Violet Radiation, and Lasers. IOP Pub. 1988 $91.00. ISBN 0-85274-166-9. On a wide range of physical characteristics, biological effects, and medical applications of electromagnetic radiations.

BOOK ABOUT MOSELEY

Heilbron, John L. *H.G.J. Moseley: The Life and Letters of an English Physicist, 1887–1915.* U. CA Pr. 1974 o.p. Presents a balanced account of Moseley's brief, but spectacular career. Covers Moseley's scientific achievements as well as other aspects of his life; half the volume is devoted to reprinting Moseley's letters.

MÖSSBAUER, RUDOLF LUDWIG. 1929– (NOBEL PRIZE 1961)

Born in Munich, Germany, Rudolf Mössbauer received his Ph.D. from the Munich Technical University in 1958. Mössbauer is noted for the significant advancements he made in the study of gamma radiation. In particular, he observed the resonance emission and absorption of nuclear gamma radiation (known as the Mössbauer effect), provided a theoretical explanation for this discovery, and devised an apparatus that enhanced the study of these extremely narrow gamma resonances. The sharp resonances of the Mössbauer effect have allowed many observations in physics, including studies of the properties of solids and a laboratory test of the theory of relativity. For his research, Mössbauer shared the 1961 Nobel Prize with Robert Hofstadter. Mössbauer's Nobel Prize-winning research on gamma absorption was conducted in the 1960s at the California Institute of Technology, Pasadena. He is now a professor of physics at the California Institute of Technology and at the Munich Technical University in Germany.

BOOKS ABOUT MÖSSBAUER

Frauerfelder, Hans, ed. *The Mössbauer Effect.* W. A. Benjamin 1963 o.p. A collection of early reprints on applications of the Mössbauer effect that includes English translations of Mössbauer's original papers and other early applications of the Mössbauer effect to problems in physics; includes an introduction that presents both a classical physics approach to the Mössbauer effect and a quantum interpretation.

Wertheim, Gunther K. *Mössbauer Effect: Principles and Applications.* Acad. Pr. 1964 o.p. Presents the simplest available introduction to the Mössbauer effect and the apparatus used to observe it; requires some physics background.

MOTT, SIR NEVILL FRANCIS. 1905– (NOBEL PRIZE 1977)

Born in Leeds, England, Nevill Francis Mott was the son of two physicists at the Cavendish Laboratory at Cambridge. Mott studied at Cambridge University, where he received his M.A. in 1930, never pursuing his Ph.D. Despite this lack, Mott made significant contributions to the development of the theory of atomic collisions and scattering in the early 1930s while lecturing at Gonville and Caius College in Cambridge, as Melville Wells Professor of Theoretical Physics.

As a professor of theoretical physics at Bristol University, Mott wrote three classic texts: *The Theory of Atomic Collisions* (1934), *The Theory of Properties of Metals and Alloys* with H. Jones (1936), and *Electronic Processes in Ionic Crystals* with R. W. Gurney (1940). Each text marked a significant phase of active research.

By the mid-1950s, Mott returned to Cambridge, where he studied problems of disordered materials, liquid metal, impurity bands in semiconductors, and the glassy semiconductors. His models of the solid state included an analysis of electronic processes in metal-insulator translations, often called Mott transistors. Mott was knighted in 1962 and shared the 1977 Nobel Prize in physics with PHILIP W. ANDERSON and John van Vleck for his fundamental contributions to the theoretical understanding of the differences between conductors, insulators, and semiconductors. His theories about the transition between conductors and insulators made of disordered or amorphous material, such as glasses, were especially influential.

BOOKS BY MOTT

Atomic Structure and the Strength of Metals. Franklin 1956 $40.00. ISBN 0-08-013765-2

Electronic Processes in Ionic Crystals. (coauthored with R. W. Gurney). Clarendon Pr. 1940 o.p.

Electronic Processes in Non-Crystalline Materials. (coauthored with E. A. Davis). 1971. OUP 1979 $98.00. ISBN 0-19-851288-0

Elementary Quantum Mechanics. Spr.-Verlag 1972. o.p.

Elements of Wave Mechanics. Cambrige U. Pr. 1952 o.p.

A Life in Science. Taylor & Francis 1986 $44.00. ISBN 0-85066-333-4. An autobiography.

Metal-Insulator Transitions. 1974. Taylor & Francis 1990 $99.00. ISBN 0-85066-783-6

The Theory of Atomic Collisions. (coauthored with H.S.W. Massey). 1934. OUP 1987 $28.95. ISBN 0-19-852030-1

The Theory of the Properties of Metals and Alloys. (coauthored with Henry Jones). Dover 1936 $8.95. ISBN 0-486-60456-X

Wave Mechanics and Its Applications. (coauthored with I. N. Sneddon). 1948. Franklin 1973 $108.00. ISBN 0-08-016979-1

NEWTON, SIR ISAAC. 1642–1727

A British physicist and mathematician, Sir Isaac Newton is universally regarded as one of the greatest scientists of all time. In physics, he discovered the laws of motion that are named after him and was the first to explain gravitation. He made fundamental discoveries in optics and invented the reflecting telescope. In mathematics he formulated the calculus and derived the binomial theorem.

In 1665–66, Newton was forced by an outbreak of the bubonic plague to leave Cambridge University, where he was a professor of mathematics, for his country home. Many of Newton's discoveries were made in mathematics, dynamics, celestial mechanics, and gravitation theory, as well as his first optics experiments, during this so-called annus mirabilis (miraculous year). However, most of the results of this work were not published until 20 years later. In 1687 his greatest single work appeared, the *Philosophiae Naturalis Principia Mathematica (Mathematical Principles of Natural Philosophy*, commonly known as the *Principia)*. It took even longer for Newton to publish much of his work in optics, which he finally compiled in his *Opticks* of 1704.

Newton's work on gravitation, dynamics, and mechanics provides the foundation for classical physics. When he was inspired by a falling apple to consider the problem of gravity, it occurred to Newton that the force that pulled the apple might also extend into space and pull the moon into orbit about Earth. He conjectured that two bodies attract each other with a force that depends on the product of their masses and decreases in strength relative to the square of their distance. In 1679 an accurate value for the radius of Earth became available. This permitted Newton to calculate the moon's motion on the basis of his theory of gravitation. The correct result he obtained verified his conjecture. He also found that his theory explained JOHANNES KEPLER's empirically derived laws of planetary motion, discovered earlier in the seventeenth century.

In his *Principia* of 1687, Newton created the subject of classical mechanics by stating, proving, and applying his first three laws of motion. The first law states that an object remains at rest or in motion in a straight line unless acted on by a force. This is the concept of inertia, which finally replaced ARISTOTLE's (see Vols. 3 and 4) notion that constant force is required to keep an object in motion. The second law states that a force accelerates a body by an amount inversely proportional to its mass. This was the first clear definition of force and the first time mass was distinguished from weight. The third law states that action and reaction are equal and opposite, which demonstrates how objects move. By stating and applying these laws, Newton established a unified system that explained physical phenomena on Earth and in space.

To facilitate his studies of mechanics and dynamics, Newton created the differential and integral calculus, or as he called it, the "method of fluxions." This was the basis not only for much of modern mathematics but also for the most famous priority dispute in the history of science between Newton and GOTTFRIED WILHELM LEIBNIZ.

Newton's *Opticks* provided a systematic and highly organized account of his theory of the nature of light and its effects. For example, in a series of elegant experiments in 1666, Newton used prisms to show that white light is a mixture of colored light. Moreover, each color had a different index of refraction. Newton thought that light rays were corpuscular in nature and therefore capable of being analyzed by the universal forces discussed in the *Principia*. Yet, he insisted on integrating the concept of periodicity into his theory. This view showed tremendous physical intuition, since light has since been shown (by ALBERT EINSTEIN) to have a dual wave-particle nature.

Newton's supreme achievement was his indisputable demonstration that scientific principles can be universally applied. In the *Principia* he built a model of the universe from mathematical premises and experimental evidence that is still valid. Moreover, his example initiated an explosion of discovery in modern science that continues to the present.

BOOKS BY NEWTON

Demonstrations of Some of the Principal Section of Sir Isaac Newton's Principles of Natural Philosophy. Ed. by John Clarke. Johnson Repr. 1972 o.p. Features selections from the *Principia.*

Mathematical Papers of Isaac Newton, Vol. 8: Sixteen Ninety-Seven to Seventeen Twenty-Two. Cambridge U. Pr. 1981 $265.00. ISBN 0-521-20103-9

Mathematical Principles of Natural Philosophy and His System of the World. 2 vols. 1687. Trans. by Andrew Motte. U. CA Pr. 1962 $13.95 ea. ISBNs 0-520-00928-2, 0-520-00929-0. Includes Volume 1, *The Motions of Bodies,* and Volume 2, *The System of the World*; translated text of the *Principia.*

Newton's Philosophy of Nature: Selections of His Writings. 1687. Ed. by H. S. Thayer. Free Pr. 1974 $12.95. ISBN 0-685-43029-4. Selections from the *Principia.*

The Optical Papers of Sir Isaac Newton: Vol. 1: The Optical Lectures, 1670–1672. Ed. by Alan E. Shapiro. Cambridge U. Pr. 1984 $185.00. ISBN 0-521-25248-2

Opticks. 1704. Dover 1952 $9.95. ISBN 0-486-60205-2

BOOKS ABOUT NEWTON

Andrade, E. N. *Sir Isaac Newton.* Greenwood 1979 $55.00. ISBN 0-313-22022-0. Presents a brief, but thorough biography; written by a modern physicist.

Brodetsky, Selig. *Sir Isaac Newton.* Richard West repr. of 1927 ed. o.p. A brief biography that emphasizes Newton's scientific work; written for the general reader.

Burtt, Edwin A. *Metaphysical Foundations of Modern Physical Science.* Humanities 1982 $15.95. ISBN 0-391-01742-X. Classic intellectual history of early modern science, featuring Newton.

Christianson, Gale E. *In the Presence of the Creator: Isaac Newton and His Times.* Free Pr. 1984 $27.50. ISBN 0-02-905190-8. Presents the first popular biography of Newton in 50 years. Incorporates modern scholarship and the author's study of original sources; fails to offer serious descriptions of Newton's philosophical work.

Cohen, I. Bernard. *The Newtonian Revolution.* Cambridge U. Pr. 1983 o.p.

Graneau, Peter, and Neal Graneau. *Newton Versus Einstein.* Carlton 1992 $14.95. ISBN 0-8062-4514-X

Hall, A. Rupert. *All Was Light: An Introduction to Newton's Opticks.* OUP 1993 $58.00. ISBN 0-19-853985-1

Westfall, Richard S. *The Life of Isaac Newton.* Cambridge U. Pr. 1993 $24.95. ISBN 0-521-43252-9

OPPENHEIMER, J. ROBERT. 1904–1967

An American physicist, born in New York City, Robert Oppenheimer graduated from Harvard University summa cum laude in 1925. He made significant contributions to the development of quantum mechanics and was the key figure in the rapid development of the first atom bomb. After extensive study with key researchers in Britain and Germany (he received his Ph.D. in 1927 from the University of Göttingen), Oppenheimer returned to the United States to establish and run simultaneously two influential schools of theoretical physics, at the California Institute of Technology and the University of California, Berkeley. Theoretical physics had never before been studied with such intensity in the United States. During the 1930s, he made numerous contributions to atomic and nuclear physics. Oppenheimer and his students developed almost all consequences of the Dirac theory of the electron, including the predicted positively charged electron, discovered by Carl Anderson in 1932 and named the position. Oppenheimer also published early papers, theoretically discussing black holes and neutron stars. These papers were ignored by astronomers for many years.

Oppenheimer is best known to the general public as the leader of the successful American effort to develop the atom bomb at Los Alamos, New Mexico (1942–45). In 1947 he was appointed director of the Institute of Advanced Study at Princeton, New Jersey. After the war, Oppenheimer made powerful enemies by his opposition to the development of the hydrogen bomb and by his public proposals for international control of atomic energy. In 1954, during the McCarthy era, the Atomic Energy Commission (AEC) declared him a "security risk," thereby greatly disturbing many scientists. In 1963, AEC reversed its position, nominating Oppenheimer for its Fermi Prize in recognition of his many achievements.

BOOKS BY OPPENHEIMER

Atom and Void: Essays on Science and Community. Princeton U. Pr. 1989 $29.95. ISBN 0-691-02434-0. An anthology of previously published essays on science, philosophy, and society by Oppenheimer, with a preface by Freeman Dyson.

Science and Common Understanding. S&S Trade 1966 o.p. A series of six lectures delivered in 1953 over the BBC on the development of modern physics, with conclusions drawn on the role of science in the modern world.

Robert Oppenheimer: Letters and Recollections. HUP 1980 $32.50. ISBN 0-674-77605-4. Includes 167 letters, all but a few written by Oppenheimer himself, covering the years from 1922 to 1945. A parallel narrative draws on reminiscences of friends and a series of oral history interviews recorded in 1963. There is little scientific material.

Uncommon Sense. Ed. by N. Metropolis and others. Birkhauser 1984 $25.00. ISBN 0-8176-3165-8

BOOKS ABOUT OPPENHEIMER

Curtis, Charles P. *The Oppenheimer Case: The Trial of a Security System.* S&S Trade 1955 o.p. A journalistic and declamatory account of Oppenheimer's 1954 hearing.

Davis, Nuel P. *Lawrence and Oppenheimer.* Da Capo 1986 $11.95. ISBN 0-306-80280-5. Based on published documents and personal interviews with about 100 associates of American physicist Ernest Lawrence and Oppenheimer; Davis gives an account of the roles they played in the development of the atom bomb.

Goodchild, Peter J. *Robert Oppenheimer: Shatterer of Worlds.* Fromm Intl. Pub. 1985 o.p. Competent biography, brisk, readable, well illustrated.

Kunetka, James W. *Oppenheimer: The Years of Risk.* P-H 1982 o.p. Enjoyable first introduction to Oppenheimer's life story, but contains little on the nature and significance of his own scientific work.

Major, John. *The Oppenheimer Hearing.* Stein & Day 1983 o.p. Analysis of the secret hearings held in 1954 that resulted in Oppenheimer's removal from his post as AEC consultant. Oppenheimer's political and ethical motivations as well as the hearings' procedural shortcomings are detailed.

Szasz, Ferenc Morton. *The Day the Sun Rose Twice: The Story of the Trinity Site Nuclear Explosion.* U. of NM Pr. 1984 o.p. Short history of the first test of the atom bomb; not about Oppenheimer per se, but deals with his role during the test.

U.S. Atomic Energy Commission. *In the Matter of J. Robert Oppenheimer: Transcript of Hearing before Personnel Security Board and Texts of Principal Documents and Letters.* Greenwood 1993. ISBN 0-275-94429-8. Complete transcript of the dramatic secret hearings.

PAULI, WOLFGANG. 1900–1958 (NOBEL PRIZE 1945)

Born in Switzerland, Wolfgang Pauli was the son of a professor of physical chemistry at the University of Vienna and godson of ERNST MACH. He was a child prodigy, writing an outstanding paper on the theory of relativity at age 19, and receiving his Ph.D. from the University of Munich in 1922. After further study with NIELS BOHR and MAX BORN, Pauli taught at the Federal Institute of Technology in Zurich, where he remained until his death in 1958.

His discovery of the exclusion principle enabled Pauli to explain the structure of the periodic table of elements, formulate fundamental theories of electrical conductivity in metal, and investigate magnetic properties of matter. For this discovery, Pauli received the Nobel Prize in 1945.

Pauli's second great accomplishment was resolving the "problem" of beta decay. In 1930 he addressed this question of the 'missing energy" of electrons by suggesting that an emitted electron was accompanied by a neutral particle carrying an excess of energy. ENRICO FERMI suggested the name "neutrino" for this particle, which was first observed in 1953 by Fredrich Reines. Pauli's intellectual ability was not matched by his manual dexterity; his colleagues laughed at the so-called Pauli effect, whereby accidents seemed to happen whenever he worked in the laboratory.

BOOKS BY PAULI

Pauli Lectures on Physics. 3 vols. Ed. by C. P. Enz. MIT Pr. 1973 $9.95 ea. ISBN 0-262-66032-6

Theory of Relativity. Dover 1981 repr. of 1958 ed. $6.95. ISBN 0-486-64152-X

BOOKS ABOUT PAULI

Born, Max. *My Life: Recollections of a Nobel Laureate.* Taylor & Francis 1978 $60.00. ISBN 0-85066-174-9. Born was Pauli's supervisor at the University of Göttingen. Admires Pauli's genius, but also indicates his weaknesses; clearly written.

Fierz, Marcus, and V. F. Weisskopf. eds. *Theoretical Physics in the Twentieth Century: A Memorial Volume to Wolfgang Pauli.* Bks. Demand repr. of 1960 ed. $85.00. ISBN 0-317-08596-4. A technical work in which 14 authors recount personal memories of Pauli as they discuss their scientific work in relation to his. Three of the articles are in German; the others are in English; includes a complete bibliography of Pauli's work.

Hermann, A., and K. V. Meyenn, eds. *Wolfgang Pauli: Scientific Correspondence with Bohr, Einstein, Heisenberg, Vol. 1: 1919–1929.* Spr.-Verlag 1979 $194.00. ISBN 0-387-08962-4

Mehra, Jadish, and Helmut Rechenberg. *The Historical Development of Quantum Theory.* 5 vols. Spr.-Verlag 1987 $109.00. ISBN 0-387-96377-4. Chronicles the rise of quantum mechanics from 1900 to 1926. Although somewhat technical, the layperson will find it interesting as a considerable amount of history is included between the technical points. There are numerous references to Pauli in each volume, and part of Volume 2 is devoted to Pauli's life and works up to 1921.

PENROSE, ROGER. 1931–

Born in England, the son of a geneticist, Roger Penrose received a Ph.D. in 1957 from Cambridge University. Penrose then became a professor of applied mathematics at Birkbeck College in 1966 and a Rouse Ball Professor of Mathematics at Oxford University in 1973.

Penrose, a mathematician and theoretical physicist, has done much to elucidate the fundamental properties of black holes. With STEPHEN HAWKING, Penrose proved a theorem of ALBERT EINSTEIN's general relativity, asserting that at the center of a black hole there must evolve a "space-time singularity" of zero volume and infinite density, in which the current laws of physics do not apply. He also proposed the hypothesis of "cosmic censorship," which claims that such singularities must possess an event horizon.

In 1969 Penrose described a process for the extraction of energy from a black hole, as well as how rotational energy of the black hole is transferred to a particle outside the hole. In addition, Penrose has done much to develop the mathematics needed to unite general relativity, which deals with the gravitational interactions of matter, and quantum mechanics, which describes all other interactions.

BOOKS BY PENROSE

The Emperor's New Mind: Concerning Computers, Minds, and the Laws of Physics. Viking Penguin 1991 $14.00. ISBN 0-14-014534-6. Argues that some aspects of the mind will never be duplicated by artificial intelligence.

Quantum Concepts in Space and Time. OUP 1986 $80.00. ISBN 0-19-851972-9

Quantum Gravity 2: A Second Oxford Symposium. OUP 1981 $90.00. ISBN 0-19-851952-4

Spinors and Space-Time. 2 vols. Cambridge U. Pr. 1987–1988 $47.95 ea. ISBNs 0-521-33707-0, 0-521-34786-6. Volume 1 studies differential geometry and relativistic fields. Volume 2 provides a detailed account of the "twister methods" original to Penrose.

Techniques of Differential Topology in Relativity. CBMS-NSF Regional Conference Ser. Soc. Indus.-Appl. Math. 1972 repr. of 1983 ed. $13.00. ISBN 0-89871-005-7

PLANCK, MAX. 1858–1947 (NOBEL PRIZE 1918)

Max Planck, a German physicist, received his Ph.D. in physics from the University of Munich (1879) and taught at the University of Berlin from 1891 to 1928. By studying black-body radiation, he discovered that energy is not continuous, but is emitted or absorbed in fundamental, individual units called quanta. Quantum theory originated from his 1900 paper, representing a radical break with classical physics that even Planck could not wholly accept. For his work in quantum theory, Planck was awarded the 1918 Nobel Prize in physics.

Other physicists were able to apply the quantum concept by following up on his revolutionary idea. ALBERT EINSTEIN's 1905 paper, explaining the photoelectric effect, and NIELS BOHR's 1913 model of the hydrogen atom were two applications of Planck's theory.

Along with Einstein, Planck ranks as one of the two founders of modern physics. He was the acknowledged leader of German science in the 1930s, as president of the Kaiser Wilhelm Institute. However, he resigned this post in 1937 to protest the Nazi treatment of Jewish scientists. He remained in Germany throughout World War II. After the war the Institute was renamed the Max Planck Institute, and he again served as its president until his death.

Planck's personal life contained many tragedies: death of a wife, two sons (one was killed in World War I, the other was executed in 1944 for participation in an unsuccessful conspiracy to assassinate Hitler), and two daughters (in childbirth).

BOOKS BY PLANCK

Scientific Autobiography and Other Papers. Greenwood 1968 repr. of 1949 ed. $22.50. ISBN 0-8371-0194-8. Presents an autobiography and reprints philosophical essays on topics such as causality, the meaning and limits of science, and religion and natural science.

The Theory of Heat Radiation. Trans. by Morton Masius. *History of Modern Physics and Astronomy Ser.* Am. Inst. Physics 1989 $45.00. ISBN 0-88318-597-0. Reprints of the original Leipzig edition of 1906, and the English of 1914 published by P. Blakiston. A work that had a large influence on American physics.

Where Is Science Going? AMS Pr. 1981 repr. of 1932 ed. $19.50. ISBN 0-404-14696-1. Discusses many philosophical topics, such as free will, causality, and the reality of the external world, from the viewpoint of an important theoretical physicist.

BOOKS ABOUT PLANCK

Heilbron, J. L. *The Dilemmas of an Upright Man: Max Planck as Spokesman for German Science.* U. CA Pr. 1986 $25.00. ISBN 0-520-05710-4. Emphasizes Planck's courageous efforts to oppose Nazi policies on behalf of German science.
Rosenthal-Schneider, Ilse. *Reality and Scientific Truth: Discussions with Einstein, von Laue, and Planck.* Ed. by Thomas Braun. Bks. Demand repr. of 1980 ed. $38.80. ISBN 0-318-39785-4. The author-editor corresponded with Einstein, Planck, and Max von Laue for many years on the nature of scientific truth and physical reality, as well as on lighter topics; includes selections of the correspondence with connecting text.

RAMSAY, SIR WILLIAM. 1852–1916 (NOBEL PRIZE 1904)

William Ramsay, a British physicist and chemist, was the son of an engineer and the nephew of geology professors. He was probably most well known for his work in chemistry, although he made significant contributions to nuclear physics. In 1904 Ramsay received the Nobel Prize in chemistry for his demonstration that helium is continually produced during the radioactive decay of radium. This research and its subsequent explanation by ERNEST RUTHERFORD laid the foundation for the emerging discipline of nuclear physics.

After completing his education at Glasgow University in chemistry, and receiving his Ph.D. in 1872 from the University of Tübingen, Ramsay taught at University College in Bristol until 1880 and then at University College in London until his retirement in 1912. His research studies of helium led Ramsay to search for new gases on the periodic table. With the help of Morris Travers, Ramsay discovered the elements neon, krypton, and xenon. In 1904 Ramsay discovered radon.

BOOKS BY RAMSAY

Elements and Electrons. Harper 1912 o.p.
The Gases of the Atmosphere, the History of Their Discovery. Macmillan 1902 o.p.
Stoichiometry. Longmans Green 1908 o.p.

BOOK ABOUT RAMSAY

Travers, Morris William. *A Life of Sir William Ramsay.* Arnold 1956 o.p.

RÖNTGEN, WILHELM (KONRAD). 1845–1923 (NOBEL PRIZE 1901)

Wilhelm Röntgen was born in Lennep, Prussia (now Germany), and studied in Holland and Switzerland. He received his Ph.D. in physics in 1869 from the University of Zürich. After teaching at several German universities, he became a professor of physics at Wurzburg. On November 8, 1895, Röntgen noticed that a sheet of paper coated with barium platinocyanide glowed when he switched on a nearby cathode-ray tube entirely covered with black cardboard. In a cathode-ray tube, electrons are accelerated in a vacuum by an electric field. The impact of these electrons on the glass end of the tube produced penetrating "X" (since their nature was then unknown) rays, which caused the salt to glow. Soon X-rays were being widely used in medicine and were stimulating research in new directions; Becquerel's discovery of radioactivity followed within a year. In 1901, Röntgen received the first Nobel Prize in physics for his discovery of the remarkable penetrating radiation that were named Röntgen rays, or X-rays.

Refusing to benefit financially from his work, Röntgen died in poverty in the German inflation that followed World War I.

Books about Röntgen

Glasser, Otto. *Dr. W. C. Röntgen.* Charles C. Thomas 1958 o.p. Focuses on Röntgen's life. Much shorter than the 1934 volume, but features some of the same material, such as the list of Röntgen's publications, a translation of the original discovery article, and some of his original X-ray photographs.

_____. *Wilhelm Conrad Röntgen and the Early History of the Röntgen Rays.* 1934. Norman SF 1993 $115.00. ISBN 0-930405-22-6. Provides a complete list of publications by Röntgen, as well as a list of books, pamphlets, and scientific papers written about X-rays during 1896. Features a complete English translation of Röntgen's original paper and of many other contemporary documents; includes many photographs of colleagues and family, buildings, apparatus, papers, and early X-ray pictures.

Nitske, W. Robert. *The Life of Wilhelm Conrad Röntgen, Discoverer of the X-Ray.* Bks. Demand repr. of 1971 ed. $91.50. ISBN 0-317-28634-X. Contains details about Röntgen's life. Some of the material from the earlier Glasser work is restored here, such as the response by contemporary newspapers and magazines to Röntgen's winning the Nobel Prize; incudes reproductions of excerpts from many personal letters.

Oibner, Bern. *The New Rays of Professor Röntgen.* Burndy Lib. 1963 o.p. An easy-to-read book in a series aimed at interesting students in the careers of great scientists.

Shapiro, Gilbert. *A Skeleton in the Darkroom: Stories of Serendipity in Science.* HarpC 1986 o.p. Seven narratives designed to illustrate the role of chance in scientific discovery. The title story is an account of Röntgen's experiments with X-rays, focusing on the moment of discovery; suitable for high school students and general readers.

RUTHERFORD, ERNEST. 1871–1937 (Nobel Prize 1908)

The New Zealand-born physicist Ernest Rutherford was one of the dominant figures of early modern physics, perhaps one of the greatest experimental physicists of all time. Born in Spring Grove (later Brightwater), the fourth of 12 children, Rutherford won scholarships to Nelson College and Canterbury College, Christchurch. His first research projects involved the magnetization of iron by high-frequency discharges and magnetic viscosity. In 1895 Rutherford was admitted to the Cavendish Laboratory and Trinity College, Cambridge University, and in 1898 he became professor of physics at McGill University in Canada. From McGill he went back to England to Manchester University and then to the Cavendish Laboratory again. As director of the Cavendish Laboratory, he attracted some of the best young physicists in the world.

Rutherford's achievements are many. He was the first to explain that radioactivity is produced by the disintegration of atoms, distinguishing among three types of radioactive emission—alpha rays, beta rays, and gamma rays. For this achievement, he was awarded the Nobel Prize in chemistry in 1908. In 1911 Rutherford conceived a new model that clarified the structure of the atom. Rutherford's nuclear model predicted that almost all of the mass of an atom is concentrated in a very small central region (the nucleus), while most of the remaining area consists of empty space. Rutherford also did extensive work with the natural and artificial transmutation of radioactive elements, and was the first to suggest the presence of a neutral particle in all atomic nuclei (although neutrons were not isolated until 1932).

When Rutherford began exploring the phenomenon of radioactivity, little more was known than that it was a phenomenon that characterized uranium and other elements. Working with the English chemist Frederick Soddy at McGill University, he explained radioactivity as a phenomenon caused by the breakdown of atoms in a radioactive element to produce a new element. The two men discovered that the intensity of the radioactivity decreases at a rate determined by the element's half-life. The notion that atoms could change their identity was a revolutionary idea, yet Rutherford's explanation was so satisfactory that it found immediate acceptance in the scientific community. Rutherford utilized the notion of natural transmutation of elements to calculate the ages of mineral samples, arriving at figures greater than a billion years. This was the first proof of the great age of the Earth's rocks, and the process of radioactive dating has since been developed and applied to fossils and archaeological remains as well. With Hans Geiger, Rutherford developed a particle counter to measure the radioactivity released by elements.

Perhaps his greatest discovery concerned the structure of the atom. Before Rutherford's work, an atom was pictured as a sphere of positive charge occupying the whole volume of the atom. Negatively charged electrons were thought to be embedded in this space, rather like raisins in a raisin cake. This model had to be abandoned when a student of Geiger and Rutherford, Ernest Marsden, made a series of measurements of the unexpected scattering of alpha particles by thin metal foils. It was observed that a few of the particles bombarding the foil were reflected back. As Rutherford remarked, "It was as incredible as if you fired a 15-inch shell at a piece of tissue paper and it came back and hit you." Rutherford was forced to assume that most of the atom's mass was concentrated in a small space, or nucleus. Gradually, this new model of the atom came to be the accepted one among scientists.

BOOK BY RUTHERFORD

Rutherford and Boltwood: Letters on Radioactivity. (coauthored with Bertram Boltwood). Ed. by Lawrence Badash. Yale U. Pr. 1969 o.p. Features letters exchanged between Rutherford and Bertram Boltwood, an American chemist and physicist, for more than 20 years. Discusses scientific matters and comments on their private lives and on other scientific giants of the early twentieth century; also includes a brief history of radioactivity, and biographies of Rutherford and Boltwood.

BOOKS ABOUT RUTHERFORD

Andrade, E. N. *Rutherford and the Nature of the Atom.* Peter Smith repr. of 1964 ed. $11.25. ISBN 0-8446-2053-X. An outstanding biography by a contemporary and colleague; emphasizes the Manchester years.

Feather, Norman. *Lord Rutherford.* Priory Pr. 1973 o.p. Classic and definitive biography that shows how Rutherford and his work were regarded by contemporaries; includes interesting anecdotes, written with authority and personal knowledge by a coworker at the Cavendish Laboratory.

Oliphant, Mark. *Rutherford: Recollections of the Cambridge Days.* Elsevier 1972 o.p. Features reminiscences by a coworker at Cavendish Laboratories; includes letters and photographs.

Shea, William R., and M. A. Bunge, eds. *Rutherford and Physics at the Turn of the Century.* Watson Pub. Intl. 1979 $20.00. ISBN 0-88202-184-2. A collection of essays that describe Rutherford and his times; includes Feather's Memorial Lecture, chronicling the discovery of the alpha particle.

Wilson, David. *Rutherford: Simple Genius.* MIT Pr. 1983 $45.00. ISBN 0-262-23115-8. Offers a wide-ranging and interesting account of Rutherford's life and work; written by a former science correspondent for BBC television news.

SALAM, ABDUS. 1926– (NOBEL PRIZE 1979)

Abdus Salam received an M.A. in 1946 from Government College, Punjab University, in Lahore, where he later was a professor of mathematics. After receiving his Ph.D. from the Cavendish Laboratory in Cambridge in 1952, this Pakistani physicist went on to make significant contributions in the theory of particle physics, in particular, for his theory that unified the weak force and the electromagnetic force of nature. For this theory, Salam shared the 1979 Nobel Prize with SHELDON LEE GLASHOW and STEVEN WEINBERG, although each researcher did his work independently. Salam was the first Pakistani to win a Nobel Prize.

In 1964 Salam established the International Center for Theoretical Physicists in Trieste, Italy, to encourage scientists in emerging countries. Salam divides his time between the International Center and the Imperial College of Science and Technology in London, where he has been a professor since 1957. Salam also has promoted scientific training and research in developing countries. He has been active in UN and UNESCO committees and panels since the 1950s.

BOOKS BY SALAM

Aspects of Quantum Mechanics. (coauthored with E. P. Wigner). Cambridge U. Pr. 1972 o.p.

Ideals and Realities: Selected Essays. World Scientific Pub. 1983 $41.00. ISBN 9971-950-87-1. Essays on physics and the promotion of science in the developing countries.

Notes on Science Technology and Science Education in the Development of the South. World Scientific Pub. 1991 $7.00. ISBN 0-9625118-6-2

Unification and the Fundamentals of Quantum Mechanics: The First of the 1988 Dirac Memorial Lectures. Cambridge U. Pr. 1990 $17.95. ISBN 0-521-37140-6. A brief book of lectures by three of the most important physicists of the century. Salam gives an overview of all of physics with an emphasis on the unification of physical forces.

BOOKS ABOUT SALAM

Crease, Robert P., and Charles C. Mann. *The Second Creation: Makers of the Revolution in Twentieth Century Physics.* Macmillan 1985 o.p. A personal saga of discovery in modern physics, from the Einstein revolution to the super atom smashers. Describes the physicists who made the discoveries, including Abdus Salam. Written for the individual with some knowledge of physics and for the general reader who can grasp the technical aspects of the work; includes an index, many illustrations, and a complete glossary.

Dalafi, H., M. H. Salam, and M. H. Hassan. *Renaissance of Sciences in Islamic Countries—Muhammad Abdus Salam.* World Scientific Pub. 1993 $38.00. ISBN 9971-50-946-6

Ferris, Timothy. *Coming of Age in the Milky Way.* Morrow 1988 $19.95. ISBN 0-688-05889-2. Surveys astronomy and cosmology from ancient Egypt to the present. Relates the place of Salam among his peers and against the backdrop of history. Features many illustrations, a detailed glossary, and a bibliography; written for the general reader.

Hawking, Stephen W.. *A Brief History of Time: From the Big Bang to Black Holes.* Bantam 1990 $13.95. ISBN 0-553-34614-8. Reveals the details of space and time in terms of a physical reality that is accessible to the layperson; discusses Salam's contributions to the concept of the modern universe.

Pagels, Heinz E. *The Cosmic Code: Quantum Physics as the Law of Nature.* Bantam 1984 $5.95. ISBN 0-553-24625-9. Explores the meaning and importance of quantum physics—all without mathematics and in a language easy to understand by readers who have some grounding in the sciences. Features a historical relevancy to the work, which makes it interesting and meaningful to the layperson; includes illustrations, an index, and a bibliography.

_____. *Perfect Symmetry: The Search for the Beginning of Time*. Bantam 1986 $4.95 ea. ISBN 0-553-24000-5. Examines the history of modern physics, beginning with nineteenth-century astronomer William Herschel. Discusses the revolution in physics at the beginning of the twentieth century by discussing Einstein and his inheritors, including Abdus Salam. Describes how physics moved from general knowledge of the atom to the specific process that identified its most elementary parts; written for the general reader, with a bibliography, illustrations, and an index.

SCHRÖDINGER, ERWIN. 1887–1961 (NOBEL PRIZE 1933)

Born and educated in Vienna, Erwin Schrödinger received his Ph.D. in 1910 from the University of Vienna. He developed the theory of wave mechanics (1925–26). For this theory, which furnished a solid mathematical explanation of quantum theory, Schrödinger shared the Nobel Prize in 1933 with PAUL DIRAC.

Schrödinger was dissatisfied with NIELS BOHR's early quantum theory of the atom, objecting to the many arbitrary quantum rules imposed. Building on Louis-Victor De Broglie's idea that a moving atomic particle has a wave character, Schrödinger developed a famous wave equation that describes the behavior of an electron orbiting the nucleus of an atom. When applied to the hydrogen atom, the equation yielded all the results of Bohr and De Broglie, and was also used as a tool to solve a wide range of new problems in which quantization occurs.

In 1927 Schrödinger succeeded MAX PLANCK at the University of Berlin but resigned in 1933 when the Nazis came to power. He left then for England, becoming a guest professor at Oxford University. In 1936 he returned to Austria, but then fled in 1938 under the threat of Nazi arrest and was invited to Dublin's newly established Institute for Advanced Studies. He remained there from 1940 until his retirement in 1956, when he returned to his native Austria and to the University of Vienna, where he held his last chair in theoretical physics.

In 1944 Schrödinger published *What Is Life? The Physical Aspects of a Living Cell*, a book that had a tremendous impact on a new generation of scientists. The book directed young physicists who were disillusioned by the Hiroshima bombing to an unexplored discipline free of military applications—molecular biology. Schrödinger proposed the existence of a molecular code as the genetic basis of life, inspiring an entire generation to explore this idea.

BOOKS BY SCHRÖDINGER

My View of the World. Ox Bow 1983 $12.00. ISBN 0-918024-30-7. Discusses the limits of science and the value of its study.

Space-Time Structure. Cambridge U. Pr. 1985 $17.95. ISBN 0-521-31520-4. Features addresses and essays on science and society; includes his Nobel Prize acceptance speech, "The Fundamental Idea of Wave Mechanics."

What Is Life? Mind and Matter. 1944. Cambridge U. Pr. 1992 $9.95. ISBN 0-521-42708-8

BOOKS ABOUT SCHRÖDINGER

Kilmister, C. W., ed. *Schrodinger: Centenary Celebration of a Polymath*. Cambridge U. Pr. 1989 $74.95. ISBN 0-521-34017-9. Presents a collection of technical and biographical essays.

Mehra, Jagdish. *Erwin Schrödinger and the Rise of Wave Mechanics*. Spr.-Verlag 1987 o.p. Part 1: Schrödinger in Vienna and Zurich, 1887–1925. The first of two volumes on Schrödinger planned for this outstanding series. Part 1 details Schrödinger's youth and education, early scientific work, and research leading to the development of wave mechanics.

Scott, William T. *Erwin Schrödinger: An Introduction to His Writings*. U. of Mass. Pr. 1967 $22.50. ISBN 0-87023-023-9. The first comprehensive study of Schrödinger's scientific and philosophical works. Features a biographical sketch, several interpretive chapters on the foundations of wave mechanics and quantum mechanics, and a discussion of Schrödinger's other diverse intellectual endeavors.

SCHWINGER, JULIAN SEYMOUR. 1918–

Julian Schwinger, an American physicist, developed his prowess for mathematics and physics at a very early age. At the age of 17, he received his B.A. from Columbia University and his Ph.D. three years later. By 1946 Schwinger had become a full professor at Harvard University.

Schwinger's most notable contribution to physics was uniting electromagnetic theory and quantum dynamics into the theory of quantum electrodynamics (the foundations of which had been laid by PAUL DIRAC, WERNER HEISENBERG, and WOLFGANG PAULI). During World War II, Schwinger, RICHARD FEYNMAN, SIN-ITIRO TOMONAGA, and FRANK DYSON developed the mathematical formulation of quantum electrodynamics to conform with ALBERT EINSTEIN's theory of relativity. This new theory, which proved to be useful in measuring and explaining the behavior of atomic and subatomic particles, resulted in a Nobel Prize in physics for Feynman and Tomonaga in 1963.

Schwinger also conducted significant research into the properties of synchrotron radiation, produced when a rapidly moving charged particle is diverted by a magnetic field.

BOOKS BY SCHWINGER

Discontinuities in Wave Guides. (coauthored with D. Saxon). Gordon & Breach 1968 $94.00. ISBN 0-677-01840-1
Einstein's Legacy. W. H. Freeman 1986 $32.95. ISBN 0-7167-5011-2. Complete analysis of Einstein's theory of relativity.
Particles and Sources. Gordon & Breach 1969 $70.00. ISBN 0-677-02060-0
Particles, Sources, and Fields. Classics Ser. 3 vols. Addison-Wesley 1989 Vol. 1 $27.95. ISBN 0-201-09470-3. Vol. 2 $27.95. ISBN 0-201-09472-X. Vol. 3 $42.95. ISBN 0-201-19479-1
Quantum Kinematics and Dynamics. Addison-Wesley 1991 $29.75. ISBN 0-685-50038-1
Selected Papers on Quantum Electrodynamics. Dover 1958 $10.95. ISBN 0-486-60444-6

BOOK ABOUT SCHWINGER

Deser, S., and R. J. Finkelstein. eds. *Themes in Contemporary Physics II: Essays in Honour of Julian Schwinger's 70th Birthday.* World Scientific Pr. 1989 $43.00. ISBN 0-9971-50-961-X

THOMSON, SIR JOSEPH JOHN. 1856–1940 (NOBEL PRIZE 1906)

The British scientist Sir Joseph Thomson is best known in the world of physics for discovering the electron. Thomson studied and taught mathematics, physics, and chemistry at Trinity College, Cambridge University, from 1876 until his death in 1940. He became director of the Cavendish Laboratory at the early age of 27. Of those who eventually worked under him at the laboratory, seven won the Nobel Prize.

Thomson won a fellowship to Trinity College with a dissertation showing how a number of physical and chemical effects could be predicted from the laws of mechanics without detailed knowledge. After intensive study of vortex rings and cathode rays, he pioneered the field of subatomic particle physics with his work on the electron. Thomson's experiments showed that cathode rays were made up of particles with a measurable mass. This research resulted in a Nobel Prize for Thomson in 1906.

Thomson was an excellent mathematician. However, he made his discoveries primarily by an insight into the physical nature of the world, which the mathematics made more precise. Thomson also had an outstanding ability to devise ingenious experiments that went straight to the point. He is important in science not only for his own work but also as the leader of a group of research workers, including many great physicists of the following generation. Thomson's son G. P. Thomson won the 1937 Nobel Prize in physics.

BOOKS BY THOMSON

Conduction of Electricity through Gases. Cambridge U. Pr. 1903 o.p.
Electricity and Matter. Scribners 1904 o.p.
Elements of the Mathematical Theory of Electricity and Magnetism. Cambridge U. Pr. 1897 o.p.
Rays of Positive Electricity and Their Application to Chemical Analyses. 1913. Gordon Pr. 1991 $79.75. ISBN 0-8490-4925-3
Recollection and Reflections. 1936 o.p. Covers his education, the people who influenced his life and work, and his visits to the United States; includes an entire chapter on physical research.
A Treatise on the Motion of Vortex Rings: An Essay to Which the Adams Prize Was Adjudged in 1882. Cambridge U. Pr. 1853 o.p.

BOOKS ABOUT THOMSON

Crowther, J. G. *The Cavendish Laboratory, 1874–1974.* Sci. Hist. Pubs. 1974 o.p. Covers the history of the laboratory, emphasizing the person who laid the facility's foundations and determined its research; features Thomson's early years, his initial work as the director, his assistants and students, his work on the electron, and the later period through the end of World War I. Two early chapters discuss his predecessor, John William Strutt, and eight subsequent chapters provide information on his successor, Ernest Rutherford.
Segre, Emilio. *From X-Rays to Quarks: Modern Physicists and Their Discoveries.* W. H. Freeman 1980 o.p. Covers the discoveries and theories of physicists who produced a coherent picture of the atom. Highlights the significance of Thomson's contribution to the field of nuclear physics; written by a physicist who not only participated directly in nuclear physics (he received a Nobel Prize for his work) but also wrote a number of popular books on the history of physics.
Strutt, Robert John, fourth Baron Rayleigh. *The Life of Sir J. J. Thomson, O. M., Sometime Master of Trinity College.* Cambridge U. Pr. 1942 o.p. Describes Thomson's life and professional activities, such as presidency of the Royal Society, the mastership of Trinity College, his views on education, and aspects of his personal life. Features a firsthand account of the events that took place since Rayleigh (the son of Thomson's predecessor at Cavendish Laboratory) was at Cambridge and a friend of Thomson.
Thomson, George Paget. *J. J. Thomson and the Cavendish Laboratory in His Day.* Thomas Nelson 1964 o.p. Describes the work done by Thomson and his colleagues. Although the bulk of the information in this volume is covered by Crowther and Rayleigh, it provides detailed descriptions of the experiments, excellent drawings of the experimental equipment, and photographs of the experimental results. The illustrations are useful for readers who have difficulty following verbal description of complicated equipment and experiments.

TOMONAGA, SIN-ITIRO. 1906–1979 (NOBEL PRIZE 1965)

Born in Tokyo, the son of a philosophy professor, Sin-Itiro Tomonaga studied quantum mechanics with HIDEKI YUKAWA at Kyoto University. After attending lectures at Kyoto by PAUL DIRAC and WERNER HEISENBERG, Tomonaga did research for the Japanese Navy on microwave theory, while continuing his research in quantum theory. From 1937 to 1939, he worked under Heisenberg in Germany.

As early as 1942, Tomonaga suggested a new formulation of many ideas in the quantum field theory. Moreover, it was Tomonaga's theoretical work in developing a completely relativistic quantum field theory that led to the first successful form of quantum electrodynamics. Other forms were later developed independently by JULIAN SCHWINGER and RICHARD FEYNMAN, who shared a Nobel Prize in physics with Tomonaga in 1965.

In 1955 Tomonaga established the Institute for Nuclear Studies at the University of Tokyo and became president of the Tokyo University of Education in 1956. Later, he headed the Science Council for Japan and wrote popular books on quantum mechanics.

BOOK BY TOMONAGA

Spin the Spin. World Scientific Pub. 1993 repr. $51.00. ISBN 9971-50-330-1

BOOKS ABOUT TOMONAGA

Brown, Laurie M., and Lillian Hoddeson, eds. *The Birth of Particle Physics: Proceedings of the International Symposium on the History of Particle Physics, May, 1980.* Cambridge U. Pr. 1983 o.p. Discusses Tomonaga's approaches with those of Yukawa and other Japanese scientists. In chapter 22, Julian Schwinger describes the similarity of his research to Tomonaga's work.

Brown, Laurie M., M. Konuma, and Z. Maki, eds. *Particle Physics in Japan 1930–1950.* U. of Kyoto 1981 o.p. Features an extensive discussion with Tomonaga and translations from Tomonaga's Japanese writings by Funiko Tanihara and Noriko Esuchi; sponsored by the Research Institute for Fundamental Physics at the University of Kyoto.

Heitler, Waleter. *The Quantum Theory of Radiation.* Dover 1984 repr. of 1954 ed. $10.95. ISBN 0-486-64558-4. Offers a highly technical review of quantum field theory, from its classical origins to the successful culmination of quantum electrodynamics; discusses the methods developed by Tomonaga and his contemporaries.

Schwinger, Julian, ed. *Selected Papers on Quantum Electrodynamics.* Dover 1958 $10.95. ISBN 0-486-60444-6. Presents a collection of the most important scientific articles on the topic of electrodynamics; includes two articles by Tomonaga and a paper by Dyson, "Radiation Theories of Tomonaga, Schwinger, and Feynman," that shows the mathematical equivalence of the three laureates' work.

TOWNES, CHARLES H(ARD). 1915– (NOBEL PRIZE 1964)

Charles Townes was born in Greenville, South Carolina, and attended Furman University. After graduate study at Duke University and the California Institute of Technology, he spent the years from 1939 to 1947 at the Bell Telephone Laboratories designing radar-controlled bombing systems. Townes then joined the physics department of Columbia University. In 1951, while sitting on a park bench, the idea for the maser (microwave amplification by stimulated emission of radiation) occurred to him as a way to produce high-intensity microwaves. In 1953 the first maser became operational. In a maser, ammonia (NH_3) molecules are raised to an excited vibrational state and then fed into a resonant cavity, where (as in a laser) they stimulated part of the spectrum. "Atomic clocks" of great accuracy are based on this concept, and solid-state maser amplifiers are used in radioastronomy. In 1964 Townes and two Soviet laser pioneers, Aleksander Prokhorov and Nikolai Basov, shared the Nobel Prize. Since 1966 Townes has been at the University of California, Berkeley.

BOOK BY TOWNES

Microwave Spectroscopy. (coauthored with A. L. Schawlow). Dover 1975 repr. of 1955 ed. $14.95. ISBN 0-486-61798-X

BOOKS ABOUT TOWNES

Bertolotti, M. *Masers and Lasers: An Historical Approach.* IOP Pub. 1987 $39.00. ISBN 0-85274-437-4. Offers a detailed account of the development of the maser and laser. Townes's work is discussed and compared with the research that was being done simultaneously in the Soviet Union. Outlines the contributions of minor figures in the field; somewhat technical and may be difficult for the reader without a background in physics.

Hecht, Jeff, and Dick Teresi. *Laser: Supertool of the Eighties.* Ticknor & Fields 1982 o.p. Describes the various applications of lasers and covers their uses in medicine, manufacturing, the arts, energy production, defense, and communications; provides explanations suitable for the layperson on the principles of laser action and the design of various types of lasers and masers. Also discusses Townes's contributions to laser development and the conflicts that arose among American scientists over patent rights.

Weber, Robert L. *Pioneers of Science: Nobel Prize Winners in Physics.* Ed. by J.M.A. Lenihan. IOP Pub. 1988 $30.00. ISBN 0-85274-267-3. Presents brief biographies of all the Nobel physics laureates to 1980; useful for charting Townes's career.

WEINBERG, STEVEN. 1933– (NOBEL PRIZE 1979)

Born in New York City, Steven Weinberg was a high school and college classmate of SHELDON GLASHOW; both attended the Bronx High School of Science and Cornell University. Although Weinberg has made contributions as a theoretical physicist in cosmology, quantum scattering, and the quantum theory of gravitation, he is most widely known for his work with Sheldon Glashow and ABDUS SALAM, with whom he shared the 1979 Nobel Prize in physics. Weinberg received a share of this honor for his formulation of the theory that unifies the relationship between the weak force and the electromagnetic force, including the capability to predict the weak neutral current.

After receiving a Ph.D. from Princeton University in 1957, Weinberg held postdoctoral positions at Columbia University from 1957 to 1959, the Lawrence Berkeley Laboratory from 1959 to 1960, the University of California at Berkeley from 1960 to 1966, Harvard University from 1966 to 1967, and the Massachusetts Institute of Technology from 1967 to 1969. He is married to a law professor, and they have one daughter.

BOOKS BY WEINBERG

The Discovery of Subatomic Particles. W. H. Freeman 1983 $14.95. ISBN 0-7167-2121-X. Developed from a course intended to introduce nonscientists to the achievements of twentieth-century physics, the book covers the discoveries made prior to World War II; uses "flashbacks" to explain physics concepts and history. Well written and illustrated; concludes with a brief survey of specific research areas in contemporary particle physics.

Dreams of a Final Theory. Pantheon 1992 $24.50. ISBN 0-679-41923-3. A summary of how far theory has gone toward uniting gravity, electromagnetism, and the weak and strong nuclear forces into a final theory.

The First Three Minutes: A Modern View of the Origin of the Universe. Basic 1988 $7.95. ISBN Details the "standard model" of what is known about the first moments of the universe; features a mathematical supplement for those who want to see the basic computations. Although dated, the book was the first of its type, and remains useful.

Gravitation and Cosmology: Principles and Applications of the General Theory of Relativity. Wiley 1972 $74.95. ISBN 0-471-92567-5

WHEELER, JOHN ARCHIBALD. 1911–

A native of Florida, John Wheeler contributed greatly to the field of nuclear physics as a result of his work with NIELS BOHR. Bohr and Wheeler elucidated the mechanism of nuclear fission and predicted facts about plutonium production, a vital ingredient in nuclear weapons. After supplying the mathematical formalism necessary for constructing nuclear wave functions in 1937, Wheeler formulated and described the scattering matrix, a concept applied to elementary particle physics by WERNER HEISENBERG and other nuclear physicists.

With D. L. Hill in 1953, Wheeler proposed the collective model of the atomic nucleus, which proved to be an extremely important model in particle physics. During the thermonuclear crisis of 1949–50, he helped improve thermonuclear devices by using different fuel sources.

After this work, Wheeler researched the consequences of ALBERT EINSTEIN's geometrical theory of gravitation, which led to his description of a black hole in 1968. By tying quantum theory with geometrodynamics, Wheeler concluded the varying nature of space-geometry relations. Further, he described space as having a foamlike character, leading other investigators to develop mathematical methods to give a detailed formulation of this "space foam."

BOOKS BY WHEELER

Between Quantum and Cosmos: Studies and Essays in Honor of John Archibald Wheeler. Princeton U. Pr. 1988 $65.00. ISBN 0-691-08490-4

Black Holes, Gravitational Waves and Cosmology: An Introduction to Current Research. Gordon & Breach 1974 $138.00. ISBN 0-677-04580-8

Geometrodynamics. Acad. Pr. 1962 o.p.

Gravitation. W.H. Freeman 1973 $57.50. ISBN 0-7167-0334-3

Gravitation Theory and Gravitational Collapse. (coauthored with B. Kent Harrison). 1965 o.p.

A Journey into Gravity and Spacetime. W. H. Freeman 1990 $32.95. ISBN 0-7167-5016-3.
Describes and explains gravity and space-time in an engaging and interesting way.

Mind in Nature/Nobel Conference. Harper 1982 o.p.

Quantum Theory and Measurement. Princeton U. Pr. 1982 $99.50. ISBN 0-691-08316-9

Spacetime Physics. W. H. Freeman 1971 $17.95. ISBN 0-7167-0336-X

BOOK ABOUT WHEELER

Wojciech, Hubert Zurek, Alwyn van der Merwe, and Warner Allen Miller, eds. *Between Quantum and Cosmos: Studies and Essays in Honor of John Archibald Wheeler.* Princeton U. Pr. 1988 $65.00. ISBN 0-691-08490-4.

WIGNER, EUGENE PAUL. 1902– (NOBEL PRIZE 1963)

Born in Budapest, Hungary, Paul Wigner earned a Ph.D. in engineering in Berlin in 1924. During the 1930s he became one of a group of Hungarian scientists who left Europe and settled in the United States. He became a U.S. citizen in 1937. Married three times (his first two wives died), Wigner has two children.

From 1935 to 1937, Wigner served as visiting professor at the University of Wisconsin, an experience that inspired in him a deep love for his adopted country. He then moved on to Princeton University (where he was named Thomas D. Jones Professor of Mathematical Physics in 1938) and began an association that lasted the remainder of his career. While at Princeton, Wigner played a major role in persuading the U.S. government to establish the Manhattan Project.

Wigner has been called one of the greatest physicists of the twentieth century as a result of his contributions to many fields of physics and his profound influence on the field. His pioneering application of group theory to the atomic nucleus established a method for discovering and applying the principles of symmetry to the behavior of physical phenomena and earned him a Nobel Prize in 1963 (a prize he shared with Maria Goepert Mayer and J. Hans D. Jensen).

Although he won the Nobel Prize for his work in nuclear physics, Wigner's contributions are not limited to this area. For example, he and Pascal Jordan published an important basic paper in field theory. And his definitive work with Victor Weisskopf on the relationship between line shape and transition became an integral part of theoretical physics. Moreover, with his student Fredrick Seitz, Wigner also contributed substantially to solid-state physics.

BOOKS BY WIGNER

Aspects of Quantum Theory. Cambridge U. Pr. 1972 $54.95. ISBN 0-521-08600-0
The Collected Works of Eugene Paul Wigner. Ed. by Alvin M. Weinberg. Spr.-Verlag 1992 $129.00. ISBN 0-387-55343-6
Reminiscences about a Great Physicist: Paul Adrien Dirac. Cambridge U. Pr. 1987 o.p.
Survival and the Bomb: Methods of Civil Defense. (ed.). Bks. Demand repr. of 1969 ed. $79.30. ISBN 0-317-12974-0

YANG, CHEN NING. 1922– (NOBEL PRIZE 1957)

Chen Ning Yang was born in China, the son of a mathematics professor. He adopted "Franklin" as his first name in 1945 after reading the autobiography of BENJAMIN FRANKLIN (see Vol. 1). Eventually, Yang studied under ENRICO FERMI at the University of Chicago, where he earned his Ph.D. (1948) and then went on to make significant contributions to the theory of weak interactions in the field of particle physics and statistical mechanics.

Yang is most widely known, however, for his work with Tsung-Dao Lee, for which they shared a Nobel Prize in 1957. Yang and Lee made a fundamental theoretical breakthrough by demonstrating the nonconservation of parity. As a result of their research, all scientific theories based on parity had to be reexamined. In 1964 Yang became an American citizen and assured the public in his Nobel Prize acceptance speech that he would never leave the United States because of his devotion to science, which, he believes, is primarily of Western origin.

BOOK BY YANG

Selected Papers Nineteen Forty-Five to Nineteen Eighty with Commentary. W. H. Freeman 1983 $29.95. ISBN 0-7167-1407-8

BOOK ABOUT YANG

Bernstein, Jeremy. *A Comprehensible World.* Random 1967 o.p. Includes a chapter that is invaluable for its month-by-month explanation of the scientific work conducted by Yang and Lee in 1957. Descriptions of the scientific conversations they had at a Chinese restaurant and of Yang's view that his work reflects Chinese philosophy are essential to an understanding of the human side of this brilliant scientist; written by a colleague of Yang and Lee.

YUKAWA, HIDEKI. 1970–1981 (NOBEL PRIZE 1949)

Hideki Yukawa, the son of a Kyoto University geology professor, has done important theoretical work on elementary particles and nuclear forces. In particular, he predicted the existence of the pi-meson(pion) and the short-range nuclear force associated with this particle. For his contribution, he received the 1949 Nobel Prize in physics, the first Japanese to receive this honor.

In the early 1930s, Yukawa searched for the force that holds the atomic nucleus together. He eventually proposed an explanation in terms of an exchange between nucleons of a similar intermediate mass observed in studies of cosmic rays. However, this particle, later named the muon, did not interact strongly with nuclei as required by the theory. In 1947 the pion was discovered, possessing Yukawa's predicted properties. The pion was additionally observed to undergo rapid decay to the muon, which clarified the issue. Yukawa was a professor at Kyoto and Osaka universities, as well as at Columbia and Princeton universities.

BOOKS BY YUKAWA

Quantum Theory and Nonlocal Fields. Cambridge U. Pr. 1952 o.p.

Tabibito (the Traveler). World Scientific Pub. 1982 $18.00. ISBN 9971-950-10-3. Originally appeared in 1957 in a major Japanese newspaper to commemorate Yukawa's fiftieth birthday; after 36 printings, the autobiography has been translated for Western audiences.

CHAPTER 21

Chemistry

Maureen Welling Matkovich

> Chemistry is an intermediate science. Its universe is defined not by reduction to a few elementary particles, or even the hundred or so elements, but by a reaching out to the infinities of molecules that can be synthesized. . . . The beauty I would claim for chemistry is that of richness and complexity, the realm of the possible.
> —ROALD HOFFMAN, *Chemistry Imagined: Reflections on Science*

Chemistry is the physical science that studies the composition, properties, and structure of matter at the atomic and molecular levels. Chemists also measure the energy changes that cause and result from the changes in composition and structure of matter. An experimental science, chemistry constantly tests results of experiments against the results predicted by theory. Traditionally, there are four major branches of chemistry: analytical, inorganic, organic, and physical.

Modern chemistry was preceded by the medieval practice of alchemy. Alchemists used a synthesis of fakery, experimentation, and mysticism that rested on the classical Greek theories in which earth, water, air, and fire were the basic elements of the universe. PHILIPPUS AUREOLUS PARACELSUS (see also Vol. 4) added the principles of sulfur, mercury, and salt to these basic elements.

Most people associate alchemy with chemistry. Yet at least one chemical historian, Aaron J. Ihde, in *The Development of Modern Chemistry*, has argued that medieval medicine and technology (particularly that area now called metallurgy—the obtaining of metals from ores) contributed more to the science of modern chemistry than did alchemy. From metallurgy came the attempt to quantify the amounts of precious metals that can be obtained from a particular ore. Distillation, a basic method of purifying substances, came from medieval medicine. Quantification introduced another important scientific concept, the necessity for measurement. The necessity to measure and quantify was expressed eloquently generations later by the English physicist William Thompson, Lord Kelvin: "When you can measure what you are speaking about, and express it in numbers, you know something about it; but when you cannot measure it, when you cannot express it in numbers, your knowledge is of a meager and unsatisfactory kind: It may be the beginning of knowledge, but you have scarcely, in your thoughts, advanced to the stage of Science" (*Popular Lectures and Addresses, 1891–1894*).

From the period of the alchemists through the formulation of the periodic table, chemists struggled to develop the basic tools of modern chemistry, to understand the true nature of the chemical elements, and to postulate how chemical compounds were produced from these elements. The brief biographies of representative contributors to chemical knowledge clearly show that some scientists not only contributed to chemistry but also were active political or religious leaders.

Chemical compounds are different in their chemical composition, molecular structure, and stereochemistry. Chemists represent these compounds by using specific types of chemical formulas and by a highly complex and structured system of nomenclature. With its accompanying conventions necessary to represent and univocally identify the myriad of chemical compounds, chemical nomenclature is a significant stumbling block to the understanding of chemistry. This problem often is associated with organic chemistry. Therefore, several basic study guides to organic chemistry nomenclature are included in the reading list.

Chemists use three types of formulas to describe the chemical composition of matter: Empirical formulas identify the elements present and the correct proportions; molecular formulas identify the elements, the proportions, and the size of the molecule; and structural formulas (represented as diagrams) give all the above information as well as indicate how the atoms are linked to each other. A compound that has the same molecular but a different structural formula is an isomer. Isomers can differ substantially from each other in physical properties, chemical reactivity, and effects on organic substances.

Modern chemistry is interdependent with other sciences. Chemistry is indebted to many of the concepts of modern physics and uses mathematical models to express its theories. Chemistry and biology meet in biochemistry, which is among the most exciting fields on the scientific frontier. Chemists also contribute to toxicology, the study of poisons, and the newest analytical chemistry techniques are applied in modern geology and archaeology.

GENERAL BIBLIOGRAPHY

There are many general reference sources for the various fields of chemistry. Scientific and chemical encyclopedias and dictionaries are used by the chemist and the general reader. However, the professional chemist requires handbooks with physical and chemical data on many chemicals. Special handbooks on chemical toxicity and lists of regulations covering chemical use have been published during the last 25 years. Many standard sources contain biographical data on notable chemists, and histories of the development of chemistry exist but are rare. Because of the increasing importance of the chemical industry, encyclopedias on chemical technology and industrial processes as well as sourcebooks of chemical suppliers are available. Finally, there are guides to the literature of chemistry designed for the bench or laboratory chemist.

Careful attention to these general sources of information might enlighten the general reader about chemistry more than dogged persistence in reading the more detailed texts.

Directories, Dictionaries, and Encyclopedias

The ACS Directory of Graduate Research 1991. Am. Chemical 1991 $60.00. ISBN 0-8412-2104-9. Wealth of information about faculty members of institutions granting graduate degrees in the chemical sciences; includes their current research projects.

American Men and Women of Science: A Biographical Dictionary of Today's Leaders in Physical, Biological and Related Sciences, 1992–1993. 8 vols. Bowker 1992 $750.00. ISBN 0-8453-4074-0. The standard biographical directory of approximately 125,000 living scientists in the United States and Canada. "Continues to be the standard reference tool in its field" (*Booklist*).

Ash, M., and I. Ash. *Encyclopedia of Industrial Chemical Additives*. 4 vols. Chem. Pub. $93.50 ea. Vol. 1 *A–F*. 1984. ISBN 0-8206-0299-X. Vol. 2 *G–O*. 1984. ISBN 0-8206-0308-2. Vol. 3 *P–Z*. 1984. ISBN 0-8206-0309-0. Vol. 4 1987. ISBN 0-8206-0320-1

———. *Encyclopedia of Plastics, Polymers and Resins*. 3 vols. Chem. Pub. 1981–83 o.p. Compiles practical information on trade-name plastic, polymer, and resin products. Entries are arranged by trade name and include manufacturers, brief chemical descriptions, and mechanical properties.

Asimov, Isaac. *Asimov's Biographical Encyclopedia of Science and Technology*. Doubleday 1982 $29.95. ISBN 0-385-17771-2. An alphabetical index of individuals and a subject index; includes living and dead scientists.

Bennett,H., ed. *Chemical Formulary*. 31 vols. Chem. Pub. 1933–1993 $60.00 ea.

———. *Chemical Formulary Series: Cumulative Index, Vols. 1–25*. Chem. Pub. 1986 $85.00. ISBN 0-8206-0319-8

———. *Concise Chemical and Technical Directory*. Chem. Pub. 4th ed. 1986 $125.00. ISBN 0-8206-0310-4. Covers trademarked chemical products.

———. *Encyclopedia of Chemical Trademarks and Synonyms*. 3 vols. Chem. Pub. 1981–83 o.p. Covers trademarked products. One of several sets by this publisher identifying these hard-to-find products.

Best's Safety Directory. A. M. Best 1993 $39.00. ISBN 0-685-43285-8. Intended for use as a buyer's guide for safety products and as a safety training aid. Summaries of the federal Occupational Safety and Health Administration (OSHA) requirements; includes advertising for products.

Bretherick, Leslie. *Handbook of Reactive Chemical Hazards*. Butterworth-Heinemann 1990 $195.00. Compilation of reports from the literature of hazards encountered while using these chemicals. Useful in determining conditions under which chemicals have exploded. Well indexed. Necessary for chemists, but the National Fire Protection Association (NFPA) manual might be adequate for others.

Chemcyclopedia. Am. Chemical 1993 $60.00. ISBN 0-8412-25087. Another buyer's guide for chemicals in the United States. Chemicals are arranged alphabetically within large divisions by use.

Chem Sources International. 33rd ed. Chem. Scs. Intl. 1992 $250.00. ISBN 0-939020-17-6. Provides similar information for the international marketplace as *Chem Sources U.S.A.* provides for the domestic market.

Chem Sources U.S.A. Chem. Scs. Intl. 1992 $250.00. ISBN 0-937020-16-8. The most comprehensive buyer's guide for chemicals of all types sold in the United States. Contains an alphabetical list of 104,400 chemicals produced or distributed by 855 firms; codes indicate bulk and high-purity chemical producers.

Clansky, Kenneth B., ed. *Suspect Chemicals Sourcebook: A Guide to Industrial Chemicals Covered under Major Regulatory and Advisory Programs*. Roytech 1993 o.p. Federal regulations for more than 4,000 industrial chemicals arranged by CAS registry numbers. Cross indexes and mid-year supplement. The best ready reference available to answer the question "Is this chemical federally regulated?"

Considine, Douglas M., and Glenn D. Considine. *Van Nostrand's Scientific Encyclopedia*. 7th ed. 2 vols. Van Nos. Reinhold 1988 $195.00. ISBN 0-442-21750-1. "Probably the best scientific encyclopedia available" (*Library Journal*).

Dean, J. A. *Lange's Handbook of Chemistry*. McGraw 1992 $79.50. ISBN 0-07-016194-1. Physical and chemical data of chemical compounds, nomenclature guides and cross-references for trivial and mineral names.

Directory of American Research and Technology, 1994. Bowker 1993. ISBN 0-8352-3395-2. Contains more than 11,000 research laboratories in the United States. The standard directory of the work place for chemists and allied scientists.

Encyclopedia of Physical Science and Technology. Ed. by Robert A. Meyers. Acad. Pr. 1992 $2100.00. ISBN 0-12-226930-6. More scholarly and mathematical treatment than the *McGraw-Hill Encyclopedia*. Because this publication's emphasis is on the physical sciences, chemistry subjects constitute a higher percentage of the overall material. Good combination of mathematics, physics, and chemistry.

Farm Chemicals Handbook. Meister 1987 o.p. Intended primarily for the agricultural industry. Useful in answering basic questions about fertilizers and pesticides. Describes toxicity, handling and storage cautions, and recommended uses, with extensive coverage of trade names; includes information about pesticides currently banned in the United States.

Gardner's Chemical Synonyms and Trade Names. Ed. by Jill Pierce. Gower 9th ed. 1987 o.p. Covers trade-named chemicals in commerce in Britain and chemicals produced or sold in the United States; includes alphabetical list of trade names and synonyms, with brief descriptions and manufacturers' designations.

Gerhartz, Wolfgang, ed. *Ullmann's Encyclopedia of Industrial Chemistry.* 5th ed. 36 vols. VCH Pubs. 1984–89 $235.00 ea. Standard set on industrial chemistry published in English. Coverage is similar to *Kirk-Othmer Encyclopedia of Chemical Technology.* The division of *Ullmann's* into two series (A: chemicals, product groups, etc., and B: basic principles) make this encyclopedia more difficult to use than *Kirk-Othmer*; 25 volumes of this 36-volume set currently are available in English.

Kent, James A., ed. *Riegel's Handbook of Industrial Chemistry.* Van Nos. Reinhold 1992. ISBN 0-442-00175-4. Excellent summary of chemical technology; emphasizes economic aspects of the chemical and related industries.

Kirk-Othmer Concise Encyclopedia of Chemical Technology. Ed. by Martin Grayson. Wiley 1985 o.p. Covers the subjects of the complete *Kirk-Othmer Encyclopedia* in abbreviated form; the best substitute for the larger encyclopedia.

Kirk-Othmer Encyclopedia of Chemical Technology. 27 vols. Wiley 1991–95 $250.00 ea. The classic encyclopedia on industrial chemical processes. Comprehensive articles introduce each subject, covering the industrial production and uses of the chemical and discussing it in greater depth. Excellent reference set for specialist and general reader; includes bibliographies.

Lewis, Richard J., Sr. *Lewis: Sax's Dangerous Properties of Industrial Materials.* 3 vols. Van Nos. Reinhold 1992 $399.95. ISBN 0-442-01132-6. Compilation of data on chemical hazards written for the specialist or serious amateur. Some classes of data were eliminated to allow for the inclusion of 21,000 chemicals.

Lide, David R., Jr., and Christian Martin. *Handbook of Chemistry and Physics.* CRC Pr. 74th ed. 1993 $99.50. ISBN 0-8493-0472-5. The best known and most widely used of the compilations of physical data of compounds. Covers boiling points, melting points, densities, solubilities, and refractive indexes of many compounds; issued annually.

McGraw-Hill Concise Encyclopedia of Science and Technology. McGraw 1989 $114.50. ISBN 0-07-045512-0. Substitute for the *McGraw-Hill Encyclopedia of Science and Technology.* The publisher notes that the material in this title was taken from the longer set.

McGraw Hill Encyclopedia of Chemistry. McGraw 2nd ed. 1993 $95.50. ISBN 0-07-045455-8. Provides good coverage of basic chemical terms; material has been published previously in the *McGraw-Hill Dictionary of Scientific and Technical Terms.*

McGraw-Hill Encyclopedia of Science and Technology. 20 vols. McGraw 7th ed. 1992 $1,900.00. ISBN 0-07-909206-3. Excellent general reference for adults for most phases of science and technology, including chemistry. Coverage is of current mainstream science only.

Merck Index: An Encyclopedia of Chemicals, Drugs, and Biologicals. Merck 1989 $35.00. ISBN 0-911910-28-X. Indispensable compendium of information about chemicals, drugs, and biological substances; includes a section on named organic chemical reactions.

National Fire Protection Association. *Manual of Hazardous Chemical Reactions.* NFPA 1991 $29.75. Compiles reports about hazardous chemicals and reactions; not as comprehensive as Bretherick's book.

Nickon, Alex, and Ernest F. Silversmith. *Organic Chemistry: The Name Game; Modern Coined Terms and Their Origins.* Pergamon 1987 $75.00. ISBN 0-08-034481-X.

Entertaining discussion of a number of interesting chemical names; useful also as a chemical dictionary.

Orchin, Milton, and Hans Zimmer. *The Vocabulary of Organic Chemistry*. Wiley 1980 $79.95. ISBN 0-471-04491-1. Useful for learning the vocabulary and concepts of organic chemistry.

Oxford Illustrated Encyclopedia. 8 vols. OUP 1989 $49.95 ea. Vol. 1 *The Physical World*. Ed. by Sir Vivian Fuchs. ISBN 0-19-869129-7. Vol. 6 *Invention and Technology*. Ed. by Monty Finniston. ISBN 0-19-869138-6. Vol. 1 covers the physical sciences, including chemistry; Vol. 6 covers the applications of science. Superbly illustrated encyclopedia for the general reader.

Reagent Chemicals. 8th ed. Am. Chemical 1993 $149.95. ISBN 0-8412-2502-8. Specifications for procedures and chemicals used in analytical chemistry.

Sax, N. Irving. *Dangerous Properties of Industrial Materials*. 3 vols. Van Nos. Reinhold 8th ed. 1988 $395.00. ISBN 0-442-28020-3. Written for the specialist or serious amateur.

Sax, N. Irving, and Richard J. Lewis, Sr., eds. *Hawley's Condensed Chemical Dictionary*. 12th ed. Van Nos. Reinhold 1992 $69.95. ISBN 0-442-01131-8. Covers chemical processes, equipment, and famous chemists. The best chemical dictionary available for general collections.

Science and Technology Desk Reference: 1500 Answers to Frequently Asked or Difficult-to-Answer Questions. Ed. by Carnegie Library of Pittsburgh, Science and Technology Department. Gale 1992 $39.95. ISBN 0-8103-8884-7. Chemistry questions appear in two chapters in this book, "Chemistry and Physics" and "Metals and Materials." The choice of questions is sensible, the layout is attractive, and the included references are appropriate.

Walker, John, and Michael Cox, eds. *The Language of Biotechnology: A Dictionary of Terms*. Am. Chemical 1988 $49.95. ISBN 0-8412-1489-1. Specialized dictionary for biotechnology specialists, but also useful for the general reader.

World of Learning 1993. Gale 43rd ed. 1993 $370.00. ISBN 0-8103-9747-1. Covers learned organizations and universities in a range of disciplines, including chemistry.

Young, Jay A., ed. *Improving Safety in the Chemical Laboratory: A Practical Guide*. Wiley 1991 $84.95. ISBN 0-471-53036-0. Fast becoming the standard book for basic chemical laboratory safety; useful for academic and industrial laboratories.

Chemistry in Perspective

Asimov, Isaac. *Asimov's New Guide to Science*. Basic 1984 $40.00. ISBN 0-465-00473-3. Chapters on the elements and the molecule summarize two basic concepts of chemistry. The remainder of the book covers fundamental concepts from other branches of science.

Cavalieri, Liebe F. *Double-Edged Helix: Genetic Engineering in the Real World*. Ed. by Ruth N. Anshen. Col. U. Pr. 1984 $12.95. ISBN 0-275-91783-5. Examines the interaction between science and society.

National Research Council. *Opportunities in Chemistry*. National Acad. Pr. 1985 $34.95. ISBN 0-309-03633-X. Discusses the benefits to society provided by chemistry and the current scientific frontiers. Identifies priority areas and opportunities in chemistry and makes recommendations for federal involvement (particularly the National Science Foundation) in these areas.

Office of Technology Assessment, U.S. Congress. *Regulatory Environment for Science: A Technical Memorandum*. USGPO 1986 o.p. Examines the social and legal forces that restrict or regulate scientific and engineering research in the United States. Describes regulations on the use of animals in experiments and land-use prohibitions on the storage, use, and disposal of toxic and flammable chemicals.

Porterfield, William W. *Concepts of Chemistry*. Norton 1972 o.p. "A must for all college libraries, public libraries, and collections dealing with chemistry" (*Choice*).

Weber, Robert J., and David Perkins, eds. *Inventive Minds: Profiles of Creativity in Science and Industry*. OUP 1992 $39.95. ISBN 0-19-507170-0. Contemporary inventors discuss how they created their inventions, and historians and psychologists speculate on the creative mind and its thought processes.

Guides to the Chemical Literature

Aluri, Rao, and Judith S. Robinson. *Guide to U.S. Government Scientific and Technical Periodicals.* Scarecrow 1976 $19.00. ISBN 0-8108-0888-9. Traces the information flow from research proposal to the production of the secondary sources, such as abstracting and indexing services.

Dodd, Janet S., ed. *The ACS Style Guide: A Manual for Authors and Editors.* Am. Chemical 1985 $24.95. ISBN 0-8412-0917-0. Discusses the ethical obligations of editors, authors, reviewers and scientists publishing outside the scientific literature.

Maizell, Robert E. *How to Find Chemical Information: A Guide for Practicing Chemists, Teachers, and Students.* Wiley 1987 $69.95. ISBN 0-471-86767-5. Useful discussion on patents and chemical marketing information; intended for the professional but accessible to the general reader.

Schoenfeld, Robert. *The Chemist's English: Say It in English, Please!* Fr. & Eur. 1986 $22.95. ISBN 0-8288-0849-X. "It is strongly recommended that everyone contemplating the preparation of a scientific article should first purchase and study this splendid little book" (*Carbohydrate Research*).

Warr, Wendy, and Claus Suhr. *Chemical Information Management.* VCH Pubs. 1992 $90.00. ISBN 1-56081-180-3. Covers traditional sources, such as journals, but emphasizes database use and construction.

Wiggins, Gary D. *Chemical Information Sources.* Ed. by Kirk Emry. McGraw 1991 $42.35. ISBN 0-07-00030-4. The best current compendium on chemical information. Thoroughly covers the old (trade literature) and the new (online techniques). "Recommended very highly for libraries serving chemistry students at all levels" (*Choice*); includes two diskettes.

HISTORY OF CHEMISTRY AND THE CHEMICAL INDUSTRY

Modern chemistry evolved mainly from alchemy, primitive metallurgy, and medicine. Chemistry is an experimental science firmly established on theoretical concepts developed by physicists and mathematicians. As with all modern sciences, the study of chemistry is a cooperative endeavor. Individuals can make outstanding contributions to theory or practice, but they rely on the body of scientific knowledge that already had been compiled. Or as SIR ISAAC NEWTON (see also Vol. 4) wrote to Robert Hooke (1634–1703) in 1676, "If I have seen further [than you and Descartes], it is by standing on the shoulders of giants." One of ROBERT BOYLE's outstanding contributions to chemistry was his clear grasp that the secrecy, fakery, and sorcery so prevalent in medieval alchemy was antithetical to modern science. JONS JAKOB BERZELIUS and JUSTUS VON LIEBIG (1803–1873), in addition to their own substantial scientific contributions, also founded important scientific journals to circulate the results of scientific research.

The following references do not emphasize individual chemists. Instead they focus on the development of chemical concepts, industrial processes, and experimental methods as well as a major theme in the history of chemistry—the discovery of the elements.

Asimov, Isaac. *The Search for the Elements.* Basic 1962 o.p. Easy-to-read history of chemistry; somewhat dated.

Bertsch, Sharon McGrayne. *Nobel Prize Women in Science: Their Lives, Struggles and Momentous Discoveries.* Carol Pub. Group 1992 $24.00. ISBN 1-55972-146-4. "At the onset, Bertsch asks, 'Why so few?'—at the conclusion, given the trials and tribulations, one wonders how so many endured. Highly recommended" (*Library Journal*).

Dictionary of Scientific Biography. Ed. by Charles C. Gillispie. Macmillan 1981 $1,080.00. ISBN 0-684-16962-2. 2 supplements. Covers the careers of scientists from antiquity to the present in many scientific endeavors, including chemistry. Living scientists are excluded; bibliography for each entry.

Farber, Eduard. *Evolution of Chemistry: A History of Its Ideas, Methods, and Materials*. Ronald Pr. 1952 o.p. Describes the development of specific ideas and concepts; requires some knowledge of chemistry.

Goran, Morris. *Story of Fritz Haber*. U. of Okla. Pr. 1967 o.p. Describes how Haber developed a method of combining nitrogen from the air with hydrogen to produce ammonia, which could be used for the production of chemicals from fertilizers to gunpowder.

Great Chemists. Ed. by Eduard Farber. Wiley 1961 o.p. More than 100 biographies of chemists; excludes living chemists.

Haber, L. F. *Chemical Industry during the Nineteenth Century: A Study of the Economic Aspect of Applied Chemistry in Europe and North America*. OUP 1958 o.p. Well-documented study of the rise of the chemical industry.

———. *Chemical Industry, 1900–1930: International Growth and Technological Change*. OUP 1971 o.p. Continuation of the preceding title. The coverage is comparatively better for the European and British chemical industries than for the rapidly growing American chemical industry.

Hochheiser, Sheldon. *Rohm and Haas: History of a Chemical Company*. U. of Pa. Pr. 1985 $37.95. ISBN 0-8122-7940-9. One of the best historical studies of an American chemical company.

Hudson, John. *The History of Chemistry*. Routledge Chapman & Hall 1992 $59.95. ISBN 0-412-03641-X. Text that introduces "historical material into the teaching of chemistry, both at school and undergraduate level" (preface). Concisely written, with attractive format and numerous illustrations; not as comprehensive as Ihde.

Ihde, Aaron J. *The Development of Modern Chemistry*. Dover 1983 repr. of 1964 ed. $17.95. ISBN 0-486-64235-6. History of chemistry from before 1750 to the mid-twentieth century; fine bibliography and appendices that cover the chemical elements (1982) and Nobel Prize-winners in chemistry, physics, and medicine (1983).

Leicester, Henry M. *Historical Background of Chemistry*. Dover 1971 repr. of 1956 ed. $6.98. ISBN 0-486-61053-5. Covers the ideas and practices before the era of modern chemistry, focusing on the history of iron extraction.

———. *Source Book in Chemistry, 1900–1950. Source Bks. in the History of Science*. 2 vols. HUP 1968 $27.50. ISBN 0-674-82231-5. Selections from writings of the major contributors to chemical thought, with short synopses of the lives and times of the contributors.

Li Ch'iao-p'ing. *The Chemical Arts of Old China*. AMS Pr. 1979 repr. of 1948 ed. $24.50. ISBN 0-404-14482-9. Covers the development of applied chemistry from approximately 400 B.C. to the early twentieth century; includes chapters on the production of gunpowder, ceramics, and dyes.

Magill, Frank N., ed. *Nobel Prize Winners, Chemistry*. 3 vols. Salem Pr. 1990 $210.00. ISBN 0-89356-557-1. Part of a series that, when completed, will include all Nobel Prize categories. "Despite a glut of reference works on the Nobel Prize, this set stands out as perhaps the best comprehensive source now available for reference information devoted to the Nobel Foundation. . . . " (*Choice*).

Morss, L. R., and J. Fuger, eds. *Transuranium Elements: A Half Century*. Am. Chemical 1992 $99.95. ISBN 0-8412-2219-3. Developed from an ACS Symposium in Washington, D.C. (1990), commemorating the fiftieth anniversary of the synthesis of a new series of elements. Contains papers from participants in the symposium; accessible to the general reader.

Multhauf, Robert P. *Neptune's Gift: A History of Common Salt. Studies in the History of Technology*. Johns Hopkins repr. of 1978 ed. $89.50. ISBN 0-8357-4033-1. History of the technology and production of common table salt and related compounds from antiquity to the mid-twentieth century.

―――――. *The Origins of Chemistry*. 1967 *Classics in the History and Philosophy of Science Ser*. Vol. 13 Gordon & Breach 1993 $48.00. ISBN 2-88124-594-3. A "most engaging book" (*Library Journal*) on the history of scientific knowledge to the seventeenth century. Begins with the use of iron and manganese oxides in paleolithic paintings.

Partington, James R. *A History of Chemistry*. 4 vols. St. Martin 1961–64 o.p. Scholarly and heavily referenced work on the history of chemistry from the early Greek philosophers to G. N. Lewis and his generalized theory of acids and bases.

Salzberg, Hugh W. *From Caveman to Chemist: Circumstances and Achievements*. Am. Chemical 1991 $24.95. ISBN 0-8412-1786-6. From the beginnings of chemistry until the end of the nineteenth century, showing the influence of history on the development of chemistry. "Strongly recommended" (*Choice*).

Seeman, Jeffrey L., ed. *Profiles, Pathways, and Dreams: Autobiographies of Eminent Chemists*. 22 vols. Am. Chemical 1990–present $24.95 ea. Series of autobiographies of eminent organic chemists.

Seymour, Raymond B., and Charles H. Fisher. *Profiles of Eminent American Chemists*. *Discovering the Discoverers Ser*. Vol. 1 Litarvan Lit. 1988 $29.95. ISBN 0-937557-05-6. Summaries of the lives and work of contemporary American chemists. Eclectic mix of subjects provides biographical information on important scientists not easily obtained elsewhere.

Sherwood, M. *The New Chemistry*. Basic 1973 o.p. Describes the discovery of industrial chemical products, such as nylon, plastics, and food products; accessible to the general reader.

Skolnik, Herman, and Kenneth M. Reese, eds. *Century of Chemistry: The Role of Chemists and the American Chemical Society*. Am. Chemical 1976 o.p. History commemorating the centennial of the founding of the American Chemical Society.

Smith, Richard Furnald. *Chemistry for the Millions*. Macmillan 1972 o.p. "Chapters cover such themes as ancient origins and alchemy, metals, Lavoisier, oxygen, inert gases, the Periodic Table, halogens, nonmetals, and carbon" (*Library Journal*).

Stillman, John Maxson. *The Story of Alchemy and Early Chemistry*. Dover 1960 o.p. Examines the development of chemistry from the early use of metals through the time of Lavoisier, with liberal use of quotations describing laboratory procedures and accompanying explanations; first published as *The Story of Early Chemistry* in 1924.

Thackray, Arnold. *Atoms and Powers: An Essay on Newtonian Matter—Theory and the Development of Chemistry*. HUP 1970 o.p. Thought-provoking examination by a leading historian of science.

Wasson, Tyler, ed. *Nobel Prize Winners*. Wilson 1987 $90.00. ISBN 0-8242-0756-4. Comprehensive one-volume dictionary covering Nobel Prize-winners from 1901 to 1986. Supplement volume covers 1987 through 1991 ($35.00).

Weeks, Mary Elvira. *Discovery of the Elements*. Bks. Demand repr. of 1968 ed. $160.00. ISBN 0-317-09341-X. Scholarly summary of the discovery of the elements, beginning with the precious metals discovered during antiquity and ending with elements synthesized by controlled radioactive methods.

GENERAL CHEMISTRY

The following books are suitable for either the general reader or the individual who needs to refresh his or her grasp of the language and principles of chemistry. Several self-study texts are included.

Bliss, Anne. *A Handbook of Dyes from Natural Materials*. Macmillan 1981 $14.95. ISBN 0-684-16502-3. Illustrates how an elementary knowledge of chemistry, chemical formulas, and techniques is employed in one of the earliest forms of chemical technology.

Davies, Geoffrey. *Forensic Science*. Am. Chemical 1986 $64.95. ISBN 0-8412-0918-9. Basic coverage of forensic science.

Groom, Nigel. *The Perfume Handbook*. Routledge Chapman & Hall 1992 $29.95. ISBN 0-412-46320-2. Discusses the art of making perfumes—from the raw materials through the finished product; includes biographies of great perfume makers and instructions on making perfumes at home.

Hess, Fred C. *Chemistry Made Simple*. Ed. by Arthur L. Thomas. Doubleday 1984 $12.00. ISBN 0-385-18850-1. Explains basic concepts including the gas laws, oxidation-reduction reactions and chemical equilibria; slightly more elementary than *Chemistry Made Easy*.

Lippy, John D., Jr., and Edward L. Plader. *Modern Chemical Magic*. Stackpole 1959 o.p. Describes experiments that no longer are considered safe for amateurs to perform but includes interesting recipes for invisible inks, colored flames, and materializing ghosts.

Nentwig, Joachim, Manfred Kreuder, and Karl Morgenstern. *Chemistry Made Easy*. 2 vols. VCH Pubs. 1992 $59.95. ISBN 1-56081-549-3. Self-study course with programmed instruction techniques to teach basic chemistry.

Pauling, Linus, and Roger Hayward. *Architecture of Molecules*. W. H. Freeman 1970 o.p. Explains chemical bonding and how it determines molecular structure; for the general reader.

Richards, W. Graham. *The Problems of Chemistry*. OUP 1986 $8.95. ISBN 0-19-219191-8. Brief introduction to some of the basic concepts of chemistry and how they apply to everyday life; designed for the general reader.

Ryschkewitsch, George E. *Chemical Bonding and the Geometry of Molecules*. Bks. Demand repr. of 1963 ed. $32.30. ISBN 0-317-09188-3. Discusses chemical bonding and molecular geometries and their dependence on electrovalent structure.

Sisler, Harry H. *Electronic Structure, Properties, and the Periodic Law*. Reinhold 1963 o.p. Useful introductory book that explains the chemical properties of elements in terms of their electronic structure.

Steiner, Richard P., ed. *Folk Medicine: The Art and the Science*. Am. Chemical 1985 $24.95. ISBN 0-8412-0939-1. Discusses folk medicine scientifically; relates the virtues of folk medicines to the chemical composition of their ingredients.

ORGANIC CHEMISTRY

Organic chemistry can be defined as the study of chemicals that contain, or are analogous to, compounds that have at least one carbon-carbon bond. However, this definition includes carbides, which usually are not considered organic compounds. Another definition states that organic chemists study only hydrocarbon derivatives. The first definition stresses the unique property of carbon—its ability to form chains—that makes possible the seemingly infinite variety of organic compounds. Organic chemicals are categorized broadly by the type of molecular structures present, either rings or chains.

All living organisms contain and synthesize organic chemicals. At one time, this distinction was used to separate chemistry into two major classes: inorganic (not derived from living species) and organic (containing carbon and derived from living species).

Carbon has the ability to make four bonds—a fact that the German organic chemist Friedrich August Kekulé von Stradonitz (1829–1896) published in 1858. Because these bonds are covalent rather than ionic, carbon can bond with up to four other carbon or other element atoms to form straight, branched, and cyclic chains containing single, double, and triple as well as aromatic bonds. Almost all organic chemicals contain hydrogen in addition to carbon. Nitrogen, oxygen, and sulfur also frequently occur bonded to carbon.

In 1800, organic chemistry already had begun research on the medicinal properties of some naturally occurring compounds. People had developed methods of extracting these naturally occurring chemicals for use. A theory called vitalism postulated that a vital force, which was present only in living organisms, was necessary to produce organic chemicals. JONS JAKOB BERZELIUS believed in vitalism and that a chemist in the laboratory could not produce an organic chemical from inorganic material—until he was proved wrong by German chemist FRIEDRICH WÖHLER. Before Wöhler's laboratory synthesis of urea in 1828, chemists believed that organic chemicals could be synthesized only by living organisms. Today, most organic chemicals are made in a laboratory or chemical manufacturing plant. Many of these chemicals do not occur naturally.

Because of the multitude of organic chemicals, chemists have developed elaborate classification schemes. Chemicals are classified by structure because chemicals of like structure tend to react in similar ways. The functional group concept is the most widely used classification scheme. For example, acetic acid contains the carboxyl group, which means that it should behave as a weak acid and ionize to the anion (negatively charged ion) and the cation (a positively charged hydrogen ion). One can predict that acetic acid will react with an alcohol to produce an ester. The major functional groups are discussed below.

Hydrocarbons are compounds of only carbon and hydrogen. Because of the multiple bonding capability of carbon, there are thousands of hydrocarbons with several main forms. They can be straight chains (butane), branched chains (isooctane), and cyclic structures (cyclohexane). Because of this diversity in structure, chemists often use structural formulas to represent organic compounds, and an elaborate system of nomenclature has been formulated for naming these compounds according to their structure. In addition, hydrocarbons are classified based on their molecular bonds. Alkanes contain single bonds, alkenes contain one or more double bonds, and alkynes contain one or more triple bonds. Aromatic hydrocarbons contain one or more rings with a unique mixture of single and double bonds. The primary source of aromatic hydrocarbons is the processing of petroleum.

Many organic chemicals have oxygen in the molecule as well as hydrogen and carbon. For example, alcohols (including ethyl alcohol) have a hydroxy or (OH) group. Ethers, such as diethyl ether, have an oxygen atom with single bonds to two carbon atoms. Aldehydes have a carbon atom at the end of the chain with a double bond to an oxygen and a single bond to a hydrogen. Ketones have a carbon atom with a double bond to an oxygen and other bonds to other carbon atoms. Carboxylic acids consist of a terminal carbon atom with a double-bonded oxygen and a singly bonded oxygen bonded to a hydrogen atom.

Carboxylic acid derivatives consist of acyl halides, which are composed of a carbon atom double-bonded to an oxygen atom, with a single bond to the halide atom; acid anhydrides have two carbon atoms double-bonded to oxygen atoms, with an oxygen atom bonded between them; esters are produced by the reaction of an alcohol and an acid; and amides have a carbon atom double-bonded to an oxygen atom and with the same carbon single-bonded to a nitrogen atom.

Nitrogen-containing organic compounds are classified as nitriles, amines, and nitro compounds.

Benfey, O. Theodor, ed. *Kekulé Centennial.* Am. Chemical 1966 $21.95. ISBN 0-8412-0062-9. Collection of 10 papers on various historical aspects of Kekulé's benzene ring postulation.

Fessenden, Ralph J., and Joan S. Fessenden. *Organic Chemistry*. Brooks-Cole 1990 $74.25. ISBN 0-534-12252-3. Shows the relationship between organic chemistry and biology by the selection of problems and material.

Morawetz, Herbert. *Polymers: The Origins and Growth of a Science*. Wiley 1985 o.p. "A well-documented chronology of the origins and growth of polymer science based on obviously careful readings, excerpts, and annotation of the original literature—more than 1,000 references in all, and all mostly important references, coupled with a lifetime of experience between the author and contemporary scientists and their work" (*Choice*).

Morrison, Robert T., and Robert N. Boyd. *Organic Chemistry*. P-H 1992 $71.00. ISBN 0-13-643669-2. Emphasizes reaction mechanisms and functional groups.

Pine, Stanley H., and George S. Hammond. *Organic Chemistry*. McGraw 1987 $51.30. ISBN 0-07-050118-1. Emphasizes chemical structures and reactions.

Traynham, James G. *Organic Nomenclature: A Programmed Introduction*. P-H 1991 $14.95. ISBN 0-13-639394-2. Excellent self-study program for the beginning student of organic nomenclature.

BIOCHEMISTRY

Biochemistry is the chemistry of living organisms. It has been established on the twin foundations of biology and organic chemistry. Possibly the most exciting work occurring in science today is being done in biochemistry. The basic textbooks on this reading list approach biochemistry from the perspective of chemistry.

Abeles, R. H., P. A. Frey, and W. P. Jencks. *Biochemistry*. Jones and Bartlett 1992 $60.00. ISBN 0-86720-212-2. Comprehensive text for a college course; requires a knowledge of organic chemistry and cell biology.

Cairns-Smith, A. G. *Seven Clues to the Origin of Life: A Scientific Detective Story*. Cambridge U. Pr. 1990 $8.95. ISBN 0-521-39828-2. Examines the origin of life using the concept of a detective story; entertaining and informative.

Coombs, Jim. *The Biotechnology Directory 1990*. Groves Dict. Music 1993 $235.00. ISBN 1-56159-061-4. Directory of suppliers and biotechnology products worldwide.

Fruton, Joseph S. *A Skeptical Biochemist*. HUP 1993 $29.95. ISBN 0-674-81077-5. Easy-to-read book on the scientific method and biochemistry.

Gregory, Richard P. *The Biochemistry of Photosynthesis*. Wiley 1989 $69.95. ISBN 0-471-91899-7. "Stimulating comparisons between analogous systems in plant and animal life, e.g., processes in the chloroplast and in the mitochondrion" (*Choice*).

Holum, John R. *Elements of General and Biological Chemistry: An Introduction to the Molecular Basis of Life*. Wiley 1991 $49.95. ISBN 0-471-51757-7. Text for students of chemistry in the allied health care fields.

Stryer, Lubert. *Biochemistry*. W. H. Freeman 1988 $57.95. ISBN 0-7167-1843-X. Standard text in college biochemistry.

Watson, James D. *Double Helix: Being a Personal Account of the Discovery of the Structure of DNA*. Atheneum 1980 repr. of 1968 ed. $11.95. ISBN 0-689-70602-2. First-person account of the research and personalities that earned the author a Nobel Prize (1962) and started the biotechnology revolution.

INORGANIC CHEMISTRY

Inorganic chemistry studies more than 100 noncarbon elements and the properties and reactions of those elements in forming compounds. The reactions are primarily of an ionic type in which compounds dissociate into positively or negatively charged ions, which then react to form new compounds held together by ionic bonds. These chemicals usually are acids, bases, or salts.

Acids and bases are two of the most important chemical classifications. Sulfuric acid is the major manufactured chemical in the world, used to produce such items as fertilizers, hydrochloric acid, detergents, and other household products. Bases, such as ammonia and sodium hydroxide, also are produced in large quantities. Acids display some common properties. For example, all acids are sour to the taste; acetic acid (an organic acid) gives vinegar its sour taste, and citric acid (another organic acid) gives lemon its characteristic taste. Acids also dissolve many metals and liberate hydrogen in the process. (Early chemists studied this reaction thoroughly.) In contrast, bases tend to precipitate metals.

Another property shared by acids and bases is the ability to change the color of certain naturally occurring, and some synthetic, dyes. For example, litmus paper, which is paper impregnated with litmus, turns red on exposure to acids and blue when exposed to bases. The ability to change color when exposed to acids or bases makes the litmus an indicator. Indicators, such as litmus, phenophthalein, bromothymo blue, and bromocresol, still are widely used to identify acids. Acids are defined as chemicals that can donate hydrogen ions. Incidentally, many dyes used to color textiles are indicators and can suffer permanent color changes when exposed to acids or bases.

In the late 1800s, the Swedish chemist SVANTE ARRHENIUS developed a theory of acids and bases based on the ability of a chemical to conduct electricity. An acid in water dissociates into hydrogen ions and the remaining characteristic anion. Because these particles are charged, the water then can conduct electricity efficiently.

Bases were postulated to contain the hydroxide ion (OH^-) and to behave similarly when dissolved in water. The base dissociated into a hydroxide ion and the corresponding base cation. For example, potassium hydroxide dissociates in water to potassium ions with positive charges and hydroxide ions with negative charges. The hydroxide ions give the base its characteristic properties.

The Arrhenius theory of acids and bases was useful, but it did not explain some observed phenomena. For example, ammonia was known to be a base even though it did not possess a hydroxide group. Hydrochloric acid and ammonia dissolved in benzene still reacted to form a salt (ammonium chloride) just as these two chemicals would if they had been dissolved in water. In the early 1920s, Johannes Bronsted (1879–1947) and Thomas Lowry (1874–1936) modified Arrhenius's theory. According to Bronsted and Lowry, an acid was a hydrogen ion donor and a base was a hydrogen ion acceptor. Thus, ammonia (without a hydroxide group) was a base because it could accept a hydrogen ion and acid-base reactions could occur without water. Later, GILBERT NEWTON LEWIS (1875–1946) further modified the acid-base theory in respect to electron pair donors and acceptors.

The formation of salts from acids and bases, such as ammonium chloride, is an important chemical reaction. Salts are important commercially. For example, the salts of such acids as nitric and phosphoric acids are used as fertilizers. Salts do not have the same properties as the acids or bases from which they are derived but instead display properties characteristic of salts. Salts cannot dissolve or precipitate metals, do not taste sour or bitter, and can conduct electricity when dissolved in water. The latter demonstrates that salts also dissociate or ionize when dissolved in water to the corresponding negatively and positively charged ions. For example, ammonium chloride in water dissociates to the ammonium ion and the choride ion. Sodium chloride, or common table salt, dissociates to the sodium ion and the chloride ion.

Asimov, Isaac. *The Noble Gases.* Basic 1966 o.p. Among the many books on science for the general reader by this author and one of the few books devoted to the noble gases. A historical account from their discovery by Ramsey and Rayleigh to the preparation of the first noble gas compounds in 1962.

Brown, Theodore L., and others. *Chemistry: The Central Science.* P-H 1990 $57.00. ISBN 0-13-126202-5. College chemistry text that shows the relevance of chemistry to everyday life.

Coulson, Charles. *Coulson's Valence.* Ed. by Roy McWeeney. OUP 1979 $59.00. ISBN 0-19-855144-4. One of the classic descriptions of chemical bonding.

Holden, Alan, and Phyllis S. Morrison. *Crystals and Crystal Growing.* MIT Pr. 1982 repr. of 1960 ed. $10.95. ISBN 0-262-58050-0. Fascinating book for the general reader that describes crystal symmetry, cleavage, and classification as well as vacancies and grain boundaries.

Kieffer, William F. *Mole Concept in Chemistry.* Krieger 1973 o.p. Explains thoroughly the fundamental concept of the "mole," or Avogadro's number of molecules; intended for undergraduate chemistry students.

Pauling, Linus. *The Nature of the Chemical Bond and the Structure of Molecules and Crystals: An Introduction to Modern Structural Chemistry.* Cornell Univ. Pr. 1960 $59.95. ISBN 0-8014-0333-2. Reprint of his classic 1939 work on behavior of the electron in chemical bonding.

PHYSICAL CHEMISTRY

Physical chemistry clearly illustrates the theoretical and mathematical basis of modern chemistry. Physical chemists solve scientific problems by using mathematical models to quantify and predict the behavior of matter. Brief illustrations of two questions that have concerned physical chemists and physicists follow.

In the early 1800s, JOHN DALTON first proposed the modern atomic theory. Throughout much of the nineteenth century, scientists thought that the atom was indivisible. Later in the century, scientists began to consider the possibility that the atom consisted of even smaller particles. In the early 1900s, experimental work by physicist ERNEST RUTHERFORD and his coworkers indicated that a nuclear atom had a positive charge at the nucleus surrounded by a negative charge. NIELS BOHR, another physicist, using his knowledge of Rutherford's work and MAX PLANCK's quantum theory, developed a model for the electronic structure of the atom. Later, the work of LOUIS DE BROGLIE on the wave theory of matter and WERNER HEISENBERG's postulate that it is impossible to know both the position and velocity of the electron at the same time contributed to the current quantum mechanical view of the electronic structure of the atom.

Theories of chemical equilibrium and thermodynamics have significantly influenced the development of modern chemistry. During the nineteenth century, the caloric concept of heat was abandoned and replaced by the concept of the interconvertibility of heat and mechanical work. Julius Mayer first calculated the mechanical equivalent of heat. HERMANN HELMHOLTZ postulated the principle of the conservation of energy and that the universe had a constant amount of energy. Rudolf Clausius (1822–1888) defined a term for the disorder in the universe—*entropy*—and claimed that the entropy of the universe always tends to increase. The law of mass action, proposed by Cato Guldberg and Peter Waage, defined an equilibrium constant in terms of the concentrations of reactions and products. The development of the Clausius-

Clapeyron equation applied thermodynamic principles to chemical equilibria. JOSIAH WILLARD GIBBS, the first significant American chemist, developed the phase rule, which allowed calculation of the degrees of freedom in a heterogeneous system. In 1884, Henri Louis le Châtelier (1850–1936) stated that imposed changes on a system in equilibrium causes the equilibrium to readjust in the direction necessary to offset the change.

Many of the physical chemistry texts are difficult for the reader without a strong mathematical background. However, much useful information can be gleaned from the introductory material contained in even the most complex mathematical treatments.

Alberty, Robert A., and Robert J. Silbey. *Physical Chemistry*. Wiley 1992 $54.95. ISBN 0-471-62181-1. Remains the classic text for undergraduate chemistry majors; requires a knowledge of calculus and physics.

Prigogine, Ilya, and Isabelle Stengers. *Order Out of Chaos: Man's New Dialogue with Nature*. Bantam 1984 $10.95. ISBN 0-553-34363-7. "The 1977 Nobel laureate in chemistry and a former co-worker and scientific journalist have written a dazzling and profoundly optimistic book . . . in which . . . they envisage a universe where chance becomes a partner of determinism—a universe [that might] under certain conditions become spontaneously self-organizing, achieving 'order out of chaos'" (*Library Journal*).

Spielberg, Nathan, and Byron D. Anderson. *Seven Ideas That Shook the Universe*. Wiley 1987 $32.95. ISBN 0-471-85974-5. One of the best current explanations of the concepts of energy and entropy and the quantum theory for the general reader.

ANALYTICAL CHEMISTRY

Analytical chemistry, the fourth traditional branch of chemistry, defines the techniques used to obtain knowledge of the chemical composition of materials. Improved instrumentation has made possible the detection of trace quantities of chemicals. The advancement of analytical techniques has greatly improved the ability of chemists to determine minute contaminants in industrial processes, such as semiconductor manufacture, and to trace amounts of chemicals in the environment. Because of the current use of improved analytical techniques in toxicological studies, several titles related to toxicology are included in this section.

Bender, Gray T. *Principles of Chemical Instrumentation*. Saunders 1987 $33.50. ISBN 0-7216-1834-0. Describes instrumental analysis in clinical chemistry and molecular biology. Useful to the general reader because it does not require knowledge of either physics or calculus.

Christian, Gary D. *Analytical Chemistry*. Wiley 1986 $54.95. ISBN 0-471-88574-6. Fundamental undergraduate text on analytical chemistry; includes a useful elementary chapter on data handling.

Furman, N. Howell, and Frank J. Welcher. *Standard Methods of Chemical Analysis*. 3 vols. Krieger 1975 repr. of 1962–66 ed. $548.50 set. ISBN 0-88275-940-X. Comprehensive set of fundamental analytical separations and methods. Discusses methods of preparation for many reagents and standard and indicator solutions; somewhat dated.

Official Methods of Analysis of the AOAC. [Association of Official Analytical Chemists]. Ed. by S. Williams. 2 vols. AOAC 1990 $281.00. ISBN 0-935584-42-0. Compendium of analytical methods used in the enforcement of the food, feed, and pesticide laws by federal and state departments of agriculture.

Szabadvary, Ferenc. *History of Analytical Chemistry*. Trans. by Gyula Svehla. Pergamon 1992 repr. of 1976 ed. ISBN 02-88-124569-2. Describes the importance of analytical

chemistry to the development of modern chemistry and postulates that the
development of suitable analytical methods was necessary for most discoveries in
chemistry. Discusses the contributions of Lavoisier, Berzelius, and Ostwald, among
others.

ENVIRONMENTAL CHEMISTRY AND APPLICATIONS OF CHEMISTRY

Berger, Melvin. *Hazardous Substances: A Reference*. Enslow Pubs. 1986 $17.95. ISBN 0-
89490-116-8. "A concise, alphabetically arranged guide to 230 dangerous materials
and other environmental hazards that are encountered at home and in the
workplace. . . . Technical terms are kept to a minimum, and a handy glossary at the
front of the volume defines those [that] are used in the annotations" (*School Library
Journal*).

Committee on Science, Engineering, and Public Policy. *Policy Implications of Greenhouse Warming: Mitigation, Adaptation, and the Science Base*. Natl Acad. Pr. 1992
$89.95. ISBN 0-309-04386-7. Examines all aspects of the greenhouse effect.

Crone, Hugh. *Chemicals and Society: A Guide to the New Chemical Age*. Cambridge U. Pr.
1987 o.p. Discusses benefits and disadvantages of current chemical use; one of the
few books for the general reader that covers improvements in analytical techniques.

Gough, Michael. *Dioxin, Agent Orange: The Facts*. Plenum Pub. 1986 $19.95. ISBN 0-306-
42247-6. Scholarly examination of the studies on the health of people exposed to
dioxin. Concludes that the effects of dioxin on human health have been exaggerated.

Harte, John. *Toxics A to Z: A Guide to Everyday Pollution Hazards*. U. CA Pr. 1991 $75.00.
ISBN 0-520-07223-5. Covers many of the same subjects as *A Consumer's Dictionary of
House, Yard and Office Chemicals* but is somewhat more scholarly. "A much-
needed, comprehensive reference for the lay reader, this book should be in all public
libraries" (*Library Journal*).

McCann, Michael. *Artist Beware*. Lyons & Beerford 1992 $29.95. ISBN 1-55821-175-6.
Describes correct ventilation and safety equipment and the hazards of chemicals
used in dyes and pigments.

_____. *Health Hazards Manual for Artists*. N. Lyons Bks. 1985 $9.95. ISBN 0-941130-
06-1. Compendium of information about naturally occurring compounds that can be
poisonous. Documents naturally occuring teratogens and carcinogenic toxins, as
well as the compounds that cause contact dermatitis; somewhat technical for the
general reader.

National Research Council. *Pesticides in the Diets of Infants and Children*. Natl Acad. Pr.
1993. ISBN 0-309-04875-3. Recommends changes in current regulatory practice to
protect children from unsafe levels of pesticides.

_____. *Regulating Pesticides in Food: The Delaney Paradox*. Natl. Acad. Pr. 1987 $29.95.
ISBN 0-309-03746-8. Examines the contradictions inherent in barring any pesticide
residue that has been found to cause cancer in animals and the law's requirement for
"an adequate, wholesome, and economical food supply"; from a study by the Board
of Agriculture (National Research Council) on the impact of the Delaney Clause of
the Food, Drug, and Cosmetic Act on the Environmental Protection Agency's
methods for allowing pesticide residues in food.

O'Neill, Peter. *Environmental Chemistry*. Routledge Chapman & Hall 1993. ISBN 0-412-
48490-0. Overview of the operation of natural systems and the movement of the
chemical elements and their compounds; similar to a freshman chemistry text but
does not include problems and exercises.

Ottoboni, M. Alice. *The Dose Makes the Poison: A Plain-Language Guide to Toxicology*.
Van Nos. Rheinhold 1991 $24.95. ISBN 0-442-00660-8. Balanced discussion for
general readers on the basic principles of toxicology and their application to
chemical exposures.

Rushefsky, Mark. *Making Cancer Policy*. State U. NY Pr. 1986 $64.50. ISBN 0-88706-
406-X. Examines the controversies surrounding cancer policy and risk-assessment

procedures and describes significant choices and the assumptions used in making those choices. Introductory chapter discusses "science, uncertainty, and politics."

Sittig, Marshall. *Handbook of Toxic and Hazardous Chemicals and Carcinogens.* 2 vols. Noyes 1992 $197.00. ISBN 0-8155-1286-4. Another compendium of industrial chemicals and their hazards and regulations; includes health and safety data on more than 1,300 chemicals.

Winter, Ruth. *A Consumer's Dictionary of Household, Yard and Office Chemicals.* Crown Pub. Group 1992 $12.00. ISBN 0-517-58722-X. List of consumer chemicals with their associated hazards; includes a section on the basics of toxicology.

REPRODUCTIVE HAZARDS AND CHEMICALS

Recently, the public has become concerned about the effects of some chemicals on human reproduction. These substances, called teratogens, include such things as lead and mercury. Under some circumstances such teratogens can cause fetal and developmental deformities. A famous example is the deformities suffered by Japanese children in Minimata, Japan, as a result of mercury poisoning. The following titles cover this subject well for the general reader and are highly recommended.

Office of Technology Assessment, U.S. Congress. *Reproductive Health Hazards in the Workplace.* USGPO 1985 o.p. Excellent and balanced discussion of the current knowledge of hazards and suspected hazards to the reproductive health of American men and women. Reviews the basic principles of reproductive biology and development as well as related legal and ethical issues; not a catalog of suspected teratogens.

Shepard, Thomas H. *Catalog of Teratogenic Agents.* Johns Hopkins 1992 $95.00. ISBN 0-8018-4414-2. Definitive list of agents that have been studied as possible teratogens in human beings and animals. For use in answering the question "Does this agent cause congenital defects?" Complements the preceding title. Seventh edition of a book describing such nonchemical agents as emotional stress and the rubella virus, as well as chemicals.

CHRONOLOGY OF AUTHORS

Paracelsus, Philippus Aureolus. 1493?-1541
Boyle, Robert. 1627-1691
Priestley, Joseph. 1733-1804
Lavoisier, Antoine Laurent. 1743-1794
Dalton, John. 1766-1844
Davy, Sir Humphry. 1778-1829
Gay-Lussac, Joseph-Louis. 1778-1850
Berzelius, Jons Jakob. 1779-1848
Faraday, Michael. 1791-1867
Wöhler, Friedrich. 1800-1882
Cannizzaro, Stanislao. 1826-1910
Mendeleev, Dmitrii Ivanovitch. 1834-1907
Perkin, Sir William Henry. 1838-1907

Gibbs, Josiah Willard. 1839-1903
Ramsay, Sir William. 1852-1916
Arrhenius, Svante. 1859-1927
Lewis, Gilbert Newton. 1875-1946
Langmuir, Irving. 1881-1957
Beckman, Arnold Orville. 1900-
Pauling, Linus. 1901-
Libby, Willard Frank. 1908-1980
Flory, Paul John 1910-1985
Calvin, Melvin. 1911-
Seaborg, Glenn Theodore. 1912-
Woodward, Robert Burns. 1917-1979
Djerassi, Carl. 1923-
Corey, Elias James, 1928-
Ernst, Richard Robert. 1933-
Hoffmann, Roald. 1937-

ARRHENIUS, SVANTE. 1859–1927 (NOBEL PRIZE 1903)

Born near Uppsala, Sweden, Svante Arrhenius graduated from the University of Uppsala in 1878, after studying chemistry, physics, and mathematics. He also pursued graduate studies at Uppsala. His dissertation, however, was poorly rated by the faculty despite his extensive research on ionic dissociation, because it did not conform to the current theory. Arrhenius became professor of physics at Stockholm in 1895. While there he developed the idea of the reaction rate coefficient and investigated osmosis, toxins, and antitoxins. For his lifetime of research on electrolytic dissociation of ions he received the Nobel Prize in chemistry in 1903. In 1905 he became a director of the Nobel Institute for Physical Chemistry in Stockholm.

BOOKS BY ARRHENIUS

Chemistry in Modern Life. 1925. Crowell 1956 o.p.
Quantitative Laws in Biological Chemistry. 1915. Johnson repr. of 1928 ed. o.p.

BOOK ABOUT ARRHENIUS

Stiller, W. *Arrhenius Equation and Non-Equilibrium Kinetics.* VCH Pubs. 1989 $25.00. ISBN 3-322-00714-6. Examines past and current theories on the temperature-dependence of chemical reactions; published on the centennial of the Arrhenius equation.

BECKMAN, ARNOLD ORVILLE. 1900–

Born in Illinois, Arnold Beckman attended the University of Illinois and the California Institute of Technology. His career has focused on the applied aspects of instrument design and manufacture. Among his first patents was a design for a pH meter (1936). This development triggered an era in which electronics would be used routinely in chemical instrumentation. Beckman also developed a quartz photoelectric spectrophotometer and a precision helical potentiometer. He founded and was associated with several instrument manufacturing companies.

BOOK BY BECKMAN

Collected Works. U. Ch. Pr. 1990 $34.95. ISBN 0-226-04135-2

BERZELIUS, JONS JAKOB. 1779–1848

Although JOHN DALTON used certain symbols to represent elements and compounds, Jons Jakob Berzelius introduced the series of chemical nomenclature used today. He performed many analyses to prove Joseph Louis Proust's law of multiple proportions. Perhaps to facilitate his own record keeping, he invented a system of abbreviations for the elements and compounds. He published this system of chemical nomenclature as part of a work entitled *Essay on the Cause of Chemical Proportions, and Some Circumstances Relating to Them, Together with a Short and Easy Method of Expressing Them.* Berzelius recommended that the elements be expressed as letters and that the combining ratios be included in the formula. He dominated the new science of chemistry from 1815 to 1835, publishing the journal *Jahres-Bericht,* in which he reviewed the chemical reports of the year.

BOOK BY BERZELIUS

Essay on the Cause of Chemical Proportions (Essai sur la Theorie des Proportions Chimiques et sur l'influence Chimique de l'Electricité). Johnson Repr. repr. of 1819 ed. o.p.

BOOKS ABOUT BERZELIUS

Jorpes, J. Erik. *Jakob Berzelius: His Life and Work.* Trans. by Barbara Steele. U. CA Pr. 1970 o.p. Emphasizes his research and discoveries rather than his personal life; lavishly illustrated.

Melhado, Evan M. *Jacob Berzelius: The Emergence of His Chemical System.* U. of Wis. Pr. 1982 repr. $45.00. ISBN 0-299-08970-3. Provides an understanding of the personality and the talent of Berzelius as a chemist.

BOYLE, ROBERT. 1627–1691

Born in Munster, Ireland, of English parents, Robert Boyle was among the earliest scientists who studied nature and drew conclusions justified by experiments. A son of a wealthy man, he received a good education. In 1654 he set up a laboratory in Oxford, England, and hired Robert Hooke (1634–1703) as his laboratory assistant. Boyle and Hooke designed a greatly improved air pump, which enabled them to study the behavior of air by creating a sufficient vacuum. In 1660 Boyle published *Spring and Weight of the Air* in which he articulated Boyle's Law, describing the inverse relationship between the temperature and the pressure of a gas.

In 1661 Boyle published *The Sceptical Chymist* in which he challenged the alchemists' belief in the four elements of earth, air, fire, and water. He also attacked the three principles of PARACELSUS: salt, sulfur, and mercury. In this work he described an element as follows: "Certain Primitive and Single, or perfectly unmingled bodies which not being made of any other bodies, or of one another, are the ingredients of which all those called perfectly mixed bodies are immediately compounded." Boyle also studied the relationship between air and combustion and the respiration of animals, and reported his findings in *Suspicions about Some Hidden Qualities of the Air* (1674). However, the discovery of oxygen would wait for JOSEPH PRIESTLEY.

Boyle experimented with the calcination of tin in a sealed container, but, because he weighed only the resultant tin oxide, he did not get sufficient data to interpret the results accurately. When the tin oxide weighed more than the original tin, he theorized that a substance had passed into the glass container. LAVOISIER later repeated the experiment, weighed the container, and realized that something in the air had combined with the tin.

With his discovery of Boyle's Law, Boyle became somewhat of a celebrity and enjoyed King Charles II's favor. He contributed to the founding of the Royal Society of London for Improving Natural Knowledge in 1662, and he died in London.

BOOKS BY BOYLE

Experiments and Considerations Touching Colours. Johnson Repr. 1964 repr. of 1664 ed. o.p.

Origin and Virtues of Gems. 1672. Macmillan 1972 o.p. "This facsimile reprint . . . makes a valuable addition for historians of geology, historians of science and medicine, and for the general historian of the 17th century" (*Choice*).

Robert Boyle on Natural Philosophy: An Essay with Selections from His Writings by Maria Boas Hall. Greenwood 1980 repr. of 1965 ed. $45.50. ISBN 0-313-22394-7. "Hall places Boyle's contributions in the stream of scientific thought. This essay also serves as a prelude to the wide selection of Boylean writings [that] constitute the second part of the volume" (*Library Journal*).

Robert Boyle's Experiments in Pneumatics. Ed. by James Bryant Conant. Bks. Demand repr. of 1967 ed. $20.00. ISBN 0-317-08773-8

The Sceptical Chemist. 1661. Kessinger Pub. 1992 repr. of 1661 ed. $36.00. ISBN 0-922802-90-4

BOOKS ABOUT BOYLE

Hall, Maria Boas. *Robert Boyle and Seventeenth-Century Chemistry.* Kraus repr. of 1958 ed. o.p. Biography by an eminent historian of science who spent most of her career studying Boyle.

Scootin, Harry. *Robert Boyle: Founder of Modern Chemistry.* Watts 1962 o.p. Detailed discussion of the personal life and scientific contributions of Robert Boyle; includes diagrams of Boyle's experimental apparatus.

CALVIN, MELVIN. 1911– (NOBEL PRIZE 1961)

American chemist Melvin Calvin was born in St. Paul, Minnesota, of Russian immigrant parents. After earning his B.S. from the Minnesota College of Mining and Technology in 1931 and his Ph.D. from the University of Minnesota in 1935, Calvin became a researcher at the University of Manchester, England. He remained there until 1937, when he joined the chemistry department at the University of California at Berkeley. As a professor at Berkeley, he helped form the research group that later became the Lawrence Radiation Laboratory of the University of California.

Calvin's early research focused on the chemical and physical properties of organic compounds. His investigation of organic molecules proved particularly important, providing a solid foundation for his work in biological chemistry. Using radioisotope carbon-14, Calvin and his colleagues at Berkeley began investigating complex organic systems. Calvin employed this radioisotopic tracer technique in studying the biochemical mechanisms of plant photosynthesis. He described his findings in two treatises, *The Path of Carbon in Photosynthesis* (1957) and *Photosynthesis of Carbon Compounds* (1962). Calvin later was awarded the Nobel Prize in chemistry in 1961 for his work in this area.

Calvin focused his later research on his theories of the chemical evolution of life by studying ancient rocks and by simulating the atmosphere of earth that was thought to exist at that time. He published this research in 1969 in *Chemical Evolution.*

BOOKS BY CALVIN

Grass Systematics and Evolution. Coedited by Thomas A. Soderstrom and others. Smithsonian 1988 $52.00. ISBN 0-87474-300-1. The International Symposium on Grass Systematics and Evolution, July, 1986 at the Smithsonian. General topics include structural and biochemical diversity, and evolution.

The Path of Carbon in Photosynthesis. P-H 1957 o.p.

Photosynthesis of Carbon Compounds. W. A. Benjamin 1962 o.p.

CANNIZZARO, STANISLAO. 1826–1910

Born in Palermo, Sicily, Italian scientist Stanislao Cannizzaro began studying medicine when he was 15 years. Four years later, however, he changed to the study of chemistry when he was given the opportunity to study with Raffaele Piria at Pisa. In 1858, Cannizzaro published his atomic theory and presented it at the Karlsruhe Congress in 1860. His theory explained how atomic weights could be determined on the basis of Avogadro's law and thus distinguished from molecular-weights. The theory validated Amedeo Avogadro's law by showing that the applicable particles can be molecules or atoms. A professor of chemistry at Genoa, Palermo, and Rome, Cannizzaro is also known for his discovery of cyanamide and for his method of synthesizing alcohols, a reaction that was named after him.

BOOK ABOUT CANNIZZARO

Rocke, Alan J. *Chemical Atomism in the Nineteenth Century: From Dalton to Cannizzaro.* Ohio St. U. Pr. 1984 $52.50. ISBN 0-8142-0360-4. Scholarly history of the development of a concept central to modern chemistry.

COREY, ELIAS JAMES. 1928– (NOBEL PRIZE 1990)

Elias James Corey is an American organic chemist whose research in synthesizing complex molecules won the Nobel Prize for chemistry in 1990. Born in Methuen, Massachusetts, Corey earned both his B.S. and Ph.D. degrees from M.I.T. In 1951, he became professor of chemistry at the University of Illinois and remained there until 1959, when he moved to Harvard University. His subsequent academic career and research in organic chemistry has been conducted at Harvard.

It was at Harvard that Corey began his ground-breaking research into making organic synthesis more systematic. He began to look for the basic, underlying principles of synthesis in order to develop a logical, coherent approach to forming organic molecules from simpler precursors. His approach was to work backward from the desired molecule to its starting ingredients, observing how the molecule can be split into progressively smaller and smaller pieces until ending up with the basic building blocks for the synthesis. His successful strategies of organic synthesis enabled chemists, for the first time, to achieve total syntheses of complicated biologically active compounds. Corey's research, because it grasped the power of working with the "big picture" instead of trying to solve problems one at a time, also empowered other chemists to try new ways of attacking problems and to focus on large classes of problems rather than single molecules.

Corey's research and his discovery of ways to synthesize nearly 100 natural products also have had important pharmaceutical applications. Corey and his researchers, for example, have devised ways of synthesizing a variety of substances that play a crucial role in regulating many of the body's activities, such as immune responses, including inflammation, blood pressure, and blood coagulation. His 1990 Nobel prize was for his many major achievements in the field of molecular chemistry.

BOOK BY COREY

The Logic of Chemical Synthesis. Wiley 1989 $44.95. ISBN 0-471-50979-5

DALTON, JOHN. 1766–1844

Born at Eaglesfield, in Cumberland, England, John Dalton was a practicing Quaker who studied many areas of physical science, including chemistry and physics. In 1794 he published the first study of color blindness, *Extraordinary Facts Relating to the Vision of Colors.* (Dalton himself was color blind.) Dalton is best remembered for his ideas on atomic theory, which he began formulating about 1800. In 1808 he published *A New System of Chemical Philosophy*, in which he expounded the basic laws of the atomic theory: 1) Small particles, called atoms, exist and compose all matter. 2) Atoms are indivisible and indestructible. 3) Atoms of the same chemical element have the same chemical properties and do not transmute or change into atoms of a different element; atoms of one element differ from the atoms of another element because their masses are different. 4) Elements form compounds in constant combining ratios consisting of integral ratios of one type of atom to another.

Because of his religious beliefs, Dalton initially refused to be nominated to the Royal Society. Later, in 1822, he was elected without his knowledge.

BOOK BY DALTON

A New System of Chemical Philosophy, 1808–1827. 2 vols. Beekman Pubs. 1953 repr. of 1827 ed. o.p.

BOOKS ABOUT DALTON

Millington, John P. *John Dalton.* AMS Pr. repr. of 1906 ed. $19.45. ISBN 0-404-07896-6

Patterson, Elizabeth C. *John Dalton and the Atomic Theory: The Biography of a Natural Philosopher.* Doubleday 1970 o.p. Easy-to-read biography of Dalton's life and scientific achievements; includes ample notes and illustrations.

Thackary, Arnold. *John Dalton: Critical Assessments of His Life and Science.* HUP 1972 $17.00. ISBN 0-674-47525-9. An exacting look at Dalton's scientific achievements and his influence on later scientists.

DAVY, SIR HUMPHRY. 1778–1829

An indifferent student, Humphry Davy pursued his interest in hunting, fishing, and hiking in the great outdoors of his native Cornwall, England, as a young man. He began to study medicine but spent much time composing poetry. Then he discovered chemistry and his life's work became clear.

He brought remarkable energy and intellectual gifts to his studies. Davy frequently experimented on himself in his study of gases. In one careless experiment with water gas—a mixture of mainly hydrogen and carbon monoxide—he nearly lost his life. Work in agricultural chemistry culminated in a book that was the standard text in the field for more than 50 years. His studies in electrochemistry produced the first arc lamp and the first incandescent electric light (THOMAS EDISON's was the first "practical" one), as well as the discovery of sodium and potassium, among other elements.

In 1815 Davy invented the miner's safety lamp. He refused to take out a patent for the lamp so that it might be manufactured and used without impediment. He was already one of the most popular lecturers of his day, and this selfless act won him even greater public esteem.

Illness in the last few years of his life forced Davy to abandon many activities, including the presidency of the Royal Society. He finally withdrew from England itself and sought unsuccessfully to restore his health on the European Continent. One of his last works was a lyrical examination of the joys of fishing called *Salmonia*, a final demonstration to the world of his lifelong love for nature and his great writing ability.

BOOKS BY DAVY

Collected Works. Ed. by John Davy. 9 vols. Johnson Repr. 1972 repr. of 1839–40 ed. o.p. Edited by Davy's brother. "Davy was one of the great 19th-century chemists, known especially for his discovery of sodium and potassium, his electrochemical analyses, his standard text on agricultural chemistry, and his invention of a safe miner's lamp. These volumes originally appeared in 1839–40 and contain the major parts of his scientific writings and lectures" (*Choice*).

Salmonia. Freshet Pr. 1970 $10.75. ISBN 0-88395-004-9

BOOKS ABOUT DAVY

Fullmer, June Z. *Sir Humphrey Davy's Published Works.* HUP 1969 $14.95. ISBN 0-674-8096-0. "This annotated bibliography 'lists all of Davy's published writings, including translations, critical reviews, and reports of experimental findings printed prior to the official versions'" (*Library Journal*).

Hartley, Sir Harold. *Humphrey Davy.* Morrow 1970 o.p. "Davy's place in the history of science is secure. From the discovery of nitrous oxide ('laughing gas') at Bristol in 1799 to the invention of the miner's safety lamp in 1815 there stands to his credit an immense record of achievement [that] is not merely of theoretical interest but has also had a profound effect upon the modern world. . . . Hartley's . . . excellent assessment of Davy's life and achievement leave nothing to be desired in orderliness of presentation, freshness of writing and sureness of judgment" (*TLS*).

Siegfried, Robert, and Robert H. Dott, Jr., eds. *Humphrey Davy on Geology: The 1805 Lectures for the General Audience.* U. of Wis. Pr. 1980 $27.50. ISBN 0-299-08030-7

DJERASSI, CARL. 1923–

Born in Vienna, Austria, Carl Djerassi immigrated to the United States in 1939. He received a B.A. from Kenyon College in Ohio and a Ph.D. from the University of Wisconsin. Djerassi is best known for his development of the first commercial oral contraceptive. As an organic chemist, he also has contributed to the study and synthesis of a number of antihistamines and alkaloids, and his theoretical work has focused on optical rotatory dispersion and circular dichroism. He has spent most of his professional life at Stanford University. In addition, he has served as president of the Syntex Research Division (1968–72) and president (1968–83) and chairman of the board (1983–88) of the Zoecon Corporation.

BOOKS BY DJERASSI

Interpretation of Mass Spectra of Organic Compounds. (coauthored with Herbert Budzikiewicz). *Holden-Day Series in Physical Techniques in Chemistry.* Bks. Demand repr. of 1964 ed. $72.00. ISBN 0-317-09615-X. Written early in the development of mass spectral analysis.

The Pill, Pygmy Chimps and Degas' Horse: The Remarkable Autobiography of the Award-winning Scientist Who Synthesized the Pill. Basic 1992 $25.00. ISBN 0-465-05758-6. "This memoir is a reflection of Djerassi's idiosyncratic personality, offering a mix of serious treatises on chemistry . . . lighthearted accounts of his mishaps abroad; thoughtful essays on birth control and world population growth; and revelations of personal tragedies and triumphs" (*Kirkus*).

Steroid Reactions: An Outline for Organic Chemists. (ed.). Prepared by 16 graduate students at Stanford University. Holden-Day 1963 o.p. Compilation that resulted from a class assignment in June 1962; reproduced and used in a course taught by Djerassi.

Steroids Made It Possible. Profiles, Pathways, and Dreams: Autobiographies of Eminent Chemists Ser. Am. Chemical 1990 $24.95. ISBN 0-8412-1773-4

ERNST, RICHARD ROBERT. 1933–   (NOBEL PRIZE 1991)

Born in Winterthur, Switzerland, Richard Ernst developed an enthusiasm for chemistry by the age of 14, encouraged by his father who was a professor of architecture at the Winterthur Technical School. Ernst's pioneering research has led to the greater effectiveness of magnetic resonance imaging (MRI) as a diagnostic tool in medicine. MRI is especially useful in studying the brain and other tissues that may be injured or destroyed by harmful x-rays or exploratory surgery. For his accomplishments, Ernst received the 1991 Nobel Prize in Chemistry.

Ernst attended the Swiss Federal Institute of Technology in Zurich, earning a B.S. in chemistry (1956) and a Ph.D in physical chemistry (1962). He was awarded the Silver Medal by the Institute for his doctoral thesis on nuclear magnetic resonance spectroscopy. In 1966, Ernst introduced Fourier-transform nuclear magnetic resonance, a process that took only a fraction of the time of older methods used since the 1940s. Since 1968, Ernst has taught physical chemistry at the Institute and served on its Research Council. During this period, he has amassed 15 patents related to MRI technology.

In addition to winning the 1991 Nobel Prize, Ernst has been awarded the Benoist Prize by Switzerland (1986), the John Gamble Kirkwood Medal by Yale University (1989), the Ampere Prize (1990), and the Horwitz Prize by Columbia University (1991). In 1989, he was awarded an honorary doctorate from the Munich Technical School.

BOOKS BY ERNST

Dictionary of Engineering and Technology: English-German, Vol. II. OUP 1985 $125.00. ISBN 0-19-520485-9.

Principles of Nuclear Magnetic Resonance in One and Two Dimensions. (co-authored with G. Bodenhausen and A. Wokann.) OUP 1990 repr. of 1987 ed. $110.00. ISBN 0-19-855629-2. Uniquely comprehensive and up-to-date. Written by a leading NMR research team.

FARADAY, MICHAEL. 1791–1867

Michael Faraday contributed the basic concepts of electrochemistry now known as Faraday's laws. Born in Newington Butts near London, Faraday came from a poor family and had little formal education. Apprenticed to a bookbinder, he was noticed by SIR HUMPHRY DAVY, who carried out a variety of studies on chemistry and its relationship to electricity. Faraday became Davy's assistant and accompanied him on a year and a half long European tour, during which he met top scientists and gained a rather substantial scientific education. In 1827 he succeeded to Davy's chair of Chemistry at the Royal Institution; that same year he published *Chemical Manipulation*, a landmark work for its time.

Faraday's scientific achievements surpassed those of Davy when he related the quantity of electricity to electrochemical equivalents. Faraday's two laws describe the relationships in which the mass of an element involved in an electrolysis reaction is directly proportional to the quantity of electricity employed and the same quantity of electricity produces chemically equivalent quantities of all substances.

Throughout his career, Faraday had no apprentices and worked with only one assistant. Nevertheless, his contributions are significant, and he is generally acknowledged as perhaps the greatest experimental physicist.

BOOKS BY FARADAY

The Achievements of Michael Faraday. Ed. by L. Pearce Williams. Johnson Repr. 1973 o.p. Letters and other documents.

The Chemical History of a Candle. Cherokee 1978 repr. of 1861 ed. $9.95. ISBN 0-87797-209-5. Lectures for young people presented at the Royal Institute.

Chemical Manipulation. 1827. Wiley 1974 o.p. "A reproduction of the copy Faraday presented to the Royal Institution, with his own handwritten dedication and corrections. Nobel Prize-winner Sir George Porter has written a new foreword for this edition. As he points out, this book was a landmark in chemical techniques. Much of what Faraday describes is still applicable today, and what is no longer applicable is well founded for its time and lends a bit of nostalgia for chemists trained before World War II" (*Choice*).

Experimental Researches in Chemistry and Physics. Taylor & Francis 1990 $65.00. ISBN 0-85066-841-7. Reprint of the original volume of a collection of papers Faraday had brought together. The papers had appeared over the preceding 40 years in

Philosophical magazine, *Philosophical Transactions of the Royal Society* and *The Journal of the Royal Institution.*

Experimental Researches in Electricity. 1839–55. 3 vols. in 2 Dover 1962 o.p. "This work is one of the masterpieces of scientific literature, setting forth with wonderful clarity and in explicit detail the step-by-step records of Faraday's investigations and discoveries, among them electromagnetic induction, . . . the laws of electrolysis, the identities of different forms of electricity, the electrical capacities of various substances, the effect of magnetism on polarized light and diamagnetism" (*Scientific American*).

The Forces of Matter. Prometheus Bks. 1993 $5.95. ISBN 0-87975-811-2. Basic explanation of Faraday's laws relating to mass and electricity.

On the Various Forces of Nature (A Course of Six Lectures on the Forces of Matter and Their Relations to Each Other). 1860. Crowell 1961 o.p. Lectures for young people on gravity, electricity, and magnetism.

BOOKS ABOUT FARADAY

Agassi, Joseph. *Faraday as a Natural Philosopher.* Bks. Demand repr. of 1971 ed. Interesting biography by a leading philosopher and historian of science.

Cantor, Geoffrey. *Michael Faraday: Sandemanian and Scientist: A Study of Science and Religion in the Nineteenth Century.* St. Martin 1991 $45.00. ISBN 0-312-06669-4. Discusses how Faraday's religious beliefs affected his scientific researches.

Gooding, David, ed. *Faraday Rediscovered: Essays on the Life and Work of Michael Faraday, 1791–1867.* Groves Dict. Music 1986 o.p. "Research on Faraday can draw on an enormous manuscript record of correspondence and laboratory notebooks as well as his experimental apparatus itself. . . . Though not quite an industry in itself, this excellent volume, which brings together essays by some dozen scholars, could claim to have 'rediscovered' Faraday in three basic ways: as experimentalist, as member of the Royal Institution, and as Sandemanian" (*Science*).

Jeffreys, Alan E. *Michael Faraday: A List of His Lectures and Published Writings.* Acad. Pr. 1961 o.p. "The bibliography is a model of clarity, both in the presentation as a whole and in that of the individual items. The latter, which are arranged in chronological order under each year, are numbered from 1 (1816) to 489 (1932), the last seven being works, e.g. the *Diary*, published subsequently to Faraday's death in 1867. Titles are given in full, followed by bibliographical details (in smaller type) and brief notes by the author, including references to later reprints, e.g. in the *Experimental Researches*" (*Annals of Science*).

Ludwig, Charles. *Michael Faraday: Father of Electronics.* Herald Pr. 1978 $7.95. Well-written and insightful biography focusing on Faraday's contributions to electro-chemistry.

Thomas, J. M. *Michael Faraday and the Royal Institution.* IOP Pub. 1991 $25.00. ISBN 0-7503-0145-2. Story of Faraday's life, work, and legacy.

Williams, L. Pearce. *Michael Faraday: A Biography.* S & S Trade 1971 o.p. "Dr. Williams has written a definitive study of the man and his work. Although the subject matter is necessarily of a technical nature, the book's clear and vivid prose style should make it appealing to a wider audience" (*Library Journal*).

FLORY, PAUL JOHN. 1910–1985 (NOBEL PRIZE 1974)

Born in Illinois, Paul Flory received his Ph.D. from Ohio State University. Throughout his career, he has divided his energies between the university and industry. Since beginning his professional career in 1934, he has worked in chemical research at E.I. DuPont, the Standard Oil Company, the Goodyear Tire Company, and the Mellon Institute. In addition, he has served as chair of chemistry at Cornell University and at Stanford University.

In the 1930s, Flory was one of the people who began working on the properties of polymers, chemical compounds of high molecular weight consisting of a number of smaller structural units linked together. He contributed many insights into polymerization mechanics, including using statistical methods to determine ways of expressing the distribution of chain lengths of polymer molecules. Flory also developed a theory of nonlinear polymers, which involved cross-linkages between molecular chains. One important innovation of Flory's was the concept of "Flory temperature"—a temperature for a given solution at which meaningful measurements can be made of the properties of polymers. For his work in the physical chemistry of the macromolecules [polymers], he was awarded the Nobel Prize in 1974.

BOOKS BY FLORY

Principles of Polymer Chemistry. The George Fisher Baker Non-Resident Lectureship in Chemistry. Cornell Univ. Pr. 1953 $68.00. ISBN 0-8014-0134-8. Notes from a series of lectures presented at Cornell University.

Selected Works of Paul J. Flory. 3 vols. Ed. by Leo Mandelkern, James E. Mark, Ulrich W. Suter, and Do Y. Yoon. Stanford U. Pr., 1985 $199.50 set. ISBN 0-8047-1277-8. Comprehensive set of Flory's writings.

Statistical Mechanics of Chain Molecules. OUP 1989 $52.00. ISBN 0-19-520756-4. Highly mathematical treatise that requires an advanced background in statistics.

GIBBS, JOSIAH WILLARD. 1839–1903

Possessor of one of the greatest minds of American science, Josiah Gibbs led the most unassuming of lives. The son of a Yale Divinity School professor, he showed early promise as a scholar, winning prizes in Latin, Greek, and mathematics during his undergraduate days at Yale University. In 1863 Yale awarded Gibbs the first Ph.D. in engineering in the United States. After serving several years as a tutor, he traveled to Europe in 1866 for three intensive years of postdoctoral study. Returning to New Haven and the house where he was born, he took up his teaching duties at Yale, never to leave again. His studies behind him, he began single-handedly to develop several new fields of science.

His *On the Equilibrium of Heterogeneous Substances* formed the basis of chemical thermodynamics. The phase rule, one of the principal and enduring tools of this new field, opened up new and lucrative avenues of industrial production and metallurgy and earned him the reputation as a founder of physical chemistry. For the first time, chemists were able to calculate precisely, and thus vary, the conditions under which different forms of compounds could exist. For example, great strides were made in the development and production of alloys. Gibbs was aware of the potential value of his work but made no effort to gain wealth from it, preferring instead to lead the quiet life of a bachelor scholar.

His diffidence and the complex nature of his papers resulted in his being largely unrecognized by the scientific community of his time. When he developed vector analysis, a mathematical tool of critical importance to physics and engineering, he did not publish his work but merely circulated several papers among his students.

His final legacy was the development of statistical mechanics, which found wide application in physics, chemistry, and engineering, and also prepared the way for the great developments in quantum mechanics in the early decades of the twentieth century.

BOOKS BY GIBBS

Elementary Principles in Statistical Mechanics. 1902. Ox Bow 1982 $32.00. ISBN 0-918024-19-6. The only book (excluding his writings in collections) published by Gibbs; appeared in the Yale Bicentennial Series a year before his death.

Scientific Papers of J. Willard Gibbs. 1906. Ox Bow 1993 repr. of 1906 ed. ISBN 0-918024-77-3. "That Josiah Willard Gibbs advanced science the world over more than it has ever been given to any other American researcher to do, can hardly be questioned. [Except for] 'Elementary Principles in Statistical Mechanics' . . . his only other printed remains are the papers now collected, which are few but fundamental. They are substantially limited to three, not counting an unusually small number of preliminary and supplementary outputs" (*The Nation*).

BOOKS ABOUT GIBBS

Seeger, Raymond J. *Josiah Willard Gibbs: An American Physicist Par Excellence. Men of Physics Ser.* Pergamon 1974 $123.00. ISBN 0-08-018013-2. Easy-to-read book by an established writer of scientific biography.

Wheeler, Lynde Phelps. *Josiah Willard Gibbs: The History of a Great Mind.* Shoe String 1970 repr. of 1962 ed. o.p. The definitive biography of Gibbs; includes an extensive bibliography.

GAY-LUSSAC, JOSEPH-LOUIS. 1778–1850

French chemist and physicist Joseph-Louis Gay-Lussac was born at St. Leonard-de-Noblat. After graduating from the École Polytechnique in Paris in 1800, he served as assistant to Claude-Louis Berthollet, the noted French research chemist. Working at Berthollet's laboratory outside Paris, which was home to a group of bright young chemists known as the Arcueil Circle, Gay-Lussac began his major work in the investigation of the behavior of gases. His early research in this area established a common thermal expansion coefficient that enabled scientists to define a new temperature scale with important thermodynamics applications.

During several successful balloon ascensions in 1804, Gay-Lussac measured the thermal expansion of gases and compared correlations of earth's magnetic intensity with altitude variations. Using samples of air to analyze pressure and temperature, he demonstrated that the chemical composition of the atmosphere and earth's magnetic intensity were constant up to 20,000 feet. The following year, he joined with the Prussian naturalist and scientist ALEXANDER VON HUMBOLDT (see Vol. 3) in experiments to demonstrate that volume rather than weight determined the relative proportions with which oxygen and hydrogen combine to form water.

By 1808 Gay-Lussac had become professor of chemistry at the University of Paris, where he remained until 1832 when he was appointed to the chair in chemistry at Paris's Musée d'Histoire Nationale. During these years, Gay-Lussac completed the major research on which he formulated the law carrying his name that explains the way in which gases combine. He also collaborated with Louis-Jacques Thenard, using English chemist SIR HUMPHRY DAVY's electrochemical reserch to conduct studies of electric current and its chemical effects. This collaboration helped Gay-Lussac identify the properties of potassium and led to the discovery of the element boron. Continuing his research, he studied the nature of prussic acid, hydrogen chloride, hydrogen fluoride, and other acids. His findings here paralleled JUSTUS VON LIEBIG and FRIEDRICH WÖHLER's discovery that groups of atoms in compound acids act as a single unit in chemical reactions.

BOOK ABOUT GAY-LUSSAC

Crosland, Maurice. *Gay-Lussac: Scientist and Bourgeois.* Cambridge U. Pr. 1978 $54.95. ISBN 0-521-21979-5

HOFFMANN, ROALD. 1937–   (NOBEL PRIZE 1981)

Born in Zloczow, Poland, Roald Hoffmann escaped the annihilation of Polish Jews by the Germans during World War II and immigrated to the United States in 1949. He received a B.A. from Columbia University and a Ph.D. from Harvard University. While at Harvard, he and ROBERT BURNS WOODWARD developed the Woodward-Hoffmann rules on the conservation of orbital symmetry during a chemical reaction by applying principles of quantum theory. These rules enabled scientists to predict an important class of organic reactions. Hoffmann went to work at Cornell University in 1965. In 1981 he shared the Nobel Prize for chemical reaction theory with Kenichi Fukui (who independently had developed an orbital theory in the 1950s).

BOOKS BY HOFFMANN

Chemistry Imagined: Reflections on Science. (coauthored with Vivian Torrence). Smith-sonian 1993 $19.95. ISBN 1-56098-214-4. Unusual blend of full-color collages and Hoffmann's prose or poetry on the meaning of chemistry; one of the few recent books on chemistry and philosophy.
Solids and Surfaces: A Chemist's View of Bonding in Extended Structures. VCH Pubs. 1989 $30.00. ISBN 0-89573-709-4. Discusses the electronic structures and the bonding that occurs in extended structures.

LANGMUIR, IRVING. 1881–1957 (NOBEL PRIZE 1932)

Born in Brooklyn, New York, Irving Langmuir, like many American scientists of his day, went to Europe to obtain a scientific education, receiving a Ph.D. from the University of Göttingen in 1906. Most of Langmuir's career was spent at the General Electric research laboratory in Schenectady, New York. While at General Electric, he developed a better light bulb—one filled with nitrogen, rather than a partial vacuum. He also invented the hydrogen welding torch and mercury vacuum pump, and he studied surface phenomena, initially by studying the tungsten filament in light bulbs. In 1932 Langmuir received the Nobel Prize for his discoveries in surface chemistry.

BOOK BY LANGMUIR

Langmuir the Man and the Scientist. The Collected Works of Irving Langmuir. Vol. 12 Ed. by C. Suits and H. Way. Franklin 1960–62 $200.00. ISBN 0-08-009364-7. All of Langmuir's significant works.

LAVOISIER, ANTOINE LAURENT. 1743–1794

Born in Paris of a well-to-do family, Antoine Lavoisier received a good education, and, at an early age, became interested in science. He had an extraordinary ability to make accurate measurements and conduct careful experiments. Lavoisier made the measurement that ROBERT BOYLE had neglect-ed by weighing the tin oxide and the retort (particularly the air inside the retort), and noted that the total system did not gain or lose weight; he then concluded that during the calcination the metal received a substance from the air. Lavoisier realized that the true state of JOSEPH PRIESTLEY's "dephlogistonat-ed air" consists of at least two substances—one that supports combustion, *oxygen*; and another, *nitrogen*.

On May 8, 1794, Lavoisier was sent to the guillotine because he was part owner of a tax-collecting firm. According to tradition, the presiding judge responded to a plea on Lavoisier's behalf by saying, "The Republic has no need for scientists. Let justice take its course."

BOOKS BY LAVOISIER

Elements of Chemistry in a New Systematic Order, Containing All the Modern Discoveries. 1790. Dover 1984 $14.95. ISBN 0-48664624-6. "Scientists tend to assume that present theories are substantially correct whereas older assumptions were obviously erroneous. This accurate 1790 Kerr translation is a valuable antidote. It demonstrates Lavoisier's ability to create a practical science on experimental facts. It also underscores difficulties still encountered in the interpretation of nature" (*Choice*).

Essays: Physical and Chemical. Trans. by H. Thomas Pope. Biblio NY 1970 repr. of 1776 ed. $45.00. ISBN 0-7146-1604-4. "The *Essays* are therefore historically valuable, as a sort of uncalcinated Lavoisier; but they are not for the uncommitted. They are not for those who are likely to be taken unawares by the theory that there might be either fixed or indeed fixable air in calcareous earths. The reader must know his phlogisticated air from mephitic gas, his acidum pingue from spiritus sylvestris. Granted a very little chemical knowledge, and a vocabulary, however, one can study not only Lavoisier's chemistry, but the man himself—a much more complicated affair" (*Times Literary Supplement*).

Memoir on Heat. (coauthored with Pierre Simon LaPlace). Ed. by Henry Guerlac. Watson Pub. Intl. 1981 $14.95. ISBN 0-88202-195-8

BOOKS ABOUT LAVOISIER

Guerlac, Henry. *Antoine-Laurent Lavoisier: Chemist and Revolutionary.* Macmillan 1975 o.p. The best general text on the life and scientific achievements of Lavoisier. Drawn from Gillispie's *Dictionary of Scientific Biography.*

Holmes, Frederic L. *Lavoisier and the Chemistry of Life: An Exploration of Scientific Creativity.* History of Science and Medicine Ser. U. of Wis. Pr. 1987 $17.50. ISBN 0-299-09984-9. Emphasizes Lavoisier's interest in physiological chemistry.

LEWIS, GILBERT NEWTON. 1875–1946

Born in Weymouth, Massachusetts, Gilbert Lewis received his B.S. and Ph.D. from Harvard University and did postdoctoral work in Germany at the University of Göttingen and the University of Leipzig. While teaching at the Massachusetts Institute of Technology, he began his research on thermodynamics. He later moved to the University of California at Berkeley as the chair of the chemistry department. There he collected thermodynamic data—free energy and entropy data. Lewis also developed his shared electron pair theory of chemical bonding and his theory of acids and bases.

Though a great physical chemist who contributed much to the science of thermodynamics, Lewis never was honored with the Nobel Prize.

BOOKS BY LEWIS

Thermodynamics. (coauthored with Merle Randall). McGraw 1961 $59.70. ISBN 0-07-037622-0. The classic exposition on the interconvertibility of heat and work; a highly mathematical treatment for the specialist or for the general reader with a science background.

Valence and the Structure of Atoms and Molecules. Kraus 1965 repr. of 1923 ed. o.p. An early textbook that describes chemical bonding.

LIBBY, WILLARD FRANK. 1908–1980   (NOBEL PRIZE 1960)

Born in Grand Valley, Colorado, American chemist Willard Libby was educated at the University of California at Berkeley, where he received his Ph.D. in 1933. In 1941, he went to Columbia University to work on the development of the atom bomb. After World War II, Libby was appointed professor of chemistry at the University of Chicago's Institute for Nuclear Studies. Then in 1959, he returned to the University of California as director of the school's Institute of Geophysics.

Libby is most noted for his contributions to dating techniques. In 1947, he and his students at the University of Chicago developed a radiocarbon dating technique using a highly sensitive geiger counter. The test proved reliable in dating objects up to 5000 years old. Later improvements extended the range of dating to about 70,000 years. This radiocarbon dating technique proved extremely useful in the earth sciences, archaeology, and anthropology. Libby was awarded the Nobel Prize for chemistry in 1960 in recognition of this achievement.

BOOK BY LIBBY

Radiocarbon Dating. 1952. Bks. Demand repr. of 1955 ed. $46.80. ISBN 0-317-08415-1. Discussion of the dating technique developed by Libby and his colleagues.

MENDELEEV, DMITRII IVANOVITCH. 1834–1907

Born in Tobolsk, Siberia, Dmitrii Mendeleev was educated at the University of St. Petersburg and became a professor of chemistry there. While at the university he wrote *Principles of Chemistry* (1868–71), which long remained a standard text. Unfortunately, Mendeleev's liberal political views kept him from receiving full credit for many of his scientific discoveries. One exception was the periodic table of elements he devised in 1869. This table showed a clear repetition of the properties of the elements and classified them in a concise and orderly way. From this table and Mendeleev's understanding of the law of periodicity, he correctly predicted the properties of a yet undiscovered element, which he called ekaaluminum (1871). Gallium, discovered in 1875, closely resembled the element that Mendeleev had predicted.

Mendeleev's periodic table, unlike the natures of the elements themselves, has been dynamic. Throughout the years it has been rearranged as new elements have been synthesized (in the case of the transuranium elements) or revised in response to changing views on the correct presentation of chemical information. Today's periodic table contains 103 elements. Element number 101, mendelevium, is named in honor of Mendeleev.

BOOK BY MENDELEEV

Principles of Chemistry. 1868–71. 2 vols. Ed. by Thomas H. Pope. Trans. by George Kamensky. Kraus repr. of 1905 ed. o.p. Standard text for many generations.

BOOK ABOUT MENDELEEV

Petryanov, I. V., and D. N. Tifonov. *Elementary Order: Mendeleev's Periodic System.* Imported Pubns. 1985 o.p.

PARACELSUS, PHILIPPUS AUREOLUS. 1493?–1541

Despite the fact that he left a large number of influential writings on medicine and chemistry, scholars have sharply divided opinions on the value of Paracelsus's contributions to modern chemistry. This Swiss physician was born Theophrastus Bombastus von Hohenheim in Einsieden, Switzerland. He coined his pseudonym, which means "beyond Celsus," from the ancient Roman physician Aulus Cornelius Celsus, whom he admired greatly. The chemical historian Aaron J. Ihde minimizes Paracelsus's contributions, claiming that he did not add empirical knowledge but only introduced incorrect theoretical concepts. Burland postulates that Paracelsus left "books and ideas behind him

[that] sealed the fate of the chemical side of alchemy." In the chapter "Medical Chemistry" from *The Origins of Chemistry* (see the section "History of Chemistry and the Chemical Industry"), Multhauf discusses many of the activities of sixteenth-century European medical practitioners. An illustrative footnote describes the use of sulfuric acid by Paracelsus for treating a variety of ailments. Multhauf notes that Paracelsus might have described the preparation of diethyl ether (the anesthetic gas) from sulfuric acid and wine. However, Multhauf ascribes to Valerius Cordus (1515–1544) the honor of first having noted clearly the preparation of diethyl ether from sulfuric acid and alcohol. In conclusion, much of the problem in assessing Paracelsus's contributions lies in the confusing and obtuse nature of his numerous writings. This style, of course, was standard for the alchemists of his time.

BOOK BY PARACELSUS

Selected Writings. Ed. by J. Jacoby. Trans. by Norman Gutterman. Princeton U. Pr. 1958 $49.50. ISBN 0-691-09810-7. Covers selections from Paracelsus's major works; includes *Archidoxes*, his most important work.

BOOK ABOUT PARACELSUS

Pachter, Henry M. *Magic into Science: The Story of Paracelsus.* Arden Lib. 1982 repr. of 1951 ed. o.p. A reasoned approach to his work.

PAULING, LINUS (CARL). 1901– (NOBEL PRIZE 1954, 1962)

This American winner of two Nobel Prizes—the first in chemistry for his discoveries on the structure of the molecule and the nature of the chemical bond; the second for peace—did pioneering work in many areas of his field, including medical applications. His books on chemistry are basic to understanding the subject. He did research and taught at the California Institute of Technology (1922–64), was research professor at the Center for the Study of Democratic Institutions in California (1963–67), and taught at the University of California, San Diego. Understanding the threat to the human system from radioactive fallout in the postwar days of indiscriminate atomic-bomb testing, he conducted a personal crusade in the 1950s and early 1960s, seeking a halt to the tests. Because of his views on atomic bombs, Pauling suffered considerable persecution at the hands of the U.S. government in the form of denial of passport—and similar limitations—as a dangerous radical. He was one of the people most responsible for the change in American public opinion that resulted in the 1963 international ban on above-ground testing. In 1962, he received the Nobel Prize for peace in recognition of his efforts—from an international community that had admired him throughout the threat it felt from fallout experiments by the two major nuclear powers. His *No More War* (1958) is still a valuable primer on the nature of the three giant nuclear bombs—atomic, hydrogen, and thermonuclear—and of the effects of radiation on human beings. He was instrumental in securing the signatures of 52 Nobel laureates for the "Mainau Declaration of Nobel Laureates" in 1955, which ended: "In extreme danger no nation will deny itself the use of any weapon that scientific technology can produce. All nations must come to the decision to renounce force as a final resort of policy. If they are not prepared to do this they will cease to exist."

BOOKS BY PAULING

Centennial Lectures. (ed.) Oreg. St. U. Pr. 1969 o.p.

Chemistry. (coauthored with Peter Pauling). W. H. Freeman 1975 $52.50. ISBN 0-8371-7460-0. "Although much is borrowed from the elder Pauling's texts, there is also much that is new in the way of recent advances, especially in biochemistry. Coverage of the Watson-Crick model and its ramifications is the clearest and most thorough this side of a course in biochemistry. The excitement of modern molecular biology, conveyed through excellent illustrations as well as text, will captivate any intelligent student with some bent in that direction" (*Choice*).

Introduction to Quantum Mechanics with Applications to Chemistry. (coauthored with E. Bright Wilson). Dover 1985 repr. of 1935 ed. $10.95. ISBN 0-486-64871-0. Classic text for chemists. Lucid but heavily mathematical.

The Nature of the Chemical Bond and the Structure of Molecules and Crystals: An Introduction to Modern Structural Chemistry. Cornell Univ. Pr. 1960 $59.95. ISBN 0-80140-333-2

No More War. 1958. Greenwood 1975 repr. of 1962 ed. $34.95. ISBN 0-7167-0176-6

BOOK ABOUT PAULING

White, Florence M. *Linus Pauling: Scientist and Crusader.* Walker & Co. 1980 $9.95. ISBN 0-8027-6389-8

PERKIN, SIR WILLIAM HENRY. 1838–1907

Born in London, William Perkin showed an aptitude and interest in science at an early age. He enrolled in the Royal College of Science at age 15 and soon became the assistant of one of his lecturers, the German chemist A.W. von Hoffman. At age 17, Perkin synthesized the first aniline dyestuff, mauve. A short time later, he patented the manufacturing process for the material, which was useful for dyeing silk. The process was later applied to cotton and wool as well. With financial backing from his father, a builder and contractor, and other investors, Perkin built a factory in Greenford Green in 1957 to manufacture this new dyestuff.

Perkin's discovery founded a new industry devoted to manufacturing dyestuffs from coal tar, but he never received full credit for his achievement from his contemporaries. Nor did they build upon his achievement and, as a result, leadership of the dyestuff industry soon moved to Germany.

At age 36, Perkin sold his dyestuff factory and devoted his time to research in pure chemistry. Among his many contributions was the discovery of a material for synthesizing unsaturated acids by a process now known as "Perkin's synthesis." For the last 25 years of his life, his research focused on the physical aspects of organic chemistry, and he is considered one of the pioneers in the field.

BOOKS ABOUT PERKIN

Meldola, R. *Jubilee of the Discovery of Mauve and of the Foundation of Coal-Tar Industry by Sir W. H. Perkin.* Routledge 1906 o.p.

Travis, Anthony S. *The Rainbow Makers: The Origin of the Synthetic Dyestuffs Industry in Western Europe.* Lehigh U. Pr. 1993 $49.50. ISBN 0-934223-18-1. Since Perkin founded the European dyestuff industry, his career is covered in detail in this exhaustive book. Also discusses the growth of German dye producers, including the companies that later became major chemical manufacturers.

PRIESTLEY, JOSEPH. 1733–1804

Born in Leeds, England, Joseph Priestley received an education for the dissenting ministry. However, throughout his life, his religious views were far more liberal than those of his fellows, and part of the time he earned his living as a schoolmaster, and later, as the librarian for Sir William Petty, the second

Earl of Shelbourne. During those six years, Priestley systematically studied a variety of gases, including nitrogen oxides, ammonia, and oxygen. In 1774 he prepared and collected oxygen by heating mercuric oxide and collecting the gas over mercury. During separate experiments with mice and burning candles in closed systems, he noted that the "dephlogistonated air" or oxygen supported combustion and respiration better than air or nitrogen. Priestley was an amateur scientist; he focused much of his effort on the religious and political issues of late eighteenth-century England. During the Birmingham riots of 1791, he was a target of the mobs because of his liberal religious views. Finally, in 1794, he immigrated to the United States and for the last 10 years of his life lived in Northumberland, Pennsylvania.

BOOKS BY PRIESTLEY

Autobiography of Joseph Priestley. Fairleigh Dickinson 1971 $25.00. ISBN 0-685-37308-8. "Starts . . . from the time of his birth, including a brief account of his family's background, and continues it in chronological order up to the time of his self-imposed exile in the United States. . . . [It] ends with a short account of the last few years before his death, given by his son. This book can be appreciated not only by historians of science but also by the general reader interested in Priestley or in the beginnings of Unitarianism" (*Library Journal*).

Considerations on the Doctrine of Phlogiston and the Decomposition of Water. Ed. by William Foster. Kraus 1968 repr. of 1929 ed. o.p.

Experiments and Observations on Different Kinds of Air. 3 vols. Kraus repr. of 1790 ed. o.p.

The History and Present State of Discoveries Relating to Vision, Light and Colours. Ed. by Bernard I. Cohen. Ayer 1981 $70.00. ISBN 0-405-13897-0

The History and Present State of Electricity, with Original Experiments. 2 vols. Johnson Repr. repr. of 1975 ed. o.p.

Priestley in America, 1794–1804. Ayer 1980 repr. of 1920 ed. $16.00. ISBN 0-405-12557-7. Priestley's noteworthy experimental work was done nearly two decades earlier in England, but nevertheless this is an interesting tract.

A Scientific Autobiography of Joseph Priestley. MIT Pr. 1966 o.p. Good discussion of Priestley's scientific contributions, with several letters from his correspondence with his friend Benjamin Franklin.

BOOKS ABOUT PRIESTLEY

Hoecher, James J. *Joseph Priestley and the Idea of Progress.* Ed. by Peter Stansky. Garland 1987 $15.00. ISBN 0-8240-7816-0. Assesses Priestley's achievements and their effect on scientific advancement.

Kieft, Lester, and Bennett R. Willeford, Jr., eds. *Joseph Priestley: Scientist, Theologian, and Metaphysician.* Bucknell U. Pr. 1980 $15.00. ISBN 0-8387-2202-4. Collection of papers revealing the diverse interests of this man. "Three recognized authorities from Harvard University . . . give a renewed appreciation of the contributions of Joseph Priestley . . . Unitarian minister, theologian, teacher, historian, chemist, and physicist. . . . 'His life's objective,' says Erwin N. Hiebert [one of the contributors], 'was to generate a polymorphic synthesis of natural science and revealed religion.' To him 'religion and science were compatible domains'" (*Zygon*).

Thorpe, Thomas E. *Joseph Priestley.* AMS Pr. 1976 repr. of 1906 ed. $21.00. ISBN 0-404-07893-1

RAMSAY, SIR WILLIAM. 1852–1916 (NOBEL PRIZE 1904)

Born in Glasgow, Scotland, William Ramsay attended the University of Glasgow, where he studied mathematics and literature. After graduating in 1869, he began his study of chemistry, first at Glasgow and then at the University of Heidelberg, where he was taught by Robert Bunsen. He then attended the

University of Tubingen, where he received his Ph.D. in 1872. When Ramsay returned to Scotland, he taught chemistry at Anderson's College and then at the University of Glasgow. In 1880 he was appointed professor of chemistry at University College, Bristol, and then in 1887 became chair of chemistry at University College in London, where he remained until his retirement.

Ramsay's doctoral work was in organic chemistry, but by 1880 his interest had shifted to inorganic and physical chemistry. He began investigating the volume and boiling points of pure liquids and demonstrated the complexity of their molecular structure. His research then turned to determining the density of gases. In 1894 Ramsay discovered the new element argon, for which he was later awarded the Nobel Prize in chemistry in 1904. This finding then led to his intensive research into a group of elements characterized by chemical inertness that he believed were not included in the periodic table. In 1898, while working with Morris W. Travers, Ramsay reported the discovery of three new elements: neon, xenon, and krypton. Then in 1903, Ramsay and Frederick Soddy identified a fourth inert element, radon. Two years later, Ramsay announced his discovery of helium in the atmosphere. Continuing his research, Ramsay discovered that the newly found inert elements were present in radioactive minerals. He also determined that radium disintegrates with the emission of charged helium nuclei, or alpha particles, a significant finding to later researchers.

BOOK BY RAMSAY

System of Inorganic Chemistry. 1891. Ayer repr. of 1902 ed. o.p.

BOOK ABOUT RAMSAY

Travers, Morris W. *A Life of Sir William Ramsay.* Acad. Pr. 1956 o.p.

SEABORG, GLENN THEODORE. 1912– (NOBEL PRIZE 1951)

Born in Ishepeming, Michigan, Glenn Seaborg received a degree in chemistry from the University of California at Los Angeles. He then studied at the University of California at Berkeley, where he received a Ph.D. and taught until World War II. During the war Seaborg worked at the University of Chicago on the Manhattan Project. He was a leader of the team that discovered the transuranic elements plutonium, americium, and curium. This work led to the development of a method of separating plutonium from uranium in quantities large enough to make an atomic bomb. After World War II Seaborg continued his research on the creation of the transuranium elements. In 1951 he shared the Nobel Prize for discoveries in the chemistry of these elements with Edwin McMillan. Seaborg is codiscoverer of the elements Berkelium, Californium, Einsteinium, Fermium, Mendelevium, and Nobelium. He has spent most of his postwar professional life at the Lawrence Radiation Laboratory. From 1961 to 1971 he also served as chairman of the U.S. Atomic Energy Commission.

BOOKS BY SEABORG

The Chemistry of the Actinide Elements. (coedited with J. J. Katz and L. R. Morss). 2 vols. Routledge Chapman & Hall 1986 $210.00 ea. The definitive set on the actinides.
The Elements beyond Uranium. (coauthored with Walter D. Loveland). Wiley 1990 $59.95. ISBN 0-471-89062-6. Description of the transuranium elements by one of the most important living scientists of the era.
Modern Alchemy: Selected Papers of Glenn T. Seaborg. World Scientific Pub. 1993 $78.00. ISBN 981-02-1440-5

Transuranium Elements: Products of Modern Alchemy. (ed.). Van Nos. Reinhold 1978
$64.95. ISBN 0-87933-326-X. Selection of the original papers on the production of
the transuranium elements; somewhat technical, but the editor's comments are
extensive and placed throughout the book, which makes it interesting to the general
reader.

WÖHLER, FRIEDRICH. 1800–1882

Born at Eschersheim, Germany, Friedrich Wöhler, a pioneer in the field of
organic compounds, was educated at the Frankfurt Gymnasium, where he first
became interested in chemistry. In 1820 he enrolled at the University of
Marburg to pursue a medical career and then transferred to the University of
Heidelberg, where he received his medical degree. At Heidelberg, however, he
became fascinated with chemistry, and in 1823 he gave up medicine to study in
Stockholm under the guidance of one of Europe's leading chemists, JONS JAKOB
BERZELIUS. After returning to Germany in 1825, Wöhler taught chemistry at
Berlin's municipal technical school, remaining there until 1831.

While teaching in Berlin, Wöhler was successful in synthesizing urea from
ammonium cyanate, an inorganic compound. At about the same time, he also
pioneered a method for preparing metallic aluminum, a method later developed into an industrial process to produce this new metal. It was also at this
time that Wöhler began collaborative research with famed German chemist
JUSTUS VON LIEBIG. Studying the chemistry of benzaldehyde, they discovered the
theory of radicals, which enabled scientists to begin understanding the
structure of organic compounds. Their investigation demonstrated that groups
of atoms hold together in organic substances and act like elements in their
reactions.

In 1836 Wöhler was named professor of chemistry at the University of
Göttingen, where he continued his research in organic and inorganic chemistry.
While there, he isolated several elements and investigated uric acid, cocaine,
and other compounds. An excellent teacher, his lectures at Göttingen attracted
a generation of outstanding students. Despite his landmark research achievements in organic and inorganic chemistry, Wöhler preferred teaching and the
interaction of the classroom to laboratory research. He was the author of
several important textbooks in organic, inorganic, and analytical chemistry.

BOOK BY WÖHLER

Outlines of Organic Chemistry. 1840. Johnson repr. of 1873 ed. o.p.

WOODWARD, ROBERT BURNS. 1917–1979 (NOBEL PRIZE 1965)

Born in Boston, Massachusetts, Robert Woodward received his Ph.D. from
the Massachusetts Institute of Technology, and for most of his professional life,
taught at Harvard University. He was a superb synthetic organic chemist. He
and ROALD HOFFMANN developed the Woodward-Hoffmann rules of the conversion of orbital symmetry during chemical reactions. In 1965 he received the
Nobel Prize for his contributions to organic synthesis.

BOOK BY WOODWARD

The Conservation of Orbital Symmetry. (coauthored with Roald Hoffmann). VCH Pubs.
1970 o.p. Describes in deceptively simple terms the theory of the conservation of
orbital symmetry in chemical reactions.

Book about Woodward

Bowden, Mary E., and Theodor Benfey. *Robert Burns Woodward and the Art of Organic Synthesis. BCHOC Publication Ser.* Chem. Heritage Fnd. 1992 $5.00. ISBN 0-941901-08-4. Useful description of Woodward's work (even without the exhibit). Preface by Arnold Thackray.

CHAPTER 22

Biological Sciences

Kathleen Kehoe Glass

I have ever felt persuaded that there is nothing impossible to Nature.
—PLINY THE ELDER, *Natural History*

Biology is the study of living things, including the origin, history, physical characteristics, life processes, and habits of plants, animals, and other organisms. Traditionally, biology is divided into two branches—zoology and botany, which are subdivided according to the plant or animal studied. Recently, areas of study in the biological sciences have been redefined. The specialties now correspond to different levels of structural organization of living organisms and the focus of the work is defined by the specific concepts and methods used. Two important fields of biology that reflect this redefinition are molecular biology and ecology. Molecular biology is the microscopic study of structures within an organism. Thus, genetics is included in this field of biology. In contrast, ecology is the study of individual organisms and their relationships with the environment and other living things.

Biology informally dates back to prehistoric times, with the observation and handling of plants and animals by early human beings. As a systematic science, biology existed in ancient Egypt, Babylonia, and Greece. The decline of Greek civilization was followed by a long period of scientific inactivity in Europe and a loss of codified knowledge, which lasted until the mid-seventeenth century. The development of the microscope then sparked an interest in the observation of cells and tissues, which now could be seen for the first time. The eighteenth century was characterized by the collection, classification, and analysis of exotic fauna and flora brought to Europe by the many expeditions of explorers. The nineteenth century saw the development of modern biology as we know it. The Darwinian theory of evolution revolutionized biology, determining its course for the next century.

During the first half of the twentieth century, Mendelian genetics dominated biological research. By the 1950s another revolution had occurred in biology—the discovery of deoxyribonucleic acid (DNA) and the growth of molecular biology. We may now be in another "Golden Age" of biology. For example, biological advances are providing the basis for enormous progress in medicine. This is contrary to the earlier history of biology, when medicine provided the impetus and understanding that promoted the growth and development of the biological sciences. As a result of the great activity in biological research, the literature is vast and continually growing. More than 70 percent of the literature is highly technical and is published as journal articles. Fortunately, there are a number of scientists and science writers who write books that are designed for the general reader. The general bibliography below contains reference books and a representative group of recent titles from all specialties of biological literature.

BIOLOGY

Reference Works

Adelman, George. *Encyclopedia of Neuroscience.* 2 vols. Birkhauser 1987 $195.00. ISBN 0-8176-3335-9. Covers all the fields of study in neuroscience. Serves as a valuable tool for specialists and nonspecialists; contributors include distinguished researchers, such as Francis O. Schmitt.

Ainsworth, G. C. *Ainsworth and Bisby's Dictionary of the Fungi.* CAB Intl. 1983 $31.50. ISBN 0-85198-515-7. Represents the most authoritative dictionary on the fungi and lichens written in English.

Allaby, Michael. *Oxford Dictionary of Natural History.* OUP 1985 o.p. An excellent dictionary for the layperson, featuring 12,000 concise, jargon-free definitions. "This dictionary will clearly help us to better understand our natural world, and will make it possible for us to communicate that understanding to others" (*Choice*).

Anderson, Sydney, and J. Knox Jones, Jr., eds. *Recent Mammals of the World.* Wiley 1984 o.p. An invaluable reference on mammalogy that includes authoritative summaries on 21 orders and 131 families of living mammals.

Aristotle. *Aristotle: History of Animals, Bks. VII–IX.* Trans. and ed. by D. M. Balme. HUP 1990 $15.50. ISBN 0-674-99483-3. Aristotle describes the 500 animal species known to the Greeks, some of which were mythical creatures.

Asimov, Isaac. *Asimov's New Guide to Science.* Basic 1984 o.p. "An updating of the author's 1972 version, consisting of a series of chapters collectively covering the physical sciences, the biological sciences, and mathematics" (*Library Journal*).

Audubon Society Field Guide to North American Fishes, Whales and Dolphins. Knopf 1983 $15.95. ISBN 0-394-53405-0. An excellent identification guide.

Banister, Keith, and Andrew Campbell. *Encyclopedia of Aquatic Life.* Facts on File 1985 $45.00. ISBN 0-8160-1257-1. Illustrated encyclopedia that surveys animals of many species, in fresh- and salt-water habitats. "Although the ground has been covered before, the excellent presentation makes this book special. . . . One of the best encyclopedias on this topic" (*Library Journal*).

Barnes, R.S.K. *A Synoptic Classification of Living Organisms.* Blackwell Sci. 1984 o.p. A pocket guide to the classification of living things that includes kingdoms, phyla, classes, and orders of plant and animal life.

Barrett, James, ed. *Contemporary Classics in Plant, Animal and Environmental Sciences.* ISI Pr. 1986 $39.95. ISBN 0-89495-066-5. A collection of classic science articles; includes a useful bibliography with many references to recent botanical works.

Barrett, Paul H., and others, eds. *A Concordance to Darwin's "Expressions of Emotions in Man and Animals."* Cornell Univ. Pr. 1986 $62.50. ISBN 0-8014-1990-5. A thorough and invaluable reference to Darwin's *Expressions of Emotions in Man and Animals.* Each of Darwin's words is indexed with references to every occurrence in that work.

Bodner, John Tyler. *Life Cycles: Reflections of an Evolutionary Biologist.* Princeton U. Pr. 1993 $19.95. ISBN 0-691-03319-6. Offers a well-written series of essays on evolution.

Bull, John. *Audubon Society Guide to North American Birds: Eastern Region.* Knopf 1977 $18.00. ISBN 0-594-41405-5. The standard field guide to eastern birds.

Campbell, Bruce, and Elizabeth Lack, eds. *A Dictionary of Birds.* Harrell Bks. 1985 $75.00. ISBN 0-931130-12-3. Lists bird species and provides extensive information, photographs, and illustrations for each species; includes short bibliographies and biographies of amateur and professional ornithologists.

Chadwick, Douglas H. *Fate of the Elephant.* Sierra 1992 $25.00. ISBN 0-871-56635-4. Describes the current struggle by conservationists to protect the African elephant from extinction.

Chambers Biology Dictionary. Chambers 1989 o.p. Standard source, covering a broad range of topics in biology. Very helpful for the layperson.

Coombs, J. *Dictionary of Biotechnology.* Groves Dict. Music 1992 $90.00. ISBN 1-56159-074-6. A useful reference for understanding the terminology of the recently developed area of biotechnology.

Corbet, G. B. *World List of Mammalian Species.* OUP 1991 $72.00. ISBN 0-19-854017-5. A useful list that includes more than 4,000 species of living and recently extinct mammals; gives Latin names, common names, and habitats for each species.

Cox, C. Barry. *Biogeography: An Ecological and Evolutionary Approach.* Blackwell Pubs. 1993 $34.95. ISBN 0-632-02967-6. Introduces biogeography and biodiversity and discusses species such as the plaintain, dragonfly, and magnolia to illustrate the process of population, evolution, and distribution.

Del Hoyo, Joseph, and others. *Handbook of the Birds of the World.* Vol. 1 *Ostrich to Ducks.* ICBP 1992 o.p. The first volume in a series of 10 that will cover all bird species worldwide; well written and illustrated.

Dulbecco, Renato. *Encyclopedia of Human Biology.* 8 vols. Acad. Pr. 1991 $1,950.00. ISBN 0-685-48179-4. Provides more than 600 article-length entries on concepts in human genetics, biochemistry, physiology, and anatomy by 700 contributors.

Encyclopedia of Evolution. Ed. by Richard Milner. Facts on File 1990 $45.00. ISBN 0-8160-1472-8. Comprehensive. Five hundred entries, 150 photographs.

Eversman, Sharon, and Mary Carr. *Yellowstone Ecology: A Road Guide.* Mountain Pr. 1992 $12.00. ISBN 0-87842-278-1. A field guide to the plants, trees, and animals that live along the roads in Yellowstone National Park.

Farrand, John, Jr., ed. *Audubon Society Master Guide to Birding.* 3 vols. Knopf 1984 $49.35. ISBN 0-394-54121-9. Vol. 1 *Loons-Sandpipers*; Vol. 2 *Gulls-Dippers*; Vol. 3 *Old World Warblers-Sparrows.* A well-organized and comprehensive work on American birds; designed for serious birders.

Fischer, David W., and Alan E. Besette. *Edible Wild Mushrooms of North America: A Field to Kitchen Guide.* U. of Tex. Pr. 1992 $35.00. ISBN 0-292-72080-7. Provides descriptions and photographs of 99 species, with 76 recipes for their preparation; includes tips on mushroom hunting and identifying poisonous species.

Freeman, Richard Burke. *British Natural History Books, 1495–1900: A Handlist.* Archon 1977 o.p. Lists all the books written on the fauna and flora of Britain, Ireland, and the Channel Islands during this period.

Friday, Adrian, and David S. Ingram, eds. *Cambridge Encyclopedia of the Life Sciences.* Cambridge U. Pr. 1985 o.p. Excellent encyclopedia that covers all organisms, in authoritative and well-written articles; illustrated with fine drawing, micrographs, and photographs.

Frost, Darrel R. *Amphibian Species of the World: A Taxonomic and Geographical Reference.* Assn. of Syst. Coll. 1985 o.p. The most authoritative guide to amphibian life forms; includes 4,014 species, giving the scientific name, locality, distribution, protected status, and authority.

Gray, Peter. *The Encyclopedia of the Biological Sciences.* Van Nos. Reinhold 1970 o.p. Somewhat dated, but still a fine reference work for the biological sciences.

Grzimek, Bernhard. *Grzimek's Animal Life Encyclopedia.* Van Nos. Reinhold 1974 o.p. A comprehensive encyclopedia that covers lower animals, insects, mollusks and echinoderms, fishes, fishes and amphibia, reptiles, birds, and mammals.

———. *Grzimek's Encyclopedia of Evolution.* Van Nos. Reinhold 1976 o.p. Includes articles covering paleontology, paleogeology, and the evolution of human beings.

———. *Grzimek's Encyclopedia of Mammals.* 5 vols. McGraw 1990 $500.00. ISBN 0-07-909508-9. Offers the best reference on mammals to date; lavishly illustrated with color photographs, line drawings, graphs, and tables.

Harrison, Peter. *Seabirds: An Identification Guide.* HM 1991 $24.45. ISBN 0-395-60291-2. "A definitive guide to more than 300 species of seabirds found the world over, this volume is designed to become a classic" (*Library Journal*); includes color photographs, line drawings, distribution maps, and keys to the identification of each species.

Holliday, Paul. *Dictionary of Plant Pathology*. Cambridge U. Pr. 1992 $24.95. ISBN 0-521-42475-5. Covers botany, emphasizing plant and crop disease terms; includes the names of the bacteria, fungi, viruses, and insects that cause plant diseases.

Holt, John G., and others, eds. *Bergey's Manual of Systematic Bacteriology*. 4 vols. Williams & Wilkins Vol. 1 1984 $98.95. ISBN 0-683-04108-8. Vol. 2 1986 $81.95. ISBN 0-683-07893-3. Vol. 3 1989. ISBN 0-683-07908-5. Vol. 4 1989. ISBN 0-683-09061-5. Definitive manual of bacterial taxonomy; provides uniform conventions for the naming of newly discovered organisms; extremely useful as a source of information on specific types of bacteria; for the nonscientist.

Hora, Bayard. *Oxford Encyclopedia of Trees of the World*. OUP 1981 $27.50. ISBN 0-19-217712-5. An introduction to trees for the general reader; includes information on 2,200 species and color photographs to aid in the identification of trees.

Hoyt, Erich. *Whale Watcher's Handbook*. Doubleday 1984 o.p. A fine field guide for the novice observer; includes a worldwide list of species, their locations, and drawings to aid in identification.

Hull, Roger. *Virology: Directory and Dictionary of Animal, Bacterial and Plant Viruses*. Groves Dict. Music 1989 $80.00. ISBN 0-935859-59-4. Presents biological data on the viruses that prey on animals, plants, and bacteria; arranged taxonomically.

Information Sources in the Life Sciences. Ed. by H. V. Wyatt. K. G. Saur 4th ed. 1994 $65.00. ISBN 1-85739-032-6. Enables research workers and librarians to find the most efficient methods and materials available today.

International Dictionary of Medicine and Biology. 3 vols. Churchhill 1986 $495.00. ISBN 0-471-01849-X

Jolivet, Pierre. *Insects and Plants: Parallel Evolution and Adaptations*. Sandhill Crane 1992 $25.00. ISBN 1-877743-10-0. "This fascinating handbook covers in an abbreviated manner almost all types of insect and plant relationships. . . . Some of the topics discussed are diets and food selection, biological control of weeds, galls, carnivorous plants, myrmecophilous and myrmechorous plants, and insect pollination" (*Choice*).

Jones, Steven, and others, eds. *Cambridge Encyclopedia of Human Evolution*. Cambridge U. Pr. 1992 $95.00. ISBN 0-521-32370-3. Provides essays on major issues in the field of human evolution; foreword by Steven Dawkins.

King, Robert C. *Dictionary of Genetics*. OUP 1990 $39.95. ISBN 0-19-506370-8. Standard in college and university reference collections.

King, Wayne. *Audubon Society Field Guide to North American Reptiles and Amphibians*. Knopf 1979 $18.00. ISBN 0-394-50824-6. A reliable field guide to reptiles and amphibians.

Kress, Stephen W. *Audubon Society Guide to Attracting Birds*. Macmillan 1985 $24.95. ISBN 0-684-18362-5. Offers tips on how to attract local bird species to your yard or windowsill.

Kulik, Stephen, and others. *The Audubon Society Field Guide to the Natural Places of the Northeast*. 2 vols. Pantheon 1984 o.p. "These volumes aim to provide information to enhance a reader's enjoyment and exploration of selected sites in the northeast, organized by geological and ecological region. After comments on the geology, vegetation, and wildlife found in the region, practical information is provided about each site" (*Library Journal*).

Lackie, J. M., ed. *Dictionary of Cell Biology*. Acad. Pr. 1989 $43.00. ISBN 0-12-432560-2. A standard dictionary for the field of cell biology; requires a basic background in biology.

Lampe, Kenneth F., and Mary Ann McCann. *AMA Handbook of Poisonous and Injurious Plants*. AMA 1985 $28.00. ISBN 0-89970-183-3. A useful field guide to poisonous plants and their toxic effects on humans.

Landau, Sidney,, and others, eds. *International Dictionary of Medicine and Biology*. Churchill 1986 $495.00. ISBN 0-471-01849-X. The most extensive dictionary of medicine and biology currently available (more than 159,000 definitions and 30,000 etymologies). Covers cell biology, anatomy, botany, ecology, biochemistry, genetics, histology, microbiology, and marine biology, among others.

Lawrence, Gale. *A Field Guide to the Familiar*. P-H 1984 $9.95. ISBN 0-13-314063-6. Presents the fauna and flora that characterize each season of the year; designed for the amateur naturalist.

Leatherwood, Stephen, and Randall R. Reeves. *The Sierra Club Handbook of Whales and Dolphins*. Random 1983 $25.00. ISBN 0-87156-341-X. Provides a wealth of information on the many dolphin and whale species and an excellent guide for learning how to identify these animals in the field; written by biologists.

Lederberg, Joshua. *Encyclopedia of Microbiology*. 3 vols. Acad. Pr. 1992 $695.00. ISBN 0-12-226890-3. A revised and expanded edition of the comprehensive reference book for microbiology.

Lellinger, David B. *A Field Manual of the Ferns and Fern Allies of the United States and Canada*. Smithsonian 1985 $29.95. ISBN 0-87474-603-5. An excellent field guide to ferns and related plants; includes ample color photographs to aid in identifying ferns.

Levy, Charles K. *A Field Guide to the Dangerous Animals of North America*. Stephen Greene Pr. 1983 o.p. Illustrated with photographs and pictures of dangerous animals of the American wilderness.

Lincoff, Gary F. *Audubon Society Field Guide to North American Mushrooms*. Knopf 1981 $17.50. ISBN 0-394-51992-2. A guide to edible and inedible mushroom species.

Little, R. John, and C. Eugene Jones. *A Dictionary of Botany*. Van Nos. Reinhold 1980 o.p. Provides concise definitions of 5,500 botanical terms.

Macdonald, David, ed. *The Encyclopedia of Mammals*. Facts on File 1984 $65.00. ISBN 0-87196-871-1. A comprehensive reference to mammalia that presents a vast amount of detailed information on the major mammalian orders. The 700 articles by research scientists are well written and elegantly illustrated.

Maclean, Norman. *Dictionary of Genetics and Cell Biology*. NYU Pr. 1987 o.p. A useful, basic dictionary for understanding technical literature.

Macura, P., ed. *Elsevier's Dictionary of Botany II: General Terms*. Fr. & Eur. 1982 $295.00. ISBN 0-8288-9211-3. A polyglot dictionary of botanical, horticultural, agricultural, and taxonomic terminology in English, French, German, and Russian.

Martin, E. A. *A Dictionary of the Life Sciences*. Macmillan 1984 o.p. Concise, authoritative, and well written; illustrated with helpful line drawings, diagrams, and charts.

Meinkoth, Norman A. *Audubon Society Field Guide to North American Seashore Creatures*. Knopf 1981 $18.00. ISBN 0-394-51993-0. A standard guide to fiddler crabs, snails, and others.

Medawar, Peter, and J. S. Medawar. *Aristotle to Zoo: A Philosophical Dictionary of Biology*. HUP 1983 $27.50. ISBN 0-674-04535-1. An unconventional dictionary for browsing; includes descriptions and commentary on biological phenomena and concepts.

Nelson, Joseph S. *Fishes of the World*. Wiley 1984 $64.95. ISBN 0-471-86475-7. An updated and revised edition of the excellent 1977 work; includes basic information and many photographs of all types of fishes.

Nowak, Ronald M. *Walker's Mammals of the World*. Johns Hopkins 1991 $89.95. ISBN 0-8018-3970-X. Presents an authoritative and easy-to-read reference that includes descriptions of 1,100 recent mammals; 800 descriptions are illustrated with black and white or color photographs.

Oraf, Alfred D. *Tropica: Color Cyclopedia of Exotic Plants and Trees*. Roehrs 1992 repr. of 1978 ed. $165.00. ISBN 0-911266-24-0

Peterson, Roger Tory. *Peterson's First Guide to Birds*. HM 1986 $4.80. ISBN 0-395-40684-6. A reprint of the well-known bird guide.

_____. *Peterson's First Guide to Wildflowers*. HM 1986 $4.80. ISBN 0-395-40777-X. A reprint of Peterson's well-known wildflower guide.

Pyle, Robert M., ed. *Audubon Society Field Guide to North American Butterflies*. Knopf 1981 $17.95. ISBN 0-394-51914-0. An excellent field guide for butterfly watchers.

_____. *The Audubon Society Handbook for Butterfly Watchers*. Macmillan 1984 o.p. "A confirmed butterfly watcher shares his knowledge. . . . Entertaining anecdotes illustrate his points as Pyle moves through chapters on butterfly biology, watching equipment, names and identification, field notes, behavior, butterfly gardening, and conservation, to name a few" (*Library Journal*).

Rehder, Harold A. *Audubon Society Field Guide to North American Seashells*. Knopf 1981 $17.95. ISBN 0-394-51913-2. An invaluable companion for beachcombing.

Ride, W.D.L., and others. *International Code of Zoological Nomenclature*. U. CA Pr. 1985 $45.00. ISBN 0-520-05546-2. The international standard for nomenclature conventions. Provides maximum universality and continuity in the naming and classification of animals.

Roe, Keith E., and Richard G. Frederick. *Dictionary of Theoretical Concepts in Biology*. Scarecrow 1981 $32.50. ISBN 0-8108-1353-X. Lists major concepts and laws by the names used to identify them in the biological literature. Each entry is accompanied by a bibliographic citation; a useful reference for the general reader.

Scott, James A. *The Butterflies of North America: A Natural History and Field Guide*. Stanford U. Pr. 1986 $65.00. ISBN 0-8047-1205-0. The author fulfills his goal "to write a book that would give all the important natural history information for all the species of North American butterflies in a scientifically accurate form, but would present it in such a fashion that it is accessible to everyone."

Smith, Roger C., W. Malcolm Reid, and Arlene E. Luchsinger. *Guide to the Literature of the Biological Sciences*. Burgess 1980 o.p. A useful guide to the literature for students and general readers; includes coverage of primary and secondary sources, ready reference sources, databases, thesis preparation, and thesis writing.

Sugden, Auden. *Longman Illustrated Dictionary of Botany*. Dearborn Trade 1984 $8.95. ISBN 0-582-55696-1. Covers morphology, plant physiology, evolution, ecology, and classification; illustrated with extensive charts, tables, and diagrams to facilitate the understanding of the concepts defined.

Terres, John K., ed. *The Audubon Society Encyclopedia of North American Birds*. Outlet Bk. Co. 1991 repr. of 1982 ed. $39.95. ISBN 0-517-03288-0. A comprehensive one-volume encyclopedia on the birds of North America; includes contributions by distinguished ornithologists.

Thompson, Ida, ed. *The Audubon Society Field Guide to North American Fossils*. Knopf 1982 $18.00. ISBN 0-394-52412-8. An excellent tool for the novice interested in identifying fossils; includes photographs (many in color), maps, and line drawings.

Thoreau, Henry David. *Faith in a Seed: The Dispersion of Seeds and Other Late Natural History Writings*. Ed. by Bradley P. Dean. Island Pr. 1993 $25.00. ISBN 1-55963-181-3. Presents a compilation of observations on seeds, tree, fruits, weeds and grasses.

Toothill, Elizabeth. *The Facts on File Dictionary of Biology*. Knopf 1988 $16.95. Presents comprehensive coverage of biological terminology and concise, lucid definitions.

Toothill, Elizabeth, and Stephen Blackmore. *The Facts on File Dictionary of Botany*. Facts on File 1990 $12.95. ISBN 0-8160-2368-9. An excellent dictionary of botanical terms for the scientist or general reader.

Udvardy, M. D. *Audubon Society Guide to North American Birds: Western Region*. Knopf 1977 $18.00. ISBN 0-394-41410-1. The standard field guide to western birds.

U.S. Department of Agriculture Soil Conservation Service. *National List of Scientific Plant Names*. USGPO 2 vols. 1982 o.p. Includes species names, plant distribution, and other general information for plants of the United States and Canada.

Wye, Kenneth R. *Encyclopedia of Shells*. Facts on File 1991 $45.00. ISBN 0-8160-2702-1. Each entry has color photographs of an example of the species, anatomical data, and geographical distribution.

General Bibliography

Adams, Jonathon S. *Myth of Wild Africa: Conservation without Illusion*. Norton 1992 $21.95. ISBN 0-393-03396-1. Written by two members of the World Wildlife Fund. Suggests coexistence between the African wildlife and the African people themselves, thereby refuting the belief that the native peoples are responsible for the downfall of African wildlife.

Ahmadjian, Vernon, and Surindar Paracer. *Symbiosis: An Introduction to Biological Associations.* U. Pr. of New England 1986 $40.00. ISBN 0-87451-371-5. A good introduction to the concept of symbiosis in all organisms.

Bleier, Ruth. *Science and Gender: A Critique of Biology and Its Theories on Women.* Pergamon 1984 $45.00. ISBN 0-08-030972-0. A critique of the role that science has played in supporting the myth that women are biologically inferior. Provides an objective background for the biological and evolutionary basis of sexual differences.

Bowler, Peter J. *The Eclipse of Darwinism: Anti-Darwinism Evolution Theories in the Decades around 1900.* Johns Hopkins 1993 repr. of 1992 ed. $13.95. ISBN 0-8018-4391-X. "The 1982 centenary of Darwin's death renewed interest in the scientific thought of his day. . . . Bowler discusses the many alternate theories of the day, including Lamarckism, mutation theory, and others, introducing some of the noted scientists of the late 19th Century." (*Library Journal*).

Cairns-Smith, A. G. *Seven Clues to the Origin of Life: A Scientific Detective Story.* Cambridge U. Pr. 1990 $8.95. ISBN 0-521-39828-2. "A clear, readable overview of evolutionary thinking as it is applied to the origins of life that will appeal to the informed reader" (*Library Journal*).

Campbell, Neil A. *Biology.* Benjamin-Cummings 1993 $59.95. ISBN 0-8053-1880-1. Presents basic material in a meaningful way.

Catton, Chris, and James Grey. *Sex in Nature.* Bks. Demand repr. of 1985 ed. $60.50. ISBN 0-8357-3489-7. Popular introduction to reproductive biology.

Cohen, I. Bernard. *Revolution in Science.* HUP 1985 $37.50. ISBN 0-674-76777-2. An outstanding introduction to the history of science, with exceptional coverage of the changes in biology brought about by Darwin's theories.

Cox, C. Barry. *Biogeography: An Ecological and Evolutionary Approach.* Blackwell Pubs. 1993 $34.95. ISBN 0-632-02967-6. Introduces biogeography and biodiversity and discusses species, such as the plaintain, dragonfly, and magnolia to illustrate the process of population, evolution, and distribution.

Dawkins, Richard. *The Blind Watchmaker: Why the Evidence of Evolution Reveals a Universe without Design.* Norton 1987 $10.95. ISBN 0-393-30448-5. "A lovely book. Original and lively it expounds the ins and outs of evolution with enthusiastic clarity, answering at every point the cavemen of creationism" (Isaac Asimov).

Depew, David J., and Bruce H. Weber. *Evolution at a Crossroads: The New Philosophy of Science.* MIT Pr. 1985 $32.50. ISBN 0-262-04079-4. A collection of essays by 10 acclaimed biologists, addressing the conceptual side of their work. "Knowledgeable readers will find this challenging and worthwhile" (*Library Journal*).

Douglas, Matthew M. *The Lives of Butterflies.* U. of Mich. Pr. 1986 $32.50. ISBN 0-472-10078-5. "The perfect book for someone who wants to learn about butterflies without becoming bogged down in the technical literature. It is not long; it is written in very readable and lucid English; and the reader is referred to the literature at every point in case one wishes to pursue a topic further. Glossary of terms; 18-page bibliography; species index; subject index" (*Choice*).

Douglas-Hamilton, Iain, and Oria Douglas-Hamilton. *The Battle for the Elephants.* Viking Penguin 1992 $30.00. ISBN 0-670-8400-3. Describes the struggle to protect elephant herds from poachers; written by two active conservationists.

Dunne, Peter. *Tales of a Low Rent Birder.* Rutgers U. Pr. 1986 $15.95. ISBN 0-8135-1139-9. An amusing and engaging collection of reminiscences of interest to all birders.

Eldredge, Niles. *Life Pulse: Episodes from the Story of the Fossil Record.* Facts on File 1987 $21.95. ISBN 0-8160-1151-6. "Eldredge (and his frequent collaborator S. J. Gould) may be approaching Darwin himself for the total number of words produced concerning topics relating to evolution. This spicily written volume concentrates on paleontological vignettes that, for the most part, emphasize the apparent cyclical phenomenon of widespread periodic extinctions" (*Choice*).

Farish, Donald. *Human Biology.* Jones and Bartlett 1993 $47.50. ISBN 0-86720-114-2. A basic textbook that focuses on the human organism in terms of evolution and physiology.

Forsyth, Adrian, and Ken Miyata. *Tropical Nature: Life and Death in the Rain Forests of Central and South America*. Macmillan 1987 $11.00. ISBN 0-684-18710-8. "An introduction to the natural history of the New World tropical forests that provides the most recent information available on tropical biology. The authors, who did most of their field study in Costa Rica and Ecuador, give an overview of essential ecological features of rain forests, with closer examination of topics they found particularly interesting, epithytes, the forest floor, army ants, etc." (*Library Journal*).

Garstand, William. *Larval Forms and Other Zoological Verses*. U. Ch. Pr. 1985 o.p. A collection of rhymes and writing about phylogeny and ontogeny.

Gould, Stephen Jay. *Eight Little Piggies: Reflections in Natural History*. Norton 1993 $22.95. ISBN 0-393-03416-X. Presents the sixth volume of essays in Gould's *This View of Life* series; more personal and contemplative than his earlier books.

———. *Ever Since Darwin*. Norton 1992 $9.95. ISBN 0-393-30818-9. The first of Gould's collections of essays for the general reader, which won him acclaim as a writer of popular science.

———. *The Flamingo's Smile: Reflections in Natural History*. Norton 1987 repr. of 1985 ed. $10.95. ISBN 0-393-30375-6. Well-written and thought-provoking collection of Gould's essays on evolutionary theory.

———. *Hen's Teeth and Horse's Toes: Further Reflections in Natural History*. Norton 1993 $10.95. ISBN 0-393-31103-1. Another excellent collection of essays by Gould on evolution and related topics. "The essays range widely, from a discussion of the evolution of the Hershey bar or an appraisal of Teilhard de Chardin's role in the Piltdown forgery to the parental behavior of Galápagos Island boobies" (*Library Journal*).

Grant, Peter R. *Ecology and Evolution of Darwin's Finches*. Princeton U. Pr. 1986 $73.50. ISBN 0-691-08427-0. "Can anyone with an interest in biological science not have heard of Darwin's finches? . . . Because they are so central to evolutionary theory, numerous studies of behavioral, morphological, and biochemical aspects of their life histories have been made. . . . The volume provides a description of the [Galápagos] islands, and the characteristics of the finches with emphasis on their beak size and shape, the two features critical to Grant's long-term study of their evolution" (*Choice*).

Griffin, Robert D. *The Biology Coloring Book*. HarpC 1986 $14.00. ISBN 0-06-460307-5. Presents the fundamental concepts of biology, with diagrams for the reader to color. The author believes that coloring the diagrams aids in the retention of information, as well as entertaining the reader.

Heinrich, Bernd. *In a Patch of Fireweed*. HUP 1984 $22.00. ISBN 0-674-44548-1. Discusses the general motivation for nature studies and author's own entomological interests and experiences.

Janovy, John, Jr. *On Becoming a Biologist*. HarpC 1986 $6.95. ISBN 0-06-091363-0. A very readable book about life in the biological sciences. "Provides a realistic view of its topic" (*Library Journal*).

Kanigel, Robert. *Apprentice to Genius: The Making of a Scientific Dynasty*. Macmillan 1986 o.p. Clearly written book about several outstanding neuroscientists and their mentors. Biologic principles discussed in the context of the scientist's work are accessible to the general reader.

Keeton, William, and James L. Gould. *Biological Science*. Norton 1993 $59.95. ISBN 0-393-96223-7. Lucid and well-organized text that is the standard by which new biology textbooks are judged.

Kurten, Bjorn. *How to Deep Freeze a Mammoth*. Col. U. Pr. 1986 $23.50. ISBN 0-231-05978-7. A collection of 14 essays on prehistoric life, the title is derived from the essay about a bison discovered in Alaska in 1979 that had died and been frozen 36,000 years ago.

Levins, Richard, and Richard Lewontin. *The Dialectical Biologist*. HUP 1985 $27.00. ISBN 0-674-20281-3. Presents essays that illustrate dialectical thinking, written for biologists, but accessible to the informed general reader.

Lopez, Barry. *Arctic Dreams: Imagination and Desire in a Northern Landscape*. Bantam 1985 $11.00. ISBN 0-553-34664-4. "Lopez presents a whole series of raptures and riffs on the subject of musk oxen, ivory gulls, white foxes, polar bears, icebergs and sea currents" (*New York Times Book Review*).

Luria, Salvador E. *A Slot Machine, A Broken Test Tube*. HarpC 1985 $6.95. ISBN 0-06-091213-8. "Forthright and appealing memoir [of the] pioneering molecular biologist . . . the sections on his work and on serendipity in the scientific process are particularly engrossing" (*Library Journal*).

———. *Thirty-Six Lectures in Biology*. MIT Pr. 1975 $24.00. ISBN 0-262-62029-4. A collection of the author's classic lectures on biology and genetics.

Luria, Salvador E., Stephen Jay Gould, and Sam Singer. *A View of Life*. Benjamin-Cummings 1981 o.p. A fine introductory textbook for general biology; written by three distinguished scientists—a microbiologist, paleontologist, and physician.

Maienschein, Jane. *Defining Biology: Lectures from the 1890's*. HUP 1986 $30.00. ISBN 0-674-19615-5. Offers a collection of ten lectures that were delivered at the Woods Hole research center by famous biologists during the 1890s. An introduction provides a historical perspective for each lecture; includes photographs of each lecturer.

Mayr, Ernst. *The Growth of Biological Thought: Diversity, Evolution, and Inheritance*. HUP 1982 $45.00. ISBN 0-674-36645-7. A classic work on the history of biology. Covers theories and the philosophical views that have developed within the discipline.

McKown, Delos B. *Mythmaker's Magic: Behind the Illusion of "Creation Science"*. Prometheus Bks. 1992 $23.95. ISBN 0-87975-770-1. Examines creationist arguments and assumptions in a systematic way.

Medawar, Peter. *Memoir of a Thinking Radish: An Autobiography*. OUP 1988 $9.95. ISBN 0-19-282083-4. "In this autobiography the Nobel-prize winning scientist provides a witty and discerning view of biological research" (*Library Journal*).

Montagu, Ashley, ed. *Science and Creationism*. OUP 1984 $35.00. ISBN 0-19-503252-7. Features essays that refute the creationist viewpoint and strongly oppose the teaching of creationism in the public schools; includes contributions by such notable scientists as Isaac Asimov and Stephen Jay Gould.

Morowitz, Harold J. *Mayonnaise and the Origin of Life*. OxBow 1991 repr. of 1985 ed. $14.95. ISBN 0-918024-82-X. "Morowitz is a sage celebrant at heart and we share his pleasure as he contemplates the beauty of biochemistry, mathematics, beetles, bacteria" (*Publisher's Weekly*).

Panchen, Alec L. *Classification, Evolution and the Nature of Biology*. Cambridge U. Pr. 1992 $80.00. ISBN 0-521-30582-9. Describes the basic principles of biology for the general reader.

Poinar, George O. *Life in Amber*. Stanford U. Pr. 1992 $45.00. ISBN 0-8047-2001-0. Describes recent experiments in paleontology that inspired *Jurassic Park*—the extraction and analysis of DNA from fossils encased in amber.

Preston, Douglas J. *Dinosaurs in the Attic: An Excursion into the American Museum of Natural History*. St. Martin 1986 $18.95. ISBN 0-312-21098-1. Provides a fascinating insider's view of the collectors and collections, the explorers and the expeditions, instrumental in amassing the museum's treasures.

Purves, William K., and Gordon H. Orians. *Life: The Science of Biology*. W. H. Freeman 1992 $59.95. ISBN 0-7167-2276-3. A comprehensive, introductory text to biology.

Quammen, David. *Natural Acts: A Sidelong View of Science and Nature*. Dell 1986 $6.95. ISBN 0-440-55696-1. "Well-informed, witty, irreverent and sometimes outrageous" (*Quarterly Review of Biology*).

Re, Richard Noel. *Bioburst: The Impact of Modern Biology on the Affairs of Man*. La. State U. Pr. 1986 $24.95. ISBN 0-8071-1289-5. Describes the advances made by modern biology and the resulting impact on medicine, agriculture, and technology.

Shapiro, Robert. *Origins: A Skeptic's Guide to the Creation of Life on Earth*. Bantam 1987 o.p. "Shapiro, a professor of chemistry and an expert on DNA research, takes the reader on a quest to explain 'what science does and does not understand about how life first began.' Rejecting both the belief that a supernatural power endowed life and also that life evolved from clay, Shapiro describes other explanations and manages to entertain and educate in the process" (*Library Journal*).

Skutch, Alexander F. *Life Ascending*. U. Tex. Pr. 1985 $10.95. ISBN 0-292-74644-X. An overview of "life ascending" from its simplest beginnings to human beings. Selected by *Library Journal* as one of the best sci-tech books of 1985.

Smith, John Maynard. *The Problems of Biology*. OUP 1986 $19.95. ISBN 0-19-219213-2. Presents the fundamental ideas of biology and its major unsolved problems.

Thomas, Lewis. *Late Night Thoughts on Listening to Mahler's Ninth Symphony*. Bantam 1984 $8.95. ISBN 0-553-34533-8. "An especially interesting chapter is concerned with the 'Seven Wonders'—not the usual Seven Wonders of the World but with such wonders as a certain bacterial species, a species of beetle, a virus, an olfactory receptor cell, the termite, a human child, and the greatest wonder of all: the planet Earth. The short chapters of the book reflect the usual 'Thomas style'—captivating, unusual, provocative. The book is again meant for the curious reader who appreciates original, interesting, and probing writing mainly in the area of science" (*Choice*).

————. *The Lives of a Cell: Notes of a Biology Watcher*. Bantam 1984 $4.95. ISBN 0-553-27580-1. "A brilliant but humble scientific mind is at work in this collection of 29 short essays by the president of the Sloan-Kettering Center for Cancer Research. Thomas can look at recent biological discoveries on tiny microorganisms and relate them to the totality of human society. He has perceptive and surprising things to say. . . . A National Book Award winner" (*Publisher's Weekly*).

————. *Medusa and the Snail: More Notes of a Biology Watcher*. Bantam 1983 $4.99. ISBN 0-553-25913-X. Another collection of engrossing essays on nature; illustrates that all forms of life are interconnected.

Weissmann, Gerald. *The Woods Hole Cantata: Essays on Science and Society*. Raven 1985 $18.50. ISBN 0-88167-181-9. "Written by a man who is both a physician and an experimental marine biologist, these 18 essays aimed at general readers explore issues touching on modern biology and the inadequacies of our social organization" (*Library Journal*).

Wilson, Edward Osborne. *The Diversity of Life*. Norton 1992 $29.95. ISBN 0-393-31047-7. Well-written analysis of the impending loss of many of Earth's organisms and the consequences of this improverishment.

Wolken, Jerome J. *Light and Life Processes*. Van Nos. Reinhold 1986 $58.95. ISBN 0-442-29348-8. A comprehensive overview of photobiology that explores light in relationship to living things and physiologic processes.

Young, Allan M. *Sarapiqui Chronicle: A Naturalist in Costa Rica*. Smithsonian 1991 $40.00. ISBN 1-56098-014-1. A personal account of the author's years in the Costa Rican rain forest; includes science, travel, and discovery.

BOTANY

Botany is the study of plant life—marine, terrestrial, one-celled, many-celled, living, and fossilized. Botanists study individual plants and groups of plants, in relationship to one another and the environment.

Early botanists primarily collected, described, and classified plants. Modern botanical science had evolved by the nineteenth century, when the first work in plant cell biology was done and Mendelian genetics was rediscovered and pursued by botanists. At this time, the experimental method was employed in plant physiology and botanists began to use biochemical techniques.

Today, biotechnology has revolutionized botanical research. Molecular biologists are pursuing research that could dramatically change agriculture. Plants already developed through genetic engineering are resistant to specific crop diseases and herbicides. Researchers also are studying ways to improve the nutritional quality of certain plants, to increase plant size, to heighten different species' resistance to drought, and to make crops more resistant to fungal diseases.

Reference Works

Allaby, Michael. *Concise Oxford Dictionary of Botany*. OUP 1992 $11.95. ISBN 0-19-286094-1. An excellent dictionary for the general reader.

Beales, Peter. *Roses: an Illustrated Encyclopedia and Grower's Handbook of Species Roses, Old Roses, and Modern Roses, Shrub Roses, and Climbers*. H. Holt & Co. 1992 $60.00. ISBN 0-8050-2053-5. A well-illustrated, comprehensive reference on the care of roses.

Brookes, John. *The Indoor Garden Book*. Crown 1986 o.p. Offers a general guide to house plants for apartment or house dwellers; a well-organized, informative, and well-illustrated book.

Cox, Donald D. *Common Flowering Plants of the Northeast: Their Natural History and Uses*. St. U. of NY Pr. 1984 $39.95. ISBN 0-87395-889-6. Provides general information on the flowering plants of the American Northeast.

Cullen, J. *Orchid Book*. Cambridge U. Pr. 1992 $49.95. ISBN 0-521-41856-9. A comprehensive guide to orchid species; includes information on the care of orchids.

Elias, Thomas S., and Peter A. Dykeman. *Field Guide to North American Edible Wild Plants*. Van Nos. Reinhold 1983 $19.95. ISBN 0-442-22254-8. "Amateur botanists will enjoy this authoritative treatment of more than 200 native species and the good color photographs that support it. . . . Includes helpful guides to the identification of toxic and inedible plants that closely resemble those that can be eaten" (*Library Journal*).

Heil, Kenneth D. *Familiar Cacti of North America. Audubon Society Pocket Guides Ser.* Knopf 1993 $8.00. ISBN 0-679-74149-6. Covers the major American cacti species with color photos, accompanying species descriptions, and range; valuable field guide for the desert visitor.

Kramer, Jack. *The New Gardener's Handbook and Dictionary*. Wiley 1992 $28.50. ISBN 0-471-52090-X. An excellent handbook for the novice or experienced gardener; well illustrated.

Phillips, Roger, and Martyn Rix. *The Random House Book of Early Perennials*. Vol. 1 Random 1991 $25.00. ISBN 0-679-73797-9. A beautifully illustrated reference on the care of perennials.

———. *The Random House Book of Late Perennials*. Random 1991 $25.00. ISBN 0-679-73798-7. A second volume by the author on perennials.

General Works

Barth, Friedrich G. *Insects and Flowers: Biology of a Partnership*. Princeton U. Pr. 1985 $14.95. ISBN 0-691-02523-1. Covers basic pollination biology; written in a sprightly and engaging manner and illustrated with excellent color plates, line drawings, and electron micrographs.

Bell, Peter Robert. *Green Plants: Their Origin and Diversity*. Timber 1992 $39.95. ISBN 0-931146-20-8. Presents a general introduction for the student or general reader.

Burgess, Jeremy. *An Introduction to Plant Cell Development*. Cambridge U. Pr. 1985 $57.50. ISBN 0-521-30273-0. A useful, introductory textbook for undergraduates or the nonspecialist.

Cumminghan, Isabel Shipley. *Frank N. Meyer: Plant Hunter in Asia*. Iowa St. U. Pr. 1984 $29.95. ISBN 0-8138-1148-1. Well-written book that documents the dangers and rigors of plant exploration at the turn of the twentieth century.

Freethy, Ron. *From Agar to Zenry: A Book of Plant Uses, Names, and Folklore*. Hollowbrook 1985 $24.95. ISBN 0-58072-072-7. An entertaining book for reference or browsing.

Gibson, Arthur C., and Park S. Noble. *The Cactus Primer.* HUP 1986 $44.95. ISBN 0-674-08991-X. An authoritative book on primitive cacti that includes a new generic taxonomy of Cactaceae, and the biology, chemistry, and evolutionary relationships of members of this family; written by two biology professors.

Hobhouse, Henry. *Seeds of Change: Five Plants That Transformed Mankind.* HarpC 1986 $18.95. ISBN 0-06-015631-7. Focuses on the role of sugar, quinine, tea, opium, and the potato in terms of their impact on history and society. "Highly recommended" (*Library Journal*).

Johnson, Warren T., and Howard H. Lyon. *Insects That Feed on Trees and Shrubs.* Cornell Univ. Pr. 1988 $52.50. ISBN 0-8014-2108-X. A comprehensive work on pests and pest damage to ornamental plants; excellent for the amateur or professional horticulturalist.

Margulis, Lynn, and Karlene V. Smith. *Five Kingdoms: An Illustrated Guide to the Physics of Life on Earth.* W. H. Freeman 1987 $37.95. ISBN 0-7167-1912-6. An overview of all life forms. Organized by phyla, and the material on each phylum includes a brief essay, photographs, and an anatomical drawing.

Meeuse, Bastiaan, and Sean Morris. *The Sex Life of Flowers.* Facts on File 1984 $24.95. ISBN 0-87196-907-6. Wonderful book for the general reader who wants a better understanding and appreciation of floral ecology.

Prance, Ghillean Tolmie. *Leaves: The Formation, Characteristics, and Uses of Hundreds of Leaves Found in All Parts of the World.* Crown 1985 o.p. Discusses leaf structure, function, fossil leaves, leaf identification, and leaf collecting; illustrated with 300 magnificent color transparencies. The first leaf book of its kind.

Reveal, James L. *Gentle Conquest: The Botanical Discovery of North America.* Starwood Pub. 1992 $39.95. ISBN 1-56373-002-2. Illustrated with beautiful reproductions of early American botanical drawings.

Rost, T. L., and others. *Botany: A Brief Introduction to Plant Biology.* Wiley 1984 $52.95. ISBN 0-471-87454-4. Well-written textbook for introductory botany.

Rudall, Paul. *Anatomy of Flowering Plants: An Introduction to Structure and Development.* Cambridge U. Pr. 1992 $19.95. ISBN 0-521-42154-3. A basic text for readers with a minimal background in biology.

ZOOLOGY

Zoology is the study of animal life. Early zoologists, like botanists, were primarily interested in describing and classifying fauna. The zoological specialties were defined by the phylum studied. These included herpetology (the study of reptiles), icthyology (the study of fishes), ornithology (the study of birds), entomology (the study of insects), and mammalogy (the study of mammals).

By the late nineteenth century, zoology had taken on its modern form as a discipline. The experimentalists changed the focus of zoology from the study of species types to the study of biological processes, structures, and their functions. The processes of inheritance and development became important areas of inquiry.

Today, a broad range of research issues is being studied in zoology. Traditional pursuits, such as the classification of animals, continue, using new techniques developed by molecular biologists, such as the analysis and comparison of the amino acid sequences of two species. Zoologists are working in genetic engineering research, developing new animal subspecies by transferring cloned DNA from one animal species to another. Others work on live animal populations, studying phenomena such as communication in whales' songs and dolphin language.

Reference Works

Allaby, Michael, ed. *Concise Oxford Dictionary of Zoology*. OUP 1992 $10.95. ISBN 0-19-286093-3. An excellent dictionary for the general reader.

Clark, Alisa McGown. *Starfishes of the Atlantic*. Routledge Chapman & Hall 1992 $250.00. ISBN 0-412-43280-3. Represents the only comprehensive guide to starfish.

Collar, N. J. *Threatened Birds of the Americas: the ICBP/IUCN Red Data Book*. Smithsonian 1992 $75.00. ISBN 1-56098-267-5. Updated edition of the list of endangered bird species; includes the current population and distribution of each species.

Cranbrook, Earl of. *Mammals of South-East Asia*. OUP 1991 $24.95. ISBN 0-19-588568-6. Originally published as *Riches of the Wild: Land Mammals of South-East Asia*.

Ehrlich, Paul R., David S. Dobkin, and Darryl Wheye. *Birds in Jeopardy: The Imperiled and Extinct Birds of the United States and Canada, Including Hawaii and Puerto Rico*. Stanford U. Pr. 1992 $45.00. ISBN 0-8047-2967-5. Provides the latest data on 184 species of rare and extinct birds.

Grenard, Steve. *Handbook of Alligators and Crocodiles*. Krieger 1991 $49.50. ISBN 0-89464-435-1. A useful introductory guide to the subject; includes fine color photographs.

Halstead, Bruce. *Poisonous and Venomous Marine Animals of the World*. Darwin Pr. 1988 $250.00. ISBN 0-87850-050-2. An impressive reference on poisonous marine plants, reptiles, and fishes.

Jobling, James A. *A Dictionary of Scientific Bird Names*. OUP 1992 $29.95. ISBN 0-19-854634-3. Lists 8,500 names of bird species worldwide; includes a brief history of taxonomy and nomenclature, and a bibliography.

Lee, Phyllis C. *Threatened Primates of Africa: The IUCN Red Data Book*. St. Martin 1989 $30.00. ISBN 0-685-27045-9. A comprehensive handbook of African primate species; includes descriptions of the species, their distribution and range, ecology, and nature of threats that confront them.

Miller, Jacqueline Y. *Common Names of North American Butterflies*. Smithsonian 1992 $14.95. ISBN 1-56098-122-9. A useful reference for the naturalist or general reader.

Nowak, Ronald M., and John L. Paradiso. *Walker's Mammals of the World*. Johns Hopkins 1991 $89.95. ISBN 0-8018-3970-X. The most recently revised edition of the basic reference book on mammal systematics, description, and natural history; includes 17 new genera.

O'Toole, Christopher, ed. *The Encyclopedia of Insects*. Facts on File 1985 $24.95. ISBN 0-8160-1358-6. Not an encyclopedia or reference book, but a good introductory text on entomology with excellent illustrations.

Walls, Jerry G. *Encyclopedia of Marine Invertebrates*. TFH Pubns. 1982 $69.95. ISBN 0-86622-141-7. An excellent reference for general readers; well illustrated with a minimum of technical language.

Wright, Albert Hazen. *Handbook of Snakes of the United States and Canada*. Cornell Univ. Pr. 1957 $85.00. ISBN 0-8014-0463-0. A comprehensive, standard reference for North American snakes.

General Works

Anderson, E. W. *Animals as Navigators*. Van Nos. Reinhold 1983 o.p. "Discusses various external influences on animal migration behavior (predation, seasonal weather, etc.) and describes how different animal groups respond to external and internal stimuli by changing their habitats" (*Library Journal*).

Barash, David P. *Marmots: Social Behavior and Ecology*. Stanford U. Pr. 1989 $55.00. ISBN 0-8047-1534-3. Provides an overview of woodchuck biology.

Barth, Friedrich G. *Neurobiology of Arachnids*. Spr.-Verlag 1985 $128.00. ISBN 0-387-15303-9. "Most of the chapters provide well researched reviews as well as detailed accounts of each author's own work. Distinguished by bountiful half-tone illustrations and a beautiful layout" (*Science*).

Bright, Michael. *Animal Language*. Cornell Univ. Pr. 1984 o.p. A well-written, nontechnical book that summarizes the research on animal sounds.

Carr, Archie. *The Sea Turtle: So Excellent a Fishe*. U. of Tex. Pr. 1986 o.p. A revised edition of this classic work on the biology of sea turtles.

Churchfield, Sara. *Natural History of Shrews*. Cornell Univ. Pr. 1991 $35.95. ISBN 0-8014-2595-6. Presents a natural history of shrews for the general reader; includes the biology, ecology, and behavior of the shrew species.

Cook, L. M., ed. *Case Studies in Population Biology*. Longwood 1985 $55.00. ISBN 0-7190-1740-8. A good overview of population biology, based on material drawn from the work of field zoologists.

Davidson, R. H., and W. F. Lyon. *Insect Pests of Farm and Orchard*. Wiley 1986 o.p. A wealth of information on pests that afflict agricultural crops, humans, domestic animals, and the home.

Dietz, Tim. *Call of the Siren: Manatees and Dugongs*. Fulcrum Pub. 1992 $15.95. ISBN 1-55591-104-8. Offers a natural history of aquatic animals, commonly called sea cows; for the general reader.

Duellman, William E., and Linda Trueb. *Biology of Amphibians*. McGraw 1985 $59.95. ISBN 0-07-017977-8. A delightful, accurate, informative, and lively book.

Dukelow, Richard W., and J. Erwin. *Reproduction and Development*. Vol. 3 in *Comparative Primate Biology*. Wiley 1986 $198.00. ISBN 0-471-62517-5. A comprehensive compilation of all the primates in terms of reproduction and development.

Ewer, R. F. *The Carnivores*. Cornell U. Pr. 1985 $47.50. ISBN 0-8014-0745-1. "To anyone who likes carnivores and wants to learn interesting facts about them, whether the size of the home range of a wolf or the hunting methods of lions, this book will be interesting."

Goodall, Jane. *The Chimpanzees of Gombe: Patterns of Behavior*. HUP 1986 o.p. Synthesizes Goodall's 25 years of chimpanzee research working in the field at Lake Tanganyika, as well as recent laboratory work with chimpanzees. Illustrated with attractive photographs of chimpanzees; also includes tables of data to help organize the information presented.

Gorman, Martyn L., and David Stone. *Natural History of Moles*. Cornell U. Pr. 1990 $29.95. ISBN 0-8014-2466-6. Summarizes mole species biology, ecology, and behavior for the general reader.

Halstead, Bruce W. *Dangerous Aquatic Animals of the World*. Mosby Yr. Bk. 1992 $59.95. ISBN 0-8016-6981-2

Harris, C. Leon. *Concepts in Zoology*. HarpC 1992 $65.50. ISBN 0-06-042659-4. An undergraduate textbook in zoology that is accessible to the general reader.

Holldobler, Bert, and Edmund O. Wilson. *Ants*. Belknap Pr. 1990 $70.00. ISBN 0-674-04075-9. A comprehensive work on ants that covers their anatomy, physiology, behavior, ecology, and evolution; includes a 45-page bibliography.

Hoyt, Erich. *Riding with the Dolphins: The Equinox Guide to Dolphins and Porpoises*. Firefly Bks. Ltd. 1992 $17.95. ISBN 0-921820-55-0. An excellent reference for the general reader.

Johnsgaard, Paul A. *Diving Birds of North America*. U. of Nebr. Pr. 1987 $45.00 ISBN 0-8032-2566-0. Covers three bird families—loons, grebes, and auks. Focuses on comparative biology and species accounts. Although technical, the book is accessible to serious birders.

Jones, Dick. *Spider: The Story of a Predator and Its Prey*. Facts on File 1986 $15.95. ISBN 0-8160-1587-2. A general overview of spider biology and behavior.

Jones, Mary Lou, and Stephen L. Schwartz. *The Grey Whale, Eschrichtius Robustus*. Acad. Pr. 1984 $90.00. ISBN 0-12-389180-9. Current review of the research and summary of knowledge on the grey whale.

Kevles, Bettyann. *The Female of the Species: Sex and Survival in the Animal Kingdom*. HUP 1986 $12.95. ISBN 0-674-29866-7. Examines the behavior of females of all species in the animal kingdom.

King, Carolyn M. *Natural History of Weasels and Stoats.* Cornell Univ. Pr. 1990 $28.50. ISBN 0-8014-2428-3. Presents an overview of the biology, behavior, and ecology of the weasel and stoat (ermine) species.

King, J. E. *Seals of the World.* Cornell Univ. Pr. 1983 $16.95. ISBN 0-8014-9953-4. An authoritative introduction to seals, sea lions, and walruses; includes geographical and subject indexes, and is illustrated with color and black-and-white illustrations.

Kirevald, Barbara C., and Joan S. Lockhart, eds. *Behavioral Biology of Killer Whales.* Wiley 1986 $109.00. ISBN 0-471-62641-4. A thorough overview of the biology and behavior of killer whales.

Mattison, Chris. *A to Z of Snake Keeping.* Sterling 1993 $17.95. ISBN 0-8069-8297-0. Offers advice on how to care for snakes.

Metcalf, Robert L., and Robert A. Metcalf. *Destructive and Useful Insects: Their Habits and Control.* McGraw 1993 $85.00. ISBN 0-07-041692-3. A standard text for agriculture and horticulture.

Moss, Sanford A. *Sharks: An Introduction for the Amateur Naturalist.* P-H 1984 $10.95. ISBN 0-13-808304-5. "Serious study of sharks began in 1958 and this book brings together what has been learned about shark biology since that time. A primary focus is the ways in which sharks, skates, and rays have adapted to their varied environments. Well-labelled black and white illustrations add to the educational value" (*Library Journal*).

Moyle, Peter B. *Fish: An Enthusiast's Guide.* U. CA Pr. 1993 $25.00. ISBN 0-520-07977-9. Summarizes the current research in fish biology, behavior, ecology, and conservation; written by a leading icthyologist and conservationist.

Murray, John A., ed. *The Great Bear: Contemporary Writings on the Grizzly.* Alaska Northwest 1992 $14.95. ISBN 0-88240392-3. An anthology of essays on bear behavior, ecology, and conservation; includes a chronology of important events in grizzly bear history, a list of readings, and an index.

Napier, J. R., and P. H. Napier. *The Natural History of the Primates.* MIT Pr. 1985 $25.00. ISBN 0-262-14039-X. A fine introduction to primates that covers anatomy, characteristics, classification, diet, distribution, evolution, and social behavior; includes illustrations, glossary, references, and a list of books for further reading.

O'Connor, Raymond J. *Growth and Development of Birds.* Wiley 1984 $99.00. ISBN 0-471-90345-0. The most current review of the literature on avian growth patterns and the factors that regulate them.

O'Toole, Christopher, and Anthony Raw. *Bees of the World.* Facts on File 1992 $24.95. ISBN 0-8160-1992-4. An illustrated overview of bee biology and behavior for the general reader.

Putnam, Rory. *Natural History of Deer.* Cornell Univ. Pr. 1989 $27.50. ISBN 0-8014-2283-3. An overview of deer biology, ecology, and behavior for the general reader.

Schaller, George B. *The Deer and the Tiger: A Study of Wildlife in India.* U. Ch. Pr. o.p. A classic study of predator-prey relationships.

———. *The Last Panda.* U. Ch. Pr. 1993 $24.95. ISBN 0-226-73628-8. Written by an expert on pandas and a major figure in the international efforts at panda conservation. "He writes superbly—the book is quotably lively, varied and jumbled, riveting and often depressing, but essential reading to find out what the world out there is really like." (*Nature*).

Schaller, George B., and others. *The Giant Pandas of Wolong.* U. Ch. Pr. 1985 $25.00. ISBN 0-226-73643-1. Gives a detailed account of the biology and natural history of the panda; beautifully illustrated.

Seeley, Thomas. *Honeybee Ecology: A Study of Adaptation in Social Life.* Princeton U. Pr. 1985 $52.50. ISBN 0-691-08391-6. "A masterly statement of what we know about honeybee behavior" (*Science*).

Sheldon, Jennifer W. *Wild Dogs: the Natural History of the Nondomestic Canidae.* Acad. Pr. 1992 $49.95. ISBN 0-12-639375-3. Presents the biology and behavior of wild dogs.

Sinclair, Sandra. *How Animals See.* Bks. Demand 1985 $44.30. ISBN 0-8357-3495-1. Summarizes current knowledge about vision in animals such as fishes, mammals, amphibians, reptiles, and insects; includes excellent photographs of the eyes of these animals.

Stone, John L. S. *Keeping and Breeding Butterflies and other Exotica.* Sterling 1992 $24.95. ISBN 0-7137-2293-2. Offers advice for the amateur lepidopterist.

Swindler, Daris R., and J. Erwin, eds. *Systematics, Evolution and Anatomy.* Vol. 1 in *Comparative Primate Biology.* Alan R. Liss 1987 $298.00. ISBN 0-471-62644-9. The first in a series of books that covers an area of primate research for use by specialists and nonspecialists. The second and third volumes are *Behavior, Conservation and Ecology* and *Reproduction and Development.*

Terborgh, John. *Five New World Primates: A Study in Comparative Ecology.* Princeton U. Pr. 1983 $55.00. ISBN 0-691-08337-1. "This is one of the most well reasoned and thoughtful studies of primate ecology ever written. It is also delightful reading" (*Quarterly Review of Biology*).

Tyrrell, Esther Quesada, and Robert A. Tyrrell. *Hummingbirds: Their Life and Behavior, A Photographic Study of American Species.* Crown Pub. Group 1984 $35.00. ISBN 0-571-55336-8. A beautiful and invaluable work that includes 235 photographs of hummingbirds.

Wharton, David A. *A Functional Biology of the Nematodes.* Johns Hopkins 1986 $32.50. ISBN 0-8018-3359-0. Offers a general overview of the biology of worms.

Wootton, Anthony. *Insects of the World.* Facts on File 1984 $24.95. ISBN 0-87196-991-2. Offers a brief introduction to the world of insects; designed for adult readers with no prior knowledge of entomology.

Zug, George R. *Herpetology: An Introductory Biology of Amphibians and Reptiles.* Acad. Pr. 1993 $50.00. ISBN 0-12-78262-0. An undergraduate text that covers all the amphibians and reptiles except the Ornithosuchia (certain herbivorous dinosaurs); includes the lineage of birds and dinosaurs; accessible to the general reader.

ANATOMY, HISTOLOGY, AND PHYSIOLOGY

Anatomy is the science of the structural organization of organisms. General anatomy combines the macroscopic and microscopic anatomy of the organs, tissues, and fluids of the body. In general, anatomy involves the dissection or microdissection of an animal or plant to determine the position or specific structure of its parts. Anatomy includes such subspecialties as developmental anatomy (the structures of embryonic organism) and comparative anatomy (the systematic comparison of structures within groups of plants or animals).

Another subfield of anatomy is histology, or the study of plant or animal tissues. Histologists study the molecular cellular and intracellular structure of the tissues, the chemical processes that take place in the tissues, and the function of particular tissues in the physiology of an organ or entire organism.

In the eighteenth century, Albrecht von Haller described physiology as a "vitalized anatomy." This remains a succinct description of the discipline. Physiology encompasses the physical structures and internal processes that maintain life in the plant or animal organism. General physiology studies functions common to all organisms, such as respiration, circulation, and ingestion of nutrients. Cell physiology studies the intracellular processes without regard to the whole organism. Molecular biology, biophysics, and biochemistry are all related to physiology.

Clemente, Carmine D., ed. *Gray's Anatomy of the Human Body.* Lea & Febiger 1984 $89.50. ISBN 0-8121-0644-X. Remains the definitive general anatomy text after 125 years. The writing is elegant, succinct, and appropriate to the general reader.

Crapo, Lawrence. *Hormones: The Messengers of Life.* W. H. Freeman 1985 o.p. A witty, literate, authoritative account of the substances that regulate life.

Despopoulus, Agamemnon, and Stefan Silbernagl. *Color Atlas of Physiology*. Thieme Med. Pubs. 1991 $25.95. ISBN 0-86577-382-3. An economical and concise overview of physiology; includes helpful charts, anatomical maps, and illustrations.

Eckert, Roger, and David Randall. *Animal Physiology: Mechanisms and Adaptations*. W. H. Freeman 1988 $47.95. ISBN 0-7167-1828-6. An introduction to the physiology of animals as a reflection of biological adaptation.

Eroschenko, Victor. *D. Fiore's Atlas of Histology with Functional Correlations*. Lea & Febiger 1992 $34.50. ISBN 0-8121-1560-0. Significant changes in this seventh edition. Composite, precise, and beautiful color drawings of basic histologic structures.

Gartner, Leslie P., and James L. Hiatt. *Atlas of Histology*. Williams & Wilkins 1987 o.p. Designed for beginning students, also useful to readers without a background in histology.

Johnson, Leonard R., ed. *Essential Medical Physiology*. Raven 1992 $59.50. ISBN 0-88167-738-8. Covers essential material in medical physiology as it is taught in most major medical schools.

Kristic, R. V. *Illustrated Encyclopedia of Human Histology*. Spr.-Verlag 1984 $64.00. ISBN 0-387-13142-6. A general reference guide to histology; includes very brief general entries and accompanying illustrations.

Leeson, C. Roland, and others. *Text-Atlas of Histology*. Saunders 1988 $60.95. ISBN 0-7216-2386-7. Presents basic human histology and relevant background information on the cell and microscopy.

Restak, Richard M. *The Brain*. Bantam 1991 $17.50. ISBN 0-553-35307-1. Presents a history of research on the brain and its functions. Well written and appropriate to the nonspecialist, the book is "an outgrowth and expanded version of the popular, eight-part public television series on the brain. . . . The information, presented in an interesting manner, includes discussions of right brain/left brain research, biological rhythms, learning and memory, stress and emotions, vision and movement, and mental illness. The text is nicely complemented by over 150 color and black and white illustrations" (*Library Journal*).

Romer, Alfred S., and Thomas S. Parsons. *The Vertebrate Body*. Saunders 1986 $56.00. ISBN 0-03-058446-9. A revised edition of the classic textbook on comparative vertebrate anatomy.

Ross, Michael H., and Edward J. Reith. *Histology: A Text and an Atlas*. HarpC 1989 $52.00. ISBN 0-683-07368-0. An introductory text that covers histology and relevant material in cell biology.

Sadler, T. W. *Langman's Medical Embryology*. Williams & Wilkins 1990 $31.00. ISBN 0-683-07493-8. A concise but comprehensive text and atlas to prenatal human development; includes photographs, drawings, and anatomical maps to illustrate the fetus and body systems in different stages of development.

Thompson, Richard F., ed. *Progress in Neuroscience: Readings from Scientific American*. W. H. Freeman 1986 $14.95. ISBN 0-7167-1727-1. A collection of articles from recent editions of *Scientific American* that provides an overview of new discoveries and theories in neuroscience.

Tortora, Gerard J., and Nicholas Anagnostakos. *Principles of Anatomy: Physiology, 6th ed.* HarpC 1993 $61.50. ISBN 0-06-046704-5. Latest edition of an anually revised text.

Vander, Arthur J., James H. Sherman, and Dorothy S. Luciano. *Human Physiology: The Mechanism of Body Function*. McGraw 1990 $43.95. ISBN 0-07-066969-4. A beginning text for human physiology; accessible to the general reader with or without a background in biology.

BIOCHEMISTRY

Biochemistry is the study of the chemical reactions and substances that occur within living organisms. Biochemists identify chemical substances in plants and animals and analyze their structures, explain their function, and investigate the roles they play in physiological processes. The process of nitrogen fixation in plants and the structure of proteins in DNA are examples of biochemical problems. Biochemists have helped molecular biologists significantly in recent years by describing the molecular machinery of heredity and the action of enzymes.

Allport, Susan. *Explorers of the Black Box: The Search for the Cellular Basis of Memory*. Norton 1986 o.p. "Allport, a science writer, has provided a very interesting account of the inroads made by neurobiologists to explain the mechanisms of memory" (*Library Journal*).

Baker, Jeffrey, and Garland E. Allen. *Matter, Energy and Life: An Introduction to Chemical Concepts*. Addison-Wesley 1980 $20.50. ISBN 0-201-00169-1. Presents the basic principles of chemistry and physics necessary to understand biology; designed for beginning students in biology and medicine.

Goodsell, David S. *The Machinery of Life*. Spr.-Verlag 1992 $29.00. ISBN 0-387-97846-1. An introduction to biochemistry for the general reader; extensively illustrated with black-and-white line drawings and color plates.

Lehninger, Albert L. *Principles of Biochemistry*. Worth 1993 $65.95. ISBN 0-87901-500-4. The best basic textbook in biochemistry; requires a background in general chemistry and biology.

Oparin, Aleksandr Ivanovich. *The Origin of Life*. Dover 1965 o.p. The first exploration of the problems related to determining the origins of life from a materialistic point of view; originally published in 1924 (in Russian).

Palmer, Trevor. *Understanding Enzymes*. P-H 1991. ISBN 0-13-932534-4. A general introduction to the theoretical and applied aspects of enzyme biochemistry.

Smith, Emil L. *Principles of Biochemistry: General Aspects*. McGraw 1983 o.p. A good introductory text in biochemistry; accessible to readers with a background in general chemistry and biology.

———. *Principles of Biochemistry: Mammalian Biochemistry*. McGraw 1983 $42.00. ISBN 0-07-069763-9. A good general textbook for mammalian biochemistry; requires some background in biology and chemistry.

BIOCLIMATOLOGY

Bioclimatology is an interdisciplinary field that combines biology, climatology, and ecology. Bioclimatologists study the relationship between climate and living organisms, especially the seasonal variations in atmospheric conditions that affect the lives of animals and plants and limit their geographical distribution. Two of the most important limiting factors for terrestrial organisms are air temperature and rainfall. Marine organisms are studied, as well as terrestrial life forms. Salinity, temperature, and light are among the limiting factors that affect marine life. In the 1960s, bioclimatology became prominent due to an increasing awareness of the environment and environmental concerns.

Desjardins, R. L., and others. *Advances in Bioclimatology, Vol. 1*. Spr.-Verlag 1992 $89.00. ISBN 0-387-53843-7. Reviews developments in all research areas concerned with the effect of climatic factors on living organisms.

Johnson, H. D. *Progress in Animal Biometeorology: The Effects of Weather and Climate on Animals*. 2 pts. Taylor & Francis 1976. Pt. 1 $140.00. ISBN 0-685-26764-4. Pt. 2 $70.00. ISBN 0-685-544681-6. A good review of research on the effect of weather on animal life.

Monteith, J. L. *Vegetation and the Atmosphere*. Acad. Pr. 1976 o.p. A good overview of basic bioclimatology.

Peters, Robert L., and Thomas Lovejoy. *Global Warming and Biological Diversity.* Yale U. Pr. 1992 $45.00. ISBN 0-300-05056-9. Twenty-six essays presented at the 1988 conference of the World Wildlife Fund concerning consequences of the greenhouse effect.

Schneider, Stephen H., and Randi Londer. *The Coevolution of Climate and Life.* Sierra 1984 $25.00. ISBN 0-87156-349-5. An authoritative and easy-to-read account of theories regarding the coevolution of climate and living life forms. "This is a a thoroughly professional, sparkling piece of writing that will bring pleasure as well as enlightenment to the person interested in bioclimatology or paleobioclimatology" (*Quarterly Review of Biology*).

BIOPHYSICS

Biophysics applies theories and methods from chemistry and physics to biological problems. The development of biophysics is due to the development of technological innovations such as X-ray diffraction equipment, which enables research at the molecular level. In fact, X-ray diffraction techniques and equipment made it possible for molecular biologists to discover the double-helix structure of DNA in the early 1950s. Subspecialties are molecular, radiation, physiological, and mathematical (theoretical) biophysics.

Berg, Howard C. *Random Walks in Biology.* Princeton U. Pr. 1983 o.p. A fine introduction to biophysical phenomena; requires some background in biochemistry and biology.

Cerdonio, M., and R. W. Noble. *Introductory Biophysics.* World Scientific Pub. 1986 $33.00. ISBN 0-9971-966-33-6. Emphasizes the application of chemical and physical methods to the study of biological systems.

Perrycuick, C. J. *Newton Rules Biology: A Physical Approach to Biological Problems.* OUP 1992 $39.95. ISBN 0-19-854020-5. Draws a relationship between physics and biology by proposing a Newtonian approach. Unorthodox but worthwhile.

CELL BIOLOGY

Cell biology is now commonly called cytology, which is concerned with the structure, function, pathology, and life history of cells. The main subdisciplines of cytology are cytochemistry and cytophysiology. Cytochemistry is the study of chemical processes within the cell, such as digestion, and cytophysiology is the study of physiologic processes within the cell, such as diffusion and osmosis. The most closely related fields are molecular biology, biochemistry, and biophysics.

Becker, Wayne M. *The World of the Cell.* Benjamin-Cummings 1991 $58.25. ISBN 0-08053-0870-9. A comprehensive introduction to molecular and cell biology with substantuial background material on microscopy.

De Duve, Christian. *Blueprint for a Cell: An Essay on the Nature and Origin of Life.* Carolina Biological 1991 $19.95. ISBN 0-89278-410-5. Delineates the current thinking on how life could have evolved and developed in stages into the first cell.

———. *A Guided Tour of the Living Cell.* W. H. Freeman 1985 $59.95. ISBN 0-7107-5002-3. 2 vols. Discusses the eucaryotic cell and presents what is currently understood in cell biology; suitable for reading by the student or layperson.

Karp, Gerald. *Cell Biology.* McGraw 1984 $38.99. ISBN 0-07-033365-3. An introductory text that emphasizes the experimental approach to cell biology.

Lackie, J. M. *Cell Movement and Cell Behavior.* Routledge Chapman & Hall 1986 $34.95. ISBN 0-04-574035-6. The best current introduction to research in this field of biological research.

McKinnell, Robert Gilmore. *Cloning of Frogs, Mice and Other Animals.* U. of Minn. Pr. 1985 o.p. An overview of how nuclear transfer and related experiments are performed; designed for the general reader.

Margulis, Lynn. *Symbiosis in Cell Evolution.* W. H. Freeman 1981 $19.95. ISBN 0-7167-1256-3. Presents the idea that eucaryotic cells evolved from bacterial ancestors; well written and accessible to the general reader.

Margulis, Lynn, and Dorion Sagan. *Microcosmos: Four Billion Years of Evolution from Our Microbial Ancestors.* S&S Trade 1991 $10.00. ISBN 0-671-74798-3. "A beautifully written explanation of evolutionary theory now emerging regarding the origins of life on earth. . . . Margulis and Sagan provide the general reader with an excellent overview of current thought on evolution as informed by research in the areas of biochemistry, paleontology, and microbiology. A short glossary will help readers, while in general the writing style works well and should please and inform those new to this area of biology" (*Library Journal*).

DEVELOPMENTAL BIOLOGY

Although developmental biology was formally founded at a conference in 1939, the first independent journal was not established until 1959. Thus, it is a relatively new area of research. Developmental biologists go beyond the mechanics of fertilization to understand the processes that govern the development of living things.

A major field of developmental biology is embryology, which studies the formation and development of embryos from a microscopic, unicellular stage to 90 days in human beings. Embryologists have contributed knowledge that has resulted in the application of life-saving techniques, such as fetal electrocardiography and ultrasound, by which pediatricians can treat illnesses in the developing fetus. Moreover, embryology provides scientific explanations for congenital deformities.

Dworkin, Martin. *Developmental Biology of the Bacteria.* Benjamin-Cummings 1986 o.p. An excellent overview of the developmental biology of bacteria; written for readers with a general background in biology and biochemistry.

Feduccia, Alan, and Edward McCrady. *Torrey's Morphogenesis of the Vertebrates.* Wiley 1991 $7.95. ISBN 0-471-62314-8. Revised edition of Theodore W. Torrey's book on the physical development and evolution of the vertebrates.

Gilbert, Scott F. *A Conceptual History of Modern Embryology.* Plenum Pub. 1991 $69.50. ISBN 0-306-43842-9. Presents the history of the field for the general reader.

_____. *Developmental Biology.* Sinauer Assocs. 1991 $53.95. ISBN 0-87893-245-3. The best developmental biology textbook now available at the introductory level. Presents descriptive and analytic aspects of animal embryology at the organismal, biochemical, and molecular biologic levels.

Gilbert, Steven G. *Pictorial Human Embryology.* U. of Wash. Pr. 1989 $20.00. ISBN 0-295-96631-9. Covers the human embryo from a blastula to a mature fetus.

Guidics, Giovanni. *The Sea Urchin Embryo: A Developmental Biological System.* Spr.-Verlag 1986 $103.00. ISBN 0-387-15353-5. A review of the problems studied and literature published by developmental biologists who used the sea urchin embryo as a model; representative of developmental research and accessible to readers with a general biology background.

Raff, Rudolph A., and Elizabeth C. Raff, eds. *Development as an Evolutionary Process.* Wiley 1987 $89.95. ISBN 0-471-62922-7. A collection of papers that summarize the work in a new area of study—the experimental study of developmental mechanisms in evolutionary development, the product of a symposium of developmental biologists held at Woods Hole, Massachusetts, in 1985.

Rossant, Janet, and Roger A. Pedersen. *Experimental Approaches to Mammalian Embryonic Development.* Cambridge U. Pr. 1987 $37.95. ISBN 0-521-36891-X. Provides a review of the recent work done in cellular, molecular, and biochemical aspects of research in mammalian development.

GENETICS

Genetics, or the study of heredity, attempts to answer the fundamental questions about the variety and variability of living things. This field traces its origins to GREGOR JOHANN MENDEL, who through his systematic experimentation and observation proposed a theory of heredity in 1865. Unfortunately, Mendel's work was ignored until 1900, when three botanists, Hugo de Vries (1848–1935), Carl Correns (1864–1933), and E. Von Tschermak (1871–1962), essentially repeated his experiments and revived interest in his theories. During the early twentieth century the term *genetics* was coined (by William Bateson, 1861–1926) and Mendelian laws were applied to humans (by W. E. Castle and A. E. Garrod). Studies of fruit flies, corn, bacteria, and viruses have added to the body of genetic knowledge. The delineation of the molecular structure of DNA by JAMES WATSON, FRANCIS CRICK, and MAURICE WILKINS was a milestone, paving the way for the present intense interest in molecular genetics.

There has been a burgeoning interest in human genetics (including medical genetics) in recent years, and over 4,000 inherited disorders have been cataloged. Prenatal diagnosis is now possible for many of these disorders, as well as for many chromosomal abnormalities. The potential for genetic testing both prenatally and postnatally will certainly increase, raising a host of legal and ethical issues. Because of the increasing role that genetic technology has in medicine and agriculture, a basic knowledge of genetics has become a necessity for professionals in these fields.

General Bibliography

Readers new to the field of genetics will find that a good grasp of issues involved in medical genetics, genetic counseling and genetic engineering, and the ethical and legal quandaries that arise from these, requires an understanding of the basic principles and terminology of genetics.

Berg, Paul. *Dealing with Genes: The Language of Heredity.* Univ. Sci. Bks. 1992 $34.00. ISBN 0-935702-69-5. A good introduction to genetics for the general reader or beginning student.

Bishop, Jerry E. *Genome: The Story of the Most Astonishing Scientific Adventure of Our Time—the Attempt to Map All the Genes in the Human Body.* S&S Trade 1990 $21.95. ISBN 0-671-67094-8. A history of the Human Genome Project for the general reader.

Brennan, James R. *Patterns of Human Heredity: An Introduction to Human Genetics.* P-H 1985 $31.95. ISBN 0-13-654245-X. A textbook, clearly written and well illustrated; includes suggested readings, review questions, chapter summaries, and a glossary.

Carlson, Elof Axel. *Human Genetics.* Heath 1983 $28.00. ISBN 0-669-05559-X. A basic genetics text that covers material on the ethical issues of genetics and the political history of eugenics.

Davern, Cedric I., ed. *Genetics: Readings from Scientific American.* W. H. Freeman 1981 o.p. These articles selected from the pages of *Scientific American* "comprise a series of vignettes that capture the essence of significant problems that have characterized the field of genetics" (Introduction); also includes Mendel's classic 1866 paper "Experiments in Plant Hybridization."

Davis, Joel. *Mapping the Code: The Human Genome Project and the Choices of Modern Science.* Wiley 1990 $19.95. ISBN 0-471-50383-5. A summary of the goals and potential of the Human Genome Project; written for the general reader.

Dronamraju, Krishna R., ed. *History and Development of Human Genetics: Progress in Different Countries.* World Scientific Pub. 1992 $50.00. ISBN 981-02-0900-2. A compilation of papers that covers such topics as the history of human genetics, medical genetics, and cross-cultural comparisons of genetic research performed in various countries.

Dunn, L. C. *Short History of Genetics: The Development of Some Main Lines of Thought, 1864–1939.* Iowa St. U. Pr. 1991 $15.95. ISBN 0-8138-0447-7. This is a reissue of L. C. Dunn's 1964 work; written in a clear and engaging style.

Hartl, Daniel L. *Our Uncertain Heritage: Genetics and Human Diversity.* HarpC 1989 $52.00. ISBN 0-06-04264-5. Approaches genetics topics as a lively and challenging part of any student's general education. This edition has incorporated many suggestions of students and teachers, resulting in a shorter but more current and readable text; written by a genetics professor.

Judson, Horace Freeland. *The Eighth Day of Creation.* S&S Trade 1980 $15.00. ISBN 0-671-25410-3. The result of extensive interviews with leading contemporary scientists. Provides a history of molecular biology's investigation of DNA from 1930 to 1970, covering the careers of T. H. Morgan, Francis H. C. Crick, and James D. Watson; includes photographs, illustrations, notes, and index.

Klug, William S., and Michael R. Cummings. *Essentials of Genetics.* Macmillan 1993 $42.75. ISBN 0-02-364797-3. Provides a good overview of genetics for the nonscientist.

Kowles, Richard V. *Genetics, Society and Decisions.* Scott F. 1985 $42.50. ISBN 0-673-18678-8. Provides the basic concepts of genetics and examines the course of events in genetics and society that lead to controversial issues and problematic situations. Unique to this volume are chapters on the genetic consequences of inbreeding, heredity and aging, and genetics and politics; intended for students majoring in disciplines such as psychology, anthropology, and philosophy.

Lawrence, Peter A. *Making of a Fly: The Genetics of Animal Design.* Blackwell Pubs. 1992 $29.95. ISBN 0-632-03048-8. A text for basic drosophila genetics that requires a background in basic biology.

McConkey, Edwin M. *Human Genetics: Molecular Revolution.* Jones & Barlett 1993 $40.00. ISBN 0-86720-854-6. A textbook that emphasizes an understanding of genetics in molecular terms; designed for advanced students of biology or medicine.

Pai, Anna C. *Foundations of Genetics: A Science for Society.* McGraw 1984 $29.95. ISBN 0-07-048094-4. Covers basic genetic principles thoroughly in nontechnical language for the nonscientist.

Russell, Peter J. *Genetics: The Past and the Present.* HarpCollege 1992 $62.00. ISBN 0-673-52143-5. A basic text that summarizes genetics and its history; accessible to the beginning student or general reader.

Singer, Sam. *Human Genetics: An Introduction to the Principles of Heredity.* W. H. Freeman 1985 $18.00. ISBN 0-7167-1648-8. Presents the fundamentals of human genetics.

Suzuki, David T., and others. *An Introduction to Genetic Analysis.* W. H. Freeman 1993. ISBN 0-7167-2285-2. In the first half of this balanced view of current genetics, classical genetics is treated in general; the second half introduces molecular techniques and information. Emphasizes techniques of analysis and modes of inference rather than the various uses of genetic information.

U.S. Congress, Office of Technology Assessment. *Mapping Our Genes: Genome Projects— How Big, How Fast?* Johns Hopkins 1988 $35.00. ISBN 0-8018-3755-3. An overview of the conflicting scientific viewpoints on the goals, cost, and value of the Human Genome Project.

Varmus, Harold. *Cells, Development, and the Biology of Cancer. Scientific American Library Series.* W. H. Freeman 1992 $32.95. ISBN 0-7167-5037-6. A well-written and lucid account of the relationship between genes and cancer; written for the general reader.

Voeller, Bruce R., ed. *The Chromosome Theory of Inheritance: Classic Papers in Development and Heredity.* Bks. Demand repr. of 1968 ed. $62.50. ISBN 0-317-26294-X. Presents reprinted papers of historic significance in the study of the chromosome theory of inheritance, from the eighteenth though the early twentieth centuries, many translated for the first time.

Wallace, Bruce. *Search for the Gene.* Cornell Univ. Pr. 1992 $37.95. ISBN 0-8014-2680-4. A popular account of the history of genetics.

Winchester, A. M. *Human Genetics.* HarpCollege 1986 $31.00. ISBN 0-673-18669-5. Presents a well-organized discussion of genetics topics, beginning with the nature of genes and ending with some of the more complicated aspects of population genetics; emphasizes the medical application of genetics.

Heredity and Evolution

Heredity and evolution explain both constancy and change in the history of life on earth, and comprise much of the core of biological theory. Heredity is the transmission of characeristics from parent to offspring by means of genes located inside the chromosomes. As a result, offspring tend to resemble their parents or ancestors. Evolution is the development of a species, organism, or particular organ from its embryonic stage into its adult form. According to DARWIN's theory, all species of plants and animals developed from primitive forms by the hereditary transmission of slight variations (mutations) in successive generations. Heredity and evolution are the fields of biology most often referred to by philosophers, anthropologists, sociologists, political scientists, and other social scientists.

Berra, Tim. *Evolution and the Myth of Creationism: A Basic Guide to the Facts and the Evolution Debate.* Stanford U. Pr. 1991 $29.50. ISBN 0-8047-1548-3. A brief and simplified explanation of the theory of evolution that presents the shortcomings of the creationist view of evolution from a scientific standpoint.

Cain, A. J. *Animal Species and Their Evolution.* Princeton U. Pr. 1993 repr. of 1954 ed. $10.95. ISBN 0-691-02098-1

Dawkins, Richard. *The Selfish Gene.* OUP 1990 $27.95. ISBN 0-19-286092-5. Attempts to ground ethology (the study of animal behavior) in genetics, by means of the idea that "an organism is just a gene's way of making another gene"; written for the general reader.

Dobzhansky, Theodosius. *Genetics and the Origin of Species. Classics of Modern Evolution Ser.* Ed. by Niles Eldredge and Stephen Jay Gould. Col. U. Pr. 1982 $22.00. ISBN 0-231-05475. A classic of basic genetics that integrates genetics and evolutionary theory; based on lectures delivered in 1936.

Grant, Peter R., and Henry S. Horn, eds. *Molds, Molecules and Metazoa: Growing Points in Evolutionary Biology.* Princeton U. Pr. 1993 $32.50. ISBN 0-691-08768-7. Examines the current specialties within evolutionary research; written by six prominent biologists who have contributed articles on different areas of evolutionary research, including paleontology and molecular evolution.

Haynes, Gary. *Mammoths, Mastodons, and Elephants: Biology, Behavior and the Fossil Record.* Cambridge U. Pr. 1991 $69.50. ISBN 0-521-38435-4. Discusses how the behavior of extinct species can be inferred from their remains and the behavior of living, related species.

Howells, William. *Getting Here: The Story of Human Evolution.* Howells Hse. 1993 $36.00. ISBN 0-929590-10-4. Summarizes the data and thinking on evolution to date for the general reader; written by an evolution expert.

Keller, Evelyn Fox, and Elisabeth A. Lloyd. *Keywords in Evolutionary Biology.* HUP 1992 $45.00. ISBN 0-674-50312-0. Contains 51 essays on topics in evolutionary biology and ecology by scientists, philosophers, and historians of science.

McIver, Tom. *Anti-Evolution: A Reader's Guide to Writings before and after Darwin.* Johns Hopkins 1992 $16.95. ISBN 0-8018-4520-3. Examines how Darwin's theory of evolution shook the European world and stirred debate that continues to the present.

Provine, William B. *Sewall Wright and Evolutionary Biology.* U. Ch. Pr. 1989 $30.00. ISBN 0-226-68474-1. "Best known for developing the theory of genetic drift, Wright was one of a select few who helped flesh out Darwin's theory of evolution by natural selection. . . . Provine has done an exceptionally good job of presenting Wright's contributions to this field" (*Library Journal*).

Ridley, Mark. *Evolution.* Blackwell Pubs. 1993 $39.00. ISBN 0-86542-226-5. A text that not only provides basic descriptions of evolution and its mechanisms but also covers the many conflicting viewpoints related to theories on evolution.

Schwartz, Jeffrey H. *The Red Ape: Orang-utans and Human Origins.* HM 1987 o.p. "Schwartz is one of the principal proponents of the close relationship of the orang and *Homo.* His account of the origins and relationships of primates covers a vast range of studies including paleontological, biochemical, anatomical, and behavioral. The book could and should be read with ease and pleasure by readers interested in human evolution" (*Choice*).

Schwartz, Jeffrey H. *What the Bones Tell Us.* H. Holt & Co. 1992 $25.00. ISBN 0-8050-1056-4. Describes how social and behavioral facts can be inferred from bones and the materials that are found with them.

Stebbins, G. Ledyard. *Darwin to DNA, Molecules to Humanity.* W. H. Freeman 1982 o.p. A nontechnical volume that takes novel approaches to the discussion of evolution. For example, natural selection and heredity are interwoven. The author compares the framework of the book to a classical symphony.

Medical Genetics and Genetic Counseling

Virtually every week a different human ailment is revealed to have a genetic aspect. Disorders including senility and mental illness and diseases such as Huntington's disease and cystic fibrosis have a genetic component. Medical genetics seeks to identify the mechanisms that underly these disorders and diseases and to develop interventions to cure or improve them. Genetic counseling and genetic screening are new allied health fields that have developed as a result of new diagnostic procedures that identify genetic abnormalities. Currently, these fields focus on diagnosing genetic traits in prospective parents and their unborn offspring. The routine use of genetic screening to assess an individual's risk of developing various pathologies is a controversial issue that is currently being debated from moral, ethical, economic, and medical viewpoints.

Applebaum, Eleanor G., and Stephen K. Fierstein, eds. *A Genetic Counseling Casebook.* Free Pr. 1983 $32.95. ISBN 0-19-504932-2. An annotated collection of 24 varied genetic counseling cases provided by 26 practitioners and one client; gives excellent insights into the work of the counselor and the different responses of patients to the counseling experience.

Atkinson, Gary M., and Albert S. Moraczewski, eds. *Genetic Counseling, the Church, and the Law.* Pope John Ctr. 1980 $9.95. ISBN 0-935327-06-7. Examines the moral issues engendered by genetic counseling; the result of an interdisciplinary Task Force on Genetic Diagnosis and Counseling assembled by the Pope John Center in Massachusetts.

Capron, Alexander M., and others, eds. *Genetic Counseling: Facts, Values and Norms.* March of Dimes 1979 $41.00. ISBN 0-685-03289-2. An anthology of articles on genetic counseling that covers concepts in human medical genetics, roles and qualifications of genetics counselors, and moral and legal issues.

Emery, Alan E. H., and Ian Pullen, eds. *Psychological Aspects of Genetic Counseling.* Acad. Pr. 1984 $76.00. ISBN 0-12-238222-6. A comprehensive presentation of various components of genetic counseling; emphasizes the psychological impact of genetic disease on the family.

Hsia, Y. Edward, and others, eds. *Counseling in Genetics.* March of Dimes 1979 o.p. Provides a comprehensive view of genetic counseling; includes a chapter on basic human genetics.

Hubbard, Ruth, and Elijah Wald. *Exploding the Gene Myth.* Beacon Pr. 1993 $24.00. ISBN 0-8070-0418-9. Harvard biologists examine socio-political ramifications of modern biotechnological research.

Kelly, Thaddeus E. *Clinical Genetics and Genetic Counseling.* Mosby Yr. Bk. 1986 o.p. A clinically oriented text written for health professionals; chapters on genetic screening, genetic counseling, and case studies are useful for the general reader.

Kessler, Seymour, ed. *Genetic Counseling: Psychological Dimensions.* Acad. Pr. 1979 $63.00. ISBN 0-12-405650-4. A well-written collection of papers on the psychosocial aspects of genetic counseling. The editor writes that "the book is based on two premises: first, genetic counseling deals with human behavior and psychological functioning, and . . . a strong kinship exists between genetic counseling and other forms of counseling."

Simopoulos, Artemis P., and others. *Genetic Nutrition.* Macmillan 1993 $22.00. ISBN 0-02-611295-7. Examines the correlation between nutrition and diet and one's susceptibility to disease and illness.

Thompson, James S., and Margaret W. Thompson. *Genetics in Medicine.* SCP 1986 o.p. Presents an introduction to medical genetics with photographs, illustrations, glossary, references, name and subject indexes, and chapter review questions that are answered in an appendix. Covers heredity, structure and function of chromosomes and genes, single-gene inheritance, biochemical genetics, chromosomal aberrations, sex chromosomes, immunogenetics, blood polymorphisms, somatic cell genetics, linkage and mapping, multifactorial inheritance, genetic aspects of development, mathematical and population genetics, twin studies, dermatoglyphics, prenatal diagnosis, and genetic counseling; written by a professor of anatomy and a professor of medical genetics and pediatrics.

Genetic Engineering and Bioethics

The process of producing altered DNA, usually by breaking apart a DNA molecule and inserting new genes, is called genetic engineering. For example, the new medical technique of gene therapy involves correcting genetic defects by transferring normal genes to cells that lack them. When DNA from two species are joined, it is called recombinant DNA. The production of interferon is a way that genetic engineering helps human beings combat viruses. Genetic engineers insert the human gene for interferon into bacteria, which can then produce large amounts of interferon rapidly. The interferon is collected and administered to people suffering viral diseases. Other valuable substances produced in this way are insulin and the clotting factor.

Genetic engineering represents a union of high theory and high technology and a rejection of science as contemplation. The results are several new types of individuals and institutions: the scientist-businessperson, the professor-consultant, and the corporation-affiliated and -funded university laboratory. The seventeenth-century natural philosophers who gave the original impetus to modern science proposed to "render ourselves as masters and possessors of nature." Genetic engineering raises special ethical and political issues because the nature at whose mastery and possession it chiefly aims is that of human beings.

British Medical Association. *Our Genetic Future: The Science and Ethics of Genetic Technology.* OUP 1992 $12.00. ISBN 0-19-286156-5. "A valiant and highly successful attempt to present to the general public a comprehensive picture of the enormous and rapidly developing field of molecular genetics, its present and potential applications for the good of mankind, and the complex and bewildering ethical and social issues arising." (*Trends in Genetics*).

Cavalieri, Liebe F. *The Double-Edged Helix: Science in the Real World.* Col. U. Pr. 1981 $37.50. ISBN 0-231-05306-1. A critical evaluation of recombinant DNA technology and its impact on society.

Davis, Bernard D. *Genetic Revolution: Scientific Prospects and Public Perceptions.* Johns Hopkins 1991 $45.00. ISBN 0-8018-4235-2. "I would enthusiastically recommend Genetic Revolution to all persons who are concerned with issues that affect the application of molecular genetic technologies to human health and development" (*Quarterly Review of Biology*).

Gros, François. *Gene Civilization.* Trans. by Lee F. Scanlon. McGraw 1989 $9.95. ISBN 0-07-02496-3. Provides an enduring biological perspective on the genetic revolution and its social implications.

Kevles, Daniel J., and Leroy Hoods, eds. *Code of Codes: Scientific and Social Issues in the Human Genome Project.* HUP 1992 $29.95. ISBN 0-674-13645-4. Introduces the reader to the Human Genome Project and its social and ethical implications.

Krimsky, Sheldon. *Genetic Alchemy: The Social History of the Recombinant DNA Controversy.* MIT 1982 $12.95. ISBN 0-262-61038-8. Describes the possible hazard of releasing new and lethal bacteria into the environment, as well as offering more lurid speculations about the manipulation of the genetic endowments of higher species, including humans; examines the need to regulate recombinant DNA research.

Lappe, Marc. *The Broken Code: The Exploitation of DNA.* Sierra 1985 $17.95. ISBN 0-87156-835-7. Discusses environmental and other dangers of recombinant DNA technology; written by a pathologist and professor of public health.

Lutherer, Otto L., and Margaret Sheffield. *Targeted: The Anatomy of an Animal Rights Attack.* U. of Okla. Pr. 1992 $22.95. ISBN 0-8061-2492-X. Presents an overview of the animal rights movement's efforts to hinder scientific research by targeting research laboratories. Covers the history of the animal rights movement, common denominators in the attacks against specific researchers, protection against these attacks, and the legislative issues involved.

Morowitz, Harold J., and James S. Trefil. *The Facts of Life: Science and the Abortion Controversy.* OUP 1992 $19.95. ISBN 0-19-507927-2. Offers some relevant facts to help in establishing or revising a thoughtful position on abortion; written by a physicist (Trefil) and a biophysicist (Morowitz).

Nossal, G.J.V. *Reshaping Life: Key Issues in Genetic Engineering.* Cambridge U. Pr. 1990 $16.95. ISBN 0-521-38969-0. Detailed coverage of current and prospective uses of genetic technology; includes recent areas such as AIDS vaccine research.

Paton, William. *Man and Mouse: Animals in Medical Research.* OUP 1993 $14.95. ISBN 0-19-286146-8. Offers a balanced review of the concepts and ethical issues involved in the controversy over animal experimentation.

Rollin, Bernard E. *The Unheeded Cry: Animal Consciousness, Animal Pain, and Science.* OUP 1990 $14.95. ISBN 0-19-286104-2. The author's goal is to show "that denial of subjective states in animals is not an essential feature of the scientific stance, but rather a contingent, historical aberration which can be changed to make science both coherent and morally responsible."

Spallone, Patricia. *Beyond Conception: The New Politics of Reproduction.* Greenwood 1988 $49.95. ISBN 0-89789-199-6. Covers feminist objections to new reproductive technologies and embryo research.

Zimmerman, Burke K. *Biofuture: Confronting the Genetic Era*. Plenum Pub. 1984 $19.95. ISBN 0-306-41315-9. Clearly explains genetics in nonscientific terms. Covers current technology and contemporary controversies, evaluates the ethical issues, and concludes with a history of recombinant DNA research.

MICROBIOLOGY AND VIROLOGY

Microbiology is the study of microorganisms, such as bacteria, algae, fungi, and rickettsiae. Microbiologists study the organisms' structures, physiology, biochemistry, and pathology. Virology, the study of viruses, is an independent subdiscipline, although originally it was a subspecialty of microbiology. Viruses are not complete cells; they are DNA fragments that require a host cell in order to multiply. Viruses were not "discovered" until the twentieth century because they were too small to see with a light microscope; the electron microscope, which uses electrons instead of light to create the images seen, made it possible to view viruses for the first time.

Brock, Thomas D., David W. Smith, and Michael T. Madigan. *Biology of Microorganisms*. P-H 1990 $58.00. ISBN 0-13-08381-7. Covers basic microbiology, as well as material on immunology, biotechnology, and biochemistry.

De Kruif, Paul. *Microbe Hunters*. HarBraceJ 1986 repr. of 1924 ed. o.p. An entertaining classic on the history of early biology.

Gallo, Robert M. D. *Virus Hunting: AIDS, Cancer and the Human Retrovirus: A Story of Scientific Discovery*. Basic 1991 $15.00. ISBN 0-465-09806-1. An interesting biographical account by one of the scientists who identified the AIDS virus.

Herbert, R. A., and G. A. Codd. *Microbes in Extreme Environments*. Acad. Pr. 1986 $69.00. ISBN 0-12-341960-1. A collection of papers on how microorganisms adapt to different types of extreme environments, a topic of increasing research interest in academic and biotechnological study.

Leadbetter, Edward R., and Jeanne S. Poindexter, eds. *Bacteria in Nature, Vol. 1: Bacterial Activities in Perspective*. Plenum Pub. $69.50. ISBN 0-306-41944-0. *Bacteria in Nature, Vol. 2: Methods and Special Applications in Bacterial Ecology*. Plenum Pub. 1986 $79.50. ISBN 0-306-42346-4. *Bacteria in Nature, Vol. 3: Structure, Physiology and Genetic Adaptability*. Plenum Pub. 1989 $79.50. ISBN 0-306-43173-4. The first in a series of books intended to provide a survey of the issues in bacteriological research; covers all classes of bacteria.

Lee, John J., and others, eds. *An Illustrated Guide to the Protozoa*. Allen Pr. 1985 o.p. "For the nonprotozoologist this book serves as a valuable reference to identify organisms, learn about their biology, and the relations of the genera" (*Quarterly Review of Biology*).

Linton, Alan H., and Mary P. English, eds. *Microbes, Man and Animals: The Natural History of Microbial Interactions*. Wiley 1982 $50.00. ISBN 0-471-10083-8. Presents basic host-parasite relationships in medical and veterinary microbiology.

Postgate, John. *Microbes and Man*. Cambridge U. Pr. 1992 $49.95. ISBN 0-521-42355-4. Discusses microbes and human disease for the general reader.

Scott, Andrew. *Pirates of the Cell: The Story of Viruses from Molecule to Microbe*. Blackwell Pubs. 1987 $12.95. ISBN 0-631-15637-2. Offers an outstanding introduction to viruses.

MOLECULAR BIOLOGY

Molecular biology is one of the most recently developed specialties in biology. Molecular biologists study cellular processes in the form of molecular behavior. The major questions that specialists in this discipline address are the cell's uptake and transformation of energy, the intracellular production and use of energy, and the molecular representation of information that governs the cell's metabolic activities. Biochemistry, biophysics, and genetics overlap with molecular biology.

Calladine, Chris, and Horace Drew. *Understanding DNA: The Molecule and How It Works.* Acad. Pr. 1992 $65.00. ISBN 0-12-155085-0. A well-illustrated, introductory text on the structure and function of DNA; includes an introduction to molecular biology for the nonscientist.

Crick, Francis. *What Mad Pursuit?* Basic 1988 $16.95. ISBN 0-465-09137-7. Focuses on Crick's personal life and philosophy in broad terms; does not emphasize Crick's role in discovering the structure of DNA but rather encompasses a view of his scientific career.

Darnell, James, Harvey Lodisch, and David Baltimore. *Molecular Cell Biology.* W. H. Freeman 1990 $56.95. ISBN 0-7167-1981-9. Integrates basic material from cell biology, biochemistry, and genetics to form the basic introduction to the study of molecular biology.

Denton, Michael. *Evolution: A Theory in Crisis.* Adler & Adler 1986 $19.95. ISBN 0-917561-05-8. Explains evolutionary theory from the viewpoint of molecular biologists.

Freifelder, David. *Essentials of Molecular Biology.* Ed. by George M. Malacinski. Jones & Bartlett 1992 $40.00. ISBN 0-86720-137-1. A good introductory text in molecular biology; designed for students with a minimal background in biology and chemistry.

Goodsell, David S. *The Machinery of Life.* Spr.-Verlag 1992 $29.00. ISBN 0-387-97846-1. An introduction to biochemistry for the general reader; extensively illustrated with black-and-white line drawings and color plates.

Kay, Lily E. *The Molecular Vision of Life: Caltech, the Rockefeller Foundation, and the Rise of the New Biology.* OUP 1993 $49.95. ISBN 0-19-505812-7. "As a contribution to the history of the American involvement in molecular biology, Kay's book is a work of considerable value, and it is written with clarity and elegance" (*Science*).

Li, Wen-Hsiung. *Fundamentals of Molecular Evolution.* Sinauer Assocs. 1991 $25.95. ISBN 0-87893-452-9. An introductory text to the field of molecular evolution; requires some background in biology.

Nei, Masatoshi. *Molecular Evolutionary Genetics.* Col. U. Pr. 1989 $86.00. ISBN 0-231-06320-2. "Nei has made a significant scholarly contribution, presenting the leading edge of evolutionary thought" (*Quarterly Review of Biology*). Recommended for readers with a background in basic biology and chemistry.

Scientific American. *The Molecules of Life.* W. H. Freeman 1985 o.p. Describes the range of instruments and techniques now available in electron microscopy and illustrates how these techniques are employed; accessible to the general reader.

Wills, Christopher. *Exons, Introns and Talking Genes—The Science behind the Human Genome Project.* OUP 1991 $15.00. ISBN 0-19-286154-9. A well-written book on the various aspects of the Human Genome Project; requires a basic background in genetics.

CHRONOLOGY OF AUTHORS

Pliny the Elder. c.a.d. 23–a.d. 79
Leeuwenhoek, Anton van. 1632–1723
Linnaeus, Carolus. 1707–1778
Lamarck, Jean Baptiste. 1744–1829
Cuvier, Baron Georges. 1769–1832
Audubon, John James. 1785–1851
Agassiz, Louis. 1807–1873
Darwin, Charles Robert. 1809–1882
Bernard, Claude. 1813–1878

Mendel, Gregor Johann. 1822–1884
Pasteur, Louis. 1822–1895
Fabre, Jean Henri. 1823–1915
Wallace, Alfred Russel. 1823–1913
Huxley, Thomas Henry. 1825–1895
Koch, Robert. 1843–1910
Ramon y Cajal, Santiago. 1852–1934
Bailey, Liberty Hyde. 1858–1954
Morgan, Thomas Hunt. 1866–1945

Frisch, Karl von. 1887–1982
Huxley, Julian Sorrell. 1887–1975
Sinnott, Edmund Ware. 1888–1968
Muller, Hermann Joseph. 1890–1967
Haldane, John Burdon Sanderson.
  1892–1964
Krebs, Hans Adolf. 1900–1981
Dubos, René Jules. 1901–1982
McClintock, Barbara. 1902–1992

Beadle, George Wells. 1903–1989
Levi-Montalcini, Rita. 1909–1989
Crick, Francis Harry Compton. 1916–
Wilkins, Maurice Hugh Frederick.
  1916–
François, Jacob. 1920–
Cohen, Stanley. 1922–
Watson, James Dewey. 1928–
Bishop, John Michael. 1936–

AGASSIZ, LOUIS (JEAN LOUIS RODOLPHE AGASSIZ). 1807–1873

"The exact description of things seen, on which so many twentieth-century writing is found, was a craft developed as recently as the nineteenth century, and not by men of letters but scientists. Agassiz was quite possibly the greatest master of this art who ever lived" (Hugh Kenner). Born at Motier, Switzerland, Louis Agassiz was taught by his father (a clergyman) and his mother (the daughter of a physician) until the age of 10. As a penurious student and professor in Paris, this Swiss naturalist and geologist studied fish classification and produced the monumental five-volume treatise on extinct marine organisms, *Recherches sur les poissons fossiles* (1833–43). His second period of research was devoted to the study of Swiss glaciers (the results published as *Etudes sur les glaciers*, 1840); he made important discoveries about the Ice Age in Europe. The widespread hunger for scientific knowledge in the early nineteenth century took him to the United States in 1846, where he became a professor of zoology and geology at Harvard University. A skillful lecturer and popular and devoted teacher, Agassiz revolutionized the study of natural history by promoting the openminded observation and interpretation of nature, as opposed to reliance on traditional classification systems. The Agassiz approach was adopted by an entire generation of scientists. With his usual industry and enthusiasm he established a museum of comparative zoology, now the Agassiz Museum at Harvard. His second wife, Elizabeth Cabot Cary, a pioneer in the higher education of women, played a major role in the founding of Radcliffe College. His famous "Essay on Classification" is included in his four-volume *Contributions to the Natural History of the United States* (1857–62). EZRA POUND (see Vol. 1) once said to him, "Agassiz, apart from his brilliant achievement in natural science, ranks as a writer of prose, precise knowledge of his subject leading to great exactitude of expression."

BOOKS BY AGASSIZ

Geological Sketches. Rprt. Serv. 1985 repr. of 1885 ed. $39.00. ISBN 0-7812-0855-6
*The Intelligence of Louis Agassiz: A Specimen Book of Scientific Writings; Selected, with
  an Introduction and Notes*. Ed. by Guy Davenport. Greenwood 1983 repr. of 1963 ed.
  $55.00. ISBN 0-313-24249-6
Louis Agassiz: His Life and Correspondence. 2 vols. Somerset 1885 o.p.

BOOKS ABOUT AGASSIZ

Gould, Alice B. *Louis Agassiz*. Folcroft 1981 repr. of 1900 ed. o.p.
Lurie, Edward. *Louis Agassiz: A Life in Science*. Johns Hopkins 1988 $15.95. ISBN 0-8018-
  3743-X
———. *Nature and the American Mind: Louis Agassiz and the Culture of Science*. Watson
  1974 o.p.
Marcou, Jules. *Life, Letters and Works of Louis Agassiz*. Gregg Intl. repr. of 1896 ed. o.p.

Paton, Lucy A. *Elizabeth Cary Agassiz: A Biography.* Ayer 1974 repr. of 1919 ed. $32.00. ISBN 0-405-06117-X. Features the accounts of Elizabeth Cary Agassiz's travels with her husband. She was the first president of Radcliffe College.

Robinson, Mabel L. *Runner of the Mountain Tops: The Life of Louis Agassiz.* Gale 1971 repr. of 1939 ed. o.p.

Tiner, John H. *The Ghost Lake: The True Story of Louis Agassiz.* Baker Bk 1983 o.p.

AUDUBON, JOHN JAMES. 1785–1851

The great American ornithologist John James Audubon was born in Haiti, educated in France, and went to the Audubon estate ("Mill Grove") near Philadelphia in 1803. As a youth, Audubon enjoyed observing birds and organizing bird-banding flights, the first in this country. He began by painting portraits and teaching drawing, then conceived the idea of painting every species of American bird in its native habitat. Audubon spent years traveling through the wilderness and enduring incredible hardships. His drawings and paintings of birds and other animals "represent a rare combination of artistic talent and scientific observation and remain one of the great achievements of American intellectual history" (*Columbia Encyclopedia*). Despondent at being unable to provide financially for his family, he went to Great Britain in search of a publisher in 1826. Not only did he succeed in getting his work published in England, Audubon also was made a member of the Wernerian Natural History Society and of the Royal Society. *The Birds of America*, in elephant folio size, was published in parts between 1827 and 1938. The accompanying five-volume text, called *Ornithological Biography* (1831–39), was prepared largely in Edinburgh in collaboration with William MacGillivray. *The Viviporous Quadrupeds of North America*, which he began in collaboration with John Bachman, was completed by Audubon's two sons.

Returning to the United States in 1836, Audubon dined with President Jackson and received a warm welcome from Daniel Webster and WASHINGTON IRVING (see Vol. 1). The latter praised Audubon for achievements that "were highly creditable to the nation," and deserved "national patronage." While Audubon's drawings of birds and other animals were exceptional as art, they also influenced ornithologists and other zoologists to observe wildlife in natural settings.

BOOKS BY AUDUBON

Audubon and His Journals. 2 vols. Ed. by Maria F. Audubon. Dover 1986 repr. of 1897 ed. $8.95 ea. ISBNs 0-486-25143-8, 0-486-25144-6.

The Audubon Notebook. 2 vols. Ed. by Maria F. Audubon. Ayer repr. of 1897 ed. o.p.

Audubon Reader: The Best Writings of John James Audubon. Ed. by Scott R. Sanders. Ind. U. Pr. 1986 $29.95. ISBN 0-253-20384-0. Includes such memorable pieces as Audubon's report of the huge earthquake of 1811 and his life of the passenger pigeon.

The Birds of America. 1827–38. 7 vols. Peter Smith 1985 repr. of 1840 ed. o.p.

Delineations of American Scenery and Character. Ed. by F. H. Herrick. Ayer 1970 repr. of 1926 ed. o.p. Extracts from Audubon's pictures of American frontier life.

The 1826 Journal of John James Audubon. Ed. by Alice Ford. Abbeville Pr. 1987 repr. of 1966 ed. o.p. The first unabridged version of Audubon's journal, describing his search in England and Scotland to find a publisher for *Birds of America*. Audubon was a painstaking diarist, and this eight-month memoir, written in the form of letters to his wife in Louisiana, shows him at his best—naive, sincere, proud, and above all, ebullient. "Ford's notes . . . are excellent, but it should be added that the index is not perfectly reliable. Illustrated with sketches and drawings done by Audubon during his trip" (*The New Yorker*).

BOOKS ABOUT AUDUBON

Alexander, Pamela. *Commonwealth of Wings: An Ornithological Biography Based on the Life of John James Audubon.* U. Pr. of New Eng. 1991 $22.50. ISBN 0-8195-2191-4. Poems about Audubon based loosely on his letters and journals.

Dock, George, Jr. *Audubon's Birds of America.* Abrams 1979 o.p.

Durant, Mary, and Michael Harwood. *On the Road with John James Audubon.* Dodd 1980 o.p. "Durant and Harwood have given us a fascinating journal. They manage, at every step, to evoke the time past to supply us with interesting facts and to guide us through the inconsistencies in Audubon's work" (*Natural History*).

Fries, Walderman H. *The Double Elephant Folio: The Story of Audubon's Birds of America.* ALA 1973 o.p. Features 30 plates of the engravings for the elephant folio in color with a simple accompanying text.

Herrick, F. H. *Audubon the Naturalist.* 2 vols. 1917. Peter Smith 1980 o.p.

Peterson, Roger Tory. *Audubon Birds.* Abbeville Pr. 1980 o.p.

Warren, Robert Penn. *Audubon: A Vision.* Random 1969 o.p. "With irony Warren develops Audubon's passage in time—his birth, life and death—into a story of deep delight, a story both intellectually and emotionally moving" (*Library Journal*).

BAILEY, LIBERTY HYDE. 1858–1954

Born in South Haven, Michigan, Liberty Bailey is noted for his basic works in botany and horticulture. He was instrumental in raising the stature of horticulture to an applied science and in improving the living conditions and education of farmers. Bailey became a professor of horticulture at Michigan State University (1885) and at Cornell University (1888–1903). In 1920 he established the Bailey Hortorium of the State University of New York. "Bailey was a man of driving energy. As a diversion from administrative burdens and research in science he wrote two volumes of poetry and nine in the fields of sociology, religion, and philosophy" (*Encyclopedia Britannica*). Bailey wrote more than 60 books on botany, horticulture, and agriculture. He is credited with coining the term *cultivar.*

BOOKS BY BAILEY

Cyclopedia of American Agriculture: A Popular Survey of Agricultural Conditions, Practice and Ideals in the United States and Canada. 2 vols. 1907–09. Ayer 1975 repr. of 1912 ed. o.p. A collection of articles with bibliographies written by agricultural specialists; outdated as a reference.

Cyclopedia of American Horticulture. 6 vols. Gordon Pr. 1972 $1800.00. ISBN 0-87968-247-7. This book is a "complete record of the status of North American Horticulture as it exists at the close of the nineteenth century" (Preface).

The Holy Earth. NY State Coll. of Ag. 1980 repr. of 1915 ed. $5.55. ISBN 0-9605314-6-7

Hortus Third: A Concise Dictionary of Plants Cultivated in the United States and Canada. (coauthored with Ethel Z. Bailey). Macmillan 1976 $150.00. ISBN 0-02-505430-8. The standard American horticultural reference work; includes the description and correct botanical name, with its author or authors, for 281 families, 3,301 genera, and 20,397 species of North American plants.

How Plants Get Their Names. Dover 1963 repr. of 1933 ed. $4.50. ISBN 0-486-20796-X

Manual of Cultivated Plants. Macmillan 1949 $40.00. ISBN 0-02-505520-8. The standard manual of cultivated plants commonly grown in North America.

Nursery Manual. Macmillan 1967 o.p. The classic plant nursery manual, still useful as a guide to plant cultivation.

Pruning Manual. Ed. by E. P. Christopher. Macmillan 1954 o.p.

Sketch of the Evolution of Our Native Fruits. Scholarly Res. Inc. 1973 repr. of 1898 ed. $39.00. ISBN 0-8420-1473-X

BOOK ABOUT BAILEY

Rodgers, Andrew D., III *Liberty Hyde Bailey*. 1949. Hafner 1965 o.p. "Mr. Rodgers
alternates between the romantic and the pedantic. Documents and letters are
lavishly quoted and footnoted. But through this musty material steals the soft breath
of orchards in bloom and of fields turning green in the spring. Especially is this true
in the description of Bailey's Michigan boyhood" (*New York Times*).

BEADLE, GEORGE WELLS. 1903–1989 (NOBEL PRIZE 1958)

George Wells Beadle was one of the founders of biochemical genetics.
Building upon earlier work primarily by Archibald Edward Garrod and JOHN
BURDON HALDANE, he defined and systematically demonstrated the "gene
enzyme hypothesis," which explains how genes control the cells' metabolic
processes. A single gene controls the production of each enzyme. A genetic
mutation can result in the alteration or blocking of its enzyme and thus alter the
cell's metabolism. These alterations subsequently result in changes in the
organism's phenotype.

Born on his parents' farm in Wahoo, Nebraska, Beadle attended the
University of Nebraska's College of Agriculture and Cornell University. At
Cornell, he did his graduate work in the Department of Cytology and Genetics
and worked as a research assistant in R. A. Emerson's maize genetics
laboratory. Beadle took a postdoctoral position in THOMAS HUNT MORGAN's
drosophila laboratory at the California Institute of Technology and worked with
Boris Ephrussi on a series of drosophila experiments designed to support the
"gene enzyme" hypothesis. Later, he became a professor at Stanford University,
continuing his research on the "gene enzyme" hypothesis with a new series of
experiments using a fungus, Neurospora Crassa. These experiments led to the
Nobel Prize, which he shared with Edward Tatum and Joshua Lederberg in
1958. In 1946 Beadle accepted the chairmanship of the Biology Department at
the California Institute of Technology. In 1962 he became the president of the
University of Chicago, serving in this position until his retirement in 1968.
Following his retirement, Beadle returned to research in genetics until his
death.

BOOKS BY BEADLE

Genetics and Modern Biology. Bks. Demand repr. of 1962 ed. $20.80. ISBN 0-317-27906-8.
An introductory text accessible to the general reader or beginning student that
reflects the knowledge of the 1960s; outdated.

An Introduction to Genetics. (coauthored with A. H. Sturtevant). Garland 1988 o.p.
A reprint of the 1962 classic textbook; written by two of the twentieth century's great
biologists.

Language of Life: An Introduction to the Science of Genetics. (coauthored with Muriel
Beadle). Doubleday 1966 o.p. An introductory text that does not reflect the advances
in molecular biology during the last 20 years.

BERNARD, CLAUDE. 1813–1878

Born in France, Claude Bernard is the founder of modern experimental
physiology. As a student in Lyon, he studied to become a playwright. His work
was rejected by critics, which ended his dramatic aspirations. Instead, after
serving for several years as a pharmacist's assistant, he became a physician and
an exceptional biological scientist.

Bernard's investigations in physiology were very fruitful and broad in scope.
In 1855 he was appointed full professor of medicine at the Collège de France.

By this time he had explained the chemical and nervous system control of digestion, demonstrated the role of the pancreas in fat metabolism, and discovered the role that bile plays in the digestion of proteins. In the years that followed, he identified the liver as the site of glycogenesis and explained the processes governing vasodilation.

His most important theoretical contribution was proposing the concept of homeostasis, which he called the *milieu interieur*. Homeostasis is the principle that all of the body's systems are in a constant state of adjustment and that these adjustments maintain equilibrium within the body. Bernard also was the first physiologist to demonstrate that the theories and methods of chemistry and physics could contribute to the study of biology. This first use of interdisciplinary techniques broadened the base of physiology and foreshadowed the form that future research in biology would take.

BOOKS BY BERNARD

The Cahier Rouge of Claude Bernard. Trans. by Hebbel E. Hoff, Lucienne Guillemin, and Roger Guillemin. Schenkman 1967 o.p. Presents the translated notebooks of Claude Bernard; the original is held by the archives of the Collège de France.

An Introduction to the Study of Experimental Medicine. 1865. Trans. by Henry C. Greene. Dover 1957 $6.95. ISBN 0-486-20400-6. This work is accessible to the general reader.

Lectures on the Phenomena of Life Common to Animals and Plants. Trans. by Hebbel E. Hoff, Roger Guillemin, and Lucienne Guillemin. C. C. Thomas 1974 o.p. Features Bernard's treatise on biology and general physiology.

Memoir on the Pancreas and on the Role of Pancreatic Juice in Digestive Processes: Particularly in the Digestion of Neutral Fat. Trans. by John Henderon. Acad. Pr. 1985 $102.00. ISBN 0-12-092880-9. Bernard's classic work elucidating the functioning of the pancreas; very technical for the general reader.

BOOKS ABOUT BERNARD

Bergson, Henri. *An Introduction to Metaphysics: The Creative Mind.* Littlefield 1975 repr. of 1965 ed. $11.50. ISBN 0-8226-0164-8

Hirst, Paul O. *Durkheim, Bernard and Epistemology.* Routledge Chapman & Hall 1980 repr. of 1975 ed. o.p.

Holmes, Frederic L. *Claude Bernard and Animal Chemistry.* HUP 1974 $45.00. ISBN 0-674-13485-0. A fine scholarly account of the life of Claude Bernard, based largely on his diaries and notebooks.

Parvez, H., ed. *Advances in Experimental Medicine: A Centenary Tribute to Claude Bernard.* Elsevier 1980 o.p. This is a collection of addresses, essays, and lectures on Claude Bernard's work by distinguished biologists.

Robin, E. D. *Claude Bernard and the Internal Environment: A Memorial Symposium.* Bks. Demand repr. of 1979 ed. $83.00. ISBN 0-8357-6056-1

BISHOP, JOHN MICHAEL. 1936– (NOBEL PRIZE 1989)

Molecular biologist and Nobel Prize winner in physiology and medicine, John Bishop was born in York, Pennsylvania, and educated at Gettysburg College and Harvard University. After completing his residency at Massachusetts General Hospital in 1964, he was medical researcher with the National Institute for Health from 1964 to 1968. In 1968 he became professor in the Department of Microbiology and Immunology at the University of California, San Francisco.

At the University of California, Bishop collaborated with Harold E. Varmus, his colleague and fellow department member, in virology research. During the 1970s, they investigated the decades-old problem of the mechanisms by which certain retroviruses were thought to induce cancer. In investigating how a viral gene, or oncogene, caused tumors in chicks, they developed a nucleic acid probe capable of identifying the oncogene that existed in chicken tumor cells transformed by the virus. While doing so, they made the remarkable discovery that an almost identical version of the gene was also present in normal cells.

In 1976 Bishop and Varmus published their findings: "The oncogene in the virus did not represent a true viral gene but instead was a normal cellular gene, which the virus had acquired during replication in the host cell and thereafter carried along." The discovery that oncogenes are abnormal versions of normal cellular genes, for which Bishop and Varmus shared the Nobel Prize for physiology and medicine in 1989, altered the way in which scientists view cancer, the normal growth of cells, and the growth of tumors.

BOOK BY BISHOP

Natural Agency: An Essay on the Causal Theory of Action. Cambridge U. Pr. 1990 $54.95. ISBN 0-521-37430-8. Engaging defense of the thesis that the actions of persons are mentally caused behavior.

COHEN, STANLEY. 1922– (NOBEL PRIZE 1986)

The American biochemist and Nobel Prize winner Stanley Cohen was born in Brooklyn, New York. A graduate of Brooklyn College, he received his M.A. from Oberlin College and in 1948 his Ph.D. from the University of Michigan. Soon after, he became a researcher at Washington University, where he began his notable collaboration with RITA LEVI-MONTALCINI. Cohen's biochemical background enabled him to help isolate the nerve growth factor (NGF) in the area of Levi-Montalcini's own research, namely, the neurogenesis of the growth of nerve cells and fibers.

Working with Levi-Montalcini from 1953 until 1959, Cohen discovered another cell growth factor in chemical extracts. Through experiments, he showed that this growth factor caused the eyes of newborn mice to open and their teeth to emerge several days sooner than normal. He labeled this substance the epidermal growth factor, or EGF, analyzing its exact chemical properties and the mechanisms by which it is taken into cells and acts upon them. Continuing his research, Cohen demonstrated that EGF influences a great range of bodily developmental processes. In 1959 Cohen was appointed professor of biochemistry at Vanderbilt University. In 1986 he shared the Nobel Prize in physiology and medicine with Levi-Montalcini.

BOOKS BY COHEN

Chemical Mediators of Inflamation and Immunity. Acad. Pr. 1986 $71.00. ISBN 0-12-179065-7
Lymphokines and the Immune Response. CRC Pr. 1989 $179.95. ISBN 0-8493-6427-2

CRICK, FRANCIS HARRY COMPTON. 1916– (NOBEL PRIZE 1962)

Born in Northampton, England, Francis Crick received a B.S. from University College in London and a Ph.D. from Cambridge University in 1955. Crick began his career as a physicist, but in 1949 he began research in molecular biology at Cambridge. In 1951 he and the American biologist JAMES WATSON began working intensively to learn the structure of the DNA molecule. Using research findings that the British scientists MAURICE WILKINS and Rosalind Franklin had reached on the structure of nucleic acids, including DNA, they succeeded in building a model of the molecule in 1953. The Watson-Crick model for DNA was hailed by biologists worldwide, ushering in a new era of research and understanding in cell biology and genetics. Crick, Watson, and Wilkins were awarded the 1962 Nobel Prize in physiology and medicine in recognition of their great achievement. The same year, Crick became director of Cambridge's Molecular Biology Laboratory, where he went on to do further work on the genetic code. In 1977 he became a research professor at the Salk Institute in San Diego.

BOOKS BY CRICK

Life Itself. S&S Trade 1981 $12.95. ISBN 0-671-25562-0. Discusses the origin of life by directed panspermia, his theory that life came from outer space.

What Mad Pursuit: A Personal View of Scientific Discovery. Basic 1988 $16.95. ISBN 0-465-09137-7. Describes his life as a scientist and his part in discovering the structure of DNA.

BOOKS ABOUT CRICK

Holton, Gerald, ed. *The Twentieth-Century Scientists: Studies in the Biography of Ideas.* Norton 1972 $15.00. ISBN 0-393-06384-4. Collection of essays on contemporary science topics; includes an essay on Crick.

Judson, Horace F. *The Eighth Day of Creation: Makers of the Revolution in Biology.* S&S Trade 1979 $15.95. ISBN 0-671-22540-5. History of the discoveries in molecular biology and the scientists involved from 1930 to 1970.

Moore, Ruth E. *The Coil of Life: The Story of the Great Discoveries of the Life Sciences.* Knopf 1961 $8.95. ISBN 0-394-41966-9. Discusses the discoveries related to the chemical basis of heredity; includes information about Crick.

Olby, Robert. *The Path to the Double Helix.* U. of Wash. Pr. 1974 $23.50. ISBN 0-295-95359-4. History of molecular biology: the ideas, methods, and people that contributed to the discovery of DNA's structure.

Watson, James D. *The Double Helix: A Personal Account of the Discovery of the Structure of DNA.* 1968. Atheneum 1985 $6.95. ISBN 0-689-70602-2. Watson's account of the events and people involved in determining the structure of DNA.

CUVIER, BARON GEORGES (GEORGES LEOPOLD CHRETIEN FREDERIC DAGOBERT CUVIER). 1769–1832

Born in France, Georges Cuvier, the great paleontologist and zoologist, regarded as the founder of comparative anatomy, had no formal scientific training. He studied at the military academy at Stuttgart in order to qualify for the French civil service.

Cuvier worked as a tutor on the north coast of France, while he waited for a civil service appointment. There, he became fascinated with the marine life that he saw on the beaches and began to study it. He dissected mollusks and fishes and made drawings of their various parts. Cuvier's understanding of anatomy and his drawings were so well-executed that he was offered a chair at the University of Paris in the Department of Comparative Anatomy.

At the University of Paris, he began studying the great apes as a way of understanding human anatomy. As a result of his studies, he proposed the revolutionary idea that all life forms descended from a single species. His most notable theory of comparative anatomy was the correlation theory. Cuvier recognized that all body structures are related to one another. Thus, he concluded that a single organ or structure could be used to predict the form of the rest of the animal's parts. Because this concept provided the basis for future work in the reconstruction of fossils, Cuvier is credited with originating modern paleontological theory and method.

Cuvier's work led him to reject theories of continuous evolution. He developed a theory whereby all evolutionary changes were caused by "cataclysmic" geological events, an idea that was disproved by CHARLES DARWIN and later evolutionists.

During later life, Cuvier was recognized by Napoleon as one of France's foremost thinkers. Napoleon conferred a baronetcy on him (1819) and appointed Cuvier director of the Department of Education of France. As director, Cuvier made many reforms and innovations in the French educational system and founded many new universities.

BOOKS BY CUVIER

The Animal Kingdom, Arranged after Its Organization: Forming a Natural History of Animals and an Introduction to Comparative Anatomy. Kraus Repr. 1979 repr. of 1863 ed. o.p. Illustrates the use of Cuvier's principle of the correlation of body parts.

The Class Mammalia: The Animal Kingdom Arranged in Conformity with Its Organization by the Baron Cuvier. Ed. by Keir B. Sterling. 5 vols. Ayer 1978 repr. of 1827 ed. $43.00 ea. set $217.00. ISBN 0-405-10746-3. This set includes an English translation of volume 1 and the entire French editions (1827–35) of *Regne Animal.*

Essay on the Theory of the Earth. Ayer 1978 repr. of 1817 ed. $32.00. ISBN 0-405-10439-1. The text of this reprint is in English and French.

Memoirs on Fossil Elephants and on Reconstruction of the Genera Palaeotherium and Anoplotherium (Recherches sur les ossemens fossiles des quadrupèdes). Ed. by Stephen Jay Gould. Ayer 1980 repr. of 1812 ed. $80.00. ISBN 0-405-12709-X. This is a reprint of volumes 2 and 13 of the 1812 edition, including memories I–II; the text is in French.

BOOK ABOUT CUVIER

Outram, Dorinda. *Georges Cuvier: Vocation, Science and Authority in Post-Revolutionary France.* St. Martin 1988 $55.00. ISBN 0-7190-1077-2

DARWIN, CHARLES ROBERT. 1809–1882

Charles Darwin, born in Shrewbury, England, became interested in the study of evolution when he was official naturalist on the HMS *Beagle*, which sailed around the world from 1831 to 1836. After his return, he continued his research on animal and plant forms, concluding that "selection was the key to man's success." His theory of evolution, soon known as Darwinism, stated that beneficial variations of species were preserved, while others, unfavored by their environments, were eliminated in the struggle for existence. Darwin used findings from anatomy, geology, embryology, and paleontology. Although later research required modification of some of Darwin's statements, his discoveries were corroborated by Mendelian genetics and became the "prime cornerstone of modern scientific teaching." The controversy triggered by the first publication of *On the Origin of Species* (1859) and its sequel, *The Descent of Man*, 12 years later is still raging in some parts of the world.

Darwin was a warm and modest man. Always in poor health, he spent the last 40 years of his life studying and writing at his home in Down, Sussex. Darwin had the faculty of writing simply on abstruse matters; his use of reminiscence or a discursive anecdote lending great color to his scientific expositions.

BOOKS BY DARWIN

Autobiography of Charles Darwin. Ed. by Nora Burlow. Norton 1969 repr. of 1959 ed. $8.95. ISBN 0-393-00487-2. Restores Darwin's comments on religion, omitted from the original 1887 version because of family sentiment. "Some of the passages formerly suppressed are the most revealing he ever wrote concerning his own estimate of the bearing of his famous theory on religion, morals and philosophy" (*New York Times*).

The Collected Papers of Charles Darwin. 2 vols. Ed. by Paul H. Barrett. U. Ch. Pr. 1980 $13.50. ISBN 0-226-13658-2

The Correspondence of Charles Darwin: Vol. 1, 1821–1834. Ed. by Frederick Burkhardt and Sydney Smith. Cambridge U. Pr. 1985 o.p. "The 338 letters in this first volume begin when Darwin was 12 years old and end as he returns from the *Beagle* voyage. . . . Includes letters from family and friends as well as scientific colleagues, giving the reader a full view of Darwin's personal life, the social mores of the time, and the nature of his particular creative genius. Enriched with a list of books on the *Beagle* and a biographical register of the correspondents" (*Library Journal*).

The Descent of Man and Selection in Relation to Sex. 1871. Princeton U. Pr. 1981 repr. of 1871 ed. $90.00. ISBN 0-691-02369-7. In *The Descent of Man,* Darwin applied the principles of evolution and natural selection to human beings. "Natural selection" is replaced by the concept of "sexual selection."

The Different Forms of Flowers on Plants of the Same Species. 1877. U. Ch. Pr. 1986 $13.95. ISBN 0-226-13664-7

The Effects of Cross and Self-Fertilisation in the Vegetable Kingdom. AMS Pr. 1972 repr. of 1889 ed. $42.50. ISBN 0-404-08413-3. Demonstrates the advantages of cross-fertilization, which involves the interchange of different sets of genes, in terms of developing adaptations.

The Essential Darwin. Ed. by Kenneth Korey. Little 1984 $19.95. ISBN 0-31645826-0. "This will be welcomed by readers who want to understand more precisely what Darwin said and where his theories stand today. Excerpts from Darwin's *Autobiography, The Voyage of the Beagle, The Origin of Species,* and *The Descent of Man* are interspersed with overviews and critical notes" (*Library Journal*).

The Expression of the Emotions in Man and Animals. U. Ch. Pr. 1965 $15.00. ISBN 0-226-13656-6. The first work in the field of ethology, the study of comparative animal behavior; includes an introduction by Konrad Lorenz.

The Formation of Vegetable Mould, through the Action of Worms with Observation of Their Habits. 1881. AMS Pr. 1972 $42.50. ISBN 0-404-08416-8. One of the first complete treatises on plant ecology; characterizes and quantifies the changes in soil that are brought about by earthworms and that benefit plants.

Foundations of the Origin of Species. Ed. by Francis Darwin. Kraus Repr. repr. of 1909 ed. o.p.

Geological Observations on the Volcanis Islands and Parts of South America Visited during the Voyage of the H.M.S. Beagle. 1844–46. AMS Pr. 1972 $42.50. ISBN 0-404-08403-8. Presents Darwin's work on geology and geological evolution.

Insectivorous Plants: Works of Charles Darwin. 1893. 2 vols. AMS Pr. 1972 $42.50. ISBN 0-404-08412-5. Focuses on the adaptations of meat-eating plants, such as "fly-catching" plants; covers the various anatomical and physiological features of these plants, which are specific to snaring and consuming prey.

Journal of Researches into the Natural History and Geology of the Countries Visited during the Voyage of the H.M.S. Beagle round the World under the Command of Captain Fitz Roy. 1839. AMS Pr. 1972 $42.50. ISBN 0-404-08401-X. Focuses on his geological observations and on natural history.

Metaphysics, Materialism, and the Evolution of the Mind: Early Writings of Charles Darwin. U. Ch. Pr. 1980 $6.95. ISBN 0-226-13659-0

Natural Selection. Ed. by Robert C. Stauffer. Cambridge U. Pr. 1975 o.p. "This book is probably the publishing event of the decade in the history of science. . . . I cannot praise highly enough the meticulous work of Stauffer and a staff of assistants in rendering the text right down to the details of Darwin's misspellings. . . . *Natural Selection* is a joy to read. It is full of insights and subtle observations" (*Science*).

On the Movements and Habits of Climbing Plants. 1865. AMS Pr. repr. of 1891 ed. $42.50. ISBN 0-404-08411-7. Explores the specific adaptations of plants to climbing, such as tendrils that enable plants to help them reach light.

On the Origin of Species: A Facsimile of the First Edition. Ed. by Ernst Mayr. HUP 1964 $11.95. ISBN 0-674-63752-6. Six editions were issued under Darwin's direction between 1859 and 1872. Each edition embodied the author's revision of his theory based on new evidence. By 1872, about 75 percent of the first edition had been rewritten.

On the Structure and Distribution of Coral Reefs. U. of Ariz. Pr. 1984 repr. of 1842 ed. $12.95. ISBN 0-8165-0844-5. Discusses Darwin's theories on the development of coral reefs, based on his observations and theorizing during the *H.M.S. Beagle* voyage.

The Power of Movement in Plants. 1880. AMS Pr. 1972 $42.50. ISBN 0-404-08415-X

The Substance of the Descent of Man. Richard West 1978 repr. of 1926 ed. o.p.

Variation of Animals and Plants under Domestication. 1867. 2 vols. AMS Pr. 1972 o.p. Offers a detailed study on the origins of cultivated plants and domesticated animals.

The Various Contrivances by Which Orchids Are Fertilised by Insects. 1862. U. Ch. Pr. 1984 $20.00. ISBN 0-226-13661-2. Illustrates the principle that all changes in the form of a species are adaptations that improve the plant's chances of survival. Orchids and all other plants fertilized by insects show physical adaptations different from the adaptations of plants fertilized by wind-borne pollen.

The Voyage of Charles Darwin: His Autobiographical Writings. Ed. by Christopher Ralling. Parkwest Pubns. 1986 o.p.

BOOKS ABOUT DARWIN

Alland, Alexander, Jr. *Human Nature: Darwin's View.* Col. U. Pr. 1985 o.p.

Armstrong, Patrick. *Charles Darwin in Western Australia.* International Specialized Bk. 1986 o.p.

Berry, R. J. *Charles Darwin: A Commemoration, 1882–1982.* Acad. Pr. 1982 $36.00. ISBN 0-12-093180-X

Clark, Ronald W. *The Survival of Charles Darwin: A Biography of a Man and an Idea.* Avon 1986 o.p. An excellent biography of Darwin's life and summary of Darwin's ideas on evolution.

Darwin, Francis, ed. *The Life and Letters of Charles Darwin.* 1887. 3 vols. Johnson 1969 repr. of 1888 ed. $110.00. ISBN 0-384-10900-4. Features extensive personal information about Darwin and his family; written by his son, Francis.

Gale, Barry G. *Evolution without Evidence: Charles Darwin and the Origin of Species.* U. of NM Pr. 1982 o.p.

Ghiselin, Michael. *The Triumph of the Darwinian Method.* U. Ch. Pr. 1984 repr. of 1969 ed. $9.95. ISBN 0-226-29024-7. Covers an important but neglected subject—Darwin's methodology; written by a research biologist.

Gillespie, Neal C. *Charles Darwin and the Problems of Creation.* U. Ch. Pr. 1982 o.p.

Grene, Marjorie, ed. *Dimensions of Darwinism: Themes and Counterthemes in Twentieth Century Evolutionary Theory.* Cambridge U. Pr. 1986 o.p.

Hull, David L. *Darwin and His Critics: The Reception of Darwin's Theory of Evolution by the Scientific Community.* U. Ch. Pr. 1983 $17.00. ISBN 0-226-36046-6. "Writing clearly and cogently, [Hull] skillfully combines five of his own brief essays with an anthology of 16 contemporary reviews of 'The Origin of Species' and adds helpful comments" (*Choice*).

Irvine, William. *Apes, Angels, and Victorians: The Story of Darwin, Huxley, and Evolution.* U. Pr. of Amer. 1983 o.p. Presents a combination of information and humor about Charles Darwin, T. H. Huxley, and the impact of Darwinism on the nineteenth-century world.

Livingstone, David N. *Darwin's Forgotten Defenders: The Encounter between Evangelical Theology and Evolutionary Thought.* Eerdmans 1987 $10.95. ISBN 0-8028-0260-5

Parker, Steve. *Charles Darwin and Evolution.* HarpC 1992 $14.00. ISBN 0-06-020733-7. Objective and exciting presentation of this all-too-controversial scientist.

Porter, Duncan, and others. *The Portable Darwin.* Viking Penguin 1993 ISBN 0-14-015109-5. Another in the Viking Penguin series which has proven its comprehensive coverage of various figures in history.

Richards, Robert J. *The Meaning of Evolution.* U. Ch. Pr. 1993 $9.95. ISBN 0-226-71203-6. Argues that Darwin believed evolution to be progressively producing more-advanced forms of life.

Smith, John M., ed. *Evolution Now: A Century after Darwin*. W. H. Freeman 1982 $13.95. ISBN 0-7167-1427-2. A fine collection of review articles originally printed in *Nature* and other journals.

Young, Robert M. *Darwin's Metaphor: Nature's Place in Victorian Culture*. Cambridge U. Pr. 1985 $21.95. ISBN 0-521-31742-2

DUBOS, RENÉ JULES. 1901–1982

René Dubos was a famous microbiologist, as well as a writer, educator, and environmentalist. Born and educated in France, Dubos came to the United States in 1924 to join the research staff of Rutgers University. In 1927 he was invited to join the staff of Rockefeller University, where he spent practically his entire career. At Rockefeller University, Dubos pioneered research in antibiotics for commercial use during the 1940s. In 1939 he discovered tyrothricin, the first commercially produced antibiotic. As he grew older, his interests shifted from microbiology to humanistic and social-environmental issues. He devoted much of his writing to environmental problems and their impact on human beings.

Dubos served as president of several professional organizations in the sciences, wrote 20 books, and was awarded more than a score of prizes by the scientific community. As an emeritus professor at Rockefeller University he continued to write until his death.

BOOKS BY DUBOS

Celebrations of Life. McGraw 1981 o.p.

Dreams of Reason: Science and Utopias. Col. U. Pr. 1961 o.p. "Dubos develops his theme with wit, irony, art and facts" (*The New Yorker*).

God Within. Macmillan 1984 $25.00. ISBN 0-684-17979-2

Louis Pasteur: Free Lance of Science. Da Capo 1986 repr. of 1960 ed. $11.95. ISBN 0-306-80262-7

Man Adapting. 1965. Yale U. Pr. 1980 $47.00. ISBN 0-300-02581-5. "An incisive analysis of the situation in organized medicine, which continues to define all minute particulars of life without adapting to the new problems posed by the modern social conflict" (*Atlantic*).

Only One Earth: The Care and Maintenance of a Small Planet. (coauthored with Barbara Ward). Norton 1983 o.p. Provides background information on the "fact of environmental interrelationships—air, water, land, energy resources—and the consequences of policies which ignore these interrelationships" (*America*).

The Professor, the Institute, and DNA. Rockefeller U. Pr. 1976 $15.00. ISBN 0-87470-022-1

Reason Awake: Science for Man. Col. U. Pr. 1970 $44.00. ISBN 0-231-03181-5. "Dubos attempts to determine the role of science in human life and the growth of civilization . . . [and] indicates new attitudes and directions that could help man to find his place within nature" (*Library Journal*).

So Human an Animal. Macmillan 1968 $10.95. ISBN 0-684-71753-0. Dubos "asserts that we are as much the product of our total environment as of our genetic endowment . . . that we can change our suicidal course by learning to deal scientifically with the living experience of man" (Publisher's note).

Torch of Life. S&S Trade 1962 o.p.

The Unseen World. Rockefeller U. Pr. 1962 o.p. "The story of microorganisms, both disease producing agents and 'domesticated' microbes that yield beer, cheese, antibiotics, etc." (*New York Times Book Review*).

The Wooing of Earth. Scribner 1980 o.p. "In a rebuttal to those who equate ecological and environmental purity with unspoiled wilderness, Dubos argues in this extended essay that humankind irretrievably changes the natural world and that the results do not have to be detrimental" (*Library Journal*).

World of Rene Dubos: A Collection of His Writings. H. Holt & Co. 1992 $16.95. ISBN 0-
   8050-2110-8. A collection of Dubos's writings for the nonscientist that focuses on
   ecological issues and future directions of science.

FABRE, JEAN HENRI. 1823–1915

Born at Saint-Léons, a small town in southern France, the French entomolo-
gist Jean Henri Fabre worked directly from nature. After a period teaching at
French schools and universities, he spent all his time observing and writing
about insect behavior. His well-known essays on the life and habits of various
insects are imaginative and charming. Now out of print is his well-known *The
Marvels of the Insect World* (1938), selected translations from his main 10-
volume work *Souvenirs entomologiques* (1879–1907). Fabre's greatest accomplishment in biology was his research that illustrated the crucial role of
instinctual behavior in insects.

BOOKS BY FABRE

The Insect World of J. Henri Fabre. Ed. by Edwin Way Teale. Beacon Pr. 1991 $12.95.
   ISBN 0-8070-8513-8. Contains some of the most vivid and perceptive insect studies
   ever written; a fine overview of Fabre's studies, accessible to the general reader.
The Life of the Spider. Norwood 1912 o.p. Selections in English from his principal work,
   Souvenirs entomologiques.
Social Life in the Insect World. Ayer repr. of 1912 ed. $23.50. ISBN 0-8369-6646-5. Covers
   familiar insects, their habits, and life stages. Fabre presents his observations in a
   romantic and "humanized style." A good popular introduction to insect life.

FRISCH, KARL VON. 1887–1982 (NOBEL PRIZE 1973)

The Austrian zoologist Karl von Frisch achieved international recognition for
his pioneer research on sense functions in fish and for his discovery of the
"language" of bees. In *The Dancing Bees*, von Frisch explains how these insects
are able to communicate the direction, quantity, and quality of food through
dances.

As a student, von Frisch studied medicine and zoology in Vienna and Munich.
In 1910 he joined the faculty of the University of Munich and was associated
with it intermittently until his retirement as professor of zoology in 1958. He
also spent many years as the director of the zoological institutes in Rostock,
Breslau, and Munich and was active in the international scientific community,
lecturing in the United States and Europe.

In 1959 von Frisch was awarded the Kalinga Prize and in 1963 a Balzan Prize.
In 1973 he shared the Nobel Prize for physiology or medicine for his
contributions in sociobiology. Von Frisch died at the age of 96, ending a
productive and rewarding life.

BOOKS BY VON FRISCH

Bees: Their Vision, Chemical Senses and Language. Cornell Univ. Pr. 1971 o.p.
Dance Language and Orientation of Bees. HUP 1967 $45.00. ISBN 0-674-19050-5. This is
   still the major source on bee communication.
The Dancing Bees: An Account of the Life and Senses of the Honey Bee. Trans. by Dora Ilse
   and Norman Walker. HarBraceJ 1961 o.p.
Man and the Living World. HarBraceJ 1963 o.p. A fine introduction to biology for the
   general reader.
Twelve Little Housemates. Pergamon 1979 $60.00. ISBN 0-08-021959-4. A book on insects
   that are common household pests; written for general readers.

HALDANE, JOHN BURDON SANDERSON. 1892–1964

The son of a noted British physiologist, J. B. Haldane was an eccentric genius, described as "the last man who might know all there was to know." A student of classics at Oxford University, he became a brilliant biochemist, physiologist, geneticist, and Marxist revolutionary (until he broke with the Communist party during the 1950s over its uncritical reverence for the Russian geneticist Trofim Denisovich Lysenko). During his Communist period, Haldane did important work in science for the British government. An officer in World War I, he later taught at the University of London (1933–1957) and made remarkable discoveries in the application of mathematics and statistics to biology. Upset by the British attack on Egypt over Suez, Haldane spent his last years researching and holding various scientific posts in India, though he traveled back to England on several occasions. On one of his visits to England, Haldane saw his obituary on BBC television.

Haldane was known for trying dangerous experiments on himself and for his lucid and enthusiastic expositions for the general reader. "This ability to entrance," writes Ronald Clark, "was due partly to his humble wonder at the world around him [and partly to] his facility for linking the facets of one science with those of all of the rest: beneath this there lay the touchstones of personal integrity, honesty and courage" (*Journal of Biological Sciences*).

BOOKS BY HALDANE

Causes of Evolution. Princeton U. Pr. 1990 $7.95. ISBN 0-691-92442-1. Summarizes the genetic evidence on variation and the theory of natural selection; includes a new introduction by E. G. Leigh, which puts Haldane's work in context with the ongoing research in evolution.

Daedalus, or Science and the Future. 1923. Quaker City Bks. o.p. Prophesizes about the future of the sciences and the subsequent impact on human life. "Mr. Haldane's is a brilliant little book, sparkling here and there with a witty thought or turn of phrase, often daring in some casual statement" (*New York Tribune*).

Keeping Cool and Other Essays. Richard West repr. of 1940 ed. o.p.

Marxist Philosophy and the Sciences. Ayer repr. of 1939 ed. $15.00. ISBN 0-8369-1137-7. Covers mathematical, biological, and sociological problems from a Marxist point of view.

On Being the Right Size and Other Essays. Ed. by John M. Smith. OUP 1985 $9.95. ISBN 0-19-286045-3

The Philosophical Basis of Biology. Richard West 1931 o.p. Presents his view of the "nature of life" based on his own observations as a biologist; based on a series of lectures Haldane delivered at Trinity College in 1930.

The Philosophy of a Biologist. Richard West 1955 o.p.

Possible Worlds: and Other Papers. Ayer repr. of 1928 ed. $18.00. ISBN 0-8369-2452-5. A collection of lectures, broadcasts, and essays expressing a Marxist point of view on biological and sociological issues.

Science and Everyday Life. Ayer 1975 $25.50. ISBN 0-405-06595-7

Science and Human Life. Ayer repr. of 1933 ed. $19.00. ISBN 0-8369-2161-5. The concept that unifies this collection of essays, addresses, and lectures is how science affects human life. "Only a man of independent thought, originality of view and exceptional literary gifts could be sure that a miscellany of this type would be read with interest. He is as fascinating to himself as any of the dahlias, fruit flies, mice and other organisms with which he experiments" (*New York Times*).

BOOKS ABOUT HALDANE

Clark, Ronald. *JBS: The Life and Work of J.B.S. Haldane*. OUP 1984 o.p. "J.B.S. Haldane loomed larger than life in so many ways that is difficult to compress his accomplishments and personality into a brief biography. Ronald Clark, who based his work on primary sources . . . has met the challenge, however, in this delightful, balanced, well-written study of both the man and his work. He presents scientific explanations with a lucidity likely to have pleased Haldane himself. He includes the details of Haldane's often flamboyant life without sensationalism but also without sloughing over highly controversial works. . . . I cannot recommend this book too highly" (*Library Journal*).

Dronamraju, Krishna R., ed. *Haldane and Modern Biology*. Johns Hopkins 1968 o.p. A fascinating collection of essays by an international group of scientists.

———. *Selected Genetic Papers of J.B.S. Haldane*. Garland 1993 $120.00. ISBN 0-8240-0473-6. The introductions by the editor place each essay in the context of Haldane's life and work.

Smith, Maynard, ed. *On Being the Right Size and Other Essays*. OUP 1985 $9.95. ISBN 0-19-286045-3. Presents a compilation of Haldane's essays written between 1920 and 1950.

HUXLEY, SIR JULIAN SORRELL. 1887–1975

Sir Julian Huxley, elder brother of novelist ALDOUS HUXLEY (see Vol. 1), was born in London, the eldest son of Leonard Huxley, biographer and historian; "the nephew of Mrs. Humphrey Ward"; the grand nephew of MATTHEW ARNOLD (see Vol. 1); and the grandson of the great scientist THOMAS HENRY HUXLEY. Julian Huxley began gathering honors while at Balliol College, and Oxford University, where he lectured on zoology for two years (1910–1912). One of the leading popularizers of science, he was a gifted master of lucid prose and wrote innumerable articles and books, many on science for the layperson on subjects ranging from "the evolutionary conception of God to the politics of ants." Huxley is credited with coining the term *ethology* to indicate the science of animal behavior. He advocated a scientific humanism as a substitute for the mysticism of the past. Huxley was interested in politics, as well as science, serving as the first director-general of UNESCO (1946–48). In January 1960, Huxley received the New York University Medal following his lecture entitled "Evolution in Our Time." "My final belief is life," was his stated philosophy.

BOOKS BY SIR JULIAN HUXLEY

Africa View. Greenwood 1968 repr. of 1930 ed. o.p. Huxley spent four months traveling in East Africa, during which time he kept a daily record of his thoughts, activities, and observations. Written from his daily record, enriched with his views on imperialism, education, and science.

Ants. AMS Pr. 1985 repr. of 1930 ed. $20.00. ISBN 0-404-03467-5. Huxley's view of ants and his essays on the various aspects of ant life are informative, as well as gracefully written.

Essays of a Biologist. Telegraph Bks. repr. of 1923 ed. $19.00. ISBN 0-8369-1613-1. A collection of addresses, lectures, and essays on progress in biology and sociology and on the relationship of science and religion. "The book covers a wide field and Mr. Huxley shows himself to be a man of many parts . . . attractive style of writing" (*New York Times*).

Heredity, East and West: Lysenko and World Science. Kraus Repr. 1969 repr. of 1949 ed. o.p.

Man Stands Alone. Ayer repr. of 1941 ed. $22.00. ISBN 0-8369-1961-0. A collection of essays on natural science, evolution, humanism, and religion; originally published in London under the title *The Uniqueness of Man*.

Religion without Revelation. Greenwood 1979 repr. of 1967 ed. $35.00. ISBN 0-313-21225-2

Science and Religion. Ayer repr. of 1931 ed. $14.25. ISBN 0-8369-1106-7

BOOKS ABOUT SIR JULIAN HUXLEY

Baker, J. R. *Julian Huxley: Scientist and World Citizen, 1887–1975: A Bibliographic Memoir.* UNIPUB 1978 $7.00. ISBN 92-3-101461-7

Dronamraju, Krishna R. *If I Am to be Remembered.* World Scientific Pub. 1993 $38.00. ISBN 981-02-1142-2. A biographical account of Julian Huxley that presents a selection of his letters and writings; includes a biographical summary and a complete bibliography.

HUXLEY, THOMAS HENRY. 1825–1895

Born at Ealing (a suburb of London), England, Thomas Henry Huxley, "the great agnostic," the living example of the high ethical standard of the true evolutionist and the true rationalist, devoted himself almost exclusively to the defense and exposition of CHARLES DARWIN's theory of evolution. Like Darwin, he started his scientific investigations while on a long voyage to distant places. He was assistant surgeon on the *H.M.S. Rattlesnake*, sent to explore Australia and the Great Barrier Reef, and stayed with the ship throughout the voyage (1846–50). Although he was one of the foremost anatomists of his time, his lectures and books were predominantly on Darwinism. He had the "gift for the apt and acid phrase" and his "pure, rapid, athletic English" has stood as a model for all scientific writers. Huxley was later secretary and president of the Royal Society and a member of many royal commissions. His period on the London school board significantly influenced British educational reform.

BOOKS BY THOMAS HENRY HUXLEY

Autobiography and Essays. Ed. by Brander Matthews. Kraus Repr. 1969 repr. of 1919 ed. o.p.

Collected Essays. 1894. 9 vols. Greenwood 1979 repr. of 1902 ed. $138.00. ISBN 0-8371-0491-2. Presents Huxley's thought on science, religion, and education.

Critiques and Addresses. Ayer repr. of 1873 ed. $15.50. ISBN 0-8366-2908-X

Darwiniana. AMS Pr. repr. of 1896 ed. $39.50. ISBN 0-404-03468-3. A collection of articles and essays that Huxley wrote in defense of Darwin's theory of evolution.

Diary of the Voyage of the H.M.S. Rattlesnake. Kraus Repr. repr. of 1936 ed. o.p. Documents *Rattlesnake*'s voyage in the Pacific waters north of Australia, which provided a natural laboratory that Huxley used to study medusae and plankton. On this voyage, Huxley's work led him to be a master at invertebrate zoology, and his later work and thought stem from this trip.

Huxley: Selections from the Essays. Ed. by Aubrey Castell. Harlan Davidson 1948 o.p. Huxley's essays are valuable to anyr eader interested in the history and philosophy of science.

Man's Place in Nature and Other Essays. 1863. Richard West 1979 repr. of 1906 ed. o.p. Refutes the anatomist Richard Owen's view that human beings differ from other animals in brain structure.

BOOKS ABOUT THOMAS HENRY HUXLEY

Ainsworth-Davies, James R. *Thomas H. Huxley.* AMS Pr. 1974 repr. of 1907 ed. $21.50. ISBN 0-404-07829-3

Clodd, Edward. *Thomas Henry Huxley.* AMS Pr. repr. of 1902 ed. $20.00. ISBN 0-404-14023-8

DiGregorio, Mario A. *T. H. Huxley's Place in Natural Science.* Yale U. Pr. 1984 o.p.

Irvine, William. *Thomas Henry Huxley.* British Bk. Ctr. o.p.

Jensen, J. Vernon. *Thomas Henry Huxley: Communicating for Science.* U. Delaware Pr. 1991 $38.50. ISBN 0-87413-379-3. A collection of the author's essays about Huxley's public lectures.

Landau, Misia. *Narratives of Human Evolution.* Yale U. Pr. 1991 $25.00. ISBN 0-300-04940-4. A lucid and well-written book that summarizes the theories of Darwin, Haeckel, and Huxley.

Marshall, A. J. *Darwin and Huxley in Australia.* Verry 1971 o.p.

Paradis, James, and George C. Williams. *Evolution and Ethics.* Princeton U. Pr. 1989 $45.00. ISBN 0-691-98535-8. Places Huxley's famous lecture "Evolution and Ethics" in a Victorian context and in a biological perspective; written by an expert in Victorian studies (Paradis) and a biologist (Williams).

Peterson, Houston. *Huxley: Prophet of Science.* AMS Pr. repr. of 1932 ed. $26.00. ISBN 0-404-14040-8

JACOB, FRANÇOIS. 1920– (NOBEL PRIZE 1965)

Born in Nancy, France, François Jacob is a major figure in modern genetics. He shared the Nobel Prize with two other Frenchmen, Andre Lwoff and Jacques Monod, for explication of the "lac operon" (a gene regulation mechanism) in the bacterium E.Coli. The "lac operon" responds to information from outside the cell by activating (or inhibiting) certain genes that govern the production of enzymes involved in the metabolism of lactose and other sugars. This was the first gene regulation system to be fully understood, representing a major breakthrough in the field.

Jacob spent his youth and attended medical school in Paris. In 1940, when the Germans invaded France, he left medical school and joined the Free French Army. He fought the Germans in North Africa for four years and was injured during the Normandy invasion. After a long period of hospitalization, Jacob finished medical school. He did not recover sufficiently from his injuries to become a surgeon, so after graduation he accepted a job in an antibiotics laboratory. In 1950 he worked in Andre Lwoff's laboratory at the Pasteur Institute and began his research in genetics. In 1960 he became chairman of the Department of Cellular Genetics at the Pasteur Institute and in 1964 was appointed professor of the Collège de France. Since winning the Nobel Prize in 1965, Jacob has continued his research and has written scientific and popular books.

BOOKS BY JACOB

The Logic of Life. Trans. by Betty E. Spillman. Princeton U. Pr. 1993 repr. of 1973 ed. $12.95. ISBN 0-691-00042-5. Presents the history of genetics and molecular biology for the beginning student or general reader; includes bibliographical references and an index.

The Possible and the Actual. Pantheon 1982 $3.95. ISBN 0-394-70671-4. Features Jacob's Danz lecture on biological variation and evolution.

The Statue Within. Trans. by Franklin Phillip. Basic 1988 $22.95. ISBN 0-465-08223-8. "There are few scientists who will reveal the core of their personalities and then describe their emotions, strivings, hopes, and fears as felicitiously and elegantly" (*Journal of the American Medical Association*).

KOCH, ROBERT. 1843–1910 (NOBEL PRIZE 1905)

Born in Clausthal, Germany, Robert Koch first studied the natural sciences at Göttingen University and then switched to the medical school. In 1866 he graduated, went to Berlin, and worked in charity clinics.

Koch practiced medicine in a rural community for a short time and then joined the army to serve as a field physician. He gained valuable experience serving on the battlefield during the Franco-Prussian War. Upon leaving the army, he obtained a post as district physician in Wollstein, Austria. There, in

1876 during a severe anthrax outbreak, Koch made his first important discovery. He identified the bacillus that causes anthrax—the first time a specific pathogen was proven to cause a specific disease. This breakthrough earned Koch an appointment to the Imperial Health Service in Berlin.

Koch's next achievement was the identification of the tuberculosis bacillus and the explanation of its mode of transmission. In 1905 Koch won the Nobel Prize for physiology and medicine for his work on tuberculosis.

Berlin was Koch's headquarters for most of his lifetime, and he was promoted to higher ranks in the Imperial Health Service. Throughout his lifetime, he traveled extensively to the sites of different epidemics in Europe and Africa. He identified the organism that causes cholera in 1883, as well as bacteria that cause other human and animal epidemics.

Koch's work established him as the founder of modern bacteriology, tropical medicine, and public health. Among his major contributions are "Koch's Postulates," the principles that have been used to diagnose disease agents. He also developed the methods used for culturing and staining bacteria, growing pure bacterial cultures, and using steam as a sterilizer. Koch had an enormous impact on the development of the field of public health, serving as the first director of the Berlin Institute for Infectious Diseases (1891). He was responsible for much early public health legislation in Europe and for developing public awareness of disease control through hygienic and immunologic measures.

BOOK BY KOCH

Founders of Modern Medicine. 1939. Ed. by Ilia Ilich Mechnikov, Louis Pasteur, Joseph Lister, and Robert Koch. Trans. by D. Berger. Ayer repr. of 1939 ed. $21.00. ISBN 0-8369-2119-9. Contains three essays, one by Pasteur, one by Lister, and "The Etiology of Wound Infections" by Koch.

BOOKS ABOUT KOCH

Brock, Thomas D. *Robert Koch: A Life in Medicine and Bacteriology.* Sci. Tech. Pubs. 1988 $35.00. ISBN 0-910239-19-3. Description of the life and the tremendous accomplishments of Koch.

DeKruif, Paul. *Microbe Hunters.* HarBraceJ 1966 $6.95. ISBN 0-15-659413-7. Stories of scientists who made great discoveries with a microscope; includes discussion of Koch.

Dolan, Edward F., Jr. *Adventure with a Microscope.* Dodd 1964 o.p. Story of Koch's achievements, beginning with the gift of a microscope from his wife.

Riedman, Sarah R. *Shots without Guns: The Story of Vaccination.* Rand 1960 o.p. Story of the fight against epidemics of diseases from smallpox to polio.

Walker, M. E. *Pioneers of Public Health: The Story of Some Benefactors of the Human Race.* Ayer repr. of 1930 ed. $20.00. ISBN 0-8369-0965-8. Sketches of the lives and works of scientists who greatly influenced medicine and public health.

KREBS, HANS ADOLF. 1900–1981 (NOBEL PRIZE 1953)

Born in Hildesheim, Germany, Hans Adolf Krebs studied medicine at the universities of Göttingen, Freiburg, Munich, and Berlin. In 1925 he received a medical degree from the University of Hamburg and then became a laboratory assistant at the Kaiser Wilhelm Institute of Biology in Berlin. In 1930 Krebs began a private practice and did research. As Adolf Hitler rose to power, Krebs left Germany and went to England, where he received an M.S. in biochemistry from Cambridge University. In 1935 he became a lecturer at the University of Sheffield, where he carried out research in cell metabolism. In 1937 Krebs discovered the citric acid cycle, a complex set of reactions that take place continuously in cellular respiration. This cycle, commonly called the Krebs cycle, is an essential part of the process in which organisms obtain energy from food. Krebs received a share of the 1953 Nobel Prize in physiology and medicine for this discovery. In 1954 Krebs became a professor at Oxford University, where he remained until 1967. After his retirement from Oxford, he continued his investigations of cell metabolism.

BOOKS BY KREBS

Otto Warburg: Cell Physiologist, Biochemist, and Eccentric. OUP 1981 $36.00. ISBN 0-19-858171-8

Reminiscences and Reflections. OUP 1982 $35.00. ISBN 0-19-854702-1

LAMARCK, JEAN BAPTISTE (JEAN BAPTISTE PIERRE ANTOINE DE MONET, CHEVALIER DE LAMARCK). 1744–1829

Jean Baptiste Lamarck made significant contributions to the disciplines of botany, zoology, and paleontology. Born in Picardy, France, he studied at a Jesuit seminary, but he never completed his training for the priesthood. Lamarck joined the army and fought in the Seven Years' War. During this time, he developed an interest in Mediterranean flora and began to do botanical research. As a result of his work, he was appointed Keeper of the Royal Garden in 1774. The first recognition Lamarck received as a scientist was for his design of a new classification scheme for plants, which was published in 1778 as *Flore française*. His other major botanical works were *Dictionnaire botanique*, an encyclopedic work finished in 1795, and *Introduction à botanique*, published in 1803. Lamarck had begun work in zoology and paleontology in the 1790s. In 1801 he published his most significant work on invertebrate zoology—*Système des animaux sans vertèbres*. His major paleontological work, *Memoires sur les fossiles des environs de Paris*, was written between 1802 and 1806.

Lamarck's evolutionary theories were presented in *Recherche sur l'organisation des corps vivans* (1802). Lamarck claimed that over long periods of time, life forms evolved and grew increasingly complex. He attributed these changes in form to the inheritability of acquired traits. This theory was widely publicized and had great impact on the future of biology. Although his theories were proven fallacious by the work of other evolutionists, Lamarck paved the way for CHARLES DARWIN and ALFRED RUSSEL WALLACE, by establishing the conceptual basis for the theory of descent.

During his later years, Lamarck's reputation declined. He proposed theories in chemistry and physics that were ridiculed. Ten years before his death, Lamarck went blind but continued to work despite poverty and blindness. In fact, he was beset by tragedy throughout his life. Lamarck was widowed three times and had two sons: one was deaf and the other was insane.

BOOK BY LAMARCK

Zoological Philosophy: An Exposition with Regard to the Natural History of Animals. Trans. by Hugh Elliot. AMS Pr. repr. of 1914 ed. $57.50. ISBN 0-404-19353-6

BOOKS ABOUT LAMARCK

Barthelemy-Madaule, Madeleine. *Lamarck the Mythical Precursor: A Study of the Relations between Science and Ideology.* Trans. by Michael Shank. MIT Pr. 1982 $25.00. ISBN 0-262-02179-X. "The thesis is established that Lamarck was an heir of the enlightenment and founder of a new science, but the many references make the book difficult to read" (*Choice*).

Burkhardt, Richard W., Jr. *The Spirit of System: Lamarck and Evolutionary Biology.* HUP 1977 $25.00. ISBN 0-674-83317-1. "All in all Burkhardt has given us an important and reliable study, no doubt the major source now on the topic" (*Science*).

Cannon, H. Graham. *Lamarck and Modern Genetics.* Greenwood repr. of 1959 ed. $45.00. ISBN 0-8371-8173-9

Jordanova, L. J. *Lamarck.* OUP 1984 $14.95. ISBN 0-19-287587-6. "Jordanova provides not only an effective introduction to Lamarck's work, but also a highly original interpretation" (*Times Literary Supplement*).

McKinney, H., ed. *Lamarck to Darwin: Contributions to Evolutionary Biology, 1809–1859.* Coronado Pr. 1971 $7.50. ISBN 0-87291-019-9

Packard, Alpheus S. *Lamarck: The Founder of Evolution: His Life and Work; with Translations of His Writings on Organic Evolution.* Ayer repr. of 1901 ed. $39.00. ISBN 0-405-12562-3

Palmer, Katherine. *The Unpublished Velins of Lamarck, 1802 to 1809: Illustrations of Fossils of the Paris Basin Eocene.* Paleo Res. 1977 $15.00. ISBN 0-87710-373-9

LEEUWENHOEK, ANTON VAN. 1632–1723

Anton van Leeuwenhoek, the famed Dutch microscopist and naturalist, was born in Delft and spent his life there. After receiving informal schooling, which probably included mathematics and science, he was apprenticed to a draper for six years. In 1654 he opened his own drapery shop, but after receiving an appointment as a minor city official in 1660, he devoted most of his time to microscopy.

Leeuwenhoek's major scientific achievements centered on the simple but remarkably accurate short-focus lenses that he produced. He carefully ground these single lenses and mounted them between metal plates to make his observations. During his career, he built nearly 250 microscopes, which had magnifying powers ranging from 50 to as high as 270 times. Employing these microscopes, Leeuwenhoek harnessed his insatiable scientific curiosity to his talent for careful, systematic observation.

Leeuwenhoek used his microscopes to study nearly 200 biological species, including aphids, birds, frogs, and fish. His most important discoveries included the minute circulation system of the blood vessels and the capillary connections between arteries and veins. He studied and clearly described red blood cells, noting their distinguishing characteristics in humans and mammals, as well as those in birds and fish. He also described and illustrated human and animal spermatozoa.

In about 1764 Leeuwenhoek began his extraordinary work in the field of microorganisms, becoming the first scientist to study and identify protozoa and bacteria under the microscope. His study of human anatomy revealed the microscopic structure of the eye, skin, teeth, and muscle. He also accomplished important work in comparative anatomy and carried out a series of microdissections on insects.

Although Leeuwenhoek wrote no scientific articles or books, he recorded and reported nearly all of his observations in more than 200 letters to the Royal Society of London and to friends and fellow scientists such as GOTTFRIED WILHELM LEIBNIZ (see Vol. 4) and CHRISTÍAN HUYGENS. Elected to the Royal Society and the French Academy of Science, Leeuwenhoek's many remarkable discoveries and observations helped refute the theory of spontaneous generation that was then widely accepted.

BOOKS BY LEEUWENHOEK

The Collected Letters of Antoni van Leeuwenhoek. 1939–67. 11 vols. Swets North Am. 1939–1984 $180.00 ea.

The Select Works of Antony van Leeuwenhoek. Ed. by Frank Egerton. Ayer 1978 repr. of
   1807 ed. $54.00. ISBN 0-405-10405-7

BOOKS ABOUT LEEUWENHOEK

Dobell, Clifford. *Antony van Leeuwenhoek and His "Little Animals."* 1932 o.p.
Ford, Bran J. *The Leeuwenhoek Legacy.* Lubrecht & Cramer 1991 $60.00. ISBN 0-
   948737-10-7. Touches on nearly every aspect of Leeuwenhoek's history.

LEVI-MONTALCINI, RITA. 1909–1989 (NOBEL PRIZE 1986)

The American biologist Rita Levi-Montalcini was born in Turin, Italy, and
earned her M.D. from the University of Turin in 1936. After she became a
clinical neurobiologist, Italy's anti-Jewish laws forced her to work in Belgium.
After Germany occupied northern Italy in World War II, she went into hiding in
Florence and then served as physician to the Allied invaders. When the war
ended, Levi-Montalcini joined Viktor Hamburger, a pioneer in experimental
embryology and a German expatriate who was chair of the department of
zoology at Washington University in St. Louis, Missouri. Together they began
experimental research on the regulatory mechanisms controlling motor and
sensory nerve cells. This research launched Levi-Montalcini's own pioneering
work in the mechanisms of neurogenesis.

During the early 1950s, Levi-Montalcini visited the Institute of Biophysics in
Rio de Janeiro; its innovative in vitro culture unit helped shape the course of
her future research. Soon after returning to Washington University, she was
joined by the biochemist STANLEY COHEN, who collaborated with her from 1953
to 1959 on research into the nerve growth factor (NFG), a natural substance that
stimulates the growth of nerve cells and fibers, and its chemical and biological
properties. Using immunological methods, they discovered the determining
role of NFG in cell differentiation and survival. For this pioneering work, they
later shared the Nobel Prize in physiology and medicine in 1986.

By 1961 Levi-Montalcini was dividing her research career between Washington University and her own Center of Neurobiology in Rome, a research center
supported by the Italian government. Later renamed the Laboratory of Cell
Biology, it has departments of cell biology, immunology, and physiological
genetics. Thanks to the efforts of Levi-Montalcini, by the late 1980s and 1990s,
NFG research had become a major area of interest for scientists engaged in
genes coding, recombinant DNA technology, and genetic engineering.

BOOKS BY LEVI-MONTALCINI

In Praise of Imperfection: My Life and Work. Basic 1989 $9.95. ISBN 0-465-03218-4. Her
   autobiography.
Nerve Cells: Transmitters and Behavior. Elsevier 1980 o.p.

LINNAEUS, CAROLUS. 1707–1778

Carolus Linnaeus was a botanist, physician, teacher, writer, and administrator. He was the most influential naturalist of his time and the founder of
biological taxonomy. His eminence is due to the development of biological
classification systems for plants and animals.

Born in Rashult, Sweden, Linnaeus, also known as Carl von Linné, studied at
the universities of Lund and Uppsala and at Harderwyck, where he received a
degree in medicine. At the age of 25, Linnaeus undertook an expedition to
Lapland to collect exotic plants. This expedition marked the beginning of a

project that would involve him for 20 years in naming, describing, and classifying every organism known to the Western world.

While pursuing his botanical and taxonomic research, Linnaeus practiced medicine to earn a living. As his research progressed, he published numerous works, including 12 editions of *Systema Naturae* (1735), *Species Plantarum* (1753), *Philosophia Botanica* (1751), and *Genera Plantarum* (1737). In 1741 he was appointed to a chair at Uppsala, and in the following year he accepted a chair in botany at the same institution. By 1758, Linnaeus had completed his taxonomic project by classifying 4,400 species of animals and 7,700 species of plants. In middle age, he became a university administrator. In 1770 Linnaeus became ill and remained sick until his death.

Linnaeus's enduring contributions were the development of the principles and methods for defining taxonomic groups and the establishment of uniform taxonomic systems. His systems are still used with some modifications and revisions.

BOOKS BY LINNAEUS

Bibliotheca Botanica. Lubrecht & Cramer 1968 $12.00. ISBN 0-934454-13-2. The second important bibliography of botany to be compiled and printed.
Carl von Linnaeus' Travels. Ed. by David Black. Scribner 1984 o.p.
Caroli Linnaei: A Photographic Facsimile of the First Volume of the Tenth Edition (1758) Regnum Animale. British Mus. of Natural History 1978 repr. of 1956 ed. o.p. The first use of Linnaen zoological classification, which became internationally accepted.
Hortus Cliffortianus. 1737. Lubrecht & Cramer 1968 repr. of 1751 ed. $162.50. ISBN 3-7682-0543-6
Index Kewensis Plantarum Phanerogarum (Linnaeus to the Year 1885). 2 vols. Ed. by J. D. Hooker and B. D. Jackson. Lubrecht & Cramer 1977 o.p.
Mantissa Plantarum, 1767–71. 2 vols. Lubrecht & Cramer 1960 $97.50. ISBN 3-7682-0037-X
Miscellaneous Tracts Relating to Natural History, Husbandry, and Physick: Calendar of Flora Is Added. Ayer 1978 repr. of 1762 ed. $29.00. ISBN 0-405-10406-5
Philosophia Botanica. 1751. Lubrecht & Cramer 1960 repr. of 1751 ed. $197.50. ISBN 3-7682-0350-6.
Select Dissertations from Amoenitates Academicae: Supplement to Mr. Stillingfleet's Tracts, Relating Natural History. Ayer 1978 repr. of 1781 ed. $38.50. ISBN 0-405-10407-3
Species Plantarum: A Facsimile of the First Edition 1753. 2 vols. British Mus. Natural History 1956 o.p. The Linnaen classification system applied to all known plants; represents the starting point for internationally accepted nomenclature.
Systema Naturae: Tomus II Vegetabilia. 1759. Lubrecht & Cramer 1964 repr. of 1759 ed. $112.50. ISBN 3-7682-0219-4. *Systema Naturae Regnum Vegetable* introduced the Linnaen classification system.

BOOKS ABOUT LINNAEUS

Broberg, Gunnar, ed. *Linnaeus: Progress and Prospects in Linnean Research*. Hunt Inst. Botanical 1980 o.p.
Frangsmyr, Tore, and others, eds. *Linnaeus: The Man and His Work*. U. CA Pr. 1983 o.p. "This book is important reading for all biologists and science historians and will interest informed layreaders" (*Library Journal*).
Gjertsen, Derek. *The Classics of Science: A Study of Twelve Enduring Scientific Works*. Barber Pr. 1984 $24.95. ISBN 0-936508-09-4
Lewis, Arthur M. *Evolution—Social and Organic: Linnaeus, Darwin, Kropotkin, Marx*. C. H. Kerr 1984 $17.95. ISBN 0-88286-088-7

Smith, James E., and Keir B. Sterling. *A Selection of the Correspondence of Linnaeus and Other Naturalists: From Original Manuscripts.* 2 vols. Ayer repr. of 1821 ed. 1978 $99.00. ISBN 0-405-10730-7

Soulsby, Basil H., ed. *A Catalogue of the World of Linnaeus Preserved in the Libraries of the British Museum of Natural History.* British Mus. of Natural History 1933–36 o.p.

Stearn, W. T. *Three Prefaces to Linnaeus and Robert Brown.* Lubrecht & Cramer 1962 o.p.

Weinstock, John. *Contemporary Perspectives on Linnaeus.* U. Pr. of Amer. 1985 $50.50. ISBN 0-8191-4697-8. Presents expanded papers from a biological history symposium and a bibliography.

West, Luther S., and Oneita B. Peters. *Annotated Bibliography of Musca Domestica Linnaeus.* N. Mich. U. Pr. 1973 $38.95. ISBN 0-7129-0536-7

MCCLINTOCK, BARBARA. 1902–1992 (NOBEL PRIZE 1983)

The American geneticist Barbara McClintock was trained as a botanist, receiving a Ph.D. in botany from Cornell University (1927). McClintock discovered anomalies in pigmentation and other features of corn (Zea Mays) that led her to question the prevailing model of the chromosome as a linear arrangement of fixed genes. Her model of the chromosome involved a process of "transposition." In this process, the chromosome released genes and groups of genes from their original positions (this subprocess is named "dislocation") and reinserted them into new positions. Although her original research was published in the 1930s and 1940s, it was not until research in molecular biology confirmed her theories that she received wide professional recognition. McClintock was elected to the National Academy at the age of 42 and was elected president of the Genetics Society of America a year later. She received many honorary degrees and other awards, including the Lasker Award and a Nobel Prize. McClintock died after a brief illness at the Carnegie Institution's Cold Spring Harbor Laboratories, where she had lived and worked for 50 years.

BOOK BY MCCLINTOCK

The Discovery and Characterization of Transposable Elements: The Collected Papers of Barbara McClintock. Garland 1987 o.p. A collection of research papers; requires an advanced knowledge of genetics.

BOOKS ABOUT MCCLINTOCK

Federoff, Nina, and David Botstein, eds. *Dynamic Genome: Barbara McClintock's Ideas in the Century of Genetics.* Cold Spring Harbor Pr. 1992 $65.00. ISBN 0-87969-422-X. A collection of essays about McClintock's personality, life, and work; written to commemorate McClintock's ninetieth birthday by a group of her peers in genetics.

Keller, Evelyn Fox. *A Feeling for the Organism: The Life and Work of Barbara McClintock.* W. H. Freeman 1983 $20.95. ISBN 0-7167-1433-7. Features a brief psychobiology of the reclusive McClintock. Also describes her giftedness, unconventional parents, and inherent capacity to be alone, self-entertained, and absorbed in whatever project she pursued.

MENDEL, GREGOR JOHANN. 1822–1884

Gregor Mendel was an Austrian biologist and a Roman Catholic monk whose classic article on the breeding of peas (1866), published in an obscure journal, was ignored in his lifetime and only rediscovered at the turn of the twentieth century, 16 years after his death. It described Mendel's crucial discoveries in genetics, based on intensive experimentation; these discoveries, now known as Mendel's laws, concern the incidence of dominant and recessive characteristics and other factors in the offspring of plant and animal families. Besides their importance for understanding human biological inheritance, they have been applied extensively in the breeding of animals and plants.

BOOK BY MENDEL

Experiments in Plant–Hybridization. 1866. HUP 1965 $4.95. ISBN 0-674-27800-3. Mendel's original paper recounting the experiments that led him to formulate his laws of inheritance. This translation is easily accessible to the undergraduate. The foreword gives a brief history of the rediscovery of Mendel's work.

BOOKS ABOUT MENDEL

Olby, Robert C. *The Origins of Mendelism.* U. Ch. Pr. 1985 $38.00. ISBN 0-226-62593-3. Covers the history of hybridization experiments and related studies before Mendel by Georges Louis LeClerc du Buffon, Rudolph Camerius, Carl Linneaus, Johann Hedwig, Augustin Sageret, and especially Joseph Gottlieb Koelreuter and Carl von Gaertner. Also discusses the work of Mendel, Darwin, Naudin, and Galton and the rediscovery of Mendel's work by De Vries, Correns, and Tshermak; includes photographs, illustrations, notes, appendices, and an index.

Stern, Curt, and Eva R. Sherwood, eds. *The Origin of Genetics: A Mendel Source Book.* W. H. Freeman 1966 o.p. An anthology of the original papers and correspondences of Mendel and one of those who rediscovered his work 34 years after its publication; includes the papers of Hugo De Vries of Holland and Carl Correns of Germany.

MORGAN, THOMAS HUNT. 1866–1945 (NOBEL PRIZE 1933)

A pioneer of genetics research in the first half of the twentieth century, Thomas Morgan won the Nobel Prize in 1933 for research that he had begun in 1910 with the fruit fly (*Drosophila melanogaster*). Reaching sexual maturity 12 to 14 hours after birth, the fruit fly had a number of heritable traits, primarily variations of wing shape and eye color, as well as large chromosomes easily visible under the microscopes of the time. The results of the experiments conducted in "The Fly Room," Morgan's laboratory at Columbia University, showed that two apparently different explanations of heredity, the chromosome theory (which identified the chromosomes of the cell nuclei as agents of heredity) and the Mendelian laws of inheritance were closely related. Morgan's contributions to genetics included the ideas that GREGOR MENDEL's factors or determinants of characteristics (now called genes) were grouped together on chromosomes, that some characteristics are sex-linked, and that the position of genes on chromosomes can be mapped.

BOOKS BY MORGAN

Embryology and Genetics. Greenwood 1975 repr. of 1934 ed. o.p. Covers such topics as the gametes, egg cleavage, gastrulation, twinning, parthenogenesis, sex determination, and larval and foetal types; includes illustrations, notes, and an index.

The Mechanism of Mendelian Heredity. (coauthored with Hermann Joseph Muller). 1915. Johnson Repr. 1972 repr. of 1915 ed. $35.00. ISBN 0-384-40136-8

The Theory of the Gene. Richard West 1985 repr. of 1926 ed. o.p. Covers Mendelian principles, particularly theories of mechanism in heredity, the relationship of chromosome to gene, mutation, tetraploids, haploids, triploids, polyploids and heteroploids, sex determination, intersexes, and sex reversal.

BOOKS ABOUT MORGAN

Garland, Allan E. *Thomas Hunt Morgan: A Scientific Biography.* Princeton U. Pr. 1978 $65.00. ISBN 0-691-08200-6

Maienschein, Jane. *Transforming Traditions in American Biology.* Johns Hopkins 1991 $48.00. ISBN 0-8018-4126-7. Presents a collective biography of four pioneers in biology: Edmund Beecher Wilson, Edward Grant Conklin, Thomas Hunt Morgan, and Ross Granville Harrison.

Shine, Ian B., and Sylvia Wrobel. *Thomas Hunt Morgan: Pioneer of Genetics*. U. Pr. of Ky. 1976 $20.00. ISBN 0-8131-0095-X. A brief biography accessible to high school students; includes an illustration of the Morgan family tree, photographs, a chronology, notes, and index.

MULLER, HERMANN JOSEPH. 1890–1967 (NOBEL PRIZE 1946)

An American geneticist, Hermann Muller was one of THOMAS HUNT MORGAN'S students at Columbia University (receiving a Ph.D. in 1916), and a coauthor with Morgan of *The Mechanism of Mendelian Heredity*. In this book, they codified their view that chromosomes contained GREGOR MENDEL's factors, or determinants of the characteristics of organisms. Muller received the Nobel Prize in 1946 for research that grew out of Morgan's "Fly Room." Muller demonstrated that radiation was mutagenic—that it caused changes in the genes of irradiated cells. During the 1950s, Muller campaigned against the testing of nuclear weapons. He was a professor of biology for more than 40 years, teaching at the University of Texas (1920–1932) and at the University of Indiana (1945–1964).

BOOKS BY MULLER

Genetics, Medicine, and Man. Cornell Univ. Pr. 1947 o.p.

Man's Future Birthright: Essays on Science and Humanity. 1973. Ed. by Elof Axel Carlson. St. U. of NY Pr. 1973 o.p. Includes nine papers from 1939 to 1967 in which Nobel laureate Muller discusses the eugenics movement and mutagenic dangers of radiation and speculates on the prospects for extraterrestrial life.

The Mechanism of Mendelian Heredity. 1915. (coauthored with Thomas Hunt Morgan). Johnson Repr. 1972 repr. of 1915 ed. $35.00. ISBN 0-384-40136-8

The Modern Concept of Nature: Essays on Theoretical Biology and Evolution by H. J. Muller. Ed. by Elof Axel Carlson. St. U. of NY Pr. 1973 o.p. Presents 10 scientific papers published from 1922 to 1958; includes a chronology of Muller's life, a list of his honors and awards, and a glossary of genetics terminology.

Out of the Night: A Biologist's View of the Future. Ed. by Charles Rosenberg. Garland 1984 repr. of 1935 ed. o.p.

Studies in Genetics: The Selected Papers of H. J. Muller. Ind. U. Pr. 1962 o.p. An anthology that covers the chromosome basis of heredity and linkage, genotype-phenotype relations, gene theory, spontaneous mutation, radiation-induced mutations, chromosome properties, heterochromatin, evolution, and human genetics; includes an index.

BOOK ABOUT MULLER

Carlson, Elof Axel. *Genes, Radiation and Society: The Life and Work of H. J. Muller.* Cornell Univ. Pr. 1981 o.p. Discusses Muller's criticism of the American eugenics movement, proposal for a reformed eugenics movement, Communist party activities in the United States, and sojourns abroad; includes his life in the Soviet Union, where he debated with T. D. Lysenko, Soviet biologist and agronomist, and other leaders of the antigenetics movement.

PASTEUR, LOUIS. 1822–1895

Although his father was a tanner and his mother was the daughter of a gardener, Louis Pasteur became one of the most famous biologists of the nineteenth century. This scientific genius spent most of his life teaching at various universities through France, including the Sorbonne (1868–69) and the École Normale (1857–67) in Paris. Pasteur had a passion for work, whose virtues he liked to extol, and was able to combine his teaching with research of tremendous consequence. His discoveries about bacteria demolished once and for all the ancient belief in the "spontaneous generation" of disease. His "pasteurization" process became the widely used method of decontaminating milk and saved the wine and beer industries of France from endemic souring. Pasteur did valuable research on diseases of the silkworm (which threatened the French silk industry) and on rabies, to which the Pasteur Institute in Paris was devoted. He lived to receive many honors but declined all temptations to become wealthy.

BOOKS BY PASTEUR

Founders of Modern Medicine. Ed. by Ilia Ilich Mechnikov, Louis Pasteur, Joseph Lister, and Robert Koch. Trans. by D. Berger. Ayer repr. of 1939 ed. $21.00. ISBN 0-8369-2111-9. Offers three essays, one by Pasteur, one by Lister, and "The Etiology of Wound Infections" by Robert Koch.

Studies on Fermentation. 1879. Trans. and ed. by James B. Conant. HUP 1952 o.p. Describes his discovery of yeast as the cause of fermentation in beer and the microorganism that ferments wine. The pasteurization process was an outcome of these fermentation studies.

BOOKS ABOUT PASTEUR

Conant, James B. *Pasteur's and Tyndall's Study of Spontaneous Generation.* HUP 1953 o.p. Discusses Pasteur's fermentation research that enabled him to conclude that the yeast in fermented beer did not arise spontaneously. This provided conclusive evidence to refute the spontaneous-generation belief.

Dubos, René. *Louis Pasteur: Free Lance of Society.* Da Capo 1986 repr. of 1960 ed. $11.95. ISBN 0-306-80262-7. A look at Pasteur's life and contributions to medicine and other fields.

Eastman, Fred. *Men of Power: Thomas Jefferson, Charles Dickens, Matthew Arnold, Louis Pasteur.* 5 vols. Ayer repr. of 1938 ed. ea. $18.00. ISBN 0-8369-1991-2

Hume, David. *Bechamp vs Pasteur.* Blackwell Pubs. 1981 o.p.

Keim, Albert, and Louis Lumet. *Louis Pasteur.* Folcroft 1981 repr. of 1914 ed. o.p. Provides an illustrated biography of Louis Pasteur and a summary of his scientific work.

Koprowski, Hilary, and Stanley A. Plotkin. *World's Debt to Pasteur.* Alan R. Liss 1985 o.p.

Radot, René V. *The Life of Pasteur.* Richard West 1923 o.p.

Wood, Laura N. *Louis Pasteur.* Messner 1948 o.p. Emphasizes Pasteur's scientific work and his contributions to medical and industrial research.

PLINY THE ELDER (CAIUS PLINIUS SECUNDUS). c.a.d. 23–a.d. 79

Born into a wealthy north Italian family, Pliny the Elder was a Roman scholar and naturalist who wrote many books in the fields of natural science and military tactics. At 23, he entered the army and served in Germany, becoming an officer of a cavalry regiment. Only his great work, *Natural History*, the oldest encyclopedia (in 37 books), is extant. It covers the nature of the physical universe: geography, anthropology, zoology, botany, mineralogy, and allied subjects. Pliny was credulous; his *History* contains many unsubstantiated marvels and factual errors. He hated to waste time and his prolific output was considered authoritative for several centuries after his death. *Natural History* offers information on ancient art and general culture found nowhere else. He died of asphyxiation near Naples, while observing a massive eruption of Mount Vesuvius.

Books by Pliny the Elder

The Elder Pliny's Chapters on Chemical Subjects. 2 vols. Scholarly repr. of 1929 ed. o.p.
   Presents translated excerpts from Pliny's *Naturalis Historia.*
The Elder Pliny's Chapters on the History of Art. Rprt. Serv. 1988 repr. of 1896 ed. $59.00.
   ISBN 0-7812-0568-9
Natural History. Trans. by John I. Healy. Viking Penguin 1991 $9.95. ISBN 0-14-04413-0

Books about Pliny the Elder

Beagon, Mary. *Roman Nature: The Thought of Pliny the Elder.* OUP 1992 $59.00. ISBN 0-
   19-814726-0. Includes bibliographical references.
French, Roger, and Frank Greenaway. *Science in the Early Roman Empire: Pliny the
   Elder, His Sources and Influence.* B&N Imports 1986 $53.00. ISBN 0-389-20634-2

RAMÓN Y CAJAL, SANTIAGO. 1852–1934 (NOBEL PRIZE 1906)

Santiago Ramón y Cajal was among Spain's greatest scientists. A century ago,
his work laid the foundations for the field of modern neuroanatomy. In 1906
Ramón y Cajal shared the Nobel Prize with the Italian anatomist Camillo Golgi
for the development of the revolutionary neuron theory, which established the
neuron as the basic unit of the nervous system.

Born in Petila de Aragon in rural northeastern Spain, Ramón y Cajal was a
bright but restless child and a poor student. His father, a surgeon, apprenticed
him to a barber and later to a carpenter because he showed little academic
promise. Both of these apprenticeships were failures. Surprisingly, Ramón y
Cajal was admitted to the medical school at the University of Zaragoza,
graduating in 1873. Upon receiving his license to practice medicine, he went to
Cuba and worked as an army surgeon.

In 1875 Ramón y Cajal returned to Spain, married, and became a professor at
the University of Zaragoza. There, he began his neuroanatomical research,
which became his main interest. Soon after, he was promoted to the rank of
Extraordinary Professor and then to the directorship of the University's Medical
Museum. In 1887 he became Extraordinary Professor at the University of
Barcelona. In the following year, he published his first significant work on the
nervous system, an analysis of the structure and development of the cerebral
cortex.

In 1892 Ramón y Cajal accepted the position of chairman of the Department
of Histology and Pathological Anatomy at the University of Madrid. In 1922 he
formally retired from the University but continued to conduct research, teach,
and write his final book, *The World Seen at Eighty: Impressions of an
Ateriosclerotic.*

Books by Ramón y Cajal

Cajal on the Cerebral Cortex: An Annotated Translation of the Complete Writings. Ed. by
   Javier DeFelipe and Edward G. Jones. OUP 1988 $79.00. ISBN 0-19-505280-3. Offers
   a translation of all of Ramón y Cajal's writings on the structure and organization of
   the cerebral cortex; includes historical material on Cajal, his methods, and the
   importance of his work.
New Ideas on the Structure of the Nervous System in Man and the Vertebrates. Trans. from
   the French by Neely Swanson and Larry W. Swanson. MIT Pr. 1990 $29.95. ISBN
   0-262-18141-X. Represents Ramón y Cajal's greatest work. First published in 1899,
   Cajal translated it into French and published the enlarged edition in 1911; it was
   subsequently translated into English and German.
Precepts and Counsels on Scientific Investigation. Pacific Pr. Pub. Assn. 1951 o.p.
   Presents a classic work on scientific theory and method; written for scientists.

Recollections of My Life. MIT Pr. 1989 $17.95. ISBN 0-262-68060-2. Presents an entertaining account of the development and flowering of one of the most creative individuals in modern biology.

BOOKS ABOUT RAMÓN Y CAJAL

Cannon, Dorothy F. *Explorer of the Human Brain: the Life of Santiago Ramón y Cajal.* H. Schuman 1965 o.p. Includes a memoir by Sir Charles Sherrington.

Craigie, E. Horne, and William C. Gibson. *The World of Ramón y Cajal, With Selections from his Nonscientific Writings.* Thomas 1968 o.p.

Williams, Harley. *Don Quixote of the Microscope: An Interpretation of the Spanish Savant, Santiago Ramón y Cajal.* 1852–1934. Cape 1954 o.p.

SINNOTT, EDMUND WARE. 1888–1968

Among the world's leading botanists, Edmund Sinnott specialized in the morphology (physical form) of vascular plants. He was particularly interested in problems of biological philosophy. In *The Biology of the Spirit*, his main thesis is that "protoplasm, the basic stuff of plants and animal life, has a biological purpose." In human beings, this "goal-seeking" protoplasm, which seems to direct human motivation, is an extension of a universal reality—"God" ("Spirit," "Force," or "Personality"). In *Matter, Mind and Man*, Sinnott provides answers to the perennial questions that human beings ask about themselves and the world to form a unified and logically harmonious framework of concepts about our relationship to life and to the universe. "Our aim," he writes, "has been to fit man into the universe of matter, mind, and spirit without the necessity of dismembering him." He claimed that "only in God can man be fulfilled" (*Saturday Review*). Sinnott is the author of many textbooks.

BOOKS BY SINNOTT

Matter, Mind and Man: The Biology of Human Nature. Atheneum 1963 o.p.

Plant Morphogenesis. Krieger 1979 repr. of 1960 ed. o.p. Presents a comprehensive discussion of the phenomena of morphogenesis in plants and the main physiological factors governing plant development.

WALLACE, ALFRED RUSSEL. 1823–1913

Born in Usk, Wales, Alfred Wallace had a very limited education, yet he became a noted naturalist and independently developed the theory of evolution, which is most commonly associated with the name of CHARLES DARWIN. Wallace's formal education was completed with his graduation from grammar school at the age of 14. Having developed an interest in natural history, he avidly pursued this study during his years as a teacher in Leicester, England.

In 1848 Wallace went to Brazil to study animals of the Amazon. Returning to England in 1853, he departed a year later on an expedition to the East Indies, where he remained for nine years. It was during this time that he developed his theory of evolution, essentially the same theory of natural selection and survival of the fittest that Darwin had developed and had been painstakingly perfecting before making his views known. Wallace sent his paper setting forth his theory to Darwin, who recognized that his and Wallace's theories were the same. The theory was presented in a joint paper before the Linnaean Society, an organization of scientists, in London in 1858. With Wallace's agreement, Darwin was given the major credit for developing the theory because of the wide-ranging body of evidence that he had amassed in support of it.

BOOKS BY WALLACE

The Action of Natural Selection on Man. 1871. AMS Pr. repr. of 1871 ed. o.p.

Contributions to the Theory of Natural Selection. 1870. AMS Pr. 1978 $33.00. ISBN 0-404-08181-9

Darwinism: An Exposition of the Theory of Natural Selection with Some of Its Applications. 1891. AMS Pr. 1975 repr. of 1871 ed. $39.50. ISBN 0-404-08182-7

The Malay Archipelago. 1869. Dover 1978 $9.95. ISBN 0-486-20187-2

My Life, a Record of Events and Opinions. 2 vols. Gregg Intl. repr. of 1905 ed. $240.00. ISBN 0-576-29128-5

A Narrative of Travels on the Amazon and Rio Negro. 1853. Greenwood 1969 $35.00. ISBN 0-8371-1641-4

BOOKS ABOUT WALLACE

Fichman, Martin. *Alfred Russel Wallace.* Twayne 1981 o.p. A biography of Wallace that emphasizes his biogeographical system.

Smith, Charles H., ed. *Alfred Russel Wallace: An Anthology of His Shorter Writings.* OUP 1991 $79.00. ISBN 0-19-857725-7

WATSON, JAMES DEWEY. 1928– (NOBEL PRIZE 1962)

Born in Chicago, Illinois, James Watson is an American biologist and educator. He was a graduate of the University of Chicago and received his Ph.D. from the University of Indiana, where he was a pupil of HERMANN JOSEPH MULLER. At the Cavendish Laboratory of Cambridge University, England, Watson and the British molecular biologist FRANCIS HARRY COMPTON CRICK discovered the molecular structure of DNA in 1953. The 1962 Nobel Prize in medicine and physiology was awarded to them and to MAURICE HUGH FREDERICK WILKINS (an Irish biophysicist on whose work their studies were partly based) as a result of their published research findings. In 1988 Watson actively supported the effort to establish a unified international project to sequence and map the Human Genome, serving as head of the project for three years. Since then, he has returned to the Cold Spring Harbor Laboratories, where he has served as the director since 1968.

BOOKS BY WATSON

The Double Helix: Being a Personal Account of the Discovery of the Structure of DNA. Ed. by Gunther S. Stent. Norton 1980 $8.95. ISBN 0-393-95075-1. Includes Watson's account of the decipherment of DNA, as well as articles, correspondences, and reviews of the original volume. "Watson's account of the events leading up to the discovery unabashedly discloses the competitive atmosphere within the scientific community, the amoral tactics employed, and the less-than-logical procedures that eventually led to the discovery of the double-helical structure of DNA" (*Choice*).

The DNA Story: A Documentary History of Gene Cloning. (coauthored with John Tooze). W. H. Freeman 1983 o.p. Provides a documentary history of the debates about recombinant DNA and cloning that began in the 1960s; includes memoranda, articles, letters, and photographs.

Molecular Biology of the Gene. Benjamin-Cummings 1987 $48.95. ISBN 0-8053-9612-8. Derived from introductory undergraduate course lectures in biochemistry and molecular biology. Topics covered include Mendelian laws, cell chemistry, the chemistry of *E. coli*, weak chemical interactions, coupled reactions and group transfers, template surfaces, gene arrangement, structure and function, DNA replication, RNA transcription, protein synthesis, the genetic code, viral replication, embryology at the molecular level, cell proliferation, antibody synthesis, and the viral origin of cancer.

Recognition and Regulation in Cell-Mediated Immunity. Ed. by John Marbrook. Dekker 1985 $139.00. ISBN 0-8247-7268-7. An anthology that covers cell biology and the thymus, development of recognition and the T cell receptors, mediators and T cell maturation, and regulation of T cell induction.

Recombinant DNA: A Short Course. (coauthored with John Tooze). W. H. Freeman 1992 $49.95. ISBN 0-7167-1994-0. Covers the role of genes in the life of the cell, the nature of DNA, the genetic code, gene expression, recombinant DNA methods, viral vectors, cloning, in vitro mutagenesis, and the use of recombinant DNA in treating genetic diseases; includes illustrations, a reading list, dateline (with photographs), appendixes on enzymes, and an index.

BOOKS ABOUT WATSON

Holton, Gerald, ed. *The Twentieth-Century Scientists: Studies in the Biography of Ideas.* Norton 1972 o.p. Collection of essays on contemporary science topics; includes information about Watson.

Judson, Horace F. *The Eighth Day of Creation: Makers of the Revolution in Biology.* S & S Trade 1979 $15.95. ISBN 0-671-22540-5. History of the discoveries in molecular biology and the scientists involved during the period 1930–1970.

Moore, Ruth E. *The Coil of Life: The Story of the Great Discoveries of the Life Sciences.* Knopf 1961 o.p. Discussion of the discoveries pertaining to the chemical basis of heredity; includes information about Watson.

Olby, Robert. *The Path to the Double Helix.* U. of Wash. Pr. 1974 o.p. History of molecular biology: the ideas, methods, and people that led to understanding the structure of DNA.

WILKINS, MAURICE HUGH FREDERICK. 1916– (NOBEL PRIZE 1962)

Born in Pongaroa, New Zealand, Maurice Wilkins received a B.A. in physics from St. John's College at Cambridge University and received a Ph.D. from the University of Birmingham in England in 1940. His doctoral research led to improvements in radar screens during World War II. During the war, Wilkins worked on the Manhattan Project at the University of California, Berkeley. This group, a unit of the U.S. Army Corps of Engineers, administered the research team that developed the atomic bomb.

At Berkeley, Wilkins became interested in biology. In 1945 he became a lecturer in biophysics at St. Andrews University in Scotland and in 1946 at King's College, University of London. At King's College, he became an authority on the structure of nucleic acids and began studying DNA. He and the British scientist Rosalind Franklin used X-ray diffraction analysis to determine the shape of DNA. These X-ray studies of DNA were the basis for the model of DNA structure developed by the American biologist JAMES WATSON and the British molecular biologist FRANCIS HARRY COMPTON CRICK. In 1962 Wilkins shared the Nobel Prize in physiology or medicine with Watson and Crick for his contributions to their findings. Franklin had died six years previously, and thus could not be awarded a share of the Nobel Prize.

BOOKS ABOUT WILKINS

Judson, Horace F. *The Eighth Day of Creation: Makers of the Revolution in Biology.* S&S Trade 1979 $15.95. ISBN 0-671-22540-5. History of the discoveries in molecular biology and the scientists involved from 1930 to 1970.

Olby, Robert. *The Path to the Double Helix.* U. of Wash. Pr. 1974 o.p. History of molecular biology that covers the ideas, methods, and people that led to understanding of the structure of DNA.

Watson, James D. *The Double Helix: A Personal Account of the Discovery of the Structure of DNA.* 1968. Atheneum 1985 $6.95. ISBN 0-689-70602-2. Watson's account of the events and people involved in determining the structure of DNA.

CHAPTER 23

Ecology and Environmental Science

Robert Merideth

The ecologist is the most recent of science's prophets. He offers not only a credible explanation of the way nature works, but also something of a metaphysical insight, a set of ethical precepts—perhaps even a revolutionary program.

—DONALD WORSTER, *Nature's Economy*

The study of the relationships between living organisms and the environment is called ecology. Although modern ecology is slightly more than 100 years old, groups of early human beings, several million years ago, relied on their knowledge of ecology to survive. For example, by observing the relations of plants and animals with each other and with the environment, hunters could predict where and when their prey could be found, and gatherers would know where and when edible plants would appear. In fact, ecology may have been the subject matter of the first teachers as one generation attempted to prepare the next to survive.

The first step in the development of the science of ecology, at least in the Western world, occurred in Greece. ARISTOTLE (see Vols. 3 and 4) gathered a tremendous amount of information (and misinformation) about animals, which he divided into four categories. One of them—*bioi*, or "modes of living"—was ecological information. However, neither the Greek philosophers nor the average Greek citizen attempted to apply ecological principles to themselves or their surroundings; following the pattern of many other people, they used their environment as if it were an inexhaustible resource. The thistle-covered, eroded hills of Attica are their descendants' heritage.

Ancient Rome, *Roma aeterna*, failed to last eternally, at least in part, because its citizens, too, had no concern for their environment. Trees were removed, erosion filled irrigation canals with silt, and farming became more and more difficult. At one time, so many people left the land that farms were offered free to those who would work them.

Ecology shared the fate of other sciences during the Middle Ages. When truth is dictated rather than discovered, science has no place. The first tentative steps of the modern science of ecology were not taken until individuals, many of them trained in theology, decided that studying nature was another way to learn about God.

REFERENCE BOOKS

This section contains useful reference books on ecology and environmental sciences, including dictionaries, encyclopedias, bibliographies, directories of organizations, statistical sources, and biographical references.

Allaby, Michael. *Dictionary of the Environment.* NYU Pr. 1989 $75.00. ISBN 0-8147-0591-X. Comprehensive work by a prolific author of scientific reference books.

Art, Henry W., ed. *The Dictionary of Ecology and Environmental Science.* H. Holt & Co. 1993 $60.00. ISBN 0-8050-2079-9. Useful collection of definitions of environmental terms and concepts.

Ashworth, William. *The Encyclopedia of Environmental Studies.* Facts on File 1990 $60.00. ISBN 0-8160-1531-7. Good source of information about environmental organizations and agencies, legislation, famous individuals, and biological and chemical processes.

Cump, Andy. *Dictionary of Environment and Development: People, Places, Ideas and Organizations.* MIT Pr. 1993. ISBN 0-262-03207-4. Useful guide to the scope of the emerging world interest in environmental science and economic development.

Darnay, Arsen J., ed. *Statistical Record of the Environment.* Gale 1992 $89.50. ISBN 0-8103-8374-8. Some 800 tables and charts, providing statistical information on such topics as pollutants, laws and regulations, costs and expenditures, and public attitudes.

Davis, Donald Edward. *Ecophilosophy: A Field Guide to the Literature.* R & E Miles 1989 o.p. Good introduction to the literature on environmental ethics, philosophy, and values.

Deal, Carl. *The Greenpeace Guide to Anti-Environmental Organizations.* Odonian Pr. 1993 $5.00. ISBN 1-878825-05-4. Descriptions of numerous organizations with "environmentally friendly" names that were created by private interests to counter the activities of "real" environmental groups.

Earth Journal, 1993: Environmental Almanac and Resource Directory. Buzzworm Magazine Editors. Buzzworm 1992 $9.95. ISBN 0-9603722-7-X. Annual review of environmental highlights for the previous year, including cultural, political, and social events.

The Environmental Careers Organization. *The New Complete Guide to Environmental Careers.* Island Pr. 1993 $29.95. ISBN 1-55963-179-1. Essential reference for students, faculty advisers, or others wanting information about environmental career opportunities.

Environmental Data Research Institute. *Environmental Grantmaking Foundations: 1992 Directory.* Environ. Data Res. 1992 $40.00. ISBN 0-9631943-0-5. Guide to 250 foundations that make grants available to environmental projects and programs.

Franck, Irene, and David Brownstone. *The Green Encyclopedia: An A–to–Z Sourcebook of Environmental Concerns and Solutions.* P-H Gen. Ref. & Trav. 1992 $35.00. ISBN 0-13-365685-3. Excellent, well-organized source of information on a variety of environmental topics; includes appendixes.

Hall, Bob, and Mary Lee Kerr. *1991–1992 Green Index: A State-by-State Guide to the Nation's Environmental Health.* Island Pr. 1991 $29.95. ISBN 1-55963-115-5. Rankings of the 50 states based on some 200 environmental indicators.

Hill, Karen, and Annette Piccireli, eds. *Gale Environmental Sourcebook: A Guide to Organizations, Agencies, and Publications.* Gale 1992 $75.00. ISBN 0-8103-8403-5. Comprehensive guide to associations, government agencies, universities, magazines, newsletters, and books that pertain to environmental studies.

Jester, John L., and Rick Piltz. *Environmental Success Index 1992.* Brick Hse. Pub. 1992 $25.00. ISBN 0-931790-61-1. Directory of grassroots organizations making a positive difference in their communities in a number of environmental areas; excellent resource and source of inspiration for citizen activists.

Katz, Linda Sobel, Sarah Orrick, and Robert Honig. *Environmental Profiles: A Global Guide to Projects and People.* Garland 1993 $125.00. ISBN 0-8153-0063-8. Extensive descriptions of environmental nongovernment organizations, government agencies, private companies, and universities in 115 countries.

Lanier-Graham, Susan D. *The Nature Directory: A Guide to Environmental Organizations.* Walker & Co. 1991 $22.95. ISBN 0-8027-1151-0. Listing of 120 environmental groups, with detailed descriptions of the history, goals, past achievements, ongoing projects, membership information, and contacts for each group.

Levine, Michael. *The Environmental Address Book: How to Reach the Environment's Greatest Champions and Worst Offenders.* Putnam Pub. Group 1991 o.p. Names, addresses, and telephone numbers for individuals, organizations, companies, and government agencies having an interest in or impact on the environment.

Makower, Joel. *The Nature Catalog.* Random 1991 $18.00. ISBN 0-679-73300-0. Exhaustive compilation of information on products, services, organizations, and facilities related to nature and the environment.

Mason, Robert J., and Mark T. Mattson. *Atlas of the United States Environmental Issues.* Macmillan 1990 $80.00. ISBN 0-02-897261-9. Thorough graphical presentation of environmental conditions in the United States. Extensive supporting, descriptive, and analytical text.

Merideth, Robert. *The Environmentalist's Bookshelf: A Guide to the Best Books.* Macmillan 1993 $40.00. ISBN 0-8161-7359-1. Describes the 500 best books on nature and the environment as determined by a questionnaire survey of 230 environmental leaders from around the world. Ranks the "Top 40" environmental books; includes author, title, and subject indexes.

National Wildlife Federation. *1993 Conservation Directory.* Natl. Wildlife 1993 $18.00. ISBN 0-945051-54-9. Excellent resource, especially about state and regional environmental and conservation groups and agencies; best and most complete environmental directory available.

Parker, Sybil P., and Robert A. Corbitt, eds. *McGraw-Hill Encyclopedia of Environmental Science and Engineering.* McGraw 1993 $85.00. ISBN 0-07-051396-1. Significant reference dealing with technical areas of environmental issues.

Rittner, Don. *Ecolinking: Everyone's Guide to Online Environmental Information.* Peachpit Pr. 1992 $18.95. ISBN 0-938151-35-5. Guide to data bases, electronic bulletin boards, networks, and other information services accessible through computer/telephone systems.

Rodes, Barbara K., and Rice Odell. *A Dictionary of Environmental Quotations.* S&S Trade 1992 $35.00. ISBN 0-13-210576-4. Very useful compilation of some 3,700 quotations taken from proverbs, poems, speeches, scientific articles, books, and even bumper stickers; organized into 143 categories with indexes.

Seager, Joni. *The State of the Earth Atlas (Atlas Survey of the State of the Earth).* S&S Trade 1990 $27.95. ISBN 0-671-70523-7. Describes the global environmental situation through a series of maps and graphs.

Seredich, John, ed. *Your Resource Guide to Environmental Organizations.* Smiling Dolphins Pr. 1991 $15.95. ISBN 1-879072-00-9. Describes more than 150 environmental organizations.

Sinclair, Patti, ed. *E for Environment: An Annotated Bibliography of Children's Books with Environmental Themes.* Bowker 1992 $39.95. ISBN 0-8352-3028-7. Describes hundreds of children's books on nature and the environment; includes extensive author, title, and subject indexes.

Stein, Edith. *Environmental Sourcebook.* Lyons & Burford 1992 $16.95. ISBN 1-55821-165-9. Another reference for information about environmental organizations.

Stroud, Richard H., ed. *National Leaders of American Conservation.* Smithsonian 1985 $27.50. ISBN 0-87474-867-4. Collection of biographies for nearly 500 American conservationists and environmentalists.

Wild, Peter. *Pioneer Conservationists of Eastern America.* Mountain Pr. 1986 $14.95. ISBN 0-87842-126-2

_____. *Pioneer Conservationists of Western America.* Mountain Pr. 1979 $12.95. ISBN 0-87842-107-6. In these two books, Wild describes the lives and deeds of 30 famous conservationists.

World Resources Institute. *1993 Information Please Environmental Almanac*. HM 1992 $21.45. ISBN 0-395-63767-8. Basic facts and figures on all aspects of the environment.

World Resources Institute, International Institute for Environment and Development, and IUCN-The World Conservation Union. *1993 Directory of Country Environmental Studies: An Annotated Bibliography of Environmental and Natural Resources Profiles and Assessments*. World Resources Inst. 1992 $19.95. ISBN 0-915825-880. Extensive descriptions of some 350 national reports assessing environmental conditions in 130 countries.

World Resources Institute, United Nations Environment Programme, and United Nations Development Programme. *World Resources: 1992–93*. OUP 1992 $32.50. ISBN 0-19-506230-2. Perhaps the most complete assembly of a wide range of environmental data for nearly every country on the planet.

The Yale School of Forestry and Environmental Studies. *The Island Press Bibliography of Environmental Literature*. Island Pr. 1993 $48.00. ISBN 1-55963-189-9. Compilation of more than 3,000 entries (books, journal articles, and reports) on a variety of topics related to the natural and human environment.

NATURAL HISTORY

A naturalist differs from an ecologist in that the work of the naturalist is primarily descriptive—whereas that of the ecologist is quantitative. One observer has asserted that the difference is that ecologists consider what they do to be work, whereas naturalists insist that they are having fun. Many of the authors listed here have been effective combinations of ecologist and naturalist.

Attenborough, David. *Life on Earth: A Natural History*. Little 1983 $24.95. ISBN 0-316-05747-9

———. *The Living Planet*. Little 1986 $17.95. ISBN 0-316-05749-5

———. *The Trials of Life; Vol. 1*. Little 1991 $29.95. ISBN 0-316-05751-7. Excellent trilogy of books that coincided with the BBC-produced television series. Offers an impressive overview of the diversity and dynamics of life on this planet; richly illustrated with stunning photographs.

Bass, Rick. *Winter: Notes from Montana*. HM 1992 $9.70. ISBN 0-395-61150-4. Chronicles the discoveries and adventures of a young couple's first year of wilderness life in northern Montana.

Bates, Marston. *The Forest and the Sea*. Lyons and Burford 1988 $11.95. ISBN 1-55821-009-1. Discusses the place of biology in the whole of human knowledge and the place of the human species in nature. Also deals with organisms in a variety of habitats, the natural history of disease, and aspects of animal behavior.

Bonta, Marcia Myers. *Women in the Field: America's Pioneering Women Naturalists*. Texas A & M Univ. Pr. 1991 $29.50. ISBN 0-89096-467-X. Documents the lives and work of 25 women who made important contributions to the field of natural history.

Campbell, David G. *The Crystal Desert: Summers in Antarctica*. HM 1992 $21.45. ISBN 0-395-58969-X. Describes the landscape, wildlife, and natural history of Antarctica based on three summers of research.

Carr, Archie. *The Windward Road: Adventures of a Naturalist on Remote Caribbean Shores*. U. Press Fla. 1979 repr. of 1955 ed. $15.95. ISBN 0-8130-0639-2. Recollections by a noted biologist of his work in the Caribbean region to study and protect sea turtles; originally published in 1955.

Carrighar, Sally. *One Day on Beetle Rock*. U. Neb. Pr. 1978 repr. of 1956 ed. $6.95. ISBN 0-8032-6301-5. Peaceful account of the natural history found on a mountain in the Sierra Nevada; first published in 1944.

Connor, Jack. *Season at the Point: The Birds and Birders of Cape May*. Grove-Atlic. 1992 $11.95. ISBN 0-87133-456-X. Records the special attraction that the Cape May peninsula in southern New Jersey presents to migrating birds and bird watchers.

Dillard, Annie. *Pilgrim at Tinker Creek*. HarpC 1988 $12.00. ISBN 0-06-091545-5. Beautifully written chronicle of the natural and spiritual character of the Blue Ridge mountains in the eastern United States; winner of the Pulitzer Prize in 1975.

Durrell, Gerald, and Lee Durrell. *The Amateur Naturalist*. McKay 1989 $25.00. ISBN 0-679-72837-6. Helps the reader to do what a naturalist does and to think as a naturalist thinks. Nothing would help the preservation of our natural resources as much as having more people become amateur naturalists.

Finch, Robert, and John Elder, eds. *The Norton Book of Nature Writing*. Norton 1990 $29.95. ISBN 0-393-02799-6. An extensive anthology, consisting of more than 125 selections from the best of American nature writing.

Fisk, Erma J. *The Peacocks of Baboquivari*. Norton 1987 $8.95. ISBN 0-393-30419-1. Fisk's diary of her winter on Baboquivari Peak in southwestern Arizona counting birds for The Nature Conservancy.

Gould, Stephen Jay. *Wonderful Life: The Burgess Shale and the Nature of History*. Norton 1990 $10.95. ISBN 0-393-30700-X. One of many excellent books by the noted Harvard professor and prolific natural history writer.

Hubbell, Sue. *A Country Year: Living the Questions*. Random 1986 $17.95. ISBN 0-394-55146-X. Describes the activities and interactions of reptiles, mammals, insects and other arthropods, and birds; illustrates Hubbell's keen eye and knack for description. Includes many comments about her personal life. Another charming book.

Kastner, Joseph. *A World of Watchers*. BDD Promo. Bk. 1983 $2.98. ISBN 0-7974-8207-7. Covers the history of birding, the people who have encouraged birders, organizations of birders, and the contributions of birders to avian biology.

Lopez, Barry. *Arctic Dreams: Imagination and Desire in a Northern Landscape*. Macmillan 1986 $22.95. ISBN 0-684-18578-4. Presents one man's fascination with the land, wildlife, and people of the arctic; beautiful prose.

Lyon, Thomas J., ed. *This Incomperable Lande: A Book of American Nature Writing*. Viking Penguin 1991 $14.95. ISBN 0-14-014441-2. Excellent collection of natural history writings with an thorough explanatory and analytical introductory piece by the editor.

Nabhan, Gary. *The Desert Smells like Rain: A Naturalist in Papago Indian Country*. FS&G 1987 $10.95. ISBN 0-86547-050-2. Beautifully written book, concerning the "ethnobotany" of the Sonoran desert in the United States and Mexico.

Norwood, Vera. *Made from This Earth: American Woman and Nature*. U. NC Pr. 1993 $37.50. ISBN 0-8078-2062-8. History of the role of American women in nature study, gardening and landscape design, the natural sciences, and environmental activism.

Olson, Sigurd. *The Singing Wilderness*. Knopf 1956 $24.95. ISBN 0-394-44560-0. Olson's most famous tribute to the wonder of the north country in Minnesota and Ontario.

Owens, Mark, and Delia Owens. *Cry of the Kalahari*. HM 1992 $9.70. ISBN 0-395-64780-0. Fascinating book about the daily life and adventures of two researchers who study lions in the semi-arid plains of Botswana.

Peterson, Roger Tory. *A Field Guide to the Birds: A Completely New Guide to All the Birds of Eastern and Central North America*. HM 1980 $21.45. ISBN 0-395-26621-1

———. *A Field Guide to Western Birds*. HM 1990 $22.50. ISBN 0-395-51749-4. Essential field guides for bird watching, based upon Peterson's "field marks" system for bird identification; first introduced in 1934.

Teale, Edwin Way. *Autumn across America*. St. Martin 1990 $12.95. ISBN 0-312-04455-0

———. *Journey into Summer*. St. Martin 1990 $12.95. ISBN 0-312-04456-9

———. *North with the Spring*. St. Martin 1990 $12.95. ISBN 0-312-04457-7

———. *Wandering through Winter*. St. Martin 1990 $12.95. ISBN 0-312-04458-5. Reprints of the four classics that won Teale great admiration and a Pulitzer Prize in 1966.

Tuttle, Merlin D. *America's Neighborhood Bats: Understanding and Learning to Live in Harmony with Them*. U. of Tex. Pr. 1988 $19.95. ISBN 0-292-70403-8. A record of his achievements by a naturalist who has gone a long way to change public perceptions of bats.

Warner, William W. *Beautiful Swimmers: Watermen, Crabs, and the Chesapeake Bay*. Little 1976 $22.50. ISBN 0-316-92326-5. Captures the fragility of the human and natural ecology of the tidewater region; winner of the Pulitzer Prize for general nonfiction.

White, Gilbert. *The Natural History of Selborne.* OUP 1993 repr. of 1789 ed. $6.95. ISBN 0-19-282928-9. Observations of the natural history of his native village recorded in letters by one of the early naturalists whose example helped give rise to ecology.

Wilson, Edward O. *Biophilia.* HUP 1984 $18.95. ISBN 0-674-07441-6. Expresses the fascination with life that has motivated this highly reknowned entomologist to dedicate himself to understanding, appreciating, and preserving the flora and fauna of our planet.

ECOLOGY

The word *ecology* was first applied to this branch of biology in 1886 by Ernst Haeckel. From the Greek *oikos* meaning "home" or "household," ecology deals with the relationships among animal and plant communities and their surroundings. The first college courses in ecology in the United States were established in the 1930s by H. C. Cowles at the University of Chicago, Charles C. Adams and Victor E. Shelford at the University of Illinois, and J. E. Weaver and Frederic E. Clements at the University of Nebraska. (Clements was later at the University of Minnesota.) Students learned the fundamental concepts of ecology in these courses, including succession, adaptation, interdependence, and limiting factors. Another important goal of these early ecology courses was the instruction of laboratory and field techniques and the proper use of sampling equipment.

Allee, Warder C., and others. *Principles of Animal Ecology.* Saunders 1949 o.p. Classic, easy-to-read text. Section 1 presents a good summary of the history of ecology.

Altieri, Miguel. *Agroecology: The Scientific Basis of Alternative Agriculture.* Westview 1987 $39.00. ISBN 0-8133-7284-4. Describes the biological basis for and practical approaches to alternative, or sustainable, agriculture.

Andrewartha, H. G., and L. C. Birch. *The Ecological Web: More on the Distribution and Abundance of Animals.* U. Ch. Pr. 1986 $40.00. ISBN 0-226-02033-9. An expansion and update of the first volume, with neither being easy reading.

_____. *Selections from Distribution and Abundance of Animals.* U. Ch. Pr. 1982 $25.00. ISBN 0-226-02031-2. Includes the "envirogram," a graphic representation of modifiers in an animal's environment.

Botkin, Daniel B. *Discordant Harmonies: A New Ecology for the Twenty-First Century.* OUP 1990 $22.95. ISBN 0-19-505491-1. Suggests that nature realistically can only be preserved through management by humans and calls for a better understanding of the biosphere through improved research and field studies.

Bramwell, Anna. *Ecology and History: The Greening of the West Since 1880.* Yale U. Pr. 1989 $20.00. ISBN 0-300-04521-2. Draws connections between the popularization of ecological ideas by activist scientists and the development of environmentalism.

Browne, Janet. *The Secular Ark: Studies in the History of Biogeography.* Yale U. Pr. 1983 $42.00. ISBN 0-300-02600-6. "A history of the study of the distribution of species around the world and how that early thought contributed to Darwin's evolution theories" (*Library Journal*).

Clements, Frederic E. *Plant Competition: An Analysis of Community Functions.* Ed. by Frank N. Egerton. Ayer 1978 repr. of 1929 ed. $37.50. ISBN 0-405-10380-8. As the title indicates, text deals with the interactions of plants in a community; technical.

Cox, C. Barry, and Peter D. Moore. *Biogeography: An Ecological and Evolutionary Approach.* Blackwell Pubs. 1993 $34.95. ISBN 0-632-02967-6. One of the more popular textbooks on the topic.

Craighead, Frank C., Jr. *Track of the Grizzly.* Peter Smith 1985 $18.75. ISBN 0-8446-6131-7. Describes the life history and ecology of grizzly bears and makes some suggestions about management.

Craighead, John J., and Frank C. Craighead, Jr. *Hawks, Owls, and Wildlife.* Dover 1969 repr. of 1956 ed. $8.95. ISBN 0-486-22123-7. A look at the relationships between these carnivorous birds and other wildlife.

Crosby, Alfred W. *Ecological Imperialism: The Biological Expansion of Europe, 900–1900.* Cambridge U. Pr. 1987 $42.95. ISBN 0-521-32009-7. Well-written and interesting account of the ecological impacts of exploration and colonialism by Western European nations in both the New World and the Old World.

Crowcroft, Peter. *Elton's Ecologists: A History of the Bureau of Animal Population.* U. Ch. Pr. 1991 $35.00. ISBN 0-226-12146-1. Documents the life and work of British ecologist Charles Elton, author of *The Ecology of Invasions by Animals and Plants* (1958) and other highly regarded monographs.

Huxley, Anthony J. *Green Inheritance: The World Wildlife Fund Book of Plants.* FWEW 1992 $26.95. ISBN 0-94123-70-0. Lavishly illustrated book documenting the variety of plants around the world and their importance to humans.

MacArthur, Robert H. *Geographical Ecology: Patterns in the Distribution of Species.* Princeton U. Pr. 1984 $17.95. ISBN 0-691-02382-4. Early explanation of the patterns of plant and animal distributions, focusing on such causal factors as physiography and behavior.

MacArthur, Robert H., and Edward O. Wilson. *Theory of Island Biogeography.* Princeton U. Pr. 1967 $15.95. ISBN 0-691-08050-X. Dated but classic statement on island biogeography.

McIntosh, Robert P. *The Background of Ecology: Concept and Theory.* Cambridge U. Pr. 1986 $27.95. ISBN 0-521-27087-1. Thorough overview of the emergence and development of ecological ideas. Examines the work and contributions of numerous scientists; includes an excellent bibliography.

McNeill, William H. *Plaques and Peoples.* Peter Smith 1992 $19.50. ISBN 0-8446-6492-8. Looks at the "ecology" of diseases and parasites and the impact on human populations.

Margulis, Lynn, and Karlene V. Schwartz. *Five Kingdoms: An Illustrated Guide to the Phyla of Life on Earth.* W. H. Freeman 1987 $26.95. ISBN 0-7167-1912-6. Comprehensive, well-illustrated introduction to the various life forms found on earth.

Mollison, Bill. *Permaculture: A Practical Guide for a Sustainable Future.* Permaculture 1992 $34.95. ISBN 0-317-04874-0. Reviews the ecological principles and practices related to permanent agriculture, or "permaculture," whereby humans live more harmoniously and sustainably within their landscapes.

Odum, Eugene P. *Fundamentals of Ecology.* Saunders 1971 $50.75. ISBN 0-7216-6941-7. Elaborates the systems approach—the flow of energy and materials—to understanding ecological interactions; a pioneering textbook.

Peattie, Donald C. *Flowering Earth.* Ind. U. Pr. 1991 $27.50. ISBN 0-253-34308-9. Reprint of Peattie's 1939 botanical classic.

Perry, Donald. *Life above the Forest Floor: Tree Top World.* S&S Trade 1986 $16.95. ISBN 0-685-16651-1. Personal first-hand observations of the little-known community that exists among the understory and canopy trees of a tropical rain forest; descriptions are as colorful as the photographs with which the book is illustrated.

Rambler, Mitchell B., Lynn Margulis, and René Fester. *Global Ecology: Towards a Science of the Biosphere.* Acad. Pr. 1989 $44.00. ISBN 0-12-576890-7. Call for a new understanding of the biosphere through the interdisciplinary linkages of various scientific disciplines.

Rickets, Edward, and Jack Calvin. *Between Pacific Tides.* Stanford U. Pr. 1985 $55.00. ISBN 0-8047-1229-8. Popular guide to the marine life, especially invertebrates, in the tidal zone of the Pacific coast of North America.

Robinson, William L., and Eric Bolen. *Wildlife Ecology and Management.* Macmillan 1988. ISBN 0-299-402251-9. According to a survey reported in *Wildlife Society Bulletin,* one of the essential volumes of a wildlife professional's library.

Shelford, Victor E. *The Ecology of North America*. U. of Ill. Pr. 1978 o.p. Shelford's monumental work provides a look at the ecology of a continent. No small task.

Soule, Michael E., ed. *Conservation Biology: The Science of Scarcity and Diversity*. Sinauer Assocs. 1986 $33.95. ISBN 0-87893-795-1. Elaborates on the concerns, concepts, and methods that are now engaging biologists in the race to preserve endangered species.

Stokes, Donald W. *A Guide to Nature in Winter: Northeast and North Central North America*. Little 1979 $18.95. ISBN 0-316-81720-1. The ecologist anxious to study living things under a variety of conditions will appreciate this guide during the severe conditions of winter.

Westman, Walter E. *Ecology, Impact Assessment, and Environmental Planning*. Wiley 1985 $54.95. ISBN 0-471-80895-4. Takes an ecological approach to analyzing and interpreting potential changes caused by human activities; a useful textbook and reference.

Wilson, Edward O. *The Diversity of Life*. HUP 1992 $29.95. ISBN 0-674-21298-3. Exceptionally brilliant presentation on why humans should protect plant and animal species from extinction.

Wilson, E. O., ed. *Biodiversity*. Nat. Acad. Pr. 1988 $24.50. ISBN 0-309-03739-5. Collection of papers presented by distinguished experts at a national conference on biological conservation.

Worster, Donald E. *Nature's Economy: A History of Ecological Ideas*. Cambridge U. Pr. 1985 $54.95. ISBN 0-521-26792-7. Traces the development of ecological ideas from the eighteenth century through the contemporary period; written by a distinguished environmental historian.

ENVIRONMENTALISM

Any scheme of classification presents difficulties. Separating naturalists, ecologists, and environmentalists is especially difficult. An environmentalist may or may not also be a naturalist or an ecologist. The environmentalists listed here have displayed particular concern for the maintenance and intelligent use of natural resources for the protection and preservation of key elements of the biosphere, for the prevention of environmental hazards that threaten life on this planet, for certain aspects of quality of life, and for equity and social justice for all citizens of the planet. A number of the titles below address these issues.

Berger, John, ed. *Environmental Restoration: Science and Strategies for Restoring the Earth*. Island Pr. 1990 $37.00. ISBN 0-933280-94-7. Describes how people in different parts of the United States are involved in restoration; edited by the author of *Restoring the Earth: How Americans Are Working to Renew Our Damaged Environment* (1985).

Berry, Wendell. *The Unsettling of America: Culture and Agriculture*. Sierra 1986 repr. of 1977 ed. $9.00. ISBN 0-87156-772-5. Reflection on the nature of agriculture in America and how public and private interests have shaped it into an activity that has a significant harmful impact on the environment.

Blaikie, Piers M., and Harold C. Brookfield. *Land Degradation and Society*. Routledge Chapman & Hall 1987 o.p. Examines the role of political, social, and economic forces in causing environmental degradation.

Caufield, Catherine. *In the Rainforest: Report from a Strange, Beautiful, Imperiled World*. U. Ch. Pr. $11.95. ISBN 0-226-09786-2. Dramatically documents how tropical rainforests are being destroyed by unrelenting human activities in Asia, Africa, and Latin America.

Chase, Alston. *Playing God in Yellowstone: The Destruction of America's First National Park*. HarBraceJ 1987 $13.95. ISBN 0-15-672036-1. Discusses and evaluates the management policies of government agencies in wilderness areas and what it means to manage a natural area.

Commoner, Barry. *Making Peace with the Planet*. Pantheon 1990 $19.95. ISBN 0-394-56598-3. Looking at how our technological society is devastating the planet, Commoner suggests that we should not turn our backs on technological development, per se, but should choose more appropriate technologies that can be in harmony with the natural world; by the author of *The Closing Circle* (1971).

Cronon, William. *Changes in the Land: Indians, Colonists, and the Ecology of New England*. Hill & Wang 1983 o.p. Shows the ecological impacts on the New England landscape both from European colonists and from the native people of the region; a classic in the field of environmental history.

————. *Nature's Metropolis: Chicago and the Great West*. Norton 1991 $15.95. ISBN 0-393-30873-1. Looks at the environmental changes that occurred as a result of the economic linkages between late nineteenth-century Chicago and its hinterland in the upper Midwest.

Daly, Herman, and John Cobb, Jr. *For the Common Good: Redirecting the Economy toward Community, the Environment, and a Sustainable Future*. Beacon Pr. 1991 repr. of 1989 ed. $16.00. ISBN 0-8070-4703-1. Innovative look at the way society values and consumes nature with recommendations for alternative economic approaches.

Devall, Bill, and George Sessions. *Deep Ecology: Living as if Nature Mattered*. Gibbs Smith Pub. 1987 $11.95. ISBN 0-87905-247-3. Expresses and urges society to adopt a biocentric viewpoint of the world, where humans are merely one of many equally valued components of nature.

Durrell, Lee. *State of the Ark: An Atlas of Conservation in Action*. Doubleday 1986 $17.95. ISBN 0-385-23668-9. Shows in splendid illustrations the status of wildlife around the planet and documents the impact of humans on the fragile habitats upon which these animals depend.

Ehrenfeld, David. *The Arrogance of Humanism*. OUP 1975 $11.95. ISBN 0-19-502890-2. Critiques human-centered thinking and shows how this viewpoint has dominated for centuries the relationship between humans and the rest of the biosphere.

Epstein, Samuel S., Lester O. Brown, and Carl Pope. *Hazardous Wastes in America*. Sierra 1983 $12.95. ISBN 0-87156-807-1. Looks at the wide range of interests involved in hazardous waste production.

Evernden, Neil. *The Social Creation of Nature*. Johns Hopkins 1992 $38.00. ISBN 0-8018-4396-0. Examines the concept of "nature" and what it has meant to cultures at different times; by the author of *The Natural Alien: Humankind and Environment* (1985).

50 Simple Things You Can Do to Save the Planet. Earthworks Group. Earthworks Pr. 1990 $4.95. ISBN 0-929634-06-3. A small but useful guide that answers the question: "What can one person do to help protect the environment?"

Fox, Stephen R. *John Muir and His Legacy: The American Conservation Movement*. Little 1981 $29.95. ISBN 0-316-29110-2. Excellent history of the conservation movement in the United States.

Gore, Al. *Earth in the Balance: Ecology and the Human Spirit*. NAL-Dutton 1993 $13.00. ISBN 0-452-26935-0. Personal and reasoned discussion about the global situation and how we might begin to deal with some of the major problems.

Hardin, Garrett. *Living within Limits: Ecology, Economic, and Population Taboos*. OUP 1993 $25.00. ISBN 0-19-507811-X. Suggests that human overpopulation is the primary environmental problem facing the world and that we are already extending beyond the earth's limited carrying capacity; the most recent book by a prolific writer.

Hays, Samuel P. *Beauty, Health, and Permanence: Environmental Politics in the United States, 1955–1985*. Cambridge U. Pr. 1989 $19.95. ISBN 0-521-38928-3. Looks at the emergence of the modern environmental movement and a shift of priorities from notions of conservation to those of concern for pollution prevention and wilderness preservation; by the author of *Conservation and the Gospel of Efficiency* (1959).

Hecht, Susanna, and Alexander Cockburn. *The Fate of the Forest: Developers, Destroyers, and Defenders of the Amazon*. Routledge Chapman & Hall 1989 $24.95. ISBN 0-

86091-261-2. One of the earliest popular books to look at deforestation in Brazil and at the political and social context within which it occurs.

Jackson, Wes, Wendell Berry, and Bruce Colman, eds. *Meeting the Expectations of the Land: Essays in Sustainable Agriculture and Stewardship.* FS&G 1984 $12.50. ISBN 0-86547-172-X. Important contribution to the dialogue on sustainable agriculture.

Jorgensen, Eric P. *The Poisoned Well: New Strategies for Groundwater Protection.* Island Pr. 1989 $35.00. ISBN 0-9-33280-56-4. Excellent resource for citizens and local governments; prepared by the staff of the Sierra Club Legal Defense Fund.

Lewis, Martin W. *Green Delusions: An Environmentalist Critique of Radical Environmentalism.* Duke 1992 $24.95. ISBN 0-8223-1257-3. Well-reasoned argument that society should not embrace the anti-technology ideas espoused by radical environmentalists, but rather should be selective in choosing and using technology as a means to solving ecological crises.

Lovelock, J. E. *Gaia: A New Look at Life on Earth.* OUP 1987 $9.95. ISBN 0-19-286030-5. Presents the intriguing hypothesis that the earth is a self-regulating entity and that its biosphere, air, oceans, and land respond in a coordinated fashion to global changes to help maintain certain ideal states for the planet.

Lovins, Amory B., and others. *Energy Unbound: A Fable for America's Future.* Sierra 1986 $17.95. ISBN 0-87156-820-9. As the author of *Soft Energy Paths: Toward a Durable Peace* (1977), Lovins makes another pitch about wasteful energy consumption by our contemporary society and offers many useful recommendations for conservation practices and technologies.

McHarg, Ian L. *Design with Nature.* Wiley 1991 $55.00. ISBN 0-471-55797-8. Elaborates principles of landscape planning that harmonize the human with the natural element. First published in 1969, this book introduced the concept of "multiple attribute overlay analysis" for environmental planning.

McKibben, Bill. *The End of Nature.* Random 1989 $19.95. ISBN 0-394-57601-2. Suggests that humans have so completely transformed the planet that there is no longer any place that can be called "natural."

McPhee, John A. *Encounters with the Archdruid.* FS&G 1977 $9.00. ISBN 0-374-51431-3. Describes the encounters between environmental leader David Brower, then director of the Sierra Club, and three of his main antagonists.

Mannion, Antionette M. *Global Environmental Change: A Natural and Cultural Environmental History.* Halsted Pr. 1991 $48.95. ISBN 0-470-21678-6. Introductory textbook on the causes and impacts of global environmental changes, both natural and human induced.

Martinez-Alier, Juan, and Klaus Schlupmann. *Ecological Economics: Energy, Environment, and Society.* Blackwell Pubs. 1987 $45.00. ISBN 0-631-15739-5. Useful introduction to the relationship between ecological theory and economics.

Meadows, Donella H., Dennis L. Meadows, and Jorgen Randers. *Beyond the Limits: Confronting Global Collapse, Envisioning a Sustainable Future.* Chelsea Green Pub. 1992 $19.95. ISBN 0-930031-55-5. Reviews the authors' computer forecasts of population growth, resource consumption, and environmental problems; update to the authors' classic *The Limits to Growth* (1972).

Merchant, Carolyn. *The Death of Nature: Women, Ecology and the Scientific Revolution.* Harper SF 1990 $12.00. ISBN 0-06-250595-5. Feminist and historical analysis of science and its relationship to nature; a pioneering work.

Miller, G. Tyler. *Living in the Environment: An Introduction to Environmental Science.* Wadsworth Pub. 1992. ISBN 0-534-16560-5. Perhaps the most widely used environmental science textbook at the college level.

Miller, Kenton, and Laura Tangley. *Trees of Life: Saving Tropical Forests and Their Biological Wealth.* Beacon Pr. 1991 $27.50. ISBN 0-8070-8508-1. Interesting and easy-to-read overview of the complexity of issues pertaining to deforestation in the tropics; produced by the World Resources Institute.

Myers, Norman. *The Primary Source: Tropical Forests and Our Future.* Norton 1992 $10.95. ISBN 0-393-30828-6. Discusses the many threats that tropical forests are facing and the social, economic, and political causes of these problems; written by an environmental writer and consultant from England.

———— ed. *Gaia: An Atlas of Planet Management.* Doubleday 1992 $22.95. ISBN 0-385-19072-7. Abundantly illustrated and interestingly written citizen's guide to global environmental issues.

Nash, Roderick F. *The Rights of Nature: A History of Environmental Ethics.* U. of Wis. Pr. 1989 $35.00. ISBN 0-299-11840-1. Reviews the emergence of different philosophies and attitudes of respect for nature.

————. *Wilderness and the American Mind.* Yale U. Pr. 1982 $15.00. ISBN 0-300-02910-1. One of the most important accounts of how the American view of nature has changed through history.

National Research Council. *Global Environmental Change: Understanding the Human Dimensions.* Natl. Acad. Pr. 1992 $29.95. ISBN 0-309-04494-4. Comprehensive look at the human causes of and response to global environmental change.

————. *Sustainable Agriculture and the Environment in the Humid Tropics.* Nat. Acad. Pr. 1993 $49.95. ISBN 0-309-04749-8. Intensive examination of land use activities in the humid tropics and their impacts on the environment; includes lengthy case studies for Brazil, Ivory Coast, Indonesia, Malaysia, Mexico, the Philippines and Zaire.

Reisner, Marc P. *Cadillac Desert: The American West and Its Disappearing Water.* Viking Penguin 1987 $13.00. ISBN 0-14-01432-1. Chronicle of the development, use, and waste of water resources in California, Arizona, and other states in the arid American West.

Richards, John F., and Richard P. Tucker, eds. *World Deforestation in the Twentieth Century.* Duke 1989 repr. of 1988 ed. $15.95. ISBN 0-8223-1013-9. The companion to *Global Deforestation and the Nineteenth Century World Economy* (1983). Together they offer a thorough analysis of the causes and impacts of deforestation around the world during the past two centuries.

Rifkin, Jeremy. *Biosphere Politics: A New Consciousness for a New Century.* Crown Pub. Group 1991 $20.00. ISBN 0-517-57746-1. Offers a new way of looking at the world and an alternative view of humans in that world.

Sagoff, Mark. *The Economy of Earth: Philosophy, Law, and the Environment.* Cambridge U. Pr. 1988 $54.95. ISBN 0-521-34113-2. Looks at individual and social values related to scientific decisions that affect the environment.

Sale, Kirkpatrick. *Dwellers in the Land: The Bioregional Vision.* New Soc. Pubs. 1991 $39.95. ISBN 0-86571-224-7. Presents the author's position that because the impact of the human animal on the global environment is greater than that of all other animals taken together, it is time for us to stop thinking and acting like "just another animal"; asserts that it is time for the human species to shift from domination to preservation.

Schaller, George B. *The Last Panda.* U. Ch. Pr. 1993 $24.95. ISBN 0-226-73628-8. A personal and sometimes pessimistic look at what might be the last attempts at protecting the giant panda in the wild areas of China; by the author of *Golden Shadows, Flying Hooves* (1983) and *The Year of the Gorilla* (1964).

Schneider, Stephen. *Global Warming: Are We Entering the Greenhouse Century?* Sierra 1989 $20.00. ISBN 0-87156-693-1. A reknowned climatologist examines the role of citizens and government in the global warming debate and in contributing to the development of appropriate policy strategies.

Schumacher, Ernst F. *Small Is Beautiful: Economics As If People Mattered.* Borgo Pr. 1991 $25.00. ISBN 0-8095-9115-4. Reprint of the 1973 classic that became the bible of the appropriate technology movement.

Shiva, Vandana. *Staying Alive: Women, Ecology, and Development.* Humanities 1989 $49.95. ISBN 0-86232-822-5. Feminist and non-Western look at environmental and developmental issues in the Third World; focuses specifically on examples in India.

Stone, Christopher D. *The Gnat Is Older Than Man: Global Environment and Human Agenda.* Princeton U. Pr. 1993 $21.95. ISBN 0-691-03250-5. Reviews international policy responses to the global environmental dilemma, suggesting creation of a global monitoring entity and a global environmental remediation fund; by the author of *Should Trees Have Standing? Toward Legal Rights for Natural Objects* (1974).

Turner, B. L., II, and others, eds. *The Earth as Transformed by Human Action: Global and Regional Changes in the Biosphere over the Past 300 Years.* Cambridge U. Pr. 1991 $105.00. ISBN 0-521-36357-8. Comprehensive and scholarly look at the human impact on the environment.

Turner, Tom. *Sierra Club: 100 Years of Protecting Nature.* Abrams 1991 $49.50. ISBN 0-8109-3820-0. Richly illustrated with the works of several highly regarded nature photographers; celebrates the centennial of the Sierra Club.

World Commission on Environment and Development. *Our Common Future.* OUP 1987 $12.95. ISBN 0-19-282080-X. Widely publicized report that looks at how nations could combine economic development with environmental protection.

Worster, Donald. *Dust Bowl: The Southern Plans in the 1930s.* OUP 1982 $10.95. ISBN 0-19-503212-8. Looks at the political and economic influences that led to widespread environmental devastation during the Dust Bowl era.

Wright, Angus. *The Death of Ramon Gonzalez: The Modern Agricultural Dilemma.* U. of Tex. Pr. 1990 $29.95. ISBN 0-292-71560-9. Reviews the deadly impacts of pesticide use on farm workers in Mexico and California.

ANIMAL BEHAVIOR

Animal behavior has been one of the most rapidly developing fields of ecology for the last 25 years. The discipline was given legitimacy in 1973 when KONRAD LORENZ, KARL VON FRISCH, and NIKOLAAS TINBERGEN shared the Nobel Prize in physiology and medicine. A by-product of the study of animal behavior has been an increasing understanding of human nature. Three terms used over and over in discussions of animal behavior are *territory, display,* and *imprinting.* Territories are of different kinds and have different functions, but in all circumstances they are areas that are defended by an organism or a pair of organisms against members of the same species. A display is a behavior pattern an animal carries out hoping to influence another member of the same species. Displays can be involved in courtship, defense of territory, or some other interactive behavior. Imprinting is the process by which an organism learns what organism it is. At a certain critical period while it is quite young, the organism becomes imprinted on whatever is moving or is making a sound near it. Usually this will be the mother, but ducks and geese have been imprinted on wooden blocks, cats, and humans. The process can be carried on with other animals. Ethology, the study of animal behavior, examines these and other aspects of animal activities related to feeding, avoidance, aggression, reproduction, migration, and dormancy.

Alock, John. *Animal Behavior: An Evolutionary Approach.* Sinauer Assocs. 1993 $46.95. ISBN 0-87893-017-5. Approaches the study of animal behavior through the theoretical framework of natural selection.

Altman, Stuart A., ed. *Social Communication among Primates. Midway Repr. Ser.* U. Ch. Pr. 1982 $18.00. ISBN 0-226-01597-1. Vocalization is only one way by which animals can communicate with other members of their species. Altman indicates that other primates also have many ways of keeping in touch.

Burton, Robert. *Bird Behavior.* Ed. by Bruce Campbell. Knopf 1985 $18.95. ISBN 0-394-53957-5. Presents new ideas about what to watch in order to observe various aspects of bird behavior. A good book to read after reading *A World of Watchers* by Joseph Kastner for interesting new facets of bird biology.

Caplan, Arthur L., ed. *The Sociobiology Debate.* HarpC 1985 $10.00. ISBN 0-06-131995-3. One of the best presentations of firsthand information available about the sociobiological debate.

Caras, Roger. *The Endless Migrations: The Epic Voyages of Living Things across the North American Continent*. NAL-Dutton 1985 o.p. Birds are only one of many species of animals that migrate. Tells about insects, reptiles, birds, and mammals that migrate and discusses some factors that may trigger migration.

Dewsbury, Donald A., ed. *Studying Animal Behavior: Autobiographies of the Founders*. U. Ch. Pr. 1989 repr. of 1985 ed. $19.95. ISBN 0-226-14410-0. Collection of some 20 essays by animal behavior experts from around the world. *Be Eldredge, Niles, and Marjorie Grene. *Interactions: The Biological Context of Social Systems*. Columbia U. Pr. 1992 $40.00. ISBN 0-231-07946-X. Argues against the genetic and reproductive reductionism of sociobiology and the neo-Darwinism.

Eldredge, Niles, and Marjorie Grene. *Interactions: The Biological Context of Social Systems*. Col. U. Pr. 1992 $40.00. ISBN 0-231-07946-X. Argues against the genetic and reproductive reductionism of sociobiology and neo-Darwinism.

Errington, Paul L. *Of Predation and Life*. Bks. Demand repr. of 1967 ed. $75.70. ISBN 0-317-58131-7. Presents Errington's thesis that predation is a natural phenomenon and that predators are important in any community.

Hahn, Emily. *On the Side of the Apes*. T. Y. Crowell 1971 o.p. Covers the many research projects dealing with primates other than man that are being conducted in the United States as well as in other parts of the world. Based on on-site visits and interviews with many of the researchers. Includes an especially good discussion of behavior studies.

Kitcher, Philip. *Vaulting Ambition: Sociobiology and the Quest for Human Nature*. MIT Pr. 1987 $35.00. ISBN 0-262-11109-8. Presents a fairly complete picture of this controversial subject.

Lewontin, R. C., and Leon J. Kamin. *Not in Our Genes*. Pantheon 1985 $11.95. ISBN 0-394-50817-3. Challenges the sociobiolgists who hold that genetics exerts an inexorable influence on behavior.

Lockley, Ronald M. *Flight of the Storm Petrel*. Eriksson 1983 o.p. Portrays a British naturalist's love for and interaction with the storm petrel, a very small seabird. Illustrations by Noel Cusa add a great deal to the book.

McFarland, David. *Animal Behavior: Psychobiology, Ethology and Evolution*. Benjamin-Cummings 1985 $39.95. ISBN 0-8053-6740-X. Comprehensive, well-organized introduction to animal behavior.

———, ed. *The Oxford Companion to Animal Behavior*. OUP 1987 $19.95. ISBN 0-19-281990-9. Information on topics from abnormal behavior to wildlife management; useful to the animal behaviorist, professional or amateur. Among the many other topics included are imprinting, territoriality, conditioning, operant behavior, and releaser mechanisms.

Markowitz, Hal, and Victor Stevens, eds. *Behavior of Captive Wild Animals*. Nelson-Hall 1978 $33.95. ISBN 0-88229-385-0. Technical reports by several scientists who conduct research on captive wild animals; deals with topics such as the control of predatory behavior; operant research in a zoo; vocal communication of sea lions, fur seals, and walruses; and a variety of others.

Maxwell, Mary, ed. *The Sociobiological Imagination*. State U. NY Pr. 1991 $57.50. ISBN 0-7914-0767-5. Introduces the major principles of sociobiology and presents its uses in diverse disciplines.

Mead, Christopher. *Bird Migration*. Facts on File 1983 o.p. Comprehensive study on the topic of bird migration by a man who has been with the British Trust for Ornithology for more than 20 years, working primarily in its bird-banding programs. Includes quotations referring to migration from the Bible, Aristotle, and Pliny, and information about observing migration, as well as more technical material. Discussion covers American as well as European species, and the maps are very useful.

Nollman, Jim. *Dolphin Dreamtime: The Art and Science of Interspecies Communication*. Bantam 1987 $8.95. ISBN 0-553-34427-7. Interesting approach to looking at animal behavior, showing what humans can learn from other species.

Stokes, Donald, and Lilian Stokes. *A Guide to Animal Tracking and Behavior.* Little 1986 $18.95. ISBN 0-316-81730-9. Excellent resource for getting to know wild animals and their habits a little better.

Teleki, Geza. *The Predatory Behavior among Wild Chimpanzees.* Bucknell U. Pr. 1975 $35.00. ISBN 0-8387-7743-3. Discusses in great detail the role of chimpanzees as predators.

Wilson, Edward O. *Sociobiology: The New Synthesis.* HUP 1975 $45.00. ISBN 0-674-81621-8. Thorough, technical discussion of the entire field of sociobiology. "Man: From Sociobiology to Sociology" is worth reading by itself if one lacks the time to tackle the entire book.

CHRONOLOGY OF AUTHORS

Darwin, Charles Robert. 1809–1882
Thoreau, Henry David. 1817–1862
Muir, John. 1838–1914
Frisch, Karl von. 1887–1982
Leopold, Aldo. 1887–1948
Krutch, Joseph Wood. 1893–1970
Lorenz, Konrad. 1903–1989

Carson, Rachel Louise. 1907–1964
Tinbergen, Nikolaas. 1907–1988
Abbey, Edward. 1927–1989
Ehrlich, Paul Ralph. 1932–
Ehrlich, Anne. 1933–
Brown, Lester Russell. 1934–
Goodall, Jane van Lawick. 1934–

ABBEY, EDWARD. 1927–1989

Edward Abbey, who became one of the most popular contemporary writers of the American West, was born in Pennsylvania. He received a B.A. from the University of New Mexico in 1951 and an M.A. in 1956, and attended the University of Edinburgh on a Fulbright Fellowship in 1951–52. He served in the U. S. Army (1945–47) and worked as a seasonal U. S. Park Service ranger from 1956 to 1968 and as a Forest Service fire lookout from 1969 to 1980. As a park ranger in Arches National Monument, Utah, Abbey not only learned to love the canyon land of the desert southwest but also learned about the commercialization and development of America's wilderness areas.

Through his novels and works of nonfiction, Abbey has come to represent the voice of anger for many who have watched the destruction of parts of the American western landscape. Many people would suggest that his literature has inspired many environmentalists to become so-called eco-radicals, operating much in the same fashion as Abbey's fictional monkey wrenchers, sabotaging billboards, bulldozers, and other infringements upon the natural landscape. Perhaps a more lasting legacy is that Abbey is also responsible for teaching a whole generation how to appreciate the land more by just getting outside and hiking around.

BOOKS BY ABBEY

Desert Solitaire: A Season in the Wilderness. 1968. U. of Ariz. Pr. 1988 $28.50. ISBN 0-8165-1057-1. Abbey rails against bureaucrats and developers who promote "automobile tourism" in America's wilderness areas.

Hayduke Lives! Little 1990 $18.95. ISBN 0-316-00411-1. The sequel to Abbey's earlier "monkey wrenching" novel.

The Journey Home: Some Words in Defense of the American West. NAL-Dutton 1991 $10.00. ISBN 0-452-26562-2. Abbey summons forth the multitudes of hikers, backpackers, mountain climbers, and others to experience the wilderness of the American Southwest and to learn about what can be lost.

The Monkey Wrench Gang. 1976. Avon 1992 $12.50. ISBN 0-380-71339-X. Describes the
   exploits of fictional environmental activists who take on developers and other
   destroyers of the wilderness of southern Utah and northern Arizona using guerrilla-
   style tactics.

BOOKS ABOUT ABBEY.

Hepworth, James R., and Gregory McNamee, eds. *Resist Much, Obey Little: Some Notes
   on Edward Abbey.* Harbinger AZ 1989 repr. of 1985 ed. $10.95. ISBN 0-943173-45-0
Ronald, Ann. *The New West of Edward Abbey.* U. of Nev. Pr. 1988 repr. of 1982 ed. $11.95.
   ISBN 0-87417-131-8

BROWN, LESTER RUSSELL. 1934–

   Lester Brown, whose parents were farmers, was born in New Jersey and
attended Rutgers University, receiving a B.S. in agricultural science in 1955. He
earned an M.S. in agricultural economics from the University of Maryland in
1959 and an M.P.A. from Harvard University in 1962. He worked as adviser on
foreign agricultural policy for the secretary of the U.S. Department of
Agriculture, served as administrator of the International Agricultural Development Service, and helped establish the Overseas Development Council. In 1974
he founded the Worldwatch Institute, a private, nonprofit, environmental think
tank designed to act as a "global early warning system" and to study
overpopulation, famine, and other world problems. Located in Washington,
D.C., the institute publishes the Worldwatch Papers series, *Worldwatch Magazine*, and the annual *State of the World* report. Although sometimes criticized for
his emphasis on population control, this author of more than a dozen books and
the recipient of a MacArthur Foundation fellowship has been highly praised for
his understanding of the threats to the ecology of our planet.

BOOKS BY BROWN

State of the World. (coauthored with the Worldwatch Institute staff). Norton 1993 $19.95.
   ISBN 0-393-03439-9. Annual assessment of the world's progress toward a sustainable
   society. Examines such topics as solid waste recycling, renewable energy, deforestation, extinction of species, toxic chemicals, and population; deemed one of the three
   most influential books on the environment in a recent poll of environmental leaders
   worldwide.
Vital Signs 1993: The Trends That Are Shaping Our Future. (coauthored by the staff of the
   Worldwatch Institute). Norton 1993 $19.95. ISBN 0-393-03517-4. Assembly of
   diagrams, tables, and data, with accompanying text, that analyzes key indicators of
   global environmental conditions.
The Worldwatch Reader. Norton 1991 $20.95. ISBN 0-393-03007-5. Anthology of the best
   articles and reports prepared by the staff of the Worldwatch Institute over the past
   decade.

CARSON, RACHEL LOUISE. 1907–1964

   Rachel Louise Carson was born in Springdale, Pennsylvania. She received a
B.A. from the Pennsylvania College for Women in 1929 and an M.A. from Johns
Hopkins University in 1932. After undertaking postgraduate work at the Woods
Hole Marine Biological Laboratory, she assumed a position as staff biologist at
the University of Maryland in 1931. Five years later, Carson was appointed
aquatic biologist in the U.S. Bureau of Fisheries (which later became the Fish
and Wildlife Service) and became editor-in-chief of its publications in 1949. In
1941 Carson published her first book, *Under the Sea Wind*, for which she
received acclaim as an accomplished science writer. Her next book, *The Sea
around Us*, published in 1951, won the National Book Award. With her

increased success as a popular writer, she resigned from her position with the Fish and Wildlife Service in 1952 to devote all her time to writing. In 1956 she published her third book about the ocean, *The Edge of the Sea*. Soon thereafter, she began work on the book that would become an environmental classic.

When Carson became concerned about pesticide pollution and its effects on ecosystems and human health, she spent years reading scientific reports, interviewing scientists, and pulling together thousands of bits of data about the use and impact of pesticides on the soil, in the water, and on plants, animals, and people. In 1962 she published *Silent Spring*, which immediately caused a stir. The book soared in sales, staying 31 weeks on the bestseller list. In all, *Silent Spring* sold 500,000 copies in hardcover and millions of copies in paperback. The popularity of her book was in part generated by the outraged response from the chemical industry, which created a substantial debate within scientific, industrial, and governmental circles. The more industry criticized Carson's interpretation of the facts, the more support she seemed to gain from the public, subsequently leading to legislation, such as the ban on the use of DDT in 1972. It would seem that Carson ignited the match that caught the environmental movement on fire. Her impact in the environmental community is significant. Among her many honors are the John Burroughs Medal from the John Burroughs Memorial Association; the Frances K. Hutchinson Medal of the Garden Clubs of America; the Distinguished Service Award of the U.S. Department of Interior; the Audubon Medal of the National Audubon Society; the gold medal of the New York Zoological Society; and the conservationist of the year award from the National Wildlife Federation. She died of cancer in 1964. In 1969 the U.S. Department of the Interior named the Rachel Carson National Wildlife Refuge in Maine in her honor.

BOOKS BY CARSON

The Edge of the Sea. 1956. HM 1979 $10.70. ISBN 0-395-28519-4. Entire book devoted to descriptions of many of the myriad organisms that live in the tidal zone despite the great challenges. Also describes how animals protect themselves from wave action, sand, and silt; how they time their reproductive cycles to enhance the survival rates of offspring; and how predator and prey interact with each other.

The Sea around Us. 1961. OUP 1991 $9.95. ISBN 0-19-506997-8. Deals primarily with the physics, chemistry, and geography of the oceans. As one cannot write of these characteristics without indicating how they affect living organisms, the book is a study of the oceans as ecological biomes as well.

The Sense of Wonder. 1965. HarpC 1987 $10.95. ISBN 0-06-091450-5. Discusses how to help parents learn to teach their children about nature, using the example of her own teachings of her grandnephew.

Silent Spring. 1962. HM 1987 $19.45. ISBN 0-395-45389-5. The book that alerted the world to the dangers of the overuse of pesticides and other chemicals, helped invigorate the emerging environmental movement, and played a major role in the shift from a parks-and-conservation perspective to one concerned with pollution.

Under the Sea Wind. 1941. NAL-Dutton 1992 $11.00. ISBN 0-452-26918-0. Explores the diversity of natural wonders that occurs just below the ocean's surface as well as within its depths.

BOOKS ABOUT CARSON

Brooks, Paul. *The House of Life: Rachel Carson at Work*. HM 1989 $9.70. ISBN 0-395-51742-7. Personal biography by Carson's editor and friend at Houghton Mifflin; includes material from unpublished papers and letters and from interviews with many of Carson's colleagues and friends.

Hynes, H. Patricia. *The Recurring Silent Spring.* Pergamon 1989 $30.00. ISBN 0-08-037117-5. Looks at the contribution Carson made to feminism in science and to the establishment of the U.S. Environmental Protection Agency.

DARWIN, CHARLES ROBERT. 1809–1882

Born in Shrewsbury, England, Charles Darwin was descended from two noted families. His grandfather Erasmus Darwin was a noted physician and naturalist who had proposed a theory of evolution in the 1790s. In his early schooling, Darwin showed so little promise that his father, also a well-known physician, told him, "You care for nothing but shooting, dogs, and rat catching, and you will be a disgrace to yourself and all your family."

Darwin first went to the University of Edinburgh to study medicine. Here again he was a poor student and could not stand the operating theater, where surgery was performed without an anesthetic. When he returned home, there appeared only one career choice left open—the ministry. Darwin thus went to Christ's College, Cambridge University, to study theology. The British biologist SIR JULIAN HUXLEY observed that, if Darwin were living today, he would not get into a good university. He may have entered Cambridge a poor student, but while he was there the faculty made sure that he learned something. Darwin had extra tutoring, special assignments, and whatever else was necessary for him to know something before he was granted his A.B. degree.

Darwin's interest in natural history, stimulated by people he met at Cambridge, led to his big break, which came shortly after graduation in 1831. A nonpaying position as a naturalist on His Majesty's Ship *Beagle* was available, and Darwin was recommended for the post by John Henslow, botany professor at Cambridge. The *Beagle* was involved in surveying the coast of South America, and Darwin had plenty of leisure ashore to make observations. It was his observations of natural history on this five-year voyage that led eventually to Darwin's theory of evolution and the publication of *The Origin of Species* (1859). After his famous voyage, Darwin returned to England and married Emma Wedgewood in 1839. For the next 20 years, he developed his theory, while raising a family of 10 children at his country home in Down, England. When he died, Darwin was buried in Westminster Abbey—England's final resting place for its greatest heroes. The works presented here are those having an ecological component. For a fuller list of Darwin's works, see also Chapter 22.

BOOKS BY DARWIN

Darwin on Earthworms: The Formation of Vegetable Mould through the Action of Worms. Bookworm Pub. 1976 repr. of 1881 ed. $7.95. ISBN 0-916302-10-5. Darwin's detailed study of the way earthworms use leaves as food or to line or cover the openings of burrows, as well as his estimate of the rate at which worm castings can cover objects lying on the surface of the field.

Fertilization of Orchids by Insects. 1862. E. M. Coleman. 1980 repr. of 1862 ed. o.p. Interesting observations of the ways in which flowers are adapted to profit from the visits of bees.

Journal of Researches into the Natural History and Geology of the Countries Visited during the Voyage of the H.M.S. Beagle round the World under the Command of Captain Fitz Roy. 1839. 2 vols. AMS Pr. 1972 repr. of 1892 ed. $42.50. ISBN 0-404-08401-X. Enthusiastic descriptions of his personal observations of the natural history of South America; presented in an interesting fashion with a keen eye for detail.

Books about Darwin

Appleman, Philip, ed. *Darwin*. Norton 1979 $24.95. ISBN 0-393-95009-3. Volume dealing with the impact that Charles Darwin's theory of evolution has had on all aspects of life. Includes papers selected from outstanding people in many fields, some comprising interesting observations on animal behavior and human relationships.

Desmond, Adrian, and James Moore. *Darwin*. Warner Bks. 1992 $35.00. ISBN 0-446-51589-2. Extensively researched work, tracing Darwin's development and interests from childhood to death. Incorporates materials from Darwin's diaries, letters, and other personal papers.

Irvine, William. *Apes, Angels, and Victorians: The Story of Darwin, Huxley and Evolution*. U. Pr. of Amer. 1983 o.p. Vividly communicates the intellectual and social atmosphere of the time in which Charles Darwin lived. The book has both heroes and villains as did those times—or any times. Also has a tender love story between Huxley and Henrietta Heathorn; worth reading—by men or monkeys.

Montagu, Ashley. *Darwin: Competition and Cooperation*. Greenwood 1973 repr. of 1952 ed. $35.00. ISBN 0-8371-6657-8. Clearly demonstrates the differences between Darwinism and the theory of evolution and beliefs that often have no relationship to the actual content of the theory. Probably the most important book, pointing to the fallacies of popular ideas about Darwinism and providing a warning to those who would read their own psychic hungers into the theories of sociobiology.

EHRLICH, PAUL RALPH, 1932– and EHRLICH, ANNE. 1933–

Paul Ehrlich, founder and first president of the Zero Population Growth organization, was born in Philadelphia, Pennsylvania. He received a B.A. in zoology from the University of Pennsylvania in 1953 and an M.A. and Ph.D. from the University of Kansas in 1955 and 1957, respectively. He became a member of the faculty at Stanford University in 1959 and was named Bing Professor of Population Studies in 1976. He is a recipient of a MacArthur Foundation fellowship, and in 1990 he was awarded Sweden's Crafoord Prize, created by the Royal Swedish Academy of Sciences to honor researchers in those disciplines not covered by the Nobel Prize. An expert in population biology, ecology, evolution, and behavior, Ehrlich has published more than 600 articles and scientific papers. He is perhaps best known for his environmental classic *The Population Bomb* (1968).

Paul Ehrlich and his wife Anne began working together shortly after their marriage in 1954. Anne Ehrlich received her B.S. in biology from the University of Kansas. As senior research associate in biology and associate director of the Center for Conservation Biology at Stanford University, she has lectured widely and written on various environmental issues, including the environmental consequences of nuclear war. Together, the Ehrlichs have written six books and dozens of magazine articles.

Books by the Ehrlichs

The Birder's Handbook: A Field Guide to the Natural History of North American Birds. (coauthored with David S. Dobkin and Darryl Wheye). S&S Trade 1988 $17.00. ISBN 0-671-62133-5. Exhaustive reference on all aspects of North American birds; designed to be used in the field as a supplement to identification guides.

Birds in Jeopardy: The Imperiled and Extinct Birds of the United States and Canada: Including Hawaii and Puerto Rico. (coauthored with David S. Dobkin and Darryl Wheye). Stanford U. Pr. 1992 $45.00. ISBN 0-8047-1967-5. Documents the former distributional ranges and reasons for extinction of each of the species listed.

Extinction: The Causes and Consequences of the Disappearance of Species. Random 1981 $16.95. ISBN 0-394-51312-6. Although many species have become extinct through-out the history of life on earth, the process has never occurred on a global scale or as the result of the activities of a single species of organism as it is happening at the present time. This book makes us aware of the disaster and of possible consequences.

Healing the Planet: Strategies for Resolving the Environmental Crisis. Addison-Wesley 1991 $22.95. ISBN 0-201-55046-6. Set of recommendations on how to grapple with planetary problems that threaten the quality of life for humans as well as the rest of nature.

The Machinery of Nature: The Living World around Us—And How It Works. S&S Trade 1987 $12.00. ISBN 0-671-63312-0. Explains ecological concepts and principles for a popular audience by showing how plants, animals, and humans interact, and how ecologists go about their work in the field.

The Population Bomb. Amereon Ltd. 1975 $17.95. ISBN 0-89190-861-7. Points out the consequences of uncontrolled increase in the human population. Ehrlich was another prophet without honor in his own country.

The Population Explosion. S&S Trade 1991 $11.00. ISBN 0-671-73294-3. Thoroughly researched update to Paul Ehrlich's earlier book *The Population Bomb* (1968); observes that our planet is approaching the extreme limits of being able to support human society.

FRISCH, KARL VON. 1887–1982 (NOBEL PRIZE 1973)

Born in Vienna, Austria, the youngest son of a surgeon, Karl von Frisch explored his interest in nature at his family's summer home. At an early age, he kept careful records of his wildlife observations and submitted papers to journals for amateur naturalists. He received a Ph.D from the University of Munich and later became professor at the Zoological Institute of Munich. Because of his poor vision, von Frisch was not conscripted into the army during World War I. He worked at a military hospital until 1919 and then returned to Munich.

In 1917 von Frisch married Margarethe Mohr, a nurse and artist whom he had met while working at the military hospital. She subsequently illustrated the published collection of his lectures; they raised three daughters and a son.

For his research on the behavior of honeybees, von Frisch received honorary degrees and awards from many institutions, foundations, and colleges. In 1973 von Frisch shared the Nobel Prize for physiology with KONRAD LORENZ and NIKOLAAS TINBERGEN.

BOOKS BY VON FRISCH

A Biologist Remembers. Trans. by Lisbeth Gombrich. Pergamon Pr. 1967 o.p. Von Frisch's autobiography about his life and work as a pioneer in ethology.

Dance Language and Orientation of Bees. HUP 1967 $49.50. ISBN 0-674-19050-5. Extensive monograph, elaborating von Frisch's theories on how bees communicate the location of food sources to other bees in the hive.

The Dancing Bees: An Account of the Life and Senses of the Honey Bee. Trans. by Dora Ilse. HarBraceJ 1961 o.p. Reports the results of von Frisch's discoveries about honeybees by using simple equipment, essentially saucers and colored water, to perform some very elegant experiments.

GOODALL, JANE VAN LAWICK. 1934–

Jane Goodall, a well-respected English zoologist, is famous for her fieldwork with chimpanzees in Africa. An early interest in African wild animals and the opportunity, at age 18, to stay on a friend's farm in Kenya, led her to Dr. Louis Leakey, then curator of the National Museum of Natural History in Nairobi. Almost immediately Leakey hired Goodall as his assistant secretary, and she was soon accompanying Leakey and his wife on their expeditions. Following

Leakey's suggestion that a field study of some of the higher primates would be a major contribution to the understanding of animal behavior, she began studying the chimpanzees of the Gombe Stream Research Center in Tanganyika (now Tanzania) in 1960. Although she had no undergraduate degree, Goodall earned a Ph.D. from Cambridge University in 1965, based on her first five years of research at the Gombe center. After more than 20 years of extensive study and direct contact with wild chimpanzees in their natural habitat, Goodall continues to research, teach, and write about primate behavior today.

BOOKS BY GOODALL

The Chimpanzees of Gombe. HUP 1986 $39.95. ISBN 0-674-11649-6. Technical account of Goodall's 25 years of work with chimpanzees. Information is presented in charts and graphs as well as in narrative form. Readers of Goodall's other books will encounter old friends among the chimpanzees discussed here.

In the Shadow of Man. 1967. HM 1983 $9.70. ISBN 0-395-33145-5. Goodall's report on the lives of chimpanzees including a poignant account of a male stricken with polio and the devotion of a younger male.

Through a Window: My Thirty Years with the Chimpanzees of Gombe. HM 1990 $21.45. ISBN 0-395-50081-8. Goodall's reflections on the three decades of her work and her many colleagues and associates at the Gombe chimpanzee reserve in Tanzania.

Visions of Caliban: Of Chimpanzees, Humans and the Honored Shape. (coauthored with Dale Peterson). HM 1993 $22.45. ISBN 0-395-53760-6

BOOK ABOUT GOODALL

Montgomery, Sy. *Walking with the Great Apes: Jane Goodall, Dian Fossey, and Birute Galdikas.* HM 1991 $19.45 ISBN 0-395-51597-1. Personal look at and comparison of the work of three pioneers in the field of primate behavior studies: Goodall and the chimpanzees of Tanzania; Fossey and the mountain gorillas of Rwanda; and Galdikas and the orangutans of southeast Asia.

KRUTCH, JOSEPH WOOD. 1893–1970

Joseph Wood Krutch demonstrated that the Renaissance man was not someone merely to read about. Born in Knoxville, Tennessee, he studied science and received his B.A. from the University of Tennessee. Afraid that society's emphasis on science and technology was a threat to our wilderness and wildlife, he went on to study humanities. After receiving his M.A. and Ph.D. degrees from Columbia University, he remained there to teach as a member of the English department and later occupied an endowed chair of dramatic literature. He was also an editor and a drama critic. When Krutch retired in 1952 because of respiratory problems, he moved to the southern Arizona desert, where, inspired by the natural beauty of the desert and its wildlife, he began to write about nature and conservation. Although his biographical work includes books on EDGAR ALLAN POE (see Vol. 1), SAMUEL JOHNSON (see Vol. 1), and HENRY DAVID THOREAU (see Vol. 1), here we will be concerned with some of his writings in natural history.

BOOKS BY KRUTCH

The Desert Year. 1952. U. of Ariz. Pr. 1985 $11.95. ISBN 0-8165-0923-9. Allows the reader to take a close look at a desert environment and to see the beauty that is a part of that ecosystem.

The Forgotten Peninsula: A Naturalist in Baja California. 1961. U. of Ariz. Pr. 1986 $12.95. ISBN 0-8165-0987-5. Description of Baja California, a land of interesting environments from the nursery waters of the gray whale along the shore to the rugged areas of the interior.

Grand Canyon. 1958. U. of Arizona Pr. 1989 $12.95. ISBN 0-8165-1112-8. Using the Grand Canyon to illustrate many of the great principles of ecology, Krutch points out aspects of the succession of aspen and pine trees, divergent species of squirrels on opposite sides of the canyon, and other biological processes.

The Twelve Seasons. 1949. Ayer repr. of 1949 ed. $16.00. ISBN 0-8369-1970-X. Krutch's first book on natural history.

The Voice of the Desert: A Naturalist's Interpretation. Morrow 1971 $9.95. ISBN 0-688-07715-3. A magnificent portrayal of life and death in the desert.

LEOPOLD, ALDO. 1887–1948

Aldo Leopold, who has become the most esteemed ecologist of this century, is best remembered for his articulation of the "land ethic," which demonstrates a respect and reverence for all life. His landmark book *A Sand County Almanac*, published in 1949, is considered by many to be the most significant book published on nature and the environment.

Born in Burlington, Iowa, Leopold attended the Yale Graduate School of Forestry (newly established in 1900 by Gifford Pinchot) and graduated in 1909. He immediately began his career with the U.S. Forest Service as a forest assistant in Arizona and later became supervisor of Carson National Forest in New Mexico in 1912. During his stint in the Southwest, he encouraged interest in establishing the Gila Wilderness Area in southwest New Mexico, the first in the national forest wilderness system. He later moved to Madison, Wisconsin, to help direct the Forest Products Laboratory from 1925 to 1927. He worked for a while as a game consultant and completed his book *Game Management* in 1933. Soon thereafter, he became professor of game management at the University of Wisconsin and held that position until his death in 1948. Leopold was one of the founders of The Wilderness Society in 1935 and an organizer of The Wildlife Society in 1937, which later created the Aldo Leopold Award, which has been awarded annually since 1950 for significant achievements in wildlife biology and conservation. The Leopold Memorial Reserve, a private 1,400-acre tract near Baraboo, Wisconsin, is dedicated to his memory. The landmark of the reserve is the Shack, Leopold's country retreat in one of central Wisconsin's "sand counties," a place which he describes so vividly in his journals.

BOOKS BY LEOPOLD

Game Management. 1933. U. of Wis. Pr. 1986 $14.00. ISBN 0-299-10774-4. Reissue of one of the earliest textbooks to shape the emerging field of wildlife ecology.

The River of the Mother of God and Other Essays by Aldo Leopold. Ed. by Susan L. Flader and J. Baird Callicott. U. of Wis. Pr. 1991 $24.95. ISBN 0-299-12760-5. Collection of heretofore unpublished essays by Leopold; assembled by two noted scholars of Leopold's work.

A Sand County Almanac, and Sketches Here and There. 1949. OUP 1987 $25.00. ISBN 0-19-505305-2. Collection of essays recording Leopold's awareness of and appreciation for the wild things around him; perhaps the most highly regarded book on nature and the environment.

BOOKS ABOUT LEOPOLD

Callicott, J. Baird, ed. *Companion to a Sand County Almanac: Interpretive and Critical Essays.* U. of Wis. Pr. 1987 $12.95. ISBN 0-299-11234-9. Set of articles examining Leopold's life and ideas, particularly those presented in *A Sand County Almanac* (1949).

Flader, Susan L. *Thinking Like a Mountain: Aldo Leopold and the Evolution of an Ecological Attitude toward Deer, Wolves, and Forests.* U. of Mo. Pr. 1974 $27.50. ISBN

0-8262-0167-9. Traces the development and conversion of Leopold from game manager to natural philosopher.

McCabe, Robert A. *Aldo Leopold: The Professor*. Palmer 1987 o.p. A more personal account of Leopold by one of his wildlife ecology students; contains numerous photographs taken by the author and other Leopold students.

Meine, Curt. *Aldo Leopold: His Life and Work*. U. of Wis. Pr. 1988 $29.50. ISBN 0-299-11490-2. By far the most extensive biography of Leopold, covering his life from childhood to his adulthood as wildlife conservationist and university professor; includes a lengthy bibliographic listing of references about Leopold and his work.

Tanner, Thomas, ed. *Aldo Leopold: The Man and His Legacy*. Soil & Water Conserv. 1987 $10.00. ISBN 0-935734-13-9. Collection of papers prepared by several of Leopold's biographers, colleagues, friends, and family members, commemorating his birth.

LORENZ, KONRAD. 1903–1989 (NOBEL PRIZE 1973)

Born in Vienna, Austria, Konrad Lorenz, the son of a wealthy orthopedic surgeon, studied medicine at the University of Vienna and Columbia University, before receiving a Ph.D. in zoology from the University of Munich. Acknowledged as one of the pioneers of modern ethology, he has served in various academic and research positions and has been involved in the study of animal behavior for most of the last 40 years. His studies with Oscar Heinroth led to the discovery of imprinting, an early and centrally important learning process for many animal species. In 1936 at a symposium in Leiden, Netherlands, Lorenz met NIKOLAAS TINBERGEN. Over the next few years, they developed the concept of instinctive behavior that became the foundation of modern ethology. In 1973 he shared the Nobel Prize for physiology or medicine with Tinbergen and KARL VON FRISCH "for their discoveries concerning organization and elicitation of individual and social behavior patterns."

Some of his views about animal behavior have been criticized as being speculative and anthropomorphic, to which Lorenz once responded, "To call the animal jealous is just as legitimate as to call an octopus' eye an eye or a lobster's leg a leg." His works benefit from his rare talent of being able to write for both general and technical audiences.

BOOKS BY LORENZ

The Foundations of Ethology. Trans. by Konrad Lorenz and Robert Warren Kickert. Spr.-Verlag 1981 $52.00. ISBN 0-387-81623-2. History of the development of the field of ethology, the study of animal behavior in relation to habitat.

King Solomon's Ring. 1952. HarpC 1982 $12.00. ISBN 0-06-131976-7. Lorenz believes that the way to study animal behavior is to have intimate contact with animals as they are "doing what comes naturally." Many hilarious events about Lorenz's interactions with the animals he studied give this book a real sparkle.

On Aggression. 1966. Trans. by Marjorie K. Wilson. Peter Smith 1986 $20.00. ISBN 0-8446-6213-5. Presents Lorenz's beliefs that we must study the aggressive drives of other animals in order to understand them in ourselves and that understanding these drives in ourselves may be essential to our survival as a species.

BOOK ABOUT LORENZ

Nisbett, Alec. *Konrad Lorenz*. HarBraceJ 1976 o.p. Biography of the noted scientist who had great enjoyment working closely with animals.

MUIR, JOHN. 1838–1914

The naturalist John Muir was born in Dunbar, Scotland. When he was 11 years old, he moved to the United States with his family and lived on a Wisconsin farm, where he had to work hard for long hours. He would rise as

early as one o'clock in the morning in order to have time to study. At the urging
of friends, he took some inventions he had made to a fair in Madison,
Wisconsin. This trip resulted in his attending the University of Wisconsin. After
four years in school, he began the travels that eventually took him around the
world.

Muir's inventing career came to an abrupt end in 1867, when he lost an eye in
an accident while working on one of his mechanical inventions. Thereafter, he
focused his attention on natural history, exploring the American West,
especially the Yosemite region of California. Muir traveled primarily on foot
carrying only a minimum amount of food and a bedroll. In 1880 Muir married
Louie Strentzel, the daughter of an Austrian who began the fruit and wine
industry in California.

One of the first explorers to postulate the role of glaciers in forming the
Yosemite Valley, Muir also discovered a glacier in Alaska that later was named
for him. His lively descriptions of many of the natural areas of the United States
contributed to the founding of Yosemite National Park in 1890. His urge to
preserve these areas for posterity led to his founding of the Sierra Club in 1892.

BOOKS BY MUIR

My First Summer in the Sierra. 1911. Sierra 1990 $35.00. ISBN 0-87156-600-1. Account of
    Muir's explorations while overseeing a shepherd who was taking a flock into the high
    country for the summer.
Our National Parks. 1901. Sierra 1991 $10.00. ISBN 0-87156-626-5. Muir's description of
    the four national parks and numerous national forests that had been established in
    the United States by 1900 and his call for more people to seek solace in the
    wilderness. New forward by Alfred Runte.
The Story of My Boyhood and Youth. 1913. Sierra 1989 $9.95. ISBN 0-87156-749-0.
    Especially interesting account of Muir's early experiences.
A Thousand-Mile Walk to the Gulf. 1916. Sierra 1992 $10.00. ISBN 0-87156-591-9.
    Records Muir's journey from Indiana to the Gulf of Mexico, which initiated his life-
    long wilderness travels.
Travels in Alaska. 1915. Sierra 1988 $9.95. ISBN 0-87156-783-0. Muir shows his keen
    observational and literary style in this amazing adventure in a remote wilderness.
Wilderness World of John Muir. HM 1975 $9.70. ISBN 0-395-24083-2. Fifty selections
    from Muir's various books. Introduction and interpretation by Edwin Way Teale.
The Yosemite. 1912. Sierra 1989 $40.00. ISBN 0-87156-653-2. Volume describing some of
    the many hikes during which Muir explored the Yosemite area.

BOOK ABOUT MUIR

Cohen, Michael P. *The Pathless Way: John Muir and American Wilderness.* U. of Wis. Pr.
    1984 $35.00. ISBN 0-299-09720-X. In this book dealing with the great naturalist, the
    author is primarily interested in interpreting or revealing Muir, not in writing his
    biography. Might mean more to the reader who had just finished two or three of
    Muir's own books.

THOREAU, HENRY DAVID. 1817–1862

Born in Concord, Massachusetts, Henry David Thoreau developed an early
interest in the woodlands and meadows near his home. After graduating from
Harvard College in 1837, Thoreau became a teacher and established a small
school in 1838. During the 1840s, he became associated with RALPH WALDO
EMERSON (see Vol. 1) and others who were influential in the Transcendentalism
movement. Thoreau aspired to be a writer, and under the influence of Emerson
and the other transcendalists, his talent developed. In 1845 he built a small
cabin on the shore of Walden Pond, spending much time enjoying the natural

beauty nearby or tending to his garden and other household tasks. He continued writing about his experiences there and published *A Week on the Concord and Merrimack Rivers* in 1849. Later he published *Walden; or Life in the Woods* (1854), a series of essays that describe his meditations and lifestyle at Walden Pond. Although he left Walden Pond in 1847, he continued writing and became involved in other projects in Concord, including the abolitionist movement. *Walden* sold only a few thousand copies during Thoreau's lifetime, but it has become a bestseller in modern times and is highly regarded for its literary, philosophical, and aesthetic qualities. In *Walden*, Thoreau exhibited the romantic perspective toward nature, which emphasizes that the natural environment is valuable for its ability to stimulate the human imagination rather than serving solely as a resource for food and the extraction of natural resources, such as minerals and timber. Thoreau also strongly objected to the traditional study of dead plants and animals in museums and laboratories. His belief in the reverence of life is evident in his observations of wildlife in their native habitats. His influence can certainly be seen and felt on such naturalists and writers of the late nineteenth and twentieth centuries as JOHN MUIR, John Burroughs, and Annie Dillard.

BOOK BY THOREAU

Walden and Other Writings of Henry David Thoreau. 1854. Ed. by Brooks Atkinson. Random 1992 $18.50. ISBN 0-679-60004-3. The classic book that has rallied so many persons to become interested in nature and the environment. Thoreau's simple and peaceful living has served as a model for generations, especially for those in the back-to-land movement of the 1960s and 1970s; has an intimate influence on its reader and leads to inspired thoughts and actions.

BOOKS ABOUT THOREAU

Baron, Robert, and Edmund Schofield, eds. *Thoreau's World and Ours: A Natural Legacy.* Fulcrum Pub. 1993 $26.95. ISBN 1-55591-903-0. Examines Thoreau's influence on the modern environmental movement.

Harding, Walter. *Thoreau, as Seen by His Contemporaries.* Dover 1990 $6.95. ISBN 0-486-26160-3

TINBERGEN, NIKOLAAS. 1907–1988 (NOBEL PRIZE 1973)

Born in The Hague, Netherlands, Nikolaas Tinbergen developed an early love of nature and enjoyed collecting seashells and observing birds. He received a Ph.D. from the University of Leiden in 1932 and remained there to teach, becoming professor of zoology in 1947. Two years later he moved to Oxford University, where he taught until 1974. Some of Tinbergen's earlier studies were done under and with KONRAD LORENZ. However, it is Tinbergen's thorough, in-depth field and laboratory research that distinguishes his work from Lorenz's and that has given validity and respect to the science of ethology. The majority of Tinbergen's work during the 1950s and 1960s focuses on gull behavior, especially in the area of aggression and attraction. More recently, and until his death in 1988, he was concerned mainly with applying his expertise to the solution of the human problem.

BOOKS BY TINBERGEN

Curious Naturalists. 1956. U. of Mass. Pr. 1984 $15.95. ISBN 0-87023-456-0. Recounts some of Tinbergen's experiences in the field with various observers studying the behavior of many types of animals. Easy-to-read account of some interesting events in the lives of curious naturalists.

Social Behavior in Animals: With Special Reference to Vertebrates. Routledge Chapman
   & Hall 1965 $12.95. ISBN 0-412-20000-7. Discusses animal behavior and describes a
   variety of social behaviors.
The Study of Instinct. 1951. OUP 1990 $30.00. ISBN 0-19-857740-0. Describes Tinbergen's
   classic experiments with fish, birds, and other animals to determine the innate
   behavioral responses known as *instinct*.

BOOK ABOUT TINBERGEN

Dawkins, M. S., T. R. Halliday, and R. Dawkins, eds. *The Tinbergen Legacy*. Routledge
   Chapman & Hall 1991 $56.50. ISBN 0-412-39120-1. Collection of essays delivered in
   Tinbergen's honor by his colleagues and students.

Name Index

In addition to authors of books, this index includes the names of persons mentioned in introductory essays, section introductions, biographical profiles, general bibliographic entries, and "Books about" sections. Throughout, however, persons mentioned only in passing—to indicate friendships, relationships, and so on—are generally not indexed. Editors, translators, and compilers are not indexed unless there is no specific author given for the work in question. Writers of the introductions, forewords, afterwords, and similar parts of works are not indexed. The names of individuals who are represented by separate biographical profiles appear in boldface, as do the page numbers on which their profiles appear.

Barnes, Mildred A., 627
Barnes, R.S.K., 758
Barnes, Virgil E., 627
Barnett, Lincoln, 682
Barnhart, B., 77
Baron, Jason D., 403
Baron, Naomi S., 549
Baron, Robert, 837
Barondess, Jeremiah, 364
Barr, Avron, 569
Barret, Robert B., 100
Barrett, Edward, 561
Barrett, James, 758
Barrett, Paul H., 758
Barrett, Stephen, 346
Barrett, William, 69
Barrow, John D., 11, 196,
594, 654
Barry, John A., 536
Barry, John M., 373
Barry, Robert, 196
Barry, Roger G., 633
Barstow, David R., 549
Barth, Friedrich G., 767, 769
Barth, John, 563
Barth, Michael C., 633
Barth, Richard B., 403
Barthelemy-Madaule, Made-
leine, 802
Bartholomew, Fletcher, 196
Bartlett, John G., 386
Bartusiak, Marcia, 593
Baruch, Dorothy W., 421
Bascom, Willard, 631
Basile, Robert M., 635
Bass, Rick, 817
Bassin, A., 451
Bateman, Alan M., 636
Bates, Marston, 817
Bates, Robert L., 616, 635
Bates, William, 539
Batschelet, Margaret W., 27
Batshaw, Mark L., 321, 375
Battan, Louis J., 633
Bauer, Henry H., 9, 150, 589
Baum, Andrew, 321, 339
Baum, Joan, 578
Baum, Robert J., 73, 127
Baxandall, Michael, 191
Bayer, Edward J., 129
Bayles, Michael D., 106
Baylin, Frank, 228
Bayliss, R.I.S., 381
Bayliss-Smith, T. P., 262
Baynes, Ken, 191, 212
Beadle, George Wells, 788
Beagon, Mary, 810
Beakley, George C., 227
Beales, Peter, 767
Bean, William N., 312
Bear, John, 536
Beasley, Joseph D., 327
Beatty, J. Kelly, 592

Beatty, William K., 314
Beauchamp, Dan E., 401
Beauchamp, Thomas L.,
106, 118, 120, **131**
Beaver, Paul, 238
Beck, Aaron T., 432
Becker, M., 240
Becker, Robert O., 318
Becker, Wayne M., 775
Beckett, Derrick, 250
Beckler, Alfred W., 368
Beckman, Arnold Orville,
738
Beckman, William A., 284
Bedini, Silvio A., 43
Beigel, Hugo G., 413
Beiser, Arthur, 652
Belitsos, Byron, 559
Belkin, Lisa, 118, 343
Bell, Arthur E., 695
Bell, Daniel, 150, 572
Bell, Eric T., 30, 527
Bell, Peter Robert, 767
Bell, Robert, 9, 106
Bell, Roger, 327
Bell, S. P., 216
Bell, Whitfield J., 312
Bellack, Alan S., 417
Bellak, Leopold, 417, 421
Bellamy, Edward, 563
Bellamy, John, 301
Bellina, Joseph H., 357
Belloni, Lanfranco, 27
Benacerraf, P., 492
Ben-David, Joseph, 150
Bender, Arnold E., 261
Bender, Gray T., 735
Benderly, Beryl L., 379
Benfey, O. Theodor, 731, 756
Beniger, James R., 125
Benjamin, Ben, 399
Benjamin, Martin, 118
Bennett, Arnold, 330
Bennett, E. A., 455
Bennett, H., 724
Bennett, Hal Z., 342
Bennett, J. H., 528
Bennett, William, 344
Benson, Ezra Taft, 267
Benson, Herbert, 400, 401
Benton, Neville, 262
Bereano, Philip L., 150
Beresford, Larry, 378
Berg, Howard C., 775
Berg, Paul, 777
Berger, John, 264, 821
Berger, Karen, 371
Berger, Melvin, 736
Berger, Peter L., 69, 128
Berger, Stuart M., 344
Berghorn, Forrest J., 316
Bergman, Abraham B., 375
Bergman, David, 219

Bergman, Jules, 219
Bergmann, Peter G., 664
Bergson, Henri, 96, 789
Berke, J., 426
Berkley, George, 339
Berkow, Robert, 405
Berkson, William, 99
Berland, Theodore, 386
Berlin, Laura, 566
Berliner, Arthur K., 447
Bernal, J. D., 24
Bernard, Claude, 788
Bernauer, James W., 88
Berndt, Bruce C., 488
Berne, Eric Lennard, 424,
433
Bernice, Daniel D., 480
Bernoulli, Jakob, 525, 527
Bernstein, Jeremy, 536, 650,
654, 668, 672, 682, 720
Bernstein, Richard, 89
Berquist, Thomas A., 396
Berra, Tim, 779
Berry, Adrian, 567
Berry, Arthur, 31
Berry, Brian J., 619
Berry, R. J., 794
Berry, Thomas, 657
Berry, Wendell, 113, 132,
265, **268**, 821, 823
Bersani, Leo, 447
Bertolotti, M., 666, 718
Bertsch, Sharon McGrayne,
4, 187, 727
Berzelius, Jons Jakob, 727,
731, **738**, 755
Besancon, Robert M., 652
Besette, Alan E., 759
Bester, William S., 35
Beth, E. W., 493
Bethe, Hans Albrecht., 133,
605, **671**
Bettelheim, Bruno, 434
Betts, Richard K., 184
Beven, Keith, 626
Beveridge, W. I., 389
Bevlin, Marjorie Elliott, 191
Beyer, Karl H., 350
Beyerchen, Alan D., 47
Biagio, John Melloni, 311
Bianchina, Paul, 225
Bickel, Leonard, 270
Bier, Robert A., Jr., 625
Bigelow, W. G., 370
Biggs, Donald A., 417
Bijker, Wiebe E., 24, 150,
151
Billings, Charlene W., 577
Billington, David P., 191
Bills, Donald D., 222
Binder, Arnold, 417
Binder, Virginia, 417
Bingham, John A. C., 302

Title Index

Titles of all books discussed in *The Reader's Adviser* are indexed here, except broad generic titles such as "Complete Works," "Selections," "Poems," "Correspondence." Also omitted is any title written by a profiled author that also includes that author's full name or last name as part of the title, such as *The Collected Papers of Charles Darwin*. The only exception to this is Shakespeare (Volume 1), where *all* works by and about him are indexed. To locate all titles by and about a profiled author, the user should refer to the Name Index for the author's primary listing (given in boldface). In general, subtitles are omitted unless two or more works have the same main title, or the main title consists of an author's full or last name (e.g., *Marie Curie: A Biography*). When two or more works by different authors have the same title, the authors' last names will appear in parentheses following the title.

Subject Index

This index provides detailed, multiple-approach access to the subject content of the volume. Arrangement is alphabetical. The names of profiled, main-entry authors are not included in this index; the reader is reminded to use the Name Index to locate these individuals. For additional information, the reader should refer to the detailed Table of Contents at the front of the volume.